MW00514438

Financial Services Offered by Different Institutions

	Banks		S & Ls		Insurance Companies		Retailers		Security Dealers	
Checking	A	B		B		B		B		B
Savings	A	B	A	B		B		B		B
Time Deposits	A	B	A	B		B		B		B
Installment Loans	A	B		B		B		B		B
Business Loans	A	B		B		B		B		B
Mortgage Loans		B	A	B		B		B		B
Credit Cards		B		B		B	A	B		B
Insurance					A	B		B		B
Stocks, Bonds		C				B		B	A	B
Mutual Funds		C				B		B	A	B
Real Estate						B		B		B
Full Interstate Facilities						B		B		B

Key: A—1960
         B—1985
         C—Available to well-capitalized-banking institutions by use of separate subsidiaries or via trust department funds, 1991

Financial Institutions, Markets, and Money

FINANCIAL INSTITUTIONS, MARKETS, AND MONEY

Fifth Edition

David S. Kidwell
University of Minnesota

Richard L. Peterson
Texas Tech University

David W. Blackwell
University of Georgia

The Dryden Press

Harcourt Brace Jovanovich College Publishers

Fort Worth   Philadelphia   San Diego   New York   Orlando   Austin
San Antonio   Toronto   Montreal   London   Sydney   Tokyo

Editor in Chief:	Robert A. Pawlik
Acquisitions Editor:	Michael Roche
Developmental Editor:	Millicent Treloar
Project Editor:	Jon Gregory
Assistant Project Editor:	Matt Ball
Production Manager:	Marilyn Williams
Book Designer:	Sue Hart
Permissions Editor:	Van Strength

Copyright © 1993, 1990, 1987, 1984, 1981, by The Dryden Press.

All rights reserved. No part of this publication may be reproduced or transmitted in any form or by any means, electronic or mechanical, including photocopy, recording, or any information storage and retrieval system, without permission in writing from the publisher.

Requests for permission to make copies of any part of the work should be mailed to: Permissions Department, Harcourt Brace Jovanovich, Inc., 8th Floor, Orlando, FL 32887.

Permissions acknowledgments appear on page 819, which constitutes a continuation of the copyright page.

Address for Editorial Correspondence
The Dryden Press, 301 Commerce Street, Suite 3700, Fort Worth, TX 76102

Address for Orders
The Dryden Press, 6277 Sea Harbor Drive, Orlando, FL 32887
1-800-782-4479, or 1-800-433-0001 (in Florida)

ISBN: 0–03–075478–X

Library of Congress Catalogue Number: 92–70697

Printed in the United States of America
3 4 5 6 7 8 9 0 1 2   039   9 8 7 6 5 4 3 2 1

The Dryden Press
Harcourt Brace Jovanovich

The Dryden Press Series in Finance

Amling and Droms
Investment Fundamentals

Berry and Young
Managing Investments: A Case Approach

Boyet
Security Analysis for Investment Decisions: Text and Software

Brigham
Fundamentals of Financial Management, *Sixth Edition*

Brigham and Gapenski
Cases in Financial Management, *Second Edition*

Brigham and Gapenski
Cases in Financial Management: Module A,
Second Edition

Brigham and Gapenski
Cases in Financial Management: Module B

Brigham and Gapenski
Cases in Financial Management: Module C

Brigham and Gapenski
Financial Management: Theory and Practice, *Sixth Edition*

Brigham and Gapenski
Intermediate Financial Management, *Fourth Edition*

Brigham, Gapenski, and Aberwald
Finance with Lotus 1-2-3, *Second Edition*

Campsey and Brigham
Introduction to Financial Management, *Third Edition*

Chance
An Introduction to Options and Futures, *Second Edition*

Clauretie and Webb
The Theory and Practice of Real Estate Finance

Cooley
Advances in Business Financial Management: A Collection of Readings

Cooley and Roden
Business Financial Management, *Second Edition*

Curran
Principles of Corporate Finance

Evans
International Finance: A Markets Approach

Fama and Miller
The Theory of Finance

Gardner and Mills
Managing Financial Institutions: An Asset/Liability Approach, *Second Edition*

Gitman and Joehnk
Personal Financial Planning, *Sixth Edition*

Harrington
Case Studies in Financial Decision Making, *Third Edition*

Hayes and Meerschwam
Financial Institutions: Contemporary Cases in the Financial Services Industry

Johnson
Issues and Readings in Managerial Finance, *Third Edition*

Kidwell, Peterson, and Blackwell
Financial Institutions, Markets, and Money, *Fifth Edition*

Koch
Bank Management, *Second Edition*

Kohn
Money, Banking and Financial Markets, *Second Edition*

Lee and Finnerty
Corporate Finance: Theory, Method, and Application

Maisel
Real Estate Finance, *Second Edition*

Martin, Cox, and MacMinn
The Theory of Finance: Evidence and Applications

Mayo
Finance: An Introduction, *Fourth Edition*

Mayo
Investments: An Introduction, *Third Edition*

Pettijohn
PROFIT +

Reilly
Investment Analysis and Portfolio Management,
Third Edition

Reilly
Investments, *Third Edition*

Sears and Trennepohl
Investment Management

Seitz
Capital Budgeting and Long-Term Financing Decisions

Siegel and Siegel
Futures Markets

Smith and Spudeck
Interest Rates: Principles and Applications

Stickney
Financial Statement Analysis: A Strategic Perspective,
Second Edition

Turnbull
Option Valuation

Weston and Brigham
Essentials of Managerial Finance, *Tenth Edition*

Weston and Copeland
Managerial Finance, *Ninth Edition*

Wood and Wood
Financial Markets

The HBJ College Outline Series

Baker
Financial Management

Preface

BUSINESS SCHOOLS AND ECONOMICS DEPARTMENTS have long recognized the importance to their curriculums of courses on money and banking and financial institutions. Often these courses have been taught with a macroeconomic emphasis, which stresses the effects of monetary policy on the U.S. economy and places only a secondary emphasis on the institutions and markets that form the economy's financial system.

Because of the dramatic changes that have occurred in the U.S. financial system in recent years, we believe that a student at the introductory level should receive a balanced view of the system and its major participants. By a balanced view, we mean that emphasis should be placed on the student's understanding of all financial institutions, financial markets, and financial instruments, not just banks and monetary policy. We believe that such an approach will accommodate the educational and professional needs of a greater number of students. Those who are majoring in finance or economics can take specialized courses, such as monetary theory or management of financial institutions, at a more advanced level. Our book provides the background for students to pursue more advanced training in finance, economics, and the management of financial institutions.

Thus, the goal of this textbook is to give the student a broad introduction to the operation, mechanics, and structure of the financial system in the United States, emphasizing its institutions, markets, and instruments. The Federal Reserve System and monetary policy are also given special attention. We stress monetary policy's effect on the economy and on financial institutions. We also emphasize ways in which managers of financial institutions can adjust their operations to reduce risk caused by changes in monetary policy and the interest rate environment.

This book is intended for use as a primary text in a school of business administration for a first course on financial institutions or the financial system. The book is also appropriate for an introductory money and banking course in a professionally oriented economics department. The text assumes that the student has taken an introductory economics course, preferably one with some coverage of macroeconomics. A knowledge of mathematics, other than high school algebra, is not required. Any college student or informed business person should feel comfortable reading this book.

Features of the Book

Pedagogically, the book attempts to blend a descriptive narrative of the operations of the financial system with a sufficient amount of theory to enable the reader to understand the underlying principles of the financial system. Utilizing the theory and analytical tools presented in this book, the student should have the background to understand and evaluate events in the financial world and therefore be able to make intelligent, real-world decisions concerning the management of money and the operation of financial institutions and markets.

This book has several unique characteristics that distinguish it from other texts. First, and most important, it provides a balanced view of the financial institutions and markets that form our nation's financial system. In the past, introductory courses have given only cursory attention to banking practices and nonbank financial institutions while emphasizing the Federal Reserve System and monetary policy. Our book goes beyond this, devoting five in-depth chapters to commercial banking, five to nonbank financial institutions, and five to financial markets, including a chapter on international banking and a chapter on foreign exchange and international credit markets. In addition, five chapters are devoted to the history of the financial system in the United States, the Federal Reserve System, the money supply and monetary policy, and the regulation of financial institutions. The text contains two chapters on contemporary issues that are likely to affect financial markets and institutions in the future. Those chapters discuss numerous issues related to the growth of electronic funds transfer systems, the globalization of financial markets, the effects of regulation on financial markets and institutions, regulatory arbitrage, and present and future regulatory problems.

Second, this book differs from other texts in that monetary policy is also examined from the perspective of the firm. The model of national income determination is used to discuss the direct and indirect effects of monetary policy on financial institutions and the general level of interest rates. Then the book considers ways in which different macroeconomic policies are likely to affect interest rates and the profitability of various institutions. It also describes ways in which firms can monitor and control their exposure to interest-rate risk. This approach serves to integrate the descriptive materials on financial markets and institutions with the changes in monetary policy that affect the entire economy.

Finally, we have provided numerous tables and diagrams to augment each topic covered in the text. Each chapter opens with an overview of the material to be covered and ends with a detailed summary recounting the major concepts and points covered within that chapter. Questions are included at the end of each chapter for discussion and review. For instructors and students who wish to explore a topic in more detail, suggested annotated readings are listed at the end of each chapter. An instructor's manual is also available.

Changes in this Edition

The 1980s and 1990s have brought about deregulation and rapid change in the structure of the U.S. financial system. The Depository Institutions Deregulation and Monetary Control Act of 1980 (DIDMCA) and the Garn-St. Germain Depository Institutions Act of 1982 made far-reaching changes in the nation's financial system. Commercial banks can now enter lines of business previously closed to them, and the distinction between banks and nonbank financial institutions is rapidly becoming blurred. In addition, historical restrictions against interstate banking have been all but abolished. Financial institutions have adapted to the changed regulatory environment by changing their asset and liability structures, their capital structure, and their corporate status. Some institutions have taken excessive risks, causing dramatic increases in failure rates and jeopardizing their deposit insurance funds. Congress has responded by passing new laws, such as the Financial Institutions Reform, Recovery, and Enforcement Act of 1989; and the Federal Deposit Insurance Corporation Improvement Act of 1991, that changed the structure of regulation and the funding of deposit insurance agencies. Major changes have occurred in both the form of financial institutions and in their regulatory environment. Because of deregulation, reregulation, and increasing risks, many financial institutions' costs have risen. When they have tried to pass on their increased costs by raising loan rates, many large corporations have found that they could obtain lower interest rates by borrowing directly from the financial markets rather than from banks and other depository institutions. In addition, development of the "junk bond" market extended direct financing opportunities even to relatively risky corporations. Thus, this fifth edition has been substantially revised and reorganized to keep current with the hazardous milieu in which financial markets and institutions operate.

In this dangerous economic environment, it is important for future managers of financial institutions to navigate the intricacies of financial markets and interest rates. The book has been reorganized to provide a stronger coverage of interest rates and financial markets. The new organization places greater emphasis on understanding interest rate risk and moves the description of the various financial markets so they now come *before* the chapters on financial institutions. The logic for the change in chapter order is that many of the assets and liabilities of financial institutions are traded in financial markets; thus, it is critical that students understand the markets within which institutions operate before studying the management problems of institutions. The book begins with a general description and history of the financial system, including a discussion of the Federal Reserve System. Then the book moves to an expanded treatment of interest rates and interest rate risk, continues with a discussion of the financial markets, and finally embarks on a treatment of the management of important bank and nonbank financial institutions. The book concludes by discussing the effects of monetary policy on financial markets and institutions.

The theme for the financial institutions chapters is the management of the fundamental risks that financial institutions face: liquidity risk, credit risk, and interest-rate risk. These unifying concepts allow students to see how the same set of financial tools (i.e., risk management tools) can be used to manage different financial institutions. Liquidity risk is the risk that a financial institution will be unable to generate sufficient cash inflow to meet required cash outflows. Credit risk represents the possibility that a borrower fails to pay promised cash flows to a lender at the time and in the amount promised. Interest-rate risk is the risk of fluctuations in the values of a financial institution's assets and liabilities caused by changes in interest rates. These key concepts are developed early in the book and they then provide the framework for analyzing commercial banks and other financial institutions later in the book.

Another major change is the way we deal with international issues; in this edition we integrate the international topics directly into relevant sections and chapters of the book. For example, in this edition of the book the chapter on international banking (Chapter 16) now follows the four banking chapters. Likewise, the international markets chapter (Chapter 12) now follows the financial markets chapters. Furthermore, the chapters on money and capital markets now contain sections on the globalization of the financial markets.

There are several other significant organizational changes and additions. First, the material on deposit expansion and the money supply has been condensed and combined with the chapter on the Federal Reserve System to form the new Chapter 4. It provides the basic material necessary to understand how the Fed controls the money supply. For those students interested in forecasting *what* the Fed is likely to do in different circumstances, the chapters on the theory of monetary policy and on monetary policy's effects on financial markets and institutions have been moved to Chapters 25 and 26. They can be read after Chapter 4 has been completed.

Second, the material on asset and liability management has been distributed among the relevant chapters on financial institutions. For example, the material on maturity and duration GAP is now introduced in Chapter 14, "Bank Management and Profitability." Chapter 14 also provides a detailed example of how interest rate risk affects the cash flows of commercial banks and shows how financial futures, options, and swaps can be used to manage the interest rate risk of commercial banks.

Third, we introduce the concepts of interest-rate risk and duration much earlier in the book. Chapter 5 now contains a more detailed treatment of bond prices, bond yields, and interest rate risk. The chapter explains the time value of money and then applies present value mathematics to bond pricing. Then, after describing various bond yield measures, the chapter explains how the characteristics of a bond affect bond price volatility. This leads to a discussion of interest rate risk and how duration can be used to measure and manage interest rate risk.

Fourth, Chapter 23, "Contemporary Issues Affecting Financial Institutions" has been updated to capture issues raised by the FDIC Improvement Act of 1991, including market value accounting and regulatory definitions of capital adequacy and deposit insurance risk. In addition, a new Chapter 24 "Contemporary Issues Affecting Financial Markets," has been added to discuss major regulatory issues affecting financial markets. That chapter first describes the way that various financial markets function. It then discusses issues related to "specialist" vs. "dealer" markets screen-based, 24-hour, and global trading; markets' information requirements and information access; margin requirements and risk-based capital requirements for financial risk exposures; trading limits; risk assessment procedures and guarantees; and regulatory arbitrage. It also discusses London's deregulatory "Big Bang" and the Olympia and York real estate bankruptcy.

Finally, every other chapter in the book has been updated or expanded to reflect current developments. For instance, Chapter 17 describes the major new regulations that were required by the 1991 FDIC Improvement Act and Chapter 18 discusses the operations of the Resolution Trust Corporation (RTC) in liquidating failed thrift institutions' assets. In addition, Chapter 11 now includes a section on swap markets and Chapter 12 includes a section that discusses factors determining exchange rates. Chapter 6, which covers the level of interest rates, now contains a section on the forecasting of interest rates. This section allows students to see how the theoretical determinants of interest rates lead to forecasts that are useful to financial institutions. Chapter 7, on the structure of interest rates, now has a section that discusses the effects of put options and conversion features on bond yields, in addition to the usual discussion of the call provision.

Chapter 9, on capital markets, has several new features. The chapter now contains detailed discussion of the informational, operational, and allocational efficiency of capital markets. Next, the chapter discusses the role of third-party financial guarantees in the capital markets. In addition, the chapter contains new sections on the globalization of equity markets, the beginnings of 24-hour trading in the U.S., and the success of the stock market as a predictor of economic activity. Chapter 20 on insurance companies and pension funds has been completely remotivated and updated. Rather than simply describing the balance sheets of insurance companies, the chapter now provides more detailed discussion of the economic role of insurance, pricing of insurance, and the management problems facing insurance companies. Chapter 21 now covers venture capitalists in addition to investment banks and investment funds. The venture capital firm is a new financial intermediary emerging in the last decade. In the 1970s, these firms managed only $3 billion of investments; now they manage over $30 billion. Venture capital firms are important sources of capital for new, rapidly growing firms.

Pedagogy

From a student viewpoint, the text contains a number of pedagogical points to make it more educational and interesting. Each chapter opens with a practical application of chapter concepts. Legends explain each figure and chart in the text. Two types of boxed items – "People and Events" and "Did You Know?" – pique student interest and provide interesting background or current events material for each chapter. Furthermore, each part opener of the book contains a profile in finance. The profiles describe successful young executives of various financial institutions and regulatory bodies. They show the dynamic world of finance as a potential arena for future careers and offer practical advice on achieving success in the financial world.

Finally, this edition has been printed in two colors, making headings, key concepts, box items, and graphic presentations easier to read.

Ancillary Package

For this edition of the book, we offer updated, complementary materials that should help both the students and the instructors who use the book. These include the following.

Instructor's Manual and Test Bank

This volume contains a wealth of useful teaching aids, including chapter-by-chapter objectives, key points, answers to end-of-chapter questions, and an outline of changes from the previous edition. Also, the *Instructor's Manual* offers transparency masters for instructors to use in illustrating their lectures. Finally, the *Test Bank*, including over 1,000 questions, has been updated.

Computerized Test Bank

The *Test Bank* is also available on disk for IBM PC and compatible computers. The program allows instructors to create and print their own tests from a pool of multiple-choice and true/false questions.

Study Guide

Written by David R. Durst of the University of Akron, students will find this tool to be a valuable part of the learning package. Each chapter provides a detailed summary, topic outline, key terms review, true/false and multiple-choice questions, problems, and solutions. Each chapter also includes a short "Career Planning" section designed to encourage students to begin thinking about their careers. There is a special "Supplementary Material" section that expands and applies each chapter's concepts to the real world by providing library reference and assignments and flow-of-funds data analyses assignments. In addition, each of the early chapters features a "How to Use *The Wall Street Journal*" section intended to acquaint students with the organization of the *WSJ*. In later chapters, specific sections, data tables, and other features that appear regularly in the *WSJ* are explained and assignments are made.

Organization of the Book

The organization of this book reflects the way we would teach an introductory course in the financial system. The book is designed so that, after Parts 1 and 2, some chapters can be omitted or sections assigned in alternative sequence without adversely affecting the flow of discussion. The book is organized into seven major sections.

Part 1 (Chapters 1-4) introduces the basic concepts and vocabulary necessary to understand the operation of the financial system. The first chapter introduces the student to the course and discusses the fundamentals of money, prices, and inflation. The basic elements of the financial system are presented in Chapter 2. These elements, when integrated, form a conceptual model of the financial system. Chapter 3 explains the economic, political, and regulatory forces that have shaped our current financial system; Chapter 4 explains the Federal Reserve System, how it manages the money supply, and the deposit expansion process of money for all financial institutions holding checkable deposits.

Part 2 (Chapters 5-7) provides a comprehensive introduction to interest rates, bond pricing, bond yields, and interest rate risk. Chapter 5 reviews present value mathematics and bond pricing. It then explains yield calculations, bond price volatility, interest rate risk, and how duration can be used to reduce interest rate risk. Next, Chapter 6 shows how firms' investment opportunities and consumers' time preferences interact to determine the equilibrium real rate of interest. Chapter 6 then discusses the effects of inflation on interest rates, the cyclical behavior of interest rates, and interest rate forecasting. Finally, Chapter 7 discusses how interest rates on financial instruments are influenced by their default risk, term to maturity, marketability, tax treatment, and option-like features such as call provisions, put options, and convertibility.

Part 3 (Chapters 8-12) describes the major financial markets in which commercial banks and other financial intermediaries participate, presenting discussions of money markets in Chapter 8, capital markets in Chapter 9, mortgage markets in Chapter 10, and futures, options, forward and swap markets in Chapter 11. Chapter 11 also stresses financial institutions' use of the futures markets to reduce interest or exchange rate risk. Chapter 12 discusses international flows of funds, the Eurodollar market and exchange rates.

Part 4 (Chapters 13-17) presents the operation, regulation, and structure of the commercial banking system. Banks have been selected for particular study because of the diversity of their business activity and because they are the primary transmitters of monetary policy. Once bank operations are understood, it is easier to understand the operations of other specialized, nonbank financial institutions. Chapter 13 describes bank operations by examining balance sheets. Chapter 14 then looks at how banks resolve the conflict between bank profitability and bank safety through the careful management of their assets and liabilities. Chapter 15 discusses important issues in bank structure, such as economies of scale, bank holding companies, bank branching, and interstate banking. Chapter 16 explains the regulatory environment affecting banks and other financial institutions, emphasizing the deposit insurance system and regulations adopted to try to prevent financial institution failures. Chapter 17 discusses international banking both from the perspective of U.S. banks operating abroad and foreign banks operating in the United States.

Part 5 (Chapter 18-22) is devoted to a description of important nonbank financial intermediaries in the nation's economy. The institutions discussed are savings and loan associations and mutual savings banks (Chapter 18); credit unions (Chapter 19); insurance companies and pension funds (Chapter 20); investment banks, venture capitalists, and investment funds (Chapter 21); and finance companies and financial conglomerates (Chapter 22).

Part 6 (Chapters 23-24) discusses issues that are of importance to contemporary managers of financial institutions. Chapter 23 discusses value-exchange and electronic funds transfer systems. It also discusses the regulatory environment in which depository institutions operate and some of the major regulatory issues that are of current interest, such as risk-based deposit insurance premiums, alternatives to deposit insurance, market value accounting, and capital adequacy requirements. Chapter 24 describes alternative ways in which financial markets function and describes issues related to their regulation and development. Computerized trading systems, 24-hour trading, risk-based capital requirements, margin requirements and trading limits, and international regulatory arbitrage processes are discussed.

Part 7 (Chapters 25-26) explains the effect of monetary policy on the financial system. Chapter 25 presents various theories of how monetary policy works. Chapter 26 discusses monetary policy's impact on financial markets and the economy as well as political influences on policy.

Possible Course Outlines

We have organized this book with a financial markets and institutions approach, which is the way we would suggest teaching an introductory financial systems course. However, depending on individual preference and course emphasis, there are alternative ways to organize the course. We have therefore written this book to allow a different ordering of the chapters. The only constraint in our flexible design is that Parts 1 and 2 should be assigned first, since these sections provide the conceptual foundation and vocabulary for the financial system regardless of subsequent topic emphasis. The following are some possible organizational sequences that we think could be successfully employed in using this book. Exhibit 1 shows a flow chart outlining possible alternative courses.

Financial Institutions Emphasis

After Parts 1 and 2 are completed, financial institutions can be introduced by turning directly to Part 4, *Commercial Banking.* Following completion of Parts 1, 2, and 4; Part 5, *Financial Institutions,* Part 6, *Contemporary Problems and Issues,* and Part 3, *Financial Markets,* can be covered. Part 7, *Monetary Policy,* need not be covered.

Money and Banking Emphasis

After Parts 1 and 2, the instructor may emphasize monetary policy by going directly to Part 7, *Monetary Policy.* Then the emphasis turns to banking by covering Part 4, *Commercial Banking.* Parts 5 and 6 follow and the course ends with Part 3, *Financial Markets.* As an option, some instructors may also wish to include Chapter 8, "Money Markets," before Part 7 in the sequence just described.

Financial Market Emphasis

This organization follows the current sequence of the text. Part 7, *Monetary Policy,* can be used to explain ways in which the financial markets are likely to be affected by changes in national economic policies.

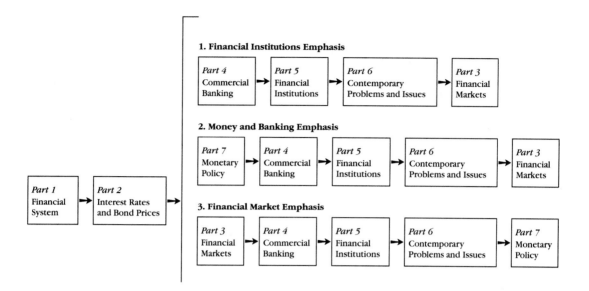

Note of Appreciation

As with any textbook, the authors owe an enormous debt of gratitude to many people. First, we would like to thank those who have taught, trained, and encouraged us throughout our academic careers: John B. Harbell, California State University at San Francisco; Michael H. Hopewell, University of Oregon; George G. Kaufman, Loyola University, Chicago; Dudley G. Luckett, Iowa State University; Jonas E. Mittelman, California State University at San Francisco; Joseph F. Sinkey, Jr., University of Georgia; the late Warren L. Smith, University of Michigan; Wolfgang Stolper, University of Michigan; Erik Thorbecke, Cornell University; James A. Verbrugge, University of Georgia; and Richard B. West, New York University. Special gratitude goes to Robert W. Johnson, Director of the Credit Research Center, Krannert Graduate School of Management, Purdue University, who provided valuable encouragement and advice during the inception of the book. We would also like to extend special thanks to I. Wylie Briscoe, who funded the I. Wylie and Elizabeth Briscoe Chair of Bank Management at Texas Tech University. In addition, we would like to thank our friends at Chemical Bank who provided valuable assistance in preparing the manuscript: Edward A. O'Neal, Jr., Tom Jacobs, Bill Linderman, Jeffrey Culpepper, Paul Nichols, John Lewis, and Gene Philippi. Also, we extend our thanks to David Durst of the University of Akron for preparing the teacher's manual and study guide, and to Marianne Pritchard and Vicki Peden of Touche Ross, who provided helpful information on thrift industry accounting and failures. A note of special thanks goes to the individuals from the financial community who kindly made time in their busy schedules to be interviewed for our career profiles. They include Sidney R. Bundrage, The Northern Trust Company; Charles Wickens, Iowa Grain Company; Darrell W. Naquin, Dai-Ichi Kangyo Bank; Ronald E. Alston, Trust Company Bank; Anthony S.W. Yeung, Daiwa International Capital Management; David Kelso, Office of Thrift Supervision; Mary Rosenbaum, Federal Reserve Bank of Atlanta.

We are also grateful to those who have painstakingly reviewed the various editions of this book and provided many helpful suggestions that have substantially improved our final product. For their work, we thank J. Amanda Adkisson, Sam Houston State University; Theodore A. Andersen, University of California, Los Angeles; Vincent P. Apilado, University of Texas,

Arlington; Nasser Arshadi, University of Missouri, St. Louis; James C. Baker, Kent State University; Howard W. Bohnen, St. Cloud State University; Sheldon D. Balbirer, University of North Carolina, Greensboro; Antony C. Cherin, San Diego State University; William Christiansen, Florida State University; Richard Dowen, Northern Illinois University; Gunter Dufey, University of Michigan at Ann Arbor; David Durst, University of Akron; Philip Friedman, Boston University; Joyce Furfero, St. John's University; Edward Gill, Boise State University; James Halloran, University of Notre Dame; John H. Hand, Auburn University; Paul Handorf, George Washington University; Chaman L. Jain, St. John's University; James Kehr, Miami University, Ohio; James M. Kelly, LaSalle College; H.C. Li, Bryant College; Michael Long, University of Illinois, Chicago; James Ludke, University of Massachusetts; Inayat U. Mangla, Western Michigan University; Joseph Mascia, Adelphi University; Ronald W. Masulis, Southern Methodist University; Robert C. McLeod, University of Alabama; Melanie McNeil, Northern Illinois University; Hormoz Movassaghi, Ithaca College; Theodore Muzio, St. John's University of Virginia; Vivian Nazar, Ferris State University; John Olienyk, Colorado State University; Robert Rogowski, Washington State University; Dexter R. Rowell, Old Dominion University; David Schauer, University of Texas at El Paso; Robert Schweitzer, University of Delaware; G.L. Suchanek, University of Iowa and University of Arizona; Ellen Torrance, First Colony Life Insurance Company; Peter Van Den Dool, University of Santa Clara; Richard B. Voss, Western Illinois University; William Wilbur, Northern Illinois University; Shee Wong, University of Minnesota, Duluth.

At the Dryden Press, we are very grateful to Millicent Treloar who once again provided many helpful suggestions and much support and guidance. Her persistence and patience are greatly appreciated. She also prepared the profiles in finance in this edition. We also thank Mike Roche, acquisitions editor and Ann Heath, formerly of Dryden Press, for her assistance during the developmental stage of the book. Jon Gregory performed superbly as project editor, and our thanks to Michael J. O'Neal, the copy editor on the fifth edition. We gratefully acknowledge the work of Carol A. Jordan, Eastern Kentucky University who revised Chapter 20 on insurance companies and pension funds; William L. Megginson, University of Georgia, who revised Chapter 16 on international banking; and John C. Yeoman, University of Georgia, who revised Chapter 21 on investment banks, venture capitalists, and investment funds. In addition, Rolando Pelaez of the University of Houston provided helpful comments on Chapter 3. Also, Bryant L. Brooks, Brian Greene, and Michael F. McRoberts, MBA students at the University of Georgia, permitted us to use their class project as a basis for our Bank of New England boxed item. Our thanks go to those who supplied valuable research assistance, especially Kathleen A. Farrell, University of Georgia and William Chittendem at Texas Tech University.

Finally, we would like to thank our families for their encouragement and for putting up with our many hours at the writing table. To all, thank you for your support and help.

David S. Kidwell
Minneapolis, Minnesota

Richard L. Peterson
Lubbock, Texas

David W. Blackwell
Athens, Georgia

Contents in Brief

Contents

FINANCIAL INSTITUTIONS, MARKETS, AND MONEY

1 THE FINANCIAL SYSTEM

PROFILE/Sidney Bundrage

SHE IS

Vice-president, Commercial Banking, The Northern Trust Company, promoted in 1991 from second vice-president. She manages banking services for large corporate accounts, companies with revenues of $125 million or more, in the Chicago area. In this capacity, she typically works with the client corporation's treasurer or vice-president of finance.

WHAT SHE DOES

She is responsible for arranging credit and credit extensions for her clients, work which entails financial analysis, assessment of client business strengths and weaknesses, assessment of client industry climate, and determination of client creditworthiness. She also oversees all bank services provided to her clients, including corporate cash management, payroll deposits and disbursements, and trust services such as administration of pension and profit-sharing programs. She manages twenty-three accounts covering the range of single to full bank services and spanning a diversity of industries from utilities and transportation to manufacturing and services. While managing her twenty-three current accounts, she actively pursues an average of twenty new business prospects from bringing in new clients to expanding services provided for existing clients.

HOW SHE GOT THERE

B.A.: Stanford University
M.BA: Northwestern University
First job: Kidder Peabody, New York, intern in investment research.

BACKGROUND

She grew up in Chicago, where she was a gifted student in the Chicago public schools through the seventh grade. Her parents—her mother a restaurant food and beverage director and her father a welder—were unhappy with the education she was receiving despite her being in a gifted program. Through friends of the family they arranged to transfer her in the eighth grade to the Evanston school system, one of the most prestigious in the country. There she found herself trailing her peers and resolved to catch up, which she did. She graduated from Evanston High School with honors and with the skills needed to propel her to both Stanford and Northwestern universities. Over the 5 years she spent in the Evanston schools, commuting back and forth to her home an hour and a half each way on the L system, she developed adroit time-management and reading skills along with her outstanding academic achievements. She now lives in Chicago in a Hyde Park brownstone she is rehabilitating, close to the neighborhood where she grew up. Her commute to her job in downtown Chicago is 10 minutes by car.

WHAT SHE LIKES BEST ABOUT HER JOB

The versatility and challenge of using all of her business skills: strategic planning, analytical, sales and marketing, management, and critically important business social skills. In addition to her daily responsibilities on the job, the Northern Trust encourages community involvement, enabling her to be very active, both in her sorority and in the National Black MBA Association. The Association's efforts focus on developing the best African-American business leaders and managers through a commitment to education. It also provides consulting services to small businesses, networking, and advice to minorities on issues pertinent to working in a corporation.

WORST NIGHTMARE

That one of her clients would file for bankruptcy. In managing the bank's risk on her accounts, she should be able to anticipate a client's problems and be proactive in solving them.

HOW SHE UNWINDS

Working out three or four times a week. Concerts and dinner with a core of college friends living in Chicago. Vacations to Jamaica and the Bahamas. She is considering taking up other building rehab projects in her community.

ADVICE

Utilize summers during college to gain exposure to formal business environments. Talk to people about their work to gain a better understanding of what career would be a good fit for you. Don't make yourself a specialist too early in your career. Make a difference, in your job and in your community.

3

MONEY AND THE FINANCIAL SYSTEM

1

THROWN INTO TURMOIL BY UNUSUALLY high inflation and interest rates in the late 1970s and by deregulation in the 1980s, the U.S. financial system faces in the 1990s the frustrating task of structural reorganization in an unstable environment. Shaping the new environment are formidable forces: economic, regulatory, and technological developments. The spoils of the volatile interest rates, disastrous bank and thrift failures, and two back-to-back recessions that formed the plots of the 1980s dramas have not yet been resolved. Exacerbating the search for solutions to these problems are new challenges spawned by massive levels of leveraged buyout activities on an international scale, by the collapse of the stock market in 1987, the subsequent collapse of the junk bond market, and the recession in the early 1990s. Thus, the fluid reconfiguration of the financial system—financial institutions, markets, and their products—continues to be an important element of the system's response to these forces.

To give you some idea how fluid the financial system has been, beginning in the early 1980s, for example, banks began to pay interest on checking accounts, thrifts offered checking accounts (called NOW accounts) for the first time, and interest rate ceilings were removed from all consumer deposit accounts. As the decade progressed, thrifts gained expanded business powers, and the distinction between banks and thrifts was blurred. States began to allow banks from other states to cross their borders to conduct banking business. Emboldened by their victories over regulation, banks entered into security underwriting, insurance, and retail brokerage businesses. At the same time, bank competitors, such as life insurance companies and Wall Street investment banking firms, entered the banking business, serving both consumer and commercial customers.

The purpose of the book is to help students intelligently and systematically sort out what will certainly be the sheer madness of the 1990s. The book will provide a comprehensive overview of the financial institutions, markets, and instruments that make up the U.S. financial system. The financial system is important to our economy because it facilitates the flow of funds from savers to borrowers, and efficient allocation of funds is necessary for the economy to reach its maximum output. Also, in the process of transferring funds, the financial system produces a myriad of financial services that businesses and consumers use daily. The products range from simple checking accounts and consumer loans to complex insurance and pension fund contracts.

This first chapter deals primarily with money. Money is a controversial topic in financial circles. Some economists argue that money is the "root of all evil," though not in a biblical sense. They blame money for high rates of inflation, high interest rates, economic recessions, and even swings in presidential elections. Powerful stuff, money! Given this panoply of potential sins, it is clear that money is an important variable in the economy and one worthy of study. The remainder of the chapter examines the nature and role of money in the U.S. economy.

What Is Money?

In one form or another, people have always used money. Grains, cattle, salt, wool, arrowheads, beads, shells, fishhooks, and metals all have been valued as money. Whale teeth served as currency in the Fiji Islands; in colonial America, tobacco functioned as money; during World War II and the Korean and Vietnam wars, cigarettes served as money in POW camps. These commodities served as money because people had confidence in their value and were willing to accept them as payment for debts. Much of the confidence resulted from a reasonable assurance that the supply of the substance used as money was limited. Thus the characteristic these primitive monies shared was scarcity. Two other traits of primitive monies were durability and divisibility. Because metal best meets these three requirements, metal coins have served as the primary form of money throughout recorded history. A discussion of the types of money follows.

Types of Money

Full-Bodied Money.   Early commodity-type monies are called *full-bodied money* because they were also valued for their own sake. Wool was valued as an exchange item, but it also had intrinsic value because it could be used to make clothing. Thus the holders of full-bodied money always held something of value should the commodity cease to be accepted as money. As long as the commodity's exchange value was above its intrinsic value (value as a commodity), it would serve as money. When the exchange value dropped below the intrinsic value, it could be used for its own sake.

Representative Money.   Representative money is money that is fully convertible into full-bodied money. It is usually made of paper but "represents" in circulation an amount of a commodity equal to the value of the money. An example of representative money was certified tobacco warehouse receipts that circulated in Virginia during colonial times; the receipts were fully backed and fully exchangeable for tobacco. The public was willing to accept the receipts as money because of its backing, and it was certainly more convenient to transact with than tobacco. Government-issued representative money is usually backed by precious metals (usually gold and silver), but the backing is often something less than 100 percent of the paper money's face value.

Credit Money.   Most modern monies are credit money in that they are backed by the government's promise to pay. The most common credit monies in our economy are issues of paper and checkable accounts at commercial banks. Paper monies have almost no intrinsic value, and modern coins with their reduced precious metal content do not fare much better. Credit monies circulate as money only because people are willing to accept them for purchases of goods and services or for debt payments. In the United States today, all money in circulation is credit money. Prior to 1933 there were gold coins in circulation with gold content equal to the face values of the coins. These coins would be classified as full-bodied money. Today they do not circulate and are held primarily by collectors.

Currency.   Any form of money that can be passed from hand to hand in an exchange transaction is currency. Thus, most representative and credit monies are currencies. Full-bodied monies, such as cattle, usually are not currency; however, cigarettes are.

The Role of Money in an Economy

What important function does money perform for society that makes its existence so enduring? Early civilizations discovered that the use of money allowed for division of labor and specialization. It had become apparent that a community's total output was greater if an individual could specialize in a few tasks rather than being the proverbial jack-of-all-trades and master of none. An individual specializing as a cobbler, for instance, could become more expert and productive if that person did not also have to function as a blacksmith. Thus some people would specialize as hunters, others as farmers, and so on. In general, people would engage in whatever tasks were necessary for the community's well-being. Specialization is not without problems, however. No one could specialize in a particular good or service unless it could easily be exchanged for food and other necessities of life.

The primary function of money, then, is to facilitate exchange. Of course, exchange could always take place by barter, but barter exchange is complicated and relatively inefficient. In a barter economy, for example, a shoemaker who wants wheat for bread must find a farmer who wants shoes. If the shoemaker has just made a pair of $16\frac{1}{2}$ triple-E shoes, it may prove difficult to find a person who is both a giant and a farmer. Thus a major problem in a barter economy is that of double coincidence—finding two people each desiring the other's output.

Another problem is how to price goods and services. In the preceding example, suppose the shoemaker found two giants who wanted the $16\frac{1}{2}$ triple-E shoes but who had commodities other than wheat to trade. The first giant offers two chickens for the shoes, and the second giant offers a complete set of the 1986 Chicago Bears Superbowl champion bubble gum trading cards. The cobbler quickly recalls that ten loaves of bread trade for one chicken, and the bubble gum cards trade for fifteen loaves of bread. The astute shoemaker goes for the two chickens. Anyway, if he's made a bad deal, at least he can eat the chickens.

In following this example, it is easy to see how one can quickly become confused by the growing number of prices. The problem with a barter economy is that every good must be priced in terms of every other good, resulting in a large number of exchange rates (prices) that make trade difficult. For example, in a primitive society with only 10 commodities, we would need to keep in mind 45 prices in a barter economy but only

---

Exhibit 1–1

Relationship between the Number of Commodities and Prices in Money and Barter Economies

	Number of Prices	
Number of Commodities	**Money Economy**	**Barter Economy**
5	5	10
10	10	45
1,000	1,000	499,500
1,000,000	1,000,000	499,999,500,000

In a barter economy, the number of prices increases rapidly as the number of commodities sold increases. In a money economy, in contrast, there is one price for each commodity.

---

10 different prices in a money economy (see Exhibit 1-1).[1] With 1,000 goods in a barter economy, the total number of prices would skyrocket to 499,500, and in a highly developed economy such as ours, the number of prices would be inconceivably large.

In sum, the introduction of money in trade increased the welfare of both users and the community in two ways. First, money reduced the time and effort involved in exchange. Second, it allowed for division of labor and specialization.

The Properties of Money

Money is usually defined as anything used to make payment for goods, services, or debt obligations. This definition of money is not a legal one, but it emphasizes the behavioral or psychological aspects of money. In a sense, money is whatever people believe others will accept as payment. However, economists generally identify three basic properties of money. Money must serve as a:

1. Medium of exchange;
2. Store of value;
3. Unit of account.

Medium of Exchange.   The most self-evident property of money is that it is used to purchase goods and services. Most people acquire money by engaging in a specialized skill and use it to purchase goods and services from others. Actually, goods and services are exchanged for other goods and services; money merely facilitates the exchange process.

Store of Value.   People today want money not only for exchange but also for goods and services they may want to purchase in the future. In addition, people may

---

[1] The formula for computing the number of possible combinations of N things taken two at a time is:

$$C = N(N-1)/2,$$

where C is the total number of combinations and N is the number of items.

hold money as a precaution for such contingencies as loss of a job or medical emergencies. Thus money serves as a means of temporarily storing purchasing power. That is, we would like a unit of money to buy the same amount of goods and services in the future as it does today. If money were to lose its purchasing power rapidly, households or businesses would not want to save and they would find it difficult to buy goods or services for large dollar amounts over time.

Of course, money is not the only way to store value. Stocks, bonds, savings accounts, and life insurance policies also store value and may provide a higher return. Unfortunately, many of these items do not serve well as a medium of exchange. There are also significant transaction costs in converting these assets back into money. It is not critical that money serve as the optimal means of storing purchasing power, but it must at least serve as a reasonable store of value.

Unit of Account.   In a complex economy, the exchange price of all goods and services is expressed in units of money. For example, in the United States all prices are expressed in terms of the dollar and in England in terms of the pound sterling. Examples of other units of account are the peso, lira, franc, deutsche mark, yen, and ruble. These are all abstract units of measure, just as kilogram and ounce are abstract units of weight. The property of money as a unit of account permits the pricing of goods and services in terms of the same standard of value.

Definition of Money Today

What is money? Theoretically, money should possess the three properties discussed in the previous section. Unfortunately, no single substance perfectly satisfies all three functions. Furthermore, there is no agreement by economists about which property is the most important. Some emphasize the medium of exchange property and define money as coins and currency in circulation and checkable accounts at financial institutions. Others view money as the group of financial assets most closely related to aggregate levels of economic activity. As a result, a number of definitions of money are used by economists and government officials. The following are the alternative definitions of money used by the Federal Reserve System (the Fed):

M1 = Currency; checkable deposits at commercial banks; checkable deposits at credit unions and thrift institutions (NOW, ATS, and share-draft accounts); and traveler's checks outstanding.[2]

M2 = M1 + noncheckable savings accounts and small-denomination time deposits (less than $100,000) at depository institutions, money market deposit accounts, shares in money market mutual funds, and retail repurchase agreements.

M3 = M2 + large-denomination time deposits ($100,000 and over) at depository institutions, shares in institution-only money market funds, and large-denomination repurchase agreements.

L = M3 + all other liquid financial assets such as banker's acceptances, commercial paper, short-term Treasury securities, and U.S. savings bonds.

[2] Thrift institutions are defined as savings and loan associations and mutual savings banks.

The Transaction Approach

M1 is the narrowest definition of money and reflects money's property as a medium of exchange. Proponents of the transaction approach believe that money is the only asset held by the public that is generally accepted for payment of goods and services. They stress that this is the important difference between money and other assets. That is, although all assets serve as a store of value, only a few are accepted as a medium of exchange.

The Store of Value Approach

Some economists prefer broader definitions of money, such as M2 and M3, definitions that reflect money's role as a store of value. They recognize that financial market innovations, such as money market mutual fund shares and repurchase agreements, can serve as money.

These financial market innovations offer investors liquidity and rates of return comparable to open market rates.[3]

The economists who advocate the broader definitions of money do so because empirical evidence suggests that these definitions are most closely related to national income. Such economists are called *monetarists*. Monetarists like Milton Friedman believe that controlling the money supply is critical to government policies in controlling unemployment, inflation, and the economy's rate of output.

Monetarists reason that in a money economy, the sale of one commodity is separated from the purchase of another commodity. During the time between the sale and purchase, the seller does not always have to retain the sale proceeds in the form of the medium of exchange (M1); other financial assets that are close substitutes for the medium of exchange can be held, and these assets may be a superior store of purchasing power. Thus, if these assets are considered by the public to be close substitutes for the medium of exchange (M1), then the relevant variable for conducting monetary policy includes both the medium of exchange (M1) and the close substitutes (M2 or M3).

The Money Supply

A natural question at this point is: Where does this money come from? The actual mechanism of generating the nation's money supply and controlling its level is quite complex and will be discussed later in this book. As Exhibit 1–2 shows, as of April 1991 the nation's money supply varied from $853 to $4,986 billion, depending on which definition of money one selected. The supply of money at any time is the result of the interaction of (1) the Federal Reserve System, (2) the commercial banking system, (3) the public, and (4) thrift institutions. The ultimate control over the nation's money stock, however, is considered to reside with the nation's central bank—the Federal Reserve System. By controlling the money supply, the Federal Reserve System helps stabilize economic activity.

---

[3] An *open market* is an economic area of exchange in which all qualified buyers and sellers can participate. The number of participants is large, and the market rate of interest is determined impersonally by the forces of supply and demand.

Exhibit 1–2	**Money Supply, April 1991**			
Definition	**Billions**	**Percentage of L**	**Degree of Liquidity**
Currency and travelers checks	$ 265	5.3	Highest
Demand deposits	276	5.5	•
Other checkable deposits	302	6.1	•
M1	853	17.1	•
M2	3,397	68.1	•
M3	4,180	83.8	•
L	4,986	100.0	Lowest

M1 and M2 are the measures of money most widely used by economists and the Fed.
Source: Federal Reserve Bulletin, July 1991.

Liquidity of an Asset

When we discuss the operation and management of financial institutions later in this book, an important concept will be the ease with which an asset can be converted into money. The difficulty of converting an asset into money depends on the *liquidity* of the asset. Liquidity is defined as the ease of converting an asset (either financial or real) into money (M1) quickly without loss of income or principal. M1 is regarded as the most liquid of all financial assets, for it represents immediate command over goods and services in the marketplace. Other definitions of money (M2, M3, and L) that contain assets such as savings accounts or Treasury securities are less liquid than M1. Generally speaking, real assets, such as housing or inventories, are less liquid than financial assets.

There are two dimensions to liquidity: (1) the transaction costs of converting to money, and (2) the risk that the investor will sell an asset for less than the price at which it was purchased (price risk). Transaction costs are broadly defined and refer to the costs of search, information, transportation, and time, plus any fees involved in converting the assets into money. In functional notation, the liquidity of an asset can be expressed as:

$$L = f(\overline{TC}, \ \overline{PR}), \tag{1-1}$$

where TC = transaction costs and PR = price risk. The sign above the factor tells the direction of causation. The higher the transaction cost of converting an asset into money, the lower the liquidity of that asset; similarly, the higher the price risk of rapid conversion into money, the lower the asset's liquidity.

The Value of Money

Everyone complains that a dollar just isn't worth what it used to be, that the value of the dollar has declined. What is the value of money people speak about so frequently?

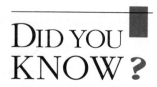

DID YOU KNOW?

Marx and Conservative Politicians on Gold

For most of recorded history, gold has served as money. Gold has reigned supreme as *the* standard of value because of its persistent scarcity and extreme durability. There has been a persistent feeling in some quarters that money cannot be "good" unless it is tied to some commodity—namely, gold.

When a country's currency is defined in terms of a specific amount of gold and the currency is freely convertible into gold, the country's monetary system is said to be on the *gold standard*. Interestingly, the critical use of gold as money seems to know no political boundaries. Marx (Karl, not Groucho) dryly commented that "only in so far as paper money represents gold...is it a symbol of value." More recently, some conservative economists and politicians have called for the United States to return to the gold standard.

The United States officially went on the gold standard with passage of the Gold Standard Act of 1900. The act defined the dollar in terms of gold—23.22 grains to a dollar. However, paper money began to lose its glitter as the percentage of gold reserves backing paper money was repeatedly lowered by Congress. Finally, in 1968, gold was no longer required to back paper money.

Today, the question of returning to the gold standard is being given serious consideration. A return to the gold standard would back U.S. money by gold so that the U.S. monetary gold stock would regulate the money supply. Critics of the gold standard charge that the nation's money supply would be substantially influenced by the production of gold, gold discoveries, or other economic forces affecting the price of gold. These persons prefer to have the quantity of credit adjusted by a central bank to meet the needs of the economy rather than having it be left to the precarious whims of a commodity market.

Proponents of the gold standard contend that the "flexibility" or ease with which credit money can be created (issued) is precisely the problem. They argue that the free-wheeling and expansionary monetary policy pursued by the Federal Reserve System since the late 1960s was the primary cause of the persistent and higher rates of inflation that plagued the U.S. economy during the late 1970s and early 1980s. They see a return to the gold standard as the best practical way to keep inflation under control.

Does the value of money refer to the amount of gold in Fort Knox or the worth of other resources owned by the federal government? The answer is no. The value of money is what you can buy with it—its purchasing power.

The value of money may change over time. For example, if $100 buys a case of quality California wine today and a year from now $100 buys only three-fourths of a case of the same wine, the value of money has declined by 25 percent relative to the value of wine. Of course, we value money in terms of the full spectrum of commodities it can purchase. At the same time the value of the dollar is declining with respect to wine, it may be increasing with respect to automobiles or television sets. Thus the value of money is determined by the prices of a broad range of goods and services it will buy in the economy. The spectrum of goods and services that money will buy is measured by a *price index*. An inverse relationship exists between price levels and the value of money. This relationship can be summarized in functional form:

$$VM = f(\overline{PL}),\qquad\qquad(1\text{-}2)$$

where VM = value of money and PL = a price index. Thus as price levels increase (decrease), the value of money decreases (increases).

Inflation

A great deal of public rhetoric has been advanced regarding *inflation*. *Inflation* is defined as the continuing rise in the average level of prices. In other words, inflation occurs when more prices rise than fall. In the United States, inflation dominated trends in price movements in the 1970s and early 1980s, as shown in Exhibit 1–3. Specifically, in 1973–1974 prices accelerated, and in 1979 the rate of inflation was 13.3 percent, the highest rate in U.S. peacetime history. Then two back-to-back recessions in 1980 and 1982, caused primarily by restrictive monetary policy, reduced inflation to the 4 percent range by the mid-1980s. Inflation then began to creep upward in the late 1980s and during the early 1990s recession.

The major problem with inflation is that it causes wealth transfers between parties of a financial contract if the inflation is unanticipated or if the parties are unable to adjust to the anticipated inflation. An example is people on fixed incomes, who may anticipate inflation but cannot alter their income stream. Retired people are particularly likely to experience such difficulties. On the other hand, if inflation is anticipated correctly and the appropriate adjustments are made, no wealth transfer occurs and inflation has no economic effect. Unfortunately, in the real world, this is rarely the case.

The reasons for inflation will be examined in greater detail later in the book. At this point, it is important to understand that inflation is the result of excessive growth in

Exhibit 1–3   Annual Rates of Inflation (CPI) for the Economy (1965–1990)

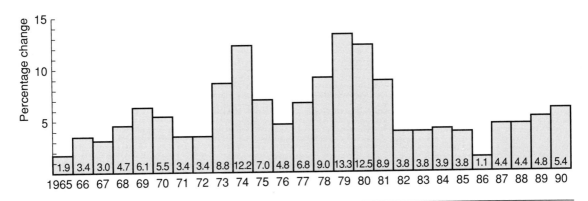

The inflation rate for the U.S. economy peaked in 1979. Then two back-to-back recessions (1980 and 1982) dramatically reduced the inflation rate, but at the expense of high unemployment. Inflation crept higher during the late 1980s and early 1990s.

Source: Economic Report of the President. 1991.

aggregate demand relative to aggregate supply. When the quantity of goods and services demanded at prevailing prices exceeds the available supply, prices tend to rise. When the supply of goods and services available for consumption at prevailing prices exceeds the quantity demanded, prices tend to decline. Thus the fundamental cause of inflation is an imbalance between supply and demand. Finally, we need to distinguish between the causes of inflation and the symptoms of inflation. The fundamental cause of inflation is the imbalance between supply and demand; the symptom of inflation is rising prices. Rising prices do not cause inflation.

Price Indexes

Economists and the public are concerned about whether prices are rising or falling and by how much. This information is an important input for economic decision making with respect to revenues and expenditures. It is particularly important to consumers. Changes in prices tell something about the cost of living and what is happening to the purchasing power of the dollar. Changes in the general level of prices are easiest to measure by converting individual price changes into a price index. A price index is constructed by selecting a representative group of commodities, called a *market basket*, and tracing the commodities' price changes from period to period.[4] For each time period, the index is constructed by dividing the cost of the market basket at the present time by its cost in a period selected as the base period. Prices in the base period are typically established at 100 percent. The resulting price index shows relative price changes from period to period. If prices rise, the price index will be greater than 100; if they fall, prices will be less than 100; if prices stay the same, the index will remain at 100.

Percentage changes in price levels relative to the base year can be computed easily. For example, if a price index rises from 100 to 120, we know that the average price of the commodities composing the index has increased 20 percent $(120 - 100/100)$. If the index increases in the next period from 120 to 140, the increase is only 16.7 percent $(140 - 120/120)$ because the starting period for our calculation was 120. The change of the entire two periods is 40 percent $(140 - 100/100)$. Note that changes from the base period are automatically shown as percentages, whereas changes between other time periods must be calculated. Percentage change calculations are computed as:

$$\Delta P = \frac{(P_t - P_{t-1})}{P_{t-1}} \times 100, \qquad (1-3)$$

where ΔP = percentage change in prices between periods, P_t = price in period t, and P_{t-1} = price in the past period, period $t - 1$.

---

[4] Most price indexes are fixed-weight indexes, in which the weights are relative quantities as of some base period. The formula for this type of index is

$$PI_t = \Sigma p_t p_0 / \Sigma p_0 q_0$$

where PI_t is the value of the price index in the current period, p_t are the various component prices in the current period, p_0 are component prices in the base period, and q_0 are the component quantities in the base period. Both the consumer price index and the producer price index are examples of this type of index.

Widely Used Price Indexes

There are three widely used price indexes: the consumer price index (CPI), the producer price indexes (PPI), and the national income deflators. Two deflators based on national income are currently used: the GNP (Gross National Product) deflator and the GDP (Gross Domestic Product) deflator. Each of these price indexes is estimated by the federal government and represents the average behavior of prices of the goods and services that compose the index. Exhibit 1–4 shows the CPI, PPI, and national income deflators for the years 1970 through 1990. For the CPI, the base period is 1982–1984, for which the index is set equal to 100 percent; for the PPI and GNP deflator, the base period is 1982; for the GDP deflator, the base period is 1987.

Exhibit 1–4

Consumer Price Index, Producer Price Index, and National Income Deflators (1970–1990)[a]

Year	CPI	PPI[b]	GDP Deflator	GNP Deflator
1970	38.8	39.3	35.1	42.0
1971	40.5	40.5	37.0	44.4
1972	41.8	41.8	38.8	46.5
1973	44.4	45.6	41.3	49.5
1974	49.3	52.6	44.9	54.0
1975	53.8	58.2	49.2	59.3
1976	56.9	60.8	52.3	63.1
1977	60.6	64.7	55.9	67.3
1978	65.2	69.8	60.3	72.2
1979	72.6	77.6	65.5	78.6
1980	82.4	88.0	71.7	85.7
1981	90.9	96.1	78.9	94.0
1982	96.5	100.0	83.8	100.0
1983	99.6	101.6	87.2	103.9
1984	103.9	103.7	91.0	107.7
1985	107.6	104.7	94.4	110.9
1986	109.6	103.2	96.9	113.9
1987	113.6	105.4	100.0	117.7
1988	118.3	108.0	103.9	121.7
1989	124.0	113.6	108.4	126.3
1990	130.7	119.2	112.9	131.5

Prices have increased almost every year since 1970. Inflation is virtually a fact of life.

[a] The base years for the CPI are 1982–1984, and the base year for the PPI and the implicit GNP deflator is 1982. The base year for the GDP deflator is 1987.

[b] Producer price index for finished goods.

Source: Bureau of Labor Statistics, Department of Commerce, various issues of *Economic Indicators*, prepared for the Joint Economic Committee by the Council of Economic Advisors, and The Economic Report of the President, 1991 and 1992.

As can be seen from the exhibit, in recent years there has been a persistent upward trend in prices (inflation) and a corresponding decline in the value of money. We shall now briefly describe each of these indexes.

Consumer Price Index

The CPI is the most quoted of all price indexes. It measures the change in prices of goods and services purchased by a typical urban working-class family. The CPI measures the total cost of a market basket of some 400 goods and services. These come from six broad categories: food, housing, clothing, transportation, medical care, and entertainment. The items and their relative weights in constructing the CPI are shown in Exhibit 1–5. The prices are collected monthly from about 18,000 retail stores in 56 cities. The national CPI is computed by weighting the indexes of the 56 cities according to population. Because the items included in the CPI market basket are representative of most household purchasing patterns, the CPI is considered to be the most reliable measure of the cost of living for most American families.

Producer Price Index

The PPI focuses on the prices paid by businesses rather than those paid by consumers. The prices used are those charged on large-volume transactions in wholesale markets in which the buyers and sellers are primarily business firms. Prices are collected monthly from establishments that voluntarily return questionnaires on about 2,800 commodities classified into three stages of processing: crude materials, intermediate materials and supplies, and finished goods. Price indexes are published for each stage of processing and by commodity. Exhibit 1–4 shows the producer price index for finished goods.

Because producer price movements tend to be more volatile than price movements in retail markets, the PPI is considered to be a more sensitive measure of price pressures than the CPI. In addition, because many items measured in the PPI are

---

Exhibit 1–5   **Relative Importance of Items Included in the Consumer Price Index**

Category	Percent
Housing	42.7
Transportation	18.7
Food and beverages	17.8
Clothing	6.5
Medical care	4.8
Entertainment	4.4
Other goods and services	5.1
Total	100.0

Source: U.S. Department of Labor, Bureau of Labor Statistics, "The Consumer Price Index: 1987 Revision," Report 736, January 1987.

measured in the CPI, changes in the PPI have tended to precede changes in the CPI. However, this is not always true. The primary reason that the PPI is more volatile lies in the difference in the composition of the market baskets of the two indexes. Because the producer price index does not include services, the movement of the two indexes may differ when price changes for services differ materially from other price changes.

National Income Deflators

Two widely quoted national income deflators are used in the United States. Both are calculated by the Department of Commerce and are by-products of the national income and production accounts. First is the Gross National Product (GNP) deflator, which represents an adjustment of all final goods and services included in the GNP estimate. GNP is an estimate of the dollar value at current market prices of all final goods and services produced by the residents of a country both at home and abroad in a given year. The GNP deflator is used to adjust GNP data for price level changes so GNP data can be compared in real terms.

Second is the Gross Domestic Product (GDP) deflator, which was introduced by the Commerce Department in 1992. The GDP deflator is a price index derived from GDP estimates. The GDP is the dollar value at current market prices of all final goods and services produced within a country in a given year. Although different in concept, GNP and GDP for the United States show essentially the same pattern of past cyclical and trend movements. Note that the GDP of a country includes the goods and services produced within the geographical boundaries of that country, whereas the GNP includes the goods and services produced by a country's residents regardless of location. Because of their comprehensiveness, the GDP and the GNP deflators are the best measures of overall price changes in an economy.

The Commerce Department is shifting its emphasis to the GDP over the GNP for a number of reasons. First is that conceptually the GDP is more consistent with other indicators of U.S. economic performance such as employment, industrial production, and retail sales. Second, the GDP is the primary measure of production in most of the rest of the world. Whether the GDP is greater or less than the GNP depends primarily on the amount of foreign investment in a country relative to the amount the country has invested abroad. For most major industrial countries that invest heavily abroad, the GDP tends to be less than the GNP, although the differences are small. For example, in 1990 the ratio of GDP/GNP for the United States was 99.8 percent, and for Germany and Japan the ratios were 98.9 and 99.3 percent, respectively. In developing countries such as Mexico and Chile, the GDP is larger than the GNP by 5 percent or more.

How to Use Price Indexes

Price indexes tell us something about the purchasing power of the dollar. Looking at Exhibit 1–4, we see that in 1990 the CPI was 130.7. This means that from the base period of 1982–1984 to 1990, prices rose 30.7 percent. Changes in the purchasing power of the dollar can be computed by taking the reciprocal of the CPI times 100. Thus the purchasing power of a dollar in 1990 was $\frac{1}{130.7}$, or .77 of a dollar during the base period (1982–1984). That is, a dollar in 1990 purchased 77 percent of the goods and services that it would have purchased during the base period.

The fluctuating purchasing power of the dollar suggests that decision makers should base economic decisions on *real* rather than *nominal* values. *Nominal values* are those observed in the market and reflect price-level changes. *Real values* are nominal values adjusted for price-level changes and thus reflect only changes in physical output. If there are no price-level changes during a period, the nominal and real values will be the same. However, if prices change during a period, the nominal value will differ from the real value by the amount of the price-level change.

To illustrate the importance of using real terms in decision making, take the example of two individuals during the high-inflation years of the early 1980s. Each earned a salary of $20,000 in 1980 and received a $1,500 raise at the beginning of 1981. How should they have responded to this "good" news? Mr. Nominal was delighted—$1,500 is a lot of money anytime and, anyway, bigger is always better. Ms. Real, however, understood that the reason we want money is for what we can buy with it. A person is economically better off only when his or her purchasing power is increased. A quick calculation using the CPI figures from Exhibit 1–4 shows that in terms of 1980 dollars, the two individuals' real income decreased from $20,000 to $19,490 even though their nominal income increased from $20,000 to $21,500:

$$
\begin{array}{ll}
\text{1980} & \text{1981} \\
\text{dollars} & \text{dollars} \\
| & | \\
\$20{,}000 & \$21{,}500 \\
\$19{,}490 \leftarrow\!\!\!\!\!-\!\!\!-\!\!\!-\!\!\!-\!\!\!-\!\!\!-\!\!\!-\!\!\!\!\rfloor &
\end{array}
$$

That $21,500 when converted into 1980 purchasing-power dollars is equivalent to only $19,490. Thus $21,500 in 1981 bought fewer goods and services than did $20,000 in 1980. Therefore, to compare dollars of one time period against dollars of another period, the dollars must be converted to a common purchasing base. In that way the dollars are comparable because they represent the same amount of purchasing power.

To convert dollars into real terms or a common base period, the following formula can be used:

$$D_1 = D_2 \times \frac{PI_1}{PI_2}, \tag{1–4}$$

where:

$$
\begin{aligned}
D_1 &= \text{dollars in Period 1 purchasing-power units;} \\
D_2 &= \text{dollars in Period 2 purchasing-power units;} \\
PI_1 &= \text{price index for Period 1;} \\
PI_2 &= \text{price index for Period 2.}
\end{aligned}
$$

In our example, we convert 1981 income to 1980 dollars as follows:

$$\$19{,}490 = \$21{,}500 \times \frac{82.4}{90.9}.$$

Finally, note that if economic decision makers are aware of price-level increases, they will attempt to adjust nominal values for the increases and will base all decisions on deflated, or real, values. If price-level changes are not anticipated or adjusted for, they will cause wealth transfers between the parties of a contract. In our example, the salaried workers needed to have an increase in nominal income of 10.3 percent $((90.9 - 82.4)/82.4)$ just to maintain their standard of living.

The Importance of Money

We have stressed the importance of money. First, money is a prerequisite for establishing a highly industrialized economy. Money frees society from the time-consuming double coincidence of wants and from an incomprehensible number of prices that earmark a barter economy. Second, money is the keystone to establishing a financial system that allows money-earning income units to achieve purchasing power that can be spent or saved. In such a financial system, funds are transferred between those wishing to save and those wishing to spend more than their current-period income. Finally, money has an important effect on the level of aggregate economic activity. Evidence suggests that increases in the supply of money lead to increases in the aggregate level of income, prices, and employment. Conversely, decreases in the supply of money reduce aggregate levels of income, prices, and employment. Although most economists generally agree that "money matters," there is disagreement about the precise relationship between money and economic activity and about the proper role of the Federal Reserve System in managing the nation's money supply.

To illustrate how money affects the economy, suppose that the money supply is reduced. With less money, the demand for goods and services will be reduced. Retailers and other merchants may reduce prices to some extent, but they will also reduce orders for inventory from suppliers. These suppliers will have to reduce production, lay off workers, and reduce orders to their suppliers. If workers have fewer job possibilities and smaller incomes, they will cut their spending, causing other retailers and businesses to face a reduction in the demand for their goods. As these effects are transmitted throughout the economy over time, the result will be a decline in the nation's output of goods and services as measured by GNP (or GDP). Prices will decline because of reduced demand by consumers, and unemployment will increase.

The Federal Reserve System controls the size of the nation's money stock through monetary policy actions. The major variables in the linkage scheme (or road map) along which monetary policy travels through the economy from the time policy actions are taken by the Federal Reserve are shown in Exhibit 1–6. Suppose the

---

Exhibit 1–6   **Transmission Mechanism for Monetary Policy**

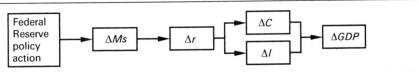

Money is an important economic variable. Changes in the rate of growth of the money supply affect key economic variables such as interest-rate levels, inflation, GDP, and unemployment.

Federal Reserve decides to stimulate the economy by increasing the money supply (ΔMs). This action leads to a temporary decrease in the level of interest rates (Δr), and these lower interest rates stimulate both business investment (ΔI) and consumer spending (ΔC), which, in turn, lead to higher production and lower unemployment in the economy. The net effect is an increase in nominal gross domestic product (ΔGDP). If the money supply is decreased, the reverse is true.

Though our discussion at this point is highly simplified, history provides ample evidence that an insufficient amount of money hampers business activity, induces a slowdown of spending, and results in a decline in income. On the other hand, too much money stimulates spending that outstrips the current supply of goods and services, which results in inflation. In sum, money is one of the most important economic variables in the economy, and, as a result, contemporary governments consider monetary management an integral part of their economic responsibilities. In the United States, the Federal Reserve System has the responsibility of managing the nation's money supply.

Summary

This chapter presents some background information on money, prices, and inflation.

Money is defined as any substance that is used to make payment for goods and services or debt obligations. Items that successfully serve as money must function as a medium of exchange, a store of value, and a unit of account. There is controversy among economists about which substance best serves these three functions. The supply of money is determined by the public, the commercial banking system, and the Federal Reserve System. However, the Federal Reserve System—our nation's central bank—has the ultimate control over the money supply.

The value of money is its purchasing power—what you can buy with it. An inverse relationship exists between general price-level movements and the value of money. Thus, the value of money is not always constant, and its value may change over time. The CPI, PPI, and the national income deflators (GNP or GDP) are the most widely used measures of price levels. Inflation is defined as the continuous rise in the average price level. The major problem with inflation is that it causes wealth transfers between parties of financial contracts. The fundamental cause of inflation is an imbalance between aggregate supply and demand.

The supply of money is one of the most important economic variables in an industrial economy. There is strong evidence that changes in the supply of money have a substantial effect on the level of aggregate economic activity: Too much money causes inflation, and too little money causes recession. Monetary management is an important part of government economic programs. Monetary policy is conducted by the Federal Reserve System by increasing or decreasing the nation's money supply.

Questions

1. How does the introduction of money into a barter economy affect the welfare of society?
2. What are the principal properties that allow a good to successfully serve as money? Which of these properties is most important? Defend your choice.

PEOPLE
& EVENTS

Bolivia's Hyperinflation: Money to Burn

Long notorious for political coups and cocaine deals, Bolivia became a "celebrity country" among economists when its inflation rate averaged 12,000 percent during 1985. And during the chaotic hyperinflation years of 1982–1985, inflation reached a cumulative rate of 24,000 percent, the seventh highest inflation rate recorded in the world!

What did hyperinflation mean to the average Bolivian? Truck drivers in La Paz carried their money in burlap sacks, because the devalued pesos were too bulky to fit into their pants' pockets. Housewives rushed to market to do their weekly shopping, because food prices were marked up daily, and sometimes more often. The price of bread could go up 10 percent or more in a matter of hours, not days. Movie ticket prices would often rise while patrons were waiting in line. That's inflation. In short, a great deal of productive time was spent by the average Bolivian trying to adjust to inflation and protect their purchasing power. Not a good use of time.

Bolivia pulled itself out of the hyperinflation morass with tough economic policies imposed by the government of then-president Victor Paz Estenssoro. The government announced a tight monetary policy, and resolved it would not spend more pesos than it collected in revenues. Furthermore, it devalued the Bolivian peso by a massive 90 percent, and then let the peso float in a daily dollar auction.

Within months, the hyperinflation abated and the annual rate of inflation for 1986 was less than 10 percent. The cost of fighting inflation was not free, however, because economic growth crept at a sluggish 2 percent annual rate during the 1986–1987 period and unemployment hovered near 20 percent.

There were other hidden and unexpected costs to hyperinflation. During the hyperinflation years, so much money was in circulation physically that the central bank had to rent a series of huge warehouses to store over 900 tons of bank notes. Bankers complained to the central bank that the bulk of money bags lying around the banks impeded day-to-day banking operations. When the hyperinflation was over, the central bank had to spend $130,000 to burn money in the state smelting plant at Vinto in Ororo State; the ovens were in operation around the clock in 8-hour shifts for 34 days, were manned by 40 employees of the central bank, and were fed by 30-ton railcars carrying 15,000 sixty-kilo bags of money. After all of this, it was necessary to dig a large hole near the plant to bury the ashes.

Though hyperinflation has its lighter sides, it is intolerable economically. At the limit, domestic money ceases to mean anything and transactions become increasingly conducted in foreign currencies, such as the dollar. Following Bolivia's hyperinflation period, 68 percent of all Bolivian bank deposits were in U.S. dollars.

3. Discuss the controversies over the definitions of money.
4. List five assets that you own and rank them in order of their liquidity. Justify your ranking scheme.
5. What is the value of money? How can it be measured? What is the relationship between prices and the value of money?
6. What are the major problems of using full-bodied money rather than paper money?
7. What characteristics distinguish money from other stores of wealth?

8. Explain the meaning of the following terms: (a) full-bodied money, (b) representative money, (c) credit money, and (d) currency.
9. In 1983, Kathy Farrell's income was $30,000. In 1990, after several promotions, her income has risen to $40,000. Is Kathy better off in 1990 than in 1983? (Hint: Exhibit 1–4 may prove to be helpful.)
10. Why do many economists consider money to be such an important economic variable? Explain why too much money in the economy leads to inflation and why too little leads to recession.
11. What is the fundamental cause of inflation? Since economists tell us that we all have insatiable wants for goods and services, does this mean that consumers are really the cause of inflation?

Selected References

Avery, Roberts, et al. "The Use of Cash and Transaction Accounts by American Families." *Federal Reserve Bulletin*, February 1986, pp. 87–108.
The results of a comprehensive study of the payment habits of American families.

Bordo, Michael D. *The Classical Gold Standard: Some Lessons for Today*. Federal Reserve Bank of St. Louis, May 1981.
A review of the controversy surrounding the gold standard.

Carlson, Keith M. "Do Price Indexes Tell Us about Inflation? A Review of the Issues." *Economic Review*. Federal Reserve Bank of St. Louis, November 1989, pp. 12–29.
This article reviews the fundamentals of price indexes as a measure of inflation, and discusses some of their shortcomings.

Carlstrom, Charles T., and Edward N. Gamber. "Does the Fed Cause Christmas?" *Economic Review*. Federal Reserve Bank of Cleveland, January 1, 1990, pp. 1–4.
This article examines the relationship between the money supply and national income and puts forth the argument that the Fed should commit to a fixed monetary policy rule.

Christiano, Lawrence, J. "P*: Not the Inflation Forecaster's Holy Grail." *Quarterly Review*. Federal Reserve Bank of Minneapolis, Fall 1989, pp. 3–17.
The article examines a new method of forecasting inflation developed by the Board of Governors of the Federal Reserve System called P-Star (P*). The new method (P*) may not be much better than existing methods to forecast inflation.

Hoskins, Lee W. "Breaking the Inflation-Recession Cycle." *Economic Commentary*. Federal Reserve Bank of Cleveland, October 15, 1989, pp. 1–4.
This article argues that a monetary policy which leads to zero or low rates of inflation, even if it risks a recession, is the country's best opportunity for long-term economic growth.

Humphrey, Thomas M., ed. *Essays on Inflation*. Federal Reserve Bank of Richmond, 1986.
A collection of articles on inflation. Most are quite readable.

Judd, John P., and Brian Motley. "Ending Inflation." *Weekly Letter*. Federal Reserve Bank of San Francisco, May 31, 1991, pp. 1–3.
The article states that controlling inflation is recognized as the most appropriate goal of monetary policy. Monetary policy targets and operational roles for monetary policy are then discussed.

Lee, Susan. "Gold, the Ultimate Burglar Alarm." *Forbes*, September 23, 1985, pp. 127–133.
An overview of the historical and current controversy surrounding the desire of many politicians and economists to return to the gold standard.

Mauskopf, Eileen. "The Transmission Channels of Monetary Policy: How Have They Changed?" *Federal Reserve Bulletin,* **December 1990, pp. 985–1008.**
The article discusses important structural changes in the economy that have taken place over the last two decades and examines the impact they have had on the channels through which monetary policy affects the level of economic activity.

Tatom, John A. "The Effect of Financial Innovations on Checkable Deposits, M1 and M2." *Economic Review.* **Federal Reserve Bank of St. Louis, July/August 1990, pp. 37–53.**
The article suggests that the financial innovations of the 1980s, especially NOW accounts, have seriously distorted the effectiveness of M1 as a tool of monetary policy; the effect on M2 is much less.

Wallace, William H., and William E. Cullision. *Measuring Price Indexes.* **Federal Reserve Bank of Richmond, June 1992.**
A comprehensive booklet on the construction and use of the consumer price index and the controversy surrounding the index.

Walter, John R. "Monetary Aggregates: A User's Guide." *Economic Review.* **Federal Reserve Bank of Richmond, January/February 1989, pp. 20–28.**
Monetary aggregates are measures of the nation's money supply. This article is a primer on how the money supply is measured and how aggregate monetary data is used.

THE FINANCIAL SECTOR: OVERVIEW

2

THE U.S. FINANCIAL SYSTEM, NOW as throughout its entire history, functions to gather and allocate funds in the economy. The larger the flow of funds and the more efficiently the funds are allocated, the greater the accommodation of individual preferences and the greater the output and welfare of the economy.

For example, suppose you receive your student loan of $2,500 at the beginning of the school year in the fall but need only $1,500 of it right away. You deposit the $1,000, needed for the winter term, into a three-month certificate of deposit. You can purchase this high-interest savings certificate because you are willing to invest your money for a fixed time period. Also, you purchase this instrument through a local bank located near campus. The bank then pools your $1,000 with funds from other students and makes a large loan to the local pizza shop to expand its home delivery service. Given the cost of funds and its profit-maximizing goal, the pizza shop owner selects only the most profitable projects and drops other projects whose returns would be below the firm's cost of capital. Other firms with projects that promise low returns will also find money too expensive to finance those projects. If the financial system is working properly, the interest you receive will be the highest possible interest rate for your money for a three-month period, the pizza shop will have borrowed money at the lowest possible cost, and only those projects with the highest rate of return will have been financed. The more efficient our financial system, the more likely this is to happen.

This chapter presents an overview of the components of the U.S. financial system. The purpose of the financial system is to facilitate the flow of funds from savers to borrowers in the most efficient manner. The chapter begins by providing basic definitions of surplus and deficit spending units, and describes the characteristics of financial claims. It then describes how surplus and deficit spending units are brought together, either directly or indirectly. Next, the chapter identifies the types of financial institutions and the benefits financial institutions provide to consumers. Included in this discussion is an explanation of disintermediation and the conditions for its occurrence. Following this, financial markets are discussed and classified according to a number of characteristics. Finally, major trends in the financial system are introduced. When integrated, these components make up a model of the financial sector. More detailed discussion of financial institutions and markets will be presented in later chapters.

Surplus and Deficit Spending Units

All economic units can be classified into one of the following groups:

1. Households;
2. Business firms;
3. Governments (local, state, and federal).

Each economic unit must operate within a budget constraint imposed by its total income for the period. Households typically receive income in the form of wages and make frequent expenditures for durable and nondurable consumer goods and services and for real estate in the form of home mortgage payments or rents. Businesses sell goods and services to households and businesses for revenues, and their expenditures are for wages, inventory purchases, and other production costs. Occasionally, businesses make capital expenditures in the form of new buildings and equipment. Governmental units obtain income by collecting taxes and fees and make expenditures for myriad services, such as health, welfare, education, and police and fire protection.

Budget Positions

For a given budget period, any unit within a group can have one of three possible budget positions: (1) a *balanced budget* position, where income and expenditures are equal; (2) a *surplus* position, where income for the period exceeds current expenditures; or (3) a *deficit* position, where expenditures for the period exceed receipts. The financial system is concerned with funneling purchasing power from *surplus spending units (SSUs)* to *deficit spending units (DSUs)*. DSUs include some households, some state and local governments, the federal government in most periods, and a large number of businesses. Other economic units may be SSUs. Taken as groups, however, business firms and governments are typically DSUs and, somewhat surprisingly, households are SSUs.

Financial Claims

The problem is how to transfer the SSUs' excess purchasing power to the DSUs that wish to borrow to finance current expenditures. The transfer can be accomplished by an SSU lending money to and accepting an IOU from a DSU. An IOU is a written promise to pay a specific sum of money (the principal) plus fee (an interest rate) for the privilege of borrowing the money over a period of time (maturity of the loan). IOUs are called *financial claims*. They are claims against someone else's money at a future date.

To a DSU, a financial claim is a liability, and the interest rate payments are the penalty for consuming before income is earned. To the SSU, the financial claim is an asset, and the interest earned is the reward for postponing current consumption. The fact that financial claims (IOUs) are liabilities for borrowers (DSUs) and are simultaneously assets for lenders (SSUs) illustrates the two faces of debt. That is, total financial liabilities outstanding in the economy must equal total financial assets.

Once a financial claim is outstanding, the lender (SSU) may hold the claim until it matures. Alternatively, the SSU may sell the financial claim to someone else before it matures. The DSU continues to have use of the funds even though the lender is now a different party.

The ability to resell financial claims allows the SSU to purchase claims with maturities that do not exactly match its time preference. If an SSU purchases a financial claim with a longer maturity than its investment period, the claim can be resold to another SSU at the appropriate time. Likewise, an SSU can purchase a financial claim with a maturity shorter than its time horizon, if additional claims, either new or outstanding, can be easily purchased. The ease with which a financial claim can be resold is called its *marketability*.

There are wide-ranging financial claims in this country, all designed to meet the preferences of both SSUs and DSUs. Financial claims differ according to maturity, risk of default, marketability, and tax treatment. At any time, these factors interact to determine the interest rate of a financial claim. Interest rates and the pricing of financial claims are the topics of Chapters 5–7.

Transferring Funds from SSUs to DSUs

The purpose of the financial system is to transfer funds from DSUs to SSUs in the most efficient manner possible, either for investment in real assets or for consumption. The job of bringing DSUs and SSUs together can be done by (1) *direct financing* or by (2) *indirect financing*, or, as it is more commonly called, *intermediation financing*. Regardless of the financing method, the goal is to bring the parties together at the least possible cost and with the least inconvenience. An efficient financial system is important, because it ensures adequate capital formation for economic growth. Thus, if the system works properly, firms with the most promising investment opportunities will receive funds. and those with inferior opportunities will not receive funding. In a similar manner, consumers who are willing and able to pay the current market rate of interest can purchase on credit goods and services when they desire them.

Direct Financing

In *direct financing*, DSUs and SSUs exchange money and financial claims directly. DSUs issue financial claims on themselves and sell them for money to SSUs. The SSUs hold the financial claims in their portfolios as interest-bearing assets. The financial claims are bought and sold in *financial markets*. The transactions appear as changes in the balance sheets (asset and liability holdings) of the two parties as follows:

SSU		DSU	
Assets	**Liabilities**	**Assets**	**Liabilities**
— Money		+ Money from SSU	+ Direct claims sold
+ Direct claims of DSU			

The claims issued by the DSU are called *direct claims* and are typically sold in direct credit markets, such as the money or capital markets. Direct financing gives SSUs an outlet for their savings, which provides an expected return, and DSUs no longer need to postpone current consumption or forgo promising investment opportunities for lack of funds. Thus direct credit markets increase the efficiency of the financial system.

There are some problems with the direct credit markets, however. For one thing, because they are wholesale markets, the denominations of securities sold are very large (usually $1 million or more), and thus few consumers can transact in these markets. Another problem is that DSUs must find SSUs that want primary claims with precisely the characteristics they can and are willing to sell. The flow of primary claims from SSUs to DSUs by way of direct financing is illustrated in the top portion of Exhibit 2–1. We shall now discuss some of the institutional arrangements that facilitate the transfer of funds in the direct credit markets.

Private Placements.   The simplest method of transferring funds between SSUs and DSUs is a *private placement*. Here a DSU, such as a corporation, sells an entire security issue to a single institutional investor or small group of such investors. The advantages of a private placement sale over a public offering are the speed with which funds can be committed, the low transaction cost of bringing the securities to market, and the fact that the issue need not be registered with the Securities and Exchange Commission (SEC).

Exhibit 2–1   **Transfer of Funds from Surplus to Deficit Spending Units**

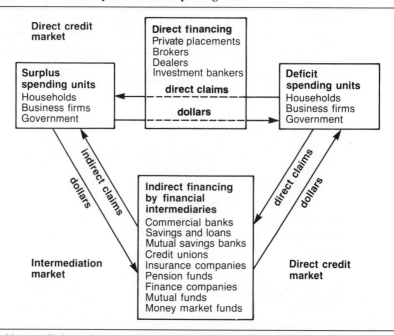

Financial intermediaries such as commercial banks tailor financial claims to meet the investment needs of SSUs while simultaneously buying a variety of financial claims from DSUs. In the direct credit markets, SSUs buy whatever type of claims DSUs sell.

Brokers and Dealers.   To aid in the search process of bringing buyers and sellers together, a number of market specialists exist. *Brokers* do not actually buy or sell securities; they only execute their clients' transactions at the best possible price. Thus brokers provide a pure search service in that they act merely as matchmakers, bringing SSUs and DSUs together. Their profits are derived by charging a commission fee for their services.

A *dealer's* primary function is to "make a market" for a security. Dealers do this by carrying an inventory of securities from which they stand ready either to buy or sell particular securities at stated prices. For example, a dealer making a market in IBM stock might offer to buy shares from investors at $80 and sell shares to other investors at $81.50. The *bid price* is the highest price offered by the dealer to purchase a given security ($80); the *ask price* is the lowest price at which the dealer is willing to sell the security ($81.50). The dealer makes a profit on the *spread* between the bid and the ask price ($1.50).[1] Most dealers also operate as brokers and typically specialize in a particular type of market, such as the commercial paper market, bond market, or equity market.

Investment Bankers.   Another direct market participant is the investment banker who helps DSUs bring their new financial claims to market. An important economic function of the investment banker is risk bearing. The investment banker purchases an entire block of securities to be issued by a DSU at a guaranteed price and then resells the securities individually to investors. The investment banker's gross profit (spread) is the difference between the fixed price paid for the securities and the price at which they are resold on the open market. Investment bankers provide other services, such as helping prepare the prospectus, selecting the sale date, and providing general financial advice to the issuer. Issuers who enter the direct financial markets infrequently or have complicated financial deals find these services valuable. In addition to these services, most investment banking firms act as dealers and brokers. Investment banks are the most important players in the direct credit market.

Some examples of direct financing include the following:

1.   A household (SSU) purchases a newly issued share of AT&T (DSU) stock from a stockbroker whose firm underwrote the issue.
2.   A business with excess cash (SSU) purchases commercial paper directly from General Motors Acceptance Corporation (DSU).
3.   A commercial bank (SSU) purchases from a security broker tax-exempt bonds issued by the state of New Hampshire (DSU).

Intermediation Financing

Until now we have considered only the direct flow of funds from SSUs to DSUs. Flows can be indirect if financial intermediaries are involved. Financial intermediaries transform financial claims in ways that make them more attractive to the ultimate

---

[1] More technically, the *spread* is the difference between the price at which a security is sold minus the price at which it was purchased. The spread represents the dealer's gross profit; it does not include the costs related to selling the security.

DID YOU KNOW?

Smart Cards: Credit Cards with Brains

The U.S. payments system may be altered by a new "credit" card with a built-in brain—the so-called "smart card." The new card, which contains a microprocessor and micromemory chip, is changing the way the world's banks and their customers pay bills, keep records, and fight fraud. The first patent on chip-bearing cards, filed in 1970, belonged to IBM. However, the first marketable microchip card was developed in 1974 by Frenchman Roland C. Moreno, a journalist and self-taught tinkerer. Since then, scientists have developed smart cards that can store 64,000 bits of data, can talk to other computers through electronic contacts so that information may be entered into or retrieved from the cards, run on their own batteries, and have a screen that talks to you and lets you talk back. Not only that, these cards are only 3 millimeters thick.

Currently, less exotic cards that cost about $2 to $4, and supersmart cards, with their displays and keypads, cost $25 to $30. Smart cards are being used to capture information about retail and bank transactions. For example, by using a special machine that reads smart cards, an electronic cash register is able to capture data about the consumer and a particular transaction. A communication device then reports the transaction to the customer and a merchant bank via an automatic clearinghouse. This speedy process eliminates a money management strategy enjoyed by consumers called "float." Float, however, can be programmed into retail transactions so that the consumer's checking account may be debited, say, three days after a purchase.

Smart-card transactions are also more secure than other types of transactions because the consumer's password registered on the chip cannot be copied. Other recent updates in smart-card technology include the addition of a mini-keyboard on the card itself. With this keyboard, a person can transfer money from checking to savings or make a payment on a credit card. This can all be accomplished with just the card itself, without the aid of any special coding machine.

The smart card's ability to store data has other useful applications aside from banking transactions. For soldiers, the smart card could replace the ubiquitous dogtag; a card could be sewn into the soldiers' uniforms and could contain more information than just their name, rank, and serial number. Similarly, medical histories could be stored and updated on a smart card, thereby eliminating the need for bulky files and insuring complete and accurate medical information at all times. College students could register, buy books, eat in the cafeteria, and check out books from the library—all with one smart card.

investor. Financial intermediaries include commercial banks, mutual savings banks, credit unions, life insurance companies, and pension funds. These and other financial intermediaries emerged because of inefficiencies found in direct financing. For direct financing to take place, the DSU must be willing to issue a security with a denomination, maturity, and other security characteristics that match exactly the desires of the SSU. Unless both SSU and DSU are satisfied simultaneously, the transfer of money will probably not take place. A household with a six-month temporary excess cash balance of $400 will have very little interest in buying a $5,000, 20-year bond issued by IBM.

To overcome these problems, financial intermediaries intervene between the borrower (DSU) and the ultimate lender (SSU). Financial intermediaries purchase direct claims (IOUs) with one set of characteristics (e.g., term to maturity, denomination) from DSUs and transform them into indirect claims (IOUs) with a different set of characteristics, which they sell to the SSU. This transformation process is called *intermediation*. Firms that specialize in intermediation are called *financial intermediaries* or more commonly, financial institutions. The changes in balance sheets describing financial intermediation are as follows:

SSU		Financial Intermediaries		DSU	
Assets	**Liabilities**	**Assets**	**Liabilities**	**Assets**	**Liabilities**
− Money		+ Direct claim	+ Indirect claim	+ Money	+ Direct claim
+ Indirect claim					

Notice that the balance sheet of the financial intermediary consists entirely of financial claims—indirect claims as a source of funds (liabilities) and direct claims as a use of funds (assets). Furthermore, notice that in the financial intermediation market, the SSU's residual claim is against the financial intermediaries rather than the DSU, as is the case with direct financing. The financial intermediation market is typically a retail market, and the indirect financial claims issued by financial intermediaries are often given names such as NOW accounts, savings accounts, or money market fund shares.

The bottom half of Exhibit 2–1 illustrates the flow of money through the intermediation market and identifies the more important financial intermediaries.

Some examples of intermediation transactions include the following:

1. Households (SSUs) deposit excess cash balances in passbook savings accounts of a savings and loan association (financial intermediary), which in turn makes home mortgage loans to other households (DSUs).
2. Households (SSUs) purchase life insurance policies from an insurance company (financial intermediary), which in turn invests the funds in bonds of a corporation (DSU).
3. Corporations (SSUs) purchase the commercial paper of a consumer finance company (financial intermediary), which in turn makes personal loans to households (DSUs).

The Benefits of Financial Intermediation

Financial intermediaries are firms that produce specialized financial products such as business loans, consumer installment loans, NOW accounts, life insurance policies, pension fund shares, and money market mutual fund shares. They produce financial claims in such a way as to make them more attractive to both DSUs and SSUs. If they did not do this, financial intermediaries would not exist. Financial intermediaries produce financial products whenever they can sell them for prices that are expected to cover all of their production costs and provide the firm with a profit.

Financial intermediaries enjoy three sources of comparative advantage over others who may try to produce similar services. First, financial intermediaries can achieve *economies of scale* because of their specialization. Because they handle large numbers of transactions, they are able to spread out their fixed costs. Also, specialized equipment allows them to further lower operating costs. Second, financial intermediaries can reduce the *transaction costs* involved in searching for credit information. A consumer who wishes to lend directly can also search for information, but usually at a higher cost. Finally, financial intermediaries may be able to obtain important but sensitive information about a borrower's financial condition, because they have a history of exercising discretion with this type of information. Furthermore, the intermediary may be able to reduce the problem of unreliable information because of their intimate knowledge of the borrower's operations, personal history, and character.

Intermediation Services

For the previously mentioned reasons, financial intermediaries are often able to produce financial commodities at a lower cost than individual consumers. If they did not, individuals would produce their own financial commodities and thus would transact in the direct credit markets. Financial intermediaries exist, therefore, because of the high transaction costs involved in producing many financial commodities in small quantities. If transaction costs are relatively low or if individual consumers use the service in large quantities, achieving economies of scale, the commodity may be produced by the individual consumer.

In producing financial commodities, intermediaries perform four basic services:

1. **Denomination Divisibility.**   Financial intermediaries are able to produce a wide range of denominations—from $1 to many millions. They can do this by pooling the funds of many individuals and investing them in direct securities of varying sizes. Of particular importance is their acceptance of the deposits of small savers who do not have an adequate amount of money to engage in the large-denomination transactions found in direct financial markets.
2. **Maturity Flexibility.**   Financial intermediaries are able to create securities with a wide range of maturities—from 1 day to more than 30 years. Thus they are able to buy direct claims issued by DSUs and issue indirect securities with precisely the maturities (usually shorter) desired by SSUs. For example, savings and loan associations obtain funds by issuing passbook accounts and savings certificates and invest the funds in long-term consumer mortgages.
3. **Credit Risk Diversification.**   By purchasing a wide variety of securities, financial intermediaries are able to spread risk. If the securities purchased are less than perfectly correlated with each other, the intermediary is able to reduce the fluctuation in the principal value of the portfolio.[2] Portfolio diversification is an

---

[2] The extent to which diversification reduces risk for a given portfolio depends on how the returns on individual securities are correlated with one another. Diversification will reduce portfolio risk only if returns on individual securities are not perfectly correlated. For example, if two securities have the same rate of return and riskiness, the one that is less perfectly correlated with the rest of the portfolio will be the more attractive. Thus it is possible that a security with a lower rate of return will be a useful addition to a portfolio if it is imperfectly correlated with the rest of the portfolio.

application of not putting "all of your eggs into one basket," where they might be "broken" simultaneously. For example, the return on a portfolio with a large number of securities would not be affected much if one security were to go into default. The individual who held only the defaulted security would be greatly affected, however.

4. **Liquidity.** For most consumers, the timing of revenues and expenses rarely coincides. Because of this, most economic units prefer to hold some assets that have low transaction costs associated with converting them into money. Many of the financial commodities produced by intermediaries are highly liquid. For example, a checking account permits consumers to purchase an asset or repay a debt with minimal transaction cost.

Financial intermediaries, therefore, tailor the characteristics of the indirect securities they issue to the desires of SSUs. They engage in one or more distinct types of intermediation: (1) denomination intermediation, (2) risk intermediation, (3) maturity intermediation, and (4) liquidity intermediation. They provide these and other services to earn a profit. SSUs and DSUs use these services as long as the cost of doing so is less than in direct credit markets.

SSUs' or DSUs' choices between the direct credit market or the intermediation market depend on which market best meets their needs. Typically, consumers whose transactions are small in dollar amount (retail transactions) find that the intermediation market is most cost effective. In contrast, economic units that deal in large dollar amounts (wholesale transactions) can switch back and forth between the two markets, selecting the market that offers the most favorable interest rate.[3] For example, many large businesses take out loans from commercial banks, an intermediation transaction, and also raise money by selling commercial paper in the direct credit market.

Intermediation and Disintermediation

Since World War II, the trend in the United States has been a growth in funds flowing through the financial intermediation market rather than the direct credit market. This trend occurred primarily because financial intermediaries catered to the rapidly growing consumer credit market. Consumers deal in small transaction amounts and, hence, cannot transact in the direct credit market. In the United States, 70 to 85 percent of total funds are normally channeled through the intermediation market. Funds shift between the two markets—direct or intermediation—depending on market conditions and where SSUs and DSUs get the best deal. The shift of funds that were previously routed through the intermediation market to the direct credit market is called *disintermediation.*

Historically, disintermediation occurred when market rates of interest rose above the interest rate that depository institutions could legally pay on their liability accounts, such as savings accounts and consumer time deposits. During these periods,

---

[3] Wholesale transactions are usually defined as transactions in which the dollar amount is $1 million or more.

consumers could earn higher yields by purchasing direct credit claims such as Treasury bills. These periodic misalignments of interest rates occurred in the United States because of legal limits on deposit rates set by government regulations. These ceilings are popularly referred to as Regulation Q, after the Federal Reserve regulation that sets the maximum rate commercial banks can pay on time deposits.[4] In 1980, a law was passed requiring a phaseout of Regulation Q by April 1986.

Regulation Q and the resulting disintermediation caused enormous hardship for depository institutions and consumers. For example, in the 1960s, direct credit market rates rose substantially above the Regulation Q limit. During this time, depositors at thrift institutions found it worthwhile to withdraw their deposits and buy direct securities, causing a net outflow of funds from thrifts. As a result, thrift institutions had to cut back on their mortgage lending and sell off part of their mortgage portfolio to meet deposit withdrawals. At the same time, consumers whose funds remained in thrift institutions earned less than the fair market rate on their savings.

With the emergence of money market mutual funds in the early 1970s, another type of disintermediation occurred, technically called *gross disintermediation*. This term describes the outflow of funds from one financial intermediary subject to deposit rate ceilings to another financial intermediary not subject to deposit rate ceilings. Thus, there is no net disintermediation between the direct credit market and the intermediation market. There is, however, a shift of funds between financial institutions within the intermediation market. For example, in the 1970s, when market rates of interest rose above deposit rate ceilings, consumers withdrew their funds from commercial banks and thrift institutions and began buying shares in money market mutual funds that paid the market rate of interest. Money market mutual funds went from an obscure segment of the mutual fund industry in 1970 to an $80 billion asset business by the early 1980s. Gross intermediation because of money market mutual funds declined in 1983, when commercial banks and thrift institutions were permitted to issue money market deposit accounts that were not subject to an interest rate ceiling. However, MMMFs still hold $415 billion in assets, roughly 9.5 percent of total bank and thrift deposits.

As previously discussed, disintermediation was something that "happened" to banks because of market forces. However, beginning in the mid-1980s, banks themselves began to initiate gross disintermediation because of increasing deposit insurance costs and increasing capital standards imposed by bank regulators. Thus, banks were "voluntarily" reducing their asset sizing by selling commercial loans to nonbank purchasers such as prime rate funds and privately placed institutional loan funds. These funds are specialized mutual funds that purchase diversified pools of bank loans. In addition, banks have been selling off loans by securitizing real estate loans, credit card receivables, and consumer installment loans. *Securitization* is the process of pooling and repackaging loans so they have the characteristics of security instruments, which enables them to be more easily resold.

---

[4] The term Regulation Q has no deep or mystic meaning. The Fed called its first regulation "Regulation A" and had reached Q at the time it regulated deposit rates. Unfortunately for the banking system, federal regulations have not been hampered by the number of letters in the alphabet.

Types of Financial Intermediaries

There are many types of financial intermediaries that coexist in our economy. Though different, financial intermediaries all have one function in common: They purchase financial claims with one set of characteristics from DSUs and sell financial claims with different characteristics to SSUs. Exhibit 2–2 shows the major financial intermediaries in our economy and their growth rates between 1950 and 1989. During this period, the assets of all financial intermediaries grew at a compound annual rate of 9.6 percent. This rate of growth was faster than the economy as a whole, which had grown at an annual rate of 7.7 percent. The rapid growth rate of financial intermediaries reflects both the growth in indirect securities issued and the increase in the proportion of funds being channeled through the intermediation market.

Financial intermediaries are classified as (1) deposit-type institutions, (2) contractual savings institutions, or (3) other types of intermediaries.

Exhibit 2–2   **Size and Growth of Major Financial Intermediaries in the United States (1950–1989)**

Intermediary	Rank	1989 Total Assets (billions)	1989 Percentage of Total	1950 Total Assets (billions)	1950 Percentage of Total	Annual Growth Rate
Commercial banks	1	$ 3,231	32	$150	52	8.2%
Savings and loan associations	2	1,233	12	17	6	11.7
Life insurance companies	3	1,268	13	63	22	8.0
Private pension funds	4	1,164	12	7	2	14.1
State and local government pension funds	5	727	7	5	2	13.7
Mutual funds	6	555	5	3	1	14.4
Finance companies	7	519	5	9	3	11.0
Casualty insurance companies	8	491	5	12	4	10.1
Money market funds	9	428	4	a	a	a
Mutual savings banks	10	284	3	22	8	6.8
Credit unions	11	200	2	1	b	14.6
Total		$10,100	100	$289	100	9.6%

Commercial banks are the largest and most important financial intermediaries in the U.S. economy. Credit unions and mutual funds, however, are the fastest growing.

a Did not exist until 1972.

b Less than 1 percent.

Source: Board of Governors, Federal Reserve System. *Flow of Funds Accounts, Financial Assets and Liabilities, Year-End, 1963–89*, September 1990.

Deposit-Type Institutions

Deposit-type financial institutions are the most commonly recognized intermediaries because most people use their services on a daily basis. Typically, deposit institutions issue a variety of checking or savings accounts and time deposits, and they use the funds to make consumer, business, and mortgage loans. The interest paid on deposit accounts is usually insured by one of several federally sponsored insurance agencies. Thus, for practical purposes, the deposits are devoid of any risk of loss of principal. Also, these deposits are highly liquid because they can be withdrawn on very short notice, usually on demand. The use of funds attracted by the deposit-type financial intermediaries is shown in Exhibit 2–3.

Commercial Banks.   Commercial banks are the largest and most diversified intermediaries on the basis of range of assets held and liabilities issued. They are referred to as the "department stores of finance." Their liabilities are in the form of checking accounts, savings accounts, and various time deposits. Most bank deposits are insured up to a maximum of $100,000 by the Federal Deposit Insurance Corporation (FDIC), thus carrying no default risk to the holder. On the asset side, commercial banks make a wide variety of loans in all denominations to consumers, businesses, and state and local governments. Many commercial banks have trust departments and leasing operations, and may underwrite certain classes of securities. Because of their vital role in the nation's monetary system and the effect they have on the economic well-being of the communities in which they are located, commercial banks are among the most highly regulated of all financial institutions.

Savings and Loan Associations.   Savings and loan associations are specialized financial institutions, obtaining most of their funds by issuing NOW accounts, savings accounts, and a variety of consumer time deposit accounts, then using the funds to

| Exhibit 2–3 | **Major Asset Holdings of Deposit-Type Intermediaries (1989)** |

	Percentage of Total Assets			
Assets	**CB**	**SLA**	**MSB**	**CU**
U.S. government securities	12	16	13	9
Municipal bonds	4	—	1	—
Corporate and foreign bonds	3	4	4	—
Consumer loans	12	4	4	46
Business loans	27	3	5	—
Real estate loans	24	61	59	23
Other assets	18	12	14	22
Total	100	100	100	100

CB = commercial banks, SLA = savings and loan associations, MSB = mutual savings banks, and CU = credit unions.

The types of assets that depository institutions own differ because of regulatory constraints and the institutions' tax status.

Source: Board of Governors, Federal Reserve System. *Flow of Funds Accounts, Financial Assets and Liabilities, Year-End, 1963–89*, September 1990.

purchase long-term mortgages. They are the largest provider of residential mortgage loans to consumers. In addition, they are now allowed to make a limited amount of consumer and commercial loans. In effect, savings and loan associations specialize in maturity and denomination intermediation, because they borrow small amounts of money short-term with checking and savings accounts and lend long-term on real estate collateral. Most deposits are insured up to $100,000 by the Federal Savings and Loan Insurance Corporation (FSLIC). Currently, savings and loan associations are the second largest type of financial intermediary in the economy, with more than three thousand located in every state.

Mutual Savings Banks. Mutual savings banks are similar to savings and loan associations. They issue consumer checking and time savings accounts to collect funds from households, and they invest primarily in residential mortgages. Their deposits are insured by the FDIC or by state insurance plans. To consumers, the difference between a mutual savings bank and a savings and loan association is largely technical; the two institutions are virtually interchangeable. At present only 18 states charter mutual savings banks, and most of these are along the northern Atlantic seaboard. Of the 400 mutual savings banks, about 300 are located in three states—Massachusetts, New York, and Connecticut.

Credit Unions. Credit unions are small, nonprofit, cooperative, consumer-organized institutions owned entirely by their member-customers. The primary liabilities of credit unions are checking accounts (called *share drafts*) and savings accounts (called *share accounts*); their investments are almost entirely short-term installment consumer loans. Credit union share accounts are federally insured to a maximum of $100,000. Credit unions are organized by consumers having a *common bond*, such as employees of a given firm or union. To use any service of a credit union—for example, to open a passbook account or to obtain a loan—an individual must be a member. The major regulatory differences between credit unions and other depository institutions are the requirement of a common bond and the restriction of most loans to consumer loans. In addition, credit unions generally are exempt from federal income tax because of their cooperative nature.

Contractual Savings Institutions

Contractual savings institutions obtain funds under long-term contractual arrangements and invest the funds in the capital markets. Firms in this category are insurance companies and pension funds. These institutions are characterized by a relatively steady inflow of funds from contractual commitments with their insurance policyholders and pension fund participants. Thus liquidity is not a problem in the management of these institutions. They are able to invest in long-term securities, such as bonds, and in some cases in common stock. The use of funds for contractual savings institutions is shown in Exhibit 2-4.

Life Insurance Companies. Life insurance companies obtain funds by selling insurance policies that protect against loss of income from premature death or retirement. In the event of death, the policyholder's beneficiaries receive the insurance benefits, and with retirement the policyholder receives the benefits. In addition to risk protection, many life insurance policies provide some savings.

Exhibit 2–4   **Major Asset Holdings of Contractual Savings Institutions (1989)**

| | Percentage of Total Assets | | | |
Assets	LIC	CIC	SLGPF	PPF
U.S. government securities	12	20	27	12
Municipal bonds	1	28	—	—
Corporate and foreign bonds	41	16	27	12
Mortgages	19	1	2	1
Corporate stocks	11	19	40	61
Other assets	16	16	4	14
Total	100	100	100	100

LIC = life insurance companies, CIC = casualty insurance companies, SLGPF = state and local government pension funds, and PPF = private pension funds.

Liquidity is not a problem for contractual savings institutions because of their steady inflow of funds and predictable outflow. As a result, they invest heavily in long-term securities, such as bonds, and in some cases in common stock.

Source: Board of Governors, Federal Reserve System. *Flow of Funds Accounts, Financial Assets and Liabilities, Year-End, 1963–89*, September 1990.

Because life insurance companies have a predictable inflow of funds and their outflows are actuarially predictable, they are able to invest primarily in higher-yielding, long-term assets, such as corporate bonds and stocks. Life insurance companies are regulated by the states in which they operate, and, compared to deposit-type institutions, their regulation is less strict.

Casualty Insurance Companies.   Casualty insurance companies sell protection against loss of property from fire, theft, accident, negligence, and other causes that can be actuarially predicted. The major source of funds for these firms is premiums charged on insurance policies. Casualty insurance policies are pure risk-protection policies; as a result, they have no cash surrender value and thus provide no liquidity to the policyholders. As might be expected, the cash outflows from claims on policies are not as predictable as those of life insurance companies. Consequently, a greater proportion of these companies' assets are in short-term, highly marketable securities. To offset the lower return typically generated by these investments, casualty companies have substantial holdings of equity securities. Casualty insurance companies also hold many municipal bonds to reduce their taxes.

Pension Funds.   Pension funds obtain their funds from employer and employee contributions during the employees' working years and provide monthly payments upon retirement. Pension funds invest these monies in corporate bonds and equity obligations. The purpose of pension funds is to help workers plan for their retirement years in an orderly and systematic manner. The need for retirement income, combined with the success of organized labor in negotiating for increased pension benefits, has led to a remarkable growth of both private pensions and state and local government pension funds in the postwar period. Because the inflow into pension funds is long-term and the outflow is highly predictable, pension funds are able to invest in higher-yielding, long-term securities. To increase earnings and reduce the amounts of monthly payments needed to support a retirement income, pension funds have in recent years invested heavily in equity securities.

Other Types of Financial Intermediaries

There are several other types of financial intermediaries that purchase direct securities from DSUs and sell indirect claims to SSUs. Exhibit 2–5 shows the use of funds for finance companies, mutual funds, and money market mutual funds.

Finance Companies. Finance companies make loans to consumers and small businesses. Unlike commercial banks, they do not accept savings deposits from consumers. They obtain the majority of their funds by selling short-term IOUs, called *commercial paper*, to investors. The balance of their funds comes from the sale of equity capital and long-term debt obligations.

There are three basic types of finance companies: consumer finance companies specializing in installment loans to households, business finance companies specializing in loans and leases to businesses, and sales finance companies that finance the products sold by retail dealers. Finance companies are regulated by the states in which they operate and are also subject to many federal regulations. These regulations focus primarily on consumer transactions and deal with loan terms, conditions, rates charged, and collection practices.

Mutual Funds. Mutual funds sell equity shares to investors and use these funds to purchase stocks or bonds. As intermediaries, they tend to specialize in denomination

---

Exhibit 2–5   **Major Asset Holdings of Other Types of Financial Intermediaries (1989)**

Assets	Percentage of Total Assets		
	FC	MF	MMF
Government securities	—	22	8
Commercial bank CDs	—	—	10
Commercial paper	—	4	44
Corporate and municipal bonds	—	30	16
Corporate equities	—	43	—
Consumer loans	32	—	—
Business loans	50	—	—
Mortgages	16	—	—
Other assets	2	1	22
Total	100	100	100

FC = finance companies, MF = mutual funds, and MMF = money market mutual funds.

The asset holdings of financial institutions in this category primarily reflect the type of business activities in which they engage.

Source: Board of Governors, Federal Reserve System. *Flow of Funds Accounts, Financial Assets and Liabilities, Year-End, 1963–89*, September 1990.

and default-risk intermediation. The advantage of a mutual fund over direct investment is that it provides small investors access to reduced investment risk that results
from diversification, economies of scale in transaction costs, and professional financial
managers. The value of a share of a mutual fund is not fixed; it fluctuates as the prices
of the stocks its investment portfolio comprises change. Most mutual funds specialize
within particular sectors of the market. For example, some invest only in equities or
debt, others in a particular industry (such as energy or electronics), others in growth
or income stocks, and still others in foreign investments.

Money Market Mutual Funds.   Money market mutual funds emerged on the
financial scene in 1972, and since that time they have been one of the fastest-growing
financial intermediaries. Currently over 80 money market funds (MMF), with assets
totaling more than $316 billion, are operating in the United States. A MMF is simply
a mutual fund that invests in short-term securities with low default risk. These
securities sell in denominations of $1 million or more, so most investors are unable to
purchase them. Thus MMFs provide investors with small money balances the
opportunity to earn the market rate of interest without incurring a great deal of
financial risk. Most MMFs offer check-writing privileges, which make them close
substitutes for the NOW accounts and savings accounts offered at most depository
institutions. This advantage is limited, however, in that most MMFs restrict the
minimum withdrawals to $500, and the funds are not insured by a federal government
agency, such as the Federal Deposit Insurance Corporation (FDIC).

Federal Agencies.   The U.S. government is a major financial institution through
the borrowing and lending activities of its agencies. Since the 1960s, federal agencies
have been among the most rapidly growing of all financial institutions. With the
reordering of federal priorities in the 1980s, however, it has been uncertain whether
this trend will continue. The primary purposes of federal agencies are to reduce the
cost of funds and increase the availability of funds to target sectors in the economy.
The agencies do this by selling debt instruments (called *agency securities*) in the direct
credit markets at or near the government borrowing rate, then lending those funds to
economic participants in the sectors they serve. Most of the funds provided by the
federal agencies support agriculture and housing because of the importance of these
sectors to the nation's well-being. It is argued that these and other target sectors in the
economy would not receive adequate credit at reasonable cost without direct
intervention by the federal government. Exhibit 2-6 shows the debt outstanding for
some of the largest borrowing agencies.

To summarize, Exhibit 2-7 lists the principal assets and liabilities issued by the
various types of financial intermediaries. In examining the exhibit, it is important to
review the reasons that a particular intermediary holds certain types of assets and
incurs certain types of liabilities.

Financial Markets

Financial intermediaries buy the financial claims of others and sell their own claims in
financial markets. As one might expect, there are many different types of financial
claims issued by financial intermediaries and a large number of markets in which these

Exhibit 2–6   **Debt Outstanding of Selected Federally Sponsored Agencies (1990)**

Agency	Amount Outstanding (billions)
Federal Home Loan Bank	$117.9
Federal National Mortgage Association	123.4
Farm Credit Bank	53.6
Tennessee Valley Authority (TVA)	23.4
Federal Home Loan Mortgage Corporation	30.9
Student Loan Marketing Association	34.2
Export-Import Bank	11.4
Postal Service	6.9
Total	$409.9

The three largest federally sponsored agencies are engaged in supporting the housing and agricultural credit markets.

Source: Federal Reserve Bulletin.

claims are bought and sold. In this and the following sections, we shall briefly describe the different types of financial markets.

Primary and Secondary Markets

Financial markets can be divided into primary and secondary markets. A *primary market* represents the point at which financial claims are first produced by DSUs. All financial claims have primary markets. An example of a typical primary market transaction is a corporation raising external funds by issuing new stocks or bonds.

A *secondary market* is one in which initial buyers resell their securities before maturity. In effect, a secondary market is a secondhand market for previously sold securities. Securities can be sold only once in a primary market; all subsequent transactions take place in secondary markets. The New York Stock Exchange is an example of a well-known secondary market. Though all securities have a primary market, not all securities have a secondary market. The function of secondary markets is to provide liquidity to individuals who acquire securities in the primary market. The primary market would be seriously hampered in its function of bringing new issues to market if investors believed they would not subsequently be able to resell a security quickly at a fair price in a secondary market.

Organized and Over-the-Counter Markets

Once issued, a security may be traded in the secondary market *on the floor* of an organized security exchange or traded *over the counter*. Organized markets, commonly referred to as *security exchanges*, provide a physical meeting place and communication facilities for members to conduct their transactions under a specific set of rules and regulations. Only members of the exchange may use the facilities, and

---

Exhibit 2–7   **Principal Financial Assets and Liabilities Owned by Financial Intermediaries**

Type of Intermediary	Assets (Direct Securities Purchased)	Liabilities (Indirect Securities Sold)
1. *Deposit-type institutions*		
Commercial banks	Business loans	Checkable deposits
	Consumer loans	Savings deposits
	Mortgages	Time deposits
Savings and loan associations	Mortgages	Savings deposits and time deposits
Mutual savings banks	Mortgages	Saving deposits
Credit unions	Consumer loans	Saving deposits
2. *Contractual savings institutions*		
Life insurance companies	Corporate bonds	Life insurance policies
	Mortgages	
Casualty insurance companies	Municipal bonds	Casualty insurance polices
	Corporate stock	Pension funds' reserves
	Government securities	
Private pension funds	Corporate stock	Pension funds' reserves
	Corporate bonds	
State and local government pension funds	Corporate bonds	Pension funds' reserves
	Corporate stock	
	Government securities	
3. *Other financial institutions*		
Finance companies	Consumer loans	Commercial paper
	Business loans	Bonds
Mutual funds	Corporate stock	Shares in fund
	Government securities	
	Municipal bonds	
	Corporate bonds	
Money market funds	Money market securities	Shares in fund
Federal agencies	Government loans	Agency securities

This exhibit presents a summary of the most important assets held and liabilities issued by the financial institutions discussed in this book.

only securities listed on the exchange may be traded. The largest and most important organized exchange in the United States is the New York Stock Exchange (NYSE).

Securities not listed on one of the exchanges are sold over the counter. Listed securities may also be sold over the counter. In contrast to organized markets, dealers and brokers trade directly with one another in over-the-counter markets rather than in a central location. To *make a market* for a security, dealers and brokers throughout the United States are connected in an elaborate communications network.

Money and Capital Markets

Financial markets may be classified by the maturity of financial claims traded. The *money market* trades short-term debt instruments with maturities of one year or less. Money market instruments also have very low financial risk for investors. Transaction sizes are usually quite large, typically $1 million or more. The function of money market instruments is to help economic units to adjust their liquidity—bridge the gap between their cash receipts and cash expenditures. The money market is not a single physical location but a group of markets linked nationwide by telephone.

In *capital markets* financial claims with maturities greater than one year are traded. The purpose of capital markets is to channel savings into long-term productive investments. Capital markets encompass all long-term debt instruments and equity obligations.

International and Domestic Markets

Financial markets can be classified as either domestic or international markets. The most important international financial markets for U.S. firms are the short-term Eurodollar market and the long-term Eurobond market. In these markets, domestic or overseas firms can borrow or lend large amounts of U.S. dollars that have been deposited in overseas banks. These markets are closely linked to the U.S. money and capital markets. Large financial institutions, business firms, and institutional investors, both in the United States and overseas, conduct daily transactions between the U.S. domestic markets and the international markets.

Spot Market and Futures Market

The *spot market* is the market in which securities are traded for immediate delivery and payment. The term "immediate" can mean the same day or a week later depending on the particular market. The spot market is also called the *cash market*.

The *futures market* is the market in which securities are traded for future delivery at a specified price. The instruments traded in this market are called *futures contracts*. Futures contracts trade on organized exchanges such as the Chicago Board of Trade, and their contracts are standardized. If the futures contract is negotiated and sold over the counter, it is referred to as a *forward contract* and the market is referred to as a *forward market*. For example, currencies such as the dollar or yen are sold as forward contracts negotiated between two parties. Currencies are also sold as futures contracts on futures exchanges. Futures contracts in foreign exchange markets are similar to forward contracts, except that they are standardized and sold on an organized exchange.

Option Market

The *option market* is the market in which securities are traded for conditional future delivery. The instruments traded are called *option contracts*. The option contract calls for one party (the option writer) to perform a specific act if called upon by the option holder. Typically, an option gives a party the right to buy or sell a security such as a

PEOPLE & EVENTS

A Criminal's Guide to Stashing the Cash

It sounds bizarre, but former Kidder Peabody investment banker and convicted felon Martin Siegel kept $700,000 from Ivan Boesky in a closet and used it to pay his child's nurse. Aren't there better ways to stash cash? You would expect a sophisticated Wall Street criminal with an MBA to do better than this.

The truth of the matter is that recent changes in the law have made it next to impossible for white-collar criminals to hide cash from the authorities. Using computers, the IRS matches up against individual taxpayers virtually all of the $664 million in wage and other income that come in. The IRS also has other tools to discourage cash sheltering, such as new penalties for wrong Social Security numbers on bank accounts.

Okay, you say, but how about putting cash into my friendly neighborhood bank? This alternative is closed out by the law requiring your local bank to tattle on people who deposit or withdraw more than $10,000 in currency. Although the law has been on the books since 1970, the IRS has only recently begun to enforce it, as evidenced by recent fines against the Bank of Boston and 23 others for failing to report such transactions. To make matters worse, in October 1987 Congress added a 20-year sentence to the penalty for bankers or others who abet money laundering.

Well, why not then hire runners to open accounts at 75 different banks and deposit just under $10,000 in each? The new law makes this practice—called "smurfing" by drug dealers—a felony. Also, each deposit increases the chance of getting caught, since banks are also required to report deposits under $10,000 made by people who look "suspicious."

Buy stock? This won't work either, because brokers also are required to report deposits over $10,000. Firms like Charles Schwab won't take cash at its teller cages, whereas Merrill Lynch will take no more than $100. And, if you sell your stock, the proceeds are reported to the IRS on form 1099.

Why not spend your money? Live it up—buy meals, clothes, and an expensive imported car. The lunches are okay, but don't buy a car for more than $10,000, as car dealers must file form 8300 with the IRS to report all car purchases over $10,000. Winnings and purchases of gambling chips are also reported when large.

Shipping your money overseas is not such a hot idea either. Not admitting an overseas account on the 1040 tax return is a felony. Even old tax havens like Switzerland, Panama, and the Cayman Islands are hard to use. Not only do you leave a paper trail by wiring money abroad, but the United States is using political leverage to cause these countries to release bank data on evidence of any criminal activity.

Certainly, big-time drug dealers and seasoned criminals with international connections and a chain of pizza parlors in which to launder profits can and do get away with stashing money. But for the amateur criminal, it is increasingly difficult to avoid the IRS, and the stiffer penalties diminish the benefits of sheltering cash.

particular stock or bond. The option contract stipulates the price at which the security is to be bought or sold and the date on which the ability to exercise the option expires. For example, a *put option* allows an investor to sell (put) a security back to the issuer at a predetermined price by a certain date. A *call option* allows the issuer of a security to purchase (call) a particular security for a predetermined price by a certain date. Option contracts on securities are traded on most major organized exchanges such as the American Stock Exchange (AMEX), and options on commodities are traded on commodity exchanges such as the Chicago Board of Trade.

Foreign Exchange Market

The foreign exchange market is the market on which foreign currencies are bought and sold. Foreign currencies such as the British pound, Japanese yen, German mark, or French franc are traded against the U.S. dollar or are traded against other foreign currencies. Foreign currencies are traded either for spot or future delivery; foreign currencies are traded over the counter at large commercial banks or investment banking firms, or they are traded on organized exchanges such as the Chicago Mercantile Exchange.

Major Trends in the Financial System

As commented on in Chapter 1, the U.S. financial system has seen some of the most profound changes in its history since the late 1970s. New kinds of investment and credit instruments have proliferated at a bewildering pace.

As a first major change, electronic information processing is reducing the cost of gathering, managing, and transmitting the data needed to produce financial services. This trend reduces costs and makes new financial services possible, thereby altering ways of raising and investing funds. For example, at the consumer level, automatic teller machines and point-of-sale terminals are altering the consumer payment system. At the wholesale level, business firms are doing more of their financial transactions in the direct credit market because of new financial products and a more favorable cost structure. The shift to direct-credit-market transactions is straining the traditional market relationship between investment banking firms and large commercial banks. Commercial banks, who are prohibited from engaging in many investment banking activities by the Glass-Steagall Act of 1933, are calling for the act's repeal so that they can remain competitive with their largest customers.

Second, the growth in wealth and level of business activity worldwide is increasing the number, size, and type of transactions in financial markets. The growth of international trade and the declining cost of information appear to be increasing the optimal geographic scope of firms in banking and finance. As a result, there is a trend towards internationalization of money and capital markets, along with interstate delivery of domestic financial services.

Finally, the greater volatility of interest rates, exchange rates, and asset prices that began during the late 1970s is expanding the demand for risk-management services. The importance of risk management is exemplified by the importance to financial firms of asset and liability management techniques and by the growth in the options and futures markets. Although our discussion of these trends has been relatively brief thus far, the balance of the book will provide the detail and analytical tools necessary for a comprehensive understanding of them.

Summary

This chapter presents an overview of the financial sector of the economy that will serve as the starting point for our discussion of financial institutions in later chapters. SSUs are economic units whose total receipts exceed expenditures for a given period; DSUs are economic units whose total expenditures exceed receipts. The basic role of the financial system is to facilitate the efficient transfer of funds from SSUs to DSUs. There are two ways the transfer can take place: (1) direct financing and (2) indirect (intermediation) financing. Most funds flow through the intermediation market, because intermediaries provide financial services at lower costs than most people can obtain in the direct financing market.

Commercial banks are the largest and the most important financial intermediaries in the economy. They, along with savings and loan associations, mutual savings banks, and credit unions, are classified as deposit-type institutions. These institutions typically receive their funds from checkable accounts and time deposits and use the funds to make consumer, business, and mortgage loans. Because of the short-term nature of their liabilities, liquidity is a major management problem for these institutions.

Life and casualty insurance companies and pension funds are classified as contractual savings institutions. These institutions usually obtain funds under long-term contractual arrangements and invest the funds in capital markets. They can invest in long-term securities because of the relatively stable inflow of funds and the actuarial predictability of their outflows.

Financial markets can be classified by whether they trade new (primary) or used (secondary) securities, whether they have formal trading locations (organized exchange) or operate informally in many locations (over-the-counter) at the individual offices of traders, whether the securities' maturities are short-term (money markets) or long-term (capital markets), whether they operate within the United States (domestic) or overseas (international), and whether spot, futures, options, or foreign exchange contracts are sold.

Questions

1. Explain the concept of financial intermediation. How does the possibility of financial intermediation increase the efficiency of the financial system?
2. What are the major services provided by financial intermediaries? Identify products through which commercial banks provide these services.
3. What is disintermediation? Under what conditions might it occur?
4. General Motors Corporation needs $100,000 for two months. Using T-accounts, explain how GMC might obtain the $100,000 through a transaction in the direct credit market and in the intermediation market.
5. Explain the statement, "A financial claim is someone's asset and someone else's liability."
6. Compare and contrast the major operating and regulatory differences between savings and loan associations and credit unions.
7. Why do contractual savings institutions typically hold long-term securities and deposit institutions do so less frequently?

8. Explain the economic importance of secondary markets. How do secondary markets aid the primary market?
9. Explain why Treasury securities are popular short-term investments for commercial banks and other corporations.
10. What is the economic purpose of funds channeled into the money market versus those channeled into the capital market?

Selected References

Benston, George J., and Clifford W. Smith, Jr. "A Transaction Cost Approach to the Theory of Financial Intermediation." *Journal of Finance,* **May 1976, pp. 215–232.**
This classic article explains why financial intermediaries exist, and their role in reducing transaction costs when creating financial services.

Bloch, Ernest. *Inside Investment Banking.* **Homewood, IL: Dow Jones–Irwin, 1987.**
A good introduction to investment banks, the firms that dominate the direct credit market.

Gutfreund, John H. *The State of the U.S. Financial Service Industry: Testimony Before the U.S. Senate Committee on Banking, Subcommittee on Securities.* **New York: Salomon Brothers, March 6, 1990.**
An overview of the problems facing the financial service industry in the 1990s.

Logue, Dennis E., ed. *Handbook of Modern Finance.* **Boston: Warren, Gorham & Lamont, 1990.**
Comprehensive book that has a chapter devoted to various financial institutions and markets. A good reference book.

Napoli, Janet, and Hebert L. Baer. "Disintermediation Marches On." *Chicago Fed Letter.* **Federal Reserve Bank of Chicago, January 1991, pp. 1–3.**
Historically, disintermediation was something that "happened" to banks. Since the 1980s, banks have promoted some disintermediation by selling commercial loans to nonbank purchasers.

Pardee, Scott E. "Internationalization of Financial Markets." *Economic Review.* **Federal Reserve Bank of Kansas City, February 1987, pp. 3–7.**
The article discusses an evolutionary process that is globalizing financial markets, transferring old kinds of debt into new kinds of securities, and blurring the distinction between commercial banks and investment banks.

Rose, Peter S., and Donald R. Fraser. *Financial Institutions.* **Dallas: Business Publications, 1988.**
A comprehensive book discussing each of the major financial institutions in the U.S. economy. Emphasis is on commercial banking.

Simpson, Thomas D. "Developments in the U.S. Financial System Since the Mid-1970s." *Federal Reserve Bulletin,* **January 1988, pp. 1–13.**
The article chronicles the dramatic changes that have occurred since the mid-1970s within the U.S. financial system. An excellent overview.

Stigum, Marcia. *The Money Market.* **Homewood, IL: Dow Jones–Irwin, 1990.**
The definitive book dealing with all aspects of the money markets.

Theobald, Thomas C. "Restructuring the U.S. Banking System for Global Competition." *Journal of Applied Corporate Finance,* **Winter 1991, pp. 21–24.**
A view of how the U.S. financial system is being restructured by regulatory, economic, and technological forces.

HISTORICAL DEVELOPMENT OF AMERICAN COMMERCIAL BANKING

3

IT HAS BEEN SAID THAT those who do not learn from history are doomed to repeat it. The Federal Reserve wants to be sure there will not be a repeat of the wave of bank failures that took place in the 1930s, and thus it is actively studying the history of banking. With rapid changes occurring in bank structure and products, researchers hope historical analyses will help them anticipate the effects of interstate banking, deposit insurance reform, and the globalization of banking markets.

The American financial system is complex and at times appears bizarre to outsiders. The history of commercial banking explains the economic and political forces that shaped the structure of our current financial system. Against this historical background it becomes easier to understand why banks are chartered by both the federal and state governments, why we have so many small banks, why branch banking is prohibited in many areas of the country, and why there are so many bank regulations. This chapter will also provide insight into the regulatory and operating characteristics of nonbank financial institutions, which are discussed in Part 5.

The Development of Modern Banking

Although archaeologists have uncovered stone tablets that apparently served as loan contracts in ancient Babylon, modern commercial banks probably evolved from European institutions that provided depository or safekeeping services. In the Middle Ages, goldsmiths and silversmiths, having protective facilities in which to keep their own valuable inventories, found that they could earn additional income by storing valuables (often gold coins) for others for a fee. When the metalsmith received valuables for deposit, he typically issued a depository receipt to his customer as proof of ownership. Whenever an individual made purchases, he would redeem his valuables and physically transfer the appropriate amount of coins to the seller. The seller would then redeposit the coins, possibly with the same metalsmith. Trade in this manner was burdensome and time consuming. However, before this crude system of transactions could develop into our modern commercial banking system, several important innovations were necessary. Though our account of the developments is somewhat fictitious, it illustrates the important steps.

Innovative Elements

Standardized Receipts as Money.   It gradually became apparent to both the goldsmiths and their customers that business transactions could be simplified by transferring deposit receipts rather than redeeming receipts and physically transferring gold. Goldsmiths, to further expedite business transactions to gain customers, began to standardize their deposit receipts with respect to value, color, and form. Holders of these standardized receipts soon discovered that they could directly exchange receipts for goods and services, provided that the recipient knew the receipt would be redeemed by the goldsmith (bank) for gold coins. As this practice became widespread, deposit receipts were increasingly used as a medium of exchange and soon became a form of money. Gradually the role of goldsmiths began to change from custodians of precious metals to issuers of deposit receipts that began to serve as early currency.

Lending and Fractional Reserve Banking.   Over time, some astute goldsmiths observed that not all coins were withdrawn simultaneously. This meant that the goldsmiths could hold only a fraction of the total amount of gold coins received on deposit in their vaults; the remainder could be loaned out to individuals in need of temporary purchasing power. Better yet, goldsmiths could print additional standardized deposit receipts and loan them out to individuals, since these notes were now accepted as a medium of exchange. Borrowers gave the goldsmith a note promising to repay by a certain date and paid interest on the loans, providing the goldsmiths with additional income. The balance sheet of a goldsmith before and after making loans in the described manner is shown below in the format of T-accounts. Bank assets (uses of funds) are shown on the left-hand side, and bank liabilities (sources of funds) are shown on the right-hand side:

Before loan		After loan	
Assets	**Liabilities**	**Assets**	**Liabilities**
Gold $1,000	Receipts $1,000 (money)	Gold $1,000 Loans $4,000	Receipts $5,000 (money)
Total $1,000	Total $1,000	Total $5,000	Total $5,000

In our example, the goldsmith has printed $4,000 in additional standardized receipts that he has loaned out to earn interest. Notice that before the loans, the goldsmith had $1,000 in gold for $1,000 of standardized receipts; after the $4,000 in loans, there are $5,000 in receipts but still only $1,000 in gold to accommodate redemption of receipts for gold.

The example illustrates two important concepts. First, by issuing the additional $4,000, the goldsmith has in effect "created" money. Second, the goldsmith has ushered in the age of fractional reserve banking. *Fractional reserve banking* occurs when a bank's reserves (gold) amount to less than 100 percent of total deposits. In our example, the goldsmith went from 100 percent reserve banking to 20 percent ($1,000/ $5,000). Today, as then, money creation is based on the concept of fractional reserve banking.

Bank Safety. With the advent of fractional reserve banking, goldsmiths quickly found that it was more profitable to lend their standardized receipts (money) than to craft precious metals. Gradually, goldsmiths became known as *banks* and their receipts (liabilities) became know as *bank notes*. Bank notes are no more than unsecured IOUs issued by a bank.

Fractional reserve banking is not without problems, however. The concept is predicated on the fact that at any one time, only a small fraction of gold coins deposited will be needed to satisfy note redemptions. If, however, more note holders than usual were to attempt to convert their notes to gold coins, the bank might have to call for immediate repayment of some loans to gain additional gold or be faced with the prospect of failing. Because many note holders recognized that banks held insufficient funds to redeem all deposits, the slightest rumor of a bank's inability to convert notes into gold precipitated requests by large numbers of depositors to obtain gold coins for their bank notes before the supply of gold was exhausted. This is called a *run on the bank*. Bank panics occur when depositors lose confidence in banks in general and "run" many banks. Such bank panics, frequent in early American bank history, are marked by substantial declines in the money stock, which contribute to a general decline in employment and economic activity.

Deposit Banking. A final step necessary for the development of modern banking was for bankers to recognize that it was in their mutual self-interest to honor depository receipts issued or drawn on other banks. This development allowed bank notes and checking accounts to expand geographically and increase in popularity as a medium of exchange. Bank demand deposits emerged because bank customers found it more desirable to transfer ownership of their bank deposits by writing an order to the bank than to physically transfer bank notes. This practice led to the development of checking accounts as we know them today.

The First Banks

The first American bank to begin operations was the Bank of North America, established in Philadelphia in 1782. The bank was granted the power to issue bank notes, which were freely convertible into *specie* (gold or silver coins). That is, holders could exchange a note for its equivalent value in gold or silver coins. The bank and its currency (bank notes) proved to be profitable for the owners and popular with the public. The success of the Bank of North America prompted banks patterned after it to open in New York and Boston in 1784 and in a number of other cities before 1800.

Banks were controversial during the colonial period. Commercial forces in the country favored a strong banking industry. They viewed banks as stimulating capital formation and promoting trade by providing credit and a more generous supply of money. Conversely, agrarian interests denied that banks were productive at all. They viewed banks as lowering the quality of the nation's money because bank notes and deposits displaced metal coins from circulation. More fundamentally, the agricultural sector believed that banks favored industry and commerce at the expense of the agricultural and frontier areas of the country.

There was also deep-seated antagonism towards banks by the general public, which made banks politically vulnerable. Many colonists, when they were living in

Europe, had accumulated debts beyond their means to repay, and they were forced to either leave their homelands or go to debtor prison. Thus banks and a strong banking system were feared because of the economic power of banks as creditors and creators of money. Finally, the religious beliefs of many Americans were the basis for attitudes toward moneylenders that were less than favorable. One need only turn to biblical references to the immorality of usury or to the story of Jesus evicting the money changers from the temple to see why this was so. Though times have changed, banks in their role as creditors still draw much unfavorable attention, as attested by the vivid press and television coverage given credit card rates, credit restrictions, and bank foreclosures during the 1980s and 1990s.

In the early years of the new republic, there was controversy over who should charter banks—the federal government or the state governments. The Federalists, who favored centralized political power, thought that only the federal government had the power to create and supervise banks. They questioned the constitutionality of state activities in this field. Anti-Federalists and their supporters, who championed states' rights, believed that the chartering and supervision of banks should reside entirely with the individual states and that state control of banking would serve the best interests of each region of the country.

Although much of the controversy over banking was political, some of it arose from the way in which banks created money (bank notes) by extending loans. To many it appeared that banks were duping the public with worthless paper money or, at best, unsound money. When a bank loan was made, the borrower usually would receive loan funds in the form of bank notes rather than specie. As the notes were spent, they passed into general circulation. The individual bank notes were legal liabilities of the issuing bank, redeemable into gold or silver upon demand by the bearer. The hypothetical balance sheet of a typical bank before and after making a loan by issuing bank notes is shown in the following T-accounts:

Before loan		**After loan**	
Assets	**Liabilities**	**Assets**	**Liabilities**
Coins $1,000	Deposits $1,000	Coins $1,000	Deposits $1,000
		Loans $4,000	Bank
			Notes $4,000
Total $1,000	$1,000	$5,000	$5,000

Using fractional reserve banking in a manner similar to our hypothetical goldsmith, the bank is able to create $4,000 of bank note money while maintaining $1,000 in specie reserves. Modern banks use a similar process to create demand deposits rather than bank notes.

If the issuing bank was known for sound redemptions, the bank notes were readily accepted by the general public as a medium of exchange. However, if a bank had a poor business reputation, with large amounts of bank notes outstanding relative to its cash reserves (specie), or if the bank made it difficult to redeem its currency into gold or silver, its bank notes were *discounted*—that is, accepted for less than their face value in business transactions. For example, a New Yorker buying an item priced at $10 might be able to pay for it with a $10 bank note issued by a reputable and well-known

Exhibit 3–1   **Bank Note from Pawtuckaway Bank, Epping, New Hampshire**

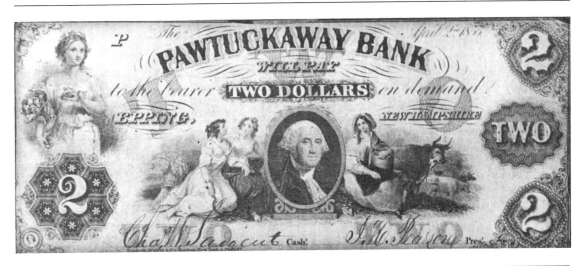

Historically, individual bank liabilities (called bank notes) served as money. The fact that so many different monies existed made trade difficult. A person never knew if the bank note was from a sound bank or from a failed or disreputable bank. It's no wonder that bank notes from lesser-known banks were heavily discounted.

Source: Courtesy of the Public Service Department, Federal Reserve Bank of Boston.

New York City bank. On the other hand, if the customer offered to pay with a bank note of a lesser-known Connecticut bank, the merchant might require $12 worth of notes—a 16.7 percent discount. The reason for the discount is the higher transaction cost of converting the Connecticut bank notes into specie and the risk of not being able to redeem the notes into gold at all. Exhibit 3–1 shows an example of a bank note issued by a New England bank.

Early Central Banking

First Bank of the United States

The first *central bank*, chartered by the federal government in 1791, was the Bank of the United States. A central bank is an institution charged with the responsibility of regulating the supply of money in the best interests of the public. The Bank of the United States was nationwide in scope, with eight branch offices in principal cities of the country and headquarters in Philadelphia. The bank was unique in that it performed both public and private functions. Privately, it operated as a commercial bank, making business loans, taking deposits, and issuing bank notes. Publicly, it served as a central bank for the federal government by controlling the amount of bank notes state banks could issue, transferring funds from one part of the country to another, and acting as fiscal agent for the federal government.

Opposition to the bank was strong. Defenders of state banks believed that the new federally sponsored bank created unfair competition by acting both as a controlling central bank and as a competing commercial bank. Anti-Federalists opposed the bank on constitutional grounds. Rural and agricultural interests feared that the bank would curb the relatively easy lending policies of state-chartered banks, siphoning funds away from rural areas and directing them to the cities for industrial investment.

The Bank of the United States made some of its bitterest enemies through its practice of draining reserves from state banks in order to limit their volume of loans and bank notes. This was achieved by accumulating a large quantity of a particular bank's notes and then presenting the notes to the bank for redemption, thus decreasing that bank's specie reserves. With lower reserves, the bank was forced to contract its bank notes or run the risk of failure. If the Bank of the United States was satisfied with a state bank's operating policy, it would hold that bank's notes or pay them out into circulation rather than redeeming them, thus allowing the bank to retain its specie reserve. As the largest bank in the system, the bank's own lending policies also increased the reserves of other banks. When it expanded its loans, some of the proceeds flowed to them. Bank notes of the Bank of the United States could be held by state banks to augment their gold and silver reserves. With additional reserves, they could extend more loans.

The bank appears to have functioned fairly well, especially when compared to other banks of the time. However, Congress refused to renew the charter of the Bank of the United States when it expired in 1811. The arguments advanced against the bank were mostly political: (1) the bank was unconstitutional, (2) it did not encourage the growth of state banking, (3) it encouraged the use of paper money, and (4) much of the bank's stock was foreign owned.

Second Bank of the United States

After five years, Congress reestablished a central bank in the United States by chartering the Second Bank of the United States in 1816. The period between the first and the second central banks was marked by high rates of inflation caused in part by the financial demands of the War of 1812 and in part by the gross abuse of banking privileges by state-chartered banks. The primary motivation for the establishment of the Second Bank was to curb the excessive inflation that followed the demise of the First Bank in 1811. The Second Bank's operations were similar to those of the First Bank, with it serving both as a private commercial bank and as a central bank. The Second Bank of the United States also received a 20-year charter from the federal government. Its operations were national in scope, and at its zenith it had as many as 25 branches throughout the country and controlled nearly one-third of all bank assets.

The Second Bank failed in its primary purpose of curbing the inflationary spiral of 1817 and 1818. The economic depressions of 1818 and 1820 came during periods when the bank was following a policy of restricting the quantity of state bank notes. Although other factors contributed to these sharp downturns in economic activity, the Second Bank received almost all the blame for these depressions. The wrath against the bank was so strong that opponents went so far as to organize a movement to revoke its charter, an action that proved unsuccessful. The Second Bank's demise

The Downfall of the Second Bank of the United States

Source: Courtesy, New York Historical Society, New York.

came shortly after Andrew Jackson, a populist president and states' rights advocate, vetoed a bill to renew its charter in 1832. Jackson's veto put an end to central banking in the United States until the establishment of the Federal Reserve System in 1913.

Early State Banking

Banks chartered by individual states dominated the American banking scene during the 1811–1816 period, as well as from 1836 until the establishment of a national banking system in 1863. The state banking eras, although free from domination by a federal central bank, were not without financial difficulties. Major financial panics and business recessions occurred regularly.

The scenarios preceding the financial panics were similar. First, the economy would expand rapidly, creating heavy demand for bank credit. Then, as interest rates increased, banks would meet their loan demands by issuing more and more bank notes. This would increase the money supply, further stimulate the economy, and lead to inflation. As banks continued to expand, many would overextend themselves by issuing too many bank notes relative to their reserve holdings. A slight downturn in economic activity would cause overextended banks to fail and the bank note component or the money supply to contract. People would panic, knowing that banks carried only fractional reserves. When the public demanded the conversion of its paper money into hard currency, banks were forced to "call in loans" from their customers. (Most bank loans at the time were *call loans*, which are loans due when the bank calls and asks for the money.) Bank panics would spread, leading to massive numbers of bank failures and further contractions in the money supply and credit availability; businesses would fail as their loans were called, and a recession would ensue. Exhibit 3–2 shows the often repeated cycle of financial panics, bank failures, and recessions.

Throughout the state banking eras, business activity fluctuated widely as banks alternated between liberal loan policies coupled with the rapid creation of bank notes and reduced lending activity followed by a shrinking of the money supply. Furthermore, a large number of banks entered and left the market, making it difficult to tell which bank notes were redeemable and which originated from failed banks. With so many different banks issuing bank notes, the period became a counterfeiter's paradise. For example, in 1860 there were more than 1,600 different banks operating under the diverse laws of some 30 states, and each bank issued a variety of notes. As a result, monthly registers were published describing which notes were (1) genuine notes of banks in operation, (2) genuine notes of failed banks, and (3) counterfeit notes. In one such publication, the *Bank Note Reporter and Counterfeit Detector*, more than 1,000 counterfeit bank notes were listed. Interestingly enough, because the public spent time and effort ascertaining which bank notes were sound, bank failures were concentrated among banks with the poorest assets (see *People and Events*).

State Banking Abuses

Without condemning all banks of the time, it can be said that the early state banks left much to be desired from the standpoint of depositors and note holders. The abuses in

---

Exhibit 3–2   **Financial Panics and the Business Cycle**

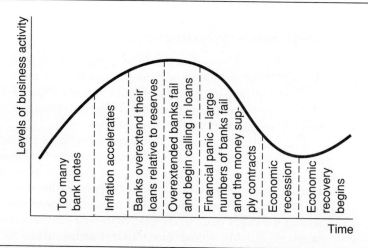

Large numbers of failures always seem to precede a business recession. Thus, bank failures were viewed as harbingers of bad economic news.

banking were so widespread that they had grave implications for the public's confidence in the banking system. Some of the most serious excesses of the times are outlined in this section; not all of them were permanently eliminated by subsequent regulation.

Bank Chartering.   Bank charters were often granted by special acts of the state legislatures. As today, not all state legislators were free of corruption. In fact, it was difficult to obtain a bank charter without some degree of political favoritism or bribery. Favored banks could also exercise political manipulation to ensure that applications of potential competitors were rejected. Thus favored banks could obtain geographic monopoly power.

Insufficient Bank Capital.   Many banks failed to acquire adequate capital (net worth) to protect their depositors from losses arising from bad loans or poor investments. Because losses are written off against capital, a bank will fail if it lacks adequate capital to absorb such losses. Bank failures result in losses to bank depositors and note holders.

High-Risk Loans.   Many banks made high-risk loans without adequate security or engaged in speculative lending activities. These practices were especially prevalent in land development schemes and real estate lending. Moreover, some banks lent imprudently and excessively to their stockholders and officers. Losses on high-risk loans, combined with inadequate capital, resulted in numerous bank failures and serious losses to depositors and note holders.

Inadequate Reserves.   Reserve requirements varied widely among states. In some states, reserve requirements were inadequate or absent altogether. Banks could issue a large quantity of bank notes without any regard for the amount of specie reserves held. Without adequate specie reserves or liquid assets, banks were vulnerable to failure if large numbers of depositors or note holders demanded gold or silver coin payments. Banks with inadequate reserves found their notes discounted by varying amounts.

Excessive Issuance of Bank Notes.   In good economic times, many banks financed their aggressive lending or speculative activities by issuing excessive amounts of bank notes, then suffered severe contractions during poor economic times. These periodic fluctuations in the money supply corresponded closely with inflationary and deflationary periods. Though bank policies were not the sole cause of these fluctuations, public opinion accused the banks of being a major contributor to them. Exhibit 3-3 shows the wide swings in the money supply that occurred during the state banking eras.

State Banking Experiments

Even though banking abuses were widespread during the state banking eras, many state banks were sound. Attempts to reform and regulate the banking system were primarily regional efforts. Most notably, New York and Massachusetts enacted highly protective banking laws and implemented them with strict bank supervision and examinations. State programs did little to alleviate the nationwide banking situation,

Exhibit 3–3   **Percentage of Expansion (+) and Contraction (−) in the Money Supply (1834–1861)**

Period	Percentage of Change in the Money Supply
1834–1837	+61
1837–1843	−58
1843–1848	+102
1848–1849	−11
1849–1854	+109
1854–1855	−12
1855–1857	+18
1857–1858	−23
1858–1861	+35

With lax state banking regulations and no central bank, there were wide swings in the money supply that led to disruptions in the economy. Even though they were not the only cause, banks were blamed by the public for these problems.

Source: John J. Knox. *A History of Banking in the United States* (New York: Bradford Rhodes, 1903).

but they did in some cases act as the forerunner of modern legislation. Three important state-initiated programs were (1) the Suffolk System, (2) free banking, and (3) the New York State Safety Fund.

The Suffolk System

In the early 1800s, Boston was the major trading center in the New England area. When business transactions were settled using notes of banks outside the Boston area, the notes usually were discounted 1 to 5 percent because of difficulties in redeeming them. Notes of Boston banks circulated at par because they were readily redeemable into gold and silver. Thus, in conformity with *Gresham's Law*—bad money drives out good money—people hoarded the notes of Boston banks and used the currency of country banks to pay their bills.[1] However, the public's preference for Boston bank notes was costly for the Boston banks. These banks were forced to hold large amounts of noninterest-bearing gold and silver reserves to meet potential redemptions of paper money. In addition, the New England economy could not function at maximum efficiency because of the lack of a sound currency and a widely accepted medium of exchange.

To remedy this situation, the Suffolk Bank of Boston adopted the policy of redeeming at par the bank notes of any New England bank that agreed to maintain specie deposits (reserves) with it large enough to meet the redemption of their notes. Country banks did not like this arrangement because the reserve requirements imposed by the Suffolk Bank limited their ability to make loans and create bank notes simultaneously. To coax country banks to participate in the system, the Suffolk Bank would accumulate a large volume of a nonmember bank's notes and then present

---

[1]*Gresham's Law* is named after Sir Thomas Gresham, who founded Martins Bank in 1563 when he converted his goldsmith business into a commercial bank. The bank still operates today.

them to the bank on a surprise visit for immediate redemption into gold or silver. Naturally, any bank with inadequate specie reserves was in a awkward position when it was unable to meet note redemptions. Most New England banks soon "saw the light" and joined the Suffolk's banking system.

By 1825, almost all New England banks were members, giving New England one of the soundest currencies in the country. Bank notes circulated freely throughout the area, facilitating trade. Furthermore, because of the threat of large-scale redemption by the Suffolk Bank, other New England banks avoided issuing excessive amounts of bank notes. This gave New England a sounder banking system than most other areas of the country and freed the area from many of the perils associated with state banking. It should be added that the Suffolk Bank's motives were not entirely altruistic; a portion of the deposits held with them could safely be loaned out for a profit. In sum, the Suffolk banking system achieved some of the results of a central banking system by providing a sound currency and controlling the size of the money supply. It underscored the importance of a central bank such as our present Federal Reserve System.

Free Banking

Prompted by the abuses suffered in the granting of bank charters, the Michigan Act of 1837 established a system of chartering banks called *free banking*. Free banking meant that any group that met preestablished legal requirements could operate a bank without obtaining special legislative approval. Many free banking laws required, however, that all bank note issues be backed with bank holdings of state bonds. The idea of free banking met with wide popular acceptance. Other states soon adopted free banking laws, and by 1860, 18 states had them. The public's response was astounding. In just six years, the number of banks almost doubled, increasing from 500 in 1834 to more than 900 in 1840. Exhibit 3–4 shows this dramatic increase in the number of

Exhibit 3–4   **State Bank Growth Following Free Banking Laws**

Year	Number of State Banks	State Bank Notes Outstanding (millions)	Total State Bank Notes and Deposits (millions)
1834	506	$ 95	$171
1835	704	104	187
1836	713	140	255
1837	788	149	276
1838	829	116	201
1839	840	135	225
1840	901	107	182

Following the enactment of free banking laws by states in 1837, the number of banks increased dramatically. Many of these new banks were undercapitalized, poorly managed, or held poor-quality assets, and many failed as a result.

Source: Board of Governors, Federal Reserve System, *Banking Studies* (Washington, DC, 1941).

DID YOU KNOW?

Private Clearinghouses' Public Functions

In the period from 1837 through 1913, the United States did not have a functioning central bank. However, private institutions, in the form of bank clearinghouses, developed functions that were de facto central banking functions. Because some of those functions were illegal under the national banking acts, banks supported the formation of the Federal Reserve System, since it was set up to perform legally the central banking functions that bank clearinghouses had performed during emergencies.

Before the formation of the Fed, during trying times bank clearinghouses had made loans by issuing clearinghouse "loan certificates" to member banks that were short of specie (coin) when it came time to clear their balances. A borrowing bank pledged loans or other assets as collateral with the clearinghouse association in exchange for clearinghouse "loan certificates." It then used those certificates to pay its debts to other clearing banks. This lender of last resort function of the clearinghouses anticipated the Federal Reserve's discount window loan policy. Banks can now honor their check payments and reserve requirements by borrowing additional reserves at the Fed discount window and posting suitable collateral to secure their short-term debts to the Fed.

During the panics of 1893 and 1907, bank clearinghouses also issued "clearinghouse certificates" in small denominations in exchange for the collateralized loan certificates deposited by banks. These clearinghouse certificates in turn were issued to the public by the banks and circulated as currency

during the panics. During the panic of 1893, these clearinghouse certificates added $2\frac{1}{2}$ percent to the money stock and in 1907, they added $4\frac{1}{2}$ percent. In this way the bank clearinghouses provided an elastic currency supply during crisis periods. However, under the national banking acts, their actions were illegal as the clearinghouse currency was not backed by government bonds. Thus, commercial banks supported provisions in the 1913 Federal Reserve Act that gave Federal Reserve banks the power to provide an elastic currency supply and also to serve as lenders of last resort to fight stresses caused by financial panics and crises.

Finally, because clearinghouse loans were backed by member banks in the clearinghouse associations, all members were potentially exposed to losses from the default of any one member—not only because such defaults could degrade the value of loan certificates, causing losses to other clearinghouse members, but also because the default could cause the public to lose confidence in the solvency of all clearinghouse member banks. Consequently, member banks required that all bank members provide regular detailed financial statements to the clearinghouse and be subject to examination by clearinghouse representatives. These provisions also carried over to the Fed. The Federal Reserve Act required that the Fed regularly examine banks that were accepted as "member banks" in the federal system. In addition, bank regulators today require that all federally chartered and federally insured banks submit quarterly call reports that provide detailed data on each bank's financial condition.

banks. Unfortunately, free banking was not without its problems. Many of the laws were too lenient, leading to cases of unsound or unscrupulous banking.

Although free banking eliminated some banking abuses, such as graft, political patronage in receiving bank charters, and monopolistic protection from competition, it exacerbated other abuses found in state banking that we have previously discussed.

The lack of uniform currency and a central bank led to financial chaos in some states. Many free banks failed, and people found themselves holding bank notes having little or no value. The situation became so serious that the federal government was forced to set up an independent Treasury payment system that completely bypassed the banking system. The Treasury Department maintained this system for nearly 20 years, until it was forced to rely on commercial banks to finance the Civil War in 1862. The free banking period again emphasized the need to regulate banking and the negative effect that an unhealthy banking system has on the economy as a whole.

The Safety Fund System

An innovation in American banking was the establishment of the New York Safety Fund in 1829. The purpose of the fund was to protect creditors (note holders and depositors) in the event of a bank failure. The fund greatly reduced the likelihood that large numbers of depositors and note holders would redeem their bank liabilities at the slightest rumor of a bank's inability to convert notes or deposits to coins. Without such protection, many sound banks could fail in the event of a bank run.

New York banks financed the fund by paying annually to the state's treasury department one-half of 1 percent of the bank's capital until the total contribution equaled 3 percent of the bank's capital. The Safety Fund worked until a wave of bank failures in the 1840s exhausted it.

The lessons from the New York Safety Fund are clear. First, only deposit insurance backed by the federal government has the financial resources to withstand large numbers of bank failures and thereby engender public confidence during crisis situations. Second, state or private insurance systems do not have the necessary diversification that is possible under a national plan, nor do they have the supervisory and examining powers necessary to maintain the strength of the insured institutions. Although state and private insurance programs can succeed in preventing individual bank failures, they cannot succeed in preventing bank panics and the resulting widespread bank failures that are so damaging to the economy.

Regrettably, the lessons from the past are still being learned. Some states still allow some depository institutions to obtain private deposit insurance—or worse, operate without any insurance. A recent example illustrating this problem was the collapse of Home State Saving Bank of Cincinnati, Ohio, a privately insured institution. Its closing in March 1985 led to the temporary closing of 70 Ohio thrifts whose deposits were insured by a state-sponsored private insurance fund. The losses suffered by Home State were believed to be large enough to exhaust the insurance reserves. As a result, depositors in the privately insured thrifts had little confidence that their funds were safe, and they began a run on Home State's deposits. Subsequently, the state declared a bank holiday that temporarily prevented depositors from withdrawing their funds. This was the first bank holiday that had been declared since the Great Depression of the 1930s.

Another example was the failure of the Rhode Island Share and Deposit Indemnity Corporation in 1991. Because of the large losses at an insured bank, the governor closed the fund, leaving many depositors at small credit unions and banks without insurance. In both Ohio and Rhode Island, taxpayers were unwilling to pay for the losses incurred by the insurance fund, so many depositors lost money.

In sum, despite the limited success of the New York Safety Fund and similar state programs, these programs were the forerunners of our present-day federally insured deposit programs. Their historical record underscored the advantage of deposit insurance and the pitfalls of private insurance programs.

The Civil War and National Banking

The National Bank Acts

The shortcomings of state banking were painfully obvious to most observers of the times. Although there was considerable pressure for bank reform, various political factions and interest groups could not coalesce behind any single legislative proposal. The federal government's need to finance the Civil War in 1862 finally brought positive action with the passage of the National Bank acts of 1863 and 1864. Although these acts did not reinstate federal centralized control of banking, as some desired, they did correct some of the major deficiencies that existed with state banking.

Congress had two broad goals when designing the National Bank acts: (1) to provide the nation with a safe and uniform currency system and (2) to provide a new source of loans with which to finance the Civil War. The acts allowed the establishment of a system of federally chartered banks owned and operated by private individuals. These new "national" banks were required to hold United States government bonds as security against any bank notes they issued. The purchase of government securities would provide additional funds to finance the war. The national bank notes were printed by the U.S. Treasury and were redeemable at par at any national bank. It was hoped that the new national bank notes would provide the country with a safe and uniform national currency that could not be easily counterfeited.

The National Bank acts remain one of the foundations of American banking practice. The following are some of the more important provisions.

Chartering.   The National Bank acts allowed any group of five or more persons to apply to the comptroller of the currency in Washington, DC, for a bank charter. Anyone meeting the basic requirements would receive a charter and permission to open a national bank. A *national bank* was to be distinguished from a *state bank*, which received its charter from state banking authorities. The existence of both a national- and a state-chartered banking system is known as the *dual banking system*. The distinction between state and national banks remains today.

Capital Requirements.   One of the major improvements of the National Bank acts was the establishment of higher minimum capital requirements for the protection of depositors. The minimum capital requirement for a national bank ranged from $50,000 for a small-community bank to up to $200,000 for banks in larger communities. The acts' capital requirements, though not harsh by today's standards, represented a substantial improvement over bank capital standards of the times.

Assets.   The National Bank acts placed restrictions on the type and amount of loans that could be made by national banks. To promote liquidity and safety, the banks were prohibited from lending on real estate or lending to any one borrower an amount exceeding 10 percent of the bank's capital stock.

Reserve Requirements.   The acts also set up minimum reserve requirements against the banks' deposits and bank notes outstanding. The amount of reserves required ranged from 15 percent of notes and deposits for rural banks to 25 percent for banks in large metropolitan areas. Reserve requirements for banks continue today.

Bank Notes.   First, national bank notes were printed by the Treasury Department to ensure standardization and quality of printing and to thereby reduce the possibility of counterfeiting. Second, national bank notes could be issued only against U.S. government securities deposited with the comptroller of the currency, and each bank had to maintain a redemption fund with the comptroller equal to 5 percent of its outstanding notes. Finally, national banks were required to accept at par the notes of other national banks. Although bank note holders could still suffer losses because of bank failures, the National Bank acts were the first step in developing a uniform and safe national currency.

Bank Supervision.   A major problem with state banking was that many states had poorly constructed and inadequately enforced banking laws. The National Bank acts allowed the Treasury Department to establish the Office of the Comptroller of the Currency, whose responsibility was to supervise and administer the law. To this end, the comptroller had a corps of bank examiners who were generally better trained than their state counterparts.

Rise of Deposit Banking

The National Bank acts, for the most part, succeeded in providing a safer national currency. Their framers also hoped that most state banks would switch to the more attractive national charters, thus eliminating dual banking. This would further ensure a more uniform national currency and, more importantly, eliminate the abuses perpetrated by state banks in the issuance of paper money. However, this was not to be the case.

After the National Bank acts, state banks continued to issue excessive amounts of paper money. To correct this apparent deficiency, Congress passed an additional act in 1865 that placed a 10 percent annual tax on all state bank notes. This tax was so prohibitive that it made the issuance of state bank notes unprofitable. As a result, within a few years most state bank notes were withdrawn from circulation and the number of state banks declined sharply.

However, the bank notes tax did not spell an end to state banking, as some had expected. Following the Civil War there were marked changes in the character of American economic life as business firms grew larger, communications and transportation improved, and the volume of regional and national business transactions increased. To facilitate these transactions, people increasingly found checks written on bank deposits payable on demand to be a more convenient payment mechanism than paper currency. State banks soon found that they could continue operations by issuing demand deposits rather than bank notes when making loans. Once banks and their customers became accustomed to these new instruments, the number of state

PEOPLE & EVENTS

Wildcat Banking and Public Prescience

Most "free" banking acts in the 1800s allowed newly chartered banks to issue currency only if it was backed by state bonds deposited as collateral with the state banking commissioner. If a bank subsequently failed to redeem its bank notes with specie, the bank could be shut down and the bonds sold to provide funds to repay holders of the bank's notes.

Abuses of the free banking privilege could occur if a state allowed banks to deposit securities with a "par" value equal to the value of the bank notes, but with market values that were considerably less than par. In particular, organizers of fraudulent "wildcat banks" sometimes intentionally posted bonds worth less than par as collateral to back their bank note issues, and then quickly went out of business, keeping any surplus funds (the difference between the bond's par value and market value) for themselves.

However, in investigations of free banking era bank failures, Rolnick and Weber found that most occurred not because bank organizers intentionally posted discount bonds to back their bank note issues, but rather because the bonds used to back their bank note issues had fallen in price. Thus free banking bank failures tended to be correlated with factors such as regional hard times or financial crises that caused bond backing for bank notes to lose value and, thus, precipitated note holder runs on affected banks. Since not all banks held the same collateral to back their bank notes, Rolnick and Weber concluded that there was little evidence that bank runs were contagious across states during the free banking era.

Rolnick and Weber also noted that bank failures were strongly correlated with the value of collateral used to back bank notes. For instance, Minnesota's 7 percent railroad bonds lost value after railroad construction was suspended in early 1859. Subsequently, most Minnesota banks that collateralized their bank notes with those bonds failed. However, the Minnesota "free" banks that collateralized their bank notes with Minnesota 8 percent bonds (which

were backed by tax revenues, not railroad revenues) or Ohio 6 percent bonds (which also were of good quality) did not fail.

These free banking era experiences provide several important lessons for today's banking. First, they show that bank assets should, insofar as possible, be valued on a "market value" basis, rather than a "book value" or "par value" basis, so the public can ascertain the true value of bank assets. Second, it suggests that regulators should make information on the true value and composition of bank assets used to back transactions deposits available to the public. In that way, bankers will have an incentive to hold high-quality assets that retain their value to assure the public that their transactions deposits (which are fundamentally similar to 1800s bank notes) are safe. Clearly, the public showed in the 1800s that it was smart enough to want to hold bank notes only of banks with good-quality assets, as banks that held such assets survived while those that held the poorest-quality assets experienced "runs" and failed. In the 1800s the public was able to ascertain the quality of bank assets used to back bank notes because those assets were held on deposit with state officials. Now the public can only observe quarterly "call report" statements that provide limited information on the quality of bank assets and no information on discrepancies between their market value and book value (or par value). A private public-interest group called the "Shadow Financial Regulatory Committee," therefore, has suggested that these present-day policies be changed to provide today's depositors with better information on the current market value of financial institutions' assets. They believe this would encourage financial institutions to hold higher-quality assets. Many officers of financial institutions oppose such policies, however, as they fear that such full disclosure would once again cause the public to "run" to withdraw their deposits from weak institutions.

Exhibit 3–5   **National and State Banks in the United States (1800–1914)**

Year	National Banks	State Banks	Total
1860	—	1,529	1,529
1865	1,294	349	1.643
1870	1,612	325	1,937
1875	2,076	586	2,662
1880	2,076	650	2,726
1890	3,484	2,250	5,734
1900	3,731	5,007	8,738
1910	7,138	14,348	21,486
1914	7,518	17,498	25,016

Following the National Bank acts of 1863 and 1864, it appeared that state banks might be driven from the marketplace. The acceptance of checks as a medium of payment by the public, however, kept the dual banking system intact.

Source: Board of Governors, Federal Reserve System, *Banking Studies* (Washington, DC, 1941).

banks increased rapidly. Exhibit 3–5 shows the beginning of national banks and the decline and subsequent rebirth of state banking.

Defects in the National Banking System

The Inelasticity Problem.   Although the national banking system unquestionably improved the quality of American banks, it had a number of serious shortcomings. Most notable was the lack of a flexible or "elastic" currency supply. The National Bank acts did not provide for increases in the money supply as the economy expanded or as seasonal needs arose during the agricultural cycle. Furthermore, as we have already discussed, the amount of bank notes that could be issued was based on a percentage of the market value of the Treasury securities that a bank owned. Consequently, the supply of national bank notes depended solely on the U.S. government bond market. From 1888 to 1891, for example, the volume of national bank notes outstanding fell by one-third, from $247 million to $165 million, causing a reduction in the money supply and contributing to a recession. Thus critics rightfully maintained that the nation's money supply was "inelastic" to economic needs. As we shall see later, one of the major purposes of the Federal Reserve Act of 1913 was to establish an elastic currency.

The Illiquidity Problem.   Another deficiency in the national banking system was that it allowed legal *pyramiding of reserves*, which was responsible for the tendency of the banking system to precipitate financial panics. Pyramiding resulted from smaller country banks counting their deposits in large city banks as part of their reserves. Under the pyramiding system, big city banks competed vigorously for the reserve deposits of country banks because these reserves could be loaned out for additional income. Country banks viewed these deposits as reserves that could be exchanged for cash when they were faced with cash needs. This frequently happened during the harvest season, when farming-area banks distributed large amounts of currency. As the agricultural banks exchanged their reserves for cash, the large banks found their cash holdings depleted. Once this occurred, the large banks were forced to liquidate loans, such as call loans made to brokers, that could be liquidated at the bank's request.

The forced reduction in bank credit and the drawing of reserves from central reserve cities often led to a *liquidity squeeze* as the public and businesses found they had less cash than they desired. As a result, many people sold financial assets at reduced prices in order to gain a share of the diminished supply of cash. As financial asset prices fell sharply, people panicked, selling more of their assets in an attempt to gain a portion of the ever-diminishing supply of cash. Financial panics, which led to violent disruptions in the economy, were caused by a banking system with limited cash reserves that could be easily drained off. Though the pyramiding of reserves may appear to have been the root problem, the absence of any degree of flexibility in providing reserves and currency permitted this structural weakness to be translated into numerous banking crises.

The Payment System Problem.   A final deficiency in the national banking system was the lack of an efficient national payment system. There was no central check-clearing and collection mechanism comparable to that maintained today by the Federal Reserve System. Instead, there existed thousands of individual banks that cleared checks through an extensive correspondent banking network. The cost of

---

America Needs an Elastic Currency

Source: Courtesy, *Philadelphia Record* as appeared in *Historical Beginnings ... The Federal Reserve*, Federal Reserve Bank of Boston, 1982, p. 13. Reprinted with permission.

transferring funds between regional locations was great, and there frequently were long delays in check clearing. Thus many banks would redeem out-of-town checks at discounts rather than at par.

Panics and Change

The shortcomings of the national banking system became apparent with the occurrence of frequent and successive financial panics. The financial crises of 1873, 1884, and 1893, and finally the disastrous 1907 crisis brought people of differing political and economic views to the realization that some sort of centralized control over the nation's monetary system was needed. During the last of these panics, private bank clearinghouses had found it necessary to print their own "currency" (see *Did You Know*), even though that was illegal under the National Banking acts. Thus, they favored the formation of a central bank that could legally perform that function.

The passage of the Federal Reserve Act in 1913 marked the return of central banking to the United States after a 77-year absence following the demise of the Second Bank of the United States. The new central banks had a decentralized structure that involved a combination of public and private interest. This unique structure dispelled widespread concern over a concentration of economic power in the hands of the nation's banks (especially the large Eastern banks) or the nation's politicians. After the enactment of the Federal Reserve Act in 1913, no major changes were made in the banking system until the 1930s. Then a major depression, starting in 1929 and aggravated by massive bank failures, led to the enactment of a number of measures to protect banks and their depositors. These and other banking regulations are discussed in Chapters 4 and 17.

Summary

This chapter examines the development of the American banking system. Understanding this development should provide insight into current regulatory and operating practices of commercial banks as well as into some of the illogical aspects of the American banking system. Commercial banks as we know them today probably originated in Europe from gold- and silversmiths, who stored precious metals and coins for their customers.

The early banks in this country were controversial. The controversy, in part, was centered on industrialization versus agrarianism and on centralization of political power versus states' rights. The Federalists wanted to develop a strong, industry-based economy and favored banking, whereas states' rights proponents viewed banks as favoring industry at the expense of the agricultural and frontier sections of the country. The attempts to establish a central bank in this country were caught up in the same political turmoil. The United States had two central banks prior to 1913. Both were politically controversial and lost their charters.

The state banking eras covered the years 1811–1816 and 1836–1863. Free from domination by a federal central bank, these periods were generally marked by wide-open banking practices and lax state regulation. The country suffered a major economic crisis almost once every decade. Financial panics and business recessions appeared to be ignited or reinforced by a large number of bank failures. The shortcomings of state banking were apparent to most observers of the time. Unfortunately, the country was unable to coalesce behind any single legislative proposal that might have stabilized the financial system.

The catalyst that brought about national banking legislation was the government's need to finance the Civil War. The result was the passage of the National Bank acts of 1863 and 1864, which corrected some of state banking's major deficiencies. Unfortunately, these acts had a number of shortcomings, the most notable of which were the lack of a flexible currency supply and the pyramiding of reserves. Furthermore, checks were often cleared only with a discount, and bank notes periodically became suspect. These deficiencies often led to financial panics and ultimately to economic depressions. To correct these deficiencies, Congress established the Federal Reserve System in 1913.

Questions

1. What is a central bank? What is its primary purpose? Does the United States have a central bank?
2. How did early banks create bank notes? What were the problems associated with too many bank notes and too few bank notes?
3. Why weren't the charters of the First and Second Banks of the United States renewed? Do you believe Jackson's veto of the charter of the Second Bank was good for the country?
4. Why were runs on banks frequent occurrences in American banking history? What is their cause? Why are runs on banks infrequent today?
5. What were the major abuses of state banking? Describe how these abuses affected the public and the economy.
6. What important lessons were learned from the Suffolk System? How did the system operate?
7. Explain the importance of the New York Safety Fund. What important banking problems did it try to eliminate? Why did it fail to work as designed?
8. One of the intentions of the National Bank acts was to eliminate state banking in the United States. Explain how state banks were able not only to survive but also to prosper.
9. Explain how the pyramiding of reserves led to financial panics.
10. What events led to the establishment of the Federal Reserve System in 1913?

Selected References

Benston, George J. "Why Continue to Regulate Banks?: An Historical Assessment of Federal Banking Regulations." *Midland Corporate Finance Journal*, Fall 1987, pp. 67–82.
An excellent article that examines from a historical perspective the reasons banks are regulated.

Duprey, James N., and Clarence W. Nelson. "A Visible Hand: The Fed's Involvement in the Check Payment System." *Quarterly Review*. Federal Reserve Bank of Minneapolis, Spring 1986, pp. 18–29.
This article examines the role of the Federal Reserve System in establishing the national payment system.

Gilbert, Alton, and Geoffrey E. Wood. "Coping with Bank Failures: Some Lessons from the United States and the United Kingdom." *Economic Review*. **Federal Reserve Bank of St. Louis, December 1986, pp. 5–14.**

A historical examination of bank failures and issues related to bank failures. Looks at experiences in both the United States and the United Kingdom.

Hammond, Bray. *Banks and Politics in America from the Revolution to the Civil War*. **Princeton, NJ: Princeton University Press, 1957.**

A good view of the political nature of early U.S. banking. A winner of a Pulitzer Prize in history.

Huertas, Thomas F. "The Regulation of Financial Institutions: A Historical Perspective on Current Issues." In *Financial Services: The Changing Institutions and Government Policy*, **ed. George J. Benston. Englewood Cliffs, NJ: Prentice-Hall, 1983.**

An overview of the historical origins and development of current bank regulations. Very readable.

Johnson, Roger T. *Historical Beginnings: The Federal Reserve*. **Boston: Federal Reserve Bank of Boston, 1979.**

A well-written illustrated account of the history and development of the Federal Reserve System.

McCarthy, F. Ward. "The Evolution of the Bank Regulatory Structure: A Reappraisal." *Economic Review*. **Federal Reserve Bank of Richmond, March–April 1984.**

A comprehensive analysis of the origin and development of the bank regulatory structure in the United States, covering the colonial period through the financial reforms of the 1930s.

Prager, Jonas. *Fundamentals of Money, Banking, and Financial Institutions*. **New York: Harper & Row, 1987.**

A readable presentation on the development of American banking up to the Federal Reserve Act. See Chapter 5.

Rolnick, Arthur J., and Warren E. Weber. "Banking Instability and Regulation in the U.S. Free Banking Era." *Quarterly Review*. **Federal Reserve Bank of Minneapolis, Summer 1985.**

This article examines whether the free banking era caused the bank failures and closures that swept the nation in the nineteenth century. It indicates that contagion was not prevalent in free banking era bank failures because the public was aware of the quality of state bonds backing each bank's notes.

Studenski, Paul, and Herman E. Kross. *Financial History of the United States*. **New York: McGraw-Hill, 1963.**

A comprehensive and well-documented history of the U.S. financial system.

Veazey, Edward E. "Evolution of Money and Banking in the United States." *Business Review*. **Federal Reserve Bank of Dallas, December 1975.**

A brief but well-written history of the development of commercial banking in the United States.

THE FEDERAL RESERVE SYSTEM

4

H AS YOUR LOCAL BANK EVER given you dollar bills so new that they stuck together? And have you ever wondered where they came from? The printing of new bills is one of the responsibilities of the U.S. Treasury Department. But who tells the U.S. Treasury Department how many new bills to print?

Regulation of the amount of money and credit in the economy is the responsibility of the Federal Reserve System. It is a heavy responsibility indeed. The amount of money and credit in the marketplace is a factor that influences inflation, recession, interest rate levels, unemployment, and foreign trade problems. While Fed policy is known to influence the structure of the economy, control is another matter. Many people do not understand what the Fed is or what it realistically can or cannot be expected to do.

In this chapter we first describe how the Federal Reserve developed and how it is now structured. We then review the Fed's balance sheet and note how its financial behavior allows it to affect total financial institution reserves and the money supply. We also describe the Fed's major regulations, which allow it to have a substantial effect on practically all of the nation's financial institutions and financial markets.

The Federal Reserve Act

The passage of the Federal Reserve Act in 1913 was meant to correct some of the shortcomings of the national bank system that became apparent during the severe financial crisis of 1907. The goals of the legislation were to establish (1) a monetary authority that would expand and contract the nation's money supply according to the needs of the economy, (2) a lender of last resort that could furnish additional currency to banks in times of financial crisis, (3) an efficient payment system for clearing and collecting checks throughout the country, and (4) a more vigorous bank supervision system.

The Federal Reserve System's ability to provide currency was established to eliminate the financial panics that had plagued the country when the public feared currency would not be available on demand. An elastic money supply was achieved by authorizing the Federal Reserve banks to issue a new type of bank note— the Federal Reserve note. Member banks of the Federal Reserve System could obtain

Federal Reserve notes whenever they needed extra currency. Today Federal Reserve notes are the principal form of currency in circulation.

Because people were wary of centralized power, the Federal Reserve Act provided for 12 largely autonomous regional Federal Reserve banks coordinated by a Board of Governors in Washington, DC. As originally conceived, each regional bank was responsible for the economic needs of a particular geographic area of the country.

Over the years the goals and role of the Federal Reserve System have changed with the changing economic environment. Today most authority in the system resides with the Board of Governors rather than with the regional Federal Reserve banks. The primary function of the Federal Reserve is economic stabilization through the management of the nation's money supply.

Structure of the Federal Reserve System

The modern-day Federal Reserve System consists of a seven-member Board of Governors, 12 regional Federal Reserve banks (and their branches) located throughout the country (see Exhibit 4–1), and thousands of member commercial banks. It also includes the Federal Open Market Committee (FOMC), which plays a major role in shaping the nation's monetary policy.

Member banks include all nationally chartered commercial banks, plus approximately 10 percent of all state-chartered commercial banks, which joined the Fed voluntarily. Member banks buy stock in their regional Federal Reserve banks and help elect each regional bank's board of directors. Prior to 1980, only member banks had unrestricted access to the Federal Reserve's free check-clearing services. In 1980 Congress gave access to Federal Reserve services to all depository institutions, but it required that the Federal Reserve impose service charges.

Federal Reserve banks in each region assist in clearing and processing checks and certain electronic funds payments in their respective areas of the country. They also issue Federal Reserve notes, monitor local economic conditions, provide advice to the Federal Reserve Board, help implement Federal Reserve regulations, and participate (through the Federal Open Market Committee) in the making of monetary policy.

When first established, Federal Reserve banks were intended to represent regional interests in Washington and to provide for the credit needs of their regions. Thus they were given power to issue currency and establish discount rates applicable to all institutions in their regions that wished to borrow from them. Historically, discount rates occasionally have varied from one Federal Reserve bank to another. In recent years, however, the Federal Reserve Board has used its power to review discount rates to enforce uniformity.

Over time the regional banks have relinquished powers to the Board of Governors. Not only can the Board review and disapprove the banks' discount rates, thereby causing the banks to change their discount rates to satisfy the Board, but also it appoints the top officers of each Federal Reserve bank and determines their salaries. Nonetheless, through their periodic representation on the Federal Open Market Committee (11 banks rotate four FOMC memberships while the Federal Reserve Bank of New York has a permanent representative), Federal Reserve bank presidents help establish monetary policy.

Exhibit 4–1   **The Federal Reserve System**

The Federal Reserve System consists of the Board of Governors and 12 Federal Reserve districts. Each district is served by a Federal Reserve bank that is named after its headquarters city. Each district bank may have one or more branches that assist in funds transfers within the district. For example, the Federal Reserve Bank of Chicago has a branch bank in Detroit. Each district Federal Reserve bank also issues its own Federal Reserve notes, with its name and seal on the notes.

The FOMC

The Federal Open Market Committee (FOMC) consists of the seven members of the Board of Governors of the Federal Reserve System plus five presidents of Federal Reserve banks. The FOMC is extremely important because it determines the nation's monetary policy (and financial institutions' reserve balances). It can affect the amount of money in circulation and the level of economic activity by controlling the monetary base.

The Board of Governors

Because it sets the nation's monetary policy, the Board of Governors of the Federal Reserve System is among the most powerful of all governmental bodies. It is financially and administratively independent of both Congress and the president.

In many countries, rather than raise taxes, politicians use their country's central bank to finance excessive deficits, thereby creating substantial inflation. To preserve the Fed's political independence, Congress established overlapping terms for Federal Reserve Board members, with one 14-year term expiring every 2 years. However, governors frequently resign from the Board to earn higher pay. Thus presidents can often appoint a majority of the Board quickly—for instance, President Carter needed only two years to appoint a majority of the Board. In addition to appointing Board members, the president names one of the Board members to a four-year term as chairman. All presidential appointments must be confirmed by the Senate.

Independence of the Fed

Because of the president's appointive power and Congress's power to change or abolish the Federal Reserve's authority, the Federal Reserve is less independent in fact than it is on paper. Strong political pressures from Congress or the president often are brought to bear on the Fed (see People and Events). It is doubtful, however, that Congress really wants to set Fed policies, for then Congress could no longer blame the Fed for the nation's economic problems. Still, congressional threats and presidential pressure alter Fed policies at times.

The Chairman of the Fed

The chairman of the Board of Governors is one of the most powerful people in the United States. The chairman influences the nation's monetary policy by controlling the agenda and meetings of both the Federal Reserve Board and the FOMC. He also is the principal spokesman for the Fed both before Congress and to the national press.

The structure of the Federal Reserve System is diagramed in Exhibit 4-2.

The Fed's Balance Sheet

The assets and liabilities of the Federal Reserve System are extremely important because they largely determine the nation's *monetary base*, which equals currency in circulation plus financial institution deposits at the Fed. The Fed's major assets and liabilities are shown in Exhibit 4-3.

Liabilities of the Fed

Federal Reserve Notes.   As shown in Exhibit 4-3, the largest single liability of the Fed consists of Federal Reserve notes in circulation. Look at the bills (if any) in your pocket. You will find that each has a seal of the Federal Reserve bank that issued it. You can take the bill to that bank and ask for lawful money in exchange, but you will get back only another Federal Reserve note. Federal Reserve notes are lawful money, because they are "legal tender for all debts public and private." That means you can repay any debt in this country by offering the proper amount of Federal Reserve notes.

Depository Institution Reserve Deposits.   The second largest liability of the Fed consists of *reserve and clearing deposits held by depository institutions*. These deposits are useful because they can be transferred from one institution to another when checks and wire transfers are "cleared" from one institution to another. They

Exhibit 4–2   **Organization of the Federal Reserve System**

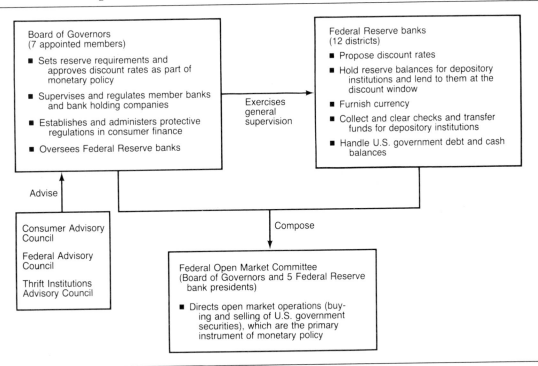

The Federal Reserve System has overlapping lines of authority. Even though the Board of Governors oversees the Federal Reserve banks and approves the appointment of their top officers, all members of the Board of Governors and five of the twelve Federal Reserve bank presidents vote equally on monetary policy decisions made by the FOMC.

Exhibit 4–3   **The Federal Reserve Balance Sheet (December 31, 1991)**

Assets (percent)			Liabilities (percent)		
Loans		0.1%	Federal Reserve notes		81.5%
Government and agency securities		81.6	Deposits:		14.1
Coins		0.2	Depository institution reserves	8.3%	
Cash items in process of collection (CIPC)		2.3	U.S. Treasury deposits	5.0	
Other Assets:		15.8	Foreign and other	0.8	
Gold certificates and SDRs	6.0%		Deferred availability cash items (DACI)		2.1
Foreign-denominated assets	7.8		Other liabilities and accrued dividends		0.8
Other assets and premises	2.0		Capital and surplus		1.5
Total ($353 billion)		100.0%	Total ($353 billion)		100.0%

The Fed's assets consist primarily of holdings of securities issued by the federal government and agencies of the federal government. Its liabilities consist primarily of Federal Reserve notes. The nation's total money supply is greatly affected by the Fed's balance sheet, because Federal Reserve notes and depository institution reserves account for nearly all of the nation's monetary base.

PEOPLE & EVENTS

The Fed Is Independent: or Is It?

The Fed is less independent than it appears because both the administration and the Congress often bring pressure to bear on it. In 1990 and 1991 the economy entered a recession that may have been aggravated by the Fed's desire to reduce inflation expectations in the economy. Thus, as the economy weakened, the Fed let the money supply grow slowly throughout 1991. Furthermore, several Federal Reserve Bank presidents gave speeches extolling the virtues of price stability for abetting business and personal planning and improving economic efficiency. Congress and the president, who had to stand for election in 1992, were not enamored of concepts such as economic efficiency if the only way that the economy could achieve the desired price stability was to create a serious recession that would cost them their jobs. Thus, Congress introduced bills that, if passed, would remove Federal Reserve Bank presidents (including the outspoken "zero-inflation" advocates) from the FOMC. Furthermore, the president delayed his renomination of Alan Greenspan as chairman of the Fed until July 1991, even though Greenspan's term expired in early August. Also, Congress did not act on his reappointment until February, 1992—by which time the Fed had eased monetary policy substantially by cutting the discount rate three times from $5\frac{1}{2}$ percent to $3\frac{1}{2}$ percent, the Fed Funds rate from 6 percent to 4 percent, and announced a reduction in reserve requirements on transactions deposits from 12 percent to 10 percent effective in April. These steps were designed to kick-start monetary growth, and hopefully, the economy prior to the 1992 election.

also are useful to the Fed for controlling the nation's money supply. *Depository institutions* are limited as to the amount of deposits they can hold by the fact that they must back a portion of all customer transactions deposits either with cash in their vault or with deposits held as *reserves* at the Federal Reserve banks.

Treasury and Other Deposits.   Another important class of Federal Reserve deposits consists of *U.S. Treasury deposits*. The Federal Reserve acts as the fiscal agent for the U.S. Treasury, as you can see if you ever get a check from the federal government. If you read the fine print, you will find that the check was written on a deposit at a Federal Reserve bank. When the Treasury collects money from you, it first puts the money in "tax and loan" accounts at the depository institutions, then transfers the money to the Fed when it wants to spend it. Large payments into or out of Treasury deposits at the Fed will cause large shifts in depository institutions' reserves as the checks are deposited and collected. Thus the Treasury tries to minimize fluctuations in its deposits at the Fed. It also tries to coordinate any large fluctuations in its deposits with the Fed so that depository institutions' reserve deposits will not fluctuate violently.

A few other institutions, mainly foreign banks, hold relatively small deposits at the Fed.

Deferred Availability Cash Items (DACI). *Deferred availability cash items (DACI)* represent the value of checks deposited at the Fed by depository institutions that have not yet been credited to the institution's accounts. For instance, if a bank in New York deposits a $200 check written on a bank in California, it will get a $200 deferred availability cash item for two days. At the end of that time, the New York bank's reserve deposit will be increased by $200. The Fed does not give the New York bank instant credit because it takes time to ship the check to California and collect on it from the California bank. If all goes well, the Fed expects to collect the check in two days, and usually it is cheaper and more desirable to transfer the funds to the New York bank's account automatically than to wait for a message saying the check was finally collected from the California bank. (See Exhibit 4–4 for details on the check collection process.)

Other Liabilities and Capital. Other Fed liabilities include Federal Reserve checks outstanding and miscellaneous items. Fed "capital" primarily represents stock paid in by Fed member banks. The Fed pays a 6 percent dividend on that stock regardless of its earnings, and it returns the lion's share of its earnings (nearly $18 billion in 1987) to the U.S. Treasury each year.

Assets of the Fed

Loans. When first established, the Fed was designed to be a lender of last resort. Thus, when a depository institution needs additional funds, it can borrow at the Fed's "discount window." Because the discount rate is often lower than other interest rates, one would expect depository institutions to borrow from the Fed. However, the Fed has discouraged borrowing unless an institution is in need. Thus the stigma attached to discount-window borrowing restricts its use. As a result, loans account for only a tiny portion of the Fed's total assets.

Government Securities. The Federal Reserve System's primary asset is its portfolio of government securities. U.S. Treasury and U.S. government agency securities, plus repurchase agreements covering both, account for four-fifths of the Fed's assets. The Fed can buy and sell government securities in the securities market at will through *open market operations.* By buying or selling government securities, the Fed can change the monetary base.

Cash Items in Process of Collection (CIPC). *Cash items in process of collection (CIPC)* are items the Federal Reserve is clearing but for which it has not yet obtained funds. In our earlier example, the $200 check deposited by the New York bank is a CIPC item until it is actually subtracted from the account of the California bank on which it was written. (See Exhibit 4–4.) Because the Fed clears many checks, the number of CIPC items is large.

Float. Float represents a net extension of credit from the Fed to depository institutions. It is the difference between CIPC and DACI. For instance, if it took the Fed three days to collect the check from the California bank instead of the two days assumed by the deferred availability credit schedule, the New York bank would receive a $200 deposit to its reserve account at the Fed the day before the money was withdrawn from the California bank's reserve account—so, DACI would fall but CIPC would not; as a result "float" would rise by $200.

Coinage and Other Assets.   Other assets of the Fed are varied. The Fed holds a small amount of coinage issued by the Treasury so that it can accommodate depository institutions that wish to exchange some of their reserve deposits for coin. The Fed still holds Treasury gold certificates, redeemable at the U.S. Treasury for gold, as a carryover from the days when it formerly backed Federal Reserve notes with gold certificates. It holds Special Drawing Rights (SDRs) and foreign-denominated assets because it frequently engages in foreign currency transactions or currency "swap" agreements with other nations' central banks. Finally, it owns buildings, computers, vehicles, and other assets needed to house its operations and conduct its business.

The Fed's Role in Check Clearing

Many checks and electronic transfers are "cleared" by local banks exchanging them through local clearinghouse associations. Those clearinghouses net out the value of checks and transfers drawn on or received by each depository institution in the association and make only net payments of the net balances due among members in the association. This saves much time and expense since payments do not have to be made for each transaction individually.

The Fed plays a major role in check clearing, particularly in clearing checks drawn on depository institutions located in other market areas or different parts of the country. The Fed clearing process is facilitated by the fact that most depository institutions either directly or indirectly hold reserve deposits or clearing deposit balances with the Fed. These deposits can then be easily transferred from one institution to another by making appropriate entries on the Fed's books.[1]

An example of the check-clearing process, which also shows how it can give rise to float, is illustrated in Exhibit 4–4. For instance, assume a consumer in California wants to buy something priced at $200 from a mail-order merchant in New York City. The consumer could send currency through the mail, but that would be cumbersome and the money might be lost or stolen. Instead, the consumer writes a check on his or her bank (Bank A) in California and mails it to the merchant. In turn, the merchant sends the goods when the check is received. This process is illustrated as step 1 in Exhibit 4–4.

A merchant who receives a check in payment for goods typically deposits the check in his or her bank and receives credit for the deposit in his or her account (step 2 in Exhibit 4–4). If the check is not drawn on the account of another customer at the

---

[1] The Fed clears a check by subtracting the amount of the check from the reserve account balance of the bank (Bank A) on which the check was written and by adding the amount to the reserve account balance of the bank (Bank B) that presents the check to the Fed for clearing. Before the check clears, it is a cash item in the process of collection (CIPC) for the Fed. Before Bank B's reserve account is credited, the Fed gives Bank B a deferred availability credit item (DACI) for the length of time it expects to take collecting the check from Bank A.

Exhibit 4–4   **Check Clearing through the Fed**

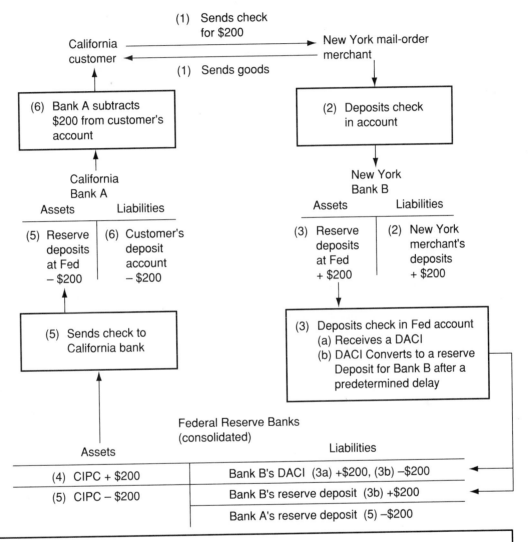

(3a) & (4) The Fed gives Bank B a deferred credit item, (3a) in exchange for the check and adds cash item in the process of collection (CIPC) to its assets.

(3b)   After a predetermined delay, the Fed credits Bank B's reserve account by the amount of the check and eliminates the DACI.

(5)   The Fed sends the check to California and collects it from Bank A by reducing Bank A's reserve deposit by the amount of the check. When the check is collected, the Fed also reduces its CIPC account by the same amount.

bank, the bank must collect from another financial institution. In our example, since the other financial institution is located in California, rather than send the check back to the California bank directly, the New York bank (Bank B) deposits the check at the Fed (step 3). The Fed initially credits Bank A with a deferred availability credit item (step 3a). The deferred availability credit item is eliminated and the value of the check is added to the bank's reserve deposit at the Fed according to a predetermined time schedule—zero days if in the same city and up to two days if Bank A is far away (step 3b). When there is a delay in check collection, the Fed first adds the check to its "cash items in the process of collection" (CIPC) account (step 4), then sends the customer's check back to Bank A for collection (step 5). When the check is collected, the Fed eliminates the CIPC item and subtracts $200 from Bank A's reserve deposit at the Fed. Finally, in Step 6, Bank A in California receives the check and subtracts the $200 from its customer's checking account. The transaction is complete.

Note in this example how easy it is to transfer funds from California to New York. In essence, all the Fed had to do was subtract $200 from Bank A's reserve deposit account and add $200 to Bank B's reserve deposit account. Even though the actual transaction is slightly more complicated when the "deferred availability credit item" schedule comes into play between Fed districts, because the district banks keep separate books, that is the Fed's problem. For Bank A and Bank B, the transfers are quite simple. Deposited checks are added to the reserve balances of the depository institution that deposited them (Bank B), and collected checks are subtracted from the reserve balances of the depository institution on which they were written (Bank A).

It is important to remember that reserve balances are transferred from one bank to another when checks are cleared between them. They do not disappear from the banking system, only from the account of the bank on which the check was drawn.

The check-clearing process gives rise to "float," which is a form of credit extended by the Fed when the deferred availability credit item (DACI) account is reduced before the check is collected. That means the Fed has added to Bank A's reserve balances before it has subtracted from Bank B's reserve balances. Thus an increase in Fed "float," which equals CIPC − DACI, causes banks' total reserve balances at the Fed to increase.

Float is important because it adds to bank reserves and is hard to predict. For instance, if there is a postal or an airline strike or bad weather in New York, float will increase because it will take longer for checks deposited in New York banks to be withdrawn from the reserve deposit of the banks in other parts of the country on which the checks were drawn. The Fed has reduced float greatly in recent years by shortening deferred availability credit schedules and by running its own air courier service to deliver checks across the country.

Federal Reserve Tools of Monetary Policy

As noted earlier, the Federal Reserve System is the most important financial institution in the economy because it controls the nation's monetary policy. It does so with three major tools: (1) reserve requirements, (2) open market operations, and (3) discount rate policy.

Reserve Requirements

The Federal Reserve can establish *reserve requirements* within limits set by Congress. These requirements are important because they determine how many funds financial institutions must hold (either in cash or in reserve deposits at the Fed) in order to back their deposits. For instance, a depository institution that is subject to a reserve requirement of 10 percent on its transactions deposits must back every dollar of those deposits with 10 cents of reserve assets. If the institution also has other reservable accounts, such as Eurodollar deposits, its reserve requirements may be increased.

The power to establish reserve requirements gives the Fed part of its power to control the nation's total money supply. Reserve requirements applicable in 1992 are shown in Exhibit 4–5. In addition to reserves on their transactions accounts (accounts from which the public can transfer or withdraw funds on demand), financial institutions may be required to hold small reserves, either in vault cash or deposits at the Fed, against their holdings of short-maturity, nonpersonal time and savings deposits. Also, at the discretion of the Federal Reserve, banks may be required to hold reserves against certain other liabilities—such as Eurodollar borrowings from their overseas branches or certain liabilities issued by bank holding companies.

The example given in Exhibit 4–6 illustrates the way in which individual banks compute both their actual reserves (AR) and their required reserves (RR). First, a

---

Exhibit 4–5   Reserve Requirements, 1992

Type of Deposit	Total Amount of Deposits of That Type in Institution	Reserve Requirement (percentage)	Allowable Range (minimum/maximum percentage)[a]
Transactions deposits	Under $42.2 million[b]	3	3/3
	Over $42.2 million[b]	10[c]	8/14
Nonpersonal time deposits (CDs) maturing in less than $1\frac{1}{2}$ years		0[d]	0/9
Nonpersonal time deposits (CDs) maturing in over $1\frac{1}{2}$ years		0	0/9
Consumer savings deposits (under $100,000)		0	
Eurodollar deposits		0[d]	

[a] The allowable ranges are set by Congress. However, institutions with under $3.2 million in total reservable liabilities are exempt from all reserve requirements. The exemption grows by 80 percent of the growth in total reservable liabilities each year. At the other extreme, the Fed may impose a supplementary reserve requirement of up to 4 percent provided that it pays interest on the additional reserve deposits held at the Fed.

[b] The $42.2 million limit applied in 1991. It is increased annually in step with 80 percent of the growth in the nation's money supply in the previous year.

[c] Maximum reserve requirements were reduced from 12 percent to 10 percent on April 2, 1992.

[d] Reserve requirements were changed from 3 percent to 0 percent on December 17, 1991.

The Fed establishes reserve requirements consistent with the guidelines and allowable ranges established by Congress in the Depository Institutions Deregulation and Monetary Control Act of 1980.

Exhibit 4–6   **Bank Reserve Computations**

Hypothetical Bank Balance Sheet (Average values over a two-week period)

Assets		Liabilities and Net Worth	
Vault cash on hand (VC)	$2 million	Transactions deposits (D) (checking accounts, NOW accounts, and other reservable transactions accounts)	$150 million
Reserve deposits at the Federal Reserve bank (RD)	$18 million		
Fed Funds sold	$1 million	Eurodollar deposits (ED)	$10 million
Other assets: (loans and investments, buildings, etc.)	$200 million	Savings deposits	$44 million
		Borrowed reserves (BR)	$2 million
		Net worth (capital)*	$15 million
Total assets	$221 million	Total liabilities and net worth	$221 million

Note: U.S. Depository institutions must hold net worth (capital) equal to at least 3 percent of their total assets, and all depository institutions must hold net worth equal to 8 percent of their risk-adjusted assets (loans count 100 percent in the risk weighting, so they must be backed with 8 percent capital, while Treasury bills count 0 percent and require no explicit capital backing as long as the overall 3 percent requirement is met). Because of these capital limits, at times some banks and other depository institutions may not be able to expand their assets and deposit liabilities unless they are first able to add to their net worth. Financial institutions can add to their net worth by selling stock or by earning profits that they retain in their retained earnings or surplus accounts and do not pay out as dividends.

bank computes its *actual reserves*, by summing its holdings of vault cash (VC) with its holdings of reserve deposits (RD) at Federal Reserve Banks. In Exhibit 4–6, the bank's actual reserves equal $2 million in vault cash plus $18 million in deposits held in the bank's reserve account at the Fed, or $20 million, that is, $AR = VC + RD = \$2$ million + $18 million = $20 million. Because cash and deposit holdings fluctuate from day to day, the Fed allows banks to calculate their actual reserves based on their average cash and deposit holdings over a two-week "reserve maintenance" period.

Individual banks compute their *required reserves* (RR) by computing the amount of reserves they are required to hold to back each type of reservable deposit liability they have; the banks then sum their required reserves for each type of deposit to compute their total reserve requirements (RR). For instance, in Exhibit 4–6, assume that reserve requirements, denoted r_D, on transactions deposits, denoted D, are 12 percent; then total reserves required to back the bank's average transactions deposits over a two-week period are 12 percent of $150 million, or $18 million. Further, suppose that reserve requirements on the bank's Eurodollar deposits, denoted r_{ED}, are 3 percent. The required reserves for the bank's Eurodollar holdings, denoted ED, are 3 percent of $10 million, or $0.3 million. Its total *reserve requirements*, then, are $18.3 million. In terms of a formula, $RR = r_D \times D + r_{ED} \times ED = .12 \times \$150$ million +

.03 × $10 million = $18.3 million. If the bank had no Eurodollar deposit liabilities, its required reserves would just be $RR = r_D \times D$, or $18 million.

The difference between a bank's actual reserves and free reserves equals its *excess reserves (ER)*. In Exhibit 4-6, the bank's excess reserves are given by $ER = AR - RR = 20 million $- 18.3 million $= 1.7 million. Banks usually try to hold few excess reserves because they do not earn interest on them. Thus, if they have excess reserves, they will often try to lend them out (possibly to other banks by selling Fed Funds to them) and transfer some of their reserve deposits to the borrowing bank through the Fed's wire transfer system. The next day the selling bank will get its reserve deposits back when the borrowing bank repays the Fed Funds loan plus interest by redepositing the money in the selling bank's reserve deposit at the Fed. Because "Fed Funds sold" are lent to other banks, they are no longer available to meet a bank's reserve requirements and are not considered part of a bank's actual reserves.

If a bank doesn't use its excess reserves to sell Fed Funds (that is, lend) to other banks, it may use them to lend to people in its community or to buy interest-bearing investments so it can earn an interest return on its excess funds. Thus many people total the excess reserves for the banking system as a whole to see if total excess reserves are high or not. If excess reserves are high, they expect that banks will be more willing to make loans and will bid up the price of securities so credit will be "easier" and interest rates will tend to fall.

However, a bank with excess reserves may not be inclined to lend them out or invest them if it has a loan from the Fed that it must pay back. Banks may borrow extra reserve deposits from the Fed at its "discount window" so they can meet their reserve requirements; such "adjustment credits" usually are for 15 days, provided that the Fed approves the loan request. Since there is a stigma to borrowing from the Fed, and banks don't want to encounter embarrassing "discount window scrutiny" from the Fed, most banks try to avoid borrowing from the Fed and repay their debts as soon as possible. As a result, many banks with excess reserves will not lend freely if they have borrowed from the Fed and need to repay their debt soon. Thus many analysts prefer to look at banks' *net free reserves* (NFR) rather than excess reserves. Net free reserves equal the total of excess reserves of all banks minus their total *borrowed reserves* (BR), which they obtained by borrowing from the Fed discount window. In Exhibit 4-6, the bank in question has net free reserves equal to $- 0.3 million, calculated as $NFR = ER - BR = 1.7 million $- 2 million $= - 0.3 million. Thus the bank illustrated in Exhibit 4-6 is unlikely to expand its loans and investments aggressively because it soon must repay more to the Fed (when it repays its Fed borrowings) than it currently holds in actual reserves.

While we assume in Exhibit 4-6 that all banks must hold a 12 percent reserve requirement to back their transactions deposits, in the past, the Fed frequently imposed substantially different reserve requirements on large and small banks. Because large banks often clear checks for smaller banks, they are more likely to be subject to unexpected drains of funds and must hold much higher reserves. Although reserve requirements were substantially simplified by the 1980 Depository Institutions Deregulation and Monetary Control Act (DIDMCA), large banks still have to hold higher reserve requirements (see Exhibit 4-5).

Open Market Operations

Reserve requirements alone do not give the Fed sufficient power to control the nation's money supply. It must also control the total amount of assets that are available for depository institutions to use to meet their reserve requirements.

The Fed is the only institution in the country that can expand or contract its liabilities at will. To expand them, it need only issue Federal Reserve notes or write a check on itself.

The Fed usually expands or contracts its liabilities by engaging in open market operations. These involve the Fed's buying or selling of securities in the open market. As payment when the Fed buys securities, it writes a check on itself. When the check is cashed, the Fed credits the reserve deposit account of the institution that presented it for payment, thereby increasing the bank's actual reserves. When the Fed sells securities, it collects each check it receives in payment by reducing the balance in the reserve account of the depository institution on which the check was written. Thus, by selling securities in the open market, it decreases depository institutions' reserve account deposits at the Fed, whereas buying securities has the opposite effect.

Discount Rate Policy

The *discount rate* is the rate a financial institution must pay to borrow reserve deposits from its regional Federal Reserve bank. When the rate is low, financial institutions can inexpensively meet their reserve requirement obligations by borrowing from the Federal Reserve, provided they don't mind the discount window scrutiny of their operations. In this case they will expand their assets and deposits more readily, because it will not cost them as much to obtain the reserves required to back their new deposit or asset holdings if they must borrow to obtain additional reserves. When the discount rate is high, the institutions are more reluctant to borrow reserves, and hence they are more careful about expanding their assets and deposit holdings if that means borrowing from the Fed.

In the early days of the Federal Reserve System, changing the discount rate was the major way in which the Fed attempted to affect national monetary policy. Changing the rate affected a bank's willingness to borrow from the Fed, the total amount of Federal reserve credit outstanding, and the nation's money supply. However, it is difficult to predict how much bank discount window borrowing will increase or decrease when the discount rate is changed. Also, such changes may be misinterpreted by "Fed watchers," who believe they foretell alterations in Fed policy. In recent years, therefore, the Federal Reserve has relied mainly on open market operations involving purchases and sales of securities for its own portfolio to influence the nation's money supply.

Federal Reserve Control of the Money Supply

Control of the Monetary Base

The most important powers of the Fed, cited above, are important because they allow the Fed to control the money supply. The Fed's control of the money supply depends on its ability to control the monetary base and its ability to set reserve requirements. The components of the monetary base—cash (held as vault cash) and reserve balances held by financial institutions at the Federal Reserve System—are the only financial institution assets that can be used to satisfy Federal Reserve reserve requirements. By controlling the monetary base (the total amount of currency in circulation plus reserve balances outstanding), the Federal Reserve can control the total amount of assets that financial institutions can use to meet their reserve requirements. The Federal Reserve uses its power over these reserves to control the amount of money and other monetary aggregates outstanding in the country.

Balance Sheet Sources of the Monetary Base

The primary sources of the monetary base can be determined by analyzing the Federal Reserve balance sheet, a simplified version of which is presented in Exhibit 4–7. This shows that Federal Reserve notes outstanding and depository institution reserve deposit liabilities of the Federal Reserve System are the largest components of the monetary base. In addition, a truncated balance sheet for the U.S. Treasury shows

Exhibit 4–7   Sources of the Monetary Base (December 31, 1991)

Simplified Federal Reserve Balance Sheet

Assets (billions)		Liabilities (billions)		
Loans	$0.2	Federal reserve notes	$287.9	Base Liabilities
U.S. government and agency securities	$288.4	Financial institutions' reserve deposits	$29.4	Base Liabilities
Other assets	$64.4	U.S. Treasury, foreign, and other deposits; other liabilities and capital accounts	$35.7	Nonbase Liabilities

Monetary base $333.6

U.S. Treasury Balance Sheet

Assets (billions)	Liabilities (billions)		
	Treasury currency issued and held by public	$16.3	Base Liabilities
	Treasury currency, coin, and certificate issues held by the Federal Reserve		
	Other liabilities and Treasury cash (computed as a residual)		

The monetary base ($333.6 billion) consists of financial institutions' reserve deposits at the Fed ($29.4 billion), Federal Reserve notes outstanding ($287.9 billion), and U.S. Treasury coin and currency held by banks and the public ($16.3 billion). All else being equal, the monetary base increases whenever the Fed increases its assets, and it decreases whenever the Fed's nonbase liabilities increase.

that Treasury currency held by the public accounts for the remainder of the monetary base.

Note in the Federal Reserve balance sheet depicted in Exhibit 4–7 that, because both sides of a balance sheet change at the same time, increases in Federal Reserve asset holdings increase the monetary base. For instance, if the Federal Reserve makes $2 billion worth of additional loans to depository institutions, the Fed's assets will increase by $2 billion, and so will the reserve deposits of the institutions that received the loans. Similarly, if the Fed buys government securities or other assets with checks drawn on itself, when those checks are cashed it will credit (increase) the reserve deposits of the depository institutions that presented the checks for payment. Therefore, its assets and reserve deposits will increase by the same amount. Conversely, contractions in Federal Reserve assets will cause the monetary base to contract. When the Federal Reserve sells some of its assets to the public (or makes fewer loans), payment for those assets (or repayment of outstanding loans) will cause the monetary base to shrink. As the Federal Reserve collects checks drawn on depository institutions, those institutions' deposits at the Federal Reserve are reduced.

On the other side of the balance sheet, note that if total assets and total liabilities remain the same, the monetary base will be reduced if nonbase liabilities of the Federal Reserve increase. For instance, if the U.S. Treasury increases its deposits at the Fed by $1 billion by reducing its deposits at commercial banks, those banks' reserve deposits (and the monetary base) will decrease by $1 billion. The affected banks will have to surrender $1 billion of their deposits at the Fed to the Treasury when the Treasury withdraws its funds. Transfers of reserves from banks to foreigners' deposits at the Fed will have the same effect.

Conversely, when the Treasury writes checks on its deposits at the Federal Reserve and those checks are cashed, the deposits of the financial institutions cashing the checks are increased by the same amount that the Treasury deposits at the Fed are reduced. For instance, if the Treasury writes Social Security checks worth $3 billion on its account at the Fed, Treasury deposits at the Fed will fall by $3 billion and bank reserve deposits at the Fed will increase by $3 billion when those checks are cashed. Thus contractions in the Federal Reserve nonbase liabilities will cause the monetary base to expand.

In brief, if no offsetting effects occur, (1) the monetary base will increase or decrease directly with changes in Federal Reserve asset holdings, and (2) the monetary base will increase or decrease oppositely from changes in Federal Reserve nonbase liabilities. The monetary base will also expand if the public acquires more Treasury-issued currency, while Federal Reserve Treasury currency holdings remain unchanged.

Monetary Base and Money Supply Changes: The Deposit-Expansion Process

When the Fed changes either the monetary base or reserve requirements, the money supply will usually change in a predictable manner. The reason this is so is that banks' ability to expand their transactions deposits (which comprise the major part of the money supply) is limited by their holdings of actual reserves. In particular, transactions deposits, D, multiplied by their reserve requirements, r_D, will determine banks' required reserves, RR. Because of the Fed's Regulation D, actual reserves, AR, that banks must hold must at least equal their required reserves, RR. If banks hold no reservable liabilities other than transactions deposits, this relationship is given in Equation 4–1:

$$AR = RR = r_D \times D. \tag{4-1}$$

Assuming that banks hold no excess reserves, actual reserves will equal required reserves, and Equation 4–1 can be manipulated by dividing both sides by r_D and reversing sides to get Equation 4–2:

$$D = \frac{AR}{r_D} = \frac{1}{r_D} AR. \tag{4-2}$$

Equation 4–2 is important because it shows that the maximum amount of transactions deposits banks can issue is determined by their actual reserve holdings and the reserve requirement on deposits. Thus deposit holdings will change whenever banks' actual reserves change or whenever the reserve requirement changes. This is illustrated in Exhibit 4–8.

In Exhibit 4–8, panels A and B correspond to cases where the reserve requirement for all banks, r_D, is assumed to equal 10 percent. Panels C and D correspond to cases where r_D equals 5 percent.

Exhibit 4–8 **Relationships of Bank Transactions Deposits to Reserve Requirements, and Their Actual Reserve Holdings**

Reserve Requirement, 10%

	A			B	
Assets	**Liabilities**		**Assets**	**Liabilities**	
Actual reserves $60 billion	Transactions deposits $600 billion		Actual reserves $90 billion	Transactions deposits $900 billion	
Loans and investments $540 billion			Loans and investments $810 billion		

Reserve Requirement, 5%

	C			D	
Assets	**Liabilities**		**Assets**	**Liabilities**	
Actual reserves $60 billion	Transactions deposits $1,200 billion		Actual reserves $90 billion	Transactions deposits $1,800 billion	
Loans and investments $1,140 billion			Loans and investments $1,710 billion		

Note: Bank balance sheets were simplified by deleting net worth and items not directly related to the transaction deposit expansion process.

In Panel A we assume that all banks have $60 billion in actual reserves available to them. By using Equation 4–2 we can determine that banks could hold $600 billion in transactions deposits (since $60 billion divided by 0.10 equals $600 billion) before the whole $60 billion in actual reserves would be "used up" as "required reserves." In fact, banks will tend to expand their transactions deposits to $600 billion in that case.

The reason that banks tend to expand their deposits until they have no excess reserves, as Equation 4–2 implies, is that banks do not earn interest on any actual reserves they hold over and above their reserve requirements. Thus they try to "spend" any excess reserves they hold by making more loans and buying investments that pay an interest return. When a bank makes a loan, it gives a transactions deposit to the borrower or gives the borrower a check. When the check is cashed, either the borrower's transactions deposits increase or the transactions deposits of the person the borrower gave the check to increase. *In all cases, total transactions deposits in the banking system increase when a bank uses some of its excess reserves to make a loan.* Conversely, if a loan is repaid, the checking account of the person who repays the debt decreases when the bank cashes the check, and so will total transactions deposits unless the bank makes more loans.

When a bank uses excess reserves to expand investments, a similar process occurs. When a bank buys investments for its own account, it pays with a check or a wire transfer. When the check or wire clears, the demand deposit of the person who sold the investment securities will increase, and so will total deposits in the banking system. Conversely, when the bank sells some of its investment securities to the public in exchange for a check, when the check clears, the public's transactions deposits will decrease along with the bank's holdings of investment securities.

Because of the process just described, banks expand their loan and investment holdings until all their actual reserves are required reserves. This occurs in Panel A when loans and investments equal $540 billion. At that point, total transactions deposits equal $600 billion, required reserves and actual reserves both equal $60 billion, and banks no longer have any excess reserves with which they can expand their loans and investments.

Now suppose the Fed buys $30 billion in government securities and pays for them by giving banks $30 billion more in reserve deposits at the Fed. Thus banks' actual reserve holdings increase from $60 billion to $90 billion, and initially, banks hold $30 billion in excess reserves if they hold only $600 billion in transactions deposits (that is, their actual reserves are $90 billion and their required reserves are only $60 billion, so $30 billion of their actual reserves are "excess reserves").

Therefore, banks expand their loans and investments so they can earn extra income. At the same time, by making more loans and by acquiring investments, they expand the public's holdings of transactions deposits. This process continues until they reach the state depicted in Panel B in Exhibit 4–8. In Panel B, banks hold $900 billion in transactions deposits, so their required reserves are $90 billion (which equals their actual reserves and leaves them with no excess reserves with which they could buy additional investment securities or make loans). Thus their deposit expansion stops at $900 billion. At that point, they back their $900 billion in deposits with $90 billion in reserves and $810 billion in loans and investments.

Reserve Requirement Changes

The Fed also can stimulate deposit expansion by reducing banks' reserve requirements. The effect of a reserve requirement cut from 10 percent to 5 percent is shown in Panels C and D of Exhibit 4–8 when they are compared to Panels A and B, respectively. If reserve requirements are reduced, depository institutions find that they hold more actual reserves than they need to meet the new reduced reserve requirements. Since excess reserves pay no interest, depository institutions start to make loans and buy more investments to increase their interest returns.

Once again, the end result of the expansion process can be predicted by using equation 4–2. If reserves are $60 and the reserve requirement is 5 percent, as shown in Panel C, banks can expand their loans and investments until transactions deposits total $1,200, which will equal $1/0.05 \times \$60$ billion. (To calculate this, remember $r_D = 5\% = 0.05$ so $1/r_D = 20$.) At that point, the expansion process halts because banks have no more free reserves. In the case of Panel D, the expansion process halts when total transactions deposits equal $1,800, which will equal $1/0.05 \times \$90$ billion. The end results can all be calculated using Equation 4–2.

If the Fed wishes to cause transactions deposits to decrease, it can reverse the process just described. For instance, suppose the initial situation is given by Panel D in Exhibit 4–8, where actual reserves equal $90 billion, transactions deposits equal $1,800 billion, and loans and investments equal the difference, or $1,710 billion. If the Fed sells $30 billion in government securities to the public, when the public's checks clear to the Fed, the Fed reduces banks' reserves to collect on the checks. Thus actual reserves fall by $30 billion, to $60 billion, As a result, banks hold too few reserves and have to make fewer loans and sell investments in order to get more funds. They are under pressure to reduce their loans and investments until they reach the state depicted in Panel C of Exhibit 4–8. At that point their transactions deposits have fallen to $1,200 billion, so once again their actual reserves (now $60 billion) equal their required reserves, and they no longer have an incentive to decrease their holdings of interest-bearing loans and investments.

Similarly, if reserve requirements are raised from 5 percent to 10 percent, the banks in Panel D find they need to hold $180 billion in actual reserves rather than the $90 billion they actually hold. Because of their reserve deficiency, they are forced to reduce their loans and investments until they reach the state depicted in Panel B.

The Deposit-Expansion Multiplier

In all cases shown, the reserve expansion or contraction can be computed by using Equation 4–2. Equation 4–2 can also be adapted to calculate *changes* in transactions deposits that are likely to result from *changes* in actual reserves. This form is shown as Equation 4–3:

$$\Delta D = \frac{1}{r_D} \times \Delta AR = X_{AR}^{D} \times \Delta AR. \qquad (4-3)$$

In Equation 4–3, Δ means "change in" and X_{AR}^{D} is a shorthand way of defining the "expansion multiplier for deposits that results from a change in actual reserves." The term X_{AR}^{D} is used instead of $1/r_D$ because it can be generalized to account for more complicated cases later. In this case, though, it just equals $1/r_D$. Thus if $r_D = 10\%$, $X^D_{AR} = 1/10\% = 1/.10 = 10$, so the expected change in deposits is 10 times the expected change in actual reserves. If $r_D = 5\%$, $X^D_{AR} = 1/5\% = 1/.05 = 20$, so a small change in actual reserves has a much greater impact on deposits than was true in the previous case (that is, the expansion ratio is larger when reserve requirements are smaller). This can be observed in Exhibit 4–8. When reserves expand from $60 to $90 billion, the resulting change in deposits is $300 billion when reserve requirements are 10 percent (as banks move from Panel A to Panel B). However, when reserve requirements are 5 percent, the same reserve expansion causes total deposits to expand by $600 billion (from $1,200 billion in Panel C to $1,800 billion in Panel D).

Monetary Expansion with Cash Drains

The actual monetary expansion process is somewhat more complicated than shown previously because the Fed basically controls reserve requirements and the monetary base (which equals cash plus banks' reserve deposits), and the money supply basically consists of cash plus transactions deposits. However, deposit-expansion ratios can still be computed if, (1) the public holds predictable ratios of cash to demand deposits, and (2) once again, banks are assumed to hold no noninterest-bearing excess reserves.

Assume for instance that the public typically holds 15 cents in cash holdings (CH) for each dollar it holds in transactions deposits. Call the cash holding ratio c, so $CH = c \times D$, where c = the ratio of cash holdings to deposits. Then the M1 money supply is given by $M1 = D + CH = D + c \times D = (1 + c)D$. Thus we have Equation 4–4:

$$\Delta M1 = (1 + c)\Delta D. \tag{4-4}$$

Again Δ means "change in," so the change in $M1 = (1 + c)$ times the change in deposits.

However, cash drains have another effect. They cause a "leakage" between the change in the monetary base and the change in banks' holdings of actual reserves. In particular, cash holdings by the public "use up" the monetary base so it is not available to banks as actual reserves. This is expressed in Equation 4–5:

$$\Delta AR = \Delta MB - \Delta CH. \tag{4-5}$$

Thus, the change in actual reserves of banks equals the change in the monetary base minus the change in the public's cash holdings. Combining Equations 4–5 and 4–2 in "change" form we get:

$$\Delta D = \frac{1}{r_D} \times (\Delta MB - \Delta CH). \tag{4-6}$$

By substituting $\Delta CH = c\Delta D$ and solving for ΔD as a function of the change in the monetary base, we get Equation 4–7:

$$\Delta D = \frac{1}{r_D + c} \times \Delta MB = X^D_{MB} \times \Delta MB. \tag{4-7}$$

Because of the cash drain "leakage," we now have a new expansion multiplier, X^D_{MB}, which tells us how much deposits will change for each one dollar change in the monetary base. That new multiplier equals $1/(r_D + c)$. Thus, if reserve requirements are 10 percent and cash holding ratios are 15 percent,

$$X\frac{D}{MB} = \frac{1}{r_D + c} = \frac{1}{.10 + .15} = \frac{1}{.25} = 4.$$

Therefore, deposits expand by 4 times the amount of the change in the monetary base. The monetary base deposit-expansion multiplier is lower than the reserve deposit-expansion multiplier because of cash drains.

However, our primary interest is in the way the Fed can change the money supply. By noting that $\Delta M1 = \Delta D + \Delta CH = (1 + c)\,\Delta D$, we can convert Equation 4–7 to a money supply expansion equation, as shown in Equation 4–8.

$$\Delta M1 = \frac{1 + c}{r_D + c} \times \Delta MB = X\frac{M1}{MB} \times \Delta MB \qquad (4\text{–}8)$$

In this case, the expansion multiplier, X_{MB}^{M1}, tells how much the M1 money supply will increase for each dollar change in the monetary base. If r_D equals 10 percent and c equals 15 percent, then X_{MB}^{M1} equals $(1 + .15)/(.10 + .15) = 1.15/.25 = 4.60$. Thus, for each \$1 billion increase in the monetary base, the M1 money supply would be expected to rise by \$4.6 billion. Conversely, a \$2 billion decrease in the monetary base would be expected to cause the M1 money supply to fall by \$9.2 billion ($= 4.6 \times -\$2$ billion). These results can all be obtained by using Equation 4–8.

These expansion ratios can be used by the Fed to calculate the impact that various changes in the monetary base are likely to have on the nation's money supply. Thus they are highly useful when the Fed plans its monetary policy. The world, however, is more complicated than we have assumed here. Thus the Fed must wrestle with the question of whether banks will hold some excess reserves and whether some of the monetary base will be used up in reserves for nontransactions deposits (such as Eurodollar deposits). In addition, the Fed must worry about whether the public holds its deposits at banks with high or low reserve requirement ratios for their transactions deposits. Furthermore, the Fed must worry about whether the public will change its propensity to hold cash either seasonally or secularly. Finally, the Fed must worry about whether banks hold enough net worth or capital to expand their deposits as much as planned without violating their legally required net-worth-to-capital ratios. Some of these issues are addressed in Appendix A. The Fed must also worry about whether the changes in the money supply will affect the economy in the expected manner. That issue is addressed briefly in Appendix B to this chapter and more extensively in Chapters 25 and 26.

Other Powers of the Fed

The Fed's primary function is to effect changes in the nation's money supply and credit conditions so the economy can grow in a stable, noninflationary manner. However, it also has important regulatory functions that it performs in supervising banks, the nation's payments system, and credit markets in general. The most important powers of the Fed, and the regulations under which they implement those powers, are presented in Exhibit 4–9. Some key regulations to know are: Regulation

Exhibit 4–9   **Federal Reserve Regulations**

Regulation	Topic of Regulations	Institutions Affected
Money Control, Money Transfer, and General Banking Regulations		
A	Establishes Fed discount window policy	Borrowers from discount window
D	Establishes reserve requirements	All depository institutions
E	Regulates electronic funds transfer	All institutions providing EFT
J	Regulates check collection and wire transfers of funds	All institutions clearing checks and transfers through the Fed
F,H,I,L.N,O,P	Regulations for member banks and Federal Reserve banks	Member banks and Federal Reserve banks
Q	Used to set deposit interest rate ceilings, and now regulates advertising of interest on savings accounts	All commercial banks
International Banking Regulation		
K	Regulates international banking in United States and by U.S. banks abroad	Domestic and foreign banks
Bank Holding Company Regulation		
Y	Sets rules applicable to bank holding companies	Banks and their affiliates
Securities Credit Regulations		
G,U,T,X	Establishes securities margin requirements for exchange-listed stocks and list of OTC stocks subject to margin regulations	Brokers, dealers, banks, individuals, and others
Consumer Financial Regulation: Disclosure of Credit and Leasing Terms, Credit, and Funds Availability Regulation		
W(now lapsed)	Controls consumer credit at banks and other institutions	All institutions offering consumer credit
Z,B,C,AA,BB	Regulates consumer credit and mortgage credit transactions	Institutions offering consumer credit
CC (new, 1988 on)	Expedited funds availability for deposits	Depository institutions

Fed regulations cover a wide range of financial activities. In addition to banking, the Fed regulates consumer credit, securities margin requirements, and bank holding companies.

Q, which used to regulate the maximum interest rate that banks could pay on time and savings deposits, but which caused so many problems that all deposit rate ceilings were abandoned in the 1980s' banking reform acts; Regulation D, which sets depository institution reserve requirements; Regulation Y, which regulates bank holding companies and their subsidiary operations; Regulation Z, which requires that full disclosure of interest costs and billing terms be made on all consumer loans; and Regulations G, U, T, and X, which regulate the maximum percent of the purchase price that banks, security dealers, and others can loan people as "margin credit" used to finance the purchase of all exchange-listed stocks and Fed-specified over-the-

DID YOU KNOW?

The New Definitions of Money Confused the Fed

Because of the growth of transactions deposits at nonbank financial institutions, the Fed changed its definition of the money supply in 1980. Previously, M1 had included only currency in circulation and (noninterest-bearing) demand deposits held at commercial banks. People only held that type of money if they wanted to buy something soon. M1 now also includes traveler's checks and all customer balances held in depository institutions' transactions accounts that allow unlimited checks to be written. The problem is that people now hold some of their savings in transactions accounts (such as NOW and share-draft accounts) that pay interest. As a result, the new definition of M1 includes both money that people want to hold for transactions purposes and money that they hold for savings purposes.

Because people now have mixed motives for holding different M1 balances, the new definition of M1 is not as closely related to gross domestic production (GDP) as M1 was prior to 1980. In fact, after the Fed changed its definition of money, the ratio of M1 to income rose substantially. The Fed couldn't explain why increases in the money supply didn't cause GDP to increase more.

Economists at St. Louis Fed suggested that the new definition of M1 was the problem. They suggested that the Fed should look instead at only the relationship between GDP and the noninterest-bearing components of M1. Since people only want to hold noninterest-bearing money to engage in transactions, there should be a closer link between noninterest-bearing money (which is called M1A, or "adjusted" M1) and GDP levels than there is between the Fed's new definition of M1 and GDP.

This suggestion makes sense. Furthermore, research has shown that the relationship between M1A and GDP is closer than the relationship between M1 and GDP. However, rather than change the definition of M1 again, the Fed just stopped looking at it. Now the Fed sets policy targets for the annual growth rate of M2 and M3, but it ignores M1. Unfortunately, M2 and M3 both contain interest-sensitive components. Thus, right after the Fed cut the discount rate sharply in late 1991, depository institutions lowered the rates they paid their customers, so their customers withdrew their savings deposits and M2 and M3 fell sharply. That was opposite to what one would expect would happen to the money supply if the discount rate fell and bank reserves increased. Because the 1980s' monetary aggregates often respond strangely, because of changes in their savings components when interest rates change, the Fed still needs to monitor bank reserves, the monetary base, and M1A to see how the economy's noninterest-bearing monetary aggregates are affected by changes in Fed policy.

counter traded stocks. Many of the Fed regulations will be discussed in more detail in Chapter 17 or in other chapters, as appropriate.

As can be seen in Exhibit 4–9, the Fed exercises a wide range of specific powers and, therefore, has an important impact on all financial institutions and markets both directly (through specific regulations) and indirectly (through its ability to control monetary policy). In addition, the Fed directly examines and supervises bank holding companies and all state-chartered banks that are members of the Federal Reserve System. Because the Fed has such power, the chairman of the Federal Reserve Board is often called the "second most powerful" person in the United States.

Summary

The Federal Reserve System was formed in 1913 to remedy defects that had appeared in the National Banking Acts. Because people distrusted central authority, it consisted of 12 regional Federal Reserve Banks plus a Board of Governors in Washington. At first, each separate Federal Reserve bank had considerable discretion regarding the discount rate it charged and the way it conducted some of its other operations. However, in the 1930s, the Federal Open Market Committee (FOMC) was set up to coordinate monetary policy among the banks; the Board of Governors hold 7 of the 12 positions on the FOMC, while the Federal Reserve Bank presidents rotate the other 5 spots. Thus the nation's monetary policy is now unequivocally executed by the FOMC and the Board of Governors of the Federal Reserve System. The primary tools of monetary policy involve changes in the Fed's reserve requirement regulations (Regulation D), the Federal Reserve Bank's discount rates, and the Fed's open market operations (which affect the nation's monetary base).

By changing the monetary base and depository institutions' reserve requirements, the Fed can change depository institutions' net excess reserve positions and either induce them to lend and invest (thereby increasing credit availability and bank deposits) or cause depository institutions to restrict lending and sell investments (thereby shrinking the nation's money supply and credit availability). The approximate effect of changes in Fed policy on the money supply can be computed using the deposit and money supply expansion equations developed in this chapter.

In addition to changing the nation's money supply and credit conditions by changing depository institutions' reserve requirements and the monetary base, the Fed can change the discount rate to "signal" its policy intent as well as to encourage banks to borrow more or fewer reserves from the Fed. The Fed also plays a very important role in banking and credit market regulation in general. Besides regulating and examining some banks and bank holding companies directly, it regulates international banking, electronic funds transfers, consumer credit and leasing transactions, and securities market margin credit.

Questions

1. What were the major reasons why the Fed was established?
2. How have Fed powers become more centralized over time? Who now has the most influence at the Fed?
3. What are the three major tools that the Fed uses to manipulate the nation's money supply? How do they work?
4. What other major areas of our financial system are subject to Federal Reserve regulation? What are the applicable regulations for each area?
5. How is the monetary base affected in each case if:
   (*a*) the Fed buys government securities?
   (*b*) the Fed makes loans to depository institutions?
   (*c*) the U.S. Treasury sells bonds to the public?
   (*d*) U.S. citizens spend dollars held in their U.S. bank accounts to buy foreign currencies from other countries' banks so they can buy foreign "goods"

(and the foreign central banks that receive the dollars hold the dollars they receive from U.S. citizens in the foreign central banks' deposit accounts at the Fed)?

    (e) the public cashes checks to get cash from their banks to take on vacation?

    (f) the U.S. Treasury mints more coins, which it deposits in its account at the Fed?

6. Answer Question 5 again, only this time explain how each of the actions cited will affect banks' actual reserve holdings.

7. Refer to Appendix B, then define the velocity of money (M1). Explain why velocity either may or may not be important for predicting how the economy is likely to respond to changes in the Fed's monetary policy.

8. (a) What do you think would happen to the transactions deposit-expansion multiplier, X_{MB}^D, if cash holdings equaled 15 percent of deposits and reserve requirements, r_D, increased from 12 percent to 15 percent?

    (b) What would happen to the deposit-expansion multiplier, X_{MB}^D, if r_D equaled 10 percent and cash-holding propensities increased from 15 percent to 20 percent of the total amount of transactions deposits?

    (c) What would happen to the M1 expansion multiplier, X_{MB}^{M1}, in case (a) above?

    (d) What would happen to the M1 expansion multiplier, X_{MB}^{M1}, in case (b) above?

    (e) Why does an increase in cash-holding propensities, c, have less of an impact on M1 expansion than on deposit expansion?

9. Referring to Appendix A, explain how the M2 multiplier, X_{MB}^{M2}, will be affected if:

    (a) people decide to hold more savings deposits relative to their transactions deposits?

    (b) people decide to hold more cash relative to their transactions deposits?

10. Why has the inclusion of interest-bearing deposits in the definition of money made it harder to tell how the money supply is related to the economy?

Selected References

Board of Governors, Federal Reserve System. *The Federal Reserve System: Purposes and Functions.* **Washington, DC: Federal Reserve Board, 1984.**
A comprehensive view of the structure and functions of the Federal Reserve System. Easy to read. Excellent for students.

Board of Governors, Federal Reserve System. *Annual Report.*
Annual reports submitted to Congress summarize the financial condition, regulatory actions, and monetary policy actions of the Federal Reserve for each year.

Capsule. **Federal Reserve Bank of New York, January 1983.**
A pamphlet explaining the key provisions of the Garn–St. Germain Depository Institutions Act of 1982.

50 Years of the Federal Reserve Act. **Federal Reserve Bank of Philadelphia, 1964.**
A straightforward description of the historical development and evolution of the Federal Reserve System. Shows how the Fed's present structure and powers have evolved over time.

Groton, Gary. "Private Clearinghouses and the Origins of Central Banking." *Business Review.* **Federal Reserve Bank of Philadelphia, January–February 1984.**
This interesting article notes that many of the initial powers given the Fed were powers (such as lending, currency issue, and supervisory powers) that bank clearinghouses had exercised—not always legally—prior to the establishment of the Federal Reserve System.

Hafer, R. W. "The Money–GNP Link: Assessing Alternative Transaction Measures." *Review.* **Federal Reserve Bank of St. Louis, March 1984, pp. 19–27.**
A discussion of the implications of the interest-bearing (NOW and SuperNOW) components of the money supply for the velocity of M1 and of the link between money and GNP. Points out that M1A is more closely linked to GNP than M1.

Johnson, Roger T. *Historical Beginnings . . . The Federal Reserve.* **Federal Reserve Bank of Boston, 1977.**
A lucid and interesting description of the historical background of the Federal Reserve Act and the development of the Federal Reserve System in its first few years.

Nichols, Dorothy M. *Modern Money Mechanics: A Workbook on Deposits, Currency, and Bank Reserves.* **Federal Reserve Bank of Chicago, 1971.**
An excellent explanation of how deposit expansion occurs and how it is related to Federal Reserve behavior and to the Fed's balance sheet.

Sellon, Gordon H., Jr. "The Instruments of Monetary Policy." *Economic Review.* **Federal Reserve Bank of Kansas City, May 1984, pp. 3–20.**
An examination of monetary policy techniques since 1979, when the Fed began to use reserve aggregates (a part of the monetary base) to affect the rate of growth of the money supply. It notes that reserve requirement adjustments and discount rate changes can also be helpful in achieving monetary policy objectives.

Thorton, Daniel L. "Why Does Velocity Matter?" *Review.* **Federal Reserve Bank of St. Louis, December 1983, pp. 5–13.**
A good explanation of why monetarists consider an understanding of velocity essential to understanding the link between money and national income. It also explains how velocity can be altered by various factors.

Whitehead, David. "Explaining the Cash Explosion." *Economic Review.* **Federal Reserve Bank of Atlanta, March 1982, pp. 14–18.**
Documentation of the rapid growth of cash in circulation using charts and graphs for bills of different denominations. Suggests that tax avoidance, illegal activity, cash hoarding, or foreign use of U.S. currency may contribute to the extraordinary increase in demand for U.S. cash.

Appendix A

Complications Affecting Monetary Expansion

The Fed's job of controlling the money supply is not easy. For one thing, while the Fed supplies the monetary base to the banking system, it cannot control cash drains. Because cash drains from the banking system reduce actual reserves held by banks, the Fed must try to anticipate when people are likely to withdraw cash from banks. The Fed then tries to expand the monetary base to offset the cash drains so depository institutions' reserves will not fall and their loans, investments, and deposits will not contract as cash leaves the banking system. Conversely, the Fed must anticipate when people will put cash back in depository institutions and offset that addition to reserves, lest depository institutions expand their loans, investments, and deposits in an inflationary manner. Because seasonal fluctuations in cash flows are large, the Fed often must engage in open market operations to offset these flows (see Exhibit 4A–1).

A second problem the Fed faces is to analyze the effect that variations in required reserves used to back Eurodollar deposits or other reservable deposits have on changes in transactions deposits and money supply expansion in general. The effect can be calculated if one assumes that other types of deposits have a predictable relationship to transactions deposits. We will consider two types of complications: (1) where Eurodollar deposits have reserve requirements applied to them and are assumed to be a constant ratio of total depository institutions transactions or deposits, and (2) where depository institutions' nontransactions deposits included in M2 (or M3) are a constant ratio to transactions deposits.

First, we consider the case where "leakages" other than cash drains occur from the monetary base. In particular, the monetary base can be used in the following manner: (1) as reserves used to meet requirements for transactions deposits, (2) as reserves used to meet reserve requirements for Eurodollar deposits or other reservable deposits, (3) as cash held by the public, or (4) as excess reserves held by depository institutions. This is summarized in Equation 4A–1,

$$MB = r_D \times D + r_{ED} \times ED + CH + ER, \qquad (4A-1)$$

Exhibit 4A–1   Currency in Circulation

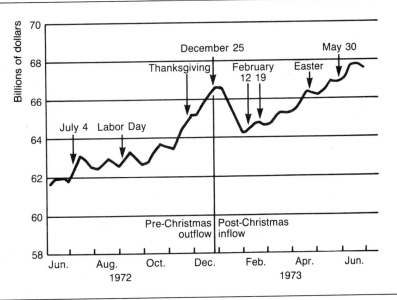

Note: Weekly averages of daily figures.

The amount of currency in circulation varies substantially over the course of a year. People typically withdraw money from the banks before holidays, particularly during the Christmas shopping season, and redeposit it afterwards. Because cash withdrawals reduce depository institutions' actual reserves, the Fed has to supply additional reserves to banks before holidays and drain the additional reserves from the banking system after holidays. Otherwise the deposit expansion multiplier (and the money supply) would vary greatly in response to the cash drains.

where all variables are defined in the chapter. To simplify things we will assume that banks hold zero excess reserves since they earn no interest on them. (If they do, in fact, hold excess reserves, it would have the same effect as a "cash drain leakage.") Now assuming that Eurodollar deposits generally are a constant ratio to transaction deposits, e, where $e = \dfrac{ED}{D}$ or $ED = e \times D$, and that excess reserves equal zero, so $ER = 0$, then Equation 4A–1 can be manipulated to obtain a new expansion ratio. In particular, first remember that $CH = c \times D$ and then substitute $c \times D$ for CH, $e \times D$ for ED, and 0 for ER into Equation 4A–1, to get Equation 4A–2:

$$MB = r_D \times D + r_{ED} \times e \times D + c \times D + 0. \tag{4A–2}$$

Then combine all terms with a D in them and delete the 0 to get:

$$MB = D\,(r_D + r_{ED} \times e + c). \tag{4A–3}$$

Dividing both sides by $(r_D + r_{ED} \times e + c)$ and switching sides we get:

$$D = \frac{1}{r_D + r_{ED} \times e + c} \times MB \tag{4A–4}$$

or, in "change" form:

$$\Delta D = \frac{1}{r_D + r_{ED} \times e + c} \times \Delta MB = X_{MB}^{D} \times \Delta MB, \tag{4A–5}$$

where, once again, X_{MB}^{D} is the expansion multiplier for transactions deposits given a change in the monetary base. This version of the expansion multiplier will be slightly smaller than the version presented in the chapter since a positive value for $r_{ED} \times e$ will *increase the denominator* of the fraction, and thereby *reduce* the multiplier.

As in the chapter, Equation 4A–5 can be converted to a monetary expansion multiplier by multiplying by $(1 + c)$. This gives:

$$\Delta M1 = \frac{1 + c}{r_D + r_{ED} \times e + c} \times \Delta MB = X_{MB}^{M1} \times \Delta MB. \tag{4A–6}$$

Different deposit and money-expansion multipliers can be computed for different levels of reserve requirements, different ratios of cash holdings or other reservable deposit holdings to transactions deposits. By so doing, the Fed can calculate the approximate impact that a change in the monetary base will have on the money supply (M1).

The Fed also can calculate the approximate impact that a change in the monetary base will have on other measures of the money supply if it assumes that the ratios of monetary aggregate components to deposits tend to be constant over time. For instance, assume that the savings deposits and other nontransaction deposit components of M2 (other than cash) equal a constant ratio of transactions deposits, or $S = s \times D$ where s is the ratio in question and S is the time and savings deposit component of M2. M2 can then be defined as:

$$M2 = M1 + S = D + CH + S. \tag{4A–7}$$

By substituting $s \times D$ for S and $c \times D$ for CH we get:

$$M2 = D + c \times D + s \times D. \qquad (4A\text{-}8)$$

Then we can observe that:

$$M2 = D(1 + c + s). \qquad (4A\text{-}9)$$

Therefore, an expansion multiplier for M2 can be written as:

$$\Delta M2 = X^{M2}_{MB} \times \Delta MB = (1 + c + s)X^{D}_{MB} \times \Delta MB = \frac{1 + c + s}{r_D + r_{ED} \times e + c} \times \Delta MB$$
$$(4A\text{-}10)$$

where X^{M2}_{MB} gives the expected change in M2 that is likely to result from a change in M1. Basically, that expansion ratio is the same as the expansion ratio for M1 except for the added s in the numerator.

As can be seen, if monetary aggregates tend to be held in fixed proportions, the Fed can calculate many expansion ratios to predict how much each of the monetary aggregates is likely to change for a given change in the monetary base. The same expansion ratios will tend to apply for either increases or decreases in the monetary base.

Appendix B

Money, Velocity, and the Economy

We have seen that the Fed can change deposit expansion multipliers by changing reserve requirements and can change deposit expansion by changing the monetary base. The Fed does this so that it can control the nation's money supply. At different times the Fed may want to control the M1, M2, or M3 definitions of money.

Velocity.   *Velocity* measures the relationship between money and the level of economic activity. The velocity of M1 is denoted V_1. It is computed as the ratio of national income, Y, to the money stock as follows:

$$M1 V_1 = Y \quad \text{or} \quad V_1 = Y/M1. \qquad (4\text{-}B1)$$

Velocity measures can also be defined for M2 and M3 as follows:

$$M2 V_2 = Y \quad \text{or} \quad V_2 = Y/M2 \qquad (4\text{-}B2)$$
$$M3 V_3 = Y \quad \text{or} \quad V_3 = Y/M3 \qquad (4\text{-}B3)$$

The importance of velocity is that it relates the money supply to the level of economic activity. If velocity is constant, or at least predictable, the Fed may be able to change the level of economic activity by changing the money supply. That is why it is so important for the Fed to know both (1) how much the money supply is likely to change when it changes reserve requirements or the monetary base and (2) how much the level of national income is likely to change when the money supply changes.

Major arguments exist among economists as to how the Fed can change the level of economic activity by changing the money supply. Those arguments are explained in detail in Chapters 25 and 26. For now, however, it is sufficient to note that economists of the monetarist (or quantity theory) school believe that velocity is predictably stable. Thus they advocate changing the money supply to change levels of economic activity. Economists of the Keynesian school, in contrast, believe that monetary policy does not necessarily work because velocity is unstable and unpredictable.

In fact, the velocity of money has changed over time. Also, changes in velocity can be difficult to predict. Although V_1 has grown, on average, by around 3 percent per year since World War II, it fell sharply from 1981 on as NOW accounts became available to the public on a nationwide basis. The addition of these interest-bearing transactions accounts to M1 has made the prediction of velocity much less certain. The public no longer has as large an incentive to switch from M1 to interest-bearing investments when interest rates rise (see "Did you Know?"), and may shift away from the interest-bearing components of the money supply when interest rates fall.

Finally, while velocity usually grows by several percentage points per year, it is not highly predictable in the short run. These facts indicate that even though the stock of money and the level of economic activity tend to be correlated, the correlation may be sufficiently variable that it is difficult to use changes in the money stock to influence the economy in the short run.

Appendix C

Deposit Expansion in the Banking System

The deposit-expansion process depicted in the chapter applies to the final deposit expansion (or contraction) that can be expected if the monetary base changes. It should be noted that the deposit-expansion (or contraction) process works the same both in a single bank and in a multibank banking system. The only difference is that the deposit expansion process in a multibank banking system may take more steps. This is shown in the example given in this appendix.

To illustrate the multibank expansion process, let us assume that the Federal Reserve System offers an attractive price and, after bidding in the open market, purchases an extra $100,000 in securities for its asset holdings from a customer of Bank A. When the Fed's check is deposited in the customer's account, Bank A acquires $100,000 more in legal reserves (deposits at the Federal Reserve) and $100,000 more in deposit obligations. Because the bank's deposits have increased, its legally required reserves also increase. Thus 10 percent of the $100,000 increase in reserves is needed to meet reserve requirements and the other $90,000 constitutes excess reserve holdings.

Because excess reserves do not earn interest, a financial institution will not hold any substantial amount of reserves idle for long. Rather, it will acquire interest-bearing investments or loans equal in value to those excess reserves. This is the only way in which a monopoly bank and a multi-institution financial system differ. The monopoly bank knows that if it creates new demand deposits or writes checks to acquire new loans and investments, none of those deposits will be checked away (i.e. deposited in another bank). Thus it can immediately expand its loan, investment, and deposit holdings by several times the amount of excess reserves. However, if Bank A writes a check or makes a loan greater in value than its excess reserves, the chances are that the checks written by the bank or by its new borrower (who needed the money to purchase something) will be deposited with one of the 30,000 other depository institutions in the country. When that happens, Bank A will lose reserves to other institutions that equal the value of the checks written on its accounts. If the reserves lost exceed its excess reserves, Bank A could experience severe problems as it scurries to cover its reserve deficiency. Thus, ordinarily, *Bank A will acquire additional new loans and investments equal in value to, but not greater than, its excess reserves.* In the process, it creates new deposits.

To illustrate how deposits are expanded in multi-institution banking, let us assume that Bank A uses its $90,000 in excess reserves to make a loan by purchasing $90,000 in notes payable from Corporation X.

If Corporation X deposits the check in Bank B, the balance sheets of Banks A and B and of Corporation X will change as follows:

Bank A		**Corporation X**		**Bank B**	
Assets	**Liabilities**	**Assets**	**Liabilities**	**Assets**	**Liabilities**
Vault cash plus reserve deposit changes = +$100,000 − $ 90,000 = +$10,000 Note payable from Corporation X +$90,000	Deposits +$100,000	Deposit at Bank B +$90,000	Note payable to Bank A +$90,000	Vault cash + reserves (including reserves obtained from Bank A) +$90,000	Deposits of Corporation X +$90,000

Note that of the initial $100,000 in additional reserves received by Bank A, it retains only $10,000, which is required to back its additional deposits. Its $90,000 in initial excess reserves were checked away to Bank B after it made the loan to Corporation X. Bank B, in turn, has acquired $90,000 in additional reserves and $90,000 more in deposits. *The loan (note purchase) by Bank A caused total deposits to increase by $90,000, even though those deposits did not remain at Bank A.*

To continue with our example, once Bank B receives the deposit from Corporation X and cashes the check drawn on Bank A, it has $90,000 more in total reserves and $90,000 more in deposits. Because it has $90,000 more in total deposits, its required reserves increase by 10 percent of $90,000, or $9,000. Thus it finds itself with excess reserves of $90,000 minus $9,000, or $81,000.

If Bank B should decide to invest its new excess reserves (in order to earn a positive rather than zero return on them), it will make a loan or acquire an investment. Suppose that it purchases $81,000 in Treasury securities from Government Security

Dealer Y, who then deposits the check from Bank B in a transactions account in Savings Bank C. As before, the net changes show up in the depository institutions' balance sheets as follows:

Bank B		Government Security Dealer Y		Savings Bank C	
Assets	**Liabilities**	**Assets**	**Liabilities**	**Assets**	**Liabilities**
Vault cash plus reserves at the Fed +$90,000 − $81,000 = +$9,000 Government security holdings +$81,000	Deposits of Corporation X +$90,000	Government security holdings − $81,000 Deposits at Savings Bank C +$81,000	No change	Reserves at Fed +$81,000	Transactions deposits of Security Dealer Y + $81,000

Note that the demand deposits created by Bank B when it acquired additional securities have again been checked away (to Savings Bank C) along with its excess reserves. However, for the financial system as a whole, transactions (demand) deposits continue to expand. At this point, the cumulative expansion is $271,000 (= $100,000 + $90,000 + $81,000). Furthermore, Savings Bank C now holds excess reserves of $72,900 ($81,000 in additional reserves minus $8,100 in reserves required on its new deposit holding of $81,000), so it too can acquire additional interest-bearing loans and investments.

Let us assume that Savings Bank C acquires new earning assets and that, in the process, its excess reserves are checked away to Financial Institution D. Exhibit 4C-1 summarizes the expansion process for (transactions) deposits, required reserves, and excess reserves as this process continues from one financial institution to the next. This gives us insight into how far the deposit creation process will continue.

Several points should be observed in Exhibit 4C-1. First, at each stage in the *deposit expansion* process, required reserves increase along with the increase in deposits. Thus each succeeding institution receives fewer additional deposits and fewer additional reserves and can make only smaller acquisitions of new loans and investments. Second, as required reserves increase with the cumulative increase in deposits, excess reserves decrease and the total change in reserves stays the same. Third, the process has an upper limit. Successive increases in deposits are smaller and smaller. By the time the expansion process reaches 80 institutions, the cumulative increase in deposits is nearly (but not quite) ten times the amount of the increase in reserves. If the process were to proceed through an infinite number of institutions, all of the additional $100,000 in reserves would be converted to required reserves. Thus the deposit expansion process would cease when $1 million in new deposits had been created. At that point, all reserves would be converted to required reserves, and no institution would hold excess reserves that it could use to acquire new earning assets.

Exhibit 4C–1   Expansion of Transactions Deposits at Financial Institutions

Financial Institution	Initial Effects				Actions		Cumulative Effects		
	(1) Increase in Deposits	(2) Increase in Reserves	(3) Increase in Required Reserves	(4) Increase in Excess Reserves	(5) New Loans and Investments	(6) Reserves Checked Away	(7) Cumulative Change in Reserves	(8) Increases in Required Reserves	(9) Increases in Deposits
1[a]	$100,000	$100,000	$10,000	$90,000	$90,000	$90,000	$100,000	$ 10,000	$ 100,000
2[b]	90,000	90,000	9,000	81,000	81,000	81,000	100,000	19,000	190,000
3[c]	81,000	81,000	8,100	72,900	72,900	72,900	100,000	27,100	271,000
4	72,900	72,900	7,290	65,610	65,610	65,610	100,000	34,390	343,900
5	65,610	65,610	6,561	59,049	59,049	59,049	100,000	40,951	409,510
·	·							·	·
·	·							·	·
·	·							·	·
78	30	30	3	27	27	27	100,000	99,973	999,730
79	$27	$27	$2.70	$24.30	$24.30	$24.30	$100,000	$ 99,976	$ 999,757
·							·	·	·
·							·	·	·
·							·	·	·
Ultimate cumulative expansion							$100,000	$100,000	$1,000,000

[a] Bank A.
[b] Bank B.
[c] Savings Bank C.

Explanation of columns:

(1) New deposits = $100,000 for Bank A and equals the figure shown in Column (6), one row up, for all other institutions (on the assumption that all reserves checked away from the previous institution are deposited in the next institution).

(2) New reserve balances available to each bank = new deposits, Column (1), same row.

(3) Increase in required reserves = 10 percent reserve requirement times the increase in deposits, Column (1), same row.

(4) Increase in excess reserves = increase in actual reserves, Column (2), minus increase in required reserves, Column (3).

(5) New loans or investments = increase in excess reserves, Column (4), as banks try to earn a return on excess funds.

(6) Reserves checked away = Column (5), new loans and investments, assuming all checks or deposits created to acquire loans and investments are checked away.

(7) Cumulative change in actual reserves = $100,000, as all reserves introduced at Step 1 subsequently are owned by someone.

(8) Cumulative increase in required reserves = the sum of Column (3) down to and including the row in question.

(9) Cumulative increase in deposits = the sum of Column (1) down to and including the row in question.

Note: This analysis can be reproduced by students with spreadsheet programs on computers if they follow the steps in Columns (1) to (9). In a multi-institution banking system, each institution can increase its loans and investments only by an amount that is equal to its excess reserves. Nonetheless, the ultimate cumulative effect of deposit expansion in a multi-institutional system is the same as it is in a single-institution system. In both cases, it equals the deposit-expansion multiplier, X_{AR}^D, times the initial change in actual reserves. In this case, the deposit-expansion multiplier equals 10, so the ultimate expansion is ten times the increase in reserves.

It should be noted that the total deposit expansion that can occur in the multi-institution system is exactly the same as the total deposit expansion that can occur in a monopoly bank system. It still equals the expansion multiplier, X^D_{AR}, times the change in reserves, as shown by Equation 4-3 in the text. It may take somewhat more time, however, and each institution contributes only a small part to the total expansion of deposits.

RATES AND
S PRICES

es "Chip" Wickens

HE IS

Commodity broker and trader with the Iowa Grain Company, a commercial account commodities brokerage house. Previously he was a partner with Hennessy & Associates, also a commercial account commodities brokerage house, where he became a partner at age 27, one year after joining the firm. He began floor trading at Hennessy using a company-owned seat on the Chicago Board of Trade and now owns his own seat paid for out of earned commissions and personal trading.

WHAT HE DOES

Trades futures contracts on soybeans, wheat, corn, and other grains as a broker for commercial clients and for himself. Transactions range from $30,000 to $10 million in the trading pit, where he has only seconds to make his decisions. He prepares himself to operate in the chaotic environment of the pit by arriving at his office at 6:00 a.m. He spends the first hour of the day reading government reports and the business press. At 7:00 a.m. he participates in a half-hour meeting of fifteen traders in the "war room," discussing financial rumors as well as printed statements about the overall economy, the agricultural economy, the weather, and world political and economic conditions that affect the demand for and supply of agricultural commodities. Beginning at 7:30 a.m., he is on the phone with his commercial clients and grain brokers on other exchanges. Trading starts at 9:30 a.m. and finishes at 1:15 p.m., after which he spends a bit more time on reading and phone calls.

HOW HE GOT THERE

B.S.: University of Missouri

First job: Trading in the cash grain market for Continental Grain Company and Pillsbury, buying and selling barges, trains, and cargos of grain by telephone with his counterparts at other companies and in other countries, including the former Soviet Union.

BACKGROUND

He grew up in New Jersey with the lifelong ambition of being a farmer. On entering the University of Missouri, he was introduced to the field of economics and could not get enough courses. In one of his classes, he saw a film about trading at the Chicago Board of Trade and knew instantly what he wanted to do with his dual interests in farming and economics—to become a trader. He finished his degree as an agricultural economics major. He now lives in Chicago's historic Lincoln Park neighborhood, a few minutes' travel time from the CBOT.

WHAT HE LIKES BEST ABOUT HIS JOB

Being an entrepreneur in an environment of rapid change and constant challenge.

WORST NIGHTMARE

Going broke.

HOW HE UNWINDS

He owns land in Colorado, his favorite skiing spot, and a summer vacation house in St. Joseph, Michigan. While in Chicago, his spare time is occupied with gardening and gourmet cooking, interests he shares with his fiancée.

ADVICE

Find something you really enjoy and do it well.

BOND PRICES, BOND YIELDS, AND INTEREST RATE RISK

5

THE DECADES OF THE 1980s and 1990s were difficult periods for financial institutions—record numbers of them failed or were forced to merge by regulators. Historically, financial institutions failed because of credit risk or inadequate liquidity. More recently, however, financial institutions have failed because of interest rate risk, which is caused by the volatile and unpredictable behavior of interest rates.

The purpose of this chapter is to explain how interest rate movements affect the prices of assets and liabilities of investors and financial institutions. We first focus on bonds because their behavior in the face of interest rate changes is similar to that of other financial instruments, including many of the assets and liabilities of commercial banks and other financial institutions that we study in this book. Once you understand the mechanics of bond prices and how interest rates affect them, you can apply these concepts to understanding the critical management problems faced by financial institutions in the 1990s.

We begin our treatment of bond pricing and interest rate risk with an examination of the concepts of future and present value. Next, we develop the bond pricing formula and explain how to calculate various yield measures of bonds. We then discuss the characteristics of a bond that influence its price volatility and explore the concept of interest rate risk. Finally, we discuss the concept of duration and how it can be used by financial institutions and other investors to reduce or eliminate the damaging effects of interest rate risk.

The Time Value of Money

Before we can understand interest rates and how bonds are priced, we need to understand the concept of the time value of money. The *time value of money* is based on the belief that people have a positive time preference for consumption; that is, people prefer to consume goods today rather than consume similar goods in the future. Thus, the time value of money can be simply stated as *a dollar today is worth more than a dollar received at some future date*. This makes sense, because if you had the dollar today, you could invest it and earn interest. In contrast, the further the dollar is in the future, the less it is worth. Let's see how finance theory values both dollars today and dollars in the future.

Future Value

Future-value or compound-value problems ask this question: If a person has a certain amount of money today (present value), how much will it be worth in the future (future value) at a given rate of interest? The future value formula is:

$$FV = PV(1 + i)^n, \tag{5-1}$$

where:

FV = future value of an investment n periods in the future;
PV = present value of an amount of money (the value of money today);
i = interest rate;
n = number of interest-rate compounding periods.

To illustrate, suppose you have \$100 and put it in a savings account at a local bank, expecting to keep it there for five years. The bank pays 4 percent interest on savings accounts and compounds interest annually. Applying Equation 5–1, we have:

$$FV = \$100(1 + 0.04)^5$$
$$= \$100(1.04)^5$$
$$= \$100(1.2167)$$
$$= \$121.67.$$

If the bank decided to pay interest quarterly, the number of compounding periods increases to 20 periods (5 years × 4 periods) and the annual interest rate converted to a quarterly interest rate is 1.00 percent (4 percent/4 periods). Applying Equation 5–1 to the new situation, the future value is:

$$FV = \$100(1.01)^{20}$$
$$= \$100(1.2202)$$
$$= \$122.02.$$

Notice that the dollar amount is slightly larger because we have increased the number of compounding periods and are now earning more interest on interest. For a given interest rate, the more frequent the compounding, the larger the future value. This explains why banks like to advertise daily compounding rather than annual or quarterly compounding.

If you have a calculator available, it is easy to calculate the interest factor, $(1 + i)^n$, with just the touch of a few buttons. As the number of periods becomes large, however, the calculation of the interest factors becomes difficult, even with a calculator. To avoid these messy calculations, not to mention mistakes, tables have been constructed for values of $(1 + i)^n$ for a wide range of values of i and n. Exhibit 5–1 is illustrative. Also, these calculations are easily made with financial calculators or spreadsheets software.

We define the term future value *interest factor*, *IF*, as being equal to $(1 + i)^n$. Then Equation 5–1 can be rewritten as:

$$FV = PV(IF). \tag{5-1a}$$

Now it is only necessary to look up the appropriate *IF* value from Exhibit 5–1 rather than calculate it by hand. Turning to our original example, the correct interest

Exhibit 5–1   **Future Value of \$1 at the End of *n* Periods: $IF = (1 + i)^n$**

Number of Periods	1%	2%	3%	4%	5%	6%	7%	8%	9%	10%	12%	14%	15%
1	1.0100	1.0200	1.0300	1.0400	1.0500	1.0600	1.0700	1.0800	1.0900	1.1000	1.1200	1.1400	1.1500
2	1.0201	1.0404	1.0609	1.0816	1.1025	1.1236	1.1449	1.1664	1.1881	1.2100	1.2544	1.2996	1.3225
3	1.0303	1.0612	1.0927	1.1249	1.1576	1.1910	1.2250	1.2597	1.2950	1.3310	1.4049	1.4815	1.5209
4	1.0406	1.0824	1.1255	1.1699	1.2155	1.2625	1.3108	1.3605	1.4116	1.4641	1.5735	1.6890	1.7490
5	1.0510	1.1041	1.1593	1.2167	1.2763	1.3382	1.4026	1.4693	1.5386	1.6105	1.7623	1.9254	2.0114
6	1.0615	1.1262	1.1941	1.2653	1.3401	1.4185	1.5007	1.5869	1.6771	1.7716	1.9738	2.1950	2.3131
7	1.0721	1.1487	1.2299	1.3159	1.4071	1.5036	1.6058	1.7138	1.8280	1.9487	2.2107	2.5023	2.6600
8	1.0829	1.1717	1.2668	1.3686	1.4775	1.5938	1.7182	1.8509	1.9926	2.1436	2.4760	2.8526	3.0590
9	1.0937	1.1951	1.3048	1.4233	1.5513	1.6895	1.8385	1.9990	2.1719	2.3579	2.7731	3.2519	3.5179
10	1.1046	1.2190	1.3439	1.4802	1.6289	1.7908	1.9672	2.1589	2.3674	2.5937	3.1058	3.7072	4.0456
11	1.1157	1.2434	1.3842	1.5395	1.7103	1.8983	2.1049	2.3316	2.5804	2.8531	3.4785	4.2262	4.6524
12	1.1268	1.2682	1.4258	1.6010	1.7959	2.0122	2.2522	2.5182	2.8127	3.1384	3.8960	4.8179	5.3503
13	1.1381	1.2936	1.4685	1.6651	1.8856	2.1329	2.4098	2.7196	3.0658	3.4523	4.3635	5.4924	6.1528
14	1.1495	1.3195	1.5126	1.7317	1.9799	2.2609	2.5785	2.9372	3.3417	3.7975	4.8871	6.2613	7.0757
15	1.1610	1.3459	1.5580	1.8009	2.0789	2.3966	2.7590	3.1722	3.6425	4.1772	5.4736	7.1379	8.1371
16	1.1726	1.3728	1.6047	1.8730	2.1829	2.5404	2.9522	3.4259	3.9703	4.5950	6.1304	8.1372	9.3576
17	1.1843	1.4002	1.6528	1.9479	2.2920	2.6928	3.1588	3.7000	4.3276	5.0545	6.8660	9.2765	10.761
18	1.1961	1.4282	1.7024	2.0258	2.4066	2.8543	3.3799	3.9960	4.7171	5.5599	7.6900	10.575	12.375
19	1.2081	1.4568	1.7535	2.1068	2.5270	3.0256	3.6165	4.3157	5.1417	6.1159	8.6128	12.056	14.232
20	1.2202	1.4859	1.3061	2.1911	2.6533	3.2071	3.8697	4.6610	5.6044	6.7275	9.6463	13.743	16.367

Future value is the amount to which a dollar amount will grow when compounded by a given interest rate.

Copyright © 1984 The Dryden Press. A division of CBS College Publishing.

factor (*IF*) for the five-year bank deposit earning 4 percent is found by looking down the "number of periods" column to 5, then across this row to the "4 percent" column to find the interest factor of 1.2167. Using this factor, the future value of \$100 after five years at 4 percent is:

$$FV = PV(IF)$$
$$= \$100(1.2167)$$
$$= \$121.67,$$

which is identical to our hand-calculated value using Equation 5–1.

Present Value

Suppose that you could buy a financial claim that would pay \$121.67 in five years and there is no doubt the amount will be paid. Furthermore, assume that your only other investment opportunity is to put your money in the bank at 4 percent (is this starting to sound familiar?). How much would you pay for this financial claim? You know from the previous example that \$100 deposited in the bank for five years at 4 percent will be worth \$121.67—the same amount as the five-year financial claim. Therefore, in a strictly financial sense, you would be indifferent in your choice between $100 today or $121.67 at the end of five years. In our example, the $100 is the *present value (PV)* of $121.67 to be received five years in the future. Let's examine this idea in a more analytical framework.

Finding the present value of some future sum of money (called discounting) is simply the reverse of compounding. To illustrate this point we can use Equation 5–1:

$$FV = PV(1 + i)^n.$$

The equation as it now stands allows us to solve for the future value (*FV*) of a given sum of money today (its present value). To solve for the present value (*PV*), we solve Equation 5–1 by dividing both sides of the equation by the interest factor, $(1 + i)^n$, which results in the following equation:

$$PV = FV\left[\frac{1}{(1 + i)^n}\right].\qquad(5\text{–}2)$$

The term in brackets is called the *discount factor, DF*, and it is equal to the reciprocal of the interest factor $(1/IF)$. Just as with the interest factor, tables have been constructed for various values of i and n, where $DF = 1/(1 + i)^n$. A table of discount factors is shown in Exhibit 5–2.

Exhibit 5–2 shows the present value of $1 paid at the end of various future years at different rates of interest. For example, at a market rate of interest of 10 percent, the present value (price) of a dollar not received until one, two, three, five, and ten years from now is $0.9091, $0.8264, $0.7513, $0.6209, and $0.3855, respectively.[1] Notice that the value of the amount becomes smaller the further into the future the money is to be received. Of course, that is the whole idea of the time value of money.

Using the discount factor (*DF*), Equation 5–2 can be written in modified form as:

$$PV = FV(DF).\qquad(5\text{–}2a)$$

Now, going back to our original question, how much would we pay for $121.67, to be received five years in the future, if our opportunity cost were 4 percent? Using Exhibit 5–2, we can find the discount factor by looking down the "number of periods" column to 5 and then across this row to the "4 percent" column to find the discount factor, 0.8219. We then compute the present value of $121.67 received in five years as:

$$\begin{aligned}PV &= FV(DF)\\ &= \$121.67(0.8219)\\ &= \$100.00.\end{aligned}$$

As a drill, you may want to make this calculation using Equation 5–2. We now turn to how bonds are priced, a process that is merely an application of the present value formula.

---

[1]The calculation of the values from the present value table for $1 discounted at 10 percent are as follows: one year, $0.9091 = $1/(1.10)^1$; two years, $0.8264 = $1/(1.10)^2$; three years, $0.7513 = $1/(1.10)^3$; five years, $0.6209 = $1/(1.10)^5$; and ten years, $0.3855 = $1/(1.10)^{10}$.

Exhibit 5–2   **Present Value of a Dollar Due at the End of _n_ Periods: _DF_ = 1/(1 + _i_)^n**

Number of Periods	1%	2%	3%	4%	5%	6%	7%	8%	9%	10%	12%	14%	15%
1	.9901	.9804	.9709	.9615	.9524	.9434	.9346	.9259	.9174	.9091	.8929	.8772	.8696
2	.9803	.9612	.9426	.9246	.9070	.8900	.8734	.8573	.8417	.8264	.7972	.7695	.7561
3	.9706	.9423	.9151	.8890	.8638	.8396	.8163	.7938	.7722	.7513	.7118	.6750	.6575
4	.9610	.9238	.8885	.8548	.8227	.7921	.7629	.7350	.7084	.6830	.6355	.5921	.5718
5	.9515	.9057	.8626	.8219	.7835	.7473	.7130	.6806	.6499	.6209	.5674	.5194	.4972
6	.9420	.8880	.8375	.7903	.7462	.7050	.6663	.6302	.5963	.5645	.5066	.4556	.4323
7	.9327	.8706	.8131	.7599	.7107	.6651	.6227	.5835	.5470	.5132	.4523	.3996	.3759
8	.9235	.8535	.7894	.7307	.6768	.6274	.5820	.5403	.5019	.4665	.4039	.3506	.3269
9	.9143	.8368	.7664	.7026	.6446	.5919	.5439	.5002	.4604	.4241	.3606	.3075	.2843
10	.9053	.8203	.7441	.6756	.6139	.5584	.5083	.4632	.4224	.3855	.3220	.2697	.2472
11	.8963	.8043	.7224	.6496	.5847	.5268	.4751	.4289	.3875	.3505	.2875	.2366	.2149
12	.8874	.7885	.7014	.6246	.5568	.4970	.4440	.3971	.3555	.3186	.2567	.2076	.1869
13	.8787	.7730	.6810	.6006	.5303	.4688	.4150	.3677	.3262	.2897	.2292	.1821	.1625
14	.8700	.7579	.6611	.5775	.5051	.4423	.3878	.3405	.2992	.2633	.2046	.1597	.1413
15	.8613	.7430	.6419	.5553	.4810	.4173	.3624	.3152	.2745	.2394	.1827	.1401	.1229
16	.8528	.7284	.6232	.5339	.4581	.3936	.3387	.2919	.2519	.2176	.1631	.1229	.1069
17	.8444	.7142	.6050	.5134	.4363	.3714	.3166	.2703	.2311	.1978	.1456	.1078	.0929
18	.8360	.7002	.5874	.4936	.4155	.3503	.2959	.2502	.2120	.1799	.1300	.0946	.0808
19	.8277	.6864	.5703	.4746	.3957	.3305	.2765	.2317	.1945	.1635	.1161	.0829	.0703
20	.8195	.6730	.5537	.4564	.3769	.3118	.2584	.2145	.1784	.1486	.1037	.0728	.0611

The present value table illustrates the principle of the time value of money. A dollar today is worth more than a dollar in the future.

Copyright © 1982 The Dryden Press. A division of CBS College Publishing.

The Mechanics of Bond Pricing

This section focuses on how bonds and other financial claims are priced. The method employed involves an application of the present value concept. We begin, however, by defining the important terms of a bond contract.

Bond Definitions

A _bond_ is a contractual obligation of a borrower to make periodic cash interest payments to a lender for a fixed number of years. Upon maturity, the lender is paid the original sum borrowed. The periodic interest payment is called the _coupon_, the number of years over which the bond contract extends is called the _term to maturity_, and the number of dollars paid to the lender upon maturity is called the _par value_, or _principal_ amount. The coupon payment is typically expressed as a percentage of the principal amount and is known as the _coupon rate_. The coupon rate (_c_) is computed by

DID YOU KNOW?

"Does Bo Know Finance?"

Bo Jackson, the 1985 Heisman Trophy winner, had more offers than you could shake a sneaker at when he first put his services as a professional athlete on the market. Bo had his choice of football or baseball. In 1986, the Kansas City Royals (baseball) offered Bo a three-year package reported in the press as "worth" $1.086 million. The package included $200,000 in the first year, $353,000 in the second, and $533,000 in the third. Further, Bo agreed to return half of his salary if he switched to football. Bo's competing offer from the Oakland Raiders (football) included $2 million in the first year and an average salary of $1.35 million over the next four years, a package the press reported as "worth" $7.4 million. Which package would you have picked? The answer isn't so simple unless you consider the *present value* of the two offers. Assuming an 8 percent discount rate, the present value of the baseball deal is $910,938 and the present value of the football deal is $6 million. In both cases the value of the deals is worth less than that reported in the press because the journalists did not account for the time value of money.

Did Bo account for the time value of money, given that he initially chose baseball, apparently ignoring the huge difference in present value? Perhaps not. Bo most likely figured that a pro baseball career would last much longer than a career as an NFL running back. Thus, even though Bo earned less money initially from baseball, he probably estimated his career earnings would be higher. To quote the owner of the Kansas City Royals, Ewing Kauffman: "Football guaranteed him $2 million; we guaranteed him $200,000. I think it shows his self-confidence and character. In the long run he'll make more money from us than football, and he'll be able to walk when he's 50."

Did Kauffman's argument make sense? To arrive at some "ballpark" (pun intended) figures, let's assume that Bo's salary would grow at a 10 percent annual rate on average for as long as he played either sport. At a 10 percent growth rate in salary, Bo would have to play baseball for over 20 years before the present value of the baseball salary exceeded the present value of a 10-year football career. If we were willing to assume that Bo's baseball salary grows twice as fast as his football salary (that is, at a 20 percent annual rate) he would have to play baseball for 15 years to equal the present value of a 10-year football career. The moral of the story is that Bo will have to play baseball a lot longer to achieve the same wealth from playing football. We do need to recognize, of course, that our calculations assume Bo lasts 10 years in the NFL without a career-ending injury. It is somewhat rare for an NFL running back to last that long. On the other hand, not many pro baseball players last 15 or 20 years either. Bo obviously had a complicated decision.

To finish the story, Bo ultimately played *both* football and baseball and along the way picked up a string of product endorsements that have made him a multimillionaire. Bo recently suffered a painful hip injury from football that has kept him out of *both* sports and hurt his earning power as a product endorser. Perhaps Bo is now wishing he would have stuck with baseball, where the chance of severe injury is lower. In any event, he continues to work hard to rehabilitate his hip and return to the playing field. Bo's appeal as a pitchman, however, has certainly provided him with some financial security. We are thus left with the question, "Does Bo know finance?" Given the complexity of Bo's deals, the product endorsements, and the hip injury it is difficult to answer that question. One thing is certain, however, Bo *knows* money!

$c = C/P$, where C = annual dollar coupon payment and P = par or maturity value of the bond.

It is important to keep in mind that for most bonds the coupon rate, the par value, and the term to maturity are fixed over the life of the bond contract. When most bonds are first sold, they are sold in $1,000 or $5,000 denominations. Coupon rates are typically set at or near the *market rate of interest* or *yield* on similar bonds available in the market. By similar, we mean bonds nearly identical in term to maturity and credit risk. Also note that the coupon rate and the market rate of interest are different. The coupon rate is fixed throughout the life of a bond. The market rate or yield on a bond varies when changes in supply and demand for credit alter the market price of existing bonds.

The Bond Price Formula

Because a bond is a borrower's contractual promise to make future cash payments, the pricing of a bond is an application of the *present value formula*. Thus the price of a bond is the present value of the future cash flow (coupon payments and principal amount) discounted by the interest rate that people place on the time value of money. The formula for the present value, or price of a fixed-coupon-rate bond with n periods to maturity, is:

$$PB = \frac{C_1}{(1 + i)^1} + \frac{C_2}{(1 + i)^2} + \cdots + \frac{C_n + F_n}{(1 + i)^n}, \tag{5-3}$$

where:

PB = price of the bond or present value of the stream of cash payments;
C_t = coupon payment in period t;
F_n = par amount or face value to be paid at maturity;
i = interest rate (discount rate) or yield to maturity;
n = number of periods to maturity.

Notice that a bond is a series of cash payments (coupon payments and principal) of a fixed amount for a specified number of years. Thus, each future cash payment must be individually discounted from the date received back to the present using Equation 5-2. In words, the formula says that the present value, or market price of a bond, is the sum of the discounted values of all future cash flows (coupon payments and principal). Also note that in applying the bond-pricing equation, there are five unknowns, and if we know any four of the variables, the fifth can be found from the formula.

Consider a three-year bond with a face value of $1,000 and a coupon of 8 percent so that the coupon payments are $80. If coupon payments are made annually and the current market rate of interest is 10 percent, the price of the bond, using Equation 5-3, is:

$$PB = \frac{\$80}{(1.10)^1} + \frac{\$80}{(1.10)^2} + \frac{\$1,080}{(1.10)^3}$$
$$= \$72.73 + \$66.12 + \$811.42$$
$$= \$950.27.$$

Notice that the final cash payment, consisting of the final coupon payment ($80) and the face value of the bond ($1,000), is $1,080.

Using the present value tables, we can use a modified version of Equation 5-3 that uses the discount factors in Exhibit 5-2:

$$PB = FV_1 DF_1 + FV_2 DF_2 + \cdots + FV_n DF_n. \tag{5-3a}$$

The bond price of the 8 percent coupon bond in the previous example is:

$$
\begin{aligned}
PB &= \$80(0.9091) + \$80(0.8264) + \$1,080(0.7513) \\
&= \$72.73 + \$66.11 + \$811.40 \\
&= \$950.24.
\end{aligned}
$$

The slight difference between our two answers is due to four-digit rounding in the preparation of the present value table.

Properties of the Bond Price Formula.   One of the properties of the bond formula is that whenever a bond's coupon rate is equal to the market rate of interest (the bond's yield), the bond will *always* sell at par. Such bonds are called *par bonds* because they sell at face value. For example, consider a three-year bond with a face value of $1,000 and an annual coupon rate of 5 percent, when the current yield or market rate of interest on similar bonds is 5 percent. The price of the bond, using Equation 5-3, is:

$$
\begin{aligned}
PB &= \frac{\$50}{(1.05)^1} + \frac{\$50}{(1.05)^2} + \frac{\$1,050}{(1.05)^3} \\
&= \$47.62 + \$45.35 + \$907.03 \\
&= \$1,000.
\end{aligned}
$$

As predicted, our bond sells at its par value. Notice that you would have gotten the same answer if you had computed the bond price using the present value table.

Now assume that the market rate of interest immediately rises to 8 percent. What will be the price of the bond? Will it be below, above, or at par? For i equal to 8 percent, the price of the bond declines to $922.69. The bond sells below par; such bonds are called *discount bonds.* Whenever the market rate of interest on similar bonds is above a bond's coupon rate, a bond will sell at a discount. The reason is the fixed nature of a bond's coupon. If bonds with similar characteristics are yielding 8 percent and our bond is paying 5 percent (the coupon rate), no one will buy our bond at par since its yield is only 5 percent. To increase the bond's yield, the seller must reduce the price of the bond to $922.69. At this price the bond's yield will be precisely 8 percent, which is competitive with similar bonds. Through the price reduction of $77.31 ($1,000 − 922.69), the seller provides the new owner with additional interest in the form of a capital gain.

If the interest rate on similar bonds were to fall to 2 percent, the price of our bond would rise to $1,086.52. The bond now would sell at a *premium*. Whenever the market rate of interest is below a bond's coupon rate, a bond will sell at a premium. The premium price adjusts the bond's yield to 2 percent, which is the market rate that similar bonds are yielding.

Semiannual Compounding. If interest payments are made more than once a year, Equation 5–3 is modified as follows:

$$PB = \frac{C_1/m}{(1 + i/m)^1} + \frac{C_2/m}{(1 + i/m)^2} + \frac{C_3/m}{(1 + i/m)^3} + \cdots + \frac{C_{mn}/m + F_{mn}}{(1 + i/m)^{mn}}, \quad (5\text{--}4)$$

where m is the number of times interest is compounded each year. For example, if our three-year, 5 percent coupon bond paid interest semiannually and the current market yield was 6 percent, the price of the bond would be:

$$PB = \frac{\$25}{(1.03)^1} + \frac{\$25}{(1.03)^2} + \cdots + \frac{\$1,025}{(1.03)^6}$$
$$= \$972.91.$$

Note that the market yield is 3 percent semiannually (6 percent yearly), the coupon payment is $25 semiannually ($50 per year), and the total number of interest payments is six (two per year for three years). Quarterly and monthly compounding periods are computed in a similar manner.

Bond Yield Measures

The coupon rate on a bond reflects only the annual cash flow promised by the borrower to the lender. The actual rate of return the lender earns, however, depends on several key risks. First is the chance that the borrower fails to make coupon or principal payments in the amount or at the time promised. This is called *credit* or *default risk.*[2] Second, market interest rates may change, causing the lender to have to reinvest coupon payments at interest rates different from the interest rate at the time the bond was purchased. This is called *reinvestment risk.* Finally, interest rate changes cause the market value of a bond to rise or fall, resulting in capital gains or losses to the investor.[3] This is called *price risk.*

The purpose of this section is to explain various ways to measure bond returns—or as they are more commonly called, *bond yields.* In general, a yield on any investment, such as a bond, is the interest rate that equates the market price of an investment with the discounted sum of all cash flows from the investment. The ideal yield measure should capture all three potential sources of cash flow from a bond: (1) coupon payments, (2) interest income from reinvesting coupon payments, and (3) any capital gain or loss. We now discuss three yield measures: yield to maturity, realized yield, and expected yield.

[2] We will thoroughly discuss the effect of default risk on bond returns in Chapter 7. For the remainder of this chapter we will assume that borrowers make all cash flows as promised so that we can focus our attention on interest rate risk.

[3] More technically, a capital gain (or loss) is the difference between the purchase price and the principal if the bond is held to maturity or the difference between the purchase price and the sale price if the bond is sold prior to maturity.

Yield to Maturity

If a bond's purchase price is known, the bond-pricing formulas (Equations 5–3 and 5–4) can be used to find the yield of a bond. A yield calculated in this manner is called the *yield to maturity* or *promised yield*. It is the yield promised the bondholder on the assumption that the bond will be held to maturity, all coupon and principal payments will be made as promised, and the coupon payments will be reinvested at the bond's promised yield for the remaining term to maturity. If the coupon payments are reinvested at a lower rate, the bondholder's actual yield will be less than the promised yield. This type of risk is called *reinvestment risk*.

An example of a bond yield calculation is as follows. If a person purchased a three-year, 5 percent coupon (semiannual payments) bond for $951.90, the yield to maturity is found by solving the following equation for the interest rate (i).

$$\$951.90 = \frac{\$25}{(1 + i/2)^1} + \frac{\$25}{(1 + i/2)^2} + \cdots + \frac{\$1,025}{(1 + i/2)^6}.$$

Unfortunately, the yield to maturity (i) cannot be determined algebraically but must be found by trial and error. That is, the calculation is done by selecting different values of i until the present value of the cash flows on the right-hand side of the equation equals $951.90. Solving the preceding equation in this manner results in a yield of 3.40 percent semiannually, or 6.80 percent annually. The calculation of the final value of i (the yield) is cumbersome and difficult to make by hand because many iterations usually are required. Most financial calculators are programmed to provide the answer at the touch of a button.

Realized Yield

The yield to maturity tells us what return we will earn on a bond if the borrower makes all cash payments as promised, if interest rates do not change over the bond's maturity, and if the investor holds the bond to maturity. Quite frequently, however, one or more of these events will not occur. For example, an investor may sell a bond before maturity at a price below the purchase price, or the bond issuer may default. In any event, the return actually earned on a bond will likely be different from the promised yield.

The *realized yield* is the return earned on a bond, given the cash flows actually received by the investor and assuming that the coupon payments are reinvested at the promised yield. We now illustrate the calculation of realized yield with an example. Suppose you purchased a ten-year, 8 percent coupon (annual payments) bond at par. Recall that because the bond is selling at par, the yield to maturity (promised yield) equals the coupon rate. Three years later you decide to take a vacation to Cancun and you sell the bond to acquire the necessary funds. At the time you sell the bond, seven-year bonds with similar characteristics (for example, default risk) sell for yields of 10 percent.

In this case the realized yield will be different from the promised yield of 8 percent because market yields on similar bonds increased to 10 percent. We calculate the yield actually earned on the investment by solving for the interest rate that equates the price you originally paid for the bond with the discounted sum of the cash flows you actually received.

The first step is to calculate the current price of the bond. In the example you paid $1,000 for the bond. You held the bond for three years and received three annual coupon payments of $80 each. The market price of the bond is equal to the present value of the remaining seven coupon payments and final principal repayment:

$$PB = \$902.63 = \frac{\$80}{(1.10)^1} + \frac{\$80}{(1.10)^2} + \cdots + \frac{\$1,080}{(1.10)^7}.$$

The next step is to set the original purchase price of $1,000 equal to the present value of the cash flows *actually received* (three coupon payments of $80.00 and the sale price of $902.63) and solve for the interest rate:

$$\$1,000 = \frac{\$80}{(1 + i)^1} + \frac{\$80}{(1 + i)^2} + \frac{\$80 + \$902.63}{(1 + i)^3}.$$

Solving the preceding equation either by trial and error or by financial calculator results in a realized yield of 4.91 percent annually. The difference between the realized yield and the promised yield in this case is accounted for by the capital loss of $97.37 ($1,000 − $902.63) suffered when the bond was sold before maturity. In sum, realized yield is useful because it allows an investor or financial institution to evaluate the return on a bond *ex-post* (*after* the end of the holding period or investment horizon).

Expected Yield

Investors and financial institutions that plan to sell their bonds before maturity would like to know the potential impact of interest rate changes on the returns of their bond investments *ex-ante* (*before* the fact). They can use various forecasting techniques to estimate future interest rates based on information about the money supply, inflation rates, economic activity, and the past behavior of interest rates. Once armed with an interest rate forecast,[4] an investor can predict the market price of a bond at the end of a relevant holding period. Given the prediction of the future price, the investor can calculate an *expected yield* that reflects the expected sale price.

Suppose when you purchased the bond in the preceding example (a ten-year, 8 percent coupon bond), you planned to sell it at the end of two years at the prevailing market price. When you purchased the bond, your investment adviser predicted that similar bonds with eight years to maturity would yield 6 percent at the end of two years. Your interest rate forecast implies that the bond's expected price (PB_e) is $1,124.20:

$$PB_e = \$1,124.20 = \frac{\$80}{(1.06)^1} + \frac{\$80}{(1.06)^2} + \cdots + \frac{\$1,080}{(1.06)^8}.$$

Notice there are eight coupon payments and the principal payment remaining at the time of sale.

---

[4] We will discuss how financial institutions forecast interest rates in Chapter 6.

To calculate the expected yield over your two-year holding period, you solve for the interest rate that equates the original purchase price (par, or $1,000 in this example) with the discounted sum of the cash flows you expect to receive (coupon payments and the *expected* sale price):

$$\$1,000 = \frac{\$80}{(1 + i)^1} + \frac{\$80 + \$1,124.20}{(1 + i)^2}.$$

Solving the preceding equation either by trial and error or by financial calculator results in an expected yield of 13.81. In this case, the difference between the promised yield and the expected yield is accounted for by the capital gain of $124.20 earned from selling the bond before maturity.

Pricing Other Types of Securities

Although most debt securities promise both periodic coupon payments and repayment of the principal at maturity, some debt securities have different characteristics. These securities can be priced (or the yield calculated) using the bond-pricing formulas. All that is necessary is to properly identify the timing and amount of the periodic cash payments. Some examples follow.

Zero Coupon Securities

Zero coupon securities are securities that have no coupon payment but promise a single payment at maturity. The interest paid to the holder is the difference between the price paid for the security and the amount received upon maturity (or price received when sold). Common examples of zero coupon securities are U.S. Treasury bills and U.S. savings bonds. As a general rule, most money market instruments (securities with maturities of less than one year) are sold on a discount basis. Also, in recent years some corporations have issued zero coupon bonds. A major attraction of zero coupon bonds for investors is that there is no coupon reinvestment risk. That is, because there are no coupon payments to be reinvested, the bond's actual yield is equal to the promised yield.

The price (or yield) on a zero coupon bond is simply a special case of Equation 5–4, in that all the coupon payments are set equal to zero. Hence the pricing equation is:

$$PB = \frac{F_{mn}}{\left(1 + \dfrac{i}{m}\right)^{mn}}, \tag{5–5}$$

where:

PB = price of the bond;
F_n = amount of cash payments at maturity;
i = interest rate (yield) for n periods;
n = number of years until the payment is due;
m = number of times interest is compounded each year.

Thus the price of a ten-year zero coupon bond with a $1,000 face value and a 12 percent (6 percent semiannual rate) market rate of interest is:

$$PB = \frac{\$1,000}{(1.06)^{20}} = \$311.80.$$

Notice that our calculation is based on semiannual numbers because U.S. bonds pay coupon interest semiannually; thus, Equation 5–4 provides the best comparison.

Amortized Loan

An amortized loan contract repays the loan in equal payments in each period over the life of the loan, using a special rate of interest. Thus each payment includes both interest and principal. Most mortgage loans to finance residential property and consumer installment loans are *amortized loans*. For example, an individual borrows $100,000 for a home mortgage from a savings and loan association for 20 years. If monthly payments are to be $1,100, the annual percentage rate for the loan is computed from Equation 5–4 as follows:

$$\$100,000 = \frac{\$1,100}{(1 + i)^1} + \frac{\$1,100}{(1 + i)^2} + \cdots + \frac{\$1,100}{(1 + i)^{240}}.$$

Solving the equation, we find that the monthly interest rate is 1 percent, or 12 percent on an annual basis.[5] Clearly, solving equations such as this one must be done with the aid of a financial calculator.

Bond Theorems

Bond Price and Yield

For bonds or any other financial claims, a strict relationship exists between price and yield: Bond prices and yields vary inversely. Specifically, as a bond's market price rises, its yield declines; or as the price declines, its yield increases. The inverse relationship exists because the coupon rate on a bond is fixed at the time the bond is issued. The higher the price that an investor must pay for a fixed amount of interest payments, the lower the realized yield or rate of return on the investment. This inverse relationship is observed for bonds as well as for all other financial claims. It is extremely important that the reader keep in mind this inverse relationship between prices and yields.

Bond Price Volatility

Before we can meaningfully examine how the maturity and coupon rate affect the sensitivity of bond prices to interest rate changes, we need a workable definition of

---

[5] The 12 percent annual rate (12 × 1 percent) does not consider the monthly compounding effect. To compute the effective annual yield (EAY), the proper formula is: $EAY = (1 + i/n)^n - 1$, where i is the simple annual rate (12 percent) and n is the number of compounding periods. For our example, $EAY = (1 + 0.12/12)^{12} - 1 = 0.1268$, or 12.68 percent.

bond price volatility. Let's define *bond price volatility* as the percentage change in bond price for a given change in yield.

Bond price volatility is simple to calculate. Consider a 10-year bond selling at par with an 8 percent annual coupon. Suppose that yields on similar bonds increase by 25 basis points to 8.25 percent.[6] In terms of dollars, the price of the bond falls from $1,000 to $983.41, a decline of $16.59. The question answered by bond price volatility is: How much will the price change in percentage terms?

The percentage change in a bond price (price volatility) is calculated as:

$$\Delta PB = \frac{P_t - P_{t-1}}{P_{t-1}} \times 100 \tag{5-6}$$

where:

$$\Delta PB = \text{the percentage change in price;}$$
$$P_t = \text{the new price in period } t;$$
$$P_{t-1} = \text{the bond's price one period earlier.}$$

For our example, the price of the bond fell from $1,000 to $983.41. Applying Equation 5–6,

$$\Delta PB = \frac{\$983.41 - \$1,000}{\$1,000} \times 100 = -1.66 \text{ percent.}$$

Thus a bond's price volatility is a measure of how sensitive a bond's price is to yield changes.

Bond Price Volatility and Maturity

The mathematics of the present value formula have some interesting implications for the relationship between bond price volatility and maturity. Specifically, long-term bonds have greater price volatility than short-term bonds, holding other bond characteristics constant. This fact is illustrated in Exhibit 5–3, which shows the price of a $1,000, 5 percent coupon bond when the market interest rate is 5 percent (Column 2). The market rate of interest is then allowed to rise from 5 to 6 percent (Column 3) and to fall from 5 to 4 percent (Column 6). For both cases, the dollar price changes resulting from the given yield changes are recorded in Columns 4 and 7. The percentage price changes (price volatilities) are recorded in Columns 5 and 8.

As the exhibit shows, when the market yield rises to 6 percent, a one-year, 5 percent coupon bond sells at $990.57, a price decline of $9.43 or 0.94 percent. In contrast, the 100-year, 5 percent coupon bond sells at $833.82, a price decline of $166.18 or 16.62 percent. The 100 basis point increase in interest rates causes a capital loss almost 18 times larger on the long-term bond than on the short-term bond. Likewise, the price volatility of the long-term bond is 18 times greater than that of the short-term bond. Similar results are shown for interest decreases in Columns 7 and 8. In sum, the longer

---

[6] From now on, we will discuss changes in bond yields in terms of what investors on Wall Street call *basis points*. A basis point is 1/100th of one percent; that is, 100 basis points equal one percent. A change in yield of 25 basis points, for example, is equal to a change of 0.25 percent.

| Exhibit 5–3 | Relationship between Price, Maturity, Market Yield, and Price Volatility for a $1,000, 5 Percent Coupon Bond | | | | | | |

(1)	(2)	Price Change if Yield Changes to 6 Percent			Price Change if Yield Changes to 4 Percent		
Maturity (years)	Bond Price at 5 percent Yield ($)	(3) Bond Price ($)	(4) Loss from Increase in Yield ($)	(5) Price Volatility (percent)	(6) Bond Price ($)	(7) Gain from Decrease in Yield ($)	(8) Price Volatility (percent)
1	$1,000	$990.57	$9.43	−0.94%	$1,009.62	$9.62	0.96%
5	1,000	957.88	42.12	−4.21	1,044.52	44.52	4.45
10	1,000	926.40	73.60	−7.36	1,081.11	81.11	8.11
20	1,000	885.30	114.70	−11.47	1,135.90	135.90	13.59
40	1,000	849.54	150.46	−15.05	1,197.93	197.93	19.79
100	1,000	833.82	166.18	−16.62	1,245.05	245.05	24.50

This exhibit shows that the longer the maturity of a bond, the greater the bond's price volatility. Thus, long-term bonds have greater interest rate risk than short-term bonds.

the term to maturity, the greater the price volatility, and hence, longer maturity bonds have greater interest rate risk.

Bond Price Volatility and Coupon Rate

Another important factor that affects the price volatility of a bond is the bond's coupon rate. Specifically, the lower a bond's coupon rate, the greater the percentage price change (price volatility) for a given change in yield. This mathematical property of the bond pricing formula is illustrated in Exhibit 5-4, which shows the prices of three ten-year bonds: a zero-coupon bond, a 5 percent coupon bond, and a 10 percent coupon bond. Initially, the bonds are priced to yield 5 percent (see Column 2). The bonds are then priced at yields of 6 and 4 percent (see Columns 3 and 8). The dollar price changes for each bond given the appropriate interest rate change are recorded in Columns 4 and 7, and percentage price changes (price volatilities) are shown in Columns 5 and 8. As Column 5 shows, when interest rates increase from 5 to 6 percent, the zero coupon bond experiences the greatest percentage price decline, and the 10 percent bond experiences the smallest percentage price decline. Similar results are shown in Column 8 for interest rate decreases. In sum, the lower a bond's coupon rate, the greater a bond's price volatility, and hence, lower coupon bonds have greater interest rate risk.

Summary of Bond Theorems

There are three important properties of the relationship between bond prices and yields you should remember:

1. Bond prices are inversely related to bond yields.
2. The bond price volatility of a long-term bond is greater than that of a short-term bond, holding coupon rate constant.

Exhibit 5–4   **Relationship between Price, Coupon Rate, Market Yield, and Price Volatility for a $1,000, Ten-Year Bond**

(1)	(2)	Price Change if Yield Changes to 6 Percent			Price Change if Yield Changes to 4 Percent		
		(3)	(4)	(5)	(6)	(7)	(8)
Coupon Rate (percent)	Bond Price at 5 percent Yield ($)	Bond Price ($)	Loss from Increase in Yield ($)	Price Volatility (percent)	Bond Price ($)	Gain from Decrease in Yield ($)	Price Volatility (percent)
0%	$613.91	$558.39	$55.52	−9.04%	$675.56	$61.65	10.04%
5	1,000.00	926.40	73.60	−7.36	1,081.11	81.11	8.11
10	1,386.09	1,294.40	91.69	−6.62	1,486.65	100.56	7.25

This exhibit shows that the longer the coupon rate of a bond, the greater the bond's price volatility. Thus, low-coupon bonds have greater interest rate risk than high-coupon bonds.

3. The bond price volatility of a low-coupon bond is greater than that of a high-coupon bond, holding maturity constant.

We will call on these relationships to help us explain interest rate risk in the next section, and later in the book they will also help us explain how interest rate risk affects financial institutions.

Interest Rate Risk and Duration

By now, you should be catching on that investing in bonds can be risky. Market yields on bonds fluctuate on a daily basis, and these fluctuations cause bond prices to change through the mechanics of the bond pricing formula (Equation 5–1). In this section we formally present the concept of interest rate risk and show how investors and financial institutions attempt to manage it using a risk measure called duration.

Interest Rate Risk

Interest rate risk is the risk related to changes in interest rates that cause a bond's realized yield to differ from the promised yield. Two factors affect interest rate risk: (1) price risk and (2) reinvestment risk. We now discuss these two risks.

Price Risk.   Price risk is defined by the first bond theorem described in the preceding section; namely, bond prices and bond yields are inversely related. Increases in interest rates lead to capital losses that cause realized yields to decline. Conversely, decreases in interest rates lead to capital gains that cause realized yields to rise. These fluctuations in realized yield caused by capital gains and losses constitute *price risk*.

Reinvestment Risk.   Reinvestment risk is a trickier concept. Remember when we calculated yield to maturity, we noted that the bond pricing formula assumes that all coupon payments are reinvested at the bond's yield to maturity. Given that interest rates fluctuate, it is unlikely that an investor will reinvest all coupon payments at the promised yield. If, for example, interest rates increase over the life of a bond, coupons will be reinvested at higher yields, increasing reinvestment income.[7] The increase in reinvestment income will increase the realized yield of the bond. If interest rates rise, the converse is true. The change in a bond's realized yield caused by changing coupon reinvestment rates is what constitutes *reinvestment risk.*

Because of reinvestment risk, investors calculate what is called *realized compound yield.* Realized compound yield accounts for the impact of changing interest rates and, thus, changing coupon reinvestment rates on a bond's realized return. This measure is similar in spirit to the realized yield we calculated earlier in this chapter, except that realized compound yield allows for the possibility of changing coupon reinvestment rates.[8]

Exhibit 5-5 illustrates the effect of different reinvestment rates on the realized compound yield of a ten-year, 8 percent coupon bond purchased at par. Column 1 shows different interest rates at which coupon income is reinvested, and Column 2 reports the realized compound yield. Notice that when the bond's coupon income ($80 per year or 8 percent) is reinvested at exactly 8 percent, the realized compound yield equals 8 percent, the bond's promised yield. When the coupon income is spent rather than reinvested (reinvestment rate = 0 percent), the bond's realized compound yield is 6.05 percent, and if the reinvestment rate is 11 percent, the realized compound yield is 8.86 percent.

Exhibit 5-5

Different Reinvestment Rate Assumptions for an 8 Percent Coupon 10-Year Bond Purchased at Par

(1) Reinvestment Rate in Percent	(2) Realized Compound Yield in Percent
0	6.05
5	7.21
6	7.47
7	7.73
8	8.00
9	8.28
10	8.57
11	8.86

As the reinvestment rate increases, the realized compound yield increases. When all coupons are reinvested at the yield to maturity, the realized compound yield equals the yield to maturity.

---

[7] We use future value mathematics to calculate reinvestment income, which is really just the interest-on-interest from a bond. Future values behave just the opposite of present values when interest rates change. When interest rates increase, future value increases. When they decrease, future value also decreases.

[8] For an excellent discussion and example of calculating realized compound yield, see Frank J. Fabozzi and T. Dessa Fabozzi. *Bond Markets: Analysis and Strategies.* Englewood Cliffs, N.J. Prentice-Hall, 1989, Chapter 3, pp. 45–53.

Price Risk versus Reinvestment Risk.   It is very important to recognize that price risk and reinvestment risk partially offset one another. When interest rates decline, a bond's price increases resulting in a capital gain (good news!), but the bond's realized compound yield decreases because of lower coupon reinvestment income (bad news!). On the other hand, when interest rates rise, a bond's price declines resulting in a capital loss (bad news!), but the bond's realized compound yield increases because of higher coupon reinvestment income (good news!).

Duration and Interest Rate Risk

It is important for investors and financial institutions to be able to evaluate the effect of interest rate risk on their bond investments. How can we measure interest rate risk? The problem we have is that bond price volatility varies directly with maturity and inversely with coupon rate. A good measure of interest rate risk should account for both effects simultaneously. A measure of interest rate risk (or bond price volatility) that considers both coupon rate and maturity is *duration*. A bond's duration is defined as the weighted average number of years needed to fully recover the present value of principal and coupon payments. Using annual compounding, the formula for duration is:

$$D = \frac{\sum_{t=1}^{n} \dfrac{CF_t(t)}{(1+i)^t}}{\sum_{t=1}^{n} \dfrac{CF_t}{(1+i)^t}} \tag{5-7}$$

where:

D = duration of the bond;
CF_t = interest or principal payment at time t;
t = time period in which principal or coupon interest is paid;
n = number of periods to maturity;
i = the yield to maturity (interest rate).

The denominator is the price of the bond (PB) and is just another form of the bond pricing formula presented earlier (Equation 5–1). The numerator is the present value of all cash flows weighted according to the length of time to receipt. Admittedly, the formula for duration looks pretty formidable. However, we will work through some computational examples and then use the examples to illustrate the important properties of duration. We will be using the concept of duration throughout the book, so it is important that you grasp the fundamentals now.

To illustrate the calculation of duration using Equation 5–7, suppose that we have a bond with a three-year maturity, an 8 percent coupon rate paid annually, and a market yield of 10 percent. The duration of the bond is:

$$D = \frac{\dfrac{\$80(1)}{(1.10)^1} + \dfrac{\$80(2)}{(1.10)^2} + \dfrac{\$1,080(3)}{(1.10)^3}}{\dfrac{\$80}{(1.10)^1} + \dfrac{\$80}{(1.10)^2} + \dfrac{\$1,080}{(1.10)^3}} = 2.78 \text{ years.}$$

If the market rate of interest (yield) increases from 10 percent to 15 percent, the bond's duration would be:

$$D = \frac{\dfrac{\$80(1)}{(1.15)^1} + \dfrac{\$80(2)}{(1.15)^2} + \dfrac{\$1,080(3)}{(1.15)^3}}{\dfrac{\$80}{(1.15)^1} + \dfrac{\$80}{(1.15)^2} + \dfrac{\$1,080}{(1.15)^3}} = 2.76 \text{ years.}$$

To give you a chance to sharpen your computational skills, Exhibit 5–6 shows the duration for a group of bonds with different coupon rates (zero, 4 percent, and 8 percent) and different maturities (one to five years); in all cases the bonds are priced to yield 10 percent, and coupon payments are paid annually. Go ahead and do a few calculations.

Exhibit 5–6 and our examples can be used to illustrate some important properties of duration.

1. Bonds with higher coupon rates have a *shorter* duration than bonds with smaller coupons of the same maturity. This is true because the higher coupon bonds receive more of the total cash flow earlier in the form of coupon payments. For example, for any given maturity, the 8 percent coupon bonds always have a shorter duration than the 4 percent or zero coupon bonds.
2. There is generally a positive relationship between term to maturity and duration. The longer the maturity of a bond, the higher the bond's duration.[9] This is true because the bond's cash flow is received further out in time.
3. For bonds with a single payment (principal with or without a coupon payment), duration is equal to term to maturity. Thus, for zero coupon bonds (the single payment is the principal), duration equals final maturity. Likewise, the one-year bonds in Exhibit 5–6 have a duration equal to one year because

---

Exhibit 5–6   Duration for Bonds Yielding 10 Percent (Annual Compounding)

Maturity (years)	Duration in Years		
	Zero Coupon	4 Percent Coupon	8 Percent Coupon
1	1.00	1.00	1.00
2	2.00	1.96	1.92
3	3.00	2.88	2.78
4	4.00	3.75	3.56
5	5.00	4.57	4.28

Duration is a measure of bond price volatility that considers both the coupon rate and term to maturity.

[9] For bonds selling at a discount (below par), duration increases at a decreasing rate up to a fairly long maturity, such as 50 years, and then declines. Since most bonds have maturities of 30 years or less, duration increases with maturity for most bonds we observe in the marketplace.

PEOPLE
& EVENTS

Junk Bonds Can Have a Big Bite: Interest Rate Risk and the Dog

April 1990 was a tough month for Peter A. Cohen, former chief executive officer at American Express company's investment banking subsidiary, Shearson Lehman Hutton. Security analysts say his miscalculations and lack of judgment caused two firms to lose $115 million, he was unceremoniously fired from his job at Shearson, and, it was rumored, his dog bit him. That's a bad month, especially the dog bite. How did Peter accomplish all of this in a month? Simple. Bet on interest rate movements and buy long-term junk bonds, then kick the dog.

Let's turn the clock back to early 1989 when the junk bond market was just reaching its peak. Then plunk down $290 million to buy shares in seven junk bond mutual funds and another $190 million of individual junk bonds, for a whopping total of $480 million. Finally, purchase junk bonds yielding well above 12 percent by selling short-term floating-rate paper with yields of less than 9 percent. Cohen and other executives at Shearson reasoned, if I can earn 12 percent on my investment and pay 9 percent for money, that's a 3 percent spread, which is a huge return on investment compared to other alternatives. Of course, what Shearson did to earn that "high" return was to invest in bonds whose prices were very sensitive to interest rate changes (that is, high price volatility or interest rate risk). As you recall from this chapter, interest rate risk is the risk that changes in interest rates will cause a bond's

realized yield to differ from the promised yield. Interest rate risk manifests itself through changes in the market prices of bonds (price risk) or fluctuations in coupon reinvestment income (reinvestment risk).

In the case of Shearson, its timing—both the buying and selling—could not have been worse. The firm purchased the long-term junk bonds when their price was near their peak; then interest rates sprinted upward, causing bond prices to decline precipitously (recall, long-term bonds have greater price volatility than short-term bonds). Then compounding Shearson's problems, the interest cost on the floating-rate paper rose in conjunction with the general interest rate increase, increasing the firm's cost of funding the junk bonds. In early April 1990, with the price of junk bonds falling and the cost of funding rising, the firm decided to bail out their junk bond holdings. Again, its timing was off. As one analyst said, "They may not have hit the bottom with their selling, but they could not have done much worse." Of course, that was the end of the deal and end of Peter's high-salaried job.

What's the moral of the story? Simply put, long-term bonds have lots of interest rate risk compared to short-term bonds, especially high-risk junk bonds whose price volatilities are much larger than those of similar maturity higher-grade bonds. Also, never kick a dog that bites.

they pay coupon interest annually. Bonds with interim payments always have durations less than their final maturity.

4. All other factors held constant, the higher the market rate of interest, the shorter the duration of the bond. This stands to reason because the higher the market rate of interest, the faster coupon reinvestment income accumulates. This means that cash flows arrive sooner on average, resulting in a shorter duration.

One property of duration that is particularly important to managers of financial institutions is the *direct* relationship between bond price volatility and duration. The longer a bond's duration, the greater the percentage change in a bond's price for a given change in interest rates. Thus, duration is a good measure of interest rate risk since, as noted above, duration is directly related to maturity and inversely related to coupon rate. Duration, therefore, captures the effects of the second bond theorem (maturity) and the third bond theorem (coupon rate).

Uses of Duration

Probably the most important use of duration is as a tool for reducing or eliminating interest rate risk over a given holding period. For example, suppose that you are in the beginning of your junior year in college and wish to plan for a well-deserved vacation two years from now. You have a two-year investment horizon over which you must accumulate enough funds to take your vacation. You consider investing in bonds, but you are concerned about the potential impact of interest rate risk on the returns to your investment and, hence, your ability to afford the vacation. We now discuss the relative merits of three possible approaches to dealing with interest rate risk.

The Zero Coupon Approach. The simplest way to avoid the interest rate risk in this situation is to invest in a zero coupon bond that matures in two years. This strategy eliminates price risk because the bond is held to maturity, and it eliminates reinvestment risk because there are no coupon payments to reinvest. The entire return from the zero coupon bond comes from the difference between the purchase price and the maturity value. Assuming default-free bonds, there will be no risk in this strategy.

The Maturity-Matching Approach. A more naive alternative is to invest in a coupon bond with a maturity equal to the two-year holding period. With this strategy you eliminate the price risk because you hold the bond to maturity, but there is still reinvestment risk because coupons are received. Consequently, interest rate changes could potentially wreak havoc with your vacation plans should interest rates decline dramatically over the two years.

The Duration-Matching Approach. A "surefire" way of eliminating both price risk and reinvestment risk is to structure your bond investment such that the *duration* of the bond equals your holding period.[10] What happens with the duration-matching strategy that results in the elimination of both price and reinvestment risks? By matching duration with your holding period, you set up a situation in which capital gains or losses from interest rate changes are exactly offset by changes in reinvestment income. You are able to lock in on a given target return to your investment and thus ensure that you will have enough money at the end of two years to take your vacation.

---

[10]Technically, this is true only when the term structure of interest rates is flat and moves only in parallel shifts. Interest rates, unfortunately, do not usually behave this way in the real world. As a result, it is usually not possible to *completely* eliminate interest rate risk from a bond investment with this strategy, although many academic studies show that it is possible to obtain substantial *reduction* in interest rate risk. The term structure of interest rates is discussed in Chapter 7.

The duration-matching strategy has many real-world applications. Managers of pension funds use the strategy to protect from interest rate risk the value of bond portfolios used to provide workers with retirement income in the distant future. By using duration combined with a strategy of "dedicating" a bond portfolio's assets to paying a particular stream of pension fund obligations, fund managers can ensure that they will be able to pay retirees the contracted amount regardless of interest rate changes. Later in the book, we will show how managers of commercial banks and thrift institutions can use duration to reduce fluctuations in net interest income (the difference between the average return of the assets minus the average cost of liabilities) resulting from interest rate changes. Basically, banks and thrifts can protect their net income and net worth from interest rate risk by matching the average duration of the assets with the average duration of the liabilities.

Summary

In this chapter we show that both bond prices and bond yields are calculated from the present value formula. The present value formula considers the time value of money and is the proper technique by which to value a series of cash payments over time. Three important properties of the bond-pricing formula are: (1) the relationship between bond prices and bond yields is inverse; (2) the longer the maturity of a bond, the greater its percentage price change (bond price volatility) for a given change in interest rates; and (3) the lower the coupon rate of a bond, the greater its percentage price change for a given change in interest rates.

We then define and illustrate one of the book's most important concepts, interest rate risk. Interest rate risk consists of fluctuations in the bond's market price (price risk) and the bond's coupon reinvestment income (reinvestment risk) that cause realized yield to differ from yield to maturity. A measure of interest rate risk that considers both the coupon rate and the term to maturity is duration. By matching the duration of their firms' assets and liabilities, managers of financial institutions can minimize exposure to interest rate risk.

Questions

1. Write the equation expressing the present value (or price) of a bond that has an 8 percent coupon (annual payments), a four-year maturity, and a principal of $1,000 if yields on similar securities are 10 percent. Compute the price using a calculator.
2. Find the price of a corporate bond maturing in five years that has a 5 percent coupon (annual payments), a $1,000 face value, and an Aa rating. A local newspaper's financial section reports that the yields on five-year bonds are: Aaa, 6 percent; Aa, 7 percent; and A, 8 percent.
3. What is the yield to maturity of a corporate bond with a three-year maturity, 5 percent coupon (semiannual payments), and $1,000 face value if the bond sold for $978.30?
4. Explain why yields and prices of fixed-income securities are inversely related.
5. What is the relationship between bond price volatility and term to maturity? Between bond price volatility and the coupon rate?

6. An investor purchases a one-year discount bond with a $1,000 face value for $862.07. What is the yield of the bond?

7. An investor purchases a $1,000 twenty-year bond with an 8 percent coupon rate (annual payments). Yields on comparable bonds are 10 percent. The investor expects that two years from now, yields on comparable bonds will have declined to 9 percent. Find the realized yield the investor expects, assuming the bond is sold in two years.

8. Calculate the duration of a $1,000 four-year bond with an 8 percent coupon rate (annual payments) that is currently selling at par.

9. What is the relationship between duration and term to maturity? Between duration and the coupon rate?

10. Define interest rate risk. Explain the two types of interest rate risk. How can an investor with a given holding period use duration to reduce interest rate risk?

Selected References

Alexander, Gordon J., and William F. Sharpe. *Investments.* Englewood Cliffs, NJ: Prentice-Hall, 1990.
Chapter 14 provides an excellent overview of how to manage interest rate risk.

Becketti, Sean. "The Role of Stripped Securities in Portfolio Management." *Economic Review.* Federal Reserve Bank of Kansas City, May 1988, pp. 20–31.
The article provides an introduction to stripped securities and their use in investment portfolio management. The article discusses the risk and benefits to financial institutions of purchasing stripped securities for their investment portfolios.

Fabozzi, Frank J., and T. Dessa Fabozzi. *Bond Markets: Analysis and Strategies.* Englewood Cliffs, NJ: Prentice-Hall, 1989.
Chapters 1–4 provide an excellent introduction to the mechanics of bond pricing and yield measures. The book also thoroughly explains the measurement of interest rate risk and gives examples of the implications of interest rate risk for investing in bonds.

Hilliard, Jimmy, and Joseph F. Sinkey, Jr. "Duration Analysis as a Tool for Predicting Interest-Sensitive Cash Flows." *Journal of Financial Education*, Fall 1989, pp. 1–7.
This article provides excellent examples of how duration can be used as a measure of interest rate sensitivity for financial institutions. The approach is insightful because it relates duration to a pro forma statement of cash flows.

Horner, Sidney, and Martin L. Leibowitz. *Inside the Yield Book.* Englewood Cliffs, NJ: Prentice-Hall, 1972.
The classic treatise on bond prices and yields. Essential reading for serious students of bonds.

Livingston, Miles. *Money and Capital Markets: Financial Instruments and Their Uses.* Englewood Cliffs, NJ: Prentice-Hall, 1990.
Chapters 9 and 11 discuss bond pricing, bond price volatility, and the uses of duration in reducing the interest rate risk of a bond portfolio.

Morris, Charles S. "Managing Interest Rate Risk with Interest Rate Futures." *Economic Review.* Federal Reserve Bank of Kansas City, March 1989, pp. 3–20.
This article describes volatility in the bond markets in the 1970s and 1980s and also explains how interest rate futures are used to reduce interest rate risk.

Rose, Peter S. *Money and Capital Markets.* Homewood, IL: Richard D. Irwin, 1992.
Chapters 7–11 provide comprehensive coverage of bond pricing, yield calculations, and interest rate risk.

Smith, Clifford W., Jr., Charles W. Smithson, and D. Sykes Wilford. *Managing Financial Risk.* **New York: Harper & Row, 1990.**
This book is somewhat advanced, but it provides an excellent framework within which to analyze and manage interest rate risk, as well as other forms of financial risk. An outstanding book.

Van Horne, James C. *Financial Market Rates and Flows.* **Englewood Cliffs, NJ: Prentice-Hall, 1990.**
Chapter 6 provides an excellent example of how duration is used to reduce interest rate risk.

THE LEVEL OF INTEREST RATES

6

As WE MOVE THROUGH THE decade of the1990s, it is prudent for all financial decision makers to remember the aberrant behavior of interest rates in the early 1980s. Back then, high and volatile interest rates made news headlines with regularity, and justifiably so. Annual averages of monthly data on the interest rates of Federal Funds bounced from 13.36 percent in 1980 to 16.38 percent in 1981, then dropped back dramatically to 8.13 percent by 1985. On a daily basis during this period, rates sometimes went up or down a whole percentage point in less than an hour. In some cases, minutes actually determined whether or not someone could afford to purchase a house or a car or to expand business operations. Even though the late 1980s brought an abatement of the very fast and wide swings in interest rates, many financial managers, as well as consumers, remain fearful of history repeating itself.

The purpose of this chapter is to explain what factors cause the levels of interest rates to rise and fall and why interest rates were at record-high levels during the early 1980s. Our treatment of interest rates begins with an examination of the forces that establish the level of interest rates in the economy and highlight the effect of inflation on the level of interest rates. Next, we explain why interest rates vary over the business cycle. Finally, we describe how investors and financial institutions forecast interest rate movements.

What Are Interest Rates?

For thousands of years, people have been lending goods to other people, and, on occasion they have asked for some compensation for this service. The compensation is called *rent*—the price of borrowing another person's property. Similarly, money is often loaned, or rented for its purchasing power. The rental price of money is called *interest* and is usually expressed as an annual percentage of the nominal amount of money borrowed. Thus interest rates are the price of borrowing money for the use of its purchasing power.

To a person borrowing money, interest is the penalty paid for consuming income before it is earned. To a lender, interest is the reward for postponing current consumption until the maturity of the loan. During the life of a loan contract, borrowers typically make periodic interest payments to the lender. Upon maturity of the loan, the borrower repays the same amount of money borrowed (the principal) to the lender.

Like other prices, interest rates serve an *allocative function* in our economy. They allocate funds between surplus spending units (SSUs) and deficit spending units (DSUs) and between financial markets. For SSUs, the higher the rate of interest, the greater the reward for postponing current consumption and the greater the amount of saving in the economy. For DSUs, the higher the yield paid on a particular security, the greater the demand for that security but the less willing they will be to supply the security. Therefore SSUs want to buy financial claims with the highest returns whereas DSUs want to sell financial claims at the lowest possible interest rate.

The Real Rate of Interest

The fundamental determinant of interest rates is the interaction of the production opportunities facing society and the individual's time preference for consumption. Let's examine how producers (investors) and savers interact to determine the market rate of interest. Business people and other producers have the opportunity to invest in capital projects that are productive in the sense that they yield additional real output in the future. The extra output generated constitutes the *return on investment*. The higher the return on an investment, the more likely producers are to undertake a particular investment project.

Individuals have different preferences for consumption over time. All things being equal, most people prefer to consume goods today rather than tomorrow. This is called a *positive time preference*. For example, most people prefer to go on a vacation or purchase a stereo or new car now. People consume today, however, realizing that their future consumption may be less because they have forgone the opportunity to save.

Given people's positive time preference, the interest rate offered to savers will determine how thrifty those persons are. At low interest rate levels, most people will postpone very little consumption for the sake of saving. To coax people to postpone additional current consumption, higher interest rates, or rewards, must be offered. However, as the interest rate rises, fewer business projects earn an expected return high enough to cover the added interest expense. As a result, fewer investment projects are undertaken.

Therefore, the interest rate paid on savings basically depends on (1) the rate of return producers can expect to earn on investment capital, and (2) savers' time preference for current versus future consumption. The expected return on investment projects sets an upper limit on the interest rate producers can pay for savings, whereas consumer time preference for consumption establishes how much consumption consumers are willing to forgo (save) at the different levels of interest rates offered by producers.

Exhibit 6–1 shows the determination of the market equilibrium interest rate for the economy in a supply and demand framework. Aggregate savings for the economy represents the desired amount of savings for consumers at various rates of interest. Similarly, the aggregate investment schedule represents the amount of desired

---

Exhibit 6–1   **Determinants of the Real Rate of Interest**

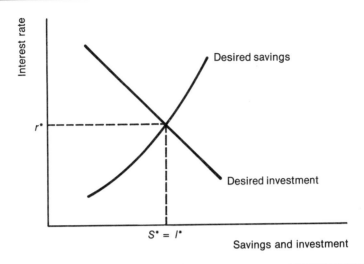

The real rate of interest is the base interest rate for the economy. It is estimated to be on average about 3 percent, and it varies between 2 and 4 percent.

investment by producers at various interest rates. The two curves show that consumers will save more if producers offer higher interest rates on savings, and producers will borrow more if consumers will accept a lower return on their savings. The market equilibrium rate of interest (r^*) is achieved when desired savings (S^*) by savers equals desired investment (I^*) by producers across all economic units. At this point, funds are allocated over time in a manner that fits people's preference between current and future consumption. The equilibrium rate of interest is called the *real rate of interest*. The real rate of interest is the fundamental long-run interest rate in the economy. It is called the "real" rate of interest because it is determined by the real output of the economy.

The real rate of interest is estimated to be on average about 3 percent for the U.S. economy, and it varies between 2 and 4 percent because of changes in economic conditions. For example, a major breakthrough in technology would cause the investment schedule to shift to the right and thus increase r^*. Other demand factors that could shift the investment schedule to the right and increase r^* are an increase in productivity of existing capital, an increase in expected business product demand, reduction in taxes affecting corporations, or reduction in the expected risk on a particular class of investment projects. Likewise, economic factors can affect the supply of savings. For example, consumer attitudes toward savings can change so that they become more thrifty. If this occurs, the savings schedule will shift to the right and the real rate of interest will decline. Other supply-side factors that could decrease r^* would be a reduction in the personal income tax rate and an increase in income.

PEOPLE
& EVENTS

Irving Fisher (1867–1947): Economist and Social Reformer

Irving Fisher was one of America's best-known economists. A man of exceptional talents and diverse interests, he was an economist, a statistician, a businessman, and a social reformer. A son of a Congregational minister, Fisher entered Yale University in 1884 and studied widely in the physical and social sciences throughout his academic career. His doctoral dissertation combined his love of mathematics and economics and is considered a classic today. Upon receiving his Ph.D., Fisher taught mathematics at Yale for four years and then switched to economics, the field in which he spent the rest of his academic career.

As an economist, Fisher is most acclaimed for his theory of the real rate of interest (presented in this chapter) and his analysis of the quantity theory of money. Regarding interest rates, Fisher articulated that two basic forces determine the real rate of interest in a market economy: (1) subjective forces reflecting the preference of individuals for present consumption over future consumption, and (2) objective forces depending on available investment opportunities and productivity of capital. Fisher also recognized the distinction between the nominal and the real rate of interest—the nominal rate of interest being composed of a real component

and an inflation premium that compensates lenders for losses in purchasing power caused by inflation. Fisher's classic treatise on interest, *The Theory of Interest Rates*, was first published in the 1930s and is still reprinted today. Fisher's views on interest are the foundation for contemporary interest rate theory.

Outside the academic realm, Fisher had his share of crackpot ideas, but he also met with some successes. One of his major achievements was a card index system he invented and sold; the company he formed merged in 1926 with other companies to form Remington Rand Corporation.

Perhaps one of Fisher's most interesting endeavors came after an attack of tuberculosis in 1898. Following his recovery, he became an ardent advocate of eugenics and public health. His zeal went so far that he wrote a book advocating a temperate and healthful lifestyle. The book, *How to Live: Rules for Healthful Living Based on Modern Science*, was enormously successful, going through more than 90 editions. Though bizarre by today's standards, the book extolled the virtues of good posture, proper shoe fit, and complete chewing of food—all as a means to a long and healthy life.

Loanable Funds Theory of Interest

Although the trade-off between productivity and thrift is the underlying force that determines interest rates, it is difficult to use this framework to explain short-run changes in the level of interest rates observed in a monetary economy (where money is the medium of exchange) such as ours. Interest rates can be viewed as being determined by the demand for and supply of direct and indirect financial claims on the primary and secondary markets during a particular time period. Thus, in the short run, interest rates depend on the supply of and the demand for loanable funds, which in turn depend on productivity and thrift. The loanable funds framework is widely used by financial analysts and economists because of its intuitive appeal and because it is easily employed as a basis for interest rate forecasting models.

Deficit spending units (DSUs) issue financial claims to finance expenditures in excess of their current income. The need to sell these financial claims constitutes the demand for loanable funds. On the other side of the market, surplus spending units (SSUs) supply loanable funds to the market. SSUs purchase financial claims to earn interest on their excess funds. Exhibit 6–2 shows the major sources of the demand for and supply of loanable funds in the economy.

The scheme outlined in Exhibit 6–2 is, for the most part, disaggregated—it shows the sources of the gross supplies of and demands for loanable funds in the economy. Household, business, and governmental units appear on both sides of the market. Thus consumer personal savings are a major source of funds and, simultaneously, most households are demanders of funds as they engage in a wide variety of consumer credit purchases. Likewise, business firms supply loanable funds through depreciation and retained earnings, and they demand loanable funds to invest in plant, equipment, and inventories. State and local governments can run surplus budgets (tax revenues exceed expenditures) that act as a supply of funds, whereas budget deficits (expenditures exceed tax revenues) create a demand for loanable funds as governmental units issue debt to cover the shortfall in revenues. The federal government is usually a demander of loanable funds because it typically runs a deficit budget.

The Federal Reserve is shown as a source of loanable funds. The supply of loanable funds is increased whenever the Federal Reserve increases the money supply (ΔM is positive). As discussed in Chapter 4, money is created through central bank policy actions, change in bank reserves and currency, and the money multiplier. The supply of loanable funds can be decreased if the Federal Reserve decides to contract the money supply (ΔM is negative). The supply of loanable funds also can be affected by the public desire to hold money balances.

The supply of loanable funds schedule is shown in Exhibit 6–3, Frame A. The aggregate schedule shown is a composite of all suppliers of loanable funds in the

---

Exhibit 6–2	**Sources of Supply of and Demand for Loanable Funds**

Supply of Loanable Funds (SSU)
Consumer savings
Business savings (depreciation and retained earnings)
State and local government budget surpluses
Federal government budget surplus (if any)
Federal Reserve increases the money supply (ΔM)
Demand for Loanable Funds (DSU)
Consumer credit purchases
Business investment
Federal government budget deficits
State and local government budget deficits

Notice that households, businesses, and governmental units are both suppliers and demanders of loanable funds. During most periods, households are net suppliers of funds, whereas the federal government is almost always a net demander of funds.

Exhibit 6–3   **Loanable Funds Theory of Interest Rate Determination**

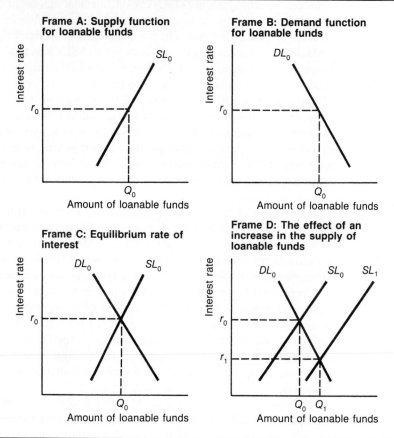

The equilibrium rate of interest is determined to be the point at which the supply of loanable funds equals the demand for loanable funds.

economy, and it is drawn sloping upward to the right. Hence, at higher interest rates, SSUs are willing to provide greater amounts of loanable funds. However, not all suppliers of loanable funds are equally sensitive to changes in interest rates.

In general, consumers will save more as interest rates rise. Higher interest rates will also stimulate business to finance investments out of internal sources (retained earnings and depreciation) rather than by issuing new debt or equity. This can be accomplished by reducing dividend payments in order to increase retained earnings or by switching to an accelerated depreciation method. Furthermore, at higher interest rates there will be a decrease in the demand to hold money balances because of the greater opportunity cost of holding noninterest-bearing money. Thus, as interest rates rise, the quantity of loanable funds supplied to the market increases.

The aggregate demand schedule for loanable funds is shown in Exhibit 6–3, Frame B. It is drawn as a downward-sloping function of interest rates. In general, the higher the interest rate, the smaller the quantity of loanable funds demanded by DSUs.

Higher borrowing costs will reduce the level of business investments in plant and equipment, cause state and local governments to postpone capital expenditures, and reduce consumer installment purchases. The federal government's borrowing is not influenced much by higher interest rates.

The equilibrium rate of interest (r_0) is shown in Exhibit 6-3, Frame C, by the intersection of the aggregate demand for loanable funds schedule and the aggregate supply of loanable funds schedule at r_0. In equilibrium, the supply of loanable funds equals the demand for loanable funds ($SL = DL$). As long as competitive forces are allowed to operate in the financial sector, the forces of supply and demand will always bring the interest rate to this point (r_0). For example, if interest rates are above equilibrium, there will be an excess supply of funds because of the higher rate. To entice borrowers to purchase the excess funds, lenders will have to lower their rates. The rates will be lowered until $DL = SL$ at r_0, which is the equilibrium rate of interest. On the other hand, if the market rate of interest is below the equilibrium rate, there will be an excess demand for funds. Higher interest rates will decrease borrowers' demand for funds and at the same time increase the supply of funds provided by lenders until the supply of and demand for loanable funds is again equal at r_0.

The equilibrium rate (r_0) in Exhibit 6-3, Frame C, is only a temporary equilibrium point. Any force that provides a shift in positions of the supply of or demand for loanable funds will produce a change in the equilibrium rate of interest. Specifically, an increase in the level of interest rates may be accomplished by either an increase in the demand for or a decrease in the supply of loanable funds. Similarly, a decline in the level of interest rates can be caused by either an increase in the supply of or a reduction in the demand for loanable funds.

Exhibit 6-3, Frame D, shows the effect on the level of interest rates of an increase in the stock of money ($+ \Delta M$) by the Federal Reserve. The Federal Reserve's policy action increases the supply of loanable funds from SL_0 to SL_1, which results in a decrease in interest rates from r_0 to r_1. Of course, other factors can account for a shift on the supply side. An increase in consumer saving caused by more favorable tax treatment of savings by the federal government would increase the supply of loanable funds and bring down interest rates. So would an increase in business saving as a result of high business profits. A change in state or federal government policy from a deficit budget to a surplus budget position because of reduced government expenditures would also shift the supply of loanable funds schedule to the right. On the demand side, downward pressure on interest rates would result from a decline in expectations about future business activities. This would result in a shift to the left in the demand schedule because of both reduced business investments and consumer credit purchases. Likewise, an increase in taxes would reduce government deficits and the government's demand for loanable funds.

Price Expectations and Interest Rates

In the loanable funds theory presented in the preceding section, no mention was made of the influence of price level changes (inflation or deflation) on the level of interest rates. We assumed that price levels remained constant over the life of the loan or investment in securities. However, price level changes affect both the realized return that lenders receive on their loans and the cost that borrowers must pay for them. For example, if prices rise during the life of a loan contract, the purchasing power of the dollar will decrease, and borrowers will be repaying lenders in inflated dollars—dollars with less purchasing power. If prices decrease, the purchasing power of the dollar will increase, and lenders will receive a windfall gain of more purchasing power at the expense of borrowers.

Protection against changes in purchasing power can be incorporated in the interest rate on a loan contract, as a simple example will illustrate. Suppose that two individuals, an SSU and a DSU, plan to exchange money and financial claims for a period of one year. Both agree that a fair rental price for the money is 5 percent and both anticipate a 7 percent inflation rate for the year. In the spirit of fair play, both would probably agree to a loan repayment contract as follows:

Item to Be Paid	Calculation	Amount
1. Principal borrowed		$1,000
2. Rent for one year's interest	$1,000 × 5%	50
3. Compensation for loss of purchasing power due to inflation	$1,000 × 7%	70
Total		$1,120

For the use of $1,000 for one year, the loan contract calls for the payment of three items at maturity: (1) $1,000, which is the nominal amount borrowed; (2) $50, which is the interest or rent for the use of the money's purchasing power for the one year; and (3) $70, which is the compensation to the lender for the loss of purchasing power incurred because of the 7 percent inflation during the one-year period. It is clear that the actual "interest" charged is 12 percent ($120): 5 percent ($50) compensation for forgoing present consumption and 7 percent ($70) compensation for anticipated loss in purchasing power.

The Fisher Effect

The preceding example suggests that complete protection against price level changes is achieved when the nominal, or market, rate of interest is divided into two parts: (1) the real rate of interest, or the rate that would exist in the absence of any price changes; and (2) the anticipated percentage change in price levels with respect to time. This can be written as follows:[1]

$$i = r + \Delta P_e, \tag{6-1}$$

where:

i = observed nominal rate of interest;
r = real rate of interest in the absence of price level changes;
ΔP_e = expected annual change in commodity prices
   = $(P_{e_{t+1}} - P_t)/P_t$.

---

[1] Technically, Equation 6-1 should be written in the following form:

$$i = r + \Delta P_e + r\Delta P_e,$$

where $r\Delta P_e$ is the inflation premium for the loss of purchasing power on the interest payment. If either r or ΔP_e is small, $r\Delta P_e$ is very small and approximates 0.

DID YOU KNOW?

The Market as An Economic Forecaster

For most of history, people have wanted to forecast future levels of economic activity. At times astrology, tea leaves, changes in sunspots, and the Super Bowl champions have been tried. In more recent years, economists have focused on financial markets such as the stock market or on composite indexes of economic variables such as the government's Index of Leading Indicators. Most forecasting techniques have proven unreliable, especially over the long run.

The stock market fell from the economists' "good graces" following the stock market crash of 1987, when the economy continued to expand rather than contract as the crash had predicted. Even before the 1987 forecasting fiasco, many economists has come to recognize that the stock market was an unreliable predictor and tended to overpredict the number of recessions. Paul A. Samuelson, the American Nobel laureate in economics, coined what has become the standard Wall Street joke that "the stock market has forecasted nine of the last five recessions." Actually the record is a bit worse than

that. From 1961 to 1991, the stock market has fallen to ten lows on a year-to-year basis, and these market lows were followed by five recessions: 1969–1970, 1973–1974, 1980, 1981–1982, and 1990–1991. Thus the stock market is batting a .500 average in recent years.

Campbell R. Harvey, an economist at Duke University, presents evidence that the slope of the yield curve as measured by the difference between the three-month and ten-year Treasury rate is a more reliable predictor than the stock market. Using data on the slope of the yield curve from 1966 through 1988, Harvey explained 40 percent of the variation in real economic growth. This was much better than the 5 percent of variation in economic growth explained by the stock market. Though the Harvey model did not successfully predict the 1990–1992 recession, it does appear that in recent years the stock market is more volatile and gives more false signals than the bond market.

The inflation premium component (ΔP_e) of the nominal rate of interest is commonly referred to as the *Fisher effect*. It is named after the economist Irving Fisher, who analyzed it in the early 1900s. When examining Equation 6-1, notice that the anticipated percentage price level change, not the observed or reported rate of inflation, is added to the real rate of interest. Thus, to properly determine the nominal rate of interest, it is necessary to first predict commodity price changes over the life of the contract. The figure arrived at in the marketplace represents the market's consensus of anticipated future price changes. Second, notice that we define the *nominal interest rate* as the rate of interest actually observed in financial markets. The real and the nominal rates of interest are equal only when market participants do not anticipate price changes ($\Delta P_e = 0$). As with all expectations or predictions, the actual rate of price level changes may or may not be equal to what was expected.

Price Level Changes

Notice that ΔP_e is the percentage rate of price level change and not the level of prices. Exhibit 6-4 illustrates the importance of this statement. In our previous example, the

Exhibit 6–4   **Expected Price Level Changes and the Nominal Rate of Interest**

Time Period	Real Rate	Expected Price Change	Nominal Rate
0	5	0	5
1	5	7	12
2	5	7	12
3	5	9	14
4	5	3	8
5	5	−2	3
6	5	−7	0

The nominal rate of interest is directly influenced by changes in the expected rate of inflation. The higher the expected rate of inflation, the higher the nominal rate of interest.

real rate of interest was 5 percent and inflation increased from zero to 7 percent. The nominal rate of interest thus went from 5 to 12 percent. For the next time period, what happens to the nominal rate of interest if prices are expected to continue to rise at 7 percent annually? As Exhibit 6–4 shows, the nominal rate stays at 12 percent. This is because in each period, new loans are made with money already protected against past changes in purchasing power. However, if the expected annual inflation rate accelerates from 7 to 9 percent, the nominal interest rate will jump to 14 percent for all new loans. Thus the nominal interest rate will become greater only if the rate of price-level increases becomes greater. Finally, if prices begin to fall (deflation), the nominal rate will be below the real rate by the amount of the expected rate of price decline. Thus, if prices are expected to decline 2 percent annually, the nominal rate in our example will be 3 percent. However, the real rate cannot decline below zero regardless of the rate of price decline. Lenders would always prefer to retain their money and purchase goods and services rather than to pay someone else (negative interest) to do the same.

The Realized Real Rate

In the preceding section, we stated that the real rate of interest can never be negative; the reason is that lenders would simple retain cash holdings rather than lend at negative interest rates. Yet the financial press abounds with discussion of "negative real rates of interest." How can this be so? Who is right? The answer is that when a loan contract is entered into, borrower and lender implicitly agree on an *expected* rate of inflation (ΔP_e) during the life of the loan. Unfortunately, as with all expectations, the actual rate of inflation more than likely will not equal what was expected. Hence the realized rate of return on a loan contract will differ from the nominal rate that was agreed on at the time the loan was made. Equation 6–1 can be modified so that the realized real rate can be expressed as:

$$r = i - \Delta P_a, \tag{6–2}$$

where r is the *realized real rate of return* and ΔP_a is the *actual rate of inflation* during the loan contract period.

For example, if the real rate of interest is 4 percent for a one-year loan and the expected annual rate of inflation is 3 percent, the nominal rate of interest on the loan would be 7 percent (4 + 3). However, if the actual rate of inflation during the year was 5 percent, the realized real rate of return would be 2 percent (7 − 5); the lender earns 2 percent less than expected as a result of unanticipated inflation. If the actual rate of inflation were 10 percent, the realized rate of return would be a negative 3 percent (7 − 10)—hence, a "negative real rate."

Exhibit 6-5 shows the unadjusted or nominal rate of interest for three-month Treasury bills plotted semiannually since 1967; also shown is the realized real rate on the three-month bills for the same time period. As can be seen, the realized real rate was negative during most of the 1970s. Lenders underpredicted the rise in price levels and, in retrospect, charged too low a nominal rate of interest. Thus unanticipated inflation caused wealth transfers from lender to borrowers. In the 1980s the reverse was true. The realized real rate was quite high because of the unanticipated disinflation that occurred during this period. More specifically, the 1980–1982 period was marked by a prolonged and deep recession (two recessions virtually back to back), which caused inflation to drop sharply from that which was expected. However, there is no evidence that, as a group, borrowers or lenders are able to outpredict each other consistently.

Exhibit 6–5   **Three-Month Treasury Bill Rates**

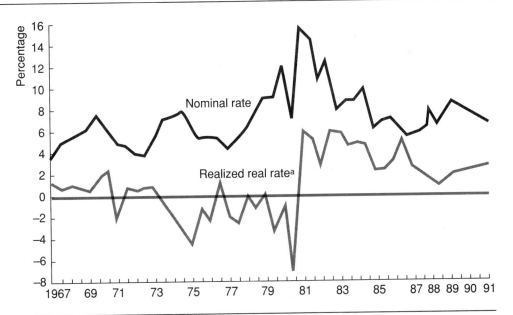

[a]Three-month Treasury bill rate minus the annualized change in the CPI in the next three months. The realized real rate of interest can be either a negative or a positive value, depending on the extent to which the actual rate of inflation exceeds the expected rate of inflation.

Inflation and the Loanable Funds Model

The loanable funds theory can be used to illustrate inflation's effect on financial markets. Assuming that both borrowers and lenders fully anticipate all increases in the level of prices, the demand for loanable funds schedule will shift upward precisely by the amount ΔP_e, as shown in Exhibit 6-6. The shift from DL_0 to DL_1 implies that borrowers are willing to pay the inflation premium of ΔP_e. Similarly, lenders, anticipating inflation, will cause the supply curve to shift to the left from SL_0 to SL_1. The shift in the curve will be such that lenders are given a higher nominal yield to compensate for their loss of purchasing power. The net effect is that the market rate of interest will rise from r_0 to i_1, where $i_1 = r_0 + \Delta P_e$. Even though the real rate of interest (r_0) remains unchanged, the nominal rate of interest (i_1) has adjusted fully for the anticipated rate of inflation (ΔP_e), and the quantity of loanable funds in the market has remained the same at Q_0.

Interest Rate Movements over the Business Cycle

The movement of interest rates for both short-term and long-term securities since 1954 is plotted in Exhibit 6-7. Periods of officially declared economic contraction (recessions) are shaded. As one can see, interest rate movements closely follow the business cycle. Interest rates rise during periods of economic expansion and decline during periods of economic contraction. In recent years, periods of economic expansion have been quite long—averaging over four years—whereas periods of

---

Exhibit 6–6   **Impact of Inflation on Loanable Funds Theory of Interest**

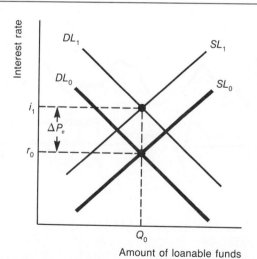

Inflationary expectations also affect the loanable funds theory of interest. The higher the expected rate of inflation, the higher the nominal rate of interest.

economic contraction have been fairly short—averaging about nine months. Thus interest rates have tended to be rising more than declining.

Exhibit 6–7 also shows that short-term interest rates experienced much wider swings than long-term interest rates. This is what we would expect if investors and financial institutions are slow to adjust required yields or loan rates to new information, such as changes in inflation expectations. For example, a financial institution might be willing to lower the rate on a short-term loan, say three months to maturity, if it observes a one-month decline in the Consumer Price Index (CPI). For a long-term loan such as a 20-year mortgage, on the other hand, the lender might be reluctant to reduce the loan rate based on a one-month decline in the CPI. The lender might want to observe the CPI for several months or even years before finally lowering the long-term mortgage rate to be sure that the decline in inflation is not temporary.

The cyclical movement of interest rates predicted by the loanable funds theory is demonstrated in Exhibit 6–7. First, as business activities expand, there is an increase in the demand for loanable funds, shifting the demand schedule to the right as

Exhibit 6–7   **Movement of Interest Rates over the Business Cycle[a]**

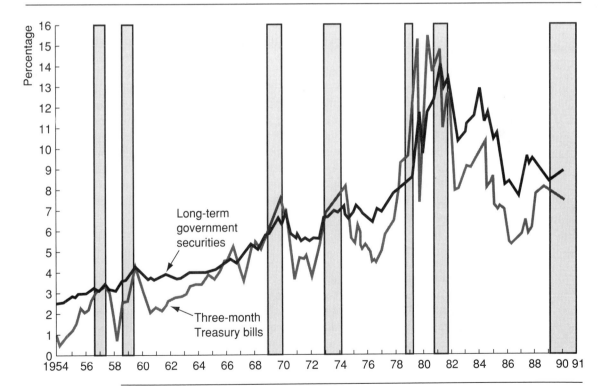

[a]Shaded areas indicate periods of economic recession.

This exhibit shows how interest rates move over the business cycle: They rise during periods of economic expansion and decline during periods of economic contraction.

aggregate income is expected to increase. Furthermore, during periods of business expansion, as the economy approaches full employment, it is reasonable to expect inflation to accelerate and for the Federal Reserve to slow the rate of growth in the money supply. All of these effects exert upward pressure on interest rates. Conversely, during recessions business activity decreases and the Federal Reserve accelerates the rate of growth in the money supply to stimulate the economy. In recessions, price levels are expected to increase at a slower rate or possibly decline. All three of these forces cause interest rates to decline.

Finally, the cyclical movement of interest rate phenomena is a long-range trend. Daily and even monthly interest rate movements are influenced by numerous short-run and seasonal forces. As a result, the movement of interest rates appears to be irregular. Nonetheless, over time cyclical forces dominate the temporary factors, and interest rates do follow the business cycle.

Forecasting Interest Rates

There has always been considerable interest in forecasting interest rate movements. The reason, of course, is that changes in the level of interest rates affect the present value of streams of future payments; that is, they affect the prices of financial assets—one's economic wealth! Moreover, beginning in the 1980s, interest rate movements became more volatile than in the past, and, therefore, firms and individual investors have faced substantial exposure to interest rate risk. For example, since 1981 the monthly three-month Treasury bill rate has ranged from 5.18 to 16.30 percent and the Baa corporate bond rate has ranged from 9.61 to 17.18 percent.

Individuals or firms can take two basic approaches to reduce exposure to interest rate risk. The first, discussed elsewhere in the book, is to *hedge* interest rate risk (see Chapters 5 and 11). The second—and the topic here—is to accurately forecast interest rate movements. In general, economists use a variety of approaches to forecast interest rates. They range from naive forecasting models based on subjective adjustments to extremely complicated financial models of the economy. We will now examine two of the popular forecasting methods used by economists on Wall Street: statistical models of the economy, and the flow-of-funds approach.

Economic Models

Economic models predict interest rates by estimating the statistical relationships between measures of the output of goods and services in the economy and the level of interest rates. The models range in complexity from single-equation models to those involving hundreds of simultaneous equations. The common element of all such models is that they produce interest rate forecasts assuming that the pattern of causality among economic variables is stable into the future.

Some of the larger economic models simultaneously forecast changes in spending on goods and services, wages and salaries, price levels, the balance of international trade, credit demand, supply of securities, capital goods, the money supply, the fiscal policy of the federal government, and interest rates. Once the relationships among these variables are modeled, expected *changes* in key economic variables are entered into the model; then changes in interest rates and output in various sectors of the economy are forecasted. For example, in the agricultural sector of the economy, changes in the prices of farm produce affect the balance of payments, farm machinery sales, the sales of capital goods used to produce farm machinery, personal income of farmers and other workers whose livelihood is tied to agriculture, and retail food prices. Increases in these factors ultimately lead to higher national income and rising price levels (inflation), which causes higher interest rates.

Prominent economic models of the economy that provide comprehensive descriptions of various sectors of the economy are those used by Wharton Econometric Forecasting Associates, Chase Econometric Associates, and Data Resources, Inc. (DRI). The DRI model forecasts about 1,000 financial and economic variables, and the Wharton model forecasts 10,000 different economic variables. A more modest but widely known forecasting model is one developed by the Federal Reserve Bank of St. Louis. This model consists of only eight basic equations and generates quarterly forecasts for a number of key economic variables, such as the change in nominal and real GNP or GDP, the change in the price level (inflation), the unemployment rate, and the market rate of interest. The key input variables into the model (called exogenous variables) are the change in the nation's money supply, the change in federal government expenditures, the potential full-employment output of goods and services in the economy, and past changes in price levels. At the very heart of the Federal Reserve Bank of St. Louis model is the effect of changes in the money supply on national income (GNP or GDP), unemployment, and the rate of inflation. In case you have not guessed by now, the Fed of St. Louis model is a monetarist model of the economy. Exhibit 6-8 shows the linkage scheme for the model, with the key input variables shown on the left side in the exhibit.

Flow-of-Funds Account Forecasting

One of the most widely used interest rate forecasting techniques makes use of the flow-of-funds framework embedded within the loanable funds theory of interest rates. The *flow-of-funds* data show the movement of savings—the sources and uses of funds—through the economy in a structured and comprehensive manner. The flow-of-funds accounts are companion data to the national income accounts, which provide information about the flows of goods and services in the real economy. Since 1955 the Board of Governors of the Federal Reserve System have published quarterly and annual data on the flow-of-funds accounts.

In forecasting interest rates, analysts look for pressure points where the demand for funds in a particular market exceeds the supply of funds, which should cause interest rates in that market to rise and ultimately spill over into other financial markets that are closely linked. Conversely, a low demand for funds relative to supply should drive interest rates down in a sector. The projections of changes in supply and demand factors are based in part on projections of changes in monetary policy, changes in fiscal policy, expected inflation, and other relevant economic variables. Clearly, a great deal of analysis, judgment, and luck are necessary for a good forecast.

Exhibit 6–8   **Schematic Diagram for the Federal Reserve of St. Louis Economic Model**

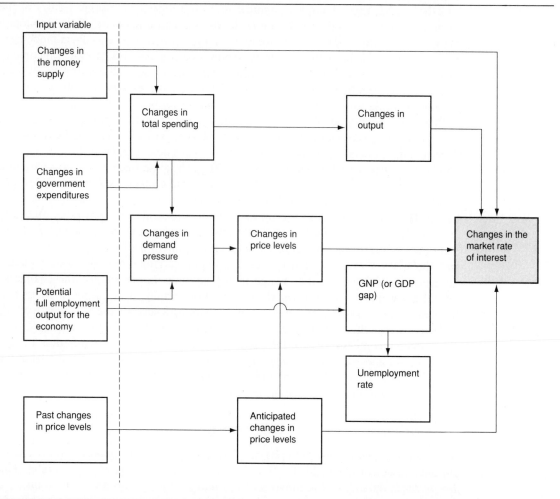

This exhibit shows how the Federal Reserve Bank of St. Louis model forecasts interest rates and the relationships between interest rates and other economic variables in the model.

How Good Are the Forecasters?

Despite the wide variety of methods and the large number of forecasters, those who publish their interest rate forecasts publicly do quite poorly. Of course, this should come as no surprise because there is no motivation for a firm or individual who can forecast interest rates accurately to make the forecast publicly available. The reason, simply stated, is self-interest. That is, accurate forecasts of interest rate movements would allow a person to transact in the credit markets for huge profits. Furthermore, the efficient-market hypothesis suggests that all publicly available information is reflected in a security's current price. If the current interest rate reflects all relevant publicly available information, it is the best prediction of the interest rate in the next period.

The efficient-market approach to analyzing the quality of interest rate forecasts begs the question: Why go to the expense and effort of building a complicated forecasting model if the best prediction of tomorrow's interest rate is today's interest rate? The answer is that above-average forecasters will ultimately be rewarded by the market with above-average returns. To quote a long-dead and forgotten finance professor, "Even a blind squirrel finds an acorn occasionally." Of course, if you don't bother searching for the "acorn," you are guaranteed to *never* find one.

A number of studies have assessed the accuracy of interest rate forecasts. One by Stephen McNees reports that forecasts by professional forecasters of the three-month Treasury rate six months into the future were within two percentage points of the actual rate 67 percent of the time.[2] Thus, in January, if the three-month Treasury rate was forecast to be 10 percent in July, there was a 67 percent chance that the rate would be somewhere between 8 and 12 percent. Other studies show that as the forecast period is lengthened, the forecast errors will be larger.[3] Another study by Michael Belongia looked at how professional forecasters did in predicting the *direction* of interest rate movements.[4] That is, if interest rates were forecast to increase, did they in fact increase? For the period 1982 to 1986, nine professional forecasters correctly predicted the direction of change of the three-month Treasury rate six months into the future 42 percent of the time. If interest rate movements were random, a 50 percent record would be expected. Sadly, only one of the nine forecasters predicted the direction of change more than 50 percent of the time; this forecaster predicted correctly on six of the ten forecasting opportunities. The worst prediction record was two correct predictions in ten chances.

Summary

Interest rates are similar to other prices in the economy in that they allocate funds between SSUs and DSUs and between financial markets. To the borrower, interest is the penalty for consuming before income is earned; to the lender, interest is the reward for postponing current consumption. Individuals' lending or borrowing patterns are determined by their time preference between present and future consumption and the return available to them on investments.

The loanable funds theory views interest rates as being determined by the equilibrium force between the demand for and supply of loanable funds. Any force that shifts the schedule of the aggregate demand for or supply of loanable funds will produce a change in the equilibrium rate of interest. The level of interest rates is also influenced by the market's anticipated rate of inflation. Interest rates tend to follow

[2] Stephen K. McNees, "Forecasting Accuracy of Alternative Techniques: A Comparison of U.S. Macroeconomic Forecasts," *Journal of Business Statistics*, January 1986, pp. 5–15.

[3] Victor Zarnowitz, "Rational Expectations and Macroeconomic Forecasts," NBER Working Paper No. 1070, January 1983.

[4] Michael T. Belongia, "Predicting Interest Rates: A Comparison of Professional and Market-Based Forecasts," *Economic Review*, Federal Reserve Bank of St. Louis, March 1987, pp. 9–15.

the business cycle, rising during periods of economic expansion and falling during periods of economic contraction. Investors and financial institutions have a keen interest in forecasting the movements of interest rates because of the potential impact on their wealth. While the models used to forecast interest rates are technically sophisticated and complex, the track record of forecasters in predicting the magnitude or direction of interest rate changes is weak.

Questions

1. What factors determine the real rate of interest?
2. If the money supply is increased, what happens to the level of interest rates?
3. What is the "Fisher effect"? How does it affect the nominal rate of interest?
4. The one-year real rate of interest is currently estimated to be 4 percent. The current annual rate of inflation is 6 percent, and market forecasts expect the annual rate of inflation to be 8 percent. What is the current one-year nominal rate of interest?
5. Explain why interest rates tend to be higher at the top of the business cycle than at the bottom.
6. What are the two basic approaches that firms can take to reduce interest rate risk?
7. Explain why it is not surprising that interest rate forecasters do so poorly forecasting interest rates.
8. Explain how forecasters using the flow-of-funds approach determine future interest rate movements.
9. An investor purchased a one-year Treasury security with a promised yield of 10 percent. The investor expected the annual rate of inflation to be 6 percent; however, the actual rate turned out to be 10 percent. What was the expected and the realized real rate of interest for the investor?
10. Carefully explain how the real rate of interest can be negative.

Selected References

Anderson, Leonall C., and Keith M. Carlson. "A Monetarist Model for Economic Stabilization." *Economic Review*. Federal Reserve Bank of St. Louis, April 1970, pp. 7–25.
The article which first presented the Federal Reserve of St. Louis economic model discussed in this chapter. A very readable and understandable model of the U.S. economy based on a monetarist point of view.

Belongia, Michael T. "Predicting Interest Rates: A Comparison of Professional and Market-Based Forecasts." *Economic Review*. Federal Reserve Bank of St. Louis, March 1987, pp. 9–15.
An interesting article that compares simple market-based forecasts to forecasts made by professional economists. Simple market-based forecasts do well.

Bennet, Paul. "The Influence of Financial Changes on Interest Rates and Monetary Policy: A Review of the Recent Evidence." *Quarterly Review*. Federal Reserve Bank of New York City, Summer 1990, pp. 8–30.
This article explores the way changes in the financial system have affected interest rates and the transmission of monetary policy. A comprehensive article.

Cecchetti, Stephen G. "High Real Interest Rates: Can They Be Explained." *Economic Review*. Federal Reserve Bank of Kansas City, September/October 1986, pp. 31–41.
The article examines factors that have contributed to high real interest rates in recent years.

Cunningham, Rosemary T., and Thomas J. Cunningham. "Recent Views of Viewing the Real Rate of Interest." *Economic Review.* **Federal Reserve Bank of Atlanta, July/August 1990, pp. 28–37.**
This paper examines theoretical and empirical approaches to assessing the influence of monetary policy on the real rate of interest.

Glick, Reuven. "Global Interest Rate Linkages." *Weekly Letter.* **Federal Reserve Bank of San Francisco, May 25, 1990, pp. 1–3.**
This article examines the factors which link U.S. and foreign interest rates.

Henning, Charles N., et al. *Financial Markets and the Economy.* **Englewood Cliffs, NJ: Prentice-Hall, 1988.**
Chapter 12 has an advanced discussion on bond pricing and the determinants of the level of interest rates. The chapter also has a good appendix on the real rate of interest.

Livingston, Miles. *Money and Capital Markets.* **Englewood Cliffs, NJ: Prentice-Hall, 1990.**
Several chapters of this book provide good coverage of interest rates.

McNees, Stephen K. "Forecasting Accuracy of Alternative Techniques: A Comparison of U.S. Macroeconomic Forecasts." *Journal of Business Statistics,* **January 1986, pp. 5–15.**

Santoni, G. J., and Courtenay C. Stone. "Navigating Through the Interest Rate Morass: Some Basic Principles." *Economic Review.* **Federal Reserve Bank of St. Louis, March 1981, pp. 11–17.**
One of the best basic articles written on the fundamentals of interest rates. Essential reading for the beginning student.

Van Horne, James C. *Financial Market Rates and Flows.* **Englewood Cliffs, NJ: Prentice-Hall, 1990.**
A comprehensive book dealing with all aspects of the determinants of interest rates. An outstanding book.

Walsh, Carl E. "Interest Rate Smoothing." *Weekly Letter.* **Federal Reserve Bank of San Francisco, April 14, 1989, pp. 1–3.**
This article evaluates the Federal Reserve System's ability to smooth interest rates.

———. "Three Questions Concerning Nominal and Real Interest Rates." *Economic Review.* **Federal Reserve Bank of San Francisco, Fall 1987, pp. 5–19.**
This article examines some empirical evidence about real and nominal interest rates, then discusses their implications for monetary policy. The article is fairly advanced.

Zarnowitz, Victor. "Rational Expectations and Macroeconomic Forecasts." **NBER Working Paper No. 1070, January 1983.**

THE STRUCTURE OF INTEREST RATES

7

ARMED WITH A BASIC UNDERSTANDING of the determinants of the general level of interest rates, we can explore the reasons interest rates vary among financial products. The variation can seem overwhelming. To get an idea of how extensively rates differ across products, take a close look at the financial section of any major newspaper. On any given day, newspapers report yields on thousands of financial instruments, and almost every product has a different market rate of interest. Exhibit 7-1 shows the diversity of interest rates that existed during May 1991. For example, why did three-month Treasury bills yield 5.46 percent and five-year Treasury notes yield 7.70 percent when both had the same issuer (the U.S. Treasury Department)? Or why did an Aaa-rated municipal bond yield 6.70 percent and an Aaa-rated corporate bond yield 8.86 percent? If you read this chapter carefully, you will be able to answer these questions.

Market analysts have identified five major characteristics that are responsible for most of the differences in interest rates among securities: (1) term to maturity, (2) default risk, (3) tax treatment, (4) marketability, and (5) special features such as call and put options. We shall now examine these factors separately to determine how each influences a security's yield.

The Term Structure of Interest Rates

The *term to maturity* of a financial claim is the length of time until the principal amount borrowed becomes payable. The relationship between yield and term to maturity on securities that differ only in length of time to maturity is known as the *term structure of interest rates*. For term-structure relationships to be meaningful, other factors that affect interest rates, such as default risk and tax treatment, must be held constant. The term structure may be approximated by graphically plotting yield and maturity for equivalent-grade securities at a point in time. The term structure relationship can best be seen by examining yields on U.S. Treasury securities because they have similar default risk (nearly none), tax treatment, and marketability.

Exhibit 7-2 shows some yield curves for Treasury securities during the 1980s. Yield curves such as those displayed are constructed by plotting the terms to maturity on the horizontal axis and the securities' yields on the vertical axis. The plots are then connected in a smooth line called the *yield curve*. Thus a yield curve shows the

Exhibit 7–1   **Selected Rates of Interest, May 1991**

Financial Security	Interest Rate (percentage)
Commercial paper, 3 months	5.92
Finance company paper, 3 months	5.81
Banker's acceptance, 3 months	5.75
U.S. government securities:	
3-month Treasury bills	5.46
12-month Treasury bills	5.76
5-year Treasury notes	7.70
10-year Treasury bonds	8.07
Aaa municipals (state and local obligations)	6.70
Aaa corporate bonds	8.86
Aa corporate bonds	9.15
A corporate bonds	9.41
Baa corporate bonds	9.86

Notice that the U.S. Treasury rate is the lowest interest rate in the economy for comparable maturities.
Source: Federal Reserve Bulletin, August 1991.

Exhibit 7–2   **Yield Curves on Treasury Securities in the 1980s**

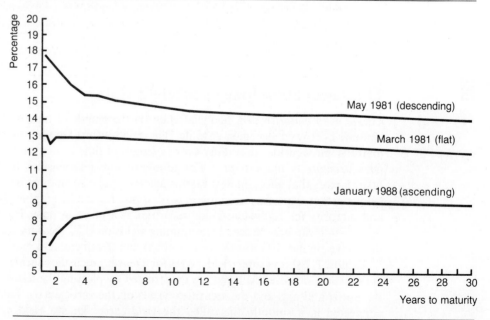

Note: Although yield curves can be upward- or downward-sloping, they are typically upward-sloping.
Source: Weekly Money Market Bulletin, Morgan Guaranty Trust Company, various issues.

relationship between maturity and a security's yield at a point in time. For example, in January 1988 two-year securities yielded about 7.2 percent, four-year securities 8.3 percent, six-year securities 8.6 percent, and so on.

As shown in Exhibit 7–2, the shape and level of yield curves do not remain constant over time. As the general level of interest rates rises and falls, yield curves correspondingly shift up and down and have different slopes. The exhibit shows the more common types of yield curves. An *ascending yield curve* is formed when interest rates are lowest on short-term issues, and it rises at a diminishing rate until the rates level out on the longer maturities. The ascending yield curve is the most common curve observed in financial markets. *Flat yield curves* are not common, but they do occur from time to time. *Descending yield curves* occur periodically, usually at or near the beginning of an economic recession. The question that has intrigued market analysis is: What economic forces explain both the shape of the yield curve and its movement over time? We shall now discuss two competing theories that explain changes in the term structure: the expectation theory and the market segmentation theory.

The Expectation Theory

The expectation theory holds that the shape of the yield curve is determined by investors' expectations of future interest rate movements and that changes in these expectations change the shape of the yield curve.[1] The expectation theory is "idealized" because it assumes that investors are profit maximizers and that they have no preference between holding a long-term security or holding a series of short-term securities. Nonetheless, economists believe the theory explains the basic force that alters the shape of the yield curve.

To see how changing expectations of interest rate movements can alter the slope of the yield curve, let us perform the following experiment. Suppose that an investor has a two-year investment horizon and that only one-year bonds and two-year bonds can be purchased. Since both types of securities currently yield 6 percent, the prevailing term structure is flat, as indicated by the yield curve shown on the left-hand side of the diagram on the following page. Now suppose that new economic information becomes available and investors *expect* interest rates to rise to 12 percent within a year. Note that the 12 percent rate is a *forward rate* in that it is the interest that will exist one year in the future. Given the new information, what portfolio of bonds should investors hold?

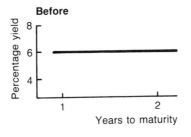

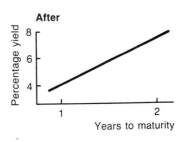

[1] The expectation theory was first stated by Irving Fisher (see Chapter 6, People and Events) and was further developed by the British Nobel laureate in economics, Sir John Hicks.

Under such circumstances, investors would want to buy one-year bonds and sell any two-year bonds they might own. Why? First of all, who would want to invest in long-term bonds and lock in the prevailing 6 percent yield when interest rates are expected to rise in the future? Most investors would prefer to buy short-term securities, wait for interest rates to rise, and then buy long-term bonds and lock in the higher interest rate.

More analytically, a profit-maximizing investor would examine the alternatives of (1) buying a two-year bond or (2) buying two successive one-year bonds for a two-year investment horizon, then selecting the alternative with the highest holding-period yield. Specifically, if an investor buys a one-year bond that currently yields 6 percent and at the end of the year buys the expected 12 percent bond, the average holding-period yield for the two-year period is 9 percent $[\frac{1}{2} (6 + 12)]$. Alternatively, if the investor purchases a two-year security, the two-year holding period yield is only 6 percent. Naturally, profit-maximizing investors begin to buy one-year bonds, driving their price up and yield down. Simultaneously, investors sell two-year bonds, driving their price down and yield up. The net effect of this portfolio adjustment is to shift the prevailing yield curve from flat to ascending, as shown in the yield curve on the right side of the diagram.

The process of buying one-year bonds and selling two-year bonds continues until any differential in expected returns over the two-year investment period is eliminated. That condition *could* occur when the yields on one-year securities equal 4 percent, the two-year securities yield 8 percent, and the one-year forward rate remains 12 percent. With this term structure, an investor who purchases a two-year bond will have a two-year holding-period yield of 8 percent. This is identical to the investor who purchases a 4 percent one-year security and then reinvests the proceeds at the end of the first year in the expected 12 percent bonds $[\frac{1}{2} (4 + 12)]$. This is an equilibrium condition because under either alternative the investor's average holding period is the same. That is, investors are indifferent between the yield on a two-year security or the average holding-period yield they can earn when investing in two successive one-year securities.

The Term Structure Formula

Although simplified, the example in the preceding section illustrates that investors can trade among securities of different maturities and, if they are profit maximizers, obtain an equilibrium return across the entire spectrum of maturities. This implies a formal relationship between long- and short-term interest rates. Specifically, the long-term rate of interest is a geometric average of the current short-term interest rate and a series of expected short-term forward rates. More formally, the yield on a bond maturing n years from now is shown as follows:

$$(1 + {}_tR_n) = [(1 + {}_tR_1)(1 + {}_{t+1}f_1)(1 + {}_{t+2}f_1) \ldots (1 + {}_{t+n-1}f_1)]^{1/n}, \quad (7\text{--}1)$$

where:

R = the observed (or actual) market interest rate;
f = the forward, or future, interest rate;
t = time period for which the rate is applicable;
n = maturity of the bond.

The postscript identifies the maturity (n) of the security, and the prescript represents the time period in which the security originates (t). Thus, $_tR_1$ is the actual market rate of interest on a one-year security today (time t); similarly, $_tR_{10}$ is the current market rate of interest for a 10-year security. For the forward rates, the prescript still identifies the time period in which the security originates, but now it represents the number of years in the future; thus, $_{t+1}f_1$ refers to the one-year interest rate one year in the future; likewise, $_{t+2}f_1$ is the one-year interest rate two years from now, and so on.

Do not panic—the geometric mean is not as difficult to apply as it looks. For example, suppose the current one-year rate is 6 percent. The market expects the one-year rate a year from now to be 8 percent and the one-year rate two years from now to be 10 percent. In our notational form, that is

$$_tR_1 = 6 \text{ percent,}$$
$$_{t+1}f_1 = 8 \text{ percent,}$$
$$_{t+2}f_1 = 10 \text{ percent.}$$

Given the market's expectations of future interest rates, we can calculate the current three-year rate of interest by applying Equation 7–1:

$$(1 + _tR_3) = [(1.06)(1.08)(1.10)]^{1/3}$$
$$_tR_3 = (1.259)^{1/3} - 1$$
$$_tR_3 = 8.0 \text{ percent.}$$

Notice that an investor with a three-year investment horizon will be indifferent between buying a three-year security yielding 8 percent or buying three successive one-year securities that will also yield, on average, 8 percent.[2]

The reason for developing Equation 7–1 was not to dazzle you with mathematical footwork but to show how investors' expectations of future interest rates determine the shape of the yield curve. For example, when short-term interest rates are expected to rise in the future (as in our previous example), the yield curve will be upward-sloping. This must be true, since the long-term interest rate is an average of the current and the future expected short-term interest rates. Likewise, if the market expects future short-term interest rates to decrease, the yield curve will be downward-sloping. If no change is expected in future short-term rates, the yield curve will be flat. The behavioral implications of the yield curve from the expectation theory are as follows:

Expected Interest Rate Movement	**Observed Yield Curve**
If interest rates are expected to increase	Upward-sloping
If interest rates are expected to decline	Downward-sloping
If interest rates are expected to stay the same	Flat

[2]For students who have difficulty understanding the behavioral implications of Equation 7–1, the geometric mean can be approximated with the following simpler arithmetic mean formula:

$$_tR_n = \frac{1}{n}[_tR_1 + _{t+1}f_1 + _{t+2}f_1 \ldots _{t+n-1}f_1]$$

For our example,

$$_tR_3 = \frac{1}{3}[6 + 8 + 10] = 8.0 \text{ percent.}$$

Equation 7–1 helps to illustrate some of the difficulties of lending long-term. For example, in setting a fixed-rate mortgage rate, a lending institution must be able to predict future interest rate movements (that is, predict $_{t+1}f_1, _{t+2}f_1 \ldots _{t+n-1}f_1$). If the interest rate cycle is reasonably stable, this can be done. But if interest rates have wide, unexpected swings, such as might happen during inflationary periods, setting long-term rates of interest may be very difficult, if not impossible. We shall return to the discussion of the inherent risk in lending long-term when we discuss the mortgage lending problems of thrift institutions in Chapter 18.

Term Structure and Liquidity Premiums.   We have seen that the expectation theory assumes that investors are indifferent between purchasing long-term or short-term securities. However, this usually is not true. Investors know from experience that short-term securities provide greater marketability (more active secondary markets) and have smaller price fluctuations (price risk) than do long-term securities. As a result, borrowers who seek long-term funds to finance capital projects must pay lenders a *liquidity premium* to purchase riskier long-term securities. Thus the yield curve must have a liquidity premium added to it. The liquidity premium increases as maturity increases, because the longer the maturity of a security, the greater its price risk. The liquidity premium therefore causes the observed market yield curve to be more upward-sloping than that predicted by the expectation theory. Exhibit 7–3 illustrates this.

The Market Segmentation Theory

The market segmentation theory, which differs sharply from the expectation approach, maintains that market participants have strong preferences for securities of

Exhibit 7–3   The Effects of Liquidity Premiums on the Yield Curve

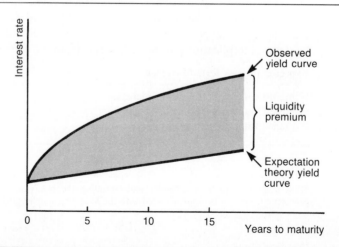

Liquidity premiums increase as maturity increases. Thus liquidity premiums cause an upward slope in market yield curves.

a particular maturity and holds that they buy and sell securities consistent with these maturity preferences. As a result, the yield curve is determined by the supply of and the demand for securities at or near a particular maturity. Investors, such as commercial banks, who desire short-term securities determine the short-term yield curve; investors with preferences for intermediate maturities determine the intermediate-term yield curve; and investors who prefer long-term securities, such as pension funds and life insurance companies, determine the long-term yield curve. On the supply side, security issuers tailor the maturities of their security offerings to the length of time they need the borrowed funds (see Exhibit 7–4). Thus both issuers and investors have a preference for securities with a narrow maturity range. Changes in interest rates in one segment of the yield curve, therefore, will have little effect on interest rates in other maturities. Although discontinuities in the yield curve are possible under the segmentation theory, in practice profit-seeking arbitrageurs will smooth out extreme irregularities. As a result, the predicted yield curves are relatively smooth and are consistent with yield curves observed in the bond markets.

Which Theory Is Right?

Available evidence is not sufficiently persuasive to establish any one theory as being totally correct in explaining the term structure of interest rates. Market participants tend to favor the segmentation theory, whereas economists tend to favor the expectation and liquidity premium approaches. Day-to-day changes in the term

---

Exhibit 7–4   **Market Segmentation Yield Curve**

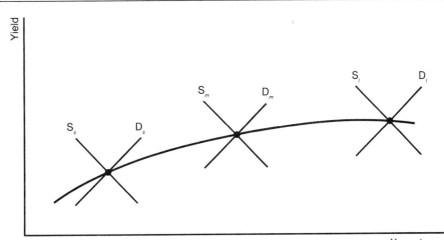

Note: Supply (*S*) and Demand (*D*) for *s* = short-term maturities, *m* = intermediate-term maturities, and *l* = long-term maturities.

Market segmentation theory suggests that borrowers and lenders have strong preferences for securities of a particular maturity. As a result, the supply and demand for securities at or near a particular maturity determine the yield for that maturity.

structure reveal patterns that are most consistent with the market segmentation theory. Changes in interest rates in one segment of the maturity spectrum appear not to be immediately transmitted to other segments. Furthermore, yield curves are not always smooth. For longer periods of time, such as month to month, interest rate changes in one maturity segment appear to be transmitted throughout the yield curve and yield curves appear relatively smooth. These observations are consistent with most published studies on the term structure that support the role of liquidity premiums and expectations of interest rates as important components of any interpretation of the term structure.

Economic Implications of the Yield Curve

The yield curve is an analytical tool widely employed by both financial analysts and managers of financial institutions. Some examples follow.

Yield Curve and the Business Cycle.   The term structure provides information about the market expectations of future business activity. If the yield curve is upward-sloping, the consensus of market participants is that interest rates will increase in the future. Since interest rates and the business cycle are procyclical, increasing interest rates imply that market participants expect a period of economic expansion. Similarly, if the yield curve is downward-sloping, the market expects interest rates to decline in the future and a period of economic contraction to ensue. Descending yield curves are common near the final phase of a period of economic expansion. Economic information can also be obtained by watching the spread between long-term and short-term interest rates. As the spread narrows, the market consensus is that the rate of economic expansion will be slowing. The relationship between the yield curve and the business cycle is illustrated in Exhibit 7–5.

A warning to the student is in order. Although yield curves do provide information about market expectations of future business activity, as with any expectations, they may not be realized. The yield curve observed at any point in time represents the market's best interpretation of the economic data available. As new information becomes available, expectations are revised.

Yield Curve and Financial Intermediaries.   The slope of the yield curve is important for such financial intermediaries as commercial banks, savings and loan associations, mutual savings banks, and finance companies. These and other intermediaries borrow funds in financial markets from surplus spending units and, after intermediation, lend the funds to businesses and consumers. An upward-sloping yield curve is generally favorable for these institutions because they borrow most of their funds short-term (transaction accounts and time deposits) and lend the funds at longer maturities. Clearly, the more steeply the yield curve slopes upward, the wider the spread between the borrowing and lending rates and the greater the profit for the financial intermediaries.

When yield curves begin to flatten out or slope downward, profits are squeezed and a different portfolio management strategy is called for. If the yield curve is near the top of the business cycle and is downward-sloping, financial institutions will typically try to shorten the maturity of their liabilities (source of funds), thereby avoiding locking in relatively expensive sources of funds for a longer period of time; simultaneously,

Exhibit 7–5   **Interest-Rate and Yield-Curve Patterns over the Business Cycle**

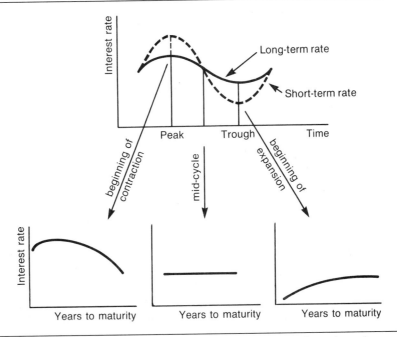

Yield curves are typically upward-sloping during periods of economic expansion and turn downward when the economy begins to contract.

financial institutions will try to lengthen the maturity of their loans. The strategy here is to get borrowers to lock in relatively high borrowing rates for long periods of time in anticipation that interest rates will decline in the future.

Default Risk

A debt security includes a formal promise by the borrower to pay the lender coupon payments and principal payments according to a predetermined schedule. Failure on the part of the borrower to meet any condition of the bond contract constitutes *default*. *Default risk* refers to the possibility of not collecting the amount of interest or principal, or both, promised at the agreed time.

It is believed that most investors are risk averters in that if the expected returns from two investments are identical except for risk, the investors will prefer the security whose return is most certain. Therefore, to induce investors to purchase securities that possess default risk, borrowers must compensate lenders for the potential financial injury they may incur by purchasing risky securities. A security's default risk can be measured as the difference between the rate paid on a risky security and the rate paid on a default-free security, with all factors other than default risk being held constant.

The *default risk premium* may be expressed as

$$DRP = i - i_{rf},$$

(7–2)

where *DRP* is the default risk premium, *i* is the promised yield to maturity on the security, and i_{rf} is the yield on a comparable default-free security. U.S. Treasury securities are the best proxy measures for the default-free rate. The larger the default risk premium, the higher the probability of default and the higher the security's market yield.

Market default risk premiums can be computed by comparing Treasury securities with risky securities of similar term to maturity and other issue characteristics. Exhibit 7–6 shows some typical risk premiums for selected securities. For example, the 59 basis point default risk premium on Aaa-rated corporate bonds represents the market consensus of the amount of compensation that investors must be paid to induce them to buy risky bonds instead of default-free bonds (100 basis points = 1 percent).[3] Also notice that as credit quality declines, the default risk premium increases. Default risk premiums are not abstract notions, as can be attested by those who owned Penn Central debt securities when that company declared bankruptcy in June 1970, precipitating the largest corporate failure in American financial history. Other well-publicized defaults include that of New York City on its municipal bonds during 1975, the Braniff Airlines default during 1982, the failure of the Washington Public Power Supply System ("Whoops") on its nuclear power plants in 1983 (the largest municipal default in history), and the LTV Steel Company default in 1986.

Default Risk and the Business Cycle

Default risk premiums, as shown in Exhibit 7–7, vary systematically over the business cycle. They widen during periods of economic decline and narrow during periods of economic expansion. Exhibit 7–7 shows this pattern for corporate bonds.

The pattern of behavior for default risk premiums is attributable to changes in investor willingness to own bonds of different credit ratings over the business cycle—the so-called *flight-to-quality* argument. Specifically, during periods of econ-

---

Exhibit 7–6   **Risk Premiums for Selected Securities (May 1991)**

Security	Security Yield (percent)	Equivalent Risk-Free Rate[a] (percent)	Risk Premium (percent)
Corporate bonds: Aaa	8.86	8.27	0.59
Corporate bonds: Aa	9.15	8.27	0.88
Corporate bonds: A	9.41	8.27	1.14
Corporate bonds: Baa	9.86	8.27	1.59

Notice that as bond rating quality declines, the default risk premium increases.

[a] Thirty-year Treasury bond yield

Source: Federal Reserve Bulletin, August 1991.

---

[3] When comparing two securities, the interest rate differential is rarely quoted in percentage terms, such as 0.43 percent. Instead, the term is converted to basis points: 100 basis points equals 1 percent. Thus 0.43 percent is equal to 43 basis points.

Exhibit 7–7   **Default Risk Premiums (Yield Spreads between Corporate Baa and Aaa Bonds)**

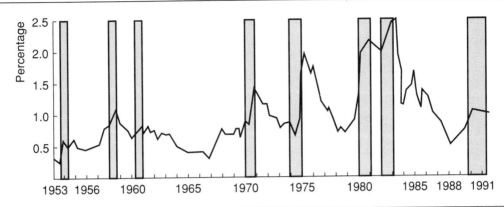

Note: Shaded areas indicate periods of economic recession.

Notice that the default risk premium increases during periods of economic contraction and decreases during periods of economic expansion.

omic prosperity, investors are willing to hold bonds with low credit ratings in their portfolios because there is little chance of default and these bonds normally have higher yields. During such times, investors tend to seek out the highest-yielding investments. On the other hand, during a recession, the prime concern of investors becomes safety. As a result, there is a flight to quality as investors adjust their portfolios—buying bonds with high credit ratings (low default risk) and selling from their portfolios bonds with low credit ratings. The increase in demand for high-grade bonds drives their price up and their yield down; correspondingly, a decrease in demand for bonds with low credit ratings drives their price down and their yield up. The result is the increase in default risk premiums during periods of economic recession.

Bond Ratings

Investors typically do not formulate the probability of default themselves but employ credit ratings assigned by investment agencies, principally Moody's Investors Service and Standard & Poor's. Both rank bonds in order of the perceived probability of their default and publish the ratings as letter grades. The rating schemes they use are shown in Exhibit 7-8. The highest-grade bonds, those with the lowest default risk, are rated triple-A. As can be seen in Exhibit 7-6, the default risk premium on corporate bonds increases as the bond rating becomes lower.

Bonds rated in the top four rating categories—Aaa to Baa for Moody's and AAA to BBB for Standard & Poor's—are called *investment grade bonds*. State and federal laws frequently require commercial banks, insurance companies, pension funds, and other financial institutions to purchase only securities rated as investment quality.

Exhibit 7–8   **Corporate Bond-Rating Systems**

Explanation	Moody's	Standard & Poor's	Default Risk Premium
Best quality, smallest degree of risk	Aaa	AAA	Lowest
High quality, slightly more long-term risk than top rating	Aa1 Aa2 Aa3	AA+ AA AA−	. . .
Upper-medium grade, possible impairment in the future	A1 A2 A3	A+ A A−	. . .
Medium grade, lack outstanding investment characteristics	Baa1 Baa2 Baa3	BBB+ BBB BBB−	. . .
Speculative issues, protection may be very moderate	Ba1 Ba2 Ba3	BB+ BB BB−	. . .
Very speculative, may have small assurance of interest and principal payments	B1 B2 B3	B+ B B−	. . .
Issues in poor standing, may be in default	Caa	CCC	.
Speculative in a high degree, with marked shortcomings	Ca	CC	.
Lowest quality, poor prospects of attaining real investment standing	C	C D	. Highest

Note: The top four rating categories are investment grade bonds. Bonds below the double rule are below investment grade.

Investment grade quality bonds are those rated Baa or above by Moody's (or BBB by Standard and Poor's). Financial institutions are typically allowed to purchase only investment grade securities.

Bond-rating agencies consider a number of factors when assigning a bond rating. Among the most important are (1) the firm's expected cash flow; (2) the amount of the firm's fixed contractual cash payments, such as interest and principal payments or lease payments; (3) the length of time the firm has been profitable; and (4) the variability of the firm's earnings.

Once a bond rating is assigned to a particular issue, the rating is periodically reviewed by the rating agency and is subject to change. A lower bond rating increases the firm's future borrowing costs and may limit its access to money and capital markets. For example, International Harvester (a major manufacturer of trucks, farm implements, and construction machinery) had its debt securities rated A in 1978. Beginning in 1980, the firm experienced large financial losses, which forced it to

DID YOU KNOW?

Poison Puts and the Crumbling Oreo Cookie

One of the most interesting financial market innovations of the 1980s was the emergence of the "poison put" option to protect investors against event risk. *Event risk* is the possibility of an increase in a firm's financial leverage or other events that increase the riskiness of the firm. For example, a leveraged buyout increases a firm's debt burden. The firm is now more risky because of the increased fixed-interest payments to bondholders. As a result, the rating agencies lower the firm's credit rating, the firm's bond prices decline, and bondholders suffer a capital loss on their investment.

The full consequences of event risk became a painful reality for some investors during October 1988, when RJR Nabisco was "successfully" taken over by perennial takeover artists Kohlberg Kravis Roberts & Company (KKR). The $25 billion takeover was the largest ever and graphically illustrated the enormous financial consequences of event risk—the value of RJR Nabisco debt declined by $800 million, or nearly 40 percent! One wiser but poorer bondholder remarked, "That's how the Oreo crumbles."

As a result of the huge capital losses suffered by bondholders in the RJR Nabisco takeover and other takeovers, investors became reluctant to purchase bonds without covenants that provided adequate protection against event risk. One type of bond covenant that provides protection is a poison put option. A *poison put* is an option that allows the investor to sell a bond back to the issuer at face value or require a coupon reset (an adjustment of the coupon rate) if a designated event occurs. For example, if the RJR Nabisco bonds had had a poison put option, investors could have sold their bonds back to the firm at par, thus avoiding an $800 million capital loss. Coupon resets are typically used when the named event is a downgrade in a firm's credit rating. For example, if a firm issued Aaa bonds and the credit rating agency subsequently downgraded the bonds to single-A because of a leveraged buyout, the bond's coupon rate would be reset to the current market rate paid by similar bonds rated A.

Because of the large number of debt issues with poison puts sold during the 1980s, Standard & Poor's developed a system to rate event risk covenants according to the degree to which they protect bondholders. The event risk rating system provides five rating categories, from E1, providing the greatest protection against event risk, to E5, providing the least protection. Before the RJR Nabisco takeover, few bonds had event risk protection or at best, weak protection (E5). Following the RJR Nabisco takeover, however, the number of bonds issued with poison put options increased dramatically, and the strength of the event risk protection increased such that most bonds carried event risk protection ratings of E3 to E1 (medium to high event risk protection).

restructure its debt payments in the latter part of 1981. During this period, International Harvester's credit ratings were successively lowered by the credit rating agencies. During January 1983, International Harvester's debt securities were rated Caa by Moody's, which suggests that the issue was extremely speculative and near default. Correspondingly, the firm's 20-year bonds had a promised yield of more than

30 percent, whereas a typical A-rated corporate bond yielded about 13.85 percent. Clearly, the market judged International Harvester bonds to be extremely risky.[4]

Tax Treatment

The interest rate most relevant to investors is the rate of return earned *after taxes*. Thus the lower the taxes on the income from a security, the greater the demand for the security and the lower its before-tax yield. It is no surprise, therefore, that tax-exempt securities have lower market yields than similar taxable securities.

Federal, state, and local governments impose a variety of taxes on income from securities, the most important of which is the federal income tax. Federal income taxes discriminate between two forms of income on securities: (1) coupon income, and (2) capital gains income. Let us consider the effect that the tax structure has on the market yield of a security.

Coupon Income

All coupon income earned on state and local government debt is exempt from federal taxes. Thus securities issued by state and local governments (called *municipal securities*) sell for lower market yields than comparable securities issued by the U.S. Treasury or private corporations. The exemption of coupon income from federal taxes stems from the separation of federal and state powers, and its primary purpose is to help state and local governments borrow at lower interest rates than would otherwise be possible.[5]

The decision by an investor to purchase either a taxable or a tax-exempt security depends on the relative yields between the two securities and the investor's marginal tax rate. To see how investors make this decision, consider the following example. Assume that the current yield to maturity on a taxable corporate bond is 10 percent, whereas the current tax-exempt yield on a municipal bond of comparable maturity and bond rating is 7 percent. The after-tax yield on the two securities can be compared using the following formula:

$$i_{at} = i_{bt}(1 - t), \tag{7-3}$$

where i_{at} is the after-tax yield on the security, i_{bt} is the before-tax yield, and t is the marginal tax rate of the investor. The equation assumes that the return on the securities is composed entirely of coupon income, with no capital gains. The after-tax yields on the two bonds are as follows for investors in a variety of different tax brackets:

---

[4]In 1987, the company reorganized itself, and the new company is called Navistar International Corporation.

[5]During April 1988, the Supreme Court ruled that Congress is free to tax all coupon interest on state and local government bonds. Overturning a major 1895 precedent, the court held that the Constitution does not protect state and local government against federal taxation of interest received by a holder of municipal bonds. Currently, there is no movement in Congress to tax municipal bonds, but the potential to do so is now there. If the federal government were to tax municipal securities, it would only apply to new bond issues and not to outstanding bonds.

Investors' Marginal Tax Rate	Municipal Yield	Corporate After-Tax Yield
0%	7%	10 (1 − 0.00) = 10.0%
10	7	10 (1 − 0.10) = 9.0
20	7	10 (1 − 0.20) = 8.0
30	7	10 (1 − 0.30) = 7.0
40	7	10 (1 − 0.40) = 6.0
50	7	10 (1 − 0.50) = 5.0

For example, an investor in the 20 percent tax bracket would buy a corporate security, because the after-tax return is 8 percent versus 7 percent for the municipal security. However, as the investor's marginal tax rate increases, the return on municipal securities becomes more favorable compared to the after-tax return on corporates. An investor in the 40 percent tax bracket would prefer a tax-exempt security yielding 7 percent to the corporate security, for which the after-tax return is only 6 percent. The rule that emerges is that investors in high tax brackets, such as wealthy and fully taxed corporations (e.g., commercial banks), usually hold portfolios of municipal securities because of their higher after-tax yield compared to taxable securities. In contrast, investors in lower tax brackets, such as persons with low incomes and tax-exempt institutions (e.g., pension funds), receive high after-tax yields from taxable securities because they pay fewer taxes. As a personal note, discussing your municipal bond portfolio at a cocktail party subtly identifies you as an upper-income person without your actually saying so.

Capital Gains Income

From 1921 through 1986, long-term capital gains were taxed at substantially lower rates than ordinary income. For example, in 1986, long-term capital gains were taxed at 40 percent of the tax rate on ordinary income. During this period, taxable bonds trading at a discount from their par value had lower market yields than comparable bonds with coupon rates selling at or above par. The reason was that part of the income to the investor on the discounted bonds—the capital gain—was subject to the lower capital-gains tax rate. However, the tax law change that took effect in 1987 eliminated the tax differential, and thus capital-gains income is currently taxed as ordinary income.

Marketability

The interest rate on securities also varies with the degree of marketability. Marketability refers to the cost and quickness with which investors can resell a security. The greater the marketability of a security, the greater the demand for it and the lower its interest rate. Marketability depends on the costs of trade, physical transfer, search, and information. The lower these costs, the greater the security's marketability.

Marketability is often gauged by the volume of a security's secondary market. For example, short-term Treasury bills have the largest and most active secondary market and are considered to be the most marketable of all securities. Investors are able to sell

PEOPLE
& EVENTS

Rating the Rating Agencies: How Are We Doing?

Investors put a lot of faith in the bond ratings of the two top rating agencies, Moody's Investors Service and Standard & Poor's (S&P). Ideally, the higher the credit rating, the lower the probability a firm will default. But a growing body of research indicates that bond ratings may provide an incomplete and out-of-date guide to credit quality. Specifically, the studies, most out of the academic community, note the following:

■ There is less correlation than might be expected between a firm's bond rating and the likelihood of default.

■ Bond ratings do not tell investors much about other measures of risk, like price volatility and market performance.

■ Bond rating changes do not convey new information to the market.

Obviously, the credit rating agencies are not happy with the publicity the research studies have gotten in recent years. It is not good for business. Collectively, the two major rating agencies provide credit ratings for more than 92 percent of the corporate and municipal debt issued each year. Also, both companies charge hefty fees for their services, which typically range between $1,000 to $50,000, depending on the size and complexity of the issues.

Critics of the rating agencies like to recount the story of the $2.25 billion of bonds sold in the late 1970s and early 1980s by the Washington Public Power Supply System. The bonds when sold were rated single-A, indicating a strong capacity to pay principal and interest. By May of 1981, analysts at some of the large brokerage houses predicted the power plants would never be built. The rating agencies were painfully slow in downgrading the issues as problems mounted publicly. It was not until the power plants were canceled some seven months later that Moody's and S&P assigned them junk debt status. The bonds defaulted in June 1982, the biggest default in the history of the municipal bond market.

The rating agencies defend their services, arguing that they do not pretend to answer all questions about a bond issue in a single alphabetical rating. The ratings they provide are independent and only assess the likelihood that a firm may default. They point out that most of the rated corporate bonds that have defaulted since 1970 were rated as junk debt (below Baa) at time of sale. In discussing the timeliness of ratings, the agencies argue that they do update credit ratings periodically to insure their accuracy and currency. They do admit, however, that they move cautiously and do not change a firm's rating until facts are conclusive.

What should the investor believe or do? It is hard to know who is right. Probably the best advice is that overall credit ratings do a reasonable, but not perfect, job of segregating firms by credit quality. However, credit ratings are not a substitute for informed judgment and do not mitigate the need to hold a well-diversified portfolio.

virtually any dollar amount of Treasury securities quickly and without disrupting the market. Similarly, the securities of many other large, well-known issuers enjoy a high degree of marketability, especially those actively traded on the New York and American exchanges. For thousands of other securities not traded actively each day, however, marketability can pose a problem. The market for these may be confined to a region or a community. As a result, trading them may occur infrequently, and it may be difficult to establish the securities' fair market price.

Options on Debt Securities

Most bonds contain options that permit the borrower or lender to change the nature of the bond contract before maturity. More specifically, an *option* is a contract that gives the holder the right, but not the obligation, to buy or sell an asset at some specified price and date in the future. If the holder of the option has the right to buy the underlying security, the option is called a *call option;* if the holder has the right to sell the underlying security, the option is called a *put option;* and if the option holder has the right to convert the security into another type of security, the option is called a *conversion option.* Options that are traded separately from the underlying security are discussed in Chapter 11.

Call Options

Most corporate and municipal bonds and some U.S. government bonds contain in their contracts a call option, or as they are often referred to, a call provision. A call option gives the bond issuer the option to buy back the bond at a specified price in advance of the maturity date. The price is known as the *call price*, and it is usually set at the bond's par value or slightly above par (usually one year's interest payment above). When bonds are called, investors are informed through a notice in a paper of general circulation, such as *The Wall Street Journal.*

Bonds that contain a call option sell at a higher market yield than comparable noncallable bonds. The reason for the penalty yield on callable bonds is that the call option works to the benefit of the issuer (borrower) and to the detriment of investors. For example, if interest rates decline significantly below the coupon rate on a callable bond, the issuer can call (retire) the old bond issue and refinance it with a new one at a lower interest rate. The result of this action is that the issuer achieves an interest cost savings, but the investor is now forced to reinvest funds at the current lower market rate of interest, suffering a loss of interest income.

The difference in interest rates between callable and comparable noncallable bonds is known as the *call interest premium* and can be written as follows:

$$CIP = i_c - i_{nc}, \tag{7-4}$$

where CIP is the call interest premium, i_c is the yield on a callable bond, and i_{nc} is the yield on a similar, noncallable bond. For proper comparison, the two bonds should be of similar default risk, term to maturity, tax treatment, and marketability. The call interest premium, therefore, is compensation paid to investors who own callable bonds for potential financial injury in the event their bonds are called. The greater the probability a particular bond will be called, the greater the call interest premium and the higher the bond's market yield. The call option is more likely to be exercised when interest rates are declining. Thus, the lower interest rates are expected to fall, the more valuable the option and, hence, the greater the CIP.

Put Options

A put option allows an investor to sell a bond back (*put* the bond) to the issuer before maturity at a predetermined price. Investors typically exercise put options during periods when interest rates are rising and bond prices are declining. A put option sets a "floor" or minimum price of a bond at the *exercise price*, which is generally at or below par value.

Because the put option is an advantage to investors, bonds that contain a put option sell at lower yields than comparable nonputable bonds. The reason for the lower yield is that investors can protect themselves against capital losses due to unexpected rises in interest rates. For example, if interest rates rise significantly above the coupon rate on a putable bond, the investor can sell (put) the bond back to the issuer at the exercise price (par of near par), then buy a new bond at the current market rate of interest. The difference in interest rates between putable and similar nonputable bonds is called the *put interest premium* and can be expressed as follows:

$$PIP = i_p - i_{np} \qquad (7\text{--}5)$$

where PIP is the put interest premium, i_p is the yield on a putable bond, and i_{np} is the yield on a similar nonputable bond. The value of the put option depends upon interest rate expectations; the higher interest rates are expected to rise, the more valuable the option and, hence, the greater the absolute value of PIP. Finally, notice that callable bonds sell for higher yields and putable bonds sell for lower yields than similar bonds without these options.

Conversion Option

Another factor that affects the yields on different securities is a conversion option. A *conversion option* allows the investor to convert a security into another type of security at a predetermined price. The most common type of conversion feature is the option to convert a bond into an issuer's stock; another popular option in volatile interest rate periods is the conversion of a variable-coupon bond into a fixed-coupon bond. The timing of the conversion is at the option of the investor. However, the terms under which the conversion may take place are agreed upon when the security is purchased.

Because a conversion option is an advantage to investors, they pay higher prices for convertible securities. In the case of convertible bonds, the higher price results in a lower yield. Thus convertible bonds have lower yields than similar bonds without this option. This difference in yield is called the *conversion yield premium* and can be expressed as follows:

$$CYP = i_{con} - i_{ncon} \qquad (7\text{--}6)$$

where CYP is the conversion yield premium, i_{con} is the yield on a convertible bond, and i_{ncon} is the yield on a similar nonconvertible bond. The conversion yield premium is the price investors are willing to pay for the conversion option.

Convertible bonds have lower yields than similar nonconvertible bonds because the investor holding a convertible bond is granted a hedge against future risk. For example, if an investor owns a bond that is convertible into common stock and the stock price falls, the investor earns a fixed rate of return in the form of interest income from the bond. If the stock price rises sufficiently, the investor can exercise the option and earn a capital gain as the stock's current market price rises above the option's exercise price. Thus the conversion option is most valuable during periods when stock market prices are rising and bond prices are declining. For another example, suppose an investor owns a variable-coupon bond convertible into a fixed-coupon bond. If interest rates are rising, the investor would hold the variable-coupon bond and earn higher interest income as the coupon rates are adjusted upward in concert with the market rate of interest. Then, if the investor believes that interest rates are near their peak, the investor would exercise the option to convert into a fixed-coupon bond and, thus, lock in the higher rate of interest. The value of this conversion option depends on interest rate expectations; the higher interest rates are expected to rise, the more valuable the option and, hence, the greater the absolute value of the conversion yield premium (CYP).

Comovement of Interest Rates

In the preceding sections we discussed why interest rates differ on different securities. We now want to explore why interest rates tend to move together. One reason is the substitutability of different types of financial securities. For example, say that an increase in the supply of one security causes a fall in its price and an increase in its yield. How do investors respond? They shift out of lower-yielding securities and into the one that now carries the greater yield. And what is the effect of this shift? The result is a rise in the yields of the securities that are being sold off. The degree and quickness of interest rate changes transmitted from one sector to another depend on the linkages connecting supply and demand variables. The tighter the linkages, the more quickly changes in supply or demand will affect yields in various sectors of the economy.

Summary

The structure of interest rates explains why large numbers of different interest rates exist in financial markets on any given day. The most important factors that determine differences in interest rates among securities are (1) term to maturity, (2) risk of default, (3) tax treatment, (4) marketability, and (5) special features such as call and put options.

Two competing theories help explain the behavior of the term structure of interest rates. The expectation theory suggests that expectations of future interest rate movements alter the slope of the yield curve. If interest rates are expected to increase in the future, long-term rates will be higher than short-term rates, and the yield curve will slope upward. The market segmentation theory suggests that the shape of the yield curve is determined by the supply of and demand for securities within a narrow maturity range.

Default risk refers to the probability that the issuer may not pay the amount of interest or principal, or both, when promised. The greater a security's default risk, the higher the market rate of interest that must be paid to investors as compensation for potential financial loss. Most investors are concerned about the after-tax yield on an investment. Thus the before-tax yield on securities that are subject to higher tax rates is higher than the yield on comparable securities with a lower tax rate. Marketability refers to the ease and quickness with which investors can resell a security. The greater the marketability of a security, the lower its interest rate.

A call option allows an issuer to retire a security before its maturity date. Because call options can lead to financial injury to investors, bonds with call options sell for higher interest rates than similar noncallable bonds. A put option allows an investor to sell a bond back to the issuer before maturity at a predetermined price. Because put options protect investors against capital losses caused by rising interest rates, putable bonds sell for lower yields than similar nonputable bonds. A conversion option allows the investor to convert a security into another type of security. Because conversion options allow investors to hedge against future risk, convertible bonds have lower yields than similar, nonconvertible bonds. Finally, all interest rates tend to move together over the business cycle because of the close interrelationship between suppliers and demanders of securities. The closer the linkages between different security markets, the more quickly changes in supply and demand will affect yields in various sectors of the economy.

Questions

1. Using the *Federal Reserve Bulletin*, plot the yield curve for U.S. Treasury securities on a quarterly basis for 1992. Given your knowledge of the term structure of interest rates, what would be your economic forecast for 1993?
2. Summarize the expectation theory and the segmentation theory of the term structure of interest rates. Are these theories in any way related, or are they alternative explanations of the term structure?
3. A commercial bank made a three-year term loan at 10 percent. The bank's economics department forecasts that one and two years in the future, the one-year interest rate will be 10 percent and 14 percent, respectively. The current one-year rate is 8 percent. Given that the bank's forecasts are reliable, has the bank set the three-year rate correctly?
4. Define *default risk*. How does the default risk premium vary over the business cycle? Explain your answer.
5. What do bond ratings measure? Explain some of the important factors in determining a security's bond rating.
6. Why do most commercial banks hold portfolios of municipal bonds and relatively few corporate bonds?
7. Explain the importance of a call provision to investors. Do callable bonds have higher or lower yields than similar noncallable bonds? Why?
8. Define *marketability*. Explain why marketability of a security is important to both investor and issuer.
9. A new-issue municipal bond rated Aaa by Moody's Investors Service is priced to yield 8 percent. If you are in the 33 percent tax bracket, what yield would you need to earn on a taxable bond to be indifferent?
10 Historically, the yield curve typically has been upward sloping. Why would you expect this to be the case?

Selected References

Cook, Timothy, and Thomas Hahn. "Interest Rate Expectations and the Slope of the Money Market Yield Curve." *Economic Review*. Federal Reserve Bank of Richmond, September/October 1990, pp. 3–26.

Furlong, Frederick T. "The Yield Curve and Recessions." *Weekly Letter*. **Federal Reserve Bank of San Francisco, March 10, 1989, pp. 1–3.**

Stevens, E. J. "Is There a Message in the Yield Curve?" *Economic Commentary*. **Federal Reserve Bank of Cleveland, March 15, 1989, pp. 1–4.**

These three papers discuss yield curves as predictors of future interest rates and future economic activity.

Henning, Charles N., et al. *Financial Markets and the Economy*. **Englewood Cliffs, NJ: Prentice-Hall, 1988.**

Chapters 13 and 14 provide a comprehensive discussion of the structure of interest rates. Readable but at a more advanced level. Good practical applications.

Livingston, Miles. *Money and Capital Markets: Financial Instruments and Their Uses*. **Englewood Cliffs, NJ: Prentice-Hall, 1990.**

Several chapters of this book provide good coverage of interest rates.

Peek. Joe, and James A. Wilcox. "Tax Rates and Interest Rates on Tax-Exempt Securities." *New England Economic Review*. **Federal Reserve Bank of Boston, January–February 1986, pp. 29–41.**

A discussion of how reductions in marginal tax rates for both individuals and corporations narrow the interest rate spread between taxable and tax-exempt securities. The size of the change depends on who the marginal investors in the municipal bond market are and how completely yields adjust to tax changes. An advanced article.

Pozdena, Randall J. "Municipal Bond Behavior." *Weekly Letter*. **Federal Reserve Bank of San Francisco, February 22, 1985.**

Analyzes the reasons for the narrowing spread between tax-exempt and taxable yields.

———. "Option Fever." *Weekly Letter*. **Federal Reserve Bank of San Francisco, December 31, 1982.**

A discussion of the emergence of the call and put options markets.

Rose, Peter S. *Money and Capital Markets*. **Homewood, IL: Richard D. Irwin, 1992.**

Chapters 7–11 provide comprehensive coverage of interest rates.

Rowe, Timothy D., et al. "Treasury Bill versus Private Money Market Yield Curves." *Economic Review*. **Federal Reserve Bank of Richmond, July/August 1986, pp. 3–12.**

This article considers what factors influence the shape of the Treasury bill and private market yield curves.

Van Horne, James C. *Financial Market Rates and Flows*. **Englewood Cliffs, NJ: Prentice-Hall, 1990.**

A comprehensive book dealing with all aspects of the determinants of interest rates. An outstanding book.

Zimmer, Steve A. "Event Risk Premia and Bond Market Incentives for Corporate Leverage." *Quarterly Review*. **Federal Reserve Bank of New York, Spring 1990, pp. 15–30.**

3 FINANCIAL MARKETS

PROFILE/Darrell W. Naquin

HE IS

Vice-president, Investment Banking Department at Dai-Ichi Kangyo Bank, where he heads the Syndications and Placement group he founded in January 1991. Previously, was a vice-president in the Corporate Finance Department of the Dai-Ichi Kangyo Bank, promoted to that position 1 year after joining the firm. The Dai-Ichi Kangyo Bank is the largest bank in the world.

WHAT HE DOES

Working with a staff of six professionals, his group first provides pricing, structuring, and market information to the bank's loan officers who are involved in making large loans to multinational corporations. After a loan is committed, the Syndications and Placement group sells a portion of the loan to other banks. This activity is often referred to as a "trading desk" in which deals are bought and sold in the interbank market. The bank assumes substantial underwriting risk from the time a loan is made to the client to the time a portion of the loan is sold. There is enormous timing and market risk during the holding period and the challenge for the Syndications and Placement group is to ensure sufficient compensation to the bank for the risk. In the first year of the group's operation, they placed over $300 million of bank loans in the primary and secondary bank market.

HOW HE GOT THERE

B.A.: Loyola University, New Orleans
Associate Degree: British Trade Board, City College of London, London, England
M.BA: Tulane University

First job: LEP Group, international distribution and finance company in London, England, specializing in international trade and development, 8 years.

BACKGROUND

He grew up in Louisiana. His father was in the retail furniture business, and his mother was a special education teacher. In his senior undergraduate year, pursuing a degree in English, he found himself in need of a part-time job and answered an ad for an office clerk. The office turned out to be a local branch of the LEP group and his part-time job grew into a career he had not previously considered. Now he lives on the Upper East Side of New York City, a short subway commute to work at the World Trade Center.

WHAT HE LIKES BEST ABOUT HIS JOB

The challenge of assessing market risk and timing in an environment where the tolerable margin of error is only one basis point (1/100th of 1 percent).

WORST NIGHTMARE

Mispricing a deal, as the deal then will not sell in the marketplace. Mispricing or mistiming a deal would translate to your bank holding an asset that it does not intend to hold. That amount can easily exceed $100 million-plus.

HOW HE UNWINDS

In New York City with racquetball, swimming, and some spectator baseball. Twice a year, he heads out to St. John, Virgin Islands. Here he camps out in a tent on the beach with no radio, no telephone, no newspapers, and no hot water while enjoying day sailing, snorkeling, and scuba diving.

ADVICE

Learn how to live before learning how to make a living. Don't be afraid to take risks in your career early on. Take some chances in life.

MONEY MARKETS

8

NINETEEN EIGHTY-EIGHT WAS THE year of the worst drought since the dustbowl days of the 1930s. There were massive crop failures of corn, oats, wheat, and soybeans that threatened to send hordes of farmers off their lands. Cattle ranchers and dairy farmers were forced to send their herds to early slaughter because they could not afford to feed livestock. To mitigate this crisis, Congress approved $3.9 billion in drought aid for farmers and ranchers. One of the ways available to Congress to raise such disaster relief funds is the sale of farm credit debt issues in the money markets.

This chapter examines the money market in which short-term credit instruments such as farm credit debt issues are bought and sold. It is the market in which commercial banks and other businesses adjust their liquidity, the Federal Reserve conducts its monetary policy, and the federal government finances its day-to-day operations. This chapter focuses on the economic reasons for money markets, the major money market participants, money market instruments, the interest rate relationships between various money market instruments, and the book entry process for handling money market transactions.

Nature of the Money Market

In the money markets, businesses, governments, and, sometimes, individuals borrow or lend funds for short periods of time—usually 1 to 120 days. Exhibit 8–1 shows that U.S. Treasury securities are the dominant money market instrument, with about $870 billion outstanding. They are followed by commercial paper, repurchase agreements, and negotiable certificates of deposit. Other money market instruments, though not as large in volume outstanding, are important in their respective markets and represent investment alternatives for money market participants. As we shall see, it is the close substitutability of market instruments that links all of the money markets.

Actually, the money market consists of a collection of markets, each trading a distinctly different financial instrument. There is no formal organization, such as the New York Stock Exchange for the equity markets. Central to the activity of the money markets are the dealers and brokers who specialize in one or more money market instruments. Dealers buy securities for their own position and sell from their security inventories when a trade takes place. Transactions, particularly in the

Exhibit 8–1   **Selected Money Market Instruments Outstanding (December 31, 1990)**

Instrument	Amount Outstanding ($ in billions)
U.S. Treasury securities	$870.2
Treasury bills	527.4
Others under 1 year	342.8
Negotiable certificates of deposit	357.5
Commercial paper	561.1
Banker's acceptances	54.8
Repurchase agreements	417.7

U.S. Treasury securities are the dominant instrument in the money market.

Source: Board of Governors, Federal Reserve System, *Flow of Funds Accounts, Financial Assets and Liabilities*, 1991.

secondary market, are almost always completed by telephone. The market is centered in New York City in downtown Manhattan because of the concentration of financial firms in that area. The major dealers and brokers are tied to each other and to their customers by direct phone lines all over the United States and in major European financial centers. Other communication devices, such as teletypes and computers, link large banks, some big corporations, and other participants in the money markets.

The money markets are also distinct from other financial markets in that they are wholesale markets because of the large transactions involved. Although some small transactions do take place, most involve $1 million or more. Money market transactions are called *open market transactions* because of their impersonal and competitive nature. There are no established customer relationships. For example, a bank trading in Federal Funds will ask for bids from a number of brokers, selling at the highest price and buying at the lowest. However, not all money market transactions are as open as the Federal Funds market. For example, money market banks often "accommodate" dealers who are good customers of the bank by selling them negotiable certificates of deposit even though the bank is not actively seeking funds at the prevailing market interest rate. Thus in the money markets we find some "give," not so much in the form of price concessions but in the form of accommodations.

The hub of money market transactions is the trading rooms of dealers and brokers. When the market is open, these rooms are characterized by tension and a frenzy of activity. Each trader sits in front of a battery of phones that link the dealer to other dealers and their major customers. Phones never ring. Instead, incoming calls are signaled by what appears to be a continuous stream of blinking lights. Huge transactions—$5, $10, or $150 million—take place in conversations that average 10 seconds. Business is conducted in a shorthand jargon discernible only to traders. The request of "$1 at $\frac{7}{8}$" with the response "the buck is yours Manny" translates to mean that Manufacturers Hanover has just purchased $1 million worth of Federal Funds from a broker at $9\frac{7}{8}$ for use overnight. Since Federal Funds brokers earn about $1 per $1 million on overnight funds, it is understandable that trading volumes must be large.

Also, because billions of dollars of business is conducted over the phone, the motto of the money markets is "My word is my bond." Participants who renege on their word or make too many errors soon find themselves unable to transact with other brokers and dealers and seeking employment in another profession. Of course, mistakes do occur, and they are typically worked out over lunch in what is agreed to be the fairest way to all concerned.

Payment for securities traded in the money market is as simple as making the transaction over the telephone. Most transactions are settled in Federal Funds, with parties involved instructing the Federal Reserve to transfer funds from the account of one customer's bank to the other party's bank. The physical transfer of securities is also simplified by the availability of safekeeping facilities in New York City banks. Securities are rarely physically shipped between buyer and seller.

Economic Role of the Money Market

The most important economic function of the money market is to provide an efficient means for economic units to adjust their liquidity positions. Almost every economic unit—financial institution, business corporation, or governmental body—has a recurring problem of liquidity management. The problem occurs because rarely is the timing of cash receipts and cash expenditures perfectly synchronized. Money market instruments allow economic units to bridge the gap between cash receipts and cash expenditures, thereby solving their liquidity problems. Exhibit 8–2 illustrates this concept. For example, a business firm has a temporary surplus of cash. Rather than leaving the funds idle in a checking account and earning no interest, the firm can invest in the money markets safely for a period of 1 to 30 days, or longer if needed, and earn the market rate of interest. In another situation, if a bank is temporarily short of cash reserves to meet its legal reserve requirements, it can go to the money markets for Federal Funds to meet this temporary need.

Characteristics of Money Market Instruments

Given the economic role of money markets—to provide liquidity adjustments—it is not difficult to establish the general characteristics of money market instruments and the types of firms that may issue them. Specifically, people who invest in money market instruments want to take as little risk as possible. Thus these instruments are financial claims that have (1) low default risk, (2) low price risk (short term to maturity), and (3) high marketability. Let us examine why this is true.

First, if you have money to invest temporarily, you would want to purchase the financial claims of firms having the highest credit standing and thus minimize any loss of principal due to default. Second, you would not want to hold long-term securities because of their greater price risk (interest rate risk) relative to short-term securities. Furthermore, for short-term securities, maturity is not far away. If you could postpone your cash needs long enough, you could redeem them for face value at maturity. Finally, temporary investments must be marketable in the event that you unexpectedly need the funds before maturity. Generally speaking, for a financial claim to have

Exhibit 8–2   **Money Markets Bridge the Gap between Intermittent Cash Flows**

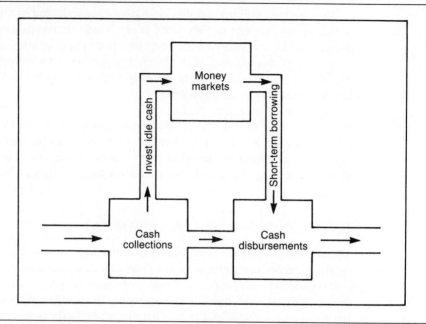

Money markets help governments, businesses, and individuals to manage their liquidity by temporarily bridging the gap between cash receipts and cash expenditures. If a firm is temporarily short of cash, it can borrow in the money market; or if it has temporary excess cash, it can invest in short-term money market instruments.

a strong secondary market and, thus, be highly marketable, it must have the following characteristics: a standardized contract, an issuer that is well known, and an issuer with a high credit rating and a large amount of debt outstanding. Exhibit 8–3 summarizes the characteristics of the money market instruments we shall study in this chapter.

Exhibit 8–3   **Characteristics of Money Market Instruments**

Instrument	Typical Maturity	Marketability	Default Risk
U.S. Treasury securities	13 to 52 weeks	Excellent	None
Negotiable certificates of deposit	14 to 120 days	Good	Low
Commercial paper	1 to 270 days	Limited	Low
Federal agency securities	Up to 1 year	Varies	Low
Banker's acceptances	30 to 180 days	Good	Low
Repurchase agreements	1 to 15 days	Good	Low
Federal Funds	1 to 7 days	Excellent	Low

Treasury securities are the most marketable of all money market instruments and also have the lowest default risk.

Money Market Participants

To gain a more explicit view of money market practices, we shall start by discussing the major "players" in the money market, why they are in the market, and what their typical balance sheet position is. Exhibit 8–4 presents, in matrix form, the major money market participants and the instruments most important to their operation.

Commercial Banks

Commercial banks are by far the most important class of buyers and sellers of money market instruments. As Exhibit 8–4 shows, banks engage actively in almost all the money markets. They are continuously in the process of adjusting their liquidity because of the short-term nature of their liabilities, wide variations in loan demand, and legal reserve requirements imposed on banks by regulations. During periods of cyclical boom, banks are typically faced with the problem of reserve deficiencies because of heavy loan demand. Needed reserves can be obtained by selling securities, such as short-term Treasury securities, from their investment portfolio; or banks can borrow reserves from other banks (Federal Funds), sell negotiable certificates of deposit, sell commercial paper, or borrow in the Eurodollar market. At other times, particularly during recessions, a major bank problem is that of investing excess reserves. During such periods, banks typically build up their secondary reserves position and also purchase quantities of long-term tax-exempt municipal bonds, as well as Treasury and government agency securities.

Exhibit 8–4   Money Market Balance Sheet Position of Major Participants

Instrument	Commercial Banks		Federal Reserve System		Treasury Department		Dealers and Brokers		Corporations	
	A	L	A	L	A	L	A	L	A	L
Treasury bills	■		■			■	■		■	
Agency securities	■		■				■		■	
Negotiable CDs		■					■		■	
Commercial paper		■					■		■	■
Banker's acceptances	■	■	■				■		■	
Federal Funds	■	■								
Repurchase agreements	■	■	■				■	■	■	

Note: A = Assets, L = Liabilities.

Commercial banks are both important investors in and issuers of money market instruments.

The Federal Reserve System

Although commercial banks are the largest class of participants in the money markets, the Federal Reserve is ultimately the most important participant because of its position as manager of the nation's money supply. The Federal Reserve System has no liquidity problems because of its ability to create money—its monetary power. Monetary policy is implemented by controlling the amount of reserve balances that member banks hold at the Federal Reserve. Changes in reserve balances are usually accomplished by *open market operations*—the sale or purchase of Treasury securities by the Federal Reserve Bank. Thus direct intervention by the Federal Reserve in the Treasury securities market affects the liquidity of the nation's banking system by altering banks' reserve positions, which indirectly affects the liquidity of all economic units in the economy by its impact on general business conditions.

The Federal Reserve System also influences money markets through its discount window operation. Banks may borrow temporary reserves from the Federal Reserve System as an alternative to selling secondary reserves or borrowing Federal Funds to cover legal reserve deficiencies. Thus the discount window is part of the mechanism for adjusting short-term reserve deficiencies.

The U.S. Treasury

Unlike the Federal Reserve System, the Treasury Department has a major liquidity problem. Tax receipts tend to be concentrated around the scheduled tax payment dates, but government expenditures tend to be more evenly distributed throughout the year. Furthermore, total government expenditures rarely equal and usually exceed total receipts. The Treasury Department is given the job of financing the federal government's large debt.

Tax receipts are usually deposited into commercial banks in tax and loan accounts. These accounts are drawn down by the Treasury periodically as the funds are needed. To even out the patterns of cash payment and receipts, the Treasury sells Treasury bills. In addition to helping meet liquidity needs, Treasury bills are used to finance much of the government's normal operating costs. Because of the ease with which the federal government can sell its debt, the financing of operating expenditures with short-term debt does not pose a problem, as it would for a private corporation.

Dealers in U.S. Securities

Although small in number, U.S. government securities dealers play an important role in the smooth and orderly operation of the money markets. There are about 40 dealers that bear the primary responsibility for buying new Treasury securities (see Exhibit 8–5): 10 dealer banks (departments of large money-center banks) headquartered primarily in New York City and Chicago; 22 diversified brokerage firms based mainly out of New York City and Tokyo; and 7 specialty bond houses. These dealers bid for securities at the weekly Treasury auction. They may keep the securities for investment or resell them to hundreds of other dealers or banks, who in turn sell retail to individual investors, pension funds, mutual funds, other (smaller) banks, and corporations.

Exhibit 8–5   **The Primary Dealers That Trade in the Money Markets**

Banks	Diversified Brokerage Firms	Bond Houses
Bank of America		
Bankers Trust	Bear Stearns	Barclays de Zoetc Wedd
Chase Manhattan Government	Dillon, Read & Co. Inc.	Securities Inc.
Securities	Donaldson, Lufkin & Jenrette	Discount Corp. of New York
Chemical Bank	Securities	Eastbridge Capital Inc.
Citibank	Drexel Burnham Lambert	Aubrey G. Lanston
First National Bank of Chicago	Government Securities	Carrol McEntee & McGinley
Deutsche Bank Government	First Boston	CRT Government Securities
Securities	Fuji Securities Inc.	SBC Government Securities,
Harris Trust & Savings Bank	Goldman, Sachs	Inc.
Morgan Guaranty Trust	Kidder Peabody	
	Lehman Government Securities	
	Merrill Lynch Government Securities	
	Morgan Stanley	
	Paine, Webber, Jackson & Curtis	
	Prudential-Bache Securities	
	Sanwa-BGK Securities Co., L.P.	
	Salomon Bros.	
	Smith Barney Government Securities	
	Dean Witter Reynolds	
	Daiwa Securities America	
	Greenwich Capital Markets	
	The Nikko Security Co.	
	Nomura Securities International	
	S. G. Warburg & Co., Inc.	
	Yamaichi International (America),	
	Inc.	

Large commercial banks are among the bond dealers that participate directly in the money markets. Such banks are known as money-center banks and most are headquartered in New York City, Chicago, and Los Angeles.

Source: Federal Reserve Bank of New York.

The primary economic function of dealers is to "make a market" for Treasury securities by maintaining an active position in most of the maturities issued. That is, dealers maintain an inventory of these securities at their own risk and stand ready to buy or sell from these inventories virtually any quantity of Treasury securities at their quoted bid-or-offer price. Making a market greatly increases the liquidity of Treasury securities, because the brokerage function of matching buyers and sellers in multimillion-dollar transactions would prove to be difficult, if not impossible, without it.

Most large dealers also trade in other money and capital market instruments. For example, some large dealers make markets in federal agency securities, banker's acceptances, negotiable certificates of deposit, and state and local government bonds.

Still others specialize in commercial paper, corporate debt obligations, and over-the-counter stocks. Thus dealers help link together the nation's money and capital markets.

The lure of becoming a dealer is based in the immense leverage available in the government securities market and the anonymity the market affords. Dealers are not required to register with any government agency, and they finance 95 percent of the securities they buy. Of course, high leverage means higher risk, and unfavorable interest-rate swings of only a few basis points can mean catastrophic losses. On the other hand, favorable interest rate movements can mean substantial profits.

There have been a number of highly publicized failures of government securities firms, such as Drysdale (1982), Lombard-Wall (1982), ESM Government Securities (1985), and Bevill Bressler and Schulman (1985). These and other failures resulted in losses to investors of more than $700 million between 1980 and 1985. Prior to 1987, there were no federal regulations on firms that did business in the government securities market as long as they restricted their activities to being a broker or dealer in exempt securities, principally U.S. government securities. Thus, many large, well-known, and prudently operated government securities firms were unregulated, including the 40 or so primary dealers who report their trading, financing, and securities positions to the Federal Reserve Bank of New York. The center of the controversy was not these firms, however, but the questionable practices and sometimes outright fraud on the part of other unregulated government securities dealers, most of whom were small firms.

As a result of these and other abuses, Congress passed the Government Securities Act of 1986. The act standardizes custody arrangements in repurchase agreements involving government securities. It also seeks to bring unregulated government securities firms under capital adequacy, financial record-keeping, and customer protection standards similar to those that already apply to brokers and dealers in other securities.

Corporations

Although not as severe as the liquidity problems facing commercial banks, liquidity management problems also plague corporations. For corporations, the inflow of cash usually comes from the collection of accounts receivable that have been generated from sales. Corporate cash disbursements take place in various forms, such as expenditures for payrolls, inventory purchases, and other services necessary to do business.

Because cash flows rarely balance, corporate treasuries are constantly juggling their cash positions. The focal point of corporate cash management strategy is the relationship with commercial banks. Some cash balances are held at commercial banks for liquidity needs and others are held as compensating balances as payment for bank services. Because compensating balance service contracts are usually based on monthly averages, corporate treasuries can use these bank balances as a day-to-day buffer for small, unexpected variations in cash flows. For larger, more persistent cash demands, corporate treasuries arrange for lines of credit or seasonal bank loans. If the corporation is large enough, it may find that commercial paper is a less expensive source of short-term credit than borrowing from a bank.

Treasury Bills

To finance the huge national debt, the U.S. Treasury Department issues various types of debt. The most important of these is Treasury bills, which is the most widely held liquid investment. Treasury bills have virtually no default risk and little price risk because of their short-term nature, and they can be readily converted into cash because of their large and active secondary market. Thus Treasury securities are considered the ideal money market instrument.

Treasury bills are sold to investors on a *discount basis*. Because they pay no coupon interest, the interest income to the investors is the difference between the purchase price and face value of the bill. Treasury bills are issued with maturities of three months, six months, and one year and in denominations of $10,000, $15,000, $50,000, $100,000, $500,000, and $1 million. Their market is basically a wholesale market; a round lot in the interdealer market is $5 million.

Auctioning New Bills

The Treasury Department has a systematic procedure for auctioning and redeeming Treasury bills. Each Thursday, the regular weekly offering of 9l-day (13-week) and 182-day (26-week) bills is announced. Bids, or tenders, must be received by a Federal Reserve bank on the following Monday by 1:30 P.M., New York time. Bidders are apprised of awards the next morning. In addition, the Treasury Department auctions 52-week (12-month) bills on a monthly basis. The regular weekly or monthly sales provide investors with a wide variety of maturities and denominations from which to select.

Bids may be competitive or noncompetitive. Competitive bids are usually made by large investors who actively participate in money markets.

In making a *competitive bid*, the investor states the quantity of bills desired and the bid price. An investor can enter more than one competitive bid. In making a *noncompetitive bid*, the investor indicates the quantity of bills desired and agrees to pay the weighted average price of the competitive bids that are accepted. Noncompetitive bids are usually entered by individuals and small commercial banks, and all noncompetitive bids are accepted up to $1 million on both three- and six-month bills. Noncompetitive bids allow small investors who are not familiar with money market interest rate movements to purchase Treasury securities to avoid the risks of (1) bidding a price too low to receive any bills or (2) bidding a price substantially above the market equilibrium.

Book-Entry Securities

An interesting innovation in the Treasury bill market occurred in 1976 when the Treasury announced that it would begin switching the entire marketable portion of the federal debt over to *book-entry securities* in lieu of engraved pieces of paper. Thus Treasury securities owned or held by banks that are members of the Federal Reserve System would exist only in the Fed's computer memory bank. All marketable government securities (Treasury and agency) may be held in book-entry form, and the bulk of the Treasury's marketable debt is now held in this form.

Most large banks typically have several book-entry accounts at the Fed. For example, one account may be securities that the bank owns for its own account, a second book-entry account may be for securities it is safekeeping for corporate and other investors, and a third account may include securities it holds for dealers who clear transactions through the bank. The Fed's computer keeps track of the amount and types of securities a bank has in each of its accounts.

In New York City, the major banks are linked by wire, and all securities transactions among them are by wire. Thus, if Chemical Bank were to sell securities to Bankers Trust, it would make delivery by instructing the Fed to debit its Treasury bill account for the amount sold and to simultaneously credit Bankers Trust's account for the same amount.

Federal Agency Securities

Since the mid-1960s, federal agency securities have been important in the secondary money markets. They have features that make them attractive to a wide variety of investors. They have low default risk and, in many cases, well-developed secondary markets. All agency securities qualify as legal investments for financial institutions, and they are acceptable as collateral for commercial bank tax and loan accounts and as security for public deposits. They can also be used as collateral by banks for borrowing at the Federal Reserve discount window. Thus federal agency securities offer many of the advantages of regular Treasury securities and usually provide higher yields.

A federal agency is an independent federal department or corporation established by Congress and owned or underwritten by the U.S. government. Federal agency securities result from selected government lending programs. Initially these programs were designed to attract private capital to sectors of the economy where credit flows were considered to be insufficient. Housing and agriculture were traditionally the principal beneficiaries of federal credit programs. In recent years, the objectives of federal credit programs have expanded to include social and economic goals and to promote conservation and resource utilization.

Types of Federal Agencies

Exhibit 8-6 provides a list of the major government agencies authorized to issue debt. Many of them issue only long-term debt; however, as these issues approach maturity, they are traded in the money markets. With regard to short-term issues, about 25 percent of all new agency issues have an original maturity of one year or less. We shall now discuss the more important federal agencies.

The Farm Credit System.   The farm credit system (FCS) is a cooperatively owned system of banks and associations that provides credit and related services to farmers and agricultural cooperatives. The system holds about one-fourth of total farm debt in the United States. The oldest government debt-issuing agency in the system is the Federal Land Bank (FLB), created by the Federal Farm Loan Act of 1916. Today there are 12 FLBs throughout the country that make credit available to farmers to purchase and develop land and to buy farm equipment and livestock. In

Exhibit 8–6   **Selected Federal Agencies Authorized to Issue Debt**

Farm Credit Agencies	*Other Agencies*
Banks for Cooperatives	Federal Financing Bank
Federal Land Banks	Community Development Corporation
Federal Intermediate Credit Banks	Environmental Financing Authority
Housing Credit Agencies	Export-Import Bank of the United States
Federal National Mortgage Association	Small Business Administration
Government National Mortgage Association	Student Loan Marketing Association
Federal Home Loan Banks	Tennessee Valley Authority
Federal Home Loan Mortgage Corporation	Maritime Administration
Federal Housing Administration	
Farm Home Administration	
Veterans Administration	

Historically, most federal agencies were involved in directing capital flows into farming or housing. In recent years, federal agency credit programs have expanded into several other areas.

addition, farmers can obtain credit from Federal Intermediate Credit Banks (FICB), established in 1923, and from Banks for Cooperatives (Coops), organized in 1933. Originally, the federal government provided all of the capital to organize the agricultural banks. At present, most of the capital for the system is obtained from its members. Farmers borrowing from the system are required to purchase capital. When the loan is paid, the farmer can redeem the capital. The financial crisis in the farm sector during the 1980s raised concern over the riskiness of debt issued by farm credit agencies. This led to the passage of the 1985 Farm Bill, which allows Congress to provide direct federal aid to the FCS through a line of credit with the Treasury. Thus the act strengthened the market's perception of an implicit federal guarantee of agency debt in the event of default.

Housing Credit Agencies.   Another major group of federal agencies is involved in financing home construction. Foremost among these agencies is the Federal National Mortgage Association (FNMA), chartered by the federal government in 1938. FNMA is now privately owned and it retains its government credit line. FNMAs objective is to provide a secondary market for home mortgages. Also of major importance are the Federal Home Loan Banks (FHLB), created in 1932 to provide credit for savings and loans. The 12 FHLBs provide loans to member thrift institutions. Other government-sponsored agencies designed to assist the home mortgage markets are listed in Exhibit 8-6.

Other Agencies.   Examples of other agencies with power to issue securities are the Community Development Corporation (CDC), established in 1970 to help private developers finance new community development projects; the Environmental Financing Authority (EFA), established in 1972 to ensure that state and local governments can borrow funds at reasonable rates to finance waste treatment facilities; the Export-Import Bank (Eximbank), founded in 1942 to help finance trade between the United States and foreign countries; the Small Business Administration (SBA), which provides financial and managerial assistance to small business; and the Tennessee

Valley Authority (TVA), created in the mid-1930s to assist in the development of power projects and other economic undertakings in the Tennessee River Basin.

Federal Financing Bank.   In the past, most agency securities were sold through financial specialists known as *fiscal agents*. Each agency had one, usually located in New York City, whose job was to assemble a group of investment banking firms to distribute the agency's securities to retail buyers. Today this method of selling new issues is used primarily by federally sponsored agencies that issue large amounts of securities, such as the housing and farm credit agencies. Other government agencies now acquire most of their funds from the Federal Financing Bank (FFB), established in 1973 to coordinate and consolidate the federal financing activities of agencies that issue small amounts of debt or infrequently enter the money and capital markets. The goal of the FFB is to lower the borrowing cost of participating agencies. The FFB purchases the securities of participating agencies and, in turn, issues it own obligations.

Short-Term Issuers

Two types of short-term debt are sold by federally sponsored credit agencies: (1) bonds, which carry a coupon; and (2) discount notes, which are sold at a discount below par and are redeemed at their par value upon maturity. Bonds are sold periodically through fiscal agents, and advance notice of their sale is required. Discount notes do not require advance notice and can be offered by an agency on a continuous basis. The procedure is similar to the manner in which large banks issue negotiable certificates of deposit. Exhibit 8–7 shows a list of federal agencies most active in issuing short-term debt and the characteristics of that debt.

Characteristics of Agency Debt

Except for GNMA, Eximbank, and FHA debentures, agency securities are *not* guaranteed by the federal government against default. These agency securities are often referred to as *nonguaranteed agency debt*. However, some form of federal backing is implied. First, it is unlikely that the federal government would allow one of its own sponsored agencies to default. Furthermore, for some issues the Treasury

---

Exhibit 8–7   **Characteristics of Short-Term Agency Securities**

Issuer	Type	Maturities	Offering Schedule	Minimum Denomination
Farm Credit Banks	Bonds	6 and 9 months	Monthly	$ 5,000
	Discount notes	5 to 270 days	Daily	50,000
Federal Home Loan Banks	Discount notes	30 to 270 days	Daily	100,000
Federal National Mortgage Association	Discount notes	30 to 270 days	Daily	5,000

The majority of the federal agencies most active in issuing short-term debt offer securities daily with maturities typically in the three- to six-month range.

Department and the Federal Reserve are authorized to purchase securities in the event that market support is needed. For other issues, the agency can borrow from the Treasury up to certain limits.

The marketability of agency securities varies with each type of security. The securities of the Federal Land Banks, the Federal Intermediate Credit Banks, Banks for Cooperatives, the Federal Home Loan Banks, and Federal National Mortgage Association have well-established secondary markets. In recent years, the yield on agency securities has been 3 to 20 basis points above the yield on similar Treasury securities (100 basis points equal 1 percent). Though some of the yield spread difference results from the agency securities' higher default risk, most is attributable to their lower marketability. Yet this may not always be the case. In 1985, for example, because of the high default rate on farm loans, there was concern that the Farm Credit Banks might default on securities they had issued to finance their farm-lending activities. As a result, Farm Credit securities traded as much as 50 basis points above equivalent Treasuries.

Negotiable Certificates of Deposit

A negotiable CD is simply a bank time deposit that is negotiable. Because the receipt is negotiable, it can be traded any number of times in the secondary market before its maturity. The denominations of CDs range from $100,000 to $10 million.[1] However, few negotiable CDs are denominated in less than $1 million because smaller denominations, although technically negotiable, are not as marketable and sell at concession prices. The normal round-lot trading unit among dealers is $1 million.

Negotiable CDs typically have maturities of one to four months. There is also a market for six-month CDs, but beyond that maturity the volume is small and there is not an active secondary market. Most negotiable CDs, regardless of where the issuer is located, are payable in New York City in Federal Funds. This eliminates the problem of customers having to ship securities out of New York City to be presented to the issuing bank for payment. A negotiable CD for the Chemical Bank of New York City is shown in Exhibit 8–8.

History of the CD Market

The idea of a certificate of deposit is not really new. CDs, in one form or another, were used by banks early in the 1900s to attract consumer and business deposits. However, before 1960, CDs were rarely issued in negotiable form. In February 1961, Citibank announced that it would issue negotiable CDs in large denominations and that major government securities dealers had agreed to make a secondary market in them. Other money center banks and dealers quickly followed Citibank's lead, paving the way for what proved to be a major innovation in the manner in which today's large banks manage their liquidity. One reason for the development of negotiable CDs was the long-term trend of declining demand deposits at large banks. Corporate treasurers

---

[1] The Federal Reserve System defines and reports negotiable certificates of deposit as those with denominations of $100,000 or greater.

PEOPLE
& EVENTS

Zero Coupon but Not Zero Risk

Zero coupon bonds are bonds that make no coupon payments; hence, their coupon rate is "zero." Of course they do pay interest, but it is all paid when the bond matures. Zero coupon investors buy these bonds at big discounts, then at maturity collect the full $1,000 face amount at once. For example, a $1,000, 20-year zero coupon Treasury bond with an 8.5 percent yield sells for $189.22. Investors in these bonds will get back more than five times the amount of their original investment. This feature led one Wall Street analyst to compare zero coupon bonds to fungus: "They don't make noise, they just multiply and grow; then one day you look in and say: Goodness, look at the size of this!"

Zero coupon bonds were first introduced in 1982 by Merrill Lynch and Salomon Brothers, and they were an immediate hit with investors. The reason is that because the bonds have no coupons, the interest earned on them is automatically reinvested at the bond's promised yield throughout the bond's life. Thus zero coupon bonds have no reinvestment risk—the possibility that coupon income might be reinvested at a lower rate. In contrast, investors in coupon bonds get periodic interest payments they have to reinvest. Investors suffer heavy transaction costs to reinvest coupons and, if they are reinvested below the bonds' promised yields, investors take a real bath on the bonds' realized yields.

The bad news about zeros is that if they are sold before maturity investors are subject to considerable price risk. That is, while their maturity value is cast in stone, the market price of zeros fluctuates wildly for given changes in interest rates. If interest rates unexpectedly rise, the drop in price of a 30-year zero coupon bond is three times that of a bond whose coupon rate is near the current market yield. A further problem with zero coupon bonds is that the interest income on them is taxable; Uncle Sam taxes the bondholder on the interest that theoretically accrues to the investor annually. Thus each year you own the bond you must pay taxes on interest income you will not receive until maturity.

Should you buy a zero coupon bond? It depends. Zero coupon bonds are best suited to situations in which you have a specific holding-period target, such as a retirement date, and where the interest earned is tax-exempt, as it is in IRA accounts or with municipal securities.

---

were becoming increasingly sophisticated in managing their cash balances. They were minimizing demand deposit balances and investing these funds in safe, income-generating money market instruments, such as Treasury bills and commercial paper. Large New York City banks, which are the principal banks for most large corporations, experienced substantial reductions in deposits. Negotiable CDs were designed to recapture lost corporate deposits by allowing commercial banks to be competitive for short-term funds.

The CD Market

The rate paid on a CD is negotiated between the issuing bank and the buyer. The underlying factors that determine the rate are current money market conditions, rates paid by competing banks on their CDs, yield on other similar short-term instruments,

Exhibit 8–8   **Negotiable Certificate of Deposit**

Negotiable Certificate of Deposit

CHEMICAL BANK

New York, N.Y. _____ July 1, 1992 _____ No. 159109 $\begin{smallmatrix}1\text{-}12\\210\end{smallmatrix}$

This certifies that there has been deposited with this Bank the sum of

2,000,000.00 _____ dollars

payable on ___ July 31, 1992 ___

to the order ___ of XYZ Corporation ___

together with interest thereon at the rate of ___ 10.25 ___ per cent per annum (calculated on the basis of a 360 day year) from the

date hereof to maturity only, upon return of this certificate, properly endorsed.

No interest will be paid on this deposit after its maturity.

Textbook Sample _____

Authorized Signature

Chemical Bank of New York is one of the nation's largest money-center banks. CDs are attractive to investors because of their safety and high marketability.

and issue characteristics, such as the default risk and marketability of the CD. Banks post an "official" CD rate that serves as an approximate guide to their actual rate. A bank will sell its CDs to any buyer at the posted rate, which is typically a bit below the rate charged in the secondary market. The implication for this apparent anomaly between the posted and actual rate charged is that commercial banks write CDs for their preferred customers at rates above those posted. However, if a bank is eager to attract funds, it may adjust its posted rate above that of other banks and, in fact, a bit above the secondary market.

Large "prime-name" banks, mostly located in New York City and Chicago, are usually able to issue CDs at lower interest rates than smaller regional banks. The reason for this *tiering* of interest rates is the lower default risk and greater marketability of prime-name banks' CDs. This difference is also justified by past federal agency handling of failing banks. The FDIC does not allow large banks to fail (most failures are small banks). A failing large bank is usually merged with another bank, and uninsured depositors rarely lose any money. In general, regional banks pay a premium of 5 to 25 basis points to sell their CDs.[2]

The primary purchasers of CDs are corporate treasurers interested in maximizing the return of their firms' excess funds while maintaining the liquidity and safety of their principal. The existence of a large secondary market is one of the major reasons prime-name banks can attract a large quantity of corporate funds. The secondary market allows corporate treasurers to enter the market at any time and on either

[2] This rate spread varies and can be reversed if the financial conditions of banks change relative to other banks. For example, in 1975, when New York City was on the verge of defaulting on its bonds, the major New York City banks, which had substantial holdings of New York City bonds, had to pay rates above those paid by the major Chicago banks.

side—selling when they want to raise cash quickly or realize profits (capital gains), or buying when they want maturities shorter than can be acquired in the primary market. Surveys by the Federal Reserve System indicate that between 70 and 80 percent of CDs are purchased by corporate customers.

Commercial Paper

Commercial paper is a short-term, unsecured promissory note typically issued by large corporations to finance short-term working capital needs. In recent years, some firms have also used commercial paper as a source of interim financing for major construction projects The basic reason firms issue commercial paper is to achieve interest rate savings as an alternative to bank borrowing. Because commercial paper is an unsecured promissory note, the issuer pledges no assets to protect the investor in the event of default. As a result, only large, well-known firms of the highest credit standing (lowest default risk) can issue commercial paper. Exhibit 8–9 presents a survey of commercial paper issuers, indicating that nearly two-thirds of all issuers are either industrial firms or public utilities.

The commercial paper market is almost entirely a wholesale money market. Most commercial paper is sold in denominations of $100,000, $250,000, $500,000, and $1 million. Maturities on commercial paper range from 1 to 270 days. Longer maturities are infrequent because issues with maturities greater than 270 days must comply with the costly and time-consuming Securities and Exchange Commission (SEC) registration and prospectus requirements.

History of Commercial Paper

Commercial paper is one of the oldest money market instruments; its use can be traced back to the early 1800s. Early issuers were mainly nonfinancial business firms,

Exhibit 8–9	**Survey of Industry Groups Issuing Commercial Paper**

Industry Grouping	Percentage of Total
Industrial	42.0
Public utilities	21.9
Finance	17.6
Bank holding	13.6
Mortage finance	1.0
Insurance	2.8
Transportation	1.1
Total	100.0

The largest issuers of commercial paper are industrial firms. Banks can also issue commercial paper through their bank holding companies.

Source: Moody's Bond Survey, 1987.

such as textile mills, railroads, and tobacco companies. Most early paper was placed by dealers for a fee. The principal buyers were commercial banks. Beginning in the 1920s, the nature of the commercial paper market began to change. The introduction of the automobile and other consumer durables created a demand by consumers for short-term personal loans. This led to the rapid growth of consumer finance companies that needed funds to finance consumer purchases. The first large consumer finance company to issue commercial paper was General Motors Acceptance Corporation (GMAC), which was established to finance the purchase of General Motors' automobiles. An innovation by GMAC was to sell its paper directly to investors rather than placing it through commercial paper dealers.

The Commercial Paper Market

Historically, commercial banks were the major purchasers of commercial paper. In the early 1950s, many other firms began purchasing commercial paper because of its combination of low default risk, short maturity, and relatively high yields. Today the major investors in commercial paper are large insurance companies, nonfinancial business firms, bank trust departments, and state and local government pension funds. Commercial banks still purchase commercial paper for their own accounts, but they are not a dominant force in the market. Commercial banks remain important to the operation of the commercial paper market, however, because they act as agents in issuing paper, hold it for safekeeping, and facilitate payment in Federal Funds.

Currently, 600 to 800 firms issue significant quantities of commercial paper. The precise amount issued varies, depending on economic and market conditions, the number being smaller during high-interest periods and greater when money is more readily available. Most of these firms sell their paper through dealers. There are about 30 commercial paper dealers, most of whom are located in New York City. In addition, in recent years large money center banks have gained expanded powers and are now allowed to underwrite and trade in commercial paper. Dealers maintain an inventory of the commercial paper they sell and stand ready to buy paper back from their customers at the going market rate plus a $\frac{1}{8}$ of 1 percent commission fee. Also, issuing firms will repurchase their own commercial paper within limits. Thus there is a secondary market for commercial paper but it is not nearly as liquid as that for negotiable bank CDs, because (1) commercial paper is much more heterogeneous than bank CDs and consequently more difficult to actively trade, and (2) most purchasers of commercial paper hold it until maturity and do not require a secondary market. Dealers report that only about 2 percent of all commercial paper is redeemed prior to maturity.

Credit Ratings.   Both Moody's Investors Service and Standard & Poor's (S&P) rate commercial paper. From highest to lowest, paper ratings run P-1, P-2, and P-3 for Moody's, and A-1, A-2, and A-3 for S&P. During the 1980s the average distribution for the three quality gradations was 75 percent in Grade 1, 24 percent in Grade 2, and 1 percent in Grade 3. For practical purposes, it is difficult to sell commercial paper with a Grade 3 rating, especially during hard economic times.

Backup Lines of Credit.   In most cases, issuers back up their commercial paper issue with a line of credit from a commercial bank. Even though the maturity on commercial paper is short, there is always the risk that an issuer might not be able to pay off or roll over the maturing paper. Rolling over paper means that the issuer sells new commercial paper to get the funds to retire maturing paper. Therefore, backup lines ensure a source of funds in the event that the firm experiences a cash flow problem or credit market conditions become tight. From a practical standpoint, most investors will not buy commercial paper unless it is backed by a bank line. Banks receive a fee for providing backup lines.

Placement.   Firms issuing commercial paper can sell it either directly to investors using their own sales force or indirectly using commercial paper dealers. At present, about 80 firms sell their commercial paper through direct placement. Most of these are large finance companies and bank holding companies, their volume accounting for about 60 percent of all commercial paper sold. Some of the major finance companies issuing paper directly are General Motors Acceptance Corporation, Sears, Ford Motors Credit, and Household International.

The major incentive for direct placement is that the issuer is able to save the $\frac{1}{8}$ of 1 percent dealer's commission. For example, if a firm places $100 million in commercial paper through a dealer, the commission cost would be $125,000. However, to achieve the $125,000 savings, the issuer must maintain a small sales force—usually three to six employees plus a manager. Thus most firms find that it pays to deal directly when the average annual amount outstanding is somewhere around $200 million.

Banker's Acceptances

A banker's acceptance is a time draft drawn on and accepted by a commercial bank. Time drafts are orders to pay a specified amount of money to the bearer on a given date. When drafts are accepted, a bank unconditionally promises to pay to the holder the face amount of the draft at maturity, even if the bank encounters difficulty collecting from its customers. It is the act of the bank substituting its creditworthiness for that of the issuer that makes banker's acceptances marketable instruments. Exhibit 8–10 shows a banker's acceptance.

Most banker's acceptances arise in international transactions between exporters and importers of different countries. In these transactions the accepting bank can be either a U.S. or a foreign bank, and the transaction can be denominated in any currency. However, the U.S. secondary market consists primarily of dollar acceptance financing in which the acceptor is a U.S. bank and the draft is denominated in dollars.

History of Banker's Acceptances

The history of banker's acceptances dates back as far as the twelfth century. Early acceptances were used primarily in Europe to finance international trade. In the United States, they were not widely used until the establishment of the Federal Reserve System in 1913. At that time the Federal Reserve wanted to develop a dollar-based acceptance market to enhance the role of New York City as a center for international trade and finance.

Until the 1960s, banker's acceptances were not a major money market instrument. Their use depended on world economic conditions and the extent of U.S. foreign

Exhibit 8-10 **Banker's Acceptance**

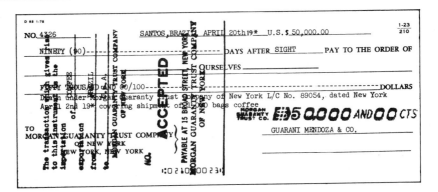

A time draft does not become a banker's acceptance until it is stamped "accepted" by a bank. The acceptance means that the draft is now a liability of the accepting bank when it comes due.

Source: Financing of Exports and Imports (New York: Morgan Guaranty Trust Company of New York, 1980).

trade. Beginning in the 1960s, with the tremendous expansion of international trade, the volume of acceptances grew rapidly. Today foreign banks and nonbank financial institutions are the most important investors in the banker's acceptance market, regarding banker's acceptances as a safe and liquid investment. For foreign holders, the income from acceptances is not subject to federal income tax, and thus foreign investors realize high yields. The next largest investors in acceptances are the issuing banks themselves. Typically, banks hold about 30 percent of all acceptances and about 85 percent of their holdings consist of acceptances drawn on themselves.

Creating a Banker's Acceptance

To illustrate how banker's acceptances are created, the following example will be helpful. The sequence of events for our transaction can be followed in Exhibit 8–11. Assume that a U.S. importer wishes to finance the importation of Colombian coffee. Furthermore, the American importer wishes to pay for the coffee in 90 days. To obtain financing, the importer has an American bank write an irrevocable letter of credit for the amount of the sale, which is sent to the Colombian exporter. The letter specifies the details of the shipment and authorizes the Colombian exporter to draw a time draft for the sale price on the importer's bank. When the coffee is shipped, the exporter draws the draft on the American bank and then discounts the draft at a local bank, thereby receiving immediate payment for the coffee. The exporter's bank then sends the time draft, along with the proper shipping documents, to the American bank. The American bank accepts the draft by stamping "accepted" on its face and signs the instrument. The the bank either returns the stamped time draft (acceptance) to the exporter's bank or immediately pays the exporter's bank for it at a discounted price reflecting the time value of money during the wating period. If the American bank pays the exporter's bank for the acceptance, it can then either hold the accepted draft

Exhibit 8–11   The Sequence of a Banker's Acceptance Transaction

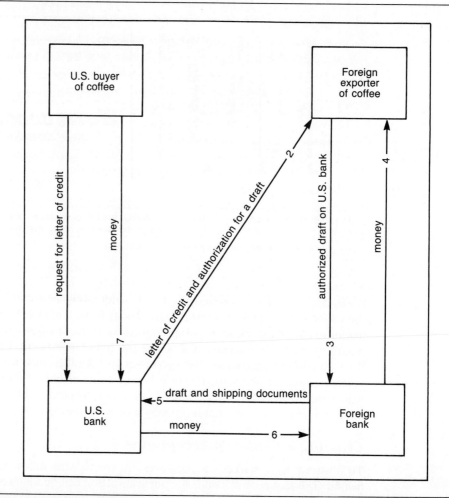

This exhibit shows a possible sequence for creating a banker's acceptance. However, there are many ways to create acceptances, and to do so requires a great deal of specialized knowledge on the part of the accepting bank.

as an investment or sell it in the open market as a source of funds. When the draft matures, the American importer is responsible for paying the accepting bank. If for some reason the importer fails to pay, the accepting bank has legal recourse to collect from the Colombian exporter.

The advantages of banker's acceptances in international trade are apparent from our simplified example. First, the exporter receives money promptly and avoids delays that could arise in international shipping. Second, the exporter is shielded from foreign exchange risk because a local bank pays in domestic funds. Third, the exporter does not have to examine the creditworthiness of the American firm because a large, well-known bank has guaranteed payment for the merchandise. Thus it is not surprising that banker's acceptances are used primarily for international transactions.

The Market for Banker's Acceptances

Creating a banker's acceptance requires a great deal of specialized knowledge on the part of the accepting bank. Consequently, there are only about 170 institutions worldwide that have specialized staff members who are knowledgeable about the banker's acceptance market. Domestically, the majority of all acceptances originate in New York City, Chicago, and San Francisco. The denomination of banker's acceptances depends on the originating transaction, which may be large or small. However, banker's acceptances trade in round lots, with $100,000 and $500,000 being the most common transaction sizes. Banks asked to finance large transactions will generally divide the amount into several drafts of $500,000. For small transactions, the bank may combine various drafts into a large, single, marketable draft. The maturities of acceptances are commonly 30, 60, or 90 days, but drafts may be acquired for any number of days up to a legal maximum of 180. The default risk involved is quite low. During the 65 years that banker's acceptances have been traded in the United States, no investor has ever suffered a loss of principal.

The secondary market for banker's acceptances is created as banks sell accepted drafts. Currently, there are 14 primary dealers in banker's acceptances who make an ongoing market in this instrument. The major dealers include most of the major Treasury securities dealers, some firms that specialize in banker's acceptances, and several large banks. In addition, there are a number of other banks and nonbank dealers who trade banker's acceptances on a less active basis. All dealers trade the acceptances generated by the major banks, and some specialize in making markets for selected groups of regional banks. Banker's acceptances are at least as marketable as commercial paper or bank negotiable CDs.

Federal Funds

The market for Federal Funds is one of the most important financial markets in the United States. It provides the means by which commercial banks and a limited number of other financial institutions trade large amounts of liquid funds with one another for periods as short as one day. The Federal Funds rate is of particular interest because (1) it measures the return on the most liquid of all financial assets; (2) it is closely related to the conduct of monetary policy; and (3) it measures directly the availability of excess reserves within the banking system, which, in turn, influences commercial banks' decisions concerning loans to businesses, consumers, and other borrowers.

Traditionally, the Federal Funds market has been described as one in which commercial banks borrow and lend excess reserve balances held at the Federal Reserve. These transactions make up the majority of all Federal Funds transactions. They are essentially one-day unsecured loans. The typical unit of trade is $1 million or more. Some banks will trade smaller amounts but will almost never trade in less than $500,000. This type of transaction is also an extremely efficient means of transferring

DID YOU KNOW?

The Collapse of ESM: Life in the Fast Lane

A $1 million-plus yacht, two airplanes, three Mercedes, two Jaguars, and a dozen polo ponies were among the assets the court seized from Ronnie R. Ewton in March 1985. Why? Because Ewton was an owner and the manager of ESM Government Securities Inc., whose financial collapse had caused $315 million in losses to 50 thrifts and municipalities. What was ESM and how did it cause such losses?

ESM was a small government securities dealer— named for its owners Ronnie R. Ewton, Robert C. Seneca, and George C. Mead—that opened in October 1976. The Fort Lauderdale, Florida, firm bought and sold securities and repurchase agreements, dealing with banks, brokerage firms, thrifts, municipalities, and individuals. To the casual observer, the firm appeared to be extremely profitable. Its top officials were living in grand style, drawing salaries of $300,000 to $500,000. But on March 4, 1985, the SEC shut down ESM, alleging fraud and claiming that the firm couldn't pay its customers the millions of dollars owed on repurchase agreements.

Normally, repurchase agreements are safe. In a "repo," an investor buys securities from a dealer who pledges to repurchase them a few days later at a higher price. But the key to safety for investors is making sure the securities purchased are available as collateral should the dealer not make good on the promise. ESM offered a high return to customers, but the collateral was held with a third party. SEC investigators discovered that ESM had pledged the same securities to several customers. Thus the customers' loans to ESM, in the form of repos, were secured not by collateral but by "thin air."

ESM had been losing money for seven years, but it had kept afloat by increasing the dollar volume of its repurchase agreements to generate new cash. Management had also been cooking the books to disguise the firm's losses. By the time it was shut down, ESM had accumulated red ink of $200 million. ESM had been able to get away with this scheme for so many years because of the lack of regulation of securities dealers.

Until the government securities industry becomes more closely regulated, customers should be cautious in trading with smaller firms. After all, a few yachts, cars, and airplanes can't compare with the hundreds of millions lost—not to mention the chain reaction of financial damage triggered by these losses. The remnants of life in the fast lane are cold comfort to creditors and depositors left behind.

or reallocating excess reserves of banks with surpluses to banks with temporary deficiencies. In most cases, the only step necessary to arrange the funds transfer is a telephone call or wire transfer. No physical transfer of funds occurs.

The recent growth and change in the Federal Funds market makes the previous description overly simplified. Today, many active participants in Federal Funds do not hold balances at the Federal Reserve, such as commercial banks that are not members of the Federal Reserve.

A more appropriate definition of the Federal Funds transaction is that of an overnight loan (one day) that is settled in *immediately available funds*. Immediately available funds are defined as (1) deposit liabilities of Federal Reserve banks and (2) liabilities of commercial banks that may be transferred or withdrawn during a business day. The liabilities of commercial banks include a portion of their demand

and time deposits as well as liabilities that are used much like demand deposits but that are classified separately for regulatory reasons. For example, a growing portion of the Federal Funds market has consisted of large banks borrowing correspondent balances from smaller banks. At one time, these correspondent balances earned no interest and were held as payment for services. Today small banks intentionally accumulate large balances to sell the excess to the correspondent for investment in the Federal Funds market. The unit amounts are usually somewhat less than needed for open market Federal Funds transactions. However, the large bank accumulates these balances from its various smaller respondent banks to reach trading-lot size. The correspondent earns a fee for this service.

Nonbank financial institutions have also become increasingly active in the market for immediately available funds. However, only a limited number of institutions are in a position to borrow in this fashion. These institutions may engage in certain types of immediate fund transactions because of federal regulations governing commercial bank funds that are subject to reserve requirements. This group includes federal agencies, savings and loan associations, mutual savings banks, branches of foreign banks, and government securities dealers. For example, a savings and loan association may lend Federal Funds to a foreign bank. The emergence of these institutions has dramatically changed the structure of the Federal Funds market. Commercial banks now borrow Federal Funds from a wide array of institutions, rather than just reallocating reserves among member banks. In recent years, the daily outstanding borrowings by member banks in the Federal Funds market have approached $50 million, or about 40 percent more than the total reserves in the banking system.

The Federal Funds rate is influenced by various special factors that cause it to fluctuate more widely in the short run than other market rates. One important factor is banks' heavy use of Federal Funds to meet their legal reserve requirements. Reserve requirements must be met weekly on a Wednesday. Banks that are deficient at the end of a statement period generally enter the Federal Funds market for reserves (or borrow from the discount window). Thus the Federal Funds rate tends to rise or fall sharply on Wednesday, depending on the availability of reserves in the banking system.

Repurchase Agreements

Closely associated with the functioning of the Federal Funds market is the negotiation of repurchase agreements (RP). A repurchase agreement consists of the sale of a short-term security (collateral) with the condition that, after a period of time, the original seller will buy it back at a predetermined price. The collateral used most frequently is U.S. Treasury or agency securities. However, it is possible to use any of the better-known money market instruments. This dual transaction, which in market jargon is called a *repo*, has developed into a meaningful money market instrument in its own right. Repurchase agreements are most commonly made for one day or for very short terms. In recent years, however, the market has expanded to include a substantial volume of one- to three-month (and even longer) transactions. The smallest customary denomination for an RP is $1 million. As with other money market instruments, transactions are settled in Federal Funds.

An RP Transaction

An illustration of a typical RP transaction will help clarify our understanding of this money market instrument. Suppose that a corporate treasurer determines that the firm has $1 million excess cash for a two-day period. The treasurer, wishing to earn interest on the funds, arranges to purchase $1 million worth of government securities from a bank with an accompanying agreement that the bank will repurchase the securities in two days. The interest paid to the corporation is the difference between the purchase and repurchase price of the collateralized securities. The transactions for both the bank and the corporation (T-account entries) are as follows:

	Bank		**Corporate Customer**	
Before RP		$1 million deposit	$1 million deposit	
Creation of RP		−$1 million deposit +$1 million RP borrowing	−$1 million deposit +$1 million collateralized loan (RP)	
Completion of RP agreement		+$1 million deposit	+$1 million deposit	
		−$1 million RP borrowing	−$1 million loan (RP)	

Notice that from the standpoint of the temporary seller of securities, repurchase agreements represent a source of funds; for the buyer they represent an interest-earning investment. As our example illustrates, a commercial bank may buy idle funds from a corporate customer by selling Treasury securities on a repurchase basis. Or a commercial bank can sell immediately available funds to a dealer in U.S. government securities by purchasing the securities on a repurchase agreement. The dealer thereby finances his or her security inventory with funds purchased by the bank, and the bank receives interest income from the dealer at money market rates of return. Repurchase agreements may also be entered into by nonfinancial corporations, insurance companies, state and local governments, and the Federal Reserve.

The unique feature that distinguishes repurchase agreements from other money market instruments is that they may be used to shorten the actual maturity of a security to meet the needs of the borrower and lender. For example, an investor may wish to invest funds for a very short period of time, say for three days. A Treasury bill maturing in three days could be purchased, but often a three-day bill is not available. A longer-maturity bill could be purchased, held for three days, and then resold in the secondary market. However, this alternative involves price risk.[3] A three-day RP provides the investor with a money market instrument with precisely the needed maturity, thus eliminating all price risk.

---

[3] If interest rates rise during the three-day interval, the investor will suffer a capital loss.

RPs are also used by the Federal Reserve in conducting monetary policy. When the Federal Reserve wishes to adjust the reserve positions of commercial banks on a long-term basis, it usually engages in direct open-market purchases of Treasury securities. However, when the adjustments are intended to be temporary, the Federal Reserve often employs repurchase agreement transactions with dealers or banks. The maturities of repurchase agreements used by the Federal Reserve are quite short, never in excess of 15 days.

The rate charged in repurchase agreements is negotiated between the buyer and seller of funds, but it must be competitive with other money market rates. Transactions are arranged by telephone either directly between the two parties supplying and acquiring funds or through a small group of market specialists, usually government securities dealers. They arrange a RP transaction with one party to acquire funds and a reverse RP with another party to supply funds. The specialists earn a profit by acquiring funds at a lower cost than that at which the funds are supplied.

The Interrelationship of Money Market Interest Rates

Although the various money market instruments have their individual differences, they serve as close substitutes for each other in investment portfolios. For this reason, the interest rates on different money market instruments are usually highly correlated with one another and tend to fluctuate closely together over time. For short periods, the traditional spreads between some money market instruments may get out of line. However, these temporary divergences set off forces that restore the rates to their normal spread. For example, if circumstances are such that corporations issue unusually large amounts of commercial paper, the commercial paper rate may rise relative to other money market rates. Sophisticated traders, noting the abnormal differential, will adjust their portfolios by selling other money market instruments, such as Treasury bills, and purchasing commercial paper. This action will cause commercial paper rates to fall and Treasury bill rates to rise until the normal or usual rate relationship is restored. This process is known as *interest rate arbitrage*. The action of arbitrageurs ensures the comovement of money market interest rates.

Money market rates can also be affected by what happens in the stock market. For example, during the stock market crashes of October 1987 and 1989, many investors liquidated their stock market holdings in favor of safer investments in money market instruments, which have lower default risk and price risk.

Exhibit 8-12 shows the yield of money market instruments over time. As expected, there is a high degree of correlation between the rates in money market securities. Also notice that the yield on Treasury securities is the lowest of all money market securities because they have the lowest default risk and are the most marketable of any security.

Globalizing Financial Markets

The process of globalizing financial markets has been taking place for some time. U.S. banks began developing worldwide branching systems beginning in the 1960s. U.S. securities firms also began to build up their operations abroad, first in London in the Eurobond market, then later in other geographic locations in Europe and Asia.

Exhibit 8–12   **The Comovement of Selected Money Market Interest Rates.**

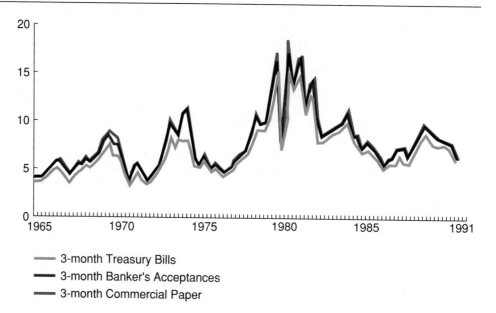

──── 3-month Treasury Bills
──── 3-month Banker's Acceptances
──── 3-month Commercial Paper

This exhibit illustrates the high degree of correlation among the yields of various money market instruments.

Foreign banks and, later on, securities firms began opening offices in the United States. Trading in individual markets has also globalized. For example, in the 1970s, the foreign exchange market became a 24-hour market, with major international and domestic bank and brokerage houses dealing with each other in offices throughout the world. In the 1980s the market for U.S. government securities became a 24-hour market, with foreign investors buying and selling huge volumes of Treasury bills, notes, and bonds. Primary dealers of U.S. securities have opened offices in London, Tokyo, and Zurich to accommodate the burgeoning business. Today, Eurodollar deposits, Eurocurrencies, Euronotes, Eurobonds, and Eurocommercial paper trade in markets that are becoming increasingly globalized. These and other financial products sold on a worldwide basis will be discussed in detail in Chapter 12.

Summary

The money market consists of a collection of markets in which short-term credit obligations are bought and sold with little chance of financial loss. The primary economic function of money markets is to provide an efficient means by which economic units may adjust their liquidity. To reduce investors' financial risk, money market instruments have certain common characteristics: (1) low default risk, (2) short term to maturity, and (3) high marketability.

Commercial banks are the largest single buyer and seller of money market instruments, participating in almost every market. The banks' dominant role in the money markets is the result of their continuous reserve adjustments necessitated by the short nature of their liabilities, legal reserve requirements, and wide variations in loan demand. The Federal Reserve is the most important market participant, because it conducts monetary policy through open market operations. Money market dealers' primary function is to help make markets by standing ready to buy and sell securities from their inventories. Corporations use money markets to invest temporarily idle cash, and if a corporation is large enough, it may be able to sell commercial paper as a source of funds.

The most important money market instrument is Treasury securities, which have virtually no default risk and the largest and most active secondary market of any market instrument. U.S. government agency securities are a close substitute for Treasury securities. Negotiable certificates of deposit are unsecured liabilities of commercial banks. Commercial paper is a short-term, unsecured liability of large corporations. Banker's acceptances, which are time drafts drawn on and accepted by a commercial bank, are used primarily in foreign trade transactions. Federal Funds transactions are overnight loans that are settled in immediately available funds. Repurchase agreements involve the sale of a short-term security with the condition that, after a period of time, the original seller will buy it back.

Questions

1. What is the economic reason that money markets exist? Explain how commercial banks, business firms, and governmental units transact in the money markets.
2. What are the three characteristics of money market instruments? Why must a financial claim possess these characteristics to function as a money market instrument?
3. Why are money markets classed as wholesale markets? Why are small borrowers and lenders excluded from direct participation in the money markets?
4. Explain why the Federal Reserve System has no liquidity problem yet is a major factor in the money markets.
5. How are Treasury bills and federal agency securities different? What difference primarily explains the yield differential between the two securities?
6. Explain the reason for the two-tiered market for negotiable CDs. Why are small banks unable to issue negotiable CDs?
7. Explain why negotiable CDs were developed by large New York City banks in the early 1960s. How did the development of negotiable CDs ultimately affect bank liquidity management and lending practices?
8. Explain why businesses issue commercial paper. Why has the dollar volume of commercial paper issued increased so dramatically since the mid-1960s?
9. Describe the steps in a typical banker's acceptance transaction. Why is the banker's acceptance form of financing ideal in foreign transactions?
10. Explain how repurchase agreement transactions provide short-term loans to businesses. Show the T-accounts for such a transaction.

Selected References

Becketti, Sean, and Gordon H. Sellon, Jr. "Has Financial Market Volatility Increased?" *Economic Review*. Federal Reserve Bank of Kansas City, June 1989, pp. 17–30.
Increased interest rate volatility has increased interest rate risk to investors. This article examines whether interest rates have become more volatile in recent years.

Cook, Timothy Q. *Instruments of the Money Market*. Federal Reserve Bank of Richmond, 1986.
An excellent booklet, available free from the Federal Reserve Bank of Richmond, that describes each money market instrument in detail—the instrument characteristics, the buyer and seller, regulations, and historical perspective.

First Boston Corporation. *Handbook of Securities of the United States Government and Federal Agencies*. New York, biannually.
A booklet describing the characteristics of each money market investment.

Furlong, Frederick T., and John M. Nielson. "FSC: At the Crossroad Again." *Weekly Letter*. Federal Reserve Bank of San Francisco, October 16, 1987.
Examines the effect of the 1985 Farm Bill on the Farm Credit System (FCS); the bill allowed Congress to provide direct federal aid to the FCS.

Hurley, Evelyn M. "The Commercial Paper Market Since the Mid-Seventies." *Federal Reserve Bulletin*, June 1982, pp. 327–344.
An excellent overview that describes the operation and participants of the commercial paper market.

Jensen, Frederich, and Patrick M. Parkinson. "Recent Developments in the Banker's Acceptance Market." *Federal Reserve Bulletin*, January 1986, pp. 1–12.
An analysis of the rapid expansion of the banker's acceptance market through the 1970s and into the 1980s and the reason for its subsequent contraction in the mid-1980s.

Lamfalvssy, Alexandre. "Globalization of Financial Markets: International Supervisory and Regulatory Issues." *Economic Review*. Federal Reserve Bank of Kansas City, January 1989, pp. 3–8.
In recent years financial markets have become internationalized. This article examines some of the implications for regulators.

Lumpkin, Stephen A. "Repurchase and Reverse Repurchase Agreements." *Economic Review*. Federal Reserve Bank of Richmond, January/February 1987, pp. 15–23.
The article provides a good overview of how the repo market works and the factors that influenced the growth and development of the market.

McCauley, Robert N., and Lauren A. Hargraves. "Eurocommercial Paper and U.S. Commercial Paper: Converging Money Markets?" *Quarterly Review*. Federal Reserve Bank of New York, Autumn 1987, pp. 24–25.
The article examines the internationalization of the commercial paper market.

Pardee, Scott E. "Internationalization of Financial Markets." *Economic Review*. Federal Reserve Bank of Kansas City, February 1987, pp. 3–7.
The article discusses how and why financial markets are becoming internationalized.

Rosengren, Eric S. "Is There a Need for Regulation in the Government Security Market?" *New England Economic Review*. Federal Reserve Bank of Boston, September/October 1986, pp. 29–40.
The numerous highly publicized bankruptcies in the government securities market in the 1980s have raised the question of whether regulation is needed for this market.

Stevens, E. J. "Seeking Safety." *Economic Commentary*. Federal Reserve Bank of Cleveland, April 15, 1987.
Analyzes the failures of government securities firms and the reasons for the passage of the Government Security Act of 1986.

Stigum, Marcia, and Frank J. Fabozzi. *The Dow Jones–Irwin Guide to Bond and Money Market Instruments.* **Homewood, IL: Dow Jones–Irwin, 1987.**

A comprehensive and authoritative book on bond and money market investments.

Walter, John R. "Short-Term Municipal Securities." *Economic Review.* **Federal Reserve Bank of Richmond, November/December 1986, pp. 25–34.**

Discusses the short-term municipal securities markets such as revenue anticipation notes and tax anticipation notes, which in recent years have become important instruments in the money market.

Zimmerman, Jonathan C., and Jonathan A. Neuberger. "Interest Rate Competition." *Weekly Letter.* **Federal Reserve Bank of San Francisco, July 27, 1990, pp. 1–3.**

This article examines the interest rate competition between money market funds and other financial institutions like commercial banks.

Capital Markets

Suppose that this morning you buy a corporate investment-grade bond, rated by Moody's as Baa or better. Suppose also that the issuing corporation is taken over this afternoon. Be sure to be sitting down tomorrow morning when you read the financial section and learn that your bond has been reclassified, overnight, to a speculative grade and that the firm's president has been given a three-year "golden parachute" vacation in the Bahamas for quitting the firm.

The previous chapter discussed money market instruments that have minimal financial risk. These instruments are reasonably homogeneous and are held by economic units as a means of adjusting liquidity. This chapter, in contrast, discusses capital market instruments whose terms and risks vary substantially.

Capital market instruments are defined as long-term financial instruments with an original maturity of greater than one year. As the name implies, the proceeds from the sale of capital market instruments are usually invested in assets of a more permanent nature, such as industrial plants, equipment, buildings, and inventory. This chapter begins with a discussion of the purpose of capital markets and capital market efficiency. Then the focus turns to the markets for corporate bonds, Eurobonds, state and local government bonds (including tax-exempt securities), financial guarantees in debt markets, U.S. government and agency securities, and equity securities.

Purpose and Functions of the Capital Markets

Individuals own real assets in order to produce income and wealth. Thus the owner of a machine hopes to profit from the sale of the products the machine turns out, and the owner of a factory hopes to earn a return from the goods produced there. Similarly, owners of apartments, office buildings, warehouses, and other tangible assets hope to earn a stream of future income by using their resources to provide services either directly to final consumers or indirectly by helping make future production possible. Real goods expected to generate a future stream of returns are called *capital goods*; they are the stock of assets used in production.

Issuers of Capital Market Claims

Economic units such as corporations or governments buy capital assets because they will aid in future production. However, the economic units may be unable or unwilling to provide the full amount of funds to purchase the capital assets. Instead, they may prefer to pay for capital assets in part out of future revenues generated by the production from the asset itself. If this is the case, the economic units must enter the capital markets as primary borrowers. *Primary borrowers* issue capital market claims such as stocks and bonds that are secured by the value of future production expected from the capital asset. As Exhibit 9–1 shows, businesses and the federal government are the largest net borrowers (deficit spending units), and individuals are the largest net suppliers of funds (surplus spending units).

Economic units may issue primary claims on capital assets for more than one reason. In some cases, a deficit spending unit (DSU) may issue debt merely because it otherwise could not afford to buy the capital asset. In other cases, it may issue debt because it does not want to take the risk of investing a large portion of its resources on a single capital expenditure. A DSU that ties up all of its resources in one capital asset or line of business is totally reliant on that asset or line of business for future cash flows. By committing some of the firm's funds to other assets or ventures, a DSU can diversify its business risk and thereby reduce the chance that cash flows from all of its investments will decline simultaneously. Spreading the risk through the sale and resale of capital market claims is an important function of capital markets.

Purchasers of Capital Market Claims

The ultimate purchasers of capital market claims are surplus spending units. As Exhibit 9–1 shows, households are the largest suppliers of funds to financial markets. Financial institutions are also important participants, even though their net position is not large relative to individuals because of their role as financial intermediaries. That is, they purchase funds from individuals and others and then issue their own securities in exchange. Hence, individuals may invest directly in the capital market,

---

Exhibit 9–1   **Net Financial Position of Major Sectors of the Economy, December 31, 1990 ($ in billions)**

Sector	Financial Assets	Financial Liabilities	Net Financial Position	
			Surplus	Deficit
Households	$14,310.7	$ 3,888.8	$10,421.9	
Nonfinancial business	2,114.4	3,152.1		$1,037.7
State and local government	556.5	683.4		126.9
Federal government	379.3	2,828.2		2,448.9
Financial institutions	10,982.1	10,749.5	232.6	
Remainder	1,665.0	848.1	816.9	
Total	$30,008.0	$22,150.1	$11,471.4	$3,613.5

Households are the largest supplier of funds to financial markets. To no one's surprise, the federal government has a large deficit position.

Source: Board of Governors, Federal Reserve System, *Flow of Funds Accounts, Financial Assets and Liabilities,* 1991.

but more likely they invest indirectly through such depository institutions as commercial banks and insurance companies.

Size of the Capital Market

The capital market is massive in scope, exceeding $14.5 trillion. Exhibit 9–2 shows its size it terms of the outstanding instruments. As shown, the mortgage market—home, commercial, and farm—represents one of the largest components, amounting to over $3.7 trillion. Corporate stocks and bonds are also large, with a combined total of $5.9 trillion; long-term government securities markets (Treasury and agency) are also quite large, totaling about $3.5 trillion. The reason is the large government deficit. Also, as can be seen, debt markets have grown faster than the equity markets. By far the fastest-growing debt market during the last 20 years is that for federal agency debt.

Capital Market Efficiency

Recall from Chapter 2 that the purpose of the financial system is to channel funds from surplus spending units (SSUs) to deficit spending units (DSUs) in the most efficient manner possible. The productivity and growth of the U.S. economy depend on the smooth functioning of the financial system. If, for example, a firm with a valuable investment project is unable to obtain financing in a timely fashion or is unable to sell its securities at a fair price because of market inefficiency, the firm may have to wait before building a new factory, hiring more workers, and ultimately increasing economic output. It is easy to see how a delay in obtaining needed financing can slow down economic growth and ultimately make everyone worse off if such inefficiency becomes pervasive. Given the critical role of the capital markets in financing economic growth, it is important that you understand the concept of market

Exhibit 9–2   Capital Market Instruments Outstanding ($ in billions)

Instrument	1965	1970	1975	1980	1985	1989	1990
Treasury debt (over 1 year)	$ 120	$ 299	$ 445	$ 742	$1,600	$ 2,268	$ 2.541
Federal agency debt (over 1 year)	15	44	107	274	627	1,244	1,415
Municipal bonds	100	146	223	342	656	821	840 ·
Corporate bonds	121	202	328	495	819	1,503	1,630
Corporate stock[a]	749	906	893	1,634	2,824	4,382	4,332
Mortgages	333	471	787	1,452	2,290	3,540	3,769
Total	$1,438	$2,068	$2,783	$4,939	$8,816	$13,758	$14,527

[a] At Market values

In recent years, federal agency debt has been the fastest growing sector in the capital markets. The reason is that agency debt is off-balance-sheet financing for the federal government.

Source: Board of Governors, Federal Reserve System, *Flow of Funds Accounts, Financial Assets and Liabilities,* 1991.

efficiency. We now discuss three types of market efficiency: allocational efficiency, informational efficiency, and operational efficiency.

Allocational Efficiency

The capital market is allocationally efficient if funds are channeled to their most productive use. This means that the funds could not have been reallocated in any other way that would have made society better off. In general, this means that business firms invest in the projects offering the highest rates of return and that households invest in direct or indirect financial claims offering the highest yields for given levels of risk. As we will now see, the allocational efficiency of the financial markets depends both on informational and operational efficiency.

Informational Efficiency

Of critical importance to allocational efficiency is the ability of investors to obtain accurate information about the relative values of different securities. In an informationally efficient market, prices of securities are the best indicators of relative value because market prices reflect all relevant information about the securities.

When new information about a security arrives in an efficient market, market prices adjust very quickly. Price adjustments occur quickly because there are thousands (or millions) of investors gathering information about securities in a quest for quick profits. Investors try to make large profits by identifying overpriced securities and selling them before the price drops or by purchasing underpriced securities before the price begins to rise. The actions of such investors ensure that market prices reflect all relevant information at any point in time.

Why is it important that market prices reflect all relevant information about securities? With accurate price information, investors can determine which investments are the most valuable (or provide the highest expected return for a given level of risk) and invest accordingly. Thus, informational efficiency helps ensure that the financial markets are allocationally efficient because households or business firms can get the information they need to make intelligent investment decisions.

Operational Efficiency

Operational efficiency is also important for the allocational efficiency of the capital markets. A market is operationally efficient if the costs of conducting transactions are as low as possible. We discussed some of the transaction costs of financial markets in Chapter 2. Brokers, who aid in the search process of bringing buyers and sellers together, charge a commission for their services. Dealers, whose primary function is to provide liquidity to market participants by maintaining an inventory of securities, stand ready either to buy or sell securities at stated prices. Dealers make a profit from the difference between the price at which they sell securities (the ask price) and the price at which they buy securities (the bid price). The difference between the bid price and the ask price is usually called the bid-ask spread. Underwriters, firms that assist other firms to raise capital through the issuance of stocks and bonds, make a profit on the difference between the price at which they buy the securities from the issuing firm and the price at which they sell the securities to the public (the underwriter's spread).

How does operational efficiency affect allocational efficiency? If transaction costs are high, fewer financial transactions will take place, and a greater number of otherwise valuable investment projects will be passed up. Thus, high transaction costs can prevent firms from investing in all desirable projects. The foregone investment opportunities mean that fewer people are employed and economic output grows at a slower rate or declines. Society becomes worse off.

Corporate Bonds

Corporate bonds are debt contracts requiring borrowers to make periodic payments of interest and to repay principal at the maturity date. Corporate bonds can be *bearer bonds*, for which coupons are attached and the holder presents them for payment when they come due, or *registered bonds*, for which the owner is recorded and payment due is mailed to the owner. Corporate bonds are usually issued in denominations of $1,000 and their coupon income is fully taxable to the investor. Corporate debt can be sold in the domestic bond market or in the Eurobond market, which is a market for foreign debt. Most are *term bonds*, which means that all of the bonds that compose a particular issue mature on a single date. In contrast, most bonds issued by state and local governments are *serial bond issues*, which means that the issue contains a variety of maturity dates.

To make sure that future payments are made as promised, bonds have an *indenture* (the bond contract) that states the rights and privileges of the lender and the borrower's obligations. The indenture usually specifies the security or assets to which bondholders have prior claim in the event of default. Mortgage bonds pledge land and buildings; equipment trust certificates pledge specific industrial equipment or "rolling stock," such as railroad cars, trucks, or airplanes; and collateral bonds are secured by stocks and bonds issued by other corporations or governmental units. If no assets are pledged, the bonds are secured only by the firm's potential to generate cash flows and are called debenture bonds.

Corporate bonds can differ in ways other than security. The debentures can be *senior* debt, giving the bondholders first priority to the firm's assets in the event of default, or *subordinated* (junior) debt, in which bondholders' claims to the company's assets rank behind senior debt. In addition, many corporate bonds have sinking fund provisions, and most have call provisions. A *sinking fund* provision requires that the bond issuer provide funds to a trustee to retire a specific dollar amount (face amount) of bonds each year. The trustee may retire the bonds either by purchasing them in the open market or by calling them, if a call provision is present. It is important to notice the distinction between a sinking fund provision and a call provision. With a sinking fund provision, the issuer *must* retire a portion of the bond as promised in the bond indenture. In contrast, a *call* provision is an option of the issuer to retire bonds before their maturity. Most security issues with sinking funds have call provisions, because that guarantees the issuer the ability to retire bonds as they come due under the sinking fund retirement schedule.

Investors in Corporate Bonds

As shown in Exhibit 9–3, life insurance companies and pension funds (private and public) are the dominant purchasers of corporate bonds. Households and foreign investors also own large quantities of them. Corporate bonds are attractive to insurance companies and pension funds because of the stability of the cash flows they experience and the long-term nature of their liabilities. That is, by investing in long-term corporate bonds, these firms are able to lock in high market yields with maturities that closely match the maturity structure of their liabilities, thereby reducing their interest rate risk. In addition, both life insurance companies and pension funds are in low marginal tax brackets, and taxable corporate bonds provide them with higher after-tax yields than do tax-exempt bonds. Finally, both federal and state laws require these companies to be "prudent" in their investment decisions. This usually translates to purchasing investment-grade bonds—bonds rated Baa and above by Moody's and BBB and above by Standard & Poor's.

The Primary Market for Corporate Bonds

New corporate bond issues may be brought to market by two methods: public sale or private placement. A public sale means that the bond issue is offered publicly in the open market to all interested buyers; a private placement means that the bonds are sold privately to a limited number of investors.

Public Sales of Bonds.   Public offerings of bonds are usually made through an investment banking firm, which purchases the bonds from the issuer and then resells

---

Exhibit 9–3   **Holders of Corporate Bonds (December 31, 1990)**

Holder	Amount ($ in billions)	Percentage of Total
Households	$ 90	5.6
Foreign investors	203	12.7
Commercial banks	91	5.7
Savings and loan associations	47	2.9
Mutual savings banks	10	0.6
Life insurance companies	582	36.4
Other insurance companies	91	5.7
Private pension funds	148	9.2
Public pension funds	246	15.4
Mutual funds	89	5.6
Brokers and dealers	1	0.1
Total	$1,598	100.0

Life insurance companies and pension funds are the largest holders of corporate bonds.

Source: Board of Governors, Federal Reserve System, *Flow of Funds Accounts, Financial Assets and Liabilities,* 1991.

them to individuals and institutions. The investment banker can purchase the bonds either by competitive sales or through negotiation with the issuer. A *competitive sale* is, in effect, a public auction. The issuer advertises publicly for bids from underwriters, and the bond issue is sold to the investment banker submitting the bid that results in the lowest borrowing cost to the issuer. In contrast, a *negotiated sale* represents a contractual arrangement between the underwriter and the issuer whereby the investment banker obtains the exclusive right to originate, underwrite, and distribute the new bond issue. The major difference between the two methods of sale is that in a negotiated sale, the investment banker provides the origination and advising services to the issuer as part of the negotiated package. In a competitive sale, origination services are performed by the issuer or an outside financial adviser. As a rule, most public entities, such as public utility companies, are required by law to sell their bond issues by competitive sale. It is generally believed that issuers will receive the lowest possible interest cost through competitive rather than negotiated sales.

Private Placement.   Private placements emerged as a distinct method of issuing securities because of the Securities and Exchange Act of 1934, which required publicly sold securities to be registered with the Securities and Exchange Commission (SEC). The provisions of the act were intended to protect individual investors by forcing issuing firms to disclose a modicum of information about their securities. Unregistered securities (that is, private placements) could only be sold to large, financially sophisticated investors (in practice, usually large insurance companies or perhaps other institutional investors) as long as fewer than 35 investors were involved and as long as the securities did not change hands for two years. The rationale for exempting private placements from registration and disclosure requirements was that large, institutional investors possessed both the resources and sophistication to analyze the risks of securities.

In recent years, there has been a trend toward private placements relative to public sales. However, the ratio of private placements to public offerings is sensitive to the business cycle. During periods of low interest rates or stable market conditions, many smaller companies of lower credit quality will enter the capital markets and obtain financing by a public sale. During these times, the volume of public sales to private sales will increase; during periods of high interest rates or unstable market conditions, these same firms will sell debt privately. On the other hand, larger, more well-known firms of high credit standing can shift between the two markets and select the market that provides the lowest borrowing cost, net of transactions costs.

Since the 1980s the securities markets have become driven by institutions, with individual investors having little influence on market movements. Also, the private placement market has grown rapidly. These trends led the SEC to adopt Rule 144A in 1990 to liberalize the regulation of the private placement market. Most significantly, Rule 144A allows secondary trading of private securities by large institutional investors. By increasing liquidity and decreasing regulatory oversight in the capital markets, the rule should lower corporations' cost of capital. Investors such as pension funds and mutual funds, which have traditionally avoided investing in private placements because of their illiquidity, will now find private placements more attractive. Further, foreign corporations, which have historically shunned the highly regulated U.S. capital markets, will find it more attractive to issue securities in the United States through the private placement market.

The Secondary Market for Corporate Bonds

Most secondary trading of corporate bonds occurs through dealers, although some corporate bonds are traded on the New York Stock Exchange (NYSE). The secondary market for corporate bonds is *thin* compared to the markets for money market securities or corporate stock. The term "thin" means that secondary market trades of corporate bonds are relatively infrequent. As a result, the bid-ask spread quoted by dealers of corporate bonds are quite high compared to those of other, more marketable, securities. The higher bid-ask spread compensates the dealer for holding relatively risky and illiquid securities in inventory.[1]

Corporate bonds are less marketable than money market instruments and corporate equities for at least two reasons. First, corporate bonds have special features such as call provisions or sinking funds that make them difficult to value. Second, corporate bonds are long term; in general, longer-term securities are riskier and less marketable. To buy or sell a corporate bond in the secondary market, one must contact a broker, who in turn contacts a dealer (or the NYSE for exchange-listed bonds) who provides bid-ask quotes.

Junk Bonds

During the 1980s junk bonds became a popular form of corporate financing. Junk bonds are corporate bonds with high default risk and, hence, low bond ratings (below Moody's Baa or Standard & Poor's BBB). Junk bonds were not common in the primary market before the late 1970s and early 1980s, although they could be found in the secondary market. These secondary-market junk bonds, the so-called fallen angels, were investment grade (Baa/BBB or greater) when originally issued, but were subsequently downgraded by the rating agencies because of a deterioration in the financial condition of issuing firms.

Why weren't many junk bonds sold in the primary market before the late 1970s? As discussed earlier in this book, higher-risk bonds tend to be less marketable. In 1977, however, Drexel Burnham Lambert, Inc., innovated the marketing of junk bonds in the *primary market* by promising investors that they would act as a dealer for junk bonds in the *secondary market*. Investors, therefore, were willing to take on the extra risk of junk bonds because they knew that Drexel would buy the bonds back at quoted bid prices, thereby providing liquidity to the market.

The supply of junk bonds in the 1980s was part of the trend toward disintermediation,[2] a process whereby firms raise capital in the direct financial markets rather than from financial intermediaries such as commercial banks. High-quality firms with investment-grade credit ratings, for example, issued more commer-

---

[1] Recall from Chapter 2 that the lower the liquidity or marketability of a security the greater the rate of return required on the security.

[2] See Chapter 2 for a discussion of financial intermediation and its effects on the financial markets.

cial paper rather than borrowing from banks. These firms were able to borrow more cheaply in the commercial paper market because their credit quality was higher than that of most commercial banks.

Low-quality firms with speculative-grade credit ratings, on the other hand, found that they could issue marketable debt in the direct market (that is, the junk bond market) with longer maturities than the debt they could obtain from commercial banks. Before the development of the junk bond market, low-quality firms relied on short-term or floating-rate bank loans. Banks prefer making short-term or floating-rate loans because such a strategy minimizes their interest rate risk by timing the cash inflows from loans with potential deposit outflows. Borrowing firms that use short-term or floating-rate instruments to finance long-term projects, however, experience increased risk because the timing of cash inflows from their projects does not match the pattern of interest payments on short-term or floating-rate debt when short-term interest rates fluctuate.

The demand for junk bonds came from financial institutions such as life insurance companies, savings and loan associations, pension funds, and mutual funds. Junk bonds were attractive investments because investors believed they consistently outperformed high-rated bonds and even Treasury securities on a risk-adjusted basis. In the growing economy of the 1980s, the performance of junk bonds can be explained by the fact that there were many fewer defaults than expected, but during the late 1980s and early 1990s the number of defaults increased substantially. Losses from these defaults reduced the capital of many financial institutions, exacerbating the thrift crisis and contributing to the failure of several major life insurance firms.

Because of these failures, many observers and policymakers associate junk bonds with the so-called financial excesses of the 1980s. More specifically, critics have blamed junk bonds for the merger mania of the 1980s, for the overall rise in corporate leverage encouraged by the 1986 tax reform, and for the increased volatility of the financial markets in the 1980s. These critics have called for laws or regulations that would limit the corporate use of junk bonds and limit the ability of financial institutions to invest in them.

The record suggests that the growth of the junk bond market was coincidental with the trends described above rather than causing them.[3] Only a small portion of mergers were actually financed with junk bonds; most were issued to finance capital investment of small, growing companies. Further, researchers have uncovered numerous other causes of the financial market volatility of the 1980s; the evidence suggests little association between junk bonds and volatility. It is true that junk bond defaults may have contributed to the failures of some financial institutions, but in many cases these institutions were in deep financial trouble before investing in junk bonds. The managers of these institutions, attempting to "hit it big" and keep their firms from going under, may not have adequately diversified their investments in junk bonds. In the end, restricting the use of junk bonds might force many small- and medium-sized companies back to the more expensive short-term intermediated credit markets, increasing their cost of capital and financial risk.

---

[3] See "The Truth about Junk Bonds," a study by Sean Becketti of the Federal Reserve Bank of Kansas City appearing in *Economic Review*, July/August 1990, pp. 45–54.

State and Local Government Bonds

State and local government bonds, often called *municipal bonds*, encompass all issues of state governments and their political subdivisions, such as cities, counties, school districts, and transit authorities. The municipal bond market is one of the largest fixed-income securities markets. Intense pressure on state and local governments to provide new services to their constituents as well as a reluctance of taxpayers to pay higher taxes account for this rapid growth. The market is unique among major capital markets in that the number of issuers is so large. Estimates indicate that more than 50,000 entities have debt outstanding and an additional 30,000 have legal access to the market. No other direct capital market accommodates so many borrowers.

Characteristics of Municipal Bonds

State and local government debt generally consists of either general obligation bonds or revenue bonds. *General obligation bonds* are backed by the "full faith and credit" (the power to tax) of the issuing political entity. These bonds are typically issued to provide such basic services to communities as education, fire and police protection, and healthcare facilities. General obligation bonds usually require voter approval and have been the slowest-growing portion of the total municipal debt in recent years. This trend can be seen in Exhibit 9-4. *Revenue bonds* are sold to finance a specific revenue-producing project, and in the event of default, these bonds are backed only by the revenue generated from the project. Typical revenue projects are toll roads and bridges, water and sewer treatment plants, university dormitories, and port facilities. Depending on the type of project, revenue bonds may be riskier than general obligation bonds. For instance, Chesapeake Bridge and Tunnel Authority bonds went into default when a section of the bridge was destroyed.

Industrial development bonds (IDB) are a controversial use of revenue bonds. IDBs were first issued to help stimulate local businesses following the Great Depression. When issuing an IDB, the municipality merely gives its approval to the sale of the bonds and assumes no legal liability in the event of default. The recipient of the fund benefits because of the lower borrowing cost associated with tax-exempt debt. The abuse of IDBs has come from commercial banks that have helped local governments set up municipal development agencies, which effectively allows banks to make tax-exempt loans to qualified borrowers at lower than normal interest rates. Because of this abuse, federal legislation passed in 1984 limited the amount of IDBs sold in each state.

The tax-exemption privilege of municipal bonds has also been abused in the issuance of mortgage-backed municipal bonds. Such bonds may be issued by a city housing authority based on mortgage pools generated under its jurisdiction. Because interest paid on the bonds is tax-exempt, the issuer can borrow funds at low interest and then make low-interest mortgage loans. However, not all of the lowest-interest funds have gone to the low- and moderate-income people they were designed to benefit. Because some municipalities have abused their tax-exempt borrowing privilege, Congress has restricted the use of mortgage-backed municipal bonds.

Exhibit 9–4   **State and Local Government Securities Issues—Annual Total Gross Proceeds**

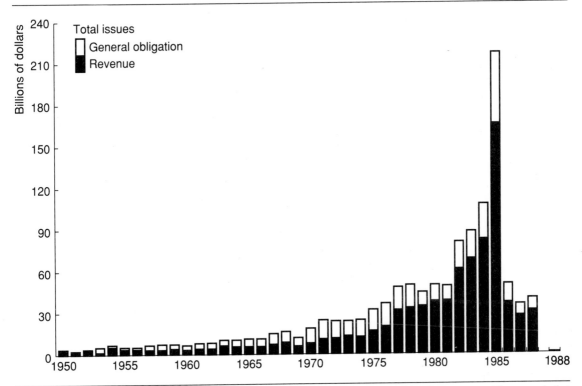

In recent years, revenue bond financing is the most important source of funds for state and local governments. The reason is that revenue bonds usually do not require voter approval as general obligation bonds do.

Source: Board of Governors of the Federal Reserve System, *1989 Historical Chart Book*.

The Tax Exempt Feature and the Demand for Municipal Bonds

Municipal securities can be distinguished from other types of securities by the fact that coupon interest payments are exempt from federal income tax. This feature lowers the borrowing cost of state and local governments because investors are willing to accept lower pretax yields on municipal bonds than on taxable securities of comparable maturity and risk. To the extent that these securities are substitutes, investors will choose the security that provides the greatest after-tax return. Recall from Chapter 7 that the appropriate yield comparison is:

$$im = it\,(1 - t), \tag{9-1}$$

where *im* and *it* are pretax yields on municipal and taxable securities of comparable maturity and risk, and *t* is the marginal tax rate that equates the after-tax yield on municipals and taxable securities.

Given t and it, the equation determines the minimum municipal yields to induce investors in tax bracket t to buy municipals rather than taxable bonds. Thus, if the investor's marginal tax rate is sufficiently high, municipal securities will yield relatively higher yields than taxable securities. If the investor's tax rate is sufficiently low, the opposite will hold—taxables will yield relatively more than tax-exempts. For the two markets to clear, tax-exempt and taxable yields will adjust so that at the margin the last investor who views these securities as substitutes will be indifferent; the after-tax yields of the two alternatives are equal. Thus it is the marginal tax rate of the last investor that determines the relative rate relationship between comparable tax-exempt and taxable securities.

Investors in Municipal Bonds.   Exhibit 9–5 shows that the demand for tax-exempt securities is concentrated among three groups of investors that face high marginal tax rates: commercial banks, property and casualty insurance companies, and high-income individuals. Note that mutual fund shares represent the indirect purchase of tax-exempt securities by individuals.

Historically, commercial banks were the major purchaser of municipal bonds. In the late 1960s and 1970s, banks typically owned more than 50 percent of all outstanding tax-exempt debt. Since then, bank ownership has declined; in 1990, banks owned only 14 percent of outstanding tax-exempt debt. In the past, bank demand for municipal securities was strongly influenced by banks' ability to engage in a form of of tax arbitrage. Unique among all other investors, commercial banks were allowed to deduct from their taxable income the interest expense on debt (for example, time deposits used to purchase tax-exempt securities). As a result, banks had incentives to borrow money and purchase tax-exempt securities as long as the after-tax cost of debt was below the tax-exempt interest rate. The Tax Reform Act of 1986 put an end to deductibility of bank interest expenses for tax-exempt securities purchased after 1986 (except for small issues). As a result, bank demand for tax-exempt securities has declined in recent years.

Exhibit 9–5   **Holders of Municipal Bonds (December 31, 1990)**

Holder	Amount ($ in billions)	Percentage of Total
Commercial banks	$118	14.0
Individuals	346	41.1
Casualty insurance companies	137	16.3
Mutual funds	110	13.1
Life insurance companies	13	1.6
Others	117	13.9
Total	$841	100.0

Individuals are the largest purchasers of municipal bonds; they buy them directly and indirectly through the purchase of mutual funds.

Source: Board of Governors, Federal Reserve System, *Flow of Funds Accounts, Financial Assets and Liabilities,* 1991.

DID YOU KNOW?

The Junk Bonds in Muni Bond Clothing

In April 1991, state insurance regulators seized the New York and California units of First Executive Corporation, a large holding company of life insurance firms. First Executive's insolvency stemmed from defaults in its junk bond portfolio. Among the unlikely victims of the failure of First Executive were investors in AAA-rated taxable municipal bonds issued by public finance authorities (PFAs) in Colorado, Louisiana, Nebraska, Tennessee, and Texas. The PFAs were supposed to issue municipal bonds and use the proceeds to finance cheap loans to farmers, finance developers of housing for low-income families, and support other socially desirable purposes. Standard & Poor's rated these municipal bonds AAA because of the strict eligibility requirements for the loans. Presumably, the strict requirements meant that the loans possessed low credit risk.

The bond underwriters (Drexel Burnham Lambert and Morgan Stanley) handling the sale of these municipal bonds got the PFAs to agree to put half of the proceeds from the bond issues into AAA-rated Executive Life GICs (guaranteed investment contracts). GICs are analogous to certificates of deposit issued by commercial banks. In effect, the underwriters got the PFAs to agree to partially collateralize the bond issues with the GIC investments. The other half of the bond proceeds would be put into another AAA-rated GIC and these funds could be drawn to make loans to farmers and developers.

Now the fun begins. The first problem was that so few potential borrowers met the strict eligibility requirements that the PFAs found it difficult to make loans. Second, the municipal bonds had coupon rates ranging from 8.3 percent to 9.5 percent but the GICs were only earning 8.5 percent, making it difficult for the PFAs to meet their coupon payments. Of course, First Executive had no trouble making the interest payments on the GICs as long as their high-yielding junk bond portfolio stayed intact. Once the junk bonds started defaulting, however, First Executive moved toward insolvency, and the resulting crisis resulted in regulatory intervention.

Once the regulators took over First Executive, they put the claims of policyholders and annuitants ahead of those of bondholders and the holders of GICs. In fact, they suspended interest payments on the municipal GICs, which the regulators classified last in priority of claims against First Executive. This move, of course, spelled doom for the PFAs, who now had virtually no income with which to make coupon payments on the municipal bonds they issued. The market price of the bonds plummeted and Standard & Poor's finally responded by lowering the rating on the PFA bonds. The sad part of the story is that many small investors purchased the AAA-rated, GIC-backed municipal bonds thinking that they were putting money away for retirement as well as providing a valuable service to the local community by helping to fund socially useful projects. A retired Nebraska farmer commented: "This has shattered my faith in AAA ratings."

Today, bank demand for tax-exempt securities is primarily influenced by bank profitability. During periods when bank income is high, demand for municipal securities is strong because the banks purchase municipal securities to shield income from taxation. Likewise, during periods when bank income is low, banks buy fewer tax-exempt securities because they have less income to shield from taxation. Finally, banks also may have incentives to purchase tax-exempt securities because of state pledging or collateral requirements for public deposits. That is, many states require banks to collateralize public deposits with in-state tax-exempt securities. In these states, banks have additional incentives to purchase tax-exempt securities issued in the bank's home state.

Demand for tax-exempt securities by property and casualty insurance companies has always varied widely over time. For example, in 1969 these companies owned only 11.3 percent of outstanding tax-exempts, and in 1980 they owned 22.9 percent. Since 1980 casualty company demand had declined, and by 1990 they owned only 16.3 percent of outstanding tax-exempts. Demand from casualty companies, like bank demand, is primarily determined by industry profitability. The recent decline in demand reflects the considerable industry-wide losses from insurance underwriting that these firms have experienced during the 1980s.

When commercial banks and insurance companies purchase tax-exempt securities, they tend to concentrate their portfolios in maturities that meet their institutional preferences. Specifically, banks tend to emphasize tax-exempts of high credit quality with short maturities for liquidity as well as those with maturities up to ten years for investment. In contrast, property and casualty insurance companies concentrate on holding securities with long-term maturities, higher yields, and lower credit ratings. Insurance companies have been especially important buyers in the market for long-term revenue bonds.

Given the supply of tax-exempt securities and the demand from banks and insurance companies, any tax-exempt securities issued in excess of those desired by firms taxed at the full corporate rate must be purchased by individuals. The greater the excess, the higher tax-exempt yields must rise relative to taxable yields to induce individuals to purchase additional tax-exempt securities. With the decline of tax-exempt holdings by insurance companies and banks since 1980, individual holdings have increased from 25 percent in 1980 to 42.5 percent of outstanding tax-exempts by 1989.

The Effect of the Tax Reform Act of 1986.   The Tax Reform Act of 1986 has notably altered the demand for tax-exempt securities by investors and the supply of new issues from municipalities. On the demand side, the act substantially reduced investors' marginal tax rates. Specifically, the act reduced the structure of individual tax rates from 14 marginal rate categories to 2, and it lowered the maximum tax rate from 50 to 28 percent. The Tax Reform Act also reduced the top corporate rate from 46 percent to 34 percent. In addition, as previously mentioned, the act put an end to deductibility of bank interest expense for tax-exempt securities purchased after 1986. Holding supply constant, the Tax Reform Act should result in an increase in the tax-exempt interest rate relative to taxable rates, especially for short maturities, which are favored by banks.

On the supply side, the Tax Reform Act significantly restricts private-purpose tax-exempt securities. Pollution-control projects of private firms, sports and convention centers, parking facilities, and industrial parks will no longer have access to the tax-exempt market. Furthermore, private colleges and universities and non-profit organizations other than hospitals are limited to a maximum of $150 million per organization in outstanding tax-exempts. Finally, other private-purpose bonds such as home mortgage bonds are subject to volume restriction. Over all, private-purpose bonds are limited by state to $50 per capita or $150 million, whichever is greater. As can be seen in Exhibit 9–4, the Tax Reform Act reduced the volume of new issues. It also appears that the act increased municipal interest rates relative to taxable rates.

The Market for Municipal Bonds

The primary market for municipal bonds is earmarked by the large number of relatively small bond issues. These bonds tend to be underwritten by small regional underwriters in the immediate area of the issuing municipality. Bond issues of well-known governmental units—states, state agencies, and large cities—attract bidding syndicates of major underwriters throughout the country and are sold in a national market. The reason for the existence of local markets is the high cost of gathering information about smaller issues and the tax treatment of these bonds (most local buyers are exempt from local as well as federal taxes on their coupons).

Secondary Market. In general, the secondary market for municipal bonds is very thin and is primarily an over-the-counter market. Although the bonds of some large, well-known municipalities do have active secondary markets, small local issues are traded infrequently, with commercial banks and local brokerage houses making the market. Because of the inactive secondary market, dealers (including local banks) find it difficult to match buyers and sellers of such bonds; thus the bid-ask spreads on municipal bonds are usually large compared to those of corporate bonds.

Financial Guarantees

The use of *financial guarantees* has grown dramatically in the 1980s. Financial guarantees cover the payment of principal and interest to investors in debt securities in the event of a default. Large, well-known insurance companies or commercial banks provide most financial guarantees. Insurance companies write insurance policies to back bond issues; commercial banks write letters of credit to back commercial paper issues or swap transactions.

The capital, assets, and reputations of these institutions back the guaranteed security. In effect, a security issuer with a lower credit standing that purchases a financial guarantee is "leasing" the reputation of the guarantor that has a higher credit standing. Thus the investor in a guaranteed security is ultimately exposed to the default risk of the guarantor or insurer, not that of the issuer. Because of the risk reduction, guaranteed securities are typically more marketable than similar non-guaranteed securities, and they also pay lower yields to investors. Of course, security issuers will only purchase financial guarantees if the price of the guarantee is less than the interest cost savings that result from the risk reduction and increased marketability.

Municipal bond insurance, developed in the early 1970s, was the first financial guarantee product. Since the 1970s, however, the market for financial guarantees has expanded to include guarantees on a variety of corporate and municipal securities. Financial guarantees are important in the commercial paper market and in the market for asset-backed securities such as securities backed by consumer credit-card receivables and mortgage-backed securities. Financial guarantees are also important in the markets for interest rate swaps and foreign currency swaps. The demand for financial guarantees seems to follow closely the level of interest rates. As interest rates rise, the potential cost savings to an issuer from enhancing a security issue with a financial guarantee increase, increasing the demand for financial guarantees.

U.S. Government and Agency Securities

Most of the characteristics of U.S. government and agency debt have been discussed in Chapter 8. We shall discuss only briefly some additional dimensions to this capital market debt.

U.S. government notes and bonds are similar to bills in that they are issued by the U.S. Treasury and are considered to be free of default risk. They differ from bills in that they are coupon issues, redeemable at face value upon maturity, and have maturities greater than one year (notes have an original maturity of one to ten years, and bonds have an original maturity of more than ten years). The primary and secondary markets for coupon issues are similar to those for bills. New issues are sold by auction by the Federal Reserve, and existing issues can be purchased or sold in the secondary market from securities dealers. In recent years, notes and bonds have become a less important financing vehicle because the federal government has increasingly relied on shorter-maturity debt (mostly bills).

Corporate Stock

So far we have focused on debt instruments; we now turn our attention to equity securities. *Equity* means an ownership claim. Thus equity securities are certificates of ownership of a corporation—the residual claim on a firm's assets after all other liabilities are paid. As owners, equity holders have the right to share in the firm's profits. There are two basic types of equity securities: common stock and preferred stock. In addition, some securities are convertible into common stock. We now discuss the various types of equity securities.

Types of Equity Securities

Common Stock.   Common stock represents the basic ownership claim in a corporation. Stockholders have one vote per share on items of major interest, such as corporate charter amendments and the election of boards of directors, and have equal claims (per share) on corporate earnings. Corporate payments to stockholders are called *dividends*. Common stock dividends are not guaranteed, and a corporation does not default if it does not pay them. For investors, equity securities offer potentially higher returns than could otherwise be obtained with debt instruments because equity holders share in the firm's profits. However, equity securities are also riskier for the same reason.

Because dividend income is taxable for most investors, corporate dividends are doubly taxed—once when the corporation pays the corporate income tax, and once when the investors pay their personal tax. To avoid double taxation, some investors hold stocks in "growth companies" that reinvest their accumulated earnings instead of paying larger dividends. Reinvestment of earnings allows the company to accumulate capital and grow faster than it otherwise might. As a firm's earnings grow, its stock price usually rises. Stockholders can sell their stock and pay capital gains taxes on their profits. Before the Tax Reform Act of 1986 capital gains were taxed at lower tax rates than ordinary income (that is, dividends), but now both capital gains and ordinary income are taxed the same. Note, however, that taxes on capital gains are paid only upon realization of the gain. Thus investors can reduce their tax bill in present-value terms by deferring the sale of securities to postpone realization of capital gains. Because investors have different portfolio preferences and corporations have different growth opportunities, corporate strategies toward growth versus current dividend payments vary widely.

Preferred Stock.   Preferred stock differs from common stock in that its cash dividends are guaranteed, do not increase as earnings rise, and must be paid before any dividends are paid to holders of common stock. Furthermore, most preferred stock is cumulative. *Cumulative preferred stock* requires that if any dividend payments are missed, they must be made up before any common stock dividends are paid. In the event of default, preferred stockholders' claims on the firm's assets come before common stockholders' claims but after debt holders' claims. Finally, preferred stockholders typically do not have a vote in the operation of the firm unless the corporation is in arrears on its dividend payments.

The main reason that individuals buy preferred stock is to obtain higher after-tax dividend returns. Many corporations invest in the preferred stock of other corporations because 85 percent of the dividends received are nontaxable. Corporate-bond interest income is taxable, however.

Convertible Securities.   *Convertible preferred stock* is stock that can be converted into common stock at a predetermined ratio (such as two shares of common for each share of preferred stock). By buying such stock, an investor can obtain a good dividend return plus the possibility that, should the common stock rise, the investment would rise in value.

Convertible bonds are bonds that can be exchanged for shares of common stock. However, until conversion they are corporate debt; thus their interest and principal payments are contractual obligations of the firm and must be made lest the corporation default. Most convertible bonds are subordinated debentures. Hence their holders have lower-ranking claims than most other debt holders, although their claims rank ahead of stockholders'.

Because convertible bonds both increase in value with rising stock prices and provide the fixed income and security of bonds, they are popular with investors, who are usually willing to pay more to acquire convertible debt than conventional debt issued by the same corporation. From the corporation's perspective, convertible bonds provide a means by which the corporation can issue debt and later convert it to equity at a price per share that exceeds the stock's present market value. This feature is attractive because it allows the corporation to "sell" stock at a higher future price.

The Market for Equity Securities

Exhibit 9-6 shows the distribution of ownership for equity securities. As can be seen, households dominate the holding of equity securities—owning almost 60 percent of all outstanding corporate securities at year-end 1990. Pension funds (private and public) are the largest institutional holder of equities, followed by foreign investors and mutual funds.

Primary Market for Equities.   New issues of equity securities may be sold directly to investors by the issuing corporation, or they may be underwritten and distributed through an investment banker. The role of investment bankers in the issuing of new equity securities parallels that described in issuing new corporate debt. Some equity securities are also distributed through private placements, but this method of sale is generally limited to investment-grade preferred stock issues of public utility companies. New issues of equity securities are subject to the regulation and disclosure requirements of the Securities Act of 1934, which is administered by the Securities and Exchange Commission (SEC). The SEC also has broad power to regulate secondary market activities in the sale of equity securities.

An important innovation in the sale of new corporate securities (equity or bonds) is shelf registration. Shelf registration permits a corporation to register a quantity of securities with the SEC and sell them over a two-year period rather than all at once. Thus the issuer is able to save money through a single registration—SEC registrations are both costly (average about $50,000) and time-consuming. In addition, with shelf registrations, the securities can be brought to market with little notice, thereby providing the issuer with maximum flexibility in timing an issue to take advantage of favorable market conditions.

The Secondary Market for Equity Securities.   The secondary market for corporate stock is the largest in dollar volume and number of trades of any security.

Exhibit 9–6   **Holders of Corporate Equity Securities (December 31, 1990)**

Holder	Amount ($ in billions)	Percentage of Total
Households	$2,558	59.1
Pension funds	994	23.0
Foreign investors	241	5.6
Mutual funds	255	5.9
Insurance companies	248	5.7
Other	36	0.8
Total	$4,332	100.0

Households are the most important holders of corporate securities.

Source: Board of Governors, Federal Reserve System, *Flow of Funds Accounts, Financial Assets and Liabilities,* 1991.

PEOPLE & EVENTS

Bursting the Speculative Bubble

The causes of the October 19, 1987, market break and subsequent sharp decline in equity prices worldwide will be debated for many years. A study by a presidential commission (the Brady Commission) and reports by several agencies and industry groups have been completed, as well as a multitude of academic studies. Interest in the October 1987 crash has been sparked by the remarkable similarity between the pattern of price movements in 1929 and 1987 and the worry that subsequent events will also be similar.

The price break of October 1987 followed a historically rapid increase in U.S. equity prices. All major stock exchanges in the world enjoyed bull markets for the better part of the period between August 1982 and October 1987. The market indexes for the 19 largest markets in the world rose an average of 296 percent during this period, and, in the United States, the Dow increased nearly 200 percent.

Eventually all things, good or bad, must come to an end. The world bull market did so with a vengeance in October 1987. From the close of trading on Tuesday, October 13, 1987, to the close of trading on Monday, October 19, the total market value of all U.S. stocks declined by approximately $1.0 trillion. In those four trading days, the Dow Jones Industrial Average fell from over 2500 to just above 1700, or 769 points. On Monday, October 19, 1987, alone, the Dow fell 22.6 percent—the largest one-day drop in history. The October 1987 events in the United States had worldwide effects. Sharp declines followed on all other world exchanges, with the Australian and Singapore exchanges falling nearly 50 percent.

This abrupt decline in equity prices has been attributed to numerous fundamental economic factors. Expectations about the status of the dollar, the trade balance, the federal budget deficit, and pending tax legislation are examples of fundamental factors that could affect U.S. corporate equity prices. The abrupt movements in the stock market indexes, however, did not coincide with changes in any of these fundamental factors. All of these components had been elements affecting the market for several years. Also, these fundamental factors were advantageous to some foreign economies and should not have caused consistent declines worldwide.

A number of technical factors have been analyzed for their role in the October 1987 decline. During the market break, those following portfolio insurance strategies tried to liquidate large portions of their stock holdings regardless of the price dictated by the formulas of their models. Another technical factor frequently cited is the failure of the market to keep pace with the transaction volume. Congestion in the stock market meant that index arbitrageurs could not be certain that they could sell while buying in the futures market, resulting in exaggerated declines in futures prices. This created further downward pressure on stock market prices. Though technical factors may have aggravated the decline, the real question is: What caused the stock market to decline so sharply in the first place?

The bursting of a "speculative bubble" is an explanation offered by some economists to explain the October 1987 market break. A speculative bubble is a movement in the price of an asset that is unjustified by changes in fundamental or technical factors. A bubble may form when it is difficult for investors to evaluate fundamental factors that affect the underlying value of the asset. Thus, individuals may hold an asset at a high price simply because it has enjoyed substantial recent capital gains. Successively higher asset prices yield expectations of even higher prices and capital gains. Speculative bubbles burst when the probability of the gains decline; the severity of the October crash can be explained by modest changes in the market fundamentals that affect this probability. Thus, the uncanny similarity between the price movements of October 1987 and October 1929 may be no more than the bursting of two speculative bubbles, and it says little about the similarities of the fundamental economic environment.

Trading is done either on organized exchanges, such as the New York Stock Exchange (NYSE), or in the over-the-counter market.

Securities not sold on one of the organized exchanges are traded over the counter (OTC). When a customer places an order to buy or sell a security in the OTC market, the broker or dealer contacts other dealers who have that particular security for sale. The broker's job is to seek out the best possible price on behalf of the client. It is estimated that from 30,000 to 40,000 various types of equity securities are traded in the OTC market. However, only about 15,000 of these securities are actively traded.

A major development in the OTC market occurred in 1971 when the National Association of Security Dealers (NASD) introduced an automatic computer-based quotation system. The system provides continuous bid and ask prices for more than 3,000 actively traded OTC stocks. The quotations are made possible by having dealers enter any change in bid and ask prices into the computer. When a dealer seeks a buy or sell quote for a customer, the memory is accessed, and all current bid or ask prices are printed out with the name of the dealer to contact.

Globalization of the Equity Markets

The secondary markets for equity securities are becoming increasingly competitive. Improved communications and computer technology have reduced transaction costs, making it easier for other financial intermediaries to compete with security firms and promoting competition among the national exchanges, regional exchanges, over-the-counter markets, and foreign exchanges. Several trends are related to the forces of technology and competition: the emergence of a so-called national market system, the move toward 24-hour trading of equity securities, and the globalization of equity markets.

The Securities Act Amendments of 1975 mandated that the Securities and Exchange Commission (SEC), the primary regulator of the U.S. financial markets, move toward implementing a national market system. In its ideal form, a national market system would include a computer system that records and reports transactions regardless of where they take place, a system that allows investors to obtain price information from any exchange instantaneously, and a means to buy or sell securities at the best price, regardless of location. Although some progress has been made toward electronically linking the national exchanges, regional exchanges, and over-the-counter markets, we are still many years away from a truly nation-wide system.

There is competitive pressure to link international equity markets electronically as well. Many U.S. firms are issuing stocks overseas to take advantage of differences in tax laws, to increase their visibility and reputation worldwide, and to avoid driving down their stock prices by flooding local markets. In 1986, the London Stock Exchange created a computer network similar to the U.S. NASDAQ system and permitted U.S. and Japanese investment firms to trade on the system. This development was important because it created virtual 24-hour global trading, given the time zone differences between New York, London, and Tokyo. Many U.S. companies are listed on exchanges in all three locations.

Stock exchanges in the United States are fearful of losing business to the overseas market. As a step toward increasing the global competitiveness of the U.S. financial markets, the SEC recently permitted after-hours trading on the NYSE. Before, trading on the NYSE took place between 9:30 a.m. and 4:00 p.m. The NYSE now has several after-hours trading sessions during which shares trade electronically at the day's closing price. The biggest beneficiary of the Big Board's move toward globalization will be U.S. companies that expect to broaden the market for their securities. The flow of capital across international boundaries will make it easier for firms to raise money and should ultimately lower the cost of capital in the United States.

The Stock Market as a Predictor of Economic Activity

In the wake of the October 1987 stock market crash there was concern as to whether a recession (or depression!) would follow. Such fears were based on memories of the 1929 stock market crash and the subsequent Great Depression.

Why do some economists and many laymen believe that the stock market can predict economic recessions? First, even if stock prices have no direct effect on the economy, changes in stock prices may precede a recession. If the market consensus is that a recession is imminent, investors may forecast lower corporate profits. Given that stock prices are the discounted sums of future corporate profits, stock prices would then decline. Second, stock price declines reduce the wealth of consumers and, therefore, may lead to reduced consumption spending and a reduction in national income (GNP or GDP). Third, if consumer confidence is adversely affected by stock price declines, consumption spending may decrease, Finally, lower stock prices may increase the cost of raising capital and result in a reduction in business investment.

Empirical evidence suggests the stock market is not very successful in predicting economic activity. A recent study by the Federal Reserve Bank of Kansas City showed that only 11 of the 27 recessions between 1900 and 1987 were successfully predicted by stock market declines.[4] Exhibit 9–7 shows the movement of the Dow Jones Industrial Average of 30 stocks since the early 1900s. As can be seen, there seems to be little correspondence between stock market declines and recessions. Note, however, that the 1990–1991 recession was successfully predicted by the stock market. The crash of 1987, on the other hand, was followed by three more years of economic expansion.

Summary

This chapter discusses the structure and functions of the U.S. capital markets. It notes that capital markets facilitate long-term capital goods financing and that both primary and secondary capital markets exist. Primary market sales include public offerings through competitive or negotiated sales and private (direct) placements. Secondary capital markets are important because they provide purchasers of capital market securities with the ability to adjust their future portfolio positions. Thus more capital flows into the capital markets for investment purposes than would otherwise be the case.

---

[4] See Bryon Higgins, "Is a Recession Inevitable This Year?" *Economic Review*, Federal Reserve Bank of Kansas City, January 1988, pp. 3–16.

Exhibit 9–7   **The Relationship between Recessions and the Stock Market**

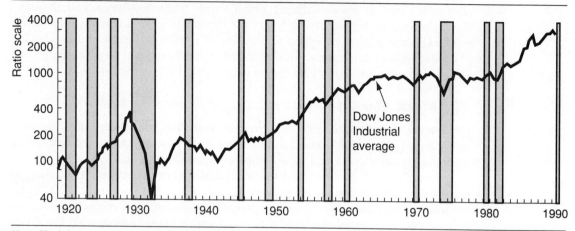

Note: Shaded areas are periods of economic recession

The stock market generally does a poor job of predicting economic recessions.

Sources: Board of Governors of the Federal Reserve System, *1989 Historical Chart Book*; 1990 Economic Report of the President; *Economic Review*, Federal Reserve Bank of Kansas City (January 1988).

Governmental units and corporations are major originators of capital market financial claims. Households are the major suppliers of capital market funds, providing them both directly and indirectly through a variety of financial intermediaries such as commercial banks, pension funds, and life insurance companies.

Several institutions make the capital markets function more effectively. Investment bankers underwrite and help market new issues of securities. Brokers and dealers bring buyers and sellers of securities together. Stock and bond exchanges and computerized trading mechanisms match the needs of buyers and sellers and provide more continuous marketability (and greater liquidity) than would otherwise exist.

Instruments traded in the capital markets include corporate, Eurobond, U.S. Treasury, federal agency, and state and local government bonds; in addition, a variety of corporate equity-related claims are traded. A bond is a contract in which the issuer agrees to make periodic interest payments and to repay the principal at the bond's maturity. Corporate bond indentures vary with respect to the security pledged and the priority of claims to the firm's assets in the event of default. The major investors in corporate bonds are life insurance companies and pension funds, which prefer them because of their variety of longer maturities and after-tax yields.

State and local government bonds, called municipal bonds, are unique because their coupon income is exempt from federal income taxes. This feature makes their after-tax yield attractive to commercial banks, property/casualty insurance companies, and high-income individuals, all of whom have high marginal income tax rates. Municipal bonds are broadly classified as either general obligation bonds, which are backed by the taxing authority of the issuer, or revenue bonds, which are backed by the reserves of a particular project. The market for municipal bonds is segmented into a national market, in which large well-known municipalities sell their bonds, and numerous local markets, in which smaller municipalities sell theirs. No other capital market accommodates so many smaller issuers.

Federal government securities in the capital market include U.S. Treasury notes and bonds and some government agency issues—especially those agencies involved in the mortgage market. However, since the major part of government and agency debt is short-term in maturity, the importance of long-term debt is diminished.

Equity refers to an ownership claim. Common and preferred stock are the principal types of equity securities, and there are also various securities that are convertible into common stock, such as convertible preferred stocks and bonds. Households are the major investors in equity securities, followed by foreign investors and pension funds (private and public). The new-issue market for equity securities is not large; however, the secondary market is the largest and most active for any capital market instrument. Large, well-known firms have their securities listed on one of the national primary markets—the New York Stock Exchange and the American Stock Exchange. Securities of other firms are traded over the counter by dealers and brokers all over the country. Stock markets are becoming increasingly globalized, increasing competitive pressures on U.S. stock exchanges. Generally, the stock market is a poor predictor of economic activity.

Questions

1. How do the capital markets play an important role in the U.S. economy?
2. Why are private placements of securities often popular with both the buyer and seller of the securities?
3. Why do government agency securities carry a slightly higher rate of interest than U.S. Treasury securities?
4. Who are the principal investors in corporate bonds and why? Why do banks hold few corporate bonds?
5. Give a concise definition of the following types of municipal bonds: (a) general obligation, (b) revenue, (c) industrial development, and (d) mortgage-backed.
6. What features make municipal bonds attractive to certain groups of investors? Why do other groups not want to hold municipal securities?
7. Define the following terms: (a) preferred stock, (b) common stock, (c) callable securities, (d) sinking fund provisions, and (e) convertible features of securities.
8. Explain how securities are brought to market under (a) a competitive sale and (b) a negotiated sale. How do the two methods of sale differ?
9. Why is common stock considered to be riskier than preferred stock?
10. Explain how the Tax Reform Act of 1986 affected interest rates in the municipal bond market.

Selected References

Chu, Franklin J. **"The Private Placement Market Comes of Age."** *The Bankers Magazine,* **September–October 1989, pp. 56–60.**
This article provides an excellent discussion of recent developments in the private placement market. It also outlines the costs and benefits of the new SEC Rule 144A.

Fabozzi, Frank, and Tessa Fabozzi. *Bond Markets: Analysis and Strategies*, **Englewood Cliffs, NJ: Prentice-Hall, 1989.**
This book provides an excellent discussion of the markets for corporate, municipal, U.S. Treasury, and agency bonds. It also discusses the pricing of bonds and various yield measures.

Fortune, Peter. "Stock Market Efficiency: An Autopsy." *New England Economic Review.* **Federal Reserve Bank of Boston, March/April 1991, pp. 17–40.**
This article assesses the current state of the efficient market hypothesis, which was conventional wisdom among academic economists in the 1970s and most of the 1980s. It concludes that the empirical evidence provides an overwhelming case against the efficient market hypothesis.

Higgins, Bryon. "Is a Recession Inevitable This Year?" *Economic Review.* **Federal Reserve Bank of Kansas City, January 1988, pp. 3–16.**
This article discusses the ability of stock market movements to predict recessions. It provides a good explanation of why some consider the stock market to be a good economic indicator. It also presents evidence that explains why the stock market does a poor job of predicting recessions.

Hirtle, Beverly. "The Growth of the Financial Guarantee Market." *Quarterly Review.* **Federal Reserve Bank of New York, Spring 1987, pp. 10–28.**
Various types of financial guarantees that have emerged in recent years are examined. Credit enhancements protect investors against default and lower borrowing costs to issuers.

Kopcke, Richard W. "Tax Reform and Stock Prices." *New England Economic Review.* **Federal Reserve Bank of Boston, March/April 1988, pp. 3–21.**
The Tax Reform Act of 1986 extensively revised the federal income tax structure for households and corporations. The article examines the effect of the tax law changes on the value of equity securities.

Lehn, Kenneth, David W. Blackwell, and M. Wayne Marr. "The Economics of Leveraged Takeovers." *Washington University Law Quarterly* **65, no. 1 (1987): pp. 163–191.**
This article examines the functional differences between debt and equity securities. It explains through examples and case studies how junk bonds are used to finance corporate takeovers. Although the article is written for lawyers, it provides a nontechnical perspective on the corporate uses of leverage.

Malkiel, B. G. *A Random Walk Down Wall Street.* **New York: Norton, 1990.**
A readable book describing the operations of the stock market and various theories of investing. Highly recommended.

Peek, Joe, and Eric S, Rosengren. "The Stock Market and Economic Activity." *New England Economic Review.* **Federal Reserve Bank of Boston, May/June 1988, pp. 39–50.**
This article examines the relationship between stock prices and recession and concludes that although stock price movements are related to economic growth, they may not be an accurate indicator of recessions.

Peek, Joe, and James A. Wilcox. "Tax Rates and Interest Rates on Tax-Exempt Securities." *New England Economic Review.* **Federal Reserve Bank of Boston, January/February 1986, pp. 29–41.**
Examines the factors that affect the yield difference between taxable and tax-exempt securities.

Perry, Kevin J., and Robert A. Taggart, Jr. "The Growing Role of Junk Bonds in Corporate Finance." *Journal of Applied Corporate Finance*, **Spring 1988, pp. 37–45.**
Discusses the growth and use of junk bonds, which constitute one of the most controversial recent developments in corporate finance.

Rosengren, Eric S. "The Case for Junk Bonds." *New England Economic Review.* **Federal Reserve Bank of Boston, May/June 1990, pp. 40–49.**
This article describes the evolution of the junk bond market and describes its development as a

natural extension of the long-run trend toward disentermediation occurring in the financial markets.

Silber, William L. "The Process of Financial Innovation." *American Economic Review*, **May 1983, pp. 89–94.**

A readable article that surveys recent innovations in the capital markets and provides a framework for understanding why they developed.

MORTGAGE MARKETS

10

PRACTICALLY NO ONE IS ABLE to afford the price of a new home by paying cash. Almost everyone who buys a home must borrow most of the money to pay for it. Typically, if a person buys a $100,000 home, he or she will borrow at least $80,000 of that amount and pledge the house as collateral, which will be forfeited if the debt is not repaid. Because there are millions of homes sold each year, home buyers need to borrow a great deal of money from the mortgage market.

Mortgage loans are loans collateralized with real property, such as houses. The mortgage market consists of all issuers and buyers of mortgages and the specialized personnel who help bring buyers and sellers together. In recent years the market has grown rapidly and become more complicated. Mortgage debt now constitutes one of the most important components of the nation's capital markets. Total mortgage debt outstanding approximately equals the total of all debt issued by the U.S. Treasury. Furthermore, total mortgage debt outstanding is nearly twice as great as the amount of outstanding corporate and foreign debt owned by United States citizens. Nonetheless, for many years, financial analysts did not concern themselves greatly with mortgage debt. Corporate debt was more interesting, as it was traded actively and revalued frequently. Mortgage debt, in contrast, was usually originated in nonstandard amounts and held by local thrift institutions who knew the local borrower and real estate market well. That, however, has all changed.

In the last 50 years, mortgage debt markets have become much more complicated and challenging. Because of government sponsorship, federally insured and, more recently, privately insured mortgages have become widely available. Insured mortgages can be sold in secondary mortgage markets in competition with bonds. In addition, the government has promoted the formation of mortgage pools that combine many mortgages, often worth many millions of dollars. Investors can purchase pass-through securities that allow them to buy participations in the pool. The participation certificates "pass through" a fraction of all payments of principal and interest made on mortgages in the pool. Initially, owners of the pass-through securities shared equally in the payments made on mortgages in the pool. More recently, however, mortgage-backed bonds and collateralized mortgage obligations have been issued that let some people obtain bondlike cash flows from their mortgage-related investments. As a result, mortgage-backed securities have begun to trade like bonds. They now compete easily with corporate and government bonds in attracting savers' funds from the capital markets.

The growth of the mortgage market has been greatly aided by government activity. Government agencies pioneered the development of mortgage insurance and "pass-through" mortgage debt obligations. In addition, government-sponsored agencies have purchased great quantities of mortgage debt.

The provision of insurance and pass-through claims greatly increased private willingness to hold direct and indirect mortgage claims. However, the growing inflation and related rise in interest rates that occurred from the mid-1960s to the early 1980s made many private institutions unwilling to hold long-term, fixed-rate financial claims of any kind. As a result, many new forms of mortgages, such as adjustable-rate mortgages, have been developed to increase their appeal to private lenders.

This chapter first describes the nature of mortgage markets and instruments. Next, it describes the major participants in the mortgage markets. Finally, it discusses key aspects of government regulation and new trends and developments in the mortgage markets.

The Unique Nature of Mortgage Markets

Mortgage markets are usually treated separately from other capital markets because of several unique differences. First, mortgage loans are always secured by the pledge of real property—land or buildings—as collateral. If a borrower defaults on the loan, the lender can foreclose on the collateral.

Second, mortgage loans are made for varying amounts and maturities, depending on the borrower's needs. Because of their lack of uniform size, they are not readily marketable in secondary markets.

Third, issuers of mortgage loans are typically small, relatively unknown financial entities. Thus only the mortgage lender will gain from investigating the borrower's financial condition fully. In contrast, corporate securities are often held by many thousands of people. Thus any changes in the financial condition of a major corporation are widely reported. In short, more people have an incentive to monitor the financial condition of General Motors than of John Jones.

Fourth, because uniform sizes and types of capital market debt instruments exist and information on the issuers of those instruments is generally widely available, secondary capital markets are highly developed and work very efficiently. Even though secondary trading in mortgage market instruments has increased recently, particularly for insured mortgages, it is much smaller relative to the value of securities outstanding than is the case in the capital markets.

Fifth, mortgage markets are both highly regulated and strongly supported by federal government policies. Federal participation in the operations of other capital markets is much more limited.

The Nature of Mortgage Instruments

Standard Fixed-Rate Mortgages (FRMs)

In a standard mortgage agreement, the lender takes a *lien* on real property and the borrower agrees to make periodic repayments of the principal amount of money borrowed plus interest on the unpaid balance of the debt for a predetermined period of time. The mortgage is *amortized* over time to the extent that the periodic (usually monthly) payments exceed the interest due; any payment in excess of interest is credited toward repayment of the debt. When the mortgage is fully amortized (that is, repaid), the borrower obtains a clear title to the property. Until then, the lien prevents the borrower from disposing of the property without first repaying the debt or agreeing to repay the lender from proceeds of the sale. If the borrower fails to make payments on the property before it is fully amortized, the lender may foreclose and, through legal processes, cause the property to be sold or obtain title to the property.

Exhibit 10–1 shows repayment patterns for two $100,000 mortgages, one with a 30-year maturity and one with a 15-year maturity. Both mortgages are fixed-rate mortgages that pay 9 percent interest. Thus the interest charge in the first month is $750 for each (which equals $100,000 × 9 percent divided by 12 since there are 12 months in a year). However, the 15-year mortgage shown in Panel A of Exhibit 10–1 has a $1,015 monthly payment requirement while the 30-year mortgage shown in Panel B has a $805 payment requirement.

The balance due on the 15-year mortgage falls by $265 in the first month, $267 in the second month, and by greater amounts thereafter (since the monthly interest due falls as the principal balance due on the mortgage declines). While the balance due falls relatively slowly at first, after 10 years it is only half the initial amount due and the mortgage is fully repaid by the end of the 15th year. In the last year the mortgage balance falls sharply because, with a small balance left, interest charges are low and almost all of the $1,015 monthly payment can be used to repay the balance due. In the last month, adjustments can be made for any discrepancies caused by rounding error since a full payment would overpay the mortgage balance in this example.

Panel B of Exhibit 10–1 shows that the monthly payment on the 30-year mortgage is substantially lower, at $805 per month, even though the interest rate and starting balance of the 30-year and 15-year mortgages are the same. The lower payment is the primary appeal of a 30-year mortgage. However, because the first month's interest is still $750, only $55 is left over to reduce the balance due on the mortgage after the first payment. Thus the second month's interest due is $749.59, and the mortgage balance falls only by $55.41 after the second payment is made. Because of the repayment of principal on the 30-year mortgage, most of the mortgage balance is still due after 10 years, and it takes 23 years before one-half of the initial balance is amortized.

In the last year of the 30-year mortgage, once again, the mortgage balance is low, so interest charges are low, and most of the mortgage payment is used to repay principal. Once again, the final payment can be adjusted if round-off error is excessive.

The mortgages are fully amortized in both cases when the initial $100,000 mortgage debt has been repaid. Note, however, that total payments are $182,400-plus on the 15-year mortgage and $289,100-plus on the 30-year mortgage. Thus total interest payments are $82,400-plus on the 15-year mortgage and twice as great at $189,100-plus on the 30-year mortgage. Thus, by making higher monthly payments for a shorter period of time, in this example, the 15-year mortgage debtor saves over $100,000 in total interest due. Consequently, even though the 30-year mortgage borrower's monthly payment is slightly more than 20 percent lower each month, that borrower's interest bill over the life of the mortgage is nearly 130 percent greater (or 2.3 times as large). These comparisons are on a pretax basis, however; for as long as

Exhibit 10–1   Mortgage Balances and Payments

A. Balance due on 15-year, 9%, $100,000 mortgage with payments of $1,015 per month made promptly.

Balance after payment number:

1	2	3	4	5	6	In
99,735.00	99,468.01	99,199.02	98,928.02	98,654.98	98,379.89	Year 1
84,377.69	83,995.52	83,610.49	83,222.57	82,831.74	82,437.97	Year 5
55,553.05	54,954.70	54,351.86	53,744.50	53,132.58	52,516.07	Year 10
10,422.85	9,486.03	8,542.17	7,591.24	6,633.17	5,667.92	Year 15

7	8	9	10	11	12	In
98,102.74	97,823.51	97,542.18	97,258.75	96,973.19	96,685.49	Year 1
82,041.26	81,641.57	81,238.88	80,833.17	80,424.42	80,012.60	Year 5
51,894.94	51,269.16	50,638.67	50,003.46	49,363.49	48,718.72	Year 10
4,695.43	3,715.65	2,728.51	1,733.98	731.98	−277.53	Year 15

Initial mortgage	$100,000	Monthly payments	$1,015	Total payments	$182,400 +
Interest rate	9%	First payment interest	$750	Total interest	$82,400 +
Maturity	15 years	First payment principal	$265	Total principal	$100,000

B. Balance due on 30-year, 9%, $100,000 mortgage with payments of $805 per month made promptly.

Balance after payment number:

1	2	3	4	5	6	In
99,945.00	99,889.59	99,833.76	99,777.51	99,720.84	99,663.75	Year 1
96,757.63	96,678.32	96,598.40	96,517.89	96,436.78	96,355.05	Year 5
90,775.16	90,650.97	90,525.86	90,399.80	90,272.80	90,144.85	Year 10
81,408.52	81,214.08	81,018.19	80,820.82	80,621.98	80,421.64	Year 15
54,215.43	53,817.04	53,415.67	53,011.29	52,603.87	52,193.40	Year 20
7,832.77	7,086.51	6,334.66	5,577.17	4,814.00	4,045.11	Year 30

7	8	9	10	11	12	In
99,606.23	99,548.28	99,489.89	99,431.06	99,371.79	99,312.08	Year 1
96,272.71	96,189.76	96,106.18	96,021.98	95,937.14	95,851.67	Year 5
90,015.93	89,886.05	89,755.20	89,623.36	89,490.54	89,356.71	Year 10
80,219.81	80,016.45	79,811.58	79,605.16	79,397.20	79,187.68	Year 15
51,779.85	51,363.20	50,943.42	50,520.50	50,094.40	49,665.11	Year 20
3,270.44	2,489.97	1,703.65	911.42	113.26	−690.89	Year 30

Initial mortgage	$100,000	Monthly payments	$805	Total payments	$289,100 +
Interest rate	9%	First payment interest	$750	Total interest	$189,100 +
Maturity	30 years	First payment principal	$55	Total principal	$100,000

the government allows mortgage interest payments to be deducted from taxable income, the federal government will absorb part of the extra interest cost.

Conventional and Insured Mortgages.   Standard mortgage contracts can either be conventional or federally insured. Mortgages whose ultimate payment is guaranteed by the Federal Housing Administration (FHA) are called *FHA mortgages*. FHA mortgages must have terms that comply with FHA requirements, and a small fee is added to cover the costs of insurance. Veterans Administration (VA) mortgages are similar, except that the mortgage and borrower must both meet the requirements of the Veterans Administration. VA and FHA mortgages usually have very low or zero down payment requirements.

Conventional mortgages are not insured by a federal government agency. Down payment requirements on conventional mortgages usually are much higher than those on federally insured mortgages. However, if conventional mortgages are privately insured, the borrower typically pays an extra "interest" charge to cover the mortgage insurance premium and, in turn, can borrow with a low down payment.

The use of private mortgage insurance is illustrated in Exhibit 10–2. That figure shows that, with insurance, the lender can extend more credit and not bear additional risk. The mortgage insurer accepts the additional risk in return for the insurance premium payment. The consumer pays the insurance premium in addition to the loan rate (and thereby pays a higher annual percentage rate, since the APR includes the insurance premium). However, the insurance feature allows the consumer to buy a house with a far lower down payment than would otherwise be possible.

Exhibit 10–2   Private Mortgage Insurance

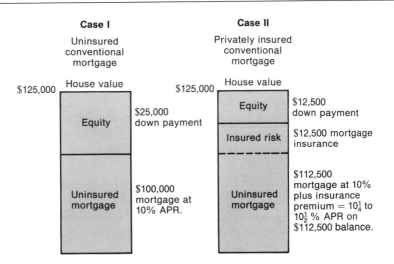

In Case I, the lender extends a $100,000 mortgage at 10 percent and is at risk in case of default only if the house value falls by more than $25,000. In Case II, the lender extends a $112,500 mortgage at 10 percent and is still at risk only if the house value falls by more than $25,000. In the second case, the private mortgage insurance company bears the risk if the house value falls by $12,500 to $25,000 and the borrower defaults, In return, the insurer receives an insurance premium equal to between $1/4$ and $1/2$ percent additional interest on the $112,500 debt.

Conditional Sale Agreements (Land Contracts)

As an alternative to a standard mortgage, many states allow property to be sold under a conditional sale agreement, or land contract. In such a case the property's sale price is agreed upon, along with the interest rate and maturity. Periodic payments are made on the contract, with payments exceeding interest due being used to amortize the debt. No lien is taken, as the property belongs to the seller until all contract terms have been fulfilled. The buyer receives use of the property while making payments, but if the buyer defaults, the sale can be nullified. Conditional sale agreements are most often used by individuals who sell their own property.

Adjustable-Rate Mortgages (ARMs)

Because of sustained inflation, inflationary expectations and market interest rates rose sharply in the 1970s and early 1980s. This posed problems for lenders who held large portfolios of fixed-rate mortgages with low interest rates. Consequently, a number of new forms of mortgages were adopted to minimize lenders' vulnerability to interest rate changes. These *adjustable-rate mortgages* (ARMs) shifted most of the risk of rate variation back to the borrowers by requiring higher monthly payments or slower mortgage amortization if market interest rates rose.

After initial experimentation with variable-rate mortgages (VRMs) starting in the mid-1970s, widespread use of adjustable-rate mortgages was first permitted in April 1981. Since then, ARMs have accounted for a large share of conventional first-mortgage originations, in part because their initial rates have been lower than rates on fixed-rate mortgages. Well over 50 percent of all new mortgages in some years have been ARMs (see Exhibit 10–3), but their popularity varies over time.

ARMs are popular with lenders because they reduce the lender's interest rate risk. Whenever interest rates rise, borrowers' adjustable-rate mortgage payments will also rise. That, in turn, will make it easier for lenders to afford the higher interest rates they will have to pay to depositors at such times. However, since higher payments come out of the borrowers' income, borrowers may have trouble making their payments if mortgage rates and payments rise too much. They may even default on their loans.

At first many ARMs had no limit to the amount by which interest rates could increase. However, such loans were not very popular with potential borrowers. They preferred "capped" ARMs, which may have either a payment cap, an interest rate cap, or both. Payment caps limit the maximum amount by which the monthly payment can increase each year or over the life of the loan. If payments greater than the cap are called for at the new interest rate, the maturity of the loan is increased. If the payment limit is less than the new interest payment, negative amortization occurs and the amount due on the loan increases each month until interest rates fall once again. If interest rates increase without limit and never fall, the borrower may never be able to repay the debt.

Interest rate caps help prevent negative amortization by limiting the amount that the interest rate on a loan can increase during each interest rate period or over the life of the loan. Interest rate caps typically limit maximum interest rate increases to 1 or 2 percent per year and to 5 percent over the life of the loan.

Because of the popularity of capped ARMs with consumers, Congress required in the 1987 CEBA law that all ARMs have a cap. Although capped ARMs have less

Exhibit 10–3   **ARMs' Share of Conventional Mortgages Issued, January 1985–January 1991**

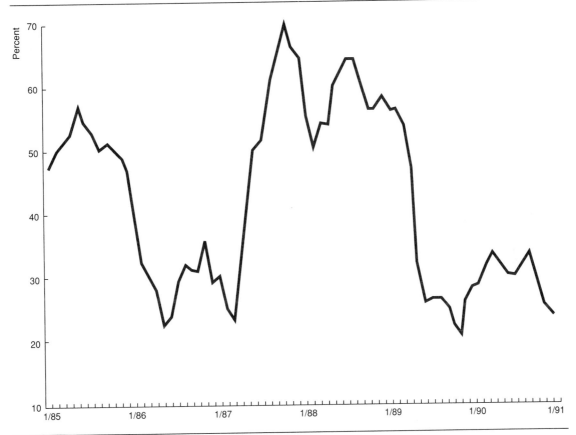

ARMs become more popular when their rates are farther below the rates on fixed-rate mortgages.

Source: Federal Home Loan Bank Bulletin, various dates

default risk than uncapped ARMs, they still leave the lender with a small amount of residual interest rate risk.

Early Payoff Mortgages: Balloon Payment, Rollover (ROMs), and Renegotiated-Rate Mortgages (RRMs)

As an alternative to ARMs, lenders have sometimes experimented with early payoff mortgages of various types. Balloon payment mortgages were frequently used in the United States prior to the Great Depression. Rollover mortgages (ROMs) are used extensively in Canada and Wisconsin. In 1980, the Federal Home Loan Bank Board authorized federally chartered savings associations to acquire renegotiated-rate mortgages (RRMs).

Balloon payment mortgages, ROMs, and RRMs basically provide a borrower with a fixed-rate mortgage that expires at a predetermined time (often in three, four, five, or seven years). The unpaid balance of the mortgage then comes due in a substantially larger *balloon payment*. When that occurs, however, the unpaid balance due can be refinanced at prevailing interest rates. This allows the lender and borrower to renegotiate the mortgage rate periodically without recourse to complicated formulas. Thus, like ARMs, these mortgages shorten the length of time a lender can be locked into low-interest-rate mortgages if market interest rates rise. It also shortens the length of time the lender will receive relatively high returns if market interest rates fall.

Balloon payment mortgages are risky for borrowers because their refinancing at maturity is not necessarily guaranteed. A borrower who cannot repay or refinance the debt at maturity could lose the property. Because of high numbers of defaults during the 1930s, balloon payment mortgages were little used in the United States for many years.

ROMs avert some of the problems of balloon payment loans by guaranteeing that the mortgage can be refinanced at prevailing interest rates. Their terms, however, can vary with the lender, and delinquent debtors might have trouble refinancing their loans.

In 1980, when the Federal Home Loan Bank Board authorized federal S&Ls to issue RRMs, it established guidelines to protect consumers. Under these guidelines, mortgage renewals would be guaranteed (even if past payments had not always been prompt), the mortgage would have a defined amortization period, and total interest rate adjustments would be limited to $\frac{1}{2}$ of 1 percent per year and to 5 percent in total.

ARM Rate Adjustments

Adjustable-rate mortgages use various measures for adjusting their rates, including Treasury security rates, current fixed-rate mortgage indexes, savings and loan cost-of-funds indexes, and the national prime rate. In addition, their rates can be adjusted with varying lags—such as monthly, quarterly, or every year or two. In no case, however, can the rate be adjusted solely at the lender's discretion, and in all cases the exact method of rate adjustment must be fully disclosed when the loan is originated. In particular, the ARM regulation of the Federal Home Loan Bank Board (FHLBB), which replaced previous regulations affecting VRMs and RRMs, gave much more flexibility to the lender and borrower. It allowed rate adjustments to be implemented through changes in payment amounts, the outstanding principal loan balance, or loan maturity, provided that the method of adjustment was specified in the contract. It allowed rates to be adjusted according to any rate index that was readily verifiable to the borrowers and beyond the control of the lender. To protect consumers, it prohibited the use of indexes tied to the lender's own cost of funds or the lender's current mortgage rate. It also required that borrowers be provided with 30- to 45-day advance notice of pending rate changes and be allowed to prepay the loan without penalties. These provisions made it possible for dissatisfied borrowers to seek alternative financing sources during the term of the loan. Because of its great flexibility and its accessibility to all federally chartered institutions, the ARM is now the most popular form of adjustable-rate mortgage loan.

Pricing Risk Transfers

Lenders like adjustable-rate loans because they reduce their interest rate risk. Thus lenders are willing to "pay" borrowers to assume interest rate risk by offering lower rates on ARMs. However, borrowers incur the interest rate risk that lenders avoid. Thus borrowers are willing to pay higher rates to have the lender assume the interest rate risk inherent in a fixed-rate, long-term mortgage. The market, then, prices risk differences in variable- and fixed-rate obligations by setting the degree of rate reduction for adjustable-rate mortgages that will satisfy both borrowers and lenders (see Exhibit 10–4).

The transfer of interest rate risk from lenders to borrowers through an ARM is not complete, however. If rates rise sufficiently, monthly payments could rise to the point that the borrower could not repay the debt at all. The credit risk of the loan would rise and a default could occur. Thus ARMs do not allow lenders to eliminate *all* risk associated with fluctuating mortgage rates. Without caps, the lender incurs greater credit risk on ARMs as interest rates rise; with caps, the lender still bears some interest rate risk.

Consumers' willingness to assume ARM obligations also varies with their expectations for future interest rate movements. If they think rates are likely to fall, they may be more willing to borrow with ARM mortgages even if ARM rates are close to FRM rates. However, if they expect interest rates to rise, they will want a larger discount from the FRM rate. At such times, the term structure of interest rates is likely to be upsloping, so lenders may be able to accommodate their wishes. However, some lenders may go further and "sweeten" the initial ARM rate discount from FRM rates

---

Exhibit 10–4   Rate Difference Needed for Borrowers to Take the Risk of an Adjustable-Rate Mortgage

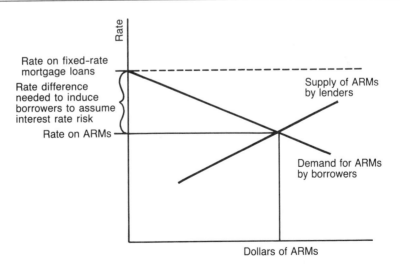

Note: When ARM rates equal rates on fixed-rate mortgage loans, it is assumed that the demand will be zero, because the borrower will receive no compensation for taking on the extra risk. As the ARM rate falls further below the fixed-rate loan rate, however, the demand for such loans will increase. At the same time, the supply of ARMs falls when lenders must give up more to reduce their risk.

Typically, lenders will offer rates on ARMs that are marked up by a certain percentage (usually 2 to 3 percent) over a short-term index rate. Consumer demand will determine the maximum markup lenders can obtain.

by offering "teaser rates." The teaser rates may apply for the first year and then adjust to whatever the rate-setting formula requires. Consumers must be cautious when they take on ARMs with "teaser rates" since rates on such loans may increase when the initial subsidy period is over even if market interest rates don't change. Exhibit 10–5 illustrates the fact that new ARM rates are always below new FRM rates.

Other Mortgage Instruments

Inflation or expected inflation in wages, salaries, and housing values has induced lenders and borrowers to develop many new varieties of mortgages at various times. We now discuss some of the most widely used.

Graduated-Payment Mortgages (GPMs and GPAMLs).   Graduated-payment mortgages (GPMs) are designed to make home purchases more affordable for people

---

Exhibit 10–5   Mortgage Interest Rates for FRMs and Capped and Uncapped ARMs
January 1985–January 1991

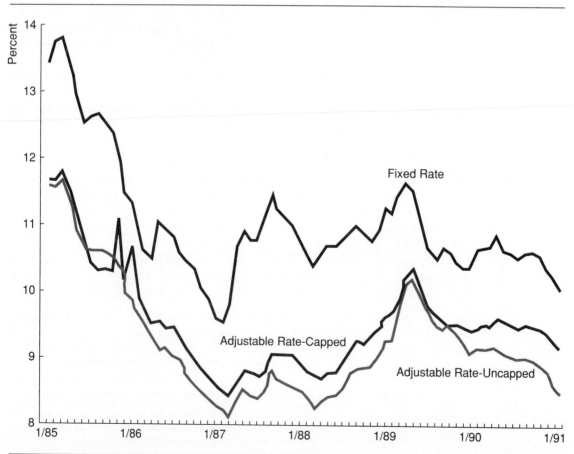

Note: Average initial effective interest rates on conventional mortgages.

Source: *Federal Home Loan Bank Bulletin*, various dates.

who expect their incomes to rise. They are similar to standard mortgages except that instead of having constant repayment streams, they have lower payments in the first few years (so low that they may not cover the full amount of interest due on the debt). However, after a few years, monthly payments on GPMs start to rise. At that time, presumably, the borrower will be better able to make higher payments.

A popular variant of the GPM is the graduated-payment, adjustable-rate loan (GPAML). Such a mortgage lets the borrower qualify for low fixed monthly payments in the early years of the mortgage, but it lets interest accrue to the lender at competitive market rates. After a few years of predetermined payments, payment rates or maturities are adjusted to account for changes in market rates.

Growing-Equity Mortgages (GEMs). Growing-equity mortgages (GEMs) are similar to graduated-payment mortgages in that they call for rising payments over time. However, the rising payments allow the loan to be paid off much faster than would otherwise be the case. GEMs are attractive to consumers who wish to repay high-interest mortgage debt quickly and to lending institutions that do not want to tie up funds in long-maturity loans. An alternative to a GEM is a 15-year FRM.

Shared-Appreciation Mortgages (SAMs). The sharp rise in interest rates in the 1970s and early 1980s was basically caused because people expected inflation to continue. Thus lenders would not lend unless they could get a rate high enough to allow them to obtain their desired "real" return after subtracting the effect of inflation on their purchasing power. SAMs provided a way that lenders could guarantee a real return without charging a higher rate. In a SAM, the borrower pays a lower rate of interest in return for agreeing to share a portion of the price appreciation in the house with the lender. Because of the low monthly payments, borrowers can qualify for SAMs more easily.

Equity Participation Mortgages. An equity participation mortgage differs from a SAM in that it is an outside investor, not the lender, who shares in the price appreciation of the property. The outside investor either provides some of the money needed to buy the house or agrees to share the payment obligation with the buyer. In either case, the buyer's payment obligations are reduced so he or she can more easily qualify to buy the property. The investor who provides money "up front" receives a share of the price appreciation in the house. The investor who helps make monthly payments may also receive valuable annual tax write-offs. However, if house prices do not rise, SAM and ERM investors may find they have made bad investments.

Reverse Annuity Mortgages (RAMs). Reverse annuity mortgages (RAMs) are designed for older people who own their homes and need additional funds to meet current living expenses but do not want to sell their homes. RAMs allow people to borrow against the equity in their homes at relatively low interest rates.

RAMs are written so that instead of making regular monthly payments, the borrower receives them. At the end of the payment term, often 10 or 15 years, the mortgage on the borrower's home equals a predetermined amount. The value of the borrower's equity in the home is also reduced by that amount—a fact that has limited the popularity of RAMs.

Second Mortgages. Second mortgages, or "junior mortgages," consist of loans secured by liens on properties that are already mortgaged. In the event of a default and liquidation, the second mortgage holder gets repaid only after the first mortgage holder has been paid.

Second mortgages can help people purchase homes with smaller down payments than they otherwise could. They can be used in creative-financing plans designed to pass on to a home buyer the benefits of a preexisting low, fixed-rate, first-mortgage loan. Second mortgages also are used by current homeowners to obtain cash by borrowing against their household equity instead of selling their home.

After the 1986 tax changes, the popularity of second mortgages increased greatly, because interest on such mortgages could be deducted (within limits) from taxes whereas interest deductions for other types of consumer credit were phased out. Subsequently, many lenders began to offer *home equity* credit lines that let consumers borrow on a credit line secured with a second mortgage on their homes. Some lenders even let borrowers use credit cards to access their credit lines.

Other Types of Mortgages.   Participants in the mortgage market are creative, constantly designing mortgages for people with special tax, inflation, or financial problems. Thus the "alphabet soup" of mortgage types is constantly expanding. Exhibit 10–6 summarizes the characteristics of the major types of mortgages.

Mortgage-Backed Securities

For many years, mortgage credit was primarily provided by local depository institutions. However, with the advent of FHA-insured mortgages in the 1930s, a secondary market for mortgages began to develop. This process was enhanced even more by the development of federally insured GNMA mortgage pools in 1968. Subsequently a wide variety of mortgage-backed securities (summarized in Exhibit 10–7) have been developed to allow mortgage lenders to obtain funds from the nation's capital markets.

Pass-Through Mortgage Securities

Pass-through mortgage securities pass through all payments of principal and interest on pools of mortgages to holders of security interests in the pool. The security interests represent a fractional share in the pool. Thus, if someone owns 1 percent of a pool of securities, that person is entitled to receive 1 percent of all principal and interest payments made.

Pass-through mortgage securities are popular because, unlike the underlying mortgages, they initially are sold in standard denominations, and, if the guarantor of the pool is well known, they are readily marketable.

Since GNMA (the Government National Mortgage Association) began guaranteeing pass-through securities in 1968, their growth has been great. They now total more than $1 trillion.

Ginnie Mae Pass-Throughs

The Government National Mortgage Association (GNMA—Ginnie Mae) was organized in 1968. GNMA issues securities that pass through all payments of interest and

Exhibit 10–6   **Mortgage Characteristics**

Type	Minimum Down Payment	Maturity	Payments	Rate
Conventional fixed-rate (FRM)	Usually 20% or more, unless privately insured	Fixed, usually 15 to 30 years	Fixed	Fixed
FHA and VA	3–10% for FHA, 0% for VA	Fixed, usually 30 years	Fixed	Fixed, cannot exceed government-set limit; insurance fee is extra
Adjustable-rate (ARM)	Same as conventional	Often 30 years, but can vary as rates change. If it does not vary, then payments will vary with rates.	Can be fixed or variable; will vary if maturity does not	Variable according to predetermined rate indexes
Balloon payment	Often the same as conventional, lower for seller financing	Usually 1 to 7 years, then the remaining balance must be refinanced at current rates	Fixed	Usually fixed
Rollover (ROM) and renegotiated-rate (RRM)	Same as balloon	Same as balloon, but the ability to refinance may be guaranteed	Fixed	Fixed for a period, then recontracted
Growing-equity (GEM)	Same as conventional	Often 15 years	Increase over time	Fixed
Graduated-payment (GPM)	5–10%	Often 30 years	Increase over time	Fixed
Adjustable-rate, graduated-payment (GPAML)	5–10%	Can vary with rates like ARMs	Increase for a few years; may vary thereafter	Variable according to rate indexes, like ARMs
Reverse annuity (RAM)	None	Fixed, usually 20 years or less	Fixed payments are made to the borrower	Fixed
Shared-appreciation (SAM)	Varies	Fixed, but usually must be refinanced in 10 years or less	Fixed	Fixed, but lender shares in property's price appreciation upon refinancing
Equity participation	Same as conventional, but the investor may pay a portion	Fixed	Fixed, but the investor may pay a portion	Fixed, but investor shares in property's price appreciation

The various mortgage types have considerably different characteristics. People who deal in the mortgage market often differentiate them by their initials (ARM, GEM, etc.).

Exhibit 10–7   Mortgage-Backed Securities

Type	Issuer	Security	Payments	Insurance
Pass throughs				
GNMA	Government National Mortgage Association	Pools of new FHA and VA mortgages— all with the same rate and originator	All principal and interest payments are passed through to security holders	FHA and VA plus GNMA guarantee
Participation certificate (PC)	Federal Home Loan Mortgage Corporation	Pools of new conventional mortgages—can have varied rates and originators	Same as GNMA	FHLMC guarantees ultimate payment of principal and interest
Privately issued pass-through (PIP)	Various private institutions	Pools of conventional mortgages— can have varied rates and originators	Same as GNMA	Privately insured
Unit investment trust	Investment banking firms	Pools of mortgages— often second mortgages	Pass-throughs of interest and principal payments	Varies wth the pool; most are insured
Mortgage mutual fund shares	Mutual funds specializing in mortgages	Mortgage-backed securities	Interest income distributed, principal repayments reinvested	Most funds hold GNMA-insured pass-throughs
Mortgage-backed bonds				
FNMA or FHLMC debt issue	FNMA or FHLMC	FNMA's or FHLMC's assets (mostly mortgages) and government credit line	Regular, contractual payments	None, except all GNMA mortgages are federally insured and some FHLMC mortgages are privately insured
FHLMC guaranteed mortgage certificate	FHLMC	Pool of mortgages	Semiannual, will be repurchased by FHLMC after 15 years	FHLMC guarantee
Privately issued mortgage-backed bonds, including CMOs (collateralized mortgage obligations) and REMICs (real estate mortgage investment conduits)	Varies with issuer, often issued by thrift institutions	Pools of mortgages held by thrifts, often overcollateralized (up to 150%) or collateralized with GNMA, FNMA, or FHLMC securities	Regular, may be on contractual basis; some tranches (subdivisions of mortgage pools) are scheduled to receive all principal payments first or second, etc., until fully repaid. Other CMOs may pay only interest to one class of security (IO) and only principal (PO) to another class. The "residual class" is repaid last.	None, but mortgages used as collateral often are insured or backed by government agency guarantees and pools may be backed with letters of credit
State or local mortgage revenue bond	State housing authorities or municipalities	Mortgage revenues earned on specific housing (finance) programs	Regular contractual payments	None

A great variety of securities have been issued that are backed either directly or indirectly by portfolios of individual mortgage loans.

principal received on a pool of *federally insured* mortgage loans. GNMA guarantees that all payments of principal and interest will be made on a timely basis. Because many mortgages are repaid before maturity, investors in GNMA pools usually recover most of their principal investment well ahead of schedule (see Did You Know?).

GNMA mortgage pools are originated by mortgage bankers, commercial banks, or other mortgage-granting institutions. Once a pool of mortgages is assembled according to GNMA specifications, pass-through securities are issued that are collateralized by interest and principal payments from the mortgages in the pool and are guaranteed by GNMA. GNMA securities are issued in $25,000 minimum denominations with $5,000 increments. Minimum pool sizes for single-family loans are $1 million.

For providing its guarantee and services, GNMA charges a fee equal to $\frac{1}{2}$ of 1 percent (50 basis points). Six basis points of its fee are retained by GNMA to cover its guarantee requirements and the other 44 are passed on to the mortgage-servicing institution. Investors are quite willing to "pay" the fee by accepting lower yields on GNMAs than on other mortgages that are uninsured and less readily marketable.

Freddie Mac PCs

The Federal Home Loan Mortgage Corporation (FHLMC—Freddie Mac) was established by Congress in 1970 as a subsidiary of the Federal Home Loan Bank System. Like its parent, it assists savings and loan associations.

Savings and loan associations primarily make conventional mortgages, which are not eligible for inclusion in GNMA pools. Furthermore, such loans often are not privately insured. Thus, before 1970, most savings and loans could not easily sell their mortgage holdings to obtain funds in the secondary markets.

Freddie Mac was established to provide a secondary market for conventional mortgages. Freddie Mac can purchase mortgages for its own account. It also issues pass-through securities—called participation certificates (PCs)—and guaranteed mortgage certificates (GMCs) that resemble bonds.

Participation certificates issued by Freddie Mac are similar to GNMA pass-throughs in that they are backed by pools of mortgages and pass through all principal and interest payments made on mortgages in those pools. However, they are unlike GNMA securities in that (1) they contain conventional mortgages, (2) the mortgages are not federally insured, (3) the pools are assembled by the FHLMC rather than by private-sector mortgage originators, (4) the mortgages in the pools may be made at more than one interest rate, and (5) the underlying mortgage pools are much larger than GNMA pools, with values ranging up to several hundred million dollars. In addition, the minimum denomination for a participation certificate is $100,000.

Guaranteed Mortgage Certificates (GMCs).   Issued by the FHLMC, these are similar to pass-through securities in that they represent an ownership interest in a particular pool of mortgages. However, they are similar to conventional bonds in that they guarantee repayment of principal and interest on a regular basis (semiannually for interest and annually for principal repayments). The FHLMC guarantees that all contractual payments due on the GMCs will be made on a timely basis and also guarantees the ultimate repayment of principal or repurchase of the GMC.

DID YOU KNOW?

GNMA Yields May Not Be What You Expect

Often one hears or sees advertisements promising high rates of return on "government-guaranteed" GNMA securities or mutual funds. Although interest and principal payments are guaranteed on GNMA securities, the yield on a GNMA security will vary according to when the individual mortgages in the mortgage pool that backs a GNMA security are repaid.

For convenience, the usual yield to maturity quoted on GNMA securities assumes that no mortgages in the pool will prepay for 12 years and then all of them will be repaid in full. Of course, this assumption is not realistic, because some mortgages will prepay the balance due and some may not prepay at all (paying back principal slowly over 30 years, as scheduled). For lack of a better assumption, however, the "12-year life" assumption roughly reflects the fact that many mortgages will be prepaid before maturity.

Let us assume that you have a choice of buying one of three GNMA securities. The first, P_L, contains mortgages that pay 8 percent interest and has a price of $86\frac{1}{2}$ and a quoted yield of 10.18 percent. The second, P_M, contains mortgages that pay 10.5 percent interest and has a price of $101\frac{6}{32}$ and a quoted yield of 10.47 percent. The third, P_H, contains mortgages that pay 15 percent interest and has a price of $114\frac{3}{4}$ and a quoted yield of 12.81 percent. It looks as if the P_H pool is the best deal because it has the highest quoted yield by far.

However, what happens if you buy one of these GNMAs and all mortgages in it prepay at the end of one year, not 12 years? The return on P_L is then 10.18 percent in interest plus 15.61 percent in capital gains as the $86\frac{1}{2}$ price investment rises to 100 (a 15.61 percent gain on each $86\frac{1}{2}$ invested) in one year. Similar calculations show that the total return on P_M if it is prepaid in one year is 9.3 percent (or 10.47

percent − 1.17 percent), and the total return on P_H is −0.04 percent (or 12.81 percent − 12.85 percent). The capital loss (resulting from early prepayment of the mortgages in the high-yield GNMA pool at face value soon after the GNMA is purchased for a premium price) causes the investor to lose money—even though P_H quoted the highest annual return.

Because GNMA yields often are not what they are expected to be, investment bankers and others who invest in GNMA securities have spent millions of dollars trying to figure out what causes mortgages to be prepaid. The investigators have clearly determined that prepayments increase if market interest rates fall, because then homeowners often obtain new mortgage financing to pay off their loans. In addition, the prepayment rate on mortgages in GNMA pools tends to accelerate a few years after the mortgage is originated, as people move and sell their house. Some people also think that they can find "fast-paying" and "slow-paying" pools of GNMA securities by identifying GNMA pools originated in certain parts of the country where people move more or less often, or by identifying GNMA pools which prepay faster or slower than the national average. Such efforts may or may not work.

Because GNMA prepayments cannot be predicted precisely, the yield to maturity is only certain on GNMA pools in which all the underlying mortgages are currently worth their face value. Other pools have variable rates of return and will be priced according to the repayment assumptions made by potential buyers. However, whenever an investment promises a higher yield than another investment with equal default risk, it is wise to assume that there is a good chance that the high quoted yield will not be realized.

For a fee, Freddie Mac will issue mortgage-backed securities under swap agreements with individual financial institutions. An institution can swap a portion of its mortgage portfolio with Freddie Mac in exchange for Freddie Mac securities (collateralized with those mortgages) that pay a slightly lower rate of interest. Because of Freddie Mac's creditworthiness, its securities can easily be sold to generate cash. However, because the swap is not treated as a sale for tax purposes, the institution does not need to record a loss if the mortgages are exchanged for FHLMC certificates worth less than their face value. Also, once Freddie Mac issues participation certificates, they can be used to collateralize issues of CMOs or REMICs.

Freddie Mac lets the originators of the mortgages service them and pays them a service fee, often 3/8 of 1 percent. In addition, the FHLMC charges an administration and insurance fee of 30 to 50 basis points. In return for that fee, it provides administrative services, guarantees the monthly pass-through of interest and scheduled principal repayments, and guarantees the ultimate repayment of the mortgages.

CMOs and REMICs

In recent years new varieties of mortgage-backed debt securities have been invented. Privately issued collateralized mortgage obligations (CMOs) consist of a series of related debt obligations, called *tranches*, which divide up the principal and interest payments made on a pool of mortgages and pay principal and interest to various borrowers with different priorities. For instance, tranche A securities usually receive a fixed interest rate plus all principal payments until the entire tranche is repaid. Each obligation in the debt series except the "residual series" has a fixed maturity priority and interest payments similar to a corporate bond (see People & Events). Wall Street investment banks sell CMOs on behalf of originating thrift institutions and their subsidiaries. As shown in the tombstone ad in Exhibit 10–8, CMO tranches typically have a variety of maturity dates that can be tailored to lender's needs. Some other CMOs may contain "interest only" (IO) tranches, coupled with "principal only" (PO) tranches; some CMOs may even have tranches that have floating rates if the tranche is backed by a pool of floating rate mortgages or is paired with an "inverse floater" tranche.

The major advantage of CMOs is that, except for the interest only or (residual) class, the size and value of their payments is more certain than payments on their underlying mortgages unless prepayments vary unexpectedly. The major problem with CMOs is that they may create tax problems for various originators, because most originators cannot pass through all interest payments tax-free when they issue multiple debt securities. To solve this problem, the 1986 Tax Reform Act authorized the creation of a new form of mortgage-backed security. The new form was called a REMIC (real estate mortgage investment conduit), which was treated like a trust that could pass through all interest and principal payments to buyers of the pass-through securities before taxes were levied. REMICs are pass-through securities in the same manner as CMOs. They differ from CMOs only in their legal structure. Often pass-through securities issued by the FHLMC or FNMA are used to back issues of CMOs or REMICs.

Exhibit 10–8   Collateralized Mortgage Obligation Offering

This announcement is neither an offer to sell nor a solicitation of an offer to buy these securities. The offer is made only by the Prospectus Supplement and the related Prospectus.

New Issue / October 2, 1985

$313,395,000

Salomon Capital Access Corporation

Collateralized Mortgage Obligations, Series 1985-3

$157,830,000 8.750% Class A, to be fully paid by October 1, 1999 @ 97.000%
$ 32,870,000 8.700% Class B, to be fully paid by April 1, 2001   @ 89.410%
$ 94,550,000 8.625% Class C, to be fully paid by October 1, 2004 @ 85.625%
$ 28,145,000 8.500% Class Z, to be fully paid by April 1, 2015   @ 64.750%

(and accrued interest from October 1, 1985)

The Bonds will be collateralized by Funding Agreements between the Issuer and Finance Subsidiaries of savings institution participants and by related Notes issued by such Finance Subsidiaries, which Notes are initially secured by GNMA Certificates and FHLMC Certificates to the extent provided in such Funding Agreements and Notes.

The Bonds represent obligations solely of the Issuer, and are not insured or guaranteed by GNMA, FHLMC or any other government agency or instrumentality or any other person or entity. The Issuer is not expected to have any significant assets other than those pledged as collateral for the Bonds and similar series of bonds.

Govaars and Associates, Newport Beach, California, has acted as investment adviser to certain of the savings institutions participating in this transaction.

Capital Access℠ is a program for savings institutions sponsored by Salomon Brothers Inc and U.S. League Investment Services, Inc., a subsidiary of the United States League of Savings Institutions.

Copies of the Prospectus Supplement and the related Prospectus may be obtained in any State in which this announcement is circulated only from such of the undersigned as may legally offer these securities in such State.

Salomon Brothers Inc

Bear, Stearns & Co.   **The First Boston Corporation**   **Goldman, Sachs & Co.**

Merrill Lynch Capital Markets   **Morgan Stanley & Co.**
                                                                       Incorporated

PaineWebber   **Shearson Lehman Brothers Inc.**
Incorporated

Savings associations form pools of mortgages that are financed by issuing series of collateralized mortgage obligations with the help of investment banking firms.

Source: Reprinted with permission of Salomon Brothers Inc.

Advantages of Mortgage-Backed Bonds. The newly developed secondary mortgage market securities all have attributes that are lacking in individual mortgages but that are desirable for capital market instruments.

1. They are issued in standardized denominations. Thus they are more readily tradable in both the primary and secondary capital markets.
2. They either are issued by large, well-known borrowers or are insured by a well-known institution whose credit standing can be checked and evaluated relatively easily. This increases their marketability.
3. They are usually insured and highly collateralized. Thus they have low degrees of risk and high credit ratings. Many have their principal and interest payments guaranteed by the U.S. government.
4. They have repayment schedules (for principal and interest) more similar to those offered on government or corporate debt issues.

Because of these considerations, secondary mortgage market instruments compete effectively for funds in the conventional capital markets and allow mortgage-lending institutions to attract funds more easily.

FNMA Pass-Throughs

The Federal National Mortgage Association (FNMA) was started in the 1930s and originally was a government agency whose primary purpose was to buy government-guaranteed (FHA) mortgages in the secondary market. In 1968, however, FNMA was turned into a private corporation, although it still retained a credit line with the Treasury and some government representatives on its board of directors. Because of its credit line, FNMA debt is considered to be government agency debt. As a privately run agency, FNMA has been able to develop a variety of pass-through securities similar to FHLMC's PCs. FNMA can issue pass-throughs for either federally insured or conventional mortgages.

Privately Issued Pass-Throughs (PIPs)

Freddie Mac's success in purchasing mortgages and issuing mortgage-backed securities sparked a number of imitators in the private sector. Some began their operations because private sellers of mortgages thought that FHLMC's insurance and administrative charges were excessively high relative to the risk of default on conventional mortgages.

Privately issued pass-through securities (PIPs) first appeared in 1977. PIPs are issued by private institutions or mortgage bankers, which pool mortgages, obtain private mortgage insurance, obtain ratings for the security issue, and sell the securities using underwriters' services to compete for funds in the bond markets.

Other Pass-Through Securities

In addition to buying formal pass-through securities, investors can buy the right to receive a share of interest and principal payments made on a pool of mortgages by buying shares in private unit investment trusts or mutual funds.

PEOPLE
& EVENTS

Watch Out for Residual Risk

The most popular financial instruments traded in the mortgage markets include CMOs and REMICs. Security issues of this type largely replicate the payment pattern of bonds. Most classes of these securities promise to make fixed semiannual interest payments and fixed-term principal payments just like corporate bonds, even though the payment of principal and interest on the underlying pool of mortgages is uncertain. The cash flows on the underlying mortgages are uncertain because some people may decide to prepay their mortgages and because, for adjustable-rate mortgages, the applicable interest rate can change. Thus, when CMOs and REMIC securities are sold for a pool of mortgages, one security class is the "residual class"—sometimes called the Z class. The residual security pays its buyers only after the payment is made on the fixed claims of the other CMO and REMIC securities backed by the same pool of mortgages. The problem with the residuals is that their ultimate payment pattern is very uncertain. Thus buyers of residuals pay a low price and *expect* to earn a high, but very uncertain, rate of return.

Some buyers have found, to their regret, that it is very hard to predict the cash flows and payout pattern of a residual class of securities. The pattern of repayment is particularly difficult to predict for residual tranches or for "principal only" mortgage-backed securities. Such securities may not be repaid in full until all mortgages are repaid in 30 years. Conversely, such securities may be repaid in only a few years if all mortgages in the pool are repaid early. Because of the difficulty in forecasting mort-

gage repayments, investment banks and others have sometimes taken large losses in their mortgage-backed security portfolios. For instance, in April 1987, Merrill Lynch suffered a $375 million loss (the largest ever trading loss by an investment bank) when interest rates rose more than 1 percent in a month and "principal only" mortgage securities plummeted in value. When interest rates rise, people slow mortgage prepayments so mortgage principal repayments, on average, are received in the more distant future. Furthermore, with rising interest rates, those future payments are more heavily discounted. Merrill Lynch's (former) trader had not adequately hedged his portfolio of "principal only" mortgage-backed securities against the possibility that interest rates would rise and principal repayments would slow. Thus, Merrill Lynch incurred gigantic losses when market interest rates spiked upward. Shortly after, in June 1988, a new firm called Residential Resources Mortgage Investments Corporation started business as a real estate investment trust whose stated objective was to earn a high (promised) rate of return by investing in residual mortgage securities. By January 1989 (only seven months later), it declared bankruptcy. Rising interest rates, coupled with an inversion in the yield curve, caused the value of its residuals to fall dramatically. When buying residual securities, the buyer must protect against both the risk that the term structure of interest rates will change shape and the risk that the level of interest rates will change. This is difficult to do, as Residential Resources found.

Unit Investment Trusts.   Investment-banking firms may buy a group of mortgages, form them into a unit investment trust, and sell units in the trust to individual investors. The trust is passively managed, passing through payments of interest and principal on the initial pool until all mortgages are repaid. Usually the mortgages in the pool are insured, often with private mortgage insurance. Individual pools may specialize in types of mortgages that have reduced interest rate risk or that promise a higher return to investors than conventional first mortgages. Unit investment trusts are particularly appealing to investors if the investment bank provides marketability by standing ready to repurchase them at current market values.

Mortgage-Backed Mutual Funds.   Because of the large minimum-purchase requirements ($25,000 or more) and the specialized knowledge needed to deal with the GNMA securities market, several mutual funds have been established to buy GNMA securities. Although GNMA securities generate higher yields than Treasury bonds, they remain federally insured. Thus many investors have been eager to invest varying amounts in order to share in the income the mutual funds generate. Investors should be careful though, to be sure that a GNMA mutual fund does not quote a high yield only because it has invested in premium-priced securities (see Did You Know?).

Mortgage-Backed Bonds

FHLMC and FNMA Debt.   General obligation securities issued by the FHLMC are basically secured by pools of mortgages that the FHLMC holds. Similarly, issues of notes and debentures by the quasi-governmental Federal National Mortgage Association basically are secured by the FNMA's mortgage holdings. Because mortgages provide excellent collateral for their note and debenture issues and they both have government credit lines, the FNMA and FHLMC are able to issue securities at very favorable rates.

Private Mortgage-Backed Debt.   Mortgage-backed bonds can be issued by any holder of mortgages. They pay interest semiannually and have a fixed maturity (often five or ten years) just like corporate, government, or federal agency bonds. However, they are collateralized by a specific pool of mortgages. The trust agreements associated with such bond issues often call for high collateral maintenance levels (150 percent or more of the value of the bonds). As a result, they obtain very high ratings (often AAA) and can compete effectively for funds in the capital markets.

Mortgage-backed bonds provide thrift institutions and commercial banks with an effective way to obtain relatively low-cost funds when their savings flows are inadequate. These bonds can be particularly helpful when a credit crunch occurs and the term structure of interest rates inverts.

In contrast with private pass-throughs (which are backed by issues of new mortgages) and new GNMA pools (which contain only mortgages written within the last year), mortgage-backed bonds allow financial institutions to borrow against the value of mortgages already in their portfolios. Such bonds greatly expand those institutions' borrowing potential and eliminate the possibility that they might have to sell (at a discount) some old, low-rate mortgages so that they can obtain more funds during financial crises. If the old bonds were sold at a discount, an institution would have to write down its net worth.

State and Local Government Housing Revenue Bonds.   Mortgage-backed bonds may be issued by particular state and local government agencies, such as state housing finance agencies or municipalities. The interest paid on housing revenue–backed bonds usually is exempt from federal taxes, as they are municipal obligations.

Thus they can be sold at advantageous rates, and the proceeds from their sale allow municipalities and housing authorities to provide mortgage credit at relatively low rates.

Participants in the Mortgage Markets

Mortgage Holders

The major holders of mortgage instruments are shown in Exhibit 10–9. They include thrift institutions, commercial banks, life insurance companies, government agencies, holders of government pool securities, pension funds, households, and others.

Thrifts and Banks.   Participation in the mortgage markets has been dramatically altered over time. Thrift institutions expanded their presence in the mortgage markets considerably after World War II. A tax and regulatory environment favorable to those institutions, coupled with the requirement that they invest a large portion of their portfolios in mortgages, contributed to that growth. However, beginning in the 1970s, high costs of funds reduced flows of funds to thrift institutions and reduced their desire to acquire long-term, fixed-rate mortgages. Consequently, thrifts' direct participation in the mortgage markets fell sharply. The decline is overstated, however,

Exhibit 10–9   **Mortgages Outstanding by Holder (1958–1990)**

	1958	1963	1968	1973	1978	1980	1983	1988	1990
Amount Outstanding (\$ in billions)	\$172.5	\$280.5	\$412.5	\$682.3	\$1,169.4	\$1,447.4	\$1.827.2	\$3,154.1	\$3,857.7
Percentage Held									
Thrift institutions	39.9	45.3	44.6	44.7	45.1	41.6	34.3	28.3	20.8
Commercial banks	14.8	14.0	15.9	17.5	18.3	18.3	18.1	20.6	21.9
Insurance companies and pension funds[a]	22.4	19.8	19.3	13.4	10.1	10.1	8.3	7.1	6.9
U.S. government	2.5	2.1	2.3	1.3	2.4	2.9	a	a	a
Government agencies	2.0	1.9	3.2	5.6	6.2	6.9	8.2	6.1	6.5
Mortgage pools	0.1	0.2	0.6	2.6	6.0	7.9	15.6	24.8	28.7
Households	16.6	14.4	11.8	9.4	8.7	8.5	a	a	a
State and local governments	0.6	0.8	0.8	1.3	1.4	2.3	a	a	a
REITs	0.2	0.2	0.2	2.3	0.5	0.3	a	a	a
Credit unions	—	—	0.2	0.2	0.3	0.3	a	a	a
Other	0.9	1.3	1.1	1.7	1.0	0.9	15.6	13.1	15.2

[a]In 1983 and later, pension funds are included in the "other" category and no separate category is given for the U.S. government per se. Also, households and other institutions are not differentiated.

The rapid growth of mortgage pools has reduced thrifts' and life insurance companies' direct holdings of mortgages, as these institutions have substituted more marketable mortgage-backed securities for individual mortgages in their portfolios.

Source: Federal Reserve Board, *Flow of Funds Accounts, Amounts Outstanding, 1957–80; Federal Reserve Bulletin*, January 1983 and December 1988 and 1991.

because thrifts swapped many of their mortgage holdings for FNMA and FHLMC participation certificates starting in late 1981. The certificates had a lower rate of return than the underlying mortgages, but because they were guaranteed by the agencies, they could be used as collateral for loans to ease thrifts' liquidity problems.

Government-sponsored agencies, households, and insurance companies picked up much of the slack as thrifts reduced their participation in the mortgage markets in the late 1970s. Banks also increased their market share somewhat—possibly because banks are more willing to hold adjustable-rate than fixed-rate loans.

Insurance Companies and Pension Funds.   Life insurance companies and pension funds often acquire mortgages to guarantee long-term returns. After World War II they held 11 percent of all mortgages outstanding, and that percentage grew in the postwar years. After the mid-1960s, however, these institutions sharply decreased their participation in the direct mortgage market. Nonetheless, they did not withdraw from the mortgage markets; they mainly acquired highly marketable pass-through securities instead of less-marketable direct mortgages.

Pools.   Pass-through securities are recorded in Exhibit 10-9 as pools. Before the establishment of the Government National Mortgage Association in 1968, pools were unimportant. By the end of 1990, however, over $1 trillion in mortgages outstanding were held in pools to back pass-through securities, participation certificates, swap certificates, and so on, and they were the largest single component of the mortgage market.

Government Holdings.   Federal as well as state and local government agencies play a direct role in the mortgage markets. Federally owned or supported institutions, such as the FNMA, the FHLMC, the Federal Land Banks, or the Farmers Home Administration, may directly acquire and hold mortgage debt. In addition, state or local housing authorities may issue housing revenue bonds and use the proceeds to acquire mortgage loans.

The mortgage markets generate several hundred billion dollars per year in new mortgages. This vast amount of financing has been facilitated by the operations of mortgage insurers, mortgage bankers, and numerous government agencies.

Mortgage Insurers

FHA Insurance.   The federal government pioneered the development of mortgage insurance during the 1930s. As real estate values plummeted and many foreclosures occurred, investors became reluctant to invest in mortgaged property without substantial down payments. Thus the Federal Housing Administration offered FHA insurance to guarantee lenders against default on mortgage loans. FHA insurance initially had a monthly premium equal to $\frac{1}{2}$ of 1 percent of the outstanding balance on a loan; now the premium is paid in advance and varies with mortgage terms.

Federally insured mortgages were popular. Lenders were willing to make FHA loans to borrowers at favorable interest rates and with the minimal down payments required by the FHA because of the insurance.

However, their popularity was hindered at times because the FHA refused to insure loans that (1) were above a certain maximum size, (2) carried an interest rate above what the FHA thought was politically expedient to allow, and (3) did not comply with

FHA appraisal and paperwork requirements. Of these, the loan size restrictions and interest rate caps caused the most problems. When FHA-approved interest rate ceilings were below market interest rates, lenders charged discount "points" on FHA loans. Loan discounts of 10 percent or more were sometimes needed before lenders could earn a market rate of return. As a result, lenders were reluctant to make FHA loans at such times.

VA Insurance.   In 1944 the Veterans Administration (VA) was allowed to insure mortgage loans to military veterans on even more lenient terms than the FHA. VA-insured loans can be made for larger amounts and require no down payment at all. However, they require cumbersome paperwork, and they too have sometimes been adversely affected by low rate ceilings.

Private Mortgage Insurance.   Because of the administrative drawbacks associated with FHA- and VA-insured mortgage lending, many institutions (particularly thrifts) prefer to make conventional mortgage loans. These are usually made with down payments that are substantially higher than those for government-insured loans in order to protect the lender against loss. However, their higher down payments make them unpopular with some borrowers.

Private mortgage insurance companies (such as PMI) have helped fill the need for low-down-payment conventional mortgages. These companies insure a portion of the total mortgage debt—the riskiest 10 to 20 percent—in return for a relatively high premium on the insured portion (see Exhibit 10–2). This can let a borrower buy real property with as little as 5 percent down. In addition, the overall interest rate on the mortgage is not substantially elevated. This is so because the insured portion is only a fraction of the total mortgage. However, when home prices stagnated in the early 1980s, many borrowers defaulted on low-down-payment loans. As a result, many private mortgage insurers suffered large losses.

Effects of Mortgage Insurance.   Mortgage insurance has facilitated the development of secondary mortgage markets. The buyer of an insured mortgage need know only the financial strength and credibility of the insurer instead of the financial strength and credibility of the mortgage issuer. This reduces the buyer's information costs considerably—from having to know about thousands of John Joneses' mortgages to merely knowing about the performance of the FHA, VA, PMI, or other mortgage insurers. As a result, more people are willing to buy mortgages, and mortgages are more marketable than would otherwise be the case.

Mortgage Bankers

Mortgage bankers have grown in importance since mortgage insurance increased the secondary market for mortgages. *Mortgage bankers*, or mortgage companies, are institutions that originate mortgages and collect payments on them. However, they generally do not hold mortgage loans in their own portfolios for long. Instead, they sell them and obtain their income from service fees that they charge the ultimate buyers for collecting payments and keeping records on each loan. The service fees, along with other fees that they receive when they make the loan, cover their costs of loan origination and collection. Most private mortgage bankers charge service fees equal to $\frac{1}{4}$ to $\frac{3}{8}$ of 1 percent of the mortgage balance. Mortgage bankers are major originators of FHA- and VA-insured mortgages and also play a substantial role in the conventional mortgage markets.

In the early 1980s, many banks and nonfinancial firms acquired mortgage-banking companies as subsidiaries. They did so to gain contact with relatively affluent, credit-using consumers on a nationwide basis.

Secondary Mortgage Markets

Mortgage bankers and other mortgage-originating institutions can sell the mortgages they originate in the secondary mortgage markets to both public and private purchasers.

Private Purchasers.   The ultimate buyers of FHA- and VA-insured mortgages originated by mortgage bankers usually have been insurance companies and pension funds. In recent years, however, investment bankers on Wall Street have marketed participation certificates in GNMA pools, mutual funds specializing in GNMA securities, mortgage-backed unit investment trust certificates, and REMIC and CMO issues to members of the public. Whereas investment bankers' trusts or GNMA may hold the underlying mortgages, the public ultimately provides the funds used to buy those mortgages.

Government Purchasers.   The federal government has established a number of institutions to promote the purchase of mortgages. They include the following:

Federal National Mortgage Association (FNMA—Fannie Mae).   This corporation was started in 1938 to provide a secondary market for government-guaranteed mortgages. It financed its purchases by issuing government-guaranteed debt. In 1954 FNMA issued common stock to obtain more funds, and in 1968 it converted to private ownership. It still issues debt in the capital markets and uses the proceeds to finance mortgage purchases, but now it issues private debt. It purchases mortgages at prearranged "commitment" prices determined at auctions held in advance of its actual mortgage purchases.

Even though the FNMA now finances its mortgage purchases by issuing various types of private debt (or capital stock), its debt is attractive to buyers in the capital markets because the U.S. Treasury has guaranteed the FNMA a large line of standby credit.

The FNMA now participates in the conventional as well as in the government-insured sector of the mortgage markets. In October 1981 it began to issue mortgage pools for conventional mortgages. At the end of 1990, FNMA held over $115 billion in mortgages for its own account and $300 billion more for mortgage pools.

Federal Home Loan Mortgage Corporation (FHLMC—Freddie Mac).   In addition to issuing pass-through securities, Freddie Mac purchases conventional mortgages for its own portfolio. Its purchases are primarily designed to help thrift institutions market their mortgages. At the end of 1990, Freddie Mac held $22 billion in mortgages for its own account and over $315 billion for mortgage pools.

Government National Mortgage Association (GNMA—Ginnie Mae).   The GNMA acquires many mortgages for its pass-through programs. In addition, it purchases mortgages for its own account under special programs. At the end of 1990, GNMA held only a few million dollars in mortgages for its own account but over $400 billion for mortgage pools.

Other Government Agencies.   Mortgages are also held by the Farmers Home Administration (FmHA), the Federal Land Banks, and other government agencies. At the end of 1990, the FmHA, which provides home financing in rural areas, held $42 billion in mortgages. At the same time the Federal Land Banks, which make mortgage loans to farmers for land purchases, held $30 billion in mortgages for their own accounts. These agencies finance their mortgage holdings by selling federal agency debt or participations in mortgage pools.

Growth and Importance of the Secondary Mortgage Markets

Because of the expansion of both federal and private mortgage insurance and the development of many new securities, the secondary markets for mortgage obligations have increased greatly in recent years. Many pass-through securities issued by federal agencies are used to back CMOs and REMICs. Because of the growing demand for these bondlike instruments in the capital markets, by year-end 1987 close to 30 percent of all mortgage debt and more than 50 percent of all new mortgage issues were used to collateralize mortgage-backed debt.

The development of secondary mortgage markets has made it easier for mortgage issuers to obtain funds from the nation's capital markets. It also has caused mortgage rates to become more uniform across the country. As different mortgage issuers compete by offering insured mortgage credit to the capital markets, those that offer the most competitive rate will attract the most funds. Because of the national competition for funds, most mortgage issuers offer similar rates. Previously, mortgage rates often were substantially higher in areas of the country where funds were in short supply.

Government's Role in the Mortgage Markets

Federal and state governments, plus regulatory agencies under their jurisdiction, play a major role in the mortgage markets. Governmental participation is at three levels. First, many government agencies directly offer mortgage credit, operating at the federal, state, and local levels. Second, federal agencies have played a major role in developing mortgage insurance and extensive secondary markets for mortgage loans. Third, legislative and regulatory bodies have adopted numerous laws and regulations that significantly affect lender and borrower obligations associated with mortgage credit contracts and the operations of mortgage market institutions.

Government Provision of Housing Credit

As previously noted, the federal government has created and supported government agencies such as the FNMA, GNMA, FHLMC, FmHA, and the Federal Land Banks, which supply substantial amounts of credit to the mortgage markets either directly or by forming pools of mortgage credit for sale to private investors. In addition to selling mortgage pool participations, the government agencies sell mortgage-backed bonds and other federal agency debt to finance their mortgage acquisitions.

Also, for a number of years state governments have provided relatively low-cost mortgage funds to borrowers that they deem qualified (under low-income, veteran's preference, welfare, or other standards). Since 1970, state housing authorities have issued tax-exempt revenue bonds secured by mortgage revenues. In 1978, municipalities began issuing similar bonds.

Government Support of the Secondary Markets

The federal government has greatly enhanced the development of secondary mortgage markets by pioneering the development of mortgage insurance and pass-through securities. In addition, the government has greatly expanded the depth of the secondary mortgage markets through the FNMA's and FHLMC's mortgage purchase programs.

Government-sponsored innovations have had spin-off effects that encouraged private-sector participation in the secondary mortgage markets. Private mortgage insurance, privately issued pass-through securities, and privately issued mortgage-backed bonds were all initiated following the government's development of the market. As a result, the secondary mortgage markets have expanded more rapidly and become more closely related to the conventional capital markets than would otherwise be the case.

Government Regulation

Government regulations have an important effect on the mortgage markets. They affect the types and terms of mortgage instruments that can be offered in the credit markets, creditors' and consumers' contractual rights and responsibilities with regard to their mortgage contracts, credit allocation in the mortgage markets, and the workings of financial institutions that operate most extensively in the mortgage markets. By standardizing the underwriting (credit risk) criteria and mortgage terms that they are willing to accept, the big government mortgage purchasers (FNMA, GNMA, and FHLMC) can, de facto, establish standards for the majority of all mortgages traded in the secondary markets.

Relationship of Mortgage Markets to the Capital Markets

In general, interest rates on mortgage obligations move in step with those on other capital market obligations, such as ten-year government securities. However, mortgage rates are somewhat higher than rates on top-grade debt issues. This is because mortgages are less marketable than government and top-grade corporate debt and because they usually can be prepaid at the borrower's option.

In recent years, interest rate differentials among mortgages issued in different parts of the country have decreased. This has occurred because mortgage markets have developed instruments that are better able to compete for funds in the nation's capital markets.

Summary

This chapter describes the U.S. mortgage markets and the major institutions that operate in both the primary and the secondary mortgage markets. Thrift institutions provide the major source of mortgage financing, but commercial banks, life insurance companies, and pension funds also furnish a substantial amount of direct and indirect financing to the mortgage markets. Governments do not hold a large portion of mortgages directly, but they have played a major role in the mortgage markets by developing mortgage insurance and secondary mortgage market financing institutions. Following the government's lead and the relaxation of restraining regulations, mortgage bankers and private financial institutions have furthered the development of secondary mortgage markets.

An important result of the development of secondary mortgage markets is that mortgage interest rates have become more uniform across the country. Mortgage markets have also become more closely linked to conventional capital markets. Thus mortgage granters can more easily use capital markets to obtain loanable funds.

Many different types of mortgage instruments now exist. Among the most important are fixed-rate mortgages, both federally insured and conventional, and adjustable-rate mortgages.

A host of regulators at both the state and federal levels regulate the terms and nature of mortgage contracts and the institutions that acquire such contracts. Probably the most important are the secondary market purchasers of mortgages, the FNMA and the FHLMC. The underwriting standards that they set for the mortgages they are willing to purchase often set the standards for all other mortgages issued in the mortgage markets.

Questions

1. Why was the development of mortgage insurance necessary before secondary mortgage markets could develop?
2. How has the development of secondary mortgage markets allowed mortgage issuers to attract additional funds from the capital markets?
3. Explain how mortgage-related securities have become more similar to capital market instruments over time.
4. Why have mortgage market interest rates become more uniform across the country in recent years?
5. How has the government encouraged the development of secondary mortgage markets?
6. What is the difference between conventional mortgages and FHA and VA mortgages?
7. How do regulations affect the functioning of the mortgage markets? Consider the effects of mortgage rate regulation, mortgage instruments (ARM and RAM) regulation, and thrift institution regulation.
8. If you expect prices to rise, what type of mortgage would you rather have on your house: conventional, GPM, ARM, SAM, or RAM? What if you expected prices to fall? Explain your answer. Also explain how your answer would differ if you were a mortgage lender.

9. Why do you think that the regulatory authorities gave thrift institutions greater powers to issue adjustable-rate (VRM, RRM, and ARM) mortgages in the late 1970s and early 1980s?

10. Why have CMOs and REMICs made it easier for the mortgage markets to compete for funds with corporate bonds? What problems do their "residuals" pose?

Selected References

Fabozzi, Frank J., ed., *The Handbook of Mortgage Finance.* **Chicago: Probus Publishing, 1988.**
This book contains an excellent set of papers by various mortgage experts that treat various aspects of the mortgage market, including pass-through securities, in considerable depth.

Federal Trade Commission. *The Mortgage Maze.* **Washington, DC, 1983.**
This 18-page pamphlet describes different mortgage options and their payment and legal requirements.

Gilbert, R. Alton, and A. Steven Holland. "Has the Deregulation of Deposit Interest Rates Raised Mortgage Rates?" *Review.* **Federal Reserve Bank of St. Louis, May 1984, pp. 5–15.**
This article analyzes the changing differential between mortgage interest rates, Treasury bond rates, and savings institutions' costs of funds. It concludes that rising default risk and prepayment risk accounted for the large rise in mortgage interest rates relative to the Treasury bond rate in the early 1980s.

Hummer, William B. "Say Hello to the CMO." *Bankers Monthly.* **December 1990, p. 54.**
This article discusses the risk associated with various CMOs and the comptroller of the currency's regulatory view of that risk.

Jones, Marcos T. "Mortgage Designs, Inflation, and Real Interest Rates." *Quarterly Review.* **Federal Reserve Bank of New York, Spring 1982, pp. 20–27.**
Presents a summary of newly authorized mortgage instruments, proposed mortgage forms, and the reasons the new instruments are necessary to cope with inflationary periods.

Konstas, Panoz. "Derivative Mortgage Securities and Their Risk/Return Characteristics." *FDIC Banking Review*, **Fall 1988, pp. 28–33.**
This article does a good job analyzing and presenting the risk attributes associated with various CMO, REMIC, and "stripped" mortgage securities. It notes that the return on the residual class of such securities is highly variable and depends on prepayment patterns and interest rate changes.

Polash, Carl J., and Robert B. Stoddard. "ARMs: Their Financing Rate and Impact on Housing." *Quarterly Review.* **Federal Reserve Bank of New York, Autumn 1985, pp. 39–49.**
This paper tries to determine if ARM mortgages have affected housing purchases and finds that they have had little effect. After pricing the value of various caps on ARMs, the authors conclude that interest rates on ARM mortgages are priced similarly (relative to securities having the same effective maturities) to FRMs. The lower rate on ARMs results primarily from the upsloping nature of the yield curve.

Sellon, Gordon H., Jr., and Deana VanNahmen. "The Securitization of Housing Finance." *Economic Review.* **Federal Reserve Bank of Kansas City, July/August 1988, pp. 3–20.**
This excellent article documents the rapid growth in the securitization of mortgages that has occurred in recent years. It also describes the new mortgage instruments in detail and discusses some of the regulatory issues associated with the new instruments and the rapidly growing market for such securities.

Sivesand, Charles M. "Mortgage Backed Securities: The Revolution in Real Estate Finance." *Quarterly Review.* **Federal Reserve Bank of New York, Autumn 1979, pp. 1–10.**
Provides an excellent discussion of different mortgage-backed securities—including GNMAs, PCs, and mortgage-backed bonds. Also discusses the valuation problem for GNMA pools when they sell at a discount and their prepayment rate is not "normal."

Stern, Richard L., and Mark Clifford. "Trouble at Home." *Forbes*, **August 12, 1985, pp. 31–34.**
Analyzes the rising trend in mortgage delinquency and foreclosure rates that resulted when housing price inflation abated in the early 1980s. Looks at the institutional arrangements for insuring, packaging, and reselling mortgages in the secondary market, and suggests that buyers of such securities may incur more risk than they expect.

FUTURES, FORWARD, SWAPS, AND OPTIONS MARKETS

11

Whatever are interest rates going to do? What about exchange rates? Should I bet that interest rates will fall or that the dollar will rise? Should I try to protect myself against the risk that interest rates or exchange rates will change? How much risk can I take? Should I gamble in order to earn a possibly high return? Will I lose my job if I lose my money? Most financial institutions hate risk and will fire people who take too much of it. How can I eliminate risk, then? How can I protect myself? Many bond traders, market makers, and managers of financial institutions must ask themselves questions like these daily, particularly because the volatility of interest rates and exchange rates has increased greatly since the early 1970s.

Because many people are concerned with controlling their exposure to interest rate or exchange rate risk, the financial futures markets have grown explosively in recent years. "Financial Engineers" have developed a wide variety of new financial instruments so various individuals or institutions can alter their risk exposure to various events and alter their potential return possibilities. The new markets for "financial derivative" securities have grown rapidly because they allow the risk inherent in the ownership of financial assets and liabilities to be transferred from risk averters to risk takers. They also generate substantial fee income for commercial banks and investment banks.

This chapter describes the nature of the most important markets for financial derivatives. It starts with forward and futures markets, then discusses the swaps and options markets. It discusses how the various markets work, what financial instruments are traded in them, who the major participants are, and how the markets are regulated. It also describes how the financial futures markets can be used to reduce risk—particularly the interest rate risk of financial intermediaries—and how new types of risk, such as "basis risk" and "counterparty risk" may be relevant to various claims traded in the financial derivative markets.

The Purpose of Futures and Forward Markets

Frequently people enter into contracts that call for future delivery of domestic or foreign currency, a security, or a commodity. The value of the contract ultimately depends on the discounted present value of the item to be received *at the time it is received*. For instance, a U.S. exporter might sell corn to a foreign importer. The contract might call for payment in British pounds in 90 days. If the pound is worth $1.50 and the agreed price is £2 per bushel, the exporter will receive a value of $3 per bushel for the corn. Based on that assumption, the person might find it worthwhile to buy corn at $2.50 per bushel, sell it, and pay the shipping costs. However, if the British pound were to fall to $1.20 in value, the exporter would receive pounds worth only $2.40 per bushel 90 days later and would lose on the transaction. The price variation in the exchange market could eliminate the profit hoped for from trade.

Futures and forward markets were designed to let people offset their price risk in transactions that call for future delivery of money, a security, or a commodity by taking a position in the futures or forward markets. The futures and forward markets let people establish their terms of exchange prior to a future delivery date.

Forward Markets

Forward markets let people arrange exchanges "forward" in time. In a forward market one entity contracts with a "counterparty" to exchange one item for another for a predetermined price at a predetermined point in time. Ordinarily, both parties to the contract are bound by the contract and will not be released from that obligation early unless they renegotiate the contract prior to its fulfillment. Also, individual parties to forward contracts are exposed to potential loss should their counterparty default rather than honor his or her obligations on the expiration date of the contract. The forward markets for foreign exchange (money) are the most active forward markets.

Markets in foreign currencies usually let people guarantee a currency exchange rate at some specific "forward" point—such as 30, 60, or 90 days or more hence. When an exporter wishes to guarantee a forward exchange rate, he or she can go to any one of a number of banks or foreign exchange dealers and write a forward contract. The contract guarantees delivery of a certain amount of foreign currency (say, 2.5 million British pounds) for exchange into a specific amount of dollars ($3.75 million, if the exchange rate is $1.50 = £1) on a specific day (90 days hence). For instance, if our corn exporter sold 1 million bushels of corn at £2 (British pounds) per bushel with payment due in 90 days, the exporter could guarantee the dollar price of the corn by entering into a forward exchange contract with a major bank or other foreign exchange dealer. The exporter might agree to sell the 2 million pounds it will receive to the counterparty for $1.45 per pound, or a total of $2.9 million. The bank or foreign exchange dealer in turn agrees to pay the exporter $2.9 million in exchange for £2 million. A risk of counterparty default exists if, for instance, the exporter does not receive prompt payment of the £2 million and is unable to keep its end of the contract, or if the bank fails (and is not bailed out) before maturity of the contract. However, potential losses will not be great if a default occurs as long as the pound–dollar exchange rate is close to $1.45 per pound on the designated delivery day, as then the unfilled end of the contract can be offset in the "spot" exchange market (the "spot market" calls for immediate delivery of foreign exchange) at a price close to the prearranged rate of exchange.

However, because the future spot rate is uncertain, exporters do not wish to risk their profits by gambling that they can predict it. Furthermore, since the risk of counterparty default on forward exchange contracts is very small, they often would rather take that risk and pay their bank a fee for arranging the forward exchange than receive a currency whose future value is uncertain. Overall, then, forward exchange contracts let importers and exporters offset the price risk inherent in future dealings by guaranteeing future exchange rates and prices.

The individual banks and foreign exchange dealers that make up the forward market balance off the supplies and demands for funds by exporters, importers, investors, and speculators in various countries and alter the forward exchange rate as necessary so that the demand and supply of funds will be equal.

Forward exchange dealers make their money on the spread between their buying and asking prices for foreign exchange. For instance, an exchange dealer might exchange dollars supplied by Japanese exporters for yen at 130 yen per dollar and exchange yen supplied by U.S. exporters for dollars at 131 yen per dollar. The dealer profits by buying low and selling high.

Futures Markets

Differences in Futures and Forward Markets

Futures markets are more formal than forward markets. They differ from forward contracts in several ways. (1) Futures contracts call for the delivery of specific commodities, securities, or currencies either on specific future dates or over limited periods of time in the future. Futures market contracts are standardized in quantities, delivery periods, and grades of deliverable items, whereas forward market contracts are not. In addition, (2) although there must be a buyer and seller when any new contract is initiated, both parties in a futures market transaction hold formal contracts with the *futures exchange*, not with each other. Thus (3) either party in a futures market transaction can liquidate its future obligation to buy (or deliver) goods by offsetting it with a sale (or purchase) of a futures contract prior to the scheduled delivery date. In the forward exchange markets, contracts are ordinarily satisfied by actual delivery of specified items on the specified date. In the futures market, almost all contracts are offset prior to delivery. Finally, (4) futures markets require that the value of all contracts be *marked to market* constantly and (5) that their owners post "margin" money (if necessary) to take account of gains or losses accruing from daily price movements. This reduces the risk of default on futures contracts. Forward contracts are riskier because one party may default if prices change dramatically before the delivery date. Defaults were common on forward contracts for oil delivery when oil prices plummeted in early 1986. Because of margin requirements, cash flows required for futures and forward contracts differ; even though these contracts are otherwise similar, this difference can affect their pricing.

Example of a Futures Market Transaction

The futures markets typically call for delivery of specific items during specific months of the year. For instance, a Treasury bill contract calls for the delivery of a $1 million face amount of a three-month (90-day) Treasury bill on a designated delivery date during the months of March, June, September, or December. A person may purchase (or sell) a futures contract for receipt (or delivery) of $1 million worth of 90-day Treasury bills for any of those months for the next year. The price for the Treasury bill futures contract equals 100 percent minus the Treasury bill interest rate; thus a contract price of 94.85 corresponds to a T-bill rate of 5.15 percent. Because a $1 million T-bill generates $10,000 in interest for each 1 percent return in a year, the value of 1 percent interest on a $1 million T-bill for one-fourth of one year equals $2,500. Thus, if the T-bill interest rate rose by 1 percent prior to the delivery, the contract's value would fall by $2,500, or $25 for each basis point (1/100 of 1 percent) change in the interest rate. The most widely traded financial futures contract, the Eurodollar interest rate futures contract, is priced similarly—only its value is determined by the average London Interbank Borrowing Rate (LIBOR) for three-month deposits quoted by London banks on the designated delivery day.

Agreeing to Trade.   Let us suppose that in December 1993, Al decides to buy a Treasury bill futures contract due in June 1994 for a price of $94.85 (which corresponds to an interest rate of 5.15 percent). At the same time, Betty decides to sell a Treasury bill futures contract if she can get a price of $94.85 or higher. Both place their orders with their brokers, who take them to the trading floor (the Treasury bill "pit") of the Chicago Mercantile Exchange. Al's broker offers to buy one contract and Betty's broker offers to sell one contract. Once they agree on the price, the brokers signal their agreement to buy and sell one June 1994 contract to each other at a price of $94.85 and record their orders with the exchange. The exchange, in turn, agrees to sell one T-bill contract to Al at $94.85 and to buy one T-bill contract from Betty at $94.85. Because there is both a new buyer and a new seller, the "open interest"—or total number of contracts to deliver a T-bill in June 1994 through the exchange—increases by one. This process is illustrated in Exhibit 11–1. Note that even though the agreement to buy and sell was between individuals, the exchange wrote separate contracts with each. This allows each participant to liquidate his or her position at will in the future.

Margin Requirements.   When they initiate their futures positions (an agreement to buy is called a *long* position and an agreement to sell is called a *short* position), Al and Betty both must deposit money with the exchange to guarantee that they will keep their part of the bargain. This deposit is called the *initial margin* requirement. The initial margin for T-bill futures is usually $750 or less, depending on the volatility of interest rates. If the market price of new contracts on the exchange moves adversely, Al or Betty will have to deposit more money with the exchange so that they can meet the *maintenance margin* requirement imposed on investors by the exchange. Maintenance margin requirements are imposed to insure that people do not default on their contracts if prices move adversely for them. The T-bill maintenance margin will be around $500 if the initial margin is $750.

Assume that Al and Betty both posted an initial margin requirement of $750 with the exchange, so the exchange holds a total of $1,500 in margin deposits. Now suppose that T-bill interest rates later rose to 5.25 percent and the price of the T-bill futures contract fell to 94.75. At that point, Al's long contract has lost $250 in value and Betty has gained an equal amount (one person's loss is always exactly offset by another

Exhibit 11–1   **Buyers and Sellers Agree on a Price through the Exchange**

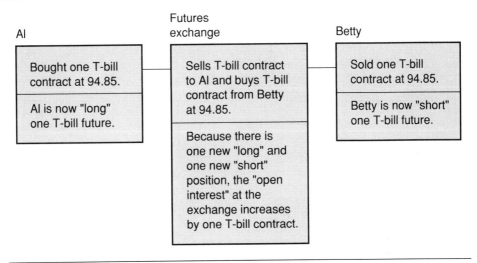

When a person buys or sells a futures contract, the futures exchange is legally the other party to the contract. However, the exchange has a neutral net position, because it always simultaneously buys *and* sells contracts to the public. The total number of long (or short) contracts outstanding in a future is called the *open interest*.

person's gain on futures contracts, because long and short positions are evenly matched). Betty's contract has gained value because it gives her the right to sell $1 million in T-bills at a price high enough to give a yield of 5.15 percent, while new sellers can sell T-bills only at lower prices because of the rise in interest rates. Thus her contract gives her the right to buy $1 million T-bills cheaply and later deliver them at a higher price for a sure gain of 0.10 percent (or $250).

Since Al's futures contract has lost $250, he has only $500 of his initial margin left, and barely meets maintenance margin requirements of $500 per contract. Because he must always post margin equal to or greater than maintenance margin requirements, any further rise in interest rates will cause him to get a "margin call," which will require him to add money to his futures margin account to offset his losses. Margin calls are necessary to ensure that futures traders will always keep a positive balance in their accounts and will not have an incentive to default on their obligations. Because futures margin requirements may at any time require interim cash outlays (or generate interim cash gains—Betty is free to withdraw her accrued gains in excess of her initial margin requirements), they pose more cash flow risk for investors than forward contracts. However, because margin requirements are continuously maintained, they also reduce the risk that a counterparty will default and one party to the transaction will suffer a loss because of credit risk.

Let us suppose that interest rates continue to rise, so the price of the T-bill futures contract continues to fall—to 94.50. At that point Al has lost $875 and must add that much to his account to restore his margin. Betty, on the other hand, has a gain of $875. She could withdraw that extra money at will or decide to sell out and take her gain and withdraw her margin money as well. In Exhibit 11–2, we assume that her broker "offsets" her short position by going to the exchange and buying one T-bill contract from Carl's broker. Since Carl's broker sold a contract to deliver one T-bill on Carl's behalf, Carl is now "short" one T-bill contract instead of Betty.

Exhibit 11–2   Transfer of Futures Contracts

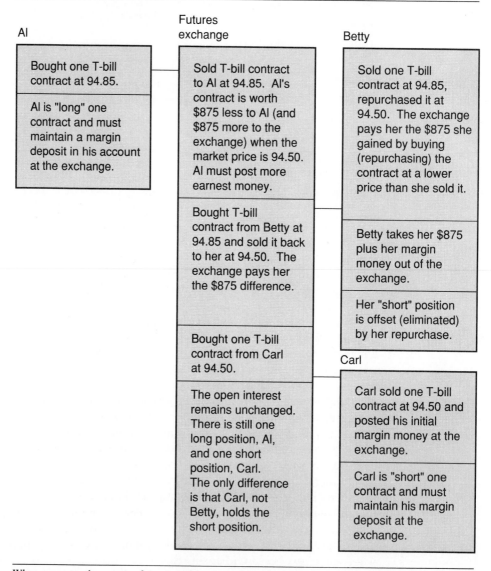

When a person closes out a futures position, a payment is made to settle the change in value that has occurred since the initial purchase, and the contract with the exchange is canceled. This procedure provides liquidity, as it allows one party to the initial trade (Betty) to liquidate her position without requiring the consent of the party who initially took the other side of the contract (A1). This is one advantage of futures over forward contracts.

Delivering on Contracts.   Although the vast majority of all contracts are offset before delivery, a few are completed by delivery from the seller to the buyer. For instance, in Exhibit 11–2, if Carl and Al continue to hold their contracts in June 1994, Carl may fulfill his contract to sell by delivering $1 million in 90-day Treasury bills on the designated delivery day. The holder of the "long" (buy side) futures position is invoiced to pay for a $1 million dollar T-bill at the current settlement price, net of gains or losses, that he or she has accrued on his futures contract. Both the long and the short contracts, then, are canceled by delivery.

Futures Market Instruments

Futures markets can be started for any type of security, foreign currency, or commodity for which a sufficient number of people want to exchange future price risk. Exhibit 11–3 lists major financial futures contracts that traded in 1992.

An interesting aspect of futures contracts is that "the fittest survive." Initially, several exchanges may issue similar contracts, or one exchange may issue several closely related contracts. However, over time one contract will tend to gain popularity at the expense of other closely related contracts, and trading will tend to be concentrated in that single contract. This happens because the contract with the highest volume generally provides the greatest liquidity and lowest bid/ask spreads. Eventually, trading in the other contracts will be discontinued. For instance, the New York Futures Exchange (NYFE) T-bill contracts were unable to compete with the Chicago Mercantile Exchange's International Monetary Market (IMM) contracts for the same instruments because the IMM had larger volumes of trading. Relatedly, the Chicago Board of Trade (CBOT) dropped its commercial paper contracts, as it was unable to attract much volume away from the IMM's Eurodollar and T-bill futures markets. The CBOT also dropped its four-to-six-year Treasury note contract, which attracted far less trading than its Treasury bond and ten-year Treasury note contracts. Later the FINEX exchange successfully began to trade a five-year Treasury note contract, so the CBOT rushed to initiate its own five-year Treasury note contract. Because of slow trading, the IMM of the Chicago Mercantile Exchange discontinued its Dutch guilder and four-year Treasury note contracts. Furthermore, the IMM never initiated trading in its six-month T-bill contract.

Because of the survival-of-the-fittest tendency of futures contracts, often only one contract is traded for each type of future, and very few contracts trade that vary in the same way (that is, have variances that are perfectly correlated). There are several exceptions, however. In particular, several similar financial futures contracts are traded on the Sydney, Singapore (SIMEX), London (LIFFE), and Chicago (IMM) futures exchanges because that allows traders to initiate or neutralize their futures positions on an around-the-clock basis. Also, different-sized units are often traded in financial futures contracts. The Midwest Commodity Exchange specializes in making markets for smaller or larger units of foreign exchange or financial instruments than the major exchanges. Multiple contracts also exist for stock index futures, because different parts of the stock market do not covary perfectly. In particular, the prices of small-company stocks, considered in the Value Line Index, often move differently than the prices of large-company stocks measured by the 20 companies in the Major

Exhibit 11–3   Most Widely Owned Financial Futures in the United States, January 31, 1992

Type of Future	Contract Size	Exchange[a]	Total Open Interest
Interest Rates			
U.S. Treasury bonds[b]	$100,000	CBOT[b]	348,506
U.S. Treasury bonds	$ 50,000	MCE	15,335
Municipal bond index	$100,000	CBOT	17,423
U.S. ten-year Treasury notes	$100,000	CBOT	123,457
U.S. five-year Treasury notes	$100,000	CBOT	117,890
U.S. two-year Treasury notes	$200,000	CBOT	16,579
U.S. Treasury bills	$1 million	IMM	47,707
Eurodollar rates[b]	$1 million	IMM[b]	1,175,125
Thirty-day interest rate	$5 million	CBOT	10,692
LIBOR—one month	$3 million	CME	20,245
Currencies[b]			
U.S. dollar index	500 × index value	FINEX	9,115
Japanese yen	12.5 million yen	IMM	65,806
W. German mark	125,000 D. mark	IMM	66,816
Canadian dollar	$100,000 Canadian	IMM	22,964
British pound	£62,500 British	IMM	24,869
Swiss franc	125,000 S. francs	IMM	27,276
Australian dollar	$100,000 Australian	IMM	1,169
European currency unit	100,000 ECU	FINEX	11
Stock Indexes			
S&P 500	500 × Index	CME	149,174
NYSE Composite Index	500 × Index	NYFE	5,346
Major Market Index	500 × Index	CBOT	5,217
K.C. Value Line Index	500 × Index	KC	2,224
K.C. Mini Value Line	100 × Index	KC	343
Nikkei 225	5 × Index	CME	16,420
Price Indexes			
Commodity Research Bureau (CRB) Index	500 × Index	NYFE	1,528

[a]Exchanges: CBOE (Chicago Board Options Exchange); CBOT (Chicago Board of Trade); CME (Chicago Mercantile Exchange); FINEX (Financial Instrument Exchange Division of New York Cotton Exchange); IMM (International Monetary Market of the Chicago Mercantile Exchange); KC (Kansas City Board of Trade); MCE (MidAmerica Commodity Exchange); and NYFE (New York Futures Exchange).

[b]International (round-the-clock) trading exists in Treasury bonds traded in the United States (on the CBOT and Midwest Commodity Exchange), in London (on the London International Financial Futures Exchange-LIFFE) and in Sydney (on the Sydney Futures Exchange). International trading also exists in Eurodollar interest rate contracts on the LIFFE, Sydney, and Singapore International Monetary (SIMEX) exchanges. Various currency futures contracts trade round the clock on numerous exchanges. The IMM contracts on the yen, German mark, and British pound can be traded on the LIFFE and SIMEX exchanges. The LIFFE exchange also has futures contracts for the German "Bund" (government bond), the British "Long Gilt" (government bond), and the Sterling Rate (British short-term rate).

The most actively traded financial futures contracts are the Eurodollar contract, the Treasury bond contracts, the S&P 500 stock index contract, and various currency futures contracts.

Market Index. The S&P 500 Futures Index responds to the price movements of 500 large companies.

Futures Exchanges

There are several futures exchanges (see Exhibit 11-3 for a listing of the major exchanges), and a great deal of competition exists among them. Because bid/ask price spreads tend to be smaller when there are large numbers of active traders in the market, each exchange tries to compete by having the greatest volume of activity in any contract for which close competition exists. To promote volume, each exchange (1) develops contracts that it thinks will have substantial market appeal because they are different from or superior to other contracts used to reduce the risk exposure of financial market participants, (2) advertises heavily, and (3) encourages local traders to trade new contracts intensively.

Each futures exchange determines the specifications for contracts traded on that exchange. The specifications show delivery dates for each contract, the value of items to be delivered when each contract is exercised, the types of items that can be delivered, and the method of delivery. The exchange also dictates the minimum price fluctuation that can occur in the contract and (to prevent panics) the maximum price change that can occur in one day. Initial and maintenance margins as well as trading rules and hours for each type of contract are also specified by the exchange. Finally, each exchange enforces trading rules, contract agreements, and margin requirements applicable to that exchange.

Futures Market Participants

There are two major types of participants in futures and forward markets: *hedgers* and *speculators*.

Hedgers.   Hedgers try to reduce price risk inherent in their balance sheets or future business dealings by guaranteeing buying or selling prices for closely related futures contracts. For instance, in our earlier forward exchange example the U.S. exporter had as an asset a 90-day note (IOU) valued in British pounds. He tried to reduce the exchange rate risk associated with that note by entering into an agreement to sell pounds in exchange for dollars 90 days forward. This transaction reduced his price risk; thus he was a hedger. Other hedgers might try to guarantee their costs of feed (by buying corn futures contracts) or the value of their livestock at market time (by selling cattle or hog futures contracts). By so doing, they can guarantee their costs of raising cattle or hogs and ensure that they will make a profit. Similarly, banks can guarantee their cost of funds over the period they make a loan by selling interest rate futures short. Also, insurance companies can guarantee a return on planned annuity policies by buying Treasury bond futures before they actually sell the policies.

In short, there are many ways that people can use futures contracts to hedge their financial and business transactions. In the process, some will be buyers and some will be sellers. Their major objective, however, is to guarantee a future price that will reduce their risk.

Speculators.   Speculators take risks in the futures markets. They are willing to enter a futures transaction in hopes that the market price will move in a favorable direction. If they are right, like Betty in our example, they can make a great deal of money in a hurry. If prices move unfavorably, however, they can also lose a great deal of money. Speculators may either speculate on a rise in prices by buying futures contracts ("going long") or speculate on a fall in prices by selling futures contracts ("going short"). They also may enter into *spreads* or *straddles*, in which they buy one futures contract and sell a closely related contract (such as a contract for the same commodity that is due in a different month, or a contract for a closely related commodity) in the hope that the price of one contract will move more favorably than the other.

Traders. Traders are a special class of speculators that speculate on very short-term changes in prices. Most operate on the floor of the exchange and try to "scalp" short-term changes in market prices by buying and selling quickly when prices seem to be changing.

Traders provide a valuable function, for their activity tends to add liquidity to markets and reduce the disparity between bid and ask prices on the exchanges. Consequently, exchanges encourage trading activity in order to broaden the market appeal of their futures contracts.

Regulation of the Futures and Options Markets

The CFTC

The primary regulator of the futures markets is the Commodity Futures Trading Commission (CFTC), a five-member federal commission whose members are appointed to staggered five-year terms by the president with the consent of the Senate. The CFTC was formed in 1974 to centralize government regulation of the futures markets. Although the federal government had regulated some futures markets as far back as the 1920s, not all futures markets were subject to consistent scrutiny.

The CFTC monitors futures trading to detect actual or potential manipulation, congestion, and price distortion. It reviews proposed contracts to see if they have an economic purpose and analyzes the terms of proposed trading contracts to ensure that they meet commercial needs and serve the public interest. It also monitors enforcement of exchange rules, registers industry professionals, and audits brokerage houses and clearing associations. Finally, it investigates alleged violations of CFTC regulations and the Commodity Exchange Act and refers apparent violations of federal laws to the Justice Department for prosecution.

The extensive enforcement responsibilities of the CFTC suggest that a major purpose of the commission is to prevent abuse of the public through misrepresentation or market manipulation. In the past such abuses have occurred with some frequency. Because of the low margin requirements relative to the value of futures contracts, it is possible for large amounts of money to be made (or lost) with only small price movements. In addition, the zero-sum nature of the commodity markets means that, unlike the stock market, if one person gains, another loses. Thus wild trading activities sometimes occur in the futures markets, and it is the CFTC's job to ensure that the public will not be harmed by violations of exchange rules or federal laws.

The SEC

The Securities and Exchange Commission (SEC) regulates options markets that have equity securities as underlying assets. Thus the SEC regulates all individual stock options traded on the Chicago Board Options Exchange as well as all stock "index options," which are based on the value of an underlying index of stocks. The CFTC, however, regulates all options that are settled with the delivery of a futures contract, even if that contract will eventually be settled based on the value of an index of stocks. For instance, the CFTC regulates the S&P 500 options contract traded on the Chicago Mercantile Exchange (CME) because that option, when exercised, involves the purchase or sale of a futures contract for the S&P 500 stock index. In contrast, the SEC regulates the S&P 500 index options contract traded on the Chicago Board Options Exchange (CBOE) because that option, when exercised, involves immediate payments based on the current value of the underlying stocks in the S&P 500 index.

The confusing state of regulation for stock-index products has caused "turf wars" between the SEC and CFTC, particularly after the October 1987 stock market crash, when the SEC maintained that it should be the sole regulator of stocks and all contracts that derived their value from stock-price movements. Congress did not go along with the SEC proposal, however.

Exchange Regulation

The commodity exchanges also impose many rules on their members. Among other purposes, the rules are designed to guarantee that members keep proper accounts, maintain sufficient funds on deposit with the exchange clearinghouse, and, in general, do not engage in practices that could affect the ability of the exchange to honor its contracts or otherwise endanger the financial solvency of the exchange. In addition, exchange rules determine trading procedures, contract terms, maximum daily price movements for commodities, margin requirements, and position limits. Position limits impose maximum contract holdings for any one speculator; they are designed to prevent manipulation of the futures markets.

Because the commodity exchanges have numerous rules designed to regulate trading behavior, they frequently argue that federal regulation of futures market activities is unnecessary. The counterargument is that the exchanges basically are organized to serve the purposes of their members, not the public. If push comes to shove, the public may lose.

The exchanges' lack of toughness in rule enforcement was illustrated in early 1989, when an FBI "sting" operation found that many exchange rules had been violated over a long period of time. As a result, many exchange members and traders were subpoenaed and numerous changes in futures market regulation and monitoring systems were proposed. Subsequently, the exchanges adapted their computer systems to be able to determine more quickly and effectively when all transactions occur and to prevent prearranged trades from taking place.

Uses of the Financial Futures Markets

Financial futures markets have grown rapidly because they provide a way for financial market participants to insulate themselves against changes in interest rates and asset prices. Financial futures can be used to reduce the systematic risk of stock portfolios or to guarantee future returns or costs. In general, financial futures prices move inversely with interest rates and directly with financial asset prices, so the sale of futures can offset asset price risk.

Reducing Systematic Risk in Stock Portfolios

In 1982, stock-index futures contracts became available that derived their value by averaging the prices of a "basket" of underlying stocks that were included in the stock index. The indexes vary in size from the Major Market Index (20 stocks) to the Value Line Index (1,700 stocks). The New York Stock Exchange Index includes all stocks listed on the New York Stock Exchange while the S&P 500 index obtains its value from the 500 stocks included in the Standard & Poor's 500 stock index. The use of stock-index futures has grown rapidly, and they now are among the most actively traded contracts in the U.S. futures markets. There are also stock-index futures (usually traded in foreign markets) that derive their value from foreign stocks. The primary advantage of stock-index futures contracts is that they let an investor alter the market risk (or systematic risk) intrinsic to his or her portfolio.

Systematic risk measures a stock portfolio's tendency to vary relative to the market as a whole. It is measured by calculating a stock's average covariance with the market, or its "beta." If a stock or stock portfolio typically moves up or down 1.2 times as much as the general stock market, it is said to have a beta of 1.2. Systematic risk is important because, unlike unsystematic risk (which measures the tendency of a stock's price to change because of factors particular to that specific stock), systematic risk cannot be diversified away. Thus before the development of stock-index futures it was difficult for investors to eliminate systematic risk from their portfolios.

Stock-index futures, however, can be used to control the systematic risk in an investor's portfolio. For instance, assume that someone has a portfolio worth $20 million that has an average beta (for all stocks in the portfolio taken as a whole) of 1. That means that, on average, the value of the portfolio will move up and down in step with the stock market as a whole. Further assume that the S&P 500 futures contract is selling at 400. Since one S&P 500 futures contract is worth $500 per point, it is worth $200,000 in stocks ($500 × 400) when it is priced at 400. Thus if the investor sold 100 contracts of the S&P 500 futures short, it would have the same effect as selling $20 million worth of stocks with an average beta of 1 (the beta of the S&P 500 is usually assumed to be 1, because that index is often used as a measure of market price movements). By selling the 100 futures contracts short, then, the investor would fully offset the systematic risk in his or her portfolio. He or she would be long $20 million worth of stocks with a beta of 1 and short $20 million worth of futures contracts (also with a beta of 1), so the net portfolio beta would be zero.

If the investor's portfolio had a beta of 1.2, he or she could still offset its systematic risk. In that case, however, the investor would sell 120 S&P 500 futures contracts short. The investor would have to sell 20 percent more contracts short because the systematic risk of his or her portfolio would be 20 percent higher than the systematic risk of the futures contract (which means that its value moves up or down by 20 percent more than the market as a whole).

By selling futures contracts short, the investor need no longer fear that the value of his or her stock portfolio would change substantially if stock market prices generally rose or fell. However, one might wonder why the investor would want to sell stock index futures short, since those short sales would cause losses that would offset part of the gain on the investor's stock portfolio if stock prices rose. For one thing, the investor might believe that the market was likely to fall, and thus would want to buy portfolio "insurance" (see People & Events) to protect against a possible market decline. However, such insurance has a cost, as it reduces investors' potential gains as well as their potential losses.

Stock investors may also desire to eliminate the systematic risk from their portfolios for several reasons unrelated to portfolio insurance. For instance, stock dealers profit by bidding to buy stocks at a lower price than they offer to sell them. However, after buying stocks at their bid price, dealers take the risk that the price of the stocks they own may decline before they can resell them. Thus, dealers may want to reduce the systematic risk of their portfolio by hedging in the futures markets. Also, investors who believe that they are superior stock pickers may want to profit by finding undervalued stocks while still protecting themselves from general stock market declines. They too might use stock futures to reduce the systematic risk of their portfolio and still let them capture the excess returns (if any) available to people with superior stock-picking abilities. Finally, stock-index futures can be used by people who wish to earn either riskless returns greater than the Treasury bill rate or returns greater than the popular stock indexes (see Did You Know? for a description of these index arbitrage strategies).

Guaranteeing Costs of Funds

When a corporation plans a major investment, it typically commits itself to major cash outlays for several years in the future. Although a project can be projected to yield a good return, it might not be profitable if interest rates unexpectedly rose and the corporation had to pay substantially more to borrow needed funds. The corporation could avoid such a risk, of course, if it borrowed all funds at the time the investment was planned and invested excess funds in short-term securities until they were needed. However, because short-term rates are often lower than long-term rates, it could be costly to borrow long term and invest the temporarily excess money at a lower rate. Thus the corporation may wish to use the futures market to guarantee its future financing costs.

If the corporation usually pays a 2 percent premium over the T-bond rate to borrow, it can use the T-bond market to hedge its cost of funds. Suppose it needs to borrow $10 million now and $10 million in another year. It could sell $10 million in long-term bonds now, possibly at $12\frac{1}{2}$ percent, and simultaneously sell 131 T-bond futures (with a face value for delivery of $13.1 million and a market value of $9.99 million) one year hence. If it sells the T-bond futures at 76–10 (or $76 and 10/32 per $100 face value) now, it could lock in an approximate interest cost of 12.94 percent on

PEOPLE & EVENTS

The Crash of October 1987

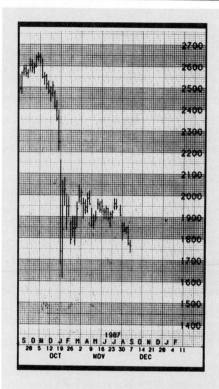

After the stock market crash of October 19, 1987, many people (particularly those in New York) blamed the futures markets for causing the crash. The facts show that that was not so, but the use of futures by some stock portfolio managers did make the crash worse than it otherwise would have been. The culprit was "dynamic portfolio insurance."

Dynamic portfolio insurance sells stock-index futures contracts short to protect portfolios from the risk of stock price declines. By selling futures short, a portfolio manager can gain on the short side (by repurchasing the future at a lower price) if the stock market falls. The gain on the futures will then offset the loss in value of the stocks in the portfolio and protect the portfolio manager against losses caused by stock market declines. Of course, if stock prices rise, the holder of the short futures position will lose on the futures (by having to repurchase the short position at a higher price, for a loss). This loss will offset the gain on the stocks he or she owns if stock prices rise.

Because people want to "have their cake and eat it too," they want to have protection against stock market declines but do not want to have offsetting losses on futures if stock prices rise. To allow them to do so, sellers of dynamic portfolio insurance sold

its future sale of corporate bonds. It would figure its probable future interest cost by adding 2 percent (the usual premium it pays to borrow over the T-bond rate) to the yield of the T-bond futures at 76–10 (which is 10.94 percent). This is illustrated in the first column of Exhibit 11–4.

If interest rates rise during the next year, the corporation will have to pay more to borrow. However, if interest rates rise, futures prices will fall. Thus the corporation will have a capital gain. The capital gain (assuming it is not taxed) can be used to reduce borrowing requirements. By so doing, total interest costs can be held to the level previously anticipated. If the corporation had not hedged, the annual interest costs on its debt would have increased in line with the change in market interest rates (see Column 2 of Exhibit 11–4).

"hedging plans" to stock portfolio managers throughout 1987. Those offering the plans essentially said, "We'll use our computer to sell stock-index futures short when the stock market starts to fall. This will protect you against downside loss. However, we'll liquidate our short positions when stock prices start to rise so that you can still gain from stock price increases." This promise of letting people win if stocks rose and not lose if stocks fell (implemented with the use of computers and sophisticated futures positions) sounded too good to pass up. Before the crash, more than $60 billion worth of stock portfolios had been signed up for dynamic portfolio insurance.

Unfortunately, when stocks fell sharply on October 15 and 16, 1987, the computers said "sell futures short" to protect against further stock market declines. As stock prices fell more, the computers said to sell more futures short. Index arbitrageurs (see Did You Know?) bought the now-cheap stock-index futures and sold their stocks. This made stocks still cheaper, so the dynamic hedgers tried to sell still more futures contracts short. Other people saw stocks declining and also tried to sell. They took their money out of mutual funds, and then the mutual funds had to sell stocks so that they could give people their cash back. Thus the decline snowballed. With so many people wanting to sell stocks and so few wanting to buy at current prices, stock prices fell more than 500 points on October 19, 1987, before they stabilized.

Dynamic portfolio insurers took their lumps on October 19 because they had mindlessly sold stock-index futures when their computers had told them to do so. As a result, futures prices plummeted more than stock prices. The dynamic portfolio insurance plans did not work when the speculative bubble burst.

The crash of 1987 was not caused by hedging in the futures market per se. If dynamic portfolio insurers had not sold futures, they would have sold their actual stocks (that is another way of obtaining "portfolio insurance"). The main cause of the crash was that too many people had tried to participate in the stock market boom when stocks became overvalued and then had tried to flee the market before it could go down. A herd of elephants cannot exit through a small door all at once or the building may collapse. Similarly, many billion dollars worth of stock cannot be sold aggressively on one day without causing the stock market to collapse.

Funding Fixed-Rate Loans

Bank customers often prefer to borrow on a fixed-rate basis so that they will know their interest costs in advance. The futures market can be used to accommodate such customers. For instance, if a bank customer wants a one-year loan at a fixed rate, a bank could sell additional certificates of deposit to finance the loan for the first six months and, following that, sell Eurodollar futures. Exhibit 11-5 illustrates such a case.

In the exhibit, a bank that traditionally pays 25 basis points more to borrow than the Eurodollar rate—which is the interest rate banks pay on dollars outside the United States—uses the Eurodollar futures market to lock in its future costs of funds.

Exhibit 11–4   **Hedging Borrowing Costs with T-Bond Futures**

Initial Position	One Year Later
Corporation X sells 131 ($10 million in market value) of T-bond futures at 76–10 for a yield of 10.94 percent. If it usually must pay 2 percent over the T-bond rate to borrow, it expects to pay 12.94 percent to borrow $10 million one year later—for total annual interest costs over 30 years of $1,294,000 per year.	Corporation X buys back 131 futures contracts at 72–22 (at a yield of 11.52 percent). Its capital gain is $3,625 per contract, or $474,875. Because of its gain, it sells only $9,525,000 worth of corporate debt at an interest cost of 13.5 percent—for total annual interest costs of $1,285,875 per year for 30 years (about what it expected). If it had not hedged, it would have incurred total annual interest costs of $1,350,000 (13.5 percent of $10 million) per year for 30 years.

It first sells a six-month CD and then sells consecutive three-month Eurodollar futures. By adding its 25 basis point premium to the rate on the Eurodollar futures, it calculates its average cost of funds for the next year as 9.6 percent. It then adds a suitable spread and makes a one-year fixed-rate loan at 11 percent.

However, interest rates unexpectedly rise, and the bank must pay more interest on its CDs. In fact, its total interest costs rise by roughly $9,600. This leaves it with an average cost of funds of 10.56 percent, which is far higher than it expected when it made the loan at 11 percent.

Nonetheless, the bank gains approximately $9,600 on its short sales of Eurodollar futures contracts. As a result, it can offset its increased interest cost and earn the spread it desired on the fixed-rate loan transaction.

Banks can use futures as shown to provide fixed-rate loans to borrowers who are reluctant to pay variable rates on loans. They also can show such customers how they can lock in their costs of funds by borrowing on a variable-rate basis and selling Eurodollar or Treasury bill futures in the forward markets. The latter approach has gained considerable popularity with banks. Consequently, many large banks have established futures-trading subsidiaries, called Futures Commission Merchants (FCMs). FCMs provide brokerage services to customers who wish to guarantee their costs of funds or use futures for other purposes.

Profiting from International Rate Differences

An individual can also take advantage of the futures market to guarantee interest returns in foreign markets. For instance, if a person could earn a 10 percent rate of return on a British one-year note but only 8 percent in the United States, the potential might exist for profitable arbitrage—by borrowing in the United States and investing in Britain. However, the extra interest return could be offset if the exchange rate deteriorated over time. For instance, if an individual initially bought British pounds at $1.70 per pound and one year later they were worth only $1.50 per pound, that

---

Exhibit 11–5   **Financing a Fixed-Rate Loan of $1 Million**

I. Bank Funding Plan

Sell a 6-month $1 million CD at 9.25% for funding January through June.

Sell a 3-month $1 million Eurodollar future in June at 90.4 (a 9.6% add-on rate) to guarantee expected funding costs of 9.85% (9.6% plus 25 extra basis points that the bank usually pays on its CDs relative to the Eurodollar futures rate).

Sell a 3-month $1 million Eurodollar future in September at 90.2 (a 9.8% add-on rate) to guarantee expected funding costs of 10.05% (9.8% plus the 25 basis point differential the bank usually pays on its CDs relative to the Eurodollar futures rate).

This gives a projected average cost of funds per quarter-year of

$$\frac{9.25 + 9.25 + 9.85 + 10.05}{4} = 9.60\%.$$

Adding a 1.4% spread, the bank offers to make a fixed-rate one-year loan for $1 million at 11.00%

II. Bank Funding Costs (after the fact)

First 6 months, 9.25% CD.

Next 3 months, 10.25% CD (40 basis points more than expected).

Last 3 months, 13.50% CD (345 basis points more than expected).

Interest costs in the third quarter, then, were $1,000 more than expected (= + 0.40% × $1,000,000 × ¼ year). Interest costs in the fourth quarter were $8,625 more than expected (= + 3.45% × $1,000,000 × ¼ year). Thus total interest expense was $9,625 more than expected.

In June, the bank repurchases the Eurodollar future at 90.01, for a gain on the short sale of 39 basis points, or $975.

In September, the bank repurchases the Eurodollar future at 86.73, for a gain on the short sale of 347 basis points, or $8,675.

Total gains on futures transactions, then, were $9,650, minus commissions of less than $100.

III Net Result

The gain on the futures transactions approximately offset the increased interest costs. Thus the bank realized its expected spread on the loan even though interest rates rose substantially.

---

individual would lose 20 cents per pound, or over 10 percent on the investment in pounds. Such a loss would more than eliminate the 2 percent extra interest earnings on British securities. However, some or all of the extra interest return could be locked in by hedging in the futures markets—provided the pound futures price for one year hence was less than 2 percent below the current pound "spot" price. This is illustrated in Exhibit 11–6.

Hedging a Balance Sheet

Financial futures can be used to protect a financial institution with an unbalanced balance sheet against changes in interest rates. For instance, assume that a thrift

---

Exhibit 11–6   **Guaranteeing Foreign Interest Returns**

I. A. An individual borrows $1.7 million at 8% and converts the dollars into 1 million British pounds by buying pounds for $1.70 per pound.

   B. The individual uses the 1 million British pounds to buy a British Security, paying 10% interest.

   C. The individual sells British pounds one year hence by selling 18 contracts (at £62,500 per contract) at $1.68 per pound in the futures markets.

II. One year later the market price of the pound might fall to $1.50. If so, when the individual converted the £1,100,000 back to dollars, he or she would receive only $1,650,000—less than he or she borrowed. Without hedging, it would not be possible to repay the $1,700,000 debt, much less the 8% interest due.

III. A. However, if the market price of the pound were $1.50, the futures price might be $1.4950 per pound. Thus there would be a gain of 18.5¢ per pound on the short sale in the futures market. The total gain in the futures market, then, would be $208,125.

   B The total gain on the transaction would be:

$1,650,000	Value of dollars received by converting £1,100,000 to dollars at $1.50/£ at year-end
+ 208,125	Gain on futures transactions (= + 18.5 × 18 × 62,500)
− 1,700,000	Repayment of principal borrowed
− 136,000	Repayment of interest due on $1,700,000 at 8%
$22,125	Net gain

Instead of taking a loss because of the decline in the value of the pound, the futures market transaction let the speculator borrow cheaply at home and guarantee a positive rate of return by investing the borrowed funds abroad. The key to making profits on this transaction was that it was possible to guarantee, by using futures, that the loss on the currency translation would be less than the interest differential earned. This was possible because "covered interest rate parity" conditions (see Chapter 12) did not hold.

---

institution has $300 million in liabilities, all with maturities of one year or less, and $15 million in capital. At the same time, assume that it holds $300 million in fixed-rate mortgages and only $15 million in assets with maturities under one year. It will have a negative one-year GAP of $285 million (since its one-year rate-sensitive assets, $15 million, less its one-year rate-sensitive liabilities, $300 million, equals − $285 million). Thus it will be extensively exposed to loss should interest rates increase. If interest rates do rise, the thrift's revenues on its mortgage portfolio will change very little and, with a higher discount rate, the value of those mortgages will fall. At the same time, its liabilities will mature, and it will find that it will either have to pay more interest to its liability holders or lose its deposits. Thus its interest costs will rise more than interest revenues (and its asset values fall). Consequently, the thrift will suffer large losses.

However, the thrift can insulate its balance sheet against interest rate risk by using interest rate futures to neutralize its long position in mortgages. In the simplest case, in which all securities are priced at par, the thrift could sell $300 million in U.S. Treasury bond or note futures to offset the interest rate risk of the $300 million in mortgages held in its portfolio. Then, if interest rates rose and prices changed in a similar manner

DID YOU KNOW?

Program Traders Are Merely Trying to Beat the T-Bill Rate

In recent years, there has been a dispute about whether program trading or "index arbitrage" should be allowed on the New York Stock Exchange. After the crash of October 1987, index arbitrage programs that used computerized order entries were prohibited if the Dow Jones stock average moved more than 50 points in one day. Program trading was thought to be disruptive to the markets because program traders typically bought or sold thousands of shares of stock almost instantaneously. These large, sudden transactions were thought to cause stock market volatility.

Yet, did you know that the purpose of program trading is not to own stocks per se, but just to obtain an investment that will generate a higher risk-free rate of return than T-bills? Program traders enter the market when the price of stock-index futures is too far out of line with the prices of the stocks that make up the stock index. For instance, if the S&P 500 future is selling at 410 and expires in three months, whereas the underlying stocks in the S&P 500 stock index are selling for an equivalent price of 400 right now, a person could buy those stocks now, sell the future short, and know that he or she would gain a "riskless" 2.5 percent (410/400 represents a 2.5 percent gain) in three months. The return is guaranteed, because the future must equal the value of the underlying stocks in the stock index when it expires in three months. In addition, by owning the stocks for three months, the investor would probably accrue dividends worth an additional $\frac{3}{4}$ percent of the stocks' value. Thus the investor who undertook this arbitrage would earn a "riskless" return of 3.25 percent (2.5 percent in capital gains plus 0.75 percent in dividends) per quarter, or 13 percent per year. If that return exceeded the T-bill rate, the index arbitrage would be a superior "risk-free" investment. As a result, when stock-index futures prices rise too far above stock prices, program traders sell the futures index and quickly buy great amounts of stock that replicate the price movement of the underlying stock index (it takes at least 50 stocks to replicate price movements in the S&P 500). This sudden buying of stocks can drive the stock market up sharply. However, the stock market rises not because the stock buyers want to own stocks, but only because they want to earn a riskless return higher than the T-bill rate.

On the downside, if an investor in stocks wants to earn a return equal to a specific stock index (as many fund managers do), that investor may sometimes be able to earn a greater return through index arbitrage. For instance, if in the previous example both stocks and the equivalent stock-index future sold at 400, a portfolio manager could buy the futures and sell his or her stocks. The proceeds from the stock sale could be invested in T-bills to earn possibly $1\frac{1}{2}$ percent a quarter. At the end of the quarter, then, the stock fund would have 101.5 percent of 400, or 406 dollars for every 400 dollars in stocks sold, but because the investor owned a futures contract purchased at a price of 400, he or she would be able to reinvest in the same stocks for a net price of 400 when the future expired. Even after allowing for a loss of dividends (of $\frac{3}{4}$ percent), in only three months the investor would still have earned $\frac{3}{4}$ percent more on the three-month period than would have been possible without entering the index arbitrage. Thus the fund manager would likely earn a nice bonus for outperforming the stock indexes during the quarter.

Index arbitrageurs, then, try to profit by earning either a riskless return that is a little greater than the T-bill rate or by selling stocks and investing in T-bills to beat the stock market. To do so, they buy and sell huge quantities of stocks whenever the value of a stock-index future is not equal to the value of its underlying stocks (adjusted for dividend yields and T-bill rate considerations). Through their actions, they tend to provide the socially valuable function of keeping stock-index futures priced in line with the value of the underlying stocks. However, when they buy or sell in quantity, they can also cause stock prices to rise or fall sharply for a few minutes.

on both its mortgages and its Treasury securities, it would receive a capital gain on the futures sufficient to offset the loss that it would take because the present value of its fixed-rate mortgages fell as interest rates rose. Its returns on capital then would vary only with the returns on its $15 million in short-term assets. If it wanted its returns on capital to vary with long-term assets, it would hedge only the GAP of $285 million (See Chapter 14 for GAP definitions).

Price Sensitivity Rule of Hedging

There are several provisos that complicate hedging scenarios. In particular, in order to hedge properly, an institution must buy or sell futures whose price will move by the same amount as the price of the asset that the institution wishes to hedge when interest rates change. This requires that the institution create a hedge that follows the following *price sensitivity rule*:

$$\Delta P_A/\Delta r_M = -N \times \Delta P_F/\Delta r_M, \tag{11-1}$$

where $\Delta P_A/\Delta r_M$ equals the change in the price of the asset that will occur for a 1 percent change in market interest rates, $\Delta P_F/\Delta r_M$ equals the change in the price of the futures contract that will occur for a 1 percent change in market interest rates, and N equals the number of futures contracts purchased to create the hedge.

If the price sensitivity rule is followed, the change in the price of the asset that occurs when market interest rates change will be exactly offset by an (inverse) change in the value of the futures position, thereby leaving the hedging institution's total portfolio value unchanged.

When creating hedges, an individual should keep in mind that the term structure of interest rates can change as well as the level of interest rates. Consequently, short-term interest rates may change by more or less than long-term rates (usually by more). Thus the hedging firm might want to try to match the durations of the asset hedged and the futures market instrument used to create the hedge fairly closely. That is why the thrift that wished to hedge a fixed-rate mortgage portfolio would probably use long-term futures contracts, such as Treasury note futures or (when they were available) GNMA futures contracts to hedge. However, an institution that wanted to hedge short-term costs of funds would be likely to use Treasury bill or Eurodollar futures contracts.

Income versus Net Worth Hedging.   Entire balance sheets can be hedged by following a basic "duration rule." The "duration rule" notes that an institution can calculate a duration gap (D_G) by comparing the market value and interest rate sensitivity of its assets to the market value and interest rate sensitivity of its liabilities. Assuming that interest rates applicable to liabilities and assets change equally when market interest rates change, the duration gap, D_G, can be expressed as follows:

$$D_G = MV_A \times D_A - MV_L \times D_L + MV_F \times D_F, \tag{11-2}$$

where

MV_A = the market value of an institution's assets;
MV_L = the market value of its liabilities;
MV_F = the market value of futures contracts purchased (this value will be negative
      if futures are sold);

D_A = the duration of its assets;
D_L = the duration of its liabilities;
D_F = the average duration (rate sensitivity) of futures contracts purchased (or sold).

An institution can calculate its duration gap on the assumption that it buys or sells no futures (that is, $MV_F = 0$). After calculating its portfolio duration on the assumption that no futures are owned (or $MV_F = 0$), the institution then can buy or sell futures contracts with appropriate durations to immunize its portfolio against interest rate changes. In general, an institution that has a positive futures-free duration GAP (because the market value–weighted duration of its assets is greater than the market value–weighted duration of its liabilities) will want to sell futures market instruments to immunize its balance sheet. An institution that has a negative futures-free GAP duration (because it has assets with a much lower duration than its liabilities) will want to buy futures market instruments in order to immunize. In general, the institution will be fully immunized when its duration gap equals zero.

Before planning its immunization strategy, however, an institution must decide whether it wishes to immunize its *earnings* or the *market value of its net worth* against rate risk, as it cannot immunize both at once. For instance, assume an institution immunizes its earnings so that they remain unchanged as interest rates vary. If interest rates rise, the discounted present value of the (constant) future earnings stream will fall. Thus the net worth of the institution will also fall. Consequently, a financial institution with immunized earnings will find that the present value of its earnings will vary inversely with interest rates.

To immunize its net worth against changes in interest rates, an institution's earnings would have to rise or fall in step with interest rates. Typically, since most institutions have more assets than liabilities, this can be done if the institution is somewhat "asset-sensitive," with more short-maturity assets than liabilities. Then, if all interest rates rise, its earnings will also rise. If the institution is properly immunized, the discounted value of its new (increased) earnings flow will be the same before and after interest rates rise; if so, its net worth will be immunized against changes in rates.

Risks in the Futures Markets

The previous illustrations have all been constructed so that investment in futures will prove to be profitable. However, there are substantial risks in the futures markets, some of which we shall now discuss.

Basis Risk

Basis risk exists because the value of an item being hedged may not always keep the same price relationship to contracts purchased or sold in the futures markets. For instance, in the corporate financing example (Exhibit 11–4), the corporation might find that its cost of borrowing was 250 basis points above the Treasury bond rate after one year. As a result, the futures hedge would only partially offset its increase in interest costs. The same would be true in the bank cost of funds example (Exhibit 11–5) if the bank had to pay 50 basis points more, rather than 25 basis points more, than the Eurodollar rate in the futures markets when it issued its CDs.

Cross-Hedges.   Cross-hedges exist when a futures market contract is used to hedge a dissimilar item. For instance, an S&L that wishes to hedge its assets for more than one year may wish to hedge in the Treasury note rather than the mortgage-backed security options or futures market, because trading in distant futures contracts is more active in the former. However, mortgage rates and Treasury note rates, although closely related, do not always move together. As the spread between the rates changes, so does the basis risk. In general, cross-hedges have more basis risk than hedges involving equivalent items.

Related-Contract Risk

Hedges can also fail because of a defect in the contract being hedged. In the bank cost-of-funds example, interest rates conceivably could fall (thereby causing a loss on the short sale of the Eurodollar contracts) and the borrower could prepay the loan. Although commercial loan contracts ordinarily do not allow for prepayments, consumer borrowers frequently prepay their debts. Thus the bank would lose on the futures contract and would not be receiving compensatory loan revenues.

Other examples of "related-contract" risk abound. For instance, our investor in British pounds could be hurt by a default on the British security that promised the 10 percent return.

Manipulation Risk

The commodity markets are federally regulated because there have been instances of manipulation in the past. Most manipulations involve "short squeezes," whereby an individual or group tries to make it difficult or impossible for short sellers in the futures markets to liquidate their contracts through delivery of acceptable commodities. Then the "shorts" will have to buy their contracts back at inflated prices.

Manipulations can take many forms and are hard to predict. In the early 1970s, a strike at grain elevators in Chicago made it impossible to deliver corn to the elevators as called for by the Chicago Board of Trade's corn contract. As a result, futures prices shot upward even though there was a bumper harvest and cash corn prices were low. In another instance, federal regulation of the pork belly market was initiated after a consortium of buyers executed a short squeeze that caused many public losses. In 1977, the activities of the Hunt family of Texas, who, because of their immense wealth held contracts for more deliverable bushels of soybeans than were readily available in Chicago, caused a short squeeze in soybeans. Then, in 1980 and 1981, the Hunts attempted to squeeze the silver market. Their activities created a short panic that sent the silver price over $50 per ounce before it collapsed following changes in exchange rules.

Because manipulations cannot be foreseen and because they cause large price movements, they add an element of risk to trading in some futures contracts. However, futures that use "cash settlement" procedures, such as Eurodollar or stock-index futures that allow cash instead of an underlying asset to be delivered at expiration, are safe from "short squeezes." With cash settlement, futures prices at expiration are simply marked to market to reflect the value of the underlying assets at the designated settlement time. Thus such contracts are safe from potential short squeezes because holders of "short" futures positions do not need to obtain physical commodities (which may be hard to obtain) to deliver to satisfy their open futures contracts' requirements on delivery day.

Margin Risk

An individual with illiquid assets can also encounter difficulty by hedging in the futures markets if the futures price moves adversely and the individual must constantly post more maintenance margin funds. For instance, if the British pound rose rather than fell, the speculator in our previous example would lose substantially on his short futures contracts in the pound. At the same time, the dollar value of the British security would rise substantially. However, the speculator would not get his pounds back to convert into dollars for one year. In the meantime he would need to deposit more dollars or government securities with the exchange to meet maintenance margin requirements. This could cause a cash shortage that might force him to liquidate his futures contracts at a loss before his security matured. If the price of the pound later fell, he could lose both on the futures and on his exchange of dollars for pounds after the security matured.

The fact that maintenance margin requirements rise when futures prices move adversely should be taken into account lest they cause an unexpected cash squeeze. Forward contracts are sometimes preferred to futures contracts because they do not cause maintenance margin problems.

Swap Markets

In the last decade a new form of financial transaction has developed called a "swap." A "swap" works much like a forward contract in that it guarantees the exchange of two items of value between counterparties at some time (or at several times) in the future. However, unlike the forward market, a swap for only a *net* transfer of funds is usually arranged. For instance, if the first party to a swap owes the second party 9 percent interest on a "notional principal" of $1,000,000 and the other party owes the first party 8 percent interest on the same "notional principal," they need only exchange the difference, or $10,000 per year, to settle the annual interest difference due on the $1 million swap. Also, unlike a forward contract, the exact terms of trade are usually not prespecified, but rather typically vary with changes in interest rates, exchange rates, or some other future price. For instance, one party may pay a 9 percent fixed interest rate on the notional principal while the other may pay "2 percent over the T-bill rate"—which would be 8 percent if the T-bill rate were 6 percent, but could vary over time.

Swaps are frequently used to offset interest rate risk by exchanging fixed interest rate payments for variable interest rate payments. Such swaps may also be used to take advantages of credit-risk premium differences for different maturities of securities (that is, the differences in yield between the debt of a Aaa firm and that of a Baa firm are likely to be much greater for long-term bonds than for commercial paper issues—but rate differences may reflect the fact that the Baa firm may have financial troubles in the future, so such "credit risk differential" swaps can be risky). In addition, swaps may also be used to offset the risk of future foreign currency flows (such as the income that a firm expects to receive from a foreign subsidiary or foreign investment) or the risk that foreign interest rates may move differently from domestic interest rates.

There is some theoretical debate as to why swap opportunities exist. It may be that some institutions have information-cost, transaction-cost, or location advantages in raising or lending funds in certain sectors of the credit markets; however, the sectors that each serves may not be well matched internally. For instance, saving associations typically have a branch structure and deposit production process that allows them to attract relatively short-term deposits at relatively low interest rates. Many savings associations also have specialized as mortgage lenders because they know both their depositors and their local mortgage markets well. However, if an S&L makes fixed-rate mortgages, its revenues will be stable even if interest rates rise. Also, if interest rates rise, the S&L has to pay more to obtain and retain its short-term deposits; thus, its profits will suffer and it will be exposed to interest rate risk when it strictly pursues its usual lines of business. As a result a savings association frequently can benefit from swap transactions, particularly if it can find a counterparty with opposite interest rate risk problems.

For example, let us assume that a commercial bank was able to sell $50 million more in a long-term (10 years) IRA certificate of deposit paying 8 percent interest than it could profitably lend out to long-term borrowers since most bank assets (such as commercial loans and T-bills) are short-term. Unless the bank could invest $50 million more in long-term assets, it would probably acquire $50 million more short-term assets. However, this would increase the "GAP" between its short-term assets and short-term liabilities by $50 million. As a result, it would be exposed to interest rate risk. Consequently, if market interest rates fell, it would earn lower rates on its short-term assets, and might not be able to afford the fixed rate of interest it had agreed to pay to its IRA depositors for the next 10 years.

The bank can offset its potential interest rate risk, however, by entering into a swap with an institution that has too many long-term assets, such as our mortgage-oriented savings association. Thus, let us assume that the bank enters into a swap agreement in which it arranges to make short-term interest payments at a rate equal to LIBOR (the London Interbank Borrowing Rate) minus 1/8 percent in exchange for a fixed-interest return of 8 3/4 percent for 10 years on a "notional principal" of $50 million. The savings bank, in turn, offers to pay a fixed rate of 8 3/4 percent for ten years in return for a variable rate of return equal to LIBOR minus 1/8 percent on $50 million. The swap is diagrammed in Exhibit 11–7.

The swap can be advantageous to both parties. For instance, a bank with good credit can usually borrow funds at the LIBOR rate, so it will earn a 1/8 percent profit on its short-term funding of the $50 million (because it pays the S&L 1/8 percent less than LIBOR). In addition, it will earn a 3/4 percent spread (an 8 3/4 percent fixed return less the 8 percent interest cost) on its long-term IRA deposits. The savings association in turn is likely to have a portfolio of mortgages on which it earns 9 3/4 percent, so it can make a sure profit by agreeing to make 8 3/4 percent interest payments for 10 years. Furthermore, because savings banks can usually pay as much as 1 percent less than LIBOR to their retail depositors, the savings bank can be assured that it will generally be able to add to its profits by issuing short-term retail deposits to fund its LIBOR minus 1/8 percent interest rate obligation. The key to making the swap work is that the savings bank has a relative cost advantage in issuing

Exhibit 11–7   Example of a Swap

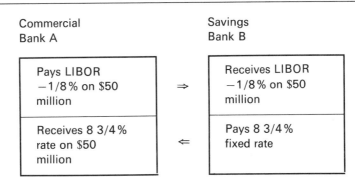

The savings bank is obligated to pay $8^3/_4\%$ of $50 million, or $4.375 million per year in interest less the amount of interest owed it by the bank. If LIBOR $-^1/_8\%$ equals $8^3/_4\%$, no net interest payment is required. However, if LIBOR averages $9^7/_8\%$, the commercial bank must pay the savings bank 1% of $50 million, or $0.50 million. Conversely, if LIBOR rates average $6^7/_8\%$ throughout the year, the savings bank must pay the net difference of $(8^3/_4\% - 6^7/_8\% + ^1/_8\%) \times$ $50 million, or $1 million to the commercial bank annually.

short-term deposits and making long-term mortgage loans, while the commercial bank has a cost advantage in making short-term commercial loans and, temporarily (in this case), in issuing long-term IRA deposits.

The risks involved in a swap are not great. Since only the net difference in interest payments is exchanged, as described in Exhibit 11–7, if one party defaults, the potential loss is just a small rate difference and not the entire notional principal. However, credit risk does exist, and defaults are more likely when the rate movement is disadvantageous to the defaulting party.

Because credit evaluation of potential counterparties is required to reduce the risks of swaps, and also because it is difficult for individual parties to agree on the exact amount, timing, and rate-determination characteristics of swaps, an extensive "dealer" market has developed in swaps. Commercial banks are among the most active participants in the swaps market, accompanied by investment banks and, to some degree, foreign exchange dealers. Within 10 years of its start, by 1992, the swaps market exceeded $4 trillion in notional principal.

The most common types of swaps involve interest rate swaps, such as the swap described in Exhibit 11–7. Sometimes such swaps are arranged to allow firms to take advantage of differential credit-risk premiums that they must pay to borrow long-term versus short-term; other times interest rate swaps allow firms to avoid special problems and/or obtain special access to markets. For instance, in the historically first interest rate swap, in 1982, ITT Financial Corporation (a finance company) agreed to receive a variable-rate payment from "Sallie Mae" (the Student Loan Marketing Association) in exchange for paying Sallie Mae a fixed-rate payment. This allowed the finance company to guarantee that it would make a profit even if its short-term cost of funds rose (if market interest rates increased) and it was unable to increase its loan revenues (since state rate ceilings limited the rate it could change on consumer loans).

Swap Dealers

Because it takes specialized skill to assess credit risk and because individual institutions' needs in a swap transaction are usually not perfectly matched with respect to desired maturities, rate indexes on which floating rates are based, or payment timing, swap dealers have developed who serve as counterparties to both sides of swap transactions. Commercial banks play a major role as swap dealers because of their easy access to money markets and foreign currency markets and their ability to assess credit risks. Investment banks also have the requisite skills and market access to serve as swap dealers.

Each dealer in the swaps market runs a "book" of swaps for which it serves as a counterparty. The dealer tries to keep its "book" as closely matched as possible with respect to short-term or long-term interest rate exposures, foreign currency exposures, or floating-rate index exposures. If its book is temporarily mismatched, the dealer will usually try to hedge any residual exposure in the financial futures or options markets.

Swap dealers take some risk running their book because they may not be able to match it perfectly or because they may experience the unexpected default of a counterparty at a time when it is expensive to replicate that counterparty's position at low cost. Because of their risks and the fact that they provide a service by matching counterparties' needs, swap dealers usually charge a fee equal to 5 to 10 basis points (0.05 percent to 0.10 percent) of the notional principal of a swap.

Swap Markets Regulation

Swap markets, in general, are subject to very little regulation. There is no central clearinghouse for swaps and no central regulatory agency. Nonetheless, while default risks on a swap are low because only one side has an incentive for default at one time, and the risk of loss is limited to the price that must be paid to rehedge the swap at current market interest rates, bank regulators are concerned with the risks banks take when acting as counterparties to a swap. Commercial banks, therefore, must apply risk-based capital requirements to swap-risk exposures. However, because most swaps are short-term and deal in low-risk assets, the risk-based capital requirements typically are low. Nonetheless, since investment banks and insurance companies, which also deal in the swap market, are not subject to bank risk-based capital requirements, commercial banks often claim that their risk-based capital requirements put them at a disadvantage in pricing swaps. Still, in spite of their capital requirements, because of their easy access to money and foreign currency markets and their expertise in evaluating credit risk, commercial banks still retain a dominant role in the swap dealer markets.

Regulators are probably correct to require that institutions provide capital to hedge against potential swap defaults. If defaults do occur, they are likely to occur in a crisis, when many defaults occur on one side of the dealer's book. However, in ordinary circumstances, defaults are not likely to be frequent. Consequently, it is difficult to ascertain just what level of capital must be maintained to protect against possible losses on swaps. Option-pricing theory is often used to determine the level of protection needed.

Options Markets

One drawback of hedging with financial futures is that the hedging process can totally insulate a firm against price changes. Not only will it reduce the firm's losses if interest rates move adversely, but it also will eliminate potential gains if interest rates move favorably. For example, in 1982 a thrift institution manager who hedged by selling short in the futures market lost his job when interest rates fell. His board of directors fired him because he had lost money in the futures markets even though, being hedged, he had offset those losses with gains on the thrift's portfolio. Because hedging eliminates gains as well as losses, some people prefer to use options rather than futures contracts to insure themselves against interest rate risk. Options have been available on stocks for many years, and they have been traded on organized exchanges since 1973. Options have been available in the United States on financial futures contracts only since October 1982. However, they have grown rapidly since that time. Exhibit 11–8 lists the financial options that were available in January 1992.

The Nature of Options

Options allow people to enter into contracts to buy or sell stocks, commodities, or other securities at a predetermined price, called the "strike" or "exercise" price, until some future time. An option is "exercised" when it is surrendered and the underlying purchase or sale transaction is made at the strike price.

Options differ from futures in three key ways. First, with an American option, the right to buy or sell and receive or deliver the underlying asset at the strike price exists over time, not at a given time. Thus an American option can be exercised prior to its expiration. However, "European" options can only be exercised at expiration. A second difference is that the buyer of the option pays the seller (called the "writer" of the option) a "premium." The writer keeps the premium regardless of whether the option is exercised. The final key difference, which is the most important, is that an option need not be exercised if it is not to the buyer's advantage to do so.

An option provides the buyer with a one-sided choice. If price movements are advantageous, the buyer exercises the option and realizes a gain. If price movements are harmful, the buyer can limit potential losses by letting the option expire unexercised. Because of this feature, options can provide their buyers with insurance against adverse price moves. If the price move is adverse, the buyer loses only the premium paid to buy the option. If the price move is favorable, however, the buyer can exercise the option and realize a gain. The option premium is the price of this "insurance."

Calls and Puts.   There are two types of options—calls and puts. *Call options* give the buyer the right to buy a security or futures contract at the strike price. *Put options* give the option buyer the right to sell a security or futures contract at the strike price. The writer of a call agrees to sell the security (or futures contract) at the strike price if the buyer exercises the option; the writer of a put agrees to buy the security (or futures contract) for the strike price if the buyer exercises the option.

Exhibit 11–8   U.S. Options Markets

Type of Options	Exchanges at which Trading Occurs	Indexes or Currencies Traded	Open Interest, January 3, 1992
Individual stock options	CBOE	Stock options on CBOE	6,438,514
	AMEX	Stock options on AMEX	3,536,352
	PHLX	Stock options on PHLX	1,970,160
	PSE	Stock options on PSE	941,717
	NYSE	Stock options on NYSE	477,399
Stock index options	CBOE	S&P 500 Stock Index, plus Leaps & Caps	1,134,710
	CBOE	S&P 100 Stock Index, plus Leaps & Caps	915,007
	AMEX	Major Market Index[a], plus caps	76,112
	AMEX	Institutional Stock Index, plus caps	139,186
	AMEX	Computer Technology Index	395
	AMEX	Oil Index	1,731
	PHLX	Gold/silver Stock Index	2,187
	PHLX	Value Line Arithmetic Index	16,017
	PHLX	Over-the-Counter 100 Index	1,532
	PHLX	Utilities Index	9,982
	PSE	Financial News Composite Index	3,346
	NYSE	NYSE Composite Index	2,633
Options on stock-index futures contracts	CME	S&P 500 Index	89,260
	NYFE	NYSE Composite Index	1,515
	CME	NIKKEI 225	539

Gains and Losses.   Potential gains and losses are quite different for buyers and writers of puts and calls. They also differ for options and futures contracts. This is illustrated by Exhibit 11-9. Part A shows how gains and losses vary as the underlying security price changes for the buyer and the writer of a call option on a security with a strike price of 40 and a premium of $5 if the option is exercised on expiration day. The call buyer's potential gain is unlimited, while the writer's potential loss is unlimited, if the security price rises. Meanwhile, if the security price falls, the buyer's maximum loss is limited to the premium paid for the option, whereas the call option writer's maximum gain is limited to the premium paid for the option. Put options are similar, as shown in Part B, except that the put buyer gains when the security price declines and loses the amount of the premium if the security price rises. In contrast with options, buyers and sellers of futures gain and lose symmetrically and without limits as futures prices vary. This is illustrated in Part C.

Covered and Naked Options.   Because the option writer's maximum loss is virtually unlimited, many option writers write *covered options*—in which they already

Type of Options	Exchanges at which Trading Occurs	Indexes or Currencies Traded	Open Interest, January 3, 1992
Interest rate options on futures	CBOT	U.S. Treasury bonds[a]	709,784
	CBOT	U.S. Treasury 10-year notes	83,411
	CBOT	Municipal Bond Index	13,536
	CBOT	5-year Treasury notes	20,745
	LIFFE	Long-Gilt	64,004
	IMM	U.S. Treasury bills	3,834
	CME	Eurodollar interest rates (3 month)[a]	849,118
	CME	LIBOR rate—1 month	6,538
Currency options—options on futures	IMM	Japanese yen	135,162
	IMM	West German mark	222,688
	IMM	Canadian dollar	26,216
	IMM	British pound	28,917
	IMM	Swiss franc	39,722
	IMM	Australian dollar	2,812
	FINEX	U.S. Dollar Index	28,721
Currency options (options for settlement by delivery of currency)	PHLX	Japanese yen, Canadian dollars, West German mark, British pound, Swiss franc, Australian dollar, French franc, various dates and amounts and types of options (American or European)	792, 598

Exchanges: AMEX (American Stock Exchange) IMM (International Monetary Market of the CME)
CBOE (Chicago Board Options Exchange) LIFFE (London International Financial Futures Exchange)
CME (Chicago Mercantile Exchange) NYFE (New York Futures Exchange)
FINEX (Financial Instrument Exchange of PHLX (Philadelphia Exchange)
the N.Y. Cotton Exchange) PSE (Pacific Stock Exchange)

[a]A number of these options are also traded in foreign countries. Major market index options are traded on the European Options Exchange in Amsterdam before the U.S. market opens. U.S. Treasury bond, Eurodollar rate, and currency options are also traded on the LIFFE exchange in London. Eurodollar rate, Japanese yen, Deutsche mark, and British pound options are traded on the Singapore Exchange (SIMEX). Also, foreign currency options of many denominations, including U.S. dollar options denominated in foreign currencies, are traded on a variety of exchanges around the world. Finally, 24-hour electronic trading should become available for interest rate, currency, and precious metals options through the CME's "Globex" automated trading system or LIFFE's Telerate Connection, while the PHLX and FINEX currency contracts trade nearly continuously through the day.

The most actively traded options series are the stock index options (particularly those based on the Standard & Poor's 100 and Standard & Poor's 500 stock indexes, both of which are traded on the CBOE).

own the security that they have agreed to sell or have already sold short the security that they have agreed to buy. Option writers may also write *naked* (that is, uncovered) *options*. In this case, they need not own an offsetting security position. However, writers of naked options typically must deposit margin requirements with the exchange to guarantee that they will honor their commitments. If the underlying security price moves adversely, writers of naked options have to deposit additional money to maintain their margin requirements.

Exhibit 11–9   **Gains and Losses on Options and Futures Contracts, if Options Are Exercised at Expiration**

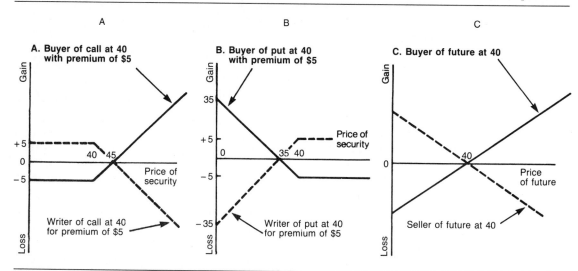

In all of these examples, the gain to the buyer of an option or future equals a loss to the seller (or writer) of the contract, and vice versa. Note that in Part A, the buyer of a call exercisable at 40 breaks even on the call but loses the $5 premium if the underlying stock is at 40 when the call expires. If the stock is at 45, the $5 gain on the call exactly offsets the $5 premium; thus the net gain is zero. Above 45, the buyer of the call gains, and the writer of the call loses more than the premium and ends up with a loss. In Part B, puts pay off at expiration in a way that is opposite to calls. Futures, however, have no premium and provide symmetric gains and losses, as shown in Part C.

Swindles and Regulation of Options Markets.   In the 1970s, some unscrupulous dealers sold options on London Commodity Futures over the phone. They took the premiums paid in by option buyers and kept them. If the commodity price moved adversely, they told the buyers that they had lost their money. If the commodity price moved favorably, they told the buyers that they had made money and urged them to reinvest it. If too many people wanted to cash out and take their gains, the dealers went out of business and kept the investors' money.

Because of the telephone swindles, options on futures received a bad name. Therefore, trading in options on U.S. futures exchanges was not allowed until 1982. Furthermore, the CFTC required that such trading be closely regulated and that margin requirements be strictly enforced for writers of options. Nonetheless, option writing can still be risky. For example, a commodities-clearing firm failed when gold prices jumped sharply in March 1985, because the price rise forced into bankruptcy several large customers who had written gold calls.

The Value of Options.   The premium "price" of options does not vary randomly. Instead, it varies positively with (1) the price variance of the underlying commodity or security, (2) the time to the option's expiration, and (3) the level of interest rates. Its value also varies with changes in the price of the underlying asset relative to the option's exercise price and, for options based on stocks, with the dividends of the underlying stocks. The more price variability a stock has, the greater the chance that the buyer can exercise the option for either a larger profit or a larger loss. However, the buyer will never exercise the option and take a loss. Thus, on average, the option's value increases because bigger gains are possible with greater price variance. Similarly, given a longer period of time, bigger cumulative price changes can be expected. Thus options have greater value when they have a longer time to expiration.

Because the purchase of an option allows the buyer to conserve capital until the option is actually exercised and the underlying stock or commodity is purchased, call options on stocks have a higher value when interest rates are high. If a buyer purchases a call option instead of a stock and then invests the money saved, the buyer still shares in the price appreciation of the stock but earns more on the invested funds when interest rates are high. Thus buyers are willing to pay more for options when interest rates are high, particularly if the option has a long time to maturity. In addition, as can be seen by analyzing Exhibit 11-9, a call on a stock will be more valuable when its strike price is lower relative to the stock's value, and a put will be more valuable when its exercise price is higher relative to the stock's value. Finally, since stock options are not protected against dividend payouts, call options will lose value (and put options will gain value) when a company distributes some of its assets as dividends to shareholders and thereby reduces its stock's price.

The value of an option changes over time in a systematic manner, as shown in Exhibit 11-10, which applies to a call option with a stock price of 100. Just before expiration, the value of a call is equal to its intrinsic value, or the value that could be realized by exercising the option immediately. An option's intrinsic value is equal to either the value of the underlying asset minus the exercise price or to zero (whichever is greater). However, before expiration an option will have an additional time value. The time value of an option usually is positive prior to expiration. Even if the option has an intrinsic value of zero (as it does in Exhibit 11-10 when the stock price is 90 and the exercise price is 90 or 100), as long as the underlying asset is sufficiently volatile and there is enough time left until expiration, the option will have a chance of becoming valuable before it expires. The time value of an option reflects this chance. Because the chances that an option will become valuable before expiration are greater the longer the time to expiration, the option value will be higher if there is a longer time to expiration. Conversely, because there is less chance that the option can still become valuable as expiration approaches, the option value will experience "time decay" and lose value. Finally, when the option is due to expire, it will retain only its intrinsic value.

Options versus Futures

The gains and losses to buyers and sellers of futures contracts are quite different from those for buyers and sellers of options contracts (see Exhibit 11-9). For futures, both gains and losses can vary virtually without limit. Therefore some buyers (or sellers) prefer options to futures contracts. For instance, suppose a portfolio manager thinks that interest rates will decline but is not sure. To take advantage of the rate decline, the manager might want to buy many long-term bonds that would increase in value as rates fell. However, if rates rose, the bonds would lose value and the manager might lose a job. If the manager hedged in the futures market by selling T-bond futures, that person would be safe if rates rose, because the loss on the bonds in the portfolio would

Exhibit 11–10   Value of a Call Option

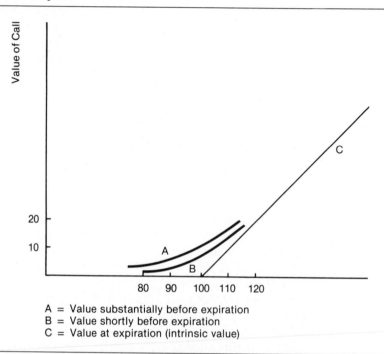

A = Value substantially before expiration
B = Value shortly before expiration
C = Value at expiration (intrinsic value)

Options have a time premium that exceeds their intrinsic value by a greater amount as the volatility of the underlying asset or the time to expiration increases. As an option approaches expiration, its value will experience time decay until it is worth only its intrinsic value.

be offset by the gain on the short sale of the T-bond futures. However, if rates fell, the loss on the T-bond futures would eliminate the gain in value of the long-term bonds. Consequently, the portfolio manager might prefer to buy a T-bond put option. If T-bond prices fell, the put option would rise in value and offset the loss on the bond portfolio. However, if rates fell, as expected, the market value of the bonds would rise and the manager could let the T-bond put expire unused—thereby losing only the premium. Similar measures could be used by thrift institution managers who want to buy protection against unexpected rises in interest rates that could lower the value of their mortgage portfolios.

Options, then, give a one-sided type of price protection that is not available from futures. However, the premiums on options may be high, and options experience time decay. The potential buyer of the protection must decide whether the insurance value provided by the option is worth its price.

Options can either be traded on organized exchanges or purchased in the over-the-counter market. Swap dealers such as commercial or investment banks frequently custom design options for their customers. Such options let customers "cap" their exposure to interest rate risk or exchange rate risk. Such caps are equivalent to "out-of-the-money" options that have no present intrinsic value but may become valuable in the future. Custom-designed options are useful to customers and provide a valuable source of fee income to the option or swaps dealers and writers. While option writers potentially take unlimited risks, they can often offset that risk by taking matched positions on their books.

Summary

Futures markets allow people to guarantee the price of future transactions with greater certainty than would otherwise be possible. Financial futures have grown rapidly in recent years as people have tried to protect themselves against increased price uncertainty in foreign exchange markets and against increased interest rate risk.

Futures markets differ from forward markets in that they involve the trading of standardized contracts on futures exchanges. Futures markets exist for commodities, metals, stock indexes, financial market instruments, foreign currencies, and other assets subject to sharp price fluctuations. Numerous exchanges exist on which financial futures contracts can be traded.

The futures markets are regulated by the Commodity Futures Trading Commission and the individual exchanges. Much of the regulation is designed to limit possibilities for fraud or manipulation in the markets.

The futures markets are used by hedgers and speculators. Financial hedgers can use the markets to lock in future costs of funds or future investment returns. They also can be used to lock in profits on mortgage market transactions and foreign security investments or to immunize the earnings or net worth of financial institutions against unexpected changes in interest rates.

Hedging in the futures markets can be risky, however. Basis risk, related-contract risk, manipulation risk, and maintenance-margin risk may all affect the returns to hedging.

Swap markets involve paired forward market contract agreements between two counterparties. Swaps can be arranged so their terms vary with future exchange rates for foreign currencies, or with changes in short-term or long-term interest rates. They can also be arranged to vary with foreign as well as domestic interest rates. Because of their great flexibility and their utility for transferring interest rate or exchange rate risk, swap markets have grown explosively since their inception in 1982. Swap transactions provide an important source of fee income for commercial banks, investment banks, and other financial institutions that act as dealers in the swap markets. Swap dealers are helpful in those markets because it often is hard for two counterparties to agree exactly on the amount, timing, and rate indexes they wish to use in a swap. However swap dealers take risk if their swap "books" are not matched exactly or if large fluctuations in interest rates, the term structure, or exchange rates occur that trigger defaults on swaps. Thus bank regulators require that commercial banks hold risk-based capital to back their riskier or longer-term swap positions. Nonbank dealers often do not incur risk-based capital requirements, because the swap market is not highly regulated.

The options markets also allow people to gain from or protect against future price movements. Moreover, the options markets provide opportunities for large one-sided gains or losses. The asymmetry of option returns lets options serve an insurance function for hedgers. However, as is true with insurance, the buyer of an option must pay a premium for protection. Because of past manipulations involving London options, options on financial futures in the United States were not authorized until late 1982. The value of option premiums generally increases with uncertainty (expected price variance), interest rates, and the time to maturity of each option. Options' values also vary as the prices of their underlying assets change relative to the exercise price of the options. Options markets are regulated either by the SEC (which regulates options whose value is based directly on stock values) or the CFTC (which regulates options on futures contracts).

Questions

1. What are the differences between futures and forward markets? What are the pros and cons associated with using each one?
2. What role does the exchange play in futures market transactions?
3. How can a thrift institution guarantee its costs of funds for a period of time by using the futures markets?
4. Why do you think some futures contracts are more widely traded than others?
5. What agency is the chief regulator of futures markets? Why is federal regulation necessary?
6. Explain the difference between a put and a call.
7. Why do you think exchanges are more concerned with writers of naked options than with writers of covered options?
8. Explain the difference in the gain and loss potential of a call option and a long futures position. Under what circumstances do you think someone would prefer the option to the future or vice versa?
9. Futures contracts on stock indexes are very popular. Why do you think that is so? How do you think they might be used?
10. Explain how futures contracts can be used to lock in returns on foreign investments. When is it profitable to do so?

Selected References

Abken, Peter A. "An Introduction to Portfolio Insurance." *Economic Review*. Federal Reserve Bank of Atlanta, November/December 1987, pp. 2–25.
Clearly explains how portfolio insurance can, in theory, protect a portfolio against substantial losses by making a portfolio's returns replicate those of a call option, in which potential upside returns are unlimited and potential losses are limited. It points out the assumptions made by portfolio insurance strategists and notes how such strategies broke down during the stock market's crash of 1987.

Belongia, Michael T., and G. J. Santoni. "Cash Flow or Present Value: What's Lurking Behind That Hedge?" *Review*. Federal Reserve Bank of St. Louis, January 1985, pp. 5–13.
This is an excellent article that uses a straightforward approach to explain different ways in which financial futures can be used by a financial institution to insulate itself against interest rate risk. It makes the important point that hedging procedures will vary according to whether the institution wishes to insulate its earnings or its net present value against interest rate risk.

Drabenstott, Mark, and Anne O'Mara McDonley. "Futures Markets: A Primer for Financial Institutions." *Economic Review*. Federal Reserve Bank of Kansas City, November 1984, pp. 17–33.

Explains simply how financial institutions can use financial futures to reduce their interest rate risk. Also provides a good bibliography.

Fieleke, Norman S. "The Rise of the Foreign Currency Futures Market." *New England Economic Review*. **Federal Reserve Bank of Boston, March–April 1985, pp. 38–47.**

This highly readable article analyzes the causes of rapid growth in the foreign currency futures market. It posits that the growth of international trade has promoted the growth of futures. It also points out that even though bid/ask spreads are about the same in both the futures and forward markets, commissions are higher and contract sizes are smaller in the futures markets.

"Futures Magazine 1992 Reference Guide to Futures/Options Markets." *Futures*, **Vol. 20, no. 14, 1991, entire issue.**

This annual *Futures* magazine publication provides useful data on all futures and options contracts authorized to trade on various exchanges around the world, including contract sizes and terms, trading dates, and trading hours. It also provides information on futures market regulators, organizations, and vendors and gives their addresses.

Gay, Gerald D., and Robert W. Kolb. "Interest Rate Futures as a Tool for Immunization." *Journal of Portfolio Management*. **Fall 1983, pp. 65–70.**

This excellent but somewhat technical article explains how futures market instruments can be used to immunize the value of a financial institution's portfolio against unexpected changes in interest rates.

Goodman, Laurie S. "New Options Markets." *Quarterly Review*. **Federal Reserve Bank of New York, Autumn 1983, pp. 35–47.**

Gives an excellent description of the new options markets and the factors that affect option pricing. Also considers the factors that determine the differences in and the continuing viability of options on futures versus the viability of options on underlying currencies, securities, or physical commodities.

Kolb, Robert W. *Understanding Futures Markets*, **3rd. ed. Miami: Kolb Publishing Co., 1991.**

This paperback text provides an excellent description of financial futures markets and their uses, as well as an introductory discussion of options markets. Its description of financial futures contracts and hedging procedures is particularly good.

Koppenhaver, G. D. "Futures Options and Their Use by Financial Intermediaries." *Economic Perspectives*. **Federal Reserve Bank of Chicago, January/February 1986, pp. 18–31.**

This interesting article describes the nature of financial options and gives examples of how they can be used by financial institutions to provide bond portfolio protection, aid in asset/liability management, or protect against losses caused by mortgage prepayments.

Smith, Clifford W., Jr., and Charles W. Smithson, eds. *The Handbook of Financial Engineering*. **New York: Harper and Row, 1990.**

This book contains 32 chapters by various experts who cover a wide variety of issues related to futures, options, swaps, forward contracts, and other financial derivative contracts and securities. It shows how financial engineering can create and value contracts that can be used to limit financial risk. It also discusses regulatory and accounting issues related to such contracts.

Wall, Larry D., and John J. Pringle. "Interest Rate Swaps: A Review of the Issues." *Economic Review*. **Federal Reserve Bank of Atlanta, November/December 1988, pp. 23–40.**

This article does an excellent job describing the theory and operation of the swap markets, the risks involved, and the regulatory issues related to swaps.

INTERNATIONAL EXCHANGE AND CREDIT MARKETS (INTRODUCTION)

IT WOULD BE NICE FOR U.S. citizens if the whole world used U.S. dollars to conduct financial transactions, just as English is used as the international language for airlines. Then U.S. citizens would never have to worry about the dollar value of the revenues they received in foreign currencies, the dollar value of assets they own abroad, or the dollar cost of supplies they obtain from foreign countries. This would make accounting and planning much easier for U.S. citizens and companies. It also would make accounting and planning much easier for foreign nationals if—and this is a big if—they were only willing to conduct transactions in a currency other than the one they have become accustomed to all their lives.

Unfortunately, most people are not willing to use a foreign currency to conduct their domestic transactions. Not only are foreign currencies "foreign" to people in their everyday affairs (since they usually use their domestic currencies to conduct transactions and keep their accounts) but also, people may distrust using a "foreign" currency whose value is not directly subject to the control of their national leaders. Consequently, the world's citizens use many currencies for their transactions.

Because people use a wide variety of currencies to conduct their transactions, "foreign exchange" markets have developed so people can convert their cash to different currencies as their needs for different currencies vary in their business affairs and business operations. Furthermore, various accounting procedures (such as "balance-of-payments" and "balance-of-trade" accounts) have been developed so people can identify flows of funds that occur when one currency is converted into another to facilitate foreign exchange and trade transactions. Finally, elaborate "credit procedures" have been developed to provide loans and financing across borders and legal jurisdictions.

Commercial banks play a major role in financing and arranging foreign exchange transactions because of their expertise in financing business, checking credit, and transferring money. Investment banks and foreign exchange dealers also play important roles in the foreign currency and investment markets. In addition, various multinational cooperative ventures have been developed to stabilize foreign exchange prices and thereby facilitate international trade. Thus the international institutional relationships used to facilitate foreign trade, investment, and exchange transactions are quite complex.

In this chapter we focus on the major forces and institutional factors that influence foreign exchange markets. First, we explain why business firms that do international business frequently enter into exchange or credit transactions designed to reduce their currency risk. Next we introduce the balance-of-payments accounts and capital accounts used to measure and account for foreign currency flows. We explain theoretically how changes in foreign currency flows can be expected to influence currency values in the long-run but also point out that considerable "exchange rate risk" exists as foreign currency values fluctuate in the short run. We also explain how commercial banks frequently arrange international credit and business-financing transactions that reduce that risk for business firms that engage in international trade. Finally, we discuss a number of the international exchange mechanisms that have been developed to stabilize international exchange rates and facilitate international trade.

Exchange Rates and International Trade

When U.S. manufacturers need to buy raw materials, they want to get the best possible deal. Hence they investigate several potential suppliers to determine the availability and quality of materials from each, how long it takes to receive an order, and the total delivered price, including transportation and other charges. When all potential suppliers are located in the United States, comparison of the alternatives is relatively easy. Both suppliers and customers keep their books, price their goods and services, and pay their employees in the same currency—the U.S. dollar. Since the federal government has authority over interstate commerce, it is unlikely that there will be any problems in shipping the order from one state to another. If a dispute arises between the buyer and the seller, both are governed by the same legal traditions and have access to the federal court system. This last characteristic, along with an extensive amount of reliable information about the trustworthiness and financial condition of both parties to the transaction, facilitates the extension of credit to finance purchases.

When potential suppliers are not located in the United States, though, comparisons are more difficult. Because both the goods and the payment for them must cross a national border, the evaluation process is complicated by at least three potential difficulties. The first problem is that the American buyer prefers to pay for the purchase with dollars, but the foreign supplier must pay employees and other local expenses with domestic currency other than U.S. dollars. Hence one of the two parties to the transaction will be forced to deal in a foreign currency. The second difficulty is that no single country or supranational organization, such as the United Nations, has total authority over all aspects of the transactions. Nations may erect barriers to control international product and capital flows so as to thwart market forces. Quotas, high tariffs, and controls on foreign exchange are examples of such barriers. Also, two countries may have distinctly different legal traditions—such as the English common law, which forms the basis for the judicial system in the United States, and the French civil law, which is encountered in many other nations. Because of concern about possible discrimination, each party to the transaction would most likely prefer not to use the other party's national court system for adjudication of disputes arising out of the transaction. But there is no supranational court to handle commercial disputes (although in some situations international arbitration panels can be used to resolve them). Thus one party to the transaction may be exposed to the jurisdiction of a foreign court. Banks and other lending agencies are also concerned about questions of legal jurisdiction; in addition they often find it difficult to obtain reliable information on which to base credit decisions in many countries. Hence, a third source of potential difficulty is associated with financing purchases of goods and services from foreign sources.

The first complicating factor—comparing suppliers who price their goods in currency units other than the U.S. dollar—is the easiest to overcome. To make such comparisons, the American buyer can check the appropriate exchange-rate quotation in the foreign exchange marked. An *exchange rate* is simply the price of one monetary unit, such as the British pound, stated in terms of another currency unit, such as the U.S. dollar. As an example of how exchange rates facilitate comparisons, assume that the American manufacturer has to pay $200 per ton for steel purchased from the most competitive supplier in the United States and £115 per ton for steel bought from a British supplier. Furthermore, a Japanese steel company is willing to sell steel to the American company for ¥24,000 per ton. Which supplier should be chosen?

If the exchange rate between dollars and pounds is $1.80/£, British steel will cost (£115) × ($1.80/£) = $207. At this dollar price, the American firm will prefer to buy steel from the American supplier. If the exchange rate between the yen and the dollar is ¥125/$, the Japanese steel will cost (¥24,000)/(¥125/$) = $192 per ton. Assuming that the price quotation of ¥24,000 includes all transportation costs and tariffs, or that the sum of those costs is less than $8, the American manufacturer will find it cheaper to purchase steel from the Japanese supplier than from the American steel company. Hence the contract will be awarded to the Japanese steel company, and dollars will be exchanged for yen in the foreign exchange market to make the purchase.

Today exchange rates are free to move up and down in response to changes in the underlying economic environment. If for some reason the exchange rate between the dollar and the pound falls from $1.80 to $1.65, British steel could be bought for (£115) × ($1.65/£) = $189.75. Because it now takes fewer dollars to buy one British pound, or, conversely, more pounds are needed to purchase one U.S. dollar, it is correct to say that the value of the pound has fallen against the dollar or that the value of the dollar has risen against the pound. These two statements are equivalent, because they both indicate that goods and services priced in pounds are now cheaper to someone holding dollars or that purchases priced in dollars are now more expensive to someone holding pounds. If the quoted price of £115 per ton were to include tariffs and transportation costs, the American manufacturer would now prefer to buy steel from the British supplier, assuming, of course, that the yen exchange rate remains at ¥125/$ and the price stays at ¥24,000 per ton.

Note that if domestic prices remain unchanged, the demand for a country's products (British steel, for instance) will be higher when the exchange rate for the country's currency is relatively lower. A reduction in the exchange rate for the pound from $1.80 to $1.65 led to a reversal of the purchase decisions: at $1.80 British steel was the most expensive, but when it fell to $1.65 it was the cheapest. When the foreign demand for a country's goods and services increases, the demand for its currency will also increase (assuming that the goods are priced in the local currency) as more people seek to obtain it in order to pay for their purchases. This is illustrated by the downward-sloping demand curve shown in Exhibit 12–1. This demand curve illustrates that the lower the dollar price of pounds, the lower the dollar price of British goods. The lower the price of British goods in terms of dollars, the higher foreigners' demand for British goods (and for pounds to pay for them).

From the point of view of a British importer, though, the lower the price of pounds, the more pounds must be given up in order to obtain dollars (or other foreign currencies) to buy foreign goods. Thus the lower the price of the pound in terms of dollars, the more likely residents of Britain are to switch from imported to domestic products. When purchases are diverted in this way to domestic goods, the demand by British residents for foreign currencies to buy imported products is reduced. This also means that they will supply fewer pounds to the foreign exchange markets because they no longer want to buy as many imports. Thus, as is shown by the upward-sloping supply curve in Exhibit 12–1, the supply of pounds in exchange for foreign currencies is low at low exchange rates for the pound and increases as the exchange rate increases.

The equilibrium exchange rate for the pound (or any other currency) can be determined when the supply and demand for it are viewed simultaneously. As illustrated by the point of intersection of the supply and demand curves in Exhibit 12–1, the equilibrium exchange rate occurs at the price at which the quantity of the currency demanded exactly equals the quantity supplied. At that rate of exchange (price), participants in the foreign exchange market will neither be accumulating nor divesting a currency they do not wish to hold.

Quotations for all currencies, similar to the rates given here for British pounds and Japanese yen, can usually be found in all foreign exchange markets. With few

Exhibit 12–1   **The Equilibrium Exchange Rate**

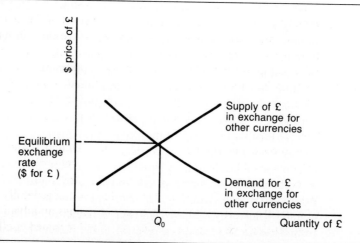

The equilibrium exchange rate for a currency is the point of intersection of the supply and demand curves for the country's currency.

exceptions, holdings of one currency can be converted into any other monetary unit in such markets. Arbitrageurs continually operate in the market to take advantage of any price disparities between currencies or between two trading centers. Thus, if a profit can be made by converting pounds into yen and then yen into dollars in New York City, then selling the dollars for pounds in London, an arbitrageur will do so and gain the profit. The action of foreign exchange arbitrageurs tends to keep exchange rates among different currencies consistent with each other (within narrow limits). Thus the equilibrium exchange rate for all currencies will be mutually and simultaneously determined at the point at which the supply of each currency in the foreign exchange markets equals the demand for it.

Factors Influencing Exchange Rates

We have seen that exchange rates are determined by the interaction of market forces that give rise to a supply of and a demand for a currency. Supplies and demands for currencies, though, depend on the underlying demand for and supply of goods and services (where financial flows result from trades of goods or services) and the underlying supply and demand for funds used to make short-term or long-term capital investments in various countries. Specifically, we examine, in turn, how exchange rates are influenced by (1) trade flows of goods and services, (2) financial factors and capital flows, and (3) government intervention in the foreign exchange market.

Trade Flows and Exchange Rates

According to the classical theory of international trade, nations produce the goods and services for which they enjoy a comparative advantage, and then they trade with foreigners to obtain other goods and services. The total volume of world trade today is worth many trillion dollars per year.

Anything that affects the demand for a country's exports or imports has the potential to alter the price of its currency in the foreign exchange market. At least six determinants of the demand for and supply of goods and services in the international economy can be identified. First, relative costs of the factors of production can give one country an advantage over another. Wage rates in many Asian nations are less than the value added to production by labor. Thus, the cost of goods imported from those nations, even after the addition of shipping costs may be less than that for comparable goods produced in the United States. Hence production of labor-intensive goods is shifting to these countries, and imports are starting to displace domestic products that require substantial amounts of unskilled labor for their production.

A second determinant of supply and demand is the relative factor endowment among nations. The Asian nations tend to have abundant supplies of cheap labor, whereas capital is relatively abundant in the more highly industrialized Western nations. Thus goods that are labor intensive can generally be produced more cheaply in Asia, the capital-intensive production enjoys an advantage in the United States.

A third aspect of supply of and demand for traded goods involves consumer tastes in the various nations. Before the OPEC oil embargo, consumers in the United States had a preference for large, powerful automobiles. Poor gas mileage was simply not an important issue to most drivers because gasoline was abundant and cheap. U.S. auto manufacturers catered to this majority demand by filling their model lines with the kind of cars most people wanted. For the small minority of consumers who were concerned about fuel economy, Detroit had little to offer. Therefore, small fuel-efficient cars represented a market niche that U.S. companies were content to leave to imports. After the oil embargo, however, the small-car niche became the dominant segment of the market, and Detroit was unable to respond in the short run. This created a tremendous demand for imported cars (and the foreign currency to pay for them) that was caused by a fundamental shift in consumer tastes. It also illustrates the fourth determinant of supply of and demand for traded goods and services—the ability of a country to satisfy its own needs domestically. Because the demand for small, fuel-efficient cars was greater than could be met from domestic U.S. sources, international trade is the only alternative available to meet the demand. When the Japanese government decided to adhere to voluntary export quotas on cars, consumer demand in the United States still existed, but it could not be fully satisfied through trade. Prices paid for Japanese automobiles were increased to absorb some of the excess demand. However, the total number of imported Japanese automobiles was reduced by barriers to international trade, in the form of export quotas, erected by the Japanese government. Barriers to trade such as this are the fifth determinant of the supply of and demand for traded goods and services that underlie the supply of and demand for foreign currencies.

A sixth factor influencing a nation's exports and imports is the rate at which national income is growing. Countries that are experiencing rapid economic growth will increase their demand for all goods and services, including imports, whereas countries that are not growing as rapidly will not experience a change in demand for imports. Therefore, rapid-growth countries will typically import more goods relative to those growing more slowly.

One theory that helps explain international trade flows is the theory of "purchasing power parity." Purchasing power parity says that exchange rates will tend to move to levels where the cost of goods in any country is the same in the same currency. For instance, if a Big Mac hamburger costs $3 in the United States and ¥450 in Japan, purchasing power parity would exist when the ¥/$ exchange rate was ¥150 for $1, as then the Big Mac would cost the same in the same currency in both countries (see Did You Know?).

If purchasing power parity holds for exchange rates, all goods cost the same in the same currency in all countries, so there would be no net cost saving from buying goods one place rather than another. However, if one currency is undervalued (possibly because of the effect of government intervention or trade barriers), goods produced in that country will tend to cost less than similar goods produced elsewhere. As a result, that country's exports will grow and its imports will diminish unless trade barriers, transportation costs, or the perishability of products make it infeasible for people to buy the same products in various places. For instance, while computer parts are easy and cheap to ship (so they will be bought from the least-cost source, such as Asian clones of IBM computers), steel prices may not be equal depending on the source because of high transportation costs, and McDonald's hamburgers might perish (or, at least, cool off) in transit. Thus steel and hamburger prices might be less closely equated in various currencies than computer prices.

Because of transportation costs, trade restrictions, and so forth, purchasing power parity is only an abstract concept. While exchange rates will tend to adjust so similar products cost the same amount in the same currency in different countries, that may not be true for many products or for many years. Thus, while purchasing power parity requires that either U.S. unskilled labor wage rates or the U.S. dollar should fall so the purchasing power of an unskilled worker's wage would be the same in the United States as in Asia, thereby reducing Asia's export surplus to the United States, that may not happen for many years, if at all.

A major reason that exchange rates do not adjust so purchasing power parity holds precisely is that short-term or long-term capital flows may substitute for flows of goods, and thereby affect exchange rates. Short-term and long-term capital flows usually are driven by financial factors, such as differences in interest rates, inflation outlooks, or financial and political stability in different countries.

Financial Determinants of Exchange Rates

In addition to the real determinants of trade flows just described, financial economic phenomena also affect exchange rates. Differential interest and inflation rates, in particular, motivate international capital flows.

Unless there are severe restrictions on the functioning of exchange markets, short-term investment funds will flow to the national money markets that offer the highest return. These funds flows are extremely sensitive to even small interest-rate movements and can be very large in absolute size. Therefore, when interest rates increase in a country (say, the United States), foreign investors will usually increase their demand for dollars to invest in the American money markets, and this increased demand will cause the dollar to appreciate relative to other currencies.

Currency appreciations caused by rising nominal interest rates may not occur if it is apparent that interest rates increased solely because of increased inflationary expectations. In that case, higher interest rates earned in a foreign country may be offset by a later decrease in the value of that country's currency because of its inflation. However, an increase in the expected *real* rate of return on investments in a country can attract investment capital from abroad and generate a substantial increase in a currency's exchange values. For example, the sharp rise in the U.S. federal government's budget in the early 1980s, coupled with an increase in private capital investment and a decline in the national savings rate, led to a dramatic increase in the real rate of return on dollar-denominated financial assets. This, in turn, caused an historic appreciation of the U.S. dollar during the first term of the Reagan administration as foreigners bought dollars aggressively so they could invest their capital in the United States and earn high real returns.

Exchange Rates and Inflation

As you know, interest rates incorporate an adjustment for expected inflation because of the Fisher effect. Because interest rates are tied closely to exchange rates, it should not be surprising that exchange rates are also materially affected by changes in a country's rate of inflation. As inflation causes prices to rise in the United States relative to other countries. American buyers are likely to switch from domestic goods to imported foreign goods. Similarly, foreigners are likely to switch from American products to those of countries other than the United States. Thus the demand for American goods (and demand for dollars to pay for them) will tend to fall at the same time that Americans supply more dollars in exchange for foreign currencies so that they can buy foreign goods. Unless there is an offsetting demand for dollars for capital account transactions, these supply and demand shifts will cause the dollar's exchange rate to fall relative to other currencies. This phenomenon is illustrated in Exhibit 12–2. As the U.S. inflation rate falls, the exchange value of the dollar rises, and vice versa.

Whether a currency rises or falls relative to a specific foreign currency, however, depends on which country is suffering the higher inflation. If prices in both countries rise at the same rate, importers and exporters will not tend to change their buying patterns. However, if one country's inflation rate is lower than another's, that country's goods become relatively cheaper. As a result, its currency will tend to rise in value relative to countries that are experiencing more rapid inflation. This fact is illustrated in Exhibit 12–3. This exhibit illustrates that when Japanese inflation was lower than U.S. inflation, from 1985 through 1987, the value of the U.S. dollar fell relative to the yen (from 250 yen/$ to 125 yen/$) as the U.S. trade balance with Japan deteriorated. From 1987 on, however, higher interest rates in the United States than in

Exhibit 12–2   Value of the Dollar and U.S. Inflation

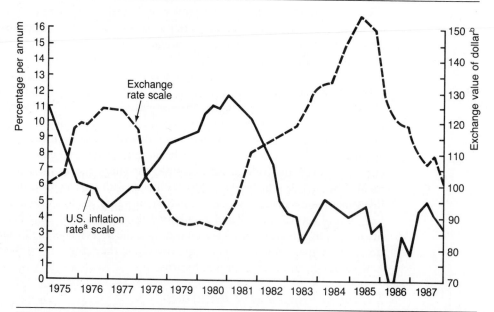

[a]Percentage change in consumption deflator from four quarters earlier.

[b]Exchange value equals 100 in the first quarter of 1975.

Exchange ratios are materially affected by changes in the rate of inflation in a country relative to other countries.

Source: Federal Reserve Bank of New York, *Quarterly Review*, Summer 1979; *Federal Reserve Bulletin*; *Economic Report of the President*; and International Monetary Fund, *International Financial Statistics*, July 1988.

Exhibit 12–3   Exchange Rates Interest Rates, and Relative Rates of Inflation

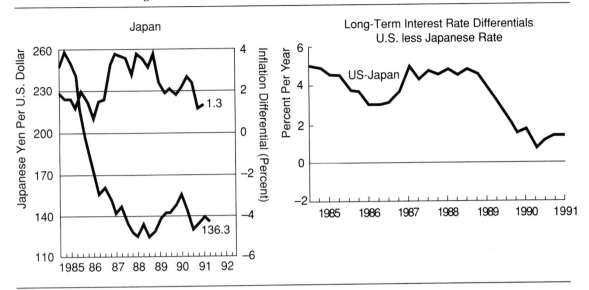

Foreign Currency/Dollar Exchange Rate (left scale)
U.S.–Foreign Inflation Differential (right scale)
The U.S. rate of inflation has generally been above the Japanese rate of inflation. As a result, the value of the dollar has fallen relative to the value of the yen. However, higher interest rates in the U.S. from 1987 on attracted Japanese capital flows and stopped the decline in the U.S. currency from continuing as the Japanese bought U.S. assets to earn a higher interest and sold the U.S. goods to pay for their investments.
Source: *International Economic Conditions*: Federal Reserve Bank of St. Louis, November, 1991.

Japan attracted capital inflows to the United States that offset the trade balance and stabilized the exchange rate.

Capital Flows

There are at least three types of international capital flows that can affect a currency's exchange rate. The first type, *speculative capital flows*, usually occur when central banks are trying to maintain a fixed exchange rate for a currency when market forces suggest that the currency's value is incorrect. If, for example, the German government was attempting to maintain an exchange rate of DM 2.00/$ (DM means deutsche mark) and market forces implied an exchange rate of DM 2.10/$, a speculator would bear very little risk by "betting against" the German government's efforts. The speculator could borrow in Germany, sell the marks obtained for dollars, invest in the United States, and then reverse this process to repay the mark, borrowing when it matured. If the speculator is correct, he or she will make a profit on the depreciation of the mark from DM 2.00/$ to DM 2.10/$ when the dollars are reconverted into marks. Even if central banks are not intervening in the market, speculative capital flows may cause exchange rates to change if many speculators bet that a country's exchange rate is or will soon be mispriced because of future changes in interest rates, inflation, or political economic conditions.

Investment capital flows are the second important type of capital flows, and these can be either the short-term money market flows motivated by differences in interest rates or long-term capital investments in a nation's real or financial assets. Changes in long-term investment flows can result either from a change in the perceived attractiveness of investment in a country or from an increase in international holdings of that country's currency. For example, foreign direct investment in the United States increased dramatically during the 1980s because of favorable taxes, a strong currency, and high expected real rates of return on investment. Foreign investors perceived the United States as both a safe and profitable place to invest. Furthermore, the ongoing U.S. trade deficits increased foreign holdings of dollars that could be returned to the United States to finance long-term direct investments made by foreigners. Thus, even though inflation was higher in the United States than in Japan, higher nominal interest rates in the United States attracted sufficient investment flows so that the dollar stopped losing value relative to the yen in the late 1980s (see Exhibit 12–3).

Changes in short-term investment flows usually respond to differences in short-term interest rates in various countries as investors seek to earn the highest possible return on their excess cash. However, high interest rates are usually associated with high expected inflation. Furthermore, higher inflation rates in one country versus another will eventually cause the value of the first country's currency to fall. Thus extra interest earnings in that country may be eliminated by possible future declines in that country's currency value before investment funds can be repatriated from investments in the high-inflation country to the investor's home currency. Consequently, short-term capital flows are most likely to occur only when investors think that *real* (expected inflation-adjusted) *interest rates* are higher in one country than another or if covered interest rate parity conditions do not hold.

Covered interest rate parity conditions imply that interest earnings in every major country will tend to be equal after adjusting for exchange rate gains or losses necessary to ensure that unexpected foreign currency transaction losses will not occur. In particular, if country A's short-term riskless interest rate were 1 percent above country B's riskless short-term interest rate, A's higher rate could be earned with certainty by someone from country B only if that person (1) bought country A's currency now, (2) invested in country A's higher-yielding securities, *and* (3) simultaneously arranged to exchange the country A money it expected to receive when the investment matured back into the investor's own (country B) currency. The future exchange rate could be ensured by entering into either futures or forward market transactions (see Chapter 11). If *covered interest rate parity holds*, however, the loss on the forward or futures market "covering" transaction will exactly offset the gain from higher interest earnings earned in country A. For instance, in this example, the investor probably would lose 1 percent per year on the exchange transaction (from, say, $1.60 per pound now to $1.584 per pound for a one-year forward exchange contract) if the interest rate were 1 percent higher in Britain than in the United States. If the investment were made for one-quarter of a year the loss probably would be 0.25 percent (or from $1.60 per pound to $1.596 per pound three months hence).

Because billions of dollars will flow from one country to another when covered interest rate parity conditions do not hold (since it then is possible to earn a "riskless" extra return), covered interest rate parity conditions generally hold. Thus forward exchange rates for a country A with high interest rates relative to another country B tend to be lower than spot exchange rates available for immediately converting currency A to currency B. If interest rate parity conditions do not hold, however, very large short-term investment capital flows will occur between countries as investors (often bank currency traders) try to earn higher (riskless) returns.

Political capital flows are the third type of capital flows that can alter exchange rates. When a country experiences political instability because of war or domestic upheavals, it will often experience the phenomenon of *capital flight*, in which owners of capital transfer their wealth out of the country. This can have a devastating impact both on a nation's economic development and on its exchange rate. A classic example of this is provided by the foreign debt experience of the less-developed countries (LDCs) during the years 1974 to 1982. It has been estimated that as much as half of the approximately $500 billion increase in external indebtedness of the LDCs during this period ended up outside of the debtor nations as a result of capital flight. More generally, when a nation adopts—or appears to be on the verge of adopting—socialist economic policies that might reduce the value of private investments, private capital flight will often occur. In addition, when people fear war or social disruption, they may transfer their investment funds to countries they deem to be safer. Thus, when an abortive coupe against Gorbachev occurred in the USSR in August 1991, European investment funds quickly flowed to the United States; as a result, the dollar's value shot upward temporarily.

Government Intervention in the Foreign Exchange Markets

By buying or selling assets, a government can affect the extent to which private-transactions pressures affect the exchange rate of its domestic currency. If a government sells assets to foreigners, it acquires foreign currencies. The government can then use these currencies to support the prices of its own domestic currency by buying its currency in the foreign exchange markets. Alternatively, foreigners can be required to pay for their asset purchases with the domestic currency. In this case, foreigners who wish to buy assets will first have to trade their currencies in the foreign exchange markets for the government's domestic currency. As more people try to buy a country's currency, its price will rise.

Governments can also seek to depress currency prices. A government that believes its currency is becoming overvalued may fear that currency appreciation will hinder its producers' abilities to export goods and will encourage imports. In this case, a government may buy assets from abroad. As the government trades its money for foreign assets, foreigners will hold more of its money, and if they sell that money in the foreign exchange markets, its value will fall.

Governments may also sell securities abroad or borrow from foreign governments to obtain claims on foreign funds. Those funds can, in turn, be used to support the exchange rate of a domestic currency by the government buying it in foreign exchange markets. If these asset flows (and net sales of government liabilities to foreigners) are reversed, the domestic funds leave the country, and the price of the domestic currency will fall in the foreign exchange markets. This is illustrated in Exhibit 12–4.

Exhibit 12–4   **Government Intervention in the Foreign Exchange Markets**

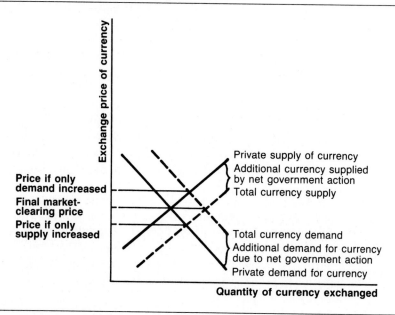

By intervening in the market for their country's currency, governments can influence its price relative to other currencies in the short run.

Exhibit 12–4 illustrates that if the net effect of government action is to increase the total demand for a currency, the currency's exchange rate will rise. If the net effect of government action is to increase the supply of domestic currency, its exchange rate will fall. Demand and supply decreases have opposite effects.

Both domestic and foreign governments can intervene in foreign exchange markets on behalf of a particular currency. If one government acts to increase the demand for the currency while the other acts to increase its supply, its price will tend to remain unchanged. For example, note that the dashed lines of Exhibit 12–4 intersect at approximately the same price that existed before government intervention. Because of this effect, governments must coordinate their actions in the foreign exchange markets so that they will not work at cross purposes to each other.

Before 1971, the world adhered to a system of fixed exchange rates known as the Bretton Woods System. Under that system, a government was obligated to intervene in the foreign exchange markets in the manner depicted in Exhibit 12–4 to keep the value of its currency within a narrow range. If the government did not have the reserve assets to sell to support the currency's floor value, either the fixed parity relationship with other currencies had to change or actions had to be undertaken to alter the fundamental forces within the domestic economy that underlie the supply of and demand for goods and services. Because of this imperative, reserve asset balances such as gold or foreign currency holdings, were key indicators of a government's ability to keep its exchange rate stable.

PEOPLE
& EVENTS

World Currency Traders: The Fleet of Foot

In today's fast-paced economy, no one moves faster than the currency traders, called "players" in the foreign exchange markets. They make their money from buying and selling currencies from around the world. If a currency is rising in value relative to other currencies, traders flock to buy it; if the currency starts to decline, they sell and swarm to a new rising star. Some round-trip deals (buy and sell) may take place in a matter of minutes. The big winners are the fleet of foot and those with the right information.

With so many currencies being exchanged around the world, a huge volume of information must be digested by traders every day to enable them to stay abreast of the market. Besides the factual information on relative currency prices, traders must be aware of how stories breaking from around the world might affect currency prices. For example, if the Saudis found out today that their oil was running out, it is obvious that tomorrow the price of their currency would plummet on the world market. Rumors are also a large portion of the trader's daily menu of information. For instance, if a trader is the first to hear a rumor (from a reliable source) that the Saudi wells are drying up, that trader has a leg up on the traders who hear it the next day. Of course, if the rumor is false, the first trader has a problem. The volume of information is so overwhelming that, according to Jeffrey Donahue, Director of International Money Management at Union Carbide, "if you can't manage 24 hours a day, you don't really stand a chance."

Another important aspect of the currency trader's job is the role of technology. Technology has progressed from quoting currency prices over the phone to providing quotations instantaneously on personal computers to giving traders up-to-the-minute information on all major currency rates —anytime and anywhere—via handheld computers. Although technology has made the trader's job easier in many ways, the increasingly rapid flow of information also makes the job more hectic.

The potential profits that can be earned from foreign exchange trading are enormous. In 1990, Bankers' Trust's key trader earned more than $300 million for the bank from foreign exchange trading. When he received "only" a $1 million bonus, instead of the usual 1 percent of profits (because Banker's Trust didn't want to pay him more than the bank president), he quit. Later, Banker's Trust found that some of the risk he had taken in establishing foreign currency option positions hadn't been fully taken into account. After allowing for those risks, foreign exchange profits were reduced to the $200 million plus range. Thus foreign exchange trading offers high potential risk as well as high potential rewards. Furthermore, banks may have a hard time determining their net risk exposure on large foreign currency futures, options, forward, and swap positions. This makes regulators, as well as bank management, wring their hands with worry. While the profit potential is so great that banks want to take risks when they participate in the foreign exchange markets, the potential risk exposure can also be great, and may not be fully understood if internal accounting systems are lax or if credit risk or option risk exposures aren't accurately computed.

Since the collapse of the Bretton Woods System in 1971, governments in general are no longer required to impose discipline on the domestic economy to maintain a stable exchange rate. Rather, any pressures can be relieved by letting the value of the currency fluctuate in the foreign exchange market to determine a new equilibrium. For most countries, this is what has happened since the early 1970s.

At times one hears that the U.S. dollar is overvalued and needs to fall substantially. In a competitive market such as the foreign exchange market, though, the value is always "fair" in the sense that it represents the equilibrium point of supply and demand. Thus what is really meant by the term "overvalued" is that the equilibrium exchange rate established in a competitive currency market results in aberrations in the domestic economy that are socially unacceptable. Today the huge deficit in the Current Account is thought to result in the "exporting of jobs" and in holding back the American economy. At a lower value for the dollar, U.S. products would be more price-competitive internationally, and both Americans and foreigners would shift from foreign products to those produced in the United States. This, it is thought, would increase American employment and stimulate the U.S. economy. Perhaps it also indicates that the discipline enforced on governments under the Bretton Woods System is coming back into vogue and that the benefits of floating exchange rates are now being seen as being double-edged.

International Payments Flows

All activities that involve transactions between residents of two countries, including those described previously, are recorded in a set of accounts known as the *balance of payments*. These accounts are kept in accordance with the rules of double-entry bookkeeping; thus debit entries must be offset by corresponding credit entries. This implies that, overall, total debits must equal total credits and that the account must always be in balance. If not, an errors and omissions account is required to balance international flows. Because of smuggling, tax evasion, poor data, and unrecorded transfers, sometimes the international errors and omissions account is quite large.

The terms *surplus* and *deficit* in the balance of payments refer to the net balances in various components of the balance of payments accounts. Depending on the items included in each component of the accounts, "surplus" and "deficit" have different implications for a country and its exchange rate.

In terms of the discussion in the previous section, indicators of particular interest are those that focus on the forces that determine the equilibrium exchange rate for a currency. Such indicators require that all transactions that lead to a demand for a foreign currency (and thus to a supply of the domestic currency) or to a demand for the domestic currency (and a supply of the foreign currency) be identified. Identifying these transactions, however, is quite difficult.

Before one can assess the motive underlying each entry in the balance-of-payments accounts, an important distinction needs to be made between the two entries required for every transaction. Originally, some event in the economy triggered the transaction that is recorded in the balance of payments. For instance, a decision by an individual in the United States to buy a new BMW instead of a Ford Thunderbird initiates a debit entry in the merchandise import account of the U.S. balance of payments. The corresponding credit entry represents a financial payment to BMW for the automobile and exists only because the debit entry must be offset to maintain the overall balance. Initiating entries, then, are motivated by events in the economy apart from the balance of payments, whereas offsetting entries are triggered by the initiating entries. Initiating flows are what give rise to a demand for foreign exchange (supply of dollars) when U.S. residents wish to acquire assets from abroad. When foreigners decide to acquire assets produced in the United States, the initiating entries give rise to a demand for dollars (and a supply of foreign exchange). In their terminology of the balance of payments, initiating transactions are called *autonomous flows* and the offsetting entries are referred to as *accommodating flows*. When autonomous debits exactly equal autonomous credits for a country, the supply of the domestic currency (demand for the foreign currency) by residents is exactly equal to the demand for the domestic currency (supply of the foreign currency) by foreigners. This equality condition describes the point of intersection of the supply and demand curves in Exhibit 12–4 and defines the equilibrium exchange rate. When autonomous debits exceed autonomous credits, the net debit position is referred to as a *deficit* in the balance of payments; it generally causes downward pressure on the exchange rate because U.S. citizens want to buy more foreign goods than foreigners want to buy from the United States. Similarly, a net credit position, or *surplus* in the balance of payments, often results in an upward pressure on the exchange rate.

Balance-of-Payments Accounts—The Current Account

Current accounts measure trade in goods and services plus investment income and gifts or grants made to other countries. As shown in Exhibit 12–5, the United States has recently run a substantial merchandise trade deficit because its imports of foreign goods have consistently exceeded its exports of goods to foreigners. U.S. consumers may prefer foreign goods for a variety of reasons such as snob appeal and/or higher quality (Mercedes and BMW cars presumably have both attributes) or lower prices (such as Chinese textiles or Southeast Asian electronics products). If the dollar exchange rate falls, however, foreign goods become more expensive and U.S. goods are relatively cheaper. Thus, as the U.S. exchange rate fell in the late 1980s and early 1990s, the U.S. merchandise trade balance improved. The 1991 recession also contributed to that improvement as domestic demand for foreign goods tends to fall during recessions (and, conversely, increase during booms). However, while the U.S. merchandise trade balance narrowed in 1991, it remained negative, where it had been for many years.

Nonetheless, the United States usually runs a surplus on the "services" component of the balance-of-payments current accounts. The services component includes royalty income, licensing fees, foreign travel and transportation, and some military expenditures and transfers. Because the U.S. services sector generates substantial fee income from transportation, insurance and other financial services, and various royalties and licensing fees, the services component usually creates a positive entry in the U.S. balance-of-payments current account.

Net investment income of U.S. citizens also has usually contributed positively to the U.S. balance of payments because of large U.S. investments abroad since World War II. However, in the late 1980s the United States changed from a net creditor nation to a net debtor nation as it sold many of its assets, in particular many U.S. government bonds, to foreigners to finance its large government deficits and its chronic deficit on its merchandise trade account. Consequently, U.S. net investment income surpluses have narrowed in recent years and may occasionally be negative.

Exhibit 12–5   **U.S. International Trade and Capital Accounts**

U.S. International Trade and Capital Accounts

I. **U.S. Current Account** (billions of dollars)	**1988 IV**	**1989 IV**	**1990 IV**	**1991 III**
A. Balance on Merchandise Trade =	− 31.61	− 28.61	− 27.73	− 20.49
+ Merchandise exports	83.94	92.49	100.58	104.53
− Merchandise imports	115.55	121.10	128.31	125.02
B. Balance on Services	+ 2.70	+ 6.48	+ 7.47	+ 9.46
+ Service exports	26.26	30.53	35.72	36.73
− Service imports	23.56	24.05	28.24	27.26
C. Balance on Investment Income =	+ 0.12	+ 2.47	+ 6.13	+ 2.50
+ Income receipts on U.S. assets abroad	28.49	33.16	34.81	28.81
− Income payments on foreign assets	28.36	30.69	28.67	26.30
D. Unilateral Transfers =	− 4.97	− 5.04	− 9.28	− 1.94
E. Total Balance on Current Account (= I.A. + I.B. + I.C. + I.D.)	− 33.76	− 24.70	− 23.40	− 10.46

II. **U.S. Capital Accounts** (billions of dollars)	**1988 IV**	**1989 IV**	**1990 IV**	**1991 III**
A. Change in U.S. Assets Abroad =	− 27.565	− 41.021	− 34.703	− 11.971
+ 1. U.S. official reserve assets	+ 1.925	− 3.202	− 1.091	+ 3.877
+ 2. Other U.S. gov't asssets	+ 3.457	+ 0.119	+ 4.759	+ 2.715
+ 3. U.S. private assets	− 32.947	− 37.938	− 38.370	− 18.564
a. Direct investment	− 4.038	− 10.168	− 3.802	− 5.875
b. Foreign securities	− 3.047	− 4.503	− 7.546	− 12.511
c. U.S. claims reported by U.S. banks	− 30.521	− 23.912	− 24.513	− 0.178
B. Change in Foreign Assets in the U.S. =	+ 77.917	+ 70.238	+ 39.033	+ 22.816
+ 1. Foreign official assets	+ 10.806	− 7.158	+ 20.301	+ 4.309
+ 2. Other foreign assets	+ 67.111	+ 77.396	+ 18.732	+ 18.507
a. Direct investment	+ 21.612	+ 22.373	+ 4.538	+ 1.403
b. U.S. Treasury securities	+ 5.412	+ 5.024	− 2.029	− 1.389
c. Other U.S. securities	+ 6.764	+ 10.588	+ 0.802	+ 9.653
d. U.S. liabilities reported by U.S. banks	+ 32.193	+ 37.365	+ 17.261	+ 8.840
C. Allocations of Special Drawing Rights	0	0	0	0
D. Statistical Discrepancy	− 16.589	− 4.517	+ 19.072	− 0.386
E. Total Capital Flows and Discrepancy (= II.A. + II.B + II.C + II.D.)	+ 33.763	+ 24.700	+ 23.402	+ 10.459

Finally, the balance of payments on current account shows that U.S. net foreign unilateral transfers such as gifts or foreign aid, for which no compensating payment is received, have consistently been negative. This adds to the net amount of U.S. dollars transferred to foreigners and makes the total balance of payments on current account more negative than it otherwise would be (see line I.E. of Exhibit 12–5).

The United States cannot continue to run a negative balance of payments indefinitely, however, as accommodation flows of funds must exactly offset autonomous flows of funds if foreign exchange markets are to have an equal flow of funds from one country to another. Thus if U.S. citizens run a deficit on their current account with other nations of the world, foreign citizens will be acquiring a net increase in their holdings of dollars and other claims on U.S. assets. If foreigners sell their extra dollars to obtain their domestic currency, the value of the dollar will fall (until U.S. goods become more attractively priced relative to foreign goods). Thus many people think that when the United States runs a deficit on its balance-of-payments current account, the dollar should fall in value relative to other currencies.

However, the dollar does not always fall when the United States runs a current account balance-of-payments deficit. The reasons for this is that foreigners can buy U.S. capital assets as well as U.S. manufactured goods and services. If real interest rates in the United States are high, and U.S. inflation is expected to be low, net foreign demand for both short-term and long-term investments may be great enough to support a high price for the dollar even if the United States runs a current account balance-of-payments deficit. In fact, if the net foreign demand for investments in the U.S. is high enough, as foreigners buy dollars to finance investments, they may bid up the value of the dollar and make the U.S. current account merchandise trade deficit even larger. The large trade deficit transfers more dollars to foreigners' hands so they can afford their desired investments in the United States. This happened in the late 1980s and in early 1990. At that time, the Japanese ran a large current account surplus with the United States, but the Japanese also bought Rockefeller Center, Pebble Beach, Hawaiian hotels, and many U.S. stocks and bonds. As a result the value of the Japanese yen fell relative to the dollar in early 1990 in spite of Japan's large trade surplus with the United States. This example shows, therefore, that it is overly simplistic to say that a large U.S. trade merchandise deficit will make the dollar fall in value. The change in the dollar value cannot be predicted unless desired intracountry investment (capital) flows are also taken into account.

Balance-of-Payments Accounts—Capital Accounts

The balance-of-payments capital accounts try to measure capital flows into or out of the country. Capital flows can be used to finance private long-term investments of more than one year, or they may be short-term flows invested in bank deposits or short-term securities. Usually short-term capital flows are thought to be accommodating flows. However, in recent years more and more of them are speculative investment flows that seek to earn higher real returns on short-term investments or to capture excess returns available if covered interest rate parity conditions do not hold. Long-term capital flows are not as liquid or as easily reversed—often they involve investments in land, plant and equipment, real estate, or stocks or bonds in other countries. Such investments occur when long-term return potentials seem to be substantially greater in one country than another. They may be driven, in part, by breakdowns in purchasing power parity that make it cheaper to buy assets in one country than another.

Government-motivated financial flows often play an important role in the flow-of-funds accounts. If a country is trying to support the value of its currency, its government can sell various reserve assets such as gold, SDRs (or "special drawing rights," also known as "paper gold"; SDRs are based on the composite value of major countries' currencies and can be transferred to other central banks through the auspices of the International Monetary Fund in exchange for domestic currency), or easily marketable foreign currencies (often called "reserve currencies") that are owned by, or can be easily borrowed by, the government in question.

The balance-of-payments capital accounts, therefore, keep track of changes in governments' reserve asset holdings, as well as any addition to their special drawing rights brought about by IMF actions—lines II.A.1, II.A.2, II.B.1 and II.C. in Exhibit 12–5. The capital accounts also record changes in private direct investment, private holdings of foreign securities, including foreigners' holdings of U.S. securities, and foreign and domestic liabilities reported by U.S. banks—lines II.A.3.a., II.A.3.b., II.B.2.a., II.B.2.b., II.B.2.c., and II.B.2.d. in Exhibit 12–5. After net flows on all capital accounts are added up, they are compared to total current account flows (line I.E., Exhibit 12–5). Since all current accounts flows must be offset by capital account flows—including accommodating changes in bank deposits—these two values should be equal. If they are not equal, the difference is called a "statistical discrepancy"—line II.D. in Exhibit 12–5—which is defined to make the balance-of-payments accounts balance exactly.

Unfortunately, because many international transactions are not reported, such as capital fleeing from socialist countries, smuggling proceeds, illegal activity transactions, tax evasion activities, and so forth, the statistical discrepancy is often quite large and it is variable in sign. As a result, substantial imprecision exists in the balance-of-payments accounts.

Exchange Rate Determination

In this chapter we have discussed a number of forces that may cause a country's currency to gain or lose value relative to other currencies (that is, cause its exchange rate to fluctuate).

As a general rule, if a country's currency is priced low so its goods are cheaper than foreigners' goods based on purchasing power parity, the country's exchange rate can be expected to appreciate. However, that will not happen if trade barriers interfere with the flow of funds and goods between countries.

Also, if country A runs a large deficit on its current account balance of payments, one might expect its exchange rate to depreciate as foreigners sell the excess currency from country A they are accumulating through the exchange of goods to obtain their own currency in the foreign exchange markets. However, if the foreigners are content holding country A's currency, or they wish to acquire that currency so they can buy assets in country A, the value of country A's currency may not fall and may even rise in value as capital flows offset country A's trade deficit.

If a country has a higher real interest rate than other countries (possibly because it is running a restrictive monetary policy), it will tend to attract investment capital flows from other countries. Those flows, if large enough, may cause the value of its currency to appreciate as foreigners buy its currency so they can finance their investments. This can cause the value of the country's currency to rise even though higher currency values may cause the country to sell fewer goods abroad, buy more goods from abroad, and experience a deficit on the current account of its balance of payments.

If a country's interest rate is sufficiently high relative to foreign interest rates, and its forward exchange rate is close to its spot exchange rate, covered interest rate parity conditions may not hold. In that case, short-term capital inflows may come into the country in order to earn a higher interest rate. Thus a strong demand for its currency may develop, thereby driving up its spot exchange rate until covered interest rate parity conditions are reestablished.

Finally, governments may intervene in foreign exchange markets to alter their exchange rate. If a country wants its exchange rate to fall it can print money and buy foreign currencies or other assets. The new money will decrease the value of its currency while its purchase activity will drive up the value of foreign currencies. Conversely, to increase the value of its money, the country can reduce its money supply by selling assets to foreigners in exchange for its domestic currency and then withdrawing the currency it receives from circulation. These are examples of "unsterilized" interventions, which are interventions in the exchange markets that are allowed to change the money supply in a consistent manner. "Sterilized interventions," in contrast, offset the foreign exchange activities by adjusting the domestic monetary supply so that it remains unchanged; sterilized interventions, however, have not been found to have a lasting effect on exchange rates.

Overall, then, many factors can affect exchange rates. For that reason it is hard to forecast exchange rate movements accurately. As a result, many businesses use forward market transactions or foreign currency options or futures to protect themselves against the risk that exchange rates will change. Such techniques may be costly, however. Thus governments often cooperate formally (as in the European exchange rate mechanism, ERM) or informally (through regular meetings of the Group of Seven largest industrial countries, which often try to coordinate intervention efforts) to prevent drastic fluctuations in exchange rates. If governments can reduce changes in exchange rates, business managers can plan better when they decide where to buy or sell goods or invest in production facilities; thus international trade will be facilitated.

The Markets for Foreign Exchange

Many references have been made in this chapter to markets for foreign exchange. In these markets, individuals, corporations, banks, and governments interact with each other to convert one currency into another for any number of purposes. It was also mentioned that these markets are quite efficient and competitive. In fact, foreign exchange transactions may total up to $1 trillion per day, and hundreds of trillions of dollars per year. In comparison, on the New York Stock Exchange's busiest day,

Black Monday, October 19, 1987, transactions totalled only $21 Billion. Whenever a market becomes as large as the foreign exchange market, it must be providing vital services to the participants. In the case of the foreign exchange markets, an ability to provide three services in particular explains their existence and growth.

The first explanation of why foreign exchange markets exist is that they provide a mechanism for transferring purchasing power from individuals who normally deal in one currency to other people who generally transact business using a different monetary unit. Importing and exporting goods and services are facilitated by this conversion service because the parties to the transactions can deal in terms of mediums of exchange instead of having to rely on bartering. The currencies of some countries, such as those of centrally planned socialist countries, are not convertible into other currencies. If a corporation chartered in another country wants to do business with a country whose currency is nonconvertible, the corporation may be required to accept locally produced merchandise in lieu of money as payment for goods and services. This practice is known as *countertrade*, and it arises largely because an efficient foreign exchange conversion mechanism does not exist.

A second reason that efficient foreign exchange markets have developed is that they provide a means for passing the risk associated with changes in exchange rates to professional risk takers. This "hedging" function is particularly important to corporations in the present era of floating exchange rates.

The third important reason for the continuing prosperity of foreign exchange markets is the provision of credit. The time span between shipment of goods by the exporter and their receipt by the importer can be considerable. While the goods are in transit, they must be financed. Foreign exchange markets are one device by which this financing and related currency conversions can be accomplished efficiently and at low cost (see Exhibit 12–6 and the related discussion).

Structure of the Foreign Exchange Markets

There is no single formal foreign exchange market such as the one that exists for the sale of stocks and bonds on the New York Stock Exchange. In fact, the foreign exchange market is an over-the-counter market that is similar to the one for money market instruments. More specifically, the foreign exchange market is composed of a group of informal markets closely interlocked through international branch banking and correspondent bank relationships. The participants are linked by telephone, telegraph, and cable. The market has no fixed trading hours, and, since 1982 when a forward market opened in Singapore, foreign exchange trading can take place at any time every day of the year. There are also no written rules governing operation of the foreign exchange markets; however, transactions are conducted according to principles and a code of ethics that have evolved over time.

The extent to which a country's currency is traded in the worldwide market depends, in some measure, on local regulations that vary from country to country. Virtually every country has some type of active foreign exchange market.

Major Participants.   The major participants in the foreign exchange markets are the large multinational commercial banks, although many investment banking houses have established foreign exchange trading operations in recent years. In the United States, the market is dominated by about 25 large banks, with about half of them located in New York City and the remainder in major financial centers such as San Francisco, Chicago, and Atlanta. These banks operate in the foreign exchange market at two levels. First, at the retail level, banks deal with individuals and corporations. Second, at the wholesale level, banks operate in the interbank market. Major banks usually transact directly with the foreign institution involved. However, many transactions are mediated by foreign exchange brokers. These brokers preserve the anonymity of the parties until the transaction is concluded.

The other major participants in the foreign exchange markets are the central banks of various countries. Central banks typically intervene in foreign exchange markets to smooth out fluctuations in a country's currency rate. Additional participants in the foreign exchange markets are nonfinancial businesses and individuals who enter the market by means of banks for various commercial reasons.

Transfer Process.   The international funds-transfer process is facilitated by interbank clearing systems. The large multinational banks of each country are linked through international correspondent relationships as well as through their worldwide branching systems. Within each country, regional banks are linked to international banks' main offices, either through nationwide branching systems or through domestic correspondent networks. In the United States, practically every bank has a correspondent relationship with a bank in New York City or with a large bank in a regional financial center, which in turn has a correspondent relationship either with a New York City bank or with its own Edge Act corporation in New York City. As a result, virtually every bank, large or small, is able to provide its customers with international payment services through checks or other financial instruments drawn on large multinational banks located in New York City or other international trade centers in the United States.

The method and financial instrument used to transfer funds varies with the purpose and time frame of the transaction involved. Most international transfers of funds for business purposes are handled by various types of orders to transfer deposits. The process is similar to domestic check payments, although there is more variety in the form of international payments orders. Most commonly, payments are made by telephone or cable, especially when speed is important or the amounts are large. As mentioned in Chapter 16, the Society for Worldwide International Financial Telecommunication (SWIFT) and the Clearinghouse Interbank Payments Systems (CHIPS) have added a new dimension to the speed and efficiency with which the payment transfer and clearing process works. These organizations were created by banks to transmit information and clear large international payments, respectively. Sight and time drafts are frequently used to make small- and medium-sized international payments. Such drafts are negotiable instruments, and their characteristics are described in a later section of this chapter.

In commercial banks, the trading in foreign exchange is usually done by only a few persons. As in the money markets, the pace of transactions is rapid, and traders must be able to make on-the-spot judgments about whether to buy or sell a particular currency. They have a dual responsibility in that on the one hand they must maintain the bank position (inventory) to meet their customers' needs, and on the other hand they must not take large inventory losses if the value of a currency falls. This is sometimes difficult, because currency values tend to fluctuate rapidly and often widely—particularly since currencies are always subject to possible devaluations by their governments. Banks are not permitted to engage in foreign exchange transactions for speculative purposes. However, if a currency is expected to fall in value, banks may want to sell it to reduce their foreign exchange losses.

Spot and Forward Transactions.   There are two basic types of foreign exchange quotations—spot and forward. The *spot market* is the market in which foreign exchange is sold or purchased "on the spot." The rate at which a currency is exchanged in this market is called the *spot rate*. Delivery of the currency in the spot market must be made within two business days, but it is usually done immediately upon agreeing to terms. Retail foreign exchange markets are mainly spot markets. In the *forward market*, the parties agree to exchange a fixed amount of one currency for a fixed amount of a second currency, but actual delivery and exchange of the two currencies occurs at some time "forward." Typically, forward contracts are written for delivery of currency 30, 60, 90, or 180 days and sometimes even longer in the future, but it is possible to tailor the maturity of the contract (as well as the amount of currency exchanged) to meet the special needs of the parties involved. This is an important feature that distinguishes the forward market from a currency futures market. The exchange rate in this transaction implied by the fixed amounts of the two currencies is called the *forward rate*. Note that the forward rate is established at the date on which the agreement is made, but it defines the exchange rate to be used in the transaction in lieu of the spot rate prevailing at the time in the future when the two currencies are exchanged. This characteristic is extremely important for facilitating international business transactions, because it permits the two parties to the agreement to eliminate all uncertainty about the amounts of currency to be delivered or received in the future.

As an example of the way in which foreign exchange markets are used by businesses, suppose than an American exporter sells farm equipment to a British firm for £100,000 to be paid in 90 days. If at the time of the transaction the spot rate is £1 = $1.70, the delivery of the farm equipment is worth $170,000. However, the actual number of dollars to be received for the machinery, which is the relevant price to the American firm, is not really certain. That is, if the American firm waits 90 days to collect the £100,000 and then sells it in the spot market for dollars, there is a risk that the dollar price of the pound sterling may have declined more than the market expected. For instance, if sterling is worth only $1.50, the American exporter will receive only $150,000. If the market did not expect sterling to fall that much, a loss in an amount up to $20,000 would be realized because of the change in the exchange rate. To eliminate this risk and ensure a certain future price, the American company can hedge by selling the £100,000 forward 90 days. If the forward rate at the time of sale is £1 = $1.68, the American exporter will deliver the £100,000 to the banks in 90 days and receive £168,000 in return. In this case, since the spot rate on the day the exchange is made is £1 = $1.70, the "savings" from hedging is $18,000 (a $20,000 "loss" without hedging minus a $2,000 "loss" with hedging).

What about the $2,000 loss incurred even with hedging? Can this be prevented? The answer is that forward contracts cannot protect against *expected* changes in exchange rates, only against *unexpected* changes. In the original pricing decision by the American exporter, the correct "price" would have to be defined in dollars. When converting this price to sterling, if the account is not to be paid for 90 days, then the 90-day forward rate should be used for the computation instead of today's spot rate. In this manner, the correct dollar price is received via the forward contract. Thus, in this example, a true loss of $18,000 is realized if the transaction is not hedged.

What would happen if the spot rate in 90 days rose to $1.90? The unhedged transaction would yield £22,000 over the expected return of $168,000, a welcome happening, but the forward contract would again provide exactly the number of dollars anticipated. Although there may be regrets after the fact because the forward contract prevented the company from receiving the benefits of the strengthening pound, most businesses would call leaving the account receivable exposed (that is, unhedged) speculation. It is generally believed that foreign exchange speculation is not a logical or legitimate function of businesses that import or export goods or services. However, there is a way to avoid large losses while not precluding the possible receipt of large gains without having to engage in speculation. This involves the use of foreign currency options.

If the American exporter were to buy a put option on the £100,000 maturing in 90 days at a striking price of $1.70, the firm would be protected against deterioration of the pound below that price. If the spot rate in 90 days is $1.60, the exporter can exercise the put and receive $170,000. On the other hand, if the rate goes up to $1.90, the American company can let the put expire and sell the sterling at the spot rate. The cost of this asymmetrical protection is the price of the option—which could be substantial. Nonetheless, if the exporter prefers an option, his or her commercial banker will usually sell the exporter one that suits the exporter's needs. Commercial banks earn fee income by selling options as well as from arranging forward currency transactions.

How Foreign Exchange Markets Link National Money Markets

The foreign exchange markets not only link foreign currency flows around the world, but they also tie together short-term capital markets in different countries. For example, if the required rate of return on risk-free British government securities is 14 percent and the rate on comparable U.S. government securities is 10 percent, every three months an investor would be better off by 1 percent (14 percent−10 percent = 4 percent per year or 1 percent per quarter) by investing in Britain rather than in the United States. From the perspective of an American investor, though, this extra return would be offset by the exchange rate risk incurred by investing in securities denominated in a different currency. To get rid of this extra risk, the investor could cover the sterling receipts from the British security with a forward contract to sell pounds for dollars. Specifically, the investor could simultaneously buy British pounds in the spot market, use them to purchase British 90-day government securities, and sell the pound-denominated receipts of interest plus return of principal in the forward market in return for dollars. (Check Chapter 11 to see how such a hedge could be structured.)

If the forward and spot rates for the pound were equal, the investor would gain an additional 1 percent per quarter in interest by engaging in such transactions. It would even be profitable to borrow money at, say, 12 percent and use it to buy more British securities. However, the activities of investors that conduct such transactions would tend to put pressure on both the securities market and the foreign exchange markets. These forces would tend to (1) drive up the price of British securities (because of higher demand), thereby reducing their yield; (2) reduce the price of American debt issues, thereby increasing their yield (since investors would prefer to buy the higher-yielding British securities, the demand for U.S. securities would fall); (3) drive up the spot rate for the pound relative to the dollar, as the demand for spot pounds and the supply of spot dollars would both increase; and (4) drive down the forward price of the pound relative to the dollar as more people entered the market to sell pounds and buy dollars 90 days hence. Even if the activities of these arbitrageurs did not affect short-term market interest rates in either country, the profit potential on the transactions would be eliminated if the future price of the pound relative to the dollar were to fall 1 percent below the spot price. In this case, because the extra 1 percent gained by the higher interest rate would be offset by the 1 percent loss in the value of the pound, the investor would be indifferent to investing in U.S. or British securities. Actually, because of transaction costs, arbitrage would cease to be profitable shortly before the forward exchange rate had fallen by the full 1 percent relative to the current spot rate. Note that from the perspective of a British investor, the 1 percent sacrifice from investing in U.S. securities would be offset by a 1 percent appreciation of the dollar in equilibrium (except for transaction costs). Thus there would also be indifference between investing in U.S. or British securities.

Financing International Trade

One of the most important services provided by international banks is the financing of imports and exports among countries. As noted earlier in the chapter, international transactions are far more complicated than equivalent domestic financing because of the additional sources of risk that are involved. Three problems in particular must be overcome before many trade deals can be executed. First, exporters often lack accurate information about the importer's current and past business practices and hence about the likelihood of payment. Importers are similarly concerned about the ability or inclination of the exporter to fulfill all contractual obligations once payment has been made. Second, before the party bearing the exchange rate risk between the times the agreement is made and payment must be delivered can hedge the risk with a forward contract (or an option contract), the exact amounts and dates of payments must be known. Finally, usually before a bank is willing to finance an international transaction, a means has to be found to insulate the bank from nonfinancial aspects of the transaction that could lead to disputes and to protracted legal proceedings, which delay recovery of its money.

A number of specialized financial instruments have been developed to overcome these three problems, thereby minimizing the risk for institutions engaging in international transactions. In particular, three types of trade documents, each with well-defined legal characteristics and each serving a specific function, have evolved over time and serve to facilitate international commerce. The three documents are the letter of credit, the draft, and the bill of lading. Commercial banks, with their multinational network of foreign branches and their international correspondent relationships, are prominent actors in this financing process, and it is the use of these three documents for most transactions that makes the process work smoothly.

The Letter of Credit

The first of the three important trade documents is the *letter of credit*, LOC or L/C. It is a financial instrument issued by an importer's bank that obligates the bank to pay the exporter (or other designated beneficiary) a specified amount of money once certain conditions are fulfilled. Legally, the bank substitutes its good faith and credit for that of the importer in that it *guarantees* payment if the correct documents are submitted.

From the perspective of the exporter, letters of credit have four primary advantages over sales on open account. First, because an exporter's knowledge about a foreign importer frequently is vague, the company is hesitant to ship merchandise without advance payment. With a letter of credit, however, the creditworthiness and financial integrity of the bank is substituted for that of the importer, and exporters see less risk of nonpayment when the bank is the guarantor. Second, as soon as the exporter meets the terms and conditions specified in the L/C, payment is assured. This is particularly important, because it eliminates the possibility that payment might be held up because of disputes arising from some alleged deficiency in the actual goods. As long as the paper documents are in order, the bank is obligated to pay, even if the importer no longer wants the merchandise. The third advantage of a letter of credit over an open account is that the exporter can usually obtain payment as soon as the necessary documentation has been provided to fulfill the contract. By shortening the collection period, fewer funds have to be tied up in working capital.

The final major advantage of letters of credit is that they eliminate a major risk facing exporters: the possibility that governments may impose restrictions on payment. There are few cases on record in which governments have prevented banks from honoring letters of credit that have already been issued, but it is not at all unusual to find restrictions placed on commercial accounts and notes payable. Hence this essentially political risk is, for all intents and purposes, neutralized by using letters of credit drawn on large commercial banks.

From the perspective of the importer, there are two definite advantages to using letters of credit. Since the L/C specifies the actions that must be taken before the exporter can be paid, the chance of noncompliance by the seller is reduced. This is most useful when the importer has little knowledge of the business practices of the exporter. The second advantage to the importer is that funds do not have to be paid out until the terms set out in the L/C have been met and the documentation is in order. Also, if banker's acceptances are created under the letter of credit, there is an additional period of financing before payment must be made to the bank.

The Draft

The second important document that serves to facilitate international trade is the *draft*. This instrument is simply a request for payment that is drawn up by the exporter (or by the exporter's bank) and sent to the bank that drew up the letter of credit for the importer. If the draft conforms to several legal requirements, it becomes a negotiable instrument that is particularly useful for financing international trade flows.

Drafts can be of two types: *sight drafts* or *time drafts*. Sight drafts, as the name implies, require the bank to pay on demand, assuming that all documentation is in proper order and that all conditions have been met. Time drafts, however, are payable at a particular time in the future, as specified in the letter of credit. When a time draft is presented to the importer's bank for payment, it is checked to make certain that all terms and conditions set forth in the letter of credit have been met, and then it is stamped "accepted" and dated on the face of the draft. The importer's bank then returns the "accepted" draft to the exporter or the exporter's bank. Alternatively, the importer's bank may elect to pay the exporter or the exporter's bank a price that reflects the discounted present value of the draft, after which it may hold the acceptance for its own account or sell it in the banker's acceptance market. In either situation, when the time draft matures, the importer must pay the amount due unless other arrangements have been made in advance. The "accepting" importer's bank must make payment if the importer does not.

The Bill of Lading

The third document of particular importance for international trade is the *bill of lading*. The bill of lading is a receipt issued to the exporter by a common carrier that acknowledges possession of the goods described on the face of the bill. The bill of lading serves as a contract between the exporter and the shipping company. In this role it specifies the services to be performed, the charges for those services, and the disposition of the goods if they cannot be delivered as instructed.

If it is properly prepared, a bill of lading is also a document of title that follows the merchandise throughout the transport process. As a document of title, it can be used by the exporter either as collateral for loans prior to payment or as a means of obtaining payment (or acceptance of a time draft) before the goods are released to the importer.

Documentation of an Import Transaction

To better understand how these three documents are used in international trade, let us examine a hypothetical transaction between an American importer and a British exporter. The steps involved in this transaction are shown in Exhibit 12–6. In Step 1, the American importer applies for a letter of credit from its American bank. In Step 2, if the bank is willing to guarantee payment for the goods upon presentation of the required documentation, it prepares a letter of credit and sends it to the exporter in England. The letter specifies the documentation and other conditions that were agreed on to receive payment. In Step 3, the British exporter ships the goods to the American importer and collects the necessary documentation. In Step 4, the British exporter prepares a draft in accordance with the terms set out in the letter of credit, and it takes the letter of credit, the draft, and all other required documentation to its London bank. The documentation required may include bills of lading, commercial invoices, certificates of quantity, and certificates of quality or grade, among others. In Step 5, the British bank examines the documents carefully for full compliance. If it is satisfied that everything is in proper order, it normally *confirms* the credit (adds its

Exhibit 12–6   **Steps in a Letter-of-Credit Transaction**

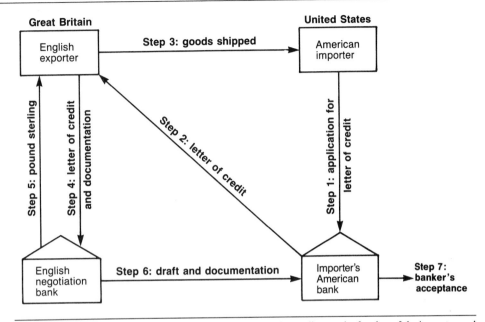

The bank that provides the letter of credit legally substitutes its credit promise for that of the importer and guarantees payment if the correct documents are submitted.

own promise to pay) and pays the exporter. Usually this payment is made in the exporter's own currency (in this case pounds sterling). Note that the British bank's inspection is limited to an examination of the documents; the bank's employees do not physically examine or even see the shipping containers or merchandise. A letter of credit transaction does not protect an importer from a dishonest exporter shipping crates of sawdust. However, the documentation may require certifications necessary to prevent such fraud.

In Step 6, the British bank sends the draft and documentation to the importer's bank. The balance the American bank examines the draft and accompanying documentation. If the draft is a sight draft, the American bank pays on demand and collects from the importer. If it is a time draft, the bank stamps it "accepted," signs it, and then either returns it to the exporter's bank or pays the exporter's bank a discounted price. If the American bank pays the exporter's bank for a time draft, the draft becomes a "bankers acceptance." The bank can either hold the acceptance and be repaid by the importer when the time draft matures (in this case, the draft acts much like a loan from the bank to the importer) or sell the banker's acceptance in the money markets (step 7) — in which case the time draft is similar to "commercial paper" issued by the importer and guaranteed by its bank. Because its bank has "accepted" the time draft it is at risk if the importer does not pay the obligation at maturity. Consequently, the banker's acceptance has no more credit risk than other bank obligations, and it might have less (if the importer has a superior credit rating).

By selling the banker's acceptance, however, the importer's bank can receive immediate cash to finance the transaction.

Collection Services

Banks also provide international collection services by acting as agents for drafts drawn by exporters and others obligated to make payment to them. In domestic banking, the situation analogous to international collection services is check clearing. Domestically, checks are cleared or collected through the facilities of the Federal Reserve System, through the correspondent banking system, and through local clearinghouses. For international banking, the main arrangements that exist for clearing items are with a bank's foreign branches and its international correspondent and clearing house relationships.

In collecting international items, banks act only as agents. That is, they will advance all or a percentage of the pending collection, but they do not accept any liability if collection problems occur. The drawer must return any advances if drafts are not honored. Banks do not take title to drafts when they collect them. They make their profits in these transactions solely from collection fees.

International collections may be *clean*; that is, the collection is made without accompanying or attached documentation. Checks, traveler's checks, and money orders are collected cleanly. They are routinely exchanged at a bank for local currency. For example, an American tourist may cash a personal check for $500 at a London bank. After the person offers proper identification, the funds are paid in pounds sterling at the bank's posted foreign exchange rate. The check is then airmailed to the British bank's American correspondent, probably in New York City, which in turn credits the British bank's account subject to collection. This type of collection by a correspondent is known formally as *cash letter services*. Collections that involve documentation are more complicated and more common in international transactions. Examples of these types of transactions are sight and time drafts generated by letters of credit.

Other Forms of Export Financing

A prominent characteristic of export financing based on letters of credit is the requirement for formal recognition of the payment obligation by the importer. Because letters of credit, although widely used, have at least a connotation of mistrust on the part of the exporter, importers may appreciate financing arrangements that avoid the need for such formal documentation. Unfortunately, however, it is the formality of the process that induces many exporters to become involved in international trade. They feel better protected from the increased risk of having to deal with a foreign firm by written evidences of indebtedness and bank guarantees.

The world is becoming increasingly competitive. New financing packages that avoid any hint of mistrust are being developed, and these often give one exporter an edge over the competition. In the United States there are two programs to help American exporters in this regard, and one additional development in the marketplace addresses longer-term capital needs for financing major projects. These three financing techniques are export credit insurance, the Export-Import Bank, and forfaiting.

Export Credit Insurance.   Export credit insurance is used by exporters as an alternative to formal letters of credit (or cash) that enables importers to buy goods essentially on open account without having to acknowledge the indebtedness formally. At the same time, the exporter is protected from most of the commercial risk of the transaction (and often all of the political risk). Thus export credit insurance is used as a marketing device to stimulate exports by making the financing package more attractive to the importer. In the United States, the unincorporated association of some 50 private insurance companies known as the Foreign Credit Insurance Association (FCIA) provides export credit insurance. This insurance provides coverage for short-, medium-, and even long-term (up to seven years) financing arrangements for individual transactions. Political risks can be insured for 100 percent of the loss, but commercial risks are only partially insured, usually up to 90 or 95 percent.

FCIA insurance differs from export credit insurance arrangements in other countries in two important ways. First, it is a private association of insurance companies rather than a formal government program. It works closely with the Export-Import Bank, but it is still a for-profit organization. The profit orientation may make it more cautious in evaluating foreign credit risks, but at the same time it sometimes is unable to make the financing arrangements for importers as attractive as competing government-run programs in other countries that are not motivated by profit. Second, FCIA regulations differ from the programs of many countries in that after a loss has been incurred, the burden of collection is borne by the FCIA.

The Export-Import Bank.   Many countries subsidize their export industries for such domestic-policy purposes as increasing domestic employment and broadening the market share so that economies of scale can be realized in key industries. These subsidies can take many forms, such as, for example, under-the-table payment of research costs in the Japanese electronics industry and low-interest loans to importers for financing the purchase of domestically produced goods and services. In the United States, the principal government agency for subsidizing export activities is the Export-Import Bank of the United States (Eximbank). The Eximbank seeks to stimulate U.S. exports by a discount loan program for foreign purchasers, various guarantee and insurance programs, direct loans on some mainly long-term contracts, and similar activities.

The Eximbank also works in cooperation with the Private Export Funding Corporation (PEFCO) to make U.S. dollar loans to foreign importers to finance the purchase of American goods and services. Although the aim of PEFCO is to mobilize private capital in the United States to support exports, all of its loans are guaranteed by the Eximbank and hence by the U.S. Treasury. It raises capital mainly in the long-term debt markets.

Forfaiting.   A third and relatively new form of medium-term export financing is called *forfaiting*. Meaning "to forfeit or surrender a right," forfaiting is the name given to the purchase of trade receivables maturing at various future dates without recourse to the exporter or to any other holder of the obligation. A specialized finance firm called a *forfaiter* buys trade receivables or other medium-term promissory notes arising out of export operations on a without-recourse basis from an exporter and then repackages them for sale to investors.

Most forfaiters are associated with large German and Swiss banks. On the one hand, a forfaiter serves as a specialist on country risk because it buys the receivables on a without-recourse basis. The exporter receives cash up front and does not have to worry about the financial ramifications of nonpayment, this risk being transferred to the forfaiter. On the other hand, a forfaiter serves as a money market firm in that it rebundles the receivables into packages of varying maturities and face amounts and supplies its own name as guarantor of the notes before selling them to investors.

The Euromarkets

The Euromarkets are vast, largely unregulated money and capital markets with centers in Europe, the Middle East, and Asia. The short-term Euromarkets are called *Eurocurrency markets*. A Eurocurrency is any currency held in a time deposit outside its country of origin. Thus, for example, a *Eurodollar* is a dollar-denominated deposit held in a bank outside the United States.

Eurocurrency markets serve three vital functions in international finance. First, they are a particularly attractive source of working capital for multinational corporations. They are attractive because the rates on Eurocurrency loans tend to be lower than for equivalent loans in the domestic economy. For Eurodollars, the rates are lower in the Euromarkets because (1) there are no reserve requirements or insurance costs associated with the deposits, and thus the overhead costs are lower; and (2) the Euromarkets are wholesale, mainly interbank markets, meaning that all participants are particularly creditworthy, the minimum transaction size is $500,000, and credit-checking and other processing costs are minimal. Because of these factors, lending rates can be lower than in the domestic U.S. market and deposit rates can be higher without sacrificing profitability.

The second function of the Eurocurrency markets is serving as storehouses for excess liquidity. Corporations, international banks, and central banks find it convenient to hold their idle funds in these markets and earn highly competitive rates of return. Also, there is less regulation in the Eurocurrency markets. This makes them attractive to investors who wish to hold securities in bearer form to preserve their anonymity. The absence of tax withholding on interest earned in the Eurocurrency markets also makes them attractive to foreigners.

Finally, the Eurocurrency markets facilitate international trade. Even when trade is financed by letters of credit, banks find it attractive to use Eurocurrency loans to make payments. Corporations sometimes borrow directly in the Eurocurrency markets and pay cash in return for discounts on goods and services. Without this source of capital at very competitive rates, the volume of international trade would probably be lower because of the higher cost of less flexible financing arrangements.

The outstanding amount of this "stateless money," as it has been called, has been extremely difficult to measure. The estimated gross size of the Eurocurrency market was $4.405 trillion at year-end 1987. Because about half of Eurocurrency deposits are interbank transfers, the net, or retail, size of this market at year-end 1987 was $2.377 trillion. In practice, Eurocurrency deposits are highly liquid, because many have maturities ranging from less than a day to a few months. Nearly one-third have a

DID YOU KNOW?

"Big Mac" Prices Can Be Used To Measure Purchasing Power Parity?

Purchasing power parity exists when exchange rates are such that the price of similar goods is the same (after adjusting for currency value differences) in different countries. Since McDonald's "Big Mac" hamburgers are now sold in every major country, *The Economist* news magazine has constructed a tongue-in-cheek purchasing power parity index based on relative prices of Big Macs in each country. It then compares implied Big Mac purchasing power parity prices with actual exchange rates to see if actual exchange rates are "overvalued" or "under-valued" based on the prices of a Big Mac. The examples in the following table, adapted from the May 5, 1990, issue of *The Economist* (p. 92) illustrate the process.

In the first column, the domestic currency price of a Big Mac is given. The second column records the amount of foreign currency that equals $1 at the official exchange rate. These numbers were taken from *The Economist*. Dividing column (1) by column (2), we get column (3), the U.S. dollar value of a Big Mac in each country.

After dividing the dollar value of the Big Mac in column (3) by $2.20, the dollar value of a Big Mac in the United States, and comparing the result to 100

percent, we obtain the number given in column (4), which shows the percentage deviation of the Big Mac price in column (3) from the U.S. value. Column (4), then, shows how much foreign prices are lower or higher than prices in the United States for a comparable good (Big Mac). If prices are lower in the foreign country, that country's exchange rate is "undervalued" because the country's goods (Big Macs) are cheaper relative to U.S. goods. Countries with "overvalued" currencies have prices higher than comparable U.S. prices.

Even though the Big Mac index is only a rough approximation for measuring purchasing power parity, it is interesting to note that the United States generally runs a merchandise trade deficit with countries such as Canada, Hong Kong, and Singapore, whose exchange rate appears to be un-dervalued relative to the U.S. dollar (so their goods are cheaper in U.S. dollar terms). At the same time, the U.S. merchandise trade balance improved in 1990 and 1991 relative to the European Community Countries (Britain, France, and Germany) whose currencies are overvalued relative to the U.S. cur-rency, or soon became overvalued—with the pound rising to 0.56£ to $1 in 1991.

	(1) Price of Big Mac in local currency	(2) Actual exchange rate	(3) Price of Big Mac in U.S. currency (after currency conversion)	(4) Over (+) or under (−) valuation of the currency currency relative to U.S.$
U.S.	$2.20	U.S.$1 = $1 U.S.	$2.20	0
Australia	A$2.30	$1.32 = $1 U.S.	$1.74	− 21%
Britain	£1.40	£0.61 = $1 U.S.	$2.30	+ 4%
Canada	C$2.19	C$1.16 = $1 U.S.	$1.89	− 14%
France	FFr 17.70	FFr5.63 = $U.S.	$3.14	+ 43%
Germany	DM4.30	DM1.68 = $1 U.S.	$2.56	+ 16%
Hong Kong	HK $8.60	HK$7.79 = $1 U.S.	$1.10	− 50%
Japan	¥370	¥159 = $1 U.S.	$2.33	+ 6%
Singapore	S $2.60	S $1.88 = $1 U.S.	$1.38	− 37%

maturity of eight days or less, and nearly 90 percent have maturities of under six months. Relatively few deposits have maturities longer than one year.

Formation of the Market

Many people use dollar deposits for settling their international payments. The dollar is used for international payments purposes because the U.S. economy is very large, politically stable, and subject to less regulation than the economies of other nations. Hence dollar-denominated deposits provide highly liquid assets that can be readily used to conduct international transactions or exchanged for other international claims.

Not all people want to hold their dollar-denominated claims in the United States, however. The Eurocurrency market started early in the 1950s when the USSR, to protect its dollar deposits in the United States from possible expropriation to repay defaulted Czarist bonds it had repudiated, withdrew its deposits from American banks and deposited them with European banks. The European banks then issued dollar-denominated deposit liabilities (Eurodollars) to the Soviets, which were backed by the deposit claims on American banks that the Soviets had transferred. This transaction is illustrated in Exhibit 12-7. The USSR, by holding the dollar-denominated claims in Europe, was able to avert the threat that the United States might freeze or expropriate its American bank deposits.

Individuals who do not fear expropriation of their funds may still wish to hold Eurodollars rather than deposits in the United States for several reasons. First, foreign banks may be able to provide essential financial services in foreign countries more readily than U.S. banks, yet the depositor may not wish to convert dollars into the currency unit of the country in which the deposits are placed. That currency unit may not be as useful as dollars for conducting international transactions, or holding that currency may expose the depositor to undesirable exchange risk or accounting complications. Second, tax regulations and periodic restrictions on capital outflows

---

Exhibit 12–7   Transfer of Funds to the Eurocurrency Market

Initial Situation

U.S. Bank		European Bank	
Assets	Liabilities	Assets	Liabilities
	U.S.S.R. deposits ($)		

Transfer of Deposits to Europe

U.S. Bank		European Bank	
Assets	Liabilities	Assets	Liabilities
	European bank deposits ($)	Deposits in U.S. banks ($)	U.S.S.R. dollar-denominated deposits ($)

The Eurodollar market allows individuals or firms to hold dollars in banks outside the United States.

by the U.S. government may make Americans reluctant to return their foreign earnings to the United States. If they held their dollars in the United States, they might subsequently be prevented from investing in certain foreign securities in the quantities and at the time that they wished. No such restrictions would be placed on their use of Eurodollar deposits. The Eurodollar markets became popular with American corporations operating abroad after the U.S. government imposed exchange controls and foreign-investment restrictions on residents in the 1960s. They also became more attractive to foreigners after the United States froze Iranian assets in 1979.

LIBOR

The Eurocurrency markets began as wholesale markets for interbank transactions. International banks sell their funds to other banks that need them. The interest rate set on these transactions is LIBOR, the London Interbank Offering Rate, a rate set much like the U.S. Federal Funds rate. LIBOR and the U.S. prime rate are the two rates used to determine the borrower's ultimate interest rate in nearly all negotiated international loans. Another phase of the LIBOR market is the retail side, as the banks then lend Eurocurrencies to corporations, government agencies, and smaller financial institutions. The interest rate commonly used is LIBOR plus a markup of from 1/8 of 1 percent to 2 1/2 percent or more.

The Eurobond Markets

The debt instruments with maturities of five years or longer that are now traded in the Euromarkets are of more recent origin than the Eurocurrency instruments discussed previously; but they are starting to play a major role in international finance. The primary long-term debt security traded in these markets is the Eurobond. A *Eurobond* is a long-term bond that is sold in markets other than the domestic market of the country in whose currency the bond is denominated. It is usually underwritten by an international syndicate of banks and securities underwriters and tends to be issued in bearer form. As is true in the short-term markets, this provision for issuing a bond in bearer form increases its marketability, because the identity of the owner is not a matter of public record. Most Eurobonds are not rated by Moody's, Standard & Poor's, or any other agency, although more and more issues are rated and the rating agencies are pushing hard to develop the market. The fact that most countries regulate securities denominated in foreign currencies only loosely, if at all, mean that disclosure requirements and registration costs for Eurobond issues are much lower than those for comparable domestic issues. Hence Eurobond issues are widely perceived as a cost-effective means of raising long-term debt capital.

The Internationalization of Financial Markets

During the past 15 years, international financial markets have witnessed exponential growth in both scale and complexity. Financial instruments and even entire markets that did not exist in the early 1970s have been developed and have grown to maturity. There have been both historical and economic factors driving this globalization of finance. Historical factors include the demise of the Bretton Woods System of fixed exchange rates; the disruption of traditional trading patterns and the concentration of financial wealth in the OPEC nations caused by the petroleum crises of 1974 and 1979–1980; the extraordinarily large budget and trade deficits experienced by the United States since 1981; Japan's rise to financial preeminence during the 1980s; and the global economic expansion that began in late 1982. Long-term economic and technological factors that have promoted the internationalization of financial markets include the global trend towards financial deregulation; the ongoing integration of international product and service markets; and breakthroughs in telecommunications and computer technology. Each of these factors will be briefly discussed in the following sections.

Floating Exchange Rates and OPEC

Under the Bretton Woods fixed exchange rate system, which lasted from 1944 to 1971, corporations had little need for protection against exchange rate movements. The floating exchange rate regime that came about in the 1970s, however, was characterized by rapid and extreme changes in currency values, and this induced an increased demand for foreign exchange advice and hedging services. International banks quickly developed large, expert (and profitable) foreign exchange trading staffs to meet the needs of their corporate clients. Currency and interest rate swaps— wherein corporations trade, say, a fixed payment obligation in one currency for a floating-rate payment obligation in a more desired currency—were developed during the 1970s and have since grown into an established international financial management tool.

International banks also played a pivotal role in recycling the OPEC financial surpluses (often called petrodollars) through the Eurodollar market. These banks bid aggressively for OPEC deposits, and they then channeled the funds to developing countries in the form of intermediate-term syndicated loans. These same banks were almost crippled when the LDC loans turned sour in the early 1980s, and the largest bank at the time, Bank of America, was dealt a near-lethal blow.

Trade Deficits, the Rise of Japan, and Global Economic Expansion

Much has been written about the economic and political consequences of the transformation of the United States from the world's largest creditor in 1980 to the world's largest debtor in 1988. Relatively little, however, has been written about the purely financial impact of this phenomenon. Three effects have predominated. First, since corporate capital spending actually rose as the budget and trade deficits mushroomed, the United States had to borrow money from foreigners on a scale never before imagined. This caused the world's most sophisticated financial system to become even larger, more efficient, and more innovative. The second effect follows from the first. As the national debt zoomed past $2 trillion, a truly global bond market (for U.S. Treasury securities) of immense size and liquidity came into being. Third, foreigners accumulated massive holdings of U.S. dollars, which they either invested in dollar-denominated financial assets or repatriated to the United States as direct investment.

As America's trade deficit widened, Japan began to run very large trade surpluses. The liquidity provided by these huge foreign currency accumulations, coupled with a high national savings rate and a slowing domestic economic growth rate, helped propel the large Japanese banks and securities firms to the top ranks of international finance. Because Japanese interest rates were far below those of other industrialized countries, these firms were able to bid aggressively for international corporate financing business, and they soon established dominance in most financial commodity markets—those where homogeneous financial instruments were traded and thus where raw financial clout could be decisive.

Paradoxically, the very prosperity enjoyed by the industrialized world during the 1980s brought stresses that helped promote the internationalization of finance. Corporations expanding their worldwide operations needed to fund expansion in deep and efficient capital markets. Foreign companies seeking to establish or expand their American operations needed dollar financing and local banking services, which they often wanted from U.S. subsidiaries of their home-country banks. Finally, stock markets around the world witnessed explosive growth in valuation and trading volume during the 1980s, and this promoted international capital flows as investors pursued diversification objectives and corporations pursued low-cost financing.

The Impact of Financial Deregulation

Long-term, secular economic forces have reinforced the historic globalizing factors just described. One powerful integrating force in finance has been the wave of deregulation, which began in the United States with the Depository Institutions Deregulation and Monetary Control Act of 1980. This subsequent legislation granted broad new powers to commercial banks and savings institutions, while changes in antitrust enforcement policies helped to trigger an unprecedented boom in mergers and acquisitions by American corporations. Other regulatory and legislative changes have weakened the Glass-Steagall Act's distinction between commercial and investment banking, and this has promoted increased competition and financial innovation.

Regulatory changes in other countries have been equally striking. Japan has taken dramatic steps to open its capital markets to foreign competition and has begun the slow, but irreversible, process of integrating its highly segmented financial markets. In France, the Mitterand government nationalized the major private banks in 1981, but France has since adopted much more market-oriented economic policies. The cycle of French deregulation was completed when the Chirac government launched a major privatization program for state-owned enterprises in 1986, and the French government has since been promoting Paris as a center of European finance.

Perhaps the most dramatic examples of deregulation in recent years have occurred in Great Britain. The Thatcher government brokered the largest public stock offerings in history, including the 1984 sale of state-owned British Telecom to the public for over $7 billion. These privatization sales more than doubled the number of British stockholders since 1979 and have given tremendous impetus to the growth of the London Stock Exchange. Also, the City (the London financial district) has been transformed by the "Big Bang" deregulation measures implemented in October 1986. London has since been firmly reestablished as the capital of international finance, although business is now dominated by Japanese and American companies. Finally,

British industrial and financial companies have positioned themselves for the birth of a fully-integrated European Common Market after 1992, as have firms all over the continent.

Other Economic and Technological Factors

As the economies of the world have become increasingly interdependent in recent years, large multinational companies have grown ever more powerful and influential. For these companies, capital is almost completely mobile, and their approach to financial management is global in scope and sophisticated in technique. Corporations that have integrated sales and production operations in 100 or more countries, as many multinational companies (particularly petroleum companies) do, require state-of-the-art systems for currency trading, cash management, capital budgeting, and risk management. The financial needs of these companies have been met by the major international banks as well as by new, specialized financial institutions such as captive finance subsidiaries.

Finally, breakthroughs in telecommunications and computer technology have transformed international finance at least as much as they have transformed our own lives and careers. Daily international capital movements larger than the gross national products of most countries have now become routine as a result of the speed, reliability, and pervasiveness of information processing technology. Computers now direct multibillion dollar program trading systems in equity, futures, and options markets around the world, and a telecommunications "global village" has become a reality for currency traders operating 24 hours a day, 365 days per year from outposts on every continent. The future will certainly bring even more rapid innovation. Because finance is but the union of three abstractions—wealth, law, and commerce—its potential when mated to technology in a world at peace is virtually unlimited.

The European Exchange Rate Mechanism and ECU

Fluctuating exchange rates make it hard for businesses to plan so they can buy supplies from the cheapest source and sell their goods for the highest possible price in terms of their domestic currency. For that reason, as the European nations have tried to integrate their economies, they have also placed great weight on keeping the exchange rates among their currencies stable. Thus they have developed the European Exchange Rate mechanism (ERM) that dictates that most European currencies should fluctuate no more than 2.25 percent on either side of a fixed exchange rate relative to each other (some currencies are given slightly more leeway, 6 percent, as a temporary measure when they join the ERM).

The European countries have also developed a joint currency unit called the European Currency Unit (ECU). The ECU is valued according to the value of its constituent European currencies. Each major currency is given a fixed weight for calculating the value of the ECU, so the ECU really represents the value of a European currency "basket." Because the values of the individual currencies are basically stable relative to each other (thanks to the ERM), the value of the ECU tends to be reasonably stable relative to its constituent currencies. Thus it has gained popularity over time as a unit for denominating exchanges between European currencies and for valuing bonds and other assets. ECU-denominated bonds have been popular because buyers can be assured that the devaluation of any one currency will not cause their bond to lose a great deal of purchasing power. At the same time, because European currencies are tied to the German deutsch mark by the ERM, most currencies, like the mark, should retain most of their purchasing power over time.

Summary

In this chapter we note that the demand for goods and services leads to a parallel demand for foreign currencies and supplies of domestic currencies to make purchases. Foreign exchange markets exist so that people can convert one country's money into monetary claims on other countries. The exchange rate is determined in the foreign exchange markets at the point at which the quantity of a country's currency supplied equals the quantity demanded. This means that the underlying demand for foreign goods and services in the domestic economy is exactly offset by foreigners' demands for domestic goods and services.

The balance of payments records all international transactions and shows exactly how inflows and outflows offset each other. Current account flows measure movements of income among countries, which affect the exchange rate by giving rise to demands for foreign currencies and supplies of domestic currency. Capital account flows, which are motivated by a desire for future gain or for prevention of future loss, represent a repositioning of a country's wealth, but they also give rise to currency supplies and demands and thereby affect the exchange rate. However, rate changes can be prevented (or induced) through government units' decisions to change their foreign asset or liability holdings and use any funds thus gained to intervene in the foreign exchange market. Any residual payments imbalance will take the form of monetary flows or "short-term" capital flows between countries. If those flows of monetary claims are willingly held by the recipients, they need not cause any change in a country's exchange rate.

Differences in interest rates and in spot and forward exchange rates between countries may provide opportunities for profitable arbitrage if covered interest rate parity conditions do not hold. Because of arbitrage, however, such opportunities will not exist for long if the securities and foreign exchange markets are competitive and unconstrained. Furthermore, the actions of arbitrageurs will generally make spot and forward exchange rates and interest rates in different countries mutually consistent.

Although different inflation rates in different countries can cause interest rates to diverge, they also will cause foreign exchange rates to change. The exchange rate for the currency of a country with a high rate of inflation will usually fall relative to the currencies of countries with lower rates of inflation. This fact will be reflected in forward exchange rates, thereby eliminating potential profits from interest rate arbitrage that attempted to take advantage of higher nominal interest rates in countries with higher inflation.

Eurodollars are U.S. dollars held on deposit in foreign banks. They are created on a one-to-one basis by transfers of U.S. demand deposit liabilities. However, the amount of Eurodollar deposits outstanding at foreign banks may exceed the amount of American bank deposit liabilities held by those foreign banks. Thus there may be some net expansion of dollar assets and liabilities by the Eurodollar market. Nonetheless, because Eurodollars are not demand deposits, they are not "money" as it is most narrowly defined.

The long-term equivalent of the Eurocurrency markets is the Eurobond market. Because the Eurobond market tends to be subjected to less regulation than domestic markets, it provides an attractive source of capital to companies needing money and to investors who want to earn high rates of interest while maintaining their anonymity.

The growth of the Euromarkets and of international banking has caused world-wide and domestic financial markets and institutions to become more closely linked. Thus international monetary policies, currency flows, spot and forward exchange rates, and domestic and international interest rates can all have major effects on the domestic financial environment and on the operating strategies of domestic financial institutions.

A number of mechanisms have been developed to minimize exchange rate fluctuations or reduce their consequences. Futures, forward, swaps, or options markets can be used to offset risks caused by exchange rate fluctuation. Aggregated currency units like the ECU or SDR fluctuate less in value then any one member currency. Furthermore, exchange stabilization activities of the G-7 countries, or through the ERM, often limit the degree to which exchange rates can change.

Questions

1. If the Japanese yen were to change from 130 per dollar to 110 per dollar, would the U.S. balance of payments be likely to improve (become more positive) or not? In answering, consider what effect the exchange rate change would have both on U.S. exports and imports to and from Japan and on purchase decisions made by manufacturers or importers located in other countries.

2. Assume that the United States and Germany are both initially in an economic recession and that the United States begins to recover before Germany. What would you expect to happen to the U.S. dollar–deutsche mark ($/DM) exchange rate? Why?

3. The newly industrializing countries (NICs) of the Far East, such as Korea, Taiwan, and Hong Kong, have dramatically increased their merchandise exports during the 1980s. Based on what you know about the determinants of international trade flows, state why this export success may have occurred and predict what this will mean for the exchange value of the NIC's currencies.

4. Explain the role that letters of credit and banker's acceptances play in international transactions. Is a banker's acceptance a sight draft? Why or why not?

5. Why do domestic governments often try to limit domestic flows of funds abroad for investment in foreign countries? How did such limitations in the United States contribute to the development of the Eurodollar markets?

6. Will the domestic balance of payments be helped or hurt if foreign investment inflows into the country increase?

7. How can government intervention affect the exchange value of a currency? Will the currency generally rise or fall if a government sells assets to foreigners? Will the effect be greater or less if the exchange market intervention is sterilized or unsterilized?
8. How can an arbitrageur make a profit if interest rates are higher in a foreign country than at home? Describe circumstances under which one could make a profit if interest rates were *lower* abroad than at home.
9. How does inflation affect a country's spot and forward exchange rates? Why? Is it absolute inflation or inflation relative to other countries that is important?
10. Describe several of the factors that have promoted the internationalization of financial markets during the last 15 years. Are any of these factors reversible?

Selected References

"Annual Financing Report." *Euromoney*, **March 1988.**
This report details the various types of international security and credit issues and gives rankings of the financial institutions underwriting each type of issue.

Chrystal, K. Alec, and Geoffrey E. Wood. "Are Trade Deficits a Problem?" *Review*. **Federal Reserve Bank of St. Louis, January/February 1988, pp.3–11.**
This article analyzes trade deficits within the context of balance-of-payments accounting. The authors suggest that concern about U.S. trade deficits is probably overstated.

Coughlin, Cletus C., K. Alec Chrystal, and Geoffrey E. Wood. "Protectionist Trade Policies: A Survey of Theory, Evidence and Rationale." *Review*. **Federal Reserve Bank of St. Louis, January/February 1988, pp. 12–26.**
This survey article neatly summarizes the arguments for and against protectionist poliices and comes out strongly for free trade.

Dornbusch, Rudiger W. "The Dollar: How Much Further Depreciation Do We Need?" *Economic Review*. **Federal Reserve Bank of Atlanta, September/October 1987, pp. 2–13.**
This excellent article examines the international trading position of the United States in 1987 and compares it to that of 1980. The author concludes that a further depreciation of the dollar is needed to restore a positive merchandise trade balance.

Eiteman, David K., and Arthur I. Stonehill. *Multinational Business Finance*. **Reading, MA: Addison-Wesley, 1986.**
Chapter 14 gives an excellent overview of trade financing.

Emminger, Otmar. "The International Role of the Dollar." *Economic Review*. **Federal Reserve Bank of Kansas City, September–October 1985, pp. 17–24.**
This is a very good article that discusses the role of the American dollar in the world economy.

Hakkio, Craig S. "Interest Rates and Exchange Rates—What Is the Relationship?" *Economic Review*. **Federal Reserve Bank of Kansas City, November 1986, pp. 33–43.**
This paper examines the relationship between interest rates and exchange rates during the 1974–1986 period. An important distinction between nominal and real interest rate changes is documented.

Humpage, Owen F. "Should We Intervene in Exchange Markets?" *Economic Commentary*. **Federal Reserve Bank of Cleveland, February 1, 1987.**
This paper discusses the reluctance of the U.S. government to intervene in foreign exchange markets and presents three theoretical channels through which exchange market intervention could influence exchange rates.

McCauley, Robert N., and Lauren A. Hargraves. "Eurocommercial Paper and U.S. Commercial Paper: Converging Money Markets?" *Quarterly Review.* Federal Reserve Bank of New York, Autumn 1987, pp. 24–35.
This article documents the growth of the Eurocommercial paper market and discusses the differences between this market and the commercial paper market in the United States.

Pardee, Scott E. "Internationalization of Financial Markets." *Economic Review:* Federal Reserve Bank of Kansas City, February 1987, pp. 3–7.
A good description of the forces that are globalizing finance.

Plaut, Steven. "The Eurobond Market—Its Use and Misuse." *Weekly Letter.* Federal Reserve Bank of San Francisco, June 10, 1988.
Brief, but excellent, overview of the workings of the Eurobond market, with an emphasis on recent developments.

Stern, Richard L. "(Dangerous) Fun and Games in the Foreign Exchange Market." *Forbes,* August 22, 1988, pp. 69–72.
This witty and informative article describes how the structure of the foreign exchange market has changed in recent years under the pressures of rapid growth and increased currency volatility.

Watson, Maxwell, et al. *International Capital Markets: Developments and Prospects.* Washington, DC: International Monetary Fund, January 1988.
This annual survey of international capital market developments provides both a descriptive framework for understanding international finance and a wealth of statistical data.

World Economic Outlook. **Washington, DC: International Monetary Fund, April 1988.**
This annual survey examines trends in world trade and economic development. It also provides a wealth of statistical information.

4 COMMERCIAL BANKING

PROFILE/Ron Alston

HE IS

Assistant vice-president, Trust Company Bank in Atlanta, promoted in January 1991 from banking officer. He has been with the bank for $4\frac{1}{2}$ years, having started in its Commercial Banking Training Program. In his current position, he manages large corporate relationships and handles credits of amounts between $5 million and $40 million. Additionally, he cross-sells other services of the bank, including cash management, corporate finance, trust, investment management, and investment banking. Although he is considered a generalist, he has developed a specialty in the insurance industry, currently one of the most financially precarious industries in the economy.

WHAT HE DOES

He manages a portfolio of 25 corporate client relationships while simultaneously pursuing 40–50 new business prospects. His clients, who are based in New England, have revenues of at least $300 million and span a number of industries, including defense, retail, apparel manufacturing, tool manufacturing, and insurance. By specializing in insurance corporate accounts, he must maintain expert knowledge and skills in reading very subtle clues about insurance company management competency and financial condition. This expertise is needed in addition to keeping up with the myriad of outside economic conditions that could affect insurance company performance. In 1991, several major insurance companies that had top industry reputations for good management and responsible financial control were taken over by state regulators. In addition to the broader insurance industry problems, the intensity of the need for vigilance is driven by the short-term nature of insurance company credit needs to cover company cash flows. Loan terms range from 3 months to a year and credit-worthiness must be assessed in a week or less.

HOW HE GOT THERE

B.A. Northeastern University

M.BA: The Wharton School

First job: Undergraduate internships in accounting and finance at Continental Forest Industries, moving to three successive internships in the Finance Division of the Bank of Boston.

BACKGROUND

He grew up in Philadelphia, graduating in 1980 with honors from Central High School, a public magnet school for the gifted. Always active in outside activities, especially choir and church-related clubs, he found he gravitated to being the treasurer of whatever organization he joined. In college, he served on the budget committee responsible for allocating student fees to campus organizations. His father, a biotech lab technician, and mother, a social worker in the public school system, always impressed on him the importance of living up to his potential. They, along with his three brothers and two sisters, provided a solid core of support and encouragement in his seeking of opportunities and setting high standards for himself. He now lives in Decatur, Georgia, a suburb of Atlanta, about a 20-minute commute to work.

WHAT HE LIKES BEST ABOUT HIS JOB

The challenge of performing credit analyses, digging into both the quantitative and qualitative information on the financial condition of companies. He also thoroughly enjoys working with his customers.

WORST NIGHTMARE

Stagnating. His greatest hope is to always feel like he is moving and growing, professionally and personally.

HOW HE UNWINDS

Reading novels, going to the movies, concerts, and the theater. His favorite vacation spots are San Francisco, California, and the Caribbean.

ADVICE

Develop a broad background in the liberal arts in addition to business knowledge. Having too narrow a focus as a whole person limits appeal in the marketplace.

COMMERCIAL BANK OPERATIONS

BACK IN THE OLD DAYS of the early 1980s, most bank depositors were accustomed to long teller lines, interrogations from loan officers, and surly comments from security guards. No longer. Now customers who maintain as little as a $100 minimum balance in their checking accounts are receiving buddy-buddy treatment from bank personnel. Now it is not uncommon for a bank officer to fill out forms, and even to stand in line to cash checks, for regular customers. Conviviality rules the conversations to be overheard between desk officer and customers. Their discussions range from automatic lines of credit to why Indiana basketball coach Bobby Knight had his last temper tantrum.

The point is that the economic environment in which banks operate is changing, and like other businesses, banks are profit-maximizing firms. As banking becomes more competitive, bank management must become more sophisticated and must more closely scrutinize revenues and expenses. The transaction costs of opening and closing accounts, advertising for new customers, and surveying lost customers are high—hence the better treatment of the ordinary citizen.

This is the first chapter on how commercial banks operate and it is intended to lay the foundation for the four chapters that follow. We begin the chapter by establishing a framework for analyzing the management of commercial banks and other financial institutions. This framework will be used in this chapter and later in the book. In our framework, we view banks and other financial institutions as business firms facing three key risks: (1) credit risk, (2) interest rate risk, and (3) liquidity risk. Next we examine the principal business activities summarized on a bank's balance sheet. We find that transactions accounts and time deposits are the major sources of funds and that investments and loans are the primary uses of funds. Included here is a discussion of the credit card industry, which is coming into its own right as a major source of consumer credit. Next, we discuss in detail how banks set the prime rate and make loans. Finally, we examine the fee-based activities that banks engage in, such as leasing, trust activities, correspondent banking, and the off-balance-sheet transactions of standby letters of credit and loan brokerage.

Banks and Financial Institutions as Business Firms

Like any privately operated businesses, financial institutions such as banks or insurance companies have as their aim the maximization of long-term profits. The profits are primarily derived from such sources as interest income on loans, income from securities, and sales of insurance contracts. Maximizing long-term profits is an appropriate goal for these firms because it considers the current year's profits as well as the magnitude and timing of future profits. For an institution whose stock is publicly traded, this goal is equivalent to maximizing the firm's stock price. A firm's stock price reflects the market's assessment of the size and riskiness of the firm's earnings stream. Also, the market price represents how well current management is performing on behalf of the shareholders. Stockholders dissatisfied with management's performance may sell the stock, putting downward pressure on the market price.

In establishing a framework to analyze how financial institutions operate, we must recognize that managers face a trade-off between risk and higher potential profits in their quest to increase the firm's long-term earnings. As moot testimony to this trade-off, the decade of the 1980s was a battleground now littered with the corpses of financial institutions that took excessive risks and failed. On the other hand, managers who took too few risks slept well at night, but their slumber reaped a reward of declining earnings and stock prices for shareholders.

In their search for higher long-term earnings, financial institutions must manage credit risk, interest rate risk, and liquidity risk. Each must be managed carefully to balance the trade-off between future profitability or potential failure. Though we have discussed these risks in the preceding chapters, we now summarize them and discuss briefly how the three risks affect the management of financial institutions.[1]

Credit Risk

When a financial institution makes a loan or invests in a bond or other debt security, the institution bears credit risk (or default risk) because it is accepting the possibility that the borrower will fail to make either interest or principal payments in the amount and at the time promised. To manage the credit risk of loans or investments in debt securities, financial institutions should (1) diversify their portfolios (don't put all of your eggs in one basket), (2) conduct a careful credit analysis of the borrower to measure default risk exposure, and (3) monitor the borrower over the life of the loan or investment to detect any critical changes in financial health.

Interest Rate Risk

Recall in Chapter 5 we defined interest rate risk as the risk of fluctuations in a bond's price or reinvestment income caused by changes in market interest rates. The concept of interest rate risk is not only applicable to bonds, but also to a financial institution's balance sheet. The savings and loan association industry (S&Ls) is the prime example of how interest rate risk adversely affects a financial institution's earnings. In the volatile interest rate environment of the late 1970s and early 1980s, many S&Ls failed because the interest rates they paid on deposits (liabilities) increased faster than the yields they earned on their mortgage loans (assets), causing earnings to decline.

---

[1]The concept of liquidity risk was discussed in Chapter 2; interest rate risk, in Chapter 5; and credit risk (default risk), in Chapter 7.

Liquidity Risk

Liquidity risk is the risk that a financial institution will be unable to generate sufficient cash inflow to meet required cash outflows. Liquidity is critical to financial institutions: banks and thrifts need liquidity to meet deposit withdrawals and pay off other liabilities as they come due; pension funds need liquidity to meet contractual pension payments; and life insurance companies need liquidity to pay death benefits. Liquidity also means that an institution need not pass up a profitable loan or investment opportunity due to a lack of cash. If a financial institution is unable to meet its short-term obligations because of inadequate liquidity, the firm will fail even though over the long run the firm may be profitable.

Balance Sheet for a Commercial Bank

We now turn our attention to examining the operation of a commercial bank. A good place to start is a commercial bank's balance sheet. The balance sheet lists what the business owns (*assets*), what the firm owes to others (*liabilities*), and what the owners have invested (*capital*) as of a given time. The basic balance sheet equation expresses the relationship between these accounts as:

$$\text{Assets} = \text{Liabilities} + \text{Capital}.$$

The capital account (or net worth) is a residual that can be calculated by subtracting liabilities owed to creditors from the total assets owned by the bank. The right-hand side of the equation can be viewed as the *sources of funds* for a bank. Funds are supplied by either creditors (liabilities) or the owners (capital). The left-hand side of the equation shows the *uses of funds* (assets) that the bank has obtained from the creditors and owners.

In Exhibit 13–1, the major liability and capital items in dollars and percentages are shown for all insured commercial banks and for samples of large and small banks.

The Source of Bank Funds

The principal source of funds for most banks is deposit accounts—demand, savings, and time deposits. Economically, deposit accounts are similar to other sources of funds borrowed by the bank. Legally, however, deposits take precedence over most other sources of borrowed funds in case of a bank failure. Furthermore, the holders of such accounts are insured against any loss up to a maximum of $100,000 per account by the Federal Deposit Insurance Corporation (FDIC).

Transactions Accounts

Demand Deposits.   Banks hold a number of different types of transactions accounts, which are more commonly called checking accounts. A *demand deposit* is a checking account in which the owner is entitled to receive his or her funds on demand and to write checks on the account, which transfers legal ownership of funds to others. Demand deposits and other transactions accounts compose 20 percent of the sources of funds of commercial banks. They serve as the basic medium of exchange in the

Exhibit 13–1

Liabilities and Capital Accounts of Insured Commercial Banks (December 1990)

Liabilities and Capital Accounts	All Insured Banks[a]		Large Banks[b]	Small Banks[c]
	Billions	Percent	Percent	Percent
Transactions accounts (domestic offices):	$684	20	19	23
Demand deposits	463	14	14	12
Other demand deposits	221	7	4	11
Time deposits (domestic offices):	1,672	49	40	65
Savings deposits	199	6	5	7
MMDA[d]	378	11	11	10
Large time deposits(> $100,000)	379	11	11	11
Other time deposits	716	21	13	38
Deposits in foreign offices	294	9	15	0
Borrowed funds	382	11	15	1
Capital notes and bonds	26	1	1	0
Other liabilities	112	3	5	1
Capital accounts:	219	6	5	9
Capital stock	33	1	1	2
Retained earnings and reserves	186	5	5	7
Total	$3,389	100	100	100

Deposit accounts are the major source of funds for most banks. Foreign deposits and borrowed funds are a more important source of funds for large banks than for smaller banks. Capital is a more important source of funds for small banks than for larger banks.

[a]This group consists of 12,345 insured commercial banks.

[b]This group consists of 234 banks with domestic and foreign offices. It includes all money-center/ multinational banks, most super-regional banks, and many regional banks. These banks have a regional, national, or global emphasis.

[c]This group consists of 9,482 banks without foreign offices and with total assets less than $100 million. It includes banks with primarily a local emphasis.

[d]Money Market Deposit Accounts.

Source: FDIC, *Statistics on Banking*, 1990.

economy, accounting for about three-fourths of the total money supply (M1). Demand deposits may be owned by individuals, government entities, and business organizations. Legally, a demand deposit is defined as a deposit that is payable on demand or issued with an original maturity of less than seven days. Because they are closely associated with consumer transactions, demand deposits are relatively more important as a source of funds for small, consumer-oriented banks than for large banks.

The demand deposits of individual corporations and state and local governments are held primarily for transaction purposes. The U.S. Treasury Department also holds deposits in commercial banks. The Treasury accounts are maintained to help banks avoid large fluctuations in reserves that would occur if the Treasury deposited consumers' and businesses' tax and loan payments directly at the Fed. Treasury deposits are called *tax and loan accounts* and are held by more than 12,000 commercial banks. Small banks also hold substantial demand deposit balances in large urban banks; these are called *correspondent balances*. Because the recipient bank can invest or loan out part of these deposits and earn income for itself, correspondent balances provide compensation to large correspondent banks for services they provide respondent banks. For example, small banks receive check-clearing, foreign exchange, and trust advisory services from large banks.

NOW Accounts.   Until 1980 most banks could not pay explicit interest on demand deposit accounts. Because these deposits provided banks with funds to lend and invest, banks competed for these "costless" funds by providing individual customers with "free" services or services sold for less than their cost. Such services include check writing, safekeeping, accounting, and the sale of traveler's checks. These constituted implicit interest payments to holders of demand deposits.

In 1972 Congress experimented by allowing financial institutions in Massachusetts and New Hampshire to pay interest on a special class of transactions account called a *NOW account* (Negotiable Order of Withdrawal). NOW accounts are just demand deposits that pay interest. They were subject to a $5\frac{1}{4}$ percent interest rate ceiling (Regulation Q). In 1976 Congress expanded the authority to offer NOW accounts to financial institutions in all of the New England states, and in 1980 the Depository Institutions Deregulation and Monetary Control Act (DIDMCA) allowed all depository financial institutions in the nation to offer NOW accounts. This type of account is currently available only to individuals, government entities, and nonprofit organizations. The $5\frac{1}{4}$ percent interest rate ceiling was removed on January 1, 1986.

Automatic Transfer Service Accounts.   In 1978 commercial banks were allowed to offer customers automatic transfers from savings accounts to checking accounts. This led to the practice of offering *automatic transfer services (ATS)*, which are essentially zero-balance checking accounts fed from savings accounts. The automatic transfer of funds from an interest-bearing savings account to a checking account is the equivalent of a NOW account or share draft. When first introduced, ATS accounts grew rapidly, but with the legalization of NOW accounts for commercial banks, their growth has slowed.

Savings Deposits

Savings accounts are the traditional form of savings held by most individuals and nonprofit organizations. They are a more important source of funds for small banks than for large banks. Since the beginning of deregulation of the financial system in 1980, these accounts are becoming a less important source of funds for all banks as consumers switch to higher-yielding and more convenient checkable accounts. Historically, savings deposits had low handling costs because of their low activity level. The basic types of savings accounts are passbook and money market deposit accounts.

Savings Accounts.   A blue or green passbook was the standard symbol of savings for generations of Americans. When funds were deposited or withdrawn from a savings account, the passbook had to be presented and the transaction recorded in it. Today most consumers do not receive passbooks. Instead, they receive quarterly statements from the bank and may do most of their savings transactions by mail. Savings accounts are most often held by individuals and nonprofit organizations. Since 1975 they may also be held by private businesses. Legally, passbook accounts require a 30-day notice before funds can be withdrawn from the bank. This requirement was instituted during the early 1930s, in the era of massive bank failures, to help curb runs on banks. The notification period was established to allow banks additional time to gain liquidity to meet deposit withdrawals. Banks today seldom insist on advance notice, and most bank customers assume that the funds can be withdrawn on demand. As of April 1, 1986, savings accounts are no longer subject to interest rate ceilings.

Money Market Deposit Accounts.   To allow banks to be more competitive with money market mutual funds (MMMFs), the Garn–St. Germain Act of 1982 authorized banks to issue accounts "directly equivalent" to MMMF accounts. In the past, MMMF accounts had grown rapidly whenever market rates of interest rose above the legal limit banks could pay on deposits (Regulation Q). MMMF accounts allowed the public to earn the market rate of interest and offered limited checking features. The regulatory response, in December 1982, was the *money market deposit account (MMDA)*.

The MMDA is federally insured and pays an interest rate set at the discretion of the issuing bank. The exact features, such as minimum balance requirements, vary from bank to bank. However, by law depositors are limited to six third-party transfers each month. The account is available to all bank customers, including for-profit corporations. MMDAs quickly proved to be popular with consumers and helped banks attract funds from MMMFs.[2]

Time Deposits

Time deposits have increased rapidly since 1960 and have become the largest source of funds for commercial banks, accounting for nearly one-third of total bank funds. Time deposits are unlike demand deposits in that they are usually legally due as of a maturity date and funds cannot be transferred to another party by a written check. Technically, a time deposit cannot be withdrawn for seven days, and if withdrawn after that an interest rate penalty must be invoked.[3] They can be owned by both

---

[2]To further allow banks to be competitive with MMMFs, banks were allowed to issue Super NOW(SNOW) accounts in January 1983. The SNOW accounts had unlimited transaction features, paid unregulated rates of interest, and required a minimum average balance of $2,500 or more. On January 1, 1986, the SNOW and NOW accounts were made a single type of account, called a NOW account.

[3]The penalty is the loss of at least three-months' interest for time deposits with maturities of less than one year and six-months' interest for time deposits of longer maturities.

consumers and corporations, and their characteristics vary widely with respect to maturity, minimum amount, early withdrawal penalties, negotiability, and renewability. Since April 1, 1986, there is no interest rate ceiling on time deposit accounts. The principal types of bank time deposits are savings certificates, money market certificates, and certificates of deposit.

Savings Certificates.   Savings certificates, which have grown in popularity during the last decade, are held primarily by consumers or other small depositors. They are an important source of funds for small, consumer-oriented banks. Savings certificates are bank liabilities issued in a designated amount, specifying a fixed rate of interest and maturity date. The interest rate is generally higher than on savings accounts.

Money Market Certificates.   To help commercial banks compete effectively with money market funds, beginning in 1978 Congress authorized banks to issue a variety of money market certificates (MMC). MMCs are designed primarily to service consumers and small businesses. For example, in June 1978, banks were allowed to sell MMCs with a six-month maturity, a $10,000 minimum, rates comparable to Treasury bills, and an early withdrawal penalty equal to three months' interest. During March 1982, banks were given the power to issue 91-day deposit certificates with a minimum balance of $7,500 and an interest rate tied to the 13-week Treasury bill rate.

Certificates of Deposit.   Certificates of deposit, commonly referred to as CDs, are very large, unsecured liabilities of commercial banks issued in denominations of $100,000 or more to business firms and individuals. They have a fixed maturity date, pay an explicit rate of interest, and are negotiable if they meet certain legal specifications. Negotiable CDs are issued by large, well-known commercial banks of the highest credit standing and are traded actively in a well-organized secondary market.

CDs are attractive both to holders of large funds and to commercial banks. They can be redeemed at any time in the secondary market without loss of deposit funds to the bank. CDs have allowed large commercial banks to attract temporary funds that had previously been invested in other money market instruments. Smaller banks can issue large CDs, but their CDs do not have active secondary markets and thus lose much of their appeal to large investors. The interest rate on CDs is competitive with the rates on comparable money market instruments. Since 1973 there has been no interest rate ceiling on CDs in denominations of $100,000 or more.

Borrowed Funds

Borrowed funds are typically short-term borrowings by commercial banks from the wholesale money markets or a Federal Reserve bank. They are economically similar to deposits but are not insured by the FDIC. Although they account for only 11 percent of all bank funds, borrowed funds have grown in importance as high levels of loan demand have increasingly provided banks with the incentive to develop exotic sources of funds. Borrowed funds are a source of funds primarily for large banks.

Federal Funds.   For liquidity reasons, banks may hold reserves in excess of those required by law. A bank with more excess reserves than it desires may lend reserves to another bank that does not have its required level of reserves or that desires additional reserves to make more loans. The buying (borrowing) and selling (lending) of reserves on deposit at the Federal Reserve banks is called trading in *Federal Funds* (or *Fed Funds*).

The maturity of Federal Funds is usually one day, but the loans may be continuously renewed with the same or other banks in the Federal Funds market. Trading units tend to be very large, generally $1 million or more. About 150 large banks participate in the Federal Funds market regularly, and a number of other large banks participate intermittently. Recently, small banks that typically hold excess reserves have become more actively engaged in the Federal Funds market as suppliers (sellers) of Fed Funds to their larger correspondent banks in amounts as small as $50,000.

Repurchase Agreements.   *Repurchase agreements (RPs)* are a form of loan in which the bank sells securities (usually government securities) to the lender but simultaneously contracts to repurchase the same securities either on call or on a specified date at a price that will produce an agreed yield. For example, a corporation with idle cash balances agrees to buy a 90-day Treasury bill from a bank at a price to yield 7 percent with a contract to buy the bills back one day later. The RP transaction is attractive to the corporation because, unlike demand deposits, RPs pay explicit interest. Most RP transactions are for $1 million or more and have a maturity of one day; however, the RP can be renewed continuously on a day-to-day basis. There are also term RP transactions that are written for maturities up to 30 days.

Eurodollars.   Short-term deposits at foreign banks or foreign branches of U.S. banks are called *Eurodollars*. They are denominated in U.S. dollars. U.S. banks may also borrow funds from individuals or other banks in the Eurodollar market for short periods of time. The interbank market is similar to the Fed Funds market except that interbank loans may be obtained for as long as six months. The base rate in this market is the *London Interbank Offer Rate* (LIBO rate, or *LIBOR*). Only large American banks actively participate in the Eurodollar market.

Banker's Acceptances.   A *banker's acceptance* is a draft drawn on a bank by a corporation to pay for merchandise. The draft promises payment of a certain sum of money to its holder at some future date. What makes such drafts unique is that a bank *accepts* them by prearrangement, thereby guaranteeing their payment at the stated time. In effect, the bank has substituted its credit standing for that of the issuer. Banker's acceptances can be held by the bank or sold in the secondary market as a source of funds. Most banker's acceptances arise in foreign trade transactions. Export and import firms find it less risky to deal in drafts guaranteed by well-known banks than those drawn against the bank accounts of firms with whom they are less familiar. Banker's acceptances are primarily a source of funds for large banks.[4]

---

[4]Federal funds, repurchase agreements, Eurodollars, and banker's acceptances are money market instruments, which are discussed in detail in Chapter 8.

Federal Reserve Bank Loans.   Banks can borrow funds from their district Federal Reserve bank for short periods of time. The purpose of this type of borrowing is to cover short-term deficiencies of reserves. The traditional term of a discount loan is 15 days, although loans may be renewed with the approval of the Federal Reserve bank. Borrowing from the discount window requires that the bank apply to the Federal Reserve Bank for the loan and receive its approval. Federal Reserve banks exercise close administrative control over this type of borrowing, and the amount of borrowing at the discount window is quite small, representing less than 1 percent of funds for all banks.

Capital Notes and Bonds

Issuing bonds to raise funds is a common practice of most industrial firms. It is only in recent years that a few large commercial banks began raising funds by selling short-term capital notes or longer-term bonds. In the early 1960s, the comptroller of the currency ruled that debentures subordinate to the claims of depositors could be used to raise funds and that a limited amount of this debt could be counted as part of a bank's capital for regulatory purposes. Capital notes and bonds account for only a small percentage of the liabilities of commercial banks.

Capital Accounts

Bank capital represents the equity or ownership funds of a bank, and it is the account against which bank loans and security losses are charged. The greater the proportion of capital to deposits, the greater the protection to depositors. Banks maintain much lower capital accounts than other businesses, and currently bank capital accounts for 6 percent of total bank funds. Notice that capital is a more important source of funds for small banks than for large banks.

There are three principal types of capital accounts for a commercial bank: capital stock, retained earnings, and special reserve accounts. Capital stock represents the direct investments into the bank; retained earnings comprise that portion of the bank's profit that is not paid out to shareholders as dividends; special reserve accounts are set up to cover anticipated losses on loans and investments. Reserve accounts involve no transfers of funds or setting aside of cash. They are merely a form of retained earnings designed to reduce tax liabilities and stockholders' claims on current revenues.

Bank Investments and Cash Assets

The earning assets of a bank are typically classified as either loans or investments, and there are important differences between these two classes. *Loans* are the primary business of a bank and usually represent an ongoing relationship between the bank and its borrowers. A loan is a highly personalized contract between the borrower and the bank and is tailor-made to the particular needs of the customer. *Investments*, on the other hand, are standardized contracts issued by large, well-known borrowers, and their purchase by the bank represents an impersonal or open market transaction; consequently, they can be resold by the bank in secondary markets. Unlike loans, investments represent pure financing, because the bank provides no service to the ultimate borrower other than the financing. Exhibit 13–2 shows the major asset accounts for all insured commercial banks in the United States and for samples of large and small banks. In this section we shall discuss bank investments and other assets, and in the next section we shall discuss bank loans.

Exhibit 13–2   **Assets of Insured Commercial Banks (December 1990)**

Asset Accounts	All Banks[a]		Large Banks[b]	Small Banks[c]
	Billions	**Percent**	**Percent**	**Percent**
Cash assets	$318	9	11	7
Investments:	752	22	17	37
U.S. Treasury securities	151	4	2	9
U.S. Government agencies	275	8	6	14
Municipal securities	84	2	2	4
Foreign and other	95	3	3	2
Federal funds sold	147	4	4	7
Loans:	2,015	59	60	52
Commercial and industrial	615	18	23	10
Agricultural	33	1	<1	5
Financial institutions	51	2	2	<1
Consumer	403	12	9	10
Real estate	829	29	22	27
Foreign	25	1	1	0
Other	59	2	3	<1
Other assets:	304	9	12	4
Lease financing receivables	38	1	2	0
Fixed assets	51	2	1	2
Miscellaneous	215	6	9	2
Total	$3,389	100	100	100

Loans are the most important earning assets held by banks. They have high yields, but for the most part they are not very liquid. Investments in securities are a much more important asset for small banks than for large banks. Large banks concentrate in commercial loans while small banks concentrate in consumer, agricultural, and real estate loans.

[a]This group consists of 12,345 insured commercial banks.

[b]This group consists of 234 banks with domestic and foreign offices. It includes all money-center/ multinational banks, most super-regional banks, and many regional banks. These banks have a regional, national, or global emphasis.

[c]This group consists of 9,482 banks without foreign offices and with total assets less than $100 million. It includes banks with primarily a local emphasis.

Source: FDIC, *Statistics on Banking,* 1990.

Cash Assets

Cash items account for 9 percent of the total assets of the commercial banking system. They consist of vault cash, reserves with the Federal Reserve banks, balances held at other banks, and cash items in the process of collection. Cash assets are noninterest-bearing funds; banks try to minimize their holdings of these idle balances within their liquidity constraints. Because large banks must hold larger amounts of legal reserves and have more checks drawn against them than small banks, cash item accounts are typically a greater percentage of total assets for larger than for smaller banks.

Vault Cash.   Vault cash consists of coin and currency held in the bank's own vault. Banks typically maintain only minimum amounts of vault cash because of the high cost of security, storage, and transfer. Vault cash does, however, perform two important functions for banks. First, it provides banks with funds to meet the cash needs of the public. Second, banks can count vault cash as part of their legal reserve requirements.

Reserves at Federal Reserve Banks.   Deposits held by banks at their district Federal Reserve bank represent the major portion of the banks' legal reserve requirements and serve as check-clearing and collection balances. Rather than physically transferring funds between banks, check clearing and collection can be done by simply debiting or crediting a bank's account at the Federal Reserve bank. Banks may also transfer funds to other banks for reasons other than check clearing. For example, transactions in the Federal Funds market are performed as bookkeeping entries between banks and are accounted for on the books of the Federal Reserve banks.

Balances at Other Banks.   Banks hold demand deposit balances at other banks for a number of reasons. In most states, small banks that are not members of the Federal Reserve System can usually meet state reserve requirements by holding balances at approved large banks. Also, many small banks use their deposits at other banks to secure correspondent services from large city banks.

Cash Items in the Process of Collection.   This account, often written as CIPC, is the value of checks drawn on other banks but not yet collected. After a check written on another bank is deposited into a customer's account, the receiving bank attempts to collect the funds through the check-clearing mechanism. This is done by presenting the check to the bank on which the check is drawn. Before collection, the funds are not available to the bank and show up in the CIPC account. At the time the funds become available to the bank, the CIPC account is decreased (reversing the original entry), and the bank's reserves are increased by the same amount. The CIPC account is analogous to the accounts receivable on the balance sheet of a nonfinancial corporation.

Investments

The investment portfolios of commercial banks are a major use of funds by the banking system, accounting for 22 percent of total assets. Bank investments consist primarily of U.S. government bonds, municipal securities, and bonds issued by agencies of the U.S. government. Bank investment portfolios serve several important functions. First, they contain short-term, highly marketable securities that provide liquidity to the bank. These short-term securities are held in lieu of noninterest-bearing reserves to the maximum extent possible. Second, the investment portfolio contains long-term securities that are purchased for their income potential. Finally, they provide the bank with tax benefits and diversification beyond that possible with only a loan portfolio.

Treasury Securities.   Commercial banks hold U.S. Treasury securities for various reasons. First, they are highly marketable. A bank in need of cash can find purchasers for its government securities nearly instantly. Second, funds held for liquidity must be safe from default, and Treasury securities are virtually default-free. Third, although yields on Treasury securities are not as high as on securities of similar maturity, they do provide banks with earned interest income on their liquid asset holdings.

Treasury securities are more important to the portfolios of smaller banks than to those of larger banks. Larger banks have access to many more sources of liquid funds than do smaller banks, and therefore they do not need to rely as heavily on Treasury securities for liquidity.

Government Agency Securities.   These are securities issued by federal agencies that administer selected lending programs of the government, such as the Federal Home Loan Mortgage Corporation. The default risk of agency securities is slightly higher than Treasury securities because most agency securities are not direct obligations of the federal government. Some have active secondary markets whereas others do not, although none have secondary markets as broad or as active as those for U.S. Treasury securities. Because agency securities have somewhat greater default risk and lower marketability, they sell at yields above comparable Treasury obligations.

Municipal Securities.   These are securities sold by city, state, and local governments to finance education, water, electricity, recreation, and other community services. The default risk varies widely from issuer to issuer. Municipal securities, except those of very short term, are not considered liquid investments.

The principal attraction of municipal securities for commercial banks is their tax-exempt status. All coupon interest payments are exempt from federal income taxes. Depending on the marginal income tax bracket of an investor, the after-tax yield on municipal bonds may be higher than that on comparable taxable securities. For example, for a commercial bank in the 34 percent income tax bracket, a 6 percent tax-exempt security is equivalent to a 9.09 percent taxable security [$6/(1 - 0.34)$]. Thus banks can generally earn higher after-tax yields by holding municpal bonds than corporate bonds.

Federal Funds Sold

Federal Funds sold correspond to the borrowing of excess bank reserves in the Federal Funds market discussed earlier. Banks that sell (lend) excess reserves in the Federal Funds market acquire assets (Federal Funds sold) and lose a corresponding amount of reserves on the balance sheet. Banks that borrow Federal Funds gain reserves but acquire a liability (Federal Funds purchased). These transactions are

Exhibit 13–3   **A Federal Funds Transaction**

Bank A (Borrower)		Federal Reserve Bank	Bank B (Lender)	
+ Reserves	+ Federal Funds purchased	− Reserves Bank B + Reserves Bank A	− Excess Reserves + Federal Funds sold	

A Fed Funds transaction is basically an unsecured loan from one bank to another, usually for a period of one day. Thus the Fed Funds rate is the interbank lending rate.

reversed when the borrowing bank returns the reserves to the selling bank. Exhibit 13–3 shows the balance sheet transaction for the sale and purchase of Federal Funds between two banks. Notice that the only role of the Federal Reserve bank is to "keep the books." As Exhibit 13–2 shows, about 4 percent of all bank funds are invested in Federal Funds for the banking system as a whole. Small banks typically have excess reserves, and, correspondingly, Federal Funds sold is a more important use of funds for them than for large banks.

Other Assets   Fixed assets are the most important group in this category and include such real assets as furniture, banking equipment, and the bank's real estate holdings. Other items are prepaid expenses, income earned but not collected, foreign currency holdings, and any direct lease financing. The Other Assets account tends to be larger for small banks because they have a higher proportion of fixed assets than do large banks. Small banks, with a greater consumer/retail emphasis, require more "bricks and mortar" than do large banks.

Bank Loans

Bank loans are the primary business activity of a commercial bank, accounting for about 60 percent of all bank assets. They generate the bulk of a bank's profits and help attract valuable deposits. Although loans are very profitable to banks, they take time to arrange, are subject to greater default risk, and have less liquidity than most bank investments. Also, they do not have the special tax advantage of municipal bonds.

Most bank loans consist of promissory notes. A *promissory note* is an unconditional promise made in writing by the borrower to pay the lender a specific amount of money, usually at some specified future date. Repayment can be made (1) periodically, in installments; (2) in total on a single date; or (3) in some cases, on demand. If the loan is due on demand, either the borrower or lender can end the contract at any time.

Bank loans can have either a fixed rate of interest for the duration of the loan commitment or a floating-rate commitment. Banks have increasingly turned toward floating- or variable-rate loans because of the high and volatile interest rates that began during the 1970s.

Bank loans may be *secured* or *unsecured*. Most are secured. The security, or *collateral*, may consist of merchandise, inventory, accounts receivable, plant and

DID YOU KNOW?

Who Gets the Most Pay and Are They Worth It?

Once again, New York banks are at the top of the heap, this time in paying their management. In its annual survey of executive compensation, *Business Week* found that in 1991, four of the five highest-paid bank executives in the country were based in New York City. Standing out against the field is Hugh McColl, CEO of NationsBank which is headquartered in Charlotte, North Carolina. The table below shows the salary, bonus, and incentive compensation for the five top bankers.

The top position in terms of salary and bonus is occupied by J. F. McGillicuddy, chairman and CEO of Chemical Banking, who earned $2,050,000 in 1991. Of the top five, only Charles Sanford of Bankers Trust appeared on the list five years ago, in 1987, when he earned $1,750,000. Don't be deceived by the salary and bonus numbers, however, because they represent only a portion of the compensation received by most executives. Much of an executive's compensation comes in the form of long-term incentive compensation which is tied directly to the bank's performance. This compensation frequently includes awarding shares of stock in the bank and stock options. In theory, incentive compensation ties the executive's pay to the fortunes of the bank's shareholders, presumably resulting in better bank performance. When we consider the *total* compensation of the five highest paid bankers to include salary, bonus, and long-term incentive compensation we get a different ranking. Among the top five in terms of salary and bonus, D. Weatherstone, chairman of J. P. Morgan earns the highest total compensation, $4,114,000 ($2,043,000 + $2,071,000).

Many among shareholders, politicians, the media, the public, and even some chief executive officers are up in arms over what they consider to be offensively exorbitant pay for America's corporate chieftains, including the nation's top bankers. The question of CEO pay has become a hot issue in the wake of the layoffs of the 1990–92 recession. Many question whether executives should receive such high salaries at the same time they are putting many of their workers in the unemployment line. Critics also question whether CEOs are worth the high salaries they command., Most empirical evidence finds that there is a positive link between executive pay and corporate performance, but many academics and policymakers question whether the link is strong enough.

Does it appear that the top five bankers have earned their pay? In their recent survey, *Business Week* ranked 500 of the country's largest firms in terms of performance measured both by shareholders' return and accounting profits. According to the survey, the banks represented in the list below ranked in the bottom 20 percent of the firms surveyed in terms of performance. This dismal performance is by no means unique to this set of banks; the entire banking industry has been suffering in the late 1980s and early 1990s. Perhaps that explains why there are no bankers to be found in *Business Week*'s list of the country's 30 highest paid executives.

Rank	Firm	Executive	Salary and Bonus	Long-term Compensation
1	Chemical Banking, New York	J., F. McGillicuddy, Chairman and CEO	$2,050,000	N/A
2	J. P. Morgan, New York	D. Weatherstone, Chairman	2,043,000	$2,071,000
3	NationsBank, Charlotte	H. L. McColl, Jr., President and CEO	2,000,000	1,353,000
4	Bankers Trust, New York	C. S. Sanford, Jr., Chairman	1,850,000	1,748,000
5	Chemical Banking, New York	W. V. Shipley, President and COO	1,716,000	563,000

Source: Business Week, May 4, 1992

equipment, and, in some instances, even stocks or bonds. The purpose of collateral is to reduce the financial injury to the lender if the borrower defaults. An asset's value as collateral depends on its expected resale value. If a borrower fails to meet the terms and conditions of his or her promissory note, the bank may sell the collateralized assets to recover the loan loss.

Types of Loan Commitments

There are three types of loan commitments that may be agreed upon by business borrowers and commercial banks: line of credit, term loan, and revolving credit. Consumers usually do not enter into these types of arrangements. The purpose of the loan commitment is to (1) provide some assurance to the borrower that funds will be available if and when they are needed and (2) provide the lender with a basic format for structuring the customer's loan request properly.

A *line of credit* is an agreement under which a bank customer can borrow up to a predetermined limit on a short-term basis (less than one year). The line of credit is a moral obligation and not a legal commitment on the part of a bank. Thus, if a company's circumstances change, a bank may cancel or change the amount of the limit at any time. With a line of credit, it is also customary for a bank to require an annual cleanup period, usually one month. This ensures the bank that funds are not being used as permanent capital by the firm. A firm does not have to use a line of credit and incurs a liability only for the amount borrowed.

A *term loan* is a formal legal agreement under which a bank will lend a customer a certain dollar amount for a period exceeding one year. The loan may be amortized over the life of the loan or paid in a lump sum at maturity. *Revolving credit* is a formal legal agreement under which a bank agrees to lend up to a certain limit for a period exceeding one year. A company has the flexibility to borrow, repay, or reborrow as it sees fit during the revolving credit period. At the end of the period, all outstanding loan balances are payable, or, if stipulated, they may be converted into a term loan. In a sense, revolving credit is a long-term, legally binding line of credit.

Fixed-Rate and Floating-Rate Loans

Banks make either fixed-rate or floating-rate loans. The interest rate on a fixed-rate loan does not change over the loan's term. The interest rate on a floating-rate loan, on the other hand, is periodically adjusted to changes in a designated short-term interest rate, usually a Treasury rate. In periods of stable interest rates and upward-sloping yield curves, banks are eager to make long-term loans at fixed rates above the rates they pay on their short-term liabilities. As long as rates do not rise too quickly, banks can roll over their deposits at relatively low rates, maintaining a positive spread. When interest rates rise quickly or become more volatile, on the other hand, banks have a preference for making short-term or floating-rate loans.

Most bank loans carry fixed rates. While many commercial loans have floating rates, consumers are generally less willing to bear the interest rate risk of a floating-rate loan. On the other hand, with a fixed-rate loan, the bank assumes all of the interest rate risk. Borrowers will shift to floating-rate loans, however, if they are offered sufficient inducement in the form of a lower initial interest rate on the floating-rate loan.

Commercial and Industrial Loans

As shown in Exhibit 13–2, loans to commercial and industrial firms constitute 18 percent of total assets. Most are short-term loans with maturities of less than one year. Business loans reflect the composition of a bank's customers and are typically more important to large banks than to small retail banks.

There are three basic types of business loans, depending on the borrower's need for funds and source of repayment. A *bridge loan* supplies cash for a specific transaction, and repayment is made from cash flows from an identifiable source. Usually, the purpose of the loan and the source of repayment are related; hence the term "bridge loan". For example, an advertising company enters into a contract to produce a TV commercial for the Ford Motor Company. The total contract will be for $350,000; however, the advertising company needs approximately $200,000 in financing to produce the commercial. The loan is a bridge loan because it supports a specific transaction (making the commercial) and the source of repayment is identifiable (completing the commercial).

A *seasonal loan* provides term financing to take care of temporary discrepancies between business revenues and expenses that are due to the manufacturing or sales cycle of a business. For example, a retail business may borrow money to build inventory in anticipation of heavy Christmas sales and may expect to repay it after the new year begins. The uncertainty in this type of loan is whether the inventory can be sold for a price that will cover the loan.

Long-term asset loans are seasonal loans with a longer term. An example would be a manufacturing company purchasing new production equipment with a seven-year expected life. The new equipment should increase the firm's cash flow in future years. The loan would then be repaid over seven years from the firm's yearly cash flow. Bank's long-term asset loans typically have maturities ranging between one and ten years.

Agricultural Loans

Agricultural loans are both short-term and long-term loans to farmers to finance farming activities. Although agricultural loans make up only 1 percent of all bank assets, they represent an important source of lending at many small rural banks. Small banks (< $100 million of assets) account for almost 60 percent of agricultural lending by all commercial banks. Short-term agricultural loans are generally seasonal and are made primarily to provide farmers with funds to purchase seed, fertilizer, and livestock. In making these loans, specialized knowledge of farm products is required, and the lending officer usually inspects the applicant's farming operation once a year.

Loans to Financial Institutions

Banks make loans to other financial institutions, such as their respondent banks, sales finance companies, savings and loan associations, and brokers and dealers in securities. These loans are usually made by large banks for a variety of purposes. Sales finance companies that engage primarily in comsumer installment lending obtain a large proportion of their funds from commercial banks. Large banks also lend to stock brokerage firms and dealers in U.S. government securities. Brokerage firms may extend credit to customers up to a certain percentage of the purchase price of the stock. These loans—called *margin loans*—are collateralized by the securities purchases.

Consumer Loans

Bank loans to individuals are known as *consumer loans.* Their maturities and conditions vary widely with the type of purchase. Maturities can be as short as one month or as long as five years for automobile loans. Longer-term loans, which are typically paid on an installment basis, are generally secured by the item purchased, as in the case of automobile loans. Shorter-term loans are usually single-payment loans.

Consumer loans account for about 12 percent of total bank assets and are an important source of lending for small retail banks. Commercial banks furnish approximately one-half of total consumer installment credit outstanding. Their emergence as a major supplier of consumer credit is a relatively new phenomenon. Prior to the 1930s, commercial banks were primarily engaged in business loans. It was in part the failure of banks to satisfy the growing demand for consumer credit that led to the emergence and rapid growth of consumer-oriented financial institutions such as finance companies, credit unions, and savings and loan associations.

Bank Credit Cards.   The first bank credit-card plan was started in 1951 by Franklin National Bank of New York. Early bank credit-card plans were local or regional in nature, were run by individual banks, did not provide revolving credit, and did not charge a membership fee. In 1958, revolving credit became a feature of bank credit-card plans. In 1966, the first nationwide card plan was started by Bank of America, using the name BankAmericard.

Before 1966, high start-up costs and the acceptance of credit cards only by merchants in the issuing bank's immediate area were obstacles to the growth and widespread use of credit cards. The advent of the nationwide clearing of bank-card slips as well as nationwide licensing of banks to issue credit cards was a turning point in the credit cards' development. These factors transformed local credit cards into national credit cards and made bank cards acceptable to a large number of merchants and consumers. Today, Visa (formerly BankAmericard) and MasterCard are the most widely known plans. Currently, more than 2 million merchants accept MasterCard, Visa, or both, and about 3,000 financial institutions issue the cards. The merchant who accepts a credit card pays a service charge ranging from 2 to 5 percent, depending on the average sale price and volume generated.

For the consumer, the holder of a credit card is guaranteed a credit limit at the time the card is issued. The dollar amount of the credit lines varies with the cardholder's income and employment record. In general, credit lines to individuals are limited to one month's income. The cardholder is entitled to purchase items up to the credit limit without prior approval of the bank. If the purchases are paid for in full within 25 days after the monthly billing by the bank, generally no interest is charged. However, the cardholder does not have to pay the full amount within the billing period and may elect to pay the balance off in installments. The bank sets a minimum monthly payment that must be paid. The interest charged for credit card installments usually varies between 1 and 2 percent per month (12 and 24 percent per annum) on the unpaid balance. The cardholder may receive the card free or may pay an annual membership fee of between $15 and $300, depending on the services the card offers to the cardholder. It is estimated that the annual maintenance cost to the bank for a credit card account ranges between $35 and $55. These costs escalate quickly with the high number of delinquent accounts or fraudulent credit card transactions.

Real Estate

Real estate loans account for 29 percent of banks' total assets. Mortgage loans finance the purchase, construction, and remodeling of both residential housing and commercial facilities. About two-thirds of all mortgage loans are for residential housing, and the remainder are for commercial and land development.

Mortgage loans are collateralized by the real estate they finance. They are long-term loans with an average maturity of about 25 years, but maturities may vary between 10 and 30 years. Historically, mortgages had a fixed interest rate, with borrowers paying the loans back in fixed monthly installments. In recent years, more mortgage loans have been variable-rate mortgages (VRMs), in which the interest rate and monthly payments vary with a market index, usually within a prescribed range. The amount of down payment affects the interest rate charged on a mortgage loan. Higher down payments reduce the risk of loss to the mortgage holder in the event that the home must be repossessed for the owner's failure to make mortgage payments or for some other breach of the contract. Down payments range from 10 to 30 percent of the purchase price.

The 1980s were a particularly turbulent period for real estate lending. High interest rates, two back-to-back recessions (1980 and 1982), the increasing use of variable-rate financing, and declining property values led to a sharp increase in mortgage foreclosures in the mid-1980s. For example, in 1981 there were 1.8 foreclosures per 1,000 mortgages, and by 1985 the figure had jumped to 2.5 per 1,000. Since 1985, mortgage foreclosures have declined for most of the country. However, the late 1980s and early 1990s have seen a continuing crisis in commercial real estate lending. Large banks have suffered the most from bad commercial real estate loans.

Loan Pricing

Because most of a bank's assets are loans, loan pricing is one of the most critical decisions made by a bank manager. There are three important facets of loan pricing. First, the bank must earn a high enough interest rate on the loan to cover the costs of funding the loan, whether the funds are from deposits, money market securities, or the capital accounts. Second, the rate on the loan must be sufficient to cover the administrative costs of originating and monitoring the loan. Finally, the loan's interest rate must provide adequate compensation for the credit (or default) risk, liquidity risk, and interest rate risk generated by the loan. Of course, the primary concern in loan pricing is the borrower's credit risk.

The Prime Rate

Historically, the role of the prime rate has gone through an evolution. In its earliest stage, the prime rate served as a benchmark, or base rate, on short-term business and agricultural loans and was the lowest loan rate posted by commercial banks. At that time, the prime rate was the rate banks charged their most creditworthy customers, and all other borrowers were typically quoted rates at some spread above prime, depending on their risk. In the 1970s and 1980s, banks would make loans below prime to firms that had the opportunity to obtain cheaper funds in the commercial paper market.

Recently, the role of the prime rate has been changing. Over the last 15 years, fewer loans have been priced using the prime rate as a benchmark. While the prime is still used as a benchmark for certain types of consumer loans, its use in business and agricultural lending has declined. Now, borrowers choose from among several other benchmark rates when obtaining loans. A common alternative benchmark for large corporate borrowers is the London Interbank Offer Rate (LIBOR), which is the price of short-term Eurodollar deposits. Other popular alternatives include Treasury rates or the bank's certificate of deposit (CD) rate. Despite the declining role of the prime rate as a benchmark for loan pricing, the popular media continue to use it as a barometer of conditions in the nation's money markets because banks are the major suppliers of commercial credit in the economy.

The Origins of the Prime   Following the collapse of the U.S. economy in 1929, interest rates declined to very low levels (see Exhibit 13-4). By 1933 the demand for business loans was so slack that commercial banks feared that interest rates would decline below their cost of funds. Congress and the Federal Reserve System shared this fear and were eager to revitalize the commercial banking system, especially by limiting "excessive" competition within the industry. As a result, banks introduced the $1\frac{1}{2}$ percent prime rate, which was considered to be the minimum return on lending after adjusting for administrative costs. The new and widely imposed floor on loans soon became an accepted feature of bank lending.

Setting the Prime Rate.   Determining the prime rate is one of many decisions large banks must make in managing their asset and liability holdings. Though the prime rate is an administered rate—set by individual banks—it is nonetheless ultimately determined by the market forces of supply of and demand for credit in the economy. That is, because banks set the prime rate to equalize their loan demand with the supply of available funds, the rate represents the price that bank management perceives will clear the market. The major market forces that determine the prime rate are:

$$\overset{+\quad+\quad+}{PR = f(CF, RI, CP),} \tag{13-1}$$

where:

$$PR = \text{prime rate};$$
$$CF = \text{cost of funds for the bank};$$
$$RI = \text{return on investments};$$
$$CP = \text{commercial paper rate}.$$

In setting the prime rate, bankers pay close attention to their cost of funds. For large banks, negotiable certificates of deposit (CDs) and Federal Funds borrowed are

PEOPLE & EVENTS

Penn Square Bank: Oil Fever Bank Failure, or How to Drink Beer from a Boot

The Penn Square Bank failure is certainly one of the most colorful in American banking history. The story begins in 1977 at a sleepy little shopping-center bank in Oklahoma City next to Shelly's Tall Girl Shop. Back then, the chairman of the bank, "Beep" (for B.P.) Jennings hired Bill Patterson, a 28-year-old assistant cashier from First National Bank of Oklahoma City. Patterson had no special credentials except the fact that Beep had known him for years and he was married to a daughter of the president of the First National Bank of Amarillo, Texas. More important, however, Jennings had five daughters and Bill was the son Jennings never had.

In short order, "son" Bill became senior vice president in charge of the oil and gas lending division. Since Jennings spent most of his time as a big civic booster, Patterson was given free reign to run the oil and gas division, often vetoing decisions made by his own loan committee and ignoring the low oil and gas reserves estimates of Penn Square's engineers. Under Patterson, the bank made lots of energy loans. When deals got too big, as they often did, the bank would invite bigger banks to participate. Unfortunately, shoddy paperwork and less than full disclosure characterized many of the bank's 3,000 energy-related loans. However, the bank's aggressive go-go approach to business seemed to work. During Beep's eight-year stewardship, the bank's assets increased 15 times to $525 million, making Penn Square the fourth largest bank in Oklahoma.

Patterson's knack for swinging oil deals was matched by his skill at wooing "upstream" correspondent banks to help finance them. Where he acquired these skills is unclear. At the University of Oklahoma, from which he graduated in 1973, Bill was nicknamed "Monkey Brain." In more sober banking circles, his style was eccentric, characterized more by guts than by judgment. Consider his penchant for closing big deals by guzzling beer out of his custom-made cowboy boots. On other occasions, Bill stunned customers and bank employees alike by strolling into work dressed in full hobo regalia, including holes in his shirt. Once he even marched in wearing a Nazi helmet emblazoned with swastikas. His favorite headgear, however, was reported to be a Mickey Mouse hat. Bill also lived with gusto. He engaged in food fights in some of the best restaurants in New York and Chicago and threw T.V.s from his hotel room on occasion. On one rather boisterous night in Chicago, he reportedly leaped from the cab he was riding in and pulled his pants down to "moon" the Continental Illinois Bank building.

Though banking with Bill was a heck of a lot of fun, all good things must come to an end. During 1982, oil prices dropped sharply, jeopardizing many of the bank's speculative oil loans. Carl W. Swan, one of the bank's biggest borrowers, had hit more dry holes than there were jackrabbits in the Texas-Oklahoma oil fields. With numerous dry holes and low proven oil reserves on too many loans, the bank's financial condition began to unravel as the bank's customers scrambled to get their money. Then, on July 5, 1982, the comptroller of the currency closed the bank. Left holding the empty boot, so to speak, with more than $2 billion in purchased loans, were Chase Manhattan, Continental Illinois, Northern Trust Company of Chicago, Seattle First National Bank, and Michigan National Bank, whose managers should have known better.

important sources of funds. Banks with international offices may attract Eurodollar deposits as a source, too. All other factors held constant, the higher the cost of bank funds, the higher the prime rate. The return on investments such as Treasury and municipal securities also affects the prime-rate decision; clearly, the higher the return

Exhibit 13–4   **The Prime Rate and the Commercial Paper Rate (1930–1990)**

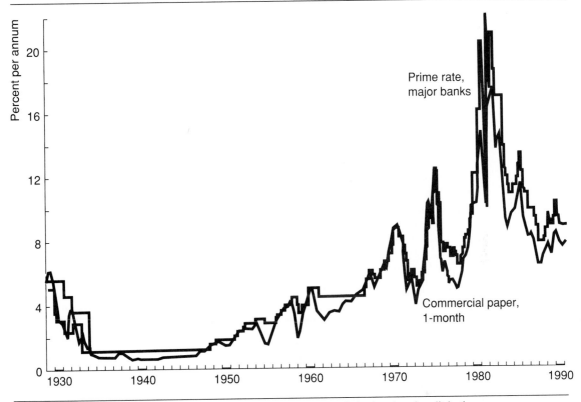

The prime rate is the lowest rate posted by commercial banks and is the wholesale price of credit in the economy.

Source: Board of Governors of the Federal Reserve System, *1989 Historical Chart Book* and The Federal Reserve Bulletin, various issues.

on investment assets, the higher the prime rate. Finally, the prime rate is also affected by the interest rates on alternative sources of borrowing for prime-rate customers. Large corporations of the highest credit standing do not have to borrow from banks; they can finance directly by selling their own IOUs in the commercial paper market. The commercial paper rates can run up to three or more percentage points below the prevailing prime rate. Thus the lower the commercial paper rate, the greater the downward pressure on the prime rate.

Historically, prime rate changes were infrequent, as shown in Exhibit 13–4. Beginning in the mid 1960s, movement became more frequent. A number of factors contributed to this phenomenon. Probably most important was the high and persistent rate of inflation, which in turn caused interest rates to become volatile and to move to record-high levels. Because of this, banks received a great deal of criticism from both the public and politicians for "setting interest rates." To help dampen this criticism, in October 1971 Citibank of New York City announced it was moving to a formula, or floating, prime rate; other large banks soon followed suit. Though formulas varied, a typical one included a spread of about $1\frac{1}{2}$ percentage points above the average cost of commercial paper in the preceding three weeks. Thus a three-week average commercial paper rate of 10 percent would bring a prime rate of $11\frac{1}{2}$ percent. The purpose of the formula prime rate was to demonstrate that the prime rate was ultimately determined by market forces and to show the linkage between it and market rates of interest. Today banks use the prime-rate formula as an indicator of the direction of prime rate changes rather than a precision rate-setting instrument.

Prime-Rate Loan Pricing

Most banks have adopted a loan-pricing procedure of setting a base interest rate for their most creditworthy customers and then using this rate as the markup base for loan rates to all other customers. The base rate is the prime rate. The prime rate includes the bank's administrative costs and a fair return to the bank's shareholders. The markups include three adjustments. The first is an adjustment for increased default risk above the prime-rate risk class. This risk assignment is determined by the bank's credit department. The second is an adjustment for term to maturity. Most bank business loans are variable rate, the rate varying with the bank's posted prime rate. Thus, as the prime is raised or lowered by the bank, the customer's loan rate is adjusted accordingly. If the customer wants a fixed-rate loan for a certain maturity period, say one year, the bank will adjust the variable-rate loan rate (short-term base rate) by an amount consistent with the current market yield curve (e.g., the Treasury yield curve). Finally, an adjustment is made that takes into account the competitive factor—a customer's ability to borrow from alternative sources. If, for example, a loan officer believes the customer has an alternative source of cheaper funding such as the commercial paper market, the bank may lower the rate to keep the customer's business. The greater the competition, the lower the loan rate. Expressed mathematically, the loan rate to a particular bank customer is:

$$r_L = PR + DR + TM, \tag{13-2}$$

where:

r_L = individual customer loan rate;
PR = bank's prime rate of interest (the base rate);
DR = adjustment for default risk above prime-rate customers;
TM = adjustment for term to maturity.

For example, a bank's prime rate is 10 percent and two customers—a small firm and a large firm—want loans. Both firms are considered medium-grade credit risks and carry a 200-basis-point penalty above the prime rate. The large firm is well known nationally, has sold commercial paper on occasion, and wants a floating-rate loan. The smaller firm wants a one-year fixed-rate loan. The bank's money market manager reports that one-year Treasury securities sell for 75 basis points above a three-month Treasury bill. Given this information, the bank's loan-pricing scheme may be as follows:

Pricing Factor	Small Firm	Large Firm
Prime rate	10.00%	10.00%
Default risk adjustment	2.00	2.00
Term-to-maturity adjustment	0.75	0.00
Competitive factor adjustment	1.00	0.00
Loan rate	13.75%	12.00%

The large firm's more favorable borrowing rate is due in part to the competitive factor—the intensity of competition from other banks or alternative, nonbank borrowing sources such as commercial paper.

Below-Prime Lending.   In the past it was commonly believed that the prime rate was a bank's lowest lending rate. In recent years, however, the competitive factor has led to the widespread bank practice of below-prime lending. Below-prime customers are usually large, financially sophisticated customers who have access to the commercial paper market or the Eurocurrency market. These borrowers do not seek customer relationships, so a loan to them is more like pure financing. The conventional borrower, on the other hand, needs the advice and counsel of a bank and has fewer borrowing alternatives. The majority of below-prime loans are made by large money-center banks because many of their customers borrow money in wholesale amounts ($1 million or more) and have access to the commercial paper market. According to a survey conducted by the Federal Reserve's Board of Governors, during the first week of November 1982, over 92 percent of all short-term business loans granted by the nation's 50 largest banks were at rates below prime.

Nonprice Adjustments.   Banks can also make nonprice loan adjustments to alter the effective loan rate. The most common of these are changes in compensating balances. *Compensating balances* are minimum average deposit balances that bank customers must maintain at the bank, usually in the form of noninterest-bearing demand deposits. Compensating balances—usually about 10 percent of the amount of outstanding loans—also encourage borrowers to use other services of the bank and raise effective loan rates. As an example, assume that a firm has a $100,000 line of credit at an 8 percent rate of interest that requires a 10 percent compensating balance. If the firm borrowed the maximum amount ($100,000) for one year, it would have to maintain $10,000 in a deposit account with the bank. Since the firm has only $90,000 ($100,000 − $10,000) available to use during the year, the annual effective rate of interest is 8.9 percent ($8,000/$90,000), rather than the stated nominal rate of 8 percent ($8,000/$100,000).

Other methods of adjusting the effective loan rate without altering the nominal rate include reclassifying borrowers from lower to higher credit-risk classes (carrying higher loan rates), increasing the amount of collateral (lowering the default risk), and changing the maturity of the loan (moving along the yield curve). Finally, the ability of banks to adjust the effective loan rate and other aspects of the customer relationship explains why the prime rate tends to be more inflexible, or "sticky," than other short-term interest rates.

Matched-Funding Loan Pricing

One way that banks can control the interest rate risk of fixed-rate loans is through matched funding of loans. Matched funding means that fixed-rate loans are funded with deposits or borrowed funds of the same maturity. If, for example, a bank makes a one-year fixed-rate loan, it might fund the loan with a one-year CD. Assuming that the cash inflows from the loan match the cash outflows on the CD, the bank is able to reduce interest rate risk because if interest rates change, the rate on the loan and the CD change by approximately the same amount since they have the same maturity.

The loan rate on a matched-funded loan is determined by adding a spread to the interest rate on the funding source:

$$r_L(t) = BR(t) + AC + DR + \pi, \tag{13-3}$$

where:

$r_L(t)$ = the interest rate on a loan with t years to maturity;
$BR(t)$ = the base rate, which is the interest rate on the funding source, which has a maturity equal to the loan maturity (t years);
AC = administrative costs of making the loan;
DR = adjustment for default risk;
π = competitive return to the bank's shareholders.

All other things constant, the loan rate will be higher, the higher the administrative costs and the default risk of the borrower. As in prime-rate pricing, banks must adjust loan rates for the customer's ability to obtain a loan from other sources. Also, the bank's managers must provide a fair return to the bank's shareholders. This formulation is similar to that for prime-rate pricing, except that the prime rate already includes administrative costs and the return to the bank's shareholders.

Analysis of Loan Credit Risk

One of a lending officer's major tasks is to analyze a customer's creditworthiness —that is, to determine a customer's default risk premium. Credit analysis determines whether or not a loan should be granted and to which credit-risk category a customer should be assigned. Of course, in making loans, it is illegal for banks to discriminate on the basis of sex, race, religion, or marital status; only economic factors can be considered.

In attempting to quantify a customer's default risk characteristics, banks typically analyze the five Cs of credit:

1. Character (willingness to pay),
2. Capacity (cash flow),
3. Capital (wealth),
4. Collateral (security),
5. Conditions (economic conditions).

Character reflects a borrower's integrity, credit history, and past business relationship with the bank. Basically, banks want to lend to persons who want to repay their debts. *Capacity* analyzes a borrower's projected income statements or cash flow generated from a job. *Capital* looks at a borrowers' balance sheet or residual wealth (e.g., stock or land ownership). *Collateral* refers to assets that can be taken by the bank and liquidated if a loan is not repaid. Finally, *conditions* refers to economic conditions at the time of the loan and a borrower's vulnerability to an economic downturn or credit crunch.

Once the five Cs are analyzed, a customer is assigned to a credit-rating category. The default risk premium for each category is determined from an analysis of the bank's credit losses over several business cycles. For example, a bank with five credit categories may develop the following loan-pricing scheme:

Credit Category	Default Risk Premium
1	Prime-rate customers
2	10 to 50 basis points
3	50 to 100 basis points
4	100 to 200 basis points
5	Reject credit

Exhibit 13–5 shows graphically a bank's loan-pricing scheme in a risk–return framework. The higher a borrower's credit risk, the higher the loan rate. At some point, however, potential borrowers become too risky, and the bank will refuse to grant them credit. Bank lending officers who set their default risk premiums too low will eventually lose their jobs as the bank's loan losses exceed the expected loan loss

Exhibit 13–5   Loan Pricing in a Risk–Return Framework

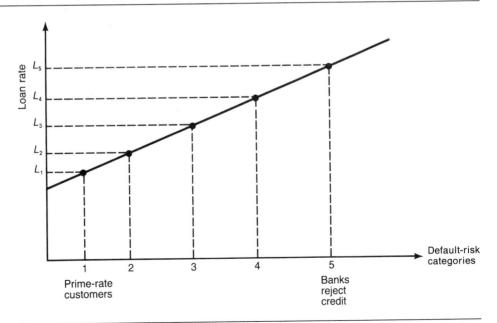

Banks analyze each loan and each customer's default risk, then assign the customer a credit ranking. Those with the best credit standing pay the prime rate; those that are riskier pay a higher rate.

rate, particularly during periods of severe economic downturn. It you don't believe these things happen, you need only ask the unemployed and "early retired" senior lending officers at Continental Bank or Sam Armacost, the former president at Bank of America. Both Banks incurred very heavy credit losses during 1984 and 1985, and many senior lending officers and officials suffered the consequences.

Pricing Bank Deposits

Because most of a bank's funds come from deposits, another critical decision of bank managers is how to determine the interest rates offered to depositors. Before the 1980s the pricing of deposits was neither a challenging nor imaginative management problem. Banks were not even permitted to pay interest on demand deposits until 1980 and the advent of NOW accounts. Further, Regulation Q set ceilings on the interest rates banks could pay on savings deposits until it was phased out in 1986. Because interest rates in the money markets exceeded the regulatory ceiling, banks had to offer rates equal to the ceiling to slow the process of disintermediation.

Since the deregulation of the 1980s, however, the pricing of deposits has been a much more interesting and difficult function of bank managers. The pricing of deposits is a complex process, but here are two factors to consider. First, the bank must offer a high enough interest rate to attract and retain deposits. If, however, it offers a rate so high that it squeezes the spread between the average return on assets and the average cost of liabilities, then the bank's profitability suffers. Second, in banking markets with intense competition, this problem is compounded. To meet competition, banks may not only have to lower rates charged on loans, but also have to increase rates paid on deposits. Thus, under extremely competitive conditions, bank managers should recognize that they ultimately have little control of deposit rates (or loan rates, for that matter) over the long run.

Why is the competition for deposits so intense? From the perspective of a depositor with less than $100,000, all deposit accounts look pretty much the same because they are insured by the FDIC; that is, the deposits are risk free. Accordingly, depositors will put their money where it will earn the highest return, all other things, such as service charges on accounts or loan relationships, held constant. Also, banks have to offer rates that are competitive with money market mutual funds. For deposits greater than $100,000, banks must compete not only with other banks, but also with other money market instruments. The money market will price large, negotiable certificates of deposit in line with the riskiness of the bank's loan and investment portfolios, given that these large CDs are uninsured. Essentially, all CDs that represent a given level of risk are close substitutes for one another in the money market and therefore must offer similar rates.

There are times when banks may price deposits above or below competitive market rates. If, for example, a bank is aggressively growing, it may offer higher-than-market rates to penetrate a new market. Such banks will attempt to make loans or sell fee-based services to new depositors in attempting to cover the higher cost of funds. On the other hand, a bank with few profitable loan or investment opportunities may lower deposit rates below market to reduce liability costs.

Fee-Based Services

Our examination of the balance sheet of a commercial bank has given us a great deal of insight into its business activities. However, some activities in which commercial banks engage are not easily classified, and they do not readily show up in balance-sheet summary accounts. Some of these services are performed directly by banks and others by subsidiaries of bank holding companies. The income from these activities comes in the form of fees rather than interest payments. In the 1980s and 1990s, banks have shifted away from the traditional services of deposit-taking and lending toward providing fee-based services. These fee-based services are subject to less interest-rate, credit, and liquidity risk and provide more stable income to banks during uncertain conditions in the economy and the financial markets.

Correspondent Banking

Correspondent banking involves the sale of bank services to other banks and to nonbank financial institutions. Correspondent banks typically act as agents for respondent banks in check clearing and collection, purchase of securities, purchase and sale of foreign exchange, and participation in large loans. Traditionally, correspondent services are sold in packages of services, with payment being made by the respondent bank holding noninterest-bearing compensating balances with the correspondent bank. For example, investing a $100,000 compensating balance from a respondent bank at 12 percent would generate $12,000 gross income for the correspondent bank. If the bundle of services the respondent receives has a fair market value of $12,000, then both parties should be satisfied. In recent years, a trend has developed to unbundle correspondent services and to pay a direct fee for each service. This trend is particularly true in the area of computer and bookkeeping services.

Correspondent banking is not a recent development; it was a common practice in this country by the 1800s. It is unique to the United States, however, and derives its origin from the structure of our financial system. In the United States there are more than 12,000 banks, most of them relatively small and operating only one office. These banks find it either impossible or inefficient to produce certain types of services needed by their customers.

Though informal in nature, the structure of correspondent banking is highly complex. Small rural banks often maintain correspondent relationships with five or more larger banks in regional financial centers. Regional financial-center banks maintain correspondent balances with 30 or more banks in national financial centers as well as with banks in other regional financial centers. The center of American correspondent banking is New York City. This is because New York is the nation's financial center, with its short-term money markets, foreign exchange markets, and long-term capital markets. Almost every important bank in the world maintains an operating office in New York, and almost every large bank in the United States maintains a correspondent relationship with at least one large bank in that city. Chicago is the second most important correspondent banking city.

The most important service that correspondent banks provide today is still check clearing and collection. Most banks, particularly nonmember banks, prefer clearing their checks through local or regional correspondent banks rather than through the Federal Reserve network of clearinghouses. One reason for this is that the correspondent banks often give immediate credit for cash items in the process of collection, whereas the Federal Reserve may withhold credit for up to two days, depending on the respondent bank's location. In addition to check clearing, correspondent banks often participate in loans arranged by respondents. The respondent bank may want outside help with some loans because demand outstrips regional supplies of funds or because the loan exceeds the bank's legal lending limit. Loan participation also helps respondents diversify their loan portfolios and reduce overall risk on their loans. Correspondent banks also provide electronic data processing for deposit accounts, installment loans, and payrolls. They provide investment and trust department advice, prepare reports on economic and financial market conditions, and allow respondent banks to participate in their group insurance and retirement programs. Correspondent banks buy and sell government securities, foreign exchange, Federal Funds, and other financial securities for respondent banks. They may also serve as clearinghouses for job applicants, assist in forming holding companies or opening new branches, or help respondents find sources of equity capital or other long-term funds.

Bank Leasing

In recent years, leasing has been a fast-growing area of business for commercial banks, particularly large banks. The impetus for bank entry into leasing was provided by a 1963 decision by then comptroller of the currency James Saxon to allow national banks to purchase property upon a customer's request and lease it to a customer. Since then, almost every state allows state-chartered banks to enter into lease-financing arrangements.

The main economic justification for leasing is taxation. When the lessee is in a lower tax bracket than the lessor (e.g., bank), leasing an asset becomes a viable alternative to borrowing and purchasing the asset. This is because with a leasing arrangement, the bank may get a larger tax deduction than the lessee and may pass part of it along to the lessee as a discount on lease payments. Banks enter into leasing because the rate of return on leasing activities is comparable (after risk adjustment) to that earned on bank lending. Leasing is viewed by most bankers as an extension of their commercial lending activities.

The market for lease equipment is quite large, and it is estimated that leasing and equipment financing account for about 25 percent of the total annual expenditures on equipment. In the United States, banks and their leasing affiliates are making major inroads into these markets. Bank leasing activities for large banks involve big-ticket items, such as commercial aircraft, ocean-going tankers, computers, and nuclear generators for utilities. Other items leased by both large and small banks include office equipment, automobiles, trucks, and machinery. The majority of bank leasing actitivies are with business firms, although the leasing of automobiles to individuals is gaining in popularity. Many bank holding companies have started or purchased equipment-leasing companies and the majority of the nation's 100 largest banks are engaged in equipment leasing. Furthermore, large correspondent banks have been increasingly involving their respondent banks in leasing activities. As these smaller banks gain knowledge of the methodology and techniques of leasing, it is likely that many will enter the leasing markets in the near future. This is because there appear to be no notable economies of scale in the leasing industry. Thus the only significant barrier to entry is knowledge and expertise in the field.

Trust Operations

Banks have been involved in trust operations since the early 1900s. Currently about one-fourth of all banks offer trust services to their customers. Trust operations involve the bank's acting in a fiduciary capacity for an individual or a legal entity, such as a corporation or the estate of a deceased person. This typically involves holding and managing trust assets for the benefit of a third party. Equity investments constitute about two-thirds of the total assets of bank trust departments. Banks administer these securities rather than own them. By law, banks are not allowed to own equity securities for their own accounts.

Banks with large trust departments tend to be large institutions located in national or regional financial centers. The largest bank trust operations are those of J. P. Morgan, Citibank, Chase Manhattan, and Bankers Trust, all located in New York City. Small banks may offer trust services to their customers through correspondent relationships with large banks. Exhibit 13-6 shows the ten largest bank trust departments.

Nearly one-half of all trust assets are managed for individual accounts. This frequently involves the settlement of estates. The trust assures that the terms and conditions of the will are fulfilled, sees that claims against the estate are settled, and manages the assets of the estate during the interim period. Banks also administer personal trusts for those not wishing or unable to undertake this responsibility for

Exhibit 13-6   Largest Commercial Bank Trust Departments (Year-end 1988)

Rank	Bank	Trust Income (millions)	Total Operating Income (millions)	Income as Percentage of Operating Income
1	J. P. Morgan, New York	$453.3	$ 7,839.4	5.8
2	Citicorp, New York	450.3	32,024.0	1.4
3	Chase Manhattan, New York	358.8	12,322.1	2.9
4	Bankers Trust, New York	321.5	5,851,3	5.5
5	State Street, Boston	292.8	896.8	32.6
6	Bank of New York	263.3	2,620.4	10.0
7	Mellon Bank, Pittsburgh	261.0	3,256.0	8.0
8	Northern Trust, Chicago	206.8	1,003.1	20.6
9	Chemical Banking Corp., New York	182.9	7,644.0	2.4
10	PNC Financial Corp., Pittsburgh	173.3	3,827.2	4.5

Large banks sell their trust services directly in addition to marketing them to smaller banks through their correspondent divisions. Morgan Guaranty Bank of New York City (the nation's fifth largest bank) has by far the largest bank trust department.

Source: American Banker: Statistical Special, 1990.

themselves. Examples of this situation would be children unable to care for an estate or a beneficiary considered to be a "spendthrift" by the originator. Banks usually follow conservative investment practices in managing personal trusts.

The second largest group of trust assets managed by banks are for pension funds. Bank pension-fund holdings account for nearly four-fifths of all pension fund assets. Bank trust departments also perform functions other than managing or investing assets. They frequently act as transfer agents, registrars, dividend disbursement agents, and coupon and bond payment agents for corporations. They also serve as bond trustees, seeing that the conditions of the bond contract are carried out by the issuer on the behalf of the bondholders.

Off-Balance-Sheet Banking

During the past decade, there has been a substantial increase in what is called off-balance-sheet banking at large U.S commercial banks. Examples of off-balance-sheet transactions are commercial loan sales (loan brokerage) and standby letters of credit. These activities have the common feature of separating, or unbundling, the traditional services associated with bank lending, such as credit information gathering, credit risk evaluation, and the funding of the loan. By separating a loan's funding from these other activities, a bank can earn fee income without the risk associated with putting an asset or corresponding liability on its balance sheet.

Standby Letters of Credit.   A *standby letter of credit* (*SLC*) is a contractual agreement issued by a bank that involves three parties: the bank, the bank's customer, and a beneficiary. In an SLC transaction, the bank acts as a third party in a commercial transaction between the bank's customer and the beneficiary by substituting the bank's creditworthiness for that of its customer. Thus, if the bank's customer fails to meet the terms and conditions of the commercial contract, the bank guarantees the performance of the contract as stipulated by the terms of the SLC. The bank's obligation under an SLC is a contingent liability, because no funds are advanced unless the contract is breached by the bank's customer and the bank has to make good on its guarantee.

Traditionally, most SLCs are used as backup lines of credit to support commercial paper offerings, municipal bond offerings, and direct loans such as construction lending. Newer applications for SLCs, such as for mergers and acquisitions, are emerging. An example of an SLC transaction would be a corporation who needs to finance inventory for three months and decides to obtain the money through the sale of commercial paper with an SLC rather than through a commercial bank loan. The SLC guarantees principal and interest payments to investors who buy the commercial paper in the event that the corporation defaults on its obligation. The SLC is payable only upon presentation of evidence of default or nonperformance on the part of the corporation. As such, most SLC's expire unused. A study by the Federal Reserve Board found that in 1978, only 2.03 percent of the SLCs outstanding defaulted, and bank losses were much smaller because 98 percent of payments due were ultimately recovered from the defaulting firms.

The benefit to a firm purchasing an SLC is that it reduces the firm's borrowing cost. In general, firms will purchase SLCs whenever the cost of the SLC is less than the discounted present value of the interest cost savings resulting from the purchase of the

SLC. The size of the interest cost savings will depend on the creditworthiness of the issuing bank relative to the firm purchasing the SLC, as well as the relative costs of obtaining information about the creditworthiness of each. For example, an SLC issued by a bank with a poor credit rating is not likely to be worth much, because its probability of defaulting on the SLC is high. Likewise, an SLC issued by a small, unknown bank of good credit standing may have little value, because the cost to the beneficiary of gathering information and evaluating the bank's creditworthiness may be high. As a result, most SLCs are issued by large, well-known banks of the highest credit standing.

In recent years, the market for SLCs has grown rapidly. SLCs soared from $11.7 million in 1970 to $175 million in 1985, but since then the growth rate has slowed somewhat. Several factors have contributed to the growth in SLCs. First, the growth in direct financing has increased the credit-risk exposure of investors who may prefer not to bear such risk. Firms have increasingly turned to direct financing, such as commercial paper, because they can obtain funds at a lower cost than through intermediary financing such as bank loans. However, this decline in financial intermediation has meant that the undiversified investors in such markets must bear more credit risk than if they were to invest their funds in deposit liabilities of commercial banks. The second reason that the use of SLCs has grown is that the overall economic risk in the economy has increased substantially since the mid-1970s. Rampant inflation of the late 1970s, two back-to-back recessions in the early 1980s, and volatile interest rates during the period have caused wide swings in the price of financial assets and returns on investment. Consequently, the demand for SLCs and guarantees that reduce risk have increased. Finally, because of a trend toward higher capital standards by bank regulators and because SLCs were initially excluded from capital requirements, banks had incentives to expand such activities in lieu of placing loans on the banks. In contrast, the size of a bank's loan portfolio is constrained by the amount of the bank's capital.

Loan Brokerage.   Banks have always sold commercial loan participations to other banks and have entered into syndicated loan agreements when a loan was too large for any single bank. Recently, however, large commercial banks have, to an increasing extent, originated loans with a view to selling them or offering participations. When acting as a loan broker, banks typically negotiate large loans through their credit departments and then sell participations to various investors, including thrifts, life insurance companies, pension funds, and other banks. Although most loan sales are business loans, some banks, with the aid of investment bankers, have structured sales of automobile loans, credit card receivables, and home mortgage loans. Exhibit 13–7 shows the ten banks that sell the most loans.

Most commercial loan sales are structured contractually as participations so that the selling bank maintains a creditor–debtor relationship with the borrower. This means that the selling bank continues to be responsible for servicing the loan, enforcing the loan covenants, monitoring the financial condition of the borrower, and handling workouts and other problems that might arise in the event of default. The bank does all of this so that it can collect origination and service fees by advancing credit to an established customer. The fees for the services are collected in the form of a "spread," which is the difference between the rate paid by the borrower to the bank

Exhibit 13–7   **The Top Ten Banks in the Sale of Loans during Second Quarter, 1989**

Rank	Bank	Total Assets, June 1989 ($ millions)	Loans Sold during Quarter ($ millions)
1	Security Pacific, Los Angeles	56,036	110,465
2	Bankers Trust, New York	58,715	44,801
3	Chase Manhattan, New York	82,014	18,169
4	Citibank, New York	152,777	18,070
5	Chemical Bank, New York	48,471	12,208
6	Mellon Bank, Pittsburgh	23,242	9,095
7	Morgan Guaranty, New York	76,685	6,326
8	Marine Midland, Buffalo	21,310	5,340
9	Continental Bank, Chicago	31,750	4,882
10	Manufacturers Hanover, New York	57,126	4,787

Banks sell loans to reduce the amount of their assets subject to capital requirements and to generate fee income from loan origination and servicing fees. These activities reduce the bank's credit, interest-rate, and liquidity risk while increasing fee income.

Source: American Banker, Top Numbers, 1990.

and the return promised to the purchaser of the loan. Typically, spreads average 15 basis points if the loan is sold without recourse.

Current bank regulations require that a loan sold with recourse (the issuing bank's guarantee against default) be treated as an asset; as a result, the bank must hold capital against the loan, and the proceeds from selling the loan are subject to reserve requirements. Thus, most bank loans are sold without recourse. To insure both the quality of the loans sold and satisfactory monitoring after the sale, purchasers will typically require the selling bank to retain a portion of the loan for its accounts. Furthermore, banks that are repeatedly in the brokered loan market realize that their future earnings as brokers depends on honest dealing.

There are several reasons, besides earning fee income, that a bank may want to broker loans. First, loan sales permit banks to invest in and diversify across a different set of loans than they originate and service. Second, a bank may sell loans because it has a competitive advantage in booking certain types of loans and, therefore, can use the funds from loan sales to fund additional similar loans. Finally, banks may sell loans to avoid burdensome regulatory taxes. Specifically, the argument is that banks have a comparative advantage in originating loans, but they are at a disadvantage in keeping loans on their books because of bank regulations. This disadvantage stems from the regulatory tax that banks must pay in the form of federal deposit premiums, forgone interest from holding required reserves, and mandatory capital requirements that exceed those that would be maintained in the absence of regulations. Thus, firms not subject to stringent banking regulations have a comparative advantage in holding loans on their balance sheet.

Securitization.   Banks have become increasingly involved in the securitization of loans in the 1980s and 1990s. The securitization process begins with banks segregating loans into relatively homogeneous pools with regard to the maturity and type of loan. These pools of loans are then transferred to a trust, which then, with the help of an underwriter, sells securities (usually called certificates) backed by the loans to ultimate investors. The originating bank usually provides some form of credit enhancement (financial guarantees similar to those discussed in Chapter 9), which pays promised cash flows to the ultimate investors in the event of default. Also, securitized issues are typically rated for default risk by one of the major rating agencies. Exhibit 13–8 illustrates the typical securitization process.

Exhibit 13–8   The Structure of a Typical Asset Securitization

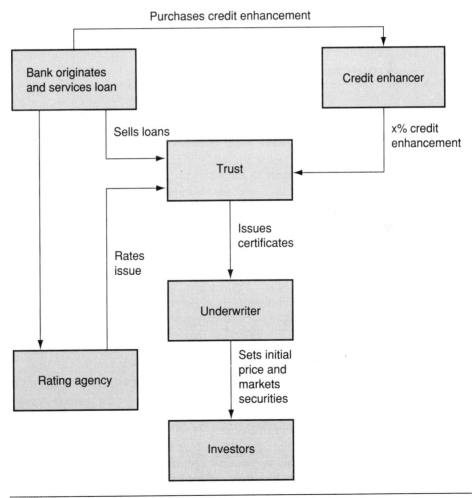

In a securitization, banks sell loans to a trust that issues securities backed by the loans. Not only does securitization improve a bank's capital and liquidity positions, but it also allows banks to generate fee income.

Asset securitization has grown dramatically in the 1980s and 1990s. While the market for residential mortgage-backed securities is the largest segment of the securitized asset market, accounting for nearly $770 billion in 1988, other types of loans, such as consumer credit card receivables, automobile loans, boat loans, commercial real estate loans, home equity loans, and student loans are increasingly securitized. The market for securities backed by consumer loans (other than mortgages) is growing the most rapidly, accounting for $140 billion in 1989.

Securitization offers several benefits to banks. First, by selling rather than holding loans, banks reduce the amount of assets and liabilities, thereby reducing reserve requirements, capital requirements, and deposit insurance premiums. Second, securitization provides a source of funding loans that is less expensive than other sources. Finally, banks generate fees from the securitization process. Banks collect origination fees and loan-servicing fees, and recently banks have been permitted to underwrite securitized issues. Thus banks can also collect underwriting fees in the securitization process.

Summary

Commercial banks, like other private businesses, aim to maximize the long-term profits of the firm's owners. Bank profits are derived principally from interest income earned on lending operations and security investments. While attempting to maximize profits, banks are subject to a number of operating restrictions, many of which are unique to commercial banking.

The balance sheet of a commercial bank is a statement showing what the business owns (assets), what it owes to creditors (liabilities), and what the owners have invested (capital) as of a given date. An examination of a bank's balance sheet tells us something about its operations and highlights important distinctions between small and large banks.

For most banks, the principal source of funds is deposit accounts. These funds are payable on demand or have very short maturities, and the owners of such accounts are insured by the FDIC against any loss up to $100,000. Historically, banks had a deposit monopoly over demand deposits until the DIDMCA of 1980 allowed thrifts and credit unions to offer NOW accounts and share drafts on a nationwide basis. Competition for depositors' transactions deposits is now far more intense than it was just a few years ago.

Over half of the funds obtained by banks are utilized in making a wide variety of loans. Loans are personalized contracts between the bank and its customers. The terms are tailor-made to meet the financing needs of the borrower. The lowest loan rate posted at banks is called the prime rate. Though set by banks, the prime rate is ultimately determined by the market forces of supply of and demand for credit in the economy.

Banks also hold large portfolios of investment securities. Short-term investments, such as Treasury securities, afford banks a source of income while also providing liquidity. Long-term securities, such as municipal bonds, are held for their higher after-tax returns. Cash assets are held to provide banks with immediate liquidity and to meet legal reserve requirements. Because cash assets earn no interest, banks keep their cash holdings to a minimum.

Questions

1. What is the primary goal of a commercial bank? Why may this goal be translated into maximizing the firm's stock share price?
2. Why are demand deposits a more important source of funds for small banks than for large banks? Why are demand deposits considered to be a more stable source of funds for small banks than for large banks?
3. Why are negotiable CDs and Federal Funds primarily sources of funds for very large banks?
4. Define *bank capital*. What is the economic importance of capital to a firm?
5. What are the important differences between investments and loans in a bank portfolio of assets?
6. Give the reasons banks hold Treasury securities and municipal bonds in their investment portfolios.
7. Explain why banks buy and sell Federal Funds. Also explain the role of the Federal Reserve System in the Federal Funds market. Show the T-accounts for a Federal Funds transaction.
8. Define *correspondent banking*. Why do banks enter into correspondent relationships?
9. What is the prime rate? Why do some banks make loans below the prime rate?
10. What are the major benefits of getting assets "off the balance sheet" through either loan sales or securitization?

Selected References

Becketti, Sean, and Charles S. Morris. "Loan Sales: Another Step in the Evolution of the Short-term Credit Market." *Economic Review.* **Federal Reserve Bank of Kansas City, pp. 22–31.**
Examines the increase in loan sales by commercial banks and discusses the effect of these sales on the safety and soundness of banking.

Berlin, Mitchell. "Bank Loans and Marketable Securities: How Do Financial Contracts Control Borrowing Firms?" *Business Review.* **Federal Reserve Bank of Philadelphia, July/August 1987, pp. 9–18.**
This interesting article explains the theory (agency theory) of how financial contracts restrict the behavior of borrowers. Applying agency theory, the article also shows the similarities and differences between bank loans and market security contracts.

Boemio, Thomas R., and Gerald A. Edwards, Jr. "Asset Securitization: A Supervisory Perspective." *Federal Reserve Bulletin,* **October 1989, pp. 659–669.**
The authors discuss the benefits of securitization to banks. They also examine the concerns that regulators have about the rising tide of securitization.

Gilbert, Alton R. "Requiem for Regulation Q: What It Did and Why It Passed Away." *Economic Review.* **Federal Reserve Bank of St. Louis, February 1986, pp. 22–37.**
An examination of Regulation Q from its inception in the 1930s to the steps to phase it out beginning in 1980. An excellent article.

Garcia, Gillian, and Annie McMahon. "Regulatory Innovation: The New Bank Accounts." *Economic Perspective*. Federal Reserve Bank of Chicago, March–April 1984.
A discussion of the new bank accounts that followed the DIDMCA of 1980 and their effect on money market mutual funds.

Johnson, Sylvester, and Amelia A. Murphy. "Going on the Balance Sheet." *Economic Review*. Federal Reserve Bank of Atlanta, September/October 1987, pp. 23–35.
Examines a number of off-balance-sheet activities that have emerged in recent years, such as standby letters of credit, futures contracts, securitization of loans, and swaps.

Keeton, William R., and Charles S. Morris. "Why Do Banks' Loan Losses Differ?" *Economic Review*. Federal Reserve Bank of Kansas City, May 1987, pp. 3–21.
Loan losses have risen significantly at many commercial banks during the last several years. The article examines why problem loans have varied greatly between banks.

Koch, Timothy W. *Bank Management*. Fort Worth, TX: The Dryden Press, 1992.
Chapters 20–24 discuss commercial bank lending and Chapter 27 covers bank trust operations. The lending chapters are particularly good. Chapter 25 provides an excellent discussion of securitization.

Koppenhaver, G. D. "Standby Letters of Credit." *Economic Perspectives*. Federal Reserve Bank of Chicago, July/August 1987, pp. 28–38.
This article examines standby letters of credit, which allow a bank to generate fee income without putting an asset or corresponding liability on its balance sheet.

Laderman, Elizabeth. "The Changing Role of the Prime Rate." *Weekly Letter*. Federal Reserve Bank of San Francisco, July 13, 1990.
The use of the prime rate as a benchmark in the pricing of commercial loans has declined. This article examines the history of the prime rate and examines why it is less frequently used.

Pavel, Christine. "Would You Buy a Car Loan from This Bank? " *Chicago Fed Letter*. Federal Reserve Bank of Chicago, May 1989.
This article provides an excellent, understandable overview of the securitization process.

Pavel, Christine, and Paula Binkley. "Cost and Competition in Bank Credit Cards." *Economic Perspectives*. Federal Reserve Bank of Chicago, March/April 1987, pp. 3–13.
Discusses the economics and cost structure of the credit card industry.

Sinkey, Joseph F., Jr. *Commercial Bank Financial Management in the Financial Services Industry*. New York: Macmillan, 1992.
An advanced text that provides excellent coverage of all facets of bank management. The discussions of credit risk, liquidity risk, and interest rate risk are outstanding.

Zimmerman, Gary C., and Jonathan A. Neuberger. "Interest Rate Competition." *Weekly Letter*. Federal Reserve Bank of San Francisco, July 27, 1990.
This article points out that interest rates on money market mutual funds and money market deposit accounts have been diverging in the late 1980s.

BANK MANAGEMENT AND PROFITABILITY

A PIVOTAL EVENT THAT WILL influence bank management practices through the 1990s and beyond was the collapse in 1984 of Continental Illinois Bank. Public announcements of millions of dollars of losses resulting from bad domestic oil loans panicked depositors and creditors large and small, domestic, and international into a run on the bank. The seventh largest bank in the nation was brought to the threshold of failure. Only after direct government support, massive injection of funds by the Fed, and an infusion of additional capital did the run stop. Although the bank was technically saved from failure, the debacle brought about a wide-scale reexamination of the management practices of large money-center banks.

The theme of this chapter is bank management's quest for profits. However, profits must be earned without sacrificing bank safety; that is, adequate liquidity and adequate capital must be maintained. Further, banks must manage interest rate risk to protect the liquidity and capital positions. An understanding of the interrelationships among these important concepts is essential to the proper management of a bank. When a bank's safety becomes endangered, the consequences can be disastrous —as was the case of Continental Illinois. The major topics covered in this chapter are asset and liability management strategies for bank liquidity, GAP management and interest rate risk, reserve position management, bank profitability, and the management of bank capital.

A Banking Dilemma: Profitability versus Safety

As profit-maximizing firms, commercial banks can increase profits by taking on more credit risk, interest rate risk, or liquidity risk, all of which jeopardize bank safety. Bank safety means that the bank survives as a going concern—staying in business. For a bank to survive it has to balance the demands of three constituencies: shareholders, depositors, and bank regulators. If stockholders believe a bank is too risky, they may become dissatisfied with management and sell their stock, driving the bank's stock price lower and making it costly for the bank to raise new capital for growth. If depositors (especially uninsured ones) become concerned with the amount of risk a bank takes, they may remove their demand deposits or not renew their certificates of deposit, creating a liquidity crisis for the bank. If bank regulators believe that the actions of managers are imprudent, they may intervene in the management of the bank, or at the extreme, revoke the bank's charter. Of course, bank managers can avoid these potential problems by taking very little risk, but then the bank would not be very profitable and in the long run it would likely not survive. In this section we discuss the trade-offs faced by bank managers in balancing profitability against liquidity and solvency.

Bank Solvency

As discussed in the previous chapter, the capital-to-total-assets ratio for a commercial bank is about 6 percent, which is low compared to other types of businesses. What are the managerial implications of commercial banks having such low capital-to-assets ratios? First, it means that the owners provide only 6 percent of the money to purchase the bank's total assets. The remaining 94 percent of the funds are furnished by the bank's creditors. Second, and more important, a slight depreciation in the value of the bank's assets could make it insolvent. A firm is *insolvent* when the value of its liabilities exceeds the value of its assets; the firm is legally bankrupt. For example, if a commercial bank invests all of its funds in Treasury bonds that fall in price by 6 percent, the bank becomes bankrupt. Thus, given commercial banks' extremely low capital position, they are vulnerable to failure if they accept excessive credit risk or interest rate risk.

Bank Liquidity

Another risk facing commercial banks is that of inadequate liquidity. *Bank liquidity* refers to the bank's ability to accommodate deposit withdrawals and pay off other liabilities as they become due. Normally, some depositors will be withdrawing funds or writing checks and others will be adding to their deposit accounts. On some occasions, however, a large number of depositors withdraw their funds simultaneously, such as occurred periodically before the 1930s. If a bank has insufficient funds to meet its depositor's demands, it must close its doors. Banks fail, therefore, because they are unable to meet their legal obligations to depositors and other creditors.

The Dilemma

Commercial banks can fail in two ways. First, a bank can become insolvent by suffering losses on its assets or investment portfolio (i.e., credit risk or interest rate risk), resulting in a depletion of its capital. Second, a bank can be a profitable business operation but fail because it cannot meet the liquidity demands of its depositors (i.e., liquidity risk). The greater a bank's expected deposit variability, the greater the proportion of liquid assets the bank should hold. Exhibit 14-1 summarizes the profitability versus safety dilemma facing bank management.

Reconciling the Dilemma.   The central problem for bank management is reconciling the conflicting goals of solvency and liquidity on the one hand and profitability on the other. Unfortunately, it is a set of conflicts not easily resolved. For example, liquidity could be achieved by holding only Treasury securities. In this strategy, bank management would sleep well but eat poorly because profits would be low. At the other extreme, the bank could shift its asset portfolio into high-yielding,

Exhibit 14–1   **Profitability Goal versus Liquidity and Solvency**

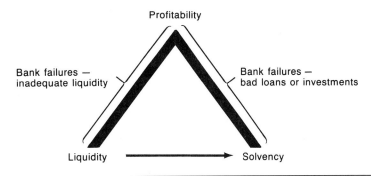

The goal of bank management is to maximize the value of the firm. However, higher profits must not be achieved at the expense of bank safety.

high-risk loans at the expense of better-quality loans or liquid investments. Bank management would eat well temporarily because of increased profits but would sleep poorly because of the possibility of a bank failure later on caused by large loan losses or inadequate liquidity. Finally, bank liquidity is ultimately related to bank solvency. That is, most bank runs are triggered by depositors' and other creditors' expectations of extraordinary losses in the bank's loan or investment portfolios.

We now turn our attention to how banks attempt to solve the problem of maximizing profits while maintaining adequate liquidity and capital. We begin with how banks manage their liquidity.

Liquidity Management

We now examine current bank strategies for maintaining sufficient liquidity and solvency while maximizing overall bank profits. The strategies discussed in the previous section emphasized the asset side of the balance sheet. Perhaps one lesson learned from the past is that reliance on a single source of liquidity is risky, be it shiftable, short-term securities or anticipated income from loans.

Several important developments in bank liquidity practices have taken place since the 1960s. The first is asset management, which is a codification of previous theories. The second is liability management—acquiring liquidity from the liability side of the balance sheet. In practice, of course, banks obtain liquidity from both sides of the balance sheet.

Asset Management

A commercial bank requires liquidity to accommodate deposit withdrawals or to pay other liabilities as they mature. Payment of withdrawals can be made only from assets. All cash accounts (except CIPC) are available to the bank for payment of immediate withdrawals at no cost to the bank. All other assets must be converted into cash assets.

The conversion process involves the time and expense to sell the assets as well as the risk that they may be sold below their purchase price (a capital loss or price risk).

We can draw the following general conclusions when examining the assets held by commercial banks: (1) Investment securities are more liquid than bank loans because of their superior marketability, and (2) short-term investments are more liquid than long-term investments because of the smaller price risk. Let us see how bank management uses these conclusions in asset management. Asset management strategy classifies bank assets into four basic groups: primary reserves, secondary reserves, bank loans, and investments for income and tax shields.

Primary Reserves.   Primary reserves are the cash assets on a bank's balance sheet. They consist of vault cash, deposits at correspondent banks, and deposits held at the Federal Reserve banks. Primary reserves are immediately available at no cost to the bank to accommodate deposit withdrawals. However, because they yield no interest, banks try to minimize their holdings of primary reserves.

Secondary Reserves.   Secondary reserves are short-term assets that can be converted quickly into cash at a price near their purchase price. Their main purpose is to provide the bank with additional liquidity while safely earning some interest income. Treasury bills and short-term agency securities make up the majority of the bank's secondary reserves. Because the securities that compose secondary reserves are highly marketable and have low default risk, they typically have yields below the yields of loans and other investment securities held by the bank.

Bank Loans.   After the bank has satisfied its unexpected needs for cash, bank management can concentrate on its primary business—making loans to business firms and individuals. Business loans are generally less liquid and riskier than other bank assets and, as a result, typically carry the highest yield of all bank assets and offer the greatest potential for profit.

Investments.   The funds remaining after the bank has satisfied its loan demand are then available for open market investments. The primary function of the investment portfolio is to provide income and tax advantages to the bank rather than liquidity. Open market investments are typically longer-term securities that are less marketable and have higher default risk than secondary reserves. These investments therefore offer greater income potential to the bank. Investments for income include long-term Treasury securities, municipal bonds, and agency securities. Banks usually prefer to hold municipal instead of corporate bonds because they offer a higher after-tax yield.

The Proper Asset Mix.   The proportion of liquid assets a bank should hold brings us back to the dilemma between bank profitability and liquidity. The greater the proportion of primary and secondary reserves the bank holds, the greater the liquidity of its portfolio. Unfortunately, highly liquid assets that are low in default risk typically have low interest returns. Overall bank strategy, then, is to hold the minimum amounts of primary and secondary reserves consistent with bank safety. Exhibit 14–2 shows assets commonly held in bank asset management strategy and the liquidity –yield trade-off that bank management must make. The table provides a useful review of the concepts involved in asset management.

Exhibit 14–2   **Summary of Asset Management Strategy**

Category and Type of Asset	Purpose	Liquidity	Yield
Primary Reserves Vault cash Deposits at the Fed Deposits at other banks	Immediately available funds	Highest	None
Secondary Reserves Treasury bills Federal Funds sold Short-term agency securities	Easily marketable funds	High	Low
Bank Loans Business loans Consumer loans Real estate loans Agricultural loans	Income	Lowest	Highest
Investments Treasury securities Agency securities Municipal bonds	Income when safe loans are unavailable and tax advantages	Medium	Medium

To maintain adequate liquidity, banks hold both primary and secondary reserves. Secondary reserves allow banks to earn some interest income while still meeting their liquidity needs.

The total amount of primary and secondary reserves that a bank holds is related to deposit variability, other sources of liquidity, bank regulations, and the risk posture of the bank's management. Deposit variability is often determined by examining past deposit behavior, particularly in regard to deposit inflows and outflows. Deposit variability also depends on the type of account and bank customer. For example, demand deposits typically are more variable than time deposits.

Liability Management

The 1960s marked the beginning of a new era in bank liquidity practices. Previously it was believed that liquidity came almost entirely from the asset side of the balance sheet. Liability management argues that banks can use the liability side of their balance sheets for liquidity. Historically, banks had always treated their liability structure as a fixed pool of funds, at least in the short run. Bank asset holdings were tailored to the deposit variability characteristics of their liabilities. Under liability management, however, banks target asset growth as given and then adjust their liabilities as needed. Thus, when a bank needs additional funds for liquidity or any other purpose, it merely buys the funds in the money markets.

Liability Management Theory.   Liability management is based on the assumption that certain types of bank liabilities are very sensitive to interest rate changes. Thus, by raising the interest rate paid on these liabilities above the market rate, a bank can immediately attract additional funds. On the other hand, by lowering the rate paid on these liabilities, a bank may allow funds to run off as the liabilities mature.

Bank liabilities employed in liability management are negotiable certificates of deposit (CDs), Federal Funds, repurchase agreements, commercial paper, and Eurodollar borrowings. These securities are sensitive to interest rates, and have markets large enough to accommodate the activities of the commercial banking system. Other bank liabilities, such as savings accounts or demand deposits, are not as interest rate sensitive, and changes in the posted offering rate will not result in notable *immediate* inflows or outflows of funds. Long-term debt and bank capital are not appropriate for use in liability management because of the time it takes to bring these securities to market.

Using Liability Management.   The liquidity gained by liability management is useful to a bank in several ways. First, it can be used to counteract deposit inflows and outflows and reduce their variability. Sudden or unexpected deposit outflows can be offset immediately by the purchase of new funds. Second, funds attracted by liability management may be used to meet increases in loan demand by the bank's customers. Customers need not be denied loans because of a lack of funds. As long as the expected marginal return of the new loans exceeds the expected marginal cost of funds, the bank can increase its income by acquiring the additional funds through liability management.

Consider the following example. A bank needs additional funds because of a sudden decrease in deposits or a sudden demand for loans. Under traditional asset management, the bank would sell Treasury bills or some other money market securities to obtain the needed funds. In contrast, using liability management, the bank could buy Federal Funds, issue negotiable CDs, or borrow in the Eurodollar markets to obtain the funds. If the bank decided to finance the loan with Fed Funds, it would have to reborrow the money on a daily basis, since Federal Funds are one-day loans. Financing loans with one-day money does expose the bank to interest rate risk, since it does not know precisely what the cost of the funds will be from one day to the next.

Summary.   Liability management supplements asset management but does not replace it as a source of bank liquidity. Asset management still remains the primary source of liquidity for banks, particularly smaller banks. If used properly, liability management allows banks to reduce their secondary reserve holdings and invest these funds in higher-yield assets, such as loans or long-term municipal bonds. Liability management is not well suited to smaller banks, because they do not have direct access to the wholesale money markets where liability management is practiced.

Liability management is not a panacea for bank liquidity problems. There may be times when banks are unable to attract or retain funds through liability management because of tight credit periods or because of uncertainty about the soundness of a particular bank. Because of some large bank failures in recent years, lenders have become particularly sensitive to the issue of bank safety. This was the case for First Pennsylvania (1980) and Continental Illinois (1984); both banks experienced financial difficulties and found themselves unable to sell their negotiable CDs or other money market liabilities.

Management of Reserve Requirements

Banks are required by law to maintain minimum reserves equal to a percentage of their deposits and designated nondeposit liabilities. The percentage varies with the deposit size of the bank and the types of deposits. Banks' legal reserves are deposits at their district Federal Reserve bank and/or cash in their own vaults.

Accounting for Reserves

Before the 1980 Depository Institutions Deregulation and Monetary Control Act (DIDMCA), banks operated under a *lagged reserve accounting system.* Under this system, banks knew at the beginning of each reserve period exactly the amount of reserves they were required to maintain. The DIDMCA changed the way banks compute their required reserves. The dollar amount of reserves a bank must hold is now based on a *contemporaneous reserve accounting system.* Under this procedure, reserves are posted two days after a two-week reserve computational period. Thus bank management does not know the exact dollar amount of reserves until the last day of the two-week reporting period. Needless to say, banks must watch their reserve position closely as they approach the end of a reporting period.

Reserve Requirements and Liquidity

Reserves permit banks to accommodate deposit withdrawals immediately and at very little conversion cost. The total reserves held by a bank at any given time consist of reserves required by law and voluntary reserves in excess of required reserves. The total dollar reserves held by a bank may be expressed as follows:

$$R = RR + ER, \tag{14-1}$$

where:

R = total bank reserves;
RR = reserves required by law;
ER = excess reserves.

To understand how reserves provide liquidity and why banks elect to hold voluntary excess reserves, the following examples will be useful. First, assume that there are *no* legal reserve requirements. Bank A, our example bank, has decided to hold non-interest-bearing reserves (R) equal to 10 percent of its deposits (D). This decision is based on the bank's past deposit behavior. Funds that are not held as reserves are invested in earning assets (EA). If Bank A has \$1,000 in deposits, its initial balance sheet condition is shown in T-account (a):

(a)		(b)	
Assets	**Liabilities**	**Assets**	**Liabilities**
\$ 100 *R*	\$1,000 *D*	\$ 50 *R*	\$950 *D*
900 *EA*		900 *EA*	
\$1,000	\$1,000	\$950	\$950

The bank's total reserves are $100 (0.10 × $1,000), and the balance ($900) is invested in earning assets.

Now let Bank A experience a deposit drain of $50. The bank can fully accommodate the withdrawal because its reserves of $100 are more than the amount withdrawn [see (b)]. Notice that the amount of earning assets remains unaffected. For the bank to return to the desired reserve position of 10 percent of deposits, it may employ either asset or liability management. If asset management is used, the bank will sell $45 of its earning assets, probably Treasury securities. The speed of the adjustment will depend on the liquidity of the assets to be sold. The less liquid the assets, the longer the time for the bank to return to its desired reserve position. Using asset management, Bank A's eventual equilibrium position is shown in T-account (c). Notice that the bank is again in reserve equilibrium with total reserves equal to $95 (0.10 × $950). Notice also that the bank's earning assets are reduced to $855, resulting in a loss of income.

	(c)		(d)
Assets	**Liabilities**	**Assets**	**Liabilities**
$ 95 *R*	$950 *D*	$ 95 *R*	$950 *D*
855 *EA*		900 *EA*	45 *FF*
$950	$950	$995	$995

If Bank A is large enough to have access to liability management, it could alternatively borrow the funds from the money markets or obtain a temporary loan from the Federal Reserve discount window. If, for example, Federal Funds (*FF*) are borrowed, the bank can adjust almost immediately to the balance sheet position as shown in T-account (d). Because there are no legal reserve requirements on Federal Funds, Bank A needs to borrow only $45 to be at its desired reserve level. Also, notice that by using liability management, the bank has no need to reduce its earning assets, as was the case for asset management.

Now let's assume that the bank is *required* by law to hold 10 percent reserves at all times. If the bank is in its initial balance sheet position, it is apparent that the bank has no liquidity on the asset side of the balance sheet even though it holds $100 in reserves. This situation is shown in T-account (e):

(e)	
Assets	**Liabilities**
$ 100 *RR*	$1,000 *D*
0 *ER*	
100 *R*	
900 *EA*	
$1,000	$1,000

The bank's excess reserve (*ER*) balance is zero. The $100 reserves are no longer legally available to pay out for deposit withdrawals. The use of required reserves (*RR*) would make the bank deficient, incurring an interest rate penalty and the possible involvement of bank regulatory authorities in the bank's internal affairs. For example, if Bank A does not have access to liability management, a $30 withdrawal would force

DID YOU KNOW?

Free Wine and Cheese on the 47th Floor with Your Private Banker

Okay, so you keep $100 minimum balance in your account, you've never bounced a check, and all of your friends have opened their accounts at your bank because of you. You're a model customer, warmly greeted by desk officers and tellers when you walk in the door. Sometimes you swap sports stories with the head loan officer. That means that the next time you leave town for a few days, you can ask your banker to water the plants and walk the dog, right? Wrong!

This privilege still belongs only to private banking customers, who can readily get not only their dogs walked but also get free tax advice, financial planning, and vault storage for their clean laundry. There's more. For example, after passing through the rich walnut doors of BankAmerica's 47th floor private bank offices with a panoramic view of San Francisco, there are no teller lines, no broken ATMs, and no surly tellers. Instead, your personal private banker offers you wine and cheese while you look at old masters' works of art. If you need a $1 million mortgage, it will be approved in a day's notice, and a large business loan may be approved in a matter of a few days. Service is not limited only to financial matters. At Bank of San Francisco, private bankers lend a hand (actually a racquet) when clients need a doubles partner for tennis. A Wells

Fargo private banker actually sent a sympathy card when a customer's hamster died. Bank policy prohibited the officer from taking a day off for mourning.

Private banking is a European tradition rooted in the Renaissance, when bankers devoted much of their time to the accounts of wealthy merchants. In the United States, banks such as J. P. Morgan provided private banking services to rich industrialists as long as 130 years ago. Today, it's still tough to qualify for private banking services. You need to earn at least $250,000 a year and have a net worth of $1 million. Typically you'll pay a high annual fee, usually $1,000 or more. If you dip below the minimum balance, usually $100,000, you'll be charged a stiff penalty. All this is done to weed out the undesirables. And forget about earning a high yield on your checking account; the bank keeps most of the interest in exchange for the tax-free services they are providing to you.

Do you qualify? If so, check out the Bank of America, Wells Fargo Bank, Chemical Bank, or Harris Trust. You may be on your way to London on the Concorde, returning via the QEII, all at a steep discount—compliments of your private banker. But, as one private banking customer said, "it's not really the services that matter, it's the rich and famous people you meet on the 47th floor."

---

it to sell $30 in earning assets. The assets must be sold immediately, even if they are liquidated at a loss, or the bank will be deficient. The less liquid the earning assets, the more costly the adjustment.

Our example illustrates two important points. First, required reserves do not provide liquidity. On the asset side of the balance sheet, immediate liquidity is provided by excess reserves. Second, surprising though it may seem, transforming voluntary reserves into legal reserves reduces banks' liquidity by reducing the amount of reserves available for withdrawal. Thus an increase in reserve requirements by regulatory authorities decreases the liquidity of the banking system. It must be understood, however, that required reserves do, in emergencies, provide liquidity to banks. For example, if bank management has incorrectly estimated the bank's liquidity needs, rather than fail because of unexpected withdrawals, it can dip into its legal reserves and satisfy the deposit withdrawals. The bank is deficient and management is penalized by the regulatory authorities instead of the bank failing and the depositors being penalized. Thus, bank safety is maintained and depositors are unaffected by management's error in judgment.

Bank Capital Management

Both bank management and regulators are concerned about banks maintaining adequate amounts of capital. Bank capital performs several important roles. First, it provides a financial cushion that enables banks to continue to operate even if they suffer temporary operating losses. Second, adequate capital helps maintain public confidence in the soundness and safety of individual banks and the banking system. This role protects the U.S. economy against the destabilizing consequences of massive bank failures. Third, adequate capital provides some protection to depositors whose bank accounts are not fully insured. Finally, capital is a source of funds for the bank's growth and the addition of new products, services, or facilities.

To see how bank capital protects banks from failure that is due to unexpected asset losses, see Exhibit 14–3. This exhibit shows the financial position of two hypothetical $100 million banks before and after each charges off an amount equal to 6 percent of its assets because of write-downs on security values or defaults on loans. Bank A, with $10 million in capital (net worth) is able to absorb the $6 million write-off and still

---

Exhibit 14–3   **Effects of Bank Charge-offs on Bank Capital**

Bank A: Initial Status		Bank B: Initial Status	
Assets	Liabilities and Capital	Assets	Liabilities and Capital
Total assets $100 million	Deposits $90 million Capital $10 million	Total assets $100 million	Deposits $95 million Capital $5 million

Bank A: After $6 Million Write-Off		Bank B: After $6 Million Write-Off	
Assets	Liabilities and Capital	Assets	Liabilities and Capital
Total assets $94 million	Deposits $90 million Capital $4 million	Total assets $94 million	Deposits $95 million Capital −$1 million

The larger a bank's capital base, the larger the losses a bank can sustain and still stay in business.

have a net worth of $4 million. Its net worth is low, but it can still meet its legal obligations and continue to operate. However, Bank B cannot absorb $6 million write-off without becoming insolvent; its net worth becomes negative because its liabilities exceed its assets. As a result, it must go out of business. The $1 million deficit then will be borne either by uninsured depositors or the FDIC.

Definition of Bank Capital

In December 1981 the principal bank regulators adopted a common definition of what constitutes bank capital. In this definition, bank capital consists of two basic components:

Primary capital
Common stock (including retained earnings)
Perpetual preferred stock
Loan loss reserves
Debt items with a mandatory conversion to common stock
Secondary capital
Subordinate notes and debentures
Sinking-fund preferred stock

Typical capital ratios (CR) used to evaluate a bank's capital adequacy are:

$$CR_P = \frac{\text{Primary capital}}{\text{Total assets}}$$

or:

$$CR_T = \frac{\text{Total capital}}{\text{Total assets}},$$

where total bank capital is the sum of primary and secondary capital.

Notice that the regulatory definition of bank capital includes debt. In the economic sense, debt is *not* capital; operating losses cannot be written off against debt. The practice of allowing certain types of debt to count as equity began in the 1960s with the Office of the Comptroller of the Currency (OCC). The procedure was initiated to bolster sagging overall capital ratios for the banking industry. The practice soon led to regulatory guidelines that permit banks to maintain up to one-third of their total capital in the form of debt with an original maturity in excess of seven years.

Trends in Bank Capital

In the early 1970s, bank regulators and public officials became concerned about the erosion of key capital ratios (see Exhibit 14-4). Their concern was heightened by the failure of several large banks in 1973 and 1974 and again during the early 1980s following two back-to-back recessions. The debate over capital adequacy focuses on how much bank capital is necessary to provide a stable and safe banking system. Although opinions differ as to the amount of capital that provides reasonable protection, there is agreement that the capital ratios of the banking system have declined appreciably since the 1960s. Exhibit 14-4 shows that CR_T declined from 8 to

Exhibit 14–4   **Ratio of Total Capital to Total Assets for Insured Commercial Banks**

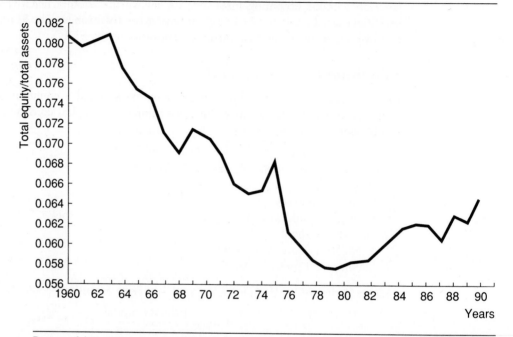

Because of the large number of bank failures in the 1980s, bank regulators have pressured banks to increase their capital positions.

Source: FDIC annual reports, 1960–1974; *Bank Operating Statistics*, 1975–1987; *Quarterly Banking Profile*, 1987–1990.

$6\frac{1}{2}$ percent from 1960 to 1974. The decline in bank capital is partly attributable to the unparalleled economic prosperity of the 1960s and early 1970s, which caused banks' assets to grow rapidly while their capital grew more slowly. After the 1974 recession, when bank regulators began to pressure banks to improve their capital positions, the ratio of bank capital to assets rose slightly for several years. However, the ratio began to decline sharply as the economy expanded once again.

Beginning in the 1980s, capital adequacy once more became an issue with bank regulators. Though the number of bank failures was less than 10 per year as recently as 1979, the number of failures reached record numbers in the 1980s, with 118 banks failing in 1985 and more than 200 in 1987. Given this environment, bank regulators started increasing bank capital requirements in a series of steps beginning in December 1981. The current capital adequacy standards, which were adopted in May 1985, require a ratio of minimum primary capital to total assets of 5.5 percent, and a ratio of minimum total capital to total assets of 6 percent.

New Capital Guidelines

On December 10, 1987, the central banks of the major industrial countries published a sweeping proposal assessing the capital adequacy of international banks resulting in the 1988 Basel accord.[1] The central banks reached this agreement as part of an effort to coordinate bank supervisory policies, with the goal of strengthening the international banking system and alleviating competitive inequities. The new guidelines define capital uniformly across all nations, apply risk weights to all assets and off-balance-sheet exposures, and set minimum levels of capital for international banks.

In the United States, the effort to develop a risk-based capital measure began in 1985. Of concern was the rapidly growing risk exposure of large money center banks stemming from their off-balance-sheet activities. For example, standby letters of credit issued by the ten largest bank holding companies had increased from 7.6 percent of total assets in 1981 to more than 12 percent by 1985. Likewise, interest rate swaps, first introduced in 1981, had increased to more than 14 percent of total assets by 1985. Neither of these or other off-balance-sheet activities were factored into existing U.S. capital guidelines, which focus on balance sheet assets.

The basic purpose of the new capital guidlines is to relate a bank's capital to its risk profile so that high-risk activities require relatively more bank capital. In making capital ratio calculations, for example, bank assets such as loans will be weighted 100 percent of their value. Less risky assets such as long-term Treasury securities will be weighted at 25 percent, short-term Treasury securities will carry a weight of 10 percent, and cash will carry no weight (zero percent) at all. Likewise, off-balance-sheet assets that carry high risk exposure to the bank, such as standby letters of credit, sales and repurchase agreements, and loan sales with recourse, are weighted 100 percent. Other off-balance-sheet items, such as commercial letters of credit, currency interest rate swaps, and interest rate options purchased are weighted 50 percent or less. The new capital standards are to be implemented in two stages: an interim risk-based capital ratio target of 7.25 percent, which took effect in 1990, and a minimum of 8 percent which took effect in 1992.

In 1992, the FDIC proposed capital guidelines much more stringent than those in the Basel accord. The FDIC acted to implement provisions of sweeping reforms enacted by Congress to stem the bank and thrift failures of the late 1980s and early 1990s. These guidelines specify five levels of capital adequacy that will determine the severity of bank regulation. As capital declines, regulators will be able to clamp down harder on bank activities. The new capital requirements are not only based on the risk-based capital ratios described above, but also on "Tier 1" capital and the so-called "leverage ratio." Tier 1 capital is analogous to the primary capital-to-total assets ratio (CR_p) shown earlier in this section. The leverage ratio is similar to the total capital-to-total assets ratio (CR_T), also shown earlier. Exhibit 14–5 presents the five levels of capital adequacy and shows the number of banks in each category.

The regulatory implications of declining capital are severe. Critically undercapitalized banks are subject to being seized by the FDIC, the worst possible penalty. All banks in the undercapitalized categories must submit improvement plans to the FDIC within 45 days of falling below the minimum. The FDIC will also restrict the asset growth of undercapitalized banks. Banks in the significantly undercapitalized category could face caps on deposit rates, forced sale of subsidiaries, or the firing of bank

---

[1]The central banks that participated in the proposal are from the following countries: Belgium, Canada, France, West Germany, Italy, Japan, The Netherlands, Sweden, United Kingdom, United States, Switzerland, and Luxembourg.

Exhibit 14–5   **The 5 Capital Categories Proposed by the FDIC, 1992**

Critically Undercapitalized Banks currently in category: 70, with $27 billion in assets	2% or lower ratio of leverage capital (tangible equity to total assets)
Significantly Undercapitalized Banks currently in category: 56, with $13 billion in assets	Total capital lower than 6% or risk- based assets. Tier 1 capital lower than 3%, or leverage ratio lower than 3%
Undercapitalized Banks currently in category: 190, with $190 billion in assets	Total capital lower than 8% of risk- based assets. Tier 1 ratio lower than 4%, or leverage ratio lower than 4%
Adequately Capitalized Banks currently in category: 709, with $1.5 trillion in assets	At least 8% total capital to risk-based assets (including 4% Tier 1 capital) and 4% leverage ratio
Well Capitalized Banks currently in category: 11.224, with $2 trillion in assets	At least 10% total capital to risk-based assets (including 6% Tier 1 capital ratio), 5% leverage ratio, and not under a regulatory order to raise capital

---

Under the 1992 FDIC proposed capital guidelines, 316 banks would be considered undercapitalized.
Source: American Banker, June 24, 1992, "FDIC Proposes 2 Ways to Limit Realty Loans," pp. 1, 13.

executives. These banks could also be forced to fire the board of directors and elect new members.

Needless to say, the new guidelines provide a strong incentive to bank managers to maintain adequate capital. Many bankers complain, however, that they will be unduly hindered in competing with large foreign banks that only have to meet the less stringent risk-based capital standards of the 1988 Basel accord. Bankers and leading financial economists have stated that the new capital standards have hampered the ability of banks to make new loans, contributing to the early 1990s credit crunch and slowing the pace of recovery from the 1990s economic recession. We will further explore the motivations for and the implications of capital requirements in Chapter 16, "Regulation of Financial Institutions."

Bank Management versus Regulators

Views on the optimal level of bank capital often differ between bank regulators and bank management because they have different objectives. The primary goal of bank management is long-term profit maximization. Bank managers may believe that this can best be achieved if their banks are highly leveraged. On the other hand, bank regulators are more interested in the risk of bank failures in general than in the profits of an individual bank. Their overriding concern is the prevention of chains of bank failures—in which one failure generates others—with their disastrous effects on the economy. Thus, because of the enormous social cost of erring on the low side, bank regulators desire the higher capital standards that promote bank safety.

Managing Interest Rate Risk

The objective of bank management is the maximization of profits consistent with bank liquidity and capital constraints. Historically, the primary risk that bank management dealt with was default risk on loans. However, because interest rates have become more volatile in the last 15 years, interest rate risk has become a concern to both bank management and regulators. The risk of unexpected interest rate changes affects both sides of a bank's balance sheet and arises because of differences in the sensitivity of bank assets and liabilities to changes in market rates of interest.

To make a profit, banks must earn higher rates of return on their loans and investments (assets) than they pay out to attract deposits and other funds (liabilities). The essence of managing interest rate risk is to ensure that the bank will always be able to profit from the spread between their borrowing (and deposit) rates and their rates of return on investment, even if market interest rates change. The focus of interest rate risk management is first on measuring interest rate risk and next on innovating ways to control it. Before discussing these two issues, however, we first show how unexpected changes in interest rates affect the earnings of a commercial bank.

Effects of Changing Interest Rates on Commercial Banks

Recall from our examination of the typical bank balance sheet in Chapter 13 that most banks operate by using shorter-term deposits to fund longer-term (or fixed-rate) loans. This strategy takes advantage of the fact that long-term interest rates usually exceed short-term interest rates (that is, the term structure is usually upward-sloping) and earns the bank a positive spread, or net interest income. But the strategy exposes the bank to decreasing earnings when interest rates rise because the liabilities reprice before the assets, on average.

To illustrate the effects of changing interest rates (interest rate risk), let us examine what happens to the cash flows of a commercial bank that borrows short and lends long if interest rates increase. We use a simple example, which is given in Exhibit 14–6.[2] Suppose that a bank makes a one-year, single-payment loan at the beginning of the year. This loan has a face value of $1,000 and pays 9 percent interest; thus, at the end of one year the borrower pays the bank $1,090 ($1,000 principal plus $90 interest). The bank funds this loan by issuing a $500 denomination, three-month certificate of deposit (CD) with the idea of renewing the CD every three months over the life of the one-year loan. The bank funds the other $500 of the loan with a $500 denomination, six-month CD with the idea of renewing the CD every six months over the life of the loan. Initially the three-month CD pays 5 percent interest and the six-month CD pays 6 percent.

---

[2] This example is adapted from Jimmy Hilliard and Joseph F. Sinkey, Jr., "Duration Analysis as a Tool for Predicting Interest-Sensitive Cash Flows," *Journal of Financial Education*, Fall 1989.

Exhibit 14–6

Net Cash Flow from Funding a $1,000 Loan with a Three-Month CD and a Six-Month CD (Assuming No Change in Interest Rates)

Action	Elapsed Time (Months)				
	0	3	6	9	12
Cash Inflows					
Issue 3-month CD	$500	$506	$513	$519	
(Percent)	(5)	(5)	(5)	(5)	
Issue 6-month CD	500		515		
(Percent)	(6)		(6)		
1-year Loan					$1,090
Total cash inflow	$1,000	$506	$1,028	$519	$1,090
Cash Outflows					
1-year Loan	1,000				
(Percent)	(9)				
Pay off 3-month CD		506	513	519	525
Pay off 6-month CD			515		530
Total cash outflow	$1,000	$506	$1,028	$519	$1,055
Net cash flow = Total cash inflow − Total cash outflow	$0	$0	$0	$0	$35

After three, six, and nine months the bank must "roll over" the three-month CD. The six-month CD rolls over after six and 12 months. Thus, every three months the bank issues a new CD in an amount sufficient to pay off the principal and interest on the old CD. At the end of the first three months of the year, for example, the bank would issue one three-month CD of $506 [$500 × $(1.05)^{.25}$] to pay off the first three-month CD (see Exhibit 14–6). At the end of six months, the bank would issue another three-month CD to retire the second three-month CD and a six-month CD of $515 [$500 × $(1.06)^{.5}$] to retire the first six-month CD. Assuming that interest rates do not change over the year, Exhibit 14–6 shows that the anticipated net cash flow (that is, the loan repayment plus interest minus the amount required to pay off the last two CDs) from funding the one-year loan with a portfolio of three-month and six-month CDs is $35, or a net yield of 3.5 percent on an investment of $1,000 over the year. Notice that the 3.5 percent figure is the difference between the average yield on assets of 9 percent and the average cost of liabilities of 5.5 percent [(5 percent + 6 percent)/2].

What happens to the bank's net cash flow if immediately after making the loan and issuing the first batch of CDs, all interest rates in the market rise by 100 basis points, or 1 percent? The bank's cash inflows from the loan will not be affected because the loan is fixed-rate; assuming no default risk, the loan will pay $1,090 after one year. Unfortunately, the rates on three-month and six-month CDs will rise by 1 percent so that when they are rolled over, the bank's cost of funds increases. Exhibit 14–7 shows that the bank's anticipated net cash flow at the end of one year falls to $28 if interest rates rise by 100 basis points. It is easy to show that the bank's cash flows would have increased had interest rates declined.

Measuring Interest Rate Risk

In the preceding example, why did the bank's net cash flow decline when interest rates increased? Because the liabilities were shorter term than the assets (4.5 months on average versus 1 year), the liabilities *repriced* before the assets. Thus the cost of liabilities increased *faster* than the yields on assets with the interest rate increase; the liabilities were more *rate sensitive* than the assets. The rate sensitivity of bank earnings can be measured by the gap between the maturity or duration of assets and liabilities (hereafter referred to as GAP).

GAP Analysis: The Basics.   In a typical GAP management process, bank management divides all assets and liabilities on the balance sheet according to their interest rate sensitivity. An asset or a liability with an interest rate subject to change within a year is considered rate sensitive. One whose interest rate cannot change for more than a year is considered fixed. The GAP between rate-sensitive assets (RSA)

Exhibit 14–7

Net Cash Flow from Funding a $1,000 Loan with a Three-Month CD and a Six-Month CD (Assuming a 1 Percent Increase in Interest Rates)

	Elapsed Time (Months)				
Action	0	3	6	9	12
Cash Inflows					
Issue 3-month CD	$500	$506	$ 514	$521	
(Percent)	(5)	(6)	(6)	(6)	
Issue 6-month CD	500		515		
(Percent)	(6)		(7)		
1-year Loan					$1,090
Total cash inflow	$1,000	$506	$1,029	$521	$1,090
Cash Outflows					
1-year Loan	1,000				
(Percent)	(9)				
Pay off		506	514	521	529
3-month CD					
Pay off			515		533
6-month CD					
Total cash outflow	$1,000	$506	$1,029	$521	$1,062
Net cash flow =	$0	$0	$0	$0	$28
Total cash inflow −					
Total cash outflow					

and rate-sensitive liabilities (RSL) is defined as:

$$GAP = RSA - RSL. \tag{14-2}$$

The GAP can be expressed either as dollars or as a percentage of total earning assets. If RSA is greater than RSL, the GAP is positive; if RSA is less than RSL, the GAP is negative; and if RSA equals RSL, the GAP is zero. Exhibit 14–8 shows the rate-sensitive GAP for a bank balance sheet and identifies the most important rate-sensitive and fixed-rate financial instruments. For the balance sheet shown, the GAP = 50% − 20% = 30%.

Controlling the size of the GAP is an important decision that depends both on the degree of risk that a bank's management is willing to accept and on its forecast of

---

Exhibit 14–8   **Rate-Sensitive GAP for a Bank Balance Sheet**

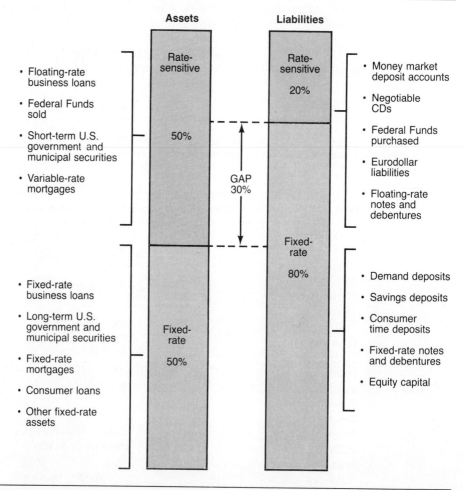

GAP management helps banks manage their interest rate risk exposure. The larger the GAP, the greater the risk exposure.

future interest rate movements. For example, assume that we are at the bottom of a business cycle and that interest rates are low and expected to rise. Under such circumstances, bank management would want a large positive GAP. The reason is that, given expected higher interest rates in the future, the bank wants to hold rate-sensitive assets in order to take advantage of future higher interest rates and to hold fixed-rate liabilities in order to lock in the current low interest rates—thus a positive GAP. On the other hand, at the top of the business cycle, when interest rates are high and expected to decline, a negative GAP is desirable. In this case the desired balance sheet portfolio consists of fixed-rate assets and rate-sensitive liabilities. Finally, if the bank's management wishes to minimize interest rate risk, a zero GAP is the desired portfolio strategy. In sum, the greater the GAP—either positive or negative—the greater the bank's exposure to interest rate risk.

The size of the GAP has a major influence on the volatility of bank earnings. If, for example, all variable interest rates changed by 1 percent, a 30 percent GAP would have a $9 million effect on the pretax earnings of a bank with $3 billion in assets. The size of a bank's GAP, then, varies with the bank management's expectations of future interest rates and the risk it is willing to take.

The tendency is for banks that are expecting higher interest rates to accept large positive GAPs and to plan to decrease the GAPs as interest rates turn down. However, because the demand for short-term (or variable-rate) loans is usually heaviest when interest rates are high, most banks cannot close the GAP when they want to. To overcome this problem, bank fund managers are increasingly turning to the use of financial futures contracts to hedge exposed asset and liability risk positions.

Maturity GAP Analysis.   The technique just discussed is maturity GAP analysis, probably the most widely used technique for assessing interest rate risk. It compares the value of assets that will either mature or be repriced within a given time interval to the value of liabilities that will either mature or be repriced during the same time period. It is possible to calculate *cumulative* GAPs for assets and liabilities due to be repriced during any period desired, such as one day, one week, one month, one quarter, six months, or one year. Large banks compute GAPs on a daily basis, whereas smaller banks often compute monthly GAPs.

In addition to cumulative GAPs, a financial institution may wish to compute *incremental* GAPs. Incremental GAPs show how much the cumulative GAP will change during a future interval. For instance, Bank A may have a cumulative GAP of +$40 million over one year, with incremental GAPs of +$30 million in the first quarter, +$15 million in the second quarter, −$10 million in the third quarter, and +$5 million in the final quarter. Incremental GAPs can be useful for determining *how* and *when* a bank should offset interest rate risk. Thus Bank A's risk-offset strategy would likely be quite different from the strategy undertaken by Bank B, which also had a cumulative GAP of +$40 million over one year but had incremental GAPs of +$10 million per quarter.

Maturity GAP analysis is widely used by banks, because it is relatively easy to compute and it makes good intuitive sense. By ensuring that its assets have maturities similar to its liabilities, a financial institution can ensure that its assets will mature or be repriced at the same time that an approximately equal amount of liabilities is repriced.

However, in recent years it has been noted that GAP analysis provides only an approximate rule for analyzing interest rate risk. Consider, for instance, a bank that issues a $10,000 zero coupon deposit that promises to double the depositor's money in seven years (i.e., pays interest at an annual compound rate of 10.4 percent) and uses the proceeds to buy a $10,000 seven-year bond paying annual interest at a 12 percent rate. Provided that the bank reinvests all interest coupons paid on the bond each year-end at a 12 percent rate, it would have $22,107 at the end of seven years—more than enough to pay back the depositor and to book a gross profit of over $2,000 before costs. However, if interest rates fell to the extent that the coupon interest could be reinvested only at a 5.5 percent rate (recall reinvestment risk from Chapter 5), at the end of seven years the institution would have accumulated only $19,920—not enough to repay the $20,000 obligation to the depositor, even before costs. Clearly, then, matching the maturities of liabilities and assets is not sufficient to guarantee that an institution will not bear interest rate risk.

Duration GAPS.   To reduce the reinvestment risk described above, banks try to match the *durations* of their assets and liabilities, not their maturities.[3] As discussed in Chapter 5, duration is a measure of the average *time* it takes for a security (or portfolio) to return its present value to the owner, and it can also be viewed as the effective time until an asset reprices.

Although duration is a complicated concept, it is quite useful for immunizing an institution's balance sheet against interest rate risk. The following are some rules applicable to duration.

1. The percentage change in value of a portfolio when interest rates change is roughly proportional to its duration times the change in rates. The longer the duration, the greater the price change when interest rates change.

2. If an institution's assets and liabilities have equal values and the same durations, their values will change similarly as interest rates change. Thus, by matching the duration of its assets to the duration of its liabilities, an institution can immunize its balance sheet against changes in value caused by interest rate changes.

3. A duration GAP is computed as the difference between the duration of an institution's assets, D_A, minus the duration of its liabilities, D_L, weighted by their respective market values. If an institution wants to use duration analysis to immunize the value of its net worth against interest rate changes, it will compute and set at zero its duration GAP, D_G. Its duration GAP accounts for differences in the respective market values of a firm's assets and liabilities, MV_A and MV_L. Thus, D_G weights the duration of liabilities by their proportion of

---

[3]See Chapter 5 for a detailed discussion of duration and its use as a measure of interest rate risk. The formula for duration is given in Chapter 5.

the institution's total assets before comparing them to the duration of assets; that is, to immunize, a firm will set D_G equal to zero, so:

$$D_G = D_A - \frac{MV_L}{MV_A} \times D_L = 0. \qquad (14\text{--}3)$$

When that is done, interest rate changes will affect the value of the firm's assets and its liabilities similarly, leaving the nominal value of its net worth unchanged. Slightly different formulas can be used to achieve other objectives.

4. Duration GAPs are opposite in sign from maturity GAPs for the same risk exposure. For instance, if an institution is asset sensitive—in other words, subject to income declines if interest rates fall—it will have shorter-duration (maturity) assets than liabilities. Thus it will have a *negative* duration GAP. At the same time, it will ordinarily have *more* rate-sensitive (short-maturity) assets than rate-sensitive liabilities, so it will have a *positive* maturity GAP.

5. Because the duration of a zero coupon security is always equal to its maturity, zero coupon securities are very useful for matching the durations of asset and liability portfolios. Consequently, as financial institutions have become more concerned with portfolio duration matching, the demand for zero coupon securities and the resultant supply of zero coupon deposits have grown substantially.

Duration matching to immunize against interest rate risk is complicated, however, because asset and liability durations change every day. Except for zero coupon securities, asset and liability durations change whenever interest rates change, just as bond present values change whenever interest rates change. Furthermore, it is difficult to assess the duration of loans on which customers have the option to prepay or the duration of deposits that customers can withdraw at any time. These customer options pose problems for computing both duration and maturity GAPs.

Because it requires a great deal of computation on a continuing basis, only the largest institutions use duration GAP analysis. Most smaller institutions prefer to use maturity GAP analysis to reduce interest rate risk because of its greater simplicity. These banks should recognize, however, that their management of interest rate risk will be less precise by using maturity GAP instead of duration GAP because maturity GAP ignores the reinvestment risk associated with intermediate cash flows.

Illustration of Duration GAP. Let us return to the example discussed earlier (see Exhibits 14–6 and 14–7) to illustrate the measurement of interest rate risk using duration GAP. Recall in our example that the bank funded a $1,000 fixed-rate, single-payment, one-year loan with a three-month and six-month CD having face values of $500.

The duration GAP calculation is simple in this case because the assets and liabilities have no intermediate cash flows (that is, they are zero coupon instruments); thus, their durations equal their maturities (0.25 years for the three-month CD and 0.5

years for the six-month CD). The duration GAP is calculated below using Equation 14-3:

$$D_G = D_A - (MV_L/MV_A) \times D_L$$
$$= 1 - (1 \times 0.375)$$
$$= 0.625$$

Note that D_L is the weighted average of the durations of the two CDs:

$$D_L = [(\$500/\$1,000) \times 0.25] + [(\$500/\$1,000) \times 0.5]$$
$$= 0.375 \text{ years.}$$

The duration of assets exceeds the duration of liabilities in this case, suggesting that the liabilities reprice before the assets. The "average" dollar of liabilities reprices after 0.375 years (4.5 months) whereas the assets do not reprice until the end of the year. Thus an interest rate increase will result in declining earnings for this bank.

On the other hand, had the bank issued a six-month CD and an 18-month (1.5 years) CD, the duration of the liabilities would have equaled one year.

$$D_L = [(\$500/\$1,000) \times 0.5] + [(\$500/\$1,000) \times 1.5]$$
$$= 1 \text{ year.}$$

Thus the duration of the assets equals the duration of the liabilities, the duration GAP is zero, and the bank's cash flows are immunized from interest rate changes. Exhibit 14–9 summarizes the effects of changing interest rates on net interest income (average yield on assets minus average cost of liabilities) for banks with different GAP positions.

Hedging Interest Rate Risk

Hedging means taking actions to reduce or eliminate risk. The simplest form of hedging is matched funding of loans, which we discussed in Chapter 13. With matched

---

Exhibit 14–9   **The Effects of Interest Rate Changes on the Net Interest Income of Banks in Various GAP Positions**

	Bank's GAP Position		
	Negative Maturity GAP or Positive Duration GAP	Zero GAP	Positive Maturity GAP or Negative Duration GAP
Rising Interest Rates	Net interest income decreases	No change in net interest income	Net interest income increases
Falling Interest Rates	Net interest income increases	No change in net interest income	Net interest income decreases

funding, the bank funds a loan with a CD (or other liability) that has exactly the same maturity (or duration, if the instruments involved have intermediate cash flows). Matched funding means that the interest rate sensitivity of the loan and the CD are identical, or that they have the same effective time to repricing. Thus changes in cash flows of the asset due to interest rate changes are matched exactly by changes in the cost of financing the asset. One should remember, however, that by hedging the bank not only eliminates *downside* risk, but it also eliminates *upside* potential.

Matched funding is a form of *microhedging*, which is hedging a specific transaction. *Macrohedging*, on the other hand, involves using instruments of risk management, such as financial futures, options on financial futures, and interest rate swaps (see Chapter 11) to reduce the interest rate risk of the firm's entire balance sheet. We will now discuss how financial futures, options on financial futures, and interest rate swaps can be used in managing interest rate risk.

Financial Futures.   The interest rate risk of a bank with a negative maturity GAP or positive duration GAP (in either case, recall that the assets are more rate sensitive than the liabilities) can be reduced through the use of financial futures. In Chapter 11 we showed that the prices of financial futures behave similarly to those of bonds when interest rates change; thus, there is an inverse relationship between the price of a financial futures contract and interest rates.

A short-funded bank will experience a decline in earnings with a rise in interest rates, as shown in our earlier example. To offset this risk, the bank should *sell* (or *short*) financial futures. Recall from Chapter 11 that if interest rates rise, a *short position* in financial futures increases in value. A short position in the futures market, therefore, offsets the decline in the bank's earnings should interest rates rise.

Exhibit 14-10 illustrates the effects of macrohedging a typical bank with financial futures. The graph shows that as interest rates increase, the bank's net cash flow declines. At the same time, the value of the short futures position increases. The logic here is simple and is just the opposite of "buying low and selling high." Recall that the bank *sold* the futures contract at a given price for the underlying security. As interest rates rise, the price of the underlying security declines, as does the value of the futures contract. To get out of the short position, the bank does not have to deliver the underlying security; it simply *purchases* the futures contract in the secondary market. With an interest rate increase (that is, a price *decrease*), therefore, the bank has "sold high and bought low" in the futures market, making a profit that offsets the decline in bank cash flows. Notice from Exhibit 14-10 that after hedging with futures, the bank's cash flows do not fluctuate with changes in interest rates. Chapter 11 provided a detailed example of how financial futures can be used to microhedge a fixed-rate loan.

Options on Financial Futures.   Banks can develop more sophisticated hedges against interest rate risk by using options on financial futures. Recall from Chapter 11 that options on financial assets can reduce downside risk without eliminating all of the upside potential. A common use of options on financial futures is to create so-called caps, floors, and collars on interest rates. A cap on interest rates is created by purchasing a put option (that is, an option to sell) on a financial futures contract. Banks can use caps to limit increases in the cost of their liabilities without sacrificing the possibility of benefiting from interest rate declines. On the other hand, a floor on

Exhibit 14–10   **Using Financial Futures to Reduce the Interest Rate Risk of a Commercial Bank**

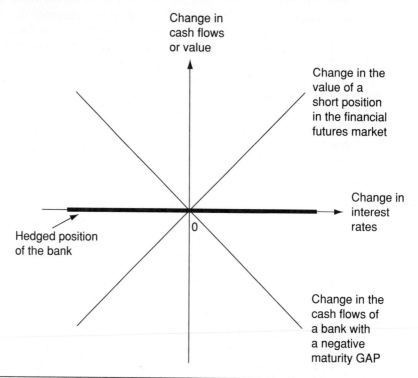

Change in
cash flows
or value

Change in the
value of a
short position
in the financial
futures market

Change in
interest
rates

0

Hedged position
of the bank

Change in the
cash flows of
a bank with
a negative
maturity GAP

Banks can reduce interest rate risk by selling short financial futures. Notice, however, that by hedging, the bank eliminates the upside potential that comes from a decline in interest rates.

interest rates is created by selling a call option (i.e., an option to buy) on a financial futures contract. The floor sets a lower limit for liability costs.

By simultaneously buying a cap and selling a floor, the bank creates a collar. Collars limit the movement of a bank's liability costs within a specified range. If, for example, a bank purchases a cap at 9 percent and a sells a floor at 5 percent, the bank's liability costs will fluctuate between 5 and 9 percent. Exhibit 14–11 shows the cash flows of caps, floors, and collars. As shown in Panel A of Exhibit 14–11, if interest rates rise above the cap rate, the bank purchasing the cap receives a cash flow from the writer (seller) of the cap (or the value of the put option on the futures contract increases). Panel B shows that if the bank has written (sold) a floor, it must pay the purchaser of the floor a cash flow if rates decrease below the floor rate. Panel C of Exhibit 14–11 shows the cash flows from the collar.

Exhibit 14–12 shows the cash flows of a bank with a negative maturity GAP (or positive duration GAP) after creating a collar. Notice that if rates increase beyond the cap rate or decrease below the floor rate, the bank's cash flows are unchanged. The caps and floors illustrated here eliminate only the effects of extreme movements in interest rates, allowing the bank's cash flows to fluctuate within a specified range.

Exhibit 14–11   Using Options on Financial Futures to Create Caps, Floors, and Collars

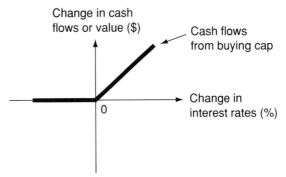

Panel A: Cash flows from purchasing
          an interest rate cap

Change in cash
flows or value ($)

Cash flows
from buying cap

Change in
interest rates (%)

0

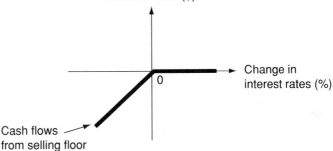

Panel B: Cash flows from selling
          an interest rate floor

Change in cash
flows or value ($)

Change in
interest rates (%)

0

Cash flows
from selling floor

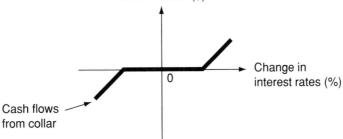

Panel C: Cash flows from simultaneously buying a cap and
          selling a floor (interest rate collar)

Change in cash
flows or value ($)

Change in
interest rates (%)

0

Cash flows
from collar

By simultaneously buying a put option on financial futures (a cap) and selling a call option on financial futures (a floor), a bank creates a collar, which limits the movements of a bank's liability costs within a specified range.

Exhibit 14–12   Using Collars to Manage Interest Rate Risk

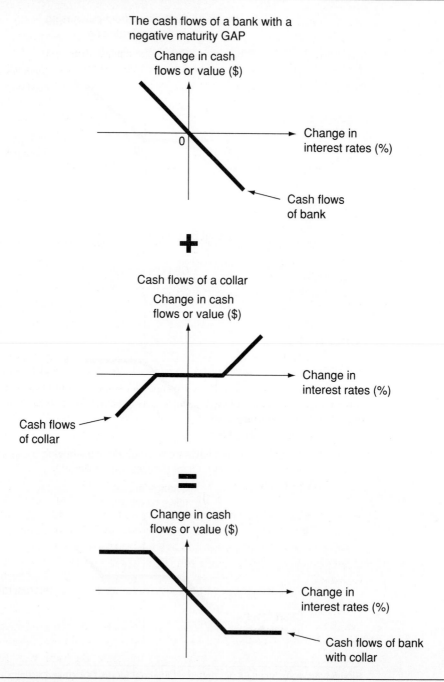

A collar eliminates the effects of extreme movements in interest rates, allowing the bank's cash flows to fluctuate within a specified range.

Exhibits 14–11 and 14–12 naturally raise the question of why a bank would want to limit reductions in its liability costs by selling a floor. To understand the answer to this question, one must understand that purchasing a cap is equivalent to buying an insurance policy against increasing interest rates and that selling a floor is equivalent to selling an insurance policy to someone who fears a decline in interest rates. As everyone knows, insurance is not free. We all must pay premiums for insurance protection. By simultaneously selling insurance (in the form of a floor) to a third party, a bank generates "premium" income that offsets the cost of obtaining the cap. Thus, banks are willing to give up some of their upside potential from decreasing interest rates as a way of reducing the cost of downside protection.

While caps, floors, and collars can be created by buying and selling options on financial futures, this strategy is difficult because exchange-traded options with sufficiently long maturities do not exist. Most caps, floors, and collars, therefore, are privately negotiated agreements (that is, over the counter) between buyers and sellers of interest rate "insurance." These privately negotiated agreements are called interest rate options.

Interest Rate Swaps. Banks also use interest rate swaps (see Chapter 11) to manage interest rate risk. Recall from Chapter 11 that in an interest rate swap, two counterparties literally swap cash flows based on relative movements of two interest rates that are agreed upon in the swap agreement. In the simplest and most common form, parties to a swap will periodically exchange cash flows (monthly, quarterly, or semiannually) based on the difference between an agreed-on fixed interest rate and a variable interest rate.

To illustrate, we shall consider the case of a short-funded bank, one whose liabilities are more rate sensitive than its assets. Such a bank has a problem with rising interest rates because liability costs are "variable" compared to the relatively "fixed" asset returns. Thus liability costs increase faster than yields on assets. The bank, therefore, pays out variable cash flows and receives relatively fixed cash flows with respect to interest rate changes. This logic leads to the same cash flow profile of a bank shown previously in Exhibit 14–10. What a short-funded bank needs to offset the risk position, therefore, is to receive a variable cash flow and pay a fixed cash flow.

To hedge interest rate risk, the bank should enter into an interest rate swap in which the bank receives cash flows based on a floating interest rate and pays cash flows based on a fixed interest rate. In an interest rate swap, the cash flows are based on what is called a *notional* amount of principal. The principal is notional in that it never actually changes hands. The counterparties to the swap simply pay each other difference checks based on the interest rate changes as applied to the notional amount of principal.

Suppose a bank enters into a swap and agrees to pay a fixed rate and receive a cash flow based on a variable rate. If interest rates rise in the first settlement period, the bank would receive a difference check because the variable interest rate increased relative to the fixed interest rate. If, for example, the variable rate is 100 basis points higher than the fixed rate on the settlement date, the bank would receive a difference check from the counterparty of $1 million on a notional principal of $100 million. If the variable interest rate declines, the bank would have to pay a difference check to the counterparty. This type of interest rate swap results in a net cash inflow to the bank if interest rates rise, offsetting the decrease in net interest income that occurs when liability costs increase faster than asset yields. Of course, the swap also eliminates the upside potential from an interest rate decline because even though a bank with a negative maturity GAP would ordinarily benefit from the decline, it must pay a difference check that offsets that benefit.

If we were to draw the cash flow profile of the type of interest rate swap just described, it would be identical to the change in value of a short position in the financial futures market shown in Exhibit 14–10. If financial futures and interest rate swaps can accomplish essentially the same objective, why do they both exist? Recall from Chapter 11 that financial futures are standardized agreements, trading on organized exchanges. Financial futures are cash-settled (or marked to market) daily. Unfortunately, there is not a corresponding financial futures contract for every financial instrument. Interest rate swaps, on the other hand, are privately negotiated agreements that can be tailor-made to fit the circumstances of particular counterparties. Swaps can be made for more varied maturities than is possible with futures, tailored to particular interest rates, and the settlement dates can be designed to fit the cash flow patterns of the counterparties. The trade-off for the increased flexibility of designing swaps is that swaps are less marketable and carry more default risk than financial futures.

Bank Earnings

Now that we have discussed the management problems banks face, let us examine the performance of commercial banks by examining the bank income statement. The major items on the income statement for all federally insured commercial banks and for samples of large and small banks are shown in Exhibit 14–13. The large banks consist of money-center and superregional banks with an international or national emphasis. The small banks have a more regional or local emphasis. The table is similar to the balance sheet presented in Chapter 13 in Exhibits 13–1 and 13–2.

The major source of revenue for commercial banks is interest earned on loans, accounting for 62 percent of operating income. Large banks and small banks obtain roughly the same proportion of revenue from loans (large banks, 61 percent and small banks, 60 percent), but small banks earn nearly all of their loan income from domestic loans while large banks receive 14 percent of their revenue from foreign loans.

Bank ownership of securities—U.S. government and municipal—provide another 15 percent. This source of revenue is much more important for small banks than for large banks because small banks hold proportionately more U.S. government securities (see Exhibit 13–2). Small banks rely more on the asset side of the balance sheet for liquidity than large banks, who are able to obtain liquidity directly in the money markets.

A source of revenue of growing importance in the 1990s, especially for large banks, is fees and service charges. These account for 17 percent of the revenues of large banks and 8 percent for small banks. Fees and service charges are important to banks because they are sources of revenue not subject to credit risk, liquidity risk, or interest rate risk.

Exhibit 14–13   Income for All Commercial Banks and Samples of Large Banks and Small Banks, 1990

	All Banks[a]		Large Banks[b]	Small Banks[c]
	Billions of Dollars	**Percentage of Operating Income**	**Percentage of Operating Income**	**Percentage of Operating Income**
Operating Income				
Interest on domestic loans	$203.6	54	47	60
Interest on securities	56.5	15	13	25
Interest on foreign loans	30.7	8	14	N/A
Interest due from depository institutions	12.7	3	5	2
Interest on Fed Funds sold and repurchase agreements	12.5	3	3	5
Service charges on deposit accounts	11.4	3	3	4
Income from lease financing	4.4	1	2	< 1
Other noninterest income	43.6	12	14	4
Total	$375.4	100	100	100
Operating Expenses				
Interest on domestic deposits	$127.4	34	26	52
Interest on foreign deposits	34.1	9	16	N/A
Interest on Fed Funds purchased and repurchase agreements	22.7	6	8	< 1
Interest on other bank funds	20.6	6	8	< 1
Salaries and wages	51.7	14	14	16
Occupancy expenses	17.4	5	5	5
Other noninterest expense	46.7	12	11	12
Provision for Loan Losses	32.0	8	9	4
Total	$352.6	94	96	90
Net Operating Income	$22.8	6	4	10
Income taxes	7.7	2	1	3
Security gains (losses)	0.5	< 1	< 1	< 1
Extraordinary items, net	0.6	< 1	< 1	< 1
Net Income	16.2	4	2	7

Banks earn most of their income from loans and investment securities, and their largest expense item is interest paid on liabilities.

[a] This group consists of 12,345 insured commercial banks.

[b] This group consists of 234 banks with domestic and foreign offices. It includes all money-center/multinational banks, most superregional banks, and many regional banks. These banks have a regional, national, or global emphasis.

[c] This group consists of 9,482 banks without foreign offices and with total assets less than $100 million. It includes banks with primarily a local emphasis.

Source: FDIC, *Statistics on Banking*, 1990.

PEOPLE
& EVENTS

Bank of New England: How Credit Risk Killed the Goose that Laid the Golden Egg

On January 6, 1991, the FDIC seized the Bank of New England (BNE), resulting in the third-largest bank bailout in U.S. history. The seizure occurred because the bank recorded a loss in 1990 of $650 million, a loss twice the size of the bank's capital base. The 1990 loss followed a disastrous year in 1989, when BNE lost $1.1 billion. Between 1985 and 1989 BNE's total assets grew from $7 billion to $30 billion, a whopping 44 percent annual growth rate over the period!

Credit risk killed the once profitable and growing "Golden Goose." Part of the problem can be attributed to Chief Executive Officer Walter Connolly, who was in charge of the bank from 1985 to 1989. His sole ambition was to overtake Bank of Boston as the largest bank in the region. Connolly's aggressive management style led to an attitude on the part of BNE loan officers to take on high risk in hope of huge returns. Exacerbating the problems with excessive credit risk was the lack of controls for evaluating credit. As BNE grew, it acquired smaller regional banks that were allowed a high degree of autonomy. The lack of controls meant that subsidiary banks were free to pursue growth at the expense of credit risk, a strategy in line with that of BNE's top management.

In early 1990, the New England economy was the first to feel the effects of the 1990–92 recession, and many of the low-quality loans came home to roost. Nonperforming loans rose from $419 million (1.7 percent of total assets) in 1988 to $2.85 billion (12.4 percent of total assets) in 1990. By late 1989 capital was a scant 1 percent of total assets, and by 1990 the bank was down to a razor-thin $225 million in equity. In March 1990, Connolly resigned under fire and the FDIC handed down a cease-and-desist order that severely curtailed the bank's operations. To raise much needed cash, the firm began furiously selling assets and as quickly as it had grown, the bank began to downsize, losing more than $7 billion in assets in 1990. Of course, depositors began to close ranks, forcing BNE to the Fed's discount window, a sure sign that the goose was about to die. On the bright side, interest rate risk was only a minor concern for BNE because the bank's loans were failing so rapidly there was little time for repricing of liabilities before assets to become a problem. After the seizure, the FDIC sold about $12 billion of BNE's assets to Fleet/Norstar-KKR for $626 million in April 1991. The FDIC assumed the problem assets of about $8 billion. In the end, BNE's goose was cooked.

As expected, the largest expense of commercial banks is the interest paid to obtain bank funds, taking 55 percent of all operating income. Interest on deposits is a greater proportion of operating income for small banks than large banks (52 percent versus 42 percent) because small banks rely more heavily on deposits as a source of funds than do large banks (see Exhibit 13–1). Large banks, which are better able to obtain funds directly in the money markets, rely more heavily on Fed Funds purchased and repurchase agreements (see Exhibit 13–1). Thus interest expense on Fed Funds and repurchase agreements account for a higher fraction of operating income for large banks than small banks (8 percent versus less than 1 percent).

After interest expense, salaries and wages are the next most significant expense, accounting for 14 percent of operating income. Salaries and wages are more important for small banks than for large banks. Small banks are less automated and have a greater retail emphasis than large banks; therefore, small banks have more employees per dollar of assets than large banks. Occupany expenses are low for commercial banks compared to other types of businesses because of the low amount of fixed assets held by commercial banks (see Exhibit 13–2).

Important Trends

Exhibit 14–14 shows some of the more important trends in bank income and expenses since 1950. Notice that the percentage of income earned from loans has grown relative to all other sources of income. This reflects in part the strong demand for loans and the more aggressive lending policies of commercial banks since World War II. Also, the development of liability management has allowed commercial banks to place larger proportions of their asset portfolios into high-yielding loans rather than into lower-yielding secondary reserves. The latter point can be seen by the continued decline in importance of earnings from securities investments.

On the cost side, interest payments on time deposits and borrowed funds have become the main cost element for commercial banks. This trend can be seen by looking at the rapid increases of total interest expense to total bank expense over time. The trend of increasing interest expense has put additional pressure on bank

Exhibit 14–14   Trends in Operating Income and Expenses for Commercial Banks (1950–1990)

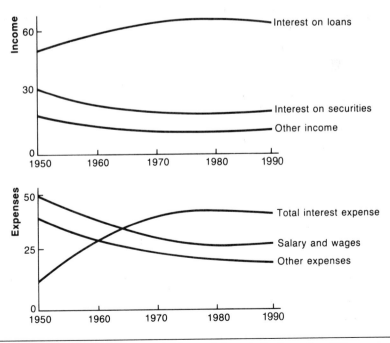

Because banks have become more automated, labor costs have declined over the years.

Source: FDIC annual reports.

management to reduce other costs and to acquire assets that earn enough to make the bank a profitable business. This again illustrates the constant conflict facing bank management—to maintain adequate liquidity and yet generate adequate profits. Since 1950, banks' wage and salary costs have fallen relative to other expenses, which reflects the growing utilization of more capital and less labor in the production of bank output. This has been particularly true for large banks in the processing of demand deposits by computers and high-speed machines that replace humans.

Bank Profitability

Although net income for banks has varied over the years, the general trend in bank profitability has been upward. Bank operations are characterized by low profit margins and a large volume of business. Profitability can be measured in several ways. The rate of return on assets (net income/total assets) allows the comparison of one bank with another. The return on assets (ROA) is the key ratio in evaluating the quality of bank management, because it tells how much profit bank management can generate with a given amount of assets. Bank management is responsible for the utilization and selection of a bank's assets, and in recent years, return on total assets for commercial banks has varied between 0.13 and 0.87 percent. This return has been somewhat below that of other industries and has contributed to banks' high cost of obtaining new capital.

Another measure of bank profitability is the rate of return on capital (net income/capital). Return on equity (ROE) tells the bank owners how management has performed on their behalf—the amount of profits in relation to their capital contribution to the firm. Because banks are very highly leveraged (low capital-to-assets ratios), their ROEs are quite respectable even though their ROAs are very low. In recent years, banks' ROEs have ranged between 2.56 and 13.02 percent. Exhibit 14–15 shows the return on total assets and the return on capital from 1975 to 1990.

Exhibit 14–15	**ROA and ROE for Insured Commercial Banks (1975–1990)**

Year	Return on Total Assets (percentage)	Return on Capital (percentage)
1975	0.77	10.56
1980	0.75	13.02
1985	0.70	11.31
1986	0.64	10.18
1987	0.13	2.56
1988	0.80	12.69
1989	0.47	7.63
1990	0.87	10.00

A typical bank has an ROA of 0.75 percent and an ROE of 12 percent. Commercial bank earnings in 1987 were down nearly 80 percent in their worst year for profitability since the Great Depression. Performance has improved in the early 1990s.

Source: FDIC, *Bank Operating Statistics*, various issues, and *Statistics on Banking*, 1990.

Exhibit 14–16 gives an idea of the substantial variation in earnings that can occur among large money center banks. As can be seen, ROA varied between −1 percent and 1.03 percent in 1991. Of the ten largest banks, six experienced declining ROA between 1990 and 1991. This overall decline in bank earnings is partially explained by the increased credit risk during the 1990–92 recession. As can be seen, eight of the ten banks in Exhibit 14–16 experienced increases in net loan charge-offs. Some of the increases were quite dramatic.

Summary

Commercial banks are profit-maximizing business firms whose primary source of income is interest earned on loans and investment securities. Like all business firms, banks strive for higher profits consistent with safety. The trade-off between profitability and safety is more acute for banks than for most other businesses because banks have low capital-to-assets ratios and because most bank liabilities are short-term.

Banks have two basic tools for maintaining sufficient liquidity: (1) asset management and (2) liability management. Asset management classifies bank assets into four basic groups. Primary and secondary reserves are held for liquidity needs. Once these are satisfied, banks make higher-yielding loans and invest the remaining funds in open market investments. Liability management is predicated on the assumption that

Exhibit 14–16   Variation in Performance for the Ten Largest U.S. Banks in 1991

Bank	Total Assets in 1991 (millions)	ROA in 1990 (percentage)	ROA in 1991 (percentage)	Net Charge-offs as Percentage of Loans in 1990	Net Charge-offs as Percentage of Loans in 1991
Citicorp, New York	$216,922	0.08	−0.50	1.8	3.2
Chemical Banking, New York	138,930	0.21	0.01	2.2	2.7
BankAmerica, San Francisco	115,509	0.77	0.93	1.0	1.3
NationsBank, Charlotte	110,319	0.47	0.15	0.6	1.9
J. P. Morgan, New York	103,468	0.73	1.00	2.9	1.7
Chase Manhattan, New York	98,197	−0.39	0.42	2.4	2.8
Security Pacific, Los Angeles	76,411	0.14	−1.00	1.4	2.4
Bankers Trust, New York	63,959	0.99	1.03	2.3	2.6
Wells Fargo, San Francisco	53,547	1.34	0.00	0.3	1.2
First Chicago, Chicago	48,963	0.41	0.15	2.7	2.1

Note: In 1991, C&S/Sovran and NCNB merged to form NationsBank, and Chemical Banking and Manufacturers Hanover merged. ROA and net charge-offs for NationsBank in 1990 are weighted averages of C&S/Sovran and NCNB. ROA and net charge-offs for Chemical Banking in 1990 are weighted averages of Chemical Banking and Manufacturers Hanover.

Performance varies widely among the country's largest banks. In general, the late 1980s were disastrous for many large money center banks because of large loan losses on their international loan portfolios. The 1990–92 recession led to further loan losses and declines in ROA for many large banks.

Source: *Business Week*, April 22, 1991, and April 27, 1992.

certain types of short-term bank liabilities are interest rate sensitive. Thus, if a bank wants to attract funds for liquidity needs or for loans, it can do so by issuing these types of liabilities at slightly over the market rate of interest. Liability management supplements asset management as a source of bank liquidity and is used by large banks that have direct access to the money markets.

Banks are required by law to maintain minimum reserves equal to a percentage of their deposits and designated as nondeposit liabilities. The dollar amount of reserves a bank must hold is a weekly average based on the average amount of deposits held during a two-week period. Banks that fail to meet their required reserves must pay a penalty fine, and frequent violators are subject to management intervention by regulatory authorities. Banks also hold excess reserves. Excess reserves provide banks with day-to-day operating liquidity since required reserves are not legally available for liquidity needs. However, required reserves do provide emergency liquidity in the event that bank management fails to hold the proper amount of excess reserves.

Bank capital serves as a cushion against losses suffered by bank operations. Bank regulators are concerned about adequate bank capital primarily to protect the U.S. economy against the destabilizing consequences of massive bank failures. In recent years, bank capital has declined below the level regulators believe is necessary for bank safety.

Banks manage interest rate risk by controlling the maturity or duration GAP between the bank's rate-sensitive assets and liabilities. The greater the size of the GAP, the greater the bank's interest rate exposure. When interest rates are expected to rise, the proper strategy is to have a positive maturity GAP; if interest rates are expected to decline, there should be a negative maturity GAP; and if bank management wishes to minimize interest rate risk, it should strive for a zero GAP. Banks use futures, options on futures, and interest rate swaps to manage interest rate risk.

Questions

1. Explain the profitability versus solvency and liquidity dilemma facing bank management.
2. Liquidity management can be practiced on either side of the balance sheet. How are asset and liability management similar and how do they differ? Why do smaller banks have limited access to liability management?
3. Discuss the debt instruments used in liability management. What are the common characteristics of these debt instruments and what type of bank is most likely to issue them?
4. How do banks decide on the proper amount of primary and secondary reserves to hold?
5. Why do banks hold reserves in excess of those required by law? To what extent do required reserves provide liquidity?
6. What are the major sources of revenue and expenses for commercial banks? What has been the trend in these accounts in recent years?
7. Explain how interest rate futures are used to reduce bank interest rate risk. How does the value of a futures contract change when interest rates change?
8. A bank economist projects that interest rates in the future are expected to decline. What is the bank's proper funds management strategy? Why?

9. Why is capital adequacy more of a problem for commercial banks than for most other businesses?
10. Explain why bank regulators are so concerned about capital adequacy for the banking system?

Selected References

Abken, Peter. "Beyond Plain Vanilla: A Taxonomy of Swaps." *Economic Review*. Federal Reserve Bank of Atlanta, March/April 1991.
The article describes the market for swaps and details the types of swaps from the simplest to the most complicated versions.

Abken, Peter. "Interest-Rate Caps, Collars, and Floors." *Economic Review*. Federal Reserve Bank of Atlanta, November/December 1989.
Provides a thorough description of the market for options on financial futures. The article describes the pricing of caps, collars, and floors and how they are used for interest rate risk management.

Brewer, Elijah. "Bank GAP Management and the Use of Financial Futures." *Economic Perspectives*. Federal Reserve Bank of Chicago, March–April 1985, pp. 12–22.
An explanation of how interest rate futures can be used to reduce bank interest rate exposure.

Goodfriend, Marvin, and Monica Hargraves. "A Historical Assessment of the Rationales and Functions of Reserve Requirements." *Economic Review*. Federal Reserve Bank of Richmond, March/April 1983, pp. 3–21.
A detailed and carefully written article that discusses the reasons for and functions of reserve requirements. Excellent and comprehensive.

Gup, Benton E., and John R. Walter. "Profitable Large Banks: The Key to Their Success." *Midland Corporate Finance Journal*, Winter 1988, pp. 24–29.
An excellent article examining the factors that determine why some banks are highly profitable and others are not.

Henderson, Yolanda K. "The Taxation of Banks: Particular Privilege or Objectionable Burdens?" *New England Economic Review*. Federal Reserve Bank of Boston, May/June 1987, pp. 4–18.
Examines the taxation of banks, and looks at the effective tax rate for banks compared to other industries. The article also has a good discussion of the provisions of the Tax Reform Act of 1986 that affect commercial banks.

Hilliard, Jimmy, and Joseph F. Sinkey, Jr. "Duration Analysis as a Tool for Predicting Interest-Sensitive Cash Flows." *Journal of Financial Education*, Fall 1989.
This article demonstrates how duration can be used to measure the interest rate sensitivity of the bank balance sheet. The authors provide excellent examples of how interest rate changes affect the net cash flows of the bank.

Keeton, William R., and Charles S. Morris. "Why Do Banks' Loan Losses Differ?" *Economic Review*. Federal Reserve Bank of Kansas City, May 1987, pp. 3–21.
Good examination of various factors that affect loan losses at different banks.

Luckett, Dudley G. "Approaches to Bank Liquidity Management." *Economic Review*. Federal Reserve Bank of Kansas City, March 1980, pp. 11–27.
Comprehensive treatment of banks' current liquidity practices, with emphasis on liability management. Contains some case studies to illustrate principles discussed in article.

Morris, Charles S. "Managing Interest Rate Risk with Interest Rate Futures." *Economic Review*. **Federal Reserve Bank of Kansas City, March 1989.**

This article provides an excellent description of financial futures and how banks use them to control interest rate risk.

Moulton, Janice M. "New Guidelines for Bank Capital: An Attempt to Reflect Risk." *Business Review*, **July/August 1987, pp. 19–33.**

A look at the new federal regulations on bank capital that attempt to adjust capital standards to reflect the riskiness of a bank's balance sheet. Of particular interest is the adjustment for off-balance-sheet items, such as standby letters of credit.

Santoni, G.J. "The Effects of Inflation on Commercial Banks." *Economic Review*. **Federal Reserve Bank of St. Louis, March 1986, pp. 15–24.**

Studies the effect of inflation on commercial banks by analyzing the relationship between inflation and the market value of bank capital. A good article.

Smith, Clifford W., Jr., Charles W. Smithson, and D. Sykes Wilford. *Managing Financial Risk*. **New York: Harper and Row, 1990.**

Anyone contemplating a career in banking must read this book. It provides excellent, simple descriptions of forward contracts, futures contracts, options, and swaps. It describes the pricing and the credit risk of the various contracts. The examples of how these instruments are used in risk management are very understandable.

Toevs, Alden. "GAP Management: Managing Interest Rate Risk in Banks and Thrifts." *Economic Review*. **Federal Reserve Bank of San Francisco, Spring 1983, pp. 20–35.**

An explanation of how proper GAP management can be used to control interest rate risk at depository institutions.

Wall, Larry D. "Commercial Bank Profitability: Some Disturbing Trends." *Economic Review*. **Federal Reserve Bank of Atlanta, March/April 1987, pp. 24–36.**

Examines why bank profitability for banks of all sizes declined so sharply during the 1985–1986 period.

BANK STRUCTURE AND COMPETITION

15

T HERE WAS A TIME WHEN major highway intersections in urban areas sported four gas stations, one on each corner. Now, in densely populated areas, it is not uncommon to see at least two of those gas stations replaced by banks. One of them may be a branch of an out-of-state bank; the other may be a local state bank. Consumers may keep their checking accounts at a local bank, where there is free checking, and simultaneously keep their savings accounts at a large out-of-state bank, where the interest is higher. This is one result of the wave of bank restructuring and intensified competition in the late 1980s and early 1990s. Will it work out profitably for both banks in the long run?

Bank structure has always been one of the most widely debated and controversial topics in American banking. The term *bank structure* refers to the distribution of banks operating in a particular market in terms of number, location, and size. The problem that has long vexed economists and bank regulators is determining the optimal structure for the banking industry—that is, the bank structure that will furnish an effective level of competition resulting in low prices but that will not permit large numbers of bank failures. This chapter examines the structure of American banking and tackles difficult questions concerning bank structure, competition, and regulation at the federal and state levels.

An Overview of Bank Structure

There are about 12,000 banks in the United States. Although this number may seem large, Exhibit 15-1 shows that more than twice as many banks were operating in the 1920s. Frequent bank panics and the collapse of the nation's financial system during the Great Depression (1930–1933) reduced the number of banks from more than 30,000 at the beginning of the 1920s to about 15,000 by 1933. After the Great Depression, the number of banks continued to decline gradually until the 1960s, primarily because of bank mergers rather than bank failures. After 1960, the number of banks increased slightly, stabilizing at around 15,000 until the late 1980s. Then, in the late 1980s and early 1990s the number of banks declined as a result of failures and mergers. Since the early 1980s, however, the number of total banking offices (branches plus main offices) has been increasing despite the downward trend in the number of banks. The reason is the increase in the number of branches. Even though the number

Exhibit 15–1   **Number of Banks, Branches, Offices, and Deposits: Commercial Banks (1920–1990)**

Year	Number of Banks	Number of Branches	Total Offices	Total Deposits (billions)
1920	30,909	1,281	32,190	$ 43
1929	25,568	3,353	28,921	60
1933	14,771	2,784	17,555	42
1940	14,399	3,593	17,992	66
1950	14,693	5,518	19,851	155
1960	13,484	10,619	24,103	230
1970	13,688	21,643	35,331	314
1975	14,633	30,262	44,895	798
1980	14,870	38,779	53,649	1,194
1985	14,809	46,081	60,890	1,774
1990	12,345	50,815	63,160	2,632

After the 1960s, the number of banks and bank offices increased until the late 1980s. With the beginning of interstate banking and the emergence of electronic banking, the number of banks declined. The number of branches per bank, however, began increasing in the late 1980s and early 1990s.

Source: Board of Governors, Federal Reserve, *Annual Statistical Digest*, various issues; FDIC, *Statistics on Banking*, various issues.

of banks has decreased, geographic restrictions on banking have relaxed in the past 15 years, resulting in more branches per bank. We now briefly discuss branch banking and holding companies. Later in the chapter we will discuss the economic implications of branch banking and holding companies for the performance of the banking industry.

Branching and Bank Holding Companies

Although the number of banks has remained fairly stable, the number of banking offices has grown dramatically because of a sharp increase in the number of branches. In 1941, there were only 3,564 branch offices in this country. By the 1990s, there was a total of more than 60,000 banking offices, and more than 50,000 of these were branch offices. This rapid growth during the postwar period was a result of banks following their customers as they moved from the cities to the suburbs and of the easing of state branching restrictions.

Historically, states with similar branch structures tended to be in the same region of the country: unit banking dominated the Midwest, limited branching the East, and statewide branching the West. This arrangement was no accident. It reflected both the political and the economic development of the United States, which we discussed in Chapter 3. Unit banking dominated the Midwest because of farmers' deeply rooted distrust of banks and the fear of economic control by Eastern banks. Statewide branching was necessary in the West because banks served relatively small populations scattered over large territories. Branch offices were the only economically viable means to serve small, distant, and often mobile communities, such as logging and mining camps.

In contrast to other business firms, commercial banks face regulatory restrictions on the number and location of offices. Exhibit 15–2 summarizes the current regulatory status of branch banking in the United States. Statewide branch banking is the most prevalent branch structure, covering over 85 percent of the states. The next most common branching regulation is limited branching, covering approximately 14 percent of the states. Three states permit interstate branch banking. Currently, there are no unit banking states. In recent years, states have been relaxing their branching laws, and depending on state laws, banks can also achieve geographic expansion by

Exhibit 15–2 **State Branching Laws (1992)**

States permitting statewide branch banking		States permitting limited branch banking[3]
Alabama[1]	New Hampshire	Arkansas[4]
Alaska	New Jersey	Georgia
Arizona	New Mexico	Illinois
California	New York	Iowa
Connecticut	North Carolina	Kentucky
Colorado[2]	North Dakota[1]	Minnesota
Delaware	Ohio	Montana
District of Columbia	Oklahoma[1]	
Florida	Oregon	
Hawaii	Pennsylvania	
Idaho	Rhode Island	
Indiana[1]	South Carolina	
Kansas	South Dakota[1]	**States permitting inter-state branch banking[5]**
Louisiana	Tennessee	
Maine	Texas	
Maryland	Utah	Delaware
Massachusetts	Vermont	Rhode Island
Michigan	Virginia	Utah
Mississippi	Washington	
Missouri	West Virginia	
Nebraska[1]	Wisconsin	
Nevada	Wyoming[1]	

Most states allow either limited or statewide banking.

Source: Federal Reserve Bank of Kansas City, *Financial Industry Trends*, 1992, p. 30.

[1]In these states, statewide branching may only occur through mergers or acquisitions of existing banking offices. Many of these states allow some de nova branching, but confine it to the limits of a city or county.
[2]Colorado began phasing in branch banking in 1991. Initially, limited de novo branching and branching by merger is permitted. Unlimited branching will be phased in by 1997.
[3]Branching laws differ widely in these states. Some states allow branching throughout a region of the state, while others restrict it to county of city limits. Also, several states place a limit on the number of branches a bank can operate or restrict branching to "facilities" or other types of bank offices.
[4]Arkansas will allow statewide branching after December 31, 1998.
[5]Delaware permits Delaware chartered banks to branch to other states. Rhode Island allows reciprocal interstate branching. Utah financial institutions may be acquired and converted to branches of out-of-state banks.

the formation of multibank holding companies. Multibank holding companies come into existence when two or more banks join together under common ownership through a holding company. Later in the chapter we discuss the implications of bank holding companies for bank performance.

Size Distribution of Banks

We can further increase our understanding of the structure of commercial banking by examining the size distribution of banks. As shown in Exhibit 15-3, the overwhelming majority of U.S. banks are very small. Currently, the smallest 9,257 banks (or about 75 percent of all banks) in this country hold only 25 percent of the total assets of the banking industry. Most of these small banks are located in small one- or two-bank towns. In contrast, the largest 172 banks (about 1.5 percent of all banks) control 60 percent of the total assets of the industry. The apparent inverse pyramid involving the number of banks on the one hand and the asset concentrations on the other raises some questions about competition in banking markets and the efficiency of the banking system. Are banking markets in the United States dominated by a few giant, economically powerful banks? Or, at the other extreme, are there too many small and possibly inefficient banks? Our analysis of bank structure will help answer these and other questions.

Exhibit 15-4 shows the largest bank holding companies (BHC) in the United States ranked by total assets. Citicorp, located in New York City, is the largest, with total assets of more than $216 billion; its far-flung operations include offices in most of the major cities of the world as well as in more than 60 cities throughout the United States. The second largest bank holding company is Chemical Banking, headquartered in New York City, with total assets of more than $138 billion. Chemical

---

Exhibit 15-3   Size Distribution of All Insured Commercial Banks (December 31, 1990)

Asset Size (dollars in millions)	Number of Banks	Number of Banks		Total Assets	
		Percent	Cumulative	Percent	Cumulative
Less than 25	3,330	27	27	2	2
25–50	3,145	25	52	3	5
50–100	2,782	23	75	6	11
100–500	2,461	20	95	14	25
500–1,000	253	2	97	5	30
1,000–3,000	202	2	99	10	40
3,000–10,000	123	1	100	20	60
10,000 or more	49	—[a]	100	40	100
Total	12,345	100			

[a]Less than 1 percent.

Although there are about 12,000 banks in the United States, the largest 1 percent of the banks control about 60 percent of all banking assets.

Source: FDIC, *Statistics on Banking*, 1990.

Exhibit 15–4	The 20 Largest Bank Holding Companies in the United States, 1991

Rank	Bank Holding Company	Assets ($Billions)
1	Citicorp, New York	$216.9
2	Chemical Banking, New York	138.9
3	BankAmerica, San Francisco	115.5
4	NationsBank, Charlotte	110.3
5	J.P. Morgan, New York	103.5
6	Chase Manhattan, New York	98.2
7	Security Pacific, Los Angeles	76.4
8	Bankers Trust, New York	64.0
9	Wells Fargo, San Francisco	53.5
10	First Chicago, Chicago	49.0
11	First Interstate Bancorp, Los Angeles	48.9
12	Banc One, Dallas	46.3
12	First Union, Charlotte	46.1
13	Fleet/Norstar Financial Group, Providence	45.4
14	PNC Financial, Pittsburgh	44.9
15	Bank of New York, New York	39.4
16	Norwest, Minneapolis	38.5
17	Suntrust Banks, Atlanta	34.5
18	Wachovia, Winston-Salem	33.2
19	Barnett Banks, Miami	32.7

Citicorp of New York is the largest bank holding company in the United States. It is more than six times as large as the nation's 20th largest bank holding company, Barnett Banks of Miami. Because of consolidation in the industry, many of the largest bank holding companies are now headquartered in the southeastern United States, whereas in the late 1980s, most of the large bank holding companies were found in the more traditional financial centers of New York, Chicago, Los Angeles, and Boston.

Source: Business Week, April 27, 1992, p. 98.

Banking's stature is the result of a 1991 merger with Manufactures Hanover of New York, a perennial money-center BHC. Vaulting into the top five largest BHCs is NationsBank, located in Charlotte, a product of the 1991 merger of C&S/Sovran and NCNB. As we will see later in the chapter, 1991 saw many mergers of large bank holding companies. Because of the recent consolidation in the industry, more of the top 20 bank holding companies are now located in the Sunbelt region, whereas previously most were found in the more traditional financial centers of New York, Chicago, Los Angeles, and Boston. Six of the top 20 are located in New York City, however, still the country's financial center. Finally, notice the startling size disparity among the largest banks in the country. Citicorp is three times as large as the tenth largest bank holding company, First Chicago.

Regulatory Structure of Banking

The American banking system is unique because of side-by-side chartering and supervision by both federal and state authorities, the so-called *dual banking system.* At the federal level, banks are regulated by the comptroller of the currency, the FDIC, and the Federal Reserve System. At the state level, banks may be regulated by one of 50 state banking agencies. In addition, some of the activities of banks and other financial intermediaries come under the purview of other federal agencies, such as the Department of Justice, the Securities and Exchange Commission, and the Federal Trade Commission. We shall discuss only the major bank regulatory agencies.

Approximately two-thirds of all banks are chartered by one of 50 state agencies. The remaining one-third are national banks chartered by the comptroller of the currency. National banks tend to be larger, together holding more than one-half of the deposits of the entire banking system. National banks are required to be members of the Federal Reserve System. State banks are given the option of joining the system if they are able to meet the requirements of membership. In practice, only a small number of state banks elect to join. Currently, only about 40 percent of all banks are member banks. Nevertheless, Federal Reserve members (both state and national) hold 75 percent of the total deposits in the banking system. Like national banks, state banks that join tend to be large.

All banks that are members of the Federal Reserve System are required to be insured by the FDIC. State-chartered banks that are not members of the Federal Reserve System have the option to be insured by the FDIC if they are able to qualify. Very few banks do not have FDIC deposit insurance, and their deposits account for only about 1 percent of all bank deposits.

The Comptroller of the Currency.   The Office of the Comptroller (pronounced 'controller') of the Currency is the nation's oldest bank regulatory agency, established in 1863 by the National Bank Act. Only banks that are federally chartered by the comptroller of the currency may use the word "national" in their name. The Office of the Comptroller of the Currency is technically under the direction of the secretary of the Treasury. Practically, however, the comptroller's office operates as if it had no official ties with the Treasury.

The Office of the Comptroller of the Currency is headquartered in Washington, D.C., and administratively divides the country into 14 different regions. The major regulatory responsibilities of the comptroller's office are approving charters and branch office applications (where permitted by state law) for national banks, evaluating applications for mergers in which the surviving bank is a national bank, enforcing operating regulations and examining national banks, and declaring national banks insolvent.

Federal Reserve System.   The Federal Reserve System was established in 1913 to manage the nation's money stock in the public interest. Besides conducting monetary policy, the Federal Reserve System has wide regulatory and supervisory powers over member banks. The Fed is responsible for granting permission for mergers and new branches, conducting bank examinations, and setting legal reserve requirements on bank deposits. The Fed also has the responsibility for regulating bank holding companies. To reduce overlap with the comptroller of the currency, the Fed's primary supervisory responsibilities are for state-chartered member banks. The Fed and its regulatory activities were discussed in greater detail in Chapter 4.

The Federal Deposit Insurance Corporation.   The Federal Deposit Insurance Corporation (FDIC) was established in 1933 to prevent individual bank failures from spreading to other banks. Deposit insurance became effective in 1934, with coverage limited to $2,500 per depositor per bank. The limit has increased periodically and currently is $100,000 per individual deposit (demand, passbook, and time) account.

The FDIC is an independent federal agency, managed by a three-person board of directors. One of the three directors is the comptroller. All three members cannot belong to the same political party. The FDIC's regulatory responsibilities pertain to insured banks. To avoid excessive duplication with the comptroller and the Fed, the FDIC is primarily concerned with state-chartered banks that are not members of the Federal Reserve System. Although the FDIC does not directly charter banks, it has an enormous effect on chartering through its approval of a bank's application for deposit insurance. Realistically, it is a competitive necessity for a bank to have deposit insurance, and some state banking agencies require FDIC approval before they will grant a bank charter.

State Banking Authorities.　Each state has its own agency that is responsible for regulating and supervising commercial banks chartered by the state. These agencies can also regulate other financial institutions in the state, such as savings and loan associations, mutual savings banks, credit unions, and finance companies. The agency officers may be named "commissioner" or "superintendent of banking," but generally the scope of their duties with respect to state-chartered banks is analogous to those of the comptroller of the currency for national banks. Although their responsibilities vary from one state to another, state banking authorities normally have several responsibilities. First, they approve the charters for new state banks, the opening and closing of branch offices (if the state permits branching), and the scope of bank holding company operations within the state. Second, they examine financial institutuions chartered by the state. The extent and thoroughness of bank examinations vary from state to state. Third, state bank agencies have powers to protect the public interest. These take the form of regulating the activities of finance companies and enforcing various consumer regulations, such as credit disclosure and usury laws.

Banking Markets

Broadly speaking, the market for any goods or services consists of the individual, business, and governmental units that buy and sell the items in question. Although our definition appears simplistic, it is quite difficult in practice to designate which buyers and sellers constitute a particular market. In defining a market, two problems arise: (1) specifying the product exchanged in the market and (2) identifying the geographic area covered by the market.

Product Markets.　Banks are what economists consider multiproduct firms —firms that produce many different products. For example, banks make business loans, accept deposits, process checks, and provide trust services. Each of these activities or products constitutes a separate product market. The amount of competition a bank faces in each product market depends on the number of competitors in that market. Not all competitors need to be banks. Nonbank financial institutions may produce products that are close substitutes for those produced by banks. For example, banks compete with credit unions for consumer loans. They also must compete with savings and loan associations for mortgage loans. Thus competition in banking cannot be discussed without first carefully identifying the product market in question.

Geographic Market.   Directly related to product market specification is the determination of the geographic pattern of banking markets. If distinct markets exist for each bank product, as we have suggested, it seems reasonable to expect geographic areas of these markets to vary considerably from one product to another. For example, the markets for consumer savings accounts, consumer loans, and small-business loans are local in character, because the customers for these types of bank services usually select institutions close to where they live or work. The market for medium-sized business and agricultural loans may be regional. Finally, the market is nationwide for large business loans to prime corporate borrowers, such as General Motors Corporation, or for the sale of money market liabilities, such as negotiable certificates of deposit.

Geographic Monopolies.   The amount of competition in a banking market is determined by both the product and the geographic markets involved. These markets are closely controlled by regulatory agencies for both commercial banks and nonbank financial institutions. Product market regulation is exemplified by the restriction that only depository institutions may offer checking accounts. Bank entry into new geographic markets is restricted by chartering requirements, branching restrictions, and limitations on acquisitions by multibank holding companies. Therefore, banks can, in some cases, have a legal monopoly on a particular product or group of products in a specific geographic market. For example, a one-bank town provides a monopoly situation for all bank products that have local markets. Most people find it inconvenient to hold a checking or savings account in a town other than that in which they live. Thus the transactions cost of doing business outside one's home area may separate markets. Such a situation is called a *geographic monopoly*. Geographic monopolies need not be restricted to one-back towns; geographic segmentation of markets occurs wherever barriers to interlocational trade exist. For example, the geographic market for consumer loans in a large metropolis is in the immediate community—an area of several square miles—and not the entire metropolitan region.

Measurements of Market Structure

There are a number of ways to measure the degree of competition in banking markets. Commonly employed statistics include (1) the number of bank offices in the market, (2) the ratio of bank offices to the population in the market area, and (3) the concentration ratios that indicate the percentage of total deposits held by the largest banks in the market.

Concentration Ratios.   The most widely used measures of monopolistic power in the banking markets are *concentration ratios*. Their popularity stems from the relative ease with which they can be computed and understood.[6] A simple example will illustrate the calculation of these statistics and their proper economic interpretations. Assume that in a particular banking market there are five banks with the following deposits:

Bank	Deposits (millions)
A	$ 30
B	25
C	20
D	15
E	10
Total	$100

Concentration ratios measure the percentage of the market controlled by any given number of the largest banks. For our example, the concentration ratio for the largest bank in the market is 30 percent (30/100). Economic theory tells us that as the concentration ratio in a market increases, competition decreases, because one bank or a small group of banks has greater influence (or market power) relative to the total size of that market.

Carrying our example forward, if Bank A and Bank B merged, the one-bank concentration ratio would rise to 55 percent (55/100), reducing the market competition. If Bank A were to acquire all the remaining banks in the market (C, D and E) by merger, the concentration ratio would increase to 100 percent—a monopoly position. Furthermore, because a few banks can conceivably coordinate their pricing policies and thereby act as a de facto monopoly, two-bank, three-bank, and four-bank concentration ratios are often calculated to measure the amount of competition in banking markets. If other financial institutions produce the same product as banks (e.g., NOW accounts at mutual savings banks), they should be included in the concentration ratio calculations.

Problems with Concentration Ratios.   Although concentration ratios are relatively simple to calculate, a major problem exists in properly defining the geographic market. For example, suppose we have a market area as picture below:

A	B
C	D

---

[6]A more complex measure of competition in banking markets is the Herfindahl-Hirschman Index (HHI), which is the sum of the squares of the market share of all competitors in a market. It has a value of $10,000 for a one-firm market and a value near zero for a market where no firm has control of prices. The Department of Justice uses the HHI as its measure of market concentration for merger approvals. Some academics and legal scholars believe that as a measure of market concentration, it is superior to simple concentration ratios.

The market is a county in which there are four towns (A, B, C, and D). Each town has a single bank, and all the banks are of equal size. How much competition exists in this banking market? First, we must be careful to define both the product and the geographic markets. If the product is consumer loans or demand deposits, which typically have a local market, citing a countrywide concentration ratio of 25 percent would be incorrect. Properly defining the market as a town, the concentration ratio for each town is 100 percent, implying that banks are operating as monopoly banks with respect to demand deposits.

Now, what if the product in question is business loans? In this case the market may well be the entire county, and the proper concentration ratio for the county would be 25 percent. Other bank products may require different market definitions. The important point is that both the product market and the geographic market must be properly defined when figuring concentration ratios.

The example also illustrates wht is known as the market paradox, which produces abuse of concentration ratios. The *market paradox* refers to the different market concentration ratios that can be obtained by incorrectly defining the product market. As our example illustrates, for consumer demand deposits there is quite a difference in reporting a concentration ratio of 25 percent when our market is incorrectly defined as the county. The correct concentration ratio is, of course, 100 percent for a townwide market.

Types of Concentration Ratios

Concentration ratios are usually calculated for three separate market areas: national, state, and local. Let's examine the meaning of each of these area statistics, bearing in mind that each must be applied to a particular product market and a particular geographic market.

National Concentration Ratios.   These ratios are usually computed for the 100 largest banks in the United States. In recent years the ratio has remained fairly stable at about 50 percent, which does not represent undue concentration in U.S. banking, as some have suggested. We are dealing with a national product market—the market for large business loans and negotiable certificates of deposit. The major customers of this market are nationwide corporations. When borrowing or lending temporary excess funds, these large firms are by no means confined to one geographic region or even to one state. They have alternative sources for obtaining funds, such as the bond market, the commercial paper market, and life insurance companies and other nonbank financial intermediaries. In short, because these large firms have numerous alternatives available, competition in these national markets is keen.

Statewide Concentration Ratios.   Since statewide concentration ratios are calculated primarily for political purposes, their economic value is questionable. Statewide ratios suggest that some bank product markets are limited to a particular state. There is no reason that markets should end at state boundaries. States are political, not economic, concepts, and one cannot assume that any two states should be identified as separate geographic markets. Such bank products as medium-sized business loans, certain agricultural loans, and loans to other banks and nonbank financial institutions typically have regional markets. For example, because Chicago is a financial center for the Midwest, Chicago banks provide stiff competition for medium-sized business loans throughout the Midwest.

Local-Market Concentration Ratios. Most consumer financial products are sold in local markets. The calculation of local-market concentration ratios can be difficult. In large financial centers, such as New York City and Chicago, the metropolitan area may encompass several hundred local submarkets. In rural areas, a local market may include more than one town. Our knowledge about local markets is limited. Nevertheless, it seems reasonable to assume that in metropolitan areas, political subdivisions and towns may constitute a reasonable approximation of local banking markets. These various political subdivisions are often selected as an approximation for local markets because of the convenience in gathering statistical data.

The Significance of Bank Structure

Economists generally conclude that the consuming public is best served by markets that are competitive; this is the theory of competitive markets. In competitive markets, firms seek to produce goods and services according to the demands of consumers, as expressed by consumers' willingness to purchase services at the offered price. The level of firms' production is determined by balancing the cost of producing the output against the price consumers are willing to pay for it. In producing goods and services, firms try to combine resources so as to provide the maximum output at the lower possible cost. This optimal use of resources occurs because firms wish to maximize their own long-term profits.

As we know, banking is a highly regulated industry. It stands to reason that bank regulations as well as economic factors determine the number and size of banks operating in a particular market. Exhibit 15–5 depicts the factors that determine bank structure and the relationship that exists between bank structure and bank performance.

Bank Structure and Competition

One of the most important conclusions of the theory of competitive markets concerns the relationship between the structure of a market and the efficient allocation of economic resources. This conclusion is that the structure of a market determines the degree of competition in the market, and that the degree of competition affects the performance of firms with respect to the quantity of goods and services produced, the efficiency of production, and the price charged in the marketplace. Of course, the key element in this chain of events is competition. For markets that are competitive, we observe (1) that greater competition exists in markets characterized by a large number of producers where no single producer controls a substantial share of the market and (2) that greater competition in a market leads to greater output at a lower price for a given level of market demand. Thus, in general, the consuming public's welfare is better served by markets that have a large number of competitors.

For the banking industry, the competitive model implies that bank structure affects performance in providing services to the public. The theory further suggests that markets with many competitors are preferable to markets exhibiting other structural characteristics. However, the validity of the competitive market theory depends on some highly restrictive assumptions. If these are not met, we cannot conclude that resources are being allocated in a manner that best serves consumers. Three of these assumptions are particularly relevant to banking.

Unrestricted Entry.   The competitive market theory assumes that entry into the market is unrestricted. If markets were restricted, poorly managed banks or banks with monopoly market positions could offer high-priced or inferior services to the public because the public would lack an alternative. If entry were unrestricted, other banks would serve these markets. However, entry into bank markets *usually is restricted* by bank-chartering requirements and by restrictions on branching and multibank holding company activities.

Ease of Exit.   The theory of competitive markets assumes that exit, either by merger or by failure, must be possible to remove inefficient or unwanted firms from the marketplace. Without unrestricted exit, the structure of the industry cannot change to meet new circumstances. For the banking industry, however, bank failures can have wide-ranging effects beyond the individual banks that fail, and this condition makes unrestrained competition among banks undesirable. The Bank Acts of 1933 and 1935 and other bank legislation passed during the 1930s include many provisions intended to reduce competition among banks.

No Natural Monopolies.   The theory of competitive markets assumes that economies of scale resulting in *natural monopolies* do not exist. Natural monopolies result when the industry cost curve is such that the firm's unit costs always decrease as the size of the firm increases. If this were true for banking, the most efficient bank size would be the largest possible, and a competitive market would result in the survival of one bank in each market.

Competition and Bank Performance

We know that competition increases bank performance. However, we need to define bank performance carefully and to specify how it is measured. The performance of a bank or any business may be evaluated in terms of either private performance or social performance. *Private performance* is concerned with the welfare of the stockholders or the owners. Typically, it is implemented by maximizing the long-term profits of the firm. On the other hand, *social performance* means maximizing the overall welfare of the community. Maximizing social performance is the principal concern of bank regulatory agencies.

Economies of Scale in Banking

The lure of greater earnings through cost reductions generated by greater size has long fascinated management in banking and other industries. The idea that a large firm can

Exhibit 15–5   **The Relationship between Bank Structure and Bank Performance**

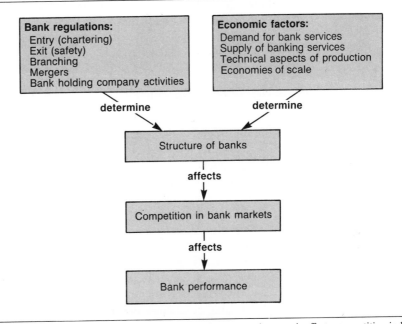

Bank regulators and economists are interested in bank structure because it affects competition in banking markets, which ultimately affects the number of bank failures.

produce the same goods or services more cheaply than a small firm is called *economies of scale*. Economies of scale suggest that as a firm's operating size becomes larger, the average cost of producing each unit decreases.

Background Information

In theory, economists believe that a firm's long-run cost curve is U-shaped. When a small firm begins to increase in size, the cost per unit of output decreases, resulting in economies of scale. As the volume of output becomes greater, however, inefficiencies begin to develop, and eventually the average cost per unit of output will rise.

Economies of scale accrue to large firms for two basic reasons. First, large firms are able to subdivide tasks, allowing employees to specialize. The efficiency gained through specialization is the basic idea behind producing automobiles on an assembly line rather than individually. Second, large firms are able to use highly efficient, specialized capital equipment, often too expensive for small firms to justify, given their lower volume of output. This is particularly true in banking, where the processing of demand deposits by computers and other mechanizations have allowed large banks to process a tremendous volume of checks at a low unit cost.

Information about possible economies of scale is of interest to both bank management and bank regulators. For management, scale economy tells what size bank can produce services at the lowest possible cost—the optimal bank size. Bank regulators use this information in merger and branching decisions because they want an efficient banking system. Because banks have begun to expand into new geographic markets as a result of deregulation and interstate banking legislation, bank regulators fear that the large multibranch firms that will emerge may drive small financial institutions from the marketplace.

Evidence on Scale Economies

The overall cost curve believed to exist for the banking industry is shown in Exhibit 15-6. These findings indicate that scale economies of size exist in some parts of the banking industry—the unit cost of bank output decreases as bank size increases— especially in the production of business and real estate loans. For most other bank services, such as time and demand deposits and installment loans, beyond some point it is unlikely that there are many, if any, economies of scale.[7]

There are some interesting implications for the banking industry if economies of scale do exist for smaller banks, those with assets of less than $75 million. As Exhibit 15-6 shows, the unit cost of output decreases as a bank size increases until a bank reaches an asset size of around $75 million. Beyond this point, the average cost of ouput may decrease as size increases, but the rate of decrease, if any, is no longer an important factor in operating efficiency.

The overall declining cost curve observed in Exhibit 15-6 has some interesting policy implications. First, it suggests that regulatory authorities and legislators need not be overly concerned that large banks will drive smaller banks from the marketplace; large banks do not have enough of a cost advantage to drive medium-sized banks from the market. Second, the cost curves indicate that *very* small banks may not be economically viable in the absence of regulatory protection. As Exhibit 15-1 indicates, more than 70 percent of all U.S. banks fall into this category.

Do the findings in Exhibit 15-6 mean that small banks will vanish without regulatory protection? A recent cost study has shown that cost differences between similar-size banks far exceed those obtainable by altering bank size (economies of scale).[8] For example, the study arrayed average cost data into 13 bank size classes and four average cost quartiles. The mean variation in average cost between the highest and lowest average cost quartiles, holding bank size constant, was 34 percent, and the mean variation in average cost across bank size classes was only 8 percent. Thus, cost savings from economies of scale, when they occur, are small in comparison to other factors that influence bank costs. These findings suggest that small banks that are

---

[7]To gain an understanding of the controversy over and complexity of the economies of scale issue in banking, see George J. Benston et al., "Operating Cost in Commercial Banking," *Economic Review*, Federal Reserve Bank of Atlanta, November 1982, pp. 6–21; David H. Humphrey, "Cost Dispersions and the Measurement of Economies in Banking," *Economic Review*, Federal Reserve Bank of Richmond, May/June 1987, pp. 24–38; and Loretta J. Mester, "Efficient Production of Financial Services; Scale and Scope Economies," *Business Review*, Federal Reserve Bank of Philadelphia, January/February 1987, pp. 15–25.
[8]David H. Humphrey, "Cost Dispersion and the Measurement of Economies in Banking," *Economic Review*, Federal Reserve Bank of Richmond, May/June 1987, pp. 24–38.

Exhibit 15–6   **The Relationship between Average Cost of Output and Size of Commercial Banks**

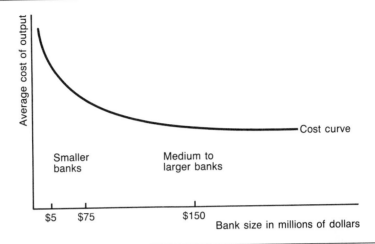

Economies of scale appear to exist for small banks, but for medium-sized and large banks, there do not appear to be significant economies of scale.

efficiently run and well managed and that identify consumer demand should prosper. Consider the analogy with the grocery industry: large, cost-efficient supermarket chains dominate, but many small grocery stores survive either by being cost efficient or by offering unique services that large stores cannot successfully provide. Small banks, for example, often provide highly personal consumer banking services that large banks find difficult to duplicate. Additionally, much new technology, such as computer systems, is available to small banks through the correspondent bank network. To operate most efficiently, however, bank management should try to achieve a size in excess of $75 million in total assets.

Bank Holding Companies

Bank holding companies have become a major form of organization for banks in the United States in recent years. The prominence of the bank holding company movement is attributable to three important desires on the part of bank management. First is the desire to achieve some form of interstate banking/branching in the face of restrictive state laws. Second is the desire by the largest banks in the country to diversify into nonbanking activities. Finally, bank holding companies can reduce their tax burden relative to the taxes they would pay if they operated as a bank. To understand the growth of the bank holding company movement, we first need to briefly discuss the history of the movement and the legislation surrounding it.

Background Information

Historically, both the number of bank holding companies in the United States and the proportion of deposits held by them were small until the 1960s. Before the 1960s, bank holding companies never controlled more than 15 percent of all bank deposits. The lack of growth of bank holding companies during this period is surprising when one considers that the holding company could establish bank systems that crossed city, county, and even state boundaries.

Despite forces that should have encouraged bank holding company expansion, other forces curtailed their growth. First, bank holding companies were not covered in the Bank Act of 1933, which prohibited banks from engaging in business activities unrelated to banking. The Board of Governors of the Federal Reserve System expressed the opinion that bank holding companies should have the same restrictions as any bank. Second, unit-banking groups waged an extensive campaign against bank holding companies as a threat to unit banking in this country, arguing that, if unchecked, holding companies held the potential to concentrate economic power and stifle competition in banking. As a result, most bankers elected not to adopt the bank holding company form of organization for fear of future restrictive legislation or outright abolition.

The Bank Holding Company Act of 1956 was intended to restrict bank holding companies' activities and expansion. However, by clarifying the status of bank holding companies, the act ultimately fostered their growth. The 1956 legislation placed responsibility for the control of bank holding companies with the Federal Reserve System. Holding companies owning 25 percent or more of the voting stock of two or more banks were (1) required to register with the Board of Governors of the Federal Reserve System as a bank holding company, (2) barred from making any new bank acquisitions across state lines (banks acquired prior to 1956 could be retained), (3) required to obtain approval of the Federal Reserve Board before the purchase of the voting stock of any banks, and (4) prohibited from owning subsidiaries engaged in nonbanking activities. As a result, many bank holding companies were required to divest themselves of their nonbanking subsidiaries.

Following the Bank Holding Company Act of 1956, the expansion of bank holding companies took one of two forms: multibank holding companies or one-bank holding companies. *Multibank holding companies*, which were included under the act, continued to be a device for banks to expand geographically. *One-bank holding companies*, which were explicitly excluded from the act, essentially gave banks carte blanche to engage in nonbanking activities. This "loophole" in the law led to a dramatic increase in the number of one-bank holding companies. In 1965, it was estimated that there were approximately 400 one-bank holding companies in the United States. By 1969, the number had nearly doubled. The loophole was closed in 1970 by the Bank Holding Company Amendment, which extended the 1956 Bank Holding Company Act to include one-bank holding companies. The number of registered bank holding companies increased sharply in 1972, the year that one-bank holding companies were required to register with the Federal Reserve System. We shall now discuss the incentives for banks to form holding companies.

PEOPLE
&EVENTS

Citicorp: Power, Innovation, and Arrogance

Enter Citicorp's headquarters at 399 Park Avenue, New York City, and "You realize you are at one of the vertexes of power in the world," said a former Citicorp executive. "It's like an aircraft carrier revving up to 30 knots. The place shakes." Although that may be a little overstated, it is definitely true that for the successful banker, Citicorp offers high salaries, prestige, excitement, and power.

Citicorp had $216 billion in assets at the end of 1991, which made it the largest bank holding company in the country. It owns Citibank, hundreds of lending offices, and savings and loan associations in five states. It is the nation's biggest bank–credit card issuer; it peddles retirement plans, mortgages, and consumer loans; and it even offers home banking. On the international scene Citicorp has a greater global presence than the large Japanese banks Dai-Ichi Kangyo and Sumitomo. Citicorp boasts 2,054 consumer and corporate banking outlets in 91 countries outside the United States. The world's largest private lender, nearly half of Citicorp's 89,000 employees work overseas. Overseas it offers many services that are prohibited to banks in the United States, including underwriting securities, owning equity in business ventures, and selling insurance.

Who is at the top of the heap, the king of Citicorpland? That extremely powerful position was handed to John S. Reed in 1984. Reed was a 44-year-old, boyish-looking, sometimes abrasive technocrat who presided over Citicorp's national consumer expansion. Under Reed, Citicorp became a world leader in the use of telecommunications and electronics for various banking applications and has since proven that electronics can be cheaper than brick-and-mortar banking. Citibank is in the process of linking all of its branches globally, allowing customers to access accounts from anywhere in the world.

Recently, Reed has come under attack from banking analysts on Wall Street for Citicorp's dismal performance in 1991. Of the ten largest bank holding companies in the United States, Citicorp turned in the worst stock price performance, with a decline in market value of 5.9 percent. In contrast, the top performer, Chemical Banking, increased its stock price by 125 percent in 1991.

The source of Citicorp's woes was a huge batch of past lending mistakes: loans to developing countries, loans to highly leveraged corporations, and—the biggest problem—real estate lending. The bad loans had security analysts calling for Reed's head. They argued that Reed lacked lending experience and that Citicorp's credit controls under his reign have been lax. Reed's critics were willing to overlook the bad loans to developing countries because he inherited them from Walter Wriston. In fact, in May 1987 Reed boldly added $3 billion to Citicorp's loan loss reserve to deal with the problem developing-country loans. Other banks quickly followed suit. Unfortunately, Citicorp's other problem loans were booked under Reed's stewardship.

The bad loans led to big losses. The slide began in the fourth quarter of 1990 when Citicorp recorded a large loss and cut its dividend. In the third quarter of 1991, Citicorp lost $885 million and eliminated its dividend, presumably under pressure from regulators because of its tenuous capital position. In the wake of the losses, Reed acted boldly, slashing costs and personnel. Citicorp's worldwide employment is down to 89,000 from a high of 95,000.

Apparently the stock market likes what it is seeing from Reed. In the first few months of 1992 Citicorp's stock price doubled, regaining $3 billion in market value for shareholders. The stock price performance is amazing in light of the small first quarter 1992 earnings. Net income was low because Reed added $3.9 billion to the provision for loan losses, a bold move to clean up the balance sheet and shore up the bank's capital position. That Citicorp had a profit despite the huge write-off is a sign of strength that the stock market apparently likes. Despite his critics, Reed believes he is the best person to serve at the helm of the nation's largest bank. In a recent interview he was asked whether he thought he deserved to be CEO. His answer was an unequivocal yes.

De Facto Branching

Although there is no longer a legal difference between one-bank and multibank holding companies, the distinction is still useful in discussing the reasons for forming bank holding companies. Multibank holdings were formed largely as a means of circumventing state branching law restrictions. Multibank holding companies allow banks to operate in larger units and thereby achieve economies of scale, and they also allow greater geographic diversification within states for greater safety. Bank holding companies give the appearance of home rule for the local bank, and, from the viewpoint of the local community, the head of the local banking office is the bank president rather than the branch manager. Some argue, however, that bank holding company groups concentrate economic power, decrease competition, and are not concerned about the communities they serve.

Nonbanking Activities

The reason many large banks formed one-bank holding companies was the opportunity to engage in a wide range of business activities. The scope of activities permitted is broader than those activities granted individual banks under the Bank Act of 1933. The Board of Governors of the Federal Reserve System has the authority to define what activities are closely related to banking activities. Exhibit 15–7 shows a list of activities approved and denied by the Board in recent years. Importantly, bank holding companies are allowed to operate their nonbank subsidiaries across state lines. For example, many bank holding companies operate finance companies and carry on credit card operations across state lines.

Another reason large banks formed one-bank holding companies was to gain access to the commercial paper market. During the late 1960s, market rates of interest had risen to such high levels that the interest rate banks could pay on deposits was at the maximum allowable under Regulation Q. However, bank holding companies could sell commercial paper at an interest rate not controlled by Regulation Q. Once the holding company had sold the commercial paper, it would deposit the money in the bank.

Tax Avoidance

One of the most important reasons for smaller banks to form a bank holding company is the tax consideration. For example, approximately 80 percent of bank holding companies are one-bank holding companies, and of these, about half are single-subsidiary companies. Product or geographic market motivation cannot account for the existence of these single-subsidiary holding companies. The principal tax benefits of a holding company organization is that interest paid on debt is a tax-deductible expense and most dividends received from subsidiaries provide tax-exempt revenues for the parent firm. In addition, nonbanking subsidiaries can be structured to avoid local taxes.

Nonbank Banks

The whimsical name *nonbank bank* springs from the confusing wording in the Bank Holding Company Act that defines a bank as a firm that simultaneously makes commercial loans and accepts deposits. Under this interpretation, for example, a bank holding company could purchase a commercial bank, sell off its commercial loan portfolio, and operate the new firm as a "consumer bank." The consumer bank, a nonbank bank, could still have its deposits insured by the FDIC and could operate in more than one state—something allowed only if a nonheadquartered state allows such expansion. In addition, the consumer bank could engage in activities prohibited to banks, such as insurance and real estate sales, and at the same time operate offices that accept deposits. The reason all of this can take place is, of course, that the nonbank bank fails to come under the Bank Holding Company Act's definition of a bank.

Bank regulators are also concerned about nonbank banks' effect on the separation of banking from other financial and business activities, such as manufacturing. For example, Gulf and Western Corporation and McMahan Valley Stores (a California furniture dealer) have received approval to operate nonbank banks. By the early 1980s there were more than 60 nonbank firms operating as limited banks, and some were owned by nonfinancial firms.

The concerns of Congress and bank regulators about the inroads of nonbank banks came to a head in 1983 when the Office of the Comptroller of the Currency (OCC) declared a moratorium on nonbank bank charters, and the Federal Reserve announced that it was interested in stopping or slowing nonbank bank growth. Since that time, the financial press has been peppered with articles on the legal jousting among various interest groups. The death knell seems to have been sounded for nonbank banks, however, with the passage of the Competitive Equality Banking Act of 1987. The legislation prohibits the creation of new nonbank banks for one year and then limits their growth to 7 percent annually; the existing 160 nonbank banks were grandfathered.

Interstate and Branch Banking

The ability of banks to expand geographically—by branching or forming a bank holding company—has been the subject of long-standing controversy in American banking. In the 1980s and 1990s the issue resurfaced in the guise of interstate banking. The controversy is being led by large U.S. banks that operate offices in countries throughout the world and now want to offer full-service banking in their own country. They cite the deregulatory spirit of the times and, more importantly, the ability of nonbank interlopers such as Merrill Lynch and Sears to sell financial products without geographic restraint and with much less regulatory hassle.

Historical View

Branch banking did not become a national issue until the passage of the National Currency Act of 1863. The act provided for the chartering of national banks and

Exhibit 15–7   Nonbank Activities for Bank Holding Companies, All of Which May Be Operated Across State Lines (June 1, 1988)

Activities Approved by the Board		Activities Denied by the Board

1. Extensions of credit
   a. Mortgage banking
   b. Finance companies
   c. Credit cards
   d. Factoring
2. Operation of industrial banks
3. Servicing of loans and other extensions of credit
4. Trust company operation
5. Investment or financial advising
6. Full-payment leasing of personal or real property
7. Investments in community welfare projects
8. Provision of bookkeeping or data-processing services
9. Action as insurance agent or broker, primarily in connection with credit extensions
10. Underwriting of credit-extension life, accident, and health insurance
11. Provision of courier services
12. Management consulting for unaffiliated banks
13. Sale at retail of money orders with a face value of not more than $1,000, traveler's checks, and savings bonds
	14. Performance of appraisals of real estate
	15. Audit services for unaffiliated banks
	16. Issuance and sale of traveler's checks
	17. Management consulting to nonbank depository institutions
	18. Buying and selling of gold and silver bullion and silver coin
	19. Issuance of money orders and general-purpose variable denominated payment instruments
	20. Action as futures commission merchant to cover gold and silver bullion and coins
	21. Underwriting of certain federal, state, and municipal securities
	22. Check verification
	23. Financial advice to consumers
	24. Issuance of small-denomination debt instruments
	25. Arrangement of commercial real estate equity financing
	26. Foreign exchange advisory and transmittal services
	27. Securities brokerage
		1. Insurance premium funding (combined sales of mutual funds and insurance)
		2. Underwriting of life insurance not related to credit extension
		3. Real estate brokerage
		4. Land development
		5. Real estate syndication
		6. General management consulting
		7. Property management
		8. Computer-output microfilm services
		9. Underwriting of mortgage guaranty insurance
		10. Operation of a savings and loan association
		11. Operation of a travel agency
		12. Underwriting of property and casualty insurance
		13. Underwriting of home-loan-life mortgage insurance
		14. Orbanco: investment note issue with transactional characteristics
		15. Armored car service
		16. Real estate advisory activities
		17. Certain contract key entry services
		18. Provision of credit ratings on bonds, preferred stock, or commercial paper
		19. Action as a specialist on foreign currency options on a securities exchange

The Fed determines the nonbanking activities in which banks may engage. In recent years there has been increasing pressure to expand the list of approved activities.

Source: Board of Governors, Federal Reserve System, 1988.

established the Office of the Comptroller of the Currency to supervise and regulate the newly created national banks. Branch banking was not mentioned in the act, and all subsequent interpretations assumed that national banks were prohibited from branching. This view was consistent with the public's concern that concentration of economic power among a few large banking organizations might allow these banks to exercise undue influence over the allocation of credit. Over time, however, this interpretation created competitive inequities between state-chartered and nationally chartered banks as states began giving branching powers to the banks they chartered.

In 1927 Congress adopted the McFadden Act, which authorized national banks to branch within their home city limits if state law permitted branching. Although the McFadden Act has become associated with the restriction of the geographic expansion of banks, it actually liberalized branching restrictions on nationally chartered banks. Even with limited branching privileges, however, national banks were still at a competitive disadvantage relative to banks in states that permitted branching beyond a bank's city limits. To remedy this inequality, the Glass-Steagall Act of 1933 included a provision to allow national banks to have branching powers identical to those of their state-chartered competitors. The act set state boundaries as the limit for banks' geographic expansion and gave the states the power to determine the structure of banking within their borders.

Because there was no legislation relating to bank holding companies prior to 1956, they often were formed to circumvent the legal restraints on geographic expansion imposed by state laws and the McFadden act. Initially, most bank holding companies focused their efforts on de facto branching within states. With time, however, some large bank holding companies began to acquire banks in other states.

The Bank Holding Company Act of 1956 (and the 1970 amendment) restricted the business activities and geographic expansion of bank holding companies. Of importance is a section of the act known as the Douglas Amendment, which prohibited a bank holding company from acquiring a bank in another state unless the laws in that state specifically authorize such acquisitions. As a vestige of the period when bank holding companies could cross state lines, seven domestic interstate bank holding companies remain in operation; the largest of these, First Interstate Bank, with total assets of $51 billion, currently controls more than 20 banks (900 branches) in 12 Western states.

Except for the grandfathering of a few interstate bank holding companies, no state took advantage of its right to allow out-of-state banks to enter its borders. Then, in 1975, the state of Maine passed the first interstate banking law allowing unrestricted entry by out-of-state bank holding companies under the provisions of the Douglas Amendment of the Bank Holding Company Act of 1956. No other state laws were enacted until 1982, when Massachusetts adopted a New England regional reciprocal banking law, and shortly after that, New York state enacted a nationwide reciprocal law. The New England regional law was challenged in the courts because it does not allow banks from *all* states equal access into the Massachusetts market. In June 1985, the United States Supreme Court ruled in favor of the New England law and reconfirmed a long-standing legal precedent that individual states control the configuration of banking within their borders.

The Major Issues

Given the new technology, banks and other firms in the financial services industry believe that they can achieve higher profits and greater market share by increasing the scope of their operations through geographic expansion. Regulators, on the other hand, are concerned about interstate banking's impact on the efficiency, competition, and safety of the U.S. financial system. We shall now discuss the issues surrounding interstate and branch banking.

Economic Efficiency.   Scale economies reduce unit cost as the level of production increases. If interstate or branch banking is allowed, larger banks are likely to develop. If larger banks can operate more efficiently than small banks, they will provide consumer services at a lower cost, thereby displacing smaller banks from the market. Except for very small banks, however, the evidence indicates that large banks do not have notable cost advantages over small banks. Thus it does not seem likely that large banks will dominate small banks if legal restrictions on geographic expansion are relaxed.

Competition and Concentration.   Perhaps the most controversial issue in the interstate and branch banking debate is the effect that multioffice banking may have on bank competition. Theory holds that competition within a market is influenced by market concentration. Some fear that if banks are allowed to expand geographically, large banks will blanket a geographic area to achieve a geographic monopoly. Indeed, some studies show that branch banking leads to increased concentration ratios. For example, both New Jersey and Virginia experienced rapid increases in statewide bank concentration ratios following the liberalization of their branching laws.

To determine the degree of competition in banking, we must consider both the products and the geographic market for the products. Banks are multiproduct firms, and their products have different geographic markets. As mentioned previously, most consumer financial services tend to be sold in local markets, the market for medium-sized business loans and agricultural loans is regional, and the market for large prime-rate loans is nationwide. Because of the local nature of consumer products, economists are most concerned about competition at the local level. Historically, entry into local markets by banks outside the market area has been restricted by regulators. Because of this protection, retail banking markets may not be as competitive as regional or national banking markets.

The effect of interstate banking on local markets depends on the manner in which entry is accomplished. If entry into a local market is de novo, a new competitor has entered the market and competition is likely to increase. If entry is by acquisition, concentration may increase in the local market, leading to less competition between firms. Because consumer financial services are sold in local markets, it is important that regulators not allow any financial institution to monopolize a local market area. Thus, if geographic expansion is allowed, banks and other financial services firms should be forced to spread out over numerous local markets and should not be allowed to concentrate in a single market.

The best evidence regarding the effect of market entry by acquisition is found in studies of holding company acquisitions. Recent studies have reported that holding company affiliations increased the market share of small banks and decreased the market share of large banks; in both cases, however, changes in concentration ratios were small.[9] Furthermore, when a small bank became affiliated with a holding company, it was able to compete more effectively with larger banks in the market. This may have occurred because the small bank could then offer additional products and services made possible through affiliation. The studies also indicate that when larger banks became affiliated with a holding company, small banks in the market competed more aggressively.

Another factor to consider is the competition that banks face from other financial services firms. Banks must compete with other banks, thrifts, credit unions, finance companies, mortgage bankers, brokerage firms, financial conglomerates, and automatic teller machine (ATM) networks. Given the variety of firms and the expanded-product powers of nonbank depository institutions, it does not seem likely that changes in bank structure will materially affect overall concentration at the local level. Simply stated, local markets are becoming increasingly competitive as nonbank firms, many of which face few legal restrictions, begin entering the local banking markets with consumer financial products. Retail banking has become a highly competitive business.

Empirical research has found that greater branching authority contributes to greater concentration at the state and local market level. Removing barriers to interstate banking is likely to produce the same results. Because state boundaries are political and by and large do not constiute market boundaries, concentration is likely to increase at the national level as well. Most economists are not alarmed by this. As Exhibit 15–8 shows, the United States is among those countries with the lowest concentration of bank deposits. More importantly, except for consumer banking, most bank products have regional markets that lend themselves to many competitors. Competition is not a concern for products with a national market, such as large business loans, because the firms dealing in these products are not confined to one geographic region or to any one bank.

Safety and Soundness of the Banking System.   Another issue of national concern is whether branching and interstate banking contribute to a higher rate of bank failures. When banks fail, there are potential ramifications for society. If the bank is small, the effect of failure is likely to be local. If a large bank fails, repercussions may be felt throughout the financial markets and the entire economy. Thus a bank may become "too big to fail," as in the case of Continental Illinois.

Supporters of interstate and branch banking, however, cite bank safety as one of their strongest arguments. Evidence over the years has shown that branch-banking

---

[9]See John T. Rose, "Bank Holding Company Affiliation and Market Share Performance," *Journal of Monetary Economics* 9 (January 1982), pp. 110–119; John T. Rose and Donald T. Savage, "Bank Holding Company De Novo Entry and Market Share Accumulation," *The Antitrust Bulletin* 26 (Winter 1981), pp. 753–767; B. Frank King, "The Impact of Local Market Entry by Large Bank Holding Companies," *Economic Review*, Federal Reserve Bank of Atlanta (November 1982), pp. 41–47; and Paul Calem, "Interstate Bank Mergers and Competition in Banking," *Business Review*, Federal Reserve Bank of Philadelphia (January/February 1987), pp. 3–14.

systems are more immune to failures than unit-banking systems. During the tumultuous years from 1921 through 1931, only seven bank failures involved banks having more than ten branches. The greater safety of multioffice banks over unit banks derives from their better geographic diversification, which results in lower business risk. On the other hand, branching bank and holding company systems are typically larger than unit banks and, as a result, usually have greater leverage and riskier loan portfolios than unit banks. The willingness of multioffice banks to assume greater business risk may offset the risk reduction of geographic diversification. However, regulators can control capital requirements and asset mix to favorably influence a bank's business risk. Finally, studies of contemporary bank failures indicate that most failures have been related to illegal managerial manipulations, not to the number of offices the bank had.

Mobility of Funds.   In today's markets, technology exists to move funds efficiently throughout the economy. At the national level this is advantageous, because it allows funds to be channeled to the best investment opportunities. Financial markets such as the Federal Funds market help achieve this economic objective, as do branching and bank holding company systems.

However, the notion of funds leaving a community to go to the highest bidder is not always politically popular. Rural and agricultural areas often see interstate and branching systems as a means of "siphoning off" needed capital to industrial or metropolitan areas. One alleged result is the chronically depressed economic condition of rural areas. This argument, originally made by farm organizations and independent banking groups, has recently been taken up by consumer groups.

To economists, an important question is whether multioffice firms allocate credit better than unit banks do. In analyzing this problem, we should consider (1) whether

---

Exhibit 15–8   **Bank Structure of the United States and Other Industrial Countries**

Country	Number of Commercial Banks	Number of Banking Offices	Average Population per Bank Office	Share of Deposits at Five Largest Banks
United States	14,451	54,235	4,177	19.2%
Germany	243	41,000	1,506	61.8
Canada	11	7,425	3,296	77.7
United Kingdom	35	14,000	4,004	56.8
Japan	86	13,420	8,835	34.5
France	206	40,200	1,347	76.1
Italy	1,170	11,970	4,787	35.1
Switzerland	432	5,501	1,153	46,7

U.S. banking has the lowest concentration of bank deposits relative to other industrialized countries.

Source: Richard F. Syron, "The 'New England Experiment' in Interstate Banking," *New England Economic Review*, March–April 1984, p. 6. Reprinted with permission of the Federal Reserve Bank of Boston.

funds are transferred from areas of low demand to high demand and (2) whether local credit needs are met. In general, research shows that multioffice banks transfer a greater proportion of loanable funds to areas of higher credit demand than do unit banks using the correspondent banking system. The probable reason for the greater transfer of funds is lower transaction costs. Furthermore, relative to unit banks, multioffice firms appear to do a larger proportion of business with local business firms than with consumers. Finally, when funds transfers do occur, funds tend to flow between nonurban areas rather than between nonurban areas and the bank's home-office city.

Service to Customers. That unit banks give better service to bank customers is an argument frequently made by unit-banking proponents. They argue that unit banks can make loans and other important decisions more quickly than managers in multibanking organizations, because decision making in unit banks is centralized, and, therefore, there is no need to consult the home office. Furthermore, the unit banker is presumably a long-time resident of the community and has a better feel for the community, its people, and its problems. Critics fault multibanking systems as often being managed by out-of-towners who act as "mercenaries" for the home office bank and do not have the best interests of the community at heart.

Multibank proponents counter that their managers are better trained and more highly educated than unit bankers and therefore are better able to service the community's financial and banking needs. More important, an office of a large bank is able to provide more complete banking services to a community than is a small unit bank. This argument is particularly true for small towns served by small unit banks. A branch of Bank of America, for example, can offer its full range of worldwide services to a small community. Unit bank advocates attempt to discredit this argument by noting that unit banks can provide many of these same services through their correspondent relationships with large banks.

Viability of Small Banks. When geographic restrictions on banking are relaxed, most economists expect many small community banks to be absorbed by larger banks. Thus the long-term survival of small banks comes under question. The viability of community banks can best be projected by examining their experience in two states with statewide branching—California and New York. If small banks are not viable, then few should exist in these states.

California is a state with a long history of statewide branching. Bank of America, which has the largest branching network in the country (over 1,000 branches), also resides in the state. Despite these facts, more than 75 independent unit banks exist in California, and the state is among the leading states each year in the number of newly chartered banks. In New York State, where branching laws were liberalized in 1962, small banks have not been derived from the market by large New York City banks. In fact, even though competition has become keener in local markets, efficient small banks have competed effectively against the larger banks that entered their market area.

The reasons for much of small banks' competitive ability can be found in the analysis already presented. One reason is that small banks do not appear to be at a significant cost disadvantage relative to large banks. Another reason is consumer

DID YOU KNOW?

Megamergers in Banking: Shake-Up at the Top

Merger mania hit banking in 1991, with more than 500 banks announcing plans to merge. The value of completed mergers in 1991 exceeded $20 billion, over four times the $4.3 billion worth of mergers in 1990. Many bankers and government policymakers view the mergers as necessary to solve the major problems of the banking industry in the United States: overcapacity, undercapitalization, lack of diversification, and declining profitably. Further, weakened U.S. banks have all but disappeared from the ranks of the top banks in the world, a list dominated by rich Japanese and European mega-banks. Mergers among the nation's largest banks, bankers argue, would permit U.S. banks to better compete on a global scale and would also result in substantial cost savings, increasing operating efficiency and shareholders' wealth, and ultimately strengthening the entire U.S. banking system. Of course, opponents of bank mergers fear that the consolidation of vast economic power, especially among the country's largest banks, would result in less competition for bank services nationally, monopoly power, and a banking system less responsive to the needs of average Joe or Jane Citizen.

Megamergers shook up the list of the ten largest bank holding companies between 1990 and 1991 (see tables below). Chemical Banking (1990 assets of $73 billion; number 6) merged with Manufacturers

Hanover (1990 assets of $61 billion; number 9) in 1991 to form the second largest bank holding company (now called Chemical Banking) with 1991 assets of $139 billion. NCNB, the country's 7th largest bank holding company in 1990 with assets of $65 billion, merged with C&S/Sovran, the country's 12th largest bank holding company in 1990 with assets of $51 billion, to form NationsBank, which is now the 4th largest bank holding company in the United States with 1991 assets of $110 billion.

As mergers go, the two mentioned above couldn't be more different, While the merging of the C&S/Sovran and NCNB organizations has proceeded smoothly, the Chemical–Manny Hanny combination has had its share of rough spots. The main problem with the Chemical deal is the agony of trying to integrate two banks operating in the same market, New York City. Over the past ten years Chemical chairman Walter V. Shipley and Manny Hanny chairman John F. McGillicuddy were able to literally (almost) wave at each other from their headquarters offices on either side of Park Avenue. The other problem is that the Chemical–Manny Hanny merger was a merger of equals, with debate over which CEO gets the final say over delicate restructing matters. For example, Manny Hanny chairman McGillicuddy prefers a centralized management system, whereas Chemical's Shipley likes

loyalty. In many cases consumers prefer to do business with their local bank rather than deal with an outsider. Local banks with officers and directors that are long-term members of the community may better know the needs of the community. These factors suggest that well-managed small community banks will continue to exist.

Banks' Interstate Business Activities

As we have seen, state boundaries have little economic meaning and, in most cases, reflect accidents of history and geography. Businesses other than banking operate decentralization and a sharing of power and authority. Observers note that the Chemical–Manny Hanny merger has been slowed by haggling over details such as whose accounting system will be adopted or whose computer software for automating branches will be used.

In contrast, the NationsBank merger has proceeded smoothly. There was little overlap between the C&S/Sovran and NCNB markets, so the merger simply joined banks in adjacent markets, creating an impressive network of 1,800 branches covering nine states. Further, there was never any question about who was in charge. Hugh McColl of NCNB has been in charge of NationsBank from the outset; clearly the NCNB–C&S/Sovran deal was not a merger of equals. NCNB was the financially stronger bank and McColl consolidated his leadership by appointing NCNB executives to six of eight top positions. McColl's unchallenged control has allowed him to take bold steps to cut costs. Cost savings from the merger are estimated to reach $450 million by 1994.

The Five Largest Bank Holding Companies in the United States, 1990			The Five Largest Bank Holding Companies in the United States, 1991		
Rank	Bank Holding Company	Assets ($ Billions)	Rank	Bank Holding Company	Assets ($ Billions)
1	Citicorp, New York	$217.0	1	Citicorp, New York	$216.9
2	BankAmerica, San Franciso	110.7	2	Chemical Banking, New York	138.9
3	Chase Manhattan, New York	98.0	3	BankAmerica San Francisco	115.5
4	J. P. Morgan, New York	93.1	4	NationsBank, Charlotte	110.3
5	Security Pacific, Los Angeles	84.7	5	J. P. Morgan, New York	103.5

freely across state lines, and, for that matter, so have many competitors of banks. It would be misleading, however, to say that banks have not participated in interstate financial activities. In fact, most of the nation's largest bank holding companies do a considerable amount of interstate business and use a variety of avenues to provide banking and financial services across state lines. We shall now discuss the more important means by which they accomplish this.

Edge Act Corporations. Since 1919, banks have been allowed to form Edge Act corporations in states other than their home state in order to engage in international business transactions. As of 1986, there were more than 150 domestic Edge Act corporations in the United States that could accept deposits and make other bank transactions without regard to state boundaries, provided that the transactions were for international business. Because an increasing number of large corporations are engaging in international business activities and because it is difficult to separate purely domestic transactions from those related to international business activities, most multinational businesses have access to interstate banking services from a single banking source.

Loan Production Offices.   National banks and many state-chartered banks expand their business activities across state lines through loan production offices (LPO). LPOs are no more than offices from which banks make loans subject to the requirement that the home office approve the loans. Banks use loan production offices mostly for commercial lending to prime-rate and middle-market customers. Currently there are more than 300 LPOs operting across state boundaries.

Nonbank Subsidiaries.   As previously discussed, bank holding companies can engage in a wide range of banklike services across state lines through nonbank subsidiaries. Mortgage banking and operating finance companies are the two most important financial activities of nonbank subsidiaries. Banks also achieve an interstate banking presence through leasing companies, companies that service loans, trust companies that underwrite credit life insurance, and data-processing companies. For example, Citicorp has more than 230 consumer and mortgage finance offices located in 55 cities throughout the United States.

Foreign Banks.   Prior to 1978, foreign banks were virtually unregulated by the federal government and could branch across state lines, whereas domestic banks could not. Currently there are more than 160 foreign banks operating in the United States, and about half of these have offices in more than one state. As an example, Barclay's Bank of London has banks in New York, California, and Massachusetts. The International Bank Act (IBA) of 1978 addressed this inequity and now requires foreign banks to choose a home state for full-service banking. Except for their banking facilities that were grandfathered under the IBA, foreign banks now operate under the same geographic restrictions as their domestic counterparts.

Acquisition through Failure.   The Garn–St. Germain Act of 1982 provides that banks can acquire failing depository institutions across state lines. For example, Citicorp of New York in September 1982 acquired Fidelity Savings and Loan of California and its ninety branches (now called Citicorp Savings). Similarly, in December 1983 Citicorp acquired two more failing savings and loan associations in two of the most attractive banking markets—Illinois and Florida. Although the number of acquisitions under the Garn–St. Germain Act is not large, they are significant because they represent footholds for relatively large banks in important banking markets.

Interstate Banking Legislation

Exhibit 15-9 shows the status of interstate banking in 1992. There are four categories of legislation. First, 13 states permit nationwide entry without reciprocity, which allows banks in their states to be acquired by bank holding companies from any other state. This so-called open-entry is the most liberal type of interstate banking legislation. Second, 21 states permit nationwide reciprocal interstate banking. Reciprocity means that out-of-state banks are permitted to acquire banks in a given state as long as the other state reciprocates. New Jersey, for example, is a national reciprocal state. This means that a bank holding company from Ohio can acquire a bank in New Jersey because Ohio is also a national reciprocal state, allowing interstate acquisitions with reciprocity. A bank holding company from Kansas, on the other hand, would not be permitted to acquire a New Jersey bank.

Third, 14 states and the District of Columbia permit regional reciprocal interstate banking. These banks are part of several regional compacts that permit interstate banking within the borders of a given group of states, for example, the Southeast of New England. The primary motivation for forming a regional compact is that it allows some banking organizations within the compact to grow to a size large enough to compete with large money-center banks and to integrate regional financial markets. Large, regionally controlled banking systems may better serve middle-market firms and may aid in attracting such firms to the region. Consumers may also find bank services more convenient as banks expand into natural markets that cross state lines. Finally, two states allow no interstate banking.

Entry and Exit

The widespread bank failures of the 1920s and the early 1930s led to a drastic change of attitudes toward easy entry into banking and, consequently, limited the degree of competition that banks could face. The rationale for restricting entry centered on preventing bank failures. The intent of the chartering process was to keep poorly capitalized and poorly managed banks from entering the market, as well as to protect existing banks from fatal competition. A study in 1960 estimated that the stiffer entry requirements initiated in the mid-1930s reduced the number of commercial banks by as many as 2,200, or 10 percent, compared to the number that would have existed in the absence of entry restrictions.[10]

A number of studies have examined the effect of new bank entry into local markets with high concentration ratios.[11] The results usually agree with economic theory. In general, the studies conclude that in local markets, the entry of new banks decreases the price of bank services, increases deposit rates, and improves banking services. Furthermore, the loan-to-deposit ratio increases for established banks, indicating a greater emphasis on business and consumer loans to the local community. And, most surprising, the benefit of competition was experienced by the public without an adverse effect on bank profitability. This suggests that new competition spurred existing banks to be more responsive to consumer demand as well as to be more efficient in their operations.

Summary

Bank structure refers to the distribution of banks in terms of number, location, and size in a particular banking market. The structure of U.S. banking is characterized by a large number of small banks, many of which are unit banks, located in one- or two-bank towns. Bank structure is important because economists believe that it affects the degree of competition in markets. Competition, in turn, affects banks' performance

---

[10]Sam Peitzman, "Bank Entry Regulation: Its Impact and Purpose," *National Banking Review*, December 1965, pp. 163–177.

[11]For example, see Donald R. Fraser and Peter S. Rose. "Bank Entry and Bank Performance," *Journal of Finance*, March 1972, pp. 65–78.

Exhibit 15–9   **State Laws Allowing Interstate Bank Holding Companies**

Nationwide entry without reciprocity	Nationwide entry with reciprocity	Regional or contiguous state entry with reciprocity	Entry not allowed
Alaska	California	Alabama	Hawaii
Arizona	Connecticut	Arkansas[13]	Montana
Colorado	Delaware	District of Columbia	
Idaho	Illinois	Florida	
Maine	Indiana	Georgia	
Nevada	Kentucky	Iowa	
New Hampshire	Lousiana	Kansas	
New Mexico	Massachusetts	Maryland	
Oklahoma[12]	Michigan	Minnesota	
Oregon	Nebraska	Mississippi	
Texas	New Jersey	Missouri	
Utah	New York	North Carolina	
Wyoming	North Dakota	South Carolina	
	Ohio	Virginia	
	Pennsylvania	Wisconsin	
	Rhode Island		
	South Dakota		
	Tennessee		
	Vermont		
	Washington		
	West Virginia		

Except for two states, all allow some form of interstate branching.

Source: Federal Reserve Bank of Kansas City, *Financial Industry Trends*, 1992, p. 31.

with respect to the quantity of goods and services produced, the efficiency of production, and the price charged in the marketplace. The optimal structure for the banking industry is the one that allows adequate competition but not to the extent that competition becomes so intense as to permit massive bank failures.

The overall cost curves for commercial banks indicate that economies of scale do exist in the banking industry, but only for banks with up to $75 million in assets. After that point, the average cost of output levels off. This finding suggests that large banks do not have enough market power to drive medium-sized banks from the market.

The geographic expansion of banks has been a long-standing controversy. Those favoring local banking argue that small community banks are more responsive to a

[12]Bank holding companies from states not granting reciprocal entry to Oklahoma banking organizations must wait four years before making additional acquisitions.

[13]Entry into Arkansas is contingent on submission, approval, and compliance with an extensive plan guaranteeing certain levels of community service and investment.

community's needs and are more likely to use deposits to develop the local economy. Others argue that whenever consumers lack alternative banking facilities, unit or community banks have monopoly powers owing to the geographic segmentation of retail banking markets. Where entry into markets is not restricted, multioffice banking provides more competitive banking markets with minimum risk of bank failure. States control the configuration of banking within their boundaries, and barriers to interstate banking are crumbling as states enter into regional banking compacts. At the commercial level, banks already compete nationwide. The protection of local retail banking markets is at the center of the interstate banking controversy.

Bank holding companies have been a controversial form of bank organization because of fear of potential concentration of economic power, which could stifle competition in banking markets, and because of the threat they pose to the survival of small unit banks. Banks are motivated to form holding companies to achieve branch banking and interstate expansion, to diversify into nonbank business activities, and to achieve tax savings.

Questions

1. Use the concepts of product market and geographic market to explain how it is possible for a bank located in a large metropolitan area to act as a monopolist.
2. What are concentration ratios, and what do they measure? How are they calculated? Discuss the proper use and the abuse of (1) nationwide concentration ratios, (2) statewide concentration ratios, and (3) local-market concentration ratios.
3. How does the theory of competitive markets allocate resources? Does this model apply readily to the banking industry? If not, explain the exceptions and implications for banking.
4. Explain the overall cost curve that is believed to exist for banks. What are the policy implications of this curve for bank management and bank regulators? What does the cost curve say about the overall efficiency of the U.S. banking system?
5. Summarize the major arguments for and against branch banking. Are you in favor of statewide branching? Of nationwide branching?
6. Give the reasons that banks select the bank holding company form of organization.
7. Under what conditions would bank mergers be beneficial to the banking system, and under what conditions would they be harmful?
8. Bentonville is a rural community with an agriculturally based economy and a population of 10,000. The town has four banks of the following size: Bank A has deposits of $100,000; Bank B, $75,000; Bank C, $40,000; and Bank D, $15,000. The banks' primary business is consumer services and agricultural loans. Banks C and D each want to merge with Bank B. Compute the appropriate concentration ratios before and after the possible mergers. Should the bank regulators allow one of the possible mergers or deny the merger requests altogether?
9. Summarize the regulations that restrict banks from crossing state lines. What avenues have banks used to achieve de facto interstate banking?

10. Banks have effectively achieved interstate banking at the commercial level. Retail banking is geographically restricted by state lines. Comment.

Selected References

Boyd, John H., and Stanley, L., Graham. "The Profitability and Risk Effects of Allowing Bank Holding Companies to Merge With Other Financial Firms: A Simulation Study." *Quarterly Review.* **Federal Reserve Bank of Minneapolis, Spring 1988, pp. 3–20.**
This article examines the debate about whether bank holding companies (BHCs) should engage in certain financial lines of business outside commercial banking. Specifically, large BHCs have argued for lower barriers of entry into investment banking, full-service security brokerage, the insurance business, and real estate investment and development.

Calem, Paul. "Interstate Bank Mergers and Competition in Banking. " *Business Review.* **Federal Reserve Bank of Philadelphia, January/February 1987, pp. 3–14.**
Looks at the effect the interstate bank mergers and acquisitions are having on competition in banking markets.

Clair, Robert T., and Paula K. Tucker. "Interstate Banking and the Federal Reserve: A Historical Perspective." *Economic Review.* **Federal Reserve Bank of Dallas, November 1989, pp. 1–20.**
This article traces the evolution of the Federal Reserve Board's stance on interstate banking. It also summarizes the current status of interstate banking legislation.

Cummings, Christine M., and Lawrence M. Sweet. "Financial Structure of the G-10 Countries: How Does the United States Compare?" *Quarterly Review.* **Federal Reserve Bank of New York, Winter 1987–88, pp. 14–25.**
This article examines the different financial structures found among the major industrialized nations.

Dunham, Constance R. "Interstate Banking and the Outflow of Local Funds." *New England Economic Review.* **Federal Reserve Bank of Boston, March–April 1986, pp. 7–19.**
Examines whether interstate banking leads to outflow of local funds. The evidence indicates that small banks tend to be conduits for a substantial outflow of funds from their local communities, whereas large banks tend to direct their funds toward areas of greatest loan demand.

Federal Reserve Bank of Atlanta. *Economies of Scale in Banking: Special Issue. Economic Review,* **November 1982.**
Special issue of *Economice Review* devoted to discussing economies of scale in banking.

Humphrey, David B. "Cost Dispersion and the Measurement of Economies in Banking." *Economic Review.* **Federal Reserve Bank of Richmond, May/June 1987, pp. 24–38.**
Compares cost economies across different size banks (economies of scale) and cost differences between similar size banks. The latter far exceeds the former in cost variation.

Humphrey, David B. "Why Do Estimates of Bank Scale Economies Differ?" *Economic Review.* **Federal Reserve Bank of Richmond, September/October 1990, pp. 38–50.**
An excellent article that compares studies of economies of scale and explores the methodological differences that may explain differing results of the studies.

Keeton, William R. "Bank Holding Companies, Cross-Bank Guarantees, and Source of Strength." *Economic Review.* **Federal Reserve Bank of Kansas City, May/June 1990, pp. 54–67.**
This article discusses the implications of bank holding companies refusing to aid subsidiary banks, allowing them to fail and be bailed out by the FDIC. A very interesting article on the adverse incentives created by government regulation.

Laderman, Elizabeth, S., Ronald H. Schmidt, and Gary C. Zimmerman. "Location, Branching, and Bank Portfolio Diversification: The Case of Agricultural Lending." *Economic Review.* **Federal Reserve Bank of San Francisco, Winter 1991, pp. 24–38.**
The authors test whether branch banking increases bank loan portfolio diversification. They find that rural banks in states permitting statewide branching hold more nonagricultural loans than similar rural banks in states that do not permit statewide branching. They also find that urban banks tend to hold more agricultural loans in states permitting statewide branching.

Mester, Loretta J. "Efficient Production of Financial Services: Scale and Scope Economies." *Business Review.* **Federal Reserve Bank of Philadelphia, January/February 1987, pp. 15–25.**
The article examines studies that look at economies of scope as well as economies of scale of operation for banks and other depository institutions.

Savage, Donald T. "Interstate Banking Developments." *Federal Reserve Bulletin,* **February 1987, pp. 79–92.**
An excellent article that examines the history, the causes, and the current status of interstate banking in the United States.

Srinivasan, Aruna. "Are There Cost Savings from Bank Mergers?" *Economic Review.* **Federal Reserve Bank of Atlanta, March/April 1992, pp. 17–28.**
A fine overview of the existing evidence on cost savings from bank mergers. The author finds that noninterest expenses decline slightly in the years following bank mergers. A good article.

INTERNATIONAL BANKING

16

Cɪᴛɪᴄᴏʀᴘ ʜᴀs ᴛᴜʀɴᴇᴅ sᴏᴍᴇ ᴏꜰ its Chilean loans into pulp. No, the people at Citicorp have not gone mad. What they did was to swap some of their loans for a 20 percent equity interest in a pulp mill being built in Nacimiento, a hillside town a few hundred miles south of Santiago, Chile's capital. Citicorp is betting that the pulp will turn into money and not a bad investment.

This action, known as an equity swap, is one of the approaches that large U.S. banks are taking to whittle down their exposure to huge third-world loans that they fear will never be repaid. More specifically, four Latin American countries owe Western commercial banks more than $161 billion as of January 1990. Those countries—Brazil, Mexico, Argentina, and Venezuela—are hard pressed to pay the $20 billion in annual interest payments, let alone the huge principal amounts. Making matters worse for U.S. banks, these countries account for only a small portion of the shaky loans made by commercial banks to third-world countries during the 1970s and 1980s.

This chapter examines international banking—that is, the banking practices, regulations, and market conditions by which we can obtain partial answers to the emergence of the third-world loan crisis. Solutions are more elusive, unlikely to reveal themselves until much later in the decade of the 1990s.

Although foreign banks have long engaged in worldwide banking activities, it was not until the 1960s that American banks began to expand aggressively overseas. Many international banking services are similar to those provided domestic customers, except that transactions cross international boundaries. Other services are unique to international trade. This chapter focuses on the development of international banking, the structure of American overseas banking, international lending, and foreign bank activities in the United States. The next chapter examines some of the other international services banks offer and the international financial markets used to provide them.

Development of International Banking

The establishment of an international presence by American banks is a relatively recent development. European financial institutions, though, have conducted overseas activities for centuries. From the twelfth to the mid-sixteenth century, Italian banks dominated international finance. With the establishment of colonial empires, British, Dutch, and Belgian banks became conspicuous by their worldwide presence. Many of them were established in colonial territories, whereas others were in countries having close trading ties to the bank's home country. During this period, Great Britain emerged as the center of international finance, a position it maintained until after World War II.

American banks did not enter the international scene with any consistency until 1914, for several reasons. First, Americans were occupied with financing the rapid industrialization of their country. Second, national banks were prohibited from establishing foreign branches and accepting bills of exchange. Though some state-chartered banks were free to engage in overseas banking, most were small and the total amount of foreign banking activity was of little consequence. Thus a large part of the banking system was precluded from engaging in international bank transactions.

The Edge Act

The legal basis for the international operation of U.S. banks was established in the period surrounding the First World War. The passage of the Federal Reserve Act in 1913 allowed American banks to establish branches outside the United States and permitted them to accept bills of exchange arising from international transactions. Although these provisions were important, American banks did not rush into the international banking arena. During the three years following the act, only one national bank established branches overseas.

To further stimulate the penetration of American banks into international finance, the Federal Reserve Act was amended in 1916 to permit national banks to invest in corporations engaged in international or foreign banking. These corporations were required to enter into an "agreement" with the Federal Reserve Board as to the type of activities in which they would engage. Hence they subsequently became known as *agreement corporations*. However, these did not prove to be popular because the Federal Reserve Act did not make provisions for them to be federally chartered.

Trying again, in 1919 Congress enacted the Edge Act, which was added to the Federal Reserve Act. The Edge Act, proposed by Senator Walter E. Edge of New Jersey, provided for federally chartered corporations to be organized that could engage in international banking and international financial operations. These activities could be entered into directly by the Edge Act corporation or through subsidiaries that owned or controlled local institutions in foreign countries. Edge Act corporations could make equity investments overseas, an activity denied domestic banks. This and other expanded powers allowed American banks to compete more effectively against stronger and better-established European banking houses.

After World War II, American corporations began to establish overseas offices and affiliates. These businesses required financial services and expertise that could best be provided by banks located in the host countries, but there was also a need to maintain a strong relationship with the companies' main U.S. banks. Frequently, because there were no American banks with local offices to serve them, the overseas affiliates had to turn to domestic banks in the host countries or to European banks with local offices that were experienced in international transactions. This trend toward substantial direct foreign investments forced some large American banks to reconsider establishing a network of foreign branches or affiliates to serve the expanding needs of their large corporate customers more fully. Although the demand was growing for international banking services, by 1960 only eight American banks had established overseas branches.

The Decade of Expansion

Beginning in 1960, a profound change took place in the international banking activities of American banks, as shown in Exhibit 16–1. At that time U.S. foreign banking was dominated by eight large banks with overseas assets totaling $3.5 billion and with considerable experience in the field. By 1965, there were 13 large banks with 211 branches and foreign assets totaling $9.1 billion. Then the rush to establish foreign branches began in earnest. By 1975, when the rush slowed, 126 U.S. banks were operating 762 branches overseas, with total assets of $176.5 billion. Since that time the number of banks with overseas operations has remained fairly constant, but in many cases the number of branches has been reduced to cut overhead and improve overall profitability. At year-end 1988, total overseas branch assets equaled about 7 percent of domestic bank assets. For large money market banks, claims on foreigners amounted to as much as one-quarter to one-half of total assets.

The Reasons for Growth

There are a number of reasons for this dramatic growth in American banking overseas, among them being the overall expansion of U.S. world trade, the growth of multinational corporations, the effects of government regulations on domestic profit opportunities, and the impetus for financing trade deficits that changes in petroleum prices generated in some foreign countries. First, the 1960s was a decade marked by rapid growth of international trade, full convertibility of most of the world's major currencies, and rapid expansion by major U.S. corporations abroad. As American firms expanded overseas, American banks found it advantageous to follow them. Corporations prefer to deal with familiar banks that understand their operations and can provide a full range of services. U.S. banks financed this expansion through letters of credit, banker's acceptances, and other credit instruments.

Exhibit 16–1   **Overseas Branches of U.S. Banks**

	1960	1965	1970	1975	1978	1984	1986	1988
Number of U.S. banks with overseas branches	8	13	79	126	130	163	151	132
Number of overseas branches	131	211	536	762	761	905	899	849
Assets of branches ($ in billions)	$3.5	$9.1	$46.5	$176.5	$257.6	$291.3	$285.0	$318.0

The 1970s marked the beginning of rapid overseas expansion for U.S. banks. During the 1980s, bank overseas expansion remained fairly constant.

Source: Board of Governors of the Federal Reserve System, reported in the 1990 *Statistical Abstract of the United States*.

Interest in foreign banking operations has also been encouraged by the regulatory environment in the United States. Specifically, a set of government programs designed to restrain the outflow of funds from the United States in 1964–1965 and help the country's balance-of-payments problems exerted a strong influence on the international activities of U.S. banks. The federal government's capital control program consisted of the Foreign Direct Investment Program (FDIP), the Interest Equalization Tax (IET), and the Voluntary Foreign Credit Restraint (VFCR) progam.

Under the FDIP, U.S. corporations were limited in the amount of funds they could transfer to their corporate affiliates overseas. Foreign affiliates were also restrained as to the amount of locally generated earnings they could retain for reinvestment purposes. The IET imposed a tax on securities of foreign origin and thus "equalized" or lowered the effective yield on such securities. As a consequence, foreign securities were made less attractive to U.S. residents. The ultimate effect of the tax was to make it more difficult for foreigners, including foreign affiliates of U.S. corporations, to finance their capital requirements in American financial markets. The VFCR program requested that the head offices of U.S. banks voluntarily limit their foreign lending to historical credit levels. The program, administered by the Federal Reserve Board, severely curtailed the capacity of home offices of U.S. banks to meet the overseas needs of their large corporate customers. As a result of these restrictions, U.S. corporations had to rely on sources outside the United States to finance their growing investments abroad. Thus, to accommodate their overseas corporate customers, many U.S. banks established networks of foreign branches to tap international sources of funds.

Other domestic regulations also accelerated the growth of American banks abroad. Regulation Q, which limited the rate that domestic banks were allowed to pay on deposits, was one such regulation. In 1966 and again in 1969, when interest rates became binding, U.S. banks were unable to pay rates that were competitive with alternative financial instruments. As a result, banks experienced large runoffs in deposits at domestic offices. To offset these lost funds, U.S. banks found it expedient to turn to foreign branches, which were not subject to interest rate ceilings. Foreign branches could attract funds because they were free to pay the market rate of interest. Deposits at overseas branches were transferred back to the United States for use by domestic offices. In 1980, the Depository Institutions Deregulation and Monetary Control Act began phasing out Regulation Q. Already, U.S. domestic banks have become more competitive in the interest rates they can offer, and the last barrier was removed in 1986.

As a reaction to restrictive domestic regulations and the internationalization of American business operations, the growth in overseas activities by U.S. banks was dramatic. Interestingly, the growth was not limited to banks located in major financial centers, such as New York and San Francisco, which are traditional international trade centers. Banks headquartered in such cities as Chicago, Pittsburgh, Atlanta, Dallas, Detroit, and other regional money centers also found it profitable to enter the foreign markets aggressively. Banks without foreign branches soon found themselves at a considerable competitive disadvantage in international as well as domestic business.

Recent Activity

By the early 1970s, the rapid expansion of international banking came to a temporary slowdown for several reasons. First, many of the regulations on the outflow of capital and foreign lending, such as the VFCR program, were being dismantled; by 1974, all U.S. controls were ended. Second, many small banks, attracted to international banking by the lure of high profits, found that they had neither the skills nor the size to compete profitably on the international scene.

In 1974, international lending jumped again, but for a different reason than in the past. The quadrupling of oil prices in 1973 created massive trade surpluses for oil-exporting nations along with correspondingly large balance-of-payment deficits for major oil-importing countries. In part, the deficits were being financed indirectly by the recycling of funds through the international banking system by the oil-exporting countries. That is, many countries financed oil imports with short- and medium-term loans from American commercial banks, which obtained the capital from the oil exporters. As a result, international lending jumped 44 percent in dollar terms between 1974 and 1976.

At the present time, American banks have a large network of international banking affiliates throughout the world. Approximately 160 U.S. banks have international banking departments. The number of U.S. banks having correspondent relationships with foreign banks is in the thousands. As Exhibit 16–2 shows, foreign branches are located throughout the world. In amounts of assets, branches in Latin America, Japan, and Europe account for half of all the assets of U.S. branches abroad. However, despite the impressive record of American banks overseas, the market remains dominated by a few giant multinational banks. Currently about 10 banks dominate the market, and more than 80 of the 160 banks operating outside the United States have only single *shell branches* in offshore money markets, such as Nassau or the Cayman Islands.

Exhibit 16–2   **Geographic Distribution of U.S. Banks' Claims on Foreigners (April 1991)**

Area	$ in Billions	Percentage
Bahamas and British West Indies	$179.9	35.7
Other Latin American and Caribbean countries	57.8	11.5
Japan	91.0	18.1
United Kingdom	52.4	10.4
Continental Europe	47.7	9.5
Asia, excluding Japan	47.9	9.5
Canada	17.5	3.5
Africa	5.4	1.1
Other	2.1	0.4
Total	501.7	100.0

Most U.S. banks' claims are on companies or individuals in Latin America, Europe, or Japan.

Source: Federal Reserve System, *Bulletin*, August 1991.

Regulation of Overseas Banking Activities

As we know, banking in the United States has traditionally been a highly regulated industry. The broad objectives of federal bank regulations have been (1) to promote bank safety, which fosters economic stability by minimizing economic disturbances originating in the banking sector; (2) to promote competition within the banking system; and (3) to maintain a separation of banking from other business activities in order to promote soundness in banking and to prevent concentration of economic power. For the most part, this overall regulatory framework has been extended to the overseas operation of American banks. This philosophy is in contrast with that of other countries, where banks are allowed to engage in a wider range of business activities than are American banks. With the important exception of Japan, which adopted most of the U.S. financial regulatory system during the postwar American occupation, most Western nations grant their banks either limited or full merchant banking powers. Furthermore, most foreign regulatory authorities have tended to focus on the domestic operations of banks, virtually ignoring activities conducted by the banks outside their own national borders. This stance has changed in recent years, however, as foreign regulatory authorities begin to understand the extremely close relationship that exists between a bank's domestic business and its international operations. In particular, the ten-nation agreement on bank capital adequacy standards worked out under the auspices of the Bank for International Standards (BIS) in July 1988 is tangible evidence that bank regulators are concerned with, and are addressing, international issues. This agreement mandates at least an 8 percent capital-to-assets ratio for all international banks by year-end 1992, and also defines precisely what will be counted as primary (Tier 1) and secondary (Tier 2) capital. At least 4 percent of the 8 percent total must be Tier 1 capital.

The Regulatory Framework

The regulatory framework for the international operations of U.S. banks can be summarized briefly: (1) The Federal Reserve Act of 1913 allowed federally chartered banks to establish branches outside the United States; (2) the 1916 amendment to the Federal Reserve Act permitted national banks to form agreement corporations; (3) the 1919 Edge Act allowed the formation of federally chartered corporations to engage in foreign banking and such financial operations as owning stock in foreign financial institutions; (4) in 1966, national banks were allowed to invest directly in the stock of foreign banks; (5) in 1970, amendments to the Bank Holding Company Act provided a regulatory framework for international activities of U.S. bank holding companies; (6) in 1978, the International Banking Act extended federal regulation to foreign banks operating in the United States; (7) in 1980, the Depository Institutions Deregulation and Monetary Control Act broadened the scope of the Federal Reserve Board's authority to impose reserve requirements on foreign banks, and permitted U.S. banks to establish international banking facilities (IBFs); and (8) the International Lending Supervision Act, passed by Congress in late 1983, mandated the reporting of country-specific loan exposure information by commercial banks and established standardized procedures for dealing with problem loans. The Financial Institutions Safety and Consumer Choice Act (FISCCA), which President Bush submitted to Congress in 1991, would likely have fundamentally altered the international competitiveness of American banks, even though the proposed law did not specifically address international banking regulations. Unfortunately, Congress rejected this legislation and prospects for passage of a similar bill in the near future seem remote.

The Federal Reserve System and the Office of the Comptroller of the Currency (OCC) have primary responsibility for supervising the activities of U.S. banks' foreign operations: the OCC examines national banks that make up the majority of banks operating overseas; and the Federal Reserve System examines state-chartered member banks, approves national banks' foreign branches, and supervises the operation of Edge Act corporations and IBFs. Also, foreign acquisitions by domestic bank holding companies come under the jurisdiction of the Federal Reserve. The FDIC has only a limited role in international banking because few purely international banks are members. However, since enactment of the International Banking Act of 1978, foreign banks operating in the United States have been allowed to establish federally chartered foreign branches, and their deposits up to $100,000 must be insured by the FDIC. Other foreign banking institutions may, at their option, obtain FDIC insurance.

In the past, regulatory authorities relied primarily on a bank's home office records in conducting examinations of overseas operations. This procedure was acceptable as long as the number of banks with overseas operations was small and foreign activities of a bank did not pose a substantial risk to the bank's domestic operations. This is not always true today. On-site examinations are becoming both more necessary and more frequent. OCC now maintains a permanent staff in London, and both the Federal Reserve Board and the FDIC are increasing the frequency of their overseas on-site examinations. These are used primarily to check the accuracy of head office records and the adequacy of internal controls. The cost of regular examinations of the quality of all foreign offices' assets would be prohibitive.

Allowable Banking Activities

In general, U.S. banks have been permitted to engage in a wider range of business activities in foreign countries than at home. For example, U.S. banks abroad have been allowed to engage in security underwriting and make limited equity investments in nonfinancial companies in connection with their financing activities. The major reason for the wider latitude in overseas markets has been to enhance the competitive effectiveness of U.S. banks in foreign markets. Most banks in foreign countries have broader powers than those possessed by American banks. Thus to promote the participation of U.S. banks in overseas markets, Federal Reserve policy has been to broaden powers as long as they did not impinge on domestic policy considerations. Furthermore, because many domestic constraints on banks are concerned with the competitive environment and the concentration of financial resources in the United States, the Federal Reserve has accordingly refrained from restricting the international activities of domestic banks.

However, certain overseas activities have been restrained. Foreign subsidiaries are not allowed to own controlling interests in nonfinancial companies. This restriction stems from the long-standing U.S. concept of separating banking and commerce.

PEOPLE
& EVENTS

Swiss Banking: Neutrality and Confidentiality

Nestled in the heart of Europe, Switzerland has historically remained neutral through more than a century of European political instability and, more recently, neutral between the tensions of Eastern Communism and Western countries. As a result, Swiss banking has always enjoyed a unique position in the international banking community as a haven for those seeking political stability and banking confidentiality. The Swiss banking formula has been extremely successful. Swiss banks hold deposits disproportionately large relative to the size of the small Swiss economy. The table shows that 5 Swiss banks ranked amoung the world's 300 largest in 1990. An additional 6 banks were among the 500 largest worldwide.

Swiss banks have long enjoyed close financial ties with the United States. For example, Swiss and American banks have worked together on participation loans, foreign exchange transactions, and in the banker's-acceptance and letter-of-credit markets. More recently, Swiss and U.S. banks often find themselves grouped together in the same Eurocredit and Eurobond syndicates. Swiss banks also work closely with other U.S. financial firms. Purchases of American stocks and bonds by Swiss banks are generally among the largest foreign security deals

transacted on Wall Street, and Swiss banks and American investment banks underwrite new issues in the Eurocurrency market with cooperative joint-venture firms, such as Credit Suisse First Boston Ltd.

The most mysterious and least understood of all Swiss bank activities is its handling of numbered deposit accounts. Banks in Switzerland, as well as in several other countries, allow bank or security safe-keeping accounts to be identified only by a number and not listed by name of the depositor. Not commonly known, however, is that Swiss banking law requires Swiss banks to identify the owner of the funds by name in order to know who the person entitled to transact with the funds is. Thus every numbered account has a name attached to it, just as every named account has a number. Furthermore, in May 1991 the Swiss government abolished "Form B" accounts, which had allowed depositors to hide their true identities by registering the accounts in the names of lawyers or other agents.

The primary purpose of a numbered account is to restrict the knowledge of the customer's identity to a small number of high-ranking bank officials. Numbered accounts merely provide protection from possible indiscretions on the part of the bank staff.

Continued

Regulatory changes announced in August 1987 weakened these restrictions somewhat by allowing banks to purchase a controlling interest in a foreign nonfinancial corporation, but only if the firm was being sold as part of a privatization program by the foreign government. Affiliates in which U.S. banks have been allowed to own a substantial minority interest have been confined to companies of a predominantly financial nature. Also, investment in foreign companies has been severely limited. It is feared that such investments could indirectly undermine domestic policy objectives, such as limiting banking and the separation of commercial banking and other lines of business. Even though it seems increasingly likely that Congress will repeal or seriously weaken the Glass-Steagall Act (which separates commercial and investment banking), such action is not guaranteed and would in any case take several years to implement.

Moreover, numbered accounts do not provide blanket secrecy for depositors, as is commonly believed, especially for those violating United States laws. In 1977 the United States and Switzerland reached an agreement whereby Switzerland would provide U.S. authorities with information about U.S. nationals suspected of having participated in securities fraud, insider trading, or income tax evasion. Swiss authorities were mortified by the role played by the Caribbean branch of Bank Leu in the Dennis Levine insider stock-trading scandal in 1986, and they have attempted to cooperate more fully with American authorities. However, the agreement has been less than successful from the American point of view. Swiss banks have been reluctant to provide client information to U.S. authorities; and because of banks' importance to the Swiss economy, Swiss regulators have been hesitant to force the banks to disclose information. The Swiss are well aware they have no monopoly on selling confidential banking services. Banks in Austria and Luxembourg are now competing head-on with Swiss banks, claiming that their services are more confidential, hence better, than those of Switzerland.

Swiss Banks That Are Among the World's 300 Largest (1990)

World Rank (by asset size)	Bank	Total Assets (U.S. $ in billions)
23	Union Bank of Switzerland, Zurich	$183.4
27	Swiss Bank Corp., Basle	151.3
39	Credit Suisse, Zurich	117.3
131	Swiss Volksbank, Bern	35.0
132	Zurcher Kantonal Bank, Zurich	34.8

Source: *American Banker*, July 26, 1991.

Delivery of Overseas Banking Services

Banks may use a number of organizational forms to deliver international banking services to their customers. The primary forms are (1) representative offices, (2) shell branches, (3) correspondent banks, (4) branch banks, (5) Edge Act corporations, (6) subsidiaries and affiliates, (7) bank consortia, and (8) international banking facilities. Exhibit 16–3 shows a possible organizational structure for the foreign operations of U.S. banks. Though possible, all these forms need not exist for any individual bank. We shall now discuss each organizational form, focusing on its advantages and disadvantages for the parent bank.

Representative Offices

Representative nonbanking offices are established in a foreign country primarily to assist the parent bank's customers in that country. Representative offices cannot accept deposits, make loans, transfer funds, accept drafts, transact in the international money market, or commit the parent bank to loans. In fact, they cannot cash a

Exhibit 16-3   Possible Organizational Structure for a U.S. Bank's International Operations

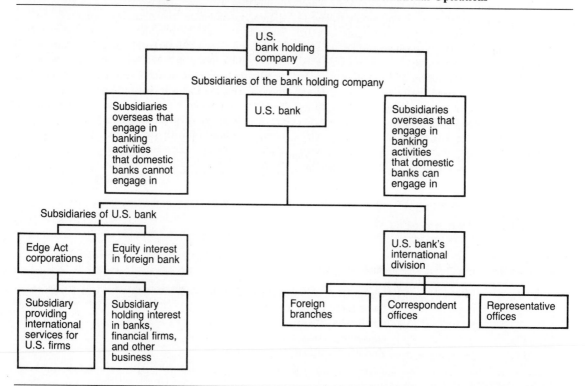

Because of regulatory changes over the years, the structure of U.S. banks' international operations vary from bank to bank. This exhibit shows one possible structure for a U.S. bank.

traveler's check drawn on the parent bank. What they may do, however, is provide information and assist the parent bank's clients in their banking and business contacts in the foreign country. For example, a representative office may introduce business-people to local bankers, or it may act as an intermediary between U.S. firms and firms located in the country of the representative office. Of course, while acting as an intermediary, it provides information about the parent bank's services. A representative's office is also a primary vehicle by which an initial presence is established in a country before setting up formal banking operations.

Shell Branches

The easiest and cheapest way to enter international banking is to establish a shell branch. This is a booking office for bank transactions located abroad that has no contact with the public. Activities of shell branches are primarily limited to interbank money market transactions (mostly in the Eurodollar market), foreign currency transactions, and the purchase of small shares of syndicate loans. In most cases, transactions at the shell branch reflect banking decisions made at the U.S. head office or at branches around the world. Thus, to some extent, the physical location of the shell branch is unimportant. What is significant, however, is that the shell's location provides an environment that is (1) almost entirely free of local taxes, (2) has liberal rules for the conversion and transfer of foreign currencies, (3) has simple and unencumbered banking regulations, (4) has modern communication facilities linked to other financial centers around the world, and (5) has a relatively stable political environment. The establishment of shell branches is not limited to small banks. All large banks operate shell branches to escape taxes and government regulations. Most U.S. banks operate their shell branches in the Caribbean Basin, with the most popular locations being the Bahamas, the Cayman Islands, and, until recently, the Republic of Panama. The seizure of Panamanian state assets in U.S. banks, and other actions taken by the U.S. government in December 1989 to topple the government of General Manuel Noriega, probably signal the demise of Panama as a major international banking center—at least until political stability is restored. According to some market analysts, offshore private bank deposits in tax havens around the world have accumulated roughly $1 trillion. Much of this activity is centered in the Caribbean, but other tax havens—such as Luxembourg and Dublin, Ireland—have grown in recent years.

Correspondent Banks

Most major banks maintain correspondent banking relationships with local banks in market areas in which they wish to do business. International correspondent relationships provide international banking services. For example, Morgan Guaranty and Trust Company of New York may have correspondent relationships with a bank in Cairo, Egypt.

Correspondent services include accepting drafts, honoring letters of credit, furnishing credit information, collecting and disbursing international funds, and investing funds in international money markets. Typically, correspondent services center around paying or collecting international funds, because most transactions involve the importing or exporting of goods. In addition, the correspondent bank will provide introductions to local businesspeople. Under a correspondent relationship, the U.S. bank usually will not maintain any permanent personnel in the foreign country; direct contact between the two banks may be limited to periodic conferences between their management to review services provided. In other cases, though, a correspondent relationship will be developed with a local institution even when the American bank has a branch or other presence in the country. This generally occurs when the U.S. bank either is precluded by local law or does not want to make the necessary investment to clear domestic currency payments in the country. For instance, until December 1984, when Citibank was granted approval to join the British Clearinghouse, U.S. banks in London were required to clear sterling payments through a correspondent relationship with one of the four clearing banks.

Foreign Branches

Branch offices of U.S. banks are widely distributed throughout the world and represent the most important means by which U.S. banks conduct overseas business. A foreign branch is a legal and operational part of the parent bank. Creditors of the branch have full legal claims on the bank's assets as a whole, and, in turn, creditors of the parent bank have claims on its branches' assets. Deposits of both foreign branches and domestic branches are considered to be total deposits of the bank, and reserve requirements are tied to these total deposits.

Foreign branches are subject to two sets of banking regulations. First, as part of the parent bank, they are subject to all legal limitations that exist for U.S. banks. Second, they are subject to the regulation of the host country. Domestically, the OCC is the overseas regulator and examiner of national banks, whereas state banking authorities and the Federal Reserve Board share the authority for state-chartered member banks. Granting power to open a branch overseas resides with the Board of Governors of the Federal Reserve System. As a practical matter, the Federal Reserve System and the OCC dominate the regulation of foreign branches.

The attitudes of host countries toward establishing and regulating branches of U.S. banks vary widely. Typically, countries that need capital and expertise in lending and investment welcome the establishment of U.S. bank branches and allow them to operate freely within their borders. Other countries allow the establishment of U.S. bank branches but limit their activities relative to domestic banks because of competitive factors. Some foreign governments may fear that branches of large U.S. banks might hamper the growth of their country's domestic banking industry. As a result, growing nationalism and a desire for locally controlled credit have slowed the expansion of American banks abroad in recent years.

The major advantage of foreign branches is a worldwide name identification with the parent bank. Customers of the foreign branch have access to the full range of the parent bank's services, and the value of these services is based on the worldwide value of the client relationship rather than just the local office relationship. Furthermore, deposits are more secure, having their ultimate claim against the much larger parent bank and not just the local office. Similarly, legal loan limits are a function of the size of the parent bank and not of the branch. The major disadvantages of foreign branches are the cost of establishing them and the legal limits placed on the activities in which they may engage.

Edge Act Corporations

Edge Act corporations are subsidiaries of U.S. banks that were formed to permit U.S. banks to engage in international banking and financing activities and to engage in activities that they could not conduct within the United States. Edge Act corporations operate under federal charter and are not subject to the banking laws of the various states. There also exist a number of agreement corporations that operate similarly to Edge Act corporations but remain under state charter. Currently, there are only six agreement corporations in operation. The principal difference between these two types of organizations is that agreement corporations must engage primarily in banking activities, whereas Edge Act corporations may undertake banking as well as some nonbanking activities. Edge Act and agreement corporations engage in two general types of activities: (1) international banking and (2) international financing.

International Banking Activities.   Edge Act and agreement corporations may engage in a wide array of international banking activities. They may accept demand and time deposits (but not savings deposits) within the United States as long as the deposits are related to identifiable international transactions. They may accept deposits from foreigners, foreign governments, and business operations overseas, provided that the deposits are not used to pay purely domestic expenses. They may also make foreign loans of up to 10 percent of the corporation's capital and surplus. In addition, Edge Act and agreement corporations can confirm letters of credit, create banker's acceptances, trade in foreign currencies, receive items for collection from abroad, hold securities for safekeeping, and act as paying agent for securities issued by foreign governments or foreign corporations.

Edge Act corporations may also own foreign banking subsidiaries. Domestic banks may have branches overseas, but they may not own foreign banking subsidiaries. Thus Edge Act corporations circumvent this legal restriction. Edge Act and agreement corporations are physically located in the United States, although their subsidiaries may be located overseas. Furthermore, these corporations may have offices located in U.S. cities outside the parent bank's own state. These offices may engage *only* in international banking activities. In recent years, Edge Act and agreement corporations have become the main vehicle by which banks may establish international banking offices throughout the United States. These offices also allow banks to circumvent the prohibition against having branch offices outside the bank's home state. Though they cannot make domestic loans, these corporations can refer customers to the parent banks, which can often make much larger loans than regional banks.

International Financing Activities. The Board of Governors of the Federal Reserve System may allow overseas Edge Act subsidiaries to engage in business activities not allowed U.S. banks. The extent to which these "nonbanking" activities are permitted depends on the host country's regulations concerning foreign banking activities. In some instances, countries allow foreign banks to engage in activities denied to their own banks. However, the Board of Governors maintains ultimate control over the activities of Edge Act subsidiaries.

The most important nonbanking activity in which Edge Act and agreement corporations may engage is investing in equities of foreign corporations. Ordinarily, U.S. banks cannot participate in investment activities. Hence this power has been the main advantage of the Edge Act and agreement corporations' form of organization; it has helped U.S. banks achieve an improved competitive position relative to foreign banks, which are typically allowed to make equity investments. The largest class of these have been investments in foreign banking institutions. Purchases have been made as an alternative to establishing a branch network or to strengthening foreign correspondent relationships. Edge Act and agreement corporations have in recent years also taken equity positions in finance and investment companies. These companies have been attractive investments as a source of funds for the parent bank. That is, finance and investment companies can effectively generate local funds by selling notes or commercial paper and by obtaining loans from local banks.

More recently, Edge Act corporations have engaged in financing commercial and industrial projects through long-term loans and equity participation. The normal procedure is for the Edge Act corporation to sell its equity investment after a period of time to free the capital for new ventures. If no local market exists in which to sell the equity portion, the existing owner will agree to buy out the Edge Act corporation's interest at a price stated by some previously agreed-upon formula.

Foreign Subsidiaries and Affiliates

A foreign subsidiary bank is a separately incorporated bank owned entirely or in part by a U.S. bank, a U.S. bank holding company, or an Edge Act corporation. A foreign subsidiary provides local identity and the appearance of a local bank in the eyes of potential customers in the host country, which often enhances its ability to attract additional local deposits. Furthermore, management is typically composed of local nationals, giving the subsidiary bank better access to the local business community. Thus foreign-owned subsidiaries are generally in a stronger position to provide domestic and international banking services to residents of the host country.

Closely related to foreign subsidiaries are foreign affiliate banks, which are locally incorporated banks owned in part, but not controlled, by an outside parent. The majority of the ownership and control may be local, or it may be other foreign banks.

International Banking Facilities

Effective in December 1981, the Federal Reserve Board permitted the establishment of international banking facilities (IBFs). These facilities may be established by a U.S.-chartered depository institution, a U.S. branch or agency of a foreign bank, or the U.S. office of an Edge Act or agreement bank. IBFs are not institutions in the organizational sense. They are actually a set of asset and liability accounts segregated on the books of the establishing institutions.

IBFs are allowed to conduct international banking operations that, for the most part, are exempt from U.S. regulation. Deposits, which can be accepted only from non-U.S. residents or other IBFs and must be at least $100,000, are exempt from reserve requirements and interest rate ceilings. The deposits obtained cannot be used domestically; they must be used for making foreign loans. In fact, to ensure that U.S.-based firms and individuals comply with this requirement, borrowers must sign a statement agreeing to this stipulation when taking out the loan. At the end of their first year of operations, IBFs' assets amounted to $47.2 billion, about evenly divided between U.S. banks and foreign bank institutions operating in the United States. They were originally intended to bring back onshore some of the substantial volume of Eurodollars that was being handled by shell branches in the Caribbean. Some of these funds have been captured by the IBFs, but not as much as was anticipated. The major explanation for this failure to attract a larger share of the Caribbean Eurodollars is that the minimum maturity on IBF deposits is 48 hours, whereas many corporations prefer to invest their money overnight. The 48-hour maturity limitation was imposed to prevent the development of an essentially unregulated parallel to the Federal Funds market, but it has also reduced the attractiveness of the IBFs as an investment medium. In fact, most of the growth in IBF assets has been in branches of Japanese and Italian banks, which are prohibited by home country legislation from operating Caribbean shell branches.

International Lending

As is the case with domestic operations, the greatest amount of income from international operations is derived from lending. The bulk of the lending is accomplished through foreign branches, subsidiaries, or affiliate banks in foreign countries. The total amount of international lending by U.S. banks is not known precisely, because published data are not available on loans made by affiliates of U.S. banks or banks owned jointly by U.S. banks and other foreign banks. However, as of year-end 1988, the Federal Reserve Board reported that foreign lending by the 178 largest U.S. banks totaled $221 billion, of which 68 percent was short-term (one year or less). Foreign banks also engage in international lending and compete with U.S. banks. Exhibit 16–4 shows the 30 largest banks in the world ranked in terms of total assets. Only one of the top 30 banks is American (down from 3 in 1987 and 9 in 1984), and BankAmerica Corp., number 2 in 1984 was ranked number 46 in 1990. It is obvious that ranking international banks by either assets or market value would show that the largest Japanese banks have emerged as being in a league by themselves.

Characteristics of International Loans

In many ways, the loans that banks make to international customers are similar to domestic business loans. Most loans are intermediate-term, floating-rate credits made to moderate- to high-quality borrowers. There are, however, important differences relating to one or more of the following factors: (1) funding; (2) syndication; (3) pricing; and (4) collateral. A further difference is that international loans can be denominated in almost any major currency, although dollars are the overwhelming favorite. International loans tend to be larger in size than typical domestic loans, and borrowers are generally sovereign governments or large multinational companies, so the perceived credit risk tends to be lower.

Most large international loans are negotiated and funded in the Eurocurrency market. International banks operating in this market accept time deposits from nonbank investors and then make short- or intermediate-term loans. Funds can be lent directly to nonbank borrowers, or they can be lent in the *interbank market* to other international banks if the original bank does not have sufficient loan demand. The interest rate paid to depositors and charged to borrowers will be related to the home-country interest rate for the currency in question, but for a variety of reasons, the spread between borrowing and lending rates tends to be smaller in the Eurocurrency market. Most Eurocurrency loans are priced with respect to the London Interbank Offered Rate (LIBOR), which is the rate at which international banks lend to each other in London, historically the center of the Eurocurrency market.

A loan to a nonbank borrower will typically be priced at some premium above LIBOR, with the premium being related to the credit risk of the borrower. For example, a loan made to a highly rated multinational company or to a European government might be priced at 0.10 percent above LIBOR, whereas a credit made to a less-well-known company or to a developing country might have a premium as high as 1.5 percent or more above LIBOR.

If the loan extends for more than one credit period (such as a month), the interest rate charged on the loan for the coming period will be determined by the level of LIBOR at the beginning of the period. These floating-rate loans allow banks to fund the credits in the Eurocurrency market at the beginning of the period and lock in a lending spread for the coming period. At the end of this period, the loan will again "roll over" and be repriced for the subsequent period. This *rollover pricing* mechan-

Exhibit 16–4   **World's 30 Largest Banks (December 31, 1990)**

Rank	Bank	Location	Total Assets ($ in billions)	Shareholders' Equity ($ in billions)	Risk-Based Capital Ratio (percent)
1	Dai-Ichi Kangyo Bank	Tokyo, Japan	$428.2	$13.7	8.76%
2	Sumitomo Bank Ltd.	Osaka, Japan	409.2	15.4	8.87
3	Mitsui Taiyo Kobe Bank	Tokyo, Japan	408.8	11.7	7.35
4	Sanwa Bank	Osaka, Japan	402.7	13.2	n.a.
5	Fuji Bank	Tokyo, Japan	400.0	13.4	9.09
6	Mitsubishi Bank	Tokyo, Japan	391.5	12.3	8.74
7	Credit Agricole Mutuel	Paris, France	305.2	14.6	8.50
8	Banque Nationale de Paris	Paris, France	291.9	9.3	8.97
9	Industrial Bank of Japan	Tokyo, Japan	290.1	9.5	8.14
10	Credit Lyonnais	Paris, France	287.3	12.1	8.46
11	Deutsche Bank	Frankfurt, Germany	266.3	10.4	10.70
12	Barclays, Plc	London, U.K.	259.0	11.7	8.30
13	Tokai Bank Ltd.	Nagoya, Japan	249.8	7.5	8.05
14	Norinchukin Bank	Tokyo, Japan	249.7	1.8	8.81
15	Mitsubishi Trust & Banking	Tokyo, Japan	237.7	5.6	10.36
16	National Westminster Bank	London, U.K.	232.5	11.3	n.a.
17	ABN Amro Holding	Amsterdam, Netherlands	231.4	8.5	n.a.
18	Bank of Tokyo	Tokyo, Japan	223.2	6.8	8.70
19	Societe Generale	Paris, France	220.0	6.2	6.68
20	Sumitomo Trust & Banking	Osaka, Japan	218.9	5.4	n.a.
21	Citicorp	New York, U.S.A.	214.8	9.7	6.52
22	Mitsui Trust & Banking	Tokyo, Japan	210.9	4.5	n.a.
23	Long-Term Credit Bank of Japan	Tokyo, Japan	200.7	7.3	n.a.
24	Dresdner Bank	Frankfurt, Germany	186.9	6.5	n.a.
25	Compagnie Financiere de Paribas	Paris, France	185.6	5.9	8.10
26	Union Bank of Switzerland	Zurich, Switzerland	183.4	13.2	n.a.
27	Yasuda Trust & Banking	Tokyo, Japan	175.6	3.6	n.a.
28	Daiwa Bank	Osaka, Japan	171.2	3.9	8.92
29	Compaignie de Suez	Paris, France	157.8	8.5	8.38
30	Swiss Bank Corp.	Basle, Switzerland	151.3	9.2	n.a.

Risk-based capital ratios are Tier 1 capital as a percentage of risk-adjusted assets, calculated using the 1992 final guidelines as defined by the Basle Committee on Banking Regulations and Supervisory Practices. It is worth noting that none of the large "megamergers" between U.S. money-center banks announced during the summer of 1991 would have ranked higher than 25th on the above list.

Source: "The World's Largest Banks," *American Banker*, July 26, 1991.

ism, which was first used in the Eurocurrency market in 1969, allows banks to make intermediate-term loans without exposing themselves to the interest rate risk inherent in fixed-rate loans. The sheer volume of credit available, the low cost of funds, and the sophistication of the banking service provided have also made the Eurocurrency market a favorite source of funds for nonbank borrowers.

Most large (greater than about $50 million) international bank loans are *syndicated*. This means that several banks participate in funding the loan, which is packaged by one or more lead banks. This allows banks to spread their risks among a large number of loans, and it allows borrowers to obtain larger amounts of capital than would be available through other means. This is especially true for sovereign borrowers (national governments). Indeed, the intermediate-term, floating-rate, general obligation (unsecured and backed by the taxing power of the government), syndicated bank loan was the principal instrument through which financial capital was channeled to the developing countries during the 1970s and early 1980s. The total level of such debt grew from essentially nothing in 1971 to over $300 billion in August 1982, when the Mexican debt moratorium effectively ended voluntary bank lending to less-developed countries (LDCs).

Finally, most international bank loans are unsecured (made without specific collateral). Business loans are generally made only to large, creditworthy multinationals and, with public sector loans, are generally backed by the "full faith and credit" of the borrowing nation. Ironically, during the period when the OPEC surplus was being recycled to the developing countries, bankers comforted themselves with the statement that "nations don't go bankrupt." Although true in a legal sense, this idea was shown to be tragically misguided when the LDCs began experiencing severe financial difficulties during the mid-1980s, and the market value of the creditor banks was knocked down to reflect the underlying value of these sovereign loans.

Risk in International Lending

In many respects, the principles applicable to foreign lending are the same as those applicable to domestic lending—that is, to define and evaluate the credit risk that the borrower will default. In international lending, bankers are exposed to two additional risks: country and currency risk. We shall now discuss each of these three risks in turn and then suggest ways in which bankers can reduce them.

Credit Risk.   Credit risk involves assessing the probability that part of the interest or principal of the loan will not be repaid. The greater the default risk, the higher the loan rate that the bank must charge the borrower. As noted previously, this is the same type of risk that bankers face on the domestic scene. However, it may be more difficult to obtain or assess credit information abroad. U.S. banks are less familiar with local economic conditions and business practices than are domestic banks. It takes time and practice to develop appropriate sources of information and to correctly evaluate such information. As a result, many U.S. banks tend to restrict their foreign lending to major international corporations or financial institutions. This policy reflects the cost of gathering reliable information. A foreign government will sometimes offer assurances against default or rescheduling of loans by private borrowers, making such loans more attractive to international lenders.

Country Risk.   Country (sovereign) risk is closely tied to political developments in a country, particularly the government's attitude toward foreign loans or investments. Some governments attempt to encourage the inflow of foreign funds whether the funds come from private or public sources. Others, however, make it difficult to maintain profitable lending operations. Minor obstacles, such as wage-price controls, profit controls, additional taxation, and other legal restrictions can inhibit the ability of borrowers to repay loans. A recent barrier is beginning to develop in some Muslim countries, where it is against the teachings of the Koran to charge interest. Although it is still possible to charge service fees, this and other unilateral changes in government policy and regulations generally raise the cost of doing business within the particular country involved.

At the extreme, foreign governments may expropriate the assets of foreigners or prohibit foreign loan repayments, either of which could drastically alter risk exposure. In a worldwide view, there are only a few cases in which countries have refused to repay or have refused permission for their citizens to repay foreign loans. The reason for this is that the borrowing country does not want to preclude the possibility of obtaining foreign credit in the future. Any nationalization or government refusals to repay international loans may virtually halt the inflow of foreign funds into the country involved. However, rebellions, civil commotions, wars, and unexpected changes in government do occur from time to time, and, as a result, risk is real and must be considered in granting international loans. Somewhat soothing to international lenders is the fact that, with the exception of Chile and Cuba, there have been few large-scale nationalizations by foreign governments in recent years. However, U.S. banks have been forced out of Iran, and some South American countries have taken the properties of some U.S. citizens.

A major problem for banks in the 1980s was the rescheduling of sovereign loans. Rescheduling refers to rolling over a loan, often capitalizing interest arrears or extending the loan's maturity. As shown in Exhibit 16–5, the debt burden of less-developed countries (LDCs) rose from $181 billion in 1975 to $1.221 *trillion* at the end of 1990. On average, this amount represents more than 183 percent of these countries' export earnings for 1989. However, the rapid growth of LDCs' external debt that characterized the late 1970s and early 1980s has slowed substantially, and most of the recent increase in outstanding debt has been involuntary, the result of capitalization of past-due and unpayable debt service obligations. With the worldwide recession in commodity prices, though, the ability of LDCs to generate export earnings with which to repay the loans has also lessened. Hence both their ability and inclination to use increasingly scarce export earnings to repay debts to American banks rather than using them for domestic purposes are eroding.

Exhibit 16–5   **Developing Countries' External Debt Positions**

	1975	1980	1983	1986	1987	1988	1989	1990
External debt ($ in billions)	$180.8	$561.8	$806.7	$1027.6	$1151.7	$1136.5	$1146.7	$1220.9
Percent of exports	105.2	133.5	201.4	241.3	231.7	200.8	186.6	183.1
Debt service payments ($ in billions)	$23.7	$91.0	$108.9	$129.3	$140.4	$151.8	$135.7	$140.5
Percent of exports	13.8	21.6	27.2	30.4	28.3	26.8	22.1	21.1

The debt burden of the less-developed countries rose dramatically throughout the 1970s. During the 1980s, the rate of growth in debt outstanding slowed, but the real burden of servicing the debt increased.

Source: International Bank for Reconstruction and Development (the World Bank), *World Debt Tables*, 1990–91, January 1991.

Because of repayment problems, multiyear rescheduling agreements were introduced in 1984. These typically involve (1) a consolidation of several individual public and private loans into a smaller number of standardized debt issues; (2) the extension of government guarantees to private-sector debts; (3) the granting of a grace period of one to several years, during which the loans do not need to be serviced; and (4) an extension of the loan maturity date to as long as 15 years. There were 24 rescheduling agreements involving $87.0 billion worth of debt in 1984, and during 1990 there were 11 reschedulings involving debt with a face value of $26.7 billion. Between $22.9 billion and $72.4 billion of debt was rescheduled in the other years since 1982. These repayment problems are cause for concern about the quality of bank earnings in the coming years.

Currency Risk. Currency risk is concerned with currency value changes and exchange controls. More specifically, some loans are denominated in foreign currency rather than dollars, and if the currency in which the loan is made loses value against the dollar during the course of the loan, the repayment will be worth fewer dollars. Of course, if the foreign currency has a well-developed market and the maturity is relatively short, the loan may be hedged. However, many world currencies, particularly those in developing nations, do not have well-established foreign currency markets; consequently, these international loans cannot always be hedged to reduce this kind of currency risk.

Another aspect of currency risk concerns exchange controls. Exchange controls, which are not uncommon in developing countries, may limit the movement of funds across national borders or restrict a currency's convertibility into dollars for repayment. Thus exchange risk may occur because of difficulties in the convertibility of a currency or in its exchange rate. Typically, if a country has an active market for its currency and its international payments and receipts are in approximate balance (or it has adequate reserves to pay deficits), currency risk is minimal. However, if a country persistently runs a deficit on its balance of payments, it may establish some form of exchange control. One such example is Mexico, which devalued its currency severely in 1982 and literally suspended exchange operations for a period of time. This was the result of its large balance-of-payments deficit and its inability to make current payments on its sizable international loans.

Risk Evaluation

When lending abroad, bankers must take into account the same economic factors that they consider domestically—government monetary and fiscal policy, bank regulations, foreign exchange controls, and national and regional economic conditions. Depending on the cost, lenders employ different means of evaluating risks in foreign lending. The most direct are in-depth studies prepared by the bank's foreign lending and economic departments. These are based on statistics and other information about a country's economic and financial condition. Information is gathered from government sources and, if available, from the bank's representatives overseas. The analyses often contain careful evaluations of expected inflation, fiscal and monetary policy, the country's trade policies, capital flows, and political stability, as well as an estimate of the credit standing of the individual borrower. Some circumstances affecting sovereign risk cannot be captured in statistical analysis, and, in such cases, practical judgment and experience play a heavy role. Here, information from government officials in this country and abroad, from branch and representative offices, and from other sources are carefully sorted out and subjectively analyzed.

When international lenders find in-depth analysis too expensive, they may turn to onsite reports, checklists, and statistical indicators to help them assess the risk of lending. One such service, provided by *Euromoney*, is shown in Exhibit 16-6. However, such methods tend not to be as reliable and may signal false alarms or a false sense of security. Part of the problem with indicators is that they often are not current, and even if current, there is no assurance that they predict the future. Thus lenders may find it expensive and difficult to gather reliable information about foreign borrowers. Lenders must decide how much information they need to negotiate a loan with a prospective borrower. The higher the cost of gathering information—or the greater the risk of lending either because of lack of information or credit quality—the higher the loan rate. If the risk of making a loan is too great, the loan applicant may be turned down.

Methods of Reducing Risk

Bankers have at their disposal several ways of reducing risk in international lending. The basic avenues open to them are to seek third-party support in the form of insurance or loan guarantees; to share risk exposure by participating in loans with other lenders; or, most important, to diversify their loans among different borrowers and countries.

Third-Party Help.   One way banks may reduce foreign-lending risk is to get a third party to agree to pay back the principal and interest in the event that the borrower defaults. Typically, this is done by either foreign governments or central banks. Of course, these guarantees are only as good as the backer's ability and intent to repay. Such a promise from a politically unstable and underdeveloped country may not mean much. Furthermore, if the same government guarantees a number of loans, its ability to repay may be strained if several of these loans were to default simultaneously.

An alternative to foreign government guarantees is an external guarantee from an outside institution. Banks can reduce foreign-lending risk by lending to exporters who insure their trade credit with the Foreign Credit Insurance Association (FCIA). The FCIA is an organization of approximately 50 insurance companies throughout the United States. FCIA insurance covers individual transactions up to a certain percentage against nonpayment arising from credit loss and political hazards. Political risks are reinsured by the FCIA through the U.S. Export-Import Bank (Eximbank). The FCIA makes thorough credit investigations of individual borrowers as well as of the sovereign risk. Typically, the insurance covers up to 90–95 percent of the credit risk and up to 100 percent of the risk associated with political hazards. The insurance premium paid by the exporter depends on the credit rating of the borrower and the rating established for each country. It typically averages about $\frac{1}{2}$ of 1 percent, but it may be higher for less creditworthy firms and less stable governments.

The Overseas Private Investment Corporation (OPIC) offers programs to insure bank loans against the risk of war, expropriation, and currency inconvertibility. The OPIC also finances some loans directly. Similarly, the Eximbank guarantees medium-

Exhibit 16–6 Country Risk Ratings

Rank 1990	Rank 1989	Country	Rating 0–100	Rank 1990	Rank 1989	Country	Rating 0–100	Rank 1990	Rank 1989	Country	Rating 0–100
1	3	West Germany	92.1	46	47	Oman	59.0	91	51	Bulgaria	34.7
2	1	Japan	91.9	47	31	India	58.7	92	75	Ghana	33.9
3	na	Luxembourg	91.1	48	63	Mexico	58.6	93	90	Iran	33.8
4=	10	Austria	89.9	49	62	Fiji	57.0	94	99	Tanzania	33.7
4=	8	Netherlands	89.9	50	43	Uae	56.0	95	101	Argentina	33.3
4=	6	France	89.9	51	49	Barbados	55.3	96	82	Nigeria	33.0
7	1	Switzerland	87.6	52	60	South Africa	55.0	97	74	Jordan	31.0
8	8	Sweden	87.4	53	69	Chile	54.4	98	98	Ecuador	30.0
9	10	Finland	86.2	54	39	Turkey	54.0	99=	na	Sierra Leone	28.9
10	6	Canada	85.8	55	23	USSR	53.4	99=	na	Gambia	28.9
11=	22	Ireland	85.7	56	86	Paraguay	53.0	99=	109	Peru	28.9
11=	17	Denmark	85.7	57	58	Pakistan	52.7	102	88	Libya	28.7
11=	4	U.S.A.	85.7	58	56	Solomon Islands	52.4	103	93	Niger	28.6
14	10	Belgium	85.4	59	88	Panama	50.8	104	109	Bolivia	28.3
15	13	Norway	84.9	60	46	Tunisia	50.0	105	86	Dominican Republic	28.0
16	16	Singapore	84.8	61	49	Israel	49.9	106	44	Kuwait	27.9
17	13	Italy	83.6	62	60	Papua New Guina	48.5	107	105	Congo	27.4
18	5	United Kingdom	83.5	63	54	Trinidad & Tobago	47.6	108	na	Chad	27.2
19	na	United Germany	82.7	64	66	Algeria	47.0	109	na	Albania	27.0
20	20	South Korea	82.0	65	59	Venezuela	46.1	110=	93	Honduras	26.0
21	15	Spain	81.9	66	69	Zimbabwe	45.0	110=	93	Guatemala	26.0
22=	25	Taiwan	79.2	67=	93	Brazil	45.0	112	105	El Salvador	25.7
22=	21	Portugal	79.2	67=	80	Colombia	45.0	113	116	Angola	25.6
24	29	Malaysia	75.8	67=	63	Swaziland	45.0	114=	na	Madagascar	25.4
25	19	Australia	74.4	67=	54	Vanuatu	45.0	114=	101	Cuba	25.4
26	28	Malta	73.9	71	47	Qatar	44.8	116=	na	Djibouti	25.2
27	17	New Zealand	73.5	72	66	Romania	43.3	116=	69	Ivory Coast	25.2
28	25	Thailand	73.5	73	65	Kenya	43.2	118	105	Myanmar (Burma)	25.0
29	29	Brunei	72.2	74	75	Poland	43.0	119	115	Haiti	23.2
30	27	Hong Kong	72.1	75	57	Morocco	42.5	120	109	Zambia	230
31	31	Cyprus	71.2	76	93	Sri Lanka	42.4	121	101	Mauritania	22.8
32	23	Iceland	70.0	77	82	Yugoslavia	42.2	122	99	Syria	22.3
33	44	Mauritius	69.0	78	75	Philippines	41.4	123	120	Zaire	21.5
34	31	East Germany	66.5	79	80	Malawi	40.0	124	109	Lebanon	19.6
35	39	Indonesia	66.4	80	75	Egypt	39.6	125=	109	Guyana	19.4
36	31	Bermuda	65.7	81	75	Bangladesh	39.3	125=	109	Uganda	19.4
37	31	Chica	65.2	82	82	Jamaica	39.0	127	109	Ethopia	19.3
38	31	Greece	65.1	83	na	Belize	38.0	128	na	Namibia	18.9
39	53	Nauru	64.7	84	90	Senegal	37.8	129	101	Iraq	18.4
40	33	Czechoslovakia	61.7	85	72	Cameroon	37.0	130	117	Liberia	17.3
41	39	Hungary	60.8	86	na	Rwanda	36.9	131=	na	Nicaragua	14.5
42	51	Botswana	60.3	87	na	Mali	368	131=	119	Sudan	14.5
43	66	Uruguay	60.1	88	82	Lesotho	36.0	133	108	Mozambique	13.6
44=	39	Bahrain	60.0	89	72	Gabon	35.8				
44=	37	Saudi Arabia	60.0	90	90	Costa Rica	35.0				

The highly industrialized nations of Western Europe, Japan, and North America are top dogs with respect to country risk. War-torn countries like Lebanon or Ethiopia are near the bottom of the list. Interestingly, this poll was taken both before and after the Iraqi invasion of Kuwait in August 1990 (the results above are the post-invasion numbers), and ratings for all countries went down. The drop was particularly severe for the United States, since it was perceived as being directly at risk.

Source: *Euromoney*. September 1990, pp. 87–88.

DID YOU KNOW?

The "Bank of Crooks and Criminals, Inc."

The year 1991 saw an unusually large number of major financial scandals around the world. First, the "Big Four" Japanese brokerage houses all admitted making illegal payments to important clients as compensation for the decline in stock prices on the Tokyo Stock Exchange in 1990. Next, several Japanese banks became involved in a massive fraud involving an Osaka restaurateur and mystic priestess. Third, mighty Salomon Brothers admitted trying to corner several U.S. Treasury bond auctions early in 1991. By far the largest scandal of 1991, however, was the one involving the Bank of Commerce and Credit International (BCCI). So outrageous and pervasive were this bank's misdeeds that one investigator labeled it the "Bank of Crooks and Criminals, Inc."

After simmering for several yeas, the BCCI scandal exploded in July 1991, when Price Waterhouse sent a report to the Bank of England documenting massive fraud and diversion of funds within the $20 billion bank. The Bank of England and other central banks then quickly moved to suspend BCCI's operations in its London headquarters, as well as in its branches and subsidiaries in approximately 70 other countries. Early reports indicate that up to half of the bank's total assets had been diverted, lost, or stolen.

Even more shocking than its financial misdeeds were BCCI's assorted criminal activities. Its self-named "black network," operating out of the bank's Karachi, Pakistan branch, had apparently been deeply involved in gunrunning, drug smuggling, money laundering, prostitution, extortion, and even murder for several years. BCCI's list of clients included Saddam Hussein, Manuel Noriega, Ferdinand Marcos, various Colombian drug lords, and assorted other shady characters. On the other hand, the U.S. Central Intelligence Agency was also a client, which valued BCCI both as an intelligence source and as an international paymaster who didn't ask too many questions. According to several reports, this busy little bank not only helped the CIA channel guns and money to anticommunist rebels in Afghanistan and Nicaragua, it also helped Saddam, Noriega, and Marcos systematically loot their national treasuries, and may have even acted as banker to the Abu Nidal terrorist group. In spite of all these activities, BCCI retained a heroic image in much of the third world (particularly in the Moslem nations) even after its closure by regulators. How one relatively small bank came to attract such a diverse and colorful client list, and to engender such strong loyalty, is an object lesson on what can go wrong in international banking. *Continued*

term loans made by commercial banks against both political and credit risks. The Eximbank deals with risk beyond the scope that private capital markets or private lenders are willing to assume. The bank's role in financing the high-risk loans may take the form of making a direct loan, participating in a loan with other lenders, or guaranteeing a loan. The Eximbank loan guarantee program is similar to the insurance provided by FCIA described earlier. As a policy matter, the Eximbank directs its international lending involvement toward the financing of capital equipment, such as hydroelectric installations, rather than consumer goods.

Pooling Risk. Banks can also reduce international-lending risk for any one institution by making participation loans. Under this kind of arrangement, banks join

BCCI was founded in 1972 by a charismatic Pakistani banker, Agha Hasan Abedi. Its avowed mission was to become the first Moslem banking powerhouse, and its operations quickly spread throughout the Middle East and beyond. BCCI was incorporated in Luxembourg, and its headquarters were in London, but it remained fundamentally a Pakistani bank throughout its life—even after nominal control of the bank was purchased by Sheik Zayed of Abu Dhabi in early 1990. It even used the Urdu language in its internal business communications, which not coincidentally made money hard to trace.

In fact, many of the bank's operations seemed designed to make money hard to trace, since its structure was in essence that of a giant Ponzi scheme. It had a voracious appetite for new deposits, but until its collapse it always had enough cash on hand to pay off withdrawal demands. Most of the money raised was, however, funneled through subsidiaries to a series of secret accounts in the Cayman Islands, where much of the money was effectively stolen using false shipping documents and other schemes. The diverted funds were then used to make ingratiating loans to governments around the world, to make unrepayable loans to business cronies, and to fund the activities of the black network. At least $5 billion of the bank's $20 billion in total assets simply disappeared.

In the United States, BCCI used front men to surreptitiously purchase three banks after it was denied permission to purchase a bank on its own. It was also in the United States that the bank first ran into legal problems. In October 1988, a federal grand jury indicted BCCI on money-laundering charges, which were settled in January 1990 with a guilty plea and payment of a $14.8 million fine. After that, follow-on investigations into BCCI's other activities progressed with unexplained slowness.

In fact, one of the enduring mysteries of the BCCI scandal is how the bank's flagrant misdeeds in so many countries could have gone unchallenged for so long. Clearly, the fact that it was chartered in Luxembourg (and thus had no major central bank accepting primary regulatory responsibility) and that it was a relatively small bank by international standards helped it escape sharp regulatory scrutiny for several years. Also, the favors BCCI did for Western intelligence services may have constrained bank regulators in those countries from asking too many embarrassing questions. Whatever the reason, BCCI's long and successful history of financial intrigue raises disturbing questions about the long-run integrity of the international banking system.

together to provide the funds for a loan and thereby directly reduce the risk exposure for individual banks. Large banks that participate in such arrangements will generally make their own assessment of the political and credit risks. Smaller lenders may rely primarily on the reports prepared by large banks. This may lead smaller banks to enter into international loans without fully appreciating or understanding the risk involved. Realistically, though, this is the only means by which smaller banks can enter the international-lending arena, but one hopes that they base their decisions on intelligent analysis of the economic returns and risks involved and not on the glamour and prestige of having an international banking department. The decline in international banking activity of some small banks suggests that they have come to the realization that they do not have the expertise necessary to compete profitably in international lending.

Diversification. Banks may reduce foreign-lending risk through portfolio diversification. That is, in the event that a borrower defaults, earnings from other investments will minimize the effect of the loan loss on the bank's total earnings. Of course, the extent that diversification reduces risk for a given portfolio of loans depends on how the returns are correlated with one another. The more highly correlated the returns, the less the portfolio risk will be reduced. Thus, in a choice between two loans having the same rate of return and riskiness, the loan that is less correlated with the bank's existing portfolio would be the more attractive loan.

Banks have pursued portfolio diversification in several ways, with geographic diversification being the most obvious means to reduce risk exposure. Geographic diversification reduces political risk, but such diversification for diversification's sake is not all good. Specifically, a bank develops expertise in certain countries and cultivates sources of primary information that may not be available to other banks. This type of information, plus long-standing experience with a particular borrower, may allow the bank to formulate better estimates of the risk involved in a particular loan. The danger is that if a bank develops expertise in an area in which the economies of all of the countries in that area depend on the same factors, specializing in the region can prove to be disastrous. This is what happened to many banks that were heavily exposed in Latin America. Although there may have been good diversification among the various countries, the whole region's fortunes were tied to a continuation of economic growth in the industrialized countries and to high prices for their export commodities. When these factors started to deteriorate, the entire region suffered, and banks were left with problem loans in many of the countries.

Loan Sales.   Although it is not a method for reducing risk per se, the sale of problem loans allows banks to "clean up" their balance sheets by disposing of nonperforming assets in exchange for cash. An active secondary market for developing-country syndicated loans has emerged since the first recorded loan sale in summer 1984, and volume was expected to exceed $70 billion (of face value) during 1990. This is an increase from $40 billion in 1988 and $6 billion in 1986. The most active bank participants in this market have been the heavily provisioned European banks and regional U.S. banks.

Until recently, the U.S. money-center banks had shunned this market as being both impractical for them, given their immense LDC loan exposure, and nonrepresentative of the true value of these loans. In fact, the secondary market value of developing-country syndicated loans has always been far below par value and has been declining steadily over time. The drop in price was especially severe after Citicorp announced the write-off of $3 billion in loans to Brazil during May 1987, but prices steadied somewhat after that. In early 1991, secondary market prices averaged 38.9 percent of face value.

Foreign Banks in the United States

Foreign banks have operated in the United States for more than 100 years. Beginning in the mid-1970s, however, they began to attract attention by their rapid expansion into major U.S. financial centers. Their rapid growth alarmed many U.S. bankers and regulators because, until the passage of the International Banking Act, foreign banks were able to escape federal control almost entirely. Exhibit 16–7 shows the increasing number of foreign banks that have established offices in the United States in recent years.

Exhibit 16–7 **Number of Foreign Banking Offices Operating in the United States (1972–1990)**

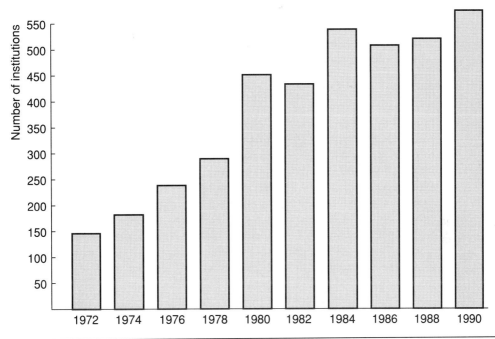

In recent years, increasing numbers of foreign banks (branches and agencies) have established offices in the United States. The International Bank Act of 1978 was intended to equalize the competitive position of foreign banks relative to U.S. banks.

Source: Board of Governors, Federal Reserve System.

Growth of Foreign Banks

Before World War II, the primary motive for foreign banks to establish banking offices in the United States was to facilitate trade and the flow of long-term investments between the United States and their home countries. Following the war, the American dollar emerged as the major world currency, primarily because of the dominance of the U.S. economy relative to the rest of the world. With the importance of U.S. money and capital markets, additional foreign banks began to locate here. By 1965, there were 41 foreign banks conducting business in the United States, with assets totaling $7 billion. Most of these foreign banks were located in New York City, the major attraction being the direct access to the city's money and capital markets. Most of the other foreign banks were concentrated in California.

The rapid expansion of foreign-banking activities in the United States began in the early 1960s. This spurt can be characterized as a worldwide response by the banking industry to the multinationalization of major manufacturing corporations, as previously discussed. For foreign corporations, the United States represented a major market, and many of these firms made sizable direct investments in the United States.

In short, foreign banks followed their corporate customers. The financial services provided were merely a continuation of long-established relationships. Similarly, U.S. corporations also provided some of the impetus for foreign banks to locate in the United States. As American corporations expanded abroad, they established relationships with major local foreign banks, which found it to be good business to extend the banking relationships to the corporate headquarters of U.S. firms by establishing offices in the United States. The banking services that were provided centered on financing the shipment of parts and semifinished products between the corporate headquarters in the United States and the affiliated suppliers of foreign countries.

However, demand was not the only factor that caused this growth. It was also fostered by both the lack of a federal regulatory framework and the ability of foreign banks to establish an interstate-banking network in a form denied U.S. banks. During this period, the entry of foreign banks into the United States was controlled by the individual states. No federal legislation governed their entry. A foreign bank's activities were regulated by federal law only if the bank joined the Federal Reserve System or if it controlled a subsidiary bank, in which case the foreign bank would be subject to the provisions of the Bank Holding Company Act. Thus, as long as the foreign bank operated branches or agencies, it was not subject to federal banking laws. Foreign banks could engage in some nonbanking activities denied to U.S. banks, and they were not required to hold reserves with the Federal Reserve System, a situation that tended to complicate monetary management. For all of the reasons previously discussed, the number of foreign banks operating in the United States increased from 85 to approximately 300 between 1965 and 1990. The growth of foreign bank assets in the United States relative to U.S. domestic bank assets is shown in Exhibit 16-8.

Exhibit 16-8   **Growth of Foreign Bank Assets in the United States (1980-1990)**

End of Year	Domestic Bank Assets ($ in billions)	Foreign Bank Assets ($ in billions)	Total Banking Assets ($ in billions)	Foreign Bank Assets as Percentage of Total
1980	$1527.0	$166.7	$1703.7	9.8
1982	1613.5	152.1	1972.2	7.7
1984	2097.8	164.8	2262.6	7.3
1986	2572.8	240.0	2812.8	8.5
1987	2580.7	266.4	2847.1	9.4
1988	2750.5	297.4	3047.9	9.8
1989	2913.6	332.2	3245.8	10.2
1990	3010.3	389.6	3399.9	11.5

Foreign banks now control over 11 percent of all banking assets in the United States. The International Banking Act of 1978 temporarily stabilized foreign bank penetration into U.S. commercial banking markets, but this share has grown rapidly since 1984.

Source: Federal Reserve System, *Bulletin*, August issues 1981-1991.

International Bank Act of 1978

The lack of regulatory control and the growth of foreign banks led to a recognition by the U.S. government that domestic banks were at a competitive disadvantage against foreign-controlled banks. The International Bank Act (IBA) of 1978 was a culmination of more than a decade of effort by Congress to effect legislation that would create a federal regulatory structure for the operation of foreign banks in the United States. Because foreign banks could operate with a minimum of regulatory controls, the broad policy objective of the IBA was to promote competitive equality between domestic and foreign banking institutions in the United States. The policy of national treatment attempts to give foreign banks operating in the United States similar power and to subject them to the same obligations as their domestic counterparts.

There are six major statutory changes implemented under the International Bank Act. First, the IBA allows federal chartering of foreign banking facilities. Second, the ability of foreign banks to accept interstate domestic deposits is limited. Foreign banks are allowed to establish branches in more than one state; however, branches outside the "home state" of a foreign bank cannot accept deposits and may only maintain customer balances as permitted for Edge Act corporations. Such multistate banking activities are not allowed for domestic banks or bank holding companies, and foreign banks' ability to engage in such activities was viewed as a competitive advantage over domestic banks. Third, the Federal Reserve Board is authorized to impose federal reserve requirements on foreign banks with worldwide assets in excess of $1 billion. This was done to help ensure the integrity of monetary policy actions as well as for competitive equality. Fourth, federal deposit insurance is required for foreign bank operations that engage in retail deposit taking. Fifth, foreign banks are allowed to establish Edge Act corporations to conduct international banking and finance activities. Sixth, foreign banks that operate in the United States are subject to the nonbanking prohibitions of the Bank Holding Company Act.

Although it is too early to assess the long-run impact of the International Bank Act, the act should help ensure the soundness of the U.S. banking system and improve the implementation of U.S. monetary policy by making foreign banks subject to many restrictions that already apply to domestic banks but from which foreign banks had been exempt. Important to American bankers, the new regulation substantially reduces the competitive advantage that foreign banks have enjoyed in the United States. Thus foreign banks should continue to enhance the competitive environment in major U.S. credit markets without an undue competitive advantage.

While the IBA leveled the regulatory playing field somewhat, foreign banking assets in the United States have continued to grow very rapidly. This is particularly true for banking in California and in wholesale banking markets, where the large Japanese banks have grabbed market share at twice the rate of other foreign banks. Japanese "city" banks, which are virtually uncontested in their home markets and which enjoyed phenomenally high market capitalizations during the late 1980s, have come to dominate several high-volume, low-margin banking markets such as issuing backup lines of credit for international trade and for commercial paper issuance facilities.

Fortunately, there are reasons to hope that the competitive balance both in the United States and in international banking may have shifted back towards American banks in the 1990s. For one thing, the crash of the Japanese stock market in 1990—which cut average market values of the city banks almost in half—forced a curtailment in the frenetic rate of growth of international asset accumulation by the large Japanese banks, and also reduced a key funding advantage these banks had enjoyed. Furthermore, American bank regulation seems set for a major, and long overdue, revision that should greatly strengthen the competitiveness of U.S. commercial banks. Already, the wave of "megamergers" that occurred during the summer of 1991 seems to signal that American regional and money-center banks are combining to achieve the size and strength that will be needed to face the fearsomely competitive world of international banking in the 1990s.

Future Directions of International Banking

The 1990s seem certain to be a time of dramatic change in international banking. The consolidation of European banking into a single market after 1992 will offer both opportunities and challenges for international banks, while the capital needs of the newly democratic nations of Eastern Europe and the republics of the former Soviet Union are likely to put pressure on world credit markets throughout the decade. Furthermore, the trend toward the securitization of bank credits seems certain to continue and perhaps even accelerate as banks everywhere scramble to build up their capital bases and derive greater fee income. Finally, banks will almost surely play a key role in financing the worldwide thrust toward privatization of state-owned enterprises, and the more general trend towards greater belief in and reliance on market economic principles.

These trends have led the major international financial institutions, such as the International Monetary Fund and the Bank for International Settlements, as well as the leading central banks, to set tighter regulatory and supervisory roles over the world's banking systems. The results have been a greater awareness of declining capital levels, some explicit regulations concerning capital adequacy and loan limits, and more supervision in such areas as international lending and foreign exchange trading. Recently the World Bank has been investigating the possibility of working with private corporations to tap larger pools of capital with which to assist countries with severe debt problems. Under one proposed arrangement, the World Bank would guarantee loans made to corporations for financing the construction of infrastructure projects in developing countries. The IMF is also looking for more ways to reduce the interest burden on the developing countries while stimulating their economies to higher levels of output.

Coupled with increased surveillance of bank operations by government supervisory agencies has been the increased use of electronic transfer systems within and among major countries and financial centers of the world. For example, the Society for Worldwide Intertelecommunications Financial Transfers (SWIFT), an electronic message system, was established in the late 1970s as a cooperative whose more than 1,500 members are the world's leading banks (although 80 percent of the total traffic is by the 300 top banks). SWIFT transfers instructions for as many as 400,000 daily financial transactions at a cost of $29\frac{1}{2}$¢ each. Although SWIFT does not directly transfer funds, it does provide a safe, rapid, low-cost means of facilitating international funds flows. Given the computer innovations being applied to electronic funds transfers, SWIFT-like institutions will increase the productivity of international banking. It is expected that stockbrokers may soon be admitted to membership in SWIFT, because banks are rapidly moving into the brokerage business.

An older competitor to SWIFT, the Clearinghouse Interbank Payments System (CHIPS), was established by the New York Clearinghouse Association in New York City in 1970. Today most New York City banks, Edge Act corporations, and branches of foreign banks located in New York City are tied into the CHIPS network, and a substantial part of the international interbank dollar transfers into or out of the city are routed through the system. There is some concern, though, that SWIFT will become so dominant that CHIPS will cease to be a significant player in the game.

Summary

U.S. banks engaged in very few international banking activities before 1914. The passage of the Federal Reserve Act in 1913 and the Edge Act in 1919 laid the legal foundation for U.S. banks to compete effectively overseas. It was not until the early 1960s, however, that the rapid expansion of U.S. overseas banking took place. The major reasons for this dramatic growth were (1) the overall expansion of U.S. world trade, (2) the growth of multinational corporations, and (3) the effect of government regulations.

The Federal Reserve Board and the OCC have primary responsibility for supervising the activities of U.S. banks overseas. In general, U.S. banks have been allowed to engage in a wider range of business activities overseas than has been permitted domestically. This policy allows U.S. banks to be competitive in foreign markets.

Banks can use a number of organizational forms to deliver banking services to their international customers. The most important are correspondent relationships, branch offices, Edge Act corporations, and international banking facilities. For large multinational banks, foreign lending is their primary international business activity, accounting for more than half of their total revenues, both domestic and international. The basic risk involved in foreign lending is the same as in domestic banking—the customer's default risk. However, there are two additional risks in lending abroad: sovereign risk and currency risk.

The growth of foreign banks operating in the United States paralleled the expansion of American banks abroad. The primary reason for the growth of foreign banking in the United States was the large amount of direct U.S. investments by foreigners in the 1960s. A second reason was the lack of federal regulations, which allowed foreign banks to operate at a competitive advantage over American banks. The International Bank Act of 1978 addressed many of the inequities that existed by subjecting foreign banks to many of the same regulations imposed on domestic banks. The intent of the act has been to maintain the competitive environment that existed between foreign and domestic banks while enhancing the soundness of the U.S. banking system.

Questions

1. What are Edge Act corporations? What advantages do they afford American banks that wish to engage in international banking?
2. Explain the major reason for the dramatic growth of American banking overseas during the 1960s.
3. What is a shell branch? What functions do banking shell branches perform in U.S. overseas banking? Why are so many located in Caribbean island nations?
4. What are the basic objectives of federal bank regulations as they apply to domestic banking? How are these basic regulatory objectives interpreted differently with respect to overseas banking? How will the new BIS capital standards affect internationally active U.S. banks?
5. What is a syndicated loan? In what ways do large international loans differ from typical domestic loans? Define the term *LIBOR*.
6. What are the risks that must be evaluated in making international loans? Which of these are unique to international lending? How may these risks be reduced?
7. Some U.S. bankers claim that the heavily indebted LDCs are merely illiquid rather than insolvent and thus that the LDC loans on their books should be carried at book value. How would you respond to this idea?
8. Do you believe that the presence of foreign banks in the United States serves the public's interest? In formulating your answer, consider the issues of bank safety and competition in banking markets.
9. What is an international banking facility? In what types of business activities can such entities engage? Why did the Federal Reserve Board create these new banking entities?
10. In international lending, what is meant by the phrase *rescheduling of sovereign loans*? Why has rescheduling of loans become a problem to international lenders? What countries are involved?

Selected References

Aliber, Robert Z. "International Banking: A Survey." *Journal of Money, Credit and Banking*, **November 1986, pp. 661–678.**
This article reviews the academic literature dealing with the theory and practice of international banking. Written by one of the leading scholars in the field, it is both rigorous and highly readable.

Baer, Herbert L. "Foreign Competition in U.S. Banking Markets." *Economic Perspectives.* **Federal Reserve Bank of Chicago, May/June 1990, pp. 22–29.**
This article documents the growth of foreign bank holdings of U.S. banking assets and analyzes the causes of this phenomenon. The author ascribes most of the increasing foreign bank market share to the superior capitalization of foreign—particularly Japanese—banks.

Frankel, Jeffrey A. "The Japanese Cost of Finance: A Survey." *Financial Management*, **Spring 1991, pp. 95–127.**
A comprehensive survey of academic research on the Japanese corporate finance system. It provides an excellent analysis of the critical role Japanese city banks play in the financing (and control) of nonfinancial corporations, and shows how this system overcomes many of the agency problems inherent in the U.S. corporate finance system.

Hirtle, Beverly. "Factors Affecting the Competitiveness of Internationally Active Financial Institutions." *Quarterly Review.* **Federal Reserve Bank of New York, Spring 1991, pp. 38–51.**
An analysis of the determinants of success in international financial markets. While U.S. commercial and investment banks still dominate important market segments, their relatively weak capitalizations make them vulnerable in the long term.

Hultman, Charles W. "The Environment of International Banking." Englewood Cliffs, NJ: Prentice-Hall, 1990.
A short but thorough textbook devoted exclusively to international banking.

Iqbal, Zubair, and Abbas Mirakhor. "Islamic Banking." Occasional Paper No. 49. Washington, DC: International Monetary Fund, March 1987.
This paper details the development of modern, noninterest-based banking in Iran and Pakistan. The basic techniques of Islamic banking are sympathetically, but objectively, described.

Keeton, William R. "The Treasury Plan for Banking Reform." *Economic Review.* **Federal Reserve Bank of Kansas City, May/June 1991, pp. 5–23.**
An analysis of the Treasury bank reform plan, which, though not focused primarily on international banking, would likely have changed the international competitiveness of U.S. banks.

Kochan, Nick. "Cleaning Up by Cleaning Up." *Euromoney,* **April 1991, pp. 73–77.**
An entertaining analysis of the competitive strivings of various tax havens to attract and keep secret deposits.

Lessard, Donald R. "Recapitalizing Third-World Debt: Toward a New Vision of Commercial Financing for Less-Developed Countries." *Midland Corporate Finance Journal,* **Fall 1987, pp. 6–21.**
This excellent study, plus a much longer predecessor article, describes the various forms of channeling capital to developing countries, and succinctly describes the problems inherent in general obligation, syndicated bank loans. Several innovative proposals for dealing with the LDC debt crisis are also presented.

Liepold, Alessandro. *International Capital Markets: Developments and Prospects.* **Washington, DC: The International Monetary Fund, May 1991.**
The IMF's annual overview of international capital markets and flows. An excellent way to get a feel for the workings of international finance.

Pavel, Christine, and John N. McElravey. "Globalization in the Financial Services Industry." *Economic Perspectives.* **Federal Reserve Bank of Chicago, May/June 1990, pp. 3–18.**
An excellent and highly readable primer on how globalization is transforming the delivery of financial services around the world.

Shapiro, Alan C. *Foundations of Multinational Financial Management.* **Needham Heights, MA: Allyn and Bacon, 1991.**
A good undergraduate textbook on all aspects of international finance. Good chapter coverage on foreign exchange risk, trade financing, international capital markets, and international banking. A more comprehensive graduate textbook by the same author is also available.

World Debt Tables: External Debt of Developing Countries. **Washington, DC: The International Bank for Reconstruction and Development/The World Bank, 1991.**
This two volume set is a must for anyone seeking hard data on developing-country debt levels or debt servicing capacity. Also available as a machine-readable data base.

REGULATION OF FINANCIAL INSTITUTIONS

17

Financial institutions are subject to an extensive web of regulation. Have you ever wondered why? One reason is that financial institutions are deemed to provide important financial services, such as loans and checking deposits, that are essential to the operation of a complex economy. Another reason is that financial institutions could excessively expand the money supply and create inflation if they were unrestricted. A third reason is that, in an attempt to make sure that financial institutions can continue to offer essential services, the government has provided "insurance" to them that helps them to survive adversity and also can potentially cost taxpayers hundreds of billions of dollars. Finally, regulators are concerned that financial institutions compete with one another so they will provide essential services at a reasonable price to customers.

Unfortunately, some regulatory objectives are contradictory. Institutions with monopolies are less likely to fail, but they may charge customers more for their financial services. Futhermore, if the taxpayer assumes more of the costs of financial institution failures, the institutions may take more risks, and, thus, increase their risk of failures. Also, regulations designed to limit institutional risks, such as capital requirements, may at times hinder the institutions' ability to expand the money supply and loans necessary to sustain economic growth.

Some of the major regulatory issues related to monetary policy are addressed in Chapters 4, 25, and 26. Some of the major issues related to bank structure and monopoly regulation are addressed in Chapter 15. This chapter addresses issues related to bank safety and soundness, deposit insurance, and the supervisory framework that regulates depository institutions. It also discusses regulatory restrictions on financial institutions' operations and balance sheets, consumer protection regulations, and depository institution examinations. It concludes with a discussion of recent regulatory initiatives and major regulatory issues. Many of the regulatory issues addressed in this chapter apply specifically to commercial banks, but, as we shall see, other financial institutions generally are subject to similar restrictions. We begin with a discussion of deposit insurance.

Deposit Insurance

Possibly the most important reason for the regulation of depository institutions is to provide for the safety and stability of the economy's financial sector. Safe financial institutions are unlikely to fail. From the viewpoint of public policy, financial institutions' failures should be avoided, if possible, because they cause individuals' deposits to be lost and a portion of their wealth and the nation's money supply to disappear. In addition, bank failures may cause hardships for local communities by reducing the amount of credit and the number of credit suppliers available to a community. Safe financial institutions are less likely to cause abrupt changes in the money supply that could disrupt the economy's overall financial stability. One of the reasons the Great Depression of the 1930s was "great" was that extensive bank failures caused credit availability to contract and the nation's money supply to fall by one-third, thereby deepening the depression.

Over time, the number of bank failures per year in the United States has fluctuated widely. They have occurred both as isolated local events and in great national waves. For instance, during the business panic of 1893, nearly 500 banks out of 9,500 suspended operations. In contrast, during the business recession of 1870, only one bank closed. As we shall see, however, it is periods of massive bank failures that are of concern and that impinge on the economy's vitality.

Exhibit 17–1 shows the number and percentage of all banks failing in the 1890–1991 period. Between 1890 and 1920, the number of bank failures averaged about 100 per year, something less than 2 percent of all banks. Beginning in the 1920s, the number of bank failures increased dramatically to an average of about 600 per year. This increase, however, was minor compared to the early years of the Great Depression. Between 1930 and 1933, more than 9,000 banks suspended operations in this country—an average of more than 2,200 bank failures per year or 43 per week.

Exhibit 17–1   **Number and Percentage of All Banks Failing (1890–1991)**

Year	Number	Annual Percentage of Active Banks	Average per Year
1890–1899	1,084	1.50	108
1900–1920	1,789	0.34	85
1921–1929	5,712	2.30	634
1930–1933	9,096	11.29	2,274
1934–1942	487	0.35	54
1943–1952	42	0.03	4
1953–1962	46	0.03	5
1963–1972	60	0.05	6
1973–1977	45	0.03	9
1978–1982	68	0.09	14
1983–1987	595	0.80	119
1988–1991	720	1.40	180

Since World War II, bank regulations have generally been successful in stopping massive bank failures. However, after rate ceilings were removed, interest rates rose, and the economy encountered a severe recession in the early 1980s, bank failures increased sharply.

Source: FDIC, *Annual Report*, various issues, and bimonthly *Regulatory Review*.

Over 40 percent of all active banks failed, and depositors sustained losses totaling $1.3 billion.

During the 1930s, Congress enacted legislation intended to prevent wholesale bank failures. The Banking Act of 1933 barred banks from paying interest on demand deposits, separated commercial banking from investment banking, and restricted the types of assets that banks could own (e.g., banks can own only investment-grade securities) on the grounds that these and other banking practices were excessively risky. Although the wisdom and effectiveness of some of these restrictions have been questioned, the establishment of the Federal Deposit Insurance Corporation (FDIC) in the 1933 Banking Act did restore confidence in the commercial banking system. By guaranteeing the safety of depositors' funds, federal deposit insurance put an end to banking panics. Thus a potential insolvency at one bank no longer threatened deposits at other banks in the same economic region, thereby putting a stop to the domino effect that had long plagued American banking

The effectiveness of federal deposit insurance in reducing bank failures can be seen in Exhibit 17-1. Between 1934 and 1942, bank failures dropped to an average of 54 per year, and many of the banks that failed did not have deposit insurance. Following World War II, the number of bank closings slowed to a trickle, averaging less than ten per year until the 1980s. In the 1980s, bank failures began to rise once again as banks' deposit interest costs rose with the phaseout of Regulation Q. In addition, regional recessions in oil and agriculture took their toll on overextended borrowers and banks. Thus bank failures reached 200 per year by the end of the decade. Overall, the establishment of federal deposit insurance had two effects: (1) it dramatically reduced the number of bank failures for the first 50 years it was available, and (2) at insured banks, it shifted the risk of financial loss from depositors to the FDIC insurance fund.

Deposit Insurance Coverage

When deposit insurance was first enacted in 1933, it only covered deposits up to $2,500. Its purpose was to protect people with small deposits. People with large deposits were assumed to be sophisticated enough to look after themselves. It was believed, however, that small depositors were more likely to be unable or unwilling to assess a bank's true financial status. Thus they were thought to be both more vulnerable to bank failures and more likely to panic and cause a run on a bank to get their deposits back quickly if they heard rumors that a bank might fail.

Over time, federal deposit insurance has been increased from $5,000 per account offered by the FDIC on deposits at insured commercial banks and savings banks in 1934 to more institutions and to $100,000 per account. In 1934, deposit insurance of $5,000 per account was extended to savings and loan depositors by the Federal Savings and Loan Insurance Corporation (FSLIC). The FSLIC was established by the National Housing Act of 1934 and continued until 1989 when the FSLIC was eliminated as a separate entity and the responsibility for thrift institutions was transferred to the FDIC. The thrift insurance branch of the FDIC, the Savings Association Insurance Fund, now insures deposits at savings and loans and at some federally chartered savings banks. Federal insurance also is extended to credit unions' depositors' "shares" through the National Credit Union Share Insurance Fund (NCUSIF) which was established in 1970. The NCUSIF provides insurance for participating credit union members' share deposits for amounts up to $100,000—the same level of insurance that the FDIC provides.

All federally chartered commercial banks, savings banks, savings and loans, and credit unions must obtain deposit insurance from one of the federal insurance funds. State chartered institutions can also obtain federal deposit insurance provided that they meet the standards imposed by the appropriate fund. Some institutions, such as savings and loans or savings banks, have sometimes changed their charters so that they could obtain insurance from the most desirable fund. In the late 1970s and early 1980s, many savings and loans and savings banks preferred FSLIC insurance in order to obtain looser regulations. After many savings and loans failed, however, the FSLIC raised its insurance premium in the mid-1980s. Subsequently, many savings institutions tried to transfer to FDIC insurance (by obtaining savings bank or commercial bank charters) so that they could pay lower rates on their deposit insurance. Such transfers are now limited, however, by the fact that institutions that transfer from the FDIC-SAIF (Savings Institution Fund) to the FDIC-BIF (Bank Insurance Fund) have to pay extra fees.

Deposit Insurance Coverage in Payoffs versus Purchases and Assumptions

The DIDMCA of 1980 raised all federal deposit insurance coverage to $100,000 per account. Some critics thought that was too high, because people with $100,000 were no longer small, unsophisticated depositors. However, the limit of coverage often was exceeded because of two policies adopted by the federal insurance funds.

The first policy was the deposit insurance funds' *purchase and assumption (P&A)* policy. When a bank fails, the insurance fund has a choice of three major ways to resolve the problem. The first approach is to *pay off* the insured deposits, take over the failed institution, *and liquidate* the institution's assets. Under a payoff and liquidate policy, if sufficient funds were not realized from the liquidation of the failed institution, the insured depositors would be paid in full only up to $100,000 per deposit. After that, the depositors would obtain only a partial settlement, or no settlement at all, when the assets of the bank were liquidated. A partial settlement often would be necessary because an insolvent bank has total assets worth less than the total value of its liabilities (see Exhibit 17–2). In such a case, insured depositors would be paid in full by the FDIC, but the uninsured depositors might receive only 50 cents on the dollar for uninsured deposits.

Instead of liquidating a failed bank, however, the insurance fund could allow another bank to enter into a purchase and assumption agreement, in which it would purchase the failed bank and assume all of its liabilities. In that case, the FDIC might provide financial assistance to the acquirer and relieve the bank of some or all of the bad assets in order to induce the new buyer to assume the failed bank's liabilities. Because the failed bank might have more value as an ongoing concern than as a failed bank, it could be less costly for the FDIC to provide financial assistance than to liquidate the failed bank. Furthermore, when all the liabilities were assumed, no depositor would lose a dime, regardless of how large or small the depositor's account was. Thus, the use of the purchase and assumption technique would provide de facto 100 percent deposit insurance.

Exhibit 17–2   FDIC Payoff Policy

Assets	Liabilities and Net Worth
Value realized from sale of assets = $75 million	Deposits under $100,000 = $50 million Uninsured liabilities and deposits over $100,000 = $100 million
	Net worth = − $75 million

In a deposit payoff, the FDIC pays off the $50 million in insured deposits and, in turn, is owed $50 million by the bank. The FDIC then takes possession of the failed bank's assets and liquidates them. It uses the proceeds to pay off the $150 million of deposits and other liabilities (including the $50 million that it is owed in return for paying off the insured deposits). After recovering $75 million from the asset liquidation, the FDIC can pay itself and uninsured liability and deposit holders 50 cents in payoff for each one dollar ($75 million/$150 million) of the bank's liabilities that they own. The owners of the bank receive zero dollars back, because the bank is insolvent and has no positive net worth.

Exhibit 17–3 illustrates a purchase and assumption in which the acquiring institution injects $5 million in new capital and pays a purchase premium of $5 million to cover past losses. In addition, the FDIC provides $20 million in financial assistance in this example to cover other losses.

Exhibit 17–3

FDIC-Assisted Purchase and Assumption Transaction:
Failed Bank Subsidiary of New Bank

Assets	Liabilities and Net Worth
$75 million, value of old bank's good assets acquired by new bank	$100 million in deposits and other liabilities of old bank assumed by new bank
$20 million in financial assistance provided by FDIC in exchange for some bad assets	
$5 million purchase premium paid by new bank's owners in the form of assumed liabilities	
$5 million in new cash injected by new bank's owners to buy capital	$5 million in new capital in new bank

In a purchase and assumption, the owners of the new bank acquire selected assets of the failed bank and assume all of its liabilities, including its uninsured as well as insured deposits. The new bank's owners may request financial assistance from the FDIC and, in turn, give the FDIC claims on some of the old bank's bad assets (defaulted or doubtful loans). Before they are allowed to acquire and operate the new bank, the owners also may have to (1) inject new money in the form of a purchase premium to make up for asset deficiencies (charged-off loans of the old bank) and (2) inject new capital into the bank. If the old bank has hidden assets, such as a valuable banking franchise, the new bank's owners may be willing to pay a substantial amount to acquire it.

The FDIC may use either a "whole bank" purchase and assumption or a "clean bank" purchase and assumption policy. In the latter case the FDIC retains some of the failed bank's assets and provides the acquirer with an FDIC promissory note to cover the value of the retained assets. Alternatively, the acquirer may acquire all the failed bank's assets but retain an option to "put" some of the assets back to the FDIC in exchange for an FDIC promissory note at some later point in time. It may exercise the put after it has a chance to evaluate the failed bank's loan portfolio better. In such a case, the FDIC is likely to receive all the failed bank's defaulted and doubtful loans when the "put" is exercised.

Finally, the FDIC may retain the failed bank's assets and transfer the insured deposits of that bank to another financial institution. Because an acquiring institution may find it cheaper to obtain additional deposit liabilities by "buying them" from the FDIC, rather than by advertising, it may be willing to pay the FDIC a small premium for being allowed to assume the failed bank's insured deposit obligations.

Deposit Insurance Coverage under the "Too Big to Fail" Policy

The second policy adopted by federal regulators that provided 100 percent deposit insurance was its "too big to fail (TBTF)" policy. For many years it appeared that the FDIC was reluctant to liquidate large banks. Instead, it generally arranged purchase and assumption transactions if a large bank failed. Then in 1984, when Continental Illinois National Bank essentially failed, the comptroller of the currency announced that Continental, as well as the 11 other largest banks in the country, were "too big to fail." Their depositors would be paid off in full regardless of how large the deposit was or how poorly the bank performed. This policy was implemented not only in resolving the Continental Illinois failure but also in conjunction with the 1988 failures of First City Bancorporation and First Republic Bank Corporation in Texas. In both cases, federal regulators guaranteed that 100 percent of deposits would be paid off, regardless of the deposits' size.

Savings and Loan Failures and Assumptions

Full deposit payoff policies also were adopted by the FSLIC before Congress abolished it and thrift deposit insurance responsibilities were transferred to the FDIC. In the early 1980s, the FSLIC arranged mergers of troubled savings and loans (S&Ls) to avoid having to liquidate them and pay off depositors. Thus no depositors lost money. Even if a willing acquirer could not be found, the FSLIC might arrange a phoenix merger of two or more troubled institutions so that the new institutions could take advantage of accounting conventions that would inflate their profits and let them keep operating without paying off their depositors. By the late 1980s, the FSLIC had insufficient funds to pay off depositors, so it arranged buyouts or mergers of failed institutions by guaranteeing future financial assistance to buyers who would agree to operate the institutions and honor their deposit liabilities. Thus, both by contrivance and by necessity, the FSLIC attempted to keep weak savings and loans operating so that their depositors' funds would technically be safe (unless everyone tried to withdraw their funds at one time) regardless of the size of the deposits.

Because the FSLIC had insufficient funds throughout the 1980s, it had no alternative but to treat all savings and loans as if they were too big to fail. Thus, S&L

depositors, like bank depositors, rarely lost funds when their depository institutions were closed down because their deposit liabilities were assumed by a new institution.

Nonfederal Deposit Insurance

In addition to federal deposit insurance plans, various private deposit insurance plans have at times been available to certain deposit-taking institutions. These plans may cover *industrial banks* (a form of finance company that accepts deposits), thrift institutions, credit unions, or other deposit-taking entities. Often, private deposit insurance funds are state sponsored. However, such funds, because they lack the ability to print money, and because state governments are not willing to bail them out if they suffer a financial emergency, are not nearly as reliable as federal deposit insurance funds. Consequently, most have failed.

In addition to the New York Deposit Safety Fund for banks, which failed many years ago (see Chapter 5), in recent years numerous state-chartered insurance funds have failed. For instance, in 1983, depositors were left with large losses when Commonwealth Savings Company of Nebraska, an industrial bank, failed, causing the Nebraska Depository Institution Guarantee Corporation to go out of existence. Fifteen other savings banks lost their deposit insurance because of that failure. In addition, the Thrift Guarantee Corporation of Hawaii was forced to close its doors in 1983 because of failures of insured institutions. Then, in 1984, the California Thrift Guarantee Corporation was unable to repay insured depositors in full after two industrial banks failed.

In 1985, most remaining state-sponsored private insurance funds closed. This occurred after the Ohio Deposit Guarantee Fund failed in March because it had insufficient resources to pay off depositors of Home State Savings and Loan for losses incurred by that institution. As a result, 70 Ohio S&Ls were left without deposit insurance, at least temporarily. Shortly thereafter, the Maryland Savings Share Insurance Corporation was brought down by the failure of Maryland's Community Savings and Loan. Consequently, all state-sponsored insurance funds became suspect, and financial institution regulators in North Carolina, Massachusetts, and other states with state-sponsored insurance funds requested that their member institutions obtain federal insurance whenever possible. Nonetheless, the Rhode Island Share and Depository Indemnity Corporation continued to provide deposit insurance to some banks and credit unions in Rhode Island until January 1991, when it was declared insolvent.

Problems with Deposit Insurance

Insurance Agencies as Police

In the 1940s through the 1960s, deposit insurance seemed to solve the problem of bank failures. However, during the 1980s, more than one-third of all savings institutions disappeared, and bank failures rose consistently to exceed 200 per year before the end of the decade. Clearly, not all problems had been solved.

One factor that changed after deposit insurance became available was that depositors with deposits under $100,000 at small banks or deposits of any size at "too big to fail" banks no longer had to fear bank failures. As a result, depositors no longer caused runs on banks based on unsubstantiated rumors. At the same time, most depositors no longer had an incentive to make sure that a depository institution was sound before they put their money in it; all they wanted to know was whether it had federal deposit insurance. Taking this to extremes, money brokers started to do business. The money brokers promised to deposit up to $100,000 of each investor's funds in whatever depository institution paid the highest rate, provided that the institution had deposit insurance.

Consequently, the development of deposit insurance caused individual investors to feel that they no longer had a responsibility to investigate the soundness of the institutions in which they deposited their funds. As a result, the deposit insurance funds had to develop a "police" mentality—as they tried to protect members of the public who (by relying on deposit insurance for protection) no longer protected themselves.

The insurance agencies, therefore, have enacted various policies designed to ensure that insured depository institutions are operated safely. They hire large forces of examiners and examine insured institutions regularly. If an insured institution is found to be violating any of a number of detailed regulations, its board of directors will be held responsible and asked to change policies. Such policy changes may include such things as hiring more guards; keeping less money in the vault; providing marked money so that bank robbers can be traced; using surveillance cameras; double-checking all transfers of funds; monitoring all loans made to employees or directors; complying fully with the disclosure and procedural requirements associated with accepting loan applications, granting loans, and documenting all aspects of all loan transactions; and so on.

If a bank is found to score poorly on the examiners' CAMEL (Capital adequacy, Asset quality, Management competence and control, Earnings, and Liquidity) rating system, it will be scheduled for more frequent examinations than other banks. If the problems are serious, the institution may be subjected to "cease and desist" orders that force it to change its operations, to change directors or principal officers, to obtain more capital contributions from stockholders, or to cease operations.

If a bank has inadequate net worth because of operating losses or loan charge-offs, examiners may force it to obtain more capital by selling more common stock or closely related securities, such as preferred stock or mandatory convertible debt. In this case, the bank must sell securities in the nation's capital markets, which entails a risk of loss for the buyers. Thus, if the bank is very risky, the buyers of those securities will buy them only if they are promised a very high rate of return. In that way, the capital market imposes a risk premium for risky banks that attempt to sell additional stock or subordinated debt to comply with the insurers' capital requirements.

Because the cost of selling the stock or debt rises with risk, the FDIC can, de facto, cause riskier banks to pay more to retain their deposit insurance by requiring them to sell more stock or debt (see Exhibit 17-4). The FDIC can also make sure that others will watch risky banks in such a case. Because stockholders and uninsured liability holders will lose a great deal if a bank fails, they will also watch the bank closely to ensure that it is operated prudently and properly.

Exhibit 17–4

Effect of Required Capital or Debt Sales on FDIC Insurance Exposure and Financing Costs at a Bank

Assets	Liabilities and Net Worth
Assets = $100 million	Insured deposits = $85 million
	Subordinated debt = $5 million
	Preferred stock = $5 million
	Common stock and retained earnings = $5 million

If the bank had additional insured deposits and no subordinated debt or preferred stock, only 5 percent of its assets would need to go bad before the common stockholders' equity would be reduced to zero and the FDIC would be exposed to loss. By requiring additional primary capital in the form of perpetual preferred stock or additional secondary capital in the form of appropriate subordinated debt, the FDIC can substantially reduce its risk of loss if more than 5 percent of the bank's assets go bad. However, the preferred stockholders and subordinated debt holders are exposed to loss, respectively, if more than 5 or 10 percent of the bank's assets become worthless. Thus they will require higher interest or dividend payout rates to compensate them for any risk that more than 5 percent or 10 percent of the bank's assets will go bad. Consequently, if the FDIC requires risky banks to acquire more capital, the risky banks will have to pay higher interest rates or preferred stock dividends to obtain the required funds and keep their deposit insurance. In that way, their costs of retaining deposit insurance will rise with their riskiness, even though the FDIC deposit insurance premium (per dollar of insured deposits) remains the same.

Moral Hazard

A major problem resulting from the provision of deposit insurance is that it reduces the incentive of depositors to monitor the health of institutions in which they place their money. This is a "moral hazard" in that the insured individual is less careful, and thus is more likely to incur a loss, than would be the case if he or she were not insured. Thus, since 1983, the FDIC has tried to ensure that *uninsured* depositors police more carefully the banks in which they deposit their funds. It has done so by arranging insured-deposit transfers in cases of bank failure. In such cases, only the insured deposits are transferred to another institution. The uninsured deposits are returned to the old bank, which is liquidated. Consequently, because uninsured depositors may lose some or all their funds, they have a greater incentive to monitor the safety of the bank than they would if they expected a purchase and assumption to occur in the event of failure.

Deposit insurance also can create a moral hazard for the managers of depository institutions. In particular, even if a depository institution is risky, if it is insured, it usually can continue to issue deposits to obtain funds at much the same rate as less risky institutions. It can do so because most deposit holders do not share the risks of loss (which are primarily borne by the insuring agency). Thus, unlike corporation managers, managers of insured depository institutions usually can take greater risk without greatly increasing the price they must pay to obtain (deposit) liabilities. If they do not bear the full cost of their risk-taking, they may be encouraged to take more risk than they would if they could only issue uninsured liabilities.

Purchase and assumption (P&A) liquidation techniques and TBTF policies aggravate moral hazard problems because they more completely break the linkage between greater risk-taking (or greater leverage) and higher costs of funds that exist in most corporations.

For example, an institution with many bad loans may fear that it will have to write them off and become insolvent. If that were done, it would be liquidated, thereby costing the management team its jobs, salaries, and perquisites. However, if the institution issues more insured deposits paying its usual insured-deposit rate, makes more loans at higher rates, and charges high loan origination fees, it may be able to report enough profits on its newly expanded loan portfolio that it will be able to absorb the losses on past loans and still appear to be profitable. This strategy can work only if losses appear on the new loans with a lag while the income from loan origination fees and higher rates on loans immediately increase reported profits. Such a "profitable" institution can continue to operate. If the new loans are, in fact, sound, the management may have true profits and survive its crisis. However, if the new borrowers were willing to pay high loan rates and large up-front fees only because the borrowers' loan requests were risky, loan losses will ultimately occur as the new loans go bad. Thus the weak institutions will have to grow still faster so that reported earnings from new loans will grow faster than reported loan losses on old loans.

This "moral hazard" problem means that managers of troubled institutions will have an incentive to gamble. If the gamble fails, they can gamble again in hopes that the gambling process will obscure their losses, buy them more time as managers, and give the institution a chance to grow out of its difficulties. Deposit insurance makes this gambling possible, as it allows remotely generated deposits to be funneled to the gamblers by deposit brokers, even if local depositors become wary of an institution that is taking too many risks.

The issue of moral hazard is not moot. A scenario like the one just described led to massive failures of Texas depository institutions in the late 1980s. The problems actually started in the early to mid-1980s as oil prices fell and the real estate market softened. However, Texas lenders, especially the thrift institutions, continued to lend. Many took advantage of the new powers given to them by the DIDMCA of 1980 and the Depository Institutions Act of 1982 to make commercial real estate construction and development loans. These loans were risky, but they paid high interest rates and large upfront fees. Also, they often provided the promise of an "equity kicker" so that the lending institutions' profits would be higher if the project financed with the borrowed money did well. By financing their lending by issuing insured deposits, the lending institutions were able to make risky loans without paying more to borrow. This was a moral hazard, but it made it easy to borrow, so many of the riskiest thrifts grew very rapidly. Often the risky thrifts lent new money to previous borrowers so the borrowers could pay the interest due on old loans, and the old loans would not default. They even counted loan origination fees on the new loans in their profits; regulatory accounting rules, since changed, let them do so.

Ultimately, however, the risky Texas thrifts could not outgrow their portfolio of risky loans and the softening real estate and oil markets. As a result, many institutions failed after suffering great losses. Yet many survived five years longer through their lending strategies than they would have survived if their early losses had been promptly recognized. Consequently, even though their managers received five more years of income, the losses to the deposit insurance fund were gigantic by the time they ultimately were realized.

Unequal Coverage for Large and Small Banks

One problem with the P&A and TBTF policies of the deposit insuring agencies is that they differentially protect depositors at large and small banks. Depositors at large institutions may receive 100 percent deposit protection whereas large deposit holders at small banks do not. The small banks often complain about this (as the Independent Bankers Association of Texas did when the FDIC promised to pay 100 cents on the dollar to all depositors at the largest bank in the state, First Republic Bank, as it approached failure). However, their complaints have had little effect on the FDIC. On the other hand, large banks sometimes complain that they pay deposit insurance premiums on all their deposits, even though the maximum coverage is $100,000 per account.

Are Deposit Insurance Premiums at the Proper Level?

In 1988, federal deposit insurance premiums varied widely. The FDIC and FSLIC assessed basic annual premiums equal to $\frac{1}{12}$ of 1 percent of deposits. However, the FDIC was empowered to rebate up to 60 percent of the premiums paid if it had a sufficient surplus (although the FDIC had had such surpluses in earlier years, it didn't have surpluses in 1988, so there was no rebate). In contrast, the FSLIC assessed an additional surcharge of $\frac{1}{8}$ of 1 percent per year on all deposits of insured institutions. As a result, many of the healthier savings and loans tried to obtain savings bank or commercial bank charters so that they could obtain FDIC insurance instead of costly FSLIC insurance. Congress, however, put a moratorium on deposit insurance switches so that the FSLIC would not be left insuring only the institutions that were too weak to qualify for a change in charter. Meanwhile, the NCUSIF stayed out of the fray. It assessed each credit union a one-time fee equal to 1 percent of its shares. When the NCUSIF's losses from credit union failures were low, no further assessment was required and rebates were made. However, when losses accrued, the NCUSIF later imposed an insurance premium of $\frac{1}{12}$ of 1 percent in addition to its initial 1 percent fee. Because banks and thrift institutions preferred their more flexible charters to a credit union charter, they had no incentive to switch to NCUSIF insurance.

Many thrifts have complained that thrift insurance premiums are too high compared to those at commercial banks. After the FIRRE act was passed in 1989, annual thrift insurance premiums equalled 0.23 percent of deposits, while commercial bank insurance premiums were raised to 0.15 percent. Shortly, thereafter, the premiums were raised to 0.25 percent and 0.23 percent, respectively, so thrifts still had to pay more. Thrifts could switch to bank charters, but still had to pay the higher thrift insurance premiums for at least 5 years. Alternatively, state-chartered institutions could choose to forgo federal deposit insurance. However, federal deposit insurance is cheap relative to the extra interest rates depositors would require on uninsured accounts. Thus almost all depository institutions obtain federal deposit insurance.

For political reasons, deposit insurance tends to be bargain priced. Because the FDIC Bank Insurance Fund was technically insolvent as a result of large losses, Congress passed the Federal Deposit Insurance Corporation Improvement Act of 1991 (FDICIA) to provide more government funds to the FDIC. The act also required that the FDIC raise deposit insurance premiums high enough to cover any losses and make the insurance premiums vary with bank risk. The FDIC-BIF proposed raising insurance premiums to 0.30 percent but deferred that action twice in 1992. Nonetheless, it did try to implement risk-based premiums in 1993, by raising insurance premiums to a range of 0.23% to 0.31% (with risky banks paying more).

Should Separate Insurance Funds Exist?

Some people advocate having multiple deposit insurance funds, including private insurance, so that competition will exist between insuring agencies. However, private deposit insurance funds are not credible in a crisis. Also, competition between regulators often can take the form of "competition in laxity." In the early 1980s, when FSLIC and FDIC deposit insurance premiums were the same, some thrift institutions preferred FSLIC insurance, because FSLIC accounting rules and examiners were more lenient than those of the FDIC.

Overall, then, a case can be made for the merger of federal deposit insurance funds. Such a merger would eliminate the incentive for depository institutions to switch charters to avoid either tough examinations and rules or higher insurance premiums. The main opposition to such a merger comes from the commercial banks and credit unions. They do not want to pay higher deposit insurance premiums to help pay for thrift institutions' past losses. Nonetheless, since all federally insured institutions benefit from reduced deposit interest costs on insured deposits, all should share the cost of keeping federal deposit insurance guarantees credible. If that cost is too high relative to the benefits, institutions should be allowed to obtain state charters in states that have no deposit insurance requirement.

Lessons from Past Bank Failures

Studies of previous bank failures provide insight into the possibility of a return of the massive bank failures of the 1930s and another Great Depression. Most evidence indicates that a major factor in the collapse of the banking system in the 1930s was the precipitous reduction of the money supply. As banks failed, bank deposits disappeared and depositors at other banks began to withdraw their funds. Given the reduced liquidity in the economy, it was not possible for banks to sell their assets to obtain the cash they needed to meet depositors' withdrawals, and the Fed did not lend the banks all that they needed to borrow. As banks began to fail in increasingly large numbers, bank deposits and the money supply contracted and helped plunge the nation into its deepest and longest economic depression. One of the lessons learned from the Great Depression is that to prevent massive bank failures, the country needs a central bank that both can and will provide the banking system with liquidity when needed. Today the Federal Reserve System understands its role as lender of last resort, as witnessed by its announcement that it would provide adequate liquidity to the economy after the stock market crash of October 19, 1987.

Another lesson was that large numbers of bank failures result from bank panics—that is, rapid withdrawals of funds by depositors who have heard rumors that their bank may fail even though the bank actually is sound. By guaranteeing depositors' funds, the FDIC has effectively prevented runs on the banks that it insures. Depositors no longer need to operate under the rule of "better first in line than sorry." If their bank fails, depositors know they will be paid in an orderly manner by the

FDIC. When bank runs have occurred in recent years, they have been limited to a single bank and have not spread to other insured banks.

Still another lesson learned from past bank failures was that regional or industry-wide depressions were a major cause of bank failures. From 1921 through 1931, most bank failures involved unit banks that were closely tied to local economies. Only seven suspensions involved banks with more than ten branches. California, the country's principal statewide branching state, experienced few bank failures during this period. The reason for unit banks' poor record with respect to bank failures is their lack of geographic diversification. Branch banking over wide geographic areas provides diversification for a bank's loan and deposit portfolio, resulting in reduced business risk as compared to a similar unit bank. Recent evidence suggests that regional or industrywide depressions still cause bank failures in states whose economies are poorly diversified. This was shown by numerous bank failures in the oil-dependent Southwest and agriculturally dependent Midwest during the 1980s. However, even in an area with weak economies, it is only the most poorly managed banks (i.e., the least diversified, most illiquid holders of the poorest quality loans) that fail.

Basically, fraud, embezzlement, and poor management are the most notable causes of bank failures. This has been particularly true since the 1940s. For example, of the 54 insured banks that failed between 1959 and 1970, 35 (65 percent) were classified by the FDIC as failing as a consequence of fraud or other irregularities. That percentage fell sharply in the 1980s, however, as bank failures ascribable to weak local economies increased. Nonetheless, among major bank failures, the FDIC blamed the failures of the United States National Bank of San Diego and Franklin National Bank of New York City on "irregular" banking practices, and the failures of Penn Square Bank of Oklahoma and United American Bank of Knoxville resulted from "unusual" loan losses.

Recent Bank Failures

The Continental Illinois "Failure"

One of the most significant recent events was the Continental Illinois National Bank crisis during the summer of 1984 and that bank's subsequent bailout by the federal government. In Continental's case, the FDIC provided open bank assistance that protected all the bank's creditors and depositors but left the original stockholders with practically nothing. Though technically not a bank failure, without direct government intervention Continental surely would have collapsed. At the time of its problems, it was the nation's seventh largest bank, with total assets in excess of $40 billion. Continental's difficulties could be traced to large anticipated loan losses in the bank's loan portfolios for energy, agriculture, and heavy industry—three industries that were suffering from serious economic problems at the time. The problems were aggravated because a senior loan officer had purchased many (bad) loan participations from Penn Square Bank after receiving a large personal loan from that Bank.

As rumors about Continental's problems began to circulate within the financial community, Continental suddenly lost $4 billion in deposits in only three days. At that time, Continental was raising about $8 billion daily in overnight funds from the domestic and world money markets. To stem the tide and to stabilize what they believed to be a potentially dangerous situation, government regulators acted quickly. First, as deposit withdrawals mounted, the Federal Reserve System provided Continental with discount-window loans. Second, the FDIC responded by guaranteeing the deposits of all of the bank's depositors and creditors (not just those with deposits up to $100,000). Finally, the FDIC added $1.5 billion to the bank's sagging capital base.

Why the extraordinary action by the government regulators? The answer, of course, is that they wanted to stabilize the banking system and avert a situation that could have resulted in another 1929-type financial collapse and depression. There was concern that if the Continental problem got out of control, it would spread to other large banks whose loan portfolios were similar to Continental's.

Nevertheless, these regulatory actions have not escaped criticism. First, the "too big to fail" policy has created a two-tiered banking system. All depositors at very large institutions have de facto 100 percent deposit insurance. This policy was reaffirmed when the FDIC promised that all depositors of First City Bancorporation and First Republic Bank Corporation in Texas would be paid in full when those institutions were saved with FDIC aid in 1988 and when the Bank of New England was closed through a federally assisted merger that protected all depositors in 1991. Depositors at small banks, however, have deposit insurance only up to $100,000 per account.

A second criticism is that if the federal government stands behind all big-bank liabilities, bank management may be tempted to make riskier loans in an effort to increase profits. This is because uninsured depositors, who are at risk, help monitor the bank's performance, and their willingness (or unwillingness) to purchase the bank's liabilities disciplines the bank to take prudent risks. In recent years the FDIC has hoped to strengthen market discipline in banking; however, with the Continental experience behind them, large bank's uninsured depositors should now be indifferent to the risks that these banks take because of the willingness of the FDIC or some other government agency to intervene and prevent the banks from suffering any loss. This has created a major moral hazard problem. To compensate, regulators must ensure that the top managers of all failed or reorganized banks lose their jobs.

The Texas and New England Failures

In the late 1970s and early 1980s, the price of oil soared. Then, in the mid-1980s, the price of oil fell from nearly $30 per barrel to $10 per barrel. As a result, many oil-drilling and oil-producing firms suffered great losses. Their lending institutions shared in those losses, as did the lending institutions that had financed real estate construction during the oil boom. The thrift institutions were hurt most badly, especially those that had made risky real estate construction and development loans. Some, such as Empire Savings and Loan, had engaged in illegal practices as well. Approximately half of all Texas, Louisiana, and Oklahoma thrifts became insolvent after the oil and real estate bubble burst in the Southwest. In addition, all of the major Texas banks either failed, required assistance from the FDIC, or were taken over by out-of-state acquisitors.

Some of the Texas failures resulted from excessively rapid growth that caused a breakdown in internal management controls so loan officers made bad loans in return for personal gain. In addition to causing a breakdown in internal controls, excessively rapid growth often caused a bank to rely excessively on high-cost purchased funds for financing as it outgrew its local deposit base. As an institution's cost of funds went up, so did its propensity to take excessive loan risks in order to earn a higher rate of return. In a study of Texas thrift-institution failures conducted by the Dallas Federal Reserve Bank, insolvent thrift institutions were found to be those that had (1) paid higher interest rates to obtain deposits, (2) acquired higher yielding loans, and, as a result, (3) incurred higher loan losses that ultimately rendered them insolvent.

Other Texas banks failed or ran to a rescuer for various reasons related to the weak oil and real estate markets. Texas Commerce was weakened by bad loans to directors and others engaged in the oil and real estate businesses; it was acquired by Chemical Bank. Interfirst Bank tried to match out-of-state banks' terms in oil lending and had to be bailed out, as did some out-of-state lenders (Continental Illinois and Seafirst), when oil prices fell and oil loans went bad. At first, Interfirst merged with Republic Bank, which had fewer oil loans, to become the largest bank in Texas. However, because Republic Bank had many real estate loans, the new bank, First Republic Bank, failed when the real estate market went sour. The remaining business was sold with FDIC assistance to Nations Bank, and all depositors were repaid in full, as the merged Interfirst/Republic Bank was deemed too big to fail.

The litany of failures in the Southwest could go on and on. However, most failures can be traced to one or more basic causes: excessively rapid growth funded with purchased money (often obtained by offering premium rates on CDs, some of which were sold through "deposit brokers" to people across the country); internal management breakdowns with insider loans and inadequate supervision of loan officers; excessive lending competitiveness, which left too little margin for error in case loan defaults rose or oil or real estate prices fell; and a vicious regional recession in the oil, real estate, and agricultural markets of the Southwest.

A few years later the Texas scenario was repeated in New England. The New England economy stagnated as defense spending was cut back and the formerly booming demand for real estate in that region "busted." As a result, banks that had lent extensively to real estate developers, building contractors, or real estate buyers on the basis of their real estate's collateral value saw that value disappear and many major loans default. By the end of 1990, 38 percent of all New England banks were incurring losses, and in January 1991, the Bank of New England and its related banks failed. Furthermore, most New Hampshire banks had to be recapitalized in 1991, and many other New England-based banks also failed. Later that year, California banks also began to suffer from a collapse in real estate prices.

Failures Due to Fraud

Excessively rapid growth, internal management breakdowns, poor diversification, and regional recessions can all cause banking failures. However, one of the largest causes of failure is still related to fraud or self-serving mismanagement. This was true in the case of United American Bank, a large bank that failed in Tennessee in 1983. The bank had made many "floater loans," which floated down to lower-ranking loan officers from top management with the request that the loans be approved. Many of the loans were to friends or political cronies of the president of the bank, and often the loans were not repaid.

In addition, United States National Bank of San Diego failed in 1973 after making loans to shell corporations that were secretly controlled by the chairman of the bank. Exhibit 17–5 explains how a fraudulent management can extract more money from a bank than it puts in, until it is caught.

Fraud, it seems, played a major part in many of the thrift institution failures of the mid- and late 1980s. Congressional committees estimated that indictable offenses had been committed in a majority of the thrift institutions that failed. In February 1990 the FBI was investigating 530 financial institution failures to determine what role, if any, law violations had played in each failure. As of July 1990, the Justice Department had indicted well over 300 people in conjunction with 243 savings and loan failures that had occurred in the previous 2 years.

Depository Institutions' Regulators

Depository Institutions are stringently regulated by a number of regulatory agencies to prevent failures because of fraud, mismanagement, or other reasons. In addition, the regulators ensure that the institutions comply with all applicable laws, and they regulate branching, mergers, and entry and exit by institutions under their jurisdiction.

Federal supervision of banks is divided between the FDIC, the Federal Reserve, and the comptroller of the currency. Exhibit 17–6 describes the regulatory responsibilities of each. In addition, state banking commissioners are responsible for the regulation and examination of banks chartered in their states.

Each state has its own agency that is responsible for regulating and supervising commercial banks chartered by the state. These agencies can also regulate other financial institutions in the state, such as savings and loan associations, mutual

---

Exhibit 17–5   **Dishonest Bankers Can Take Out More than They Put In a Captive Bank**

Assets	Liabilities and Net Worth
$50 million in good assets	Deposits and other liabilities = $93 million
$50 million in loans to shell corporations	Capital stock = $7 million

A dishonest person can buy control of a bank by buying capital worth 7 percent or less of the assets' dollar value. Then, by directing the bank to lend to a chain of secretly owned and controlled shell corporations, the dishonest party can siphon far more money out of the bank for personal use than he or she initially invested. The shell corporations, in turn, can grant loans or credit to other captive companies. As long as the shell corporations pay interest on the loans, even if they have to borrow more to do so, the process can continue until the losses are fatally large. Such a scheme caused the United States National Bank of San Diego to fail in 1973. Subsequently, the chairman of the bank was jailed.

Exhibit 17–6   **Primary Supervisory Responsibilities for Commercial Bank Regulators**

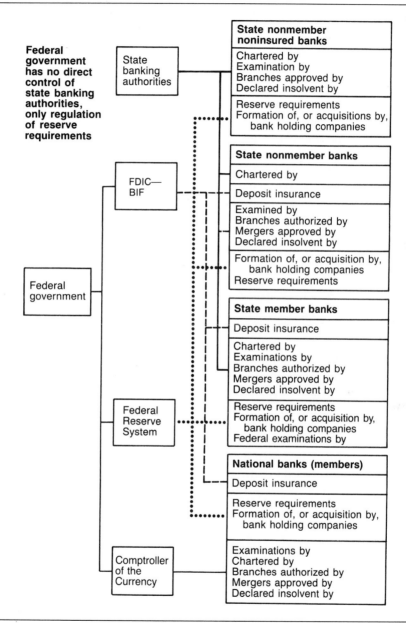

Because there are so many different bank regulators, it is often difficult to determine which regulator is responsible for which different banking activities. The FDIC regulates more banks than any other bank regulatory agency.

savings banks, credit unions, and finance companies. The agency directors may be called "commissioner" or "superintendent of banking," but, in general, the scope of their duties with respect to state-chartered banks is analogous to that of the comptroller of the currency for national banks. Although their functions vary from one state to another, state banking authorities normally have the following responsibilities. First, they approve the charters for new state banks, the opening and closing of branch offices (if the state permits branching), and the scope of bank holding company operations within the state. Second, they examine financial institutions chartered by the state. Third, state bank agencies have powers to protect the public interest. These powers take the form of regulating the activities of finance companies and enforcing various consumer regulations, such as credit disclosure and usury laws.

It is difficult to make any broad generalizations about the quality of state banking supervision. Perhaps all that can be fairly said it that the quality varies. Some state agencies are comparable to federal agencies in the quality of their bank examinations. Others, unfortunately, are weak. Administrators are selected by patronage; examiners are poorly paid, undertrained, and often controlled by the banks that they are supposed to regulate. Generally, state banking agencies are more permissive in the types of banking practices they allow. As a result, we find a large number of both large and small banks preferring state charters. For example, most large New York City banks whose operations are global in scope are state-chartered banks.

Nonbank depository institutions may also be regulated by state banking commissioners or other financial institution regulators at the state level. However, federally chartered and insured nonbank institutions often have a separate set of regulators at the federal level. Federally chartered credit unions, for instance, are chartered and regulated by the National Credit Union Administration Board (NCUAB), while federally chartered thrift institutions are now regulated by the Office of Thrift Supervision in the Department of the Treasury. Federally insured credit unions obtain insurance from the National Credit Union Share Insurance Fund (NCUSIF), while federally insured thrift institutions obtain insurance from the FDIC's savings association insurance fund (FDIC-SAIF). Also, banks and savings associations that have large proportions of mortgage-related assets in their portfolios may join a Federal Home Loan Bank, through which they can clear payments and obtain relatively low-cost "advances" when they need to borrow.

Major Regulations Affecting Depository Institutions

Historically, most bank regulations developed because of the effect that banks had on the nation's economy. In the 1970s, however, there was a trend toward legislation designed to protect consumers in credit markets. Then, in the 1980s regulations became oriented toward protecting depository institutions and their federal insurance funds. Commercial bank regulations may be classified according to their principal objective: (1) those designed to promote bank safety; (2) those designed to affect the structure of banking (the size and distribution of banks in the economy—see Chapter 15); and (3) those designed to protect the interest of consumers. Some regulations may have more than one objective. Similar regulations apply to other depository financial institutions. Exhibit 17–7 summarizes some of the major bank regulatory provisions since 1900.

Bank Safety Regulations

Bank safety regulations are directed toward preventing bank failures. In many cases, bank safety regulations are anticompetitive—that is, their enforcement by bank regulatory authorities tends to keep banks from competing with one another. This reduces the possibility of both massive as well as relatively small bank failures.

Federal Deposit Insurance.   A major cause of cumulative bank failures is the attempt by depositors to be first in converting their bank deposits into currency. Federally insuring deposits removes most of the incentive to do this, at least up to the

---

Exhibit 17–7   **Major Bank Legislation and Regulatory Provisions since 1900**

Federal Reserve Act (1913)
- Establishes the Federal Reserve System

Banking Acts of 1933 (Glass-Steagall) and 1935
- Prohibits payment of interest on demand deposits
- Establishes the FDIC
- Separates banking from investment banking
- Establishes interest rate ceilings on savings and time deposits

Bank Holding Company Act (1956)
- Regulates formation of bank holding companies (BHC)
- Allows nonbank subsidiaries to operate across state lines

Bank Merger Act (1966)
- Establishes merger guidelines and denotes competition as a criterion

Amendment to Bank Holding Company Act (1970)
- Regulates one-bank holding companies

Depository Institutions Deregulation and Monetary Control Act (1980)
- Establishes uniform reserve requirements for all depository institutions
- Phases out deposit rate ceilings by April 1, 1986
- Allows NOW accounts at all depository institutions
- Allows thrifts to make consumer loans and issue credit cards

Depository Institutions Act of 1982 (Garn–St. Germain)
- Allows possibility of interstate and interinstitutional mergers
- Gives thrifts authority to make some commercial loans

Competitive Equality in Banking Act (CEBA) of 1987
- Limits growth of nonbank banks
- Changes definition of bank to include FDIC-insured institutions

Financial Institutions Reform, Recovery, and Enforcement Act of 1989
- Changes structure of thrift institution regulation
- Changes federal deposit insurance structure and financing

Federal Deposit Insurance Corporation Improvement Act of 1991
- Provides for additional funding for federal deposit insurance
- Tightens regulations applicable to insured institutions
- Provides for greater capital regulation, early closure, and risk-based insurance

amount of the insurance. Federal deposit insurance is superior to the state-sponsored programs because state insurance is successful only in cases of relatively small local bank failures.

Federal deposit insurance effectively stopped the widespread bank failures caused by panic withdrawals by depositors. However, the cost to taxpayers for underwriting federal deposit insurance is potentially high. The web of federal regulation affecting U.S. depository institutions has been extended greatly over the last 80 years. After enactment of the Federal Reserve Act, little was done until approximately half the nation's banks failed during the early years of the Great Depression. The banking acts of 1933 (Glass-Steagall) and 1935 then developed a number of new regulations for banks and institutional frameworks that persisted until the 1980s.

Entry, Branching, and Holding Company Restrictions

Chief among the regulations imposed on banks in the 1930s was the restriction that new banks could enter a community only for the "convenience and need" of the community. Such restrictions could be used to deny entry to new banks in a community and contributed to the "cartelization" of banking in the 1940s and 1950s. Entry restrictions for federal banks persisted (at the federal level) until James Saxon became comptroller of the currency and relaxed entry restrictions in the early 1960s. The 1930s banking acts also incorporated further restrictions on bank branching. These restrictions contributed to the development of bank holding companies as a way to avoid intrastate and interstate branching restrictions. As a result, multibank holding companies were regulated by the Bank Holding Company Act of 1956 and, among other things, they were forced to divest their nonbank operations. As a result, Citicorp developed a one-bank holding-company structure to conduct nonbank operations. This exploited a loophole in the 1956 act because one-bank holding companies were not regulated. However, the 1970 amendments to the Bank Holding Company Act closed that loophole and regulated one-bank holding companies. All these restrictions tended to reduce entry of new competition into local banking markets, thereby reducing competition for existing banks and enhancing their profits.

Deposit Rate Ceilings

Additional regulations incorporated in the 1933 Banking Act were also designed to restrict risk taking by banks, reduce competition among banks, and enhance bank profitability. The Glass-Steagall Banking Act of 1933, for example, prohibited the payment of interest on demand deposits (checking accounts) and mandated that the Fed regulate maximum interest rates that could be paid on bank time and savings deposits through its *Regulation Q*. Deposit rate regulation was extended to thrift institutions in 1966. However, these rate-ceiling restrictions subsequently had very disruptive effects in financial markets as they caused financial disintermediation (as people withdrew funds from financial intermediaries) whenever market interest rates exceeded the "Reg Q" ceiling. Consequently, banks and thrifts had to drastically reduce credit availability whenever market interest rates rose. Furthermore, during the high-interest-rate period in the 1970s, disintermediated funds fled to unregulated "money market mutual funds" (MMMFs). The MMMFs began to offer checking account withdrawals and, as a result, attracted even more funds from banks and thrifts. As a result, the DIDMCA Act of 1980 provided a phaseout of deposit rate ceilings and allowed banks, thrifts, and credit unions nationwide to offer checkable interest-bearing (NOW and share draft) accounts. Because the phaseout was not fast enough and banks and thrifts had to maintain reserves to back their NOW accounts, the MMMFs still had a competitive advantage. Thus the 1982 Depository Institutions (Garn–St. Germain) Act accelerated the phaseout of rate ceilings and allowed banks and thrifts to offer checkable money market deposit accounts (MMDAs) that had no rate ceiling and no reserve requirement if check transactions were limited.

Deposit rate celings are now gone, but they led to substantial financial innovation as people sought ways to avoid them. Consequently, their legacy still exists in the form of MMMFs, MMDAs, and NOW accounts, which would not have come into existence if rate ceilings had not existed.

Another legacy of deposit rate ceilings has been a string of financial institution failures and weakened deposit insurance funds, as many institutions were unable to compete effectively once their deposit rates were deregulated. Failures were especially prevalent among depository institutions that had taken on too much interest rate risk by making long-term fixed-rate mortgage loans at rates that were not substantially above Regulation Q deposit rate ceilings. Those institutions assumed that their costs of funds would not rise above those ceilings.

Deposit Insurance Regulations

The 1933 Banking (Glass-Steagall) Act provided for the establishment of the Federal Deposit Insurance Corporation (FDIC), which began operations in 1934. Thrift institutions also obtained deposit insurance, through the Federal Savings and Loan Insurance Corporation (FSLIC), also in 1934. At first both funds were allowed to charge an annual insurance premium equal to $\frac{1}{4}$ of 1 percent per year on all deposits—and each individual deposit account was insured up to only $5,000. However, before long, insurance premiums were reduced (to $\frac{1}{12}$ of 1 percent, or lower, if the FDIC rebated the insurance premiums) and deposit insurance coverage was extended (to $100,000 per account in the DIDMC Act of 1980). Also, Federal insurance became available to credit union share accounts when the National Credit Union Share Insurance Fund (NCUSIF) was established in 1970.

Deposit insurance corporations were given the right to examine insured institutions that were not otherwise examined by federal regulators. The FDIC examines all federally insured state-chartered banks that are not members of the Federal Reserve. The Office of the Comptroller of the Currency examines all nationally chartered banks, and the Federal Reserve examines all state-chartered, Fed member banks. Bank examinations ensure that banks comply with all safety regulations. Bank examiners also investigate the quality of bank loans and ensure that institutions have adequate liquidity and capital and are soundly managed. Bank examinations have helped stabilize the banking system by insuring that potential problems are discovered in time to be corrected.

The 1980s and 1990s Acts

At first, deposit insurance and the other regulatory initiatives in the 1930s banking acts protected financial institutions against failure, but increasing interest rates, coupled with increasing competition from nonbank institutions and excessive interest rate–risk taking on the part of thrift institutions led to a sharp increase in depository institution failures in the 1980s and 1990s. As a result, a number of laws were passed in an attempt to strengthen financial institutions and their insurance funds. The laws also broke down barriers between financial institutions by giving them more powers to issue financial liabilities and diversify their assets, in hopes that this would let institutions become more profitable.

The first major law passed was the Depository Institution Deregulation and Monetary Control Act of 1980 (DIDMCA), summarized in Exhibit 17–8. Basically, DIDMCA tried to "level the playing field" for all depository institutions by giving all of them the right to issue interest-bearing transactions deposits, requiring that all back their transactions deposits with reserves, and requiring that the Fed charge them all equally for the use of check-clearing services (instead of giving such services free to Fed member banks) and give them all equal access to the discount window. Furthermore, the act phased out rate ceilings on deposits and also on certain types of loans (unless the ceilings were reimposed by individual states), and generally tried to simplify the regulatory environment. It was hoped that the new powers and relaxed loan-rate ceilings given thrift institutions and credit unions by the act would enhance their profitability and reduce their interest rate risk.

However, the DIDMCA did not do enough to help the thrift institutions. Thus Congress passed the (Garn–St. Germain) Depository Institutions Act of 1982. That act immediately deregulated interest rate ceilings by allowing depository institutions to issue checkable MMDA accounts that could pay any interest rate and had no reserve requirements as long as the depositor wrote only three checks per month. It also gave thrift institutions the power to issue limited demand deposits and the ability to make commercial loans. This let thrift institutions become more competitive with banks and also made them more attractive as merger candidates for banks. In addition, the Garn–St. Germain Act for the first time allowed bank holding companies to acquire thrift institutions, both in-state and across state lines. The only condition was that the thrift be large and failing, and that the bank be the high bidder for the institution. This increased the value of bids the FSLIC received for failing institutions, and thus added to the insurance fund. Nonetheless, because so many thrifts were in trouble as a result of past interest rate risk, the Garn–St. Germain Act also provided for additional aid to be given to troubled institutions and requested that the deposit insurance system be studied. Finally, the act allowed certain shared activities to be arranged and financed by cooperating banks.

After the Garn–St. Germain Act, few regulatory acts were passed until the Competitive Equality in Banking Act (CEBA) of 1987. The main provisions of that act were (1) to regulate the activities of nonbank banks (which were "banks" used by holding companies to evade regulatory restrictions, since they technically were not banks because they either did not have demand deposits or make consumer loans) and (2) to provide funding to bail out the failing FSLIC.

However, the aid for the FSLIC was too little and too late. Thus, in 1989 Congress passed the Financial Institution Reform, Recovery, and Enforcement Act (FIRREA). The FIRRE Act made major changes in the financing of deposit insurance and the structure of financial institution regulation. It also provided for the "bailout" of insolvent thrift institutions. The act recognized that easy accommodation of thrift

---

Exhibit 17–8

Major Provisions of the Depository Institutions Deregulation and Monetary Control Act of 1980

A. *Allowed financial institutions to become more competitive and uniformly regulated by*:
   1. Establishing identical reserve requirement standards for every institution and requiring that all institutions hold reserves to back their transactions deposits.
   2. Permitting all depository institutions to issue various forms of interest-bearing transactions accounts (NOW accounts or share drafts).
   3. Allowing all depository institutions subject to reserve requirements access to the Federal Reserve's discount window.
   4. Providing for the phase-out of deposit interest rate ceilings—including "differential" rate ceilings that existed for different types of financial institutions—under the supervision of the Depository Institutions Deregulation Committee (DIDC).
   5. Allowing all financial institutions access to the Federal Reserve's payments services, and providing for explicit pricing of those services by the Federal Reserve.
   6. Permitting savings and loan associations to acquire a larger proportion of nonmortgage loans, and eliminating or relaxing geographical lending restrictions applicable to savings and loans and mutual savings banks.
   7. Permanently overriding state usury laws that subjected state-chartered institutions to more restrictive maximum loan interest provisions than federally chartered institutions.
   8. Allowing federally chartered credit unions to charge higher rates on their loans.
B. *Attempted to reduce financial institution regulatory burdens by*:
   1. Simplifying truth-in-lending regulations (Reg. Z).
   2. Requiring all financial institution regulators to reduce the compliance burden associated with their regulations.
   3. Nullifying state rate-ceiling laws on mortgage credit (unless new ones were explicitly passed within three years) and overriding state rate ceilings on certain agricultural and business loans for three years.
C. *Enacted numerous technical provisions dealing with thrift institution powers, deposit insurance, foreign acquisition of domestic financial institutions, bank holding companies, pricing of Federal Reserve services, and other areas.*

The DIDMCA of 1980 made many major changes in the structure and function of our nation's financial system.

---

industry legislative interests, coupled with lax capital, accounting, and regulatory standards had all contributed to the high rate of failure of thrift institutions and the insolvency of the FSLIC (the thrift institution's deposit insurance fund).

The FIRRE Act tried to resolve the thrift's problems in several ways. First, it transferred chartering and some regulatory powers for the thrift industry from the Federal Home Loan Bank Board to a newly created Office of Thrift Supervision which, like the Office of the Comptroller of the Currency, is located in the Treasury Department and under the direct control of the administration. The Federal Home Loan Banks continue to exist and can still make loans (called "advances") and provide banking assistance to their member savings associations. The powers of the Federal Home Loan Bank Board (FHLBB) were stripped away, however, because it had been subject to extensive influence by the thrift industry and had not adequately protected its deposit insurance fund. Thus, the Office of Thrift Supervision assumed the FHLBB's chartering and regulatory powers, while a new federal insurance institution (the Savings Association Insurance Fund—FDIC-SAIF) assumed responsibilities for insuring thrifts' deposits.

The new thrift deposit insurance fund was made a subsidiary of the Federal Deposit Insurance Corporation, which continued to supervise the Federal Deposit Insurance fund for banks (now called the Bank Insurance Fund) as well as the new (separate) Savings Association Insurance Fund. The SAIF fund replaced the insolvent Federal Savings and Loan Insurance Corporation (FSLIC) that had been a subsidiary of the FHLBB and had incurred great losses as thrift institutions failed. The new fund was placed under the control of the FDIC because bank failures were not as serious as thrift failures and it was assumed that the FDIC's examination and insurance standards were much sounder than those of the insolvent FSLIC. Among other things, the FDIC required that its insured institutions hold much higher ratios of net worth to assets than the FSLIC had required, and its staff of examiners was larger and more professional than the FSLIC examination staff of the mid-1980s. The act also required that both banks and thrifts pay higher insurance premiums for their Federal deposit insurance.

In the FIRRE Act, the president and Congress tried to strengthen thrifts' capital (net worth) requirements by mandating higher capital standards than had been imposed in the past. They did this in two ways. First, they required that thrifts hold capital equal to at least 3 percent of their assets in order to remain in good standing with their regulators. Second, they required that thrifts not be allowed to count more than a minimum amount of capital created by intangible assets (particularly regulatory goodwill) as part of their required capital. Thrift industry lobbyists actively fought to preserve lower minimum capital requirements and to allow intangible capital to be used to meet capital adequacy standards. As a result, Congress provided for the phaseout of "goodwill" from required capital; the FIRRE Act allowed thrifts to count a limited amount of goodwill as capital for regulatory purposes but mandated that that amount be phased out before 1995. The reason Congress tightened up thrifts' capital requirements was to ensure that the thrifts' owners would lose substantial amounts of the "net worth" they invested in their institutions *before* the deposit insurance fund was exposed to loss.

The FIRRE Act also addressed the issue of how previous problems encountered by the thrifts' deposit insurance fund were to be resolved. It provided for the sale of at least $50 billion in government backed bonds. The proceeds of the bond sales were to go to a new institution called the Resolution Funding Corporation (RFC) which was also to obtain funding from deposit insurance premiums levied by SAIF and annual levies assessed the Federal Home Loan Banks. The funds were to be transferred to the Resolution Trust Corporation, which was to assume responsibility for all problem institutions shut down, merged, or assisted by the FSLIC. Failing (insolvent) thrift institutions were to be shut down, their depositors were to be paid off, and the assets acquired from the failed institutions were to be transferred to the RTC for orderly disposal. Ongoing institutions that were to receive federal assistance according to prior agreements with the FSLIC would now receive assistance from and be monitored by the RTC. The RTC also was to supervise the assets of the former Federal Asset Disposition Association—which was to be sold or liquidated. The RTC was to use the $50 billion obtained from the sale of the bonds plus the funding provided directly or indirectly by thrift institutions to pay for losses on assets acquired from failing thrifts.

Insured institutions (by paying deposit insurance premiums), the taxpayer (by underwriting and helping service the new issues of government debt), and the Federal Home Loan Banks (through assistance they provided to weak savings institutions, the deposit insurance fund, and the debt service requirements of the RFC) would all share in the losses incurred when failing thrifts were shut down and the insolvent FSLIC was liquidated. The estimated cost to the taxpayer ranged from a minimum of $50 billion (the cost of newly authorized government backed debt) to nearly $300 billion (a figure that also included the cost of interest on that debt as well as an allowance for future possible losses). Those estimates have now increased several fold.

Needless to say, the taxpayers were not happy when presented with the bill for FIRRE. To placate them, if possible, Congress also used the FIRRE Act to toughen the penalties for managers and directors of dishonest savings institutions, establish tougher standards for appraisals, and provide for more vigorous enforcement of regulations and laws related to the operation of all federally chartered or insured financial institutions. Finally, it let banks buy healthy thrifts as well as failing ones, thereby further blurring the distinction between banks and thrifts.

The deposit rate premium increases embodied in FIRREA were not sufficient to keep the bank deposit insurance fund solvent, however. Thus, in 1991 Congress passed the Federal Deposit Insurance Corporation Improvement Act (FDICIA). The major purpose of the act was to provide additional funding provisions for the FDIC. However, the act also mandated that major changes be made in financial regulation and compliance procedures in order to reduce the probability of failure and any ensuing cost to the taxpayers.

Key provisions of the FDICIA included the following: (1) The act increased the line of credit available to the FDIC from the U.S. Treasury and allowed the FDIC to borrow additional funds as needed to resolve bank failures. (2) The act mandated that the FDIC increase deposit insurance premiums as necessary to ensure that it could repay all principal and interest on any debts it incurred. (3) The act mandated that the FDIC start to charge risk-based deposit insurance premiums so riskier banks (that is, those less well capitalized or those with high interest rate or credit risk) would have an incentive to reduce their risk and would better compensate the insurance fund for their increased risk of loss.

The FDICIA also increased emphasis on bank capital adequacy. (4) It required that the FDIC establish capital adequacy categories ranging from "well capitalized" and "adequately capitalized" to "severely undercapitalized" and "critically undercapitalized." It then provided a carrot and a stick to encourage banks to be well capitalized. In particular, (5) it allowed regulators to grant additional powers to "well-capitalized' banks or bank holding companies. This ratified the Federal Reserve's decision to let J. P. Morgan Corporation enter investment banking (in a relatively small way) through a subsidiary separate from the bank, and also encouraged other large bank holding companies to strive to become better capitalized so they too could enter investment banking in the United States. In addition, it only allowed "well-capitalized" banks and regulator-approved "adequately-capitalized" banks to issue brokered deposits. On the "stick" side, (6) "undercapitalized banks" were required to develop capital restoration plans that would explain how they would restore their capital adequacy to satisfactory levels by selling stock, cutting dividends, divesting risky assets, and so forth. The FDIC was then required to monitor the implementation of the restoration plans to ensure that "undercapitalized" banks were, in fact, returning to "adequately" capitalized status. (7) Critically undercapitalized banks were given only a short period of time to correct their problems or they would be closed. (8) The FDICIA also required that any institution with capital below 2 percent of assets would be declared "critically undercapitalized" and would be subject to the act's "early closure" requirements. By closing weak institutions early, it was hoped that losses to the insurance fund would not accumulate as the institution continued to struggle along in a weakened status. In order to reinforce its "early closure" requirement, the FDICIA also required (9) that the Federal Reserve could not extend long-term adjustment credits at its discount window to banks that were weak and likely to fail. This procedure was also intended to provide early resolution of bank problems so they would not continue to create losses that would ultimately be borne by the taxpayers.

The FDICIA also (10) mandated much more complex and burdensome reporting requirements for financial institution officers and directors. These requirements were intended primarily to insure that officers and directors were monitoring the institutions to make sure that no serious problems existed and, if any were found, that they were taking appropriate actions to correct them. Furthermore, the act, like the Financial Accounting Standards Board, (11) encouraged financial institutions to move toward "market value" rather than "book value" accounting for their assets and liabilities so they could see where problems were developing and could move quickly to offset them. However, the institutions claimed that it was hard to value bank loans because each loan was unique, and usually was nonmarketable; in addition, it was hard to value certain contingent claims such as lines of credit or forward foreign-exchange agreements that might or might not expose the bank to risk. Thus the "market value" accounting provisions were not immediately implemented.

Finally, the FDICIA contained numerous specific regulations that were important to various congressional representatives and in some cases imposed additional reporting and compliance burdens on depository institutions. For instance, reporting requirements for the Community Reinvestment Act were increased substantially, funds were provided to Rhode Island to help depositors who lost money when the state's deposit and share insurance fund failed, and numerous other provisions were added that benefited or restricted the operations of one or more banks.

Additional Regulations Affecting Bank Commercial Operations

Separation of Commercial and Investment Banking.   The Glass-Steagall Act of 1933 tried to reduce bank risk-taking by separating commercial banking from investment banking. That way commercial banks would not be exposed to price-risk fluctuations in the value of securities that they had underwritten but had not yet sold.

The Glass-Steagall prohibitions against investment banking also prevented banks from acquiring equity securities for their own accounts and from acting as equity securities dealers. The prohibition against owning equity securities not only prevents banks from carrying certain potentially risky assets on their balance sheet, which could increase their risk of failure, but also lessens potential conflicts that can arise

DID YOU KNOW ?

The Failing "Empire" Abused Its New Powers

Savings and loan associations received many new powers in the early 1980s. Empire Savings and Loan of Mesquite, Texas, with assets of only $19.7 million in July 1982, used those powers to become, on paper, one of the nation's most profitable savings and loans. Then the "Empire" crumbled. On March 14, 1984, it was declared insolvent. It became possibly the most expensive failure of any depository institution up to that time—costing the FSLIC $300 million in losses.

Empire got into trouble because it didn't confine itself to home mortgage loans. Instead, it made a large number of loans for land acquisition and condominium development projects. These business loans were far riskier than home mortgage lending—particularly when Empire used appraisers who had a vested interest in projects in the area and therefore appraised the properties for up to four times what they were worth. Empire funded its loans by offering high rates on CDs and buying deposits through money brokers. It also borrowed money wherever it could. By mid-1983 it held $179 million in assets and $139 million in deposits (a ninefold

increase in only one year). It also reported an annual rate of return on average assets of 1.1, a very high ratio for an S&L in 1983.

Much of Empire's profit, however, came from fees paid by developers who 'flipped' properties by reselling them to related groups at rapidly increasing prices. The developers financed the properties at the new prices, as well as the borrowing fees, by borrowing from Empire. Thus, on paper, both Empire and the developers, whose properties "appreciated" in value, showed large profits. Because final buyers were few and far between, however, the value of the properties securing the mortgages was vastly overstated. Eventually the regulators sorted through Empire's faulty records and shoddy appraisals to prove that its loans were poorly made and that the institution was, in fact, insolvent. By the time Empire was finally closed, it had made over $400 million in bad loans—financing most of them with sales of federally insured, brokered deposits. Because most of its borrowers didn't repay their debts, the FSLIC became the owner of a 12-year supply of condominiums at Lake Ray Hubbard, Texas.

---

when the ownership and creditor functions of banks are combined. Thus the prohibition reflects, in part, a long-standing American fear that unscrupulous manipulation and exercise of creditor powers could ultimately lead to ownership.

The Glass-Steagall restrictions have been relaxed in stages over the years. For instance, banks can underwrite both federal and municipal government securities. In addition, the Competitive Equality in Banking Act of 1987 and Federal Reserve interpretations of the law have also allowed banks to expand their investment banking activities in recent years by underwriting pass-through securities, corporate commercial paper, and a wide variety of other debt or equity offerings. The Fed and FDICIA have also allowed well-capitalized bank holding companies to engage in full-service domestic investment banking through separate subsidiaries as long as the activities do not constitute a major portion of their business. In addition, most major U.S. bank holding companies have subsidiaries with foreign charters that can engage in investment banking in other countries, and domestic bank holding companies are allowed to engage in discount stock brokerage activities and provide separate investment advice to investors. Furthermore, bank trust departments are allowed to buy or sell stocks for their custodial accounts. Thus the largest U.S. banks have been able to engage extensively in investment banking in spite of the Glass-Steagall Act's restrictions.

Balance Sheet Restrictions.   In addition to restrictions against equity ownership, commercial banks' balance sheets are restricted in other ways. In particular, banks can loan no more than 15 percent of their capital to any one borrower. This restriction is intended to prevent the default of any one customer from imperiling the bank and also forces the bank to diversify its assets. Also, most banks are not allowed to invest in sub-investment-grade securities (that is, securities rated lower than BBB or Baa by the major rating agencies). Furthermore, banks are required to hold adequate liquid assets by the Federal Reserve and adequate capital to comply with the restrictions imposed by regulators. Thus banks' balance sheets and operations are frequently constrained by various regulations.

In recent years, additional laws have been passed that impose substantial restrictions on bank customer relationships as well as on their balance sheets. These take the form of "consumer protection regulations."

Consumer Protection Regulations

The final class of regulations to be discussed are those designed to protect consumers in their transactions with commercial banks and other credit-granting institutions. Since 1968 there has been a trend toward legislation designed to protect consumers in the credit market, precipitated by an active and growing consumer movement. The regulatory philosophy behind many of the consumer regulations is twofold: (1) consumers as a class have unequal market power relative to credit and other market participants, and (2) consumer markets, when left to their own devices, may not allocate credit in the most socially desirable manner. It often is not clear, however, that the regulations have their intended effects.

Loan Rate Ceilings.   Loan rate ceilings vary widely from state to state and historically have usually applied to consumer and mortgage credit. The DIDMCA of 1980 suspended state rate ceilings on all real estate loans and on business and agricultural loans exceeding $25,000. However, states had until April 1, 1983, to adopt new rate ceilings. In most instances they did not elect to do so.

Rate ceilings pose no problem for banks or consumers as long as the ceiling exceeds the rate of interest that would be charged in a competitive market. When rate ceilings become binding, they may cause serious problems. For instance, it is well documented that mortgage rate ceilings seriously impede the flow of mortgage credit and reduce housing starts when market interest rates rise above the maximum ceiling rate. In the consumer credit markets, because prices of goods sold on credit can be raised, credit is not usually cut off entirely as a result of rising market rates of interest, but it may become unprofitable for banks to make direct loans that are subject to the rate ceilings.

Truth in Lending.   In 1969 Congress passed the Consumer Credit Protection Act (popularly known as the Truth in Lending Act) with the intent of assuring every borrower meaningful information about the cost of credit. The act applies not only to banks but also to all lenders who extend credit to consumers for personal or agricultural use up to a limit of $25,000. For commercial banks, truth in lending is administered by the Board of Governors of the Federal Reserve System under Federal Reserve Regulation Z.

The two most important disclosures required by Regulation Z are (1) the annual percentage rate and (2) the total finance charges on a loan. The purpose of the Truth in Lending Act is to increase consumers' awareness of true loan rates and charges. The desired result is that consumers shop more wisely for credit and obtain credit from the lowest-rate source. This has helped banks, as they often have the lowest rates on consumer loans.

Fair Credit Billing Act.   The Fair Credit Billing Act (FCBA) of 1974 requires that creditors provide detailed information to consumers on the method of assessing finance charges and also that billing complaints be processed promptly. The purpose of the Fair Credit Billing Act is to deal with some of the problems created by the increasing automation of credit and the proliferation of credit card transactions. The act requires that banks and other suppliers of consumer credit send their customers a detailed description of their rights and of the procedures they must follow in making complaints about billing errors. The act is administered by the Federal Reserve System under Regulation Z.

The FCBA raises costs to creditors by increasing legal complexities and mandating quick formal responses to complaints. However, by formalizing procedures for filing and handling complaints, it has also simplified operations and reduced some costs. In addition, because there is no longer a threat of litigation as long as the act is complied with, lenders report that they are now less charitable in awarding disputed claims and can do so in a less costly (more routine) manner than before.

Equal Credit Opportunity Act.   In 1974 Congress passed the Equal Credit Opportunity Act (ECOA), which requires that credit be made available to individuals without regard to sex or marital status. In 1976 Congress broadened the scope of that act to forbid discrimination by creditors based on race, age, national origin, or whether credit applicants received part of their income from public assistance benefits. It also requires women's incomes to be treated equally with men's in evaluating credit. The act is implemented through Regulation B of the Federal Reserve Board.

By reducing the information available to creditors, ECOA reduces creditors' ability to make valid credit decisions, which in turn may increase their losses. Also, by mandating that creditors follow certain procedures and provide appropriate forms, Regulation B imposes direct costs of compliance. These cost increases may reduce creditors' overall incentives to extend credit to consumers or induce some to raise charges on consumer loans. On the other hand, the act may generate greater credit availability to the target consumer groups as well as psychic benefits for consumers in the form of more desirable treatment of loan applicants.

The Community Reinvestment Act (CRA).   The Community Reinvestment Act (CRA) was created to prevent "redlining," where a lender draws a hypothetical red line on a map around one part of the community and refuses to make loans in that area. While it is not clear that "redlining" existed, Congress passed the CRA to make sure that banks made credit available to all people in their market area regardless of where they lived. Thus, under the CRA, banks must be able to show that they attempt to serve the credit needs of all people in their area and they must be able to document their efforts and make the documentation available to regulators and the general public. The upside of the act is that it does ensure that credit will be generally available to all people who qualify. The downside of the act is the documentation requirements of CRA are very expensive to perform, especially after the requirements were increased by the FDICIA of 1991. Furthermore, if banks cannot show that they have complied with the act, regulators may reject their applications to engage in mergers, branching, or new activities.

Issues in Bank Regulation

Trade-offs exist between bank regulation, bank risk-taking, and service to the public. Thus numerous debates exist regarding the degree of regulation that should be imposed on depository institutions. Many of these issues are discussed in Chapter 23. Basically, the issues revolve around whether financial institutions should be free to compete and also free to fail, or whether they should be given restrictive monopolistic franchises and special regulation to reduce their chances of failure. Because the public has borne the costs of failure of deposit insurance funds, an argument can be made for stiff regulation. However, if the banks risked their own capital and liability holders knew they would lose when a bank failed, failures might be less frequent as both stockholders and liability holders would try to make sure that the institution did not take too much risk. Nonetheless, stockholders and liability holders still must be able to ascertain whether a depository institution is sound or not. This raises the issue of whether private examinations of banks are sufficient or whether public examinations might be required.

Bank Examinations

Historically, regulatory examinations did not become widespread until the National Bank Act of 1863. The then newly created Office of the Comptroller of the Currency examined annually all banks chartered under the federal statute. By the early 1900s, every state had instituted some sort of bank examination procedure. Today all commercial banks in the United States are examined by a bank regulatory agency (federal or state). Examinations are more frequent if a bank is believed to be particularly risky.

Regulatory examinations are not equivalent to an audit by a CPA firm. A public accounting firm audit verifies the bank's financial statements and ensures that generally accepted accounting principles are followed consistently from one period to the next. Regulators' examinations are intended to promote and maintain safe and sound bank-operating practices and to ensure that all applicable regulations are followed.

The Examination Procedure

The principal purpose of bank examinations is the prevention of bank failures resulting from poor management or dishonesty. There are two principal ways in which information is gathered for bank examinations. First, *call reports* (detailed statements of the operating and financial condition of the bank) are prepared by bank management four times a year. Second, on-site bank examinations are conducted by the examination staffs of the various bank regulators. Those visits are unannounced and the examiners remain at the bank or its branches until the examination is completed. Generally, the examiners first control the records of the bank and such assets as cash and marketable securities by securing or taking physical possession of them. At this point in the examination procedure, the examiners are concerned with the possible detection of embezzlement or fraud. Next, the securities portfolio is examined to see if the securities claimed are on hand and if control procedures comply with regulations. Finally, the market value of bonds is determined, with particular attention given to bonds considered to be speculative or in default.

The most important part of the examination, and the one to which most time is devoted, is the evaluation of the creditworthiness of the bank's loan portfolio. Loans are examined for compliance with or violation of laws or regulations — such as limits on the maximum size loan that may be made to any one borrower or loans to bank officers. Next, loans are examined on a sampling basis as to their quality and are classified in one of four categories: satisfactory, substandard, doubtful, or loss. Loans classified as "loss" are thought to be uncollectible, and the bank is required to write them off (but not to stop trying to collect them). "Doubtful" loans are expected to result in some loan losses, though the exact amount is not precisely determinable. Loans classified as "substandard" have some element of risk and, if not watched closely, may result in losses to the bank. "Satisfactory" loans are those that meet the standards of prudent banking practice and appear to be in no danger of defaulting.

Another important part of the bank examination procedure is the evaluation of the quality of the bank's organizational structure. The supervision by top management and the board of directors, internal controls over bank operations, and, most important, the abilities of management are all appraised.

Finally, a summary of the bank examination report is presented and discussed with the bank's management. If the bank's operations are in violation of the law, if poor operating procedures are detected, or if the bank's capital is below capital requirements, management is requested to bring the violation into compliance over a period of time. The bank's progress in correcting the difficulties is closely monitored. If a bank has a problem that could seriously jeopardize its safety, regulatory agencies can serve *cease and desist* orders on it. These require immediate or speedy compliance under penalty of law.

Federal examiners have an advantage over private examiners such as CPA firms because (1) they can schedule examinations for several related institutions simultaneously and (2) they do not depend on the bank's goodwill for continued employment.

Thus private CPAs were giving United American Bank (UAB) of Knoxville a clean bill of health while federal examiners were in the bank to shut it down. Because they conducted simultaneous examinations of all banks in the UAB holding company, the federal examiners were able to find the bad floater loans that the bank sold to holding company affiliates, whereas the private examiners did not.

Summary

The financial services industry is one of the most heavily regulated industries in this country. Pervasive regulation exists because it is believed that massive bank failures ignite or reinforce major downturns in economic activity. The majority of existing bank regulations were enacted in reaction to the many bank failures of the Great Depression. Furthermore, after the establishment of deposit insurance, the public had a substantial financial stake in the enactment of bank safety regulations. As depository institution failures have persisted, Congress has passed more and more regulations affecting banks, nonbank financial institutions, and their insurance funds.

Bank regulations may be classified as those (1) promoting bank safety, (2) affecting bank structure, and (3) protecting the interest of consumers. Bank safety regulations, such as national deposit insurance, bank balance-sheet restrictions, and bank examinations, are thought to be important in promoting bank safety. Bank structure is believed to affect the degree of competition within banking markets (see Chapter 15). Consumer regulations are those designed to protect consumers in their transactions with commercial banks and other credit-granting institutions. The basic philosophy underlying these regulations is (1) that consumers have unequal market power relative to financial institutions and (2) that when left to their own devices, consumer markets may not allocate credit in the most socially desirable manner.

All insured depository institutions in this country are examined frequently by a regulatory agency. The principal reason for examination is the prevention of depository institution failures as a result of poor management, dishonesty, or both. Bank examination procedures focus on evaluation of the creditworthiness of the bank's loan portfolio and the quality of the bank's management.

In recent years, economists and regulators have turned more of their attention toward the preservation and promotion of a more competitive financial system. However, the goals of a high degree of bank safety and a high degree of competitiveness are in conflict. More competitive institutions will offer lower-cost services to consumers, but they must be carefully managed lest they take too many risks in competition for loans and deposits and subsequently fail. The challenge for regulators is to find the proper balance between bank safety and economic stability on the one hand and competition and an efficient banking system on the other.

Questions

1. Why are bank failures considered to have a greater effect on the economy than other types of business failures? Do you agree with this conclusion?
2. What are the major lessons that have been learned from past bank failures? Do you think that history can or will repeat itself?

3. What are possible advantages and disadvantages of having multiple federal insurance funds?
4. Although the FDIC does not grant charters for banks to operate, it is said to have an enormous influence on the charter process. Explain.
5. Which of the bank safety regulations enacted in the 1930s do you believe are most important in actually achieving bank safety? Which of the safety regulations would you classify as being anticompetitive?
6. Why do federal deposit insurance funds have an advantage over private funds?
7. How would you assess the success of consumer regulation? In what areas has it failed its stated objectives?
8. Bank regulation is considered to be in the public interest. Thus the more regulation, the better. Explain why you agree or disagree with this statement.
9. What is the purpose of bank examinations? How do they differ from CPA audits?
10. How do failing bank resolution policies differ between large and small banks? Why the difference?
11. Why has Congress had to pass more and more regulatory acts for financial institutions in recent years? Cite major acts passed since 1980 and the major provisions of each.

Selected References

Blair, Christine E., and Gary S. Fissel. "A Framework for Analyzing Deposit Insurance Pricing." *FDIC Banking Review* 4 (Fall 1991), pp 25–38.
This article notes the complexities associated with determining depository institution risk and the problems associated with moving toward risk based deposit insurance premiums.

Bovenzi, John F., and Arthur J. Murton. "Resolution Costs of Bank Failures." *FDIC Banking Review* 1 (Fall 1988), pp. 1–13.
This excellent article describes the five major types of bank-failure resolutions: (1) deposit payoffs, (2) purchase and assumptions, (3) insured-deposit transfers, (4) open bank assistance, and (5) bridge banks. It also describes the purchase and assumption bidding process and the way the FDIC determines minimum acceptable bids.

"Depository Institutions, Deregulation and Monetary Control Act of 1980." *Economic Perspectives.* Federal Reserve Bank of Chicago, September–October 1980.
The entire issue is devoted to a discussion of this historic bank deregulation act.

Flannery, Mark J., and Aris A. Protopakadakis. "Risk Sensitive Deposit Insurance Premia: Some Practical Issues." *Business Review.* Federal Reserve Bank of Philadelphia, September–October 1984, pp. 3–10.
An examination of the controversies over risk-adjusted deposit insurance premiums. The system provides a fixed rate for all banks and may encourage banks to take additional risks.

Forrestal, Robert P. "Bank Safety: Risk and Responsibilities." *Economic Review.* Federal Reserve Bank of Atlanta, August 1985, pp. 4–11.
Examines the trade-off that bank regulators must make between bank safety and competition in the financial sector.

"The Garn–St. Germain Depository Institutions Act of 1982." *Economic Perspectives.* Federal Reserve Bank of Chicago, March–April 1983, pp. 10–31.
The entire issue is devoted to an analysis of the history, the legislation, and the impact of the Garn–St. Germain Act of 1982.

French, George F. "Early Corrective Action for Troubled Banks." *FDIC Banking Review* **4 (Fall 1991), pp. 1–12.**
Explains ways in which the FDIC liquidates failed banks and the costs to the FDIC of various options. Also, considers the pros and cons of "early closure" proposals.

Gilbert, R. Alton. "Supervision of Undercapitalized Banks: Is There a Case for Change?" *Review.* **Federal Reserve Bank of St Louis, May/June 1991, pp. 16–30.**
In this paper, Gilbert analyzes whether the capital restoration rules proposed by the 1991 FDICIA would have had a beneficial effect on banks that were "undercapitalized" in the past. He finds no significant difference in survival rates for undercapitalized banks that either did or did not grow slowly, restrict dividend payouts, or make more insider loans. Thus his findings suggest that the FDICIA capital restoration might have less of a beneficial impact in preventing bank failure than desired.

Hetzel, Robert L. "Too Big To Fail: Origins, Consequences, and Outlook." *Economic Review.* **Federal Reserve Bank of Richmond, November/December 1991, pp. 3–15.**
This article notes development of the de facto "too big to fail" policy of bank regulators and the adverse effect that policy had on risk-taking by large banks. This led to increased instability in the U.S. banking system that may or may not be rectified by the 1991 FDICIA.

Saulsbury, Victor L. "The Current Status of Non-Federal Deposit Insurance Programs." *Issues in Bank Regulation* **8 (Spring 1985), pp. 3–19.**
Reviews the status of nonfederal deposit insurance funds shortly after the collapse of the Ohio Deposit Guarantee Fund. Describes both existing funds and recent failures of private deposit insurance funds.

Short, Eugene D. "FDIC Settlement Practices and the Size of Failed Banks." *Economic Review.* **Federal Reserve Bank of Dallas, March 1985, pp. 12–20.**
A discussion of the bank failure practices of the FDIC, including the deposit payoff and purchase and assumption approaches. A good article.

Short, Genie D., and Jeffrey W. Gunther. *The Texas Thrift Situation: Implications for the Texas Financial Industry.* **Occasional Paper No. 1, Financial Industry Studies Department, Federal Reserve Bank of Dallas, September 1988.**
Does an excellent job of describing the problems of Texas financial institutions in general and of the Texas thrift industry in particular. Uses statistical analysis to show that the problem institutions grew faster, charged higher interest rates on loans, and suffered greater losses than the healthier thrifts.

Watro, Paul R. "Closely Watched Banks." *Economic Commentary.* **Federal Reserve Bank of Cleveland, January 30, 1984.**
An examination of the CAMEL bank-rating system.

5 FINANCIAL INSTITUTIONS

PROFILE/Anthony S. W. Yeung, CFA

HE IS

Daiwa International Capital Management (DICAM) Asian equity markets specialist. DICAM is one of the largest Japanese fund management companies with offices in Tokyo, Hong Kong, Singapore, New York, and London. He joined DICAM in 1987 as its first employee to explore the emerging Asian stock markets.

WHAT HE DOES

As the senior portfolio manager at DICAM Hong Kong, he is the fund manager of the London-listed Malaysia Equity Fund. This fund consistently outperforms the market index and the peers average (Lipper Report N.Y.). He is also the adviser of the New York-listed Thai Capital Fund. Besides managing the listed country funds, he also manages pension funds investing in Taiwan, Hong Kong, Singapore, and other Pacific Rim countries. Crunching numbers and visiting companies are part of the job to find out firsthand information that is not widely known. He travels extensively to meet with managements of different companies located in the Pacific Rim countries. By doing so, he finds out what goes on in the business world and knows who is doing well and who is not. From time to time, he advises other fund managers from Tokyo, Singapore, and London about the Asian economy, investment strategy, stock selection, and market timing.

HOW HE GOT THERE

B.BA.: Texas Tech University, Lubbock, Texas
M.S.BA.: Texas Tech University, Lubbock, Texas
First job: Financial analyst, Hewlett Packard Asia, He was recruited later to join Continental Illinois Capital Markets Group in Chicago.

BACKGROUND

He was born in Fujian, China, and grew up in Hong Kong with a businessman father and a mother who is a medical doctor. As a student, he thought investing was a science. One plus one equals two. Over the years of investing, he has learned that investing is partially science and partially an art. One plus one sometimes does not equal two.

WHAT HE LIKES BEST ABOUT HIS JOB

The tremendous opportunity in the Asian equity markets. Many Asian countries are newly industrialized, and the equity markets are still in the early stages of development. Countries like the People's Republic of China are developing stock markets, for example, at Shanghai and Shenzhen in China. Also, because Asian stock markets have not reached the maturity of other industrialized countries, there are still a lot of inefficiences to be explored.

In addition to the investment management activity, he is a firm believer in professional integrity and training. As a pioneer Asian gone through the Chartered Financial Analyst program, he is one of the founding members of the Hong Kong chapter of the International Society of Financial Analysts. The goal of the Hong Kong Chapter is to raise the professional quality of the investment industry in Asia.

WORST NIGHTMARE

During the 1987 world market crash, the Hong Kong market was closed for 4 days and was the hardest-hit. That was a lesson not to work against market forces.

ADVICE

Investment is not a nine-to-five job. To be successful, you need to be very dedicated to what you are doing. There is no one formula that works all the time and in all markets. One needs to anticipate events early rather than follow the crowd. Language skill is very important, particularly if you are investing in the international markets. Successful investing is common sense that is sometimes not so common.

THRIFT INSTITUTIONS

18

THROUGHOUT THE 1980s, THE NATIONAL press was full of comment on the problems of thrift institutions. Savings banks and savings and loan associations experienced severe problems throughout the decade, and many said that the cost to the taxpayer for bailing thrifts out of their difficulties would far exceed $100 billion. This chapter discusses the mortgage-oriented thrift institutions and the problems they have given their regulators.

In the early 1980s, thrift institutions' problems resulted from their emphasis on mortgage lending funded with savings deposits. For many decades Congress and regulators encouraged thrifts to issue savings accounts to consumers and to finance housing activity by making long-term mortgage loans. Congress gave them large tax breaks to encourage mortgage lending. Furthermore, because thrifts financed housing, their regulators supported thrifts' activities and let them hold far less net worth than banks. Then, starting in the late 1970s, the bubble burst. Because of inflation, interest rates rose. The mortgage-oriented thrift institutions found that if they did not pay higher interest rates, their depositors would take their money elsewhere. Moreover, when interest rates rose, the low-rate mortgages the thrifts had made in previous years dropped in value. With rising costs of funds, stable revenues, and declining asset values, their losses accumulated. Between 1980 and 1983, nearly one-quarter of all thrifts failed or were merged out of existence.

To help thrifts out of their troubles, Congress gave them many new powers (in the DIDMCA and Garn–St. Germain Act) to enable them to compete better with banks and money market funds. Also, the thrifts' regulators tried their best to help by relaxing regulations and providing financial assistance wherever possible.

The thrifts' new powers have enhanced their appeal as merger candidates for commercial bank holding companies and strengthened their ability to compete in the financial markets. However, many thrifts did not have experience in using their new powers. Some made mistakes when making consumer and business loans for the first time and in offering other financial services. In addition, many experienced a moral hazard problem because they were weakened by the high-interest rate environment of the early 1980s. Already technically insolvent, some gambled on high-yield, high-risk investments in an attempt to become solvent once again.

The gambling incentive of thrifts was aggravated by the fact that the thrift deposit insurance fund was so broke in the early 1980s that it sold many weak thrifts to anyone with cash rather than liquidate them, since it could not afford to pay off all depositors. Unfortunately, some of the people who bought thrifts on such generous terms were "fast operators" (See Did You Know? and People and Events). Because of the thrifts' access to deposit insurance, depositors did not fear losses, so thrifts issued deposits and grew rapidly in the early 1980s, even those that were not operated in a sound manner. Furthermore, regulators had too little enforcement authority to prevent the thrifts from taking excess risks. Many of the risky investments subsequently went bad. Thus, a new wave of thrift failures jeopardized the entire industry in the late 1980s. Even though the majority of thrift institutions remained solvent and well managed, they had to pay high deposit insurance premiums to bail out the minority that had become insolvent as a result of loan defaults. High deposit insurance premiums, in turn, prompted healthier thrifts to try to convert to commercial bank or savings bank charters so they could pay lower rates for deposit insurance. As healthier thrifts tried to change charters, the burden on the thrifts' principal deposit insurance fund became greater.

Congress, at first, tried to stop the exodus of healthy thrifts from their insurance fund, but ultimately Congress had to face up to the growing insolvency of the thrift industry and its regulators. Thus, in 1989, Congress passed the Financial Institutions Reform, Recovery, and Enforcement Act, which provided financial assistance to the thrift industry, at a cost to the taxpayer that will eventually far exceed $200 billion. That Act also totally reorganized the thrift industry's deposit insurance and regulatory system. Because the cost of the thrift bailout kept growing, Congress made additional major changes in deposit insurance requirements, accounting standards, and regulation in the 1991 FDIC Improvement Act. As a result, the regulatory environment for thrifts has changed greatly in recent years.

This chapter addresses, in turn, the nature and history of mutual savings banks and savings and loan associations, the balance sheets of thrift institutions, the regulatory environment in which thrifts operate, and the major management problems of thrift institutions.

History and Development of Thrifts

Thrift institutions developed because commercial banks, until this century, largely lived up to their name. They primarily made loans to and accepted deposits from commercial businesses. Consumers in general and small savers in particular were not served by commercial banks. Consequently, mutual savings banks were established to provide small savers with institutions in which they could accumulate funds and earn interest, and savings and loan associations were established to serve consumer's needs for housing finance.

Savings Banks

The first mutual savings banks in the United States were established in 1816, and their number increased rapidly thereafter. The orientation of the early savings banks toward small savers was often reflected in their names, such as the Dollar Savings Bank, the Dime Savings Bank, and the Five Cents Savings Bank.

Initially, each mutual savings bank was organized by a group of incorporators, who in turn appointed a board of trustees. The trustees appointed the principal bank officers. Legally, depositors in a mutual savings bank are creditors and have no voice in the management of the institutions. Thus they differ from depositors in a mutual savings and loan association, who theoretically have an equity interest. However, mutual savings and loan depositors usually grant their voting rights to the institution's management when they make their first deposit. Thus, in both mutual savings banks and mutual savings and loan associations, managers (or trustees) exercise effective control.

Historically, mutual savings banks were state-chartered in 17 states, mostly in the Northeast. Until 1980, mutual savings banks could accumulate net worth (surplus) accounts only out of retained earnings. They could not issue stock, and that fact limited their growth. In 1980, savings banks were allowed to obtain federal charters and convert to stock form. In 1982, federal savings and loan associations were allowed to convert to federal savings banks and vice versa. Federal savings banks can be headquartered in any state and may issue capital stock to obtain funds. Stock savings banks are controlled by their elected boards of directors.

Savings and Loan Associations

Savings and loan associations began as building associations designed to provide their members with funds for housing construction. Savings and loan (S&L) members made deposits and pooled their funds until they could afford to erect housing. Members could borrow money to finance housing construction and purchases. Sometimes members obtained borrowing privileges by lot. When all members had houses and all borrowed funds were repaid, the association might dissolve.

The Oxford Provident Building Association, founded in Philadelphia in 1831, was the first S&L in the United States. Possibly because S&Ls started there, Pennsylvania still has some of the most lenient regulatory laws.

Because of the self-liquidating nature of many early S&Ls and the fact that initially they did not solicit deposits from the general public, S&Ls grew relative slowly at first. Nonetheless, by 1928, the thrift industry held $8 billion in assets. During the Great Depression, more than 1,700 thrifts failed, and public confidence in them was badly shaken. To restore confidence in thrifts as well as funding for the housing industry, Congress enacted the Federal Home Loan Bank Act in 1932 to channel cash to savings and loan institutions through 12 regional Home Loan Banks that were empowered to make loans (called "advances") to thrifts that needed extra funds. Congress also passed the Home Owners Loan Act of 1933, which provided for an institution that would purchase problem loans from thrift institutions and allowed the Federal Home Loan Bank Board to charter federal savings and loan associations (previously all S&Ls were state-chartered). Furthermore, in 1934 Congress passed the National Housing Act, which established the *Federal Savings and Loan Insurance Corporation (FSLIC)* to provide deposit insurance for savings and loan depositors. Initially the deposit insurance covered $5,000 per account, and insured institutions paid a premium equal to $1/4$ of 1 percent of all deposits.

Following World War II, S&Ls gained powerful lobby support in Congress as the provisions of decent housing became a national goal. As a result of Regulation Q restrictions on commercial banks, for many years S&Ls were able to compete aggressively with banks for consumers' savings by offering interest rates $^1/_4$ percent (or more) higher than banks could offer on equivalent deposits. Thus S&Ls found it relatively easy to attract deposits. In addition, favorable tax treatment let them expand their net worth rapidly by accumulating pretax loss reserves. Consequently, their assets grew by well over 10 percent per year from 1939 to the end of the 1970s.

Recent History

Many of the regulatory advantages of S&Ls have disappeared in recent years. The 1969 and 1976 tax reform laws phased out many of their tax advantages, and their $^1/_4$ percent interest payout differential was eliminated by 1984. Furthermore, their net-worth position was seriously eroded as interest rates rose during the late 1970s and early 1980s. In that period, thrifts' cost of funds rose more sharply than their returns on their largely long-term assets (see Exhibit 18-1). Because their assets fell in value as interest rates rose and they accrued losses, many thrifts or were merged out of existence in the 1980s (see Exhibit 18-2). Many of the remainder had very weak net-worth positions that had to be bolstered by "regulatory additions" to meet minimum standards.

Because of the plight of the thrifts, in 1980 and 1982 Congress removed many of the regulatory restrictions that had helped create their problems. With continuing regulatory support, many thrifts ignored their weak net-worth positions and used their new powers to expand rapidly. A large number of them took high risks, hoping that rapid expansion would provide new high-yield assets to offset the low yields on their old mortgage loans. Unfortunately, their rapid expansion in 1983 and 1984 stretched their net worth thin and created more problems. Thus the proportion of unprofitable thrifts remained high, and many remained insolvent with negative net-worth ratios. Eventually, the failures of weak thrifts caused their deposit insurance to become insolvent. Thus, in 1989, Congress passed the FIRRE Act to create a new insurance fund, the FDIC-SAIF (FDIC savings association insurance fund). The weak and failed thrifts were then assigned to the Resolution Trust Corporation for resolution or dismemberment. As a result, the number of thrifts shrunk drastically once again. By the end of 1990, there were only 2,342 thrifts operating under OTS supervision, and 194 of those (designated as Class IV thrifts) were expected to be closed once funding became available (see Exhibit 18-3).

Assets of Thrift Institutions

Exhibit 18-4 presents aggregate measures of assets and liabilities held by all FDIC-SAIF insured savings associations at the end of 1990. Its most striking aspect is that thrifts' assets are heavily oriented toward mortgage loans and related assets. Those mortgages are primarily funded by the issuance of deposits.

Mortgages.   The major assets of both savings banks and savings associations consists of loans or securities secured by real estate. Thrifts must hold 70 percent of their assets in mortgages and mortgage-related securities in order to be classed as qualified home mortgage lenders. If so qualified, they are eligible to join and borrow from regional Federal Home Loan Banks. Also, after 1986 thrifts could deduct up to 8

Exhibit 18–1   **Income and Expense Ratios for All FSLIC-Insured Savings Associations (1970–1990)**

Year	Revenues/ Assets	Interest Paid/ Assets	Spread (Revenues- Interest)	Operating Expense/ Assets	After-Tax Income[a]/ Assets (ROA)
1970	6.26%	4.49%	1.77	1.11%	0.54%
1971	6.33	4.44	1.89	1.06	0.66
1972	6.43	4.42	2.01	1.05	0.71
1973	6.90	4.76	2.14	1.12	0.72
1974	7.28	5.31	1.97	1.19	0.51
1975	7.18	5.34	1.84	1.20	0.44
1976	7.36	5.35	2.01	1.20	0.59
1977	7.53	5.35	2.18	1.18	0.71
1978	7.91	5.59	2.32	1.20	0.76
1979	8.56	6.42	2.14	1.25	0.64
1980	8.91	7.53	1.38	1.26	0.12
1981	10.01	9.72	0.29	1.38	−0.71
1982	10.22	10.04	0.18	1.44	−0.61
1983	9.76	8.26	1.50	1.50	0.24
1984	10.77	9.04	1.73	1.64	0.16
1985	10.80	8.55	2.25	1.91	0.39
1986	9.90	7.45	2.45	2.05	0.01
1987	8.96	6.68	2.28	2.02	−0.56
1988 4th qtr	9.07	6.83	2.24	2.12	−0.87
1989	10.11	8.26	1.85	2.14	−1.66
1990 4th qtr	9.62	7.28	1.92	2.10	−0.38

Thrifts' costs of funds rose substantially into the early 1980s as they obtained fewer funds from low-rate passbook accounts and as interest rates rose. Because their mortgage yields changed more slowly than their costs of funds, thrifts experienced large net losses during high-interest-rate periods. Also, as thrifts have undertaken more complex activities, their operating expenses have increased from barely 1 percent of assets to over 2 percent. High service costs on new types of deposits coupled with falling yields on assets and large losses on new types of loans—particularly in certain parts of the country—caused thrifts' profits to fall sharply again in 1986 and 1987, even though their spreads had increased substantially after the early 1980s.

[a]After-tax income is computed by subtracting operating expenses from spreads and then adjusting for taxes and nonoperating gains and losses (loan losses were particularly important for reducing income in recent years).

Source: Federal Home Loan Bank Board and United States League of Savings Associations before 1988, Office of Thrift Supervision after 1988.

percent of their taxable income as a bad-debt deduction if they held more than 60 percent of their assets in qualifying forms, mainly in mortgage-related assets. Prior to the 1986 tax revisions, thrifts received tax breaks of up to 40 percent of income if they held up to 82 percent of their assets in mortgages.

Thrifts' holdings of mortgage-backed securities have grown sharply in recent years. If thrifts need cash, mortgage-backed securities can be sold more easily than mortgages. Furthermore, since 1981 thrifts have been able to swap pools of mortgages with government agencies to obtain easily marketable government agency securities backed with the same pool of mortgages. Mortgage swaps of this sort inexpensively provide thrifts with both liquidity and bookkeeping advantages. At year-end 1990, thrifts held more than 15 percent of their assets in mortgage-backed securities.

Exhibit 18–2   Numbers of Thrift Institutions (Year-End 1979–1991)

| | Total Thrifts | Total S&Ls (FDIC-SAIF Savings Banks) | Federal Home Loan Bank Members | | State-Chartered Nonfederally Insured | Savings Banks | |
			Federally Chartered, Federally Insured (FSLIC or FDIC-SAIF)	State-Chartered, Federally Insured (FSLIC or FDIC-SAIF)		Federally Insured by (FDIC-BIF)	State Insured
1979	5,147	4,684	4,039		645	324	163
1980	5,076	4,613	4,002		611	323	162
1981	4,740	4,292	3,779		513	331	159
1982	4,249	3,825	1,727	1,616	482	315	155
1983	4,036	3,645	1,696	1,487	462	294	146
1984	3,995	3,591	1,689	1,447	455	291	130
1985	3,893	3,535	1,721	1,525	290	392	2
1986	3,960	3,487	1,744	1,476	267	472	0
1987	3,945	3,385	1,768	1,379	238	485	0
1988	—	3,175	1,720	1,229	226	—	0
1989	—	3,011	1,788	1,090	133	—	0
1990	—	2,342	—	—	—	—	0
1991	2,554	—				—	0

The number of thrift institutions in existence declined sharply in the early 1980s because of increased failures and mergers. At the same time, the proportion of federally insured thrifts rose and thrifts found it increasingly important to have federal deposit insurance in troubled times and as several state insurance funds discontinued operations. Also, the number of federally insured savings banks rose as savings and loans converted to savings bank charters and private state insurance funds were phased out.

Source: United States League of Savings Associations, Savings Institution Sourcebooks, and various Office of Thrift Supervision publications, 1991.

Cash, Deposits, and Investment Securities

Savings banks and S&Ls are subject to reserve requirements on their transactions deposits. These reserves must be held as vault cash or be on deposit with the Fed. In addition, most thrift institutions hold some clearing deposits with correspondents and additional liquidity balances and investments.

Insured S&Ls must meet liquidity requirements established by their regulators. They must do so by holding cash, deposits due from depository institutions, or eligible investment securities, such as Treasury bills. Liquidity requirements are low, usually around 5 percent of associations' withdrawable savings deposits and borrowings due in one year or less. In the past, regulators increased liquidity reserve requirements to discourage excessive lending, or reduced them to free additional funds for mortgage financing. Since most thrifts have relatively small transactions accounts, the liquidity requirement typically exceeds deposit reserve requirements imposed by the Federal Reserve.

Exhibit 18-3

Characteristics of Thrifts by OTS Strength Classification in the Strongest (Group I) to Weakest (Group IV) Classifications, 4th Quarter, 1990

	Number of Associations	Consolidated Assets ($ Billions)	Net Income for 1990 4th Quarter ($ Millions)	Return on Average Assets (ROA)	Goodwill and Other Intangibles/ Assets	Consolidated Tangible Capital (% of Assets)
Group I	1,069	$ 323	$ 399	0.51%	0.7%	6.6%
Group II	710	300	246	0.33	0.7	4.6
Group III	369	264	−693	−1.04	1.5	2.4
Group IV	194	131	−917	−2.72	1.9	−2.6
Total	2,342	$1,018	−$965			3.7%

	1 to 4 Family Mortgages/ Assets	Brokered Deposits/ Total Deposits	Noncurrent Loans/ Total Loans	Repossessed Assets/ Total Assets	Below-Investment-Grade Debt/ Total Assets
Group I	55.1%	0.88%	1.20%	0.70%	0.7%
Group II	44.0	2.64	1.66	2.59	0.7
Group III	38.6	5.86	3.24	1.63	1.5
Group IV	31.6	9.90	5.30	4.82	1.9

Classifications as of December 31, 1990. Group I thrifts are well capitalized and profitable; Group II thrifts meet or are expected to meet capital requirements; Group III thrifts are troubled with poor earnings and low capital; and Group IV thrifts are expected to be transfered to the RTC.

All data are unconsolidated except where noted.

Source: Office of Thrift Supervision, March 1991.

Savings banks have traditionally held some long-term, nonmortgage investments, such as corporate bonds and government agency securities. Furthermore, after the DIDMCA was passed in 1980, and especially after the Garn–St. Germain Act was passed in 1982, some S&Ls used their new investment powers to expand their holdings of corporate bonds (including low-rate, high-yielding junk bonds) and corporate equities. Consequently, since the early 1980s thrifts' investment accounts have grown relative to their mortgage holdings.

Consumer and Commercial Loans

Savings banks have long had the power to make a broad range of consumer loans, and most have done so. Prior to 1980, S&Ls were able to make consumer loans, but only if they were home improvement loans, mobile home loans, education loans, or loans secured by deposits. However, the DIDMCA let all savings associations make a broad range of consumer loans. Previously, only state-chartered S&Ls in Texas, Maine, and Ohio had broad consumer-lending powers. At year-end 1987, consumer loans accounted for 4.4 percent of thrifts' assets.

Exhibit 18–4   **Private Sector Savings and Loan Balance Sheets, 1990**

Assets (in $ billions and %)			Liabilities and Net Worth (in $ billions and %)			
Cash, deposits and investment securities	$ 91.7	13.3%	Total deposits*		$767.2	76.4%
Consumer loans	43.7	4.4	Under $100,000	$684.1	68.1%	
Commercial loans	22.0	2.2	Over $100,000	83.1	8.3	
1–4 family mortgages	446.8	44.5	Borrowings		167.4	16.7
Mortgage pool securities	145.9	14.5	Advances from FHLBs	89.7		8.9
Multifamily mortgages	66.7	6.6	Reverse repo agreements	40.1		4.0
Nonresidential mortgages	68.7	6.8	Other borrowings	37.6		3.8
Land loans	22.0	1.1	Other liabilities		19.0	1.9
Other assets	91.7	2.2				
Less: contra asset valuation Allowances	−25.5	−2.5	Equity Capital		50.9	5.0
Total	$1,004.5	100%	Total		$1,004.5	100%

*The breakdown of thrift deposits by type at the end of 1989 was: transactions deposits 5.9 percent of total deposits; MMDA accounts, 9.3 percent; fixed-maturity deposits, 77.2 percent (including 1.4 percent in variable rate deposits and 46.8 percent in deposits maturing in under one year), and other deposits, 7.6 percent. Thus, only 19 percent of deposits had maturities of over one year unless the other deposits (such as IRAs etc., were assumed to be long term in nature). Consequently, thrifts still obtain the predominant shares of their liabilities (approximately half) from deposits with maturities under one year.

Note: Reported data are for December 1990 for 2,342 private thrifts. Footnote source: *1989 Combined Financial Statements SAIF Insured Thrifts*, Office of Thrift Supervision, Washington, D.C.

Source: *News*, Office of Thrift Supervision, March 14, 1991.

The DIDMCA and the Garn–St. Germain Act also gave thrifts broad powers to make commercial real estate loans, to acquire commercial paper and corporate debt securities, and to hold up to 10 percent of their assets in direct commercial loans. However, as was the case with consumer loans, only a few thrifts quickly took full advantage of their new powers. Thus, by the end of 1990, nonmortgage commercial loans accounted for only 2.2 percent of thrift's assets. Nonetheless, some thrifts made additional commercial loans through their service companies. Some thrifts also held more than 10 percent of their assets in commercial mortgage loans.

Service Companies and Other Assets

S&Ls are allowed to hold a controlling equity interest in subsidiaries called *service companies*. These service companies, in turn, can invest in a wide variety of enterprises, such as mortgage servicing, commercial lending, and real estate projects. Some state-chartered savings associations can allocate a large amount of assets to service companies and other nonmortgage activities. In addition, the DIDMCA of 1980 allows all federally chartered savings associations to allocate up to 3 percent of their assets to service companies.

At the end of 1984, federally-insured savings institutions held 1.7 percent of their assets as investments in service companies. However, the importance of service companies is far greater than that. For instance, service companies can buy a savings association's mortgages and sell them to investors under a mortgage-servicing contract. Also, finance subsidiaries can buy large amounts of assets from a savings association and finance them by selling debt, such as collateralized mortgage agreements (CMOs—see Chapter 10), in the capital markets.

In addition to acquiring equity interest in subsidiaries, federal savings associations must buy stock (worth slightly less than 1 percent of their assets) in the Federal Home Loan Bank System. Finally, savings institutions own buildings, computers, repossessed real estate ("real estate owned"), and other assets. Some state-chartered associations in California, Texas, and other states with lenient laws have held a variety of other assets, including real estate developments, fast-food outlets, barbecue food chains, funeral homes, and equity and bond interests in all types of corporations. However, most savings associations do not speculate or engage in investments far removed from mortgage lending. Furthermore, the FIRRE Act of 1989 required that state chartered savings associations be subject to the same asset restrictions as federally chartered associations. Thus, for savings institutions as a whole, other assets and securities investments amount to only a small portion of their total assets.

Liabilities and Net Worth

Deposits

The liabilities of both mutual savings banks and S&Ls primarily consist of time and savings deposits. Thrift institutions as a whole obtain 76 percent of their liabilities by issuing time and savings deposit accounts to consumers (see Exhibit 18–4). Historically, they obtained funds by issuing passbook savings accounts. Now, however, such accounts make up only a small percentage of their liabilities. Thrifts obtain larger amounts of their liabilities by issuing checkable deposits, such as NOW accounts or MMDAs, and certificates of deposit. Some thrifts also obtain a large amount of funds by issuing large-denomination certificates of deposit (CDs) in the money markets. Large CDs have drawn the wrath of regulators when problem or rapidly growing thrifts have issued them through money brokers. Money brokers pool deposits from many sources to buy CDs, thereby guaranteeing that no one investor exceeds the $100,000 federal insurance limit. Consequently, the FDIC Improvement Act of 1991 restricted the use of deposit brokers to "well-capitalized" and (regulator-approved) "adequately capitalized" depository institutions.

Borrowings

A relatively small portion of thrifts' deposits are for one year or more. Because of the long-term nature of their assets, however, many thrifts want to obtain long-term funds. Some do so by borrowing.

S&Ls can borrow either by obtaining advances from Federal Home Loan Banks or from private sources. They can tap national and international money markets by purchasing Fed Funds, issuing commercial paper, entering into reverse repo agreements, and selling mortgage-backed bonds. At year-end 1990 private borrowings and other liabilities equaled 9.7 percent of thrifts' assets, and advances from the Federal Home Loan Banks equaled another 8.9 percent.

FHL bank advances may be made with maturities up to 20 years. They provide a major source of funds for savings associations that need liquidity. The large quantity of outstanding advances reflects the fact that the FHL banks make loans on favorable terms. Rates on advances are tied to the relatively low government agency borrowing rate. Under legislation enacted in 1989, FHL bank advances are available to institutions that held 70 percent of their assets in residential mortgage related loans and securities.

Net Worth

The net worth of thrifts is extremely small relative to their assets. At year-end 1990, FDIC-SAIF-insured savings associations held total regulatory net worth equal to 5.0 percent of their total assets; however, they held even less, 3.7 percent, when only tangible capital was counted, and most of that capital was held by the best-performing thrifts (see Exhibit 18–3). The worst-performing thrifts held proportionately more goodwill and other intangible assets in their regulatory capital accounts. Furthermore, many thrifts' net-worth ratios were far less than the average.

In fact, at the end of 1990, of the 194 Group IV private thrifts over half had negative tangible capital, and Group IV thrifts' total tangible capital was a negative 2 percent of their assets. The insolvent thrifts would have been closed, but the regulators could only afford to liquidate the very worst savings and loans until Congress authorized more bailout funding for the RTC. As a result of their low net worth, many thrifts are highly leveraged and run considerable risk of insolvency if the value of their assets should decline by even a small amount.

In the early 1980s, rising interest rates caused the market value of thrifts' mortgages to fall below their book value by at least $100 billion. Consequently, most thrifts were technically insolvent. This fact was disguised, however, because the regulators let the thrifts value their mortgages at book value, and they developed a number of new strategies to augment thrifts' regulatory net worth positions. Subsequently, many thrifts reported improvements in their net worth as they took advantage of regulatory accounting practices and as market interest rates fell. However, a few abused their new powers to make excessive numbers of bad loans (See Did You Know?). As a result, thrift institutions as a whole still had low net worth as the 1980s ended. Thrift institutions' net worth primarily consists of undivided profits, surplus, and reserve accounts. Many thrifts also can include certain subordinated notes and debentures in their net worth calculations, and some have issued common and preferred stock.

In 1980, mutual savings banks were allowed to obtain federal charters and convert to stockholder-owned corporations. In 1982, such conversions were made easier for all thrifts. The sale of stock adds to the net worth of thrift institutions that convert to stock charters. Consequently, several hundred thrifts converted to stock ownership in the early 1980s, and common and preferred stock now accounts for a substantial portion of thrifts' total net worth. In addition, since 1980, mutually owned thrifts have been allowed to issue "mutual capital certificates." These can have fixed or variable dividend payments. Because they are subordinate to other debt and deposit liabilities

Vernon Savings and Loan Made Mostly Loans

So many of the S&L problems of the late 1980s were centered in the Southwest that the FSLIC developed its "Southwest Plan" to liquidate them. Although many of the liquidated institutions developed problems because of the mid-80s crash in oil prices and the ensuing deterioration of the Southwest's economic base, others developed problems because of their "fast and loose" lending practices. Because of its casual lending records, for instance, Sunbelt Savings was often jocularly removed to as "Gunbelt Savings" before its management was removed by the FSLIC. The most dramatic example of S&Ls' problems of the late 1980s, however, is exemplified by Vernon Savings and Loan. Vernon's case is typical of many savings and loans run by fast operators, but in true Texas style, it created bigger and more flamboyant problems than any other S&L.

Vernon Savings and Loan was initially headquartered in the small town of Vernon, Texas. It experienced interest rate management problems like many other S&Ls in the early 1980s. Thus, in 1982 the FSLIC was happy to sell it to a new buyer who could infuse a little capital and, it was hoped, fix its problems.

The sale of a problem S&L to a new buyer was one of the FSLIC's favorite methods of problem resolution. However, Vernon's new buyer, Don R. Dixon, was attracted to the new powers S&Ls had gained and S&Ls' ability to branch anywhere in Texas (a power not given to banks). He decided to grow out of the past problems by moving Vernon's headquarters to Dallas and by bidding for funds by issuing FSLIC-insured CDs in the national brokered money markets. During the next four years, Vernon Savings and Loan's assets grew by over 1,600 percent—even though federal regulators did not want S&Ls to grow by more than 25 percent per year.

Unfortunately, after Dixon's acquisition, the federal regulators were ill equipped to restrict Vernon's excessively rapid growth or to prevent problems from developing. In addition to selling weak institutions to questionable operators who wished to exploit the S&Ls new powers and deposit insurance, the regulators made another mistake in the early and mid-1980s. They let their examination force decline. The total number of examiners declined to the point that some S&Ls went three years with no federal examination. This problem was particularly severe in the Southwest, because most examiners quit when the head office of the Southwest region's Federal Home Loan bank was moved from Little Rock, Arkansas, to Dallas.

Thus, there were few examiners to keep Vernon from taking excess risks. Consequently, it adopted a loan policy that emphasized making loans to borrowers who would pay large up-front loan-origination fees. Because of lax accounting rules for S&Ls, the S&Ls could immediately book loan-origination fees as profits. However, borrowers who were willing to pay large up-front fees were unlikely to be good credit risks. When Vernon was closed by the federal regulators in 1988, 96 percent of its loans were nonperforming.

Nonetheless, the fat accounting profits reported by Vernon Savings and Loan let Don R. Dixon live a lavish life-style. The S&L provided him with corporate jets, a beachhouse in California, and a corporate yacht for his travel and relaxation. Vernon also entertained politicians well and paid its key officers handsomely. Reportedly, it even hired prostitutes for a board meeting.

By the time the FSLIC woke up to the problem and obtained the funding and authority necessary to shut Vernon Savings and Loan down, it had to pay off $1.3 billion in deposits (the FSLIC's greatest loss up to that date). In return, it acquired Vernon's portfolio of almost totally nonperforming loans.

Vernon was the worst case of a promotor's abuse of S&L deposit insurance, accounting arbitrariness, and regulatory laxity, but it was not the only one. There are many other sagas of S&L failures in the mid- and late 1980s. The failures were particularly scandalous in Texas, California, and other states that granted state-chartered S&Ls greater powers and looser regulation than federally chartered S&Ls. The sad thing is that the well-managed institutions now have to pay higher deposit insurance rates to pay for the mess.

of the savings associations that issue them, they are counted as part of the institutions' net worth.

Finally, to shore up thrifts incurring losses, in 1982 the Garn–St Germain Act allowed troubled thrift institutions to increase their net worths by issuing "net worth certificates" of "income capital certificates" to the FSLIC or FDIC. The interest paid on a certificate was equal to the interest paid on the promissory note that the FSLIC or FDIC issued to purchase the certificate. Thus, in essence, the troubled thrift would simultaneously add an asset (a promissory note from the FSLIC or FDIC) and a net worth account (the net worth certificate) to its balance sheet. Net worth certificates could be used only by mortgage-oriented thrifts that had a net worth of less than 3 percent and were currently incurring losses. Thrifts could not acquire net worth certificates in excess of their losses. In essence, these certificates allowed institutions on the brink of insolvency to remain technically solvent in the expectation that interest rates would fall and their situation would improve.

Conversions from Mutual to Stock Form.   Until 1980, savings banks could only be state-chartered and could not be stockholder-owned. The DIDMCA allowed them to be federally chartered so that they could be either mutually owned or stockholder-owned. Similarly, before 1982 most S&Ls could only be mutually owned. Although some states did charter stock associations, federal policy restricted the ability of S&Ls to convert from mutual to stock form. However, the Garn–St. Germain Act allowed such conversions, and several hundred mutual savings associations subsequently converted to stock form and raised billions of dollars of capital by doing so.

A mutual institution that converts to stock form gains two advantages: it can obtain additional net worth by selling stock, and can more easily become part of a financial holding company. However, costs of conversion are high, partly because all depositors are given a chance to obtain stock so they won't carelessly surrender their potentially valuable ownership claims.

After the Financial Institutions Reform, Recovery, and Enforcement Act was passed in 1989, thrifts were required to hold "tangible" net worth equal to $1^1/_2$ percent of assets immediately, and equal to 3 percent of assets after 1994. Their net worth calculation could no longer contain goodwill accounting gimmicks in the measurement of "tangible" capital. Thus many thrifts were forced to sell stock or merge with better capitalized institutions. Those that had serious capital or earnings problems were taken over by the newly created Resolution Trust Corporation under a conservatorship arrangement that would ultimately lead to the thrifts' sale or liquidation (see Exhibit 18–6). Because the RTC had only limited funds and had to return repeatedly to Congress to obtain more financing, some thrifts with negative tangible capital were still allowed to operate (as shown in Exhibit 18–3).

Thrift Income Statements

Thrifts' gross earnings come primarily from interest earnings (as shown in Exhibit 18–5), particularly from interest on mortgage loans and related securities. Similarly, their greatest expense consists of interest payments on their deposits and borrowed funds. In recent years they have earned a net interest spread equal to $1^1/_2$ percent to 2

| Exhibit 18–5 | Private Sector Savings and Loans' Keys Income Statement Variables, 1989 and 1990 (as Annualized Percent of Assets) |

	1989	1990					
	4th Qtr	1st Qtr	2nd Qtr	3rd Qtr	4th Qtr		
Interest income	9.33%	9.15%	9.06%	9.14%	9.21%	(1)
– Interest expense	–7.81	–7.35	–7.22	–7.29	–7.28	(2)
= Net interest income	1.52	1.80	1.84	1.85	1.92	(3)
+ Noninterest income	1.07	0.59	0.63	0.66	0.41	(4)
– Noninterest expense	–2.34	–2.00	–1.89	–1.96	–2.10	(5)
= Net operating income before losses	0.25	0.39	0.58	0.55	0.23	(6)
– Provision for loan losses	–1.48	–0.47	–0.72	–0.88	–0.68	(7)
+ Gain (Loss) on sale of assets	0.11	0.08	0.12	0.11	0.17	(8)
= Pretax operating income	–1.12	0	–0.02	–0.23	–0.27	(9)
– Taxes	+0.04	–0.16	–0.11	–0.08	–0.13	(10)
+ Other income	0	0	0.02	0	0	(11)
= Net income after taxes	–1.08%	–0.16%	–0.11%	–0.30%	–0.40%	(12)
Number of S&Ls reporting	2,597	2,505	2,435	2,388	2,342	

Note: After the Office of Thrift Suprvision replaced the Federal Home Loan Bank Board in late 1989, the number of private-sector thrifts fell sharply and net private-sector thrift earnings increased somewhat as thrifts with the worst losses were shifted to the RTC for resolution.

Source: News, Office of Thrift Supervision, March 14, 1991.

percent of their assets (see Exhibit 18–5, first three lines). They also earned noninterest income equal to approximately 0.6 percent of assets in 1990. The amount of noninterest income was smaller in previous years (before thrifts offered transactions deposits on which they levied fees), but as shown in Exhibit 18–1, in *most* years the difference in total revenues less interest expense has given thrifts a positive spread of 1.75 percent to 2.4 percent before expenses and losses. The only exception occurred in the early 1980s when thrifts' cost of funds rose faster than their interest income and fees (see Exhibit 18–1).

Thrift operating expenses have risen in the 1980s, as thrifts have offered a wider variety of services, including transactions deposits, and have invested in a wider variety of assets—some of which, like consumer loans, are relatively expensive to service. Thus, operating expense ratios have risen from a range of 1 percent to 1 $\frac{1}{4}$ percent of assets in the 1970s to a little over 2 percent of assets in the late 1980s and early 1990s. Their increased costs have reduced their profitability, but the major causes of losses in the late 1980s were loan losses and losses on other types of assets. Thus Exhibit 18–5 shows that thrift profits have generally been positive even after

Exhibit 18–6   The RTC Liquidation Process

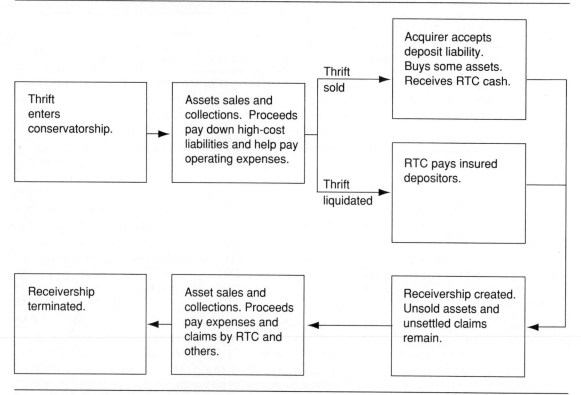

Source: Resolution Trust Corporation Briefing Materials, July–August, 1991

After a thrift enters RTC conservatorship, it is either sold or liquidated. Unsold assets are placed in a receivership and subsequently are disposed of by the RTC.

operating expenses are taken into account; however, because of large loan losses, thrifts overall were unprofitable in the early 1990s.

Details given in Exhibit 18–3 show that the low profits tended to be concentrated among the Group III and Group IV thrifts in 1990 (as both those groups had negative ROAs). Additional details given in that Exhibit also show that the weakest thrifts tended to hold disproportionately large amounts of "noncurrent" (questionable) loans, repossessed assets, and poor-grade debt securities. Obviously, disproportionate holdings of subpar assets by the weakest thrifts contributed to their losses in 1990. Furthermore, the weakest thrifts also obtained the largest portion of their assets from brokered deposits—which frequently carry higher interest rates and, therefore, are more costly to obtain than core deposits.

Because of the poor performance of the weakest two classes of thrifts, thrifts as a whole lost money in 1990. However, after the RTC received more funding from Congress in 1991, it was able to close more poorly performing thrifts. Furthermore, deposit interest rates fell throughout 1991. Consequently, by the end of 1991, private sector thrifts in total were able to eke out a small profit once again.

Agency Problems and Thrift Capital

Net Worth and Agency Problems

In the field of corporate finance, one of the most important topics involves "agency theory." The basic problem addressed by agency theory is the question of whether or not the manager of a firm (the agent in charge of the firm's assets) will take actions that are in the best interest of the firm's security holders and stockholders. Because the managers of firms are likely to pursue their own best interests rather than those of the security holders and stockholders, some action may be needed to change the managers' behavior. In particular, debt holders may require restrictive covenants that prohibit certain actions and stockholders may structure management compensation plans that use stock options and incentive bonuses to reward managers for serving the interests of the stockholders. Stockholders, acting through a firm's board of directors, also may remove ineffective or dishonest managers. Stockholders, in particular, have an incentive to monitor the behavior of managers closely because stockholders have the most to gain if a firm generates extra profits and the most to lose if a firm incurs losses. Stockholders' maximum potential losses, however, are limited to the amount of capital they have invested in the firm.

Once a firm suffers losses that exceed its net worth, the firm will be insolvent, and deposit and liability holders also will lose a portion of their investment unless their deposits are insured. Owners of subordinated debt in the firm will lose once the firm's net worth is exhausted unless an insurance plan covers their losses along with the losses that otherwise would be borne by owners of insured liabilities (deposits). Subordinated debtors may, de facto, be protected if the insuring agency arranges a "purchase and assumption" form of liquidation or provides "too big to fail" guarantees that guarantee all the liabilities of a failing financial institution (see Chapter 17).

Because of its guarantees that protect depositors and, de facto, protect some subordinated debtors of financial institutions, the agency that insures financial institutions' deposits will be exposed to substantial risks of loss if the net worth of the firm should become exhausted through losses. Thus, the insuring agency, like subordinated debtholders, has a strong incentive to require that the firm's managers comply with restrictive covenants that will protect the liability holders against loss.

The Insurers' Agency Problem

The insurer of a firm's liabilities, then, will impose restrictions on a firm's activities that are designed to protect the insurer against loss. One such restriction is that the insured firm provide regular detailed reports to the insuring agency. Another is that the firm be subject to unannounced examinations by representatives or employees of the insuring agency. A third requirement is that the management be subject to "cease and desist" orders issued by the insuring agency. In the most extreme cases the insuring agency may require that the firm's managers be replaced; for instance, the savings and loan insuring agency replaced existing thrift managers of poorly managed institutions under its management consignment program initiated in April 1985.

Finally, the insuring agency can protect itself against loss by requiring that the insured firm obtain and maintain larger net worth (capital) accounts. That is why the FIRRE and FDIC Improvement Acts increased thrift net worth requirements.

Net Worth as a Solution to the Insurers' Problem

If an institution holds more net worth (capital), its losses can be greater before its liability holders (and the insurer of those liabilities) will suffer losses. Furthermore, with more capital at risk, the institution's stockholders will have a greater incentive to monitor the actions of the firm's managers so they will not take actions that cause the stockholders to incur a loss. Because of the importance of capital for protecting deposit insurers against loss, when thrift institution deposit insurance was debated in 1989, the required level of thrift net worth (capital) was one of the most hotly debated subjects in Congress. The Bush administration initially proposed that thrifts should eventually be required to hold 6 percent of their assets as capital, and that they should hold at least 3 percent of their assets as net worth by 1991. The Senate reduced the 3 percent capital requirement to $1^1/_2$ percent but required that the "net worth" account could only consist of "tangible capital." Tangible capital consists of GAAP capital recognized as such under generally accepted accounting principles (GAAP), less goodwill and other intangible assets, such as the capitalized value of mortgage servicing income.

The thrift institutions wanted to count "goodwill" and the value of future servicing fee income contracts as capital; they did not want to raise a great deal of capital in a hurry. Since many of them were mutual associations, they could not sell stock to accumulate additional net worth and the process of net worth accumulation through the retention of earnings was expected to be slow. Thus, they prevailed upon the House of Representatives to defer the time when they would have to hold substantial amounts of tangible capital. The House, however, heeded President Bush's request and required that thrift institutions hold capital equal to at least three percent of their assets. Furthermore, the House stated that no more than half of the capital requirement could be met with intangible assets (such as goodwill) in 1990, and that no intangible assets could be counted when computing thrifts' capital adequacy after 1994. Institutions that did not meet the capital requirements would be subject to regulatory sanctions and would not be allowed to expand until their capital was adequate.

In 1991 the FDIC Improvement Act provided additional funds to finance the RTC's liquidation of weak thrifts and also tried to further restrict thrifts' ability to operate with low or intangible capital.

It provided that all depository institutions with less than 2 percent net worth be declared critically insolvent and be liquidated quickly if their problems were not redressed. In addition, it required that regulators move toward evaluating thrift balance sheets (or investment securities) on a market value rather than book value basis; that would eliminate the potential for "gains trading" (see People and Events). Also, the act (along with the FIRRE Act) required that depository institutions use GAAP accounting, thereby eliminating some of the "regulatory accounting" abuses that had let thrifts overstate their incomes and net worth in the past. In addition, the act prohibited the issuance of brokered deposits by thrifts that were not at least adequately capitalized. It also required that all insured institutions that were not adequately capitalized immediately develop and start implementing plans to restore their capital to adequate levels. Through these requirements, the regulators acknowledged that the best way to resolve agency problems was to have stockholders of thrifts have a substantial amount of capital at stake that would be lost before the thrift caused losses to the deposit insurance fund.

Agency Problems in Mutual Versus Stockholder-Owned Thrifts

The congressional actions, however, highlighted one of the primary weaknesses of the thrift institutions and their insurance funds; that is, the thrift industry has been dominated by mutual institutions. That poses a problem for accumulating the capital needed to protect the deposit insurance fund. It also poses a problem because the mutual thrifts do not have stockholders monitoring firms' management to ensure that they would not take imprudent risks. The stockholder interest in ensuring that management would be prudent is absent in mutual associations. Thus, the entire burden of monitoring the performance of mutual thrift institutions fell on the deposit insurance fund. Consequently, mutual thrift institution managers could retain their jobs as long as they did nothing dishonest enough or rash enough to incite the regulators to impose a cease and desist order or implement a management consignment program.

Because the regulators only pursue management removal as a last resort, they placed only 80 thrift institutions under management consignment programs from 1985 through 1987. Thus the managers of mutual institutions had little to fear either from regulators or from stockholder supervision.

This analysis suggests that it is not enough to require that thrifts obtain more capital. In addition, the extra capital should ideally come from stockholders who can provide it quickly and who will closely monitor the performance of management in order to protect their investment. Furthermore, the regulators must closely monitor the performance of thrift managers and quickly remove bad managers, so that the thrifts' managers will work to reduce risks and, thereby, protect the deposit insurance fund against loss. This is particularly the case with mutual associations since there will not be stockholders monitoring mutual associations to protect themselves and (as a byproduct) the deposit insurance agency against losses caused by the depletion of the firm's net worth (capital) accounts.

There is, however, one self-correcting mechanism that applies to mutual institutions. If their managers have their "human capital" (lifetime value of their labor income) tied closely to the value of the thrift, they will not want to see it fail. Thus studies have shown that managers of well-capitalized thrifts often behave conservatively—as they did in the 1930s. However, if the thrift has low capital and is likely to be liquidated soon unless it restores its earnings quickly, managers may have a perverse incentive to gamble in hopes that if they win, they can keep the thrift alive longer; if they lose, they will be out of a job anyway. Thus, in the 1980s managers of weak thrifts often gambled by buying junk bonds, taking equity interests in real estate developments (where permitted) and making weak loans with high up-front fees that (at the time) they could book as immediate fee income to inflate profits. Thus, once thrifts became weak, the agency problem gave them a greater incentive to gamble.

That is one reason the FDIC Improvement Act of 1991 requires that thrifts with critically low capital either restore it quickly or be closed by the regulators.

The Regulatory Environment

Most thrift institutions are regulated at both the state and the federal levels. Most thrifts are now federally insured, although only about half are federally chartered. Until the FIRRE and FDIC Improvement Acts were passed, state-chartered thrifts often were subject to laxer regulations than federally chartered thrifts. Now, however, the state-chartered thrifts generally must comply with minimum standards of federal regulators. Savings banks can either be insured by the FDIC-BIF or the FDIC-SAIF. However, if an institution wishes to transfer from one insurer to another, it now must pay an exit fee in the form of continued higher premiums to the fund it is leaving. Previously, in the early 1980s when transfers were easier, some savings banks sought FSLIC (savings and loan) insurance because its regulations were more lenient, while others sought FDIC insurance because the premiums were lower. Now the FDIC operates both the savings association insurance fund (FDIC-SAIF) and the bank insurance fund (FDIC-BIF).

Savings institutions are supervised and regulated both by their chartering authorities and their insurance funds. State agencies with regulatory responsibilities usually include the state banking commissioner (or the state department of financial institutions) and the state attorney general's office. At the federal level, the Office of Thrift Supervision charters S&Ls and they are examined and supervised by the FDIC's Savings Association Insurance Fund or Bank Insurance Fund. In addition the Justice Department can intervene if a proposed merger or acquisition will materially reduce competition.

The FHLBS

The Federal Home Loan Banks.   The Federal Home Loan Bank (FHLB) System was established in 1932 to provide liquidity to thrifts. Formerly it was the most important regulator of thrifts. It is similar to the Federal Reserve System in some respects, consisting of 12 regional banks with which savings associations and other mortgage-oriented depository institutions can be affiliated. All federally chartered S&Ls must join, and state-chartered S&Ls may join. Each institution that joins the system must buy sufficient stock in its regional Federal Home Loan Bank to equal 1 percent of its loan portfolio. Member institutions may borrow from their local Federal Home Loan Banks through advances, provided that they are primarily engaged in mortgage lending. Federal Home Loan Banks, in turn, issue government-agency debt obligations. They also have a credit line at the U.S. Treasury. Since 1989 the Federal Home Loan banks have been coordinated by the Federal Housing Finance Board.

The Federal Home Loan Bank Board.   Until 1989, the Federal Home Loan Bank Board (FHLBB) was located in Washington and supervised the activities of the regional Federal Home Loan banks. Unlike the Fed, it served as an advocate for its member institutions, drafted regulations that affected *all* federally chartered and insured savings associations, and supervised both the Federal Savings and Loan

Insurance Corporation and the Federal Home Loan Mortgage Corporation. It was the most important regulator of thrift institutions. However, because it favored thrifts with relatively lax regulation, it was blamed for the 1980s thrift crisis by Congress, which abolished it in the 1989 FIRRE Act and replaced it with the Office of Thrift Supervision.

The Office of Thrift Supervision (OTS).   In 1989, the FIRRE Act replaced the FHLBB with the Office of Thrift Supervision. The OTS was not an independent agency, however, but was part of the U.S. Treasury Department, like the Office of the Comptroller of the Currency. The OTS is the principal federal regulatory agency for thrift institutions. It charters federal savings associations and supervises them and their holding companies. In general, it took over the administrative duties of the FHLBB, but was subject to more direct control by the executive branch of the federal government.

The Federal Savings and Loan Insurance Corporation (FSLIC).   The FHLBB received much of the blame for the thrift failures of the 1980s because it had advocated more powers for thrift institutions. Some powers, like those involved in commercial lending, were subsequently misused. It also provided an insufficient number of thrift examiners, despite expansion efforts by 1985 chairman, Ed Gray, and over the initial objections of Congress and the administration. Furthermore, the FHLBB let its FSLIC deposit insurance subsidiary engage in creative mergers and accounting gimmicks to hide the extent of the thrift institution problems in the early and mid-1980s. However, many of its actions were taken in response to requests by Congress. On many occasions congressmen and senators had intervened in an attempt to stop FSLIC or FHLBB regulators from imposing sanctions on poorly managed or poorly funded thrift institutions located in their states. In fact, one reason that the FHLBB had no choice but to let the FSLIC use creative accounting was because Congress refused to provide the FSLIC with enough funding to cover losses that it would incur by shutting down as many insolvent savings and loans as was necessary. Additional funding was not authorized until 1987; by then, it was a case of "too-little-too-late" to solve the FSLIC's problems.

Congressional interference with the action of FHLBB regulators and the delay of funding by Speaker of the House Jim Wright contributed to the thrift institutions' problems. Rather than admit that Congress had contributed to the problem, however, Congress laid the blame for the thrifts' problems solely on the FHLBB and the FSLIC and abolished both institutions altogether in 1989. Until 1989, the Federal Savings and Loan Insurance Corporation (FSLIC) was similar to the FDIC. It insured savings associations' deposits up to $100,000 each. It also examined and supervised all federally insured savings associations, and it supervised mergers and liquidations of failing savings associations.

FSLIC obtained funds for its operations by levying an insurance premium on insured associations' deposits. Like the FDIC, the base premium was $1/12$ of 1 percent. However, the FSLIC also could levy additional premiums up to the full amount of its losses and expenses. In 1985, it imposed a supplemental premiums of $1/8$ of 1 percent, payable in four quarterly installments. Even though many thrifts complained about the premium, saying that it hurt their ability to compete with banks for deposits, the total deposit insurance premium they paid was still less than the $^1/_4$ of 1 percent charged when the FSLIC started in 1934.

Unfortunately, FSLIC deposit insurance premiums were too low relative to the risks taken by insured institutions. In the early 1980s, many thrifts failed because they had taken on too much interest rate risk. In the mid-1980s (after the federal administration had reduced the number of savings-institution examiners), many thrifts failed because they had taken too many credit risks. Thus, as of December 31, 1987, the FSLIC had a negative net worth in excess of $13 billion. It could continue to operate only because people continued to accept FSLIC notes and guarantees that it would make future payments in lieu of cash when the FSLIC recapitalized bankrupt savings and loans. The FSLIC, in turn, hoped that Congress would stand behind its promises to make future payments—even though it had given out far more promises of that sort than it had assets.

The insolvency of the FSLIC was an embarrassment and caused many problems for Congress, for thrift institutions, and for the FSLIC itself. Congress did not want to raise taxes to repay the FSLIC's debts. Thrifts institutions did not want to pay higher deposit insurance premiums, and many tried to obtain FDIC insurance so that they could avoid doing so. The FSLIC was hurt because it could not afford to liquidate many insolvent and badly run thrift institutions. Therefore, it had to let them keep operating and keep generating losses that would eventually have to be paid out of the deposit insurance fund.

Because of its low reserves, from the early 1980s on, the FSLIC let thrifts engage in creative accounting to augment their reported income and asset values. This reduced the number of thrift failures but did not increase their cash flows. In addition, the FSLIC invented new ways to creatively finance the regulatory mergers and acquisition of troubled S&Ls. Net worth certificates were one such invention, approved by Congress in October 1982. Furthermore, rather than liquidate failing savings association, the FSLIC allowed them to operate with minimal capital or, if they became insolvent, merged several into a new association called a "phoenix" (after a bird in Greek mythology that arose from ashes), which was administered by the FHLBB.

Also, rather than immediately cover the full loss associated with a failing institution, the FSLIC arranged mergers and promised to pay the acquiring institution an annual amount to compensate for the fact that the acquired portfolio of low-rate mortgages would generate inadequate earnings in future years. In that way, it could make a stream of future payments rather than large current outlays that might jeopardize the liquidity of FSLIC itself. However, as these promises to pay accumulated, the FSLIC eventually became insolvent.

To help the thrift industry, the FHLBB supported the granting of more banking powers to savings associations. At the same time, it approved cross-state and cross-institution mergers to bail out failing savings and loans. The new thrift powers made the franchises of the failing thrifts worth more than before—particularly to commercial banks and out-of-state institutions. In essence, regulators simultaneously sold the thrifts' assets and the regulatory exemptions that let acquiring institutions establish interstate branches in fast-growing banking markets. For instance, Citicorp paid $143 million more than the next highest bidder to acquire Fidelity Savings in San Francisco in 1982. By so doing, Citicorp evaded restrictions against interstate banking that had previously prevented it from acquiring depository institutions in other states. Furthermore, when Citicorp's action was legalized by the Depository Institutions Act of 1982, Citicorp also gained the right to acquire failing savings association in other states —which it promptly did.

Nevertheless, the FSLIC's problems continued to grow. Because it could not afford to liquidate most weak thrifts, the FHLBB and Congress took a number of steps to lessen the FSLIC's problems. From 1984 through 1987, the FHLBB's examination and supervisory budget tripled, and, beginning in 1985, its supervisory and examination staff more than doubled. In 1985 the regulators adopted a "management consignment program" in which the bad management of weak thrift institutions was replaced by managers hired by the regulatory authorities. In that way, it was hoped that the management of weak thrifts would be strengthened and that fraudulent activities would be stopped.

Other steps taken to help the FSLIC were the formation of the Federal Asset Disposition Association (FADA) and the Financing Corporation (FICO). FADA was an institution designed to allow the FSLIC to dispose of assets acquired from failed savings associations, and FICO was established to provide liquidity for the FSLIC. It would sell bonds in the nation's capital markets, then loan most of the money to the FSLIC. The FSLIC, in turn, pledged to repay the interest on the loans by granting FICO first claim on the deposit insurance premium payments paid by institutions. The principal repayment for FICO bonds was guaranteed by investments in U.S. Treasury securities. FICO was able to borrow money to help fund the FSLIC, but because FICO's guarantees were not ironclad, it had to pay a much higher rate to borrow than the U.S. Treasury. Also, because of Congressional delays and possible vested interests, FICO was not authorized to start operations until the Competitive Equality in Banking Act (CEBA) was passed in 1987. Furthermore, FICO initially was allowed to borrow only $3.8 billion a year for three years. Thus, the FSLIC did not have enough funding available quickly enough to close all the problem savings institutions before their losses escalated, and the FSLIC became even more indebted.

The financial weaknesses of the federal insurance fund during the S&Ls' financial crisis in the 1980s had many effects. Most important, the fund's problems helped induce Congress to break down legislative distinctions between commercial banks and S&Ls and to reduce legislative restrictions against interstate banking activities. Ultimately, however, the fund's problems became so severe that it was abolished by the 1989 FIRRE Act. Its insurance activities were then given to the FDIC's newly created "Savings Association Insurance Fund" while its bad assets, bad savings and loans, and FADA and FICO operations were transferred to the newly formed Resolution Trust Corporation (RTC).

The Savings Association Insurance Fund (FDIC-SAIF).   The 1989 FIRRE Act replaced the FSLIC with the Savings Association Insurance Fund (SAIF). The new fund was placed under the jurisdiction of the FDIC rather than the thrift institution regulators. That way it was less subject to political influence and it could draw on the experience of the FDIC staff in supervising the insured institutions. Financially, however, the FDIC-SAIF fund was kept separate from the FDIC's Bank Insurance Fund. Also, SAIF's deposit insurance premium rates were initially higher at 0.23 percent, than the insurance premiums charged for commercial bank deposit insurance, at 0.15 percent.

PEOPLE
& EVENTS

High Living at CenTrust Bank

One of the problems caused when the S&Ls' deposit insurance fund ran low on funds in the early 1980s was that it became eager to sell weak S&Ls to the highest bidder—even if the bidder had a questionable background and put up dubious capital to pay for the acquisition. This happened in 1983 when Dade Savings Bank of Florida was sold to David Paul, a Connecticut real estate investor. The acquisition was structured roughly as follows:

	Dade Country Savings (in $ millions, before conversion)	CenTrust (in $ millions, post conversion)
Cash	$ 37	$ 37
Investments	144	144
Loans	1,933	1,408
Goodwill	(0)	525
Fixed assets	49	49
Real estate holdings	128	128
Real estate holdings provided by Paul		26
Total assets	$2,291	$2,317
Deposits	1,969	1,969
Borrowings and other liabilities	322	322
Total liabilities	$2,291	$2,291
Capital	(0)	$ 26

Source: Exhibit I of testimony by John E. Ryan and Maria I. Richmond, of the Office of Thrift Supervision before the House Banking, Finance, and Urban Affairs Committee, March 26, 1990.

The main features of the acquisition were that (1) loan values were written down from book value to market value and the difference was recorded as "goodwill" that could be amortized over 25 years and (2) Paul exchanged his stock in his "Westport Company, a real estate investment company," for stock in Dade County Savings, thus adding $26 million (the book value of the Westport Company's net worth) to the assets (real estate holdings) of the thrift and $26 million to its capital account. Thus, with no cash outlay, Paul was able to acquire a multibillion-dollar institution.

Furthermore, the acquisition was cheaper than it looked and the investor less well secured. In particular, the Home Loan Bank Board staff twice advised against the merger because (1) the value of Westport's real estate holdings was overstated, (2) Westport was already delinquent on major real estate loans to New England thrifts, and (3) the proposed management lacked thrift experience. Nonetheless, after Paul promised that he would supply more capital to the thrift later, the acquisition was approved in September 1983, and Dade County Savings became CenTrust (Savings) Bank.

Because 1/25 of the goodwill had to be charged off each year, CenTrust tried to "grow" more earnings quickly by offering high rates to attract brokered deposits, investing in high-yielding "junk" bonds, and engaging in "gains trading'" with mortgages and mortgage-backed securities. In gains trading, losing security positions are retained on a firm's books at book value and securities with gains are sold to record profits, thereby inflating stated earnings. To prevent future gains trading, regulators are now trying to force depository institutions to record assets at market values rather than book values, so the losses on securities held cannot be hidden. CenTrust also became associated with Michael Milken's junk bond transactions group at Drexel Burnham and frequently traded bonds with other members through Drexel. On some trades with Lincoln

continued

Savings (controlled by Charles Keating who, like Milken was later sentenced to jail) both CenTrust and Lincoln Savings reported income. Because of rapid asset growth, high reported profits, and the role of brokered deposits, CenTrust was able to nearly double its size to $4.7 billion in its first two years and quadrupled in size to nearly $10 billion in assets by the end of 1988. David Paul was even featured in a *Forbes* magazine article as a highly successful S&L executive.

However, the growth was built on sand, and the management was extracting huge amounts in salaries and perks from the thrift institution. Because of gains trading, over time subpar mortgage-backed assets accumulated on the thrift's balance sheet, and when Michael Milken was indicted and Drexel Burnham collapsed, the junk bond market also collapsed—further devastating the market value of CenTrust's assets.

Nonetheless, because of high reported profits the thrift spent lavishly on salary and perks for its CEO, David Paul. Thus, in 1989, in addition to purchasing a Reubens painting and other "old master" artworks for $29 million, plus Persian rugs, table linens, Baccarat crystal, gifts from Tiffany's, and a 40-foot sloop (costing in total over $0.5 million), which were often used or enjoyed by Paul or his family, the thrift also provided Paul with the following (as listed in Exhibit IV of the OTS testimony cited earlier):

Salary	$700,000
Bonuses	310,000
Life insurance payable to wife	257,783
Car allowance, cash	6,000
Chauffeured Mercedes-lease	26,000
Guard service at residence (annual)	142,947
Security system at residence (annual)	78,289
Phone service in residence and car (annual)	33,082
Corporate jet expense (primarily used by Paul) (annual)	1,364,616
Out-of-town limousine services	16,992
Total (annualized values)	$2,935,709

These facts were determined in the OTS examination of May 1989 and extrapolated to obtain annual rates. In addition, the examiners found that the thrift purchased numerous valuable items that were housed at Paul's residence.

But 1989 was the year that the thrift's fast trading came unwound. By the end of the year, CenTrust reported losses of $119 million (wiping out 41 percent of the gains reported in the previous five years). To prevent further losses and extravagant spending, on February 2, 1990, the OTC turned CenTrust over to the Resolution Trust Corporation, and on March 2, 1990, CenTrust was declared insolvent and placed into receivership.

The Federal Deposit Insurance Corporation Bank Insurance Fund (FDIC-BIF).   The FDIC-BIF is the primary regulator of federally insured savings banks. It examines them for soundness and compliance with federal regulations. Because its deposit insurance premium was lower than the insurance premium charged by the FSLIC and FDIC-SAIF, many savings institutions tried to obtain commercial bank or savings bank charters and switch to the FDIC bank insurance fund, but Congress placed a moratorium on such changes in the 1987 CEBA Act. Finally, in 1989, Congress passed the FIRRE Act, which placed both the bank insurance fund and the new savings association insurance fund under the jurisdiction of the FDIC. Transfers between funds were allowed only if institutions qualified and also paid "exit fees" to their old fund. This reduced the incentive to transfer.

The Resolution Trust Corporation.   The Resolution Trust Corporation (RTC) was established by the FIRRE Act of 1989 to assume responsibility for failed or merged savings associations from the FSLIC and to manage the assets of the Federal Asset Disposition Association. Thus it was the designated institution responsible for resolving the thrift institution failures of the 1980s. As such, it had substantial powers for supervising and directing the management of those savings institutions that continued to operate with federal assistance.

The RTC obtains funds to acquire the assets of failed savings and loans and to assist weak savings and loans from the Resolution Funding Corporation (RFC). The RFC in turn, obtains most of its funding by issuing government backed debt to the public. It also receives a portion of the deposit insurance premia paid by the insured savings associations and annual contributions from the Federal Home Loan Banks.

Because the RTC was set up to resolve past problems only (the SAIF handles new problems), the FIRRE Act required that it be liquidated within ten years (by 1999). The RTC basically makes good on the government's obligation to insured depositors of weak thrifts by taking over control of the institution and placing it into conservatorship, then either transferring the deposits to a healthy institution—via a sale of deposits or a (possibly assisted) merger—or by paying off the insured deposits directly. The RTC prefers to sell institutions or their deposits because other financial institutions will often pay a premium to acquire additional core deposits and larger branch structures. In the case of mergers, the acquiring institution will typically acquire high-quality assets of the failed institution, such as investment-grade securities, performing home mortgages, and performing consumer loans. However, the acquiring institution may not want to acquire all the failed institution's assets. Thus most mergers require RTC assistance in the sense that the RTC must provide guarantees against losses by questionable assets or retain, or agree to repurchase, questionable assets. If the RTC acquires questionable assets to make a merger more palatable to the acquiring institution, it will provide cash instead to cover the deposit liability assumed by the acquiring institution that exceeds the amount of assets acquired (see Exhibit 18–6).

When the RTC acquires and liquidates a failed savings association, or when it acquires questionable assets that the acquiring institution in an assisted merger does not want, it acquires assets that it must resolve. For instance, Exhibit 18–7 shows that the RTC was able to obtain nearly full value for the investment-grade securities, 1–4 family mortgages, and other high-quality assets that it disposed of in the first year and a half of its operation. Its asset disposals generated more cash to fund continuing operations of the RTC. However, the assets not sold quickly generally were the poorer-quality assets. Thus, Exhibit 18–7 also shows the expected returns available from resolution of its remaining assets as of May 31, 1991. Those estimated recovery rates are lower, ranging down to as little as 45 percent of book value on real estate owned. The losses could be even greater if the problems of Olympia and York put further downward pressure on prices in the commercial real estate markets in the 1990s.

The Federal Home Loan Mortgage Corporation.   The Federal Home Loan Mortgage Corporation (FHLMC—"Freddie Mac") initially was under the direction of the FHLBB. Formed in 1970 to help savings associations sell their mortgage loans, Freddie Mac buys many mortgages originated by savings associations for its own

Exhibit 18–7   RTC Recoveries and Expected Recoveries on Receivership Assets

	Assets Sold by May 31, 1991 (in $ Billions)	Recovery (%) on Assets Sold by May 31, 1991	RTC Remaining Assets as of Dec 31, 1990 (in $ Billions)	Estimated % Recovery for Remaining Assets*
Securities	$76	97%	$ 3.6	80%
1–4 family mortgages	43	98	15.5	85
Other mortgages	20	96	18.1	75
Other loans	14	96	6.1	65
Real estate owned	7	75	8.5	45
Other assets	7	96	6.4	55

*Note: Recoveries are before indirect expenses such as contractor fees, etc. Such fees lower the overall expected recovery as a percent of original book value to approximately 65 percent.

While the RTC initially obtained a high rate of recovery on liquidated assets, the poorer assets were held for later disposal, so estimated recoveries are much lower.

Source: RTC Briefing Materials, July 1991.

account. It also forms pools of such mortgages and swaps or sells participations in those pools to investors.

By buying mortgages from savings associations, Freddie Mac allows S&Ls to continue to make mortgage loans even if their liquidity was low during tight-money periods. It also let them profit from service charges paid on mortgages they originated and serviced but did not own. After 1989, FHLMC became a quasi-independent agency. While the president of the United States appointed five of its directors, the other 13 were elected by its stock-holders, including its savings association members.

Other Regulators

State Regulators.   State-chartered thrifts are subject to state laws and regulations. They are examined by state departments of financial institutions (or state banking commissioners' offices). If a thrift violates state laws, it may be prosecuted by the state attorney general's office. Many state regulations are more lenient than federal regulations. Thus federal regulators have tried to prevent thrifts from taking excessive risks by using loopholes in state laws. The FIRRE Act and FDIC Improvement Act eliminated the loopholes by requiring that federally insured, state-chartered institutions be subject to minimum restrictions similar to those imposed on federally chartered institutions. However, states can still require that state-chartered thrifts comply with laws more strict than federal laws.

The Federal Reserve Board.   The Federal Reserve does not regulate thrifts directly, but it has great influence on their activities. It writes implementing regulations for the Truth in Lending, Equal Credit Opportunity, Home Mortgage Disclosure, Community Reinvestment, and Electronic Funds Transfer acts—all of which materially affect thrifts. Also, in 1980 the DIDMCA gave the Fed authority to establish reserve requirements for thrifts' transactions deposits and nonpersonal time deposits. That act also required the Fed to allow thrift institutions to borrow from its discount window and use its payments services.

Regulations Affecting Thrifts

Taxes. Tax laws allow thrifts to exclude an 8 percent allowance for bad debts from their taxable income if they hold a sufficient percentage of their assets in real estate-related loans and other qualifying investments.

Asset Restrictions. Most thrifts may acquire only certain types of assets. Until 1980 these asset restrictions were quite severe. Then the DIDMCA and the 1982 Garn–St. Germain Act let thrifts acquire commercial paper and corporate debt securities, make consumer loans, issue credit cards, make limited commercial loans, write leases, and acquire state and local government securities. They also allowed thrifts to hold up to 30 percent of their assets in non-real estate loans and investments and up to 40 percent in commercial real estate loans. However, because many thrifts that failed in the late 1980s had abused their new powers, the FIRRE Act of 1989 reimposed substantial asset restrictions. That Act provided the most favorable regulatory treatment only to those institutions that held nearly 70 percent of their assets in approved forms such as secured real estate and consumer loans.

In many states, thrift institutions are subject to ceilings on the interest rates they can charge on various loans. However, the DIDMCA abolished states' mortgage rate ceilings unless they were reinstated by 1983. Rate ceilings still exist on consumer loans in some states, however.

Liability Restrictions. Before the mid-1960s, thrift institutions could not issue savings certificates. NOW accounts were legalized (nationwide) in 1980. However, in 1982 thrifts were given the power to issue demand deposits or noninterest-bearing NOW (NINOW) accounts to customers with whom they had a loan relationship and also to issue money market deposit accounts not subject to interest rate ceilings. From 1966 through 1982, thrifts were subject to Regulation Q restrictions that limited the interest rates they could pay on all their time and savings deposits. Because these deposit rate ceilings prevented thrifts from offering depositors competitive rates during high-interest-rate periods, thrifts often experienced problems from disintermediation as consumers withdrew their deposits. Consequently, deposit rate ceilings were phased out from 1980 to 1986.

Capital Adequacy Restrictions. Thrift institutions are required to hold sufficient net worth so that their savings depositors (and the regulatory institutions that insure their depositors) will not be adversely affected by fluctuations in earnings or asset values. Regulators want savings institutions to meet risk-based capital requirements and hold net worth equal to at least 3 percent of their assets, while the FDIC Improvement Act defines any institution with net worth below 2 percent of assets as critically undercapitalized. However, many thrifts have fallen far short of these requirements in recent years (see Exhibit 18–3).

Institutional Protection. Thrift institutions are protected by the examination process and rules of their regulators, which are designed to protect them from engaging in unsound practices or taking undue risks. State and federal chartering and regulatory agencies oversee adherence to branching, charter, and merger restrictions. Those regulations may be used either to prevent excessive, "destructive" competition in local markets or to reduce monopolistic concentration in financial markets.

Consumer Protection.   Many of the consumer protection regulations, such as the Equal Credit Opportunity, Community Reinvestment, Truth in Lending, and Real Estate Settlement Practices acts, are designed to protect consumers by ensuring them access to credit and informing them more fully about the costs of loan transactions. Most of these regulations are drafted by the Federal Reserve Board and enforced by federal regulatory agencies or examining authorities. Also, a number of states have regulations, enforced by state regulators, that are more strict than federal regulations. Because of complaints about possible lending discrimination, Congress made compliance requirements substantially more onerous for the Community Reinvestment Act when it enacted the 1991 FDIC Improvement Act.

State versus Federal Regulation.   To some extent, state and federal regulators have engaged in regulatory competition—since lenient laws may induce institutions to switch from state to federal charters or vice versa. However, federal regulations can often be made effective through deposit insurance requirements. In addition, federal laws have frequently overridden state laws that affect thrifts, such as those setting mortgage rate ceilings, prohibiting enforcement of due-on-sale clauses in mortgages, or prohibiting standards not approved by federal regulators.

Reasons for Regulations

Basically, regulation is designed to serve the public interest. Consumer protection regulations are designed to help unsophisticated consumers, and institutional regulations are meant to protect certain institutions and ensure that their services will continually be available. Institutional protection regulations, net worth regulations, and regulators' examinations reduce potential losses both to depositors and to federal or state institutions that insure financial institution deposits.

Regulations prohibiting nonmortgage loans were designed to protect banks and other local financial institutions from competition. Past geographic restrictions on asset acquisition were meant to guarantee a reflow of funds from local depositors to local borrowers and thereby benefit local economies. Similarly, requirements that eligible assets or (most) consumer loans be restricted to housing-related loans were designed to benefit housing construction.

Rate restrictions on savings were aimed at ensuring that relatively low-cost funds were available to thrift institutions. In this case, the small saver was victimized when market rates were higher than the rate ceiling but high personal transactions costs kept him or her from shifting funds. Liability restrictions, like asset restrictions, are designed to prevent thrift institutions from competing "excessively" in particular types of financial markets, such as corporate demand deposit markets.

Effects of Regulation

All of these regulations may have unintended as well as intended effects, and some of the former may subvert a regulations's stated purpose. Many regulations raise costs or require thrifts to invest in risky or relatively unprofitable ventures. Others induce thrifts to take risks by inadequately diversifying their assets or by mismatching the maturities of their assets and liabilities. Regulators traditionally felt free to impose on thrifts many regulations designed to serve public policy, especially housing policy, because they gave thrifts tax breaks and protection against competition. However, these regulations often caused problems for thrift institution managers. Many of the restrictions were removed in the early 1980s so that thrifts would have a better chance to survive.

Thrift Institution Accounting

The steep rise in interest rates in the early 1980s caused considerable problems for savings institutions. The rising rates substantially reduced the present value (market value) of their long-term assets and had little effect on the present value of their mainly short-term liabilities. Consequently, it was estimated that if thrifts had used market value accounting instead of book value accounting, they would have had to report a *negative* net worth of between $100 and $200 billion. Almost all thrifts would have had to be declared insolvent in 1980 if they had used market value accounting.

Clearly, the regulators had a major problem in the early 1980s. They could not possibly liquidate an entire industry—for several reasons. First, they did not have the financial resources to do so. The FSLIC had less than $8 billion in assets—a far cry from the $100 to $200 billion that would be required to liquidate all insolvent savings institutions and pay off their depositors in full. Second, the FSLIC did not have the staff needed to liquidate a large number of thrifts. In fact, H. Brent Beasley, the head of the FSLIC, said that throughout 1982 he had to limit S&L failures to three per week. If state regulators wanted to liquidate any more than that, Beasley had to tell the most recent callers to wait until he had the staff available to act on their requests.

One way the regulators could avoid liquidating thrift institutions was by allowing them to use clever accounting gimmicks that let them report their assets on a face value basis. They could justify such a treatment in theory because all long-term, 6 percent mortgages that did not default would eventually return the full face value of the loan amount due. Of course, a savings institution might not be able to sell a 6 percent mortgage in the market for more than half its face value when mortgage interest rates were 16 percent.

Letting thrifts report their assets on a face value basis when they were worth considerably less did not provide a long-term solution, however. Low-rate assets could not provide a return adequate to cover the high interest rates that had to be paid on high-rate, short-term liabilities. Thus the thrifts would report negative earnings that would have to be charged off against their net worth until their net worth was exhausted. Their only hope was to inflate their earnings and asset values artificially so that it would take longer to exhaust their net worth. Over time, perhaps, interest rates on their short-term liabilities would fall below the rates of return on their assets, and their earnings would turn positive again.

Thus thrift regulators allowed thrifts to use several accounting practices that inflated the value of both their earnings and assets in the short run—while they crossed their fingers and hoped that interest rates would eventually decline. The most important regulatory accounting conventions used in the 1980s are described in the following section. Most, however, were banned by the FIRRE and FDIC Improvement Acts, as Congress realized that thrift problems would not have become as severe if generally accepted accounting principles had been used.

Net Worth Augmenting Conventions

Book Value Accounting.   This type of accounting let thrifts report their assets at face value even though their market value, if sold immediately, might be far less. However, the FIRRE Act made thrifts value their investment securities at market value, and the FDIC Improvement Act suggested that an effort should be made to value all assets at market value. The purpose of market value accounting is to prevent gains trading (see People and Events) and the overstating of net worth through the overvaluation of assets.

Appraised Equity Capital Adjustments.   This regulatory accounting technique lets thrifts book as net worth a one-time accounting adjustment that recognizes that a thrift's physical assets (building and land) had appreciated from the face value at which they were initially purchased. Prior to the regulator's allowing this treatment, in the 1980s thrifts often sold their buildings (if they had risen in price) and leased them back so that they could report the capital gain in their earnings and net worth statements.

Income Capital Certificates.   After 1981, thrifts that were experiencing problems could issue income capital certificates to the FDIC or FSLIC in return for the agencies' promissory notes. These certificates were treated as capital and were added to the net worth of the institution that issued them. They were to be repaid out of the thrifts' future income when their "temporary" problems had been resolved.

Net Worth Certificates.   In 1982, the Garn–St. Germain Act authorized the FSLIC and FDIC to acquire net worth certificates from thrift institutions that were experiencing losses. A thrift could issue net worth certificates to compensate for a major portion of the operating losses that it had to write off against its net worth. The federal agencies would "buy" the certificates by issuing promissory notes that carried a similar rate of interest. Like income capital certificates, the net worth certificates were to be repaid when the thrifts had regained profitability.

Thrift Net Worth Calculations

The regulators have allowed thrifts to inflate their reported net worths in various ways. For instance, thrifts net worth based on generally accepted accounting principles (GAAP) equals preferred and common stock, paid-in surplus, reserves, undivided profits, and net undistributed income plus deferred net losses (or gains) on other assets sold. Even this accounting measure is somewhat overstated, as it lets thrifts include as assets both deferred losses on assets sold at a loss and goodwill. Thus "tangible capital" is computed after goodwill and certain other intangible assets are excluded from the balance sheet. Regulatory accounting principles (RAP) used by the FHLBB required no exclusions of assets. They also allowed thrifts to include as capital income capital certificates, net-worth certificates, appraised equity capital (based on the reappraisal of the value of fixed assets owned by the thrift), and qualifying subordinated debentures. The effect of the lenient accounting practices in 1987 can be seen in the fact that 520 FSLIC-insured thrifts were insolvent based on GAAP accounting and only 346 were insolvent based on RAP accounting at year-end. To improve the thrifts' accounting, the 1987 Competitive Equality in Banking Act (CEBA) required that thrifts eventually adopt GAAP rather than use RAP net worth accounting. Furthermore, in 1989, the Financial Institutions Reform, Recovery, and Enforcement Act expedited the shift to GAAP accounting and required that thrifts hold at least $1^1/_2$ percent in tangible capital (GAAP capital less goodwill) in 1990, and 3 percent by 1995, and the FDIC Improvement Act of 1991 mandated movement toward market value accounting.

Throughout the 1980s most thrifts would have been technically insolvent if market value accounting had been used and all problem loans had been written down. However, various researchers have noted that thrifts have intangible assets that do not show up on their balance sheet.[1] Chief among these are the values of their charters and their deposit insurance. As a result, thrifts may have positive market values even though they are technically insolvent. Thus, unless the hidden assets are also recognized, and the value of loyal core customers is taken into account, even market value accounting may give a misleading picture. The implementation of full market value accounting has been delayed for this reason, as well as in recognition that thrifts, as long as they are prudently managed, can be viable institutions even though they have very low ratios of net worth to assets.

Goodwill Accounting

Under "purchase accounting" conventions, when one institution purchases another institution for more than the market value of its assets less the value of its liabilities, it records the difference as an asset called *goodwill* on its balance sheet (see People and Events). However, the goodwill must be amortized by deducting a fraction of it from the acquiring firm's earnings and assets each year after acquisition. However, the reported "goodwill" mainly reflects the fact that the market value of low-rate mortgage loans is below their book value at the time of a thrift acquisition. As those mortgages are repaid or prepaid (the average mortgage has a life of 12 years or less), they typically are repaid at their book value before the goodwill is fully amortized. This allows the thrifts to report an increase in reported earnings in the short-run. The reported increase in earnings is fictitious; it resulted from a markdown of mortgage values from book to market value (recognized over a long period of time) combined with an accelerated markup (from market to book value) when the mortgages are repaid. However, it made reported earnings and book values of the thrifts that acquired others look better in the short run. For that reason, the FSLIC sometimes merged two or more failing thrifts even if no ultimate acquiring institution could be found. The resulting "phoenix" institution then reported more earnings and assets than it could have reported had no merger taken place. Eventually this loophole in purchase accounting was closed, since goodwill is not included in calculations of

---

[1]See, in particular, Edward Kane's article cited in the references to this chapter.

tangible capital, but the loophole was closed only after a number of thrifts had added a large amount of goodwill to their books. Consequently, the FIRRE Act allows thrifts to meet a portion of their 3 percent capital requirement with intangible capital until 1995.

Swaps

After interest rates rose in the early 1980s, weakened thrifts often found it hard to redeploy their assets to take advantage of new opportunities and higher rates. The reason was that they did not want to generate cash by selling their old mortgages at a loss, since a loss would reduce their earnings and further erode their fragile net worth. However, many thrifts needed cash. One way to obtain it was to sell mortgage-backed bonds (see Chapter 10), which collateralized bonds with mortgages. Such bonds were hard to sell, though, unless the thrifts posted mortgages worth 150 percent of the value of the bonds as collateral to insure the bonds against default. This limited the amount of funds they could obtain. Therefore, government-sponsored agencies (the Federal Home Loan Mortgage Corporation and the Federal National Mortgage Association) began to issue swap agreements to thrifts.

Swap agreements required that the thrifts pledge all income and principal payments on a pool of mortgages to the government agency. In turn, the agency would issue a "participation certificate" to the thrift that guaranteed to pass through all payments of principal and interest on the mortgages, minus a small fee or rate differential, to the holder. The thrift then would have nearly the same amount of mortgage principal and interest payments as before. However, because they were backed by a government agency, the participation certificates could be sold easily in the financial marketplace if the thrift needed cash. The participation certificates, unlike private mortgage-backed bonds, did not need to be overcollateralized. Furthermore, unlike the underlying mortgages, participation certificates could be sold without recording a loss. Thus these swaps let thrifts obtain cash without booking losses on their low-valued mortgages (since, technically, the thrifts had merely "pledged" interest and principal payments on the mortgages to the government agencies and had not "sold" them the mortgages).

Income Accounting Conventions

The most appropriate statement about thrift institution income-accounting conventions was made in 1985 by William F. Ford, president of a large California-based thrift (and a former president of the Federal Reserve Bank of Atlanta). He said that if sports contests were scored with rules similar to thrifts' income-accounting procedures, after the game was over, no one would know who had won.

The preceding sections noted several ways that thrifts and their regulators have overstated thrift income and asset values and avoided the reporting of losses. There are many others. For instance, for a while, the regulators let thrifts record loan origination fees as current income, thereby inflating their reported income even though the loan would not be repaid in full for many years. However, accountants now require that thrifts amortize their loan origination fees over the life of the loan. Also, thrifts can lend developers money in sufficient amounts to allow the developers to pay interest on their loans for substantial periods of time, even though a project is ultimately likely to default (as is likely with an office or apartment building that cannot attract enough tenants), but thrifts may not record the loss if timely interest payments are made. Finally, if a thrift should sell a loan at a loss, it could record "deferred loan losses" as an asset that will be written down over the original life of the loan. Thus, even though a loss was already realized when the mortgage was sold for less than its book value, only a small portion of that loss would be recognized immediately, and (like goodwill) the remainder could be charged off over a long period of time. In short, there were many ways that individual thrifts varied their recognition of income and losses to their benefit. Thus, the FIRRE and FDIC Improvement Acts now make them use net worth accounting procedures that are similar to those used by banks.

Thrifts' Interest Rate Risk Problem

Maturity Intermediation

Most thrift institutions (1) spread risk over a large number of assets, (2) spread costs of information acquisition and transactions over a large volume of transactions, and (3) pool funds to provide liquid liabilities to depositors while obtaining higher yields on less-liquid, longer-maturity assets. The last function has created major management problems for thrift institutions.

Thrifts historically have engaged in maturity intermediation by issuing short-term, liquid liabilities and buying longer-maturity assets—on which they ordinarily earn a higher rate. Such intermediation is possible because only a few depositors will want their money back at once. Thus thrift institutions can hold a low proportion of liquid assets and invest the balance of their assets in long-term securities or mortgages.

The typical yield curve (see Exhibit 18–8) slopes upward for longer-maturity assets. Investors are willing to pay a premium to avoid wide fluctuations in security values caused by interest rate changes. Since short-term asset values fluctuate less than long-term asset values, most investors pay a greater premium (accept a lower rate) on short-term than on long-term assets.

By using short-term liabilities, pooling the funds so obtained, and investing in long-term assets, thrift institutions traditionally profited by taking advantage of the yield curve spread. In the process they provided maturity intermediation to savers, since savers can usually retrieve a portion of the increased rate of return available to the thrifts.

Term Structure Inversions

The term structure is not stable; the yield curve may flatten or even invert. Inversions of the yield curve occur when investors expect interest rates to fall in the future—as they often do after rates rise sharply. If rates fall, investors will obtain capital gains plus interest returns on any long-term securities they hold. Holders of short-term obligations, however, will obtain only an interest return. Thus holders of short-term securities want higher interest payments than holders of long-term securities, with the exception that people who hold securities for very-short convenience needs may accept lower returns on highly liquid assets. When investors expect interest rates to

Exhibit 18–8   **Typical Term Structure of Interest Rates**

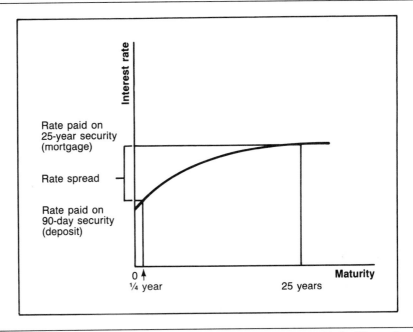

The term structure of interest rates usually slopes upward because savers with liquidity preference are willing to accept a lower rate of return on liquid assets. Thus, for many years, thrifts profited by issuing liquid liabilities to such savers, pooling their funds, and investing in long-term assets.

fall sharply, the term structure inverts. Interest rates are higher for short-maturity securities than for long-maturity obligations (see Exhibit 18-9)—with the possible exception that yields on highly liquid (very-short-term) securities may be held down by investors who need liquidity.

In the short run (as in the early 1980s), inversions of the yield curve can have a devastating effect on thrifts' earnings and operations. If a thrift tries to pay rates on its savings deposits that match other short-term interest rates, it will find itself paying rates that exceed the rates of return it can earn on its assets. Thus it will suffer losses. If a thrift tries to maintain its earnings by not raising its savings rates to stay in line with other short-term rates, it will lose deposits as savers withdraw their funds to earn higher returns elsewhere.

Disintermediation occurs when depositors take their funds out of a financial institution altogether to invest directly in securities with higher returns. Disintermediation reduces thrifts' liquid and total asset holdings. It may force them to stop making loans or to sell long-term assets, often at a loss, in order to obtain the cash needed to meet withdrawals.

Most managerial problems for thrift institutions in the early 1980s revolved around preventing or mitigating adverse consequences caused by fluctuating market interest rates and inverted interest-rate structures. Regulatory agencies tried to cushion the impact of interest rate increases and term structure inversions by letting thrifts use

Exhibit 18–9   **Inverted Term Structure**

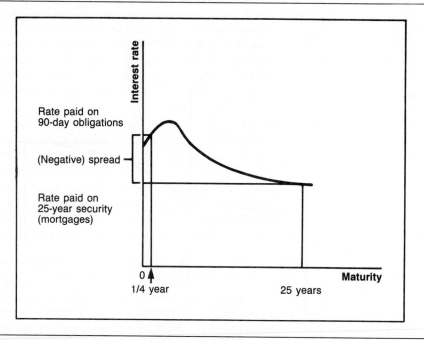

When current short-term interest rates are high and are expected to fall in the future, the term structure of interest rates will slope downward. At such times, long-term interest rates will be lower than short-term rates. Thus an institution that borrows short to fund long-term assets will lose money while short-term interest rates remain above long-term rates.

innovative accounting practices to hide their problems until, hopefully, interest rates fell once again.

Unexpected Secular Rises in Interest Rates

Rising interest rates hurt thrifts because the maturities of their assets and liabilities are not balanced. If all rates rise in step (that is , the whole yield curve moves up but does not change shape, as indicated in Exhibit 18–10), thrifts will suffer from maturity imbalance problems that cause their earnings to decline temporarily. Maturity imbalance problems hurt thrift earnings because rates on thrifts' short-term liabilities often increase quickly. As their liabilities mature, their owners will withdraw their funds and invest them elsewhere to earn higher returns, or, more likely, the thrifts will have to offer higher returns on them. However, because thrifts' low-interest mortgages will be repaid relatively slowly, particularly when interest rates are high, thrifts will not quickly obtain funds to invest in higher-rate mortgages. As a result, their usual spread between asset and liability rates will be reduced from the initial spread to the much smaller temporary spread shown in Exhibit 18–10.

Over time, as thrifts reinvest their funds in higher-rate mortgages, they can widen the rate spread between their assets and their liabilities. However, because of the long

Exhibit 18–10   General Rise in Term Structure

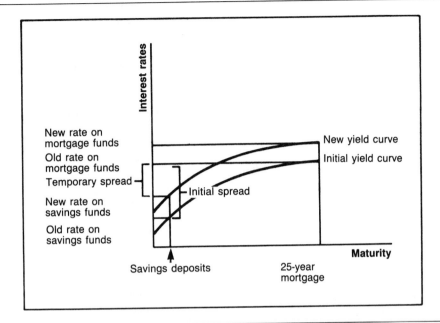

When the general level of interest rates rises, as occurs when people expect higher inflation, costs of short-term borrowings rise quickly. However, thrifts' returns on their fixed-rate, long-term assets will rise more slowly, because very few mature and can be reinvested in the short run. Over time, however, as thrifts' mortgages are repaid or prepaid, the funds thus freed can be reinvested at a higher rate. Consequently, unless rates continue to rise, thrifts eventually can become profitable again.

maturity of their mortgages and the short maturity of most of their liabilities, their earnings may be squeezed for quite a while after interest rates shift up. Furthermore, as interest rates rise, the market value of low-interest mortgages declines. Thus rising interest rates have an adverse effect on both thrifts' net earnings and the market value of their assets.

It should be noted that thrifts would benefit if all interest rates fell. In that event, thrifts would temporarily increase their earnings as their costs of funds would fall faster than the net return on their assets. Also, the market value of their assets (and their true net worth) would increase. However, if rates fell, thrifts might find that people would repay their high-rate mortgages faster and refinance their mortgage debt. If refinancing were extensive, as in 1986 and 1992, thrifts earnings would not rise greatly when rates fell.

Maturity imbalance problems arise when all interest rates rise evenly and unexpectedly. This can happen when people revise their inflation expectations upward—as often occurs during periods of rising inflation. Because interest rate problems can be severe, regulators now require that thrifts monitor their maturity GAPs. They even plan to require thrifts with greater maturity imbalances to operate with higher capital ratios—once they decide how to relate interest rate risk exposures to higher capital needs.

Credit-Risk Management

The second major problem contributing to thrift failures in the 1980s was credit risk. Credit risk causes loan defaults. In the 1980s thrifts' loan defaults developed for several reasons. First, some did not have expertise in the new areas of lending opened by the deregulation effects of the DIDMCA and Depository Institutions Acts. Thus they encountered losses in consumer and commercial lending because of a lack of expertise in evaluating such credits. For instance, consumer second-mortgage loans require much greater emphasis on an evaluation of the customer's creditworthiness (as measured by consumers' ability and willingness to repay their debts), and relatively less emphasis on valuation of underlying collateral for the loan, than a first mortgage loan. Also, while owner-occupied 1–4 family loans typically have relatively low default rates, commercial mortgage loans often are far riskier. Furthermore, while housing values rarely decline more than 20 percent or 25 percent in a short period of time (so 20 percent down payment conventional loans are relatively safe), commercial properties often fell in value by 30 percent, 40 percent, or even 50 percent in the late 1980s. Declining asset values eroded the value of the security backing many commercial loans and contributed to a high level of commercial loan defaults for both banks and thrifts in the late 1980s and early 1990s.

Inexperience in certain types of lending, overdependence on asset values as a determining factor in deciding when to make loans, and a lack of borrowers' personal liability on real estate construction and development loans made by certain S&Ls, all contributed to savings association loan defaults in the 1980s and early 1990s. Additional credit losses were caused by loans that should never have been made —such as loans made to risky borrowers by S&Ls that were hungry for profits and (under RAP accounting) could book high loan origination fees on risky loans into profits immediately. Many of those loans were made by troubled thrifts that were gambling to survive. Others were made by thrifts such as those run by fast operators (see Did You Know?, People and Events, and Chapter 17 on the Texas thrift failures). Because of inadequate loan prudence, the FIRRE and FDIC Improvement Acts required more frequent examination of thrifts coupled with stiff penalties for officers, directors, accountants, lawyers, appraisers, or consultants to thrifts engaged in wrong doing if any of those parties had approved of risky behavior.

Overall, credit-risk reduction requires that thrifts thoroughly scrutinize the creditworthiness of borrowers, accurately appraise the value of collateral, obtain adequate collateral for loans, and allow for unexpected adverse developments, that might reduce loan collateral values or borrower creditworthiness. It is interesting to note that the Group I (best) thrifts in 1990 tended to have more 1–4 family loans than other thrifts. In addition, as shown in Exhibit 18–3, they had fewer low-rated securities, fewer repossessed assets, and fewer nonperforming loans than the worse-performing thrifts. In other words, the best-performing thrifts at the end of the 1980s had stuck to markets they knew well and avoided credit risk.

Liquidity Risk

Thrifts have often had a problem with liquidity. In particular, before interest rate ceilings on deposits were removed, they often suffered from disintermediation when interest rates rose and depositors withdrew funds. As a result, at such times they had to stop making new loans and some had to sell assets (possibly at a loss) to meet depositor withdrawals. Deregulation of deposit rates has vastly improved that problem, however. So have other developments, such as the securitization of loans, access to FHL Bank advances or (for well-capitalized thrifts) access to the brokered deposit market.

Thrifts need to take some precautions to be sure that they will be able to handle potential liquidity problems, however. First, they need to make enough variable-rate loans or short-maturity loans so their interest revenues will rise if interest rates rise; they will thus be able to pay higher interest rates to attract or retain deposits at such times. Second, they also need to make sure that they meet "qualified mortgage lender" requirements and join a Federal Home Loan Bank so they will have access to Federal Home Loan Bank advances when they need them. Third, they must make sure that their mortgage loans regularly meet the underwriting standards of FHLMC, FNMA, or other entities that regularly purchase mortgages in the secondary markets. That way, if they need to sell the mortgages to obtain cash, they can do so. However, they must keep in mind that if market interest rates rise before they contract to sell the mortgages in the secondary market, they may have to do so at a loss. Nonetheless, they can make future profits by servicing mortgages that they have sold.

Management Trends and Developments

In response to previous troubles and new powers, major changes in management practices continue to occur in the thrift industry. In particular, many thrift institution managers are using interest rate futures and options as well as swap agreements to reduce interest rate risk (see Chapter 11). Some are taking advantage of new consumer and commercial loan and deposit powers. In addition, thrifts have merged at a rapid rate and have developed more joint ventures through their service and holding companies. Nevertheless, many thrifts continue to operate with low net worth positions.

Reductions in Interest Rate Risk

As previously noted, thrifts' major problems in the past have resulted from the maturity imbalance of their portfolios. This imbalance should be reduced in the future by policies designed to shorten the effective maturity of assets, increase the effective maturity of liabilities, and hedge interest rate risk in the futures market.

Reducing the Effective Maturity of Assets. The primary way that thrifts can reduce the effective maturity of their assets is by acquiring adjustable-rate rather than fixed-rate mortgages. From 1982 on, roughly half of thrifts' new mortgages have had adjustable rates. Since rates usually change on such mortgages every one to five years, their effective maturity is only one to five years. Thrifts that primarily make adjustable-rate mortgages will eventually reduce the imbalances in the effective maturities of their assets and liabilities. In addition, as thrifts make more consumer and commercial loans, they will further reduce the maturity of their assets.

Increasing the Effective Maturity of Liabilities.   If they wish, thrifts can increase the maturity of their liabilities by issuing mortgage-backed bonds or mortgage pass-through securities in the capital markets. Certificates of deposit also can lock in fixed-rate funds for several years—provided that early-withdrawal penalties are sufficiently high to prevent depositors from withdrawing funds before maturity. However, the new checking accounts, such as NOW accounts and money market deposit accounts, *increase* the interest rate sensitivity of deposit liabilities if the rates for these accounts change quickly when market interest rates change. Also, regulators reduced early-withdrawal penalties on certificates in 1983. Thus, in some ways, thrifts' liabilities have become more interest sensitive. Consequently, they must actively market more mortgage-backed bonds or pass-through securities—as they have done through their finance subsidiaries by issuing CMOs (see Chapter 10)—to reduce the imbalances in the effective maturities of their assets and liabilities.

Using Interest Rate Futures.   Savings associations may be able to neutralize some of their interest rate risk by using futures market instruments. For instance, a savings association that expected interest rates to rise might sell mortgage futures contracts. If rates rose, the contracts would fall in value and the institution could buy them back at a profit. At the same time, the value of the thrifts' existing mortgages would also fall. However, the profit on the futures could offset the loss in value of the thrifts' portfolio. It should be noted, though, that if interest rates fell instead of rising, the process would be reversed—the increase in the market value of the thrifts' mortgage holdings would be offset by a loss on the mortgage futures contracts—and the thrift would have to report the loss on the futures while it would still book its mortgages at face value.

Thrifts also can use interest rate futures to lock in their costs of funds for a short period. By selling T-bill futures, a thrift can guarantee its costs of funds from the issuance of CDs for a year or two into the future. If interest rates rise in the interim, the profit on the futures (which will fall) will offset the higher interest rates paid to depositors. Conversely, if interest rates fell, the futures would rise in price and the thrift would lose on that transaction—but that loss would be offset because the costs of borrowed funds would be lower than expected. By locking in its cost of funds, a thrift can guarantee a fixed loan rate to a potential customer. See Chapter 11 for more details.

Use of New Financial Powers

Consumer Financial Services.   The new powers given thrifts in the DIDMCA of 1980 and the Garn–St. Germain Act of 1982 allowed them to become full-service consumer financial institutions and compete with the money market funds. By combining those powers with their traditional mortgage lending, many thrifts have tried to become full-service financial institutions. They have expanded their consumer loan capabilities, have added trust departments and drive-in deposit services, and have joined ATM and credit card networks. Thus, thrifts now are able to offer full retail-banking services and can be formidable competitors to commercial banks for consumer services.

Commercial Lending.   Thrift institutions are limited in their ability to acquire commercial loans. They cannot devote more than 10 percent of their assets to unrestricted commercial lending. By making loans to finance commercial real estate or dealer holdings of consumer durable goods, however, savings associations could extend some additional loans to their commercial borrowers. Yet, because of legal restrictions, it might not pay them individually to acquire general commercial lending expertise. Furthermore, their individual abilities to extend large lines of credit may be limited. Some S&Ls have avoided these problems by forming cooperative syndicates and service companies in which a large number of S&Ls participate to originate and service corporate loans. By making variable-rate loans with maturities longer than bank financing, they have been able to offer attractive financing to corporate borrowers.

Mergers and Holding Companies

As savings associations develop more specialized expertise—in consumer and commercial lending, asset and liability maturity matching, and other specialized areas —they may be able to share overhead costs by merging into larger organizations. In addition, mergers can let them obtain geographic diversity or shore up eroded net worth.

Service companies are corporations in which thrifts can own stock and which provide financial services for them. In the past, thrift service companies have acted as data processors, bookkeepers, and mortgage bankers, and they have originated consumer loans. The Garn–St. Germain Act of 1982 gave the thrifts many additional powers that they could implement through their service corporations. Thrifts, therefore, may increasingly use these corporations to exploit their new powers.

Multi-S&L holding companies are restricted in their activities by regulator's rulings. However, in contrast to one-bank holding companies, one-S&L holding companies (such as Ford Motor Company) have not been restricted in their activities. Thus acquisition of stock S&Ls has been a popular way for nonbank institutions and even private investors to acquire de facto banking capabilities. Bank holding companies have also acquired ailing thrifts in different parts of the country. Because of the thrifts' recent difficulties and new powers, more S&Ls are likely to be acquired by holding companies in the future. At the end of 1988, many of the largest savings and loan holding companies in the nation were controlled by commercial banks (Citicorp), commercial businesses (Ford Motor), or private investors (the Bass brothers of Fort Worth, Texas).

Insurance and Insolvency

Thrift institutions have substantial insolvency risk because they have small net worth and rate-sensitive assets. They can reduce their risk by selling stock, retaining earnings, and otherwise increasing capital. They can also reduce their interest rate risk by matching the maturities of their assets and liabilities.

Actions taken to reduce risk, however, could reduce thrifts' leverage and their ability to earn a high return on assets (particularly if interest rates fell). Furthermore, Kane argues that such actions would not reduce their overall risk materially, because the deposit insurance institutions have effectively underwritten their risk.[2] Thrifts know that the FDIC-SAIF does not want them to fail and therefore regulatory agencies will make loans, buy capital certificates, and take other actions to maintain their solvency. Thus Kane argues that thrifts take more risk than would be the case if the insurers' safety net did not exist, and that thrifts will not reduce their risk substantially as long as they know their insurers will stand behind them. However, the FDICIA of 1991 tried to reduce the value of this implied safety net by requiring that critically undercapitalized thrifts be promptly closed and liquidated in the least costly manner.

Thrifts' risk-taking propensities were particularly apparent in the behavior of the failed Texas thrifts (see Did You Know? and the Short and Gunther reference). Rapid growth funded with the issuance of insured deposits and excessive risk taking in commercial lending activities contributed to the failure of many thrifts in the late 1980s.

Summary

Mortgage-oriented thrift institutions came into existence in the early 1800s to serve portions of the financial markets that commercial banks ignored. Mutual savings banks provided an outlet for small savers. Savings and loan associations specialized in housing construction finance, and since the 1930s they have grown rapidly in conjunction with growing housing markets. They have benefited from political support but also have been highly regulated at both the federal and state levels. At times, their asset and liability composition and rates have been highly restricted. In addition, they are subject to many consumer protection, institutional protection, and branching and merger restrictions.

The balance sheets of the major thrift institutions are similar. They obtain most of their funds from savings deposits and certificates and predominantly make real estate-related loans. Tax laws and regulatory restrictions impose limitations on their financial flexibility. Most thrifts are mutual institutions and hold small amounts of net worth relative to their total assets.

Thrift institutions experience major management problems at times because of the imbalance between the maturity structure of their assets and liabilities. These problems have been particularly severe from the mid-1960s on. Numerous thrifts failed in the early 1980s. As a consequence, thrifts gained extensive new powers in commercial and consumer lending, new transactions deposit accounts, and the power to make variable-rate mortgages. In addition, rate ceilings on deposits and mortgage loans were phased out or removed. The surviving thrifts have many new opportunities

---

[2]See references (this chapter).

and new powers. They are more valuable as merger candidates than before, and they can provide substantial competition for other financial institutions in the future. However, some thrifts have abused their new powers and have taken excessive risks. Self-dealing and fraud, made possible by inadequate federal examinations, have contributed to other thrift problems. Thus another large group of thrifts failed in the late 1980s. These failures jeopardized the thrifts' insurance fund and the viability of healthy thrifts. Consequently, the regulatory structure for thrifts has been materially altered—with new regulators (the OTS, FDIC-SAIF, and RTC), new accounting requirements and capital requirements (GAAP accounting, minimum tangible capital and risk-based capital requirements, and potentially, market value accounting), and new early-closure and enforcement rules (which subject managers, directors, appraisers, accountants, auditors, and others to substantial penalties if wrong doing occurs). Nonetheless, the bill for the 1980s failures is still being paid by the RTC and, in turn, the nation's taxpayers.

Management challenges for thrifts are many, but as long as they avoid taking excess liquidity, credit, or interest rate risk, and maintain adequate capital, they should be able to survive and prosper. Nonetheless, financial crises for the thrifts will recur if they rely on their regulators to underwrite their risks.

Questions

1. Why did thrift institutions receive favorable treatment from their regulators in the 1980's? What regulatory favors had unintended adverse effects on thrifts? Why?
2. What were the two major types of problems that caused thrift failures during the 1980s?
3. How did regulatory weakness contribute to some of the thrifts' problems?
4. Where do thrift institutions obtain most of their funds? What assets do they acquire?
5. What new types of assets are thrifts likely to acquire more frequently in the future? Why?
6. What changes in market interest rates can hurt thrifts? Why? What can thrifts do to minimize their problems? Explain what kind of market interest rate changes might help thrifts.
7. Explain how thrifts can control their credit risk and their liquidity risk.
8. What new types of liabilities have thrifts offered in recent years? Why?
9. What are (a) the major regulations and (b) the major regulatory bodies that affect thrift operations? How do these regulations and regulatory bodies affect them?
10. What is moral hazard? How has it been caused by government insurance and regulatory practices?

Selected References

Barth, James R., and Michael G. Bradley. "Thrift Deregulation and Federal Deposit Insurance." Federal Home Loan Bank Board, Office of Policy and Economic Research, Research Paper #150, November 1988.

This paper provides an excellent summary of regulatory changes, the recent history of the thrift industry, and the financial position of both solvent and insolvent thrifts. It notes that a thrift institution's charter is valuable even if the thrift is technically insolvent.

Dunham, Constance R. "Mutual to Stock Conversion by Thrifts: Implications for Soundness." *New England Economic Review*. **Federal Reserve Bank of Boston, January–February 1985, pp. 31–45.**

An excellent description of the process and the pros and cons involved when thrifts convert from mutual form to stock form.

Federal Home Loan Bank of San Francisco. *Managing Interest Rate Risk in the Thrift Industry.* **Proceedings of the 7th annual conference of the FHLB of San Francisco, December 1981.**

Many excellent papers on interest rate risk management by savings associations, including three on futures markets (see Chapter 11 references).

Kane, Edward J. "The Role of Government in the Thrift Industry's Net Worth Crisis." In *Financial Services: The Changing Institutions and Government Policy*, **ed. George Benston. Englewood Cliffs, NJ: Prentice-Hall, 1983.**

A thought-provoking and interesting study that provides useful background on the regulation and development of the thrift institutions—and the perverse incentives provided by deposit insurance.

Mahoney, Patrick I., and Alice P. White. "The Thrift Industry in Transition." *Federal Reserve Bulletin*, **March 1985, pp. 137–156.**

The authors of this article analyze the thrift industry's response to the trying economic times of the early 1980s and the ensuing major reductions in federal regulatory restrictions. Among other things, they find that traditional passbook accounts have declined greatly as a source of funds for thrifts but that most continue to make mortgage loans. Consumer and commercial lending is undertaken in quantity by only a few thrifts, but most have enthusiastically acquired adjustable-rate mortgages. The study also finds that the industry still has a weak capital structure and that many institutions are receiving substantial assistance from regulators.

Moore, Robert R. "Brokered Deposits and Thrift Institutions." *Financial Industry Studies Working Paper No. 1–92*, **Federal Reserve Bank of Dallas, March, 1992.**

This working paper points out that brokered deposit usage tends to be higher for thrifts with low capital/asset ratios, high asset risk, low net income, and large size. Thus, it appears that brokered deposits have been used to exploit the shortcomings of the deposit insurance system and to let high-risk thrifts expand more than would otherwise be the case.

Office of Thrift Supervision, *NEWS*, **Quarterly Publications, Washington DC.**

News releases of the OTS provide detailed information on thrift balance sheets and income statements on a monthly and quarterly basis.

Office of Thrift Supervision, *Combined Financial Statements. SAIF insured Associations,* **Washington, DC, annual.**

These reports provide detailed data on thrifts' balance sheets and income statements on an aggregate basis. Data are subdivided by institution size, district, state, and charter.

Ryan, John E., and Maria I. Richmond, Statement before the Committee on Banking, Finance, and Urban Affairs, U.S. House of Representatives, Office of Thrift Supervision, Washington DC, March 26, 1990.

This testimony by the director and deputy director of the OTS Atlanta District provides extensive details on the acquisition, operations, and subsequent failure of CenTrust Savings in Miami.

Short, Genie D., and Jeffrey W. Gunther. "The Texas Thrift Situation: Implications for the Texas Financial Industry." Federal Reserve Bank of Dallas Financial Studies Department, September 1988.

Examines the healthy and unhealthy Texas thrifts and notes that part of the problem resulted from moral hazard coupled with 100 percent deposit guarantees and federal assistance to recapitalize failed financial institutions.

U.S. League of Savings Associations, *88 Savings Institutions Sourcebook*, **annual.**
This annual publication provides excellent statistical data on all major thrift institution activities. It also provides a useful summary of applicable regulations.

White, Lawrence J. *The S&L Debacle.* **New York: Oxford University Press, 1991.**
This paperback book was written by a professor who served on the Federal Home Loan Bank Board from November 1986 to August 1989. It provides an insider's view of the S&L debacle from an academic perspective, including regulatory accounting problems, regulatory scrutiny problems, deposit insurance problems, and insider abuses. The author illustrates his points with examples and proposes reforms including: market value accounting, net worth (capital) requirements, risk-based insurance premiums, prompt disposal and early-intervention policies for weak institutions, expanded use of long-term subordinated debt, restrictions on allowable activities for thrifts, and numerous other policies. Many of the author's recommendations were incorporated in the FDIC Improvement Act passed late in 1991.

CREDIT UNIONS

19

CREDIT UNIONS ARE UNIQUE AMONG financial institutions in that they operate much like a club. Their members each have an equal voice in the selection of the credit union's board of directors. Each member has one vote, regardless of whether he or she has large or small amounts of savings with the credit union or whether he or she is primarily a borrower or a saver at the credit union. Because of their clublike nature, credit unions are generally treated as nonprofit institutions, and their earnings are exempt from federal income taxes. They also receive valuable exemptions from antitrust laws that allow them to form extensive cooperative ventures. Credit unions are not exempt from regulation, however. They are supervised and regulated by their chartering and insuring agencies. In addition, each credit union has a common-bond requirement, which, like club membership rules, defines who is eligible to be a member.

Credit unions' common bond can be narrowly defined, such as all people who work for the same employer, or broadly defined, such as all people who live in the same county. Because of the common-bond restriction, most credit unions are very small—over one-half have less than $10 million in assets each. Many others, however, such as the Navy Federal Credit Union, with close to $5 billion in assets, are larger than most banks.

The numerous small credit unions lack internal economies of scale, which could have an adverse effect on their ability to survive. However, their tax advantages and freedom from antitrust restrictions allow them to reduce their costs. The freedom from antitrust restrictions has allowed them to develop extensive cooperative arrangements so that they can share the overhead costs needed to develop specialized financial services. In addition, to let credit unions diversify and obtain economies of scale, regulators have relaxed the common-bond restrictions by letting family members and "associate" groups join or merge with credit unions.

The credit union movement has been aided substantially by its strong trade associations, which have initiated many useful cooperative ventures on both state and national levels. These have provided an essential means by which credit unions can obtain specialized services at a reasonable cost. Credit union trade associations have even developed their own central credit union, which allows them to function much like branches of a large national bank.

This chapter discusses the history and nature of credit unions, their assets and liabilities, cooperative arrangements among them, credit union regulation, and management problems and developments.

Nature and History of Credit Unions

Credit unions are small, nonprofit savings and lending institutions whose stated purposes are to encourage thrift and provide relatively inexpensive consumer credit to their members. To apply for membership, an individual must provide personal information to ensure that he or she meets the common-bond requirement and must purchase initial shares worth $5 to $10 in the credit union. A member is entitled to all financial services offered, and each member has an equal vote in the election of the credit unions' directors.

Credit unions originated in Germany in the nineteenth century. They were organized to let people pool their resources, make loans to one another, and promote thriftiness. Their goals were humanitarian in that they tried to help the average person who did not have access to other financial institutions. The first credit union in the United States was organized in 1909 in New England. In the early 1920s, Edward A. Filene, a Boston merchant and philanthropist, organized the Credit Union National Extension Bureau (CUNEB) in Boston to promote and spread the credit union movement. The bureau was formed to (1) lobby for laws allowing credit unions in all states, (2) promote the establishment of individual credit unions, and (3) form a national organization of credit unions to assume the work of CUNEB. In the next decade, credit union laws were adopted by 38 states and the District of Columbia, and CUNEB was converted to the Credit Union National Association (CUNA). Today CUNA is the major trade association for credit unions.

In 1934 the Federal Credit Union Act was passed, allowing federally chartered credit unions in all states. At that time there were only 2,500 credit unions in the United States, with a total membership of 450,000. Since then, credit unions have grown rapidly. By the early 1970s there were over 22,000 credit unions. Since then, they have consolidated and their number has declined, but their membership has increased (see Exhibit 19-1). In 1990 there were approximately 14,500 credit unions; federally insured credit unions accounted for 12,860 of those, with 56 million members and $200 billion in assets.

Credit unions emerged because they filled an unmet need. At the turn of the century, commercial banks did not provide consumer credit or accept small savings deposits. In addition, many states had unrealistically low usury laws that denied consumers access to legitimate cash credit. To meet the demand for consumer financial services and help move their merchandise, some large department stores sold on credit and began to accept and pay interest on customers' deposits. Many employers performed similar banking services for their employees. Employees recognized that the establishment of a convenient banking-type facility would make it easier for workers to conduct their financial affairs, thereby reducing absenteeism. Thus consumer-oriented thrift institutions emerged to meet the needs of small savers.

Exhibit 19–1   Credit Unions Tripled Their Loans and Shares During the 1980s

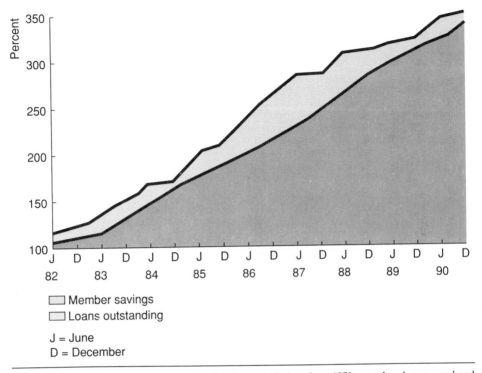

Even though the number of credit unions has been declining since 1970, as relaxed common-bond requirements have allowed mergers, credit union loans and share deposits have grown sharply in value since 1983 when additional loosening of common bond requirements let individual credit unions merge and grow in order to gain efficiency and diversification.

Source: National Credit Union Administration, *1990 Annual Report*.

Common-Bond Requirements

The common-bond requirement is one of the most important concepts of the credit union movement. Federal law provides that credit unions' membership shall be limited to groups having a common bond of occupation or association or to groups within well-defined neighborhoods, communities, or rural districts. The most frequent type of common bond applies to employees of a similar occupation; such occupational credit unions make up 85 percent of the total. Associational credit unions, based on such common bonds as members' union, religious, or professional affiliation, account for 8 percent, whereas residential credit unions make up 7 percent of all credit unions. However, associational credit unions account for a much smaller share of assets than their number might indicate. Thus, occupational credit unions control 87 percent of credit union assets, whereas residential credit unions have recently grown rapidly and now hold a larger share of credit union assets (8 percent) than associational credit unions (see Exhibit 19–2).

Exhibit 19–2   **Credit Unions by Type of Membership**

		Percentage of All Credit Unions	Percentage of All Credit Union Members	Percentage of All Credit Union Assets
Occupational	1990	85.2%	84.9%	87.1%
	1987	78.1	84.3	87.3
	1984	78.4	84.8	87.9
Associational	1990	7.9	6.8	5.3
	1987	16.2	8.4	5.9
	1984	16.6	9.7	6.9
Residential	1990	6.9	8.3	7.6
	1987	5.7	7.3	6.8
	1984	5.0	5.4	5.2

Most credit unions have an occupational common bond. However, residential credit unions have grown in recent years, while associational credit unions have shrunk. In addition, many nonresidential credit unions have extended their common bond to family members, other associational groups, and retirees.

Sources: 1984 data—Credit Union National Association, *1984 Credit Union Report*, reprinted with permission; 1987 data—National Credit Union Administration, *1987 Midyear Statistics for Federally Insured Credit Unions* (Washington, DC, 1987) and *1990 Yearend Statistics for Federally-Insured Credit Unions*.

Congressional intent has always emphasized a well-defined common bond; however, in recent years, federal and state regulatory agencies have liberalized the requirement. Residential credit unions have been allowed in urban areas, not just in rural communities. Such occupational entities as shopping centers and office buildings have formed credit unions. Also, large occupational credit unions have been allowed to merge with small, nonrelated credit unions, retiree associations, or other groups to diversify and reduce the risk involved in granting loans to all individuals employed by a single employer. Finally, credit unions are allowed to have "once a member, always a member" rules and rules that allow all individuals in a member's family to join. In general, larger credit unions tend to have more liberal membership requirements.

State statutes generally have the same requirements for chartering as federal regulations, although there are some exceptions, particularly with regard to whether or not residential credit unions are permitted in urban areas.

Size of Credit Unions

In part because many credit unions' growth potential is limited by the restrictive nature of their common-bond requirements, many remain small. Exhibit 19-3 provides details on credit unions' size distribution. As can be seen, in 1990, three-quarters of all credit unions had less than $10 million in assets, and only 3 percent had more than $100 million in assets. In spite of the small size of most credit unions, the very largest of them equal good-sized banks. Five or ten have more than $1 billion in assets.

Exhibit 19–3

Size Distribution and Operating Characteristics of Federally Insured Credit Unions (December 31, 1990)

A. Size distribution of credit unions

Asset size of credit unions	Under $500,000	$500,000 to $2 million	$2 million to $10 million	$10 million to $50 million	$50 million to $100 million	Over $100 million	Total
Total (number of credit unions)	2,295	3,232	4,160	2,376	415	382	12,860
Total (%)	17.8	25.1	32.3	18.5	3.2	3.0	100
Cumulative total (%)	17.8	43.0	75.3	93.8	97.0	100	100

B. Federally Insured Credit Unions' Income and Operating Expense as a Percent of Assets (1990)

Asset size of credit unions	Under $500,000	$500,000 to $2 million	$2 million to $10 million	$10 million to $50 million	$50 million to $100 million	Over $100 million	All Federally Insured Credit Unions
Gross income	10.76%	10.77%	10.50%	10.31%	10.27%	10.00%	10.19%
− Operating Expenses	5.40%	4.72%	4.14%	3.86%	3.76%	3.24%	3.60%
− Cost of Funds	4.39%	5.16%	5.49%	5.65%	5.72%	5.91%	5.75%
+ Nonoperating gains(−losses)	0.02%	0.02%	0.00%	0.01%	0.01%	0.02%	0.01%
= Addition to net worth (reserves + surplus) (ROAe)	1.00%	0.91%	0.88%	0.81%	0.80%	0.88%	0.85%

Most credit unions are very small; note that over 75 percent have under $10 million in assets, but the large ones dominate overall dollar statistics. Small credit unions have substantially higher operating expenses per dollar of assets than larger credit unions. As a result, they tend to charge higher rates on loans or fees on deposits to increase revenues as a percent of assets. They also tend to pay out lower dividend rates to shareholders than most of the larger credit unions. ROAe = return on assets estimate.

Source: National Credit Union Administration, *1990 Statistics for Federally Insured Credit Unions.*

Credit Union Ownership

Technically, credit unions are owned by their members. Thus funds deposited in credit unions are termed *shares* rather than deposits. Instead of interest payments, members receive dividends on their shares. As is the case with stockholders in a corporation, dividends are not guaranteed, and *uninsured* shareholders are exposed to a risk of loss if a credit union must liquidate. As a result, share insurance is highly valuable to credit union members.

DID YOU KNOW?

The Common Bond Isn't What it Used to Be

For many years, most U.S. credit unions provided financial services only to members who met a narrowly defined common bond, such as all people who worked for the same employer. However, this bond has weakened dramatically in recent years. First, the federal government became more favorably disposed toward chartering community credit unions, especially low-income credit unions, to achieve social goals. Then, regulators gradually relaxed common-bond requirements so that credit unions could obtain economies of scale by serving larger groups, such as family members who lived in the same house, former members, and retirees. Finally, because many individual firms failed in the dual recessions of the early 1980s, thereby jeopardizing the survival of credit unions that served the workers of those firms, the NCUA substantially relaxed common-bond restrictions to promote diversification and aid credit union growth and survival. Major changes that it made in 1982, 1983, and 1984 included the following: (1) Allowing credit unions to define a "family member" as any person related to a person who shared the common bond (credit unions could impose their own limits on how much "family" to accept); (2) allowing credit unions to diversify their membership base by serving nearby employee or associational groups that requested credit union service; and (3) encouraging retiree groups to join credit unions. Because of these changes, over 7,000 associated groups (potentially 3 million members) joined credit unions in 1983. After stagnating in 1981 and 1982, credit unions' assets grew rapidly from 1983 on. However, the number of credit unions declined.

Credit unions are run by managers appointed by their boards of directors. Directors are elected by the members according to a "one-person, one-vote" rule. No proxy votes are allowed, and people do not receive extra votes if they hold more shares.

Like other depository institutions, credit unions must please their customers or they will lose them and their loan business and deposits. Unlike other depository institutions, dissatisfied members can band together and vote in a new board of directors and new management. This fact makes credit unions highly responsive to members' wants and needs.

Credit Unions' Assets

Compared to other financial institutions, credit unions have a relatively simple balance sheet. Almost all of their assets consist of loans to members or investments, and almost all liabilities consist of members' savings deposits. A consolidated balance sheet for credit unions is presented in Exhibit 19–4.

Exhibit 19–4   Consolidated Federally Insured Credit Union Balance Sheet (December 31, 1990)

Assets (percentage)			Liabilities and Net Worth (percentage)		
Cash		2.2%	Savings shares		90.8%
Investments		31.2	Share drafts	8.8%	
U.S. government and agency			Share certificates	19.9	
securities	9.9%		IRAs	13.2	
Deposits in banks and S&Ls	14.2		Other savings	48.9	
Deposits (shares) in credit			Borrowings, accounts payable,		
union centrals	6.0		and dividends payable		1.6
Other	4.4		Reserves and undivided earnings		
Loans		63.6	(net worth)		7.6
New auto loans	14.8				
Used auto loans	6.6				
First and second mortgages	21.9				
Other loans	20.9				
Loan loss reserve	0.6				
Fixed and other assets		3.0			
Total		100.0%	Total		100.0%

Credit unions obtain most of their funds from regular (passbook) savings accounts and invest most of the funds in loans to members. Excess funds are invested in government securities, deposits at other financial institutions, and deposits with central credit unions.

Source: National Credit Union Administration, *1990 Yearend Statistics for Federally Insured Credit Unions* (Washington, DC, 1991).

Loans

Loans to credit union members comprise three-fifths of total credit union assets. Traditionally, these have been small, short-term consumer installment loans used either to purchase automobiles or for personal or family expenses. In recent years, however, credit unions have made an increasing number of relatively large first and second mortgage loans and new car loans.

Credit unions have increased their share of the consumer installment loan market substantially since 1950. They now are the third most important source of consumer credit. Most of their loan growth has come at the expense of higher-rate lenders, such as retailers and finance companies. Because of their emphasis on meeting consumers' personal loan needs, in 1990, the average loan outstanding at credit unions had a $4,375 balance due.

With relaxed regulations in recent years, an increasing number of the larger credit unions have made mortgage loans. Even though home equity provides good loan security, most credit unions are reluctant to hold many mortgage loans. This is because credit unions' liabilities are predominantly short-term in nature, and fixed-rate, long-term mortgages expose them to interest rate risk. As a result, many credit unions originate first mortgage loans only through mortgage bankers, who arrange to sell the mortgages to others. CUNAmortgage is a mortgage banking firm that specializes in serving credit union members. The NCUA has encouraged credit unions to avoid making fixed-rate mortgage loans that cannot be sold in the mortgage markets because it does not want credit unions to take on too much interest rate risk.

Loan Rates and Ceilings.   Loan rates that credit unions can charge were severely restricted for many years. Federally chartered credit unions could charge no more than 12 percent on any loan, and many state-chartered credit unions were subject to similar restrictions. In March 1980, the DIDMCA raised the statutory loan rate ceiling to 15 percent and, more importantly, allowed the National Credit Union Administration (NCUA) Board to permit still higher rates if it deemed them necessary. Because market interest rates were high and the NCUA did not want to limit credit unions' ability to offer loans that were risky or expensive to service, it authorized a loan ceiling of 21 percent. That ceiling has been renewed periodically. However, credit unions typically charge much lower rates. In 1990, credit unions charged an average rate of 11.24 percent on new car loans and 14.89 percent on unsecured personal loans before interest rebates.

Delinquency Rates and Losses.   Delinquency rates on credit union loans are generally low because of their close ties to their borrowers. Fewer than 2 percent of credit union loans were delinquent 60 days or more. Furthermore, loss rates have been quite low. Federally chartered credit unions have charged off only about 0.4 percent on all loans made since their origin. This is lower than the charge-off rate on consumer loans for most banks and far lower than that for finance companies.

Because of the common-bond nature of credit unions, they frequently work with delinquent debtors for many months, sometimes even years, before they charge off a debt. This increases the number of delinquent loans but defers, and may eventually reduce, the amount of loans charged off.

Other Assets

Cash.   Credit unions hold a small amount of vault cash in order to serve their members' cash-withdrawal requests. In addition, since passage of the DIDMCA of 1980, the larger credit unions have been required to hold idle reserves to back their transactions deposits. Their reserve requirements can be met by holding vault cash or by directly or indirectly depositing funds at the Federal Reserve. At year-end 1990, credit unions' cash holdings were 2.2 percent of assets.

Investments.   Credit union investments often consist of short-term, highly liquid assets, providing a secondary liquidity reserve. If deposit flows are high and loan demand low, credit unions may use their excess funds to acquire additional investments. Conversely, if loan demand is high and deposit flows low, they liquidate investments to accommodate members' loan needs. Because of liquidity needs, most credit union investments have maturities under one year.

Ordinarily, credit union investments have accounted for 10 to 20 percent of their assets. Starting in the early and mid 1980s, credit unions increased their investments to 35 percent of their assets. They did so because they could earn higher net returns on investments than on loans. However, as interest rates on investment assets declined in the late 1980s, credit unions reduced their investments to below 30 percent once again (see Exhibit 19–5).

Other Assets. Credit unions own a small amount of miscellaneous assets: vaults, office furniture and equipment, and in some cases, even buildings. These other assets are limited in value, however. Regulators do not wish credit unions to tie up too many funds in buildings or other real assets.

Credit Union Liabilities

Members' Shares

The primary source of funds for credit unions is members' share accounts. These make up over 90 percent of assets. There are several types of share accounts.

Regular Share Accounts. Credit unions' regular share accounts are similar to passbook savings accounts from which members can make withdrawals at will. Because share accounts are considered to be equity, they receive dividend payments rather than interest, and those payments are not legally guaranteed. Dividends are

Exhibit 19–5 **Credit Union Loan and Investment Ratios 1977 to 1989**

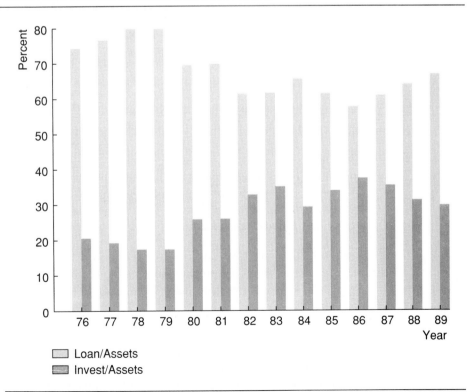

Source: National Credit Union Administration, *Annual Report, 1989*, p. 30.

declared at the end of each payment period by each credit union's board of directors. Except in the case of financial emergency or regulatory intervention, the board of directors will vote to pay the dividend rate promised. Principal balances in share accounts are insured up to $100,000 by federal share insurance. State share insurance may be available to state-chartered credit unions but, because of recent failures of state insurance funds (most recently, the Rhode Island Share and Depository Indemnity Fund in 1991) very few state insurance plans exist, and the NCUA has recommended that all credit unions apply for federal insurance. Thus less than 2,000 credit unions are no longer federally insured.

For many years, credit unions were subject to legal limits on dividend rates set by state or federal regulators. Frequently, dividend rates were limited to 6 percent. However, in 1982, the National Credit Union Administration Board eliminated all rate ceilings applicable to the liabilities of federally chartered credit unions. This has allowed credit unions to offer premium rates on accounts that contain larger balances.

Share Certificates.   Like other depository institutions' certificates of deposit, credit union share certificates pay higher interest on funds that are deposited for a longer period of time and held to maturity. Also like certificates of deposit, either a penalty is assessed for premature withdrawal or a 90-day notice may be required prior to withdrawal. Share certificates allow credit unions to lengthen the average maturity of their liabilities by offering higher interest rates. They can achieve that purpose only if premature withdrawal penalties are sufficiently high that shareholders will not readily shift their funds elsewhere if interest rates rise.

Share Drafts.   *Share draft* accounts let members write checks on their accounts. When the checks clear, the balance in the account is reduced. Balances in share draft accounts also can be accessed by debit cards or remote automatic teller machines (ATMs).

Share drafts were first developed in 1974, but their legal status was unclear until March 1980, when the DIDMCA made them legal nationwide. Since then they have spread rapidly, especially among larger credit unions. More than 80 percent of the larger ($10 million and over) credit unions offered share draft accounts within two years of their nationwide authorization. However, share drafts still account for under 10 percent of credit union shares.

At present, most share drafts are cleared through the commercial banking payment system. A credit union member's share draft follows the normal bank check-clearing process until it reaches the commercial bank on which the share drafts are payable. The bank microfilms the share draft and sends the information on it electronically to the credit union's data processor. Itemized statements showing the date, amount, and number of cleared drafts are prepared and sent to the member monthly. Because the original "check" is not returned, share drafts come in special booklets that record a carbonless copy of each draft as it is written. These statements are the legal equivalent of a canceled check. Transaction costs are reduced by eliminating the need to transport the draft physically across the country.

Debit card withdrawals can also be made from share draft accounts—either by using automatic teller machines (ATMs) or by clearing debit card receipts through bank credit-card clearing networks. When a credit union member's debit card receipt is presented for payment by another institution in the ATM or debit card network, the presenting institution is paid by drawing down the correspondent account balance that the credit union holds with that institution. At the same time, the credit union's data processor is notified that the same amount should be subtracted from the member's share draft account. Debit cards are popular with consumers because they allow people to obtain cash at any time and to obtain merchandise without having to prove that their checks are good.

Share draft accounts are important because they let credit unions compete effectively with retail-oriented banks and consumer-oriented thrift institutions that offer checking, ATM, and debit card services. Although credit unions ordinarily cannot make commercial loans, they can offer a full range of deposit and loan services to consumers. Larger credit unions have been most aggressive in doing so.

Notes Payable and Certificates of Indebtedness

Historically, credit unions have not had serious liquidity problems because their relatively high interest rates on share accounts usually allow them to compete effectively for passbook savings. However, their members' ability to supply funds may be limited at times. Thus, during high-interest periods, credit unions can attract more funds by issuing liabilities called *certificates of indebtedness* or *notes payable*. These liabilities are not subject to rate ceilings and can be issued to nonmembers as well as members. Typically, these liabilities are purchased by other credit unions or other financial institutions with excess funds. In the past, two restrictions have limited the popularity of these liabilities. First, credit unions are usually limited by various regulations from holding many certificates of indebtedness on their total balance sheet. Second, such liabilities are not insured. As a result, notes payable mount to only about 1 percent of credit unions' total liabilities.

Net Worth

Because credit unions' shares are viewed in some ways as equity, credit unions' capital is hard to measure. The best measure of a credit union's net worth is the difference between its assets and its liabilities to others (including its share account liabilities). The two major components of credit unions' net worth are reserves and undivided earnings.

Credit unions are required to maintain reserves for the protection of members' deposits against possible losses or bad debts. Before paying dividends, federal credit unions must set aside 5 to 10 percent of their gross earnings each year as additions to regular reserves until their reserves equal 10 percent of their outstanding loans and risk assets. Many state-chartered credit unions are also subject to reserve-accumulation laws. At the end of 1990, federally insured credit unions had a total net worth that equalled 7.6 percent of assets—higher than banks' or thrift institutions' average net worth.

Credit Union Cooperative Arrangements

Credit unions differ from other depository institutions in that their antitrust exemption enables them to participate in a wide variety of joint services. They are exempt from antitrust restrictions because, presumably, credit unions with nonoverlapping common-bond requirements cannot compete. Therefore, cooperative arrangements among them do not result in a restriction of competition.

Credit unions also have been favored by having strong trade associations that are devoted to furthering the credit union movement by engaging in joint ventures. Since credit unions themselves are cooperative associations, it is easy for them to see the benefits of cooperation among credit unions.

The largest credit union trade association is the Credit Union National Association (CUNA). Almost all credit unions are members of CUNA. The National Association of Federal Credit Unions (NAFCU) also represents the interests of the larger federal credit unions. Because the large federal credit unions offer a wide variety of services and are vitally affected by federal regulation, many of them consider that their legislative interests can be best served by having their own trade association in addition to CUNA.

Service Organizations

Because of credit unions' mutual interests and their relatively small size, credit union trade associations, particularly CUNA, have helped organize companies that provide specialized services to credit unions. Members are not obligated to buy services from these organizations, however.

Service companies organized by CUNA provide mortgage-banking services (helping sell mortgages originated by credit unions in the secondary mortgage markets), insurance for members' deposits and loans, data-processing and data transfer services, credit union–related supplies and promotional aids, and investment trusts and mutual funds. In addition to encouraging the development of service companies, CUNA has helped to develop banking arrangements and legal support so that credit unions could offer share drafts, IRA accounts, and Keogh plans; has negotiated credit card- and debit card–clearing arrangements; worked to develop a national ATM (automatic teller machine) system; and promoted the development and use of the state central and U.S. Central credit unions. Overall, CUNA develops and provides specialized services to credit unions that they might find too costly, or impossible, to obtain for themselves.

Corporate Central Credit Unions

The 44 state central, or "corporate," credit unions in the United States play an important role in channeling funds and information among credit union members. Corporate centrals are organized along state or regional lines. All credit unions in the area can belong (be members in) the corporate central credit union in the state. In addition to making a minimum initial contribution based on asset size, an individual credit union with surplus funds can invest in liabilities of its corporate central credit union. These liabilities can range from overnight liabilities that pay rates competitive with money market funds to jumbo certificates of deposit with maturities of one year or more. Liabilities of 31 of the corporate centrals are federally insured. The remainder are state insured or uninsured.

The corporate central credit unions use their members' funds to meet the credit needs of other member credit unions. Many credit unions, such as teachers' credit unions, have strong seasonal fluctuations in their cash flows. The existence of a central credit union makes it easy for credit unions to invest excess funds when it has them and borrow when its members all go on vacation. Other credit unions may borrow funds to cover temporary disruptions in their cash flows caused by strikes or layoffs.

In addition to loans, the corporate central credit unions may use their excess funds to invest in the financial markets or deposit them at the U.S. Central credit union, which, in turn, either loans the funds to temporarily cash-short credit unions or invests them in the financial markets. At midyear 1990, corporate central credit unions held $28 billion in shares deposited by regular credit unions and invested most of that money. Most of their investments were with the U.S. Central credit union, which held $26 billion deposited by its member corporate centrals.

Corporate central credit unions perform many services for their members. One is to hold clearing balances against which debit card receipts, ATM network transactions, or checks written on their members' share drafts can be cleared.

The corporate centrals also provide an educational function. Their staffs, along with CUNA's, help prepare cost estimates and revenue projections and provide advice to credit unions that are thinking of adopting new services, such as share drafts, debit cards, or ATMs. They also sponsor seminars so that credit union personnel and directors can learn ways to cope with common problems.

In many ways, the corporate centrals act as the head office of a bank holding company with many small regional banks. They transfer funds between surplus and deficit areas, and they provide overhead staff expertise and advice.

U.S. Central Credit Union

The U.S. Central credit union acts in many ways as a central bank for credit unions and, in fact, has a commercial bank charter in the state of Kansas. CUNA organized it in 1974 to provide banking services to the 44 corporate central credit unions. It offers a wide range of investment services to its members so that they can invest their excess funds in money market investments or longer-term certificates of deposit. It invests in liabilities of other credit unions, government securities, certificates of deposit, Euro-dollars, and a wide variety of other assets.

In 1990, the U.S. Central credit union had nearly $30 billion in assets. Its large size let it attain considerable efficiency in conducting money market transactions. It has great ability to tap national and international financial markets and to channel funds around the country in response to credit unions' needs. It also has the banking powers and contacts necessary to negotiate and organize credit card services and ATM services for its members.

Regulation of Credit Unions

Regulators

The primary regulator of credit unions is the National Credit Union Administration (NCUA) Board. Its three members are appointed by the president to overlapping six-year terms. The NCUA charters, insures, regulates, and examines all federally chartered credit unions and insures and examines all federally insured, state-chartered credit unions. The insurance activities of the NCUA are conducted through the National Credit Union Share Insurance Fund. In addition, the NCUA Board supervises the Central Liquidity Facility for credit unions. Overall, the NCUA is charged with promoting the welfare and growth of the institutions it supervises.

State credit unions can be chartered in all but three states (Delaware, South Dakota, and Wyoming) and the District of Columbia. In general, the power to charter as well as to examine and supervise credit unions resides with the same state agency that regulates state-chartered commercial banks and thrift institutions. Over one-third of all credit unions are state chartered.

Share Insurance

Federal credit unions did not have deposit insurance until October 1970, when Congress enacted legislation providing it for all eligible federally and state-chartered credit unions. The deposit insurance program administered by the National Credit Union Share Insurance Fund (NCUSIF) insures member shares up to a maximum amount of $100,000—the same limit as the FDIC. The NCUSIF received a contribution of 1 percent of all credit unions' insured assets in 1984 and 1985. It holds a reserve equal to 1.3 percent of insured assets. Because it earns interest on its assets, members often do not need to make an annual contribution to the fund, and they may even receive rebates if the fund's assets exceed 1.3 percent of insured shares. However, if the NCUSIF reserve falls below 1.25 percent of insured shares, insured credit unions may be asked to make additional contributions. In 1992 they paid an annual premium equal to 1/12 of 1 percent of their shares.

All federally chartered credit unions and most state-chartered credit unions are insured by the NCUSIF. Most of the remaining credit unions are insured by one of ten state insurance systems, since 44 states require that their credit unions have share insurance. Also, it is not uncommon for the sponsor of a liquidating credit union to volunteer the funds to return 100 percent on member shares. This occurs most frequently among occupational credit unions, where employers have a vested interest in the welfare of their employees.

The Central Liquidity Facility

Credit unions' lender of last resort is the Central Liquidity Facility (CLF). The CLF was organized because credit unions realized that even though they could shift funds among themselves, in a major liquidity crisis only a government agency could tap the nation's financial markets. Thus they lobbied Congress for the CLF, an independent agency operating under the jurisdiction of the NCUA Board. The CLF was authorized in 1978 and began operations in 1979. It is designed to provide both credit unions and state credit union insurance funds with a lender of last resort for emergency, seasonal, and protracted-assistance credit needs. The CLF has lending powers that are similar to those of the Federal Reserve System and the Federal Home Loan Banks.

Membership in the CLF is voluntary and is available to all credit unions regardless of their charter or insurance status. The CLF makes direct loans to regular members and indirect loans to credit unions through "agent" members. Agent membership is available to corporate central credit unions. When a corporate central joins the CLF, all its members gain access to the CLF through the agent. In 1983, the CLF reached an agreement with the U.S. Central credit union that extended indirect CLF membership to all 14,500 member unions through their 44 corporate centrals. In return for access to the CLF, each member credit union purchases shares in the CLF equal in value to $1/2$ percent of the credit union's unimpaired capital. Total member equity on September 30, 1990, equaled $461 million. The CLF also has made lines of credit available to private credit union share-insurance funds.

The CLF obtains its funds from its members' capital contributions and, if necessary, by borrowing through the Federal Financing Bank at the government agency rate. In a crisis, it can also borrow from the Federal Reserve discount window. It relends its borrowed funds at a spread to cover operating expenses and make a profit, as required by Congress. Thus the CLF charges slightly more than its borrowing rate on most loans.

The CLF's profitability is reduced somewhat in that it earns a very small spread on protracted-assistance loans that are intended to meet the liquidity needs of credit unions over an extended period because of "emergency" or "unusual" circumstances. Nonetheless, the CLF ordinarily pays substantial dividends to its members. In 1990 it paid a dividend equal to 7.9 percent of its members' equity interest in it.

The CLF has the legislative authority under the DIDMCA to collect credit union reserve requirements and pass them through to the Federal Reserve System. However, it has been reluctant to exercise this correspondent authority because of the bookkeeping and funds transfer costs involved. Furthermore, it has not seen the need to exercise its pass-through authority because individual credit unions can directly hold clearing balances with the Fed and can use their corporate central credit unions as correspondents when they wish to deposit required reserves with the Fed.

Management Problems and New Developments

Credit unions have several disadvantages relative to other depository institutions, as well as a number of advantages. New developments may enable them to use their strengths to overcome some of their weaknesses.

Disadvantages of Credit Unions

Credit unions' principal disadvantage is that many of them are very small. As a result, they individually find it difficult to afford the specialized skills needed to investigate and adopt new types of financial instruments and new technological procedures in a fast-changing world. Small credit unions are much less likely to offer new types of deposit accounts (such as share drafts or share certificates) or new types of services (such as ATMs or plastic cards) than large credit unions.

The small size of credit unions also causes them to incur cost disadvantages. Exhibit 19-3, Panel B shows that credit unions' annual expenses range from over 5 percent of assets to close to 3 percent as credit unions grow in size. This fact affects the smaller credit unions' ability to compete, because it means that they must earn a higher minimum spread between their return on assets and their costs of funds to remain profitable. Small credit unions achieve higher interest spreads than large credit unions by paying lower rates or charging higher fees on deposits and by charging higher rates on loans to increase gross revenues.

The overall required spread between interest earned and dividends paid is higher for credit unions than for banks because they make relatively small loans and accept small deposits, which are costly to service. Nonetheless, the experience of larger credit unions shows that substantial cost efficiencies accrue to larger institutions in providing these services. The largest institutions' costs of servicing both loans and deposits approximately equals the 3 percent service cost for consumer installment credit reported by large banks in the Federal Reserve's *Functional Cost Analysis.* Furthermore, because members value credit union services and because of tax advantages, credit unions' net incomes after dividends, expressed as a percentage of assets, compare very favorably with those of banks. See Exhibit 19–3 which shows that the equivalent return on assets (ROAe) for all credit unions averages close to 1 percent (0.85% in 1990).

Advantages of Credit Unions

Credit unions have a number of advantages that at present serve them well in competition with other financial institutions. These advantages should allow many to survive.

Sponsor Support.   Credit unions frequently are able to obtain free or low-cost office space and free personnel (or volunteers) from their sponsoring organizations— such as an employer, church, or trade union—or from their membership group. Employers may support credit unions to reduce the time employees must take off from work to obtain financial services or to make life on the job more attractive to their employees. Members may volunteer with the same esprit de corps that they devote to other community activities. In either case, free or low-cost resources reduce credit unions' expenses.

Payroll Deduction.   Payroll deduction is often provided to credit unions by sponsoring employers. It reduces the cost of obtaining both deposits and loan repayments, and it helps make loan repayments more regular and certain. In addition, if credit unions can induce their members to deposit their entire paychecks, they are also in a favorable position for selling their members other financial services.

Favorable Regulation.   Unlike banks, credit unions are in the favorable position of being regulated by an organization explicitly charged with promoting their development. Consequently, the NCUA is more likely to take a sympathetic, rather than adversarial, view toward their requests. It may also advocate legislation favorable to credit unions. Legislators are often sympathetic to credit union interests because credit unions have over 50 million members and an image of helping the small borrower by providing small loans at relatively low interest rates.

Tax Advantages.   Because credit unions are cooperative organizations, they are not subject to federal income tax on their earnings. As a result, they can accumulate "undivided earnings" more readily than other financial institutions. As the larger ones have become more effective competitors with banks and thrifts, however, their competitors have argued that credit unions should lose their tax advantages.

PEOPLE & EVENTS

Credit Unions Have Fraud Problems Too

The CAMEL rating system adopted by the NCUA in 1987 for use when examiners examine federally insured credit unions analyzes the capital, asset quality, management, earnings, and liquidity position of credit unions. Among other things, the examiners try to make sure not only that management is competent but that it uses adequate control systems so that it can guard against fraud and other losses. The examiners also try to identify fraud if it occurs.

In recent years, the NCUA has tightened its examination for fraud because it incurred large losses resulting from fraud when the Hyfin Credit Union of Brooklin failed in 1986 and the Franklin Community Federal Credit Union failed in Omaha in 1988. In the Hyfin case, because of fradulent loans and other illegal activities, the NCUSIF paid over $54 million to the Municipal Credit Union to induce it to assume Hyfin's liabilities (shares). In the Franklin case, the credit union's president and treasurer used a separate computer to establish accounts to hide $39 million in unrecorded share certificates.

They later transfered those funds to themselves, or used them to pay dividends at above-market rates on share deposits (so they could keep attracting deposits to fund their scheme). Five individuals were indicted in the Franklin case, and two others pled guilty. In the Hyfin case, eight of the top officers were convicted of fraudulent and criminal activities.

Because of the serious nature of fraud offenses, the NCUA seeks jail terms for any officers or directors who engage in fraudulent activity. It also has developed sophisticated computer programs that analyze each credit union's periodic statistical reports to see if any discrepancies exist that fit a pattern consistent with possible fraudulent activity. Because of the NCUA's vigilance, coupled with the fact that most credit unions' boards of directors are close to their members and, consequently, watch the solvency of their institutions closely, fraud has not been as large a problem at credit unions as at other financial institutions. Nonetheless, as the examples cited above show, it has occurred and it has been costly to the NCUSIF.

The Credit Union Movement.   Credit unions have the advantage of being strongly supported by people who see benefits in the social philosophy of cooperative, mutual self-help institutions. This helps them obtain both legislative support and many capable, dedicated volunteers. In addition, many depositors may be willing to accept a slightly lower return on assets, if necessary, to support their group.

Strong Trade Associations.   In part because of their antitrust exemption and in part because of their dedication to their social philosophy, credit unions have had the benefit of strong trade associations. Unlike banks, which often pursue competing interests, the credit union trade associations try to advance the mutual interests of the entire movement. Their unity has helped them obtain favorable legislation and pioneer the development of new services for credit unions.

Trends and Developments

The credit union movement is undergoing considerable change, with many new services offered and rates deregulated. As a result, three trends are apparent. First, small credit unions are merging or being liquidated. The number of credit unions has declined by one-third since 1970. The costs of coping with a high rate of technological change and elevated deposit rates have been too great for many credit unions to wish to retain their independence.

Second, the credit union movement is rapidly adopting the new technological services being developed by its trade associations and their related service corporations. This has provided many with the ability to remain technologically competitive in spite of their relatively small size.

Third, funds flows among credit unions are becoming increasingly coordinated. In many respects, CUNA and the U.S. Central function like a gigantic bank with thousands of branches. Funds flow between the branches through the central credit union system. The head office, CUNA (and its service corporation, ICU), does the development work for new services that are to be offered by the branch network. Each branch, however, decides which services to adopt and provides specialized service to its members.

Credit Union Risk Management

Credit unions potentially incur liquidity risk, credit risk, and interest rate risk. Because of their special "clublike" nature, they have adopted different mechanisms for controlling such risks than some other depository institutions.

Credit Risk

The best way to avoid credit risk is through careful risk evaluation so loans will be unlikely to default. However, another way to reduce the impact of credit risk is through diversification so multiple defaults will not occur simultaneously. Often credit unions are not able to diversify because their common bond may restrict them to serving members of one firm, one industry, and so forth. That may be one reason that credit unions are more popular in fields (such as government or military) where their members' incomes have little exposure to changes in the business cycle.

As another adoption to cyclical changes in credit risk, individual credit unions may "diversify over time" by carrying delinquent loans on their books for longer periods of time than other institutions. If an industry is in a cyclical recession, when a recovery eventually occurs, laid-off workers may be recalled and delinquent loans may be repaid if they have not previously been charged off and the collateral foreclosed upon. Credit unions also frequently provide credit life insurance on their loans. Such insurance is more likely to be used to repay long-term delinquent loans and would be less available if a loan had been charged off and the security repossessed.

Because their individual loan portfolios often are not diversified by type of employment of borrowers, credit unions have incentives to hold larger amounts of investments relative to loans, to loan money to other credit unions (indirectly) through corporate central investments, and, as noted, to carry credit life insurance for borrowers and carry delinquent loans on their books for longer periods of time.

The fact that credit unions have historically, recorded low credit losses, but carry delinquent loans on their books for long periods, may result for various reasons. (1) Credit unions often serve members with stable incomes (teachers, government employees, military people, and so forth). (2) Credit unions often have payroll deductions (so they get paid as soon as the borrower's paycheck is deposited—unless the borrower rescinds the agreement). (3) Credit unions often have a "clublike" atmosphere in which members realize that their loan performance will affect their peers' welfare, so members strive hard to repay their debts so other members of the group will not be exposed to losses. All these factors may reduce credit losses. (4) Furthermore, the widespread use of credit life insurance, coupled with their willingness to carry loans as delinquent for long periods, may marginally reduce loan losses at credit unions. Nonetheless, because credit unions' common bonds limit their loan portfolio diversification, they have strong incentives (1) to hold high capital to absorb cyclical losses, (2) to hold high liquidity in case losses slow cash inflows, and (3) to merge or otherwise relax their common bonds to achieve greater diversification.

Liquidity Risk

The National Credit Union Administration tries to reduce credit union liquidity risk by monitoring the relative liquidity of credit unions assets and liabilities. First, the examiners require that credit unions report fixed-rate investments and mortgage loans with maturities over three years as long-term assets, and encourage them to fund such assets with longer-term liabilities such as share certificates. In addition, the examiners calculate a liquidity ratio by dividing the difference between a credit union's cash and short-term investments and its short-term liabilities (including savings accounts) by the credit union's assets. The resulting percentage roughly measures a credit union's rate sensitivity "GAP" as a percentage of assets. The NCUA hopes that the liquidity ratio will deviate by less than 10 percent from zero. In 1989, the NCUA became concerned because the liquidity ratio for all credit unions combined fell from − 2.9 percent in 1987 to − 5.8 percent in 1988 to − 7.9 percent in 1989 as credit unions made more long-term loans and bought longer-term investments. Nonetheless, because most credit unions invest a large portion of their assets (nearly 30 percent) in investment securities, hold mostly consumer loans will relatively short durations, and have access to backup liquidity through loans from their credit union centrals or the CLF, in general, credit unions are not likely to have serious liquidity problems. Furthermore, the existence of NCUSIF insurance should reassure depositors and prevent panicky withdrawals that could impair a credit union's liquidity. Thus overall liquidity risk is not of great concern to most credit unions. Interest rate risk, however, is a growing concern.

Interest Rate Risk

As interest rates declined on shorter-term investments in the late 1980s, credit unions expanded their mortgage lending and bought longer-term securities to increase revenues. The 1986 Tax Reform Act enhanced this trend as it made mortgage-related borrowing more attractive to borrowers because only mortgage interest payments were fully deductible from taxable income. Thus credit unions expanded their second mortgage loans used to finance a variety of consumer activities along with their first mortgage loans used to finance homes. The results showed up in a deteriorating liquidity ratio, which the NCUA tried to rectify through pressure applied to credit unions during annual examinations. Subsequently, mortgage loan growth at credit unions slowed (from + 46 percent in 1987, and + 28 percent in 1988 to + 11 percent in 1989, and + 9 percent in 1990). In addition, the NCUA recommended that all credit unions qualify all their new mortgage loans so they could be sold in the secondary mortgage markets.

Before 1980, credit unions did not make many mortgage loans, and auto loans were usually made for three years or less. Thus credit unions, which mainly held short-duration assets, did not have serious GAP problems as their liabilities (savings shares) also were short term. However, with the advent of first- and second-mortgage lending and the lengthening of auto loan maturities in the 1980s and 1990s, credit unions now have to be more careful to avoid interest rate risk. This has been difficult, as financial institutions have a large (short-term) financial incentive to make long-term loans funded with short-term deposits when the term structure of interest rates slope sharply upward. If short-term interest rates should rise sharply once again, only the vigilance of regulators, adjustable-rate lending, credit unions' traditional emphasis on relatively short-term consumer loans, and the potential ability of credit unions to sell off mortgage loans may prevent them from incurring losses like the S&Ls did in the 1980s (after they too "lent long and borrowed short"). Thus, in the future, careful GAP management will be increasingly important for credit unions.

Summary

Credit unions are nonprofit cooperative savings and lending institutions organized by consumers having a common bond. They serve only their members. Credit unions' assets are almost entirely short- or intermediate-term consumer installment loans. Liabilities are predominantly share accounts. All credit unions offer passbook savings–type regular share accounts. Many also offer share certificates and share draft (checking) accounts.

Credit unions engage in many cooperative ventures and have strong trade associations. Among other things, their principal trade association (CUNA) has helped them organize central credit unions, debit and credit card arrangements, share draft accounts, ATM and EFT networks, insurance, data processing, and mortgage banking capabilities.

Credit unions can have either a state charter from one of 47 states of a federal charter from the National Credit Union Administration (NCUA). The NCUA also administers the NCUSIF, the federally sponsored insurance fund for credit unions, and supervises the Central Liquidity Fund.

In 1980, there were approximately 14,500 credit unions (12,860 of them federally insured) with an average asset size of less than $20 million. Their small size made it relatively expensive for them to operate and to take advantage of new technologies. However, they have been able to overcome some of the disadvantages of small size by taking advantage of employer subsidies, volunteer help, payroll deduction, tax advantages, favorable regulation, and help provided by their strong trade associations. Through CUNA, they have been able to obtain access to new technologies and financial services. As a result, many have become full-service consumer financial service organizations.

In recent years, there has been a tendency for small credit unions to merge into larger organizations so that they can obtain greater economies of scale. They also have developed an effective nationwide funds transfer network. In many ways, increased integration of services and funds transfers among credit unions have let them function much like retail branches of a giant bank holding company.

Credit unions may experience less credit risk than some other financial institutions because their members often have stable jobs and are somewhat less likely to default on loans because of payroll deduction, credit insurance, and in some cases the closeness of their common bond. Credit unions also have limited liquidity risk because they hold large amounts of liquid investments, make relatively short-term loans, and have ready access to credit through their credit union centrals and the Central Liquidity Facility. However, credit unions may increasingly have to be careful to avoid interest rate risk as they have lengthened the maturity of their loan portfolios, while they still rely on members' savings deposits for most of their funds. Careful asset/ liquidity management, adjustable rate loans, and the sale of mortgages in secondary markets may be necessary to diffuse this threat.

Questions

1. Briefly outline the historical development of credit unions. Explain which early goals of the credit union movement are still retained today.
2. What are the major asset and liability accounts for credit unions? What are the major risks credit unions face and what can they do about them?
3. What are share drafts? Why are they important to credit unions?
4. What reasons would you give for credit union loan loss rates being substantially below those of other institutions?
5. What are the advantages and disadvantages of the credit union common-bond requirement?
6. Compare and contrast the retail operations of a commercial bank with those of a typical credit union in operation today. Taking into account the expanded powers of credit unions, how will they compare in the future?
7. What are the major taxation differences between credit unions and commercial banks? Do you expect these differences to continue?
8. Identify the major positive factors that should aid future credit union growth. What factors should work against its rapid growth rate?
9. Individual credit unions are very small in size, averaging less than $20 million in assets. If there is going to be increased competition in the consumer credit market and greater regulatory equalization among competing institutions, how do you expect credit unions to survive?
10. What is the U.S. Central credit union? Why is it important to the future development of the credit union industry?

Selected References

Clair, Robert T. "Deposit Insurance, Moral Hazard, and Credit Unions." *Economic Review.* **Federal Reserve Bank of Dallas, July 1984, pp. 1–12.**
This interesting article suggests that from the time credit unions obtained federal deposit insurance in 1971, they took on more risk. After they obtained share insurance, their capital

(reserve)/risk assets ratios trended downward and their loan delinquency rates trended upward. Because credit union shareholders had less to fear from default once their accounts were insured, a moral hazard made them more willing to let credit unions add to their risk.

Cox, William N. "Southeastern Credit Unions: From Delicatessen to Supermarket?" *Economic Review.* **Federal Reserve Bank of Atlanta, June 1983, pp. 40–46.**

This article reports on a survey of southeastern credit unions to see how they intended to use their new powers. Two-thirds indicated that they wanted to move more toward a full-service financial service orientation now that they had the authority to do so. Most also saw banks and thrifts as their potential competitors, not other credit unions.

Flannery, Mark J. "Credit Unions as Consumer Lenders in the United States." *New England Economic Review.* **Federal Reserve Bank of Boston, July–August 1974, pp. 3–12.**

One of the first and best analyses of credit unions. Somewhat technical.

Heaton, Gary G., and Constance R. Dunham. "The Growing Competitiveness of Credit Unions." *New England Economic Review.* **Federal Reserve Bank of Boston, May–June 1985, pp. 19–34.**

Analyzes trends in the credit union industry in general, and New England credit unions in particular, following enactment of new regulations that let them make mortgage loans, engage in credit card lending, and offer share draft checking accounts. It points out that because the larger community-oriented credit unions have used these powers extensively, credit unions' market influence should be considered by analysts who are conducting studies of the effect of proposed mergers of bank or thrift institutions on the competitiveness of local consumer financial markets.

Kobliner, Beth. "Why Credit Unions Now Look Spooky." *Money,* **December 1988, pp. 66–67.**

This article notes that as credit unions have made more fixed-rate first and second mortgage loans, they have acquired more interest rate risk. If their deposit interest costs were to rise, some might experience problems similar to those experienced by thrift institutions in the late 1970s and early 1980s.

National Credit Union Administration, *Annual Reports, 1990* **and earlier years. Washington, DC, 1991.**

These reports provide current data and information on federally insured credit union operations and regulation.

National Credit Union Administration, *1990 Yearend Statistics for Federally Insured Credit Unions,* **and earlier years. Washington, DC, 1991.**

These reports provide comprehensive data on the operations of both federally chartered and state-chartered, but federally insured, credit unions.

Pearce, Douglas K. "Recent Developments in the Credit Union Industry." *Economic Review.* **Federal Reserve Bank of Kansas City, June 1984, pp. 3–19.**

Credit unions experienced many changes in their regulatory environment from 1977 through 1983. This article does an excellent job of summarizing those changes and analyzing the effect they have had on credit unions.

Williams, Jim. "The CU System Is a Conglomerate, Too." *Credit Union Magazine,* **September 1982, pp. 13–14.**

The president of CUNA provides a look at emerging developments in the nation's financial system. He comments on credit unions' plans to cope with the new competition by developing new shared systems for electronic data transmissions and banking.

INSURANCE COMPANIES AND PENSION FUNDS 20

SOME OF THE OLDEST FINANCIAL institutions in the United States are insurance companies. The oldest life insurer, first known as "The Fund for Pious Uses," began in 1717 in Philadelphia. That company has evolved into the Presbyterian Ministers' Fund and is still in operation. Insurance is a risk-sharing arrangement whereby one party (the insurer) agrees to indemnify another party (the insured) against certain losses specified by a contract (the policy). This chapter examines three categories of these contractual financial institutions that are characterized by inflows of funds from insurance premiums and pension plan contributions and fund outflows in the form of claims payments and related benefits: life and health insurers, property and liability insurers, and pension plans. The purpose of the chapter is to describe the operation of these organizations, the products and services they provide, their regulation, and risk exposures. Like other financial institutions discussed in this book, insurers face liquidity risk, interest rate risk, and default risk. Of course, insurers also face the risk that actual losses will deviate from expected losses once the insurer has assumed the insured's risk. This type of risk is called *objective risk*. We begin to understand insurers by developing an understanding of the insurance mechanism.

The Insurance Mechanism

Insurance is an economic device by which individuals and organizations can transfer their pure risks (that is, uncertainty about financial losses) to others. With *pure risk* the outcome can only be a loss or no loss; there is no possibility for gain. In contrast, *speculative risk* means that uncertainty about an event could result in either a gain or a loss. Pure risks arise from events over which one has little or no control. Examples of pure risk include the risk of one's home burning, the risk of a shopping mall being swept away by a tornado, the risk to a manufacturer that a particular product will cause injury to a consumer, and the risk of a working parent dying prematurely.

Self-insuring risk (as opposed to transferring risk to an insurer) is costly and burdensome. Self-insuring involves accumulating a liquid emergency fund to pay for losses and worrying about whether the fund is large enough to cover them. Society also bears costs from self-insurance. Since we each must have an emergency fund, funds are diverted from more productive, but less liquid, investments. Society may also be deprived of goods or services that were not produced because the risk was too great. For example, developers of certain important drugs may choose not to manufacture and market them, or physicians in certain high-risk specialties may not practice, if the cost of a liability suit could bring financial ruin.

Insurance reduces society's cost of bearing risk. When individuals transfer risk to insurers, the burden of risk in the aggregate decreases. Individuals and organizations exchange their uncertainty for a premium that is known for certain. After risk is transferred to the insurer, the insured no longer has to establish an emergency fund, and anxiety decreases. The insured can now invest in stocks or bonds, can develop and market new products, and can get a good night's sleep without worry. Insurers accept the risk in exchange for a premium and place the insureds in a pool with others who have transferred similar loss exposures to the insurer. For example, in property and liability insurance, owners of individual residences who purchase homeowners insurance are placed in a pool with other homeowners. The insurers then seek to reduce their own risk.

Insurers and Objective Risk

The risk that insurers face once they have accepted the pure risk of their insureds is termed objective risk. An insurer's *objective risk* is the deviation of actual losses from expected losses and can be measured statistically. Because insurers accept many loss exposures, the mathematical Law of Large Numbers applies to them. The larger the number of loss exposures, the more predictable the average losses become. For the Law of Large Numbers to work, the exposure units used to predict losses must be homogeneous, and the losses that occur must be fortuitous, meaning that the loss is unexpected and happens as a result of chance.

The insurers who do the best job of predicting losses, and who therefore have very small objective risk, are life insurers, since mortality changes very slowly over time. Mortality rates (or the number of people dying) are not as sensitive to economic conditions as are property and liability losses. For example, property and liability insurers may suffer much larger dollar losses than expected if inflation rates are very high, since the cost to rebuild a manufacturing plant that has been destroyed or to repair a wrecked car will increase with inflation. The face value that the insurer must pay upon the death of the insured under a life insurance contract, however, does not usually increase with inflation.

Requirements for Insurability

Most insurance companies insure only pure risks, not speculative risks. There are some pure risks that private insurers will not insure, however. In fact, the private insurance industry has certain requirements that a loss exposure must meet in order to be considered insurable. First, insurers require a large number of homogeneous exposure units so that losses can be predicted based on the Law of Large Numbers. Second, the losses that occur should happen accidentally and unintentionally. Since the Law of Large Numbers is based on random events, this is an important requirement. Third, the circumstances of the loss should be easily identifiable. For example, it should be easy to identify the time and location of the loss, what caused the loss, and the amount of the loss. Fourth, the insurer also requires that the probability of a loss can be calculated. This requirement is important since the insurer must be able to develop a premium that covers losses and still yields a profit. Fifth, the loss should not be catastrophic to the insurer. Ideally, this means that a large proportion of the insurance company's exposure units should not experience a loss at the same time. The final requirement for an insurable risk is that the company must be able to develop a premium that is economically feasible. If the premium is not affordable to insurance consumers, the insurance product will not be purchased or will be purchased only by those consumers who believe a loss is imminent.

Methods Used to Reduce Objective Risk

Once a risk is ascertained to be insurable, the insurer uses several methods to keep losses from the risk to a minimum. Insurers are always active in trying to reduce "underwriting losses," or the amount they pay out in claims. It is important for the profitability of insurance companies that actual losses paid are close to expected losses. Three methods are used by the industry to accomplish this goal. First, insurers actively try to prevent losses from occurring. For example, Underwriters Laboratories is an insurance-supported organization that inspects building materials for fire safety. The Insurance Institute for Highway Safety compiles research on the causes of susceptibility to highway losses, and insurers reduce premiums for cars with safety equipment such as air bags and seat belts. The National Fire Protection Association develops fire safety standards and public education programs. The Insurance Crime Prevention Institute investigates fraudulent insurance claims, and the Oil Insurance Association provides fire protection and engineering counsel for oil producers. And the list goes on.

Second, all companies underwrite prospective insureds carefully in order to assure that the individual's probability of loss is "average." Individuals applying for auto insurance will have their driving records checked to determine whether they are safe drivers. Those applying for life insurance may be required to undergo a physical exam to determine if a condition exists that could lead to a shorter life expectancy than average. Individuals applying for property insurance will have their property inspected to determine any physical hazards that could increase the probability of a loss occurring.

Third, the insured may be required to carry a deductible on the policy, so that when a loss occurs the insured participates in the loss. Deductibles are nearly always seen on property insurance policies and in health insurance, where they may be of the type called "percentage participation clauses." These deductibles help keep the insurer's costs down by reducing the administrative costs of adjusting small claims, reducing the overall loss payment, and reducing the chance of fraudulent claims. Deductibles are not ordinarily used on life insurance policies or liability policies.

The Pricing of Insurance

The goal of the insurer when developing an insurance rate is to charge enough to cover claims and administrative expenses and still make a profit. The insurer wants the rate to be competitive and, of course, meet any rate regulation. Ordinarily, the states do not regulate life insurance rates, but often automobile insurance and workers' compensation rates are regulated. Also, health insurance rates often must be "filed" with the department of insurance and approved by the state insurance commissioner. Regulators of insurance require that rates be adequate to pay losses, with the goal of insurer solvency in mind. Usually, the insurance code also requires that rates not be "unfairly discriminatory." Some observers believe that recent regulations in various states that prevent insurers from raising rates or that require them to "roll back" rates may contribute to the risk of insolvency for some insurance companies.

Actuaries who work for insurance companies or for rating bureaus that provide rates to insurance companies develop the statistics used for rate making. In the life and health insurance industry, for example, to determine the probable number of persons in a group who will die or become disabled at any age, statistics on large numbers of lives are collected and developed into mortality and morbidity tables. In the property and liability industry, past losses, premiums, and expense statistics are furnished to rating bureaus, and the bureau furnishes insurance companies with advisory rates, based on those statistics. When pricing insurance, actuaries take into consideration the investment income that will be earned on the premium dollars paid. Thus if interest rates are expected to be high and investment income is expected to be large, a lower insurance rate will be charged. If interest rates are expected to drop, investment income is expected to be less and rates will be higher.

How Interest Rate Risk Affects Insurance Companies

During the early 1980s, many insurers expected interest rates to continue rising as sharply as they had in late 1970s, and the companies charged much lower premiums than they should have for certain lines of insurance, especially commercial liability insurance. In addition, because interest rates were high, it was attractive to the companies to take in as many premium dollars as possible for investment purposes. Some exposures were written by insurers that were not good risks from an underwriting standpoint. It was said that the companies were engaging in "cash-flow underwriting," in other words, writing insurance on just about any risk in order to get the premium dollars to invest at high interest rates. Those companies experienced huge underwriting losses when investment income was insufficient to cover large claims that had to be paid under the policies. This was especially true for companies writing certain liability lines that are said to have a "long tail." Long tail lines are those in which claims may have to be paid long after the policy expiration. One such line of insurance is product liability. The practice of cash-flow underwriting contributed to some insurer insolvencies and a general "liability crisis" in the insurance business, wherein it became very difficult or impossible to purchase certain types of liability insurance in the primary insurance market.

Structure of the Insurance Industry

The American insurance industry can be categorized by type of business or by organizational form. In this section, we describe the structure of the insurance industry. We first describe the organizational forms observed in the insurance industry. We then report the number of insurance companies by both line of business (that is, life and health or property and casualty) and by organizational form (that is, stock, mutual, reciprocal, or Lloyd's).

Organizational Forms

Stock Companies.   The stock company, a corporation owned by shareholders, is one of the oldest organizational forms used by insurance companies. The oldest U.S. stock insurer is the Insurance Company of North America, which began in Philadelphia in 1792. The objective of the stock insurer is to produce a profit for the holders of the capital stock. Management of the stock company rests with the shareholders, who elect a board of directors that then elects the insurer's executive officers.

The types of insurance that a stock insurer may sell depend on the company's charter. A stock insurer must meet the minimum capital and surplus requirements of the state in which it is domiciled. Stock insurers dominate in the property and liability insurance industry, especially in the commercial lines. They write about 75 percent of all the property and liability insurance written by private insurers. Some stock companies write only nonparticipating or "nonpar" policies, while others issue "par" and "nonpar" policies. Participating policies are those that pay policyholder dividends. Thus policyholders "participate" in the profitability of the company.

Mutual Insurers.   Mutual insurers are owned by the policyholders. The objective of this type of organization is to minimize the cost of the insurance product to the policyholders. The oldest mutual insurer in the United States is The Philadelphia Contributionship for the Insurance of Houses from Loss by Fire, which began in 1752. The company continues to operate and has paid policyholder dividends continuously since 1895. Mutuals pay their policyholders dividends based on the company's performance, so their policies are participating. If the cost of providing insurance declines, policyholder dividends will increase. In life insurance, for example, if mortality is better than expected or if investment income is greater than expected, the life insurance dividend will increase. Unlike stockholder dividends, policyholder dividends are *not taxable as income* to the policyholder. The IRS regards policyholder dividends as a return to the policyholder of an overcharge of premium. Mutual insurers rarely issue nonpar policies and in fact, in some states, mutuals are prohibited by law from issuing nonpar policies. Mutual insurers dominate in the area of life insurance.

Reciprocals.   Reciprocals, or reciprocal exchanges, are another form of insuring organization. These operate like mutuals and their objective is to minimize the cost of the insurance product, but they are unincorporated. They are managed by an attorney-in-fact that is usually a corporation authorized to collect premiums, pay losses, invest the funds, and arrange reinsurance. Insurance is exchanged among the members; that is one member insures the other and vice versa. There were 43 reciprocals operating in 1990 and they usually limit the lines of insurance they write. One very successful reciprocal in the area of automobile insurance is Farmers Insurance Exchange of Los Angeles.

Lloyd's Associations.   Lloyd's associations are organizations that do not directly write insurance but provide services for members of the association who write insurance as individuals. The most famous is Lloyd's of London, where the members

DID YOU KNOW?

Pink Floyd and the Duke of Marlborough Do the Insurance "Boogie"

How do you insure against storms and fires and floods and earthquakes and other imaginable calamities, such as a space satellite being destroyed during launching or a disastrous spawning season for salmon? Ask Lloyd's of London. Its 27,000 underwriting members, who operate in syndicates, control the world's insurance and reinsurance markets.

The beginning of Lloyd's can be traced to a coffeehouse on London's Tower Street in 1688. The coffeehouse was a gathering spot for merchants, shipowners, and sea captains, who gossiped about their trade and journeys. Sharp-eyed owner Edward Lloyd realized that his establishment was the center of maritime intelligence and information. This led him to publish *Lloyd's News* in 1696, which survives today as *Lloyd's List*.

There were no formal insurance offices in those days. Each would-be vendor simply hawked his policy around the city, eventually making his way to Lloyd's Coffeehouse to hear the latest news and to assess risks. Thus insurance has been written for 300 years at Lloyd's. Lloyd's present-day insurance philosophy dates back to the eminently practical Victorians, who divided and shared insurance responsibilities to the extent that instead of being an unbearable risk for a few, they are a small risk for many.

Although maintaining its Victorian structure, Lloyd's has moved into the twentieth century by pioneering new policies for political risk, product liability, professional indemnity, and computer crime. The insurance market at Lloyd's—and it is a market like the New York Stock Exchange—has become an integral part of the world economy, providing specialist services to multinational corporations.

Great fortunes have been made at Lloyd's since the Napoleonic Wars, but the opportunity to invest is limited to invitation only. In Victorian times, Lloyd's was the investment ground for upper-crust bluebloods. In the last 50 years, however, the middle class has been sneaking into Lloyd's private investment circle. Now there is a fascinating mélange of old money and new money. The Duke and Duchess of Marlborough are there, alongside members of the rock band Pink Floyd. Jockeys, tennis stars, sheiks, Hong Kong shipowners, and Nigerian tribal chieftains all share insurance risks together.

have unlimited liability for the risks they underwrite. Lloyd's of London is admitted to do business as a primary insurer only in Kentucky and Illinois. Lloyd's was admitted first in Kentucky because of its long association with the thoroughbred horse industry. Illinois is the "backup" state for Lloyd's, in case the political winds would change in Kentucky and Lloyd's would no longer be admitted. In other states, Lloyd's may be used only when a particular coverage is not available from any primary insurer admitted in the state. In fact, Lloyd's is probably most famous for insuring the unusual risks that primary insurers consider uninsurable. Unusual loss exposures such as damage to the hands of a great pianist or the loss of a space shuttle have been insured at Lloyd's. There were 16 American Lloyd's operating in the United States in 1990 that tried to duplicate the kind of service provided by Lloyd's of London, but they had limited liability and they did not write a large premium volume.

The Size and Number of Insurance Companies

In 1990 there were about 2,350 life and health insurers doing business. Most life and health insurers are organized as stock companies, which are corporations owned by stockholders. Approximately 2,233 of the 2,350 life and health insurers were stock companies and 117 were mutuals. Even though the number of mutuals is small, they account for 46 percent of the total assets of all American life and health insurers and 38 percent of all life insurance in force. Exhibit 20-1 shows the ten largest life and health insurance companies in 1989, ranked by total assets.

In 1990, about 2,274 property and liability insurance companies were doing business in the United States, combined into 1,193 groups. The reciprocals and Lloyd's accounted for 59 of the 1,193 groups. Of the remaining 1,134, 725 were stock companies and 409 were mutuals. Although the number of firms is large, the companies tend to specialize in such areas as personal lines, commercial property or liability coverages, professional liability, aviation, or transportation insurance. Exhibit 20-2 shows the ten largest property and liability insurers in the United States in 1989, ranked by total assets.

Exhibit 20-1   **Ten Largest Property/Liability Companies, 1989**

Company	Assets ($ in billions)
1. State Farm Mutual Bloomington, IL	35.5
2. Allstate Insurance Northbrook, IL	19.9
3. Liberty Mutual Boston, MA	14.1
4. Continental Casualty Chicago, IL	13.9
5. Aetna Casualty and Surety Hartford, CT	12.5
6. State Farm Fire and Casualty Bloomington, IL	10.4
7. Nationwide Mutual Columbus, OH	9.1
8. Travelers Indemnity Hartford, CT.	9.1
9. USF & G Baltimore, MD	8.8
10. St. Paul Fire and Marine St. Paul, MN	8.4

State Farm is the largest property/liability insurance company in the United States. In recent years, property/liability companies have suffered large underwriting losses.

Source: Best's Insurance Reports, 1990.

Exhibit 20–2   **Ten Largest Life/Health Companies, 1990**

Company	Assets ($ in billions)
1. Prudential Insurance Co. of America Newark, NJ	133.5
2. Metropolitan Life Insurance Co. New York, NY	103.2
3. Aetna Life Hartford, CT	52.3
4. Equitable Life Assurance Soc. New York, NY	50.3
5. TIAA New York, NY	49.9
6. New York Life Insurance Co. New York, NY	39.9
7. Connecticut General Life Insurance Co. Hartford, CT	37.4
8. John Hancock Mutual Life Insurance Co. Boston, MA	33.7
9. Travelers Insurance Co. Hartford, CT	33.0
10. Northwestern Mutual Life Insurance Co. Milwaukee, WI	31.4

Prudential is the largest life/health insurance company in the United States. Most life/health insurance companies are mutual companies.

Source: Best's Insurance Management Reports, August 26, 1991.

Life and Health Insurance

Life and health insurance companies sell a wide variety of financial products, including mutual funds, real estate investment trusts, and money market accounts. A few traditional products, however, have accounted for a substantial proportion of life insurer revenues. These are life insurance, health insurance, and annuities. Whereas the products sold by property and liability insurers are designed to protect insureds against such perils as fire, windstorm, theft, or liability that could cause financial loss, the insurance products are designed to protect insureds against perils that can interrupt the individual's or family's stream of income. These perils include premature death, illness or disability, and old age.

The primary purpose of life insurance is to protect the economic security of an insured's dependents in the event of premature death. While it seems to most of us that our own death will most certainly be premature, in the insurance sense premature death occurs during a person's income-producing years. With life insurance, the insured is able to create an instant estate for his or her family. Term, whole life, and universal life are the three broad categories of life insurance products.

Term Insurance

Term insurance is a product that provides a death benefit to the beneficiary if the insured dies within a specified period. If the insured survives the insuring period, the contract expires and there are no further benefit rights. It is the purest form of life insurance in that it provides only death protection and no savings element. The premiums are low at young ages but increase as the insured ages. Term insurance policies may be classified broadly as to the duration of the policy, how the face amount varies, the expiration protection, and the existence of premium guarantees.

Duration.   Straight term insurance policies are written for a certain number of years and then they terminate. Typical policy durations are five-year term, ten-year term, and yearly term.

Variability in Face Amount.   Most term policies have a face amount that stays constant during the life of the policy. *Decreasing term* has a face amount that decreases yearly or monthly while the premium stays level. This type of policy is often used to cover a mortgage or other long-term loan. *Increasing term* provides coverage that increases monthly or yearly while the premium stays level. This type may be used to include cost-of-living protection for the beneficiary.

Expiration Protection.   Two provisions that are often included in term insurance policies have to do with the problem of continuing insurance coverage after the term of the policy expires. They are the renewability and convertibility provisions.

Renewable term insurance policies may be renewed at the end of the policy term without new evidence of insurability. The new premium to be charged will be the premium for the insured's attained age. The renewal privilege is usually restricted to age 65 or 70 to prevent "adverse selection." Because term insurance premiums increase with the insured's age, by the time the insured reaches age 65 the premiums are prohibitively expensive. For that reason, the only policyholders who would keep policies in force at such expensive premiums are those in bad health or who believe they will not live long. Hence the term "adverse selection."

Convertible term permits the insured to convert the term insurance policy to some form of permanent protection, such as whole life. This may be done without new evidence of insurability but must be done within some given time period stated in the policy, such as within the first five years. This is an attractive provision since often those who purchase term insurance do so because of the low premiums charged at a young age. As the family ages and income increases, insureds often desire to convert to a plan that will provide coverage for the whole life and develop a savings element.

Whole Life Insurance

Whole life insurance is designed to provide life insurance protection for those who believe they will need life insurance protection on a long-term basis. The coverage is for the insured's whole life. The most popular policy form is *continuous level-premium whole life*. The insured pays the same premium every year from the policy inception and the premium does not increase with the insured's age. Put simply, life actuaries calculate the level premium to be charged for the insured's whole life by first calculating the net single premium for all the benefits the policy will provide, then dividing that number by the insured's life expectancy. The leveling out of the premium makes the policy affordable. The policyholder pays more than the actual cost of insurance in the early policy years and less than the actual cost of insurance in the later policy years. Because of the overpayment in the early years, the premiums paid by the insured earn interest and "cash values" develop within the policy.

Also contributing to the cash value accumulation are the survivorship benefits that are attributed to the policy each year. When members of the insured's "pool" of insureds die, their cash values are divided among the survivors in the pool. Every year, therefore, the insured pays the premium, and a mortality charge is deducted for the cost of the insurance. All the mortality charges of all the individuals in the pool are accumulated and used to pay out death benefits to the beneficiaries of those in the pool who die during the year. Then, survivorship benefits from those who die are added to the account along with the interest income. The sum of the interest income and the survivorship benefit is always greater than the mortality charge, so the savings element grows. Interestingly, the interest accumulated on the cash values is not taxable as income until the cash values are taken out of the policy. This tax benefit, along with the idea of an "enforced savings" and level premiums, make the whole life product attractive to consumers. The cash value amount becomes a sort of savings account for the policyholder. It is available for borrowing at very reasonable interest rates, traditionally around 5 to 8 percent, or the insured may actually surrender the policy and receive the entire cash value.

Often whole life insurance is purchased with the idea that if the insured survives to retirement age, the cash values will be used to purchase a retirement annuity. In these situations, the life insurance protects against the peril of premature death during the income-producing years or superannuation (that is, living too long, hence outliving your income). If the policy is a participating one, dividends have also accumulated, which can be used for retirement income.

The whole life policy historically has been the most frequently purchased form of insurance for individuals. Whole life premiums proved a large source of funds for insurers because of the long-term nature of the product and the cash values that accumulate. Whole life policies pay a minimum interest rate on the cash values in the policy and are not really a lucrative investment opportunity but, of course, that is not their real purpose. The purpose of life insurance is security for the family. On the plus side, the cash values are guaranteed and are not subject to income tax.

Late in the 1970s, economic conditions lured policyholders away from whole life insurance and toward riskier investments paying higher rates of interest. Individuals were encouraged by certain insurance agents to "buy term and invest the difference." The sales scheme was to convince people that they could earn higher interest rates in the marketplace than insurers were paying them on their whole life cash values, so they should buy term insurance and invest the difference in premium (the whole life premium − the term insurance premium) in other instruments, very often some investment opportunity the agent was touting. The agents very often neglected to inform the insureds that since they were purchasing term insurance, their premiums would increase each year as they aged. They also often projected high interest rates for periods of 10 to 20 years into the future. Applicants went for the plan in a big way. Not only were they no longer buying traditional whole life insurance, but those insureds with whole life policies in force were either borrowing out all the cash values or surrendering the policies for their cash values. To stem the flow of cash from their companies, traditional insurers innovated permanent life policies, such as universal life, that paid market rates of return on policy reserves.

Universal Life

The new universal life policy design was introduced in the early 1980s, during times of very high interest rates. The policy was structured to have two distinct accounts, the insurance account and the savings or cash value account. It was a flexible-premium, nonparticipating policy, meaning that the insured could contribute to the savings account at any time and that no dividends were paid. The life insurance written was term insurance and the premium increased each year with age. The policy was designed to cover the insured for the whole life. Each month, a mortality charge was deducted from the savings account, and interest was credited to the account. The interest rates paid were very competitive with those in the market. If the insured's savings account balance fell below $1,000, then a minimum rate of interest (4 or 5 percent) was paid. The interest was not taxable as income as long as the savings amount and the life insurance amount met the requirements of the Internal Revenue Service for qualifying life insurance.

The insured had the best of both worlds with the universal life policy—insurance for the whole life and competitive interest rates being paid with deferred taxation. The policy was a huge success for the industry. By 1984, universal life accounted for 32 percent of the volume of life insurance sold. When interest rates began to fall, the product became less attractive. By 1990, the volume of universal life sold was only 20 percent of all life insurance sold.

Annuities

Annuities are a product sold by life insurers that can be thought of as the mirror image of life insurance. Whereas the function of life insurance is to create an estate, the function of an annuity is to liquidate an estate. Annuities are conservative products purchased by those who wish to guarantee that their money will last as long as they live. The insured pays a sum of money, called the capital investment, to the insurer, who scientifically liquidates it and pays the insured annuitant an annual or monthly income until death. The annuity income that is paid to the insured is made up of interest income that the insurer pays on the insured's capital, a survivorship benefit (from those in the pool who die during the year), and liquidation of the capital. Each year, the interest income becomes a smaller portion of the annuity payment and the survivorship benefit and liquidation proportion increase. The income paid will be larger than if the annuitant has placed the capital in some safe, interest-bearing instrument and lived off the interest income, because the principal is being liquidated, and the survivorship benefit is included. Also, as in whole life insurance, there are tax advantages to the annuity in that the insured doesn't pay income tax on all the income. Annuities are big business for insurers, and especially so now that the "baby boomers' are approaching retirement age. In 1986, premiums paid to insurers for individual annuities were $26.1 billion; in 1990, they were $53.7 billion.

PEOPLE
& EVENTS

Redlining Comes to Health Insurance

All during the history of insurance, some insurance companies have used "redlining" to avoid high-risk areas in property insurance or automobile insurance. For example, if the downtown area of a city experienced a high incidence of car theft, vandalism, and collision loss, insurance underwriters would figuratively draw a red line around the city on a map. They would then reject applications for insurance from automobile owners living within the red line. In recent years, with health insurance losses continuing to rise, insurers have quietly "redlined" certain occupations perceived as high-risk.

The list of occupations considered to be high-risk appears to be growing. Miners, racing jockeys, loggers, pest-control workers, bartenders, and asbestos removers have always been assumed to experience more losses than average. Lately, however, people in seemingly ordinary occupations—doctors, nurses, seasonal workers at resorts, workers at beauty salons, florists, ballet dancers, musicians, and interior

designers—have fallen within the red line. While it has always been difficult for those in some of these occupations to buy individual life or health insurance policies, they generally were able to be insured on group health insurance policies.

Representatives of the insurance industry indicate that certain occupations are excluded from coverage for several reasons. First, the very nature of the work may lead to more claims. This would be the case with jockeys, miners, hair stylists (they are exposed to toxic chemicals that lead to illness), bartenders (an occupation with a higher incidence of alcoholism and related health problems), or loggers. Second, the work may be low-paying or seasonal, attracting transient workers whose health history is difficult to document. Finally, the occupations may be those that traditionally have had a higher rate of claims, such as health-care workers who use health care more frequently than others.

Health Insurance

The perils insured against in the health insurance line are illness and disability. The medical costs associated with illness or accident can be catastrophic and the loss of income during illness or disability compounds the problem for most families. The insuring organizations that offer health insurance plans include insurance companies, Blue Cross–Blue Shield organizations (the Blues), Health Maintenance Organizations (HMOs), and Preferred Provider Organizations (PPOs). For the most part, the Blues, HMOs, and PPOs are not considered insurance companies, and are not regulated as such. Insurance companies write about 59 percent of all health insurance premiums. In 1989, life insurers took in $56.1 billion in health insurance and disability income premiums and paid out $39.4 billion in health insurance benefits—$32.7 billion for medical expenses, $4 billion for loss of income, and $2.7 billion for dental care.

The policies written include hospital expense policies, medical expense policies, surgical expense policies, major medical policies, Medicare supplement policies, disability income policies, and innovative long-term care policies. Policies may be written on individuals, families, or groups.

Underwriting in health insurance is very strict, especially for individual policies. It is much easier to become insured under a group health insurance policy than an individual one. On an individual policy, a physical examination is required and preexisting conditions are excluded from coverage, at least for a period of time, if not completely. Continuation provisions vary in health insurance, but often the insurer has the right not to renew a policy. Because medical costs have consistently increased faster than the consumer price index, the dollar amount of claims has grown rapidly and insurers are trying to control costs. Frequently insurers require that an insured get a second opinion before having surgery or have laboratory tests or minor surgery done on an outpatient basis. Insurers also reward insureds who find discrepancies on hospital bills.

The Balance Sheet of Life Insurance Companies

Life insurance funds originate primarily from the sale of life insurance policies, annuities, and pension plans that have a savings feature as part of the contract. The source of funds derives primarily from two types of liabilities—life insurance reserves, which are related to insurer obligations to policyholders and their beneficiaries, and pension reserves, which are related to insured pension plans purchased by organizations from the insurer. As Exhibit 20–3 shows, in 1990 these funds accounted for more than 80 percent of life insurance company funds.

The long-term nature of life insurance contracts and the steady cash flows they generate steer life insurance companies toward long-term investments. As Exhibit 20–3 shows, corporate bonds and mortgages are the most important investments. The tendency of life insurers toward long-term investments can create problems. When interest rates increase, the value of outstanding bonds and mortgages drops. In the event of a liquidity crunch, if an above-average number of insureds request policy loans or surrenders, for example, insurers may be required to liquidate long-term investments at substantially depressed prices, resulting in losses. With this contingency in mind, insurance regulation requires insurers to include a "deferment clause" in all life insurance policies that accumulate cash values. The clause declares the right of the insurer to defer the payment of the cash value for a period not exceeding six months from the date of the request. In some clauses, the right also applies to withdrawal of the proceeds that are being held by the company at interest. The clause is similar to a provision introduced for bank accounts as a result of the run on banks during the 1930s. Some insurers could become technically insolvent if these long-term assets were required to be liquidated or even marked to current market values.

Policy loans are monies that are loaned against the cash values of individual insurance policies. Exhibit 20–3 shows that policy loans were 4.5 percent of total assets in 1990. The importance of policy loans varies with current economic conditions. During the Great Depression, policy loans reached 18 percent of life company assets. In 1965, when interest rates and unemployment were low, policy loans made up only 4 percent of assets. In 1981, when interest rates in the market were high, policy loans accounted for 9 percent of insurer assets.

Policy loans have historically been made at low rates of interest of about 5 or 6 percent. In 1981, market interest rates greatly exceeded the low interest rates on

Exhibit 20–3   Life Insurance Companies' Balance Sheet, 1990

Type of Account	Amount ($ in billions)	Percentage
Assets		
U.S. government securities	$ 210.8	15.0
Real estate	43.4	3.0
Corporate bonds	582.6	41.4
Corporate stock	128.4	9.1
Mortgages	270.1	19.2
Policy loans	62.6	4.5
Other assets	110.2	7.8
Total	$1408.1	100.0
Liabilities and Net Worth		
Life insurance reserves	$ 348.7	24.8
Health insurance reserves	33.4	2.4
Pension fund reserves	814.6	57.8
Other liabilities	120.1	8.5
Surplus and net worth	91.3	6.5
Total	$1408.1	100.0

Life insurance companies hold long-term assets such as corporate bonds because of the long-term nature of their liabilities. They hold few municipal bonds because most of their income is exempt from federal income tax.

Source: American Council of Life Insurance, *Acquisitions and Change of Holdings, of Investments*, 1991.

policy loans, so insureds borrowed their cash values to reinvest in higher-yielding instruments. Since then, all states have enacted insurance legislation called the Model Bill on Policy Loan Rates, or a similar law, that allows life insurers to use a variable policy loan rate tied to a market interest rate.

Property and Liability Insurance

Property and liability insurers sell policies that offer protection from direct and indirect loss from such perils as fire, windstorm, theft, explosion, and negligence. Property insurance is concerned with indemnifying policyholders for the financial loss associated with the destruction and loss of use of their property. Liability insurance protects the insured who is found by a court to be negligent in causing bodily injury, property damage, or personal injury (such as libel or slander) to some person. Some examples of liability insurance include general liability, professional liability, product liability, and automobile liability.

The operations and investment practices of property and liability insurers are very different from those of life insurers for several reasons. First, property and liability insurance policies have a much shorter duration than life policies. Typically these policies are written for six months to a year. Second, the probability of loss is higher under these policies and the claim will probably have to be paid during the policy period. Thus the insurer can invest the premium revenue for a much shorter period of time. Finally, the objective risk of the property and liability insurer is greater than that of the life insurer. Claims against property and liability insurers are greatly affected by economic conditions and are often much greater than predicted. For example, inflation affects workers' compensation losses, the cost of replacing property, and amounts awarded in liability suits. Thus property and liability insurers invest a larger proportion of their funds in corporate stocks for high yield and in municipal bonds for tax advantages. The 1990 balance sheet for all property and liability insurers is shown in Exhibit 20–4.

Types of Property and Liability Insurance

Property Insurance.   Property insurance is purchased by individuals and organizations as protection against direct or indirect loss to property they own or lease. *Named peril policies* will cover loss from perils that are specifically named, such as lightning, windstorm, or theft, while *all-risk policies* protect the insured against loss from all perils except those specifically excluded from the policy. An insurer's loss exposure in property insurance is easy to predict because it is generally not difficult to determine the value of a particular piece of property.

Exhibit 20–4   Property/Liability Companies' Balance Sheet, 1990

Type of Account	Amount ($ in billions)	Percentage
Assets		
Government securities	$126.3	22.7
Municipal bonds	61.2	11.0
Corporate bonds	102.4	18.4
Corporate stocks	104.6	18.8
Special revenue bonds	145.8	26.2
Other assets	16.0	2.9
Total	$556.3	100.0
Liabilities and Net Worth		
Policy contracts	$417.9	75.1
Surplus and net worth	138.4	24.9
Total	$556.3	100.0

Property/liability insurance companies hold long-term assets such as corporate bonds because of the long-term of their liabilities. Municipal bonds are held to shield income from taxation.

Source: Insurance Information Institute, 1991 Fact Book.

Liability Insurance.   Liability insurance is purchased by individuals and organizations as protection against financial loss because of a claim of negligence against them by a third party. Liability policies agree to defend the insured against suits of negligence and to pay damages awarded by the court for bodily injury, property damage, and sometimes personal injury such as libel or slander. Liability exposure is much more difficult to predict than property exposure since there is no upper limit on damages that may be awarded. Some states have enacted tort reform statutes that may limit punitive damages, but special damages and general damages are not limited. A liability loss, therefore, is one that can be catastrophic in nature.

Marine Insurance.   Marine insurance is a special classification of property and liability insurance. Marine contracts, which cover losses related to transportation exposures, are divided into two categories: ocean marine and inland marine. *Ocean marine policies* include hull coverage for damage to the vessel and indemnity (liability) coverage. The policies can be endorsed to provide cargo coverage, longshoreman and harborworker coverage, and other supplemental coverages. *Inland marine policies* include coverage for such exposures as goods transported by rail, motor vehicles, armored cars, and such "instrumentalities of transportation" as bridges, tunnels, pipelines, lighthouses, and communication equipment. *Floater policies* covering scheduled items of high value such as fine arts, jewelry, furs, and antiques also fall under the classification of inland marine.

Multiline Policies

Certain "package policies" frequently written by property and liability insurers contain both property and liability insurance coverages. The homeowner's policy is a popular example. This policy was developed in the 1950s and continues to be widely written. For one premium, the policy offers individual homeowners property insurance for direct loss to the dwelling, other structures on the property, and personal property, as well as coverage for indirect costs resulting from loss of use of the property, personal liability insurance, and various supplemental coverages.

Like the homeowner's policy, the personal auto policy (PAP) is a popular package policy that combines a variety of coverages. Unlike the homeowner's policy, the PAP requires that the insured choose which coverages are to be included in the policy and pay separate premiums for each. Automobile liability insurance, uninsured motorists coverage, coverage for physical damage to one's own vehicle, medical payments coverage, and, in most states, no-fault coverage may be included in the policy, as well as supplemental coverages that may be endorsed.

Regulation of Insurance

Insurance companies are regulated by the states in which they do business. Insurers are regulated for several reasons. First, regulation requires capital adequacy. Premiums are paid in advance when an insured purchases an insurance policy, but the insurance coverage extends into the future. To ensure that future losses will be paid, the financial strength of insurers must be carefully monitored for the protection of policyholders, beneficiaries, and third-party claimants. Second, regulation is important because many consumers of insurance lack the ability to read and understand complicated insurance contracts, so regulations protect consumers in the drafting of policies. Third, regulation assures reasonable insurance rates, although it is arguable whether this is a good reason for regulation, especially in light of insurance company losses in recent years. Finally, insurance regulation assures that insurance is available to all who need it, either from private insurers or from government programs.

State Insurance Regulation

Insurance regulation began with states granting charters to insurance companies authorizing their formation and operation. In 1837, Massachusetts began the first formal regulation when it passed legislation requiring insurers to establish reserves for financial stability. The first state to establish a separate insurance department was New Hampshire in 1841. In 1859, New York created a separate administrative agency headed by a superintendent who had broad licensing and investigative authority. Today all states have an insurance department, usually headed by an insurance commissioner who is either appointed by the governor or elected.

All states have insurance codes, which are books of law addressing formation of insurance companies in the state, licensing of agents and brokers, financial requirements for maintaining solvency, selling practices and claims-paying practices, taxation, and rehabilitation or liquidation of insurers within the state. The New York Insurance Code is the toughest on insurers and is extraterritorial because of the Appleton Rule, a part of the code. The rule states that any insurer licensed to do business in New York must comply with the New York code in any state in which it operates. Insurance is also regulated by court decisions affecting constitutionality of state laws, policy interpretation, and actions taken by the insurance department. Insurers are also regulated by the commissioners, who have considerable power to issue, revoke, or deny licenses, to hold hearings, and to place the company in rehabilitation or liquidation.

Areas of Regulation

Licensing.   After formation, an insurer must be licensed before it can do business in a state. Insurers must meet minimum capital and surplus requirements to obtain a license.

Financial Regulation.   Every year, insurers must file a series of financial statements called "Convention Blanks" with the commissioner's office in every state of operation. An insurer must have sufficient admitted assets to offset its liabilities. Also, reserves must be shown on the balance sheet, and the states regulate the methods that may be used to calculate the reserves. The surplus position of each company is also regulated. Policyholders' surplus is the difference between the insurer's assets and liabilities. This surplus is especially important in property and liability insurance. The amount of new business an insurer is allowed to write is limited by its policyholders' surplus. For example, conservative states with more strict regulation allow only $2 of net new premiums for each $1 of policyholders' surplus. Also, surplus is necessary to offset any substantial underwriting or investment loss or deficiency in loss reserves over time. Policyholders' surplus may be less important in life insurance because of conservative interest rate assumptions and valuation of investments, safety margins in calculating premiums and dividends, and less likelihood of catastrophic loss.

States regulate the types and quality of investments that insurers make and also establish the maximum percentage of total assets that can be invested in certain instruments. Life insurers, for example, are limited in the percentage of total assets that can be invested in common stocks. In New York, common stock investments are limited to 10 percent of total assets or 100 percent of surplus, whichever is lower. Property and liability insurers are subject to fewer restrictions, but for the minimum capital requirements, for instance, the funds may be invested in federal, state, or municipal bonds. Investments in early estate are generally limited.

Also regulated are expenses of insurers: commission rates that can be paid to agents, bonuses, acquisition fees, and so forth. The New York Insurance Code is particularly limiting. For example, an insurer licensed to do business in New York may pay no more than 55 percent first-year commission to its agents.

Liquidation.   Liquidation of insurers is also regulated, and if a company becomes technically insolvent, the state insurance commissioner assumes control of the company with the intent of rehabilitating it. If it cannot be rehabilitated, it is liquidated according to the code. All states have "guaranty funds" that pay the claims of defunct property and liability insurers. Some states have guaranty funds for insolvent life and health insurers. Often the commissioner can find another insurer to buy the troubled company to avoid liquidation.

Other Regulations.   Rates, policy forms, sales practices, and claims practices are also regulated in varying degrees among the states. In some states rates must be filed and approved before they can be used by the insurer; in others they must just be filed. Some insurance policy forms must also be approved by the commissioner for readability and coverages provided. All states regulate the licensing of agents and brokers, requiring the agent to pass a license exam before selling insurance. All states have a complaint division to handle consumer complaints about unfair treatment by insurers.

The National Association of Insurance Commissioners

The National Association of Insurance Commissioners (NAIC) was founded in 1871 to set uniform regulatory standards among the states. The NAIC is not a statutory body but an organization of insurance commissioners who meet regularly for the purpose of discussing mutual problems and preparing model legislation for recommendation to their respective legislatures. By reciprocity, the commissioners have developed systems for cooperative company audits, simultaneous investigations of interstate problems, and information exchanges that increase efficiency in the regulatory process. By virtue of its high degree of cooperation, the NAIC has overcome much of the burden of conflicting regulation in the different jurisdictions within the United States.

Expansion into New Markets

No treatment of insurance company operations would be complete without reference to the changing nature of insurance markets, products, and services. The idea of "one-stop shopping" applied to insurance first received national attention in the 1960s when a number of companies explored the marketing of both life and property/liability insurance through the same agency forces. It was argued that the insuring public wanted to buy all its insurance from the same organization, but the experiment was short-lived and never accepted by most insurance consumers.

During the 1980s, one-stop shopping reemerged with renewed vigor and a new dimension—the financial "supermarket." This concept is not limited to insurance but rather has been touted as the answer to the investor's needs. The concept has referred to offering an entire range of financial services under one marketing "roof." Along with others, insurance companies have entered the broader financial marketplace in earnest. Mergers and acquisitions are the order of the day, and no one is certain of the future for these new ventures.

The Emerging Financial Services Industry

Insurance companies, the securities industries, and banks and savings and loans are currently on parallel paths in their attempts to market a broad range of financial services, including insurance policies, mutual funds, stock brokerage, money market funds, tax shelters, and other diversified financial services such as financial counseling and real estate management services. However, existing regulatory policies continue to restrict the extent to which life insurance companies can provide banking services, just as they restrict the extent to which banks can engage in insurance selling and underwriting. Banks are generally restricted from entering into the insurance business (in particular, selling and underwriting insurance directly) through the Bank Holding Company Act. Existing regulations also severely restrict the ability of insurers to enter banking areas such as trust, credit card services, and deposit taking and servicing. Because many large banks want to sell insurance and some insurers are pushing to offer a variety of banking services, there has been an accelerating trend toward consolidation within the financial services industry through mergers and acquisitions. The result has been a lowering of regulatory barriers separating these financial service activities. Despite the recent legislation that continued the separation between insurance and banking, people in both industries believe that further deregulation is likely, with the result being eventual removal of most barriers to financial services integration. Banks continue making inroads into the insurance business. A June 1991 decision of the Second Circuit Court of New York permits state-chartered subsidiaries of bank holding companies to sell and underwrite all lines of insurance. Legislation is also pending in Congress that would permit two types of holding companies: financial services holding companies that own institutions like banks and diversified holding companies that can own financial services holding companies as well as other businesses such as insurers. Under the legislation, insurance could be conducted only under the subsidiary that is not a financial services holding company. Confusing? Yes, and very risky.

The recurrent theme is "consumer service," with one agent or company orchestrating the consumer's entire financial planning program, including insurance, mutual funds, money market funds, stocks, bonds, tax shelters, and tax write-offs. Many companies contend that this movement toward integrated financial services is a response to the demands of sophisticated consumers, whereas other believe that the change in the financial services environment has occurred because of a desire to pursue more consumer protection and more investment dollars. It remains to be seen to what extent this broadening of horizons will appeal to the consumer.

Pensions

Pensions are used to protect against the peril of superannuation, a fancy word for "being disqualified for duty because of advanced age." Simply put, pensions provide income during retirement years. The movement toward providing pensions for retired people has been influenced by the increasing number of people living well into old age. In 1920, about 4.9 million people were older than 65, about 4.6 percent of the population. In 1985, 28.9 million Americans were over the age of 65, about 11.7 percent of the population. By the year 2030, it is estimated that between 18 and 25 percent of the population will be over 65. Increased life expectancy, a declining birth rate, and a curtailment of immigration has contributed to this upsurge.

Several other trends in the country have created concern about providing income to older citizens. First, there are few job opportunities for the aged. For example, in the late 1800s when the country was still largely agrarian, aged Americans made up 3.9 percent of the total population and 4.3 percent of the workforce; in 1985, only 2.5 percent of the work force was older Americans, while they made up 11.7 percent of the population.

Second, children now feel less responsible for the support of their aged parents than in the past. Because Americans are more geographically mobile and because more families own their homes rather than living with parents, grandparents, parents, and children no longer live together and take care of each other into old age. Third, it has also become increasingly difficult for individuals to save for old age. Taxes have increased, inflation has continued to erode the spending power of the dollar, and there has been a weakened propensity to save among the general population. These changes have led individuals to look more to the government and employers for income assistance in old age.

Pension plans have been among the fastest-growing financial intermediaries in the last 25 years. Like insurance, pensions are contractual agreements that provide benefits when the insured retires. Someone, either the employee, or the employer, or both, purchases the pension by way of a single lump-sum payment, or by premium payments made over a period of time. The pension fund invests the money and uses the interest earned on the money and the principal to make retirement pension payments.

History of the Pension Industry

A historical examination of the pension industry will enhance our understanding of its current structure and regulation. Industrialization is the key to the establishment of pension funds. The rise of industrialism brought about the specialization of labor and a movement of families from rural areas to the cities. No longer self-sufficient and with diminished reliance on the family unit for financial support, these people needed some systematic way of preparing financially for retirement or a means of support if disabled. The earliest pension programs were established by the railroads, the first in the United States in 1875 by the American Express Company and the second by the Baltimore and Ohio Railroad in 1880. Railroads were the first to establish pensions because they were the first business organizations to obtain large size, and, more important, because the work was hazardous and some type of relief was needed, particularly for the disabled.

Unfortunately for American workers, there was no rush by industry or government to establish pension funds. By 1929, there were only 400 assorted pension funds in operation with pension assets of less than $500 million, covering fewer than 4 million workers and their families. The Great Depression strongly affected existing pension funds. Many business firms went bankrupt and so did a large number of pension funds. Pension funds often failed because it was common practice for firms to pay benefits out of current income. In general, these nonfunded, pay-as-you-go pension plans operated without regulation, and participants had few, if any, rights. Pension plans that were underwritten by insurance companies, however, were actuarially funded and proved to be far superior in weathering the rough financial times of the 1930s.

The financial hardships of the Great Depression underscored the need for some type of universal retirement and disability program, and the passage of the Social Security Act in 1935 helped meet the need for financial security. The program's purpose was to provide minimum retirement coverage, with the balance of the coverage being supplied by the private sector. However, it was not until World War II that private pension plans became an important factor in the economy. There are several reasons for their emergence. First, during the war, employers found it exceedingly difficult to attract and retain qualified employees because of a shortage of labor and because of wage and price controls. One method to circumvent these controls was to offer generous pension plans, which were not covered by wage and price controls and were a means of increasing an employee's real income. In addition, firms were subject to excess-profit taxes during the war. Pension plan payments were tax deductible and helped firms reduce excess-profit taxes. By 1945, private pension plans covered 6.4 million workers, up 50 percent from the number that had been covered five years earlier.

After World War II, several other events contributed to the growth of pension plans. First, in 1949 the Supreme Court declined to review a ruling by the National Labor Relations Board[1] that the Inland Steel Company must bargain collectively with representatives of its employees over "conditions of employment," including pension benefits as well as wages. This ruling ended the traditional notion by employers that pensions plans were benevolent "gifts" bestowed on loyal retiring employees. Instead, the Court established that pension funds were part of the

---

[1]*Inland Steel Company* v. *National Labor Relations Board*, 170 E2d 247, 251 (1948). Certiorari denied by the Supreme Court, 336 U.S. 960 (1949).

employees' overall wage packages. Specifically, the Court viewed pension payments as deferred wages to be paid upon retirement.

Wage controls and excess-profit taxes were again imposed during the Korean conflict from 1950 to 1953 and had an effect similar to that of controls during World War II. Employers again used pension funds as a means of raising real wages and lowering their excess-profits tax liability. However, by this time pension fund plans were well accepted by both employers and unions as part of employee wage packages. Unions representing the auto workers and steel workers pioneered many pension practices that are considered standard today. The number of Americans covered by pension plans increased from 9.8 million in 1950 to more than 21 million workers by 1960.

Another major event in the development of pension plans was the enactment of the Self-Employed Individuals' Tax Retirement Act of 1962, better known as H.R. 10 or the Keogh Act, which provides for tax-sheltered pension plans for self-employed persons (Keogh Plans). The next new legislation affecting individual pension accounts was the 1978 Pension Reform Act, which established the Individual Retirement Account (IRA). The legislation concerning IRAs has changed several times since their inception in 1978. The original intent for the IRA was to provide a tax-deferred method to save for retirement for those not covered under employer pension plans. The Economic Recovery Tax Act of 1981 (ERTA) and the Tax Equity and Fiscal Responsibility Act of 1982 (TEFRA) expanded the role of IRAs, allowing virtually all taxpayers to put pretax funds into IRAs. The Tax Reform Act of 1986 substantially decreased the number of individuals eligible to put pretax funds into IRAs.

To be eligible to contribute to an IRA, an individual must be less than $70\frac{1}{2}$ years of age. Individuals can make contributions up to $2,000. Interest earned on these contributions will accrue tax-free until the funds are removed from the account. The amount of pretax funds that an individual is eligible to invest in IRAs is reduced if the individual is a participation in an employer-maintained fund. If the individual is not part of an employer-maintained fund, the contribution is tax deductible in the current tax year. For an individual filing a joint return who is not a participant in an employer-maintained plan, the maximum amount that can be deducted is equal to $2,000 − 0.2 (adjusted gross income − $40,000). Thus, individuals with joint income of less than $40,000 per year can fully deduct the contribution made to their IRA. If the individual has income in excess of $50,000 per year, the contribution to the IRA is not tax-deductible.

Despite the reduction in allowable contributions to IRAs, various other plans exist that still allow individuals to make pretax contributions to retirement plans. One popular plan is the cash or deferred arrangement (CODA). This type of plan is regulated under section 401(k) of the Internal Revenue Code. Individuals are allowed to deposit up to $7,000 of pretax wages into CODAs. If the employer makes a matching contribution, the maximum pretax deposit (by employer and employee) to the fund is limited to a total of $9,500. The limitations on pretax contributions are tied to the Consumer Price Index (CPI) for years after the 1987 base. Withdrawals from these plans are often allowed without penalty under specific conditions. The sums withdrawn are treated as regular income for the year of withdrawal.

Another type of plan that allows for pretax deposit of funds into individual accounts is the tax deferred annuity (TDA), which falls under section 403(b) of the

Internal Revenue Code. These plans are limited to those persons who are employed by nonprofit organizations or by a public school system. The maximum pretax amount that an employee can elect to deposit is limited to the lesser of 20 percent of salary or $9,500. The maximum contribution is tied to the CPI for years after the 1987 base year. Catch-up provisions exist under the law that allow individuals to deposit sums into the account to make up for previous years when an amount less than the maximum contribution was deposited. Withdrawals are often allowed under such plans, and amounts withdrawn from the plan are treated as regular income for that tax year. Additional tax penalties may occur upon withdrawal of funds under some conditions.

Other and more significant developments in the pension fund field were the enactment of the Employment Retirement Income Security Act (ERISA) in 1974 and the Tax Reform Act of 1986. The twofold purpose of ERISA was to strengthen the fiduciary responsibilities of pension fund trustees and to improve the financial soundness of pension funds. It should be noted, however, that ERISA applies primarily to private pension and other employee welfare plans but does *not* cover government pension plans. The Tax Reform Act of 1986 made some substantial changes to the laws governing pensions. The act imposed new restrictions on the size of benefits, the period of time before benefits become the property of the pensioner, and the proportion of benefits that can be paid to higher-income employees.

Types of Pension Plans

Pension funds have been among the fastest-growing financial intermediaries during the past two decades. They are contractual agreements that provide benefit payments upon the participant's retirement. Pension plans can be divided into two basic types: private pension plans and government-sponsored plans. Private pension plans are those established by private-sector groups, such as industrial, commercial, union, or service organizations, as well as certain nonprofit operations and those established by individuals that are not employment-related.

Private pension plans obtain their funds from employer and employee contributions. State and local government employee retirement funds are similar to the private plans in that funds are obtained from employee and government contributions. The largest and most important federally sponsored program is Social Security, which is funded from current tax revenues (FICA taxes). Social Security provides a prime example of the financial dangers and weaknesses of an unfunded, pay-as-you-go plan.

As shown in Exhibit 20–5, total assets held by all private and government-administered pension funds amounted to $3 trillion at year-end 1990. Private pension funds accounted for 61 percent of this total.

We now will discuss each of these types of pension plans in turn.

Private Pension Plans

There are two basic forms into which private pension funds are organized. One is an *insured* pension plan established with a life insurance company. The other is a *noninsured* pension plan managed by a trustee appointed by the sponsoring organization, such as a business or union. The trustee is usually a commercial bank or trust

Exhibit 20–5   **Total Assets of Major Retirement Programs, 1990**

Type of Pension Plan	Amount ($ in billions)	Percentage
Private Pension Plans		
With life insurance companies	$ 713.3	23.6
Other private plans	1,125.0	37.1
Total	$1,838.3	60.7
Government-Administered Plans		
Federal civilian employees	$247.5	8.2
State and local employees	707.7	23.4
Railroad retirement	9.9	0.3
Total	$965.1	31.9
Social Security	225.3	7.4
Grand total	$3,028.7	100.0

Pension funds have been one of the fastest-growing financial intermediaries in recent years. Most pension assets are held in private pension plans.

Source: American Council on Life Insurance, Assets and Reserves of Major Pension and Retirement Plans, August 14, 1991.

company, which holds and invests the contributions and pays retirement benefits in accordance with the terms of the trust. In some instances, the investment procedure is handled directly by the sponsoring organization. This is often the case with large companies or unions. Pension funds constitute more than one-third of the assets of commercial banks' trust departments, and there is intense competition among financial institutions for the business of managing these large sums of money.

The design of pension plans has caused some problems for plan participants. Design problems include underfunding, restrictive eligibility requirements (vesting), and the inability to transfer pension rights when changing jobs (portability). *Underfunding* means that employee/employer contributions are not large enough actuarially to cover the benefits promised to be paid when the employee retires or the plan terminates. Underfunded pension plans are subject to future failure when large numbers of participants reach retirement age. In many instances, underfunding becomes a problem only when a firm goes out of business. When this happens, there are no future incoming employee or employer contributions, leaving the retirement plan with inadequate funds to pay those entitled to receive benefits. If the pension plan were *fully funded*, there would be no problem. Funded pension plans formally establish charges against current income (and principal, if needed) to meet pension liabilities as they accrue in order to minimize the risk that benefits will not be available upon retirement. The Pension Benefit Guarantee Corporation (PBGC) was set up to guarantee pension benefits in case of default by private pension plans. As was previously mentioned, the PBGC guarantees benefits up to a monthly maximum for the participants in plans that default.

Vesting is one of the most important issues relating to pension plan rights. *Vesting* means that an employee owns the right to some portion of future retirement income whether or not he or she leaves the firm before retirement. In a nonvested retirement program, an employee who is fired or who leaves the firm before retirement forfeits all claim to the employer's contributions for retirement income on behalf of the employee. Prior to ERISA, most private retirement programs had either restrictive vesting provisions or none at all. As reported later in this chapter, the vesting requirements under ERISA have improved this situation substantially for covered plans. The Tax Reform Act of 1986 substantially changed the maximum vesting standards allowed under qualified pension plans. The maximum vesting period was decreased from fifteen to seven years.

A final issue is that of portability. *Portability* refers to the ability of employees to transfer vested pension benefits when they move from job to job and to combine those benefits into one pension fund. Typically, when employees leave jobs, they receive their vested benefits in a lump-sum pension payment that is often spent for current consumption. Any nonvested pension payments are, of course, lost forever. Employees who frequently switch jobs find themselves with retirement benefits (if any) substantially below those of employees who have remained with a single employer.

State and Local Government Plans

State and local government employee pension plans are designed to cover teachers, police officers, firefighters, and other employees of states, counties, and cities. Government plans typically do not conform to ERISA standards; the main differences are usually related to vesting standards, funding status, and rules concerning equity. In recent years, state and local governments have substantially increased deferred pension benefits to their employees. These increases have acted as a partial substitute for higher wage agreements. At the same time, municipal governments' pension fund contributions have not always kept pace with the amount necessary to pay the increased promised benefit. This has been done to avoid raising taxes, which is always politically unpopular. Unless there are forthcoming increases in taxes to eliminate the underfunding, many experts foresee major financial problems for many state and local government pension plans. The recent economic problems of New York City and other large city governments have led to reevaluations of funding procedures. Many economists are calling for state and local government pension systems to be required by law to actuarially fund their pension programs, thereby preventing irresponsible legislative pension increases, as have been mandated by some municipal governments.

Federal Government Plans

The federal government operates a number of pension funds. Some are large retirement funds of civil service and military employees; others are small separate funds for employees of the foreign service, federal judiciary, the Tennessee Valley Authority, and the Board of Governors of the Federal Reserve System. The largest federal government pension fund is Social Security, formally called the Old Age, Survivors, Disability, and Health Insurance System (OASDHI). Social Security is financed through employer-and employee-contributed taxes to provide payments to those who retire and to help families whose breadwinners have died or become disabled.

Social Security is intended to provide minimum retirement income for those covered by the plan, and it differs from most other pension plans in that it is a pay-as-you-go system. That is, participants do not contribute directly to their own benefits; instead, retirement benefits are paid from the Social Security taxes of those currently working. This method of financing is creating serious problems. Slowing population growth and increasing numbers of people reaching retirement age will necessitate a sharp increase in Social Security taxes to maintain current benefits. As a result, the federal government is exploring alternative ways to finance Social Security in the future. There have been numerous attempts to return Social Security to a sound financial position, including, among other changes, large tax increases for employees, employers, and self-employed individuals; increased taxation of benefits for certain groups; and an increase in the retirement age beginning in the year 2000. In addition, a recent law makes new federal employees, the president, members of Congress, and other federal officials subject to the Social Security laws and taxes. As a result of these efforts, the near-term outlook for the solvency of the Social Security system is favorable. Large surpluses are expected to accumulate in the Social Security trust funds through the beginning of the next century. The size of the surplus will diminish as the baby boom generation reaches retirement, starting about 2010. The predictions concerning the size of the Social Security trust fund are based on the most likely economic scenario. Changes in economic conditions, such as the occurrence of a major recession or unexpected economic growth, would produce results that differ substantially from the predictions.

Pension Fund Regulation

The Employee Retirement Income Security Act (ERISA) was signed into law on Labor Day, 1974. The law does not require employers to establish a pension program for its employees; it does, however, require that certain standards be observed if the plan is to retain its advantageous tax status. ERISA was passed because Congress had become concerned that many workers with long years of service were failing to receive pension benefits. In some instances, workers were forced out of employment before retirement age. In other situations, pension funds failed in their fiduciary responsibilities to their participants because the firms failed, pension plans were inadequately funded, or investment funds were mismanaged. Some of ERISA's more important provisions attempted to (1) strengthen the fiduciary responsibilities of fund's trustees, (2) establish reporting and disclosure requirements, (3) provide for insurance of the retirees' pension benefits in event of default or termination of the plan, and (4) allow self-employed persons to make tax-deferred pension contributions. Because of the importance of ERISA and its far-reaching implications for pension fund operations, we shall discuss some of its more important provisions. Because many of the provisions in ERISA were strengthened by subsequent revisions, the effect of recent modifications will be incorporated into the following discussion.

Features of ERISA

Funding Standards.   Funding refers to employers' advance preparation for setting aside money to pay pension benefits. ERISA established minimum guidelines for the funding of benefits under "qualified" plans. To remain qualified, contributions to pension plans must be sufficient both to meet current costs and to amortize past service liabilities and payments over not more than 40 years. Employers who fail to meet the funding requirements are subject to substantial tax penalties.

Portability Provisions.   Workers changing jobs may defer tax payment on a lump-sum distribution of vested credits from their employers by investing them in a tax-qualified individual annuity account (IRA) or by depositing them in the new employer's plan. The law does not require any specific portability provisions from plan to plan.

Vesting.   To remain qualified under ERISA, a pension plan must provide minimum vesting of employee retirement benefits. A variety of vesting standards are allowed, ranging from 100 percent vesting after ten years to graduated vesting so that 100 percent vesting will occur at the end of seven years of service.

Plan Termination Insurance.   A new federal insurance agency, the Pension Benefit Guarantee Corporation (PBGC), was established under ERISA. During 1987, the PBGC insured pension benefits up to a maximum of $1,857.95 per month for each pensioner. For future years, the maximum benefit will be adjusted for inflation. Only benefits that were vested under the plan prior to termination are guaranteed by the PBGC. If a plan is overfunded when it is terminated, the employer is entitled to receive a reversion of surplus assets. The Tax Reform Act of 1986 imposed a 10 percent tax on reversions to reduce the incentive for terminating such plans.

Fiduciary Standards.   *A plan fiduciary* is any trustee, investment adviser, or other person who has discretionary authority of responsibility in the management of the plan or its assets. Fiduciaries are required to perform their duties solely in the interest of plan participants and beneficiaries as defined in the pension law.

Reporting and Disclosure Requirements.   All plans are required to file a report (Form 5500) with the Department of Labor annually. This report discloses information about pension and welfare plans, their operations, and their financial conditions to the Secretary of Labor and to plan participants and their beneficiaries.

Overall, ERISA is viewed as a milestone in pension fund legislation. The creation of the PBGC was particularly important from the employee's standpoint. Before ERISA, when an employer went bankrupt, the employee could not collect anything beyond what was in the pension fund. PBGC relieves employees of the risk of losing pension benefits up to the established maximum amount per month. ERISA's provisions have been strengthened by other legislation, including ERTA, TEFRA, and the Tax Reform Act of 1986. This legislation tightens vesting standards, penalizes companies for reverting assets, and reduces discrimination in favor of highly compensated employees.

The current state of legislation is not without its critics. Criticism has been voiced concerning the failure to cover all plans; current regulation does not include public plans, leaving many employees of state and local governments with inadequate pension protection. Also, legislation does not guarantee that vested benefits will be portable between employers and does not go far enough in discouraging employers from terminating either underfunded or overfunded plans.

Summary

This chapter examines several contractual financial institutions: (1) life and health insurance companies, (2) property/liability insurance companies, and (3) pension plans. These institutions are characterized by a relatively steady inflow of funds in the form of insurance premiums or regular contributions to retirement plans. Because few people fail to pay insurance premiums or retirement payments, these institutions can estimate fairly accurately the amounts of insurance premiums and pension contributions to be paid. Thus liquidity is not a major problem. The investment policies of contractual savings institutions tend toward long-term assets with maturities that closely match their long-term liabilities.

Insurance is a contract whereby one party undertakes to indemnify another against loss, damage, or liability arising from a contingent or unknown event. The functions of insurance are to reduce anxiety and to provide protection against large, sudden financial losses. Uncertainty inhibits business and personal affairs.

Life and health insurance companies sell protection against loss of income from premature death, disability and from savings that run out when living to ages beyond expectation. These companies are regulated by the state in which they operate, and most of their income is not subjected to federal income tax. Life and health insurance companies sell several basic types of policies. Term insurance, whole life insurance, annuities, and endowments are the most common life insurance products; disability insurance and medical insurance are the major forms of health insurance products.

Property/liability insurance companies sell protection against loss of property or injury resulting from fire, theft, accident, or negligence. Their operation differs from life insurance companies in that (1) policies are usually for shorter periods of time, (2) the probabilities of the events they insure are more difficult to estimate accurately, and (3) their investment income is subject to federal income tax. These companies sell a variety of products, of which the most important are liability insurance, surety and fidelity bonds, marine insurance, fire insurance, homeowner's insurance, and automobile policies for families and businesses.

Pension funds are contractual agreements that provide benefits upon an employee's retirement. Most pension plans have benefit provisions based on earnings levels, contributions, and duration of employment. Thus the future retiree gains some sense of security from the knowledge that a certain amount of benefits awaits him or her upon retirement. Pension plans can be either private or government sponsored.

The largest and most important federal pension is the Social Security OASDHI program, which is intended to provide minimum retirement benefits for those covered by the plan. Social Security differs from most pension plans in that it is a pay-as-you-go system. At present, Social Security faces serious financial problems as the number of contributors decreases relative to the number of benefit recipients, and also as the level of promised benefits continues to rise.

A major piece of pension fund legislation was the Self-Employed Individual's Tax Retirement Act in 1962, better known as the Keogh Plan, which allows self-employed individuals to establish tax-sheltered retirement plans. A later major legislative action was the Employee Retirement Income Security Act (ERISA) of 1974, which increased the fiduciary responsibilities of trustees and provided insurance protection for pension funds in the event of default or termination. ERISA and the subsequent ERTA, TEFRA, and Tax Reform Act of 1986 have substantially strengthened pension regulations by promoting the solvency and equity of pension plans.

Questions

1. Describe the economic benefits of insurance to individuals and to the economy.
2. Explain the process by which insurance companies set their premiums. Why is investment income critical in the rate-setting process?
3. Identify the primary components of the life insurance balance sheet. The property and liability insurance balance sheet.
4. Identify the reasons for insurance regulation.
5. Define objective risk.
6. Distinguish between pure risk and speculative risk.
7. Explain the liquidity risk of life insurers. What regulation addresses this risk?
8. Why is interest rate risk important to insurers in rate-making?
9. Define policyholders' surplus and explain why it may be more important to property and liability insurers than life insurers.
10. What factors led to an increase in employer-sponsored pension plans?
11. Describe the characteristics of property and liability insurers that have become insolvent in the last 20 years.
12. What are portability and vesting provisions in pension programs? Why are they important to those being insured?

Selected References

Allen, Everett, J. Melone, J. Rosenbloom, and J. Vanderhei. *Pension Planning*. Homewood, IL: Richard D. Irwin, 1988.
A compilation of regulations and procedures concerning pensions and other deferred compensation plans.

American Council of Life Insurance. *Life Insurance Fact Book*. Washington, DC, 1991.
A good source of statistics concerning the life and health insurance industry.

Best's Review: Life and Health edition and Property and Casualty edition. Oldwick, NJ: A. M. Best, monthly.
Articles about the current state of the life/health and property/liability fields.

Fields, Joseph A. "The Role of Employee Benefits in Corporate Takeovers." *Benefits Quarterly.* Third Quarter 1986, pp. 10–14.

Greene, Mark R., James S. Trieschmann, and Sandra G. Gustavson. *Risk and Insurance*. Cincinnati, OH: South-Western Publishing, 1992.
An excellent introductory text covering all aspects of insurance, employee benefits, and risk management.

Insurance Information Institute. *Property/Casualty Fact Book*. **New York, 1991.**
A good source for information about the property/liability industry.

McGill, Dan M., and Donald S. Grubbs. *Fundamentals of Private Pensions*. **Homewood, IL: Richard D. Irwin, 1989.**

Mehr and Gustavson. *Life Insurance: Theory and Practice*. **Plano, TX: Business Publications, 1987.**

INVESTMENT BANKS, VENTURE CAPITALISTS, AND INVESTMENT FUNDS

INVESTMENT BANKING HAS THE ALLURE of allowing one to make lots of money. How would you like to make $60,000 two years out of college or $1 million a year or more as a partner in a prestigious Wall Street firm? Where else can you even come close to making that much money? Glamorous profession? Well, the job can have its downside.

"Put the handcuffs on them." These words were not spoken to common criminals but to senior executives of Goldman Sachs & Co. and Kidder Peabody & Co., two of Wall Street's classiest old-line investment banking firms. The two principals were arrested at their desk and taken out through a trading room full of open-mouthed colleagues! The scene was just part of the ongoing insider-trading bombshell that may be the Wall Street scandal of the century. The scandal involves Wall Street luminaries, and some of its brightest and best-educated young stars: Ivan F. Boesky (Ivan F. Boesky & Co.), Dennis B. Levine (Drexel Burnham Lambert), Ira B. Sokolow (Shearson Lehman Brothers), Robert M. Wilkis (Lazard Freres), David S. Brown (Goldman Sachs & Co.), and Michael Milken (Drexel Burnham Lambert), the wizard of the junk bond market, to name a few. The tragedy for Wall Street is that it cannot explain away the scandals as an outcropping of yuppie amorality or naiveté, or lay the blame on sinister outlaws operating on the fringes of Wall Street. Investment banking, the glamour business of the 1980s, harbored corruption in its very foundation.

This chapter is about Wall Street firms and highlights investment banks, which are the premier players in the capital market. Our story is also about commercial banks and their head-to-head struggle with investment banks over customers and products. We then describe venture capitalists, institutional investors that provide capital to new, thriving businesses. We also describe the functions of various specialized investment funds—unit investment trusts, mutual funds, money market mutual funds, and real estate investment trusts (REITs). We note how these specialized institutions have waxed or waned, depending on the regulatory environment and the demand for specific financial services.

Investment Banking

As we discussed in Chapter 2, there are two basic ways in which new financial claims can be brought to market: direct or indirect (intermediation) financing. In the indirect credit market, commercial banks are the most important participants; in the direct market, investment banks are the most important participants. Investment banks are firms that specialize in helping businesses and governments sell their new security issues (debt or equity) in the primary markets to finance capital expenditures. In addition, after the securities are sold, investment bankers make secondary markets for the securities as brokers and dealers.

The term *investment bank* is somewhat misleading, because those involved have little to do with commercial banking (accepting deposits and making commercial loans). The Glass-Steagall Act of 1933 separated the investment banking and commercial banking industries. The act, however, does allow commercial banks some securities activities, such as underwriting and trading in U.S. government securities, and some state and local government bonds. Thus, in the area of public securities, investment banks and commercial banks do compete.

The legislated separation of commercial banking and investment banking in the United States is somewhat unusual. In countries where there is no legislation, commercial banks provide investment banking services as part of their normal range of business activities. The notable exception to this rule is Japan, which has securities laws that closely resemble those of the United States. Countries where investment banking and commercial banking are combined have what is called a "universal banking" system. *Universal banks* are institutions that can accept deposits, make loans, underwrite securities, engage in brokerage activities, and sell and manufacture other financial services such as insurance. Most European countries allow universal banks.

In recent years, commercial banks and investment banks have come into competitive conflict. Large money center and regional commercial banks have seen their largest and most profitable customers increasingly switching from intermediation services, such as bank loans, to direct credit market transactions, such as commercial paper. As a result, large commercial banks in the United States want to break down the legal barrier to investment banking established by Glass-Steagall. As we shall see, the story of investment banking is inextricably intertwined with that of commercial banking.

Structure of the Industry

As of year-end 1990, there were about 2,500 investment banking firms doing some underwriting business in the United States. However, the industry is dominated by the 100 largest firms, of which about 55 firms have their head offices located in New York City. The balance are headquartered in major regional financial centers such as Chicago and Los Angeles. Exhibit 21–1 lists the ten largest investment banks ranked by the dollar amount of domestic securities (debt and equity) underwritten. All of these firms are headquartered in New York City. The largest investment banking firm is Merrill Lynch, which in 1990 underwrote 985 issues totaling more than $69 billion. The next four largest firms underwrote more than 350 issues each, and the total amount underwritten ranged between $32 to $54 billion.

It is important to note that in recent years, some investment banking firms have diversified or merged with other financial firms to become full-service financial firms.

Exhibit 21–1   Ten Largest Investment Banks (1990)

Rank	Firm	Underwritings ($ in billions)			
		Total	Corporate	Municipal	Number of Issues
1	Merrill Lynch	69.7	55.8	13.9	985
2	Goldman, Sachs	54.6	40.7	13.9	684
3	First Boston	41.0	33.1	7.9	612
4	Morgan Stanley	35.0	31.3	3.7	366
5	Salomon Brothers	32.7	32.7	0.0	375
6	Lehman Brothers	27.4	20.3	7.1	756
7	Bear Stearns	25.4	20.0	5.4	635
8	Kidder Peabody	23.7	22.1	1.6	735
9	Prudential Securities	17.5	13.4	4.1	599
10	Paine Webber	11.8	6.0	5.8	288

In 1990, Merrill Lynch in New York City was the top dog among investment bankers. However, competition is fierce, and positions can change substantially from year to year.

Source: *Institutional Investor*, April 1991.

Examples of recent mergers to gain a greater presence in the retail financial service industry include Prudential, American Express, and Sears. Prudential, the nation's largest life insurance company, merged with Bache Securities. The new firm is called Prudential Securities and has more than 330 offices. American Express, which is best known for its credit cards and traveler's checks, merged with Shearson, Loeb Rhodes and later purchased Lehman Brothers and E. F. Hutton. The investment banking subsidiary of Shearson Lehman Brothers is called Lehman Brothers and the firm operates 460 offices. Sears, the nation's largest retailer and grantor of consumer credit, purchased Dean Witter Reynolds and operates 350 offices.

Early History

Investment banks in the United States trace their origins to the prominent investment houses in Europe, and many early investment banks were branches or affiliates of European firms. Early investment banks in the United States differed from commercial banks. Commercial banks were corporations that were chartered exclusively to issue bank notes (money) and make short-term business loans; early investment banks were partnerships and, therefore, were not subject to the regulations that apply to corporations. As such, investment banks, referred to as *private banks* at the time, could engage in any business activity they wished and could have offices in any location. Though investment banks could not issue bank notes, they could accept deposits as well as underwrite and trade in securities.

The golden era of investment banking began after the Civil War. Following the war, America began to build a railroad system that linked the country together and provided the infrastructure for industrialization. Modern investment banking houses acted as intermediaries between the railroad firms—which needed massive amounts of capital to finance roadbeds, track, bridges, and rolling stock—and investors located primarily on the East Coast and in Europe. Because of the distance between investors and the investment project, investors found it difficult to estimate the value of the securities offered. The reputation of investment bankers to price securities fairly made these transactions possible.

With the rapid industrialization of America, companies began selling new securities publicly, and outstanding securities were traded on organized exchanges. The demand for financial services led to the growth of powerful investment banking firms like those led by Jay Cooke, J. Pierpont Morgan, Marcus Goldman, and Solomon Loeb. These organizations created some of the giant businesses of the twentieth century, such as United States Steel.

As it turned out, investment banking was a very profitable business. Firms discovered innumerable ways to make money, such as charging fees for underwriting, for financial consulting, for trading securities, for redeployment of a client's deposited funds, for private placements, for doing mergers and acquisitions, and so on. Early commercial banks, which were chartered exclusively to issue bank notes and make short-term loans, soon began to covet a wider range of financial activities, especially those that were highly profitable. Over time, because of competitive pressures, states began to permit their state-chartered commercial banks to engage in selected investment banking activities.

National banks, which were regulated by the comptroller of the currency, began pressuring the comptroller for expanded powers. At first, national banks could only underwrite and trade in securities that they were permitted to invest in, which were primarily federal and municipal securities. With time, competitive pressure from state banks, which gained expanded powers more quickly, forced the comptroller to grant national banks the authority to underwrite and trade in corporate bonds and equities. Finally, national banks were allowed to organize state-chartered security affiliates that could engage in full-service investment banking. Thus, by 1930, commercial banks and investment banks were almost fully integrated, and they or their security affiliates were underwriting more than 50 percent of all new bond issues sold.

The Glass-Steagall Act and Its Aftermath

In the 1930s, the long history of suspicion and questionable practices caught up with the investment banking industry. On October 28, 1929, the stock market declined 12.8 percent, signaling the "crash of 1929" and the beginning of the Great Depression. During the Great Depression (1929–1933), output declined 30.5 percent and unemployment rose 37.6 percent compared to the beginning of 1929. More than 9,000 commercial banks failed. The country and the financial system were devastated. To deal with the crisis at hand, Congress enacted legislation. To regulate investment banks and Wall Street, Congress enacted the Securities Act of 1933, the Securities Exchange Act of 1934, and, of course, the Glass-Steagall Act of 1933 to regulate the banking system. Thus, after years of functioning with little regulation, the financial sector—the securities industry and commercial banking system—became one of the most heavily regulated sectors in the economy.

The Glass-Steagall Act of 1933 effectively separated commercial banking from investment banking.[1] The act did the following:

- Prohibited commercial banks from underwriting or trading (for their own account) stocks, bonds, or other securities. The major exceptions were U.S. government securities, general obligation bonds of state and local governments, and bank securities such as CDs.
- Limited the amount of debt securities that commercial banks could purchase for their own account to those approved by bank regulatory authorities.
- Prohibited individuals and firms engaged in investment banking from simultaneously engaging in commercial banking.

Thus commercial banks and investment banks were given a choice of being one or the other, but not both. Most firms elected to stay in their primary line of business and divested themselves of the prohibited activity. But not all firms did this. For example, Citibank, Chase Manhattan Bank, and Harris Trust took the most common route and dissolved their security affiliates. The investment banking firm of J. P. Morgan decided to maintain a position as a commercial bank; today, the firm is known as Morgan Guaranty and Trust Co. However, some senior partners left the firm to form the investment house of Morgan Stanley. The First Boston Corporation was patched together out of the cast-off security affiliates of several commercial banks, one of which was the affiliate of the First National Bank of Boston.

The Glass-Steagall Act, when passed, had three basic objectives: (1) to discourage speculation in financial markets, (2) to prevent conflict of interest and self-dealing, and (3) to restore confidence in the safety and soundness of the banking system. Regarding speculation, the act's proponents argued that if banks were affiliated with securities dealers, banks would have incentives to lend to customers of the security affiliates, who would use the money to buy stock on credit. Thus banks engaged in investment banking were channeling money into "speculative" investment rather than into what was believed to be more productive investments. The conflict of interest rationale hinged on the fear that commercial banks might make imprudent loans to firms it had underwritten securities for in order to gain additional securities business. Thus the quality of the bank's loan portfolio could be compromised by the bank's dual role of lender and investment banker.

Perhaps the most important reason for the Glass-Steagall Act was the fear over bank safety and the desire to prevent bank failures. Simply stated, investment banking is a riskly business. Debt and equity markets are inherently subject to large price fluctuations, with the risk of such fluctuations being borne by security dealers and underwriters. The act insulated commercial banks from that risk by prohibiting them from acting as dealers, underwriters of securities, and investors in private-sector securities.

---

[1]The Glass-Steagall Act is technically known as the Banking Act of 1933. The act's popular name comes from its major sponsors, Senator Carter Glass, who sponsored the Senate bill on commercial and investment banking, and Representative Henry Steagall, who sponsored the House bill on federal deposit insurance. The Banking Act of 1933 combined the two bills.

Primary Services of an Investment Bank

Unlike commercial banks, investment banks are not restricted in the range of business activities in which they can engage. The following section describes the major business activities of investment banking firms.

Bringing New Security Issues to Market

One of the basic services offered by an investment banking firm is to bring to market new debt and equity securities issued by private firms or governmental units that require funds for capital expenditures. New issues of stocks or bonds are called *primary issues*. If the company has never offered securities to the public before, the primary issue is called an *initial public offering* (IPO). Otherwise, if the firm already has similar securities trading in the market, the primary issue is called a *seasoned offering*. One of the problems investment bankers face with IPOs is how to price them, since they are securities that have never been traded. The price a security is sold for is important to the issuer because it sets the firm's cost of capital. However, the price must be set "right" to be fair to both the issuing firm and the investment banker. For example, if a firm is selling stock and a new issue is priced too low, more shares are sold than necessary to raise the needed funds, which dilutes the firm's earnings. If the price is too high, the underwriter cannot sell the issue for the proposed reoffer price, and the investment banker suffers a loss. The correct price is called the *market equilibrium price*; this is the highest price that allows all the new securities issued to be sold quickly at the reoffer price. Seasoned offerings are typically priced at some small discount from the current market price.

In bringing securities to market, investment bankers take clients through three steps: origination, underwriting (risk bearing), and sales and distribution. Depending on the method of sale and the client's needs, an investment banker may provide all or a few of these services.

Origination.   During the origination of a new security issue, the investment banker can help the issuer analyze the feasibility of the project and determine the amount of money to borrow; decide on the type of financing needed (debt, equity); design the characteristics of securities to be issued, such as maturity, coupon rate, and the presence of a call provision and/or sinking fund for debt issues; and provide advice on the best sale date so that the issuer can get the highest possible price.

Once the decision to issue the securities is made, the investment banker can help the client prepare the official sale documents. If the securities are to be sold publicly, security laws require that a *registration statement* be filed with the Securities and Exchange Commission (SEC). This statement contains detailed information about the issuer's financial condition, business activities, industry competition, management and their experience, the project for which the funds will be used, the characteristics of the securities to be issued, and the risks of the securities. After approval by the SEC, a portion of the registration statement, called the *prospectus*, is reproduced in quantity and distributed to all potential investors. By law, investors must have a prospectus before they can invest. The prospectus contains vital information about the firm and its management, as well as financial information so that intelligent investors can make informed decisions about the proposed project and its risk. SEC approval only implies that the information presented is timely and fair; approval is not an endorsement by the SEC as to investment quality. Exhibit 21–2 shows the front page of a prospectus.

During the registration process for a debt issue, the investment banker can also help secure a credit rating; coordinate the activities of a bond counsel, who passes an opinion about the legality of the security issue; select a transfer agent for secondary market sales; select a trustee, who sees that the issuer fulfills its obligation under the security contract; and print securities so that they can be distributed to investors. For an equity issue, the investment banker can arrange for the securities to be listed on a stock exchange or traded in the over-the-counter market.

Exhibit 21–2   **The Front Page of a Prospectus**

Prospectus Supplement
(To Prospectus Dated March 29, 1989)

$150,000,000

XEROX CREDIT CORPORATION

10⅛% Notes due 1999

The Notes will mature on April 15, 1999. Interest on the Notes is payable semiannually on October 15 and April 15 of each year, beginning October 15, 1989. The Notes are not redeemable prior to April 15, 1996. Thereafter, the Notes may be redeemed at the option of the Company, in whole or in part, at any time at 100% of their principal amount plus accrued interest to the date of redemption.

THESE SECURITIES HAVE NOT BEEN APPROVED OR DISAPPROVED BY THE SECURITIES AND EXCHANGE COMMISSION NOR HAS THE COMMISSION PASSED UPON THE ACCURACY OR ADEQUACY OF THIS PROSPECTUS SUPPLEMENT OR THE PROSPECTUS TO WHICH IT RELATES. ANY REPRESENTATION TO THE CONTRARY IS A CRIMINAL OFFENSE.

	Price to Public(1)	Underwriting Discount	Proceeds to Company(1)(2)
Per Note	99.900%	.625%	99.275%
Total	$149,850,000	$937,500	$148,912,500

(1) Plus accrued interest from April 15, 1989.
(2) Before deducting expenses payable by the Company estimated to be $100,000.

The Notes are offered subject to receipt and acceptance by the Underwriters, to prior sale and to the Underwriters' right to reject any order in whole or in part and to withdraw, cancel or modify the offer without notice. It is expected that delivery of the Notes will be made at the office of Salomon Brothers Inc, One New York Plaza, New York, New York, or through the facilities of The Depository Trust Company, on or about April 24, 1989.

Salomon Brothers Inc   **Goldman, Sachs & Co.**

The date of this Prospectus Supplement is April 14, 1989.

The prospectus provides many details about the type of security and the risk of the security to prospective investors.

Underwriting. Underwriting or risk bearing is what most people think that investment bankers do. Underwriting is the process whereby the investment banker guarantees to buy the new securities for a certain price. The risk exists between the time the investment banker purchases the securities from the issuer and the time they are resold to the public. The risk (inventory risk) is that the securities may be sold at a price less than the underwriter purchased them for. The risk of unforeseen price changes as a result of changes in market conditions can be substantial. For example, in October 1979, IBM issued $1 billion in bonds through a syndicate of underwriters. As the issue was coming to market, interest rates suddenly jumped upward, causing bond prices to tumble, and the underwriters lost in excess of $10 million.

To decrease the risk of any one primary issue, underwriters form syndicates comprising other investment banking firms. Each member of the syndicate is responsible for its pro rata share of the securities being issued. By participating in the syndicate, each underwriter receives a portion of the underwriting fee as well as an allocation of the securities being sold that it can sell to its own customers. In addition, other investment banking firms, known as the selling group, can be enlisted to assist in the sale of the securities being issued. Members of the selling group bear no underwriting responsibility, but receive a commission for whatever securities they sell.

Sales and Distribution. Once the investment banker purchases the securities, they must be resold to investors. The syndicate's primary concern is to sell the securities as quickly as possible at the proposed reoffer price. If the securities are not sold within a few days, the selling syndicate disbands, and members sell the securities at whatever price they can get.

The sales function is divided into institutional sales and retail sales. Retail sales involve selling the securities to individual investors and firms that purchase in small quantities. Examples of national investment banking firms with a strong retail presence are Merrill Lynch, with an extensive network of 510 branches, and Shearson Lehman Brothers with 460 offices. Most regional investment banking firms specialize in retail sales. Institutional sales involve the sale of a large block of securities to institutional purchasers, such as pension funds, insurance companies, endowment trusts, or mutual funds. Included among the well-known institutional firms are Morgan Stanley, First Boston, and Salomon Brothers.

Trading and Brokerage

In addition to underwriting and selling newly issued securities, investment banks also provide services as brokers or dealers for existing securities in the aftermarket; that is, they make secondary markets for existing securities. Aftermarket activities may involve a simple *brokerage* function, in which the firm earns a commission for bringing buyer and seller together; or it may involve a *dealer* function, in which the investment bank carries an inventory of securities from which it executes buy and sell orders and trades for its own account. When an investment bank acts as a dealer for a security, it is said to be "making a market" in the security and is known as a "market maker." The market maker is willing to buy the security at one price, known as the bid price, and sells it at a higher price, the ask price. The market maker makes a profit based on the difference between the bid and the ask prices. The price difference is known as the bid-ask spread. Of course, with the ownership of the asset comes the risk of price fluctuations caused by changes in economic and market conditions. Because securities firms operate with a small capital base, small declines in the price of securities held can result in insolvency.

Exhibit 21–3 shows the financial assets and liabilities for security brokers and dealers. As can be seen, their largest single asset is security credit. This represents funds that brokerage firms have loaned to their customers for the purchase of securities with margin accounts. *Margin trading* simply means that the investor can buy securities partly with borrowed money. For example, if a customer uses a 25 percent margin, it means that 75 percent of the investment is being financed with the investor's own money and the balance, 25 percent, is financed with money borrowed from the brokerage house. Most types of securities can be purchased on margin—for example, common and preferred stock, corporate and Treasury bonds, convertible bonds, warrants, commodities, financial futures, and mutual funds. Margin requirements are set by the Board of Governors of the Federal Reserve System, and they currently are 50 percent for both equity and debt securities. The other principal assets of brokers and dealers are securities held as dealers' inventories or inventories held from underwriting activities.

The largest sources of funds for dealers and brokers are short-term loans from commercial banks and customer credit balances. Short-term bank financing is in the form of *call loans*, which are collateralized by the securities being financed, and of *repurchase agreements*, which involve the actual sale of the securities to the lender by the borrower, who then commits to repurchase the securities at a higher price. Call loans and repurchase agreements are usually arranged on a daily basis. Customer credit balances represent funds owed by brokers and dealers to their customers following the sale of the customers securities, as well as customers funds held in cash management accounts.

Full-Service Brokerage Firms.   Brokerage houses compete for investors' business by offering a variety of services that are sold by *stockbrokers* or account executives. Stockbrokers must be licensed by the exchange on which they place orders

Exhibit 21–3   **Financial Assets and Liabilities of Security Brokers and Dealers (1989)**

Financial Assets	($ in billions)	Financial Liabilities	($ in billions)
Demand deposits & currency	$ 9.8	Security credit	$79.6
Corporate equities	14.1	From banks	26.4
U.S. government securities	85.2	From customer	
State and local securities	7.1	credit balances	53.2
Corporate bonds	32.9	Profit taxes payable	0.6
Security credit	42.5		

Security brokers and dealers obtain most of their funds from customers' credit balances and by borrowing from U.S. and foreign banks. They use their funds to buy bonds and stocks and to make loans to their customers.

Source: Federal Reserve Board, *Flow of Funds Accounts Financial Assets and Liabilities 1963–89*, September 1990.

and must abide by the ethical guidelines of the exchange and the National Association of Security Dealers (NASD). The NASD is a self-regulating body comprising brokerage houses. For their services, stockbrokers receive commission rates that vary with the service provided. The basic services provided by a full-service brokerage firm are described below.

Storage of Securities.   Investors can leave securities with a broker for safekeeping; thus the investor does not have to rent a safety deposit box or physically transfer securities to and from the broker's office when a transaction is made. Investors are protected against loss of the securities or cash held by brokers by the Security Investor Protection Corporation (SIPC), an agency of the federal government. The SIPC insures each customer's account up to $500,000 in securities and up to $100,000 in cash balances. Note, however, that the SIPC does not guarantee the dollar value of securities but guarantees only that the securities themselves will be returned.

Execution of Trades.   A broker buys or sells all types of financial securities, from U.S. Treasury securities to speculative instruments such as futures and options. Brokers transact on all the major exchanges, such as the New York Stock Exchange; on any of the regional exchanges, such as the Cincinnati Stock Exchange and the Boston Stock Exchange; and in the over-the-counter market, where most debt instruments, such as U.S. Treasury bonds and more speculative common stocks, are traded.

Investment Advice.   Brokerage firms provide a wide range of free investment information and advice, ranging from simple stock and bond guides to detailed research reports written by a security analyst on a particular investment. In addition, some firms publish periodic publications or newsletters that analyze economic, market, and industry conditions and provide lists of securities or investments that the firm's analyst recommends investors buy or sell.

Margin Credit.   Brokerage-firm customers can obtain either a cash or margin account. Cash customers must pay cash for the security when it is purchased. Or the client can apply for a margin account, which allows the investor to borrow part of the money from the brokerage firm to pay for the security purchased. The rate of interest charged is usually marked up 1 to 2 percent above the broker's loan rate (the rate at which brokers borrow from commercial banks), which is usually slightly above the commercial bank prime rate.

Cash Management Services.   In recent years, the major brokerage houses have offered investors a variety of cash management account (CMA) programs. Although the services may vary from firm to firm, a typical CMA allows investors to write checks against credit balances and the value of securities they hold in their brokerage account. The brokerage firm may also broker savings deposits from depository institutions (commercial banks and thrifts); that is, the brokerage house sells federally insured savings deposits to investors who want to hold long-term insured deposits but do not want to bear the prepayment penalty for possible early withdrawal. Finally, some brokerage firms issue credit cards (such as Visa) to their CMA customers, which allows them to obtain funds by drawing down their credit balances or borrowing against the securities in their accounts. Thus CMA accounts allow brokerage houses to provide many of the services provided by commercial banks, but at the same time they are not subject to restrictive bank regulations.

Discount Brokerage Firms.   In recent years, a new type of brokerage firm has emerged to compete against full-service brokerage firms—the so-called *discount broker*. Discount brokerage firms compete against full-service brokerage firms by offering fewer brokerage services and passing the savings on to the investors. Specifically, most discount brokerage firms do not have a highly paid research staff producing research reports or account executives soliciting business based on the firm's current recommendation to buy and sell. Instead, they hire telephone clerks to take customers' orders. These clerks do not sell, do not offer any investment advice, and work for modest salaries. These and other savings are passed along to the investor in the form of lower commissions.

Banks as Brokers.   It is important to note that the Glass-Steagall Act does not preclude commercial banks from acting as brokers on behalf of their customers. Recall that brokers, unlike dealers, do not take title to securities but only bring buyer and seller together, an activity which was legal for commercial banks. Until the 1980s, however, commercial banks did not emphasize their brokerage powers or solicit business, except to serve a few large accounts in their trust departments. Beginning in the 1980s, commercial banks began to offer trading services to retail customers, usually in the form of discount brokerage.

Some banks started their own brokerage operations from scratch and others entered into joint-venture arrangements, whereby the bank purchased broker services from an established securities firm and marketed the services under the name of the bank. To date, more than 2,000 banks are providing active brokerage services to their customers. Even though the numbers of banks selling brokerage services is impressive, in most cases the operations have not been as profitable as expected.

Arbitrage Activities.   Closely associated with the market-making activities of investment banking firms are arbitrage activities. The essential difference between market making as a dealer or as an arbitrageur is that a risk-free *arbitrage* transaction involves the simultaneous buying and selling of a security to take advantage of a price anomaly that may exist between two markets. For example, if GMC stock is trading for $35 per share on the New York Stock Exchange (NYSE) and $34 per share on the Pacific Coast Stock Exchange (PCSE), an arbitrageur at an investment bank would buy GMC stock on the PCSE at $34 per share and immediately sell it for $35 per share on the NYSE. The process would continue until the price differential between the two exchanges was closed so that no arbitrage profits remained after transactions costs. Because investment banks have low costs for their own trades, their arbitrageurs can usually spot and exploit arbitrage opportunities before they are large enough to be profitable to the general public. Investment banks find that arbitrage activities are not only profitable but that they also serve the useful purposes of making financial markets more efficient.

Private Placements

As discussed in Chapter 9, for many businesses, the sale of securities (debt or equity) by public sale is not feasible. A private placement is a method of issuing securities in which the issuer sells the securities directly to the ultimate investors. Because there is no underwriting in a private placement deal, the investment banker's role is to bring buyer and seller together, to help determine a fair price for the securities, and to execute the transaction. For these services, the investment banker earns a fee. Firms choose between a private placement or public sale, depending on which method of sale offers to the issuer the highest possible price for the securities after transaction costs.

Mergers and Acquisitions

Since the 1960s, most investment banking firms have been active in the merger and acquisition (M&A) business. This activity is generally handled by a specialized M&A department, with highly trained personnel who specialize in specific types of mergers. Members of these groups try to identify firms with excess cash that might want to buy other firms, companies that might be willing to be bought, and firms that might be attractive to other firms as an acquisition. The primary economic motive for most mergers is to increase the value of the combined firms—so-called *economic synergy*. That is, if companies A and B merge together to form company C, the value of company C should exceed the value of companies A and B separately.

Investment banks provide a number of services to business firms in M&A work: (1) they help arrange mergers, (2) they aid firms targeted for mergers in resisting mergers, and (3) they help establish the value of target firms. In the 1980s, the volume of merger activity was substantial, and the profits from M&A work were large. For example, in the negotiations to acquire Conoco, Du Pont's investment banker, First Boston, earned fees of more than $15 million. At the same time, Conoco's investment banker, Morgan Stanley, earned $15 million defending the firm from the takeover attempt. However, in the 1990s the volume of merger activity has declined significantly from the level in the previous decade, along with the resulting fees. In recent years, large money-center banks have aggressively competed with investment banks for M&A work. M&A work complements commercial banks' private placement work and is consistent with their desire to engage in full-service investment banking.

Other Business Activities

Investment banking firms are extremely flexible organizations and will provide virtually any financial service if the firm can earn a satisfactory return. For example, given the high degree of expertise among investment bank personnel, financial consulting is a natural service for them to offer their clients. Financial consulting services include assisting clients in financial planning, determining a firm's optimal financial structure or dividend policy, and providing feasibility studies for major capital projects. The consulting reputation of some investment banks has reached the point where financial consulting is a major source of income and competitive advantage for these firms in competing for other types of business.

Another important business activity for investment banks has been real estate investment and brokerage. Beginning in the 1970s, large institutional investors became increasingly interested in purchasing real estate for investment purposes.

DID YOU KNOW?

The Fall of the House That Junk Built

At 11:07 p.m. on February 13, 1990, Wall Street's most lavish party ended and the host was left with a lot more to clear up than just a hangover. Drexel Burnham Lambert, Inc. filed for Chapter 11 bankruptcy protection. That action brought an end to what some have called the Roaring Eighties, an era of hostile takeovers, leveraged buy-outs, high living, and a disregard for huge amounts of debt.

The 55-year-old investment banking firm rose from a Wall Street also-ran in the 1970s to be the extremely profitable and prominent pioneer of what are known as "junk bonds," high-yield, high-risk bonds that back ventures with less than investment grade credit. By becoming the primary player in the junk bond market under the direction of Michael R. Milken, Drexel could take part in the takeover wars that ruled Wall Street in the 1980s. Because of Drexel's ability to raise capital for all types of firms, even very small companies could bid for and sometimes win America's largest firms. Armed with Drexel's bonds, corporate raiders swiftly made some of the largest deals the financial world had ever witnessed.

Investment bankers made billions in fees by advising both the raiders and the takeover targets. One takeover contender explained that all a raider needed to launch a bid was Milken's signature on one of Drexel's letters stating that the firm was "highly confident" of obtaining financing. At the height of his reign as king of junk bonds, Milken could charge as much as $3.5 million for such a letter.

In late 1986 things started to get sticky as Drexel became entangled in the insider dealings of convicted arbitrageur Ivan Boesky. When the smoke cleared, the Securities and Exchange Commission demanded $650 million in fines from Drexel and the ousting of Michael Milken.

Because of the scandal, Milken faced a 98-count indictment, including charges of racketeering and insider trading. In April 1990, he pleaded guilty to six felonies and was sentenced to ten years in a federal prison. As of November 1991, Milken's lawyers were appealing his sentence while he sat in a four-man cell at a minimum-security prison. Ironically, he is also one of the first in line as a Drexel creditor, being owed more than $200 million in unpaid compensation from 1987.

What could have caused one of Wall Street's largest investment houses to topple? While the hefty SEC fine certainly sapped Drexel's strength, the deathblow came as the $200 billion junk bond market slumped. Rising default rates, a slow economy, and regulations that forced S&Ls to divest junk bonds all contributed to a fall in value of almost 50 percent. Because it was holding junk bonds with a face value of nearly $1 billion, Drexel's credit rating began to slide. In an industry where trust and good faith are the stock in trade, any question about a firm's creditworthiness can cause disaster.

Disaster came calling on Drexel. Drexel's parent company no longer could use double leverage to finance its investment subsidiary. It had to buy back the stock of hundreds of laid-off employees and found itself strapped for cash. Drexel tried to arrange bank loans to no avail, as the rate at which banks would lend on junk bond collateral fell from 85 cents on the dollar to less than 50 cents. Drexel even sought a merger candidate that could infuse some cash. No one was willing to deal. The firm discovered only too quickly that confidence can vaporize when it defaulted for want of a mere $150 million, a fraction of what it could have raised only months before.

Realizing the opportunity, investment banks established real estate departments or subsidiaries that represent clients in the sale or purchase of large commercial properties, such as office buildings, shopping centers, and agricultural land. In the 1980s real estate departments generated substantial profits for investment banks as their activities were fueled by petro dollars from oil-rich countries and from the Japanese investors' interest in U.S. real estate because of the dollar's low value relative to the yen.

The Competition between Commercial and Investment Banking

In recent years, large U.S. commercial banks have increasingly pursued their desire to engage in investment banking. These banks have discovered that commercial banking is not as profitable as it once was, whereas some investment banking activities have become extremely profitable. At the same time, many of their best customers are turning to investment banks for short-term financing, the traditional business of commercial banks. Commercial banks want the flexibility, as other financial firms have, to shift to other more profitable product lines as business conditions change. Because of the lack of flexibility, some large commercial banks in New York City, most notably Chase Manhattan, are threatening to give up their banking charters so that they can operate as investment banks. Clearly, large commercial banks are trying to break down the barrier to investment banking activities established by the Glass-Steagall Act.

The primary factors changing the relationship between commercial and investment banking are (1) the interaction between economic and technological forces and (2) regulatory constraints. First, economic and technological forces comprise the development and merging of electronic computers and telecommunications. With the new technology, electronic information processing is reducing the cost of gathering data, manufacturing, and transmitting financial products to the ultimate user. The technology not only makes it possible to provide traditional financial services at reduced cost but also makes the creation of new financial products feasible. Lower transaction costs favor direct-credit-market rather than intermediation transactions.

A second reason working against intermediation financing is the regulatory taxes that commercial banks must pay relative to other financial firms. Most important are the requirement to hold noninterest-earning reserves against deposits and the mandatory capital requirements that exceed those that would exist in the absence of regulation. Banks find that they are at a disadvantage in financing and keeping loans on their books, although they still have a comparative advantage in analyzing credit risk and originating transactions. As a result of these forces (economic, technological, and regulatory), there is a trend for borrowers to place debt directly with investors and, correspondingly, to do fewer transactions with intermediaries such as commercial banks. Evidence of declining information costs is found in the shrinking amount of bank borrowing by large and middle-market corporate companies that once relied on banks as their primary source of funds.

Securities Activities of Commercial Banks

Exhibit 21-4 shows the securities activities for commercial banks that are members of the Federal Reserve System. For state-chartered banks that are not member banks, securities power varies on a state-to-state basis. The exhibit also shows that for many years, banks have been able to underwrite and trade (dealer and broker) U.S. government securities and general obligation bonds, to trade financial futures, to do private placement deals, and to do merger and acquisition work. The securities activities denied commercial banks under the Glass-Steagall Act have been underwriting and trading corporate bonds, equities, and commercial paper; underwriting and selling mutual funds; and being a full-service broker and investment adviser.

The 1980s, however, mark the beginning of the crumbling of Glass-Steagall's power to limit banks' securities activities. The most important action of the decade may be the U.S. Supreme Court decision on July 13, 1988, to let stand the Federal Reserve Board's approval for commercial banks to underwrite three new kinds of securities: commercial paper, municipal revenue bonds, and securities backed by mortages or consumer debt. The new securities activities must be handled through a separate subsidiary of a bank holding company, and underwriting activities cannot account for more than 5 percent of the subsidiary's gross revenues. The Fed's approval of the new powers was based on its interpretation that the percentage limit on underwriting would keep the bank affiliate from being "engaged principally" in securities, which is barred by the Glass-Steagall Act. Initially, 12 large commercial banks received approval, but most large money center and regional banks are expected to request approval in the near future.[2] Continuing the above trend, on June 20, 1989, the Federal Reserve Board allowed J. P. Morgan & Co. to underwrite and deal in corporate debt in the United States through its security affiliate, and on September 20, 1990, the Fed allowed J. P. Morgan & Co. to underwrite corporate equity in the United States.

Investment Banks Fight Back

Throughout this chapter we have given the impression that commercial banks have been invading Wall Street. At the same time, however, investment banks have been encroaching on activities that were traditionally the preserves of commercial banks. For example, one of the most damaging moves into retail banking was the introduction of money market mutual funds (MMMFs), which drew billions of dollars away from commercial banks during the high-interest-rate periods of the late 1970s and early 1980s. It was not until banks were allowed to offer money market deposit accounts that banks regained a portion of their customers.

At the commercial level, investment banks moved into short-term business financing with commercial paper, which drew corporate borrowers away from banks to the securities houses that issued the paper. Finally, investment banks entered the foreign exchange market, which was traditionally a bank activity.

[2]The 12 banks initially receiving approval were Bankers Trust, Chemical Bank, Chase Manhattan, Manufacturers Hanover, Citicorp, Morgan, Security Pacific, PNC Financial Corp, Marine Midland, First Interstate Banks, Bank of New England, and Bank of Montreal.

Exhibit 21–4   **Investment Banking Activities of Commercial Banks**

Activity	Year Started
Underwriting and distributing	
U.S. Treasury securities	Always
U.S. federal agency securities	Various years
Municipal securities	
General obligation	Early 1900s
School-related revenue bonds	1968
Other revenue bonds	1988[a]
Commercial paper	1988[a]
Securitized mortgage debt	1988[a]
Securitized consumer debt	1988[a]
Corporate debt	1989[b]
Corporate equity	1990[c]
Broker and dealer	
U.S. Treasury securities	Always
U.S. federal agency securities	Various years
Municipal securities	
General obligation	Early 1900s
Some revenue bonds	1968
Financial and precious metal futures	1983
Brokerage	
Limited customer	Always
Retail	1982
Trust investments	
Individual accounts	Always
IRA commingled accounts	1982
Automatic investment service	1984
Dividend investment service	Always
Sponsored closed-end funds	1974
Financial advising	
Closed-end funds	1974
Mutual funds	1974
Other investment banking activities	
Offshore dealing in Eurodollar securities	Always
Private placement	Always
Merger and acquisition	Always

In recent years, money-center and large regional banks have been gaining investment banking powers.

[a]Bank must apply to and receive approval from the Federal Reserve Board. As of June 1988, the Board had approved the application of 12 large money centers and regional banks.

[b]On June 20, 1989, the Federal Reserve Board allowed J. P. Morgan & Co. to underwrite and deal in corporate debt.

[c]On September 20, 1990, the Federal Reserve Bank allowed J. P. Morgan & Co. to underwrite corporate equity.

Other money center banks have applications pending.

PEOPLE & EVENTS

Investment Banking: High-Stakes Poker on Wall Street

On Wednesday, October 3, 1979, executives from International Business Machines (IBM) and two Wall Street investment firms—Salomon Brothers and Merrill Lynch—agreed to a security underwriting deal. Even though such decisions are routine on Wall Street, this one was not ordinary. The group agreed to the largest public borrowing in corporate history: a combined offering by IBM of $500 million in seven-year notes and $500 million in 25-year bonds, totaling an impressive $1 billion.

For the two lead underwriting firms, Salomon Brothers and Merrill Lynch, the deal was important because it represented a golden opportunity for them to break into the clubby ranks of underwriting top bluechip U.S industrial corporations. Originally, Morgan Stanley and Company, the most prestigious investment-banking firm and long-standing adviser to IBM, was involved in the deal. Both Salomon and Morgan Stanley made numerous trips to advise IBM on the type of financing needed and how best to tap the capital markets. The final financing plan was a blend of both companies' proposals. Morgan Stanley was invited to be the lead underwriter, but IBM insisted on having Salomon Brothers as a comanager. IBM reasoned that two firms could best market the large volume of bonds. Robert H. B. Baldwin, president of Morgan Stanley, rejected this arrangement, stating his firm's long-standing policy of being either the sole manager or no manager at all. Baldwin viewed any deviation from this policy as eroding Morgan Stanley's status and, over the long run, its profits as well, since comanagers split the fee. Ultimately, Merrill Lynch became the second underwriter.

The benchmark on pricing prime-rate corporate issues such as IBM's is the yield on Treasury securities of comparable maturity. IBM wanted both sets of securities priced only 5 basis points higher than comparable Treasury securities. The two lead underwriters' survey of their customers brought a negative response; a subsequent proposal of a 10-basis-point spread was also rejected. After rounds of proposals, counterproposals, and numerous high-level phone calls, a pricing agreement was reached. IBM agreed to a yield of 7 basis points above Treasury notes for the IBM notes and 12 points above Treasury bonds for the IBM bonds. The deal was closed at 12:40 p.m.

That afternoon, things quickly began to unravel as the Treasury rate moved up by 5 basis points, wiping out nearly half of the carefully negotiated spread. On Thursday (October 4), the Treasury auctioned $2.5 million worth of four-year notes. The syndicate had expected the notes to carry yields slightly above the IBM notes; instead, they yielded a shocking 17 basis points more. On Friday the credit market became unsettled as rumors circulated that Paul Volcker, chairman of the Federal Reserve Board, was about to resign. Then, over the weekend, the Fed took draconian antiinflation measures by deciding to tighten credit.

When the markets opened on Monday (October 8), the rate of interest began to spurt upward and bond prices tumbled downward. Interest rates continued to rise, and by Wednesday Salomon Brothers was forced to disband the selling syndicate —meaning that each member was no longer obligated to sell the bonds at the syndicate price, but could sell them at whatever price each could get.

How much did the underwriting syndicate lose? Nobody in the syndicate wanted to talk about it. Best estimates on Wall Street are that the members left $10 million to $15 million on the table. Morgan Stanley executives aren't talking either and why should they? That firm went from looking arrogant to appearing supersmart. As Bob Baldwin of Morgan Stanley commented about the desirability of having Salomon Brothers as comanager, "You need only one brain surgeon." Clearly, that was Morgan Stanley.

Looking Ahead

The U.S. financial markets are in a period of evolution as the technologically driven battle between large commercial and investment banks is played out. Looking ahead 10 to 15 years from now, most portions of the Glass-Steagall Act that prohibit banks from engaging in investment banking will certainly be repealed, and there will emerge a core of 10 to 15 large U.S. financial institutions—commercial banks, investment banks, and perhaps some insurance companies—that dominate this country's financial system. These firms will operate in New York and other major financial centers throughout the United States as well as in major international financial centers, such as London, Tokyo, Frankfurt, and Hong Kong. They will compete head-to-head to do business with the world's major corporations and portfolio managers. These institutions will have the capability to underwrite and trade in a wide range of financial securities: debt, equities, futures, options, and foreign exchange. They will be the flagship financial firms for the U.S. economy in the battle for world economic dominance.

Venture Capital

A new financial intermediary, the venture capital firm, emerged in the last decade. Venture capital firms managed investments totaling less than $3 billion in the 1970s. Today they manage over $30 billion. The term "venture capitalist" is usually used to denote institutional investors that provide equity financing to young businesses and play an active role in advising their managements. These funds have been a major source of equity capital for new businesses, especially in technology-based industries.

What Is Venture Capital?

New corporations raise funds from a variety of sources. Initial financing typically is provided by the firm's founders and their friends, and later financing often comes from individuals and banks. Eventually, a successful venture may raise funds from a public offering of its stock or be acquired by a larger corporation. Venture capital is yet another source of funds to finance growth. Venture capitalists are equity-oriented investors who also provide management expertise to the company. They are most likely to invest after the enterprise has exhausted capital provided by its founders, but before it is merged into a larger firm or makes an initial public offering of its stock.

Who Are Venture Capitalists?

Venture capital firms fall primarily into three categories: private independent funds, corporate subsidiaries, and publicly funded small business investment corporations. Private independent funds, typically organized as limited partnerships, are by far the largest. The typical fund manages about $30 million to $50 million, while the largest funds manage over $500 million. Private independent venture capital funds raise capital from a variety of sources, but over half comes from other financial intermediaries such as pension funds and insurance companies.

Corporate subsidiaries specializing in venture capital make investments to diversify the parent companies' activities and to gain knowledge about new technologies that may have applications in their existing businesses. Corporate venture capitalists typically prefer to invest in more mature companies and, if the company is successful, they tend to acquire the entire venture rather than take it public.

Small Business Investment Companies (SBICs) provide the least amount of venture capital. Authorized under the Small Business Investment Company Act of 1958, they operate as closed-end investment trusts licensed and regulated by the Small Business Administration. Many are subsidiaries of banks and insurance companies. The role of SBICs has varied; the federal government has sometimes used them aggressively to fill a perceived need for equity capital for small businesses, but at other times, when small businesses' need for access to the capital markets has not been large, they have played a minor role.

There are also several informal sources of venture capital. Some new businesses receive funds from large corporations not operating through a formal venture capital subsidiary. Many new ventures continue to obtain financing from individual investors. Sometimes these individuals are friends and relatives of the founders, but in many cases they are successful entrepreneurs themselves who are knowledgeable about the particular industry and have special insights into the company's chances for success.

In What Types of Businesses Do Venture Capitalists Invest?

Venture capitalists typically prefer to invest in technology-based businesses in such areas as electronics, computer software and services, biotechnology, medical care, and industrial products. For several reasons manufacturing businesses are more intense users of venture capital than most service businesses. The lag between formation of a business and initial sales is usually longer in manufacturing than in services. This development cycle is especially long for innovative products and those manufactured with high-technology processes. Also, the minimum efficient scale is typically larger in a manufacturing business. These factors increase the required level of financing and decrease the liquidity of the investment, thus increasing the need for outside equity financing.

The Structure of Venture Capital Investments

The form of investment varies from company to company, but investments tend to feature three characteristics: substantial control over management decisions, some protection against downside risks, and a share in capital appreciation. Typically, venture capitalists have a seat on the board of directors. A popular vehicle for investing in start-up companies is preferred stock that carries the right to purchase or convert into common stock. Preferred stockholders have priority over common stockholders in liquidation proceedings.

The convertibility feature enables venture capitalists to participate in the high gains associated with successful ventures that go public or are acquired.

In general, venture capitalists are less likely to provide debt financing. If they do, however, they usually combine the debt with an instrument with equity features such as warrants or convertibility into common stock at a later date.

Obtaining Venture Capital Financing

A business makes an application for financial assistance from a venture capital firm by submitting a business plan. The business plan describes the product or service the company produces, the industry in which the company operates, information on the company's management, detailed financial projections, and what the funds are to be used for. If the business plan interests the venture capitalist, and typically only 10 out of 100 do, the company receives a rigorous examination. Some venture capitalists use their own staffs for this investigation, while others depend on a board of advisers acting in a consulting capacity. Even after being investigated, a high percentage of applications is rejected, with typically only 1 out of 10 companies actually receiving funding. Thus, venture capital is not easy to obtain; out of every 100 business plans received, only 10 companies will receive serious consideration and only 1 of those will receive equity capital.

Investment Funds

Investment funds typically specialize in long-term investments. They provide investors with risk intermediation by investing in a diversified portfolio of assets, they issue liabilities in a wide variety of denominations, and they provide marketability by either issuing liabilities for which a ready market exists or repurchasing their liabilities at their current asset value. In addition, investment funds offer economies of scale in investment management and transaction costs by spreading the costs of security evaluation over a large number of investors and by taking advantage of reduced rates on large-scale transactions. Finally, the continuous flow of principal and interest payments from a diversified portfolio often will eliminate an investment company's need to incur transaction costs by selling assets to gain liquidity.

Investment Fund Organization and Fees

There are many types of investment companies, and there are considerable differences in their organization, fees charged to investors, and methods of buying and selling fund shares. Let's look at some of the types of funds.

Open-end Investment Companies.   The term *mutual fund* is commonly used to denote an open-end investment company. These funds are the most common type of investment company and account for well over 95 percent for all of the assets under professional management. Open-end investment companies stand ready to buy or sell their shares at the current market price (pro rata) at any time. When an investor buys shares in an open-end fund, the fund fills the purchase order by issuing new shares of stock. There is no limit to the number of shares, other than the market demand for the shares. Both buy and sell transactions are carried out at a price based on the current market value of all securities held in the fund's portfolio. This price is known as the net asset value (NAV). NAV is calculated at least once a day and represents the market value of a share of stock in the mutual fund.

Closed-end Investment Companies.   The term "mutual fund" technically applies only to open-end funds. As a practical matter, however, the term is used in the popular press to refer to closed-end investment companies. A closed-end investment company is a fund that operates with a *fixed* number of shares outstanding. In effect, the fund operates like any other business that has its stock publicly traded, except that the fund happens to invest in marketable securities rather than real assets. Once a closed-end fund sells its shares, it typically does not offer additional shares to investors. Any investor who wishes to buy or sell shares in the fund does so by purchasing them in the secondary market. Thus the price of a share of the fund is determined by supply and demand.

There are two important prices for shares in a closed-end investment fund. The first is the net asset value (NAV), as previously discussed. The second price is the *market price* of the fund share, which is determined by the supply of and demand for the fund's stock in the market. It is important to recognize that the two prices—NAV and market price—are almost never the same. Historically, the market price for closed-end investment companies is 5 to 20 percent below their net asset price. An interesting question is why closed-end investment companies sell for discount below their net asset value. Currently there are about 70 closed-end funds whose shares are publicly traded.

Investment Trust.   An investment trust (or unit trust) is simply a pro rata interest in an unmanaged pool of investments. More specifically, a portfolio of securities is initially purchased and held in safekeeping in accordance with a set of conditions spelled out in a trust agreement. The securities purchased are typically government notes and bonds, corporate and municipal bonds, and, on occasion, preferred stock and money market instruments. Once the securities are purchased, no new securities are added and, with rare exceptions, no securities are sold. Because there is no trading of securities by the trustee and most securities purchased have a fixed return, the return (or yield) on an investment trust is fairly predictable. Unit trusts are usually formed and sold by brokerage houses to investors with limited resources who want to acquire a diversified portfolio of fixed-income securities and to earn a monthly income. Although there is no active secondary market for trust shares, investors usually can sell them back to the sponsor at a price equal to the prevailing net asset price minus a sales commission.

Load and No-Load Funds.   When buying shares in an investment fund, investors have a choice between a "load" or "no-load" fund. With a *load fund*, the mutual fund charges a commission when shares in the fund are purchased. Load funds are usually purchased through brokers at their bid and ask price. The *bid* price represents the current pro rata net asset value (NAV) of each share of the fund, and the *ask* price refects the bid price plus a commission. Load charges on commissions can be fairly substantial and often range from 7 to 8.5 percent of the purchase price of the shares. Some mutual funds employ salespeople to sell their shares directly to the public. Others sell shares through stockbrokerage firms.

With *no-load funds*, in contrast, no sales charges are levied when the fund is purchased. Thus no-load funds buy and sell shares at the same price. The investment adviser or management company for the fund handles the purchase and sale transactions. In recent years, some no-load funds have added various charges to substitute for their lack of a "front-end" load. Some add selling costs to their annual management fees. Others impose "back-end" withdrawal charges on people who liquidate their shares in the fund.

History of Investment Companies

Investment companies were first started in Belgium in 1822 and in the United States toward the end of the nineteenth century. All the initial investment companies were closed-end companies. Once their stock was sold, there was no provision for redemption. The first U.S mutual fund, or open-end investment company, was formed in 1924. Mutual funds quickly became popular because they guaranteed that investors could always redeem their shares at their net asset value. In contrast, the shares of closed-end investment companies often sold for less than their asset value and were not always readily marketable.

The Great Depression was hard on funds. Many failed during the early 1930s. It was only after passage of the Securities Act of 1933, the Securities Exchange Act of 1934, and the Investment Company Act of 1940 that a foundation was laid for renewed investor confidence in funds. Those acts require that continuous and full disclosures be made to present and potential investors in the funds. They also regulate appointments of boards of directors and management, as well as underwriting contracts that affect fund operations and sales.

After World War II, renewed interest in mutual funds developed. By offering professional management and diversification to small- and medium-sized investors, mutual funds were able to attract more funds for investment in a generally rising stock market. As a result, from 1945 to 1965 they grew at an 18 percent annual compound rate, reaching the peak of their rapid growth curve in the late 1960s. Then rising interest rates caused the stock market to stagnate. In addition, certain abuses (such as sales commission kickbacks or ties between brokers' fund sales and brokerage commission revenues) generated bad publicity and led to the congressional amendment of the Investment Company Act in 1970. Finally, academics began to question the value of professional stock selection.

Investor reservations about the profitability of mutual fund investments, coupled with general stock-market stagnation, caused a virtual cessation of stock-oriented mutual fund growth in the 1970s.

However, mutual fund managements were astute enough to realize that when the market diminishes for one product, it may be wise to expand to another product. Investment advisers began to offer a number of new funds. They included (1) municipal bond funds (for investors who desired tax-free income), (2) government security funds (for investors who wanted their money invested in default risk-free investments), and (3) money market funds (for investors who wanted liquidity and portfolio diversification coupled with money market yields).

Composition of Investment Companies

Exhibit 21-5 presents data on the asset holdings of non-money market mutual funds. The historical data illustrate the dramatic rate of growth in mutual fund assets that occurred from 1950 to 1970 and the subsequent slackening in growth that occurred during the 1970s. Mutual funds have again experienced rapid growth, beginning during the early 1980s. It will be interesting to see if, after the precipitous stock market

Exhibit 21–5   Assets Held by Conventional Mutual Funds

Year	Total Assets ($ in billions)	Percentage Distribution of Key Assets						
		Cash and Equivalent	Corporate Bonds	Preferred Stock	Common Stock	Municipal Bonds	Government Bonds	Other
1945	1.3							
1950	2.5							
1955	7.8							
1960	17.0							
1965	35.2	5.1	7.3	1.7	85.9	NA	NA	NA
1970	47.6	6.6	9.0	2.4	80.9	NA	NA	1.1
1975	42.2	7.6	11.3	1.2	78.6	NA	NA	1.2
1980	58.4	9.1	11.3	0.9	71.2	4.9	2.5	0.2
1985	251.7	8.2	9.9	1.5	47.6	15.2	17.3	0.3
1989	553.9	8.1	9.6	0.8	43.6	15.4	21.3	1.3

Over time, mutual funds' bond holdings have increased substantially, whereas their stock holdings have declined in relative importance.

Source: Investment Company Institute, *Mutual Fund Fact Book*, 1985, 1990.

decline of mid-October 1987, their growth rate continues into the 1990s. The exhibit also reveals the considerable diversification in asset holdings that occurred from 1965 onward as mutual funds shifted away from common and preferred stock, which accounted for 88 percent of their assets in 1965 and only 44 percent of their assets in 1989. This shift reflects that as investors' enthusiasm for stock-oriented funds cooled, mutual fund managers shifted to new and more popular investment mediums, such as municipal, government, or corporate bonds.

Conventional mutual funds' holdings of cash and equivalent items can vary, ranging from 5 to 10 percent of total asset holdings. Some cash holdings are needed to redeem shares turned in for redemption. However, cash holdings may also represent liquid assets (such as bank CDs) held for later investment.

In general, mutual funds typically hold more liquid assets when market interest rates are relatively high. Then the yield on liquid assets is high and stock prices may be expected to fall. Therefore, some cash items may be held for investment at lower prices. When interest rates start to fall, however, the return on cash and equivalent holdings falls at the same time that stock prices are expected to rise. Hence many mutual funds may readjust their portfolios by reducing their cash holdings and buying stocks. When they do, they can cause temporary buying panics as many buyers simultaneously bid up the prices of stocks in order to acquire more before their prices rise further.

Because of this phenomenon, many securities analysts monitor mutual fund cash and equivalent holdings closely. They try to determine if the funds (and other investors) have sufficient liquid asset holdings to fuel a buying panic if short-term interest rates fall. Analysts also attempt to identify periods when mutual funds may wish to acquire larger cash holdings, as that means their demand for stocks will be reduced.

Types of Investment Funds

Many types of investment funds exist. The driving force that determines the types of fund is investor demand.

Aggressive Growth Funds.   Aggressive growth funds are extremely speculative investments that strive for big profits from capital gains. Their portfolios typically consist of the stocks of small companies with high price/earnings ratios or companies whose stock prices are highly volatile. These funds are extremely speculative and most appropriate for sophisticated investors.

Growth Funds.   The investment goal of a growth fund is capital appreciation. Such funds invest primarily in common stocks that are judged to have above-average growth potential. Growth funds are most suitable for aggressive investors with long-term investment horizons. The stocks in a growth fund usually pay no dividends and thus a growth fund would not be suitable for investors who need current income.

Growth and Income Funds.   Growth and income funds seek a balanced return consisting of both capital gains and current income. These funds place most of their assets in high-quality common stocks. Such funds would be appropriate for investors who need some current income, but want the opportunity to participate in the growth of the economy.

Balanced Funds.   Balanced funds hold a balanced portfolio of both stocks and bonds. They do so to generate both current income and capital appreciation. Typically, a balanced fund will generate a higher level of income than a growth and income fund and be less volatile. However, the opportunity for capital gains will be less.

Bond Funds.   Bond funds invest exclusively in various types and grades of bonds. Current income is the primary objective. The kinds of bonds include U.S. Treasury and agency securities, mortgage-backed securities, investment-grade corporate bonds, high-yield corporate bonds, municipal securities, and bonds issued by foreign governments and companies.

Specialty Funds.   Some investment funds are managed to achieve specialized objectives. Index funds are managed to match the return from a particular market index such as the S&P 500. Sector funds restrict their investments to a single segment of the market. For example, a sector fund might concentrate on the automobile or telecommunications industries. An international fund invests in foreign securities and may have a global focus or may concentrate on a single country. Such specialty funds are created in response to the demands of investors.

Regulation of Investment Companies

Investment companies are regulated by the Securities and Exchange Commission and are subject to state securities regulations. Regulations require that funds provide full and honest disclosures to actual and potential customers, diversify their portfolios, avoid questionable sales compensation or kickback schemes, and avoid conflicts of interest between advisers or management companies and fund shareholders. Federal regulations are embodied in the Investment Company Act of 1940 (as amended subsequently). Under the "conduit" theory of taxation, mutual funds are not subject to direct taxes on their income provided that they distribute to their shareholders at least 90 percent of all income received. Most distribute 100 percent (minus expenses).

Money Market Mutual Funds

Money market mutual funds (MMMFs) invest in very-short-term assets (under 120 days) whose prices are not significantly affected by changes in market interest rates. In addition, they provide shareholders with ready access to their funds—via wire transfers, transfers among stock and bond accounts, limited check writing, or unlimited credit card capabilities.

Money market mutual funds were started in the early 1970s. After five years of relatively slow growth, they grew very rapidly, from $3.7 billion in total assets in 1976 to $232.3 billion in total assets on December 1, 1982. At that point, competition from financial institutions' newly authorized money market deposit accounts (MMDAs) and Super NOW accounts terminated their rapid growth. Subsequently, their asset holdings fell by more than $60 billion in less than six months.

The rapid growth and subsequent decline of money market mutual funds depended on the existence of Regulation Q, which imposed binding deposit rate ceilings on banks and savings institutions in high-interest-rate periods. In the 1970s, as interest rates rose above Regulation Q rate ceilings on deposits at commercial banks and thrifts, their depositors had powerful incentives to withdraw funds and place them in MMMFs to earn a higher return. After Regulation Q was relaxed in late 1982, MMMFs lost market share (see Exhibit 21-6). It was only after financial institutions cut their initially high payout rates on their MMDAs that MMMFs were able to grow once again.

Transactional Convenience

In addition to offering higher rates to depositors, MMMFs offered greater liquidity and ease of access to funds than investment securities with comparable returns. In particular, most funds gave investors the right to obtain same-day wire transfers of funds from their mutual fund to their bank account. Many funds also allowed individuals or corporations to write checks (drafts) against their mutual fund assets, usually for minimum withdrawals of $100 or more. Furthermore, many MMMFs allowed free transfers between balances in stock, bond, or other mutual funds managed by the same mutual fund management company. Similarly, many brokerage firms allowed their investors to immediately transfer funds obtained from the sale of stocks or bonds to money market funds. Automatic reverse transfers allowed payments to be made for newly purchased stocks and bonds. Finally, some of the money market funds allowed depositors to withdraw funds by using either credit cards or debit cards accepted by major credit card systems (Visa and MasterCard).

Exhibit 21–6   MMMF Asset Holdings

Year	Total Assets ($ in billions)	Distribution of Assets (percentage)			
		Bank CDs and Eurodollar CDs	U.S. Government Securities and RPs	Commercial Paper and Banker's Acceptances	Cash and Miscellaneous
1974	2.4	67	4	25	4
1976	3.7	38	28	23	1
1978	10.9	49	14	34	3
1979	45.2	40	10	43	7
1980	74.4	37	19	42	2
1981	181.9	34	26	39	2
1982	206.6	31	34	33	2
1983	162.5	28	30	41	1
1984	209.7	21	31	47	1
1985	207.5	17	33	48	2
1986	228.3	18	33	46	3
1987	254.7	22	32	43	3
1988	272.3	23	26	48	3
1989	358.7	19	25	52	4

In the MMMFs' early years, their assets grew slowly. However, when market interest rates rose above the rates that financial institutions could pay on deposits in the late 1970s, their assets grew explosively until depository institutions were allowed to offer federally insured deposits exempt from rate ceilings in late 1982.

Source: Investment Company Institute, *Mutual Fund Fact Book*, various issues.

Depository Institutions Fight Back

Eventually, public resentment over the fact that money funds removed wealth from local communities led to the passage of the 1982 Depository Institutions Act. The act allowed banks and savings associations to issue new money market deposit accounts (MMDAs) starting December 14, 1982, that were exempt from both rate ceilings (for balances over $2,500) and reserve requirements. The accounts also had limited transactions privileges and were federally insured up to $100,000. Then, on January 5, 1983, the Depository Institutions Deregulation Committee (which developed the final specifications for the new MMDA accounts) authorized Super NOW accounts, which were similar to MMDAs except that they had unlimited transactions privileges and were subject to reserve requirements.[3] Both MMDAs and Super NOW accounts grew rapidly, attracting more than $300 billion in deposits within three months. Although some of these deposits came from other depository institutions' accounts, many came from money market mutual funds. The MMMFs were at a disadvantage because their accounts were not federally insured; were not readily checkable; could not offer

---

[3]Super NOW accounts (called SNOW accounts) were merged with NOW accounts on January 1, 1986, when interest rate ceilings (Regulation Q) were phased out for *all* depository accounts at banks and thrift institutions. A single account now exists, called a NOW account.

unlimited rates because they could only distribute their earnings, minus expenses; and could not match the promotional rates, up to 20 percent for short periods, that depository institutions offered.

Adjustments by MMMFs

In response to the introduction of competitive accounts by depository institutions, MMMFs took a number of actions. First, some specialized in tax-exempt securities, thereby generating income exempt from federal taxes. In contrast, interest paid by depository institutions was taxable. Second, some stressed their membership in families of funds, which allowed depositors to switch balances between stock, bond, money market, and other mutual funds at low cost. Third, many provided brokerage services to customers. Fourth, the money funds augmented their check-writing privilege by letting customers use debit cards, pay bills by phone, obtain cash from banks' ATM networks, transfer funds electronically, and, in conjunction with brokerage accounts, transfer funds automatically between accounts. Even though banks could offer similar transaction services in conjunction with NOW accounts, they were subject to reserve requirements that reduced their net earning power on such accounts.

Finally, MMMFs used various strategies to obtain insurance for customers who wanted insured accounts. Some bought or started banks, trust companies, or savings institutions. In that way they could offer federally insured MMDAs to depositors who desired them. For instance, the Fidelity Investments group started a bank so that it could offer insured accounts to its customers. The Dreyfus Fund acquired a bank so that it could offer MMDAs. Other MMMFs contracted with private insurers to insure their deposits. However, the initial private insurance fee of $\frac{3}{8}$ of 1 percent exceeded the federal insurance charge of $\frac{1}{12}$ of 1 percent.

The defensive activities of the MMMFs clearly prevented them from incurring greater withdrawals. Since they still retained several advantages in supplying transactional convenience and services, they survived the abolition of Regulation Q. They resumed their growth after many banks lowered their high introductory rates on MMDAs.

Real Estate Investment Trusts

A real estate investment trust (REIT) is a type of closed-end investment company that invests in real estate money obtained through the sale of shares. It may hold income-generating properties, acquire mortgages, finance real estate developments, provide interim financing to builders, or acquire and lease property to real estate developers. REITs must abide by the Real Estate Investment Act of 1960, which governs their formation and business operations. REITs are exempt from federal income tax provided that they derive at least three-fourths of their income from operations related to real estate and pass through at least 90 percent of their net income to shareholders.

REITs grew slowly until the late 1960s, when their growth exploded. New favorable tax treatment, federal encouragement of real estate investment, a strong economy, and rising real estate prices all contributed to their growth. However, while they were growing rapidly, many REITs took excessive risks, making highly leveraged or speculative investments on the assumption that rising real estate prices would soon increase builders' and owners' equity. Furthermore, REITs that provided construction and interim financing to speculative builders (builders who erected properties without first having firm contracts from potential users) took the most risk. Those taking the least risk provided long-term mortgage financing to ultimate users of properties or were "equity trusts" that owned and leased real properties.

When interest rates rose and housing construction sagged during the money crunch of 1973 and 1974, numerous owners could not find permanent tenants for their properties. Many construction and development projects were left uncompleted or deferred as builders saw the market for their project dry up. As a result of these developments, numerous REITs had bad loans and experienced well-publicized financial distress. Many failed. To prevent failure of REITs associated with bank holding companies bearing their names, some commercial banks knowingly purchased bad mortgage loans from their affiliated REITs. This, in turn, jeopardized the banks. Before regulators could stop this practice, several large banks failed.

The bad publicity and financial distress surrounding REITs in the early and mid-1970s halted their rapid growth and started a substantial decline. Many of those that survived the 1973–1974 money crunch were those that held relatively low-risk physical assets. Because of their decline, the nation's REITs today play only a small role as financial intermediaries. Although most survivors own sound assets, the bad publicity that REITs in general experienced in the mid-1970s has made it difficult for them to attract new shareholders and lenders. Starting in 1984, however, REITs began to play a more important role in the economy once again, in part because proposed tax reforms made other forms of real estate investment less attractive. Newly formed mortgage REITs bought pools of high-yielding mortgages. Also "finite-life REITs" (so named because they had a set termination date to insure that their shares would not sell at large discounts to asset values) obtained funds to invest in both real property and mortgages.

Summary

This chapter is about Wall Street firms. The premier players are investment banks, which dominate the direct financial markets as commercial banks dominate the intermediation market. Investment banks' major business activities are bringing new securities issues to market and making secondary markets for those securities as brokers and dealers. In addition, investment banks engage in private placements and do merger and acquisition work, real estate brokerage, and financial consulting. Although investment banking and commercial banking are legally separated by the Glass-Steagall Act of 1933, the two types of firms are locked in a head-to-head struggle for customers and products. As a result, legal barriers between the two types of business are crumbling, and many experts believe that Congress will repeal the portion of the Glass-Steagall Act that separates commercial from investment banking within the decade.

Another type of Wall Street business activity is the management of investment funds, popularly called mutual funds. These funds invest in a wide range of long-term securities (debt or equity) and provide investors with risk, denomination, maturity, and liquidity intermediation and access to professional investment management. Other specialized investment companies are the money market mutual funds, which were started in the early 1970s. They offer liquidity, portfolio diversification, and minimal transaction costs. Their growth was particularly rapid after the Regulation Q ceiling became binding on commercial banks and other depository institutions. However, they posed such a threat to depository institutions that in 1982, Congress authorized new accounts without rate ceilings for depository institutions. The new competition caused money market funds to lose assets. Nonetheless, by specializing in tax-exempt securities and providing a wide variety of funds transfer services, they were able to retain a substantial share of the deposit market.

REITs were less fortunate when their growth was cut short by real estate failures associated with the 1973–1974 credit crunch. Their assets have declined substantially since that time. Surviving REITs emphasize less risky (long-term mortgage or equity) forms of asset holdings, and many new ones have finite lives to ensure that they will be valued closer to their net asset (breakup) value.

Questions

1. Explain how investment banks and large money-center banks are similar and how they are different.
2. What are the major business activities of investment banks?
3. Why do commercial banks want to get into investment banking?
4. Explain why underwriting new securities issues can be a risky business.
5. What is a private placement? How does it differ from a deal underwritten by an investment bank?
6. What is the major difference between open-end and closed-end investment companies? Why have open-end companies been more popular?
7. How did the regulation of depository institutions contribute to the rapid growth of money market mutual funds?
8. Why are money market fund liabilities included in the broader measures of the money supply that the Federal Reserve introduced in 1980?
9. What caused the conventional mutual funds' rapid growth to cease in the 1970s, and how and why did they diversify their portfolios?
10. In what ways do some securities dealers and stockbrokers serve as financial intermediaries?
11. Give examples from this chapter to illustrate how different forms of financial institutions may either grow rapidly or decline as economic and regulatory conditions change.
12. What is a REIT? What problem did these firms experience during the 1970s?
13. What is venture capital? What types of companies seek venture capital?

Selected References

Bloch, Ernest. *Inside Investment Banking*. Homewood, IL: Dow Jones–Irwin, 1989.
A readable and comprehensive book that explores the market-making activities that differentiate investment banking firms from other financial institutions. Also provides in-depth information on the new-issue process.

Gitman, Lawrence, and Michael D. Joehnk. *Fundamentals of Investing*. **New York: Harper & Row, 1988.**
A well-written book that covers all of the firms discussed in this chapter.

Gladstone, David. *Venture Capital Investing*. **Englewood Cliffs, NJ: Prentice-Hall, 1985.**
A handbook for investing in small private companies that describes the venture capital process.

Hayes, Samuel L., and Philip M. Hubbard. *Investment Banking: A Tale of Three Cities*. **Boston: Harvard Business School Press, 1990.**
This book traces the evolution of international investment banking to the present. It examines how successful investment banking firms have responded to the changing financial environment.

Hayes, Samuel H., III, A. Michael Spence, and David V. Marks. *Competition in the Investment Banking Industry*. **Cambridge, MA: Harvard University Press, 1983.**
A good overview of investment banking that includes sections on history, innovation and product development, competition, and client relationships.

Hoffman, Paul. *The Deal Makers: Inside the World of Investment Banking*. **Garden City, NY: Doubleday & Co., 1984.**
A well-written and comprehensive book that examines the history, the firms, the trends, and the internationalization of investment banking.

Hunter, William C., and Mary Beth Walker. "Assessing the Fairness of Investment Banker's Fees." *Economic Review*. **Federal Reserve Bank of Atlanta, March/April 1988, pp. 2–7.**
This article examines whether or not the fees that investment banks charge for arranging mergers represent an equitable value.

Kaufman, George G. "Security Activities of Commercial Banks: Recent Changes in the Economic and Legal Environments." *Midland Corporate Finance Journal*, **Winter 1988, pp. 14–23.**
Examines the historical development and conflict between investment banks and commercial banks and then considers the current competitive status between the two institutions. A good article.

Lown, Cara S. "Money Market Deposit Accounts versus Money Market Mutual Funds." *Economic Review*. **Federal Reserve Bank of Dallas, November 1987, pp. 29–38.**
The article examines the extent to which depositors view money market deposit accounts and money market mutual funds as substitutes.

Parry, Robert T. "Major Trends in the U.S. Financial System: Implications and Issues." *Economic Review*. **Federal Reserve Bank of San Francisco, Spring 1987.**
This paper examines the major trends shaping the U.S. financial system. It illustrates the conflict between technology and economic forces versus an outmoded legal and regulatory framework.

Williamson, J. Peter, ed. *The Investment Banking Handbook*. **New York: John Wiley & Sons, 1988.**
A comprehensive handbook with sections on all aspects of investment banking activities, including new financial instruments, commercial banks versus investment banks, and international activities.

FINANCIAL CONGLOMERATES AND FINANCE COMPANIES

MANY PEOPLE HAVE OBSERVED THE success of department stores in selling a broad line of consumer products and have concluded that financial products can profitably be sold similarly—through "department stores of finance." Thus financial conglomerates have arisen. While commercial banks can also offer a wide variety of financial products, they are heavily regulated. Furthermore, various regulations have limited commercial banks' ability to branch nationwide, to underwrite and trade securities, and to underwrite insurance. In addition, in the United States, there has long been a regulatory separation between commerce (business interests) and banking.

Because of regulatory barriers to the offering of complete financial product lines by banks, financial conglomerates often use a holding company structure to exploit various regulatory loopholes. For instance, unlike bank holding companies, a one-S&L holding company is not regulated at the holding-company level by federal regulators. Similarly, holding companies that own "nonbank banks" (that either do not make commercial loans or do not issue transactions deposits) are exempt from holding-company regulations. Thus financial conglomerates can avoid various regulatory restrictions that apply to commercial banks but still offer a broad range of financial services nationwide.

Most major financial conglomerates have acquired various finance company subsidiaries so they can avoid some of the restrictions against interstate branching activities that have applied to commercial banks. Finance companies, in general, are less regulated than commercial or savings banks because most of them do not issue insured deposits to the public and they are not chartered or regulated at the national level. Furthermore, while consumer finance companies are subject to considerable regulation of their loan rates and collection practices, business finance companies are not heavily regulated because their borrowers are assumed to be able to look after themselves.

Also, various mergers among financial and nonfinancial institutions have enabled people to "buy their stocks where they buy their socks," buy insurance products from stockbrokers, and so forth. Not all mergers among unlike institutions have been successful, however. Evidently, people tend to think of buying particular combinations of products (such as clothing and shoes) in one place but not other combinations (such as doughnuts and auto supplies). As a result, some of the early financial conglomerates have divested some of their operations. Nonetheless, new firms are still being developed. For instance, AT&T recently introduced its "Universal" credit card to tie together communications and credit technology.

This chapter first discusses major financial conglomerates and their objectives in acquiring various financial subsidiaries. Next, the chapter discusses finance companies, noting in the process that there are substantial differences between large and small finance companies, consumer and business finance companies, and captive versus independent finance companies. Finally, some of the management challenges faced by finance companies and financial conglomerates are overviewed.

Financial Conglomerates

During the 1970s, and early 1980s, the number of financial conglomerates operating in the United States expanded substantially. Institutions acquired financial conglomerates because they hoped to increase the level and stability of their profits and obtain financial synergies with their other lines of business. Exhibit 22–1 shows the steps taken by major nonfinancial companies to enter the financial arena from 1919 to 1985. As a result of these steps, the financial markets have become more competitive, as there now are more firms providing financial services that were traditionally offered by commercial banks. In addition, many of these firms have expanded their participation in financial markets in recent years.

The entry of various firms into the financial arena differs with the type of firm. Some, particularly retailers and auto and consumer goods manufacturers, initially formed finance companies to help finance sales of their consumer goods. Others, such as industrial companies, formed finance companies to help finance their operations, their industrial sales, and their suppliers. Many brokerage firms became financial conglomerates in order to offer banking-related products to their customers and become full-service financial institutions. Similar motives induced insurance companies to become financial conglomerates.

Automobile Finance Companies

The nation's major automobile manufacturers have long had large *captive finance companies* to help finance automobile sales and dealers. These finance companies are the reason that consumers can sometimes obtain 1.9 or 2.9 percent financing on new car loans. Any loss the auto finance company takes on the cut-rate financing can be offset by extra profits earned by its parent through additional sales of new cars at good prices. Auto manufacturers also use their captive finance companies to finance automobile dealers. They provide "floorplan" wholesale financing to dealers to that the dealers can purchase new cars from the manufacturers and keep the cars on their lots until they are sold.

Because consumer financing criteria are similar for many types of credit (especially for secured credit, such as auto, mobile home, boat, or sometimes home loans), the auto finance companies have broadened their range of consumer financing products over time. In addition, because dealer financing is similar for many types of retail sales operations, and also because their suppliers may need credit, the auto finance

Exhibit 22–1	**Banking-Related Financial Services Offered by Selected Nonfinancial Companies, 1985**									

Service	General Motors	Ford	ITT	General Electric	Control Data	Borg-Warner	Westing-house	Sears	Marcor	J.C. Penney
Commercial Finance										
Commercial lending	1944	1960	1954–5	1965	1968		1961		1966	
Factoring					1968					
Accounts receivable and inventory finance	1919	1959	1971	1932	1968	1950	1954			
Venture capital				1970	1971					
Consumer Finance										
Sales finance	1919	1959	1964	1964	1968	1953	1959	1911	1917	1958
Personal finance		1966	1964	1965	1968	1969		1962	1966	1970
Credit card			1983		1983			1950	1957	1958
Real Estate										
Mortgage banking	1985		1983	1981	1982	1982		1972		1970
Residential first mortgages		1985		1981	1982	1982		1961		1981
Residential second mortgages		1972	1965		1979		1969	1961	1966	
Real estate development		1969	1970	1960	1972	1969	1969	1960	1970	1970
Real estate sales and management				1983	1981			1960	1970	1970
Commercial real estate and finance		1960	1980	1963			1969	1961	1966	1970
Insurances										
Credit life insurance	1975	1962	1964	1973	1968	1970		1960	1966	1970
Regular life insurance		1974	1964	1973	1968			1957	1966	1970
Property/casualty insurance	1925	1959	1964	1970	1968	1970		1931		1970
Accident/health insurance			1964	1973	1968			1958	1968	1967
Leasing										
Equipment and personal property	1981	1966	1968	1963	1968	1968	1968	1960	1970	1970
Real property leasing		1982	1982					1981		
Lease brokerage										
Investment Services										
Investment management			1966						1969	
Mutual fund sales		1982	1966					1969		1970
Business and Personal Services										
Travel services		1978						1961	1971	
Cash management services								1981		1985
Tax preparation services									1966–70	1969
Financial data-processing services		1985	1965		1968	1970			1982	
Credit card management services		1985		1965			1969			

Source: Christine Pavel and Harvey Rosenblum, *Economic Perspective*, Federal Reserve Bank of Chicago, May–June 1985, with some updates by authors.

companies have gradually extended their credit facilities to many other businesses. In recent years, several auto finance companies have broadened their activities to include all types of consumer and business finance, including the leasing of cars, trucks, and business equipment of various types; the provision of consumer credit cards; and the making and servicing of home mortgages.

For Ford, General Motors, and Chrysler, 1985 was a year in which they greatly extended their reach in the financial service arena. Evidently, the extensive assets held by their finance subsidiaries[1] merely whetted their appetite for more financial business—possibly because the income from such business is far more stable than the income from auto manufacturing. Thus, in 1985, all three companies acquired numerous additional financial service subsidiaries.

Ford Motor Credit acquired First Nationwide Financial Corporation, owner of the nation's ninth largest thrift, with branches in California, Florida, New York State, and Hawaii. First Nationwide also owned TransSouth Financial Corporation, which had financial offices in seven additional states, and First Nationwide Network, which provided financial services and credit card facilities to member institutions in 15 states. Thus, with one acquisition, Ford Motor Company became an even larger player in financial services—with enhanced mortgage lending, deposit-taking, and credit card capabilities. Ford's ultimate objective is to obtain 15 to 20 percent of its profits from financial services. To further that objective, Ford has continued to acquire savings and loan associations in various states and soon may be the largest savings and loan holding company in the United States.

General Motors' initial moves into financial services were slightly different. In 1985 it acquired two of the nation's largest mortgage-servicing companies and thereby became the nation's second largest servicer of mortgage loans, servicing nearly $20 billion in mortgage loans. GM planned to use the capacity of its recently acquired EDS (Electronic Data Systems) subsidiary to provide computer assistance for its mortgage servicing. It also planned to start offering transactions services related to its money market fund on a nationwide basis to its employees and, later, to its customers. Since EDS provides data-processing services for many banks, GM thought that EDS would have both the expertise and the capacity necessary to greatly expand its activities in the financial services arena. Also, because both mortgage loans and auto loans are large loans with low default risk and regular monthly payments, GM and Ford both thought that their expertise in automobile financing would help them manage their newly acquired mortgage-lending operations.

Chrysler Corporation also moved into financial services in a big way in 1985 by acquiring Finance-America, the national business finance–company subsidiary of BankAmerica. Thus both Chrysler and Ford greatly increased their ability to make loans (and, in Ford's case, to obtain funds) on a nationwide basis. Chrysler's thrust was oriented more toward business finance and leasing, whereas Ford's initiatives were more closely related to full-service consumer financial services.

---

[1]In 1988, General Motors Acceptance Corporation was the nation's second largest lender after Citicorp and held $100 billion in assets. Ford Motor Credit Corporation held $50 billion, and Chrysler Credit Corporation held approximately $20 billion.

Retailers

Sears Roebuck and Other Retailers

Like the auto finance companies, retailers initially acquired finance subsidiaries to help finance the sales of their products. However, they soon began to offer other financial services that served their customers' needs. Sears Roebuck was particularly aggressive in expanding in the financial services arena. It not only had the largest proprietary credit card operation, larger at one time than either MasterCard or Visa, but it also owned an insurance company (Allstate), thrift institutions (it expanded Allstate Savings and Loan to become one of the 20 largest in the country), and other financial subsidiaries, such as PMI (one of the first and largest private mortgage-insurance companies).

When Sears' management realized that it was obtaining most of its profits from its financial subsidiaries and that Preston Martin, the founder of PMI, was one of its highest-paid executives, the company went on an acquisition and expansion binge in the financial services arena.

In 1981, Sears acquired Dean Witter, the nation's fourth largest brokerage firm, and Coldwell Banker, the country's largest real estate broker. Subsequently it added financial services centers to sell its products (including money market funds and certificates of deposit issued by its savings bank) in many of its retail stores. In 1985, Sears' "consumer bank," Greenwood Trust Company of Delaware, introduced a general-purpose, nationwide credit card—its Discover card—to compete with the MasterCard and Visa cards offered by commercial banks. While it divested Allstate Savings and Loan, Sears retained a substantial interest in real estate finance through Sears Mortgage Corp. (which is one of the nation's largest issuers of home mortgages), in real estate development (through Homart Development Co.), and in real estate sales (through Coldwell Banker).

By 1991, Sears earned $938 million in profits from its financial subsidiaries and only $92 million in net profits from its traditional merchandise operations. During 1991, Sears' Discover card generated $17 million in profits and had 41 million cardholders with $14 billion in balances outstanding. Furthermore, Sears' credit card, with over 70 million cards and 27 million active accounts outstanding, added $394 million to the total $486 million in profit earned by Sears merchandise group in 1991, as over 60 percent of Sears' sales were made on its credit card. Thus, by year-end 1991, Sears' financial operations provided the bulk of its merchandise group's profits. At the same time, Sears' Dean Witter subsidiary managed over $50 billion in a variety of proprietary mutual funds and had a very profitable retail brokerage operation. In total, Dean Witter's operations contributed $170 million to Sears' earnings in 1991.

Sears' financial operations are profitable, in part, because of valuable synergies. For instance, the Discover and Sears credit cards share certain overhead costs and use similar risk-reduction and credit-authorization strategies to reduce credit risk. Sears also can market home insurance (Allstate) and mortgage-banking services (Sears Mortgage) through its retail real estate business (Coldwell Banker). Also, Sears can profitably exploit "good customer" lists from its various subsidiaries to cross-market appropriate products and services. Thus future profits can still be realized from Sears' already profitable entry into financial services.

Because of Sears' nationwide scope and past success, bankers feared Sears' entry into money market mutual funds through Dean Witter. They feared that Sears' sales of these products would drain funds from their customers' deposit accounts. Sears' credit services also could potentially provide considerable competition for local financial institutions. Sears' Discover card was designed not only to be a general-purpose credit card but also to provide access to a broad range of financial services. Cardholders can obtain cash through ATM networks and access their savings accounts at Sears' Greenwood Trust Company or their mutual fund accounts and individual retirement accounts at Dean Witter. Cardholders also can transfer funds between their various accounts and can make payments to Sears' Allstate Insurance Company. Sears can allow customers to access a broader array of services through its credit cards than more highly regulated banks can offer. In addition. Sears can use its mortgage expertise to allow people to obtain credit by writing checks against a home equity line of credit. Such credit is typically cheaper than commercial banks' personal loans.

Sears has other advantages not available to banks, including the ability to gather funds easily on a nationwide basis. The company has used this ability to offer cash-mangement lockbox service to business firms—a service that provides competition for banks' commercial business. That is in addition to the competition for consumer credit, deposits, savings, and investment services that the retailer already provides.

Even though, in theory, Sears is a formidable competitor for commercial banks, in practice Sears has found that not all the synergies obtainable from offering a full range of financial services and products were as great as expected. Sears' start-up costs on the Discover card were greater than it had expected, and it decided to exit the savings and loan business. Thus, by 1992, Sears decided to divest its Dean Witter and Coldwell Banker subsidiaries to pay down debt and free time to focus on its retail business. Sears also found that although many consumers purchased both stocks and socks, they didn't necessarily want to do so at the same place.

Other major retailers, such as J.C. Penney and Montgomery Ward (Marcor), have long offered credit cards. They followed Sears into the financial services business by selling insurance and allowing financial institutions to market products in their stores. However, none participated as extensively in the financial service markets as Sears (see Exhibit 22–1).

In general, the most popular financial service offered by retailers is the provision of consumer credit. Although the vast majority of retail credit outstanding consisted of revolving credit (extended largely through credit card plans) retailers also held noninstallment consumer debt obligations such as 30-day charge accounts. Thus retailers in general are one of the major suppliers of consumer credit to households.

Many retailers accept bank cards or contract with a bank or finance company to run a "private label" credit plan, but the largest retailers are able to operate their own plans profitably. However, most incur accounting losses on them, because their interest revenues often are less than the cost of their credit operations. Such losses are similar to those that retailers incur when they offer "free" customer parking—since parking fees are less than the cost of lot maintenance. However, as is the case with providing free parking, the profits earned on extra sales justify accounting losses on credit operations.

Among the retailers that offer their own credit plans, Sears Roebuck is by far the largest. However, Montgomery Ward and J.C. Penney also hold large amounts of credit card receivables. Many smaller retailers and some oil and gas companies also sell their goods on credit cards and therefore hold credit card debt.

Retailers' Sources of Funds

Retailers who finance their own credit sales obtain funds in a number of ways. Some have set up specialized subsidiaries that finance their consumer credit operations by selling commercial paper. Sears Roebuck Acceptance Corporation is the largest of these. It has terminals in the offices of major credit suppliers through which it can instantly print directly placed commercial paper obligations.

Retailers also sell bonds, equity, and commercial paper in the capital markets. In addition, some sell debt directly to the public.

Securities Brokers and Dealers

By evading restrictions against the merging of investment banking and commercial banking product lines in the United States, securities brokers and dealers were among the first firms to become financial conglomerates. They did this by offering products that were similar to, but not identical to, the products offered by commercial banks.

In particular, securities brokers and dealers offer credit facilities to commercial borrowers through subsidiaries that provide loans to corporations. They also offer checking and credit card facilities to consumers by letting the consumers write checks or use bank credit or debit cards to borrow or charge against balances held in their money market funds or securities accounts. American Express offers its own charge card, allows its customers to engage in international transactions through its international (not domestic) bank, and provides customers with traveler's checks, which, like bank checking-account balances, are part of the M1 money supply.

The first securities brokers and dealers to offer a broad range of financial services were Merrill Lynch Pierce Fenner and Smith and American Express, which are now the two largest brokerage firms in the country. Others have since followed their lead by offering equivalent products.

Merrill Lynch

Merrill Lynch Pierce Fenner and Smith was the first major brokerage firm to offer banking-related products. In particular, under its cash management account (CMA) program, Merrill Lynch allows investors to write checks against the credit balances and value of securities that they hold in their brokerage accounts. Merrill Lynch also issues bank credit cards to its CMA customers, allowing them to obtain funds for transactions purposes by drawing down their credit balances or borrowing against the securities in their accounts.

The CMA program puts brokerage firms in direct competition with more heavily regulated, deposit-taking financial intermediaries. Furthermore, the CMA program was only the beginning of Merrill Lynch's participation in the market for consumer financial services. It also brokers savings deposits for depository institutions—selling the federally insured deposits, for a small fee paid by the deposit-issuing institution, to customers who want to hold long-term insured deposits but do not want to bear prepayment penalties for possible early withdrawal. The Merrill Lynch program lets customers avoid withdrawal penalties by selling the deposits to someone else before maturity. In addition, Merrill Lynch has extensive real estate brokerage, relocation, financing, and investment services to serve the needs of affluent individuals and corporations with real estate sales or financing problems and tax shelter needs. It also has programs that let customers borrow against their household equity; offers insurance and annuity programs to its customers along with its traditional stock, bond, and commodity brokerage business; and has acquired a savings and loan association.

In 1980 Merrill Lynch became the second nonbank lender approved by the Small Business Administration (SBA). Then, in 1982, it formed a new subsidiary, Capital Resources, to sell commercial paper and long-term bonds and to lend the proceeds to certain businesses.

As a result of its initiatives, Merrill Lynch and its subsidiaries can make both commercial and consumer loans and can honor checks drawn on customers' CMA account balances. In short, Merrill Lynch offers many of the services banks provide—by serving as a broker for banks, by hiring banks to provide needed servises for a fee, or by offering the services directly. Throughout this process, however, Merrill Lynch has been careful not to get itself defined as a commercial bank, and it thus has escaped banking regulation. Merrill Lynch's successs spawned a host of imitators and induced other institutions to acquire brokerage firms.

Shearson Lehman Hutton/American Express

In June 1981, American Express Corporation (AmEx), a leading traveler's check, charge card, international banking (in 35 countries), and general financial services company, merged with Shearson, Loeb, Rhodes Inc., the nation's second largest brokerage firm. Shortly thereafter, the new firm acquired a trust company in Massachusetts, developed individual retirement account programs, and started cross-selling American Express's financial services to Shearson customers and vice veras. The new company developed its Financial Management Account to compete with Merril Lynch's Cash Management Account; developed extensive commercial lending and leasing activities; and engaged in extensive cross-marketing of services provided by its insurance, credit card, traveler's check, brokerage, international banking, and data-processing subsidiaries. In addition, it acquired a large mutual fund sales and management organization (IDS), and in 1984 it acquired a major investment banking firm—Lehman Brothers, Kuhn Loeb—to give it additional strength in corporate finance and in underwriting securities. Finally, following the stock market crash of October 19, 1987, it acquired the brokerage firm of E. F. Hutton and Company, which had suffered losses during the market drop. Many of these subsidiaries, particularly insurance and data processing, provide services to banks. Others, such as credit cards,

traveler's checks, and international banking, frequently provide services in cooperation with domestic banks. Also, like Merrill Lynch, Shearson Lehman, Inc. makes a
market in CDs and sells them to its customers.

In short, AmEx's Shearson Lehman brokerage subsidiary, like Merrill Lynch,
provides a wide range of consumer and business financial services. In so doing, it both
cooperates with and competes with commercial banks. In addition to matching
services provided by Merrill Lynch, it provides more extensive credit card, traveler's
check, and international banking services. It also offers extensive data-processing
services to banks and has experimented with home banking services.

American Express's extensive traveler's check facilities are well known, as they are
well advertised. Traveler's checks operate much like portable bank deposits. An
individual "deposits" money with a traveler's check–issuing company and receives
traveler's checks in return. The traveler's check company offers clearing mechanisms
that allow its liabilities to be redeemed at many different places. Before the cash is
withdrawn or the payment made, the company may invest the funds it receives in
exchange for the traveler's checks and earn a return on customers' "deposits" (unpaid
future liabilities to customers). Thus traveler's check companies (and also money-
order companies) act as financial intermediaries, issuing promises of future payment
in return for present cash balances that are invested. Unlike the majority of financial
intermediaries, they may charge for their remote-payment services. Furthermore, their
liabilities (deposits) are uninsured.

Because of their international payment convenience, traveler's checks enjoy
considerable popularity. Since they can be cleared by wire transfer rather than by
physical exchange, exchange rates for traveler's checks cashed abroad are often better
than exchange rates for cash.

American Express was a major financial intermediary even before it merged with
Shearson, Lehman Brothers, and E. F. Hutton. It is also a major charge card—issuing
firm. An integral part of any credit card plan is the information and funds transfer
system by which (1) a merchant receives cash in return for the credit extension at the
point of sale, and (2) the customer who used the credit card is billed for the amount of
money obtained by using the card. Typically, credit card information and funds
transfer systems work by allowing the merchant who accepts credit cards to sell credit
card sales slips to a cooperating bank. The bank pays the merchant the face value of
the slips minus a merchant discount. The discount, a few percentage points, covers the
system's cost of clearing the credit card slips. Merchants are willing to accept payment
at a discount because they obtain instant funds in return for the credit card sales slips
and sell to more people than would otherwise be possible. Moreover, merchants that
accept credit cards need not go to the trouble and expense of running their own credit
operation.

The next step in the clearing process is usually conducted by a major clearing
organization. Most banks clear their credit card slips either through Visa or through
one of the affiliates of Interbank Card Association (which clears MasterCard slips).
American Express has its own clearing subsidiary, which even processes credit card
slips for banks and other credit card issuers. The major clearing associations run a
computerized billing network that quickly credits the institution that submits a sales
slip. They then record that the card-using customer owes more money than before.
Clearing associations obtain fees for their services that usually are collected as (1) a

DID YOU KNOW?

Commercial Banks Have Competitive Disadvantages

Commercial banks have long asked to have a "level playing field." By that, the banks did not mean that they wanted others to issue credit cards and checking accounts, or have access to deposit insurance or the Federal Reserve discount window. Instead, they meant that they wanted deposit rates and loan rates deregulated so they could compete freely to attract deposits. They also wanted to engage in investment banking so they could make money by underwriting and dealing in securities for their corporate customers and by managing mutual funds. Furthermore, they wanted to underwrite insurance so they could profit from one-stop financial shopping. They also wanted to branch nationwide. Some of their wishes have been granted, such as rate deregulation, but others have been resisted by strong lobbies financed by the securities industry, insurance industry, and others who did not want to face competition from commercial banks.

At the same time, banks have lost their competitive advantages in other areas. First, many of their former best customers, such as General Motors Acceptance Corporation, began to meet their credit needs by issuing commercial paper directly rather than by borrowing from banks. Because of their good credit ratings, top-rated firms can often pay a lower rate to borrow in the money markets than banks must pay to sell their CDs. The best banks can do is to provide backup lines of credit (for a fee) to ensure that their customers can roll over their commercial paper when it matures and, in some instances, earn underwriting fees by assisting in the sale of customer commercial paper. Banks' total income, however, has been reduced by the shift of their best corporate customers from bank loans to commercial paper borrowing.

A second major problem that affects banks is that their interest-bearing deposits often do not pay more than money market funds and uninsured liabilities issued by nonbank institutions. One reason for this is that bank loan losses tended to rise (as a

percentage of loans) after the banks lost some of their best customers. Growing bank failures forced the FDIC-BIF to raise deposit insurance premiums (from 0.083 percent in the 1970s and early 1980s to 0.23 percent for the safest banks only, and to 0.31 percent or more for the riskiest banks by 1993). At the same time, risk-based capital requirements caused banks in the early 1990s to invest more of their assets in Treasury securities (which had no capital requirement) rather than loans. Consequently, a money market mutual fund that invested in Treasury bills could generally offer customers a better rate of return than a bank that invested in Treasury bills. The money market mutual fund could return to customers an amount equal to the T-bill yield less their processing and servicing costs (which are usually less than 0.25 percent). A bank that bought T-bills, in contrast, would have to subtract not only processing costs (which are much greater than 0.25 percent of assets because of banks' large investment in brick, mortar, and people), but also at least 25 basis points for deposit insurance, and a return-on-capital allowance (to compensate for bank's 3 percent minimum requirement on all investments) before it determined what rate of interest it could pay on its MMDA accounts. In addition, while the money market mutual fund could allow an unlimited number of checks to be drawn on its accounts, the bank would either have to restrict check withdrawals to three checks per month or pay an even lower interest rate to depositors (because no interest would be earned on the reserve requirements banks would have to hold to back their transactions deposits if customers wrote more than three checks per month). In short, an investor could earn a higher rate of return on deposits in money market funds that it invested in government-guaranteed paper (T-bills) than it could on government-guaranteed (insured) bank deposits used to invest in similar assets.

Continued

Finally, directors of banking institutions are subject to major regulatory restrictions on their activities and costly compliance examinations, which other financial institutions often avoid.

Consequently, many nonbank institutions are proliferating at the expense of banks. Money market mutual funds gather money from depositors and, in many cases, "lend" to the former bank borrowers by buying their commercial paper. Finance companies can issue commercial paper and use the funds so obtained to make loans to corporate and consumer borrowers in competition with banks. Because they are less regulated, can operate nationwide, have-

fewer interest rate risk problems, and are subject to fewer regulatory costs, nonbank competitors of banks such as finance companies, mutual funds, investment banks, credit card–issuing companies, and other financial institutions are often able to outcompete commercial banks. If the playing field is not leveled soon, commercial banks may well want to divest either their commercial loans or their transactions deposits so they too can become nonbank banks. Unfortunately, the misnamed Competitive Equality in Banking Act of 1987 prohibited the creation of more nonbank banks in that manner.

charge per item processed and (2) a small discount on the face value of the items processed.

When an American Express customer is billed for credit card charges, he or she may either pay the bill in full or (provided that the customer has previously obtained a credit line from a cooperating bank) make a partial payment. The rest of the payment is then automatically made by drawing on the prearranged credit line provided by the cooperating bank.

Other Brokerage Firms

Almost all other full-service brokerage firms now offer CD brokerage, corporate lending facilities, and products equivalent to Merrill Lynch's CMA account. They also offer a broad range of other financial services to both their consumer and their corporate customers. Discount brokerage firms typically offer no investment advice. However, many of them offer a wide range of financial products. For instance, Fidelity offers discount brokerage, numerous mutual funds, and a "U.S.A. account," which provides checking facilities and various financial services through a single unified account. Charles Schwab and Company is another discount brokerage firm that provides many financial services, including checking facilities, CD purchases, mutual fund purchases, discount-priced stock and bond transactions, and even computerized stock market information and order entry services to its customers. Thus many brokerage firms try to fill as many of their customers' financial needs as possible and try to provide unified check-writing and bookkeeping services as well.

Insurance Companies

Insurance companies provide both savings and investment services to individuals. Life insurance companies accept customers' payments and invest large quantities of funds for many years so that they can honor their commitments to make payments on annuity policies and life insurance contracts. They invest in stocks, bonds, and business and home mortgages, and they make "policy loans" to customers who wish to borrow against the cash value of their life insurance. Thus it is a logical step for insurance companies to use their investment expertise to offer additional, related services, such as mutual funds, IRA and Keogh account management, and lease financing. Some even offer cash management accounts. In addition, they may have mortgage banking or finance company subsidiaries that assist in their financial operations.

Insurance companies moved toward becoming full-service financial conglomerates after rising interest rates and policy-loan withdrawals forced them to offer new products with variable rates of return in the 1970s and early 1980s.

The first insurance company to enter financial services on a large scale was Prudential, which acquired Bache Securities in 1981. Prudential Securities underwrites corporate securities and now offers a full spectrum of brokerage and investment-banking services, including mutual funds and cash management accounts. It also makes many direct mortgage loans, provides banking and trust services, manages pension funds, and engages in business financing.

Other insurance companies with a major commitment to financial services include Equitable, Aetna, American General, Travelers, John Hancock, Kemper, and the CIGNA companies. Many offer mutual funds, IRAs, and cash management accounts in addition to commercial-lending, mortgage-lending, and investment services. John Hancock has started its own bank so that it can provide banking and ATM services to its customers, whereas the CIGNA companies control a thrift institution. Thus many insurance companies play a substantial role in the financial services arena.

However, not all insurance companies have found that the combination of different types of services generates profits automatically; distribution systems often are quite different for products offered by insurance companies and those offered by conventional financial institutions. In particular, stock brokers who typically sell stocks to risk-taking customers have not proved to be adept at selling insurance-related products designed for customers who wish to protect against risk. At the same time, insurance salespeople are not particularly adept at selling stocks. Nonetheless, by training their salespeople to be "financial planners" who provide their clients with a broad range of products tailored to their financial needs, insurance companies have been able to offer both equity-related products (such as mutual funds) and insurance products through a single vendor.

Other Companies

In recent years, more and more companies have been entering the financial services arena in an attempt to obtain synergy by offering complementary packages of financial services that consumers can obtain either through one-stop shopping or through a single "access" card. Sears and Household International (a major finance company that acquired numerous thrift institutions and issued a "Home Card" to customers) have used a credit card to provide access to their financial services. Most institutions that wish to offer credit card and checking services on a nationwide basis have acquired a nonbank bank or a thrift institution. John Hancock Insurance, Fidelity Investments, Dreyfus, Beneficial Finance, Associates Finance (a finance company subsidiary of Gulf and Western), Commercial Credit (a large finance company), and Prudential are some of the major institutions that have acquired nonbank banks and thrifts. Most recently, AT&T has entered the financial-services arena by issuing its "Universal" card, which allows customers to charge both phone services and other products. AT&T's linkage of credit card and telecommunications services is a logical step, since credit cards frequently are used to finance purchases made over the phone, and credit card–clearing processes make extensive use of communications links and switching services (just like phone calls).

Overall, many major industrial firms and diversified firms have extensive financial operations. As shown in Exhibit 22–1, in addition to firms previously cited, ITT, General Electric, Westinghouse, and (to a lesser extent) Borg-Warner all have extensive financial service operations. Because they are not subject to extensive federal regulation, finance companies in particular have frequently extended their credit operations by acquiring nonbank banks, thrift institutions, and other financial services operations.

Finance Companies

Basically, finance companies extend short- and intermediate-term credit to individuals and business firms that cannot obtain credit as cheaply or easily elsewhere. Often they lend to relatively risky borrowers. Approximately half their lending consists of loans to consumers, and the other half consists of loans to businesses plus leasing credit and purchases of business accounts receivable.

Finance companies obtain funds from bank loans, commercial paper sales, and issues of long-term and short-term debt. They are highly leveraged institutions. Overall, their ratio of borrowed funds to equity is nearly ten to one.

Finance companies are diverse institutions. Their business structure includes partnerships; privately owned corporations; publicly owned independent corporations; and wholly owned subsidiaries of manufacturers, commercial bank holding companies, life insurance companies, or other corporate entities. Many specialize in consumer finance, particularly small loans; others specialize in business loans, purchasing business accounts receivable (factoring), or leasing. Some primarily finance sales of products made by their parent organization.

The Federal Reserve classifies finance companies as institutions providing short- and intermediate-term credit that are not commercial banks, credit unions, mortgage banking firms, mutual savings banks, or savings and loan associations. Consumer finance companies primarily make cash loans to consumers, sales finance companies primarily buy consumer credit contracts from dealers, and "factors" buy accounts receivable from business firms.

In contrast to most depository institutions, finance companies obtain most of their funds in large amounts by borrowing from banks or selling securities in the capital markets rather than by issuing many small deposits. In addition, they often make many small loans rather than a few large ones. Some finance companies have industrial bank charters that allow them to accept deposits from the public. Others have started consumer banks, which accept deposits from the public and make loans to consumers but not to businesses (see People and Events).

Exhibit 22–2   **Size Distribution of Finance Companies (1975–1985)**

| Size | Number of Companies | | |
(millions)[a]	1975	1980	1985
$100 and over	88	148	194
$25 to 99	102	156	96
$5 to 24	204	239	161
$1 to 4	500	484	1,287
Under $1	2,482	1,749	
Total	3,376	2,776	1,738

---

[a]In business and consumer loans.

In recent years, many small finance companies have disappeared through consolidation, growth, or failure. Large finance companies have grown because they have a greater ability to cope with a complex regulatory environment.

Traditionally, finance companies have lent to consumers. However, such lending is strictly regulated by state loan rate ceilings, debt collection restrictions, and many other consumer protection or credit control regulations. This strict regulation has caused severe operating problems, especially for small finance companies. Thus, in recent years, finance companies have increasingly consolidated; as a result of their consolidation, the number of finance companies has declined sharply and their average size has increased (see Exhibit 22–2). They have also shifted their portfolios toward business lending and leasing and second mortgage credit.

Assets of Finance Companies

Gross versus Net Assets

Exhibit 22–3 presents data relating to the major assets and liabilities held by large and small finance companies at the end of 1989. As can be seen, the principal assets of finance companies consists of business and consumer receivables. Balance sheets can be somewhat misleading in that total gross receivables due can exceed total assets. This occurs because many finance companies include all scheduled payments on each loan in their gross receivables account, even though the interest due is "unearned" until time elapses (and will not be due if the loan is repaid early). Therefore, a substantial adjustment must be made to calculate their net receivables outstanding and their total assets. For instance, a 36-month loan repayable at the rate of $100 per month would be recorded as a gross receivable of $3,600. However, if the loan were made at an interest rate of 25.45 percent, the amount of credit extended (and the "net" amount receivable when the loan is made) is only $2,500. The other $1,100 represents unearned interest income that comes due only when the borrower repays the loan as scheduled. Because the unearned interest income overstates the present value of the

Exhibit 22–3   Comparative Balance Sheets of Large versus Small Finance Companies

	Assets (percentage)			Liabilities (percentage)	
	Large	**Small***		**Large**	**Small***
Cash and deposits	2.1%	2.6%	Bank loans	2.2%	12.9%
Net receivables	78.6	79.6	Commercial paper	36.4	22.8
Gross Receivables	89.2	92.7	Other short-term debt		
Consumer	50.6	90.5	and current liabilities	7.1	4.6
Business	38.6	2.2	Deposit and thrift certificates	0.6	9.7
− Unearned income	(− 9.0)	(− 11.2)	Long-term debt and		
− Loss allowance	(− 1.6)	(− 1.9)	subordinated debentures	37.8	7.3
Marketable securities	4.0	4.4	Borrowings from parent	1.5	27.6
Other investments					
and loans	1.2	2.3	All other liabilities	5.0	2.0
Other domestic assets	7.0	11.1	Capital, surplus, and		
Foreign receivalbes	7.1	0.0	undivided profits	9.4	13.1
Total	100.0%	100.0%	Total	100.0%	100.0%

Note: The data were obtained from a survey published in 1990 by the American Financial Services Association in its annual statistical report, *Finance Companies in* 1989. The large companies held over $1 billion in receivables, whereas the 63 small companies held lesser amounts of receivables. Business finance companies, including sales finance companies, responded to the survey. Thus, the 84 respondents held 73 percent of all consumer credit owned by finance companies at year-end 1989.

Source: Isabel Burns McAleer, *Finance Companies in* 1989, (Washington, D.C.: American Financial Services Association, 1990).

loan, it must be excluded from gross receivables to determine the present value of net receivables due.

A second adjustment is also commonly made to finance companies' receivables to allow for potential losses. Loan loss reserves reflect the fact that, based on past experience, 1 to 3 percent of the loan balances due will not be repaid. Thus both loss reserves and unearned income are subtracted from gross receivables before total assets are calculated.

Types of Assets

Although some finance companies make only business loans and others make only consumer loans, as a whole finance companies divide their lending about equally between consumer and business lending. After adjustment for unearned income and loss reserves, in 1989 finance companies' receivables of all types amounted to 88 percent of their net assets. Other assets consisted of cash, time deposits, investment securities, buildings, computers, and so on. Cash and deposits accounted for about 2 percent of finance companies' assets. Some of those deposits may have been held as compensating balances for bank loans; the rest provided liquidity. Investment securities, which provide both a secondary source of liquidity and direct earnings, accounted for less than 10 percent of assets. Real assets, such as real estate, computers, and equipment, and loans made to foreign borrowers accounted for the remainder of finance companies' assets.

Types of receivables held by finance companies vary greatly. Some companies, such as General Electric Credit Corporation, make all types of loans to all types of borrowers. Others, such as factors or local consumer loan companies, specialize in only a few types of loans.

Consumer Receivables

Personal Loans.   Exhibit 22–4 provides details on the types of receivables held by large and small finance companies and those specializing in personal loans versus other types of credit. Traditionally, consumer-oriented finance companies have attempted to serve consumers by extending credit with more lenient terms, making smaller loans, taking more risk, and providing more personal service than other lenders. Consequently, they make many personal loans. Consumer finance companies, in fact, specialize in personal loans. Personal loans are the largest single category of

Exhibit 22–4   **Distribution of Percentage of Gross Receivables Held by Large and Small Finance Companies (1989)**

	All Companies	Large Companies		Small Companies	
		Personal-Loan Oriented	Other Companies	Personal-Loan Oriented	Other Companies
Personal loans	18.7%	69.9%	4.4%	85.7%	14.5%
Revolving credit	4.1	15.7	1.1	7. 6	0.4
Real estate secured	1.0%	4.5%	0.1%	2.6%	0.4%
Other	3.1	11.3	1.0	5.0	0.0
Fixed term	14.6	54.2	3.3	78.1	14.1
Real estate secured	8.4	28.4	2.7	35.6	6.9
Other	6.0	24.6	0.6	42.4	7.2
Total consumer receivables	57.5	82.1	50.2	97.1	98.8
Total business receivables	42.5	17.9	49.8	2.9	1.2
Note: Automobile credit and leases (Retail + Wholesale)	45.9	8.7	56.3	1.7	44.8
Number of finance companies reporting	84	12	9	50	13

Slightly more than half of all finance company lending is to consumers. In recent years revolving credit and real estate–secured credit has grown substantially—espeically at larger finance companies that concentrate on consumer lending. Some large finance companies (GMAC, Ford Credit, Chrysler Credit) specialize in retail and wholesale automobile lending. Most smaller finance companies specialize in consumer lending, usually personal loans.

Source: American Financial Services Association, *Finance Companies in 1989*, Washington, DC 1990.

finance company receivables at smaller finance companies; they are also important at large companies. However, because of rising risks and costs of funds, in recent years many finance companies have increasingly made personal loans secured with second mortgages. Some home equity loans provide a revolving line of credit that can be used many times and often can be accessed with a credit card. Other second-mortgage consumer loans are for a fixed-term and must be renegotiated if the customer wishes to borrow more.

Automobile Credit.   Finance company subsidiaries of the major automobile manufacturers make a large number of auto loans to finance the new and used autos their dealers sell. Because the business of auto manufacturers' finance company subsidiaries is to help manufacturers profit by selling cars, they can often provide credit on more favorable terms (with 2.9 or even 0 percent financing) than consumers can find elsewhere. Smaller finance companies do little new-car financing since they do not profit from auto sales per se. However, they often finance consumers' used-car purchases.

Mobile Home Credit.   Finance companies expanded rapidly in the mobile home credit market in the early 1970s because such credit was relatively profitable. However, in the mid-1970s many finance companies experienced substantial losses from defaults on their mobile home loans. Meanwhile, their costs of funds rose. As a result, many finance companies slowed their rate of expansion of mobile home lending and others abandoned the field entirely. However, some companies with a large stake in business credit financing for mobile home dealers continued to make such loans. Therefore, mobile home loans continue to provide an important use of assets for some finance companies.

Revolving Consumer Installment Credit.   Revolving credit has become increasingly important to finance companies. Once a finance company extends credit on a revolving basis, a consumer can borrow up to his or her credit limit many times. Revolving credit origination costs are less costly per dollar of credit extended than small loans. It also may be offered through electronic funds transfer systems and can be secured through home equity lines of credit, in which a lien is taken on the borrower's home. Many finance companies also offer revolving credit to serve retailers' needs.

Several major finance companies operate private-label credit plans for retailers. Here all correspondence with the consumer is carried on using the retailer's name. However, the finance company is responsible for approving all credit card applications. In addition, the finance company bills the customers, receives all interest revenues, and incurs all losses (above a predetermined amount) applicable to credit card purchases made at the retailer's store. Thus, under such plans, the consumer who uses a credit card appears to borrow from the retailer but actually borrows from the finance company.

By offering a private-label credit plan, the retailer is able to gain customer loyalty by offering his or her "own" credit card plan. In return for providing the expertise and personnel needed to run the credit operations, the finance company usually receives a fee equal to a stated percentage of credit sales, compensation for some losses, and interest revenues on credit balances extended under the plan.

Revolving credit has been one of the most rapidly growing areas of finance company lending in recent years. Finance companies have developed dealer plans, offered credit cards directly to their customers, and offered revolving credit lines tied to second mortgages. Because such credit is compatible with electronic funds transfer systems and reduces the overhead costs of lending, it is likely to continue to grow.

Other Consumer Installment Loans.   Such loans are used to finance purchases of retail goods other than automobiles and mobile homes. Many finance companies obtain potential personal loan customers and solidify dealer relationships by buying consumer receivables from furniture and appliance dealers. Customers who have to borrow to finance a furniture or appliance purchase may also need to borrow to finance other consumer expenditures. Many such borrowers are in the stage of their life cycle where they are fairly heavily indebted. In particular, they may be young people who anticipate rising incomes in the future and have strong needs to buy particular goods (houses, cars, washers and dryers, furniture, and so on) now. Such customers may be prime candidates for finance company personal loans in the near future. Thus finance companies buy retail credit contracts and later usually try to make the borrowers aware that they can obtain additional cash credit if they need it. Because of the growth of revolving credit plans at retailers and the fact that consumer installment loans of other types are relatively small and thus not very profitable, these loans have declined at finance companies in recent years.

Rates Charged on Consumer Loans

Finance companies charge different rates on their consumer loans. Generally, they charge higher rates on loans that are not well secured, risky, small, or of short maturity, because riskier or unsecured loans are more likely to cause substantial losses. Also, because the costs of evaluating credit applicants and putting a loan on the books are substantial, a finance company will make a small, short-maturity loan only if it can set finance charges high enough to cover its costs of loan evaluation, origination, and servicing and still earn an adequate return on its invested funds. Thus interest rates on small, risky personal loans are usually quite high—ranging up to 20 percent, 30 percent, or even more—whereas rates on large, well-secured second mortgages and new-car loans are substantially lower. Used-car loans have higher rates than new-car loans because they are smaller and riskier. These rate differentials are often codified in state loan rate ceilings, which take into account the different costs and risks associated with different types of loans.

The structure of interest rates charged on consumer loans is quite sensitive to costs of loan origination and servicing. After those costs are considered, net returns on loans of small size or short maturity may well be below the net returns available on other forms of credit. This is illustrated in Exhibit 22–5, which shows that net returns on small loans (after the costs of making and servicing them but before losses) are well below contract rates. Note that a lender can earn a higher net rate of return after costs on a large loan at 15 percent (line 7) than on a smaller loan with an 18 percent rate. A lender also earns more on longer-maturity loans with the same rate (lines 4, 5, and 6). When one realizes that these computations if anything understate the cost of making and servicing loans, one can appreciate (1) why loan rates on small short-term loans

Exhibit 22–5   **Net Rates of Return on Personal Loans After Costs and Before Losses**

Type of Loan	Loan Rate (percentage)	Monthly Payment	Net Return, APR Basis[a] (percentage)
1. Loan of $1,000 for 1 year	18%	$ 91.68	− (10.20%)
2. Loan of $1,000 for 2 years	18	49.92	− (1.92)
3. Loan of $1,000 for 3 years	18	36.15	1.25
4. Loan of $2,500 for 1 year	18	229.20	6.36
5. Loan of $2,500 for 2 years	18	124.81	9.86
6. Loan of $2,500 for 3 years	18	90.38	11.21
7. Loan of $2,500 for 1 year	15	225.65	3.38
8. Loan of $10,000 for 3 years	15	346.65	13.28

[a]After loan origination costs of $100 and a collection cost of $5 per payment. These costs are similar to banks' 1986 costs of making and servicing consumer installment loans. To calculate net rates of return, origination costs are added to the loan amount, and collection costs are subtracted from each scheduled loan payment. Then an internal rate of return formula is used to calculate the monthly rate of return, and that rate is multiplied by 12 to get the APR equivalent.

Note that the net rate of return is far below the contract rate, particularly for smaller, shorter-maturity loans. Because of inflation and because finance companies' costs of loan origination and servicing are substantially higher than those of banks (because they give more personal service and spend more time on collection effort), and because their losses are substantial, finance companies now have to charge even higher rates than those shown in this exhibit to earn an adequate rate of return on their invested funds.

have to be high and (2) why revolving credit lines (where loan origination costs are incurred only once) have become increasingly popular.

Real Estate Lending

In recent years, the fastest-growing area of finance company lending has been real estate lending secured by second mortgages. Finance companies have rapidly expanded their second mortgage lending for several reasons. First, inflation increased both consumers' demands for credit and the equity value of people's homes. For many people, home equity became their largest single asset. The only way they could tap that asset, however, was either to sell their homes or to borrow against their equity with second mortgages. This phenomenon increased the demand for second mortgages. Second, revisions in consumer protection laws, particularly the Federal Bankruptcy Reform Act of 1978, made it difficult to collect defaulted debts if the debts were unsecured. Second mortgages provided excellent security for finance company loans in the event of default. As a result, losses on such loans were very low compared to those on unsecured personal loans. Consequently, many finance companies converted much of their personal lending to second mortgage lending. Third, as shown in the last line of Exhibit 22–5, by making larger, longer-maturity loans, finance companies could obtain a higher rate of return (net of costs) on their loans. At the same time they could offer lower rates and larger amounts of credit to consumers and thereby attract more customers. Finally, second mortgages now have substantial tax advantages relative to other consumer credit. The 1986 income tax reforms phased out consumers' ability to deduct consumer credit interest payments from their federal income tax; however, mortgage interest, including limited amounts of interest paid on second mortgages, retained its tax deductible status.

Business Credit

Business financing activities of finance companies include the wholesale financing of inventories held by businesses prior to sale, the retail financing of durable goods purchased by firms, lease financing, and other business financing—including the financing of customer receivables held by firms or factored (sold) to the finance company. Business credit in general has expanded much more rapidly than consumer lending in recent years. Consumer lending is highly regulated whereas business lending is not. As a result, business lending has been more profitable than consumer lending. The various types of business lending by finance companies are described in the following sections.

Wholesale Paper.   Wholesale paper is generated when a finance company helps a dealer finance the purchase of goods. For instance, retail dealers must pay for the automobiles or washers and dryers kept in stock. Dealers need the stock for display purposes and to guarantee prompt delivery, yet they receive no cash for the goods until they are sold.

A finance company may provide a dealer with interim financing called *wholesale* or *floor-plan financing*. A floor-plan financing arrangement is one in which the finance company pays the manufacturer when the goods are delivered to the dealer. The finance company then holds a lien on the goods as long as the dealer keeps them in inventory. The dealer pays interest on the value of goods financed by floor-plan financing, and when the goods are sold, the dealer uses the proceeds of the sale to repay the finance company.

Because finance companies have close ties with auto or retail goods dealers for whom they provide floor-plan financing, they may also provide retail financing for the consumers who buy the dealers' goods. In that way, their wholesale financing activities help generate retail financing business and vice versa (as a dealer is more likely to do business with a finance company that will also provide retail financing for his or her customers).

Retail Paper.   Sales of goods used for business purposes may be financed with installment sales contracts (similar to auto credit contracts) provided by finance companies. Business purchases of vans, light or heavy trucks, and other commercial vehicles are often financed this way. In addition, retail sales of industrial and farm equipment to businesses and farmers may be financed with installment contracts.

Lease Paper.   In recent years, leasing of durable goods has been popular for a number of reasons. First, accelerated depreciation and investment tax credits (when they exist) make it profitable for a firm in a high tax bracket to buy and lease durable investment goods at favorable rates to firms in low or zero tax brackets (which cannot profit as much from possible tax savings). Second, an institution that leases a durable good need not borrow the funds required to buy it outright. Third, a lessor retains an equity interest in the good and often can regain possession of it more easily and cheaply if the lessee defaults on payments than would be possible if the good were sold under an installment sales contract. This advantage is particularly valuable because consumer protection and bankruptcy laws have given far greater protection to consumers and businesses that fall behind on their debt payments. Finally, leases can be written so that the good is available when desired, and it need not be disposed of (for its residual value) by a purchaser who is relatively unsophisticated in the marketing of used durable goods.

In summary, leasing often provides greater tax advantages, protection of ownership rights, and financial flexibility or convenience. Consequently, many finance companies have rapidly expanded their leasing activities in recent years.

Other Business Credit.   Other business credit makes up a substantial portion of finance companies' total assets. Two forms of that credit are particularly interesting, as they illustrate the long and close relationship that many finance companies maintain with business firms.

First, the largest single source of other business credit is loans on commercial accounts receivable. These are secured by the accounts receivable of (bills owed to) the business firm to which the finance company extends credit. In many cases, a finance company will take possession of the accounts receivable as collateral for its loan and collect payments on them as they come due. As it collects payments, it reduces the loan balance its business customer owes.

Second, factored accounts receivable are accounts due (bills owed the business firm) that are directly purchased from the business firm by the finance company. The purchase price is discounted to allow for potential losses and also to allow for the fact that the finance company will not receive full payment until some time in the future. To make an adequate assessment of potential losses and repayment lags, a finance company dealing in factoring must have a close working knowledge of the operations of a business firm and the nature of its customers.

Once factored, the accounts receivable become the property of the finance company. It is its responsibility to collect all remaining balances due on factored accounts receivable. In return for selling its accounts receivable at a discount, the selling business firm immediately obtains cash from the finance company.

Liabilities and Net Worth of Finance Companies

Net Worth

One of the most striking aspects of finance company balance sheets, as shown in Exhibit 22–3, is that their net worth is very small relative to their total assets. Their total capital, surplus, and undivided profits account for around 10 percent of total assets. Thus finance companies are highly leveraged institutions. Consequently, their income can fluctuate substantially if they experience loan losses or if interest rate changes have different effects on their assets and liabilities.

Finance Company Debt

Even though most finance company assets are relatively short term in nature, some (such as leases and certain installment credit contracts) are basically long-term assets. On the other side of the balance sheet, finance companies hold a mixture of both short-term and long-term debt. However, the major portion of their liabilities, like the major portions of their assets, usually consists of short-term obligations. These may take several forms.

Bank Debt.   Many small finance companies that do not have access to national capital markets borrow from banks to obtain a reliable and relatively low-cost source of funds. Large finance companies often use bank lines of credit to back up their commercial paper and thereby obtain higher ratings on their commercial paper. Others may borrow seasonally from banks, or even obtain long "term" loans. Overall, at year-end 1989, bank loans made up only 2.5 percent of liabilities of large finance companies, but 15 percent of the liabilities of smaller finance companies.

Commercial Paper.   In total, finance companies obtain 30 percent of their funds by issuing commercial paper. Because commercial paper is unsecured, only large, top-rated borrowers have *direct* access to that market. Less-well-known issuers must either place their commercial paper through dealers (for a small fee) or obtain their short-term financing from other sources. In the 1989 survey of finance companies cited in Exhibit 22-3, only 24 of the 84 finance companies had any commercial paper outstanding.

There are only about 200 finance companies that regularly place their commercial paper directly with ultimate lenders. However, directly placed commercial paper accounts for most finance company commercial paper outstanding, because the borrowers are very large. They include General Motors Acceptance Corporation, Ford Motor Credit Corporation, and General Electric Credit Corporation—each of which has billions of dollars in debt outstanding.

In comparison with bank debt and commercial paper sales, other sources of short-term funds are of less consequence for finance companies taken as a whole, albeit they may be very important to some individual companies, particularly smaller finance companies. One valuable source of credit for smaller companies is "transfer credit" in the form of funding provided by their larger parent companies.

Deposit Liabilities and Thrift Certificates.   In 1989, small finance companies had outstanding deposit liabilities and thrift certificates equal to 10 percent of their assets. Finance companies may sell debt obligations directly to the public, provided that those debt issues are approved by securities regulators. In the past, finance companies often have had difficulty getting small-denomination debt issues approved, because such debt certificates would compete with savings certificates issued by thrift institutions. However, limited amounts of small-denomination debt have been sold to the public by finance companies as thrift certificates.

In 20 states, finance companies can, if they meet certain requirements, obtain charters as industrial banks. Industrial banks can accept deposits and make loans for specified purposes, such as consumer loans.

By obtaining charters as industrial banks, finance companies are better able to compete for the relatively low-cost sources of funds that are available to banks, credit unions, and thrift institutions. Nonetheless, because the largest finance companies primarily obtain their funds from other sources, at the end of 1989 deposit liabilities and thrift certificates outstanding accounted for less than 1 percent of assets for all finance companies combined.

PEOPLE & EVENTS

Household International Manages to Adapt

Consumer finance companies are particularly hard hit when sharp increases in interest rates occur. The interest rates they can charge on customer loans usually are restricted by rate ceilings. Meanwhile, since they obtain many of their funds from sales of commercial paper, their costs of funds rise quickly when market interest rates rise. Consequently, when interest rates rose sharply after October 6, 1979, Household International moved quickly to reduce its sensitivity to interest rate changes.

Among other things, Household shifted its consumer-lending orientation toward second mortgage loans. By 1982, half of its consumer loan portfolio consisted of second mortgages. Second mortgage loans are large and have low loss rates and low costs per dollar of credit extended. Thus it is possible to earn adequate profits on second mortgages even if their rates are not as high as those on smaller loans. In addition, Household reduced its rate risk by making many of its second mortgages with variable rates.

In 1981 Household closed 271 consumer finance offices in states with restrictive rate ceilings. Because of rising interest rates, lending in those states had become increasingly unprofitable.

Household also shifted its orientation away from strictly consumer lending. It made several structural changes, including the acquisition of a manufacturing company and entry into the thrift business. Household first acquired its own deposit-gathering subsidiary when it acquired a savings and loan in 1976; it then added several more in 1984. It also obtained low-cost deposits through its industrial bank subsidiaries. By the end of 1984, Household owned 53 thrifts, industrial banks, and trusts.

In 1981 Household acquired Valley National Bank in California. The bank acquisition was carefully structured so that Household would avoid bank holding company regulation. At the time of merger, Valley National sold off its commercial loan portfolio. By so doing, it became one of the first nonbank banks. The bank had consumer loans, deposits, and seven branches, but it was not considered a commercial bank because it did not make commercial loans. Nonetheless, the bank's deposit-gathering ability let Household obtain some of its funds at retail rates. In addition, it provided a base of operations for Household's credit card business. In 1985 Household became one of the few nonbank issuers of general-purpose credit cards when it issued its Home Card on a nationwide basis. That card was not only a general-purpose credit card, but it also let people access the Comp-U-Card computer-buying service.

Household has numerous other financial subsidiaries. It writes life insurance, leases capital goods, makes preferred stock investments, and buys commercial installment credit contracts. As a company, Household provides an excellent example of how finance companies have moved to become full-service financial institutions and have shifted their operations away from areas in which profits are limited by restrictive regulations.

Long-Term Debt.   Long-term debt is one of the largest liabilities of large finance companies. However, long-term debt waxes and wanes in relative importance as a source of finance company funds. When interest rates are low, finance companies may issue proportionately more long-term debt. By doing so, they hope to hold down future increases in their costs of funds if interest rates should rise. They also may sell long-term debt to reduce their interest rate risk when they acquire long-term loans or lease contracts.

Income and Expense of Finance Companies

Finance companies receive the majority of their revenues from finance-charge income associated with their lending. However, they also receive substantial amounts of income from sales of insurance, particularly credit insurance, and from other fees and charges, such as loan origination fees and fees for income tax preparation (see Exhibit 22–6).

Small finance companies, which generally make small personal loans, had higher finance-charge income and higher total income than large finance companies in 1989. However, they also had much higher expenses. In fact, small finance companies' combined operating expenses and losses were substantially greater than their interest expenses in 1989 (see Exhibit 22–6).

Large finance companies tend to make larger, better-secured loans. As a result, their interest rates are lower and their operating costs and losses are slightly smaller than their interest expenses. Nonetheless, their noninterest operating expenses still accounted for more than two-fifths of their total expenses in 1989.

		Large Companies	Small Companies
Exhibit 22–6	**Revenues and Expenses as Percentage of Assets of Large and Small Finance Companies (1987)**		
Total revenues		13.0%	18.7%
Receivables		11.1	16.0
Insurance		1.0	1.0
Other		0.9	1.7
Total expenses		11.8	16.9
Interest expense		6.6	7.1
Losses and loss reserve additions		1.2	1.5
Total operating expenses, except losses		3.5	7.5
Income taxes		0.5	0.9
Net income (ROA) from consolidated operations		1.2	1.8
(Income from foreign receivables)		0.1	—
Net income as percent of equity (ROE)		13.4	14.2
Memo:			
Losses, taxes, and operating expenses as a percent of total revenues		40.4	52.7
Interest expenses as a percent of total revenues		50.9	37.7

The operating revenues of most finance companies are enhanced by credit insurance payments and fees for other services. Noninterest operating expenses of finance companies typically are quite large, accounting for over 50 percent of the expenses incurred by small finance companies and more than 40 percent of the expenses incurred by large finance companies.

Source: American Financial Services Association, *Finance Companies in 1989*, Washington, DC, 1990.

Statistics on finance company operating costs help illustrate the point that finance companies must charge relatively high rates on their loans in order to cover the high operating costs associated with making small or risky loans and still earn an adequate return on capital. In 1989 both small and large finance companies benefited by borrowing short-term funds at relatively low rates and using those funds to make loans at much higher rates. Whereas smaller finance companies earned a higher average rate of return on their assets (ROA) and equity (ROE) in 1989, in years past the more highly leveraged large finance companies have often earned a higher average rate of return on equity (ROE). For instance, in 1987 large finance companies had an ROA of 1.6 percent and an ROE of 17.6 percent while less-leveraged smaller companies had a higher ROA of 1.9 percent but a smaller ROE of 12.4 percent.

Finance companies are not always profitable however. In 1981, many finance companies experienced severe profit squeezes because of high borrowing costs, federal regulations that raised their operating costs and increased their losses, and state loan-rate ceilings that limited their revenues. Regulatory effects on finance companies are discussed in more detail in the next section.

Regulation of Finance Companies

Finance company consumer lending is heavily regulated, although finance company business lending generally is not. The reason is that business people are presumed to be better able to act in their own interest than consumers. However, finance company business and consumer lending can both be affected by regulations affecting mergers, branching, and market entry.

Rate Ceilings.   The most influential regulations on finance company operations are those affecting rates that can be charged on loans of different types, sizes, and maturities. Most states have regulations that limit rates charged by consumer or sales finance companies. Frequently, higher rates are permitted on small loans and short-maturity loans. In addition, rate ceilings may vary with the type of loan or type of lender. Finance companies often are allowed to charge higher rates than other lenders. However, they also are frequently allowed to make only small loans. If rate ceilings are too restrictive, consumer finance companies will leave the market, as they have in several states and the District of Columbia.

Sales finance companies, however, can continue to operate in states with low rate ceilings. They can compensate for losses in interest revenues by discounting the paper they buy from retail sales outlets. By paying less than face value for consumer credit contracts, sales finance companies can earn a profitable rate of return on their invested funds.

Creditor Remedy Regulation.   Either individual states or the federal government may impose various restrictions on finance companies' abilities to collect on delinquent or defaulted debts. These restrictions include limitations on creditors' abilities to charge late fees or to garnishee (collect a portion of an employee's wages from an employer) a borrower who falls behind on payments. They also may require that certain legal processes be followed and that the lender bear the full expense of collecting on the bad debts.

Creditor remedy restrictions are of particular importance to finance companies that serve customers who are likely to default or fall behind in their payments. If finance companies have few remedies to induce customers to pay their debts (or few remedies to recover the money if a customer stops paying entirely), they will lose more whenever a customer defaults. This means that they will either have to stop serving high-risk borrowers or charge higher rates to make up for increased operating expenses and losses.

Branching, Chartering, and Merger Restrictions.   State departments of financial institutions and banks are responsible for enforcing restrictions on finance company chartering and branching within their states. Convenience and advantage (C and A) restrictions require a finance company that wishes to organize or form a new office to show that the office will offer a *convenience* to the local community and will be to the community's *advantage*. Often such restrictions reduce competition by preventing new entrants from establishing offices in a market if that market is already served by an existing finance company.

Although local market entry can be restricted by antitrust or convenience and advantage regulations, no national regulations prevent finance companies from operating across state lines. Thus the major finance companies have a nationwide presence. Because of this, many bank holding companies have acquired finance companies to gain access to interstate markets.

Consumer Protection Regulations

Since 1968, Congress and various state legislatures have passed a large number of consumer protection bills. Many of the regulations in these bills have had a considerable impact on the costs and operations of consumer finance companies. The most important regulations include Regulation Z (Truth in Lending) and the 1978 revisions in the bankruptcy laws. Regulation Z made finance companies disclose their APR rates rather than "add-on" or "discount" loan rates that understated the true rates charged. Subsequently, finance companies lost some of their market share in the consumer credit markets to banks and credit unions. Nonetheless, even though many consumers acknowledge that finance companies are not the cheapest place to borrow, many still patronize them. Because many finance companies offer fast, convenient, and personal service and grant loans on lenient terms, they attract loyal customers who are not highly sensitive to interest rate differences.

The liberalization of federal consumer bankruptcy laws in October 1979 gave increased protection to consumers who declared bankruptcy. Under the new law, consumers who declared bankruptcy could eliminate their debts and still retain many thousands of dollars of their assets. Unsecured creditors, such as finance companies, rarely were able to collect their debts once an insolvent debtor declared bankruptcy under the new law. Consequently, the law substantially increased potential finance company losses.

Because of this, finance companies could not afford to take as many risks as before without raising their loan rates (which they often could not do because of rate ceilings). As a result, many finance companies switched to second mortgage lending, since larger loans allowed them to increase their returns, net of operating costs, without raising their loan rates. Furthermore, the security provided by second mortgages reduced the finance companies' losses substantially.

Management Problems

Finance Companies

Interest Rate Risk.   Finance companies' asset/liability management problems generally are not urgent because they can match long-term assets with long-term debt financing that does not give their liability holders early withdrawal options. This gives them an advantage relative to depository institutions which may suffer premature withdrawals from long-term deposits if interest rates rise. Conversely, if interest rates fall and finance companies' long-term loans are repaid early, they usually can "call" some of their long-term debt for early redemption, thereby keeping interest expenses and returns more evenly matched than depository institutions can in similar circumstances. However, if interest rates rise dramatically, finance companies may find that they cannot raise their consumer loan rates sufficiently (because of state loan rate ceilings) to compensate for their rising costs of funds. This is why a finance company was one of the first participants in an interest rate swap. The swap allowed it to pay a fixed rate but earn higher rates of return if market interest rates rose.

Credit Risk.   Finance companies intrinsically deal in credit risk, as they often serve riskier clients than banks and other depository institutions. However, finance companies diversify their risks extensively and use sophisticated credit-evaluation models to determine which customers are likely to be most creditworthy. Furthermore, they typically charge higher rates for their credit because they often deal with people who cannot easily qualify for credit elsewhere and the extra revenues can cover a somewhat higher loss rate on their loans. This is not to say that finance companies take great risks, however. Losses typically run below 2 percent of assets because of companies' careful credit evaluation and follow-up on delinquent loans. In fact, during the early boom in second-mortgage lending in the 1980s, finance companies typically experienced far lower loss and delinquency problems on second mortgages than depository institutions (which often looked more to the value of the asset, not, like finance companies, to the creditworthiness of the customer, to provide repayment). As long as finance companies continue to diversify and emphasize careful credit evaluation and collection policies, they should continue to experience only limited credit risk.

Liquidity Risk.   Finance companies may experience liquidity risk if they rely on short-term financing, such as commercial paper or bank loans, and lose their ability to "roll over" their debts. For instance, in 1980 Chrysler Credit experienced a serious problem trying to roll over its commercial paper after Penn Central failed and shook the confidence of the commercial paper markets. Fortunately, the Fed provided liquidity to commercial banks at that time, so Chrysler and other commercial paper issuers could pay off their commercial paper when it matured by taking out bank loans. In 1991, however, only Chrysler Credit had a potential problem because lenders were unsure whether it would sell enough cars to generate cash inflows equal to its cash needs. Thus Chrysler was in danger of losing both access to the commercial paper market and to bank loans. The rapid loss of access to both sources of short-term funding could potentially precipitate a bankruptcy (as it did with the Olympia and York Corporation in 1992). However, Chrysler was able to avert problems in part by *securitizing* its assets (that is, creating pools of auto loans) and selling them in the financial markets to obtain short-term cash. Securitization of assets, then, has become attractive to finance companies as well as to financial institutions. By securitizing assets, a finance company can not only earn service fee income but also obtain liquidity, as needed, when other sources of short-term funding become expensive or difficult to obtain.

Regulatory Compliance

A major management problem for finance companies involves coping with regulations. Bankruptcy law revisions, creditor remedy restrictions, state loan rate ceilings, and merger and branching restrictions are the regulations with which they must be constantly concerned. In addition, when finance companies sell securities (other than commercial paper) in the capital markets, they also must be concerned with SEC regulations governing securities sales.

Because of the growing burden of regulation and the need to provide sophisticated products, smaller finance companies have declined in recent years whereas the large ones have become even larger. The new products offered by finance companies have included business credit, leases, second mortgage loans, revolving credit, and home equity loans. None of these products (with the exception of unsecured revolving credit) are adversely affected by bankruptcy law restrictions. In addition, by moving toward larger loan sizes, leases, and business credit, rate ceilings have become less onerous. Furthermore, the use of revolving credit has allowed finance companies to offer credit cards and to participate in EFT systems. Finally, securitization of assets has enabled finance companies to increase both their liquidity and their asset/liability management capabilities.

Because of their great flexibility, finance companies have been able to adapt to a rapidly changing financial and regulatory environment (see People and Events). They also have played a major role in the development of multipurpose financial conglomerates.

Financial Conglomerates

Financial conglomerates have expanded on the assumption that there are profitable synergies in finance that are available to firms that become full-service financial businesses. The underlying idea is that full-service firms will be better able to compete for customers because, like supermarkets, they can offer one-stop financial shopping.

Many firms that have become financial conglomerates believe that productive synergy will enable them to offer related financial services more profitably on a combined basis. The presumed synergy can occur for several reasons. First, firms can obtain synergistic advantages in marketing and sales distribution—by using nationwide advertising, developing an established and trusted name, or offering multiple products through a single salesperson. Second, firms often can obtain cost savings by using their expertise and facilities to conduct closely related operations. Ford acquired a thrift institution mortgage lender because mortgage loans (which are large and paid monthly by consumers) are similar to auto loans, which Ford already knew how to service. General Motors acquired mortgage-servicing companies in part because it recognized that its computer systems and collection procedures could be expanded inexpensively to handle a larger volume of business. Third, firms can obtain synergistic advantages by operating one-stop shopping of financial services distribution systems. Sears introduced its Discover card to facilitate offering a full set of financial services (cash access, mutual funds, insurance, savings accounts, investment vehicles, and credit) to consumers. By offering all services at a single location or through a single vehicle (its credit card), it was hoped that more people would want the services and that the costs of providing each service would be reduced. Thus the firm could obtain both marketing advantages and economies of scope at the same time.

Firms have also become financial conglomerates to avoid the various regulations that affect their main line of business. For example, commercial banks have used their holding companies to acquire a broad range of businesses related to banking (such as finance companies) that are not subject to the same regulatory restrictions (such as geographic limits on branching) as the bank per se. Conversely, nonbank financial institutions have been careful to gain access to bank-related payment services by acquiring only nonbank banks, which are exempt from federal regulation because they either do not make commercial loans or do not accept transactions deposits. State laws may allow financial conglomerates to obtain more advantageous prices or new services if they charter some of their financial subsidiaries in certain states (such as South Dakota, which has no rate ceiling on credit card loans). Thus financial conglomerates have an advantage over undiversified firms because they can shift their operations between subsidiaries to take advantage of favorable regulations in various states or jurisdictions.

The major management problem for financial conglomerates lies in identifying which products can be most successfully combined and which regulatory environments are likely to be most favorable. The bottom line is profits, and consumers have not necessarily shown that they are willing to pay more to obtain all their financial services at one place. Thus, if economies of scope are not compelling, the large, integrated financial firms may find that their profits are disappointing. The specialty shops may still be able to outcompete the financial supermarkets for many lines of business. Also, state and national regulatory environments can change over time. A firm that spends extensively to obtain a favorable regulatory regime may later find that its competitors are able to obtain equally favorable regulation without as much expense.

Consequently, strategic planning is of critical importance for financial conglomerates. They must try to determine whether particular combinations of products are likely to produce real synergies or substantive increases in product demand before they undertake large investments. Some financial conglomerates have jumped too quickly into broad-spectrum financial product development before they found that not every customer wants to deal with a financial department store.

Nonetheless, as the hand of regulation has come to fall more heavily on depository institutions, new opportunities have opened up for finance companies and financial conglomerates that are less regulated. As deposit insurance costs have gone up and bank bond and certificate of deposit ratings have declined, good-quality finance companies and other financial conglomerates have found that their net cost of funds (from issuing commercial paper and long-term debt) has declined relative to that of depository institutions. Furthermore, because finance companies have higher capital ratios and are not subject to risk-based capital requirements or strict regulatory oversight, they are often freer to take on loans and credit risk than more heavily regulated depository institutions. Consequently, alert managements may be able to capture loan and (possibly) deposit customers at the expense of banks. Unlike depository institutions, finance companies have not been subject to increased regulation, higher regulatory costs and restrictions on growth as a result of the failure of some insured institutions. As a result, finance companies may be able to expand their loans and liabilities at the expense of commercial banks and other heavily regulated institutions.

Summary

This chapter briefly describes the financial structure of financial conglomerates of various types and of finance companies in particular. Finance companies are important because almost every financial intermediary owns one. Their relative freedom from geographic regulation and from restrictions on business lending allows finance company subsidiaries to offer financial products and services that their parent companies cannot. Thus finance company subsidiaries usually expand the scope of their parents' activities.

Financial conglomerates have been formed not only to avoid geographic restrictions on product lines but also because they allow parent companies to offer a broad range of financial services. The subsidiaries' products may complement the parents', as is the case with retail credit and retailers' sales. In addition, the subsidiaries' products may provide synergy by letting the parent enter a closely related and highly profitable business by providing more of a customer's needs—as with auto credit and mortgage lending and servicing. Furthermore, financial conglomerates may be able to benefit by becoming financial supermarkets.

So far, however, the profitability of financial supermarkets is uncertain. Clearly, securities brokers and dealers have been able to gain customers by using affiliates to offer banking-related products such as brokered CDs, money market mutual funds, commercial loans, and checking accounts. However, the mixture of "socks and stocks" has not been highly profitable because it appears that consumers may prefer to shop in different places for their goods and financial products. Also, even though the merger of insurance institutions, mutual funds, and brokerage institutions has been successful if the products are marketed through financial planners, the cross-marketing of stocks and insurance products has not been as successful because of the individual products' different risk attributes.

Many securities brokers and dealers offer check withdrawals of investment funds and even issue credit cards. Thus they pose a competitive threat to more heavily regulated depository institutions. That threat has grown in recent years as mergers between securities brokers and dealers and many of the nation's largest firms have created huge financial conglomerates with extensive financial powers.

The new amalgamations of manufacturing company subsidiaries, retailers, insurance companies, credit card issuers, traveler's check companies, brokerage firms, and banks have developed extensive banking capabilities. Many use checks or credit and debit cards to provide access to their diverse financial services from all over the country. Most recently, AT&T joined the competition in the financial-services access card business by introducing its Universal card to try to exploit synergies in its telecommunications switching and credit-evaluation capabilities.

Liabilities issued by nondepository institutions are regulated by the SEC's disclosure rules and by state securities laws. However, most nondepository institutions are not heavily regulated. In general, they are not federally insured and are not directly subject to banking regulation. Many have gone to some length to avoid federal holding-company regulation by acquiring only nonbank banks or single thrift institutions when they wish to offer banking services.

Finance companies are highly diverse financial institutions. They can be partnerships, proprietorships, or corporations. Some may be chartered as industrial banks. They are best defined by what they do, which is to make short- and intermediate-term loans and leases to consumers and business firms. Generally, they obtain their funds by borrowing in the financial markets. Most of their liabilities, like most of their assets, are short term in nature. However, they do owe substantial amounts of relatively long-term debt and do make a number of relatively long-term consumer or business loans and leases.

Finance companies' capital base is thin (approximately 10 percent of their total assets). Thus short- and long-term debt fund most of their asset holdings. On the asset side of the ledger, finance companies have traditionally held large amounts of consumer credit. However, their business receivables have grown rapidly and now equal their consumer loans. One reason for the shift toward business credit is that finance companies' consumer-lending operations have become heavily regulated, and business lending has not.

Second mortgage credit, leasing (both to consumers and businesses), and revolving credit are all areas into which finance companies are expanding their operations. These forms of credit are subject to fewer drawbacks caused by regulation and enable finance companies to take advantage of new financial and technical innovations. Revolving credit may expand further as EFT systems are more extensively developed. Securitization of finance-company loans also has increased as the market for loan-pool securities has developed. Securitization of auto, mortgage, and revolving credit loans lets finance companies earn service fee income and obtain liquidity if needed.

Small finance companies have been put at a disadvantage relative to larger finance companies by the growth in regulation and the need to keep abreast of technical advances. Thus they have declined in importance. However, they may still find a niche as long as they can continue to offer profitably the personal convenience and relatively lenient loan terms that many consumers and small businesses desire.

Questions

1. Why do you think that many of the nation's largest brokerage firms were acquired by other financial services firms? Give examples to illustrate your points.

2. Why do you think that financial conglomerates are growing so rapidly? Do you prefer one-stop financial shopping yourself?

3. Explain why the major automobile manufacturers have diversified into financial services.

4. Explain how regulations, or the evasion of regulations, have contributed to or retarded the growth of financial conglomerates of various types. In particular, explain why commercial banks want regulators to "level the playing field" on which they compete with securities brokers and dealers.

5. Why are finance companies important subsidiaries both of commercial bank holding companies and of other institutions? What can finance companies do that parent companies cannot do? [Hint: For auto manufacturers, consider the relative financial leverage that is available to the parent versus the finance company subsidiary before credit ratings deteriorate.]

6. How do finance companies differ from banks, credit unions, and thrift institutions?

7. Why have finance companies shifted from consumer to business lending in recent years?

8. Why have second mortgages grown in popularity with finance company consumer lenders?

9. Consumer finance companies left Washington, DC, because it had an 8 percent rate ceiling. How can finance companies that finance retail sales made by dealers continue to operate in Washington?

10. What effect have growing consumer credit regulations had on finance companies' lines of business? What about their future opportunities?

11. How can finance companies manage their interest rate, liquidity, and credit risks? What are their advantages or disadvantages vis-à-vis depository institutions?

Selected References

"The Only Thing We Have to Fear Is Sears Itself." *ABA Banking Journal*, October 1983, pp. 58–60.
Considers the advantages that Sears has as compared to community banks in providing various financial services. Concludes that Sears has advantages in obtaining the economies of scale necessary to offer sophisticated financial services. However, it points out that Sear's effect in any one market is likely to be slight and that Sears cannot offer the kind of individualized customer services that are the essential ingredient of banking at the local level.

Benston, George. **"The Costs to Consumer Finance Companies of Extending Consumer Credit."** *The National Commission on Consumer Finance, Technical Studies*. Vol. 2. Washington, DC: U.S. Government Printing Office, 1975.
This paper is the definitive study of the costs of finance company operations. Costs per loan and average costs per office and volume of transactions are all examined. In addition, consideration is given to the effect of regulation on finance company costs. The paper is somewhat technical in nature.

Ellis, James E. **"Mighty-Sears Tests Its Clout in Credit Cards."** *Business Week*, September 2, 1985, pp. 62–63.
Reviews Sears' participation in financial services and discusses its Discover card, the key mechanism that it plans to use to link its various financial services.

Gross, Laura. "New Financial Services Scorecard Shows Who's on First." *American Banker*, **January 4, 1985, pp. 1, 6–13.**
Reports results from a survey of major firms that participate in the financial services markets. It provides information on numbers of accounts serviced and assets devoted to various financial services.

Hurley, Evelyn M. "Survey of Finance Companies, 1980." *Federal Reserve Bulletin*, **May 1981, pp. 398–409.**
This very readable study updates the 1975 survey of finance companies and provides useful statistics to document both recent and ongoing changes in finance companies' structure.

McAleer, Ysabel Burns. *Finance Companies in 1989: Research Report and Second Mortgage Lending Report, American Financial Services Association.* **Washington, DC, 1990.**
This annual publication of the AFSA provides valuable statistical information on the assets, liabilities, earnings, and expenses of finance companies of various types.

McAleer, Ysabel Burns. *Finance Companies 1977–89: Research Report and Second Mortgage Lending Report. American Financial Services Association,* **Washington, DC, 1990.**
Very useful because it makes intertemporal comparisons of finance companies' key balance sheet, earnings, and expense ratios. This report provides a valuable information source for people who want to analyze secular changes in finance companies' structure and performance.

National Commission on Consumer Finance. *Consumer Credit in the United States: Report of the National Commission on Consumer Finance.* **Washington, DC: Superintendent of Documents, 1972.**
This book provides a good history of the development of consumer credit markets and the regulations that affect them. It also summarizes empirical work relating to the consumer credit markets and their regulation. It considers convenience and advantage regulation, rate ceilings, and creditors' remedies and their effects on consumer finance.

Pavel, Christine, and Harvey Rosenblum. "Banks and Nonbanks: The Horse Race Continues." *Economic Review.* **Federal Reserve Bank of Chicago, May–June 1985, pp. 3–17.**
Provides an excellent overview of the extent to which nonbank competitors have entered lines of business traditionally served by commercial banks. It names the major players in each market and analyzes the share of the market controlled by banks, retailers, industrial firms, insurance companies, and other types of firms.

Rosenblum, Harvey, and Diane Siegel. *Competition in Financial Services: The Impact of Nonbank Entry.* **Staff Study 83–1. Federal Reserve Bank of Chicago, 1983.**
This study describes the entry of new competitors and the erosion of existing banking markets. It contains excellent appendices that describe the far-flung financial intermediary operations of many of the nation's leading nonbank firms.

6 CONTEMPORARY PROBLEMS AND ISSUES

PROFILE/David Kelso

HE IS

Associate director, Office of Thrift Supervision (OTC) for Resolution Trust Corporation (RTC) operations. He is one of five senior staff members of the OTC, reporting directly to OTC director Timothy Ryan. In position since May 1990.

WHAT HE DOES

As associate director to the RTC, David serves as Director Ryan's deputy, representing him on RTC committees. In this capacity, he serves as liaison to the RTC agency and prepares briefings for Director Ryan for board meetings and congressional testimony. Since its formation in 1989, the RTC has made an important contribution to the goal of recovering diverted assets and punishing criminal behavior. As of September 30, 1991, the RTC estimates it will have resolved 796 failed thrifts.

HOW HE GOT THERE

B.A.: Syracuse University, major in English
M.BA.: Harvard University
First job: Goldman, Sachs, 1977–1990, security sales division specializing in nontraditional investments, including raising $250 million in equity to capitalize a new bank in Texas created to acquire failed banks and their assets.

BACKGROUND

David was an elementary school teacher right after finishing his bachelor's degree, on scholarship, and before entering the Harvard M.BA program. He grew up in Syracuse, New York, with a salesman father. His mother is a nurse.

His family strongly believes in work and public service. In fact, David cannot remember not having a job.

WHAT HE LIKES BEST ABOUT HIS JOB

The challenge of finding solutions to the current problems of the financial system, problems that must and can be solved. As David puts it, the money people had entrusted to the failed savings and loans was guaranteed by the government and those guarantees must be honored. It is a solvable problem in David's eyes, albeit by slow and steady progress. There are no easy solutions.

WORST NIGHTMARE

That unforeseeable and uncontrollable events would undo the progress made by OTS/RTC efforts.

HOW HE UNWINDS

Despite his demanding schedule, David finds time to follow his favorite sport, basketball, especially the Syracuse University team.

ADVICE

Seriously consider U.S. government service, especially with the executive branch. It offers interesting careers in areas most people believe are available only in private industry.

In whatever job you are in, make a difference. Don't be just a slot in an organization chart.

CONTEMPORARY ISSUES AFFECTING FINANCIAL INSTITUTIONS 23

HOW DO YOU PAY YOUR bills —with cash, checks, a credit or debit card? Do you ever use a computer or telephone to pay your bills? If so, what happens when you make a payment? Who gets the funds, and will the transfer of funds always go as planned? Who provides the insurance guarantees that ensure that your payments will be made as planned, and who makes sure that your financial institution will not fail? What level of government regulation is required to protect the payments system, to insure deposits, or to control the money supply and economic activity? Are rate ceilings on deposits or loans a good idea?

This chapter addresses many of these issues. First, it describes electronic payments systems and the new technologies that are changing the financial markets. Second, it addresses the issue of how the payments system can be protected against risks posed by electronic breakdowns or the failure of constituent institutions. Third, it considers whether government provision of deposit insurance has been effective and notes alternative ways that deposit insurance costs could be reduced. Since increased capital requirements can reduce deposit insurance costs, the chapter looks at ways that such requirements have been altered internationally to reduce their evasion via regulatory arbitrage and off-balance-sheet financing. The chapter next addresses the question of how the regulatory authorities can affect the economy by controlling the money supply and closely related liabilities of financial institutions in a technologically changing world. Finally, it examines the effect that deposit rate ceilings and loan rate ceilings have had on financial markets.

Technological Changes in the Payments System

The Traditional Payments System

The traditional payments system uses currency, coins, and checks. Currency and coin can be used to mediate transactions by physical exchange. However, even though cash is legal tender for the payment of debts, it leaves no audit trail. Thus many people ask for written receipts to show proof of payment when they pay a debt or purchase a good with cash. As an alternative to cash payment, many people write checks that tell their depository institution to transfer funds to the person or enterprise named on the check.

Check-Clearing Process.   A major problem with present-day check systems is that they potentially require a two-way transfer of information. When a check drawn on Bank A is cashed by a merchant, the merchant, the merchant's bank (Bank B), the clearinghouse or the Federal Reserve, and any correspondent banks for Banks A and B all accept the check subject to final payment. Once the check passes through the hands of all these entities and reaches Bank A, Bank A (if there are sufficient funds in the check writer's account) subtracts the balance from the check writer's account and transfers funds to the party that presented Bank A with the check. If there are *not sufficient funds* in the depositor's account to pay the check, it is marked "NSF" and "bounced," or returned, by the way it came, to the merchant who initially accepted it. Thus information about whether or not the check is good must be conveyed through a separate set of transactions. As a result, payment on checks that have not yet cleared to the depositor's bank is always provisional on the checks being good.

Since most checks are backed by sufficient funds, the Federal Reserve Bank provides payment to banks that deposit checks drawn on banks in another Federal Reserve district according to a "deferred payment schedule," and it counts the uncollected check as a "cash item in process of collection" until it is collected (see Chapter 4).

Check Float.   The difference between the Federal Reserve's cash items in the process of collection and deferred availability credit item accounts represents float. Float is very important. It provides an interest-free source of reserves, because the Fed often gives reserves to Bank B (in payment for checks deposited for payment) before it subtracts reserves from Bank A's account (when it collects the check). Many banks fear that they will lose this free source of funds if the present checking system is altered by the introduction of electronic funds transfer (EFT) systems—where no delay need occur in the presentation of a credit to one bank and the debiting of another's bank account. Similarly, EFT will cause consumers to lose float that some obtain when they write a check a day or two before they make a deposit in their checking account.

Check Information.   When checks clear through the banking system, they carry substantial information, including who paid whom and what financial institutions assisted in their clearing. This information provides proof of payment for tax and legal purposes (in case someone claims that a contract was not fulfilled). Thus, although check clearing is cumbersome, the end product of the clearing process is (1) a transfer of funds and (2) a transfer of information pertaining to the initiating financial transaction. This second attribute is one that EFT systems may find difficult to convey and still retain their efficiency for funds transfer purposes.

Value-Exchange Systems

Value-exchange systems can work much like check-clearing systems, although they transfer assets other than claims on demand deposits. The first widespread development of value exchange involved the use of credit cards. In such systems, credit card holders' IOUs were exchanged for cash balances. Subsequently, value-exchange systems have been used to transfer debits to both demand deposit and other accounts. Accounts used for value exchange, in addition to demand deposits and credit card lines, include balances in individuals' margin accounts held with stockbrokers, balances in accounts held with money market (or even longer-term) mutual funds, and accounts held with other financial institutions. The key element necessary for a value exchange is that the value of the item being exchanged can be readily determined and agreed upon. IOUs of credit card customers and margin account customers have a fixed monetary value, as do shares in money market mutual funds (since each MMMF share is adjusted daily to equal one dollar). Shares in other funds can also be exchanged if fractional share withdrawals are allowed when the net asset value per share is not equal to an even dollar. For instance, many municipal bond mutual funds let shareholders withdraw funds by check and sell bonds, if necessary, to make the checks good when they clear. (See People and Events.)

Credit Card Systems.   Credit card systems initially used sales receipts signed at the point of purchase. After making a phone call or verifying an individual's identity or signature, a merchant would accept the credit card receipt in exchange for goods and services. The receipt would then be forwarded to the institution that issued the card (usually through a specialized credit card receipt clearing system). The card-issuing institution would then add the amount of the sale to the individual's balance due and send the credit card user a bill. Under "country club" billing systems, the credit card issuer would send a copy of the receipt along with the bill so that the cardholder could verify the debt.

The physical transfer of credit card receipts was very expensive, however. Thus credit card systems were the first to develop computerized transfer of information and computerized billing systems. Visa (initially Bank Americard) and Interbank Card Association (initially Mastercharge) developed computerized information networks to transfer credit card billing information around the country.

Computerized billing allowed credit card receipts to be "truncated." A merchant who accepted a Visa or MasterCard receipt in return for a sale could take the receipt to a cooperating bank in the appropriate card system and receive immediate credit (minus a merchant discount). The receiving bank would pass the receipt on to a clearing bank in the credit card system. That bank would then retain the credit card receipt and transmit all pertinent information (the consumer's credit card number, the amount of the charge, the date, the place, and the merchant) through the credit card data-processing network. The processing bank, in turn, would receive credit through the credit card clearing network for the funds it disbursed, plus a fee (possibly paid in the form of a smaller discount) for its services. Since the credit card receipt was retained by the processing bank, its physical movement was said to be *truncated*. However, the pertinent information on the receipt was passed on electronically.

When the electronic information reached the bank that issued the credit card, it would debit the customer's account (increase the balance due owed by the consumer) and, at the end of the billing cycle, bill the customer for the full balance due plus any applicable finance charges. The bill would indicate the amount of each charge and its date and place. This process is illustrated in Exhibit 23-1. The value that was exchanged through the clearing system, then, was the value inherent in the consumer's willingness to pay his or her debt.

PEOPLE
& EVENTS

Value-Exchange Systems Cause a Market Drop

When people write checks against the value of their demand deposits, the amount on the check causes the same number of dollars to be subtracted from their account. When a check is written against the value of shares in a money market mutual fund, once again, each dollar amount of the check causes one dollar in fund shares to be redeemed. This is so because money market mutual fund shares are always worth $1 each (any change in value is credited as earnings at the end of each day). But when a check is written against the value of shares in a municipal bond mutual fund, the fund may have to redeem a variable number of shares to redeem the check. For instance, if a person writes a $100 check, if the shares are worth $10 each on the day the check clears the fund will liquidate ten of that person's shares. However, if the share value should fall to $8 per share, the fund would have to redeem $12^1/_2$ shares in the fund to honor a $100 check.

In April 1987, many investors found that they had extraordinarily large tax bills because they had large capital gains taxes to pay for 1986. As the tax-payment due date came near, they wrote checks to the IRS to pay their taxes. Many of the checks used the value-exchange capabilities of the municipal bond mutual funds. At first, when the checks cleared, the municipal bond funds drew down their cash balances to make the checks good. However, they soon ran out of cash, and people kept writing checks on their funds' accounts to pay their taxes. To get cash to make the checks good, the municipal bond funds had to sell bonds. They all had to sell at the same time, and, as a result, municipal bond prices plummeted. From mid-March through mid-April, an index of municipal bond prices fell from nearly 102 to under 87. Bond fund shareholders watched their shares lose up to 15 percent in value. Consequently, their funds redeemed up to 15 percent more shares in mid-April than in mid-March to make each $100 check good.

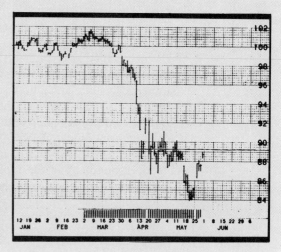

The development of computerized billing was important because once consumers became used to it, they were willing to accept the truncated check-clearing systems that are used for most NOW account and share-draft transfers of funds. The card systems also developed information transfer, clearing, and funds transfer technology necessary for EFT systems.

Exhibit 23–1   Clearing Information and Facts through a Value-Exchange System

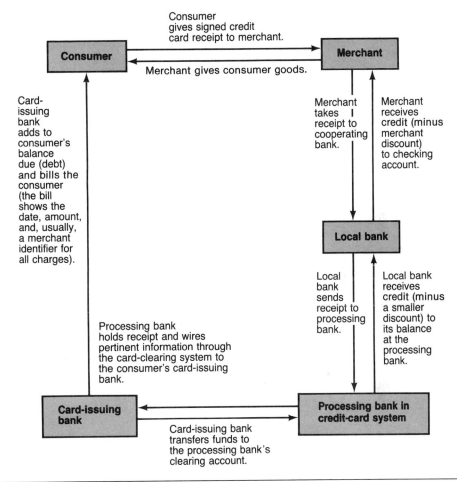

The value exchanged when a credit card slip is processed is the value inherent in the customer's promise to repay his or her debt. At each stage in the exchange process, that value is exchanged either for goods (from the merchant) or for the credits to an institution's bank or clearing balances.

Electronic Funds Transfer Systems

There is a wide variety of uses of electronic funds transfer (EFT) technologies. One of the first uses was for the transfer of computerized credit card clearing information. Other uses often require automated clearinghouses (ACHs).

The most sophisticated EFT operations are geared to ACHs. ACHs can provide either *credit transfers*, in which the initiating institution sends funds through the system to be deposited in the recipient's account, or *debit transfers*, in which the initiating institution withdraws funds from the depositor's account. Major examples of credit transfers are automatic deposits of payrolls, bill payments by telephone, and GIRO transfers (a type of payment used in Europe). Examples of debit transfers are preauthorized bill payments, transfers initiated by point-of-sale (POS) transactions, check truncation, and cash withdrawals from remote shared terminals. Bill-check payment mechanisms can be adapted to either credit or debit transfers.

Automatic Deposit of Payrolls and Social Security Payments.   Regular payments to the same individuals can be made efficiently through automated clearinghouses. As illustrated by Exhibit 23–2A, the bank of the paying organization gives the ACH a computer tape that provides information on the banks and account numbers of a firm's or agency's employees (or government pension and Social Security recipients) who are to be paid. The clearinghouse then credits the accounts of the receiving banks (or other financial institutions) with the total due and provides data indicating which depositors' accounts should be credited. The bank that submits the tape provides funds to the clearinghouse if its payments exceed its receipts at the clearinghouse from other sources.

For ACH operations to succeed, all organizations that submit tapes must use the same format and method of identifying account numbers and amounts of funds transferred. The advantages of credit transfers are that they are fast and allow both payments and related account information to make only one trip through the payments system.

Exhibit 23–2   Credit and Debit Transfers through an ACH

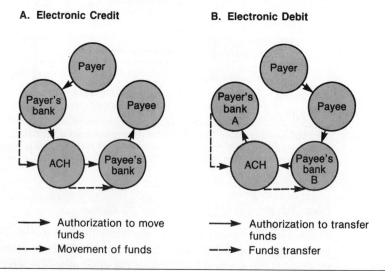

Electronic credit transfers transfer funds and information simultaneously from the payer to the payee. Debit transfers transfer funds from the payer's bank to the payee's bank, but only after the payer gives the payee valid authorization to do so.

Source: Adapted from George W. Mitchell and Raymond F. Hodgdon, "Federal Reserve and the Payments System," *Federal Reserve Bulletin*, February 1981, 112.

Bill Payments by Telephone.   Bill payments can be made efficiently through ACHs using telephones or cable television lines. To make payment, the depositor dials the bank, enters his or her account number, the amount he or she wishes to pay, and the coded bank and account numbers of the recipient of the payment. If the depositor provides data electronically (as with a touch-tone phone), the payment information can be verified and entered directly on a magnetic tape for submission to an ACH, which will make the appropriate credit transfers. Verbal information cannot be handled as cheaply or with as few errors as touch-tone information. Nonetheless, either form of bill payment by telephone can save consumers time and postage expenses and can still allow them to decide when they want to pay their bills.

GIRO Transfers.   GIRO funds transfer systems are widely used in Europe. A GIRO transfer occurs when an individual instructs a financial institution to make a payment to another individual (or company) who banks with another institution. The originating institution then transfers both funds and payment information telling which account should be credited to the receiving institution. Thus only one transfer is required for both funds and transmittal information. EFT systems can make similar transfers if appropriate payment information is entered on magnetic tape and sent to an ACH.

Preauthorized Bill Payments and Bill-Checks.   Consumers can authorize their banks or other depository institutions to make payments on their mortgages, rent, insurance, or other regularly recurring bills when they come due. Under such a system, the institution that is to receive the payment creates a tape indicating what amount it is to receive, from whom, and when. It sends the tape to an ACH to receive payment. The ACH obtains the funds from its customers' banks, which in turn subtract them from their customers' accounts.

A modified version of a preauthorized debit is the Atlanta bill-check system, which can be used to collect payments of varying amounts. In this system, the bill-check is mailed by the cooperating utility or retailer directly to the customer. The customer signs it and sends it back. The billing entity then makes up a tape to send to the ACH to debit the consumer's bank account for the amount due. In this system the consumer can still determine when to pay the bill, but the payment is made electronically. An electronic preauthorized debit is illustrated in Exhibit 23–2B. In the exhibit it is assumed that adequate funds are in the payer's account to complete the transfer.

Preauthorized bill payment can be handled more efficiently if the customer's bank has the capability to make telephone or GIRO credit transfers. For instance, if the customer took or sent all bill-checks directly to his or her bank for payment, the customer could save postage and there never would be any transfers reversed because of insufficient funds. Furthermore, the recipient of the payment could save bill-processing time and expense if the bill-checks generated credit transfers that indicated what company and account should be paid. Similarly, a consumer's bank could make preauthorized credit transfers out of the consumer's account to his or her mortgage holder, insurance company, or utility if the consumer merely told the bank which company should be paid and how much per month. Such credit transfer payments systems may be more popular than debit transfers with consumers.

Point-of-Sale (POS) Payments Systems.   Point-of-sale payments systems are more complicated than payroll, preauthorized transfer, or bill-check payments systems. They require a two-stage transfer of information and funds. One transfer requires that information on the status of the customer's account be transferred to the point of sale so that the expenditure can be authorized. The second transfer requires that funds be transferred from that account (and the institution that holds it) to the retailer's account (and the institution that holds it). See Exhibit 23–3.

Exhibit 23–3   **Point-of-Sale EFT Transfers**

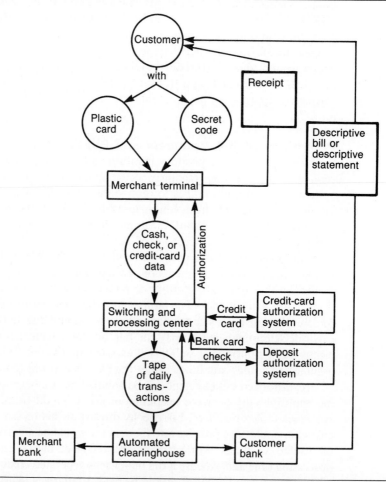

Point-of-sale transfers are more complicated than preauthorized transfers. First, a customer must prove that he or she is authorized to transfer funds from the named account. Usually this is done by providing a PIN (personal identification number) or a secret code at the point of sale. Second, the merchant must verify that sufficient funds are available to be transferred. This is done by contacting a credit-card or debit-card authorization center that has a record of the customer's account. The actual funds and goods are transferred only after the merchant receives the authorization to do so.

Source: Business Review. Federal Reserve Bank of Dallas, September 1976, 12.

Because of the complexity of the dual-information and funds-transfer functions that are required by point-of-sale systems, they have been slower to develop than other EFT functions. However, because of the great convenience they can offer consumers, numerous financial institutions have tried to position themselves so that they can offer point-of-sale credit when its use becomes widespread. They have done so by trying to ensure through legislation or regulation that all types of depository institutions and credit-granting institutions will be able to transfer funds through any developing point-of-sale system. Furthermore, they have tried to develop operations and services—such as revolving credit plans, credit cards, and debit cards—that could be used by their customers to make payments in a point-of-sale system. Finally, they have tried to simplify payment authorization and information transfer systems so that less detailed information need be transmitted to initiate and validate point-of-sale transactions.

Check Truncation.   Check truncation works like computerized billing of debit or credit card payments. When a check is cashed, it is held by the institution that received it (or, more commonly, that institution's bank). Then, by electronic means, the account on which the consumer wrote the check is debited, and the account of the merchant who deposited the check is credited. Because electronic impulses travel faster (and more cheaply) than paper, check truncation is widely used with NOW accounts and credit union share drafts.

Shared Terminal Systems

In contrast to remote terminals owned by a single institution, usually linked by telephone line directly to that institution, shared remote terminals can accommodate cross-transfers of funds between institutions or withdrawals of funds from any of several institutions. Cross-transfers of funds or pooled use of joint terminals require communications networks to be established to verify that customers have sufficient funds in their accounts so that they can be transferred according to customers' requests. Such operations are facilitated when institutions link their account-balance verification information through a single electronic "switch."

Shared systems of automatic teller machines (ATMs) have been developed for several reasons. First, they provide a way that depository institutions can obtain economies of scale in the use of their terminals. The fixed cost of ATM installations is relatively high. Depending on its expense, an ATM may need to generate several thousand transactions per month to cover its overhead costs. By sharing ATMs in networks, depository institutions can increase their rate of use and reduce their average cost of operation.

Second, ATM networks provide a means for institutions to serve customers outside their local market areas. This is a particularly important consideration in unit-banking and limited-branching states. The initial regional ATM networks expanded rapidly in such areas. ATM networks can also give depository institutions a toehold in interstate banking. For that reason many of the nation's largest financial institutions have actively engaged in developing ATM networks. However, as initially developed, ATM systems were allowed to conduct only balance inquiries or transfers or to allow cash withdrawals from out-of-state depository institutions. They could not accept deposits out of state or they would be considered interstate bank branches. The branch interpretation has changed, though, as regulatory authorities have increasingly ruled that ATMs are not branches.

National Networks.   Although many regional ATM systems were developed in the early 1980s, it was 1983 before the first nationwide hookups began. Nationwide ATM networks allow cash-dispensing systems linked to credit or debit cards to be used across the country. Generally, customers must pay an extra fee when they use an ATM that does not belong to their home depository institution, but the fees usually are small. The fee helps pay the cost of using authorization systems that link the user's withdrawal to his or her home institution account. Exhibit 23–4 illustrates the way in which EFT linkages are made between different ATM and POS networks.

Home Banking

The reduced cost of computer and communications technology has also made home banking feasible. Home-banking computers use connections over telephone lines or cable TV networks to access a depository institution's account records. Most allow people to check their account balances, pay their bills (to cooperating merchants), and transfer funds among accounts. Many also allow people to keep home budget, accounting, and tax records in an organized fashion.

Exhibit 23–4   **Point-of-Sale Network Interchange**

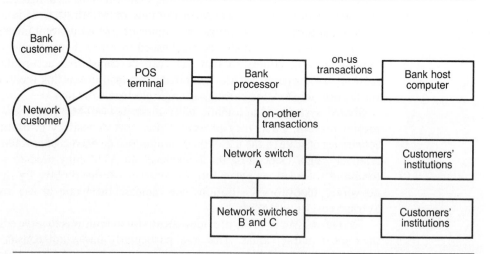

When a bank's customer uses a POS terminal, the bank's processor directly clears the transaction through the bank's computer. When a network customer uses the same POS terminal, the bank's processor forwards the funds-transfer authorization request to the proper network. That network, in turn, authorizes transfers from the customer's institution.

Source: Stephen D. Felgran, "From ATM to POS Networks: Branching, Access, and Pricing," *New England Economic Review*, Federal Reserve Bank of Boston, May–June 1985, p. 51. Reprinted with permission of the Federal Reserve Bank of Boston.

Home-banking devices frequently are used to access computerized information service systems. Such networks can provide stock and commodity market quotations, electronic shopping, current news, weather reports, airline travel information, computer games, and a host of other services.

People who use a home-banking network can select an item to buy from an electronic catalog, order the good, transfer funds to the merchant to pay for the purchase, and transfer funds from a savings to a "checking" account to replenish its balance. They may also be able to record the item in the proper home budget category and note whether it is a deductible item for tax planning.

As with ATMs, it may take some time before home banking gains public popularity. Many people are leery of computers, which basically run the system. Also, the home terminals and communications devices have initially been expensive. However, as the potential usage of such systems grows, cheaper communications techniques will become available. Preexisting telephone lines and a TV set can be used to provide home banking, provided that the consumer has appropriate interface equipment to link them together and to communicate with the depository institution's computer. With proper adjustments, home computers and video game machines could be used to provide home-banking services. Furthermore, when the generation of video game players grows up, many more people will feel comfortable operating computerized devices.

Payment Insurance

Every day in the United States, several trillion dollars in payments or electronic securities transactions are cleared by public (Federal Reserve) or private (bank clearinghouse and the CHIPS international payment ACH) payment systems. That is more than the entire M1 money supply. This means that many institutions are making payments immediately after they receive money from others or, in some cases, in the expectation that they will receive money from others later in the day.

The United States provides deposit insurance to depository institutions in part to protect the U.S. payments system. Threats to the payments system can develop if the failure of one institution makes it default on its payments due to other institutions, which in turn default on their obligations, and so on. The ultimate cause of such failures is the insolvency of the first institution. However, payments system failures can also occur because of liquidity problems. Liquidity problems rise when an institution runs out of assets that it is able to transfer to other institutions to obtain cash. Such a failure occurred in the fall of 1985, but, thanks to the Fed, a generalized payments crisis did not develop.

The potential crisis started on November 20 at the Bank of New York, which deals extensively in government securities. The securities are delivered by securities wire transfers (rather than physical delivery) that make journal entries on the books of the Fed (which keeps ownership records for all U.S. Treasury securities). When the securities are received, the bank pays for them with a wire transfer of funds (bank reserve balances). However, on November 20, the Bank of New York's computer system malfunctioned. The bank could buy government securities but it could not sell them. Thus it was obliged to pay out large amounts of funds, but it did not have comparable amounts of cash coming in. Its cash on hand was therefore quickly exhausted as it acquired more and more securities. At the close of the business day, it was more than $22 billion behind. It had to borrow $22.6 billion from the Fed in order to honor its outgoing payments for the day. The loan to the Bank of New York was by far the largest one-day borrowing at the Fed's discount window that had ever occurred.

The only reason the Bank of New York crisis did not cause problems for the entire payments system was that the bank in trouble could borrow from the Fed and thereby honor all its outgoing payments until it fixed its computer system. It was able to borrow easily because reserves held at the Fed and the Fed's wire transfer system form the heart of our nation's payments system. It might not have been able to make such facile adjustments, however, if its access to a strictly private payments mechanism had been disrupted.

A key issue regarding the payments system is whether the Fed needs to participate in it. Major correspondent banks and private clearinghouse associations say that they can clear checks faster or more inexpensively than the Fed in many cases. However, the issue does not revolve around cost alone. As the Bank of New York example shows, it pays to have the only institution in the country that can create money instantaneously—the Fed—play a major role in the payments system. Only the Fed can guarantee that payments made by a private party will be honored, if necessary, regardless of what happens.

Because it guarantees final payments, the Fed is exposed to payments system risk. To reduce its potential exposure to that risk, the Fed has limited banks' abilities to run "daylight overdrafts." Daylight overdrafts occur when the outgoing payments from a bank exceed its incoming payments by more than the amount held in its reserve account at the Fed. When that happens, the bank's reserve account is overdrawn—if only temporarily—and if the bank failed, the Fed would take a loss. To limit its risk, therefore, in 1986 the Fed set limits that would prevent banks from overdrawing their reserve accounts by too large an amount during the day. It did so because it feared that if the overdrafts were too extensive, the bank might not be able to make its reserve account balance by nightfall. Daylight overdraft regulations are interesting because when a bank is overdrawn, it must either stop payments for a while or borrow additional reserves through the Fed Funds market—if only for a few hours. As a result, banks may incur intraday interest charges in order to maintain their ability to make payments throughout the day.

Financial Market Guarantees

The Federal Reserve System is able to protect the payments system in the short run by creating liquidity—that is, by creating money when it is needed and lending those funds to people who need them to make their payments. It also is able to protect the nation's financial markets in the same manner.

On October 19, 1987, the stock market crashed. The Dow Jones Average fell more than 500 points. Many financial firms that owned stocks probably were technically insolvent at that point. As the value of their assets fell, they theoretically would have been unable to repay their debts even if they sold all their assets. Banks were reluctant to make more loans to insolvent firms. However, if banks did not make more loans, the insolvent firms and any individuals who received *margin calls* (requiring them to either sell stocks or deposit more money with their brokers) would be forced to sell more stocks. The additional selling would make stock prices fall more and would cause more people and firms to become insolvent (go broke) and face still more selling as defaults accelerated.

Thus, during the morning of October 20, 1987, the stock market fell another 200 points as many people anticipated a repeat of the great crash of 1929, with a following Great Depression. At that point, the Fed stepped in. Publicly, the chairman of the Fed guaranteed that the Fed would provide all the liquidity that the market or economy might need. All people who needed money could borrow it, without having to sell stocks. Privately, the Fed told banks to continue to lend to securities dealers, brokers and their customers. If they made such loans, the Fed would stand behind them and lend the banks any additional money that they might need. The Fed also pumped massive amounts of money into the financial markets by buying government securities. As a result, people who needed cash could borrow it. They no longer had to sell securities to obtain more funds. The stock market started to rally, and a repeat of the Great Depression was averted.

Thus, by providing liquidity when it was needed, the Fed was able to avert another crisis—just as it had done in the Bank of New York case. After the crash, as confidence returned, the brokerage firms that had suffered during the crash were quietly acquired by more solvent firms. There was no panic, and there was no repeat of 1929.

Because the Fed is able to avert financial crisis by providing adequate liquidity, one may question why we also need to protect financial institutions by providing deposit insurance.

Deposit Insurance

Deposit Insurance in the 1930s

Before 1934, this country had no federal insurance. However, after the 1929 stock market crash, banks began to fail in great numbers. By 1934, nearly half of the nation's banks had failed. Because of these massive bank failures, Congress authorized federal deposit insurance in the form of FDIC and FSLIC insurance. Both funds started in 1934 and initially charged a deposit insurance premium equal to $1/4$ of 1 percent. After the insurance became available, bank failures dropped dramatically and stayed low until the 1980s. Deposit insurance was effective because it prevented runs on insured banks. Thus banks that were basically sound no longer needed to fear that many depositors would try to withdraw all of their funds at once, thereby forcing the bank to liquidate assets at distress sale prices in order to get the cash needed to repay depositors.

There are several facts that should be noted about the 1930s experience, as they have bearing on current issues. First, if the Fed had provided adequate amounts of loans to all banks that were experiencing a run, most depositors could have been repaid in full when they "ran" to the bank, and some otherwise sound banks might have survived. Furthermore, additional bank runs would have been averted if depositors knew that all sound banks had adequate access to currency (through the Fed's provision of emergency liquidity) to repay all depositors. However, the Fed did not make as many discount window loans as needed, because banks could borrow only if they were Fed member banks and could pledge the right form of collateral.

Second, even though there were massive numbers of bank failures in the 1930s, bank depositors lost less than 1 percent of their deposits. This suggests that most banks were basically sound and had sufficient assets to repay their debts. To a lesser degree, this may also reflect the fact that many bank stockholders were liable for additional levies equal to the amount of their capital subscription if the bank experienced failure. The "double jeopardy" provision may have prevented some bank owners from taking excess risks. In addition, the tendency of the public to "run" to withdraw their deposits from any bank that they suspected was engaging in unsound banking practices may have helped to ensure that banks followed prudent practices and did not make many unsound loans. Since most bank failures in the 1930s resulted from a lack of liquidity rather than from unsound practices, losses to depositors were relatively small.

Third, when the deposit insurance funds were first started, deposit insurance covered only relatively small deposits (so people with large deposits still had an incentive to make sure that the banks in which they put their money used sound banking practices). In addition, the initial deposit insurance fee equaled $1/4$ of 1 percent—which was quite substantial relative to the extremely low loan rates (during the Great Depression, short-term prime loan rates were as low as 1 percent, and rates were even lower for safe investments like Treasury bills).

Deposit Insurance after World War II

As you know from Chapter 17, after deposit insurance became available in 1934, runs on banks and bank failures were practically eliminated. Thus, before long, deposit insurance premiums were reduced from $1/4$ to $1/12$ of 1 percent or less (since rebates of insurance premiums were often given).

More insidiously, however, after many years of having deposit insurance, depositors no longer took the time to investigate the soundness of the institutions in which they deposited their money. Their lack of care was aggravated by two changes in federal policies that occurred over time. First, Congress increased the amount of insured deposits in steps over time to equal $100,000 in 1980 (up from $40,000 in 1979). Second, the banking and thrift regulators began to adopt a de facto "too-big-to-fail" policy. Initially, they developed a strong preference for liquidating large institutions through "purchase and assumption" transactions that protected all deposits, even if those deposits exceeded the insurance limit. Regulators used deposit payoffs, which only protected depositors in full up to the deposit insurance limit, only to close smaller institutions. Possibly the examiners found that deposit payoffs posed less of a demand on their available personnel when they closed down a small instead of a large institution. Regardless of the reason, depositors in large institutions began to think that their deposits would be fully protected.

Eventually, the regulators' behavior was made explicit by the comptroller of the currency when he announced in 1984 that Continental Illinois and all similarly large banks were "too big to fail." This announcement was not surprising, since the regulators had been bailing out rather than liquidating large troubled institutions long before the announcement.

Because of the government's policies, depositors did not take an interest in making sure that they placed their deposits only in safe institutions—as long as the deposit was under $100,000 or the institution was "too big to fail." To ensure that an institution was safe, then, federal examiners had to do a better job. Yet examiners are not privy to local gossip that may indicate when an institution is engaging in self-dealing or making unsound loans. Furthermore, federal agencies did not hire enough examiners. During the first half of the 1980s, the number of federal savings and loan examiners declined. Thus, at a time when deregulation and rising interest rates placed more financial institutions under stress, federal examiners did not increase their policing activities even though the public had a diminishing incentive to monitor the performance of possibly troubled institutions. Consequently, the number of bank and thrift institution failures escalated greatly in the 1980s. By 1989, the thrift institutions' deposit insurance fund (the FSLIC) was over $100 billion in the red, and the banks' insurance fund (the FDIC) held very low reserves relative to its deposit insurance liabilities. Thus the FIRRE Act closed the FSLIC, transferred thrift deposit insurance to the FDIC, and raised insurance premiums to 0.15 and 0.23 percent of deposits for banks and thrifts, respectively. Subsequently, the government had to authorize continuing payments to keep the deposit insurance funds liquid and to cover their losses, and deposit insurance premiums were raised again.

Alternatives to Federal Deposit Insurance

Because of the technical insolvency of the nation's deposit insurance funds, alternatives to federal deposit insurance have had to be considered. Possible alternatives include private insurance, higher risk-based deposit insurance premiums, greater capital requirements for financial institutions, or more formal provision of liquidity guarantees by the government.

Private Insurance

Advocates of private deposit insurance suggest that it would be superior to federal insurance on three counts. First, competition among deposit insurance vendors would keep deposit insurance premiums in line with various institutions' actual risks of loss. For instance, institutions with fewer credit risks, less interest rate risk, and more net worth relative to their assets would probably pay lower deposit insurance premiums. Second, it is alleged that private insurers, who would stand to lose their own money if a financial institution failed, would be quicker to cancel insurance for an institution that took too much risk. In contrast, federal insurance cannot be canceled for two years and, prior to 1989, it was not uncommon for errant managers to appeal to their representatives in Congress to reduce or head off federal examiners' sanctions against their institutions. Private insurers would not be subject to political influence. Third, a private insurance firm would have an incentive to hire an adequate number of examiners and provide them with sufficient power to ensure an institution's soundness.

The major argument against private insurance is simple: it is not credible in a crisis. State-chartered deposit insurance funds have frequently failed. In Ohio and Maryland, state-chartered thrift insurance funds failed in 1985 after major thrift institutions failed. When the taxpayers of Ohio were faced with the alternative of raising taxes to bail out the Ohio Deposit Guarantee Fund after Home State Savings failed, they elected not to do so. The surviving Ohio thrifts had to obtain federal insurance. Only the federal government can easily "print money" by issuing debt in lieu of raising taxes, so only its guarantees are credible in a crisis. After the Ohio and Maryland failures, the limitations of private insurance became obvious to state-chartered insurance funds. Thus most asked their insured institutions to obtain federal insurance instead.

A second problem with private insurance is that it may not have enough examination power to ensure that misdeeds do not occur. In fact, the private insurers themselves may need to be regulated to make sure they do not underprice their products. This problem results from the fact that private insurers might find it easier to obtain business if they charged low rates for their insurance and did not impose difficult examination standards on their clients. This is analogous to the case of private CPA firms that are hired to audit financial firms. In 1983, United American Bank of Tennessee was given a clean audit by its CPA firm's examiners at the same time that the federal bank examiners were in the bank to close it down. In 1989, the FSLIC filed suit against several of the nation's largest accounting firms for not disclosing problems at failing thrift institutions. These failures of private audits resulted from the auditing firms' desire to not offend their clients and lose their business. Similar incentives could cause a private deposit insurance firm with limited liability to underprice its product or engage in possibly slack examinations.

One way that private insurance might help, however, could be in the form of "coinsurance." If federal deposit insurance covered only 80 percent of deposits, institutions could be induced to obtain "coinsurance" from private insurance companies to cover the remaining 20 percent. The coinsurance would not be cancelable without adequate notice; thus the private insurance companies would have an incentive to closely monitor bank risks. Those companies, however, could impose conditions that must be met in order for the insurance to be renewed. By imposing risk-reducing conditions or varying their insurance premiums, the private insurers would send signals to the regulators regarding which depository institutions they considered to be more risky. The regulators would then have an incentive to increase their supervision of those institutions as well. Thus coinsurance would supplement the regulatory monitoring process and might be less rigid and more innovative in monitoring and reducing risks. Furthermore, since most of the bank deposits would be insured with federal guarantees, the risk of bank runs would also be reduced as the basic deposit insurance would be credible.

Because private insurers might use different monitoring systems, and also would provide an independent assessment of risk, the FDIC Improvement Act of 1991 allowed the FDIC to obtain private reinsurance for up to 10 percent of its deposit liabilities. The risk premiums assessed for the private insurance could then be used as a guide in setting the FDIC's risk-related deposit insurance fee. That procedure would allow the FDIC to escape the thorny political thicket associated with assessing higher risk-based premiums for one institution than for another.

Higher Deposit Insurance Premiums

Only a double handful of commercial banks do not have deposit insurance. Clearly, even in states where deposit insurance is not mandatory, most banks have generally thought that the price of insurance was low relative to the benefits. The major benefit is that a federally insured institution can pay less to attract deposits than an uninsured institution. As long as reduced deposit costs more than cover the price of the insurance, an institution will willingly pay for federal insurance. However, if insurance costs become too high, depositors will move their funds to uninsured institutions (such as money market mutual funds) or abroad. Also, depository institutions will attempt to obtain more funds from sources that are not subject to deposit insurance premiums. Prior to 1989, it is clear that deposit insurance premiums were not too high, so some upward movement in deposit insurance rates was possible. In fact, the FSLIC raised its deposit insurance rate by $^1/_8$ percent in 1985. The major incentive after that was for FSLIC-insured institutions to shift to FDIC-insurance status. Such shifts were put on hold by the Competitive Equality in Banking Act of 1987, but thrifts did not drop their insurance. Thus, even the new FSLIC rate did not cost more than it was worth.

In lieu of charging higher deposit insurance premiums to all institutions the FDIC Improvement Act of 1991 required that riskier institutions should pay higher rates for deposit insurance from 1993 on. It is hard to assess risk in a nondiscriminatory manner, however, so formal differences in insurance rates were never adopted previously. Instead, the riskier institutions were subject to de facto increases in rates. More frequent examinations, cease and desist orders, and higher capital requirements often have been imposed on the riskiest insured financial institutions. All these requirements tend to raise the institutions' costs, reduce their return on equity capital, and reduce risk to the insurance funds.

Risk-based pricing of deposit insurance is hard to do explicitly because risk exposures are hard to determine before a loss occurs. In addition to credit risk (which is taken into account by risk-based capital requirements), institutions are also subject to interest rate risk—which must also be priced according to the FDICIA. Furthermore, some depository institutions may have large amounts of contingent liabilities outstanding in the form of lines of credit, swap agreements, or options transactions of various sorts. Thus explicit pricing of all risks associated with assets and liabilities may be a difficult task for regulators to accomplish. Furthermore, regulators may be reluctant to vary risk-based premiums as much as is warranted; the FDIC's first proposal would only vary rates from 0.23 percent of insured deposits for the safest banks to 0.31 percent for the riskiest ones. Thus, the use of coinsurance or reinsurance (which is priced by private insurance companies), subordinated debt and preferred stock (which is priced by the financial markets for large depository institutions), or elevated capital requirements or double jeopardy provisions (which are evaluated by shareholders) may assist the regulators in developing pricing schemes that vary with the assumed riskiness of each depository institution.

Finally, by increasing deposit insurance premiums more than in proportion to increases in depository institutions' risk, regulators may be able to discourage excess risk-taking designed to increase the institutions' returns. However, the extra premiums may also need to be assessed, in part, retroactively, (since the full exposure to risk may not be known *ex-ante*). Ex-post, de facto premium increases can be achieved by reimposing double jeopardy provisions for stockholders or by enforcing some form of personal liability penalty against officers and directors of institutions. Along these lines the FIRRE Act provided for penalties to be imposed on failed institutions' officers, directors, attorneys, consultants, and accountants if they did not adequately perform their duties to ensure that the institution complied with all applicable laws and did not take excessive risk. Over all, however, because regulators have a difficult time assessing risk exposures and ex-post penalties can be appealed, risk-based deposit insurance pricing is likely to be a contentious issue for many years.

Capital Requirements for Financial Institutions

One of the most effective ways to protect insurers of depository institutions is to require that the institutions hold adequate capital. Capital acts like a deductible on a casualty insurance policy. The greater the institution's net worth relative to its assets, the greater the loss in asset value it can incur without causing losses to the deposit insurance fund (see Exhibit 23–5). In an automobile insurance policy, if an individual elects to have a larger deductible, he or she will usually receive lower insurance rates. Similarly, in the case of deposit insurance, larger net worth requirements can substitute for an increase in insurance rates. Conversely, reducing the capital requirements necessary to obtain deposit insurance is equivalent to reducing rates.

Risk-Based Capital and Regulatory Arbitrage

If deposit insurance rates are fixed, regulators must try to vary the net cost of insurance so that it covers the risk taken by an insured institution. As previously

---

Exhibit 23–5   Bank Capital and Deposit Insurance Losses

	Bank A		Bank B	
	Assets	Liabilities and Net Worth	Assets	Liabilities and Net Worth
	Good assets— $90 million	Insured deposits— $95 million	Good assets— $90 million	Insured deposits— $90 million
	Charged-off assets— $10 million	Net worth— $5 million	Charged-off assets— $10 million	Net worth— $10 million
	Loss to deposit insurer— $5 million		Loss to deposit insurer— $0 million	

Bank A has only 5 percent of its assets funded with capital (net worth). Thus, if the value of its assets is reduced by 10 percent, the deposit insurance fund will incur substantial losses. Bank B, however, holds net worth equal to 10 percent of its assets. Thus, it can incur an equal (10 percent) loss in its assets' value without causing the deposit insurance fund to lose money.

noted, one way they can do this is by examining risky institutions more thoroughly and more frequently and by issuing cease-and-desist orders to make risky institutions change their practices. More recently, they have imposed *risk-based capital standards* that vary with the riskiness of an institution's assets and liabilities. The new requirements were necessary because many institutions had begun to assume off-balance-sheet risk by obligating themselves in swap transactions, letter-of-credit agreements, and so on to earn extra fee income from operations that did not appear on their balance sheet.

The risk-based capital requirements were proposed in 1987 by the Fed, the comptroller of the currency, the FDIC, and the Bank of England acting in concert. They were not implemented immediately because their intent was to form a basis for uniform international bank capital requirements. Thus an attempt was made to persuade the Bank of Japan and other central banks to adopt similar policies. If similar capital requirements were not adopted in all countries, a substantial risk existed that major banks would engage in "regulatory arbitrage" by shifting their operations to the countries with the least restrictive regulations. U.S. banks had done so earlier when they had shifted their investment banking business to London to avoid Glass-Steagall Act restrictions against such activities.

The new risk-based capital proposals were delayed, then, to obtain international agreements and to prevent additional regulatory arbitrage. Risk-based guidelines broke bank activities down into separate categories according to their risk and levied varying capital requirements on each. Risk-based capital requirements, for instance, are 8 percent for commercial loans and standby letters of credit, but only 4 percent for residential mortgage loans and zero for Treasury bills.

The major innovation in risk-based capital requirements is to price off-balance-sheet risk. In the past, major banks reached for fee income by arranging financial guarantees and standby letters of credit, which obligate them to pay if the client does not. Thus these financial guarantees carry as much risk as a loan, but before risk-based capital requirements they were not subject to capital requirements because they did not appear on the bank's balance sheet. Similarly, swap agreements and foreign exchange commitments have some hidden credit risk, particularly over longer periods of time. The risk-based capital requirements, therefore, assess capital charges against such contracts if they are of long duration.

Risk-based capital requirements are enforced on a local level by bank regulators. In the United States, regulators have supplemented the Bank for International Settlements (BIS) requirements with a "leverage" requirement. Under the FDICIA of 1991, depository institutions must hold capital equal to at least 2 percent of assets (even if all assets are T-bills, which have a risk-weight of zero under BIS capital requirements) or they will be deemed "critically undercapitalized." Critically undercapitalized institutions must rectify their capital deficiency promptly or be closed. Conversely, "well-capitalized" institutions are allowed by FDICIA to issue brokered deposits and to engage in limited investment banking. U.S. regulators require "well-capitalized" banks to hold leverage (Tier 1) capital equal to 5 percent of assets and total risk-based capital of 10 percent. Some "adequately capitalized" banks may also receive regulatory advantages, but only if the regulators explicitly grant them the privileges.

While local regulations can be more strict than the risk-based capital requirements, if they are more lenient, banks will not be in compliance with the international capital standards established by the BIS. As a result, their international banking activities will be restricted.

Before the BIS established mutually agreed international capital standards, local capital requirements differed widely. This led to "regulatory arbitrage" as depository institutions tried to establish subsidiaries in localities with the most lenient regulation. One form of "lenient" regulation was the Japanese practice of allowing banks to count all unrealized gains on stock they owned in related companies as an increase in their asset values (and net worth). Thus the Japanese banks had high capital ratios during the late 1980s and were very competitive worldwide. However, the BIS standards only allowed banks to count 45 percent of their unrealized gains on stock holdings as an addition to their assets. This had an adverse effect on Japanese banks, and on the Japanese stock market, when the new capital standard was imposed (see Did You Know?).

Even within a country, "capital" definitions can vary depending upon what is counted as an asset. For instance, the FIRRE Act let thrift institutions count a portion of their "goodwill" toward part of their capital requirements until 1995, but it did not let such "intangible" capital, such as goodwill, count for more than half the thrift's capital requirement. Banks, in contrast, were not given an equivalent exception.

Capital Requirements, Security Issues, Liquidity, and the Need for Deposit Insurance

The risk-based capital requirements allow perpetual preferred stock to be counted as Tier 1 capital, which must comprise at least half the capital requirement, and subordinated debt with nonmandatory interest and principal payments to be counted as Tier 2 capital on a limited basis. The idea behind this is that, in the event of problems, interest, dividend, and principal payments on such preferred stock and debt would not put a drain on the bank's cash flows. In addition, in the event of failure, the holders of those subordinated securities would lose all their funds before the bank's depositors or the deposit insurance fund lost money.

If the notion of subordinated debt were to be taken further, it could provide an alternative to deposit insurance. In particular, if a bank were to issue a sufficient amount of subordinated debt and preferred stock, it could incur substantial losses before the depositors faced a potential loss of funds. For instance, if capital, preferred stock and subordinated debt made up more than 20 percent of a bank's balance sheet, the bank's assets would have to fall in value by more than 20 percent before the depositors lost a dime. Thus, depositors in banks with substantial amounts of subordinated debt and preferred stock would have substantial protection against loss even if the bank did not have deposit insurance.

However, in the absence of deposit insurance, the bank might not receive sufficiently detailed examinations to ensure that fraud did not occur and that major losses were not incurred. Furthermore, if the bank's capital structure included only long-term subordinated debt and preferred stock, it would not necessarily have to undergo continual scrutiny of securities-rating agencies before selling more securities. Thus, it might be desirable for banks to include some short-term subordinated debt

DID YOU KNOW?

Risk-Based Capital and the Japanese Stock Market

The Japanese Nikkei stock market index peaked at nearly 39,000 at year-end 1989. At that time the value of stockholders' equity interests in Japanese companies was very high. This greatly benefited Japanese banks because they held many equity interests in other Japanese companies. Under Japanese law, banks could hold up to 5 percent of the outstanding stock of other companies. Furthermore, many Japanese companies were linked through cross-share holdings with other companies in *keiretsu* groups. Often those groups had a "lead bank" that owned stockholdings in each company in the group and provided advice and financial support to other group members.

Because Japanese banks owned stock in many other Japanese companies, the value of their assets rose sharply as the stock market rose. Prior to 1990, they could count any increase in the value of stock holdings as an increase in the value of their balance sheet assets, thereby increasing the value of their net worth. As a result, Japanese banks were very well capitalized and received very high (often AAA) credit ratings. Their high credit ratings were valuable, as they could then sell AAA-rated guarantees to other firms in the form of "standby letters of credit" and other financial guarantees where they pledged to pay creditors of the entity paying for the guarantee if that entity did not. Since most AAA-rated banks were Japanese, Japanese banks received much of the lucrative "fee income" business that could be earned from selling financial guarantees. This made other banks jealous.

However, the risk-based capital requirements imposed under international agreement by the Bank for International Settlements (BIS) soon changed

the ball game—and not to the liking of the Japanese. The BIS not only required that all international banks meet its 8 percent risk-based capital requirement by 1993 (with a phase-in period starting in 1990), but also, the BIS no longer let Japanese banks count the full value of their stockholdings in other companies toward their capital requirements. Instead, only 45 percent of their gains on equities could be counted as capital.

The new rules reduced Japanese banks' capital adequacy; they no longer held super-abundant capital. As they contemplated the new BIS requirements, Japanese banks realized that by selling some of their stocks, they could count 100 percent of their stock gains toward their capital requirements. This gave Japanese banks incentive to sell stock. Others also had incentives to sell Japanese stocks at that time (to hedge all the new Nikkei "put warrants" that had just come to market). Thus selling accelerated in the Japanese stock market.

As the Japanese stock market started down, Japanese banks' stockholdings lost value. Eventually, some of them were no longer able to meet the BIS capital requirements unless they sold stocks and realized 100 percent of their gains. As they did so, the stock market fell further. By April 1992, the Japanese stock market had fallen more than 55 percent from its high, and many people worried that many Japanese banks would be unable to meet the 8 percent risk-based capital requirement when it became fully effective one year later. They further worried that if, as a result, Japanese banks cut back on their lending to reduce their need for risk-based capital, a serious worldwide recession might result.

and limited-life preferred stock in their capital structures as well as long-term debt and preferred stock.

If a bank regularly issued short-term debt and preferred stock, it would be under continual scrutiny by the capital markets and securities-rating agencies. Because the capital market participants and rating agencies are experts at assessing risk (a primary function of capital markets is to price risk–return trade-offs properly), they would efficiently assess a financial institution's risk and price the new debt and preferred stock issues accordingly. This risk assessment, and the associate pricing of bank risk, would not necessarily rely on mechanical rules and would not be subject to political influence. Thus it would be exempt from the practical objections that have hindered regulators' abilities to price deposit insurance according to bank risk. At the same time, it would achieve the goal of making risky banks pay more for deposit protection. The major function of the preferred stock and subordinated debt is to protect depositors, and the costs of maintaining that protection would rise if the capital markets made risky institutions pay higher rates in order to sell their securities. For this scheme to work on a continuing basis, however, banks would be required to go to the capital markets repeatedly to refinance their subordinated debt or preferred stock.

The main reason that the regulators presently count only mandatory convertible subordinated debt and perpetual preferred stock as part of a bank's capital requirement is that such debt need not be refinanced regularly. Thus, if a bank experienced problems, it would not be forced to fail because the capital markets were unwilling to refinance its debt at reasonable rates. If subordinated short-term debt were included as part of the bank's capital requirement, a liquidity facility would have to be available so that banks could borrow from the Fed in a pinch. By lending to all banks experiencing liquidity problems and taking any of their assets as collateral, the Fed could have lessened the collapse of the banking system that occurred during the Great Depression. That this was true was evident in the crash of October 19, 1987. That crash did not generate a depression or even a recession, because the Fed provided adequate liquidity at that time, even (indirectly) to uninsured and technically insolvent brokerage firms. Because of the Fed's liquidity facility, damaged firms did not have to liquidate their assets at distressed prices, and they were later absorbed by stronger firms. A similar procedure could work for banks.

The major remaining problem with letting the capital market provide banks with deposit protection instead of a federal deposit insurance fund is that only large banks have easy access to the nation's capital markets. Nonetheless, small banks can issue preferred stock to their initial stockholders, and that stock could trade in local markets. Furthermore, the double jeopardy provisions of the 1930s seemed to play some role in making bank owners prudent and financially responsible with the public's funds. As long as the Fed provided liquidity to avert runs and forced sales of assets and, in addition, the management, stockholders, and debt holders of financial institutions were exposed to risks of loss in the event of a bank's failure, deposit insurance might not be necessary. Consequently, the American Assembly has proposed that deposit insurance be limited only to transactions accounts. That policy would protect the payments system but not the individual institutions that issued the accounts.[1] Institutions that wished to insure savings accounts could obtain private

[1]George J. Benston, ed., *Financial Services: The Changing Institutions and Government Policy* (Englewood Cliffs, NJ: Prentice-Hall, 64th American Assembly, 1983).

insurance, issue subordinated debt, or take other actions to assure depositors in those accounts that their savings deposits would be safe.

The Need for Bank Examinations

Even if deposit insurance were to be replaced by a system that required financial institutions to issue subordinated debt or obtain private insurance, periodic public examinations of financial institutions might still be necessary. There are two reasons for this. First, the depository institutions are subject to many laws that affect their procedures and lending practices, rate disclosures, crediting of deposits, and so on. Regular public examinations may be needed to ensure that they comply with all relevant laws.

Second, depository institutions typically operate with large liabilities relative to their capital bases. This means that it is possible for owners of an institution who have fraudulent intentions to take more out of the institution than they invested in it. This was the case in the United States National Bank failure in 1973 and the United American Banks' failures in 1983. In 1973 United States National Bank of San Diego failed when examiners found that it had made extensive loans to shell corporations that diverted the loan proceeds to benefit the bank's principal stockholder. The public examiners stopped the manipulation, but not before the bank had become insolvent (its net worth was negative) and large depositors were exposed to losses. That case illustrates financial institutions' unique vulnerability to failure through mismanagement.

Exhibit 23-6 illustrates one way in which a bank can be manipulated. Assume that an individual or group of individuals owns a bank with $8 million in capital (their cost) and $80 million in deposits. Provided that the bank holds sufficient liquidity to meet depositors' withdrawal needs, it can keep depositors happy. Thus it must remain liquid, even if it makes bad loans, or the manipulators' game will be up.

Now assume that the hypothetical bank makes $30 million in loans to shell corporations in which the bank's owners have a beneficial interest. The owners have now put $8 million into the bank and taken $30 million out. Part of the money they took out belongs to the depositors. The shell corporations can now dissipate the money borrowed, if desired, and eventually default on their loans to the bank and declare bankruptcy. It the owners of the bank received the dissipated $30 million in some way (possibly through other layers of shell corporations), when the bank collapsed they would still be $22 million ahead. Furthermore, the bank need not collapse unless it either (1) runs short of liquidity or (2) is examined by independent (possibly public) examiners that ascertain the true value of its loans. Even bad loans can look good for a long time provided that interest payments are made. Thus the looting of our hypothetical bank could continue for a long time unless careful examiners were to evaluate the soundness of the bank's loan portfolio.

The importance of public examination was illustrated when a private accounting firm certified the United American Bank of Knoxville as sound while federal examiners were preparing to close it down. The bank had made too many loans to the principal owners of the bank, and too many of those loans were unsound. Although

Exhibit 23–6   **Balance Sheet of a Hypothetical Manipulated Bank**

Assets	Liabilities
Liquid assets— $3 million	Deposits—, $80 million
All assets not elsewhere specified— $55 million	Net worth—
Loans to shell corporations— $30 million	$8 million

Because financial institutions are highly leveraged, owners can buy or start them with very little capital relative to their assets. They can then direct the institution's assets to their own uses, provided that they evade regulatory restrictions on loan limits and insider loans by lending to numerous shell corporations with disguised ownership. In this case, the owners have $8 million invested in the capital of the bank, but they have taken $30 million out through their inside loan dealings. This process, operated on a larger scale, caused the ultimate failure of United States National Bank of San Diego in 1973 and United American Bank of Knoxville in 1983. Both owners were subsequently sentenced to long jail terms.

both bank examination teams were in the bank at the same time, only the federal examiners unveiled the problems.

Because the public loses if banks fail, public regulation of financial institutions is essential. Since depositors gain most by preventing problems, a case can be made for their bearing examination costs.

Market Value Accounting and Early Closure

The FDICIA of 1991 tried to reduce the risk that insured depository institutions would cause losses to their insurance funds. One FDICIA proposal was that institutions use market value rather than book value to value assets and liabilities. Such a provision would enable regulators and depositors to monitor each institution's capital more effectively. The FDICIA also provided that each institution maintain adequate capital, and that "critically undercapitalized" institutions be promptly closed. Finally, the FDICIA let regulators define the "well-capitalized" institutions that could engage in investment banking and sell brokered deposits. Their definition was so lax that about 90% of all banks qualified—provided that they had a good examination rating. This process enhanced regulators' power. These proposals were controversial.

Market-Value Accounting

Market-value accounting would require institutions to calculate the current market value of all their assets and liabilities so the difference would reflect their true net worth. While this is an admirable goal, financial institutions complain that it is difficult and expensive to do. What is the value of a loan that has not defaulted—but might? Also, what is the value of a "core" deposit that receives a below-market rate of interest but a high level of service, regardless of the level of interest rates? Also, what is the potential value of an interest rate "cap" agreement or an interest rate "swap" agreement, or a standby line of credit? Each of these generate fee income in exchange for *possible* future payments—but the level and timing of those possible payments is unknown. Clearly, it can be difficult to determine an institution's market values accurately, but that does not mean that an attempt should not be made.

However, partial evaluation of market values may not be advisable. That issue has arisen because the SEC has tried to prohibit "gains" trading by financial institutions, in which the institutions hold their losing security investments and value them at book value while selling their profitable securities to record a capital gain. Thus the SEC has tried to require that all financial institutions that actively trade securities value all their securities at market value. Two good counterarguments to a partial market-value policy exist. First, such a policy is partial and might cause losses to be shown on securities that were used to hedge other risk exposures on the institution's balance sheet, such as mortgage loans. By only requiring disclosure of changes in security values, institutions' profits and net worths might appear to fluctuate more widely. Second, institutions might be less likely to hedge interest rate risk exposures inherent in their loans or liabilities if they had to report part of their hedge position at market value but did not report the nonsecurity portion of their hedge at market value. If partial market-value accounting discouraged institutions from buying or selling securities, futures contracts, or options to reduce their interest rate risk, their risk of failure could actually rise. A third argument, which is not good, is that institutions can hold investment securities to maturity and redeem them at face value then, so current values are not important. That argument ignores interest rate and default risk considerations.

Early Closure

The FDICIA also required that institutions that were critically undercapitalized be closed promptly—and that the Fed should not provide discount window credit to them to keep them alive for extended periods. The advantage of such a policy is that it would prevent weak institutions from gambling to make profits—thereby increasing their losses if their gambles fail. The argument makes sense, but from a practical standpoint, it might be physically impossible for an insurance agency with limited personnel and resources to take over and liquidate one of the nation's largest institutions. Also, since the FDIC lost about 30 percent of the assets of the banks it liquidated in the 1980s, closing a bank with a book value of capital of 2 percent rather than 0 percent might not reduce the FDIC's losses much. Finally, some banks that have had deficient capital in the past have recovered and become profitable again—and early closure would have prevented that good outcome from happening. On the other hand, the recovering banks might have been the banks that "won" their interest rate risk or credit risk gambles—in which case, slow closure might have encouraged gambling. Overall, it appears that the counterarguments to "early closure" are not convincing. An early closure policy will encourage insured depository institutions to rectify their problems quickly lest the managers lose their jobs.

New Technology, Velocity, and Control of the Money Supply

Controlling the Money Supply

The growth of new financial services has complicated the definition of money. Both credit card lines and the availability of money substitutes have reduced the demand for conventionally defined money. The Federal Reserve, as a result, monitors several differently defined money supplies—some of which contain liabilities issued by money market mutual funds and other unconventional intermediaries. No one definition of money is best for all purposes.

The problem of monetary control is further complicated because many components of the more broadly defined monetary aggregates are not subject to reserve requirements. Many people argue that all checkable liabilities, such as checkable money market fund accounts and deposits, should be subject to reserve requirements. However, others argue that reserve requirements per se merely serve as a "tax" that encourages new money substitutes and value-exchange systems to be developed. They claim that higher reserve requirements stimulate more financial innovation—particularly when interest rates are high and the forgone interest on required reserves is greater. As a result, greater control of the money supply could not easily be achieved in the long run by imposing higher reserve requirements. If an attempt were made to do so, more and more regulations would be needed as additional money substitutes were developed. For instance, check-related value transfers, originated against mutual fund accounts or investment portfolios, can allow people to spend money more easily than would otherwise be the case. However, no reserves are required against brokerage firms' cash management accounts. If reserves were required, human ingenuity would develop other value-transfer systems.

The existence of liabilities issued by money market mutual funds, brokerage firms, and retailers that can be used for transactions but that are not counted as M1 greatly complicates the definition of money. It also complicates monetary policy because (1) the Fed has little direct control over most nondepository financial institutions and (2) the velocity of money will generally increase, perhaps unpredictably, when additional substitutes for conventionally defined money, such as foreign deposits, become available.

An additional problem that complicates monetary control is the increasing globalization of commerce and finance. For instance, dollar-denominated deposits that are liabilities of European banks (Eurodollars) are not subject to either U.S. or foreign reserve requirements. Furthermore, a multinational firm can hold yen-denominated deposits in Japanese banks, yet hedge deposits in the futures or forward currency markets so that those deposits can be converted to dollars without loss if the firm needs to spend them on goods produced in the United States. Thus, in some respects, the global money supply is becoming more important to monitor than the domestic money supply if one wants to explain overall economic activity. Nonetheless, the domestic money supply has a large effect on domestic price expectations and price levels; thus, central banks must be concerned with its growth.

If a central bank cannot readily control the growth of its domestic money supply by changing reserve requirements, it may have to follow the Bank of England and try to control money growth by changing interest rates. Higher interest rates make people economize on their cash holdings and thus reduce growth in the demand for money, all else being equal.

Controlling Velocity

Controlling the money supply per se is not sufficient to control the level of national income. If the velocity of money changes capriciously, the linkage between money and income will be loose and the effects of monetary policy will be more problematic.

An important factor that has influenced velocity in recent years is credit card debt, which allows the velocity of money to increase. Because of credit cards, people can hold less cash relative to their income. Theories of the demand for money balances often assume that individuals hold money to meet precautionary and transactions needs. Money balance holdings allow people to (1) cope with mismatches in their flows of receipts (income) and expenditures without incurring substantial transaction costs, and (2) take advantage of unexpected investment opportunities that may arise. If greater amounts of money are held for such purposes (at any given level of income), the velocity of money will be reduced. If less money needs to be held, velocity will rise. Credit card lines reduce demand for both precautionary and transactions money. This is illustrated in Exhibits 23–7 and 23–8.

Credit card lines can reduce precautionary money demands because consumers can borrow on their credit lines in an emergency. Thus, in our example, we assume that a

---

Exhibit 23–7   **Money Balance Holdings of a Consumer Who Spends $2,000 Evenly from Payday to Payday**

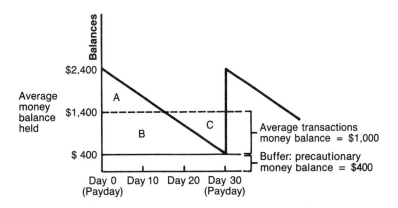

At the beginning of the month, the consumer holds $2,400 ($400 in precautionary balances and $2,000 from his or her last paycheck). As the $2,000 is spent evenly during the month, the consumer's transactions balances fall continuously from $2,000 to zero and averages $1,000. Over the course of the month, total balances (transactions plus precautionary balances of $400) average $1,400. Note that balances over $1,400 held on days when more than $1,400 was held (Area A) exactly equal the amount by which balances fell short of $1,400 (Area C) on the remaining days. Thus average total balances equal $1,400.

Exhibit 23–8

Credit Card and Money Balances Held by a Consumer Who Charges All Purchases and Repays Credit Card Debt the Day after Payday

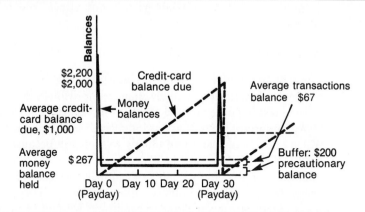

When a consumer holds a credit card, he or she can hold a lower precautionary balance because credit can be obtained as needed to finance an unexpected expenditure. Thus daily precautionary balances fall from $400 (in Exhibit 23-7) to $200 in this exhibit. In addition, although the consumer spends at the same rate as before ($2,000 per month), this time he or she does so by running up credit card debt. Then when he or she receives $2,000 in income at the end of the month, that debt is repaid. Thus the consumer's average transactions balance of $2,000 for one day is only $2,000/30, or $67 per day. As a result, the consumer's total money balances average only $267 per day, even though he or she still earns and spends as much as before.

credit card holder wishes to hold only $200 in precautionary balances whereas a person without a credit card will have a $400 precautionary demand for money.

In addition, the cardholder will have a lower transactions demand for money. If we assume that an individual has an income of $2,000 per month, and spends it all evenly during the month, his or her transactions money balances will fall from $2,000 to zero; thus that individual's daily average holdings of money for transactions will be $1,000 (half the maximum balance), as shown in Exhibit 23-7. It that individual has a credit card, however, he or she can slowly build up credit card debt throughout the month and repay it after receiving a paycheck (as in Exhibit 23-8). If we assume payment of credit card debt the next day, the person will hold $2,000 in transactions balances for one day, and zero transactions balances for the remaining days in the month. Thus daily average transactions balance holdings will be $2,000/30, or $67.

These examples show that an individual with a credit card can hold substantially lower money balances than someone without a card ($267 versus $1,400 in our example). Because income and expenditures remain the same in either case, the velocity of money will increased when money balances fall. Hence consumer use of credit cards and their related credit lines can increase the velocity of money.

At the beginning of 1980, outstanding credit card debt was small relative to the money stock ($60 + billion versus $390 billion for M1). However, a potential existed for increased consumer use of credit card lines—as well as accompanying uncontrollable increases in velocity. This could complicate monetary policy greatly. Consequently, from March to July 1980, the Federal Reserve temporarily imposed a 15 percent "special deposit" reserve requirement on any growth in credit card debt so that such debt would not expand uncontrollably at a time when the Fed wanted to reduce the money supply.

In the long run, the existence of unregulated value-exchange systems for credit card debt and consumer assets makes it very difficult for the Fed to control the economy by controlling monetary aggregates.

The Pricing and Provision of Federal Reserve Services

The Federal Reserve played an important role in the check payments system after it started to clear checks free of charge for member banks in 1918. In 1980, however, the DIDMCA required the Fed to start charging for its services in 1981. It was supposed to charge enough to cover both the incremental cost of providing the service and an allowance for overhead expenses and capital costs. When the Fed started charging for check clearing, the demand for its services fell sharply. It then cut prices on some services to retain its market share and, by so doing, incurred the wrath of private banks that offered similar services.

An argument can be made, however, that the Fed should try to maintain a position in the field of payments services. Only the Fed can guarantee payments transactions because only it can create reserves, if necessary, to honor its commitments. Thus, if a critical breakdown in a computer or other payments-processing service occurred, the Fed could give credit to the party that deposited checks before debiting the accounts of the parties on which the checks were drawn. However, if there were a failure in the private payment system, severe problems could arise. If one bank were unable to receive payment on the checks it deposited with a local clearinghouse, it could not honor payments drawn on its accounts, and the process could snowball if there were not a federal clearing system to supplement private check-clearing networks. As we have seen, the importance of Fed payment guarantees was proven in 1985 when the Bank of New York's computer failed.

Automated clearinghouse (ACH) services are also controversial. As a general rule, because their overhead costs in programming and computers are large, ACH's average costs fall as their volume expands. Thus, if the Fed operates the largest-scale ACH and EFT network, it may well become the lowest-cost producer. If it prices its services low, it may prevent competition from developing. Then the Fed itself may not feel the goad of competition to ensure that it produces its services in the most cost efficient manner.

Rate Ceilings

Deposit Rate Ceilings

Politicians often are tempted to enact rate ceilings. Shortsighted borrowers think that they can pay lower interest if rates are restricted. Thus many states have enacted rate ceilings on consumer and mortgage loans, and, in 1966, the federal government enacted Regulation Q restrictions on savings institutions, at their request, to hold down their costs of obtaining deposits. Previously, Regulation Q had imposed ceilings on banks' savings and time deposit rates from 1933 on. The Regulation Q restrictions were intended to prevent financial institutions from engaging in intense competition and to reduce their costs of funds. Over time, however, the rate ceilings (1) induced disintermediation as people took their money out of financial intermediaries to earn a higher return in money market mutual funds and T-bills; (2) encouraged "free" gifts and excessive "brick and mortar" expansion as depository institutions offered payments in goods and convenience in lieu of interest payments; and (3) brought about the development of numerous money substitutes, including NOW accounts, CDs, repurchase agreements, Eurodollars, and money market mutual fund liabilities. Eventually, deposit rate ceilings were seen to cause more trouble than they were worth, and Congress mandated that they be phased out between 1980 and 1986. Even before that time expired, depository institutions were authorized to issue new checkable deposits that were not subject to rate ceilings on higher balances.

Loan Rate Ceilings

Financial institutions are subject to a number of restrictions on the rates that they can charge on their loans. Rate ceilings are expected to protect consumers from paying high rates for credit. However, statistical studies show that, in fact, competition determines loan rates. In competitive markets, loan rates are often below rate ceilings. Furthermore, when ceilings are excessively low, as in Arkansas, where they were set at 10 percent for many years, market adjustments occur. In particular, Arkansas retailers charged higher prices for goods sold on credit (to compensate for losses incurred on their credit operations) and continued to make credit available, even to risky borrowers. Similar results occurred in Washington, DC, when it had an 8 percent rate ceiling. Thus, consumers seem to substitute goods-related credit (by buying higher-priced goods) for cash credit when rate ceilings are restrictive.

Summary

In this chapter we discuss major issues relating to new developments for and regulation of financial institutions. Technological developments in computer and communications technology have made many forms of value exchange possible. New financial instruments have been developed, and traditional regulatory structures have been avoided. EFT systems can transfer funds and information at lower costs than paper check systems. Automatic clearinghouses (ACHs) are at the heart of any EFT system. They can handle automatic deposits of payrolls, preauthorized bill payments, GIRO or bill-check transfers, and point-of-sale transactions using credit cards, debit cards, or checks. Check truncation schemes or their equivalents are necessary to make point-of-sale systems work efficiently.

The new technologies have led to the development of automated teller networks and home-banking systems. They have also changed the face of competition in the consumer financial markets. As a general rule, the most heavily regulated institutions have not fared well in competition with new unregulated institutions. Rather than develop ever-ascending layers of regulation, Congress has abolished rate ceilings and elected to deregulate the financial markets as much as possible.

Deregulation may have weakened the deposit insurance system, and because more financial institutions will fail in a deregulated world, premiums must be adjusted to cover higher risks. Both revisions in deposit insurance premiums and capital requirements based on risk have been proposed to reduce failures and to increase deposit insurance funds' ability to absorb losses. In addition, reduced federal insurance coverage has been proposed so that financial institutions will have to obtain supplementary "insurance" coverage from private insurance firms or the capital markets. Most state-supported private insurance companies closed in 1985 and 1986, however, because private insurers cannot tap the U.S. Treasury for money.

Although public regulation may lead to overregulation, it has been considered necessary because of the high leverage of most financial institutions and the essential services they provide. Nonetheless, public insurance may have created a moral hazard in that it has induced the nation's largest banks and thrift institutions to take more risk than they otherwise would, in part by selling their financial guarantees to others. If so, the very existence of federal insurance may be somewhat self-defeating. Furthermore, federal insurance may be redundant to some degree, as the financial markets excel in assessing the relative riskiness of different securities and liabilities. Perhaps the payments system would work more efficiently if most financial institutions' liabilities were uninsured—and thus had to be issued in the financial markets at their risk-adjusted rates—while the government guaranteed only that all daily payments made by qualifying institutions would be honored.

Several other regulatory issues also exist. How should the Fed define the money supply, and how can it control it? Should the Fed protect the payments mechanism by guaranteeing payments whenever necessary to prevent a potential financial crisis? Finally, given that deposit rate ceilings have been disruptive and have been phased out, is there any justification for the continuation of loan rate ceilings, which are evaded anyway?

Evolving technology has created more questions than answers. Furthermore, when answers are found, the technology will continue to evolve, and new questions will arise. That is what makes the study of financial institutions, markets, and money a challenging and interesting exercise.

Questions

1. Why do financial institutions and their regulators have differing views on how much capital the institutions should hold? Why have the regulators proposed risk-based capital requirements? Why is it difficult to price risk-based deposit insurance properly?

2. What are the pros and cons of restricting deposit rates in order to prevent financial institution failures?

3. What are the pros and cons of public examination versus private examination of financial institutions?

4. What services can be obtained through home-banking networks? Do you think they will be very popular? Why or why not?

5. What is the difference between debit and credit transfers through automated clearinghouses? Give examples of each type of transfer.

6. What are the advantages and disadvantages of EFT from the consumer's viewpoint? From a financial institution's viewpoint?

7. How has regulation of depository institutions helped new types of financial institutions grow and offer new services?

8. Why is it important that the Fed provide liquidity to the economy in a crisis, even if it indirectly provides liquidity to uninsured institutions?

9. What are the pros and cons of federal provision of deposit insurance? How should it be priced? What alternatives have been proposed?

10. How have new technological and international developments made it difficult for the Fed to control the economy by controlling the money supply?

Selected References

Benston, George J. "Deposit Insurance and Bank Failures." *Economic Review*. Federal Reserve Bank of Atlanta, March 1983, pp. 4–17.

This piece does an excellent job of describing the history and functions of deposit insurance. It also points out the limitations of federal insurance and makes a number of reform proposals.

Benston, George J., ed. *Financial Services: The Changing Institutions and Government Policy*. Englewood Cliffs, NJ: Prentice-Hall, 64th American Assembly, 1983.

Contains numerous insightful papers on current financial issues. The separate chapters are highly readable and cover major issues applicable to the regulation of financial institutions and markets.

Blair, Christine E., and Gary S. Fissel. "A Framework for Analyzing Deposit Insurance Pricing." *FDIC Banking Review* 4 (Fall 1991), pp. 25–38.

This article notes the complexities associated with determining depository institution risk and the problems associated with moving toward risk-based deposit insurance premiums.

Corrigan, E. Gerald. "Financial Market Structure: A Longer View." Federal Reserve Bank of New York, *1986 Annual Report*, June 1987.

Reviews the rapid growth of electronic payments mechanisms, the growing importance of nonbank institutions and international institutions to our domestic financial system, and the present system of regulation. Notes that much of the payment system is slipping beyond regulatory control and that the risks in the financial system are not fully understood. Therefore, Corrigan proposes far-ranging changes in the structure of the financial industry and its regulation, with the most intense regulation being reserved for only those institutions that are major participants in the payments system.

Federal Reserve Bank of Atlanta. "Special Issue: The Revolution in Retail Payments." *Economic Review*, July–August 1984.

This issue reports on papers presented by a panel of experts. The papers consider the economics and probable pricing schemes for POS and ATM systems, the development and experiences of existing systems, home banking, and the probable role of banks in the payments systems of the future.

Felgran, Stephen D. "From ATM to POS Networks: Branching, Access, and Pricing." *New England Economic Review*. Federal Reserve Bank of Boston, May–June 1985, pp. 44–62.

Discusses recent court decisions that let stand regulatory interpretations that ATM systems do not constitute branch bank networks. Also notes that ATM systems are consolidating on both a regional and a nationwide basis to obtain economies of scale. Advocates that prices for ATM and POS use be set in line with low expected long-run costs, rather than with high actual short-run costs, so that the networks can build transactions volume and take advantage of economies of scale.

Flannery, Mark J., and Aris A. Protopapdakias. "Risk-Sensitive Deposit Insurance Premiums: Some Practical Issues." *Business Review*. Federal Reserve Bank of Philadelphia, September–October 1984, pp. 3–10.

This article investigates the feasibility of risk-based deposit insurance premiums and concludes that such premiums would save few resources. As an alternative, it suggests that regulators make financial institutions' shareholders and liability holders bear more risk (by requiring higher capital ratios and insuring only those liabilities necessary to protect the integrity of the payments system). The authors support the FDIC's use of "purchase and partial payout" procedures in which depositors would be subject to possible losses on account balances in excess of $100,000. They also suggest that the $100,000 limit be lowered to encourage more depositors to analyze the riskiness of the institutions in which they place their money.

French, George F. "Early Corrective Action for Troubled Banks." *FDIC Banking Review* **4 (Fall 1991), pp. 1–12.**
Explains ways in which the FDIC liquidates failed banks and the costs to the FDIC of various options. Also, considers the pro and con arguments related to "early closure" proposals.

Gilbert, R. Alton. "Supervision of Undercapitalized Banks: Is There a Case for Change?" *Review.* **Federal Reserve Bank of St Louis, May/June 1991, pp 16–30.**
In this paper, Gilbert analyzes whether the capital restoration rules proposed by the 1991 FDICIA would have had a beneficial effect on banks that were "undercapitalized" in the past. He finds no significant difference in survival rates for undercapitalized banks that either did or did not grow slowly, restrict dividend payouts, or make more insider loans. Thus his findings suggest that the FDICIA capital restoration requirements might have less of a beneficial impact for preventing bank failure than desired.

Grandstaff, Mary G., and Charles J. Smaistria. "A Primer on Electronic Funds Transfer." *Business Review.* **Federal Reserve Bank of Dallas, September 1976, pp. 7–14.**
This paper does an excellent job of explaining how bank wire systems, point-of-sale systems, automated clearinghouses, and other electronic funds transfer systems work.

Haberman, Gary. "Capital Requirements of Commercial and Investment Banks: Contrasts in Regulation." *Quarterly Review.* **Federal Reserve Bank of New York, Autumn 1987, pp. 1–9.**
Explains the new risk-based capital requirements for banks. Contrasts those requirements with capital requirements for securities firms (investment banks). This comparison is appropriate, because with the growing securitization of traditional bank loans, competition between commercial banks and investment banks has become more intense, so differential capital requirements can help determine market shares.

Hetzel, Robert L. "Too Big To Fail: Origins, Consequences, and Outlook." *Economic Review.* **Federal Reserve Bank of Richmond November–December 1991, pp. 3–15.**
This article notes development of the de facto "too big to fail" policy of bank regulators and the adverse effect that policy had on risk-taking by large banks. This led to increased instability in the U.S. banking system that may or may not be rectified by the 1991 FDICIA.

Mengle, David L. "Daylight Overdrafts and Payments System Risks." *Economic Review.* **Federal Reserve Bank of Richmond, May–June 1985, pp. 14–27.**
Describes the process by which funds transfers are made on each of the major (Fed or private) payments-transfer systems. Also considers the problems and risks posed by daylight overdrafts and suggests that such problems could be reduced by establishing limits on allowable overdrafts, by developing an intraday Fed Funds credit market, by altering payments pricing mechanisms, or by other means.

Mitchell, George W., and Raymond F. Hodgdon. "Federal Reserve and the Payments System." *Federal Reserve Bulletin,* **February 1981, pp. 109–116.**
Describes how electronic payments systems work and how the Fed plans to upgrade them in the future.

Morris, Charles S., and Gordon H. Sellon, Jr. "Market Value Accounting for Banks: Pros and Cons." *Economic Review.* **Federal Reserve Bank of Kansas City, March–April 1991, pp. 5–20.**

This paper lays out the pros and cons of market-value accounting. Arguments against market-value accounting are that it would be costly to implement fully, while partial implementation may give a misleading picture of bank risk and increase reported earnings volatility. Arguments for market-value accounting are that it would present a more accurate picture of depository institutions' capital positions and risk exposures, and prevent "gains trading" (where institutions sell securities with gains and hold securities with losses until maturity, thereby giving a false picture of profits).

Radechi, Lawrence J., and Vincent Reinhart. "The Globalization of Financial Markets and the Effectiveness of Monetary Policy Instruments." *Quarterly Review.* **Federal Reserve Bank of New York, Autumn 1988, pp. 19–27.**

This article notes that domestic monetary policy may be harder to execute with certainty because of the globalization of world financial markets and the ease with which money can flow between countries. So far, however, it finds that domestic monetary policy instruments can still affect domestic interest rates in the desired manner.

Short, Eugenie D. "FDIC Settlement Practices and the Size of Failed Banks." *Economic Review.* **Federal Reserve Bank of Dallas, March 1985, pp. 12–20.**

This interesting article points out that the FDIC is more likely to settle large bank failures than small bank failures with various bailout arrangements or with purchase and assumption (P&A) transactions that protect all depositors' interests regardless of the size of their deposits. As a result, large banks have been able to take more risk, and large bank failures have increased relative to small bank failures since 1972.

CONTEMPORARY ISSUES AFFECTING FINANCIAL MARKETS

24

IN AN ARTICLE TITLED "BONDS, not banks," *The Economist* magazine for May 23, 1992, discussed the problems caused for banks and debt securities by the collapse of the Olympia and York real estate empire and the overblown Japanese real estate market and concluded, "If banks, as traditionally conceived, measure risk more expensively and less accurately than markets, it may soon be time to ask: who needs them?" In short, *The Economist* was suggesting that many of the functions performed by banks might better be performed by financial markets per se. Even if banks are not replaced by financial markets—and it is unlikely that they will be—it is already clear that banks and other depository institution operations are becoming more closely linked to the financial markets. Securitization and the sale of loan interests in the financial markets are becoming increasingly important as a source of liquidity and as a way for financial institutions to avoid risk-based capital requirements. Also, financial market operations provide an important source of fee income and trading income for commercial banks. For instance, recall from the People and Events in Chapter 12 that Bankers Trust's key foreign exchange trader made over $300 million for the bank in only one year. In addition, banks' holdings of futures, swaps, options, swaptions, and other related "derivative" securities—which "derive" their value from underlying movements in interest rates, exchange rates, and underlying asset prices —have exploded during the past several years. At the end of 1986, banks held approximately $0.5 trillion in over-the-counter derivative securities and $0.6 trillion in exchange-traded derivative securities. By the end of 1991, banks held $3.5 trillion in exchange-traded derivative securities and close to $4.5 trillion in over-the-counter derivative securities—such as swaps, options, forwards, and futures contracts.

Because of the rapidly growing importance of financial markets for banks and other depository institutions, this chapter describes the various ways in which financial markets function and the key issues related to their growth and regulation. The structure of financial markets is discussed first. Then, the key role played by information is described, because many regulatory initiatives relate to the open and fair disclosure of all pertinent information in order to promote market efficiency. Many regulatory issues relate to full information disclosure, information access, and insider information trading (which is generally prohibited, but is hard to define). Other regulatory initiatives relate to the question of whether market prices should be subject to price limits, or whether market traders should be subject to margin or capital requirements, and, if so, how those requirements should be determined, monitored, and enforced.

Financial Market Types and Structures

Many types of financial markets have developed and there are pros and cons associated with each. This section describes several of the major types of financial markets and mentions their strengths and limitations.

The London Gold Fix: A Walrasian Market

The London gold market is the closest market, in operation, to the theoretical market behavior described in economics textbooks. The market price for gold is established in the morning and afternoon by a consortium of dealers who consult with their customers. First, the gold dealers pick a tentative price, P_1, and ask their customers how much gold they would like to buy or sell at that price. They then tally buy and sell orders to see if the quantity purchased would equal the quantity sold at that price. If so, they "fix" the price at P_1 and execute their customers' orders. However, if the quantity offered for sale at P_1 is not equal to the quantity demanded, the dealers will check back with one another and try another tentative price, P_2. It that price still does not clear the market by equating the quantity supplied to the quantity demanded (for instance, in Exhibit 24–1, we assume that P_2 is too high so there will be an excess supply of gold at that price), another price will be tried. Usually because the gold dealers are experienced and also can offset minor imbalances by changing their gold inventories, the gold-fix price will converge to an equilibrium price (P_e) quite quickly. In Exhibit 24–1 we assume the third gold price, P_3, will be an equilibrium price, (P_e), where the quantity of gold demanded equals the quantity supplied. Thus that price will be 'fixed" and all gold will be traded at that price to clear the gold market at that time.

The gold-fix market most closely matches the supply and demand markets of economic textbooks where a "Walrasian auctioneer" tries different prices until the equilibrium market clearing price is found and all trades take place without any excess supply or demand.

Financial Markets in General

Most markets, however, do not clear in a one-time (static) manner, like a market in an economics textbook, and most do not trade only a few times a day, like the London gold-fix market. In particular, most financial markets are "continuous auction" markets in which trades occur continuously throughout each daily trading period and traders try to get the best available price at the time they trade. Prices in such markets fluctuate over time as people constantly reassess supply and demand conditions. For instance, the chart in Chapter 23's People and Events shows that municipal bond futures prices not only vary greatly from day to day, but also may vary widely from their highs to their lows on an intraday basis, as a continuous auction is conducted on the floor of the futures exchange. Trades in financial markets may be conducted either through organized exchanges or through *over-the-counter* networks of dealers, who

Exhibit 24–1   **Price and Quantity Determination in the Gold-Fix Market**

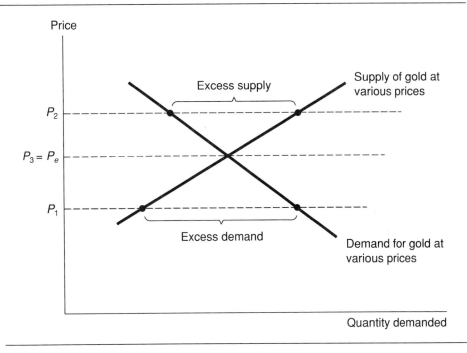

may be linked by telephone or computer networks. Increasingly, as the cost of communications and computer power has fallen, over-the-counter markets have initiated automated trading capabilities and longer trading periods in an attempt to take business from the exchanges. We discuss important variants of financial markets in turn.

Exchanges: The New York, American, and Philadelphia Stock Exchanges

The major U.S. stock exchanges use a "specialist" system to conduct a continuous auction market. Companies can get their stocks listed on an exchange if they meet exchange standards regarding company size, number of shares of stock outstanding, number of stockholders, required information disclosures, and stock voting requirements. Listed companies also must be willing to pay the required annual fee for an exchange listing and be formally approved for listing on the exchange. Exchange "listings" are often valuable because the exchange assures companies that an orderly and liquid market will exist for their stock and listed stocks are highly visible to the investment community. As a result, many companies' stocks appreciate in value when they apply for and receive an exchange listing.

One advantage of an exchange listing is that each stock is assigned to a specialist who promises to make an orderly market in the stock—with continuously listed bid and ask prices for the stocks (unless the specialist applies for and receives permission to conduct a "trading halt" because of order imbalances that cannot be quickly matched, pending news, and so on). The specialist also must make sure that the bid and ask prices are reasonably close together. If not, the specialist must enter his or her own order to ensure that the bid and ask prices will be reasonably close. In addition, the specialist is supposed to prevent large price jumps from occurring during the ordinary course of trading. In other words, the specialist's job is to keep the market "orderly," even if that means the specialist must intervene in the market by personally buying or selling stocks.

Because the specialist may have to buy or sell stocks at prices no one else is currently willing to bid or offer, the specialist potentially can take a loss from activities designed to keep an orderly market. Such potential losses must be offset by potential gains, or no one would perform the job.

One potential gain for a specialist is profits from trading at the bid-ask spread. If, in the normal course of trading, the specialist is able to buy at his or her bid and sell at a higher ask price, the specialist will be able to make trading profits from performing his or her role as a "market maker."

In addition, the specialist has an information advantage relative to other traders because the specialist keeps an order "book" containing unfilled orders. By observing a buildup of buy orders at prices below the current market price, the specialist may discern that buying interest in the stock is increasing. Thus the specialist may bid higher to accumulate stock for his or her account in the expectation that some of the potential buyers listed in the order book may get impatient and raise their bids, thereby buying the stock back from the specialist at a higher price. Similarly, a specialist may decide to sell a stock more aggressively if he or she observes sell orders accumulating in the order book at prices above the market. Thus the specialist may be able to earn trading profits by taking advantage of information recorded in the order book.

Specialists make markets in stocks listed on most of the major stock exchanges in the United States. They also make markets for options listed on the New York, American, and Philadelphia options exchanges.

Options Markets and their "Market Makers"

Individuals can trade at a price better than the specialist's bid or ask prices for a stock listed on an exchange by putting in "limit orders" to buy at a higher price than the specialists bid price or sell at a lower price than for the specialists ask price. Thus individuals may also trade at the specialist's post for a stock. An individual who regularly trades to take advantage of disparities in bid and ask prices effectively serves as a "market maker" in that stock. On the Chicago Board Options Exchange, CBOE, the market maker function is well defined as people who buy at their bid price or sell at their ask price for their own account. If a person serves as a market maker on the CBOE or Pacific Coast Exchanges, he or she cannot broker trades for others on the same day.

Market-making members of the exchange or their brokers gather at the trading post and compete to buy at the best bid or sell at the best ask price. When an order comes to the floor, the trading crowd competes to take the other side of the order and the broker executing the order tries to get the best price possible. If a limit order cannot be executed right away—for instance, if a buy order's bid price is lower than the lowest ask price offered by anyone in the trading crowd—it is entered in the order book. The order book is kept by "designated order book officials" for each option, who, unlike specialists, do not trade for their own accounts. The orders in the order book are filled when they are equal to or better than any offer made by a member of the trading crowd. For instance, if a member of the trading crowd bids higher than the best order in the order book, that member's order will be filled. However, if he or she bids the same price (or a lower price), the order in the order book will be filled when someone is willing to sell at the designated price. Orders in the order book will be given 'time priority" when filled—which means that the first limit order posted in the book at a particular price will be filled first. Small market orders will be filled automatically in the order they are received by rotation among market makers.

The Chicago Board Options Exchange, then, is basically an "open-outcry, continuous-auction market with an order book." "Open outcry" refers to the fact that market makers or traders' brokers continually call out or signal their best bid and offer prices to other members of the trading crowd at the option post. "Continuous-auction" refers to the fact that trades can take place continuously. "Order book" refers to the fact that limit orders are kept in the order book by order book officials who do not trade for their own accounts, rather than by specialists, who do trade for their own accounts. Because there are multiple market makers and brokers competing for business in open-outcry markets, they are typically very noisy and agitated, as numerous people compete to buy and sell simultaneously. Once a trade is agreed upon, both the buyer and seller fill out a trading card, time stamp the card, and drop it into a hopper for processing. Exchange rules require that all trades be recorded promptly so prices and quantities can be determined and matched up by the exchange's computers. To facilitate prompt price disclosure, exchanges also employ price reporters to enter prices of current trades into electronic reporting systems.

The Pacific Options Exchange uses a trading system with designated order book officials similar to the Chicago Board Options Exchange. However, options trading at the New York, American, and Philadelphia Stock Exchanges uses specialists to keep the order book for options. Nonetheless, members of the trading crowd that surround the specialist's post on those exchanges may also serve as market makers by trading for their own account at prices better than prices offered by the specialists.

Financial Futures Exchanges

The major stock-index interest rate and currency futures contracts are traded on futures exchanges that use "open-outcry, continuous-auction markets." Those markets are similar to the Chicago Board Options Exchange market in that multiple market makers and brokers meet in a trading pit and continuously negotiate trades at the best possible price. However, there is no order book and, therefore, there is no time priority accorded to orders. Thus, there is no guarantee that the first limit order entered at a particular price will be executed at that price, if it is executed at all. A price might be touched, another order executed, and then the market price might move away again. Furthermore, in "fast market" conditions, when trading is hectic (as it often can be in the Treasury bond futures pit, with 800 people pushing and shoving, yelling and screaming, and trying to make trades all at once), brokers may be "not held" to get the best possible price, as it may not be possible for a broker on one side of an active pit to tell what the best price is that is being bid or offered elsewhere in the pit. Nonetheless, because of the extensive competition among traders, bid-ask spreads tend to be quite small in the most actively traded futures markets. (See Exhibit 24–2 for a listing of the most active financial futures and options exchanges.)

Financial Futures Automated Trading

The intensity of open-outcry markets is exhausting, as traders cannot maintain the open-outcry pace in an active market for long. However, because the same financial instruments, such as Eurodollars, currency contracts, and U.S. Treasury bonds, are now widely traded around the world, it is highly desirable that financial futures markets be available to accommodate traders in other countries. At first, futures exchanges tried to do so by trading similar contracts around the world—for instance similar Eurodollar futures contracts were traded in Singapore (on the SIMEX exchange) in London (on the LIFFE exchange) and in Chicago (on the Chicago Mercantile Exchange—CME) at different times of the day. Similar U.S. Treasury

---

Exhibit 24–2

Trading Volume for International Exchanges' Combined Futures and Options Contracts in 1991 (millions of contracts)

Rank in 1991	Exchange*	Country	Volume		% Change
			1990	1991	
1	CBOT	U.S.	154.23	139.44	− 9.6
2	CME	U.S.	102.99	108.13	+ 5.0
3	CBOE	U.S.	80.94	75.86	− 6.3
4	LIFFE	U.K.	34.17	44.17	+ 29.3
5	NYMEX	U.S.	42.46	40.78	− 4.0
6	MATIF	France	28.06	37.13	+ 32.4
7	OSE	Japan	22.78	33.48	+ 47.0
8	BM&F	Brazil	15.85	27.39	+ 72.8
9	LME	U.K.	13.35	16.94	+ 26.9
10	ToSE	Japan	21.62	16.60	− 23.3
11	TIFFE	Japan	14.45	15.15	+ 4.9
12	COMEX	U.S.	18.29	15.12	− 17.3
13	TOCOM	Japan	14.84	14.95	+ 0.8
14	SFE	Australia	11.56	12.50	+ 8.2
15	PHLX	U.S.	10.34	11.28	+ 9.1

Note: In general U.S. exchanges are the largest, but foreign exchanges are the most rapidly growing.
*Exchanges: 1. Chicago Board of Trade, 2. Chicago Mercantile Exchange, 3. Chicago Board Options Exchange, 4. London International Financial Futures Exchange, 5. New York Mercantile Exchange, 6. Marché à Terme International de France, 7. Osaka Securities Exchange, 8. Bolsa de Mercadorios & Futuros, 9. London Metal Exchange, 10. Tokyo Stock Exchange, 11. Tokyo International Financial Futures Exchange, 12. Commodity Exchange, New York, 13. Tokyo Commodity Exchange, 14. Sidney Futures Exchange, 15. Philadelphia Stock Exchange.

Source: Futures, March 1992, pp. 52–53.

bond futures contracts were traded in London (on LIFFE) and on the Chicago Board of Trade—CBOT). To capture trading from the Asian markets, the CBOT has an evening session for Treasury bond and note futures trading that coincides with the opening of the Japanese markets.

Nonetheless, trades made on different exchanges may involve settlement complications and risk if accounts are cross-matched across the world. Also, evening trading after a long day is tiring. Thus the major Chicago futures exchanges developed the "Globex" trading system with Reuters to conduct futures trading virtually on a 24-hour basis. (See Exhibit 24–3 for information on progress made toward 24-hour trading in various financial markets.)

Exhibit 24–3   **Forward, Futures, Currency, and Option Contracts Traded "Around the Clock"**

Type of Contracts	Where Traded
1. Foreign currency forward contracts	Banks and currency dealers
2. 3-month Eurodollar interest rate	CME-IMM (U.S.)
	SIMEX (Singapore)
	LIFFE (London)
3. U.S. dollar index futures and options	FINEX (U.S.)
4. British pound, deutsche mark, yen	CME-IMM (U.S.)
	SIMEX (Singapore)
	Manilla International Futures Exchange (Philippines)
	PHLX (U.S.)
5. U.S. Treasury bond	CBOT (U.S.)
	ToSE (Japan)
	LIFFE (London)
6. a. CME deutsche mark, Japanese yen and mark/yen contracts; CME 3-month Eurodollar rates contract; 90-day T-bill and one-month LIBOR futures and options contracts.	Globex
b. CBOT—2-year and 5-year Treasury notes futures and options contracts.	
c. MATIF—MATIF 10-year notional (French) bond futures and options; 7-year ECU (European Currency Unit), CAC40 (French stock index) futures, and 3-month PIBOR (Paris Interbank Borrowing Rate)	

Note: Many contracts are traded on virtually a 24-hour basis around the world. Forward currency contracts and specialized currency option contracts are available from most major banks on a continuous basis. Linkages between the CME's International Monetary Market (or IMM) and the SIMEX and LIFFE exchanges allow Eurodollar futures to be traded around the clock. Dollar index futures can be traded virtually around the clock on the Financial Instrument Exchange (FINEX) in New York; major standardized Foreign Currency Options contracts can be traded nearly continuously on the Philadelphia Stock Exchange (PHLX) options floor; and various currency futures contracts can be traded nearly continuously on different futures exchanges around the world.

The Globex system became available in mid-1992 for use with futures contracts listed on the CME and CBOT—particularly key currencies and U.S. Treasury notes. Other futures contracts, including French 'notional" bond contracts, ECU interest rate contracts, and French (CAC40) stock index contracts listed on the MATIF futures and options exchange in France, were to be offered by early 1993. In addition, futures contracts on other major U.S. futures exchanges may be offered in the future, but no firm schedule exists as of the writing of this book.

One problem with Globex's listing of other products appears to be that the Chicago futures exchanges have been reluctant to list competitors' products on a system that they developed at great cost. In particular, they hesitated to list the FINEX exchange's dollar index futures contract, the SIMEX exchange's Eurodollar futures contract, and the LIFFE exchange's U.S. Treasury bond contract. Regulators, however, may raise the issue of whether exchanges are purely private ventures or are like public utilities that should provide access to all.

The Globex exchange network is a harbinger of things to come. Using communications networks provided by Reuters and a sophisticated computer system, it allows exchange members with access to a terminal anywhere around the world to enter limit orders for futures contracts listed on the computer. The price limit orders are stored in the computer and executed *with time and price priority*, when buy and sell orders can be matched. In addition, market price orders will execute at the best possible prices available in the computer at the time the orders are entered.

Computer matching of limit orders seems so cheap and simple that one wonders why it has not been done sooner. Advocates of open-outcry markets say that it does not allow one to judge the intensity or source of supply or demand, like trading in a futures pit does. Thus, traders do not have as good a "feel" for why the market is moving. To quiet this question the computer will list the size of limit buy and sell orders for orders close to the current market price; thus traders can roughly judge the quantities available for trade at each price. It remains to be seen if traders will find such disclosure an adequate substitute for the trading instincts they develop in the futures pits. In previous computer-automated exchanges (such as the New Zealand Futures Exchange) trading activity has been light—possibly for that reason.

A second reason that automated trading systems have been slow to develop is that pit traders fear that they will lose business to the computers. Thus they have resisted computerization of their business. As a result, the Globex system has been set up to operate only at hours when the futures trading pits are closed. For instance, the Globex CME contracts on currency trade only from 6:00 p.m. to 6:00 a.m., and the CBOT Treasury bond and rate contracts trade on Globex only from 10:30 p.m. to 6:00 a.m. At other times, trading in those contracts will be conducted in the traditional open-outcry trading pits.

Over-the-Counter Markets

The majority of stocks, forward contracts, and swap contracts are not traded on organized exchanges, where there is a single best bid or ask price for a standardized product at one point in time. Instead they usually are traded by many dealers, each of whom may have a different bid and ask price and each of whom is usually located in a different place. Since the securities or contracts are negotiated individually between the dealer and the buyer or seller, and since dealers often have separate "shops," trading between customers and individual dealers is called "over-the-counter" trading.

The most infrequently traded securities in over-the-counter markets typically do not have dealers' bid and ask prices listed on computers. Instead, in the case of stocks, the bid and ask prices of each dealer that "makes a market" (by regularly generating bid and ask prices in the stock) are listed in the daily "pink sheets" distributed to people who wish to trade in those stocks. Information on each dealer's bid and ask quotes, name, location, and phone number are given in the pink sheets and trades are executed by phone. The National Association of Securities Dealers (NASD) regulates dealers on the over-the-counter market to ensure that trades will be completed as agreed and all regulations will be honored.

In addition to smaller or infrequently traded stocks, over-the-counter markets exist for bonds, foreign currencies, swaps, forward contracts, some option contracts, and many other items. The key element in an over-the-counter market is that various dealers quote bids and asks for the securities or contracts in question and agreements to trade are generally made over the phone.

In many over-the-counter markets, dealer quotes are carried on computers and posted on video screens so they can be seen by all traders in the market. Sometimes trades can be entered and executed automatically based on the information carried on the trading screen. In other cases, the dealers or brokers shown on the screen must be contacted directly by phone, Telex or other methods to execute trades. In still other cases, such as government bond trading, the quotes carried on the screen may be posted by "screen brokers" who post the best bids and offers that they have in their order books and execute orders at those prices without revealing the counterparties' names. The advantage of brokered trades rather than direct dealer trades is that the counterparty preserves anonymity and thus can trade without giving competitors clues that may reveal a trader's strategy or impending portfolio adjustments.

NASDAQ

The National Association of Securities Dealers Automated Quotation System (NAS-DAQ) is a computerized communications system that is available for posting quotes on the most actively traded stocks. Several levels of activity are available on the system, ranging from monitoring the best bid and ask prices for each stock, through monitoring all dealers bid and ask prices for each stock. to the placing of bid and ask quotes on the NASDAQ system. Dealers who place quotes on the system are bound to honor the quotes for a minimum number of shares. However, they are not bound to honor their quotes if a large order exceeds the minimum size that must be honored, or if they have changed their quote prior to receiving their order, or if they do not answer their phones.

After the stock market fell over 500 points on October 19, 1987, some people charged that the NASDAQ dealers did not answer their phones. However, at the same time, others charged that many specialists for exchange-traded stocks did not maintain orderly markets with tight bid-ask spreads. Thus, in crisis events, both types of markets have deficiencies. Nonetheless, the NYSE later disciplined specialists who did not keep orderly markets and NASDAQ tried to rely more heavily on automated trading.

NASDAQ's Small Order Execution System (SOES)

NASDAQ has organized a "small order execution system," called SOES, that allows people to monitor dealer quotes on actively traded stocks by using computers. People can execute small orders (up to 1,000 shares) automatically by using computerized buy and sell orders. The use of the SOES system has had some interesting consequences. Some people have used the system to detect minor differences in dealers' bid-ask quotes that can be profitably exploited if they quickly buy low and sell high to exploit the differences. The consequence is that stock dealers have to be more alert and strive to keep their quotes more closely in line with other dealers' quotes. They cannot go out for a long lunch and ignore the market or they may come back and find that the computer has made many unprofitable 1,000-share trades on their account. Thus dealers' quote disparities are likely to be reduced and dealer monitoring of the market in each stock is likely to be more intensive. Because of the greater risk and monitoring costs incurred by dealers, it is possible that they may widen their bid-ask spreads to reduce their risk of having "out-of-line" quotes that can be exploited by traders on the SOES system. Higher bid-ask spreads would also allow them to earn a higher income from their trading activities to pay for their increased monitoring costs.

Thus, there are some advantages and disadvantages to the SOES system, but it does appear to be a precursor to future computerized trading.

The London International Stock Exchange

The London International Stock Exchange (ISE) offers screen-based trading through its SEAQ international system. Market makers on the system post bid and ask prices for a wide variety of international stocks. The SEAQ system is similar to NASDAQ. It was started in 1985 and expanded after London's "Big Bang" (see People and Events). By 1991, it did over half of all trades in stocks of large French and Italian companies and a third of all trades in major German companies' shares. One reason for its popularity was that it had numerous market makers who provided firm price and quantity bid and ask quotes for each stock listed on the system. Thus it provided more liquidity (and also less regulation) for stock trading than many other countries' domestic exchanges.

The U.S. Third Market—Block Trading

Because large open orders sent directly to the floor of an exchange could cause large order imbalances on the buy or sell ride, and correspondingly large price movements, a "third market" has developed for stock trading in the United States, in addition to the exchange "first" market and over-the-counter ("second") market. The third market is conducted by 'upstairs traders" who arrange matches for large "block" transactions of 10,000 shares of more and then cross the orders on the exchange where the stocks are listed. The brokers for people buying or selling large amounts of stock discreetly inquire around until they find a closely matching order on the other side. If the match is not exact, the brokerage firm (usually a major investment bank) may take a temporary position for its own account to help insure that the orders are closely matched. Then the matched orders are taken to the floor of the exchange (usually the NYSE) and "crossed" at the preagreed price at the specialist's post. Because both the buy and sell orders are presented simultaneously, a large order imbalance does not develop and there usually is not a large price movement in the underlying stock. However, if an investment banker must take a large position to help insure the trade goes through, it may be willing to do so only if the trade is made at a price sufficiently far away from the current market price so it can subsequently unload its position at a profit. Thus large block trades are sometimes accompanied by relatively large price movements and other times they are not.

Computerized Markets

Many stock exchanges are computerizing at least a portion of their trading. In addition, additional automated exchange facilities are being developed. The New York Stock Exchange uses a "SuperDot" (Super Designated Order Turnaround System) that automatically routes market orders of up to 2,099 shares to a specialist's post for rapid execution. The system can handle orders of up to 99,999 shares, but specialists are not bound to execute those orders promptly. Most other major stock exchanges have also computerized a portion of their trading. The Toronto Stock Exchange has a "computer assisted trading system" called CATS that conducts electronic auctions for less-actively traded stocks if prices match up and displays the five best buy and sell orders along with the name of the broker who posts each order. The Paris Bourse (stock exchange) uses a system similar to CATS, called CAC, but it provides less continuous trading and less liquidity for French stocks than the London International Stock Exchange (ISE) dealer market. The London ISE operates similarly to the U.S.'s NASDAQ, but its automated quote display system is called SEAQ (stock exchange automated quotation system) and small orders of up to 5,000 shares can be executed automatically on its Stock Automated Exchange Facility.

The Tokyo stock exchange also uses an automated "computer assisted order routing and execution system" (called CORES) that is similar to Toronto's CATS. The exchange has personnel who monitor the trades arranged by the computer and approve the prices. They also let the computer generate trades automatically within limited prices ranges, and can suspend trading if necessary. Most of the less-actively traded stocks on the Tokyo exchange are traded on the CORES system.

In the United States, the Cincinnati Stock exchange has long used computerized matching of orders to allow trading in stocks. It functions as an over-the-counter market with competing market makers; it uses the "National Securities Trading System," which is a computerized order-matching system. However, the volume of transactions on the exchange is typically low relative to the volumes on the NYSE and the over-the-counter market. Reuter's Holdings, PLC runs a computerized order-matching system called "Instinet" that allows exchanges of stocks at prices better than those quoted on NASDAQ. In addition, the Madoff Investment Securities firm has developed a computerized brokerage service that allows large buy and sell orders in stocks to be posted and matched by a computer for a very low cost. Madoff Securities acts strictly as a broker and does not take a position to assist such trades. Nonetheless, because of the trades' anonymity and low cost, the system has become quite popular.

In general, the automated exchange and brokerage systems have not been as popular as floor trading for the most actively traded stocks because they do not involve market makers who continuously make a market in a stock or who take positions to assist traders. Also, their popularity may be limited for large traders because those people may wish to work through block-trade brokers who will "shop" the position discreetly and not disclose the exact size of the trade until necessary. Furthermore, some traders may want to preserve their anonymity or not post the full trade quantity as well as the price when making a bid or offer.

However, because of the cost savings offered by computerized brokerage transactions, their popularity has been growing rapidly. Thus many exchange-traded stocks can now be traded by computer. Most major stock exchanges now have computer assisted order routing systems like the New York Stock Exchange's SuperDot system or Toronto's CATS system to route small orders or orders in less-actively traded stocks directly to a computer or to a specialist's posts for automatic execution. As a result, computerized trading is now offered to the public by several brokerage firms that let their customers trade with their personal computers.

Computerized trading can be offered for much more than stocks. In the loosest arrangements, computerized "bulletin boards" have developed where people can post offers to buy or sell almost anything, at any price, or in any quantity. Such offers can be posted until a match is found or trading arrangements are made by phone. Interestingly, some of the first "commodity exchanges" developed in Russia as it moved toward a free market involved computerized bulletin board systems. The exchanges would receive fees calculated as a small percentage of the value of all exchanges made. In order to be prepared for future trading possibilities, the Chicago Board of Trade is also exploring computerized bulletin board systems. One advantage that an organized exchange can bring to the development of such a system is a "clearing corporation" that keeps the books and guarantees that all parties will honor their contracts and that good currency or credit will be transferred when the exchange of goods is completed.

Other Markets and Brokerage Systems

Foreign Exchange Markets

Foreign exchange trading has long been conducted by phone or Telex by interconnecting networks of foreign exchange traders and dealers—who usually are closely connected to commercial banks or investment banks. However, Reuters, an international news corporation, provides terminals on which current price information for foreign currencies can be observed. It has around 200,000 terminals worldwide on which it provides both price quotes and market-moving news.

Nonetheless, Reuters has not been content just to provide information. It also offers computer terminals through which dealers can execute currency trades with other system subscribers. That system accounted for 40 percent of the world's trade in spot currencies in 1990, according to the *The Economist* magazine. Furthermore, starting in 1989, Reuters introduced a system called "Dealing 2000" that let dealers enter orders into the Reuters system computer, which, in turn, would match them and execute them automatically. Since the transactions can also be cleared and settled automatically, it is possible that total costs of trading foreign currencies will be reduced by more than half by use of Reuters' or other computerized trading systems.

Bond Markets

Some bonds are traded on exchanges, such as the New York or American Bond Exchanges, like exchange-listed stocks. However, the volume of trading on the exchanges is relatively light, as generally only small transactions are posted on the exchange and large transactions are made over-the-counter through phone-linked dealer networks and brokerage communications systems.

U.S. government bonds are exclusively traded over-the-counter by government dealers. The key dealers in this network are about 40 firms (including most major banks) that have "primary dealer" status. These institutions are ones with which the Fed conducts its open-market transactions. Those dealers trade with other dealers and with each other. Because they often prefer to trade anonymously so others cannot figure out their trading position or strategies, they often trade through computerized brokerage networks, such as Delta Government Securities, that list bids and offers for various issues of government bonds and arrange trades anonymously.

Because bond brokers have access to valuable trading information, they are able to sell that information to news wire networks and make profits from that information. Since some of the major dealers believe that it is their trading that gives rise to the price data sold and reported to the markets, they have tried to establish their own brokerage system so they can capture that information and earn a return on it. However, nonmembers have been reluctant to trade on that system.

Because the government bond market participants can take advantage of the Fed's government securities wire transfer and funds transfer facilities, it has been slow to adopt fully computerized trading techniques. It does not need a clearing house to settle the financial side or physical side of transactions since its users can easily transfer securities or cash to one another over the Fed's wire system. This is particularly true because, as fiscal agent for the U.S. Treasury, the Fed keeps the books that record the ownership of government securities, and "book entry" ownership of securities can be easily transferred by the Fed. Also, the major government bond market participants are "clubby" in the sense that they want to protect their special privileges and access to information; thus they are reluctant to use another firm's computerized system that would automatically disclose valuable price and quantity information to the world without compensating them. Consequently, the government bond market is less fully automated than other markets, in the sense that the trading and transfer of securities' ownership are not fully integrated into one system.

When a new, fully computerized government securities brokerage firm, EJV Government Securities, started operations, it found that only a relatively small number of trades were arranged through the firm. Traditional dealers may have been reluctant to use the firm, even though it offered lower costs, because they would give up access to information to a nonclub member. As a result, EJV sold out to the

Chicago Board of Trade in the hopes that the popularity of the Chicago Board of Trade's contracts on U.S. Treasury bonds and notes, coupled with access to the Chicago Board of Trade Clearing Corporation to settle trades (by facilitating the transfer of securities and funds), would increase its business volume. However, it still remains to be seen whether this computerized brokerage system will attract a large volume of business. Because of computerized trading's cost advantage over phone trading and EJV's tie-in with the CBOT's clearing system, it may be able to do so. However, because the CBOT and EJV are not primary dealers in the government securities markets, the primary dealers in government bonds still may not use their facilities.

Issues Related to Financial Market Information Flows

Some of the most important issues in financial markets relate to the flow of information. Efficient markets require quick, cheap, and easily accessible information. If information costs are high, as they often are in real-estate markets or over-the-counter option markets because of the nonstandardized nature of products, markets will have a more difficult time ascertaining potential rates of return or risks. As a result, market values will be less precisely determined and more variable. In short, markets may be "inefficient" in determining appropriate asset prices if information is costly. However, if the value of assets is cheap and easy to discover, as is usually the case with exchange-listed stocks, market inefficiencies will be less. Furthermore, if inexpensive information is readily available, it will not be possible for some people to gain at the expense of others. Consequently, it pays to expend resources to improve the accuracy and timeliness of financial market information available through mechanisms as diverse as real estate brokers' "multiple-listing" services or bond brokers' computerized trading screens.

This section considers several aspects of information that shape markets and influence regulation, including inside information on a corporation's performance, disclosure of trading information, sales of information, and restrictions on information access. It will be seen that in some instances, market makers will prefer to trade in markets where regulators allow them to protect private information while, in general, the public interest might (or might not) be better served if all information were readily available.

Inside Corporate Information

Securities and Exchange Commission (SEC) regulations prohibit people with inside corporate knowledge from taking advantage of that information by trading stocks. All news relevant to the performance of a company is supposed to be released to the public *first*, before corporate insiders act on it. Otherwise, corporate insiders would have an unfair advantage. The insiders could buy stock before good news was released from people who did not realize that good news was forthcoming, and who would not have wanted to sell their stock if they had known. Similarly, insiders might sell stock to unwitting members of the public who might not have wanted to buy the stock had they known that bad news was about to be announced.

DID YOU KNOW ?

Solomon Brothers Rigged the Bond Market and Paid for It

One of the problems with Treasury bond auctions up to the early 1990s was that U.S. government bonds could be purchased at auction only by one of the 40 "primary dealers" in government bonds. This meant that many bonds might be purchased by only a few dealers. To prevent any one dealer from buying too many bonds, therefore, the U.S. Treasury stated that no one buyer could acquire more than 35 percent of a new bond issue.

However, Solomon Brothers, possibly the largest government bond dealer, evaded the regulation in substance on several occasions in the early 1990s. Solomon had customers buy bonds at the Treasury security auction and then immediately resell the bonds to Solomon. It was not even clear that all customers knew bonds had been temporarily purchased on their account.

At one auction of two-year Treasury notes in early 1991, Solomon or its associates controlled over 90 percent of the new issue of securities. This caused great problems for people who had sold those securities "short" (that is, before they owned them) on a "when-issued" basis before the auction. When the notes were issued, they had to purchase some, at any price, so they could deliver them to fulfill their short sale contracts. Solomon then "squeezed the shorts" by selling them the notes at an extraordinarily high price. Because they were short the notes, the "shorts" had to pay up to get them from Solomon. Thus, Solomon made a large amount of money on the squeeze.

Solomon had squeezed the market before, but never so outrageously. This time it made people mad. Those people complained and the U.S. Treasury and Fed investigated. They found that Solomon had abused the rules on numerous occasions.

Solomon lost its prestige as a premier bond trader. Its chairman and many of its top officers lost their jobs. The company had to bring in Warren Buffet (a famous investor with a large stake in Solomon preferred stock) to rescue it and refurbish its image. Nonetheless, in 1992, Solomon had to take a $290 million charge against its earnings to pay for its market manipulation and associated lawsuits. In addition, its primary dealer privileges were suspended for several months.

To prevent insider trading before news is released to the public, the SEC continuously monitors large transactions in stocks and options and requires that insiders file reports on their trading activities. If it finds evidence of unusual trading related to corporate insiders, their friends, or relatives, it generally will prosecute the people who tried to gain from inside information. The SEC has often filed suits against corporate officers or other insiders who traded before information was disclosed on mergers, profits, or other material facts. In addition, the SEC has prosecuted corporate workers who noted that unsold inventories were accumulating in their company and, consequently, bought put options on their company's stock, as well as employees of financial printing companies who disclosed information about, for example, potential mergers that they obtained while printing prospectuses and other sensitive corporate information.

However, an issue exists regarding how far the SEC should go in prosecuting people for using inside news. In one case the SEC successfully prosecuted a broker who paid the employee of a printing plant to tell him which stocks would be favorably reported upon in the next week's issue of *Business Week*. While *Business Week* had a right to be angry that information in its publication was leaked out early, their reporters did not generate any "inside" corporate information, but rather relied on information that was already publicly available when writing their articles. Thus, it appears that the SEC may be overzealous at times in pursuing people who profit from advance knowledge. Strictly speaking, the information is "inside" only if it comes from inside the corporation and was not previously released to the public. However in the *Business Week* case, the SEC decided that even a recommendation based on previously revealed corporate information was "inside" information because the *Business Week* recommendation was not previously known by the public. By extending "inside information" prosecutions to recommendations, an issue is raised as to where to draw the line. Must every newsletter with 100 subscribers guard against the prerelease of information, or only those publications with a million subscribers? Or a billion?

Stock Trading and Bond Trading Information

If full disclosure were made of stock trades, the exchange or dealer arranging the trade would release information on the price of the transaction, the quantity traded, the identity of the buyer, and the identity of the seller. However, many people like to trade anonymously in markets so other people cannot anticipate their future actions and take advantage of them.

Anonymous Trading.   The desire for anonymous trading has shown up in many ways in financial market structure. For instance, London's International Stock Exchange has been able to attract some program stock trading from New York because many traders who trade programs involving large "baskets" of stock do not want to have to report their activities to U.S. regulators or have other people know exactly what transactions they are undertaking. In 1991, when the NYSE extended its trading hours, it tried to lure U.S. traders back from London stock trading by providing an extended program trading session for an hour after the trading day ended. Trades made in that hour would not be individually reported. Only the total amount of shares traded would be reported at the end of the session. Thus, because of lax foreign rules, the NYSE entered into limited "competition in laxity" as well.

Prompt Disclosure Issue.   Another case where market traders have resisted full disclosure involves the disclosure of trade quantities. While the New York Stock Exchange prints volume and price data simultaneously, after Britain's 1986 Big Bang (in which financial markets were extensively deregulated—see People and Events), volume disclosure became an issue in Britain. After the Big Bang, both trade prices and volumes were disclosed for Britain's International Stock Exchange. However, many market makers disliked the prompt disclosure of quantity data. If a large trade was reported, they feared that other traders would see it and deduce that a market maker had absorbed at least part of a large block of stock that they would have to resell (if they had bought stock) or repurchase (if they had sold stock) in subsequent transactions. Consequently, other traders might pressure the market by trading in the same direction as the most recent large trade. Such trading might force a market maker who had absorbed part of the transaction in his or her own portfolio to cover the position at a loss. For instance, if a stock was trading at $12.50 per share and then 100,000 shares traded at $12, traders might deduce that a market maker was holding part of that 100,000 share block hoping to make a profit by selling at prices higher than $12. However, if the other traders sold the market down further by selling short at $12, they might force the market maker to eventually sell out of his or her position at a loss, say at $11.50, where the other traders could repurchase the shares they sold short and make a gain.

Because disclosure of large block-trade volumes might expose market makers to the risk of loss, market makers on the London exchange petitioned the exchange to let them disclose the volume of stocks traded after the close, or at least after a 90-minute delay, so others would be less likely to trade against them if they took a large position in a stock. They argued that the restrictions on full information flow would allow them to bid more sharply for large blocks of stock, as they would be less likely to realize a loss if other people did not know they were disposing of a block of securities before they finished their work. As a result of these petitions, data on volume traded are released only with a delay. The issue involved, of course, is the public's right to know all pertinent information instantaneously versus the need of market makers to maintain confidentiality regarding trade volumes if they are to execute large orders at a good price.

The Specialist's Information.   As previously noted, information in stock exchange specialists' books allow specialists to monitor order flows in stocks or bonds. Consequently, they can often trade to their personal advantage by offering better prices and trading in front of a buildup of buy or sell orders. Until 1987, specialists typically earned good returns on their invested capital, and some people thought their access to "book" information was unfair. However, others point out that specialists *must* also wager their own money to keep markets orderly. As a result, they may be forced to buy or sell when no one else wants to do so. In the October 1987 stock market crash, many specialists lost large amounts of money. Thus, specialists argue that any advantage they have from having primary access to their order books is offset by the fact that they may have to take substantial risks with their own capital to keep markets orderly. Furthermore, other exchange members can also see the "book."

Treasury Bond Market Information

There are approximately 40 "primary" dealers in the U.S. Treasury bond market who can deal directly with the Fed. These dealers frequently trade with one another. However, because they don't want others to know what they are doing (lest the others trade against them), they often prefer to trade anonymously, through government security brokers. Because the brokers, in turn, sell trade information, they can earn a profit by reporting trades to news services. Thus, the dealers would like to create their own brokerage network and trade through it so they could more easily capture their own trading data and the money others pay to obtain it. The desire to capture their own trading information may be one reason that the primary dealer "club" did not use EJV Government Securities much when it first introduced computerized government bond trading.

Other Sellers of Information

Because timely financial information is valuable to transactors in the markets, many are willing to pay a high price to obtain it. As a result, exchanges make a substantial amount of money by selling price and volume information from their trading activities to news services and others. Since an exchange has first knowledge of all trades conducted on the exchange, it is in the best position to obtain and sell timely information. Futures exchanges, in fact, hire "price reporters" to record the price of the most recent trade on a continuous basis. The sale of exchange trading information is not a trivial pursuit. Information sales provide one of the major sources of revenue for the Kansas City Board of Trade, for example. Also, because timely information is valuable, the New York Stock Exchange and others charge substantial fees for providing immediate information to customers. However, 15-minute delayed information on stock trades usually is available free.

Regulators and Information

In general, regulators want to have access to all pertinent information available in the financial markets. They want to know who traded with whom, when, at what price, and why. They want to make sure that people are not trying to take advantage of inside information or manipulate markets with their trading activities. However, traders and market makers often prefer to trade privately—even if they have no inside information they do not want others monitoring their trading positions, lest it put them at a disadvantage when they try to "unwind," or get out of their positions. For example, if people know a trader has a large amount of stock to sell, they are likely to mark down the price of the stock quickly as soon as they see the trader start to sell, even in small quantity. Because access to information is valuable, to some extent information-based, regulatory arbitrage exists, whereby people seek to trade in jurisdictions that will not require full and immediate disclosure of their trading activities and information. This process has at times been a factor in luring some stock trading from New York to the London markets, as futures-related program trading need not be as fully disclosed in London. Since various jurisdictions earn fees from stock trading and securities dealing conducted in their jurisdictions, there is an incentive for regulators in various countries or states to compete in laxity to try to attract financial trading activities from other areas. This process is particularly prevalent among European countries. As a consequence of regulatory arbitrage, "competition in laxity" can also exist. For instance, the New York Stock Exchange extended trading hours in 1991 and relaxed information disclosure requirements on block trades made during the new hours. They did so in order to attract some program trading back from London.

Corporate Information Disclosure

In the United States, corporations are not allowed to list their stocks on U.S. exchanges unless they meet SEC requirements for corporate information disclosure, including the filing of both annual SEC 10-K and *quarterly* SEC 8-K reports. Many foreign firms would like to obtain listings on U.S. exchanges but do not want to comply with U.S. disclosure requirements. In particular, many European (particularly, German) firms do not want to file quarterly reports and do not want to comply with U.S. accounting standards. For that reason it is not easy for U.S. citizens to buy their stocks. At the same time, because of full-disclosure requirements it is more difficult for U.S. citizens to be defrauded by foreign firms that might not disclose full, prompt, and accurate information to their stockholders.

Summary on Information Effects

This chapter has mentioned a number of issues related to the fact that regulators try to ensure that full and fair disclosure of all pertinent information on corporations and trading activities is available to the public. At the same time, people with early access to inside information on corporate performance or market activity may be able to earn excess profits by using their information judiciously. Consequently, it is possible for "regulatory arbitrage" to occur between jurisdictions that require extensive and prompt disclosure of financial information and those that do not. It is also possible for people to earn profits by providing prompt and accurate information to other market participants.

Since the world is moving toward globally based, 24-hour trading, people are going to have increasing options regarding what financial assets they acquire and where they trade them. Consequently, it may be necessary, in the long run, to adopt uniform financial information disclosure requirements around the world to prevent "regulatory arbitrage" from degrading the availability and quality of financial information. Alternatively, if people avoid investing in stocks or markets where full and fair information is not made available promptly, no regulation will be necessary to ensure that corporations voluntarily provide accurate information. However, in the absence of strong penalties against inside information trading or market manipulation— *caveat emptor* ("buyer beware").

Other Regulatory Issues

One of the major problems in financial markets is to make sure that people will not fail to *do what they promise* to do; for example, people must deliver the stock, bond, currency, or futures contracts that they sell, or make the cash payments that they promise to make. This requires that stock and bond settlement and transfer facilities be reliable. It also implies that reliable legal systems, credit systems, money transfer systems, and so on be in place to ensure that people will be both willing and able to honor their commitments.

Regulatory Support of Payment Systems

Regulators often intervene to reduce clearing system and payments system risk in one way or another. Sometimes they directly assist in the payments system, as central banks do when they clear checks, make discount window loans, or provide credit guarantees to support entities experiencing temporary cash-flow problems—such as those problems (discussed in the preceding chapter) experienced by the Bank of New York when its computers failed or the temporary asset-value problems experienced by brokerage houses the day after the Oct. 19, 1987, 500-point stock market crash.

Regulators' direct and indirect support for world payment systems (through their support of banks and other major financial market participants) helps make cash payments more certain, timely, and reliable.

Regulators and Individual Risk Taking

Risk-Based Capital.   Regulators also intervene in the financial markets through actions designed to limit individual risk taking and excessive market volatility in asset values. They do so because people or corporations can become insolvent if the value of their assets falls below the value of their liabilities because of volatile price movements. Regulators try to prevent potential insolvencies in several ways. One way is to impose capital requirements on market participants so the value of participants' assets will exceed the value of their liabilities by a greater margin. Furthermore, regulators' risk-based capital requirements mandate larger capital requirements as asset credit risks (or, asset and liability management risks) increase. Through risk-based capital requirements, regulators try to make institutions reduce risk taking through financial leverage if the institutions take on additional asset quality or interest rate risk.

Margin Requirements.   A second type of regulatory constraint designed to protect financial market participants' solvency involves margin requirements. After the "Great Crash" of 1929, the Fed was given the power to set stock margin requirements for banks, brokerage firms, and other lenders. Stock margin requirements prohibit lenders from lending more than a certain percentage of a stock's price to a buyer. Margin requirements on stocks are now 50 percent versus as low as 10 percent before the 1929 crash. Margin requirements for less-volatile corporate bonds are lower and typically are set by self-regulatory groups, such as exchanges. Margin requirements for default-risk-free federal government securities are essentially nonexistent.

Customer Suitability Screening.   A third type of regulatory constraint involves restrictions on market participant risk taking. The SEC does not let brokerage firms invest people's money in "unsuitable investments." De facto, this means that people often must qualify on the basis of income, wealth, and risk preference before a brokerage firm will allow them to engage in highly risky investments or write options. Speculative investments can lose their value and option writing can give rise to potentially unlimited losses.

Regulations Affecting Market Volatility

In addition to regulations affecting market participants and institutions, regulators may impose, or require that exchanges impose, regulations that affect market price volatility. For instance, the New York Stock Exchange halts program trading of stocks via its automated DOT system whenever the Dow Jones average moves 50 points or more in one direction in one day. It halts trading altogether for a while if the Dow Jones average drops 200 points in one day, and if, after the market starts again, the Dow Jones average drops 400 points on the day, the market will close. Since these rules have been put into effect, volatility on the New York Stock Exchange has diminished greatly. In 1987, before the rules were operative, the Dow Jones average frequently moved by 90 or 100 points or more in a day. However, after the rules became operative, there was only one day in all of 1991 when the Dow Jones average moved more than 100 points.

It is thought that placing limits on allowable price movements will reduce market volatility because the price limits will tend to stabilize the value of investors' stock portfolios and make them less likely to sell in a panicky attempt to stem their losses when the market starts to drop. However, on the other side of the issue, price limits may prevent stocks or other assets from reaching their equilibrium values as quickly once new information becomes available. Price limits may also cause trading halts that induce people to panic if they are unsure when and at what price they eventually will be able to unwind their losing positions in the financial markets. Finally, price limits may serve as "magnets" that attract price moves because some people will wait until the trading limit is hit before they take a position in the market. Such "magnet effect" behavior may occur in the commodity markets at times—since the futures exchanges frequently impose price limits to curb excess market volatility and insure that people will not lose their wealth instantaneously.

Regulators often require or encourage the exchanges to impose rules, such as price limits or trading halt provisions, under the threat that regulators themselves will impose curbs on market behavior if the exchanges do not comply. Exchanges usually prefer to impose their own regulations rather than let the heavy hand of government set the requirements.

Regulatory Arbitrage

Unfortunately government regulators do not really care as much about maintaining the exchanges' business viability as the exchanges do. For instance, the Japanese stock market fell sharply in 1992. Thus Japanese regulators (looking for a scapegoat) cracked down on futures trading in the Nikkei futures index on the Osaka futures exchange by raising margin requirements to 30 percent of the value of the stocks in the index and restricting intraday price movements and trading hours. As a result, the Osaka exchange lost business. However, the Singapore Monetary Exchange (SIMEX), which also traded an index based on the Nikkei stock index in Japan but was outside the reach of Japanese regulators, picked up the business that the Japanese lost. Regulatory arbitrage worked and, as a result, the Japanese futures exchange lost business, while world financial markets did business as usual.

Because of fear of heavy-handed government regulations, most futures exchanges, stock exchanges, and over-the-counter stock dealers (NASD) engage in a great detail of self-regulation. One type of self regulation that affects market volatility consists of futures exchanges' margin requirements.

Exchange Margin Requirements Futures margin requirements, unlike stock margin requirements, are basically good-faith deposits. They are pledges of deposited money, securities, or bank letters of credit that ensure market participants have sufficient financial resources on deposit with the exchange that they will keep their commitments. Since no borrowed money is involved, futures margin requirements do not involve interest charges, and can be quite low. Exhibit 24–4, for instance, shows that exchange minimum margin requirements on major financial futures contracts may equal only a few percentage points of the total value of the contract. More

Exhibit 24–4   **Minimum Margin Requirements on Stocks and Stock Index Futures Contracts, January 1992**

Contract	Margin Requirement (1/1/92)	Set by*	Percent of Contract Value (1/3/92)
S&P 500 Futures	$22,000	CME	10.5
NYSE Composite Index Futures	9,000	NYFE	7.8
Value Line Arithmetic Index Futures	7,000	KCBT	4.1
Major Market Index Futures	18,000	CBOT	10.4
Nikkei Index	18,000	CME	15.0
Individual stocks (minimum equity required at purchase)	50%	FRB	50.0 at purchase

*CME, Chicago Mercantile Exchange; CBOT, Chicago Board of Trade; NYFE, New York Futures Exchange; KCBT, Kansas City Board of Trade; and FRB, Federal Reserve Board.

Note: Margin requirements for stock index futures contracts are substantially lower than (leverage) margin requirements for individual stocks. Because exchanges set their own margin requirements, those indices that represent more than 500 stocks, and therefore have less volatility, tend to have lower margin requirements. In addition, exchanges with less-active trading may try to encourage trading in their futures contracts by lowering margin requirements (see the Value Line).

volatile futures contracts, or time periods, usually have higher margin requirements than less-volatile contracts or time periods.

A futures contract margin requirement will be exhausted quickly if adverse price moves of more than a few percentage points occur. For that reason, margin requirements are higher for volatile contracts or in volatile time periods, when large adverse price movements are more likely to occur. Higher requirements make it less likely that a futures investor's initial margin money will be exhausted before he or she can provide additional maintenance margin money. Price limits prevent the initial margin requirements from being exhausted all at once, and trading halts give people more time to obtain maintenance margin money if necessary. All these restrictions reduce the chance that investors will have to engage in panicky selling or buying if a market price moves sharply against them. As a result, the price trend is less likely to be accelerated by panicky actions and market price volatility should be reduced. This argument assumes, however, that margin requirements help prevent panicky over-reactions and do not have a magnet effect that accentuates price movements.

Stock Versus Futures Contract Margin Requirements.   As shown in Exhibit 24-4 stock index futures contracts have much lower margin requirements than stocks per se. Some people think that this causes stock index futures to be more volatile than they would be if they had higher margin requirements. Further, they think that volatility is transferred from stock index futures market to underlying stocks through index arbitrage. However, studies of stock market volatility do not show that it has increased significantly since stock index futures have become available.

Nonetheless, stock price movements could be aggravated by forced selling or buying in the futures markets if people encountered margin calls once stocks moved by as much as 5 percent in one direction. Thus, while stock price volatility has declined for most days since stock index futures have become available, some people still maintain that stock futures have helped make stock price movements more volatile on days when stock prices move by a large amount. That is one reason that both the NYSE and the stock index futures markets have now imposed trading limits that restrict how much stocks or futures can move in any one day.

Capital Requirements

Risk-Based Capital Requirements for Financial Contracts.   Margin requirements apply to people and corporations who buy stocks and futures through organized exchanges. In addition, risk-based capital requirements apply to financial institutions that take certain types of risk in their financial market contracting. Exhibit 24–5 shows how the Bank for International Settlements' (BIS) risk-based capital requirements are applied to foreign currency contracts or obligations entered into by commercial banks. Basically, capital requirements are higher for contracts with longer maturities and for contracts with private rather than government counterparties.

Overall, capital requirements on foreign currency and swap contracts are very low. However, because commercial banks are subject to BIS capital requirements, holding such contracts requires that banks allocate an "opportunity cost" to the capital required to back those contracts. While it is important that banks hold a capital buffer to absorb losses before they become insolvent or insured depositors lose, the capital requirements may put banks at a bit of a competitive disadvantage. Insurance companies, pension funds, and some other institutions that engage in swap and currency market transactions are not subject to risk-based capital requirements. Thus, they do not have to allocate a "capital cost" to their swap and currency operations. Consequently, they may be able to underprice banks by a small amount.

Nonetheless, if a true risk exists in swap and currency transactions, that risk should be priced and capital should be allocated to it regardless of who enters into the transaction. Thus the effect of regulatory capital requirements may be more apparent than real. This is especially true because regulatory capital requirements are so low that prudent institutions might be well advised to hold higher requirements anyway.

Risk Assessment Accuracy

Many of the risks that financial institutions take in financial markets involve swap agreements or exchange rate agreements with "caps," "collars," or other explicit or implicit options. Most options are priced using "option pricing models" that assume that the volatility, or standard deviation, of price movements in underlying assets or interest rates completely describes the risk of the asset. However, actual asset prices are likely to be characterized by more frequent very small and more frequent very large price movements than option pricing models usually assume. This means that while most of the time an institution will make money by "writing," or selling,

Exhibit 24–5   **BIS Risk-Based Capital Requirements for Foreign Currency Contract Risks**

Contract	(1) Notional Amount (Face Value)	(2) Maturity	(3) Conversion Factor	(4) Potential Exposure	(5) Replacement Cost, Market to Market
A	$10 million	under 14 days	0%	0	$125,000
B	10 million	14 to 365 days	1	$100,000	65,000
C	10 million	over 1 year	5	500,000	375,000
D	1 million	under 14 days	0	0	12,500
E	1 million	14 to 365 days	1	10,000	6,500
F	1 million	over 1 year	5	50,000	(−37,500)

Contract	(6) Total Balance Sheet Equivalent	(7) Risk Weight	(8) Risk-Adjusted Asset Value	(9) BIS Capital Standard	(10) Total Capital Requirement
A	$125,000	50%	$62,500	8%	$ 5,000
B	165,000	0	0	8	0
C	875,000	20	175,000	8	14,000
D	12,500	50	6,250	8	500
E	16,500	0	0	8	0
F	50,000	20	10,000	8	800

Note: Capital requirements for various foreign exchange contracts are determined as follows. First, they depend on the amount of "Notional Principle" (or face value) involved. (Column 1). Next they depend on the maturity of the contracts: 0 percent for contracts under 14 days, 1 percent for contracts from 14 days to one year, and 5 percent for contracts over one year. This percentage is multiplied by the notional principal to obtain the "potential exposure" recorded in Column (4). However, if a position has a positive market value, that amount also could be lost in case of a default, so the marked-to-market replacement cost is recorded in Column (5) and, if positive, added to the "potential exposure" to get the net amount at risk calculated as "balance sheet equivalent" in Column (6). If the replacement cost is negative, 0 is added to the "potential exposure" when calculating Column (6)—see Contract F (Row 6) for an example. The balance sheet equivalent is then weighted by the risk weight applicable to the asset category. While corporate loans have a risk weight of 100 percent, currency and interest rate contracts with corporate customers have a risk weight of 50 percent, contracts with other banks have a risk weight of 20 percent and contracts with governments have a risk weight of 0 percent. Multiplying the total balance sheet equivalent (Column 6) by the risk weights (Column 7) gives the risk-adjusted balance sheet exposure (Column 8), against which banks must hold 8 percent capital according to BIS risk-based capital requirements. Thus the total calculated capital needs required for each contract are given in Column (10).

options, the chance of a disaster is greater than the institution might assume. Capital can help protect firms against unexpected bad surprises, since any loss is written off against capital account before the institution becomes insolvent and fails. That is one reason that regulators want financial firms to hold capital to back their financial asset positions. Extra capital can help cover unexpected losses that may occur if institutions have not assessed risks accurately.

Systematic Risk

The real problem with not being able to quantify financial market risks precisely before they happen is that risks may be "systematic" in the sense that adverse events may feed upon one another and cause multiple simultaneous problems. Thus, when Olympia and York got in trouble (see People and Events), not only were its banks threatened with substantial loan losses, but many others were threatened as well. If Canary Wharf and other Olympia and York properties were sold at low prices to repay at least a portion of the firm's debts, the result would be downward pressures on commercial real estate prices and rents in London, New York, Toronto, and other cities. The lower rents and real estate prices might jeopardize the financial health of other real estate firms and that, in turn, might jeopardize the financial health of the other firms' lenders. Furthermore, if the public lost confidence in financial institutions' solvency because of the growing real estate losses, they might "run" some uninsured and nonguaranteed financial institutions, thereby causing additional credit contraction and financial difficulties. Thus, when risks are systematic, many seemingly unrelated adverse events may occur simultaneously.

While the scenario described in the preceding paragraph is hypothetical, it indicates how a number of adverse events may systematically result from a single cause. In that case, financial risks may be greater than financial institutions assumed because, instead of taking on independent risks, they may find that they have taken on *interdependent risks*, where all the bad things happen at once. Option pricing models, however, do not differentiate between undiversifiable systematic (or systemic) risk, and unsystematic (or diversifiable) risk. That is another reason that regulators who must guard against systemic (systematic) risk may be more cautious in their capital requirement standards than private financial institutions think they should be.

Issues Related to Market Structure

Liquidity and Market-Maker Profits. In order for market makers to stand ready to buy or sell stocks instantaneously at their bid and ask prices, they must expect to make a profit by so doing. If they cannot make a profit, fewer people would want to be market makers in that market. For that reason, traders in London proposed, subsequent to incurring losses after the Big Bang (see People and Events), that specific "specialists" be denoted as sole market makers in thinly traded stocks. They argued that this would allow the specialists to transact more frequently, and thus they could afford to transact at lower bid/ask spreads. On the other hand, if the specialists had a market-making monopoly, why should they lower their prices? Their only incentive to do so would be if reductions in their bid-ask spreads induced a more than proportional increase in trading volume, so their total revenues from market making would be enhanced.

Computerized Trading versus Exchange Trading (Quote Driven versus Order Driven Markets). OTC and computerized markets post the best available bid and ask prices (quotes) and let people trade at those prices if they wish. In contrast, exchanges use brokers who try to obtain the best price that they can get to fill market orders. Advocates of exchange-based order-driven markets say that those markets are more efficient because people can monitor the flow of orders into and out

PEOPLE
& EVENTS

Big Boom or Big Fizzle?

In 1986, Britain substantially deregulated financial markets. Barriers between ownership of various types of financial institutions were removed, commission rates were deregulated, and major changes were made in both the regulatory structure and the permitted activities of various participants in the financial markets. London hoped that the deregulation of its financial markets would allow it to become the leading financial center of Europe and (perhaps) the world.

At first, the deregulatory tactics seemed to be highly effective. American banks gobbled up British brokerage firms at high prices. Their acquisitions let the banks obtain an international stock and bond trading presence in spite of the Glass–Steagall Act, which limited their investment banking activities in the United States European stocks came to be actively traded on London markets, and even trading of U.S. stocks picked up in the less-regulated environment of London's International Stock Exchange. The increased competition had the salutary effect of reducing stock trading commissions. Furthermore, both London-based trading activity and mergers of financial institutions increased.

Because London seemed to be well on its way to becoming a world financial center, the Olympia and York real estate development firm embarked on an ambitious project in 1987 called "Canary Wharf." That project was designed to redevelop an old run-down part of Britain called the docklands by adding large amounts of new office space to accommodate the rapidly expanding financial services business. With office rents at over $100 per square foot per year in London's financial center, called the City, Canary Wharf's developers thought they could make good profits on their vast amount of new office space with rents only half as high.

However, things did not go quite as planned. In the 1987 stock market crash, the London FT-SE100 stock index fell by 595 points (or 30 percent of its value) in one day. After that, trading dried up. With flexible commissions, many institutions competed for the reduced volume of business by cutting commissions. The combination of lower commissions and lower volume reduced profits. Furthermore, the many financial institution mergers produced less synergy and higher costs than planned because the disparate corporate cultures often clashed. Weaker firms failed or sold out. After a time, many mergers were undone at great cost to the acquirers.

As growth in the London financial markets slowed, demand grew for reregulation to restore the earnings potential of market makers in securities. For instance, stock market makers tried to put off disclosing the volume of market transactions to the end of the day so they could make profits from block trades. In addition, they also suggested that single market makers be assigned to trade infrequently traded stocks, thereby reducing competition and increasing their profits.

Because of slackened trading activity, reduced profits, and layoffs in the financial services industry, the demand for office space grew slowly in the City. As a result, London's office rents fell. The decline in rents was aggravated when Canary Wharf buildings neared completion and Olympia and York tried to bid potential tenants away from the City by offering rent concessions.

Falling rents had further consequences. The Canary Wharf project went bankrupt, causing great losses for many of the banks that financed it. Furthermore, falling rents and property values caused other major real estate firms to go bankrupt. This caused still more problems for banks and still more pressure on rents.

At this point, the biggest question about the Big Bang is whether the "bang" occurred after deregulation caused the rapid expansion in London financial market mergers and trading activity in the late 1980s, or whether the bang is yet to occur as London's real estate and financial markets near the brink of collapse.

of the market and get a better feel for supply and demand conditions than they can get by observing a price on a computer screen. Advocates of quote-driven markets say it is wasteful to pay people to jump up and down and yell at each other on the exchange floor when trying to get a better price. However, with free markets people generally get what they want at the lowest possible price. Interestingly trading volumes tend to be higher in order-driven than in quote-driven markets (perhaps because they have more "liquidity" in the form of people rapidly taking the other side of a transaction at a good price). However, computers do have a substantial cost advantage, so it remains to be seen whether computerized trading systems can hold their own or expand in competition with exchange-related markets. At present, many markets use a hybrid system, such as Globex.

Exchange Guarantees.   When individuals enter into an exchange traded options or futures contract, the exchange's clearing corporation takes the other side of the trade and guarantees the trade. Even if the other party to the trade defaults, that default would hurt the exchange, not the counterparty, unless of course the default was so severe that the exchange failed. In a forward or swap market transaction, however, if a counterparty defaults, the investor is likely to lose. At the very least, the investor may have to find a new counterparty and face the risk that the new contract would not be as advantageous as the old one. Thus, futures exchanges have tried to offer contracts on swaps and other types of financial transactions. They argue that the guarantees they offer are better than single counterparties' guarantees. Thus, exchange-based swaps and other exchange-guaranteed transactions should be safer than individual contracts. However, exchange contracts are standardized with respect to quantities and delivery dates, while individual counterparties can custom-design their forward and swaps contracts. Thus, even though exchange-based contracts may be safer, they cannot be customized to fit people's needs as specifically.

Nonetheless, the absence of counterparty risk on exchange-traded contracts could be a great advantage. When the Bank of the New England failed, it experienced great difficulty in renegotiating its forward and swaps contracts at a decent price so it could unwind them. Exchange-traded contracts, in contrast, could simply be offset by taking the opposite position on the exchange floor.

The Changing Role of Financial Institutions in Financial Markets   Traditionally financial institutions have played a relatively passive role in financial markets. They have made loans and bought investment securities at current market prices and have sold certificates of deposit and other managed liabilities, when necessary, by offering attractive rates to potential depositors or lenders. In recent years, however, financial institutions have vastly expanded their participation in financial markets by issuing forward foreign currency contracts, interest rate and currency swap contracts, and various custom-tailored over-the-counter options contracts to their customers. Some of the major commercial banks derive a majority of their income from fee income and trading income associated with their participation in financial markets. In addition, many major financial institutions have securitized large portions of their loan portfolios and sold participation interests in those portfolios to investors rather than finance the loans by selling CDs. This not only allows the institutions to avoid risk-based capital requirements applicable to the loans, but also allows them to structure the participation securities in such a way that the net cost of funds associated with selling the participation securities is lower than their net cost of funds would have been by issuing CDs.

An important factor involved in securitizing pools of loans involves the credit guarantee used to insure the safety and high credit ratings of the security participations. Some banks and insurance companies have been able to earn substantial income by pledging high-quality letter of credit guarantees or pledged deposits to protect investors against credit risk on securitized pools of loans.

In essence, in recent years major financial institutions have become much more active as financial market participants. They issue a variety of specialized options and forward, swap, and credit guarantee contracts in return for fee income. They also create and trade securities of various types very actively in the financial markets. By taking advantage of interest rate differentials across the term structure of interest rates, across credit risk grades, or across country boundaries, they can often enhance their net income through trading and fee income generating activities. Furthermore, by custom designing swaps, option, forward, and securities contracts they can often exploit market inefficiencies to earn extra profits if buyers of those contracts have limited information about the fair price of similar contracts. Finally, for "well-capitalized" institutions that are allowed to underwrite securities, additional fee income can be generated from underwriting fees and the provision of financial advice. Overall, then, major banks are likely to derive an increasing share of their income in the future from activities related to the financial markets rather than from financial intermediation per se.

These trends, however, worry regulators. Regulators worry because the linkages among financial institutions are becoming harder to identify and more difficult to assess. The holder of a participation interest in a securitized pool of loans can be jeopardized by (1) excess defaults on the underlying loan pool, or by (2) a default of the credit enhancement (letter of credit) provider or by (3) interest rate risk associated with holding part of a subordinate tranche in a loan pool, if that tranche has an uncertain payout pattern that may unexpectedly become adverse. All these risks are hard to assess and identify. Further, the risks may be cross-linked as the web of institutions that enter into swaps and other private two-party agreements with each other expands and becomes more complex. One way regulators have tried to prevent institutions from taking on too much risk is by imposing risk-based capital requirements on forward currency, swap, and option contract transactions and other contingent claim liabilities of financial institutions. However, regulatory arbitrage and the issuance of similar contracts by unregulated institutions may limit the effectiveness of the risk-based capital approach. Furthermore, systemic risk may cause problems to snowball once a problem starts in one sector of the increasingly closely linked market. As a result, it is important to have a lender of last resort available to provide backup liquidity to financial institutions in our increasingly complex credit markets. Financial institutions realize this; for instance, after Olympia and York experienced financial problems in 1992, its largest lender, Hong Kong and Shanghai Bank (which faced potentially large loan defaults and did not have access to a lender of last resort) quickly offered to buy Midland Bank of the United Kingdom (which, as one of the four major clearing banks in England, did have easy access to Britain's lender of last resort).

Summary

Financial markets trade financial instruments in a variety of ways. Each way has somewhat different implications for price flexibility, volatility, settlement, and market guarantees. Access to information frequently determines the ability of financial market participants to profit from their participation in the markets. Recently, 24-hour trading has started in many financial market instruments, and computerized trading has been extensively developed.

Issues related to financial markets include issues related to access to information. Those issues include the following: (1) What is "insider trading"? (2) How valuable is the specialist's book and who should have access to it? (3) How timely should quantity and price information reported by market makers be? (4) Should higher prices be charged for timely versus delayed market information? (5) Should regulators try to regulate market participants' solvency? (6) Should regulators try to regulate market volatility by imposing margin requirements, capital requirements, price limits, or trading halt rules on the markets?

To a great extent, regulators have let financial markets operate with relatively few restrictions. Where they have tried to impose restrictions (as with Nikkei index futures trading in Japan) regulatory arbitrage has caused market activity to flow to less regulated jurisdictions. However, it is not clear that market participants all price the risk of very bad (but very low probability) events correctly. Thus, in the absence of regulation some risk may exist in totally unregulated financial markets. Furthermore, market participants may be less concerned with systematic (systemic) risk, than regulators. As a result, some regulatory intervention in markets may be justified to help participants maintain their solvency. Regulators may also provide settlement mechanisms (such as the Fed wire) or mandate that privately guaranteed settlement procedures (such as organized exchanges) be used to execute certain types of financial transactions.

Questions

1. What are the pros and cons on order-driven versus quote-driven markets? What are the advantages and disadvantages of specialist versus over-the-counter markets?
2. What do you think should be punishable as "insider trading"? Why? Who gains and who loses in each case?
3. Would you expect to see rapidly fluctuating prices more frequently in a Walrasian market or in a continuous-auction market? Why?
4. What are the pros and cons of computerized markets? Why do you think that computerized markets often have a lower volume of trading than "people-driven" markets (like the Cincinnati Stock Exchange versus the NYSE)?
5. Why do you think that 24-hour trading is developing? What characteristics do most of the financial assets traded on a 24-hour basis have?
6. Why is it possible that financial institutions who sell explicit or implicit options to their customers may be taking more risk than regulators desire?

7. What impact are computerized markets likely to have on commercial property values in world financial centers? Why?

8. What are the reasons that the BIS imposes capital requirements on financial commitments of financial institutions? What are the pros and cons related to the capital requirements they have imposed?

9. Why is timely information so valuable in financial markets? Do more rapid information flows potentially stabilize or destabilize markets? Why? What types of information flows should be regulated and why?

10. What are the pros and cons of price-limits for stock market and other financial instrument price changes?

11. How do stock margin requirements differ from margin requirements on stock index futures? Why do some people argue that the futures market stock index margins should be raised? What are the arguments against that point of view?

12. Why do you think some regulators sometimes argue that the financial swaps market should be regulated more?

Selected References

Abken, Peter A. "Globalization of Stock, Futures, and Options Markets." *Economic Review*. Federal Reserve Bank of Atlanta, July/August, 1991, pp. 1–22.
This article provides an excellent description of the growth of international securities trading in stocks, futures, and options. It pays particular attention to technological developments that have facilitated the growth of automated exchanges and "screen trading" systems. The article also discusses issues related to market performance and regulation in some detail. It particularly considers the question of whether 24-hour worldwide trading is likely to increase market volatility or market efficiency.

"Automating Financial Markets: The Human Cost." *The Economist*, March 10, 1990, pp. 19–24.
This article documents the growing trend toward computerized trading in world financial markets and the way that the innovations are being implemented. It notes traders' objections that such markets will be less liquid and therefore less desirable than people-driven markets. However, it also notes that rather than use floor brokers, Morgan Stanley was able to obtain substantial cost savings for actively traded stocks by using automated trading (DOT) type systems on the NYSE and AMEX and sending OTC orders to the Reuters Instinet system for execution. Thus *The Economist* concludes that people will be a diminishing resource in the automated financial markets of the future. However, its conclusion strictly holds only for stocks and other investments that are already actively traded.

Domowitz, Ian. "The Mechanics of Automated Trade Execution Systems." *Journal of Financial Intermediation* 1 (1990), pp. 167–194.
This expert on automated trading systems describes in detail how they function.

"The End of Privilege." *The Economist*, December 14, 1991, pp. 86–90.
This article discusses problems encountered by London's market makers after the Big Bang and their proposals to (1) delay reports on large trade volumes, and (2) adopt a specialist system to provide a market in thinly traded stocks.

Futures Magazine, 1992 References Guide.
This highly useful annual publication lists all major futures and options exchanges, their trading hours, and the investments traded on each. It also provides phone numbers and addresses for each exchange for the benefit of people who wish to obtain more information.

"Last Orders?" *The Economist*, **March 14, 1992, p. 91.**

The Economist considers competition among European stock markets as well as the question of whether order-driven or quote-driven markets are more efficient. It notes that specialists in order-driven markets risk their own capital to offer traders liquidity, when they stand ready to accommodate orders at their bid and ask prices. However, because they risk more capital, such dealers also must have wider bid-ask spreads than quote-driven markets require—since OTC dealers can adjust their inventory position more easily than specialists. Thus *The Economist* concludes that a hybrid system might be useful.

Ma, Christopher K., Ramesh P. Rao, and R. Stephen Sears. "Volatility, Price Resolution, and the Effectiveness of Price Limits." *Journal of Financial Services Research* **3, no. 2/3 (December, 1989): 165– 200.**

This paper studies the effect that price limits have on price movements and volatility in the Treasury bond, silver, corn, and soybean futures markets. It focuses on limit price moves in those markets and notes that price changes may accelerate as they approach the limit. Subsequent to hitting the limit, prices (often) back off the next day, and (generally) are less volatile after the "cooling off" period (caused by the trading halt imposed when the limit is reached).

Roll, Richard. "Price Volatility, International Market Links, and Their Implications for Regulatory Policies." *Journal of Financial Services Research* **3, no. 2/3 (December, 1989): 213–245.**

This study analyzes stock market behavior in 23 countries before and after the October 1987 stock market crash. It tries to determine if the stock returns in each country were strongly correlated before, after, and during the crash. It also tries to determine if regulatory policies (which differed widely in various countries) had an effect on each market's behavior. It finds that correlations in various market returns were strong during the crash and positive before the crash, but weak or nonexistent after the crash. It also finds little evidence that margin requirements, transaction taxes, or price limits had their desired effect in restraining market volatility in various regulatory jurisdictions. While daily price limits may forcibly restrain measured volatility on a daily basis, over longer periods they appear to have no effect.

Salinger, Michael. "Stock Market Margin Requirements and Volatility: Implications for Regulation of Stock Index Futures." *Journal of Financial Services Research* **3, no. 2/3 (December 1989): 121–138.**

The author of this article studies stock market volatility during periods when Federal Reserve stock margin requirements were at different levels. He does not find a correlation, and therefore concludes that stock market volatility and margin requirements are not closely correlated. He extrapolates his finding to conclude that regulation of stock index futures margin requirements is not necessary.

Schap, Keith. "Bank Capital, Rules: A Boon for Exchanges?" *Futures*, **May 1992, pp. 40–42.**

This article explains how risk-based capital rules require banks to calculate capital requirements to back their forward-market risk exposures. As a result, it notes that bank trading costs may be higher than those of institutions that are not subject to the risk-based capital rules. It suggests that exchange trading of foreign currency and interest rate swap positions may benefit as a result of bank capital requirements, since bank forward positions will be more expensive to maintain.

7 MONETARY POLICY

PROFILE/Mary Rosenbaum

SHE IS

Vice-president and senior economist, Federal Reserve Bank of Atlanta, in position for 5 years. (Vice-president for 1 year, Macropolicy Group leader for 5 years.) She reports to the senior vice-president and director of research, who in turn reports to the president of the bank. The bank president is one of 12 Federal Reserve Bank presidents, who, along with the governors of the Federal Reserve Board, make up the Federal Open Market Committee (FOMC). The FOMC is the principal monetary policymaking group in the United States; its decisions impact short-term interest rates, monetary growth, and bank balance sheets. The Federal Reserve is an independent institution, created by the Congress, but not controlled by it. Because of its formal independence from the government and its mandate to pursue such goals as full employment and price stability, the Federal Reserve's monetary policy is able to focus on both the longer-run issues as well as short-term stabilization policy.

WHAT SHE DOES

She leads a macroeconomic policy group of 15 people in conducting policy analysis and drafting recommendations to the president of the bank. Using 3-year horizons, her group prepares detailed forecasts of the economic impacts of inflation, interest rate changes, growth in the money supply, and developments in the United States' major trading partners. In preparing these forecasts, her group monitors current U.S. economic conditions, evaluates long-term trends, and conducts other basic research on the fundamentals of how the economy behaves, for example, the relation between financial panics and business cycles, or ways of discerning the influence of economic policy from historical data.

This accumulated information, analysis, opinion, and forecast is used to make a policy recommendation that is formally presented to the president of the bank (that is, the policymaker). Through his participation on the FOMC, the analysis may influence policy, and thereby the financial markets, the banking system, and worldwide economic activity in general.

HOW SHE GOT THERE

B.A.: George Washington University
M.A.: Columbia University
MPhil.: Columbia University
First job: Instructor, Economics Department, Barnard College

BACKGROUND

She grew up in Washington, D.C., with a mother who is a psychologist and teacher and a father in the U.S. intelligence service. They impressed on her the importance of not limiting herself and of finding a career that would be interesting for a long time, that is not to go into something just for status or money. They also stressed the importance of developing dual capacities in mathematics and writing. She is happy with the outcome of having taken their advice. Having started college as a biology major, she switched to economics because of an excellent economics course she signed up for on a lark. She now lives in Ansley Park, in Atlanta, a 7-minute commute to work.

WHAT SHE LIKES BEST ABOUT HER JOB

The ability to bring rigorous analytic tools to bear on economic policy, being surrounded by strong, opinionated, and talented colleagues, and having the challenge of learning something new all of the time.

WORST NIGHTMARE

Losing credibility with the bank's president by being wrong or unable to communicate effectively. Once lost, credibility is difficult to earn back.

HOW SHE UNWINDS

Cooking, biking, running. Has run in the Boston Marathon since 1990.

ADVICE

If you don't want to narrow your options, develop a balance of good quantitative skills (for example, mathematics) and a good classic liberal arts background: history, literature, writing, debate.

MONETARY POLICY AND THE FINANCIAL SYSTEM

25

HAVE YOU EVER WONDERED WHY so many participants in the nation's financial markets and managers of financial institutions spend so much time "Fed-watching" and trying to foretell what the nation's monetary policies are likely to be? It is because participants in our nation's financial markets must be aware of economic theories that are held by influential members of the Fed, of Congress, and the administration. As Keynes said many years ago, the affairs of the world often are governed by the ideas of some long-dead economist. Thus a student of financial markets and institutions must understand the economic theories that influence present policymakers. With such a background, the student can anticipate what policymakers are likely to do and how different national economic policy actions are likely to affect financial markets and interest rates. Because national economic policies are so important, almost every major financial institution that operates in the U.S. financial markets has someone on staff to watch the economic policymakers, calculate the probable effects of their actions, and predict what they will do next. Because there is no single accepted theory of how money affects the economy, different policymakers may prefer to take different actions.

This chapter focuses on economic theories about how changes in interest rates and the money supply as well as changes in government tax and expenditure policies are likely to affect the economy. It first discusses the classical (quantity theory) and more modern (monetarist) theories, which emphasize the effect that changes in the money supply are likely to have on economic behavior. It then discusses the Keynesian theory, which says that government fiscal (tax and expenditure) policy may be useful under some circumstances, particularly during a great depression when monetary policy (involving changes in the money supply or interest rates) doesn't work as expected. Finally, it discusses the supply-side and rational-expectations views of optimal economic policy. The last theories draw on earlier theories but make modifications to allow for the fact that neither the Keynesian nor the monetarist theories have worked exactly as policymakers have intended in recent years. Because even the new theories do not provide all the answers, the chapter also includes a "People and Events" item that discusses Wicksellian theory, a theory to which some recent Fed governors have paid attention because it was used successfully in Sweden during the 1930s.

Classical Theory, the Quantity Theory, and Monetarism

Say's Law and the Supply of Goods

Basically, all macroeconomic theories are concerned with the factors that will affect either the total amount of income earned and goods produced (gross national product) in the economy[1] or the price level at which goods will be sold. The *classical theorists*, in general, thought that changes in money supply were likely to affect the price level rather than the physical level of production. Classical theorists who believed in Say's Law that "production creates its own demand" were not concerned that the economy would produce too much and that there would be unsold goods left over. In particular, classical theorists believed that people would work to produce goods only if they also wanted to consume an equal value of goods. Thus the total value of goods produced would equal the total value of goods people wanted to consume, and, on balance, there would be no excess production.

While classical economists believed that the economy would tend to be at full employment with no excess production, they did not believe that the level of production was rigidly fixed. In particular, by cutting taxes so that people could keep more of their income from production, people could be induced to sacrifice some leisure and produce more. Also, by providing subsidies, people would be induced to produce more of the subsidized goods. Many of these classical ideas were later adopted by "supply-side" economists. The supply-siders advocated cuts in tax rates to stimulate more work effort and output in the economy. They also advocated subsidies (or tax relief) for people who purchased capital goods (such as plants and machinery) that would allow them to be more productive in the future. Extra capital goods and extra work effort expand the supply of goods that can be produced.

Investment, Savings, and Interest Rates

In general, classical economists believed that the total amount of goods that could be produced depended on the amount of labor and capital goods used in the production process. The stock of capital goods (plant and equipment) could be increased by undertaking new investment projects. Because more investment projects are profitable when financing costs are low rather than high, producers will want to borrow more funds to finance investment projects when interest rates fall, and they will demand fewer funds to finance investment projects as interest rates rise. The investment demand for funds is shown in Exhibit 25–1 by line I_{DF}. If people expect more inflation, then the expected return on investment projects will rise by an amount approximately equal to the expected change in the price level, ΔP_e. Producers can sell

---

[1] Domestic production (GDP) and national income tend to be equal because someone has a claim on everything that is produced. Thus all production also generates income for someone who helped produce the goods. Profits are a balancing item. If the value of production exceeds the wage and salary claims, interest claims, and rental claims of people who helped produce the goods, profits will increase to reflect the excess value of production. Conversely, profits will be negative if the producer of the output pays out more income to others than the value of goods produced. In either case, the sum of all income claims (including the positive or negative profits of the owner) will equal the value of the output produced.

Exhibit 25–1   Savings Propensities

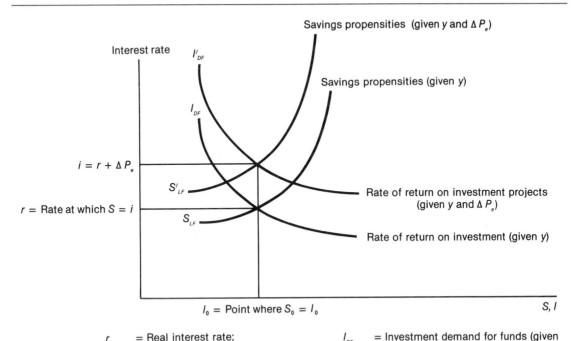

r	= Real interest rate;	I_{DF} = Investment demand for funds (given no inflation);
y	= Existing level of output and income;	
S_0	= Savings at income level y;	I'_{DF} = Investment demand for funds (given inflation of ΔP_e);
I_0	= Investment at income level y;	S_{LF} = Supply of loanable funds (savings);
i	= Nominal interest rate;	S'_{LF} = Supply of loanable funds (savings) given expected inflation of ΔP_e.
ΔP_e	= Expected change in prices (inflation);	

Note: If borrowers' demands for funds decrease as the real cost of borrowing rises, and if savers save more as their real returns on savings rise, the equilibrium real interest rate, r, will exist at the point where the amount of funds savers are willing to supply equals the amount of funds borrowers demand, If both borrowers and savers expect the same amount of inflation, ΔP_e, the nominal interest rate will equal the real rate plus ΔP_e.

their additional production at higher prices in an inflationary environment so investment projects will generate greater revenues. Thus, if inflation is expected, the demand for investment funding will rise to I'_{DF}.

Classical theorists also thought that people would save more if real interest rates rose. With higher interest rates, people could acquire more goods in the future for each dollar of income that they saved (i.e., didn't consume) in the present. Thus, the classical theorists thought that the supply of loanable funds from savers increased as interest rates rose, as shown by the curve, S_{LF} in Exhibit 25–1. However, if people expected that inflation would reduce the future purchasing power of the funds they saved, they would require a higher interest rate before they would save as much. This the curve S'_{LF} in Exhibit 25-1, which lies above S_{LF} by an amount equal to the expected rate of inflation, ΔP_e.

In the absence of inflation, the classical theorists believed that the real interest rate, r, and the level of investment, I_O, would be determined by the point (r, I_O) at which the demand for loanable funds (I_{LF}) equaled the supply of loanable funds (S_{LF}). If inflation was expected, the equilibrium point would shift upward along with the expected rate of inflation, ΔP_e. Thus, the market rate of interest, i, would rise to the level where the inflation-adjusted supply of loanable funds curve, S'_{LF}, and the inflation-adjusted demand for investible funds curve, I'_{DF}, intersected. At that point, $i = r + \Delta P_e$, approximately, and both the real interest rate and the equilibrium level of savings and investment are unaffected.

Because of their beliefs (see Did You Know?), the classical economists didn't think that a change in the money supply would affect the level of investment (or real interest rates, r). However, they did think that *monetary policy* could affect the nominal interest rate, i, by affecting the expected rate of inflation, ΔP_e.

Wages and Employment

In the opinion of many classical economists, unemployment would not be a major problem as long as wage rates were flexible. This is illustrated in Exhibit 25-2. If the money wage rate is too high (at W') relative to the price level (as it is at W'/P_0), wages

---

Exhibit 25–2   **Demand for Labor**

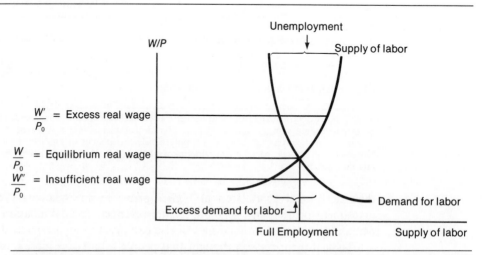

Note: The supply of labor rises as the purchasing power of wages (the real wage or the nominal wage, W, divided by the price level, P_0 rises. The equilibrium real wage exists at the point where the supply and demand for labor is equal. At that point the economy is said to be at full employment, even though some people may still be frictionallyor structurally unemployed as new businesses start up and old businesses fail. If the real wage W'/P_0 is too high, unemployment will result and unemployed workers will offer to work for a lower wage. If the real wage W''/P_0 is too low, there will be an excess demand for labor and employers will compete for workers by offering a higher wage. At W_0/P_0, the labor market will be in equilibrium at full employment, and the wage level won't change.

are too high relative to the price of goods produced with the workers' labor. Thus, demand for labor is relatively low, because few employers can afford to pay their workers a high money wage and also sell their products at a price that will generate a profit. At the same time, many people will want to work, because the real wage, W'/P_O, is high enough that they will be willing to sacrifice some of their leisure to take a job or work overtime. Thus, when the real wage equals W'/P_O, the supply of labor will exceed the demand for labor, and unemployment will result. If labor markets are competitive, this situation will not last long; unemployed workers will offer to work for less.

Similarly, if wages are too low relative to the price level, as at W''/P_O, many employers will want to hire workers at that wage so that they can produce more goods and sell them at a profit. However, fewer workers will want to work if the purchasing power of their wages falls. Thus, there will be an excess demand for labor by employers. In a competitive market, the employers who have more jobs than they can fill will bid up the wage rate that they offer in order to attract more workers. Thus, the real wage will tend to rise back toward the equilibrium level, W_O/P_O. At real wage level W_O/P_O, all workers who want to work at that wage will be able to find jobs.

Money and Price Levels (the Quantity Theory)

The classical economists generally believed in the *quantity theory of money*. That theory said that the amount of money people would demand, M_D, should be a constant function of the nominal national income level (Y). People would need more money if the level of income was higher, because the classical theorists believed that the velocity of money (V) was roughly constant. They formalized this idea by noting that if V was constant, then $1/V$ was constant as well. Thus, since $MV = Y$, $M = (1/V)Y$, or the demand for money, $M_D = kY = kPy$, where k equals a constant that is roughly the same as $1/V$, $Y =$ nominal national income (or national income measured in current dollars), $P =$ the price level expressed as a ratio to base period prices, and $y =$ real income, or the value of current income (output)[2] expressed in base period prices.

The quantity theorists' idea that people's money demand (M_D) was a constant ratio of money, k, relative to national income, Y, was similar to the notion that the velocity of money was roughly constant. However, the money-demand notion also had behavioral implications. If the central bank supplied more money, M_S, than people demanded, they would spend the excess. The additional spending (when M_S is greater than M_D) would cause either the level of real output, y, to rise or cause the price level, P, to rise as "too much money chased too few goods." Conversely, if the central bank didn't supply enough money relative to nominal income levels so that the money supply was less than money demand at current income levels, people would spend less. The money supply deficiency would then cause either the real level of output, y, to fall (as goods remained unsold and employers cut back on production) or the price level to fall (as employers cut prices so that people would buy their excess goods). In either case, a new equilibrium would be established where $M_S = M_D =$

[2]See footnote 1.

$kY = kPy$. Thus, because k was assumed to be constant, changing the money supply would change nominal national income, Y, by causing either the price level, P, or the level of real output, y, to change. However, since most classical economists believed that labor markets were competitive, they thought that all workers who wanted to work at the equilibrium real wage would be employed. Consequently, they thought that real output would remain unchanged at the level that would be produced when the economy was at full employment, y_{FE}.

Since the full employment output level would not be affected by price changes as long as labor markets were competitive, classical economists assumed that y would stay unchanged at y_{FE} and that prices and wages would adjust if the money supply changed. Thus they believed that $M_S = M_D = kPy_{FE}$. Consequently, they thought that the rate of price change (inflation) depended only on the rate of growth of the money supply.

Modern-Day Monetarists

The version of the quantity theory just presented is a little too simple to be put into practice as it is. Nonetheless, historically, during the period from 1870 to 1910, the U.S. money supply grew more slowly than full-employment output levels, y_{FE}, and, as predicted by the quantity theory, the price level fell. Furthermore, in the numerous countries that have let their money supply grow faster than their full-employment output levels, inflation has resulted. Thus the theory is generally correct for long-run policy adjustments. Milton Friedman, a famous monetarist, has suggested that our Federal Reserve System make the money supply grow at a constant rate roughly equal to the rate of growth in our economy's full-employment production capabilities. Such a policy, according to the quantity theory, should keep prices stable as long as k (and, relatedly, the velocity of money, since $k = 1/V$) is constant.

The strict quantity theory has been criticized, however, because velocity is not a constant. Velocity may expand in business cycle booms and contract in recessions. This can make the booms "boomier" and depressions more depressing.

Modern day *monetarists* differ from the quantity theorists in that they believe that velocity (and hence, k) is variable. However, they also believe that velocity is predictable. In particular, they think that the velocity of money increases over time and increases when interest rates rise. If velocity is predictable, the economy can still be managed by controlling the money supply. However, the Federal Reserve will have to alter the growth rate of the money supply not only because of changes in the economy's full-employment level of output but also because of forecast changes in interest rates and in response to increases in velocity caused by technological advances that occur over time. Still, if the Fed did its job successfully and the monetarists were right, the Fed could determine the price level and output level desired for the economy just by changing the money supply.

Keynesian Theory

The major problem with the classical theory was that it couldn't explain the massive unemployment that developed during the Great Depression of the 1930s. Although the theory allowed for a little unemployment as people leave one job and look for another in a dynamically changing economy, it certainly could not explain why our nation had unemployment rates of 20 to 30 percent or more during the Depression. That is why Keynesian theory was developed.

Keynes's Labor-Market Assumptions

Keynesian theory introduced innovations of considerable importance. First, it assumed that money wages were "sticky" in that they did not easily move downward even if people were unemployed. Wages were thought to be sticky because people had "money illusions" and thought that their real income would be lower if they were paid less; thus they would not work for lower wages even if prices fell. However, during the Depression, price levels fell by 30 percent. Since wage rates were sticky and fell more slowly than prices—in part because people had money illusions and in part because many labor contracts established rigid wages—real wages (W'/P_0) rose because of the fall in prices. Thus, massive unemployment resulted. (See Exhibit 25–2.)

Keynes's Money Demand Theory and Interest Rate Determination

Ordinarily an expansionary monetary policy during the Depression would have solved the unemployment problem (according to the quantity theorists) by allowing the money supply to expand so that people would spend more and bid up prices. However, Keynes invented the notion of a "liquidity trap," which, at times, could prevent an expansion in the money supply from having an effect on the economy.

Keynes's liquidity trap depended on his assumptions about how much money people would demand. Like the quantity theorists, Keynes said that the public's demand for money depended on their need for money to carry on income-producing transactions. He called this the *transactions demand for money*. However, he also said that people would hold additional money for investment purposes. When interest rates were very high, people would have a very low demand for money because they would invest almost all of their idle funds in securities. If interest rates were very low, however, this *speculative demand for money* would increase greatly, as investors would be afraid to commit funds to long-term investments. If interest rates were low, asset values would be very high relative to their yields. Consequently, if interest rates substantially rose, the investors in long-term assets would find that their assets' present value (price) would fall sharply. Keynes said that people would hold a great amount of money idle, rather than invest it, if interest rates were very low. Thus Keynes assumed that the demand for money would look like Exhibit 25–3.

In Keynesian theory, an increase in the money supply would cause people to hold more money relative to their transaction needs. They would invest any excess by buying securities, thereby driving up the securities' prices and driving down interest rates. This would occur as long as the economy was not in a liquidity trap. But if it were in a liquidity trap, interest rates would no longer fall, as investors would no longer invest idle cash. If interest rates were very low, the risk of loss of present value would be so great if an investment was purchased at high price and interest rates subsequently rose that Keynes assumed investors would merely hoard any excess money balances they held.

Exhibit 25–3   **The Keynesian Demand for Money and the Liquidity Trap**

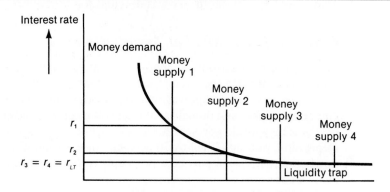

Note: In the Keynesian theory, assuming a constant income level, the interest rate is the rate at which the demand for money equals the money supply. As the money supply is increased from M_{S1} to M_{S2} to M_{S3}, the interest rate falls. However, in the liquidity trap range, the additional increases in the money supply no longer depress interest rates.

Because of his liquidity-trap assumptions, Keynes thought that interest rates were so low during the Great Depression that an expansion of the money supply would not make them go lower. As a result, no additional investment projects would be stimulated if the money supply were increased, and monetary policy could do nothing to stimulate the economy and cause prices to rise and real wages to fall. Thus, Keynes thought, monetary policy could not get us out of the Depression.

He did think, however, that government *fiscal* (tax and expenditure) *policy* could help, even in a depression. In addition, he thought that policies taken to stimulate private investment (including monetary policy, if the economy were not in a liquidity trap) could be used to change the level of national income at times.

Keynesian Theory of National Income Determination

Keynesian theory notes that final product demand comes from several sources: consumption demand (C); investment demand for plant and equipment, housing, or planned inventory changes (I); government demand (G); and export (EX), net of import (IM), demand. For simplicity, we refer to the net export demand as X (where $X = EX - IM$) instead of as EX and IM separately. If total demand in the economy equaled the total amount of production (Y), this relationship could be expressed as follows:

$$Y = C + I + G + X. \tag{25-1}$$

That is, all production is demanded by somebody.

If all production is not demanded by someone, the economy will not be in equilibrium and production levels will change. Assume, for instance, that demand is less than production. Unsold stocks of inventories will accumulate on the shelves of retailers and manufacturers. When stocks of unsold goods accumulate, retailers will reduce orders from their suppliers; so manufacturers will reduce production levels.

When production falls sufficiently that production equals demand, the economy will be in equilibrium once more.

Similar effects occur if demand exceeds production. The extra demand can be accommodated for a short time by retailers and manufacturers selling inventories from their racks and shelves. However, they will soon run out of things to sell unless retailers increase their orders for goods and manufacturers increase production. Consequently, production will rise to meet demand and restore the economy to equilibrium once again.

Because all production represents income to someone (since someone has a claim on all final products produced) economists use the symbol Y to denote total (aggregate) income in the economy as well as aggregate production. Using Y to represent income, Keynesian theory assumes that planned consumption spending in the economy as a whole is typically a function of aggregate income, or:

$$C = C_O + cY, \qquad (25\text{-}2)$$

where C_O is autonomous consumption, or consumption that does not depend on income; and c is the marginal propensity to consume, which shows the percentage of additional income that will be spent.

Keynesian theory is concerned basically with whether aggregate demand is less or more than the amount of product that can be produced at full-employment output levels. If demand is not equal to full-employment output levels, Keynesian theory believes that fiscal or monetary policy should be altered.

Keynesian Fiscal Policy

The government attempts to influence the equilibrium level of income by fiscal policy in two major ways. One is by altering government expenditure levels (G). The other is by altering tax and transfer payments policies in order to affect the income that consumers have available to spend.

Not all income generated by production accrues directly to consumers. Instead, consumers receive their personal income minus taxes, Tx. Also, some consumers' incomes are supplemented by government transfer payments, Tr. Thus consumers' disposable income, Y_d, can be represented by the following:

$$Y_d = Y - T_x + T_r. \qquad (25\text{-}3)$$

Changes in their disposable income prompt consumers to alter their expenditure plans. Thus the consumption function really should be written as:

$$C = C_O + cY_d, \qquad (25\text{-}4)$$

or, after substituting its components for Y_d,

$$C = C_O + c(Y - T_x + T_r). \qquad (25\text{-}5)$$

By increasing taxes or reducing transfer payments, the government can reduce consumers' disposable income and thereby curtail their consumption spending. Conversely, by reducing taxes or increasing transfer payments, the government can increase consumers' disposable income and hence their demand for goods. In addition, the government can increase the aggregate (total) demand for goods by increasing its expenditures, *G*, directly.

It should be pointed out that, theoretically, an increase in government expenditures will have more of a stimulative effect on the economy than the depressing effect of an equal increase in income taxes. The reason is that, since the marginal propensity to consume, *c*, is less than one, part of a tax increase is initially absorbed by reduced consumer saving in addition to reduced consumer spending. However, the full amount of a government expenditures increase is immediately reflected in an increased demand for goods and services. Consequently, it is often argued that an equal increase in government expenditures and taxation will increase total spending and output by a modest amount. This amount is called the *balanced budget multiplier*—and usually it is assumed to equal one; that is, for every dollar increase or decrease in government spending and taxation, national income is expected to increase or decrease by the same amount.

Thus the government theoretically can influence the level of national income in the short run by using fiscal policy in any of several ways:

1. The government can change the level of government expenditures. This changes national income in a similar direction. Furthermore, the effect is *multiplied*; an increase in government spending increases production and income, and, in turn, consumers consume more when they receive extra income from increasing production. Similarly, spending cutbacks reduce production and income levels and cause consumption to fall by a multiplied amount as consumers' incomes decline with the decline in production levels.

2. The government can change the level of taxes. This changes consumers' disposable income and consumption rates in the opposite direction. However, tax changes affect consumer saving as well as spending. The initial effect of a $1 change in taxes on demand for final products will be less than the effect of a $1 change in government expenditures. Consequently, tax changes have somewhat weaker multiplier effects than direct-expenditure changes.

3. The government can change the level of transfer payments. This changes disposable income and consumption in the same direction. Changes in transfer payments also can generate multiplier effects. The initial change in consumer spending causes producers to change their production levels, and this alters consumers' incomes in the same direction.

4. Finally, the government can change government expenditures and taxation equally (which can alter the level of national income modestly in the same direction because of balanced-budget multiplier effects).

Keynesian Monetary Policy

Monetary policy is incorporated into the neo-Keynesian view of the economy by assuming that as the level of income and output rises, people will need more money to carry on the elevated level of transactions. Thus the demand for money, M_D, is positively related to the level of production (income). In addition, the speculative demand for money is negatively related to interest rates.

In Equation 25-6, where the demand for money is expressed as a function, *f*, of the level of income and interest rates, the plus sign indicates that a positive association exists between changes in Y and changes in the demand for money, and the minus sign shows a negative relationship between the demand for money and interest rates. The demand for money falls as interest rates rise, because people invest their idle money balances and use their money more efficiently when conducting transactions. Thus, we have:

$$M_D = f(\overset{+}{Y}, \overset{-}{i}). \tag{25-6}$$

If the supply of money is increased in the Keynesian system, it is assumed that consumers will hold more liquidity than they need merely for carrying on transactions. Rather than hold idle money in their portfolios, it is assumed that they will use it to buy interest-bearing securities. As each consumer does so, he or she tends to bid up the price of the securities, so interest rates fall. No money is lost from the economic system, however, as the seller of securities now holds the money. Thus interest rates will continue to fall until they reach a level at which all holders of money are willing to hold it rather than use it to mediate additional transactions or invest in securities carrying the new interest rate.

In this version of the economic system, monetary policy can influence levels of economic activity by changing the money supply. Changes in the money supply will induce opposite changes in interest rates. In particular, an increase in the money supply will tend to reduce interest rates. This will happen because if people have more money than they need for carrying on their income-generating transactions, they will use the surplus to buy securities or investment goods. As they do so, they will drive up the prices of those securities and investments relative to their returns. Thus interest rates will fall until people are content to hold cash that they do not need for transactions rather than invest it. This process works except when the economy is in a liquidity trap.

Effects on Expenditures. Changes in the money supply, in a neo-Keynesian world, generate changes in interest rates. This by itself is not expected to influence economic activity. However, individuals' investment plans for plant and equipment expenditures, housing, planned inventory accumulation, and autonomous consumption (C_O) are all sensitive to interest rates. Therefore, Keynesian theorists believe that by changing the money supply, monetary authorities can change interest rates, which in turn will change spending on housing, inventories, plant and equipment investment, and consumption.

Generally, if the money supply is increased, Keynesian theorists expect interest rates to fall and investment to increase. This will cause total aggregate spending to increase and will generate a higher level of equilibrium income. Reductions in the money supply have the reverse effect. As interest rates rise, consumption and investment plans are curtailed and equilibrium income falls.

Income, Interest Rates, and the Money Supply. Any increase or decrease in equilibrium income will be reduced by the fact that, as income changes, consumers will increase their demands for money. In Exhibit 25-4 we illustrate that at higher income levels, more cash is needed to conduct transactions. Thus with a given money supply, interest rates will have to be higher, so people will reduce cash balances in their portfolios or use money more efficiently for mediating their transactions. If income rises from y_0 to y_1 and the money supply, M_S, does not increase, higher

---

Exhibit 25–4   **Short-Run Relationship of Interest Rates to the Money Stock at Different Income Levels**

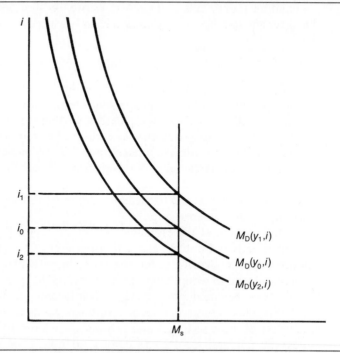

Everything else being equal, the demand for money is greater when interest rates are lower and income is higher. If the money supply remains unchanged, interest rates will rise as nominal national income rises (from y_0 to y_1) and will fall when national income falls (from y_0 to y_2).

---

interest rates will be required to induce people to use their money more efficiently in carrying on the higher volume of transactions. Numerous technological developments have enabled institutions in our economy to carry on a higher volume of transactions with a limited supply of money as interest rates have risen.

Conversely, as income levels fall, people need less money to mediate their transactions. As they invest the excess, prices of securities rise and interest rates fall. Thus if the money supply is fixed, and national income falls from y_0 to y_2, interest rates will fall from i_0 to i_2.

These effects of changing income levels on interest rates subdue but do not eliminate the effects of monetary policy changes on the economy. In particular, if the money supply is increased, after interest rates fall, consumption, C_0, and investment spending will be stimulated. The resulting increase in national income, however, will increase demand for money for transactions purposes. Thus, when the money supply increases, interest rates will fall less than they otherwise would, and national income will increase less than it otherwise would. Nonetheless, national income still will rise when the money supply increases and fall when the money supply decreases.

Because of offsetting effects of income changes on rates, a greater initial change in the money supply will be needed to change the level of national income as much as policymakers may wish. As we shall see in the next section, similar effects reduce the effectiveness of fiscal policy.

Interactions between Keynesian Monetary and Fiscal Policy

Liquidity (Interest Rate) Offset Effects.   In our previous analysis, we noted that changes in government expenditure, tax, or transfer payments policies could affect levels of national income. The effect on national income of such fiscal policy changes could be several times the amount of change in the fiscal policy instrument, depending on the strength of multiplier effects. However, if the monetary policy is not coordinated with fiscal policy, the effects of fiscal policy will be reduced.

For example, if the government wished to stimulate the economy by increasing expenditures, the level of national income would rise. With higher levels of income, however, individuals would need more money to fund the larger volume of transactions. If additional money were not forthcoming, they would be likely to sell assets to gain liquidity, thereby driving down asset prices and driving up interest rates. But with a constant money supply, one individual can gain liquidity only at the expense of another. Therefore, people would continue to be short of liquidity and would continue to sell assets. Eventually interest rates would reach a level at which people would be willing to carry on their national income–generating transactions with smaller average cash balances. At that point, a higher level of national income could be supported with a limited money stock. However, the higher interest rates would reduce investment spending, I, and possibly consumption spending, C_0, as well. As a result, national income would increase less than would otherwise have been the case. In an extreme case, interest rates would rise sufficiently high that the increase in government spending would be almost totally *offset* by decreases in investment and consumption spending. In essence, this is the view taken by the strict quantity theorists, who do not believe that Keynesian fiscal policy will work if the money supply remains unchanged.

Offsetting effects can also occur if the government tries to increase equilibrium income through its tax and transfer payments policies. As equilibrium income rises in response to the stimulative policy, without an increase in the money supply, interest rates will rise, thereby causing investment spending to fall and the resultant rise in national income to be less than would otherwise occur. These offset effects need not be total, but to the extent that they exist, they will make Keynesian fiscal policy less effective.

Offset effects can also occur when the government tries to reduce equilibrium income levels through its fiscal policies. Overall, then, regardless of the fiscal policy used, the net effect of fiscal policy would be less if the money stock remained constant than if the money stock were altered so that interest rates remained unchanged when fiscal policy changed.

Capital Market Crowding Out.   Another view of private-economy offsets to government fiscal policy involves *crowding-out* effects in the capital markets. In that view, when the government decides to run a deficit (caused when expenditures plus transfer payments exceed tax receipts) in order to stimulate the economy, it must finance the deficit by issuing debt on itself. It must either sell securities or issue new

DID YOU KNOW?

Can Monetary Policy Control Real Interest Rates? Classical Economists Didn't Think So

A basic assumption of neo-Keynesian theory is that the Fed can affect interest rates and investment incentives by controlling the money supply. Since investment incentives depend on real interest rates (i.e., interest rates adjusted for potential inflation), for neo-Keynesian theory to work the Fed must be able to control real interest rates. However, monetarists question that propostion. In his 1967 presidential address to the American Economics Association, Milton Friedman noted that monetary policy "cannot peg interest rates for more than a limited period." In fact, Friedman was reasserting what many economists had said prior to Keynes. Consider, for instance, the following quotations:

David Hume (18th century): "Money having chiefly a fictitious [i.e., nominal] value, the greater or less plenty of it is of no consequence .... The same interest, in all cases, bears the same proportion to the [capital] sum. And if you lent me so much labor and so many commodities, by receiving five *per cent* you always receive proportional labor and commodities, however represented."

David Ricardo (1811): "To suppose that any increased issues of [money by] the [Central] Bank can have the effect of permanently lowering the [real] rate of interest ... is to attribute a power to the circulating medium which it can never possess."

John C. Hubbard (1857): "I must confess my amazement at finding people censure or praise the [Central] Bank for making the rate of interest high or low, when the Bank has no possible power to make it the one or the other."

A. C. Pigou (1927): "The [real] rate of interest ... is determined by the general conditions of supply and demand of real capital; these lie outside the Central or any other Bank's controls. ...."*

In short, the classical economists believed that the supply of savings and demand for investment were the only factors that affected the real interest rate, not the monetary policy of the central bank.

* Source of quotations: Thomas M. Humphrey, "Can the Central Bank Peg Real Interest Rates? A Survey of Classical and Neoclassical Opinion," *Economic Review,* Federal Reserve Bank of Richmond, September–October 1983, 12–21.

money (such as coins) that are debt obligations of the federal government. If the money supply is not changed, the government will compete with private borrowersin its attempts to sell securities. Because the government has a prime credit rating(since it can always levy taxes or print money to repay debts), its securities are more attractive than those of private borrowers. Thus when the government is financinga large deficit, it can crowd out some potential private borrowers from the capital markets. This crowding-out effect will make it more difficult, or more expensive, for private borrowers to sell securities, and hence they may curtail their investment spending when the government is running a large deficit. The reduction in investment spending can offset some of the stimulative effects of the government spending or tax reductions. Thus crowding-out effects, like offset effects, can reduce the net effect of fiscal policy.

Unlike the case with offset effects, however, there is some dispute about whether crowding-out effects actually exist. They are hard to document historically. Possibly they exist only when government deficits are extremely large or the economy is at full employment.

Liquidity offset effects and crowding-out effects can conceivably weaken the effects of fiscal policy. As a result, pressures are frequently brought to bear on the monetary authorities by the makers of fiscal policy to accommodate the objectives of fiscal policy. This sometimes leads to bitter debate between the two sets of policymakers, since changes in monetary policy can have a considerable impact on price levels in the economy—and monetary policymakers feel it is their duty to prevent or limit inflation.

Price Levels and National Income

To this point we have been discussing the relationship between money and income in nominal rather than real terms. Nominal national income, Y, is the *dollar value of all income* produced during the relevant period of time. Real national income, y, attempts to measure the *quantity of output or income* produced in a given period of time after adjusting for price changes. The relationship between the two can be expressed as:

$$Y = P \times y, \tag{25-7}$$

where P is a price index set to compare present price levels to some base price level that is given a value of 100 percent.

Viewed from the perspective that $Y = P \times y$, it is obvious that changes in national income can be caused either by changes in price levels or by changes in levels of real output. The question is what determines how much each will change.

If real national income is relatively stable, inflated price levels can be caused by too much money chasing too few goods. In this view of the world, prices are bid up by those who possess excess money as they attempt to exchange it for the relatively fixed supply of real goods.

Real Capacity Limits

In general, price increases usually occur when there is an excess money demand for goods and when supplies are relatively limited. The supply of goods, in the aggregate, is most likely to be limited as the economy approaches the limits of its productive capacity. As the limits of the economy's productive capacity are reached, it becomes more and more difficult to increase production efficiently. Additional productive capacity must be pressed into service, possibly by activating less efficient equipment or using more wasteful procedures. Also, double- or triple-shift production schedules may be instituted, or overtime work shifts may be added—all at increased labor costs per unit of output.

Because it becomes increasingly more difficult to produce additional output at low cost once the limits of an economy's productive capacity are approached, price levels will have to rise further and further in order to induce successive increases in output. This is shown in Exhibit 25-5, which plots the price level that will be needed at any given time to induce a given real output level, y, to be produced. For instance, at price

---

Exhibit 25–5   **Short-Run Relationship between Price Levels and Aggregate Output**

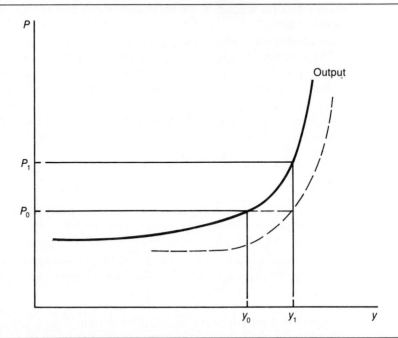

Higher prices are positively associated with national output levels. As national output approaches short-run capacity limits, prices must rise at an accelerating rate to induce people to work longer hours, employers to hire less-skilled workers, and manufacturers to defer maintenance and run their equipment overtime. When output levels are far below capacity, prices will fall as unemployed workers become willing to work for lower wages and producers cut prices to dispose of unsold stocks of goods and keep production lines running. Supply-side theorists believe that the price–output relationship can be shifted to the right, as shown by the dashed line, if governement tax and expenditure policies are designed to encourage more work, investment, and productivity.

---

level P_0, real national income will be produced at the rate y_0. If prices were to rise to P_1, real output levels of y_1 would be produced.

Price and output relationships of the type just described are stable only in the short run. In the longer run, workers will find that the overtime pay they earned was not worth as much (in purchasing-power terms) as they thought it would be. For even though their money wage increased, they can buy less with that wage when prices are at level P_1 than at level P_0. As a result, they will require higher wages. Thus, eventually, labor contracts will be rewritten, the cost of employing overtime workers will go up, and a new price level may be needed to elicit overtime production and increases in real output.

Nonetheless, for analyzing the economy's short-run responses to fiscal or monetary policy stimulus, Exhibit 25-5 can be helpful. Basically, it shows that as national income, y, increases towards real capacity limits, nominal income, Y, will increase even faster, more because of price increases than because of real-output increases.

The relationship shown in Exhibit 25-5 holds true in the short run. In the longer run, however, people will begin to discount expected price changes in their planning and wage bargains. Depending on people's price expectations, proportionately greater aggregate demand and price changes may be needed to induce the same change in real income.

In contrast to the short-run, basically Keynesian view presented previously, quantity theorists and rational-expectations theorists say that in the longer run the real output of the economy, y, will change little from full-employment levels (i.e., levels that would be obtained if workers' price expectations were correct). They believe that policies designed to change national income, y, will primarily change price levels. Thus, in the long run, they believe that the output curve is nearly vertical at y_0 unless something happens to increase capacity.

Regardless of whether price expectations adjust, real capacity limits in the economy are determined by physical manufacturing capacity, the human capital of the labor force, and the availability of labor (the size of the labor force and its willingness to work). The supply-side school of economic policy says that the focus of policy should not be on the short-run trade-off between prices and output but rather on the long-run changes in the real productive capacity of the economy. Thus supply-siders argue that policies undertaken to increase capacity limits (such as tax cuts to encourage investment in capital goods and tax rate cuts to encourage people to work rather than opt for more leisure) will be beneficial.

Supply-siders say that if the productive capacity of the economy can be increased, prices will tend to fall as the supply of goods rises relative to demand. Thus, greater output can be realized at any given price level. Hence, in Exhibit 25-5 the output curve would be shifted down and to the right, as shown by the dashed line, and more output could be produced at any given price level, such as P_0. Supply-siders argue that such noninflationary increases in output are much to be preferred to increases in output induced by price increases.

The neo-Keynesian, quantity theory, rational-expectations, and supply-side schools of economic policy take different views of the relationship between output and prices, in part because they hold different views of the relationship between employment and national income.

Employment and National Income

A major reason that the government attempts to affect the economy through its fiscal and monetary policies is to influence the employment rate. To produce higher levels of national output in the short run, either more workers are needed or employed workers must work longer hours. In the long run, higher levels of output may be obtainable if capital stock (plant and equipment) is accumulated and production processes are organized so that more output can be obtained for a given number of hours worked. In that case, the higher level of output results from improvements in labor productivity.

Politicians, however, are generally concerned with short-run problems because they wish to be elected every few years. Thus they are sensitive to their constituents' demands to increase employment opportunities. Because employment rises with national income in the short run, politicians often try to expand national income. To do this, politicians may (1) raise government expenditures, (2) reduce taxes, (3) raise transfer payments, (4) increase both government expenditures and taxes, or (5) press the monetary authorities to increase the money supply and reduce interest rates.

The theory behind these policies is that by stimulating increases in the demand for goods, nominal income, Y, and real income, y, will increase. As real income increases, either more workers will be required to produce the additional output or existing workers will need to work longer hours. As real output increases, the number of unemployed people (who wish to work but cannot find jobs) should decline.

Politicians hope that policies stimulating aggregate demand will lead to the employment of more workers. However, if people anticipate inflation or if the legal minimum wage is high, aggregate demand increases may have to be substantial to elicit price increases large enough to raise real output and income levels significantly. Furthermore, some workers may not find employment even if real income levels are raised. For example, workers who do not wish to move from a depressed area where usable minerals have already been extracted from mines and there is no industrial base may remain unemployed even if the economy as a whole prospers. Also, individuals who have no salable job skills may not be hired if they require a high minimum wage and their expected job tenure is sufficiently short that employers do not want to risk hiring and training them. In addition, some workers may be reluctant to take jobs for which they have not been trained. Beyond some point, unemployment compensation may enable workers to be choosy about the jobs they accept. Furthermore, additional workers may take jobs only if the working hours are acceptable. Thus some unemployment, called *structural unemployment*, involves people who are unemployed for special reasons, not because there is inadequate spending in the economy to stimulate higher levels of real output.

In addition to structural unemployment, *frictional unemployment* exists because different businesses are constantly starting or failing, expanding or contracting. Regardless of the level of aggregate demand, some businesses will prosper and others will fail as people shift their preferences for products or as natural resources are discovered or exhausted. Thus workers are continuously being employed or laid off. Laid-off workers are likely to be unemployed for a while. In addition, people may quit one job to seek another or move elsewhere. Such people are frictionally unemployed until they locate a different job. Some frictional unemployment will exist regardless of the level of demand for national product—albeit if the level of aggregate demand is sufficiently high, the frictionally unemployed will find suitable new jobs faster and the level of unemployment will fall.

Nonetheless, because of structural and frictional unemployment, one can never expect the level of unemployment to fall to zero. Moreover, governmental policies affecting minimum wage laws, unemployment or welfare compensation, and employment training may all affect the level of structural unemployment as much as or more than changes in aggregate demand.

Changes in Unemployment

It is hard to say exactly what constitutes an "acceptable" level of unemployment. However, if politicians try to reduce unemployment solely through policies stimulating aggregate demand, prices may have to rise substantially in order to elicit the desired decline in unemployment.

Furthermore, people can be fooled for only a short period of time. If demand increases are large, it is possible to induce some otherwise unwilling people to work more because they believe an increase in their nominal wage will substantially increase their purchasing power. However, once they find that price increases have eroded their purchasing power, they will be reluctant to work until they negotiate wage contracts to provide even larger money wage increases. In that case, it may take an even larger (unexpected) price increase to induce them to work more than they otherwise would.

Consequently, politicians may find that when they initially stimulate the aggregate demand for goods in the economy, the level of real output forthcoming with any given price increase may be relatively large. However, as people begin to anticipate inflation, increasingly larger doses of economic stimulus may be needed to generate sustained increases in real output and reductions in unemployment.

As mentioned before, Keynesian theorists believe that workers have "money-illusion"; that is, they judge the return to their work according to the number of dollars they receive and are not concerned with how much they can buy with it. Thus, if prices fall, they may prefer to be unemployed rather than work at a low dollar wage, W. This was a problem during the Great Depression, when numerous bank failures caused the U.S. money supply to shrink and prices to fall.

The flip side of money illusion is that workers will give up leisure and work more if nominal wages rise. Thus neo-Keynesians believe unemployment will fall and aggregate output will increase substantially when an increase in aggregate demand stimulates the economy and causes prices to rise.

In contrast with the Keynesian view, quantity theorists believe that people do not have money illusion for long. They believe that the levels of unemployment will hover around the full-employment level—where the only unemployment is frictional or structural in nature. The full-employment level of output will be determined by the real wage, W/P. This is the dollar wage divided by the price level to determine its purchasing power.

The real wage depends on the productivity of labor and on the willingness of workers to sacrifice leisure to earn a higher real wage. This is illustrated in Exhibit 25–2, where the supply of labor is shown to increase as the real wage, W/P, rises. The demand for labor, in contrast, falls as the real wage rises, because there are fewer jobs at which workers' productivity is sufficiently high to justify paying a high real wage rather than a low real wage.

The equilibrium real wage (price of labor) will be determined at the point where the demand for labor equals the supply of labor. This also determines the level of full employment, since all people (except those frictionally or structurally unemployed) who want to work at that wage will be able to find a job.

In the view of the quantity theorists, demand-stimulating policies can change employment levels only temporarily by changing prices (and hence W/P). However, once people realize that their nominal wage will not buy the same amount as before, they will rewrite their wage contracts to retain their purchasing power. Since the level of employment does not change substantially in the long run, neither will the level of real output.

At this point, supply-siders extend the quantity theory by noting that it is the real wage *after tax* that counts when potential workers decide how much labor to supply. Clearly, if taxes took all of a worker's wages, that person would have no incentive to work. However, if taxes were reduced, the worker would supply more labor. The supply-side theory, then, argues that the supply-of-labor curve would shift to the right and the amount of labor supplied would increase if taxes were reduced. This would increase the level of national income in a noninflationary manner.

Quantity Theory of Money and Output

Quantity Theory versus Keynesian Theory

The quantity theory's adherents believe that the level of national income, Y, is directly related to the quantity of money in circulation in the economy. Quantity theorists and monetarists also believe that, in the long run, changes in the quantity of money will primarily affect the price level, since a competitive economy will automatically move toward full employment. Moreover, quantity theorists believe that fiscal policy, unaccompanied by monetary policy changes, is unlikely to be effective because of full liquidity offset effects. In other words, they believe that unless the money supply increases, if the government spends more, private individuals will spend less and vice versa. This occurs because velocity is constant. Monetarists have similar beliefs, but acknowledge that fiscal policy can have a limited effect, but only if velocity varies in the short run or if the money supply changes.

The quantity theory assumes that over a period of time the economy will adjust toward equilibrium levels of interest rates, prices, output, and employment. It takes a long-run view of the world that does not worry greatly about fluctuations in spending, output, and income over short periods. The Keynesian theory, in contrast, is mainly concerned with predicting economic trends for the next year or two. It deals with a world in which prices, wages, and interest rates do not necessarily change instantaneously with changing economic conditions. Because Keynesian theory predicts short-term events, it is often used for business and economic forecasting.

Also because of its short-run nature, Keynesian theory often assumes that people can be fooled by price increases into working for lower real wages, Similarly, it assumes that any increase in liquidity (the money stock) in the economy must reduce interest rates and stimulate investment. However, interest rates may not fall if potential lenders associate the increased money stock with inflationary governmental policies. If so, lenders will demand higher interest rates so they can preserve their future purchasing power. Thus neo-Keynesian theory can predict precisely what will happen in the economy to demand, real output, prices, and employment in the short run only if people can be continuously fooled in the same manner. Some economists have proposed that people have rational expectations. If so, they cannot be systematically fooled about potential price changes in a predictable manner. These economists often maintain that the quantity theory of money, income, and prices is more appropriate for explaining the long-run behavior of the economy.

Strict quantity theorists believe that if the supply of money exceeds individuals' demand for money, some people will be holding more money than they want to hold. They will have a *portfolio imbalance*—too much money relative to their need for it to carry on income-generating transactions.

An individual can get rid of excess stocks of money by spending them. As this occurs, the demand for goods and services will go up. The extra spending will drive up prices, P, or induce people to expand real output, y. Note that, in contrast with the neo-Keynesian theory, excess-money balances induce spending directly. It is not necessary that interest rates fall first.

As each individual spends excess money balances, a new individual acquires those balances. As a result, the new individual may find himself or herself holding more money than desired. For instance, because of increased sales, a merchant may find that she holds more money and fewer inventories than she desires. As she spends some of the extra money to rectify her personal portfolio imbalance, another individual will acquire an extra money balance and spend it. This process will stop only when P or y have risen to the point that all money is willingly held by people who demand money balances to facilitate transactions. In short, if there is growth in the money supply, the forces just described cause total spending, price levels, and/or real output to grow until the demand for money equals its supply once again.

Reverse effects occur if the money supply is contracted. People who find that they hold too little money relative to income reduce their expenditures to conserve money balances. This drives down real output or price levels to the point at which people no longer wish to hold more money than they have. At that point, the demand for money equals the supply of money again.

The preceding is a highly simplified version of the quantity theory. Modern quantity theorists (monetarists) note that the velocity of money, V, can vary with the interest rate and other factors. However, monetarists assume that velocity (V or $1/k$) changes *predictably* over time with changes in the interest rate and other factors. Thus they think that, once allowance is made for such changes, the rate of growth in the money stock will tend to determine the rate of growth in nominal national income, Y.

Unfortunately, changes in the velocity of money, which from our formula equals Y/M, can vary substantially in the short run. Thus quantity theory relationships may be better for explaining changes in the economy that take place over long periods of time (such as years) than over short periods of time (such as the next three or six months).

Monetarists often argue that monetary policy should produce a constant growth rate of money that, after adjustment for predictable changes in velocity, should equal the growth rate of the economy's productive capacity. Even though such a policy might not stabilize the economy completely if velocity changed in the short run, it would help subdue business cycle fluctuations. People would spend more freely as they accumulated more cash relative to their income during business cycle downturns, and opposite effects would occur during business cycle upturns. Furthermore, such a policy would eliminate the need for arbitrary political influence to control the economy. Politically motivated economic actions often have an inflationary bias because politicians dislike unemployment more than inflation. Many monetarists believe constant money growth is preferable to the alternative. Many rational-expectations theorists also advocate a constant money growth rule.

Rational-Expectations Theory

The rational-expectations view of the world first developed in the 1960s and 1970s, when the economy did not behave as predicted by the neo-Keynesians. It suggests that, depending on people's expectations, discretionary changes in monetary policy may not have their desired effect on interest rates and the economy. For instance, a rapid increase in the money supply can cause people to expect inflation. As a result, market interest rates may rise, not fall, as lenders try to maintain their real rate of return by charging more to borrowers of funds. At the same time, if people expected more inflation, they would demand larger wage increases than would otherwise be the case, and the expansive monetary policy would not cause unemployment to fall as desired.

Rational-expectations theorists also suggest that fiscal policy may not have its intended effects. If people anticipate that they ultimately will have to pay higher future taxes to pay the interest and principal on government debt, they will not be fooled into spending more when the government cuts taxes and increases its deficit. As a result, neither tax cuts nor tax increases will have the full effect predicted by neo-Keynesian economists.

Because they believe that neither discretionary monetary policy nor fiscal policy may have its intended effect, depending on people's expectations, rational expectations theorists usually argue that monetary policy should at least be stable and predictable. Then, if prices rose in a stable manner, people's expectations would eventually be consistent with reality. They would no longer require an uncertainty premium in interest rates, over and above their inflationary expectations, to compensate them for their uncertainties about the real rate of return on their invested funds. In addition, if price trends were predictable, people would be more willing to enter into long-term contracts in labor markets as well as in the debt markets, and they would no longer have to waste time and effort rewriting contracts if prices did not move in accord with their expectations. Thus many rational-expectations theorists, who also adhere to the quantity theory, believe that monetary policy ideally should aim for a constant rate of growth in the money supply. Fiscal policy would not be altered in a discretionary manner.

To some extent, the views of rational-expectations theorists stimulated the development of supply-side economics. Supply-siders reasoned that if discretionary monetary and fiscal policy could not be used to stimulate the economy in a desired manner, then other techniques might be needed. Many supply-siders adopted the stable price-level objective of the rational-expectations theorists and looked for other policies that might have an effect on the economy. They concluded that efforts taken to increase productive capacity, by cutting taxes to stimulate investment spending, savings, and work effort, might have the desired effects.

Supply-Side Theory

The supply-side theory of the economy has its roots in the theories of the classical economists. It emphasizes factors that will increase the total supply of goods and is not concerned with the problems of inadequate total demand. The supply-side theory assumes that price levels are primarily determined by monetary policy, that fiscal policy is relatively unimportant, and that interest rates are determined by the productivity of investment and people's propensity to save. However, it takes an active rather than passive view toward the natural level of full-employment output, y_{FE}.

As noted earlier, supply-side theorists assume that the supply of labor can be reduced by high income tax rates. They also assume that productive investment opportunities will become more attractive if taxes are lower. Thus they believe that cutting taxes will eventually increase both the labor supply and the amount of the nation's capital stock. This will increase the economy's productive capacity and level of output without requiring that prices increase first.

During the Reagan administration, supply-side policymakers had great influence. They convinced the president to cut tax rates while maintaining a restrictive monetary policy. Unfortunately, since supply-siders did not think that, aside from taxes, fiscal policy was very important, they did not press the president to cut planned government spending as much as tax revenues in the short run. In addition, they did not think that drastic expenditure cuts would be necessary in the long run. Once the economy expanded in response to the tax-rate cuts, total tax revenues would rise once again.

However, supply-siders miscalculated. They were unsuccessful in getting Congress to cut its spending tendencies. Thus, in the 1980s, government expenditures continued to rise as a percentage of GNP even though tax revenues stabilized or fell. This increased the government deficit dramatically and put tremendous strains on the nation's capital markets.

The effect of government deficits on the capital markets is illustrated in Exhibit 25–6, which shows that an increase in government demand for a limited supply of loanable funds drives up real interest rates.

The large government deficits in the 1980s increased the total demand for loanable funds substantially, although their supply was not materially changed. As a result, real interest rates rose considerably. In addition to the deficit, real rates also rose because people born in the postwar "baby boom" years were becoming heavy borrowers and because inflation slowed faster than people expected after monetary policy turned restrictive in 1979. The increase in real rates hurt interest rate sensitive industries (such as housing, construction, and investment goods). It also had the effect of attracting foreign investment and driving up the U.S. exchange rate, thereby causing hardship for U.S. exporters as well as for U.S. firms (such as auto and steel manufacturers) that competed with foreign manufacturers of imported goods. In addition, borrowers had substantial difficulties repaying their debts. Although creditors gained at the expense of debtors, they too were jeopardized by the sharp rise in debtor bankruptcies. As a result, the economy as a whole weakened, and in

Exhibit 25–6   **Loanable Funds and the Deficit**

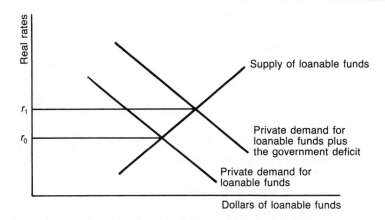

A government deficit adds to the demand for available loanable funds at any interest rate level. As a result, government deficits increase the equilibrium real rate of interest and reduce private investors' demand for borrowed funds, from right to left. Meanwhile, the total supply of savings (at the new higher rate) rises from left to right.

1981–1982, it experienced the deepest recession since the Great Depression of the 1930s.

The implementation of the supply-side policy presented several problems. First, Congress did not legislate the full policy package. Second, it should not have been expected to work instantly. Third, it should not have assumed that government fiscal policy does not matter. Clearly, the huge government deficits of the 1980s had a substantial effect on real interest rates, exchange rates, financial markets, and the economy in general. Thus it clearly was a mistake to cut taxes without cutting total government expenditures at the same time. Nonetheless, except for the large deficits and high real interest rates (which were only partially caused by the deficits), supply-side policies generally were successful. In response to tax incentives, investment spending rose rapidly after 1982 and the level of employment (total new jobs) rose rapidly while prices rose slowly throughout the Reagan administration.

Summary

The level of national income is affected by the total demand for goods and services for consumption, investment, (net) exports, and government use. It also is affected by the nation's physical and human capital stock and by individuals' willingness and ability to produce products that are in demand. At times, economic and financial policymakers may try to change the level of national income (in order to change the level of unemployment or the rate of inflation) by changing fiscal or monetary policies.

Classical economists believed in Say's Law, which holds that all goods produced will be demanded. Thus they focused on policies designed to increase total produc-

PEOPLE
&EVENTS

Wicksellian Economists Influence the Fed

Because velocity is variable, money supply definitions are changeable, and interest rates affect the economy only with long and variable lags, the Fed often has trouble telling quickly what impact its monetary policy is likely to have on the economy. For that reason, some Fed governors have adopted a Wicksellian policy.

During the 1930s depression period, Sweden was one of the few countries to experience relatively stable price levels. In the United States, in contrast, price levels fell by nearly one-third during the 1930s as numerous bank failures caused the U.S. money supply to contract sharply. Some people believe that Sweden's relative price stability resulted from its use of "Wicksellian policies" (named after Knut Wicksell, a Swedish economist). While his policies are old, they are still used to some extent today by the Federal Reserve System.

Wicksell said that the economy had two interest rates: (1) the bank rate, or "market rate," and (2) the "natural rate" of interest or real rate of return that equilibrated the supply and demand for funds. If the bank rate (such as the Fed Funds rate) were below the natural rate (which could not be observed directly), people would tend to borrow money to invest, thereby (1) increasing aggregate demand, (2) increasing commodity prices (industrial goods' prices are among the first to rise when the economy starts to accelerate), (3) increasing gold prices (which tend to rise when the market sniffs inflation), and (4) increasing foreign currency prices. These effects occur because an excess increase in the money supply will cause the bank interest rate to fall below the natural rate and thereby increase aggregate demand and prices. The dollar will fall in value as inflation proceeds; thus flexible investors will tend to sell dollars and buy gold, foreign currencies, or physical assets when they fear inflation. They will do this when they think the money supply is growing too rapidly and causing the bank rate to be too low —thereby stimulating aggregate demand and price increases.

Conversely, if the bank rate is above the natural rate of interest, the demand for goods and investments will fall and commodity prices will fall. Because of falling prices for domestic goods, inflationary expectations will be low, so gold prices will fall and the dollar will tend to rise in value relative to foreign currencies. The term structure of interest rates is also likely to slope down, as a shortage of money is likely to cause market interest rates to be high in the short run and fall in the future (if the economy enters a recession later on).

Wicksellian followers, then, tend to monitor the term structure of interest rates, commodity prices, gold prices, and the foreign exchange value of the dollar. If it appears that the bank rate (Fed Funds rate) is too low, the term structure of interest rates is upsloping (due to expected increases in future inflation), and prices of everything but the dollar are rising, Wicksellian policymakers will contract the money supply and raise the Fed Funds rate. Conversely, if the reverse conditions apply—that is, the term structure slopes down, commodity prices and gold prices are falling, and the dollar's foreign exchange value is rising—they will advocate increasing bank reserves and the money supply and lowering the Fed Funds rate.

In the early 1990s, therefore, several members of the Federal Reserve Board of Governors (Wayne Angell, John LaWare, and Manley Johnson) tended to watch changes in the slope of the term structure of interest rates as well as changes in gold, commodity, and foreign currency prices (expressed in dollars) to see if monetary policy was causing dollar prices of those items to fall or rise and determine whether monetary policy should be eased or loosened. While those governors of the Fed were not Wicksellians per se, since they also listened to other theories, they did cause the Greenspan Fed to be more eclectic in its approach than some previous Fed Boards. (See, for instance, "Dr. Wicksell, We Presume," *The Economist*, April 28, 1990, pp. 84, 86.)

tion. However, the Great Depression of the 1930s was caused, in part, by inadequate product demand. Thus neo-Keynesian policymakers usually focus on the aggregate level of demand for economic products. They believe that changes in the level of aggregate demand will affect both the price level and the employment level. Monetary policy is of importance to them only through the effect it is expected to have on interest rates or real wage levels.

Neo-Keynesian policymakers are most likely to adopt government expenditure, tax, and transfer payments policies to affect the economy. They are also likely to try to adjust market interest rates in order to affect private investment spending. Keynesian policymakers may be reluctant to tolerate wide swings in interest rates lest they cause people to overreact and cause investment spending to become too high or too low. When neo-Keynesians are in power, total credit may grow erratically but interest rates may be more stable than might otherwise be the case.

Quantity theorists, in contrast, are far less concerned with interest rates than with controlling the money supply. They are not greatly concerned about policies designed to affect investment spending, government spending or government tax and transfer payments policies. They believe that, left to its own devices, the economy will tend toward full employment. Monetary policy, therefore, will mainly affect the price level, and fiscal policy is not needed.

When quantity theorists are in power, expansion of depository institutions' deposits may proceed more smoothly over time, but fluctuations in interest rates may be greater than when the neo-Keynesians have policy influence. When quantity theorists are in power, managers of financial institutions are well advised to hedge themselves against potentially large and quick changes in interest rates.

Rational-expectations theorists are similar to quantity theorists in that they believe that changes in the money supply will affect price levels. However, they also believe that the effects monetary and fiscal policies have on the economy depend on people's expectations. To stabilize the economy, they believe that policymakers must pursue monetary policies designed to stabilize the long-run growth of the money supply and inflation. If they do so, then people can better plan for the future, and risk premiums in interest rates will no longer be needed to compensate for uncertainty about future inflation.

The supply-side school of economic policy is similar to the monetarist school in many respects. Supply-siders believe that the economy will tend toward full employment, that fiscal policy is not particularly effective, that monetary policy primarily affects price levels, and that the major problem the economy faces is to increase productive capacity. They would accomplish this by cutting income taxes and stimulating savings and productive investment. When supply-siders are in power, financial institution managers and financial market participants should take care to protect themselves against unexpected changes in market interest rates. They should also remember that supply-siders promote policies designed to increase the total flow of savings and the rate of capital formation.

If supply-side policies to promote savings and investment are successful, financial institution managers can profit by developing a way to channel individuals' increased savings flows back into the capital markets. The development of savings-oriented financial services can be profitable when supply-siders are in control. At the same time, if the supply-siders succeed in reducing marginal income tax rates, financial institutions that provide tax-sheltered income may find the demand for their services reduced.

Finally, because no one theory provides the single best explanation for how the economy behaves, practical policymakers need to be eclectic and monitor many aspects of economic development. That is why some Fed governors listen to Wicksellian views (see "Did You Know") and why many firms hire "Fed-watchers."

Questions

1. Why do Keynesian theorists think that government expenditures have multiplier effects? How do they think government fiscal policy can affect the economy?
2. How do neo-Keynesian economists believe monetary policy affects the economy?
3. How can monetary or financial considerations offset some of the effects of fiscal policy?
4. Under what circumstances can stimulation of increased economic output lead to rapid price increases? As prices rise, what is likely to happen to interest rates? What is likely to happen to employment? Why?
5. Why is it impossible to obtain unemployment rates of zero—or even close to zero?
6. How do quantity theorists get their name? Why do they think that, in the long run, changes in the money supply will affect prices rather than unemployment?
7. What is the essential difference between the neo-Keynesian and the quantity theory view of the economic world?
8. Why do supply-siders think that it is possible to increase income and employment without causing inflation? How would they do so?
9. What problems did the Reagan administration encounter when it first adopted supply-side policies?
10. If you were the manager of a financial institution, would you sleep better if Keynesians, quantity theorists, rational-expectations theorists, or supply-siders were in power? Why?
11. Why do Wicksellians think (1) the term structure of interest rates, commodity prices, and (2) the foreign exchange value of the dollar are often important?

Selected References

Anderson, Leonall C., and Jerry L. Jordan. "Monetary and Fiscal Actions: A Test of Their Relative Importance in Economic Stabilization." *Review*. Federal Reserve Bank of St. Louis, November 1968, pp. 11–24.
This important article supports quantity theorists' view that monetary policy has a substantial effect on the economy and fiscal policy does not.

Barth, James R. "The Costs of Slowing Inflation: Four Views." *Economic Review*. Federal Reserve Bank of Atlanta, January 1982.
This article does an excellent job of describing the proposals and differing views of the Keynesian, quantity theory, supply-side, and rational-expectations approaches to economic policy.

Dewald, William G. "Monetarism Is Dead; Long Live the Quantity Theory." *Review.* **Federal Reserve Bank of St. Louis, July/August 1988, pp. 3–18.**
Points out that velocity and the economy's responses to changes in monetary policy are not sufficiently predictable to allow the Fed to use monetary policy to "fine tune" short-run fluctuations in the economy, as some monetarists might wish. Notes that a constant monetary growth rule as advocated by quantity theorists is likely to provide a stable long-run basis for monetary policy.

Friedman, Milton. "The Role of Monetary Policy." *American Economic Review,* **March 1968, pp. 1–17.**
This highly readable speech clearly and succinctly presents the monetarist view of the economic world.

Friedman, Milton, and Anna Schwartz. *A Monetary History of the United States, 1867–1960.* **Princeton, NJ: Princeton University Press, 1963.**
Presents the historical statistics that document the quantity theory view that money, prices, national income, and velocity are closely related.

Holland, A. Steven. "Rational Expectations and the Effects of Monetary Policy: A Guide for the Uninitiated." *Review.* **Federal Reserve Bank of St. Louis, May 1985, pp. 5–11.**
This article provides an excellent introduction to the rational-expectations theory and its implications for monetary policy.

Roberds, William. "Forecast Accuracy and the Performance of Monetary Policy: Is There a Connection?" *Economic Review.* **Federal Reserve Bank of Atlanta, September/October 1988, pp. 20–32.**
Monetary policy's effect on the economy occurs with long and variable lags, and the economy's current state is known only with a reporting lag. Furthermore, the public may change its behavior when it anticipates changes in Fed policy, thus making the Fed's policy effects even more problematic. Thus the author suggests that a constant money growth rate, as advocated by rational expectations and monetarist theorists, may be more effective for stabilizing the economy than discretionary monetary policies.

Thornton, Daniel L. "Why Does Velocity Matter?" *Review.* **Federal Reserve Bank of St. Louis, December 1983, pp. 5–13.**
This article provides an excellent view of why monetarists think that the economy can be controlled by changing the money supply, provided that velocity is predictable. It also points out that the instability of velocity poses substantial problems for short-run monetary control.

EFFECTS OF MONETARY POLICY ON FINANCIAL MARKETS

26

WHEN GERMANY AND JAPAN INCREASE their interest rates, the U.S. Fed must react. Why? What happens when the Fed changes its policies? Obviously the policies of the central bank do something or the Fed wouldn't be so controversial, but exactly what does monetary policy do? Although the precise effect of monetary policy can vary according to people's expectations, most people agree that monetary policy actions first affect financial markets and financial institutions. Because monetary policy changes affect the public's liquid asset and wealth holdings, credit availability, and interest rates, they influence investment, consumption, and government expenditure decisions with various lags. Expenditure decisions, in turn, affect prices, the level of economic activity, and market interest rates all around the world.

This chapter describes the short-run changes that occur in the financial system when monetary authorities intervene. Also noted are the ripple effects that such changes have on the financial markets and the short-run effects that policy-induced financial market changes have on the different components of aggregate demand. It discusses the effects monetary policy has on the economy as a whole—and also, the interrelationship between our domestic monetary policy and international considerations. It points out how some of the long-run implications of monetary policy actions may be substantially different from the short-run effects. It also points out how expectations of long-run price changes can modify the short-run responses of the economy and the financial system to monetary policy. Finally, it describes some of the political complications that cause the Federal Reserve to adopt fluctuating rather than stable monetary policies as economic conditions change.

Initial Impact of Federal Reserve Policy

Changes in the Federal Reserve's monetary policy have a direct effect on depository institutions. The Fed has three main tools to influence the money supply: open market operations, legal reserve requirements, and the discount rate.

Effects of Open Market Operations and Reserve Requirement Changes

Changes in both open market operations and reserve requirements affect depository institutions' excess reserve positions. If the Fed purchases additional securities through open market operations, it will increase financial institutions' total reserves, net excess reserves, and the monetary base. Reductions in deposit reserve requirements increase excess reserves and increase the ability of the monetary base to support deposit expansion (by increasing the deposit-expansion multiplier). Conversely, Fed sales of government securities reduce reserves, net excess reserves, and the monetary base, and increases in reserve requirements reduce net excess reserves and decrease the ability of the monetary base to support deposit expansion.

When depository institutions acquire more reserves, they generally make additional loans and investments rather than hold idle, noninterest-bearing excess reserves. When depository institutions seek to acquire more investment securities, they bid up the price of securities, which reduces their yields (interest rates). In addition, as depository institutions seek to acquire more loans, they either make credit more readily available (that is, extend more credit at the same rate while taking slightly higher credit risks) or reduce interest rates to attract borrowers from other lending institutions.

Regardless of whether they acquire more loans or investments, when institutions increase their asset holdings, their liabilities also expand. Because depository institutions' liabilities form the major component of the various money supply measures, such as M1, M2, and M3, when depository institutions expand their assets, they also increase the money supply.

Exhibit 26–1 illustrates the financial effects that result from an increase in Fed open market purchases or reductions in reserve requirements. It could also illustrate the opposite effects that would result if the Fed sold government securities in the open market or raised reserve requirements. In that case, depository institutions' net excess reserves would decline, and they might even have to borrow more reserves from the Fed than they desired in the short run. To repay the borrowed reserves, they would sell off investments or make fewer loans. As a result, their asset holdings and the money supply would decline, security prices would fall and interest rates would rise, and loans would be less readily available or more expensive. Thus, in general, all the signs shown in Exhibit 26–1 would reverse if the Fed sold securities or raised reserve requirements.

Effects of Discount Rate Changes

The effect of discount rate changes is somewhat more complicated than open market operations or reserve requirement changes. Changes in the discount rate can affect financial institutions' reserves, the Federal Funds rate, or financial market psychology. This is illustrated in Exhibit 26–2.

Reserve Effects.   Lowering the discount rate relative to market interest rates will induce more depository institutions to borrow from the Fed, thereby increasing financial institutions' reserves and the monetary base. Because of the increase in depository institution reserves, the monetary base will increase, and depository institutions will expand their loans and investments. As depository institutions do so, the money supply increases, security prices tend to rise, market interest rates generally decline, and credit availability generally increases. Increases in the discount rate will have opposite effects.

Exhibit 26–1   **Financial Effects of Changes in Reserves and Reserve Requirements**

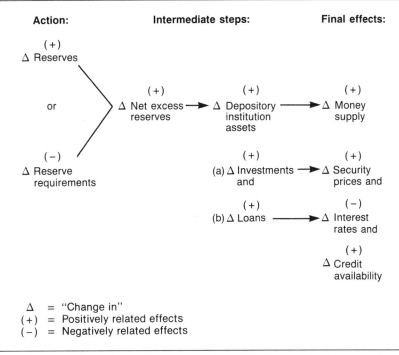

An increase in reserves (or a decrease in reserve requirements) will cause the money supply and credit availability to increase, and ordinarily it will cause interest rates to fall and security prices to rise. A decrease in reserves (or an increase in reserve requirements) will have opposite effects.

Effects on the Fed Funds Rate.   If banks borrow from the Fed, changes in the discount rate also have a direct effect on the Federal Funds rate. Bank borrowing can be influenced by the discount rate because, rather than borrow from another depository institution, a bank that needs reserves can borrow from the Fed at the discount rate. Thus, if the discount rate falls, more institutions that need reserves will borrow from the Fed rather than in the Federal Funds market. As a result, total bank reserves will increase, and the Fed Funds rate will fall (unless the Fed takes action to prevent it from falling). Conversely, an increase in the discount rate will decrease borrowing from the Fed, reduce bank reserves, and increase the demand for Federal funds, thereby causing that rate to rise.

Psychological Effects.   The final effect of a change in the discount rate involves security market psychology. The preceding paragraphs point out that depository institutions are likely to lend and invest more freely when the discount rate is low relative to other rates. Increased lending is associated with an expansionary monetary and economic policy, decreased lending with contraction. Hence, when the discount rate is low (relative to other interest rates), many financial market participants expect that depository institutions will make more loans and that monetary policy and the economy will be expansive. When the discount rate is relatively high, however, many

---

Exhibit 26–2   **Changes in the Discount Rate**

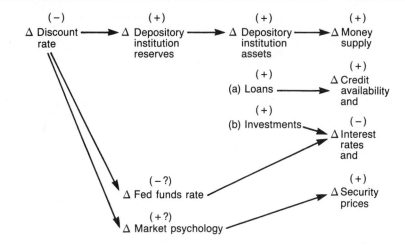

$\underline{\Delta}$ = "Change in"
(+) = Positively related effects
(−) = Negatively related effects

Changes in the discount rate often cause market interest rates to change similarly. When the discount rate falls, everything else being equal, depository institutions borrow more from the Fed and increase their loans and investments. That, in turn, causes the money supply and credit availability to increase. It also generally causes interest rates to fall and security prices to rise. Changes in the Fed Funds rate and market psychology following a discount-rate change often reinforce the interest-rate and security-price effects.

---

financial market participants expect that monetary policy will be restrictive and that the economy will decelerate.

Thus, when the Federal Reserve System changes the discount rate, many financial market participants anticipate future changes in the economy and react accordingly. Some of their reactions can have major short-run effects on financial market prices and yields. In particular, stock and bond prices often move up or down sharply in response to discount rate changes. For instance, when the Fed cut its discount rate from $4\frac{1}{2}$ percent to $3\frac{1}{2}$ percent on December 20, 1991, the stock market jumped sharply higher—nearly 10 percent within a month. Conversely, stock and bond prices often fall sharply when the discount rate rises. Consequently, the Federal Reserve System often is reluctant to change the discount rate before other market interest rates change, lest financial markets be disrupted. Therefore, changes in the discount rate frequently follow, rather than lead, other changes in interest rates. This is shown in Exhibit 26–3.

If the Federal Reserve wants to change the psychology of market participants, particularly foreign-exchange-market traders and stock- and bond-market partici-

Exhibit 26-3   Short-Term Interest Rates 1985-1991

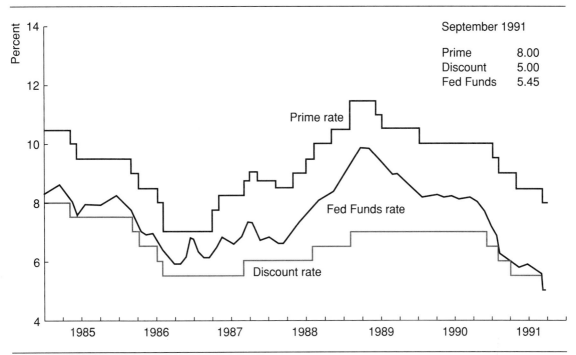

September 1991

Prime	8.00
Discount	5.00
Fed Funds	5.45

Federal Funds rate is the monthly average of daily figures.

Prime rate changed two times during May 1987, October 1987, and February 1989.

Note that changes in Fed Funds rates usually precede changes in the discount rate.

Source: Federal Reserve Bank of St. Louis, *Monetary Trends*, October 1991.

pants, it may change the discount rate to give warning of pending changes in Fed policy. Thus, if the discount rate unexpectedly increases before other interest rates rise, it signals a tightening of policy. Investors in long-term securities or foreign currencies may then try to reduce their holdings of those assets quickly before their prices fall substantially. At the same time, they may seek to borrow more long-term funds at relatively low rates before interest rates rise further. These actions drive up interest rates, particularly long-term rates, as securities prices fall, and they increase the value of the dollar relative to other currencies as foreign-exchange traders try to take advantage of rising interest rates in the United States.

Opposite effects occur when the Federal Reserve reduces the discount rate to signal plans to make monetary policy more expansive and depository institution loans easier to obtain. For example, when the Fed decided to ease monetary policy in mid-1982, it made frequent reductions in the discount rate, starting in July. Before the end of August, a strong rally in the stock and bond markets had commenced and interest rates fell sharply.

Effects of Federal Reserve Policy on the Financial System

Changes in Fed policy, then, can initially affect the money supply, security prices, credit availability, market interest rates, and market psychology. Each of these initial effects can have secondary effects on financial markets and the economy.

Effects of Changes in the Money Supply

Changes in the money supply affect the economy by affecting spending on goods and services, investment in securities, and interest rates. The first two effects work through portfolio adjustments by holders of money.

Spending Effects.   The first portfolio adjustment, emphasized by monetarists, is the adjustment that occurs between actual money balances, desired money balances, and spending on goods and services. Given the level of income, Y, quantity theorists note that desired money balances in the economy as a whole equal some predictable fraction of income. If the money supply is increased by government policy actions, then the money supply will exceed the money demanded. People will have more money than they want to hold at income level Y. They will get rid of the excess by spending it. Since the newly created money can be transferred from one person to another, but is not destroyed in the process, the increased level of spending on goods, services, and securities will continue until the new money is willingly held. This occurs when the level of output and prices rises to the point at which people need all their money to carry on transactions and have no extra liquidity in the aggregate to buy additional goods or services.

Conversely, if the Fed takes actions that cause the money supply to decrease, in the short run the demand for money will exceed the (reduced) supply of money. This will create a portfolio imbalance in which people hold less money than they desire relative to their income levels. To accumulate more money, they will reduce their spending on goods and services. Consequently, decreases in the money supply may precede slowdowns in the economy. Monetarists expect that changes in total spending and production will follow similar changes in the money supply with a lag of several quarters.

Security Price (Portfolio Imbalance) Effects.   Investors and other people may desire to hold a relatively constant portion of their wealth in the form of money. If their money holdings increase while their security holdings do not, their supply of money will temporarily exceed their demand for it. For instance, investors' money holdings will increase if they sell some securities for a high price to a depository institution that is increasing its investment holdings. As a result, investors may hold 15 percent of their assets in money. If they prefer to hold only 10 percent of their portfolio in cash, they may use their excess money to buy more securities to redress this portfolio imbalance—thereby transferring their excess cash to someone else. As this process occurs throughout the economy, security prices will be bid up. When security prices rise sufficiently, investors as a whole will find their portfolio balance is restored; their money holdings will once again equal the desired percentage (10 percent in our example) of their portfolio value.

The reverse effect will occur if the money supply shrinks. An institution or individual may use some money to buy securities from a depository institution that is contracting its investments by selling off securities at an attractive price. As a result, the individual and investors as a whole may hold less money than they desire relative to their security holdings. As each investor in turn tries to acquire more money by selling securities, security prices will fall until the desired balance between money holdings and security values is restored once again.

Interest Rate Effects.   A change in the money supply can affect interest rates in two ways. First, when security prices rise or fall, their rates of return vary inversely. Thus, if an increase in the money supply causes security prices to rise, market interest rates will fall. Conversely, a decrease in the money supply will cause security prices to fall and market interest rates to rise.

The second effect is illustrated in Exhibit 26-4, which shows that an increase in the money supply acts like an increase in the supply of loanable funds, because the new money is available to be lent to people who need to borrow funds for investment purposes. As a result, the real interest rate tends to fall and the level of investment tends to rise *while the money supply is increasing.* Conversely, if the money supply is contracted, fewer funds will be available for lending in the financial markets. Therefore, real interest rates will tend to rise and investment will tend to fall somewhat.

Changes in Interest Rates

Injections of additional reserves into the financial system can cause the Federal Funds rate to fall sharply on any given day. This is so because institutions with excess

---

Exhibit 26-4   Effects of a Change in Money Supply on Loanable Funds

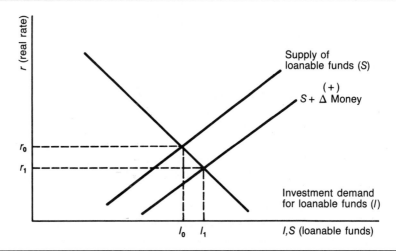

While the money supply is being increased, more funds become available to be lent to potential borrowers; thus the real interest rate declines ro r_1 and investment increases to I_1. However, this effect stops as soon as the money supply stabilizes.

reserves may be willing to accept a sharply reduced rate of return, at least for one day, while they decide how to invest their excess reserves more permanently.

If financial institutions have excess reserves, they can use them to purchase short-term securities, such as Treasury bills or commercial paper, rather than lend them in the Federal Funds market. As depository institutions do this, they will drive up the price and drive down the yield on those securities. As yields on short-term securities fall, financial institutions also will become more aggressive in acquiring longer-term securities (such as one-year Treasury notes) or will attempt to make more loans. They will do so to maintain as high a yield as possible on their loan and investment portfolios. If many institutions buy Treasury notes more aggressively, however, the notes' prices will rise and their yields will fall. Similarly, as depository institutions compete more aggressively to make loans, they will offer more attractive terms and lower rates to attract borrowers. Thus, if the Federal Reserve expands the monetary base, it will make excess reserves more readily available to depository institutions. Interest rates will fall on a broad front—particularly for short-term loans and short-term securities.

Conversely, institutions that have so many deposits that they need more reserves will incur penalties (from the Fed) if they have inadequate reserves at the end of the accounting period. If excess reserves are not readily available, these institutions will be willing to pay a substantial amount (at least for one day) in order to meet their reserve requirements by obtaining the reserves they need from other institutions with excess reserves. Thus, if the Federal Reserve sharply contracts the availability of reserves to the financial system, the Federal Funds rate will rise substantially. Interest rates on other short-term securities may also rise as financial institutions reduce their liquid security holdings in preference to borrowing Federal Funds at a high rate.

Policy-induced changes in short-term interest rates are also likely to have a notable effect on the behavior of other financial institutions and on the prices of other financial claims. In particular, if interest rates fall on short-term loans and invest-ments, nonbank financial institutions may alter their portfolio policies. They may invest more heavily in longer-term securities in order to increase the average return available on their portfolios over time. Such behavior is most noticeable with mutual and pension funds. When interest rates on highly liquid Treasury bills are relatively high, these funds may hold a larger proportion of their investment portfolios in short-term, highly liquid investments. When rates start to fall on that component of their portfolios, mutual and pension funds frequently shift toward longer-term investments, such as stocks and bonds, to guarantee that they will be able to maintain relatively high rates of return on their entire portfolios. As they accumulate relatively more stocks and bonds, they bid up the prices of those instruments; as a result, yields fall.

Other financial institutions often behave similarly. As yields fall on the short-term, highly liquid portion of their asset portfolios, they may become somewhat more willing to buy longer-term securities. Such a strategy allows these institutions to obtain higher average portfolio yields than would be available if they retained the same portion of their portfolio in short-term securities. As they buy relatively more long-term securities, they bid up their prices. Thus yields on those securities fall.

As a result of such shifts, when interest rates fall on short-term financial market instruments, interest rates generally fall on longer-term financial market claims as well. Thus monetary policy changes that increase the monetary base will, if everything else is equal, cause interest rates to fall across a broad front. Conversely, monetary policies that contract the monetary base will induce depository institutions to sell off investments and make fewer loans, thereby causing interest rates to rise on a broad front (see Exhibit 26–5).

Credit Availability

Changes in credit availability parallel changes in interest rates. When monetary policy is expansive, some creditors may increase their willingness to extend credit on lenient terms (by taking more risk and easing credit terms) rather than reducing interest rates per se. The opposite may occur when interest rates rise.

Wealth Effects

The Federal Reserve System has the power to issue IOUs against itself—in other words, checks drawn on itself, Federal Reserve notes, and receipts for member bank reserve deposits. The Fed can expand the amount of its IOUs outstanding by paying its employees with checks drawn on Federal Reserve banks. By doing so, it increases the monetary base and, at the same time, increases the amount of net claims outstanding against the government. People who hold these claims feel wealthier because they hold more government IOUs. As a result, they may increase their rate of investment or expenditure.

Such net wealth effects occur only if the Fed issues IOUs on itself in such a way that the monetary base is increased and people's holdings of other claims against the government (such as government bonds) are not reduced by an equal amount. The issuance of reserves to buy government bonds through open market operations does not increase people's net claims against the government; people merely exchange one form of claim (the government bond) for another (reserve deposits).

Even if the Federal Reserve conducts its monetary policy so that net claims against the government are not increased, it can still increase people's current purchasing power by increasing the current market value of claims they hold. Particularly in the short-run, expansions of the monetary base will generally increase the price of government securities (especially Treasury bills) as depository institutions try to convert their excess reserves into interest-bearing assets. This will lead to price increases on other financial claims through mechanisms previously described.

As prices rise on financial claims, people who hold them generally will feel wealthier. Therefore, they may spend more of their current income than they otherwise would. There is evidence, for instance, that expenditures on some consumer durable goods are correlated with movements in the stock market. Thus many econometric models incorporate stock market-related "wealth" effects to explain one method by which, in the short run, changes in monetary policy may be translated into changes in spending.

Exhibit 26–5   **Interest Rate Changes 1985–1991**

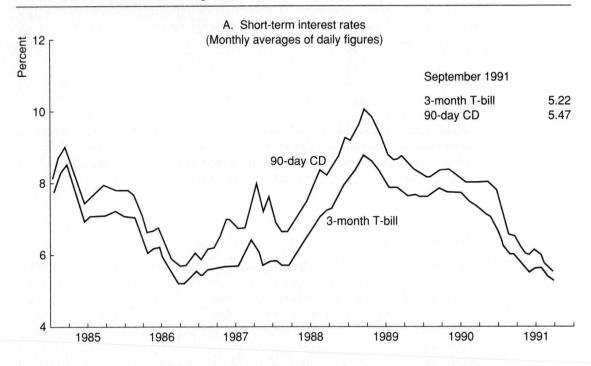

A. Short-term interest rates
(Monthly averages of daily figures)

September 1991

3-month T-bill	5.22
90-day CD	5.47

90-day CD

3-month T-bill

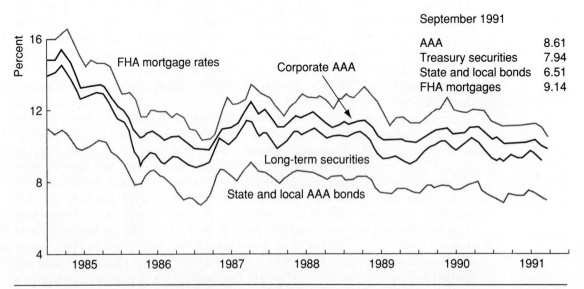

B. Long-term interest rates
(Monthly averages of daily figures)

September 1991

AAA	8.61
Treasury securities	7.94
State and local bonds	6.51
FHA mortgages	9.14

FHA mortgage rates

Corporate AAA

Long-term securities

State and local AAA bonds

Short-term and long-term interest rates often move up and down together, but short-term rates vary more.

Source: Federal Reserve Bank of St. Louis, *Monetary Conditions*, October, 1991.

Effects of Monetary Policy on Spending

Overview

In this section we discuss the channels through which monetary policy is thought to affect total spending in the economy. These channels are those usually considered by econometric model builders, who use complicated statistical models of the economy to predict an economic policy's likely effect on various sectors of the economy. It is useful for managers of financial institutions to understand these channels so that they can consider how changes in policy are likely to affect both their customers in various industries and the economy as a whole.

Monetary policy is thought to affect the economy in general through its effects on (1) investment in new housing, plant and equipment, and intended inventory accumulation; (2) consumption expenditures on such durable goods as automobiles; (3) state and local government expenditures; and (4) net exports. Changes in investment, consumption, net exports, or government spending change the level of aggregate spending in the economy. Changes in aggregate spending affect real output and price levels. These effects are summarized in Exhibit 26-6 and are discussed in more detail in the sections that follow.

Effects of Monetary Policy on Changes in Investment

Investment in housing, plant and equipment, and planned inventory accumulation traditionally has been viewed as being more sensitive to changes in monetary policy than other components of aggregate demand. Of the three, housing investment is considered to be the most sensitive.

Housing Investment.   Housing investment has been greatly affected by changes in monetary policy in the past because of institutional restrictions in the housing credit markets. Restrictions on interest rates paid on deposits (Regulation Q) often dried up flows of funds into thrift institutions when interest rates rose sharply. This happened from the mid-1960s through the 1970s. Thrift institutions provided much of the new mortgage credit financing in the country, and when their supplies of new funds fell sharply, so did their mortgage lending. Consequently, until Regulation Q was abolished so that thrifts could obtain funds to lend during periods of high interest rates, housing construction often fell off sharply because potential home buyers found mortgage financing difficult to obtain.

In recent years, changes in the structure of the mortgage credit markets have lessened pressures on housing caused by inadequate credit supplies. Deposit rate ceilings have been removed so that thrift institutions can bid more aggressively for funds during high-rate periods. In addition, growing secondary mortgage markets have allowed mortgage-lending institutions to gain more funds by selling some of their assets. New mortgage instruments, such as adjustable-rate mortgages, have allowed thrift institutions to obtain higher returns on their investment portfolios more quickly when interest rates increase, thereby allowing them to pay more for deposits. Finally, mortgage-backed bonds have allowed mortgage-granting institutions to compete for nondeposit sources of funds. Because of these changes, flows of funds to

Exhibit 26–6   **Effects of a Change in Money Supply and Interest Rates on the Economy**

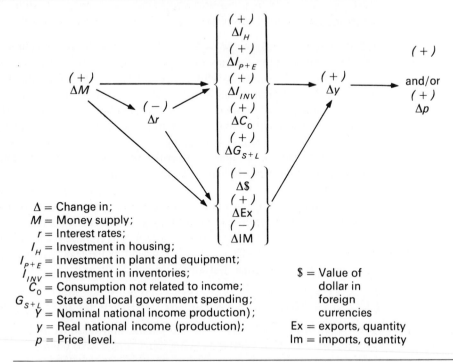

Δ = Change in;
M = Money supply;
r = Interest rates;
I_H = Investment in housing;
I_{P+E} = Investment in plant and equipment;
I_{INV} = Investment in inventories;
C_0 = Consumption not related to income;
G_{S+L} = State and local government spending;
Y = Nominal national income production);
y = Real national income (production);
p = Price level.

$\$$ = Value of dollar in foreign currencies
Ex = exports, quantity
Im = imports, quantity

Changes in the money supply affect spending both directly and indirectly. People spend more when they have excess cash. As they buy more securities, security prices rise and interest rates fall. Falling interest rates, in turn, tend to induce investors (including home buyers, business executives, and other investors), consumers, and state and local governments to spend more. Falling interest rates and increased money growth often cause the foreign currency value of the U.S. dollar to fall. As a result, U.S. exports become cheaper for foreigners to buy and foreign goods become more expensive for U.S. citizens to buy. Thus the quantity of U.S. exports will tend to increase and the quantity of goods imported into the United States will tend to fall. As boh foreigners and domestic citizens buy more domestically produced goods, spending on domestic goods increases. Additional spending from all sources stimulates additional real production and often causes domestic prices to rise. A decrease in the money supply has opposite effects.

mortgage markets are now less seriously disrupted by tight monetary policies than in the past.

Nonetheless, the housing market is still affected substantially by monetary policy changes. When interest rates rise in general, they also rise on mortgage loans. Thus some housing investment may be deterred (or encouraged) by the changes in mortgage rates that accompany changes in market interest rates.

Housing investment is particularly sensitive to interest rate changes because of the large size and long maturity of mortgage debt obligations. A relatively small change in interest rates can substantially alter monthly payments and amounts due on mortgage loans. Hence, if interest rates increase, large numbers of people will find it more difficult to finance a new home mortgage. This in turn reduces the demand for housing and the rate of housing investment. The reverse occurs when rates fall.

Housing investment is affected by changes in market interest rates with relatively short lags (one to three quarters). This is true in part because lags between planning, starting, and completing new home construction are relatively short. Thus changes in housing expenditure levels respond quickly to changes in financial market conditions.

Plant and Equipment Investment. Investors in new plant and equipment always consider the potential return on an investment and its financing costs. If costs rise or credit becomes less readily available (a particularly important consideration for small firms), these investors are less likely to undertake investment projects. When monetary policy eases, credit becomes more available and interest rates fall, so more investment projects will be undertaken. Thus, investment spending on plant and equipment is sensitive to changes in financial market conditions brought on by changes in monetary policy. It is also sensitive to changes in tax laws that affect the after-tax real cost of investment financing.

Once a decision is made to invest in new plant and equipment, it may take a long time before the details and financing of the project are fully worked out and construction is begun. As a result of the lags that exist between planning a new project and actually undertaking it, monetary policy affects plant and equipment investment spending with relatively long lags. This spending may not be substantially affected for a year or more after there is a change in monetary policy.

Planned Inventory Investment. Inventory investment is also sensitive to the cost and availability of credit. When interest rates are high, firms and retailers may intentionally reduce their inventory stocks in order to cut their costs of doing business. Since World War II, as interest rates have risen, firms have invested in computers and in inventory- and process-control management systems to ensure that they do not hold excessive stocks of idle inventories. As a result, firms have increased their sales and have not proportionately increased the stocks of goods that they keep on hand for display or production purposes.

Adjustments in production processes and operational procedures may follow interest rate changes only after relatively long lags. Shorter-term changes in planned inventory holdings may result from changes in credit availability and financing costs, however. For instance, if financing costs were to rise sharply and credit were to become difficult to obtain, a firm might sell off inventories to obtain cash. These funds could be used to meet pressing financial commitments, even if they were obtained by letting inventories temporarily fall below levels that would otherwise be desirable. Conversely, if credit were relatively inexpensive, a firm would not find the cost of holding extra inventories excessively burdensome. Thus it might move to reduce any extra inventory accumulation more slowly than would otherwise be the case.

Over time, firms are likely to establish inventory-control procedures that take into account the expected long-run cost of financing inventory investments. These procedures are not likely to be altered quickly in response to short-run monetary policy changes. However, during periods of deficient liquidity, exceptionally high interest rates, or severe credit rationing by lenders, firms and retailers may plan to reduce their inventory stocks in order to obtain additional funds to meet payrolls or finance other endeavors. Thus there may be both short-run and long-run effects of monetary policy changes on planned inventory investment. The timing and magnitude of these effects cannot be easily predicted.

Consumption Expenditures

There are several channels through which changes in monetary policy can affect consumption expenditures. First, greater (or lesser) holdings of money can cause members of the public to spend more (or less) freely. Second, when credit becomes more readily available and effective interest rates decline, consumers may borrow more readily to buy cars and other durable goods. Conversely, when credit becomes less readily available and effective interest rates rise, consumer spending on durable goods is likely to decline. Third, when consumers perceive that their current purchasing power has increased (or decreased) because of changes in their wealth holdings or in the market value of their stocks or other securities, they may spend more (or less) on durable goods.

Changes in consumer credit availability may occur relatively quickly after monetary policy changes. When policy becomes restrictive, many large commercial banks quickly curtail their consumer loan advertising or reduce their willingness to buy consumer credit obligations from dealers. Such a strategy lets them continue lending to their regular customers even if they have fewer funds to lend. Conversely, when monetary policy eases, commercial banks may seek to increase their loan portfolios in a hurry by aggressively advertising for or buying consumer credit obligations. Because commercial banks supply approximately half of all consumer installment credit in the economy, their concerted actions can have a major effect on credit availability and costs. Changes in both the cost and the availability of consumer credit influence consumers' expenditures on durable goods.

Changes in consumer credit interest rates may lag behind changes in availability. Historically, rates have changed less on consumer credit than on other debt instruments as monetary policy has alternately tightened and eased. However, effective interest rates can be increased if lenders raise loan down-payment requirements or impose other conditions that reduce the lenders' expected costs or risks and increase the borrowers' expected costs and risks. Effective interest rates also can be reduced by taking opposite actions.[1] Changes in effective interest rates (whether they reflect changes in stated rates or down-payment requirements) can affect consumers' expenditure decisions.

Stock market changes often follow changes in monetary policy with relatively short lags. However, they often precede changes in consumer durable goods expenditures by six months or more. Thus if they provide a mechanism by which consumer spending is altered in response to changes in monetary policy, they operate with a lag of six months or more.

Consumer expenditures conceivably could be affected much more quickly and directly by changes in consumers' liquidity. However, the extent to which changes in consumer expenditures lag changes in the liquidity position of the public is not easily determined.

---

[1] Effective interest rates on consumer credit may be changed even if contract rates remain the same. If, for instance, the consumer is required to pay more cash down to acquire the good, the extra cash reduces the lender's expected losses on a loan and increases its expected return. The extra cash also has an opportunity cost to the borrower that generally will increase his or her net cost of financing the good.

Overall, changes in consumer expenditures follow changes in monetary policy. Some consumer expenditures change quickly after a change in policy, whereas others may respond only after a longer period of time. In general, consumption expenditures respond to changes in monetary policy faster than plant and equipment expenditures. Some consumption responses may occur as quickly as changes in housing expenditures.

Foreign Trade Effects

Changes in monetary policy can affect foreign trade in numerous ways. All else being equal, a restrictive monetary policy tends to drive up U.S. real interest rates, dampen expected rates of U.S. inflation, and make the U.S. dollar more desirable relative to foreign currencies. Real interest rates may be elevated in the United States either because U.S. market interest rates are higher than interest rates of other countries or because the expected rate of inflation is lower in the United States than elsewhere. As the dollar rises in value, U.S. goods become more expensive relative to foreign goods. Consequently, U.S. exports fall and the United States imports more goods. These effects lead to reduced spending on domestic goods. Thus the restrictive effect that higher real interest rates in the U.S. have on domestic investment, consumption, and government spending will be reinforced by foreign trade effects.

An expansion of the money supply has the reverse effect; lower domestic interest rates relative to foreign interest rates usually cause the exchange value of the dollar to fall. If the dollar's exchange rate falls and domestic prices remain unchanged, U.S. goods will be cheaper relative to foreign goods. Eventually (possibly after a long lag), U.S. exports will increase and imports will decrease. As exports increase relative to imports, the U.S. economy will be stimulated and domestic production and income will rise. If the rising production level causes inflation to increase, however, U.S. goods no longer will be cheaper relative to foreign goods. If inflation in the United States is sufficiently great, the flow of exports and imports may reverse their direction unless the U.S. dollar's exchange rate continues to fall.

Changes in imports and exports often occur with substantial lags after the exchange value of the U.S. dollar changes, because it takes time for many importers and exporters to adjust their export patterns and sources of goods. For the same reason, export and import patterns may persist for an extended period of time after the dollar changes in value once again.

State and Local Government Expenditures

One ordinarily expects government expenditures to be insulated from contemporary changes in monetary policy. This is certainly true with federal government expenditures that are planned a year or more in advance. However, many state and local government expenditures for capital goods acquisition, such as purchases of new buildings, schools, or water works, can be put off until the future.

State and local government capital expenditure projects are usually financed through the sale of state and local government debt obligations rather than with current tax revenues. Often states and municipalities have ceilings on the interest rates they can pay on their debt. Also, as interest rates rise, so do repayment burdens and potential tax levies associated with new debt issues. Hence fewer state and local

DID YOU KNOW?

Worldwide Financial Coordination Is Required to Avert a Paradox of Thrift

Keynesian theory notes that if people attempt to save more (i.e., consumption falls relative to income, as when C_0 falls in Equation 25–4), aggregate demand for final products will fall, production will fall, and incomes will fall. Thus consumers won't be able to save more because their incomes will be reduced. This phenomenon is called the "paradox of thrift."

Although the paradox of thrift is usually assumed to apply only to one country, it also applies to world affairs. One consequence is that if the United States were to try to cut its balance of trade deficit by increasing its savings rate and reducing government spending, the world could be thrown into recession unless Japan and Germany were to spend more. Thus, it is necessary that the United States coordinate its domestic policy with other countries in the world.

Let us assume that there is a foreign country called Japany that exists with the United States in a two-country world. The inhabitants of Japany, like the present-day residents of Japan and Germany, love to save. Thus, their national product of $6 trillion is distributed as follows:

	Japany	United States
Total production (national income)	$6 trillion	$6 trillion
Equals		
Consumption	3 trillion	4 trillion
+ Government expenditures	2 trillion	2 trillion
+ Investment	$\frac{1}{2}$ trillion	$\frac{1}{2}$ trillion
+ Net exports (EX − IM)	$\frac{1}{2}$ trillion	$-\frac{1}{2}$ trillion
Excess production	0	0

Because the Japany residents save so much, consuming only half of their national incomes, their country can export $\$\frac{1}{2}$ trillion more than it imports. In contrast, because U.S. consumers spend so much, their national production does not satisfy all of their needs, so they import $\$\frac{1}{2}$ trillion more than they export. The world as a whole is in equilibrium; all goods produced are demanded by someone, so, on balance, income levels do not change.

Now let us suppose that the United States decides that it must do something about its budget deficit. It raises taxes so that consumers will cut their spending and adopts national policies to cut imports. Assume that the United States succeeds in reducing both spending and imports by $\$\frac{1}{2}$ trillion. Superficially, its problem appears to be solved. If the United States imports less, however, Japany will not be able to sell all of the goods it produces. Its workers will become unemployed, and, as they lose their jobs, they will buy fewer U.S. products as well as fewer of their own products. Because this will cause both U.S. and foreign goods to go unsold,

Continued

production levels will be cut back. As production falls around the world, consumption demand will fall still further. Thus the cutback in U.S. consumption and imports will cause a worldwide paradox of thrift.

To prevent the development of a worldwide paradox of thrift and the accompanying growth of trade barriers, such as the world experienced during the Great Depression, it is necessary to coordinate economic policies around the world. For instance, if Japany increases its government expenditures by $\$\frac{1}{2}$ trillion while the United States reduces consumption spending and imports by $\$\frac{1}{2}$ trillion, on balance, all goods produced will still be demanded, and the world economy need not deteriorate.

In fact, when the United States tried to solve its trade deficit in the late 1980s and early 1990s by letting its dollar fall in value (thereby making imported goods more expensive and discouraging their consumption), Japan cooperated by stimulating its economy with an easy monetary policy from 1985 to 1989 and increased government spending thereafter. Unfortunately, because of its fear of domestic inflation, Germany was more reluctant to cooperate.

investment projects can legally be financed through bond issues when interest rates are high. Furthermore, bond issues are less likely to be approved by local voters when interest rates are high, as taxes must be raised more to pay higher interest charges on debt. Thus changes in monetary policy have an impact on state and local government capital expenditures.

Lags between changes in monetary policy and the rate of approval of proposed state and local government capital expenditure projects may be relatively short. As with all major investment plans, however, lags between approval or disapproval of an expenditure and actual changes in governmental spending rates may be considerably longer.

Overall Effects

Changes in monetary policy can affect the levels of investment, consumption, imports and exports, and state and local government expenditures. These, in turn, affect the aggregate level of spending in the economy. The channels through which monetary policy can act are many, and some may transmit monetary policy changes to changes in economic activity with shorter or longer lags than others. Although uncertainty exists about the length of some of the lags, and although not all effects operate at the same time (see Exhibit 26-7), the channels through which monetary policy affects the economy are fairly well defined.

Exhibit 26-8 summarizes the manner in which monetary changes affect levels of aggregate spending, Y, in the economy. Relative changes in real output, y, and price levels, P, depend on various factors (including the flexibility of wages and prices and the closeness of the economy to full-employment output levels at the time the policy is initiated). Exhibit 26-8 stresses channels through which monetary policy can influence Y without differentiating between the extent to which the change in Y reflects real output changes or price changes. However, as shown in Exhibit 26-7, changes in prices usually lag changes in real income.

Exhibit 26–7   GNP Growth, Inflation, and the Past Growth of M1

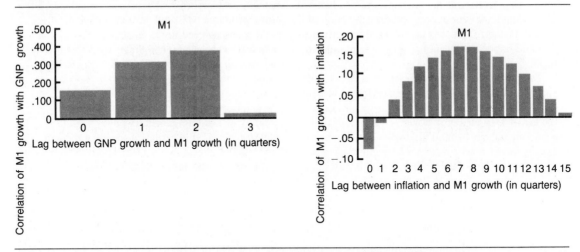

Changes in monetary growth are strongly correlated with growth in nominal GNP (and GDP) several quarters later and with inflation rates for the next several years. Thus responses of real GNP, *Y*, to money growth tend to precede responses in price levels.

Source: Richard W. Kopcke, "Inflation and the Choice of Monetary Guidelines," *New England Economic Review*, January-February 1984, 7, 9.

Reprinted with permission with permission of the Federal Reserve Bank of Boston.

Exhibit 26–8   Net Effects of an "Easier" Monetary Policy

Initial Effects	Intermediate Effects	Result
↑ Money supply (liquidity) ↑ Lending by financial institutions ↓ Interest costs for potential borrowers ↑ Market value of existing securities Possible ↑ in public's net claims on the government ↓ Exchange rate	↑ Investment spending on housing, plant and equipment, and intended inventory accumulation as credit availability ↑, liquidity ↑, and interest rates ↓ ↑ Consumption spending as liquidity ↑, interest rates ↓, credit availability ↑, net wealth possibly ↑, and the market value of existing securities ↑ ↑ Spending by some state and local governments as interest rates ↓ and credit availability ↑ ↓ Imports and ↑ exports as the U.S. dollar falls in value	↑ Y { ↑ P and/or ↑ y

Note: ↑ means increase, ↓ means decrease. Tight monetary policy has opposite effects, which can be seen by reversing all the arrows.
by reversing all the arrows.

Longer-Run Effects of Monetary Policy

The preceding discussion mainly emphasized short-run responses of the financial system and the economy to changes in monetary policy. When a long-run view is taken, some monetary policy operations may have unintended effects. As a result, some of the short-run effects of policy changes may differ from those outlined previously.

The main problem with the analysis presented is that it assumes that financial markets and economic agents react only to current conditions and not to *expected* conditions in the economy. However, the rational-expectations view of the world points out that it is irrational for economic agents to ignore current policy actions' probable future effects on the economy. In particular, it notes that excessively large rates of monetary policy stimulus will drive the economy to full employment and cause prices to rise sharply. When lenders *expect* prices to rise, however, they demand higher interest rates on their loans. Since the nominal interest rate, i, at any point in time equals the real interest rate, r, plus the expected change in price levels, ΔP_e, one expects nominal interest rates to rise whenever the price level is expected to increase sharply.

Interest Rate Effects

Because a large increase in the money supply can be expected to cause inflation, both rational-expectations theorists and many nontheoretical Wall Street investors believe that overly expansive monetary policy will lead to higher rather than lower interest rates on long-term securities. High rates of money expansion suggest that the economy will expand rapidly at some time in the future. This will lead to a situation in which, eventually, real output cannot increase rapidly and most of the increase in spending will merely reflect too much money chasing too few goods. Inflation will result, and price levels will rise. As expected inflation, ΔP_e, rises, so will long-term interest rates. Nonetheless, the monetary expansion may still cause rates to fall on short-term securities, because most of these securities will mature before prices increase significantly and lenders still wish to earn a return on their excess liquid funds.

Therefore, lenders who follow this line of reasoning will be wary of monetary policies that threaten to cause inflation. Inflation will erode the purchasing power of their money unless they obtain higher interest rates. Hence those potential lenders will not lend long term unless they obtain interest rates high enough to offset higher expected rates of inflation. In order for new buyers to obtain higher yields on existing stocks and bonds, the prices of those securities must fall.

This line of reasoning is not purely academic. Beginning in the latter half of the 1970s, financial market participants became very aware that overly expansive monetary policy would lead to inflation. Subsequently, efforts by the Federal Reserve System to hold down short-term interest rates (by expanding the monetary base and the money supply) were greeted by increases (rather than decreases) in long-term interest rates and falling (rather than rising) stock and bond prices whenever new announcements indicated that monetary policy had been excessively easy. As a result, easy monetary policy was accompanied by short-term declines in short-term rates followed quickly by increases (rather than decreases) in long-term interest rates. Long-term rates rose as financial market participants became aware that an excessively easy monetary policy would lead to higher future inflation. Thus their future price expectations, ΔP_e, rose, and so did nominal interest rates, i. Similarly, as the Fed increased the monetary base throughout 1991, short-term interest rates fell sharply. However, because the financial markets expected inflation to rise after the economy recovered from recession, long-term rates did not fall much; thus, the yield curve developed a sharp upslope because of the public's expectations for future inflation.

Investment Effects

A pure theorist would note that borrowers' price expectations will rise when monetary policy is viewed by market participants to be inflationary. Borrowers would be willing to pay more to borrow in the present if they thought that they could repay their loans with depreciated dollars in the future. As a result, long-term investment would not necessarily be decreased because of the nominal increase in interest rates.

Investment might not be increased either, as one would typically expect when monetary policy was easy. In particular, if monetary policy were easy because the Federal Reserve was expanding credit rapidly, one might expect real interest rates to fall slightly as a major new lender (the Federal Reserve) entered the credit markets (see Exhibit 26–4). As the Federal Reserve bought securities, other potential lenders in the credit markets would bid more aggressively for the remaining securities, thereby bidding up their prices and reducing their yields (interest rates). However, excessive credit (and money-supply) expansion by the Federal Reserve would cause people to expect more inflation. Thus nominal interest rates, i, would rise as expected inflation, ΔP_e, rose for both lenders and borrowers.

Even if the increase in nominal rates were such that real rates were slightly lower than before, some investment might still be discouraged. This is because a company borrowing to invest in a new plant or equipment would not be as sure that the prices of the products it sells would go up as fast as inflation as it would be sure of the interest rate that it would have to pay. Thus, if general rates of inflation were expected to rise by 5 percent and the firm had to pay 5 percent more to borrow, yet its products' price rose by only 2 percent, it would be financially strapped when it had to pay the interest and principal on the debt. Investors' uncertainties about the extent to which the prices of their goods would rise relative to all goods might make them reluctant to invest at higher nominal interest rates even if they expected inflation. Because of this increased uncertainty, it is possible that an expansive monetary policy might actually lead to less rather than more plant and equipment investment.

In addition, a monetary policy that fluctuated between rapid and slow growth of the money supply might cause real interest rates to rise and deter investment spending. Lenders would desire higher real returns when they were more uncertain about their prospective real returns, and borrowers might be less willing to invest when their price uncertainty was great.

In some Latin American countries that have experienced overly expansive monetary policies and rapid inflation for many years, plant and equipment investment rates have apparently been reduced by high nominal rates of interest. However, housing investment and investment in stocks of inventories, whose prices are expected to rise, have become relatively more important when inflationary expectations have been high. In the case of housing and certain inventory investments, there may be less uncertainty about whether prices will rise in line with general rates of inflation than is the case with industrial goods. Hence such investments increase in attractiveness relative to plant and equipment investment when inflation is expected.

Overall Effects

The implications of these peeks at "real-world" responses to changes in monetary policy are the following:

1. The monetary policy effects described earlier in this chapter are appropriate only if people have price expectations that are not affected by changes in monetary policy per se.
2. If people's expectations are influenced by changes in monetary policy, interest rates on long-term securities may move up rather than down when an expansive monetary policy is pursued.
3. Because potential borrowers as well as lenders expect price increases, the increase in long-term nominal interest rates caused by excessively expansive monetary policy may or may not inhibit long-term investment in plant and equipment. If people are more uncertain about inflation, real interest rates are likely to rise and investment in productive investment goods may be discouraged.
4. Because prices on different goods can be expected to rise at different rates or with different degrees of certainty during inflationary periods, the composition of investment may change when people expect inflation. In particular, investment in plant and equipment may be discouraged relative to investment in housing or inventories. Unfortunately, only investment in plant and equipment expands the future productive capacity of the country.
5. Because of the adverse effect of varying price levels on people's certainty, ability to plan, and willingness to take investment risks, in the late 1980s and early 1990s some reserve bank presidents on the Fed's FOMC advocated a zero inflation policy.

Practical Considerations in Monetary Policy

Practical problems of monetary policy control have been pointed out by economists who believe that investors' actions show that they have rational expectations. In addition, monetary policy works with uncertain and variable lags. Because of these facts, some economists believe that monetary policy cannot be used effectively to cause short-term changes in the level of economic activity. Instead, these economists (rational-expectations theorists, quantity theorists, and many supply-siders) advocate increasing the money stock at modest and predictable rates so that inflationary expectations will be stabilized and fewer uncertainties will disrupt the operations of the nation's financial system. Many economists also note that changes in the monetary aggregates precede similar changes in economic activity (see Exhibit 26–7). It is not certain, however, whether the forces that generate a recession also cause monetary growth to slacken or whether it is the slackening of monetary growth that causes a recession.

There is little doubt that the Federal Reserve can influence the financial markets and the economy (in the short run, before expectations adapt). Because congressional elections occur every two years and presidential elections every four years, the monetary authorities are continually under pressure to achieve politicians' short-run objectives. Even if those objectives are not consistent with long-term economic stability, the politicians may not care if the alternative is to be defeated in the next election. For example, in 1982, some politicians ran on a platform that said they would force the Fed to reduce interest rates, and in 1991 some congressmen proposed removing all reserve bank presidents from the FOMC (in part because the congressmen felt that the president's zero inflation policy caused the 1991 recession).

Because the Federal Reserve is nominally insulated from political pressures, it may take a long-range view of the nation's needs. However, high rates of turnover for members of the Federal Reserve Board, coupled with repeated threats by members of Congress to change its structure or revoke its authority, have made monetary authorities much more concerned with short-run policy objectives than might be desirable. In addition, uncertainty about what measure of the money stock (M1, M2, M3, and so on) is most appropriate has made it difficult to agree on exactly what the Federal Reserve's long-run policy objectives should be. Consequently, monetary policy often operates in fits and starts, switching from being overly expansive to overly restrictive in short periods of time. Additional policy changes have occurred as the Federal Reserve has vacillated between various policy objectives that may be mutually inconsistent. For instance, the Fed cannot control interest rates and the rate of monetary aggregate growth simultaneously, yet it has often tried to do so. At least it has often switched from interest rate control objectives to monetary aggregate control objectives and back as different problems appeared on the economic horizon.

Because of the difficulties associated with establishing and maintaining stable monetary policies, many economists have advocated that the Federal Reserve concentrate merely on stabilizing and limiting the growth rate in key measures of the money stock. The problem of controlling short-term fluctuations in the economy could then be left to fiscal policy. Congress institutionalized this line of thinking by requiring in the 1978 Humphrey-Hawkins Act that the Federal Reserve annually report to Congress on its monetary growth objectives. However, when economic troubles commence, Congress still puts pressure on the Federal Reserve to deviate from those objectives, if necessary, to alter the short-run behavior of the economy before the next election. Thus the major effect of the Fed's growth-rate disclosures has been to show that the Fed has a difficult time achieving its stated objectives for monetary growth.

Summary

Federal Reserve monetary policy can affect the nation's financial system considerably. The Fed changes policy by adjusting reserve requirements, its open market operations, or the discount rate. By so doing, it affects the rate of growth of the money supply, the level of interest rates, security prices, and credit availability. These factors, in turn, can affect the level of investment, consumption, imports and exports, state and local government spending, aggregate spending, total output, income, and price levels in the economy. Many mechanisms exist by which changes in the public's liquidity, interest rates, credit availability, net wealth holdings, and the value of financial market claims can affect expenditures.

Monetary policy mechanisms work as predicted only if people do not expect monetary policy changes. If they perceive that monetary policy changes will affect price levels, their behavior will change. For instance, under conditions of high expected inflation, people may invest more heavily in housing and inventories and less heavily in plant and equipment. Uncertainty about inflation can also affect interest rates and the composition and level of investment.

Expectations of inflation can alter, and have altered, people's behavior both in the United States and in Latin America, where inflation is endemic. Many people advocate that the United States should adopt a stable monetary policy designed to restrict the money supply's rate of growth and dampen people's inflationary expectations. However, political considerations have made it difficult to implement such a policy. As a result, discretionary policy is still used to modify the economy in an attempt to solve pressing economic problems.

Questions

1. What effects are decreases in reserve requirements likely to have on (*a*) bank reserves, (*b*) Federal Funds rates, (*c*) bank lending, (*d*) Treasury bill rates, and (*e*) the bank prime rate? Explain your answers.

2. Given your answers to Question 1, what, if anything, would you expect to happen to (*a*) housing investment, (*b*) plant and equipment investment, (*c*) intended inventory investment, (*d*) government expenditures, (*e*) consumption, (*f*) exports, and (*g*) imports? Why?

3. What are the different channels through which monetary policy can affect consumption expenditures?

4. How did Regulation Q deposit rate ceilings cause monetary policy's effect on housing investment to be greater than it might have been?

5. Why does monetary policy usually affect the economy with a lag? When are the lags likely to be shortest? When are they likely to be longest?

6. How can anticipation of monetary policy's ultimate effects cause the initial effects to differ from what is expected? Why are long-term interest rates more likely to be affected by such expectations than short-term interest rates?

7. How can expected inflation distort investment decisions?

8. Given that rational-expectations theorists dislike the use of monetary policy for business-cycle control, what do they believe that the proper role of monetary policy should be?

9. Why do you think that politicians' world view is closer to that of neo-Keynesian economists than to that of quantity theorists?

10. What do you think the proper role of monetary policy should be? Why?

Selected References

Able, Stephen L. "Inflation Uncertainty, Investment Spending and Fiscal Policy." *Economic Review.* **Federal Reserve Bank of Kansas City, February 1980, pp. 3–13.**
Statistically documents the notion that investment spending is reduced by uncertainty about the rate of inflation.

Batten, Dallas S., and Daniel L. Thornton. "The Discount Rate, Interest Rates, and Foreign Exchange Rates: An Analysis with Daily Data." *Review.* **Federal Reserve Bank of St. Louis, February 1985, pp. 22–30.**
This article suggests that unanticipated changes in the discount rate affect the foreign exchange value of the U.S. dollar. In addition, it finds that increases in U.S. interest rates relative to comparable foreign rates also increase the dollar's exchange value.

Bechter, Dan M., and Stephen Pollock. "Are Inventories Sensitive to Interest Rates?" *Economic Review.* **Federal Reserve Bank of Kansas City, April 1980, pp. 18–27.**
The relationship between inventory/sales ratios and the level of real interest rates is explored and documented.

Berkman, Neil G. "Mortgage Finance and the Housing Cycle." *New England Economic Review.* **Federal Reserve Bank of Boston, September–October 1979, pp. 54–76.**
Past cycles in housing finance are related to changes in interest rates and deposit flows to thrift institutions.

Chrystal, K. Alec, and Geoffrey E. Wood. "Are Trade Deficits a Problem?" *Review.* **Federal Reserve Bank of St. Louis. January/February 1988, pp. 3-29.**
The authors note that the U.S. trade deficit logically results from the fact that private saving is too low relative to private investment and the public deficit. Thus an import surplus is required so that U.S. residents (and their government) can buy more goods and services than they produce.

Esaki, Howard, and Judy A. Wachtenheim. "Explaining the Recent Level of Single-Family Housing Starts." *Quarterly Review.* **Federal Reserve Bank of New York, Winter 1984–1985, pp. 31-37.**
This article explains determinants of housing starts in a deregulated environment. It notes that continuing credit availability, coupled with strong demand for houses by the temporarily large 25-34 age group, led to a high demand for housing in 1983-1984 in spite of relatively high interest rates. It also considers the effect of adjustable-rate mortgages on housing starts.

Kopcke, Richard W. "Inflation and the Choice of Monetary Guidelines." *New England Economic Review.* **Federal Reserve Bank of Boston, January–February 1984, pp. 5–14.**
This study shows that changes in M1 precede changes in the level of nominal GNP with a lag of several years. It also shows that changes in the growth rate of nonfinancial institutions' total debt have similar effects but with somewhat shorter lags. It suggests that nonfinancial debt measures rather than M1, could conceivably be used to assess the probable effect of monetary policy on the economy and the overall inflation rate.

Kopcke, Richard W. "The Determinants of Investment Spending." *New England Economic Review.* **Federal Reserve Bank of Boston, July–August 1985, pp. 19–35, and September–October 1985, pp. 19–35.**
These articles look at five alternative econometric explanations of investment expenditures. They find that a cash-flow model (which implicitly considered tax breaks) and a neoclassical model that accounted for the user cost of capital (which depends in part on after-tax interest costs) had some advantages for predicting business fixed investment in the early 1980s, when both tax rates and interest rates fell dramatically.

Robinson, Kenneth J. "The Effect of Monetary Policy on Long-Term Interest Rates: Further Evidence from an Efficient Markets Approach." *Economic Review.* **Federal Reserve Bank of Dallas, March 1988, pp. 10–16.**
The author tries to determine whether an increase in the money supply will decrease interest rates (through a liquidity effect, as posited by Keynes) or increase interest rates on long-term bonds (through a price-expectations effect, as posited by rational-expectations theorists). He finds that although liquidity effects were apparent before the 1970s, people have now become more sensitive to the inflationary implications of overly rapid monetary expansion. Thus, in recent years, interest rates on long-term securities have risen, rather than fallen, when Fed monetary policy has been expansionary.

Taton, John A. "Interest Rate Variability: Its Link to the Variability of Monetary Growth and Economic Performance." *Review.* **Federal Reserve Bank of St. Louis, November 1984, pp. 31–47.**
This article points out that the uncertainty created by wide fluctuations in the money supply and interest rates after 1979 caused lenders to seek higher real rates of return. The increased real rates and greater uncertainty, in turn, had adverse effects on output and employment levels in the early 1980s.

Glossary

adjustable-rate mortgage (ARM)
A mortgage on which the contractual interest rate can be changed prior to maturity. ARMs include VRMs, RRMs, and other forms of mortgages with adjustable rates.

agency securities   Obligations of credit agencies sponsored by the U.S. government, such as the Federal Home Loan Bank.

allocational efficiency   The capital market is allocationally efficient if funds are channeled to their most productive use.

amortize   To pay the principal amount due on a loan in stages over a period of time. When the full amount is repaid, the loan is fully amortized.

annual percentage rate (APR) The method of calculating interest rates required by the Federal Consumer Protection Act (Truth in Lending Act).

arbitrage   The process of simultaneously selling overvalued assets and buying similar undervalued assets. One who engages in arbitrage is called an *arbitrageur*.

asset-liability management   A management technique designed to provide for a financial institution's

funding needs and reduce its net exposure to interest rate risk. It tries to reduce mismatches in an institution's contractual inflows and outflows of interest and principal payments.

asset management   A financial institution's management of its asset structure to provide both liquidity and desirable rates of return.

assets   The items of value that a business owns. Assets are listed on the left-hand side of the balance sheet and represent what the business has done with funds supplied by creditors and owners.

balance of payments (BOP)   The measure of the difference between the net inflow and the net outflow of domestic financial liabilities. When the balance of payments is negative, foreigners are accumulating U.S. dollars in excess of the rate that they are purchasing U.S. goods, services, and investments. If they attempt to exchange those excess dollars for foreign currency, the U.S. dollar exchange rate will fall.

balance sheet   A financial statement that presents a firm's

assets, liabilities, and net worth (capital account). Because net worth equals the difference between assets and liabilities, balance sheets always "balance" in that both sides are of equal value.

balance sheet equation   The accounting relationship that states that assets equal liabilities plus net worth, where net worth is the balancing figure.

balloon note   A loan on which the final scheduled payment is substantially larger than preceding payments.

bank insolvency   A bank is declared insolvent when the value of its liabilities exceeds the value of its assets. Typically, banks become insolvent and fail by incurring losses on their loans or investment holdings.

bank liquidy   The ability of banks to accommodate depositors' requests for withdrawals.

bank structure   The number, location, and size distribution of banks.

banker's acceptance   A promissory note drawn by a corporation to pay for merchandise on which a bank guarantees payment at maturity. In effect, the bank substitutes its credit standing for that of the issuing corporation.

basis point   One hundred basis points equals 1 percent.

bond   A long-term debt instrument.

bond price volatility   The percentage change in bond price for a given change in yield.

book value accounting   A system of accounting that values all assets and liabilities at their original cost minus scheduled depreciation or amortization and realized losses; it does not recognize changes in market values due to market interest rate changes or for other reasons. In contrast, *market value accounting* tries to value all assets and liabilities at their current market values.

borrowed funds   Short-term funds borrowed by commercial banks from the wholesale money market or the Federal Reserve. They include Eurodollar borrowings, Federal Funds, and funds obtained through the issuance of repurchase agreements.

branch banking   Branch banks can have multiple full-service offices. Some banks can engage in statewide branching; others may only be able to branch on a limited basis within their state.

broker   One who acts as an intermediary between buyers and sellers but does not take title to the securities traded.

call   An option giving the buyer the right to purchase the underlying security at a predetermined price over a stated period of time.

call loan   Usually, a loan that either the borrower or lender can terminate upon request.

call provision   The right of an issuer of a security to redeem that security for a predetermined value on or after some future point in time. Call provisions are often used by borrowers to liquidate outstanding debts that carry high interest rates after interest rates fall.

call reports   Detailed balance sheet and income statements that banks are required to prepare for federal bank examiners four times a year.

cap (on interest rates)   A cap on interest rates is created by *purchasing* a put option (i.e., an option to sell) on a financial futures contract. If interest rates rise, the value of the futures contract declines. When the value of the futures contract declines, the value of the put option increases, and purchaser of a cap receives a cash flow. Caps are used by financial institutions to limit increases in the cost of liabilities without sacrificing the possibility of benefiting from interest rate declines.

capital   On a balance sheet, an institution's net worth. In terms of physical assets, capital can be used to generate future returns.

capital adequacy   The adequacy of a financial institution's net worth enabling the institution to absorb potential adverse changes in the value of its assets without becoming insolvent.

capital gain   A gain from the sale of a capital asset at a price higher than the original cost. Special tax treatment may be given to long-term capital gains.

capital good   A good that can be used to generate future income flows. The term usually refers to physical capital, such as manufacturing plants and equipment.

capital impairment   A situation in which a financial institution holds less capital than is required by law. Such a firm may be forced to acquire new capital, merge, or cease operation.

capital loss   A loss from the sale of a capital asset at a price below the original cost.

capital markets   Financial markets in which financial claims with maturities greater than one year are traded. Capital markets channel savings into long-term productive investments.

captive finance company   A sales finance company that is owned by a manufacturer and helps finance the sale of the manufacturer's goods.

central bank   An institution that is responsible for managing a nation's money supply (monetary aggregates) in its best interest.

classical economic theory   Belief of economists prior to Keynes who emphasized the importance of aggregate supply, taxes, and the price system in making a national economy work. In contrast, Keynes and his immediate followers emphasized the importance of aggregate demand. However, in recent years supply-side economists have emphasized the classical economic arguments once again.

collar (on interest rates)   By simultaneously buying a cap and selling a floor, a collar is created. Collars limit the movement of a financial institution's liability costs within a specified range. If, for example, a bank purchases a cap at 9 percent and sells a floor at 5 percent, the bank's liability costs will fluctuate between 5 and 9 percent.

collateral   Assets that are used to secure a loan. Title to them will pass to the lender if the borrower defaults.

collateralized mortgage obligation (CMO)   A security issued by a thrift institution's finance subsidiary that is collateralized by participation certificates (issued by federal agencies) that promise to pass through principal and interest payments on pools of underlying mortgages. CMOs are attractive to many investors because they pay principal and interest like bonds and because the securities that serve as collateral are obligations of federal government agencies.

commercial paper   An unsecured, short-term promissory note issued by a large creditworthy business or financial institution. Commercial paper has maturities ranging from a day to 270 days and is usually issued in denominations of $1 million or more. Direct-placed commercial paper is sold by the seller to the buyer. Terms are negotiable. Dealer-placed commercial paper is sold through dealers with terms similar to those offered on bank CDs.

common stock   Ownership claims on a firm. Stockholders share in the distributed earnings and net worth of a firm and select its directors.

compensating balance   A required minimum balance that borrowers must maintain at a bank, usually in the form of noninterest-bearing demand deposits. The required amount is usually 10 to 15 percent of the amount of the loan outstanding. A compensating balance raises the effective rate of interest on a bank loan.

comptroller of the currency   An agency of the U.S. government responsible for regulating banks with federal charters. Only federally chartered banks may use the word *national* in their name.

concentration ratio   Measure of competition in banking markets. Typically computed as the percentage of total deposits held by the largest banks in the market. Lower concentration ratios imply greater competition.

consumer finance company   A finance company that specializes in making cash loans to consumers.

consumer price index (CPI)   A price index that measures changes in the cost of goods that represent average family purchases. The CPI measures the cost of living.

convertible bond   A bond that can be converted into a predetermined number of shares of stock at the borrower's option.

correspondent balances   Deposits that banks hold at other banks to clear checks and provide compensation for correspondent services.

correspondent banking   A business arrangement between two banks in which one (the correspondent bank) agrees to provide the other (respondent bank) with special services, such as check clearing or trust department services.

country risk   The risk tied to political developments in a country that affect the return on loans or investments. Examples of country risk are foreign government expropriation of the assets of foreigners or prohibition of foreign loan repayments.

coupon rate   The rate of interest on a bond that is determined by dividing the fixed coupon payment by the principal amount of the bond. The coupon rate is established when the bond is issued.

Covered Interest Rate Parity   In foreign exchange markets, the difference between current spot exchange rates and forward exchange rates generally reflects the difference in interest rates that can be earned in two countries over the same period of time. Thus, any gain earned by investing in the country with a higher rate will tend to be offset by equal losses in the forward exchange markets, and the net return will be equal for investing in either country.

credit money   Money backed by a promise to pay. In contrast with gold or silver coins, which are worth their face value if sold as a commodity, credit money has little intrinsic value. Paper money is an example.

credit risk   The possibility that the borrower will not pay back all or part of the interest or principal as promised. The greater the credit risk, the greater the loan rate.

crowding-out effect   The notion that large sales of government debt will make it difficult or impossible for private debtors to issue as much as they wish in the financial markets. Thus large government debts may cause some private investment to be forgone.

currency risk   Risk resulting from changes in currency exchange values that affect the return on loans or investments denominated in other currencies. For example, if the currency in which a loan is made loses value against the dollar, the loan repayment will be worth fewer dollars.

current yield   The coupon of a security divided by the security's current price. A security with a coupon of $50 that has a market value of $800 has a current yield of 50/800, or 6⅔ percent.

daylight overdraft   An overdrawn position that occurs when a depository institution, during the course of a day, transfers more funds out of its Federal Reserve account than it has received or has on balance in that account. This overdraft must be corrected by the end of the day or the Fed is exposed to default risk. Thus the Fed limits the maximum overdrawn position that an institution can have at any time during the day.

dealer   One who is in the security business acting as a principal rather than an agent. The dealer buys for his or her own account and sells to customers from his or her inventory. The dealer's profit is the difference between the price received and the price paid for a particular security.

default   The failure on the part of a borrower to fulfill any part of a loan contract, generally by not paying the interest or principal as promised.

default risk premium (DRP)   The amount of additional compensation investors must receive for purchasing securities that are not free of default risk. The rate on U.S. Treasury securities is used as the default-free rate.

deficient reserves   Reserves that fall below those required by law. Banks with deficient reserves must pay a penalty (2 percent above the discount rate) on the amount deficient to the Federal Reserve.

deficient spending unit (DSU)   An economic unit that has expenditures exceeding current income. A DSU sells financial claims on itself (liabilities) to borrow needed funds.

deflator   A price index used to convert present-day values into values with equal purchasing power in another year.

demand deposit   Deposits held at banks that the owner can withdraw instantly upon demand—either with checks or electronically.

deposit expansion   The process by which financial institutions expand their deposits. Deposit expansion occurs when financial institutions use newly received excess reserves to acquire new loans and investments.

deposit expansion multiplier   This multiplier measures the amount that financial institutions' deposits are expected to increase for each one-dollar increase in the monetary base.

deposit rate ceilings   Before April 1, 1986, legal limits were set on the interest that could be paid on financial institutions' deposits.

Depository Institutions Act of 1982 (Garn-St. Germain Bill) Extended the 1980 revisions in banking regulation by authorizing MMDA accounts, accelerating the phaseout of deposit rate ceilings, granting thrift institutions broader powers, and providing for acquisitions of failing institutions by different types of institutions located in different states.

Depository Institutions Deregulation and Monetary Control Act of 1980 (DIDMCA) The first major 1980s banking act. It deregulated financial institution deposit and loan-rate ceilings and allowed non-bank institutions to have checking accounts (NOWs) and offer other services in competition with banks. It also extended reserved requirements to all institutions that offered transactions deposits.

direct claims   Financial claims sold in the credit markets by the ultimate user of the borrowed funds. Corporate bonds are an example of a direct claim.

direct financing   Financing wherein DSUs issue financial claims on themselves and sell them for money directly to SSUs. The SSU's claim is against the DSU and not a financial intermediary.

direct loan   A loan negotiated directly by the lender and borrower.

direct placement   The direct sale by a corporation of its debt to institutional investors. Such sales do not require underwriters.

discount   A security sells at a discount when it sells for less than its face value. Treasury bills are sold at a discount and redeemed for face value at maturity.

discount bond   A bond that sells below its par or face value. A bond sells at a discount when the market rate of interest is above the bond's fixed coupon rate.

discount rate   Financial institutions can borrow from the Federal Reserve. The interest rate charged by the Federal Reserve Bank is called the *discount rate* and the act of borrowing is called *borrowing at the discount window*.

diseconomies of scale   Rising long-run average costs of operation as the level of output is increased beyond a certain point.

disintermediation   The withdrawal of funds that were previously invested through financial intermediaries so that they can be invested directly in the financial markets.

diversification   The process of acquiring a portfolio of securities that have dissimilar risk-return characteristics in order to reduce overall portfolio risk.

dual banking system   A term referring to the fact that U.S. banks can be chartered either by the federal government (national banks) or by state governments—with each system having different laws.

duration   The point in *time* when the average present value of a security (or portfolio) is repaid. Duration measures the sensitivity of securities (or portfolios) to interest rate changes. The longer the duration, the greater a security's price will change when interest rates change. It is more useful than maturity for assessing a security's price sensitivity to interest rate changes.

economies of scale   Declining long-run average costs of operation as the level of output is increased beyond a certain point.

Edge Act corporation   A subsidiary of a U.S. bank formed to engage in international banking and financial activities that domestic banks cannot conduct in the United States.

Electronic Funds Transfer System (EFTS)   A computerized information system that gathers and processes financial information and transfers funds electronically from one financial account to another.

equity   The ownership value of a business.

equity (in housing)   Housing equity equals the difference between the market value of a house and the mortgage debt outstanding on the property. If the total debt is high relative to the value of the house, the owner has low equity.

Eurodollar   A U.S. dollar-denominated deposit issued by a bank located outside the United States.

excess reserves   Cash in the vault or deposits at the Fed that exceed the amount of reserves required by law.

exchange rate, or spot exchange rate   The rate at which one nation's currency can be exchanged for another's at the present time.

exercise price (strike price)   The price at which an option allows the buyer to buy an asset (if it is a call option) or sell an asset (if it is a put option).

factor   A financial institution that regularly buys the receivables of other companies and collects the payments due on those debts.

factored accounts receivable   Receivables of a firm that have been sold to a factor in exchange for cash.

failing bank   A bank that is declared in imminent danger of being unable to meet its financial or legal obligations by the FDIC. Failing banks are allowed to merge with other banks, even though the mergers may violate the antitrust laws' competitive criteria for business mergers.

Federal Deposit Insurance Corporation (FDIC)   A government agency that provides federal insurance for depositors of qualified banks and supervises the savings association insurance fund.

Federal Funds   Financial institution deposits held at Federal Reserve banks. Banks may lend their deposits to other financial institutions through the Federal Funds market.

Federal Home Loan Bank Board (FHLBB)   Until 1989, the primary regulatory agency for savings and loan associations controlled the Federal Home Loan Bank system, the Federal Home Loan Mortgage Corporation, and the Federal Savings and Loan Insurance Corporation. Its regulations affected all federally chartered and federally insured savings associations.

Federal Home Loan Mortgage Corporation (FHLMC)   "Freddie Mac" provides a secondary market for conventional mortgages. It was established to help savings and loan associations sell their mortgages.

Federal National Mortgage Association (FNMA)   "Fannie Mae" provides a secondary market for insured mortgages by issuing and executing purchase commitments for mortgages.

Federal Reserve System (The Fed)   Our nation's central bank. Its primary function is to control the money supply and financial markets in the public's best interest. The Fed consists of 12 regional Federal Reserve banks, but primary policy responsibility resides with its Board of Governors in Washington, D.C.

Federal Savings and Loan Insurance Corporation (FSLIC—Fizzlick)   An agency that insured savings association and federal savings bank deposits until 1989, when deposit insurance responsibilities passed to the Savings Association Insurance Fund supervised by the FDIC.

fidelity bond   A contract that covers the infidelity or dishonesty of employees. Fidelity bonds protest employers and others against embezzlement, forgery, and other forms of theft.

financial claims   A written promise to pay a specific sum of money (the principal) plus interest for the privilege of borrowing money over a period of time. Financial claims are issued by DSUs (liabilities) and purchased by SSUs (assets).

financial guarantees   Guarantees by third parties such as commercial banks or insurance companies to cover the payment of interest and principal to investors in debt securities in the event of a default.

financial intermediaries Institutions that issue liabilities to SSUs and use the funds so obtained to acquire liabilities of DSUs. They include banks, savings associations, credit unions, finance companies, insurance companies, pension funds, and investment companies.

financial sector   The sector of the economy that encompasses financial institutions, financial markets, and financial instruments. The role of the financial sector is to collect savings from SSUs and allocate them efficiently to DSUs for investment in productive assets for current consumption.

FDIC Improvement Act of 1991 (FDICIA)   This act went beyond the FIRRE Act in tightening bank and thrift institutions' capital requirements. It allowed "well-capitalized commercial banks" to enter investment banking through subsidiaries. However, severely undercapitalized institutions were to be shut down quickly. The FDICIA required that deposit insurance premiums be risk-based and adequate to cover any losses covered by the deposit insurance funds (i.e., premiums were raised). It also provided for a line of credit and borrowing capacity so the FDIC's bank insurance fund would have adequate financing to close failing institutions.

Financial Institution Reform, Recovery, and Enforcement Act of 1989 (FIRREA)   This act made major changes in the structure of financial regulation. It abolished the FHLBB and FSLIC and established the OTS, FDIC-SAIF and RTC as their replacements. It required that deposit insurance premiums be raised and that thrift institutions adopt stricter accounting standards. It also imposed "tangible capital" requirements that disallowed the counting of goodwill and various other intangible assets toward a thrift's capital adequacy requirements.

fiscal policy   A national policy designed to alter the level of national income by altering the federal government's fiscal plans. Changes in the level of taxes, the rate of government expenditures, or the budget deficit are all possible instruments of fiscal policy.

floor (on interest rates)   A floor on interest rates is created by *selling* a call option (that is, an option to buy) on a financial futures contract. By creating a floor, a financial institution sets a lower limit to its liability costs.

forward exchange rate   The rate at which one nation's currency can be exchanged for another in agreements made to exchange currencies at a specific future time.

fractional reserve banking Refers to the fact that banks hold only a fraction of their deposits in the form of liquid reserves (vault cash or deposits at the Federal Reserve Bank) and loan out the rest to earn interest. For example, a bank that has deposits of $1,000 and reserves of $50 is holding 5 percent reserves (50/1,000).

full-bodied money   Money that is valued not only for its purchasing

power but also as a commodity. Gold and silver coins are examples.

futures contract   A contract to buy (or sell) a particular type of security or commodity from (or to) the futures exchange during a predetermined future time period.

futures exchange   A place where buyers and sellers can exchange futures contracts. The exchange keeps the books for buyers and sellers when contracts are initiated or liquidated.

GAP   The difference between the maturity or duration of a firm's assets and liabilities. A *maturity GAP* is calculated by subtracting the amount of an institution's liabilities that mature or are repriced within a given period of time from the amount of assets that mature or are repriced within the same period. A *duration GAP* compares the difference between the average duration of an institution's assets and its liabilities, weighted by the market value of each.

geographic monopoly   A monopoly produced by regulations restricting entry and the production of banking services by more than one financial institution in a particular geographic market.

goodwill   A hypothetical asset created when the purchase price for an institution exceeds the amount by which the market value of its assets exceeds its liabilities. Goodwill is created to reflect hidden values in the acquired institution, such as the value of a franchise location or customer relationships. Goodwill is a wasting asset that must be depreciated over time. One of the most contentious issues when the FIRRE Act of 1989 was passed was whether goodwill had to be ignored or could be counted as an asset when thrift institutions calculated their capital/asset ratios.

government bond A debt issued by the U.S. government with a maturity greater than one year.

Government National Mortgage Association (GNMA) "Ginnie Mae" helps issuers of mortgages obtain capital market financing to support their mortgage holdings. It does so by creating government-guaranteed securities that pass through all interest and principal repayments from pools of mortgages to purchasers of the pass-through securities.

gross domestic product (GDP) The dollar value at current market prices of all final goods and services produced within a country in a given year. Note that the GDP of a country includes the goods and services produced within the geographical boundaries of that country, whereas the gross national product (GNP; see below) includes the goods and services produced by a country's residents regardless of location.

gross national product (GNP) The total value of goods and services produced by the U.S. economy in a year. *National GNP* is the present dollar value of GNP. *Real GNP* is the value of GNP expressed in prices applicable to a base period. Real GNP figures are useful for determining whether the volume of production has increased. Nominal GNP may increase either if real GNP increases or if prices rise.

hedge To reduce business risk by altering one's portfolio—possibly

by buying or selling futures or option contracts—so that adverse price or interest rate changes will not cause substantial losses.

hedger An individual or firm that engages in futures market transactions to reduce price risk.

Holder-in-Due-Course Doctrine A legal principle that says that a third party to whom an installment credit contract has been sold is not liable if the product purchased with the credit does not perform as expected.

holding company A corporation operated for the purpose of owning the common stock of other companies. Most commercial banks operate as subsidiaries of holding companies.

holding period yield Rate of return on a security (considering both capital gains and principal or dividend payments) over the period that it is held. It need not be held to maturity. Holding period yields can be calculated from the present value formula when the present value (purchase price) and flow of returns are known and the interest rate is unknown.

home equity loan A revolving credit loan that is secured by a mortgage on the borrower's home.

homeowner's insurance A combination property-liability insurance coverage for individuals and families.

immunize To protect a portfolio or institution against risks and possible losses caused by changes in interest rates.

index arbitrage Involves selling or buying stock-index futures and doing the opposite with the

underlying stocks in the index in order to profit from disparities in the prices of the futures and the underlying stocks. Index arbitrage is effective because the stock-index futures contracts have the same value as the underlying stocks when the contract expires.

indirect claim A financial claim issued by a financial intermediary.

indirect loan (indirect credit) A credit contract arranged with the borrower by a third party, such as a retail dealer, and sold to the ultimate lender, such as a sales finance company.

Individual Retirement Account (IRA) A retirement plan for individuals. The pension contributions are deposited with trustees (usually banks or insurance companies).

industrial bank A financial institution chartered under industrial banking laws in a state. Industrial banks make loans and issue savings deposits. Finance companies may obtain charters as industrial banks so that they can issue savings deposits to obtain funds.

inflation A continuing rise in the average level of prices. The fundamental cause of inflation is continuing excess aggregate demand relative to aggregate supply.

informational efficiency In an informationally efficient market, prices of securities are the best indicators of the relative values of securities because current market prices reflect all available relevant information.

installment loan A loan that is repaid in a series of fixed payments.

interest rate risk The risk that changes in interest rates will cause a bond's realized yield to differ from the promised yield.

interest rate swap   The exchange of interest payments received on underlying assets. Typically, a fixed-rate interest payment stream will be exchanged for a variable-rate payment stream, or vice versa. Such swaps let institutions match the cash flows of their assets and liabilities more easily.

intermediation   Transfer of funds from surplus spending units (SSUs) to deficit spending units (DSUs) via the services of a financial intermediary. Depository institutions provide *denomination intermediation* by issuing small-denomination liabilities and buying large-denomination assets. They provide *maturity intermediation* by issuing short-maturity liabilities and acquiring long-maturity assets. They provide *risk intermediation and portfolio diversification* by pooling many assets and issuing liabilities that have pro rata claims against the pooled value of those assets.

inventories   Stocks of raw materials, semifinished goods, or finished products held by retailers and manufactures either for use in the production process or for final sale.

investment (expenditures)   In national income accounting, investment refers to the production of goods that can be used to facilitate future production. Plant and equipment investment, housing expenditures, and net inventory accumulations are classed as investment expenditures. Of the three, *net inventory investment* is the most unstable; it can become negative when stocks of goods are used up in production or sold to final purchasers and are not fully replaced.

investment (financial)   The acquisition of a financial asset (IOU) that is expected to yield future returns. A bank's investment portfolio consists of its holdings of various types of securities. Funds obtained by the sellers of those securities may or may not be used to finance real investment expenditures.

investment banker   A person who provides financial advice and who underwrites and distributes new investment securities.

Keogh Plan   A plan that allows self-employed persons to establish tax-sheltered retirement programs themselves.

Keynesian   A person who believes in the economic theories of John Maynard Keynes. Neo-Keynesians have adapted Keynes' theories to argue that fiscal policy can be effectively used to modify levels of national income, whereas the effects of monetary policy are not always certain—as monetary policy must change interest rates before it can be effective.

leverage   The ratio of funds supplied by the owner of an asset to the total value of the asset. A firm is said to be highly leveraged when its net worth is small relative to its total assets (and debts). A stock purchase is said to be highly leveraged if the buyer borrowers most of the funds used to purchase it.

liabilities   A firm's debts. Liabilities are a source of funds for the firm.

liability insurance   Insurance that protects against losses arising from liability for damages to property or personal injury to others.

liability management   A bank's management of its liability structure to increase or decrease its source of funds as needed. Liability management is based on the assumption that certain types of bank liabilities are very sensitive to interest rate changes. Examples of interest-sensitive funds are CDs, repos, Eurodollar borrowings, and Fed Funds.

LIBOR   London Interbank Borrowing Rate, the "prime rate" of international lending and the cheapest rate at which funds flow between international banks. Other international rates often are set to vary with LIBOR rates.

limited branching   State laws that restrict banks' abilities to branch to a limited geographic area, usually to a county or contiguous counties, or to a set number of branches.

line of credit   An arrangement whereby a financial institution guarantees that a business can borrow up to a specified maximum amount of funds during a period of time.

liquidity of an asset   The ease with which an asset can be quickly converted to money (M1) with negligible cost or risk of loss. The higher the potential cost of rapidly converting an asset into money, the lower its liquidity.

liquidity of an institution   An institution is liquid if it holds sufficient amounts of cash and liquid assets to allow it to easily meet requests from its liability holders for cash payment. It is *illiquid* if it has difficulty meeting such requests. Bank panics can quickly convert an institution from liquid to illiquid status as depositors withdraw their funds.

liquidity premium   Extra compensation that investors are willing to pay sellers of securities in order to buy assets with high liquidity.

long (future)   A futures contract that obligates the owner to buy a given amount of a security or commodity in the futures market. Also, a person or firm who owns more "long" than "short" futures contracts.

loss reserves   Liabilities of a firm that are accumulated, in lieu of retained earnings or surplus, to enable the firm to meet future losses. When losses on assets occur, they are written off against a firm's loss reserve accounts rather than its current profits and net worth accounts.

M1, M2, M3   Alternative definitions of the money supply as designated by the Federal Reserve System.

marginal   The term used by economists to refer to the extra (additional) increase in some variable.

margin loans   Loans that brokerage firms extend to their customers to purchase securities.

margin requirement (initial) "Good-faith" money required by a futures exchange when buyers or sellers initiate futures market purchases.

margin requirement (maintenance)   the minimum amount of "good-faith" money that a futures exchange requires all holders of futures contracts to maintain on deposit with the exchange while they own their futures contracts.

marine insurance   Insurance contracts that cover losses related to

all types of transportation. The contract may cover the means of transportation, cargo, or freight.

marketability   The ease with which a financial claim can be resold. The greater the marketability of a financial security, the lower its interest rate.

maturity   The date when the repayment of the principal amount of a financial claim is due.

maturity imbalance   A maturity imbalance occurs when an institution holds assets whose maturities are not similar to the maturities of its liabilities. If an institution suffers from a maturity imbalance, its earnings will be subject to wide swings if the term structure inverts or the general level of interest rates changes.

merger   A single business formed from two or more previously existing separate businesses.

monetarist   Economists who believe that the supply of money has a major impact on prices and the dollar value of national income (GNP).

monetary base   Currency in circulation plus financial institution reserve deposits at the Federal Reserve. The monetary base consists of all assets that can be used to satisfy legal reserve requirements. Thus, if it grows, financial institution reserves (and financial institution deposits) usually grow as well.

monetary policy   Policy of the Federal Reserve aimed at controlling the monetary supply in order to influence economic activity.

money   Broadly defined, money is a liquid store of value. Narrowly defined, money is a generally acceptable medium of exchange.

money market deposit account (MMDA)   MMDA consumer deposit accounts at commercial banks originated in 1982. MMDAs are not subject to deposit rate ceilings or reserve requirements. Customers may use them for no more than six withdrawals (including only three checks) per month.

monetary market fund   An investment company whose portfolio consists of liquid debt instruments such as Treasury bills and negotiable certificates of deposit.

money markets   Financial markets in which financial claims with maturities of less than a year are sold. The most important money market is that for U.S. Treasury bills.

mortgage   Long-term debt secured by real estate.

mortgage banker   An institution that originates and sells mortgages. Most mortgage bankers do not hold the mortgages they originate for long, but rather profit from the service fees they receive for collecting payments on each mortgage for the ultimate purchaser of the mortgage.

multibank holding companies One is formed when two or more banks join together under common ownership in a holding company.

multiplier effect   The tendency of a change in a monetary or fiscal policy instrument (the monetary base or government expenditures) to cause the stock of money or the level of national income to change by several times as much.

multiplier (money multipliers) Money multipliers are variants of the deposit expansion multiplier. They show how much the money supply changes for every one-dollar change in a monetary policy instrument (bank reserves or the monetary base). Multiplier values may change over time.

multipliers (national income multipliers)   National income multipliers measure the amount that national income is expected to change for every one-dollar change in various policy instruments. In particular, the *government expenditure multiplier* measures the change in national income that would be expected for each one-dollar change in government spending that was sustained over time. The *tax multiplier* measures the amount that national income is expected to change for each sustained one-dollar change in federal taxes. The *balanced budget multiplier* measures the amount national income is expected to change for each matched one-dollar change in both government expenditures and taxes. Neo-Keynesian economists usually assume that national income will change by several times as much as government expenditures or tax levies.

municipal securities   Securities issued by state and local government, whose coupon interest is exempt from federal income tax.

mutual company   A company that is owned and controlled by its depositors or policyholders.

National Credit Union Administration (NCUA)   The regulatory body that sets standards for all federally chartered and federally insured credit unions.

national income (Y)   The total value of goods and services produced by domestic residents in one year (see *gross national product*). National income accounting recognizes that the value

of all goods produced is available for distribution as income to producers of the gross national product.

natural monopoly   A product whose cost curve is characterized by economies of scale through the range of output demanded by the market.

negotiable certificates of deposit (CDs)   Unsecured liabilities of banks that can be resold before their maturity in a dealer-operated secondary market.

net worth   The net ownership value of a firm. Net worth equals the value of assets held by a firm minus the value of all its liabilities.

nominal income   The value of income expressed in current dollars. No adjustment is made for changes in the purchasing power of the dollar.

nominal interest rates   The interest rates that are observed in the marketplace.

Notional Principal   The face value amount for which interest payment obligations are computed under a "SWAP" agreement. Since the principal is never repaid, it is only "notional" for the duration of the SWAP.

NOW accounts   Deposit accounts that pay explicit interest and can be withdrawn "by negotiable orders of withdrawal" (checks) on demand.

objective risk   In the language of insurance, a risk that can result in either a gain or a loss.

off-balance-sheet item   An obligation or asset of a depository institution that is not listed on the

firm's balance sheet. For instance, standby letters of credit and other financial guarantees generate fee income for major banks and expose banks to risks of loss, but they do not appear on the balance sheet until a loan is made to honor the guarantee.

Office of Thrift Supervision (OTS)   Created in 1989 as a subsidiary of the Treasury Department. Assumed the chartering and many of the supervisory powers of the Federal Home Loan Bank Board, which it replaced.

offset effect   An economic effect, set into motion by government policy action, that counteracts all or part of the intended effect of the policy action.

one-bank holding company   A holding company that holds 23 percent or more of the stock of a single bank. Prior to 1970, one-bank holding companies were excluded from Federal Reserve regulations, and they could engage in a wider range of business activities than either independent banks or multi-bank holding companies.

open market   A market that is open to all qualified participants. Prices in these markets are determined by supply and demand on an impersonal basis.

open market operations   The purchase or sale of government securities by the Federal Reserve. Open market operations are used to increase or decrease bank reserves and the monetary base. When the Fed purchases securities, the monetary base expands.

operational efficiency   A market is operationally efficient if the costs of conducting transactions are as low as possible. If transactions costs are high, fewer financial transactions will take place, and a greater number of otherwise valuable real investment projects will be passed up.

option   a contractual agreement that allows the holder to buy (or sell) a specified asset at a predetermined price *prior* to its expiration date. The predetermined price is called the *strike price*. Options to buy assets are *call options*. Options to sell assets are *put options*.

option premium   The price of the option.

par bond   A bond whose market price is equal to its par or face value. A bond sells at par when the market rate of interest is equal to the bond's fixed coupon rate.

par value   The stated or face value of a stock or bond. For debt instruments, the par value is usually the final principal payment. Most bonds are sold with $1,000 or $5,000 par values.

pass-through securities   Securities that pass through the principal and interest payments made on pool of assets (mortgages) to holders of the securities. Pass-through securities have uniform denominations and set payment dates. They also may carry guarantees of timely and full payment. Thus they are more easily traded in the capital markets than mortgages per se.

pool   The collection of a number of different financial assets into a single unit. Mortgages are *pooled* before pass-through securities are issued.

portfolio insurance   A procedure designed to protect stock portfolios against large losses by systematically selling either stocks

or stock-index futures as stock market prices decline and buying them back if the stock market rises.

precautionary demand for money   Individuals and firms may hold money balances in excess of their current transactions needs to allow for unforeseen needs for readily available cash. Possible emergency expenditure needs, or the possibility that tempting but fleeting investment or expenditure opportunities may arise, may motivate people and firms to hold precautionary money balances.

preferred stock   Corporate stock that has certain "preferences" relative to the interests of common stock-holders. Usually, dividend payments are predetermined and must be made before dividends can be distributed to common stockholders.

premium   A security sells at a premium when it sells for more than its face value or more than closely comparable securities.

premium bond   A bond whose market price is above its par or face value. A bond sells at a premium when the market rate of interest is below the bond's fixed coupon rate.

present value (PV)   The value today of a future stream of cash payments discounted at the appropriate discount rate.

price index   An index constructed by selecting a representative group of commodities (called a *market basket*) and tracing their price changes from period to period. Price indexes tell us whether prices in general are rising or falling.

price risk   The greater the price fluctuation of a security, the greater the price risk. For bonds in general, the shorter their duration, the less their market price changes with interest rates. Thus short-term

bonds have less price risk than long-term bonds.

primary markets   Financial markets in which financial claims are first sold as new issues. All financial claims have a primary market.

primary reserves   Cash assets on a bank balance sheet that are immediately available to accommodate deposit withdrawals. Primary assets are the most liquid assets held by the bank, but they earn no interest income. Primary reserves are valut cash, deposits at correspondent banks, and deposits at the Federal Reserve.

prime rate   A commercial bank's lowest posted rate. The prime rate is a short-term rate granted to a bank's most creditworthy customers. Some large bank customers who have access to the commercial paper market may borrow below the prime rate. Smaller or riskier customers often pay more than the prime rate, such as "prime plus two" per percent, to borrow.

principal   The amount of money borrowed in a debt contract. Interest payments are not part of the principal.

private mortgage insurance (PMI)   A private insurance contract that agrees to make principal and interest payments on a mortgage if the borrower defaults. PMI is often required on conventional mortgage loans with low down-payment requirements.

promissory note   Unconditional promise in writing by the borrower to pay the lender a specific amount of money at some specified date.

property insurance   Insurance that provides coverage for physical damage to or destruction of personal or commercial property that results from a specified peril, such as fire, theft, or negligence.

purchased paper   Debt contracts purchased by a financial institution that did not originate the loan. Captive sales finance companies hold purchased paper acquired from their company's retail dealers.

Purchasing Power Parity   This is an economic concept that says the purchasing power of a currency should be equal in every country if goods, services, labor, capital, and other resources can flow freely between countries. However, because there are impediments to free trade, purchasing power parity conditions often don't hold. Thus, goods cost more in one country than another.

pure risk   In the language of insurance, a risk in which the outcome is either a loss or no loss; there is no possibility for gain. Pure risks arise from events over which one has little or no control. Examples of pure risk include house fire, tornado damage to a shopping mall, or the premature death of a working parent.

put   An option giving the buyer the right to sell the underlying security at a predetermined price over a stated period of time.

quantity theory   The theory that the level of nominal national income is primarily determined by the quantity of money in circulation. People who believe in the quantity theory are called *quantity theorists* or *monetarists*.

rational-expectations theorists Economists who believe that a government policy will have an uncertain or negligible effect because the public often will correctly anticipate the intent of the policy. They point out that most conventional fiscal and monetary policy theories assume that the public can be fooled if it is kept in the dark about the government's intentions.

real estate mortgage investment conduit (REMIC)   A legal entity that issues multiple classes of securities that pass through principal and interest payments made on mortgages or CMOs. Like CMOs, most REMIC securities pay predetermined principal and interest payments. However, some pay variable rates of interest and their residual payments may be very uncertain.

real GNP (real national income) A measure of GNP expressed in prices applicable to a base period. Nominal national income is deflated by the change in the price level from a predetermined base period, such as 1967. Thus real GNP may be expressed as "GNP" in 1967 dollars."

real interest rate   The nominal rate of interest prevailing in the marketplace minus the expected rate of inflation. Real and nominal rates of interest are equal when market participants have no expectation of inflation.

receivables   Balances owed a firm by its customers.

receivables, gross   The total value of principal and interest payments that are due to be paid a (finance) company over time on all loan and credit contracts owed it by its customers.

receivables, net   The present value of loan and credit contracts owed to a (finance) company by its customers. Net receivables differ from gross receivables in that they do not include interest that has not yet been earned as part of the balance due.

recession   The phase of the economic cycle during which levels of employment and economic activity decline. Recession is often defined as two consecutive periods of decline in real gross national product.

Regulation Q   A Federal Reserve regulation that set a maximum interest rate banks could charge on time and savings deposits. All interest rate ceilings were phased out on April 1, 1986, by federal law.

reinvestment risk   The risk resulting from market interest rate changes that cause a bond investor to have to reinvest coupon payments at interest rates different from the bond's promised yield.

renegotiated-rate mortgage (RRM)   A mortgage whose rate must be renegotiated periodically. Renewal at the new rate is guaranteed and the maximum rate change is limited.

repurchase agreement (repo)   A form of loan in which the borrower sells securities (usually government securities) and simultaneously contracts to repurchase the same securities, either on call or on a specified date, at a price that will produce a specified yield.

required reserves   Financial institutions are required by law to maintain minimum reserves equal to a percentage of deposits and other liabilities. Reserve requirements vary with the deposit size of the institution and the type of deposit. They are held at the Federal Reserve Banks or as cash in financial institutions' vaults.

reserves   Assets or liabilities held by an institution to provide for future contingencies. *Loss reserves* are liabilities held to absorb future losses. *Liquidity reserves* are assets held to guard against adverse cash outflows. In our fractional reserve banking system, some liquidity reserves are held in the form of vault cash or deposits at specified institutions (usually the Fed) because they are legally *required reserves*. Actual or *total reserves* held in those forms (cash or appropriate deposits) may exceed the amount required by law. Any excess is referred to as *excess reserves*.

Resolution Trust Corporation (RTC)   An institution created in 1989 to acquire and liquidate the assets of failed savings associations.

retained earnings   After-tax profits of a business that are retained by the business and not distributed to stockholders.

return on assets (ROA)   An institution's annual net profit divided by its assets. Measures the net profit per dollar of assets owned.

return on equity (ROE)   An institution's annual net income divided by the book value of its equity. Measures the return on stockholders' investment in an institution. Nonprofit institutions can calculate equivalent ROEs by dividing profits by their net worth.

risk aversion   The attitude that most investors have toward risk; that is, all other things equal, less risk is preferred to more risk. Risk aversion is one of the reasons that investors must be paid a premium to purchase risky investments.

risk-based capital requirements   These requirements allow depository institutions to hold little or no capital to back relatively riskless assets (such as government agency bonds or Treasury bills), more capital to back risky assets (such as loans), and additional capital to back off-balance-sheet items (such as standby letters of credit) that expose the institution to risks of loss.

risk-based deposit insurance   Deposit insurance that would require riskier institutions to pay higher fees for deposit insurance coverage. Alternatively, riskier institutions could be made to incur higher costs as a condition for retaining their deposit insurance.

risk discount (premium)   A security that is considered risky sells at a lower price (risk discount) relative to equivalent securities that are less risky. Because the security sells at a lower price than other securities, it will have a higher interest yield. Thus its yield (interest rate) will be adjusted upward by a *risk premium*.

risk diversification   The ability to reduce the fluctuation in the principal value of a portfolio by purchasing a variety of securities whose returns are not perfectly correlated with each other.

rollover mortgage (ROM)   A mortgage that matures before it is fully amortized. At that time, the borrower may elect to renew (roll over) the mortgage at the prevailing mortgage rate. Thus the borrower may pay several different rates on the mortgage before it is fully amortized.

run on the bank   Bank runs or "panics" occur when a large number of depositors try to convert bank liabilities into currency. Because banks hold fractional reserves, it is not possible to satisfy all requests immediately. Bank runs were a major cause of bank failures prior to the 1930s. The establishment of the FDIC has eliminated most bank runs.

sales finance company   A company that finances the credit sales of retailers and dealers by purchasing the installment credit contracts that they acquire when they sell goods on credit.

Savings Association Insurance Fund (SAIF)   Replaced the FSLIC as the federal insuring agency for savings associations in 1989. SAIF is controlled by the FDIC.

secondary market   A financial market in which existing securities are resold by one buyer to another before the security matures. The secondary market is a "secondhand" market for previously sold securities. The New York Stock Exchange is the best-known secondary market.

secondary reserves   Short-term assets (often Treasury bills) that can quickly be converted to cash at a price near their purchase price. They provide an institution with liquidity while allowing it to earn safe interest income.

secured loan   A loan secured by collateral such as merchandise, inventory or real estate.

securitization   The sale of securities backed by car loans or other IOUs of customers. By issuing securities through a separate institution, the bank can use securitization to remove assets, and the risks associated with owning them, from its balance sheet.

senior debt   In the event of liquidation of a firm, senior debt holders must be paid first.

service company   A subsidiary of a thrift institution that may engage in activities that are not allowed to thrifts because of tax considerations and regulations.

share accounts   Consumer savings accounts offered by credit unions. They are similar to passbook accounts offered by banks and thrift institutions.

share draft accounts   Checking accounts offered by credit unions that pay explicit interest. They are equivalent to NOW accounts.

short (future)   A futures contract that obligates the owner to sell a given amount of a security or commodity in the futures market. Also, a person or firm that owns more "short" than "long" futures.

speculative risk   In the language of insurance, a risk that can result in either a gain or a loss.

speculator   An individual who assumes price risk in the expectation of earning a high return.

Spot exchange rate   The current ratio of exchange between one currency and another, if the exchange is made immediately. For instance, on a given day, a person might be able to buy $1.79 U.S. dollars for each British pound he or she had to exchange.

spot market   The market in which securities are traded for immediate delivery and payment.

spread   The difference between the price that a dealer pays for a security (the bid price) and the price at which the dealer sells the security (the asking price).

standby letter of credit   A guarantee that a financial institution will make a payment (in return for advancing a loan to its customer) if the customer should fail to do so.

stock company   A company that is owned by stockholders.

stock exchange   An organization established to make purchases and sales of stocks easier. Stock exchanges may either bring buyers and sellers together through the auspices of specialists who trade in each stock, or they may use computer facilities to match buy and sell orders.

stock-index futures contract   A futures contract that is valued as a multiple of the value of the stocks in the index at the time that the futures contract expires. For instance, the S&P 500 stock-index future equals 500 times the value of the Standard & Poor's 500 stock index.

strike price   The price at which an option can be exercised.

subordinate   Junior to, or inferior to. For example, subordinated debentures do not have a claim on an institution's revenues or assets (in the event of liquidation) unless all senior debt holders have first been satisfied.

supply-siders   A group of economists and politicians who believe that government policy actions should try to increase private incentives to supply additional goods and services.

surety bond   A contract whereby one party, the surety or guarantor, guarantees the performance of a second party for the benefit of a third party. A bail bond is an example.

surplus   For a mutual institution, net profits that are not distributed as dividends are retained as surplus in the institution's net worth account.

surplus spending unit (SSU)   An economic unit whose income for the period exceeds current expenditures. SSUs often purchase financial claims issued by deficit spending units (DSUs).

swap   An exchange of assets or income streams for equivalent assets or income streams with slightly different characteristics. A typical *mortgage swap* may involve an exchange of the payments on a pool of mortgages for "participation certificates" issued by the FNMA or FHMLC that promise to pass through those same payments (minus a small service fee) to the holder of the certificates. Thrift institutions may make such swaps to gain marketable securities in exchange for mortgages that cannot be sold easily. (See also *interest rate swap*.)

syndicate   An organization of dealers formed to help underwrite and market new security issues.

tax and loan accounts   Demand deposits maintained by the U.S. Treasury Department at commercial banks. These accounts are used to collect tax receipts.

TBTF   "Too big to fail" banks include, at a minimum, the nation's 11 largest banks which were decreed by the comptroller of the currency to be TBTF after Continental Illinois Bank was taken over by the FDIC. This policy prevents major disruptions from occurring in the nation's payments system. However, it also favors large banks, because it allows them to assume more risk than small banks without paying the full cost of their risk taking.

technical insolvency   An institution is technically insolvent when the market value of its assets is less than its liabilities. However, if the institution is not forced to write off its bad debts or mark down the value of its securities portfolio to market value, the book value of its assets may still exceed its liabilities; thus it will still *appear* to be solvent. If regulatory authorities are permissive, such institutions can continue to operate, even though, if they were liquidated, not all liability holders could be paid in full.

term life insurance   An insurance contract that provides for payment of benefits to the beneficiary if the insured dies within a specified time. Term life insurance does not provide for the accumulation of any cash value (a form of savings).

term loan   A loan from a bank with a maturity greater than one year.

term structure invasion
Ordinarily the yield curve (term structure of interest rates) is upward-sloping—meaning that interest rates on longer-maturity securities are usually higher than rates on shorter-maturity securities. Term structure inversions occur when current yields on short-term securities exceed those on long-term securities. This happens when people expect interest rates on long-term securities to fall in the future (thereby generating handsome capital gains and high holding-period yields on long-term securities) to compensate for their lower current yields.

term structure of interest rates
The relationships between the yield to maturity and term to maturity of otherwise similar securities.

Graphically, this relationship is shown by the yield curve.

thrift or thrift institution   A financial institution (savings and loan association, savings bank, or credit union) that obtains a major source of its funds from consumer time and savings deposits. Often credit unions are not included. *Mortgage-oriented thrifts* refers only to savings and loan associations.

time loan   A loan that the borrower cannot pay back (except with a penalty) until the payment date(s).

trader   An individual who buys or sells futures contracts or stocks in the hope of profiting quickly from expected price movements.

transactions demand for money
Individuals and firms need to hold money so that they can conveniently carry on transactions with each other. Generally, as the dollar volume of transactions rises, the demand for money held to facilitate transactions will rise similarly.

transactions deposit   A deposit that can be used to finance depositors' transactions. Money can be withdrawn on demand by checks, electronic impulses, negotiable orders of withdrawal, share drafts, or other payment devices.

Treasury bills   Direct obligations of the federal government with initial maturities ranging from three months to one year. They are considered to have no default risk and are the most marketable of any security issued.

Truth in Lending Act   A law designed to provide consumers with meaningful information about the cost of credit. It requires that both the dollar amount of finance

charges and the annual percentage rate (APR) must be disclosed prior to extending credit.

uninsured risk   Risk that the private insurance industry is unwilling or unable to cover. These risks include such hazards as unemployment, war, insurrection, rebellion, flood, property expropriation by foreign governments, and collapse of the banking system.

unit banking   Allowing banks to operate only a single full-service banking office.

usury laws   State laws that prohibit the charging of interest above a certain limit—the *usury ceiling*. Such laws generally apply universally. However, exceptions to these laws may be enacted that establish different rate ceilings for particular types of loans or lenders.

value of money.   The value of money is what you can buy with it—its purchasing power. There is an inverse relationship between the value of money and the level of prices.

variable-rate mortgage (VRM)
A mortgage on which the rate can change (according to a predetermined formula and within certain limits) over the life of the mortgage. When VRM rates are adjusted, either the mortgage maturity is altered or the monthly payment is changed.

velocity of M2   Measures GNP divided by M2. It may be somewhat more stable and predictable than other velocity measures.

velocity of money   Measures of the number of dollars of national income that are supported with each dollar of money in circulation. When velocity rises, more income can be generated with the same amount of money in circulation. The converse holds if velocity declines. Economists debate about what measure of the money stock is most appropriate to use when calculating the velocity of money. They also debate whether changes in velocity are stable and predictable.

venture capitalists Institutional investors who provide equity financing to young businesses and play an active role in advising their managements.

vesting The rights of employees to obtain benefits in a retirement plan based on their own and their employers' contributions.

warrant A security that allows the holder to exchange it plus a predetermined amount of cash or securities for a predetermined amount of common stock or other securities at the holder's discretion. Most warrants have a life of several years. A few are "perpetual".

whole life insurance An insurance contract that provides periodic payment of premiums and protection as long as the insured lives. Upon death or a specific age (usually 65), the face amount of the policy is paid to the policyholder or beneficiary. Whole life differs from term insurance in that it has a savings feature.

yield The return on an investment. From the present value formula, the yield is the discount rate that equates the discounted value of future cash flows to the cost of the investment.

yield curve The graph of the relationship between interest rates on particular securities and their yield to maturity. To construct yield curves, bonds must be as similar in all other characteristics (e.g., default risk, tax treatment) as possible. Yield curves are most easily constructed for U.S. government securities.

yield spread The difference between the yields (rates of return available) on different types of assets. Typically, rates of return on long-maturity securities exceed those on short-maturity securities, as the latter have less price risk. The yield spread may also refer to the difference between yield (rate of return) on an institution's assets and the rate of payout on its liabilities.

yield to maturity The discount rate that equates the present value of all cash flows from a bond (interest payments plus principal) to the market price of the bond.

zero sum A set of transactions in which the winners' gains exactly equal the losers' losses. If sales commissions and fees are ignored, the futures markets are zero-sum markets.

Credits

"Top 500 Banks by Country," *American Banker,* July 26, 1991. Reprinted with permission from *American Banker.*

"The Top 100 Banking Companies in the World," *American Banker,* July 26, 1991. Reprinted with permission from *American Banker.*

"The Top 10 Banks in the Sale of Loans During 2nd Quarter, 1989," *American Banker, Top Numbers,* 1990. Reprinted with permission from *American Banker.*

Largest Commercial Bank Trust Departments (Year-end 1990)," adapted from chart entitled, "Top 100 Firms in Trust Income," from *American Banker:Top Numbers, 1990.* Reprinted and excerpted with permission from *American Banker.*

"Country Risk Ratings," *Euromoney,* September 1990. Copyright 1990 by Euromoney Publications.

"Total Assets of Major Retirement Programs," American Council on Life Insurance, *1991 Life Insurance Fact Book Update.* Reprinted with permission.

"Life Insurance Balance Sheet," American Council on Life Insurance, *1991 Life Insurance Fact Book Update.* Reprinted with permission.

"List of Ten Largest Property/Liability Companies," *Best Insurance Management Reports,* August 26, 1991. Reprinted with permission.

"Variation In Performance For The 10 Largest US Banks." Reprinted from April 22, 1991 issue of *Business Week* by special permission, copyright 1991 by McGraw-Hill, Inc.

"The 20 Largest Bank Holding Companies in the United States, 1991." Reprinted from April 27, 1992 issue of *Business Week* by special permission, copyright 1992 by McGraw-Hill, Inc.

"Assets Held by Conventional Mutual Funds," *Mutual Fund Fact Book,* 1985, 1990, Investment Company Institute, Washington, D.C. Reprinted with permission.

"Money Market Mutual Funds Asset Holdings," *Mutual Fund Fact Book,* 1990, Investment Company Institute, Washington, D.C. Reprinted with permission.

"Banker's Acceptance Check," *Financing of Exports and Imports,* (New York: Morgan Guaranty Trust Company of New York, 1980). Reprinted with permission.

"Updating the Market Basket," *The New York Times,* February 26, 1987. Copyright 1987 by the New York Times Company. Reprinted with permission.

"The Front Page of Prospectus/Xerox Credit Corporation." Reprinted with permission of Salomon Brothers Inc., New York City. All rights reserved.

"Collateralized Mortgage Obligation Offering." Reprinted with permission of Salomon Brothers Inc., New York City. All rights reserved.

"Summary of Supply and Demand for Credit," *1988 Prospects for Financial Markets.* Reprinted with permission of Salomon Brothers Inc., New York City. All rights reserved.

"Developing Countries' External Debt Positions." International Bank for Reconstruction and Development (The World Bank), *World Debt Tables,* 1990–91, January 1991. Reprinted with permission.

Index

Page numbers in italics refer to tables, graphs, and illustrations.
Page numbers followed by "n" refer to notes at the bottom of the page.

Symbols and Definitions

$=$ equals

$\rightarrow$ induces (leads to)

$\uparrow$ an increase in

$\downarrow$ a decrease in

Δ a change in

ΔP_e = expected change in prices

ΔP_a = actual change in prices

i = (nominal) market interest rates

r = real rate of return, after inflation

$= i - \Delta P_a$ (ex post real return) or

$= i - \Delta P_e$ (ex ante real return)

PV = present value (should equal market price)

C_i = cash flow in year i, where $i = 1, 2, ..., n$

n = last year a cash flow is received

i = appropriate discount rate in the present value equation

$$PV = \frac{C_1}{1+i} + \frac{C_2}{(1+i)^2} + \cdots + \frac{C_n}{(1+i)^n}$$

MB = monetary base = currency and cash outstanding plus depository institution deposits at the Fed

M = money

$M1$ = primary (transactions) money supply